THE COMPLETE WORKS OF

THE COMPLETE WORKS OF O. HENRY

FOREWORD BY HARRY HANSEN

VOLUME II

1953

DOUBLEDAY & COMPANY, INC. GARDEN CITY, N.Y.

Library of Congress Catalog Card Number 53–6098

Designed by Diana Klemin

PRINTED IN THE UNITED STATES OF AMERICA BY
KINGSPORT PRESS, INC., KINGSPORT, TENNESSEE

CONTENTS

BOOK 7 SIXES AND SEVENS

BOOK 8   ROLLING STONES

BOOK 9   POEMS

BOOK 10   WHIRLIGIGS

BOOK **11** THE VOICE OF THE CITY

BOOK **12** THE TRIMMED LAMP

BOOK **13** STRICTLY BUSINESS

BOOK **14** WAIFS AND STRAYS

THE COMPLETE WORKS OF

BOOK 7

SIXES AND SEVENS

THE LAST OF THE TROUBADOURS

Inexorably Sam Galloway saddled his pony. He was going away from
the Rancho Altito at the end of a three months' visit. It is not to be expected that a guest should put up with wheat coffee and biscuits yellow-
streaked with saleratus for longer than that. Nick Napoleon, the big Negro man cook, had never been able to make good biscuits. Once before,
when Nick was cooking at the Willow Ranch, Sam had been forced to
fly from his *cuisine,* after only a six weeks' sojourn.

On Sam's face was an expression of sorrow, deepened with regret and
slightly tempered by the patient forgiveness of a connoisseur who cannot
be understood. But very firmly and inexorably he buckled his saddle-
cinches, looped his take-rope and hung it to his saddle-horn, tied his
slicker and coat on the cantle, and looped his quirt on his right wrist.

The Merrydews (householders of the Rancho Altito), men, women, children, and servants, vassals, visitors, employés, dogs, and casual callers, were grouped in the "gallery" of the ranch house, all with face set to the tune of melancholy and grief. For, as the coming of Sam Galloway to any ranch, camp, or cabin between the rivers Frio or Bravo del Norte aroused joy, so his departure caused mourning and distress.

And then, during absolute silence, except for the bumping of a hind elbow of a hound dog as he pursued a wicked flea, Sam tenderly and carefully tied his guitar across his saddle on top of his slicker and coat. The guitar was in a green duck bag; and if you catch the significance of it, it explains Sam.

Sam Galloway was the Last of the Troubadours. Of course you know about the troubadours. The encyclopædia says they flourished between the eleventh and the thirteenth centuries. What they flourished doesn't seem clear—you may be pretty sure it wasn't a sword: maybe it was a fiddle-bow, or a forkful of spaghetti, or a lady's scarf. Anyhow, Sam Galloway was one of 'em.

Sam put on a martyred expression as he mounted his pony. But the expression on his face was hilarious compared with the one on his pony's. You see, a pony gets to know his rider mighty well, and it is not unlikely that cow ponies in pastures and at hitching racks had often guyed Sam's pony for being ridden by a guitar player instead of by a rollicking, cussing, all-wool cowboy. No man is a hero to his saddle-horse. And even an escalator in a department store might be excused for tripping up a troubadour.

Oh, I know I'm one; and so are you. You remember the stories you memorize and the card tricks you study and that little piece on the piano —how does it go—ti-tum-te-tum-ti-tum—those little Arabian Ten-Minute Entertainments that you furnish when you go up to call on your rich Aunt Jane. You should know that *omnæ personæ in tres partes divisæ sunt.* Namely: Barons, Troubadours, and Workers. Barons have no inclination to read such folderol as this; and Workers have no time: so I know you must be a Troubadour, and that you will understand Sam Galloway. Whether we sing, act, dance, write, lecture, or paint, we are only troubadours; so let us make the worst of it.

The pony with the Dante Alighieri face, guided by the pressure of Sam's knees, bore that wandering minstrel sixteen miles southeastward. Nature was in her most benignant mood. League after league of delicate, sweet flowerets made fragrant the gently undulating prairie. The east wind tempered the spring warmth; wool-white clouds flying in from the Mexican Gulf hindered the direct rays of the April sun. Sam sang songs as he rode. Under his pony's bridle he had tucked some sprigs of chaparral to keep away the deer flies. Thus crowned, the long-faced quadruped looked more Dantesque than before, and, judging by his countenance, seemed to think of Beatrice.

Straight as topography permitted, Sam rode to the sheep ranch of old man Ellison. A visit to a sheep ranch seemed to him desirable just then. There had been too many people, too much noise, argument, competition, confusion, at Rancho Altito. He had never conferred upon old man Ellison the favour of sojourning at his ranch; but he knew he would be welcome. The troubadour is his own passport everywhere. The Workers in the castle let down the drawbridge to him, and the Baron sets him at his left hand at table in the banquet hall. There ladies smile upon him and applaud his songs and stories, while the Workers bring boars' heads and flagons. If the Baron nods once or twice in his carved oaken chair, he does not do it maliciously.

Old man Ellison welcomed the troubadour flatteringly. He had often heard praises of Sam Galloway from other ranchmen who had been complimented by his visits, but had never aspired to such an honor for his own humble barony. I say barony because old man Ellison was the Last of the Barons. Of course, Mr. Bulwer-Lytton lived too early to know him or he wouldn't have conferred that sobriquet upon Warwick. In life it is the duty and the function of the Baron to provide work for the Workers and lodging and shelter for the Troubadours.

Old man Ellison was a shrunken old man, with a short, yellow-white beard and a face lined and seamed by past-and-gone smiles. His ranch was a little two-room box house in a grove of hackberry trees in the lonesomest part of the sheep country. His household consisted of a Kiowa Indian man cook, four hounds, a pet sheep, and a half-tamed coyote chained to a fence-post. He owned 3,000 sheep, which he ran on two sections of leased land and many thousands of acres neither leased nor owned. Three or four times a year some one who spoke his language would ride up to his gate and exchange a few bald ideas with him. Those were red-letter days to old man Ellison. Then in what illuminated, embossed, and gorgeously decorated capitals must have been written the day on which a troubadour—a troubadour who, according to the encyclopædia, should have flourished between the eleventh and the thirteenth centuries—drew rein at the gates of his baronial castle!

Old man Ellison's smiles came back and filled his wrinkles when he saw Sam. He hurried out of the house in his shuffling, limping way to greet him.

"Hello, Mr. Ellison," called Sam, cheerfully. "Thought I'd drop over and see you a while. Notice you've had fine rains on your range. They ought to make good grazing for your spring lambs."

"Well, well, well," said old man Ellison. "I'm mighty glad to see you, Sam. I never thought you'd take the trouble to ride over to as out-of-the-way an old ranch as this. But you're mighty welcome. 'Light. I've got a sack of new oats in the kitchen—shall I bring out a feed for your hoss?"

"Oats for him?" said Sam, derisively. "No, sir-ee. He's as fat as a pig now on grass. He don't get rode enough to keep him in condition. I'll just turn him in the horse pasture with a drag rope on if you don't mind."

I am positive that never during the eleventh and thirteenth centuries did Baron, Troubadour, and Worker amalgamate as harmoniously as their parallels did that evening at old man Ellison's sheep ranch. The Kiowa's biscuits were light and tasty and his coffee strong. Ineradicable hospitality and appreciation glowed on old man Ellison's weather-tanned face. As for the troubadour, he said to himself that he had stumbled upon pleasant places indeed. A well-cooked, abundant meal, a host whom his lightest attempt to entertain seemed to delight far beyond the merits of the exertion, and the reposeful atmosphere that his sensitive soul at that time craved united to confer upon him a satisfaction and luxurious ease that he had seldom found on his tours of the ranches.

After the delectable supper, Sam untied the green duck bag and took out his guitar. Not by way of payment, mind you—neither Sam Galloway nor any other of the true troubadours are lineal descendants of the late Tommy Tucker. You have read of Tommy Tucker in the works of the esteemed but often obscure Mother Goose. Tommy Tucker sang for his supper. No true troubadour would do that. He would have his supper, and then sing for Art's sake.

Sam Galloway's repertoire comprised about fifty funny stories and between thirty and forty songs. He by no means stopped there. He could talk through twenty cigarettes on any topic that you brought up. And he never sat up when he could lie down; and never stood when he could sit. I am strongly disposed to linger with him, for I am drawing a portrait as well as a blunt pencil and a tattered thesaurus will allow.

I wish you could have seen him: he was small and tough and inactive beyond the power of imagination to conceive. He wore an ultramarine-blue woollen shirt laced down the front with a pearl-gray, exaggerated sort of shoestring, indestructible brown duck clothes, inevitable high-heeled boots with Mexican spurs, and a Mexican straw sombrero.

That evening Sam and old man Ellison dragged their chairs out under the hackberry trees. They lighted cigarettes; and the troubadour gaily touched his guitar. Many of the songs he sang were the weird, melancholy, minor-keyed *canciones* that he had learned from the Mexican sheep herders and *vaqueros*. One, in particular, charmed and soothed the soul of the lonely baron. It was a favourite song of the sheep herders, beginning: *"Huile, huile, palomita,"* which being translated means, "Fly, fly, little dove." Sam sang it for old man Ellison many times that evening.

The troubadour stayed on at the old man's ranch. There was peace and quiet and appreciation there, such as he had not found in the noisy camps of the cattle kings. No audience in the world could have crowned the work of poet, musician, or artist with more worshipful and unflagging approval than that bestowed upon his efforts by old man Ellison. No visit by a royal personage to a humble woodchopper or peasant could have been received with more flattering thankfulness and joy.

On a cool, canvas-covered cot in the shade of the hackberry trees Sam Galloway passed the greater part of his time. There he rolled his brown paper cigarettes, read such tedious literature as the ranch afforded, and added to his repertoire of improvisations that he played so expertly on his guitar. To him, as a slave ministering to a great lord, the Kiowa brought cool water from the red jar hanging under the brush shelter, and food when he called for it. The prairie zephyrs fanned him mildly; mocking-birds at morn and eve competed with but scarce equalled the sweet melodies of his lyre; a perfumed stillness seemed to fill all his world. While old man Ellison was pottering among his flocks of sheep on his mile-an-hour pony, and while the Kiowa took his siesta in the burning sunshine at the end of the kitchen, Sam would lie on his cot thinking what a happy world he lived in, and how kind it is to the ones whose mission in life it is to give entertainment and pleasure. Here he had food and lodging as good as he had ever longed for; absolute immunity from care or exertion or strife; an endless welcome, and a host whose delight at the sixteenth repetition of a song or a story was as keen as at its initial giving. Was there ever a troubadour of old who struck upon as royal a castle in his wanderings? While he lay thus, meditating upon his blessings, little brown cottontails would shyly frolic through the yard; a covey of white-topknotted blue quail would run past, in single file, twenty yards away; a *paisano* bird, out hunting for tarantulas, would hop upon the fence and salute him with sweeping flourishes of its long tail. In the eighty-acre horse pasture the pony with the Dantesque face grew fat and almost smiling. The troubadour was at the end of his wanderings.

Old man Ellison was his own *vacïero*. That means that he supplied his sheep camps with wood, water, and rations by his own labors instead of hiring a *vacïero*. On small ranches it is often done.

One morning he started for the camp of Encarnación Felipe de la Cruz y Monto Piedras (one of his sheep herders) with the week's usual rations of brown beans, coffee, meal, and sugar. Two miles away on the trail from old Fort Ewing he met, face to face, a terrible being called King James, mounted on a fiery, prancing, Kentucky-bred horse.

King James's real name was James King; but people reversed it because it seemed to fit him better, and also because it seemed to please his majesty. King James was the biggest cattleman between the Alamo plaza in San Antone and Bill Hopper's saloon in Brownsville. Also he was the loudest and most offensive bully and braggart and bad man in southwest Texas. And he always made good whenever he bragged; and the more noise he made the more dangerous he was. In the story papers it is always the quiet, mild-mannered man with light blue eyes and a low voice who turns out to be really dangerous; but in real life and in this story such is not the case. Give me my choice between assaulting a large, loud-mouthed rough-houser and an inoffensive stranger with blue eyes sitting quietly in a corner, and you will see something doing in the corner every time.

King James, as I intended to say earlier, was a fierce, two-hundred-pound, sunburned, blond man, as pink as an October strawberry, and with two horizontal slits under shaggy red eyebrows for eyes. On that day he wore a flannel shirt that was tan-colored, with the exception of certain large areas which were darkened by transudations due to the summer sun. There seemed to be other clothing and garnishings about him, such as brown duck trousers stuffed into immense boots, and red handkerchiefs and revolvers; and a shotgun laid across his saddle and a leather belt with millions of cartridges shining in it—but your mind skidded off such accessories; what held your gaze was just the two little horizontal slits that he used for eyes.

This was the man that old man Ellison met on the trail; and when you count up in the baron's favor that he was sixty-five and weighed ninety-eight pounds and had heard of King James's record and that he (the baron) had a hankering for the *vita simplex* and had no gun with him and wouldn't have used it if he had, you can't censure him if I tell you that the smiles with which the troubadour had filled his wrinkles went out of them and left them plain wrinkles again. But he was not the kind of baron that flies from danger. He reined in the mile-an-hour pony (no difficult feat), and saluted the formidable monarch.

King James expressed himself with royal directness.

"You're that old snoozer that's running sheep on this range, ain't you?" "What right have you got to do it? Do you own the land, or lease any?"

"I have two sections leased from the state," said old man Ellison, mildly.

"Not by no means, you haven't," said King James. "Your lease expired yesterday; and I had a man at the land office on the minute to take it up. You don't control a foot of grass in Texas. You sheep men have got to git. Your time's up. It's a cattle country, and there ain't any room in it for snoozers. This range you've got your sheep on is mine. I'm putting up a wire fence, forty by sixty miles; and if there's a sheep inside of it when it's done it'll be a dead one. I'll give you a week to move yours away. If they ain't gone by then, I'll send six men over here with Winchesters to make mutton out of the whole lot. And if I find you here at the same time this is what you'll get."

King James patted the breech of his shotgun warningly.

Old man Ellison rode on to the camp of Encarnación. He sighed many times, and the wrinkles in his face grew deeper. Rumors that the old order was about to change had reached him before. The end of Free

Grass was in sight. Other troubles, too, had been accumulating upon his shoulders. His flocks were decreasing instead of growing; the price of wool was declining at every clip; even Bradshaw, the storekeeper at Frio City, at whose store he bought his ranch supplies, was dunning him for his last six months' bill and threatening to cut him off. And so this last greatest calamity suddenly dealt out to him by the terrible King James was a crusher.

When the old man got back to the ranch at sunset he found Sam Galloway lying on his cot, propped against a roll of blankets and wool sacks, fingering his guitar.

"Hello, Uncle Ben," the troubadour called, cheerfully. "You rolled in early this evening. I been trying a new twist on the Spanish Fandango to-day. I just about got it. Here's how she goes—listen."

"That's fine, that's mighty fine," said old man Ellison, sitting on the kitchen step and rubbing his white, Scotch-terrier whiskers. "I reckon you've got all the musicians beat east and west, Sam, as far as the roads are cut out."

"Oh, I don't know," said Sam reflectively. "But I certainly do get there on variations. I guess I can handle anything in five flats about as well as any of 'em. But you look kind of fagged out, Uncle Ben—ain't you feeling right well this evening?"

"Little tired; that's all, Sam. If you ain't played yourself out, let's have that Mexican piece that starts off with: '*Huile, huile, palomita.*' It seems that that song always kind of soothes and comforts me after I've been riding far or anything bothers me."

"Why, *seguramente, señor,*" said Sam. "I'll hit her up for you as often as you like. And before I forget about it, Uncle Ben, you want to jerk Bradshaw up about them last hams he sent us. They're just a little bit strong."

A man sixty-five years old, living on a sheep ranch and beset by a complication of disasters, cannot successfully and continuously dissemble. Moreover, a troubadour has eyes quick to see unhappiness in others around him—because it disturbs his own ease. So, on the next day, Sam again questioned the old man about his air of sadness and abstraction. Then old man Ellison told him the story of King James's threats and orders and that pale melancholy and red ruin appeared to have marked him for their own. The troubadour took the news thoughtfully. He had heard much about King James.

On the third day of the seven days of grace allowed him by the autocrat of the range, old man Ellison drove his buckboard to Frio City to fetch some necessary supplies for the ranch. Bradshaw was hard but not implacable. He divided the old man's order by two, and let him have a little more time. One article secured was a new, fine ham for the pleasure of the troubadour.

Five miles out of Frio City on his way home the old man met King James riding into town. His majesty could never look anything but fierce and menacing, but to-day his slits of eyes appeared to be a little wider than they usually were.

"Good day," said the king, gruffly. "I've been wanting to see you. I hear it said by a cowman from Sandy yesterday that you was from Jackson County, Mississippi, originally. I want to know if that's a fact."

"Born there," said old man Ellison, "and raised there till I was twenty-one."

"This man says," went on King James, "that he thinks you was related to the Jackson County Reeveses. Was he right?"

"Aunt Caroline Reeves," said the old man, "was my half-sister."

"She was my aunt," said King James. "I run away from home when I was sixteen. Now, let's re-talk over some things that we discussed a few days ago. They call me a bad man; and they're only half right. There's plenty of room in my pasture for your bunch of sheep and their increase for a long time to come. Aunt Caroline used to cut out sheep in cake dough and bake 'em for me. You keep your sheep where they are, and use all the range you want. How's your finances?"

The old man related his woes in detail, dignifiedly, with restraint and candor.

"She used to smuggle extra grub into my school basket—I'm speaking of Aunt Caroline," said King James. "I'm going over to Frio City to-day, and I'll ride back by your ranch tomorrow. I'll draw $2,000 out of the bank there and bring it over to you; and I'll tell Bradshaw to let you have anything you want on credit. You are bound to have heard the old saying at home, that the Jackson County Reeveses and Kings would stick closer by each other than chestnut burs. Well, I'm a King yet whenever I run across a Reeves. So you look out for me along about sundown to-morrow, and don't you worry about nothing. Shouldn't wonder if the dry spell don't kill out the young grass."

Old man Ellison drove happily ranchward. Once more the smiles filled out his wrinkles. Very suddenly, by the magic of kinship and the good that lies somewhere in all hearts, his troubles had been removed.

On reaching the ranch he found that Sam Galloway was not there. His guitar hung by its buckskin string to a hackberry limb, moaning as the gulf breeze blew across its masterless strings.

The Kiowa endeavored to explain.

"Sam, he catch pony," said he, "and say he ride to Frio City. What for no can damn sabe. Say he come back to-night. Maybe so. That all."

As the first stars came out the troubadour rode back to his haven. He pastured his pony and went into the house, his spurs jingling martially.

Old man Ellison sat at the kitchen table, having a tin cup of before-supper coffee. He looked contented and pleased.

"Hello, Sam," said he, "I'm darned glad to see ye back. I don't know how I managed to get along on this ranch, anyhow, before ye dropped in to cheer things up. I'll bet ye've been skylarking around with some of them Frio City gals, now, that's kept ye so late."

And then old man Ellison took another look at Sam's face and saw that the minstrel had changed to the man of action.

And while Sam is unbuckling from his waist old man Ellison's six-shooter, that the latter had left behind when he drove to town, we may well pause to remark that anywhere and whenever a troubadour lays down the guitar and takes up the sword trouble is sure to follow. It is not the expert thrust of Athos nor the cold skill of Aramis nor the iron wrist of Porthos that we have to fear—it is the Gascon's fury—the wild and unacademic attack of the troubadour—the sword of D'Artagnan.

"I done it," said Sam. "I went over to Frio City to do it. I couldn't let him put the skibunk on you, Uncle Ben. I met him in Summer's saloon. I knowed what to do. I said a few things to him that nobody else heard. He reached for his gun first—half a dozen fellows saw him do it—but I got mine unlimbered first. Three doses I gave him—right around the lungs, and a saucer could have covered up all of 'em. He won't bother you no more."

"This—is—King—James—you speak—of?" asked old man Ellison, while he sipped his coffee.

"You bet it was. And they took me before the county judge; and the witnesses what saw him draw his gun first was all there. Well, of course, they put me under $300 bond to appear before the court, but there was four or five boys on the spot ready to sign the bail. He won't bother you no more, Uncle Ben. You ought to have seen how close them bullet holes was together. I reckon playing a guitar as much as I do must kind of limber a fellow's trigger finger a little, don't you think, Uncle Ben?"

Then there was a little silence in the castle except for the spluttering of a venison steak that the Kiowa was cooking.

"Sam," said old man Ellison, stroking his white whiskers with a tremulous hand, "would you mind getting the guitar and playing that 'Huile, huile, palomita' piece once or twice? It always seems to be kind of soothing and comforting when a man's tired and fagged out."

There is no more to be said, except that the title of the story is wrong. It should have been called "The Last of the Barons." There never will be an end to the troubadours; and now and then it does seem that the jingle of their guitars will drown the sound of the muffled blows of the pickaxes and trip hammers of all the Workers in the world.

THE SLEUTHS

In the Big City a man will disappear with the suddenness and completeness of the flame of a candle that is blown out. All the agencies of in-
quisition—the hounds of the trail, the sleuths of the city's labyrinths, the
closet detectives of theory and induction—will be invoked to the search.
Most often the man's face will be seen no more. Sometimes he will re-
appear in Sheboygan or in the wilds of Terre Haute, calling himself one
of the synonyms of "Smith," and without memory of events up to a certain time, including his grocer's bill. Sometimes it will be found, after
dragging the rivers, and polling the restaurants to see if he may be waiting for a well-done sirloin, that he has moved next door.

This snuffing out of a human being like the erasure of a chalk man
from a blackboard is one of the most impressive themes in dramaturgy.

The case of Mary Snyder, in point, should not be without interest.

A man of middle age, of the name of Meeks, came from the West to
New York to find his sister, Mrs. Mary Snyder, a widow, aged fifty-two,
who had been living for a year in a tenement house in a crowded neighborhood.

At her address he was told that Mary Snyder had moved away longer
than a month before. No one could tell him her new address.

On coming out Mr. Meeks addressed a policeman who was standing on
the corner, and explained his dilemma.

"My sister is very poor," he said, "and I am anxious to find her. I have
recently made quite a lot of money in a lead mine, and I want her to
share my prosperity. There is no use in advertising her, because she cannot read."

The policeman pulled his mustache and looked so thoughtful and
mighty that Meeks could almost feel the joyful tears of his sister Mary
drooping upon his bright blue tie.

"You go down in the Canal Street neighborhood," said the policeman,
"and get a job drivin' the biggest dray you can find. There's old women
always gettin' knocked over by drays down there. You might see 'er
among 'em. If you don't want to do that you better go 'round to headquarters and get 'em to put a fly cop onto the dame."

At police headquarters, Meeks received ready assistance. A general
alarm was sent out and copies of a photograph of Mary Snyder that her
brother had were distributed among the stations. In Mulberry Street the
chief assigned Detective Mullins to the case.

The detective took Meeks aside and said:

"This is not a very difficult case to unravel. Shave off your whiskers, fill your pockets with good cigars, and meet me in the café of the Waldorf at three o'clock this afternoon."

Meeks obeyed. He found Mullins there. They had a bottle of wine, while the detective asked questions concerning the missing woman.

"Now," said Mullins, "New York is a big city, but we've got the detective business systematized. There are two ways we can go about finding your sister. We will try one of 'em first. You say she's fifty-two?"

"A little past," said Meeks.

The detective conducted the Westerner to a branch advertising office of one of the largest dailies. There he wrote the following "ad" and submitted it to Meeks.

"Wanted, at once—one hundred attractive chorus girls for a new musical comedy. Apply all day at No.—— Broadway."

Meeks was indignant.

"My sister," said he, "is a poor, hard-working, elderly woman. I do not see what aid an advertisement of this kind would be toward finding her."

"All right," said the detective. "I guess you don't know New York. But if you've got a grouch against this scheme we'll try the other one. It's a sure thing. But it'll cost you more."

"Never mind the expense," said Meeks; "we'll try it."

The sleuth led him back to the Waldorf. "Engage a couple of bedrooms and a parlor," he advised, "and let's go up."

This was done, and the two were shown to a superb suite on the fourth floor. Meeks looked puzzled. The detective sank into a velvet armchair, and pulled out his cigar case.

"I forgot to suggest, old man," he said, "that you should have taken the rooms by the month. They wouldn't have stuck you so much for 'em."

"By the month!" exclaimed Meeks. "What do you mean?"

"Oh, it'll take time to work the game this way. I told you it would cost you more. We'll have to wait till spring. There'll be a new city directory out then. Very likely your sister's name and address will be in it."

Meeks rid himself of the city detective at once. On the next day some one advised him to consult Shamrock Jolnes, New York's famous private detective, who demanded fabulous fees, but performed miracles in the way of solving mysteries and crimes.

After waiting for two hours in the anteroom of the great detective's apartment, Meeks was shown into his presence. Jolnes sat in a purple dressing-gown at an inlaid ivory chess table, with a magazine before him, trying to solve the mystery of "They." The famous sleuth's thin, intellectual face, piercing eyes, and rate per word are too well known to need description.

Meeks set forth his errand. "My fee, if successful, will be $500," said Shamrock Jolnes.

Meeks bowed his agreement to the price.

"I will undertake your case, Mr. Meeks," said Jolnes, finally. "The disappearance of people in this city has always been an interesting problem to me. I remember a case that I brought to a successful outcome a year ago. A family bearing the name of Clark disappeared suddenly from a small flat in which they were living. I watched the flat building for two months for a clue. One day it struck me that a certain milkman and a grocer's boy always walked backward when they carried their wares upstairs. Following out by induction the idea that this observation gave me, I at once located the missing family. They had moved into the flat across the hall and changed their name to Kralc."

Shamrock Jolnes and his client went to the tenement house where Mary Snyder had lived, and the detective demanded to be shown the room in which she had lived. It had been occupied by no tenant since her disappearance.

The room was small, dingy, and poorly furnished. Meeks seated himself dejectedly on a broken chair, while the great detective searched the walls and floors and the few sticks of old, rickety furniture for a clue.

At the end of half an hour Jolnes had collected a few seemingly unintelligible articles—a cheap black hatpin, a piece torn off a theatre programme, and the end of a small torn card on which was the word "Left" and the characters "C 12."

Shamrock Jolnes leaned against the mantel for ten minutes, with his head resting upon his hand, and an absorbed look upon his intellectual face. At the end of that time he exclaimed, with animation:

"Come, Mr. Meeks; the problem is solved. I can take you directly to the house where your sister is living. And you may have no fears concerning her welfare, for she is amply provided with funds—for the present at least."

Meeks felt joy and wonder in equal proportions.

"How did you manage it?" he asked, with admiration in his tones.

Perhaps Jolnes's only weakness was a professional pride in his wonderful achievements in induction. He was ever ready to astound and charm his listeners by describing his methods.

"By elimination," said Jolnes, spreading his clues upon a little table, "I got rid of certain parts of the city to which Mrs. Snyder might have removed. You see this hatpin? That eliminates Brooklyn. No woman attempts to board a car at the Brooklyn Bridge without being sure that she carries a hatpin with which to fight her way into a seat. And now I will demonstrate to you that she could not have gone to Harlem. Behind this door are two hooks in the wall. Upon one of these Mrs. Snyder has hung her bonnet, and upon the other her shawl. You will observe that the bottom of the hanging shawl has gradually made a soiled streak against the plastered wall. The mark is clean-cut, proving that there is no fringe on the shawl. Now, was there ever a case where a middle-aged woman, wearing a shawl, boarded a Harlem train without there being a fringe on the shawl to catch in the gate and delay the passengers behind her? So we eliminate Harlem.

"Therefore I conclude that Mrs. Snyder has not moved very far away. On this torn piece of card you see the word 'Left,' the letter 'C,' and the number '12.' Now, I happen to know that No. 12 Avenue C is a first-class boarding house, far beyond your sister's means—as we suppose. But then I find this piece of a theatre programme, crumpled into an odd shape. What meaning does it convey? None to you, very likely, Mr. Meeks; but it is eloquent to one whose habits and training take cognizance of the smallest things.

"You have told me that your sister was a scrub woman. She scrubbed the floors of offices and hallways. Let us assume that she procured such work to perform in a theatre. Where is valuable jewellery lost the oftenest, Mr. Meeks? In the theatres, of course. Look at that piece of programme, Mr. Meeks. Observe the round impression in it. It has been wrapped around a ring—perhaps a ring of great value. Mrs. Snyder found the ring while at work in the theatre. She hastily tore off a piece of a programme, wrapped the ring carefully, and thrust it into her bosom. The next day she disposed of it, and with her increased means, looked about her for a more comfortable place in which to live. When I reach thus far in the chain I see nothing impossible about No. 12 Avenue C. It is there we will find your sister, Mr. Meeks."

Shamrock Jolnes concluded his convincing speech with the smile of a successful artist. Meeks's admiration was too great for words. Together they went to No. 12 Avenue C. It was an old-fashioned brownstone house in a prosperous and respectable neighborhood.

They rang the bell, and on inquiry were told that no Mrs. Snyder was know there, and that not within six months had a new occupant come to the house.

When they reached the sidewalk again, Meeks examined the clues which he had brought away from his sister's old room.

"I am no detective," he remarked to Jolnes as he raised the piece of theatre programme to his nose, "but it seems to me that instead of a ring having been wrapped in this paper it was one of those round peppermint drops. And this piece with the address on it looks to me like the end of a seat coupon—No. 12, row C, left aisle."

Shamrock Jolnes had a far-away look in his eyes.

"I think you would do well to consult Juggins," said he.

"Who is Juggins?" asked Meeks.

"He is the leader," said Jolnes, "of a new modern school of detectives. Their methods are different from ours, but it is said that Juggins has solved some extremely puzzling cases. I will take you to him."

They found the greater Juggins in his office. He was a small man with light hair, deeply absorbed in reading one of the bourgeois works of Nathaniel Hawthorne.

The two great detectives of different schools shook hands with ceremony, and Meeks was introduced.

"State the facts," said Juggins, going on with his reading.

When Meeks ceased, the greater one closed his book and said:

"Do I understand that your sister is fifty-two years of age, with a large mole on the side of her nose, and that she is a very poor widow, making a scanty living by scrubbing, and with a very homely face and figure?"

"That describes her exactly," admitted Meeks. Juggins rose and put on his hat.

"In fifteen minutes," he said, "I will return, bringing you her present address."

Shamrock Jolnes turned pale, but forced a smile.

Within the specified time Juggins returned and consulted a little slip of paper held in his hand.

"Your sister, Mary Snyder," he announced calmly, "will be found at No. 162 Chilton Street. She is living in the back hall bedroom, five flights up. The house is only four blocks from here," he continued, addressing Meeks. "Suppose you go and verify the statement and then return here. Mr. Jolnes will await you, I dare say."

Meeks hurried away. In twenty minutes he was back again, with a beaming face.

"She is there and well!" he cried. "Name your fee!"

"Two dollars," said Juggins.

When Meeks had settled his bill and departed, Shamrock Jolnes stood with his hat in his hand before Juggins.

"If it would not be asking too much," he stammered—"if you would favor me so far—would you object to——"

"Certainly not," said Juggins, pleasantly. "I will tell you how I did it. You remember the description of Mrs. Snyder? Did you ever know a woman like that who wasn't paying weekly instalments on an enlarged crayon portrait of herself? The biggest factory of that kind in the country is just around the corner. I went there and got her address off the books. That's all."

WITCHES' LOAVES

Miss Martha Meacham kept the little bakery on the corner (the one where you go up three steps, and the bell tinkles when you open the door).

Miss Martha was forty, her bank-book showed a credit of two thousand dollars, and she possessed two false teeth and a sympathetic heart. Many people have married whose chances to do so were much inferior to Miss Martha's.

Two or three times a week a customer came in in whom she began to take an interest. He was a middle-aged man, wearing spectacles and a brown beard trimmed to a careful point.

He spoke English with a strong German accent. His clothes were worn and darned in places, and wrinkled and baggy in others. But he looked neat, and had very good manners.

He always bought two loaves of stale bread. Fresh bread was five cents a loaf. Stale ones were two for five. Never did he call for anything but stale bread.

Once Miss Martha saw a red and brown stain on his fingers. She was sure then that he was an artist and very poor. No doubt he lived in a garret, where he painted pictures and ate stale bread and thought of the good things to eat in Miss Martha's bakery.

Often when Miss Martha sat down to her chops and light rolls and jam and tea she would sigh, and wish that the gentle-mannered artist might share her tasty meal instead of eating his dry crust in that draughty attic. Miss Martha's heart, as you have been told, was a sympathetic one.

In order to test her theory as to his occupation, she brought from her room one day a painting that she had bought at a sale, and set it against the shelves behind the bread counter.

It was a Venetian scene. A splendid marble palazzo (so it said on the picture) stood in the foreground—or rather forewater. For the rest there were gondolas (with the lady trailing her hand in the water), clouds, sky, and chiaroscuro in plenty. No artist could fail to notice it.

Two days afterward the customer came in.

"Two loafs of stale bread, if you bleaze."

"You haf here a fine bicture, madame," he said while she was wrapping up the bread.

"Yes?" says Miss Martha, revelling in her own cunning. "I do so admire art and" (no, it would not do to say "artists" thus early) "and paintings," she substituted. "You think it is a good picture?"

"Der balace," said the customer, "is not in good drawing. Der bairspective of it is not true. Goot morning, madame."

He took his bread, bowed, and hurried out.

Yes, he must be an artist. Miss Martha took the picture back to her room.

How gentle and kindly his eyes shone behind his spectacles! What a broad brow he had! To be able to judge perspective at a glance—and to live on stale bread! But genius often has to struggle before it is recognized.

What a thing it would be for art and perspective if genius were backed

by two thousand dollars in bank, a bakery, and a sympathetic heart to——
But these were day-dreams, Miss Martha.

Often now when he came he would chat for a while across the show-case. He seemed to crave Miss Martha's cheerful words.

He kept on buying stale bread. Never a cake, never a pie, never one of her delicious Sally Lunns.

She thought he began to look thinner and discouraged. Her heart ached to add something good to eat to his meagre purchase, but her courage failed at the act. She did not dare affront him. She knew the pride of artists.

Miss Martha took to wearing her blue-dotted silk waist behind the counter. In the back room she cooked a mysterious compound of quince seeds and borax. Ever so many people use it for the complexion.

One day the customer came in as usual, laid his nickel on the showcase, and called for his stale loaves. While Miss Martha was reaching for them there was a great tooting and clanging, and a fire-engine came lumbering past.

The customer hurried to the door to look, as any one will. Suddenly inspired, Miss Martha seized the opportunity.

On the bottom shelf behind the counter was a pound of fresh butter that the dairyman had left ten minutes before. With bread knife Miss Martha made a deep slash in each of the stale loaves, inserted a generous quantity of butter, and pressed the loaves tight again.

When the customer turned once more she was tying the paper around them.

When he had gone, after an unusually pleasant little chat, Miss Martha smiled to herself, but not without a slight fluttering of the heart.

Had she been too bold? Would he take offense? But surely not. There was no language of edibles. Butter was no emblem of unmaidenly forwardness.

For a long time that day her mind dwelt on the subject. She imagined the scene when he should discover her little deception.

He would lay down his brushes and palette. There would stand his easel with the picture he was painting in which the perspective was beyond criticism.

He would prepare for his luncheon of dry bread and water. He would slice into a loaf—ah!

Miss Martha blushed. Would he think of the hand that placed it there as he ate? Would he——

The front door bell jangled viciously. Somebody was coming in, making a great deal of noise.

Miss Martha hurried to the front. Two men were there. One was a young man smoking a pipe—a man she had never seen before. The other was her artist.

His face was very red, his hat was on the back of his head, his hair was wildly rumpled. He clinched his two fists and shook them ferociously at Miss Martha. *At Miss Martha.*

"Dummkopf!" he shouted with extreme loudness; and then *"Tausendonfer!"* or something like it in German.

The young man tried to draw him away.

"I vill not go," he said angrily, "else I shall told her."

He made a bass drum of Miss Martha's counter.

"You haf shpoilt me," he cried, his blue eyes blazing behind his spectacles. "I vill tell you. You vas von *meddlingsome old cat!*"

Miss Martha leaned weakly against the shelves and laid one hand on her blue-dotted silk waist. The young man took the other by the collar.

"Come on," he said, "you've said enough." He dragged the angry one out at the door to the sidewalk, and then came back.

"Guess you ought to be told, ma'am," he said, "what the row is about. That's Blumberger. He's an architectural draftsman. I work in the same office with him.

"He's been working hard for three months drawing a plan for a new city hall. It was a prize competition. He finished inking the lines yesterday. You know, a draftsman always makes his drawing in pencil first. When it's done he rubs out the pencil lines with handfuls of stale bread crumbs. That's better than India rubber.

"Blumberger's been buying the bread here. Well, to-day—well, you know, ma'am, that butter isn't—well, Blumberger's plan isn't good for anything now except to cut up into railroad sandwiches."

Miss Martha went into the back room. She took off the blue-dotted silk waist and put on the old brown serge she used to wear. Then she poured the quince seed and borax mixture out of the window into the ash can.

THE PRIDE OF THE CITIES

Said Mr. Kipling, "The cities are full of pride, challenging each to each." Even so.

New York was empty. Two hundred thousand of its people were away for the summer. Three million eight hundred thousand remained as caretakers and to pay the bills of the absentees. But the two hundred thousand are an expensive lot.

The New Yorker sat at a roof-garden table, ingesting solace through a straw. His panama lay upon a chair. The July audience was scattered among vacant seats as widely as out-fielders when the champion batter steps to the plate. Vaudeville happened at intervals. The breeze was cool from the bay; around and above—everywhere except on the stage—were stars. Glimpses were to be had of waiters, always disappearing, like startled chamois. Prudent visitors who had ordered refreshments by 'phone in the morning were now being served. The New Yorker was aware of certain drawbacks to his comfort, but content beamed softly from his rimless eye-glasses. His family was out of town. The drinks were warm; the ballet was suffering from lack of both tune and talcum—but his family would not return until September.

Then up into the garden stumbled the man from Topaz City, Nevada. The gloom of the solitary sight-seer enwrapped him. Bereft of joy through loneliness, he stalked with a widower's face through the halls of pleasure. Thirst for human companionship possessed him as he panted in the metropolitan draught. Straight to the New Yorker's table he steered.

The New Yorker, disarmed and made reckless by the lawless atmosphere of a roof garden, decided upon utter abandonment of his life's traditions. He resolved to shatter with one rash, dare-devil, impulsive, harebrained act the conventions that had hitherto been woven into his existence. Carrying out this radical and precipitous inspiration he nodded slightly to the stranger as he drew nearer the table.

The next moment found the man from Topaz City in the list of the New Yorker's closest friends. He took a chair at the table, he gathered two others for his feet, he tossed his broad-brimmed hat upon a fourth, and told his life's history to his new-found pard.

The New Yorker warmed a little, as an apartment-house furnace warms when the strawberry season begins. A waiter who came within hail in an unguarded moment was captured and paroled on an errand to the Doctor Wily experimental station. The ballet was now in the midst of a musical vagary, and danced upon the stage programmed as Bolivian peasants, clothed in some portions of its anatomy as Norwegian fisher maidens, in others as ladies-in-waiting of Marie Antoinette, historically denuded in other portions so as to represent sea nymphs, and presenting the *tout ensemble* of a social club of Central Park West housemaids at a fish fry.

"Been in the city long?" inquired the New Yorker, getting ready the exact tip against the waiter's coming with large change from the bill.

"Me?" said the man from Topaz City. "Four days. Never in Topaz City, was you?"

"I!" said the New Yorker. "I was never farther west than Eighth Avenue. I had a brother who died on Ninth, but I met the cortège at Eighth. There was a bunch of violets on the hearse, and the undertaker mentioned the incident to avoid mistake. I cannot say that I am familiar with the West."

"Topaz City," said the man who occupied four chairs, "is one of the finest towns in the world."

"I presume that you have seen the sights of the metropolis," said the New Yorker. "Four days is not a sufficient length of time in which to view even our most salient points of interest, but one can possibly form a general impression. Our architectural supremacy is what generally strikes visitors to our city most forcibly. Of course you have seen our Flatiron Building. It is considered——"

"Saw it," said the man from Topaz City. "But you ought to come out our way. It's mountainous, you know, and the ladies all wear short skirts for climbing and——"

"Excuse me," said the New Yorker, "but that isn't exactly the point. New York must be a wonderful revelation to a visitor from the West. Now, as to our hotels——"

"Say," said the man from Topaz City, "that reminds me—there were sixteen stage robbers shot last year within twenty miles of——"

"I was speaking of hotels," said the New Yorker. "We lead Europe in that respect. And as far as our leisure class is concerned we are far——"

"Oh, I don't know," interrupted the man from Topaz City. "There were twelve tramps in our jail when I left home. I guess New York isn't so——"

"Beg pardon, you seem to misapprehend the idea. Of course, you visited the Stock Exchange and Wall Street, where the——"

"Oh, yes," said the man from Topaz City, as he lighted a Pennsylvania stogie, "and I want to tell you that we've got the finest town marshal west of the Rockies. Bill Rainer he took in five pickpockets out of the crowd when Red Nose Thompson laid the corner-stone of his new saloon. Topaz City don't allow——"

"Have another Rhine wine and seltzer," suggested the New Yorker. "I've never been West, as I said; but there can't be any place out there to compare with New York. As to the claims of Chicago I——"

"One man," said the Topazite—"one man only has been murdered and robbed in Topaz City in the last three——"

"Oh, I know what Chicago is," interposed the New Yorker. "Have you been up Fifth Avenue to see the magnificent residences of our mil——"

"Seen 'em all. You ought to know Reub Stegall, the assessor of Topaz. When old man Tilbury, that owns the only two-story house in town, tried to swear his taxes from $6,000 down to $450.75, Reub buckled on his forty-five and went down to see——"

"Yes, yes, but speaking of our great city—one of its greatest features is our superb police department. There is no body of men in the world that can equal it for——"

"That waiter gets around like a Langley flying machine," remarked the man from Topaz City, thirstily. "We've got men in our town, too, worth $400,000. There's old Bill Withers and Colonel Metcalf and——"

"Have you seen Broadway at night?" asked the New Yorker, courteously. "There are few streets in the world that can compare with it. When the electrics are shining and the pavements are alive with two hurrying streams of elegantly clothed men and beautiful women attired in the costliest costumes that wind in and out in a close maze of expensively——"

"Never knew but one case in Topaz City," said the man from the West. "Jim Bailey, our mayor, had his watch and chain and $235 in cash taken from his pocket while——"

"That's another matter," said the New Yorker. "While you are in our city you should avail yourself of every opportunity to see its wonders. Our rapid transit system——"

"If you was out in Topaz," broke in the man from there, "I could show you a whole cemetery full of people that got killed accidentally. Talking about mangling folks up! why, when Berry Rogers turned loose that old double-barrelled shot-gun of his loaded with slugs at anybody——"

"Here, waiter!" called the New Yorker. "Two more of the same. It is acknowledged by every one that our city is the centre of art, and literature, and learning. Take, for instance, our after-dinner speakers. Where else in the country would you find such wit and eloquence as emanate from Depew and Ford, and——"

"If you take the papers," interrupted the Westerner, "you must have read of Pete Webster's daughter. The Websters live two blocks north of the courthouse in Topaz City. Miss Tillie Webster, she slept forty days and nights without waking up. The doctors said that——"

"Pass the matches, please," said the New Yorker. "Have you observed the expedition with which new buildings are being run up in New York? Improved inventions in steel framework and——"

"I noticed," said the Nevadian, "that the statistics of Topaz City showed only one carpenter crushed by falling timbers last year and he was caught in a cyclone."

"They abuse our sky line," continued the New Yorker, "and it is likely that we are not yet artistic in the construction of our buildings. But I can safely assert that we lead in pictorial and decorative art. In some of our houses can be found masterpieces in the way of paintings and sculpture. One who has the entrée to our best galleries will find——"

"Back up," exclaimed the man from Topaz City. "There was a game last month in our town in which $90,000 changed hands on a pair of——"

"Ta-romt-tara!" went the orchestra. The stage curtain, blushing pink at the name "Asbestos" inscribed upon it, came down with a slow midsummer movement. The audience trickled leisurely down the elevator and stairs.

On the sidewalk below, the New Yorker and the man from Topaz City shook hands with alcoholic gravity. The elevated crashed raucously, surface cars hummed and clanged, cabmen swore, newsboys shrieked, wheels clattered ear-piercingly. The New Yorker conceived a happy thought, with which he aspired to clinch the pre-eminence of his city.

"You must admit," said he, "that in the way of noise New York is far ahead of any other——"

"Back to the everglades!" said the man from Topaz City. "In 1900, when Sousa's band and the repeating candidate were in our town you couldn't——"

The rattle of an express wagon drowned the rest of the words.

HOLDING UP A TRAIN

NOTE. The man who told me these things was for several years an outlaw in the Southwest and a follower of the pursuit he so frankly describes. His description of the *modus operandi* should prove interesting, his counsel of value to the potential passenger in some future "hold-up," while his estimate of the pleasures of train robbing will hardly induce any one to adopt it as a profession. I give the story in almost exactly his own words. O. H.

Most people would say, if their opinion was asked for, that holding up a train would be a hard job. Well, it isn't; it's easy. I have contributed some to the uneasiness of railroads and the insomnia of express companies, and the most trouble I ever had about a hold-up was in being swindled by unscrupulous people while spending the money I got. The danger wasn't anything to speak of, and we didn't mind the trouble.

One man has come pretty near robbing a train by himself; two have succeeded a few times; three can do it if they are hustlers, but five is about the right number. The time to do it and the place depend upon several things.

The first "stick-up" I was ever in happened in 1890. Maybe the way I got into it will explain how most train robbers start in the business. Five out of six Western outlaws are just cowboys out of a job and gone wrong. The sixth is a tough from the East who dresses up like a bad man and plays some low-down trick that gives the boys a bad name. Wire fences and "nesters" made five of them; a bad heart made the sixth.

Jim S—— and I were working on the 101 Ranch in Colorado. The nesters had the cowman on the go. They had taken up the land and elected officers who were hard to get along with. Jim and I rode into La Junta one day, going south from a round-up. We were having a little fun without malice toward anybody when a farmer administration cut in and tried to harvest us. Jim shot a deputy marshal, and I kind of corroborated his side of the argument. We skirmished up and down the main street, the boomers having bad luck all the time. After a while we leaned forward and shoved for the ranch down on the Ceriso. We were riding a couple of horses that couldn't fly, but they could catch birds.

A few days after that, a gang of the La Junta boomers came to the ranch and wanted us to go back with them. Naturally, we declined. We had the house on them, and before we were done refusing, that old 'dobe was plumb full of lead. When dark came we fagged 'em a batch of bullets and shoved out the back door for the rocks. They sure smoked us as we went. We had to drift, which we did, and rounded up down in Oklahoma.

Well, there wasn't anything we could get there, and, being mighty hard up, we decided to transact a little business with the railroads. Jim and I joined forces with Tom and Ike Moore—two brothers who had plenty of sand they were willing to convert into dust. I can call their names, for both of them are dead. Tom was shot while robbing a bank in Arkansas; Ike was killed during the more dangerous pastime of attending a dance in the Creek Nation.

We selected a place on the Santa Fé where there was a bridge across a deep creek surrounded by heavy timber. All passenger trains took water at the tank close to one end of the bridge. It was a quiet place, the nearest house being five miles away. The day before it happened, we rested our horses and "made medicine" as to how we should get about it. Our plans were not at all elaborate, as none of us had ever engaged in a hold-up before.

The Santa Fé flyer was due at the tank at 11:15 P.M. At eleven, Tom and I lay down on one side of the track, and Jim and Ike took the other. As the train rolled up, the headlight flashing far down the track and the steam hissing from the engine, I turned weak all over. I would have worked a whole year on the ranch for nothing to have been out of that affair right then. Some of the nerviest men in the business have told me that they felt the same way the first time.

The engine had hardly stopped when I jumped on the running-board on one side, while Jim mounted the other. As soon as the engineer and fireman saw our guns they threw up their hands without being told, and begged us not to shoot, saying they would do anything we wanted them to.

"Hit the ground," I ordered, and they both jumped off. We drove them before us down the side of the train. While this was happening, Tom and Ike had been blazing away, one on each side of the train, yelling like Apaches, so as to keep the passengers herded in the cars. Some fellow stuck a little twenty-two calibre out one of the coach windows and fired it straight up in the air. I let drive and smashed the glass just over his head. That settled everything like resistance from that direction.

By this time all my nervousness was gone. I felt a kind of pleasant excitement as if I were at a dance or a frolic of some sort. The lights were all out in the coaches, and, as Tom and Ike gradually quit firing and yelling, it got to be almost as still as a graveyard. I remember hearing a little bird chirping in a bush at the side of the track, as if it were complaining at being waked up.

I made the fireman get a lantern, and then I went to the express car and yelled to the messenger to open up or get perforated. He slid the door open and stood in it with his hands up. "Jump overboard, son," I said, and he hit the dirt like a lump of lead. There were two safes in the car—a big one and a little one. By the way, I first located the messenger's arsenal —a double-barrelled shot-gun with buckshot cartridges and a thirty-eight in a drawer. I drew the cartridges from the shot-gun, pocketed the pistol, and called the messenger inside. I shoved my gun against his nose and put him to work. He couldn't open the big one, but he did the little one. There was only nine hundred dollars in it. That was mighty small winnings for our trouble, so we decided to go through the passengers. We took our prisoners to the smoking-car, and from there sent the engineer through the train to light up the coaches. Beginning with the first one, we placed a man at each door and ordered the passengers to stand between the seats with their hands up.

If you want to find out what cowards the majority of men are, all you have to do is rob a passenger train. I don't mean because they don't resist —I'll tell you later on why they can't do that—but it makes a man feel sorry for them the way they lose their heads. Big, burly drummers and farmers and ex-soldiers and high-collared dudes and sports that, a few moments before, were filling the car with noise and bragging, get so scared that their ears flop.

There were very few people in the day coaches at that time of night, so we made a slim haul until we got to the sleeper. The Pullman conductor met me at one door while Jim was going round to the other one. He very politely informed me that I could not go into that car, as it did not belong to the railroad company, and, besides, the passengers had already been greatly disturbed by the shouting and firing. Never in all my life have I met with a finer instance of official dignity and reliance upon the power of Mr. Pullman's great name. I jabbed my six-shooter so hard against Mr. Conductor's front that I afterward found one of his vest buttons so firmly wedged in the end of the barrel that I had to shoot it out. He just shut up like a weak-springed knife and rolled down the car steps.

I opened the door of the sleeper and stepped inside. A big, fat old man came wabbling up to me, puffing and blowing. He had one coat-sleeve on and was trying to put his vest on over that. I don't know who he thought I was.

"Young man, young man," says he, "you must keep cool and not get excited. Above everything, keep cool."

"I can't," says I. "Excitement's just eating me up." And then I let out a yell and turned loose my forty-five through the skylight.

That old man tried to dive into one of the lower berths, but a screech came out of it, and a bare foot that took him in the bread-basket and landed him on the floor. I saw Jim coming in the other door, and I hollered for everybody to climb out and line up.

They commenced to scramble down, and for a while we had a three-ringed circus. The men looked as frightened and tame as a lot of rabbits in a deep snow. They had on, on an average, about a quarter of a suit of clothes and one shoe apiece. One chap was sitting on the floor of the aisle, looking as if he were working a hard sum in arithmetic. He was trying, very solemn, to pull a lady's number two shoe on a number nine foot.

The ladies didn't stop to dress. They were so curious to see a real, live train robber, bless 'em, that they just wrapped blankets and sheets around themselves and came out, squeaky and fidgety looking. They always show more curiosity and sand than the men do.

We got them all lined up and pretty quiet, and I went through the bunch. I found very little on them—I mean in the way of valuables. One man in the line was a sight. He was one of those big, overgrown, solemn snoozers that sit on the platform at lectures and look wise. Before crawling out he had managed to put on his long, frocktailed coat and his high silk hat. The rest of him was nothing but pajamas and bunions. When I dug into that Prince Albert, I expected to drag out at least a block of gold mine stock or an armful of Government bonds, but all I found was a little boy's French harp about four inches long. What it was there for, I don't know. I felt a little mad because he had fooled me so. I stuck the harp up against his mouth.

"If you can't pay—play," I says.

"I can't play," says he.

"Then learn right off quick," says I, letting him smell the end of my gun-barrel.

He caught hold of the harp, turned red as a beet, and commenced to blow. He blew a dinky little tune I remembered hearing when I was a kid:

> Prettiest little gal in the country—oh!
> Mammy and Daddy told me so.

I made him keep on playing it all the time we were in the car. Now and then he'd get weak and off the key, and I'd turn my gun on him and ask what was the matter with that little gal, and whether he had any intention of going back on her, which would make him start up again like sixty. I think that old boy standing there in his silk hat and bare feet, playing his little French harp, was the funniest sight I ever saw. One little red-headed woman in the line broke out laughing at him. You could have heard her in the next car.

Then Jim held them steady while I searched the berths. I grappled around in those beds and filled a pillow-case with the strangest assortment of stuff you ever saw. Now and then I'd come across a little pop-gun pistol, just about right for plugging teeth with, which I'd throw out the window. When I finished with the collection, I dumped the pillow-case load in the middle of the aisle. There were a good many watches, bracelets, rings and pocket-books, with a sprinkling of false teeth, whiskey flasks, face-powder boxes, chocolate caramels, and heads of hair of various colors and lengths. There were also about a dozen ladies' stockings into which jewelry, watches, and rolls of bills had been stuffed and then wadded up tight and stuck under the mattresses. I offered to return what I called the "scalps," saying that we were not Indians on the warpath, but none of the ladies seemed to know to whom the hair belonged.

One of the women—and a good-looker she was—wrapped in a striped blanket saw me pick up one of the stockings that was pretty chunky and heavy about the toe and she snapped out:

"That's mine, sir. You're not in the business of robbing women, are you?"

Now, as this was our first hold-up, we hadn't agreed upon any code of ethics, so I hardly knew what to answer. But, anyway, I replied: "Well, not as a specialty. If this contains your personal property you can have it back."

"It just does," she declared eagerly, and reached out her hand for it.

"You'll excuse my taking a look at the contents," I said, holding the stocking up by the toe. Out dumped a big gent's gold watch, worth two hundred, a gent's leather pocket-book, that we afterward found to contain six hundred dollars, a 32-calibre revolver and the only thing of the lot that could have been a lady's personal property was a silver bracelet worth about fifty cents.

I said: "Madame, here's your property," and handed her the bracelet. "Now," I went on, "how can you expect us to act square with you when you try to deceive us in this manner? I'm surprised at such conduct."

The young woman flushed up as if she had been caught doing something dishonest. Some other woman down the line called out: "The mean thing!" I never knew whether she meant the other lady or me.

When we finished our job we ordered everybody back to bed, told 'em good-night very politely at the door, and left. We rode forty miles before daylight and then divided the stuff. Each one of us got $1,752.85 in money. We lumped the jewelry around. Then we scattered, each man for himself.

That was my first train robbery, and it was about as easily done as any of the ones that followed. But that was the last and only time I ever went through the passengers. I don't like that part of the business. Afterward I stuck strictly to the express car. During the next eight years I handled a good deal of money.

The best haul I made was just seven years after the first one. We found out about a train that was going to bring out a lot of money to pay off the soldiers at a government post. We stuck that train up in broad daylight. Five of us lay in the sandhills near a little station. Ten soldiers were guarding the money on the train, but they might just as well have been at home on a furlough. We didn't even allow them to stick their heads out the windows to see the fun. We had no trouble at all in getting the money, which was all in gold. Of course, a big howl was raised at the time about the robbery. It was government stuff, and the Government got sarcastic and wanted to know what the convoy of soldiers went along for. The only excuse given was that nobody was expecting an attack among those bare sandhills in daytime. I don't know what the Government thought about the excuse, but I know that it was a good one. The surprise—that is the keynote of the train-robbing business. The papers published all kinds of stories about the loss, finally agreeing that it was between nine thousand and ten thousand dollars. The Government sawed wood. Here are the correct figures, printed for the first time—forty-eight thousand dollars. If anybody will take the trouble to look over Uncle Sam's private accounts for that little debit to profit and loss, he will find that I am right to a cent.

But that time we were expert enough to know what to do. We rode due west twenty miles, making a trail that a Broadway policeman could have followed, and then we doubled back, hiding our tracks. On the second night after the hold-up, while posses were scouring the country in every direction, Jim and I were eating supper in the second story of a friend's house in the town where the alarm started from. Our friend pointed out to us, in an office across the street, a printing press at work striking off handbills offering a reward for our capture.

I have been asked what we do with the money we get. Well, I never could account for a tenth part of it after it was spent. It goes fast and freely. An outlaw has to have a good many friends. A highly respected citizen may, and often does, get along with very few, but a man on the dodge has got to have "sidekickers." With angry posses and reward-hungry officers cutting out a hot trail for him, he must have a few places scattered about the country where he can stop and feed himself and his horse and get a few hours' sleep without having to keep both eyes open. When he makes a haul he feels like dropping some of the coin with these friends, and he does it liberally. Sometimes I have, at the end of a hasty visit at one of these havens of refuge, flung a handful of gold and bills into the laps of the kids playing on the floor, without knowing whether my contribution was a hundred dollars or a thousand.

When old-timers make a big haul they generally go far away to one of the big cities to spend their money. Green hands, however successful a hold-up they make, nearly always give themselves away by showing too much money near the place where they got it.

I was in a job in '94 where we got twenty thousand dollars. We followed our favorite plan for a get-away—that is, doubled on our trail—and laid low for a time near the scene of the train's bad luck. One morning I picked up a newspaper and read an article with big headlines stating that the marshal, with eight deputies and a posse of thirty armed citizens, had the train robbers surrounded in a mesquite thicket on the Cimarron, and that it was a question of only a few hours when they would be dead men or prisoners. While I was reading that article I was sitting at breakfast in one of the most elegant private residences in Washington City, with a flunky in knee pants standing behind my chair. Jim was sitting across the table talking to his half-uncle, a retired naval officer, whose name you have often seen in the accounts of doings in the capital. We had gone there and bought rattling outfits of good clothes, and were resting from our labors among the nabobs. We must have been killed in that mesquite thicket for I can make an affidavit that we didn't surrender.

Now I propose to tell why it is easy to hold up a train, and, then why no one should ever do it.

In the first place, the attacking party has all the advantage. That is, of course, supposing that they are old-timers with the necessary experience and courage. They have the outside and are protected by the darkness, while the others are in the light, hemmed into a small space, and exposed, the moment they show a head at a window or door, to the aim of a man who is a dead shot and who won't hesitate to shoot.

But, in my opinion, the main condition that makes train robbing easy is the element of *surprise* in connection with the imagination of the passengers. If you have ever seen a horse that has eaten loco weed you will understand what I mean when I say that the passengers get locoed. That horse gets the awfulest imagination on him in the world. You can't coax him to cross a little branch stream two feet wide. It looks as big to him as the Mississippi River. That's just the way with the passenger. He thinks there are a hundred men yelling and shooting outside, when maybe there are only two or three. And the muzzle of a forty-five looks like the entrance to a tunnel. The passenger is all right, although he may do mean little tricks, like hiding a wad of money in his shoe and forgetting to dig-up until you jostle his ribs some with the end of your six-shooter; but there's no harm in him.

As to the train crew, we never had any more trouble with them than if they had been so many sheep. I don't mean that they are cowards; I mean that they have got sense. They know they're not up against a bluff. It's the same way with the officers. I've seen secret service men, marshals, and railroad detectives fork over their change as meek as Moses. I saw one of the bravest marshals I ever knew hide his gun under his seat and dig up along with the rest while I was taking toll. He wasn't afraid; he simply knew that we had the drop on the whole outfit. Besides, many of those officers have families and they feel that they oughtn't to take chances; whereas death has no terrors for the man who holds up a train. He expects to get killed some day, and he generally does. My advice to you, if you should ever be in a hold-up, is to line up with the cowards and save your bravery for an occasion when it may be of some benefit to you. Another reason why officers are backward about mixing things with a train robber is a financial one. Every time there is a scrimmage and somebody gets killed, the officers lose money. If the train robber gets away they swear out a warrant against John Doe *et al.* and travel hundreds of miles and sign vouchers for thousands on the trail of the fugitives, and the Government foots the bills. So, with them, it is a question of mileage rather than courage.

I will give one instance to support my statement that the surprise is the best card in playing for a hold-up.

Along in '92 the Daltons were cutting out a hot trail for the officers down in the Cherokee Nation. Those were their lucky days, and they got so reckless and sandy, that they used to announce beforehand what job they were going to undertake. Once they gave it out that they were going to hold up the M. K. & T. flyer on a certain night at the station of Pryor Creek, in Indian Territory.

That night the railroad company got fifteen deputy marshals in Muscogee and put them on the train. Besides them they had fifty armed men hid in the depot at Pryor Creek.

When the Katy Flyer pulled in not a Dalton showed up. The next station was Adair, six miles away. When the train reached there, and the deputies were having a good time explaining what they would have done to the Dalton gang if they had turned up, all at once it sounded like an army firing outside. The conductor and brakeman came running into the car yelling, "Train robbers!"

Some of those deputies lit out of the door, hit the ground, and kept on running. Some of them hid their Winchesters under the seats. Two of them made a fight and were both killed.

It took the Daltons just ten minutes to capture the train and whip the escort. In twenty minutes more they robbed the express car of twenty-seven thousand dollars and made a clean get-away.

My opinion is that those deputies would have put up a stiff fight at Pryor Creek, where they were expecting trouble, but they were taken by surprise and "locoed" at Adair, just as the Daltons, who knew their business, expected they would.

I don't think I ought to close without giving some deductions from my experience of eight years "on the dodge." It doesn't pay to rob trains. Leaving out the question of right and morals, which I don't think I ought to tackle, there is very little envy in the life of an outlaw. After a while money ceases to have any value in his eyes. He gets to looking upon the railroads and express companies as his bankers, and his six-shooters as a cheque book good for any amount. He throws away money right and left. Most of the time he is on the jump, riding day and night, and he lives so hard between times that he doesn't enjoy the taste of high life when he gets it. He knows that his time is bound to come to lose his life or liberty, and that the accuracy of his aim, the speed of his horse, and the fidelity of his "sider," are all that postpone the inevitable.

It isn't that he loses any sleep over danger from the officers of the law. In all my experience I never knew officers to attack a band of outlaws unless they out-numbered them at least three to one.

But the outlaw carries one thought constantly in his mind—and that is what makes him so sore against life, more than anything else—he knows where the marshals get their recruits of deputies. He knows that the majority of these upholders of the law were once law-breakers, horse thieves, rustlers, highwaymen, and outlaws like himself, and that they gained their positions, and immunity by turning state's evidence, by turning traitor and delivering up their comrades to imprisonment and death. He knows that some day—unless he is shot first—his Judas will set to work, the trap will be laid, and he will be the surprised instead of a surpriser at a stick-up.

That is why the man who holds up trains picks his company with a thousand times the care with which a careful girl chooses a sweetheart. That is why he raises himself from his blankets of nights and listens to the tread of every horse's hoofs on the distant road. That is why he broods suspiciously for days upon a jesting remark or an unusual movement of a tired comrade, or the broken mutterings of his closest friend, sleeping by his side.

And it is one of the reasons why the train-robbing profession is not so pleasant a one as either of its collateral branches—politics or cornering the market.

ULYSSES AND THE DOGMAN

Do you know the time of the dogmen?

When the forefinger of twilight begins to smudge the clear-drawn lines of the Big City there is inaugurated an hour devoted to one of the most melancholy sights of urban life.

Out from the towering flat crags and apartment peaks of the cliff dwellers of New York steals an army of beings that were once men. Even yet they go upright upon two limbs and retain human form and speech; but you will observe that they are behind animals in progress. Each of these beings follows a dog, to which he is fastened by an artificial ligament.

These men are all victims to Circe. Not willingly do they become flunkeys to Fido, bell boys to bull terriers, and toddlers after Towzer. Modern Circe, instead of turning them into animals, has kindly left the difference of a six-foot leash between them. Every one of those dogmen has been either cajoled, bribed, or commanded by his own particular Circe to take the dear Household pet out for an airing.

By their faces and manner you can tell that the dogmen are bound in a hopeless enchantment. Never will there come even a dog-catcher Ulysses to remove the spell.

The faces of some are stonily set. They are past the commiseration, the curiosity, or the jeers of their fellow-beings. Years of matrimony, of continuous compulsory canine constitutionals, have made them callous. They unwind their beasts from lamp posts, or the ensnared legs of profane pedestrians, with the stolidity of mandarins manipulating the strings of their kites.

Others, more recently reduced to the ranks of Rover's retinue, take their medicine sulkily and fiercely. They play the dog on the end of their line with the pleasure felt by the girl out fishing when she catches a sea-robin on her hook. They glare at you threateningly if you look at them, as if it would be their delight to let slip the dogs of war. These are half-mutinous dogmen, not quite Circe-ized, and you will do well not to kick their charges, should they sniff around your ankles.

Others of the tribe do not seem to feel so keenly. They are mostly unfresh youths, with gold caps and drooping cigarettes, who do not harmonize with their dogs. The animals they attend wear satin bows in their collars; and the young men steer them so assiduously that you are tempted to the theory that some personal advantage, contingent upon satisfactory service, waits upon the execution of their duties.

The dogs thus personally conducted are of many varieties; but they are one in fatness, in pampered, diseased vileness of temper, in insolent, snarling capriciousness of behavior. They tug at the leash fractiously, they make leisurely nasal inventory of every door step, railing, and post. They sit down to rest when they choose; they wheeze like the winner of a Third Avenue beefsteak-eating contest; they bunder clumsily into open cellars and coal holes; they lead the dogmen a merry dance.

These unfortunate dry nurses of dogdom, the cur cuddlers, mongrel managers, Spitz stalkers, poodle pullers. Skye scrapers, dachshund dandlers, terrier trailers, and Pomeranian pushers of the cliff-dwelling Circes follow their charges meekly. The doggies neither fear nor respect them. Masters of the house these men whom they hold in leash may be, but they are not masters of them. From cosy corner to fire escape, from divan to dumbwaiter, doggy's snarl easily drives this two-legged being who is commissioned to walk at the other end of his string during his outing.

One twilight the dogmen came forth as usual at their Circes' pleading, guerdon, or crack of the whip. One among them was a strong man, apparently of too solid virtues for this airy vocation. His expression was melancholic, his manner depressed. He was leashed to a vile white dog, loathsomely fat, fiendishly ill-natured, gloatingly intractable toward his despised conductor.

At a corner nearest to his apartment house the dogman turned down a side street, hoping for fewer witnesses to his ignominy. The surfeited beast waddled before him, panting with spleen and the labor of motion.

Suddenly the dog stopped. A tall, brown, long-coated, wide-brimmed man stood like a Colossus blocking the sidewalk and declaring:

"Well, I'm a son of a gun!"

"Jim Berry!" breathed the dogman, with exclamation points in his voice.

"Sam Telfair," cried Wide-Brim again, "you ding-basted old willy walloo, give us your hoof!"

Their hands clasped in the brief, tight greeting of the West that is death to the handshake microbe.

"You old fat rascal!" continued Wide-Brim, with a wrinkled brown smile; "it's been five years since I seen you. I been in this town a week, but you can't find nobody in such a place. Well, you dinged old married man, how are they coming?"

Something mushy and heavily soft like raised dough leaned against Jim's leg and chewed his trousers with a yeasty growl.

"Get to work," said Jim, "and explain this yard-wide hydrophobia yearling you've throwed your lasso over. Are you the pound-master of this burg? Do you call that a dog or what?"

"I need a drink," said the dogman, dejected at the reminder of his old dog of the sea. "Come on."

Hard by was a café. 'Tis ever so in the big city.

They sat at a table, and the bloated monster yelped and scrambled at the end of his leash to get at the café cat.

"Whiskey," said Jim to the waiter.

"Make it two," said the dogman.

"You're fatter," said Jim, "and you look subjugated. I don't know about the East agreeing with you. All the boys asked me to hunt you up when I started. Sandy King, he went to the Klondike. Watson Burrel, he married the oldest Peters girl. I made some money buying beeves, and I bought a lot of wild land up on the Little Powder. Going to fence next fall. Bill Rawlins, he's gone to farming. You remember Bill, of course—he was courting Marcella—excuse me, Sam—I mean the lady you married, while she was teaching school at Prairie View. But you was the lucky man. How is Missis Telfair?"

"S-h-h-h!" said the dogman, signalling the waiter; "give it a name."

"Whiskey," said Jim.

"Make it two," said the dogman.

"She's well," he continued, after his chaser. "She refused to live anywhere but in New York, where she came from. We live in a flat. Every evening at six I take that dog out for a walk. It's Marcella's pet. There never were two animals on earth, Jim, that hated one another like me and that dog does. His name's Lovekins. Marcella dresses for dinner while we're out. We eat tabble dote. Ever try one of them, Jim?"

"No, I never," said Jim. "I seen the signs, but I thought they said 'table de hole.' I thought it was French for pool tables. How does it taste?"

"If you're going to be in the city for awhile we will——"

"No, sir-ee. I'm starting for home this evening on the 7:25. Like to stay longer, but I can't."

"I'll walk down to the ferry with you," said the dogman.

The dog had bound a leg each of Jim and the chair together, and had sunk into a comatose slumber. Jim stumbled, and the leash was slightly wrenched. The shrieks of the awakened beast rang for a block around.

"If that's your dog," said Jim, when they were on the street again, "what's to hinder you from running that habeas corpus you've got around his neck over a limb and walking off and forgetting him?"

"I'd never dare to," said the dogman, awed at the bold proposition. "He sleeps in the bed. I sleep on a lounge. He runs howling to Marcella if I look at him. Some night, Jim, I'm going to get even with that dog. I've made up my mind to do it. I'm going to creep over with a knife and cut a hole in his mosquito bar so they can get in to him. See if I don't do it!"

"You ain't yourself, Sam Telfair. You ain't what you was once. I don't know about these cities and flats over here. With my own eyes I seen you stand off both the Tillotson boys in Prairie View with the brass faucet out of a molasses barrel. And I seen you rope and tie the wildest steer on Little Powder in 39 1-2."

"I did, didn't I?" said the other, with a temporary gleam in his eye. "But that was before I was dogmatized."

"Does Missis Telfair——" began Jim.

"Hush!" said the dogman. "Here's another café."

They lined up at the bar. The dog fell asleep at their feet.

"Whiskey," said Jim.

"Make it two," said the dogman.

"I thought about you," said Jim, "when I bought that wild land. I wished you was out there to help me with the stock."

"Last Tuesday," said the dogman, "he bit me on the ankle because I asked for cream in my coffee. He always gets the cream."

"You'd like Prairie View now," said Jim. "The boys from the round-ups for fifty miles around ride in there. One corner of my pasture is in sixteen miles of the town. There's a straight forty miles of wire on one side of it."

"You pass through the kitchen to get to the bedroom," said the dogman, "and you pass through the parlor to get to the bathroom, and you back out through the dining room to get into the bedroom so you can turn around and leave by the kitchen. And he snores and barks in his sleep, and I have to smoke in the park on account of his asthma."

"Don't Missis Telfair——" began Jim.

"Oh, shut up!" said the dogman. "What is it this time?"

"Whiskey," said Jim.

"Make it two," said the dogman.

"Well, I'll be racking along down toward the ferry," said the other.

"Come on, there, you mangy, turtle-backed, snake-headed, bench-legged, ton-and-a-half of soap-grease!" shouted the dogman, with a new note in his voice and a new hand on the leash. The dog scrambled after them, with an angry whine at such unusual language from his guardian.

At the foot of Twenty-third Street the dogman led the way through swinging doors.

"Last chance," said he. "Speak up."

"Whiskey," said Jim.

"Make it two," said the dogman.

"I don't know," said the ranchman, "where I'll find the man I want to take charge of the Little Powder outfit. I want somebody I know something about. Finest stretch of prairie and timber you ever squinted your eye over, Sam. Now if you was——"

"Speaking of hydrophobia," said the dogman, "the other night he chewed a piece out of my leg because I knocked a fly off of Marcella's arm. 'It ought to be cauterized,' says Marcella, and I was thinking so myself. I telephones for the doctor, and when he comes Marcella says to me: 'Help me hold the poor dear while the doctor fixes his mouth. Oh, I hope he got no virus on any of his toofies when he bit you.' Now what do you think of that?"

"Does Missis Telfair——" began Jim.

"Oh, drop it," said the dogman. "Come again!"

"Whiskey," said Jim.

"Make it two," said the dogman.

They walked on to the ferry. The ranchman stepped to the ticket window.

Suddenly the swift landing of three or four heavy kicks was heard, the air was rent by piercing canine shrieks, and a pained, outraged, lubberly, bow-legged pudding of a dog ran frenziedly up the street alone.

"Ticket to Denver," said Jim.

"Make it two," shouted the ex-dogman, reaching for his inside pocket.

THE CHAMPION OF THE WEATHER

If you should speak of the Kiowa Reservation to the average New Yorker he probably wouldn't know whether you were referring to a new political dodge at Albany or a leitmotif from "Parsifal." But out in the Kiowa Reservation advices have been received concerning the existence of New York.

A party of us were on a hunting trip in the Reservation. Bud Kingsbury, our guide, philosopher, and friend, was broiling antelope steaks in camp one night. One of the party, a pinkish-haired young man in a correct hunting costume, sauntered over to the fire to light a cigarette, and remarked carelessly to Bud:

"Nice night!"

"Why, yes," said Bud, "as nice as any night could be that ain't received the Broadway stamp of approval."

Now, the young man was from New York, but the rest of us wondered how Bud guessed it. So, when the steaks were done, we besought him to lay bare his system of ratiocination. And as Bud was something of a Territorial talking machine he made oration as follows:

"How did I know he was from New York? Well, I figured it out as soon as he sprung them two words on me. I was in New York myself a couple of years ago, and I noticed some of the earmarks and hoof tracks of the Rancho Manhattan."

"Found New York rather different from the Panhandle, didn't you, Bud?" asked one of the hunters.

"Can't say that I did," answered Bud; "anyways, not more than some. The main trail in that town which they call Broadway is plenty traveled, but they're about the same brand of bipeds that tramp around in Cheyenne and Amarillo. At first I was sort of rattled by the crowds, but I soon says to myself, 'Here, now, Bud; they're just plain folks like you and Geronimo and Grover Cleveland and the Watson boys, so don't get all flustered up with consternation under your saddle blanket,' and then I feels calm and peaceful, like I was back in the Nation again at a ghost dance or a green corn pow-wow.

"I'd been saving up for a year to give this New York a whirl. I knew a man named Summers that lived there, but I couldn't find him; so I played a lone hand at enjoying the intoxicating pleasures of the corn-fed metropolis.

"For a while I was so frivolous and locoed by the electric lights and the noises of the phonographs and the second-story railroads that I forgot one of the crying needs of my Western system of natural requirements. I never was no hand to deny myself the pleasures of social vocal intercourse with friends and strangers. Out in the Territories when I meet a man I never saw before, inside of nine minutes I know his income, religion, size of collar, and his wife's temper, and how much he pays for clothes, alimony, and chewing tobacco. It's a gift with me not to be penurious with my conversation.

"But this here New York was inaugurated on the idea of abstemiousness in regard to the parts of speech. At the end of three weeks nobody in the city had fired even a blank syllable in my direction except the waiter in the grub emporium where I fed. And as his outpourings of syntax wasn't nothing but plagiarisms from the bill of fare, he never satisfied my yearnings, which was to have somebody hit. If I stood next to a man at a bar he'd edge off and give a Baldwin-Ziegler look as if he suspected me of having the North Pole concealed on my person. I began to wish that I'd gone to Abilene or Waco for my *paseado;* for the mayor of them places will drink with you, and the first citizen you meet will tell you his middle name and ask you to take a chance in a raffle for a music box.

"Well, one day when I was particular hankering for to be gregarious with something more loquacious than a lamp post, a fellow in a caffy says to me, says he:

" 'Nice day!'

"He was a kind of a manager of the place, and I reckon he'd seen me in there a good many times. He had a face like a fish and an eye like Judas, but I got up and put one arm around his neck.

" 'Pardner,' I says, 'sure it's a nice day. You're the first gentleman in all New York to observe that the intricacies of human speech might not be altogether wasted on William Kingsbury. But don't you think,' says I, 'that 'twas a little cool early in the morning; and ain't there a feeling of rain in the air tonight? But along about noon it sure was gallupsious weather. How's all up to the house? You doing right well with the caffy, now?'

"Well, sir, that galoot just turns his back and walks off stiff, without a word, after all my trying to be agreeable! I didn't know what to make of it. That night I finds a note from Summers, who'd been away from town, giving the address of his camp. I goes up to his house and has a good, old-time talk with his folks. And I tells Summers about the actions of this coyote in the caffy, and desires interpretation.

" 'Oh,' says Summers, 'he wasn't intending to strike up a conversation with you. That's just the New York style. He'd seen you was a regular customer and he spoke a word or two just to show you he appreciated your custom. You oughtn't to have followed it up. That's about as far as we care to go with a stranger. A word or so about the weather may be ventured, but we don't generally make it the basis of an acquaintance.'

" 'Billy,' says I, 'the weather and its ramifications is a solemn subject with me. Meteorology is one of my sore points. No man can open up the question of temperature or humidity or the glad sunshine with me, and then turn tail on it without its leading to a falling barometer. I'm going down to see that man again and give him a lesson in the art of continuous conversation. You say New York etiquette allows him two words and no answer. Well, he's going to turn himself into a weather bureau and finish what he begun with me, besides indulging in neighborly remarks on other subjects.'

"Summers talked agin it, but I was irritated some and I went on the street car backed to that caffy.

"The same fellow was there yet, walking round in a sort of black corral where there was tables and chairs. A few people was sitting around having drinks and sneering at one another.

"I called that man to one side and herded him into a corner. I unbuttoned enough to show him a thirty-eight I carried stuck under my vest.

" 'Pardner,' I says, 'a brief space ago I was in here and you seized the opportunity to say it was a nice day. When I attempted to corroborate your weather signal, you turned your back and walked off. Now,' says I, 'you frog-hearted, language-shy, stiff-necked cross between a Spitzbergen sea cook and a muzzled oyster, you resume where you left off in your discourse on the weather.'

"The fellow looks at me and tries to grin, but he sees I don't and he comes around serious.

" 'Well,' says he, eyeing the handle of my gun, 'it was rather a nice day; some warmish, though.'

" 'Particulars, you mealy-mouthed snoozer,' I says—'let's have the specifications—expatiate—fill in the outlines. When you start anything with me in shorthand it's bound to turn out a storm signal.'

" 'Looked like rain yesterday,' says the man, 'but it cleared off fine in the forenoon. I hear the farmers are needing rain right badly up-State.'

" 'That's the kind of a canter,' says I. 'Shake the New York dust off your hoofs and be a real agreeable kind of a centaur. You broke the ice, you know, and we're getting better acquainted every minute. Seems to me I asked you about your family?'

" 'They're all well, thanks,' says he. 'We—we have a new piano.'

" 'Now you're coming it,' I says. 'This cold reserve is breaking up at last. That little touch about the piano almost makes us brothers. What's the youngest kid's name?' I asks him.

" 'Thomas,' says he. 'He's just getting well from the measles.'

" 'I feel like I'd known you always,' says I. 'Now there was just one more—are you doing right well with the caffy, now?'

" 'Pretty well,' he says. 'I'm putting away a little money.'

" 'Glad to hear it,' says I. 'Now go back to your work and get civilized. Keep your hands off the weather unless you're ready to follow it up in a personal manner. It's a subject that naturally belongs to sociability and the forming of new ties, and I hate to see it handed out in small change in a town like this.'

"So the next day I rolls up my blankets and hits the trail away from New York City."

For many minutes after Bud ceased talking we lingered around the fire, and then all hands began to disperse for bed.

As I was unrolling my bedding I heard the pinkish-haired young man saying to Bud, with something like anxiety in his voice:

"As I say, Mr. Kingsbury, there is something really beautiful about this night. The delightful breeze and the bright stars and the clear air unite in making it wonderfully attractive."

"Yes," said Bud, "it's a nice night."

MAKES THE WHOLE WORLD KIN

The burglar stepped inside the window quickly, and then he took his time. A burglar who respects his art always takes his time before taking anything else.

The house was a private residence. By its boarded front door and untrimmed Boston ivy the burglar knew that the mistress of it was sitting on some oceanside piazza telling a sympathetic man in a yachting cap that no one had ever understood her sensitive, lonely heart. He knew by the light in the third-story front windows, and by the lateness of the season, that the master of the house had come home, and would soon extinguish his light and retire. For it was September of the year and of the soul, in which season the house's good man comes to consider roof gardens and stenographers as vanities, and to desire the return of his mate and the more durable blessings of decorum and the moral excellencies.

The burglar lighted a cigarette. The guarded glow of the match illuminated his salient points for a moment. He belonged to the third type of burglars.

This third type has not yet been recognized and accepted. The police have made us familiar with the first and second. Their classification is simple. The collar is the distinguishing mark.

When a burglar is caught who does not wear a collar he is described as a degenerate of the lowest type, singularly vicious and depraved, and is suspected of being the desperate criminal who stole the handcuffs out of Patrolman Hennessy's pocket in 1878 and walked away to escape arrest.

The other well-known type is the burglar who wears a collar. He is always referred to as a Raffles in real life. He is invariably a gentleman by daylight, breakfasting in a dress suit, and posing as a paperhanger, while after dark he plies his nefarious occupation of burglary. His mother is an extremely wealthy and respected resident of Ocean Grove, and when he is conducted to his cell he asks at once for a nail file and the *Police Gazette*. He always has a wife in every State in the Union and fiancées in all the Territories, and the newspapers print his matrimonial gallery out of their stock of cuts of the ladies who were cured by only one bottle after having been given up by five doctors, experiencing great relief after the first dose.

The burglar wore a blue sweater. He was neither a Raffles nor one of the chefs from Hell's Kitchen. The police would have been baffled had they attempted to classify him. They have not yet heard of the respectable, unassuming burglar who is neither above nor below his station.

This burglar of the third class began to prowl. He wore no masks, dark lanterns, or gum shoes. He carried a 38-calibre revolver in his pockets, and he chewed peppermint gum thoughtfully.

The furniture of the house was swathed in its summer dust protectors. The silver was far away in safe-deposit vaults. The burglar expected no remarkable "haul." His objective point was that dimly lighted room where the master of the house should be sleeping heavily after whatever solace he had sought to lighten the burden of his loneliness. A "touch" might be made there to the extent of legitimate, fair professional profits—loose money, a watch, a jeweled stick-pin—nothing exorbitant or beyond reason. He had seen the window left open and had taken the chance.

The burglar softly opened the door of the lighted room. The gas was turned low. A man lay in the bed asleep. On the dresser lay many things in confusion—a crumpled roll of bills, a watch, keys, three poker chips, crushed cigars, a pink silk hair bow, and an unopened bottle of bromo-seltzer for a bulwark in the morning.

The burglar took three steps toward the dresser. The man in the bed suddenly uttered a squeaky groan and opened his eyes. His right hand slid under his pillow, but remained there.

"Lay still," said the burglar in conversational tone. Burglars of the third type do not hiss. The citizen in the bed looked at the round end of the burglar's pistol and lay still.

"Now hold up both your hands," commanded the burglar.

The citizen had a little, pointed, brown-and-gray beard, like that of a painless dentist. He looked solid, esteemed, irritable, and disgusted. He sat up in bed and raised his right hand above his head.

"Up with the other one," ordered the burglar. "You might be amphibious and shoot with your left. You can count two, can't you? Hurry up, now."

"Can't raise the other one," said the citizen with a contortion of his lineaments.

"What's the matter with it?"

"Rheumatism in the shoulder."

"Inflammatory?"

"Was. The inflammation has gone down."

The burglar stood for a moment or two, holding his gun on the afflicted one. He glanced at the plunder on the dresser and then, with a half-embarrassed air back at the man in the bed. Then he, too, made a sudden grimace.

"Don't stand there making faces," snapped the citizen, bad-humoredly. "If you've come to burgle why don't you do it? There's some stuff lying around."

"'Scuse me," said the burglar, with a grin; "but it just socked me one, too. Its good for you that rheumatism and me happens to be old pals. I got it in my left arm, too. Most anybody but me would have popped you when you wouldn't hoist that left claw of yours."

"How long have you had it?" inquired the citizen.

"Four years. I guess that ain't all. Once you've got it, it's you for a rheumatic life—that's my judgment."

"Ever try rattlesnake oil?" asked the citizen interestedly.

"Gallons," said the burglar. "If all the snakes I've used the oil of was strung out in a row they'd reach eight times as far as Saturn, and the rattles could be heard at Valparaiso, Indiana, and back."

"Some use Chiselum's Pills," remarked the citizen.

"Fudge!" said the burglar. "Took 'em five months. No good. I had some relief the year I tried Finkelham's Extract, Balm of Gilead poultices, and Pott's Pain Pulverizer; but I think it was the buckeye I carried in my pocket what done the trick."

"Is yours worse in the morning or at night?" asked the citizen.

"Night," said the burglar; "just when I'm busiest. Say, take down that arm of your—I guess you won't—— Say! did you ever try Blickerstaff's Blood Builder?"

"I never did. Does yours come in paroxysms or is it a steady pain?"

The burglar sat down on the foot of the bed and rested his gun on his crossed knee.

"It jumps," said he. "It strikes me when I ain't looking for it. I had to give up second-story work because I got stuck sometimes half-way up. Tell you what—I don't believe the bloomin' doctors know what is good for it."

"Same here. I've spent a thousand dollars without getting any relief. Yours swell any?"

"Of mornings. And when it's goin' to rain—great Christopher!"

"Me, too," said the citizen. "I can tell when a streak of humidity the size of a tablecloth starts from Florida on its way to New York. And if I pass a theatre where there's an 'East Lynne' matinée going on, the moisture starts my left arm jumping like a toothache."

"It's undiluted—hades!" said the burglar.

"You're dead right," said the citizen.

The burglar looked down at his pistol and thrust it into his pocket with an awkward attempt at ease.

"Say, old man," he said, constrainedly, "ever try opodeldoc?"

"Slop!" said the citizen angrily. "Might as well rub on restaurant butter."

"Sure," concurred the burglar. "It's a salve suitable for little Minnie when the kitty scratches her finger. I'll tell you what! We're up against it. I only find one thing that eases her up. Hey? Little old sanitary, ameliorating, lest-we-forget Booze. Say—this job's off—'scuse me—get on your clothes and let's go out and have some. 'Scuse the liberty, but—ouch! There she goes again!"

"For a week," said the citizen, "I haven't been able to dress myself without help. I'm afraid Thomas is in bed, and——"

"Climb out," said the burglar, "I'll help you get into your duds."

The conventional returned as a tidal wave and flooded the citizen. He stroked his brown-and-gray beard.

"It's very unusual——" he began.

"Here's your shirt," said the burglar, "fall out. I know a man who said Omberry's Ointment fixed him in two weeks so he could use both hands in tying his four-in-hand."

As they were going out the door the citizen turned and started back.

"'Liked to forgot my money," he explained; "laid it on the dresser last night."

The burglar caught him by the right sleeve.

"Come on," he said, bluffly. "I ask you. Leave it alone. I've got the price. Ever try witch hazel and oil of wintergreen?"

AT ARMS WITH MORPHEUS

I never could quite understand how Tom Hopkins came to make that blunder, for he had been through a whole term at a medical college—before he inherited his aunt's fortune—and had been considered strong in therapeutics.

We had been making a call together that evening, and afterward Tom ran up to my rooms for a pipe and a chat before going on to his own luxurious apartments. I had stepped into the other room for a moment when I heard Tom sing out:

"Oh, Billy, I'm going to take about four grains of quinine, if you don't mind—I'm feeling all blue and shivery. Guess I'm taking cold."

"All right," I called back. "The bottle is on the second shelf. Take it in a spoonful of that elixir of eucalyptus. It knocks the bitter out."

After I came back we sat by the fire and got our briars going. In about eight minutes Tom sank back into a gentle collapse.

I went straight to the medicine cabinet and looked.

"You unmitigated hayseed!" I growled. "See what money will do for a man's brains!"

There stood the morphine bottle with the stopple out, just as Tom had left it.

I routed out another young M.D., who roomed on the floor above, and sent him for old Doctor Gales, two squares away. Tom Hopkins has too much money to be attended by rising young practitioners alone.

When Gales came we put Tom through as expensive a course of treatment as the resources of the profession permit. After the more drastic remedies we gave him citrate of caffeine in frequent doses and strong coffee, and walked him up and down the floor between two of us. Old Gales pinched him and slapped his face and worked hard for the big check he could see in the distance. The young M.D. from the next floor gave Tom a most hearty, rousing kick, and then apologized to me.

"Couldn't help it," he said. "I never kicked a millionaire before in my life. I may never have another opportunity."

"Now," said Doctor Gales, after a couple of hours, "he'll do. But keep him awake for another hour. You can do that by talking to him and shaking him up occasionally. When his pulse and respiration are normal then let him sleep. I'll leave him with you now."

I was left alone with Tom, whom we had laid on a couch. He lay very still, and his eyes were half closed. I began my work of keeping him awake.

"Well, old man," I said, "you've had a narrow squeak, but we've pulled you through. When you were attending lectures, Tom, didn't any of the professors ever casually remark that m-o-r-p-h-i-a never spells 'quinia,' especially in four-grain doses? But I won't pile it up on you until you get on your feet. But you ought to have been a druggist, Tom; you're splendidly qualified to fill prescriptions."

Tom looked at me with a faint and foolish smile.

"B'ly," he murmured, "I feel jus' like a hum'n bird flyin' around a jolly lot of most 'shpensive roses. Don' bozzer me. Goin' sleep now."

And he went to sleep in two seconds. I shook him by the shoulder.

"Now, Tom," I said, severely, "this won't do. The big doctor said you must stay awake for at least an hour. Open your eyes. You're not entirely safe yet, you know. Wake up."

Tom Hopkins weighs one hundred and ninety-eight. He gave me another somnolent grin, and fell into deeper slumber. I would have made him move about, but I might as well have tried to make Cleopatra's needle waltz around the room with me. Tom's breathing became stertorous, and that, in connection with morphia poisoning, means danger.

Then I began to think. I could not rouse his body; I must strive to excite his mind. "Make him angry," was an idea that suggested itself. "Good!" I thought; but how? There was not a joint in Tom's armor. Dear old fellow! He was good nature itself, and a gallant gentleman, fine and true and clean as sunlight. He came from somewhere down South, where they still have ideals and a code. New York had charmed but had not spoiled him. He had that old-fashioned, chivalrous reverence for women, that—Eureka!—there was my idea! I worked the thing up for a minute or two in my imagination. I chuckled to myself at the thought of springing a thing like that on old Tom Hopkins. Then I took him by the shoulder and shook him till his ears flopped. He opened his eyes lazily. I assumed an expression of scorn and contempt, and pointed my finger within two inches of his nose.

"Listen to me, Hopkins," I said, in cutting and distinct tones, "you and I have been good friends, but I want you to understand that in the future my doors are closed against any man who acts as much like a scoundrel as you have."

Tom looked the least bit interested.

"What's the matter, Billy?" he muttered, composedly. "Don't your clothes fit you?"

"If I were in your place," I went on, "which, thank God, I am not, I think I would be afraid to close my eyes. How about that girl you left waiting for you down among those lonesome Southern pines—the girl that you've forgotten since you came into your confounded money? Oh, I know what I'm talking about. While you were a poor medical student she was good enough for you. But now, since you are a millionaire, it's different. I wonder what she thinks of the performances of that peculiar class of people which she has been taught to worship—the Southern gentlemen? I'm sorry, Hopkins, that I was forced to speak about these matters, but you've covered it up so well and played your part so nicely that I would have sworn you were above such unmanly tricks."

Poor Tom. I could scarcely keep from laughing outright to see him struggling against the effects of the opiate. He was distinctly angry, and I didn't blame him. Tom had a Southern temper. His eyes were open now, and they showed a gleam or two of fire. But the drug still clouded his mind and bound his tongue.

"C-c-confound you," he stammered, "I'll s-smash you."

He tried to rise from the couch. With all his size he was very weak now. I thrust him back with one arm. He lay there glaring like a lion in a trap.

"That will hold you for a while, you old loony," I said to myself. I got up and lit my pipe, for I was needing a smoke. I walked around a bit, congratulating myself on my brilliant idea.

I heard a snore. I looked around. Tom was asleep again. I walked over and punched him on the jaw. He looked at me as pleasant and ungrudging as an idiot. I chewed my pipe and gave it to him hard.

"I want you to recover yourself and get out of my rooms as soon as you can," I said, insultingly. "I've told you what I think of you. If you have any honor or honesty left you will think twice before you attempt again to associate with gentlemen. She's a poor girl, isn't she?" I sneered. "Somewhat too plain and unfashionable for us since we got our money. Be ashamed to walk on Fifth Avenue with her, wouldn't you? Hopkins, you're forty-seven times worse than a cad. Who cares for your money? I don't. I'll bet that girl don't. Perhaps if you didn't have it you'd be more of a man. As it is you've made a cur of yourself, and"—I thought that quite dramatic—"perhaps broken a faithful heart." (Old Tom Hopkins breaking a faithful heart!) "Let me be rid of you as soon as possible."

I turned my back on Tom, and winked at myself in a mirror. I heard him moving, and I turned again quickly. I didn't want a hundred and ninety-eight pounds falling on me from the rear. But Tom had only turned partly over, and laid one arm across his face. He spoke a few words rather more distinctly than before.

"I couldn't have—talked this way—to you, Billy, even if I'd heard people —lyin' 'bout you. But jus' soon's I can s-stand up—I'll break your neck— don't f'get it."

I did feel a little ashamed then. But it was to save Tom. In the morning, when I explained it, we would have a good laugh over it together.

In about twenty minutes Tom dropped into a sound, easy slumber. I felt his pulse, listened to his respiration, and let him sleep. Everything was normal, and Tom was safe. I went into the other room and tumbled into bed.

I found Tom up and dressed when I awoke the next morning. He was entirely himself again with the exception of shaky nerves and a tongue like a white-oak chip.

"What an idiot I was," he said, thoughtfully. "I remember thinking that quinine bottle looked queer while I was taking the dose. Have much trouble in bringing me 'round?"

I told him no. His memory seemed bad about the entire affair. I concluded that he had no recollection of my efforts to keep him awake, and decided not to enlighten him. Some other time, I thought, when he was feeling better, we would have some fun over it.

When Tom was ready to go he stopped, with the door open, and shook my hand.

"Much obliged, old fellow," he said, quietly, "for taking so much trouble with me—and for what you said. I'm going down to telegraph to the little girl."

A GHOST OF A CHANCE

"Actually, a *hod!*" repeated Mrs. Kinsolving, pathetically.

Mrs. Bellamy Bellmore arched a sympathetic eyebrow. Thus she expressed condolence and a generous amount of apparent surprise.

"Fancy her telling everywhere," recapitulated Mrs. Kinsolving, "that she saw a ghost in the apartment she occupied here—our choicest guest-room—a ghost, carrying a hod on its shoulder—the ghost of an old man in overalls, smoking a pipe and carrying a hod! The very absurdity of the thing shows her malicious intent. There never was a Kinsolving that carried a hod. Every one knows that Mr. Kinsolving's father accumulated his money by large building contracts, but he never worked a day with his own hands. He had this house built from his own plans; but—oh, a hod! Why need she have been so cruel and malicious?"

"It is really too bad," murmured Mrs. Bellmore, with an approving glance of her fine eyes about the vast chamber done in lilac and old gold. "And it was in this room she saw it. Oh, no, I'm not afraid of ghosts. Don't have the least fear on my account. I'm glad you put me in here. I think family ghosts so interesting. But, really, the story does sound a little inconsistent. I should have expected something better from Mrs. Fischer-Suympkins. Don't they carry bricks in hods? Why should a ghost bring bricks into a villa built of marble and stone? I'm so sorry, but it makes me think that age is beginning to tell upon Mrs. Fischer-Suympkins."

"This house," continued Mrs. Kinsolving, "was built upon the site of an old one used by the family during the Revolution. There wouldn't be anything strange in its having a ghost. And there was a Captain Kinsolving who fought in General Greene's army, though we've never been able to secure any papers to vouch for it. If there is to be a family ghost, why couldn't it have been his, instead of a bricklayer's?"

"The ghost of a Revolutionary ancestor wouldn't be a bad idea," agreed Mrs. Bellmore; "but you know how arbitrary and inconsiderate ghosts can be. Maybe, like love, they are 'engendered in the eye.' One advantage of those who see ghosts is that their stories can't be disproved. By a spiteful eye, a Revolutionary knapsack might easily be construed to be a hod. Dear Mrs. Kinsolving, think no more of it. I am sure it was a knapsack."

"But she told everybody!" mourned Mrs. Kinsolving inconsolable. "She insisted upon the details. There is the pipe. And how are you going to get out of the overalls?"

"Sha'n't get into them," said Mrs. Bellmore, with a prettily suppressed yawn; "too stiff and wrinkly. Is that you, Felice? Prepare my bath, please. Do you dine at seven at Clifftop, Mrs. Kinsolving? So kind of you to run in for a chat before dinner! I love those little touches of informality with a guest. They give such a home flavor to a visit. So sorry; I must be dressing. I am so indolent I always postpone it until the last moment."

Mrs. Fischer-Suympkins had been the first large plum that the Kinsolvings had drawn from the social pie. For a long time, the pie itself had been out of reach on a top shelf. But the purse and the pursuit had at last lowered it. Mrs. Fischer-Suympkins was the heliograph of the smart society parading corps. The glitter of her wit and actions passed along the line, transmitting whatever was latest and most daring in the game of peep-show. Formerly, her fame and leadership had been secure enough not to need the support of such artifices as handing around live frogs for favors at a cotillion. But, now, these things were necessary to the holding of her throne. Besides, middle age had come to preside, incongruous, at her capers. The sensational papers had cut her space from a page to two columns. Her wit developed a sting; her manners became more rough and inconsiderate, as if she felt the royal necessity of establishing her autocracy by scorning the conventionalities that bound lesser potentates.

To some pressure at the command of the Kinsolvings, she had yielded so far as to honor their house by her presence, for an evening and night. She had her revenge upon her hostess by relating, with grim enjoyment and sarcastic humor, her story of the vision carrying the hod. To that lady, in raptures at having penetrated thus far toward the coveted inner circle, the result came as a crushing disappointment. Everybody either sympathized or laughed, and there was little to choose between the two modes of expression.

But, later on, Mrs. Kinsolving's hopes and spirits were revived by the capture of a second and greater prize.

Mrs. Bellamy Bellmore had accepted an invitation to visit at Clifftop, and would remain for three days. Mrs. Bellmore was one of the younger matrons, whose beauty, descent, and wealth gave her a reserved seat in the holy of holies that required no strenuous bolstering. She was generous enough thus to give Mrs. Kinsolving the accolade that was so poignantly desired; and, at the same time, she thought how much it would please Terence. Perhaps it would end by solving him.

Terence was Mrs. Kinsolving's son, aged twenty-nine, quite good-looking enough, and with two or three attractive and mysterious traits. For one, he was very devoted to his mother, and that was sufficiently odd to deserve notice. For others, he talked so little that it was irritating, and he seemed either very shy or very deep. Terence interested Mrs. Bellmore, because she was not sure which it was. She intended to study him a little longer unless she forgot the matter. If he was only shy, she would abandon him, for shyness is a bore. If he was deep, she would also abandon him, for depth is precarious.

On the afternoon of the third day of her visit, Terence hunted up Mrs. Bellmore, and found her in a nook actually looking at an album.

"It's so good of you," said he, "to come down here and retrieve the day for us. I suppose you have heard that Mrs. Fischer-Suympkins scuttled the ship before she left. She knocked a whole plank out of the bottom with a hod. My mother is grieving herself ill about it. Can't you manage to see a ghost for us while you are here, Mrs. Bellmore—a bang-up, swell ghost, with a coronet on his head and a cheque book under his arm?"

"That was a naughty old lady, Terence," said Mrs. Bellmore, "to tell such stories. Perhaps you gave her too much supper. Your mother doesn't really take it seriously, does she?"

"I think she does," answered Terence. "One would think every brick in the hod had dropped on her. It's a good mammy, and I don't like to see her worried. It's to be hoped that the ghost belongs to the hod-carriers' union, and will go out on a strike. If he doesn't there will be no peace in this family."

"I'm sleeping in the ghost-chamber," said Mrs. Bellmore, pensively. "But it's so nice I wouldn't change it, even if I were afraid, which I'm not. It wouldn't do for me to submit a counter story of a desirable, aristocratic shade, would it? I would do so, with pleasure, but it seems to me that it would be too obviously an antidote for the other narrative to be effective."

"True," said Terence, running two fingers thoughtfully into his crisp brown hair; "that would never do. How would it work to see the same ghost again, minus the overalls, and have gold bricks in the hod? That would elevate the spectre from degrading toil to a financial plane. Don't you think that would be respectable enough?"

"There was an ancestor who fought against the Britishers, wasn't there? Your mother said something to that effect."

"I believe so; one of those old chaps in raglan vests and golf trousers. I don't care a continental for a Continental, myself. But the mother has set her heart on pomp and heraldry and pyrotechnics, and I want her to be happy."

"You are a good boy, Terence," said Mrs. Bellmore, sweeping her silks close to one side of her; "not to beat your mother. Sit here by me, and let's look at the album, just as people used to do twenty years ago. Now, tell me about every one of them. Who is this tall, dignified gentleman leaning against the horizon, with one arm on the Corinthian column?"

"That old chap with the big feet?" inquired Terence, craning his neck. "That's great-uncle O'Brannigan. He used to keep a rathskeller on the Bowery."

"I asked you to sit down, Terence. If you are not going to amuse, or obey me, I shall report in the morning that I saw a ghost wearing an apron and carrying schooners of beer. Now, that is better. To be shy, at your age, Terence, is a thing that you should blush to acknowledge."

At breakfast on the last morning of her visit, Mrs. Bellmore startled and entranced every one present by announcing positively that she had seen the ghost.

"Did it have a—a—a——?" Mrs. Kinsolving, in her suspense and agitation, could not bring out the word.

"No, indeed—far from it."

There was a chorus of questions from others at the table. "Weren't you frightened?" "What did it do?" "How did it look?" "How was it dressed?" "Did it say anything?" "Didn't you scream?"

"I'll try to answer everything at once," said Mrs. Bellmore, heroically, "although I'm frightfully hungry. Something awakened me—I'm not sure whether it was a noise or a touch—and there stood the phantom. I never burn a light at night, so the room was quite dark, but I saw it plainly. I wasn't dreaming. It was a tall man all misty white from head to foot. It wore the full dress of the old Colonial days—powdered hair, baggy coat skirts, lace ruffles, and a sword. It looked intangible and luminous in the dark, and moved without a sound. Yes, I was a little frightened at first —or startled, I should say. It was the first ghost I had ever seen. No, it didn't say anything. I didn't scream. I raised up on my elbow, and then it glided silently away, and disappeared when it reached the door."

Mrs. Kinsolving was in the seventh heaven. "The description is that of Captain Kinsolving, of General Greene's army, one of our ancestors," she said, in a voice that trembled with pride and relief. "I really think I must apologize for our ghostly relative, Mrs. Bellmore. I am afraid he must have badly disturbed your rest."

Terence sent a smile of pleased congratulation toward his mother. Attainment was Mrs. Kinsolving's, at last, and he loved to see her happy.

"I suppose I ought to be ashamed to confess," said Mrs. Bellmore, who was now enjoying her breakfast, "that I wasn't very much disturbed. I presume it would have been the customary thing to scream and faint, and have all of you running about in picturesque costumes. But, after the first alarm was over, I really couldn't work myself up to a panic. The ghost retired from the stage quietly and peacefully, after doing its little turn, and I went to sleep again."

Nearly all listened, politely accepted Mrs. Bellmore's story as a made-up affair, charitably offered as an offset to the unkind vision seen by Mrs. Fischer-Suympkins. But one or two present perceived that her assertions bore the genuine stamp of her own convictions. Truth and candor seemed to attend upon every word. Even a scoffer at ghosts—if he were very observant—would have been forced to admit that she had, at least in a very vivid dream, been honestly aware of the weird visitor.

Soon Mrs. Bellmore's maid was packing. In two hours the auto would come to convey her to the station. As Terence was strolling upon the east piazza, Mrs. Bellmore came up to him, with a confidential sparkle in her eye.

"I didn't wish to tell the others all of it," she said, "but I will tell you. In a way, I think you should be held responsible. Can you guess in what manner that ghost awakened me last night?"

"Rattled chains," suggested Terence, after some thought, "or groaned? They usually do one or the other."

"Do you happen to know," continued Mrs. Bellmore, with sudden irrelevancy, "if I resemble any one of the female relatives of your restless ancestor, Captain Kinsolving?"

"Don't think so," said Terence, with an extremely puzzled air. "Never heard of any of them being noted beauties."

"Then, why," said Mrs. Bellmore, looking the young man gravely in the eye, "should that ghost have kissed me, as I'm sure it did?"

"Heavens!" exclaimed Terence, in wide-eyed amazement; "you don't mean that, Mrs. Bellmore! Did he actually kiss you?"

"I said *it*," corrected Mrs. Bellmore. "I hope the impersonal pronoun is correctly used."

"But why did you say I was responsible?"

"Because you are the only living male relative of the ghost."

"I see. 'Unto the third and fourth generation.' But, seriously, did he—did it—how do you——?"

"Know? How does any one know? I was asleep, and that is what awakened me, I'm almost certain."

"Almost?"

"Well, I awoke just as—oh, can't you understand what I mean? When anything arouses you suddenly you are not positive whether you dreamed, or—and yet you know that—— Dear me. Terence, must I dissect the most elementary sensations in order to accommodate your extremely practical intelligence?"

"But, about kissing ghosts, you know," said Terence, humbly, "I require the most primary instruction. I never kissed a ghost. Is it—is it——?"

"The sensation," said Mrs. Bellmore, with deliberate, but slightly smiling, emphasis, "since you are seeking instruction, is a mingling of the material and the spiritual."

"Of course," said Terence, suddenly growing serious, "it was a dream or some kind of an hallucination. Nobody believes in spirits, these days. If you told the tale out of kindness of heart, Mrs. Bellmore, I can't express how grateful I am to you. It has made my mother supremely happy. That Revolutionary ancestor was a stunning idea."

Mrs. Bellmore sighed. "The usual fate of ghost-seers is mine," she said, resignedly. "My privileged encounter with a spirit is attributed to lobster salad or mendacity. Well, I have, at least, one memory left from the wreck—a kiss from the unseen world. Was Captain Kinsolving a very brave man, do you know, Terence?"

"He was licked at Yorktown, I believe," said Terence, reflecting. "They say he skedaddled with his company, after the first battle there."

"I thought he must have been timid," said Mrs. Bellmore, absently. "He might have had another."

"Another battle?" asked Terence, dully.

"What else could I mean? I must go and get ready now; the auto will be here in an hour. I've enjoyed Clifftop immensely. Such a lovely morning, isn't it, Terence?"

On her way to the station, Mrs. Bellmore took from her bag a silk handkerchief, and looked at it with a little peculiar smile. Then she tied it in several very hard knots, and threw it, at a convenient moment, over the edge of the cliff along which the road ran.

In his room, Terence was giving some directions to his man, Brooks. "Have this stuff done up in a parcel," he said, "and ship it to the address on that card."

The card was that of a New York costumer. The "stuff" was a gentleman's costume of the days of '76, made of white satin, with silver buckles, white silk stockings, and white kid shoes. A powdered wig and a sword completed the dress.

"And look about, Brooks," added Terence, a little anxiously, "for a silk handkerchief with my initials in one corner. I must have dropped it somewhere."

It was a month later when Mrs. Bellmore and one or two others of the smart crowd were making up a list of names for a coaching trip through the Catskills. Mrs. Bellmore looked over the list for a final censoring. The name of Terence Kinsolving was there. Mrs. Bellmore ran her prohibitive pencil lightly through the name.

"Too shy!" she murmured, sweetly, in explanation.

JIMMY HAYES AND MURIEL

Supper was over, and there had fallen upon the camp the silence that accompanies the rolling of corn-husk cigarettes. The water hole shone from the dark earth like a patch of fallen sky. Coyotes yelped. Dull thumps indicated the rocking-horse movements of the hobbled ponies as they moved to fresh grass. A half-troop of the Frontier Battalion of Texas Rangers were distributed about the fire.

A well-known sound—the fluttering and scraping of chaparral against wooden stirrups—came from the thick brush above the camp. The rangers listened cautiously. They heard a loud and cheerful voice call out re-assuringly:

"Brace up, Muriel, old girl, we're 'most there now! Been a long ride for ye, ain't it, ye old antediluvian handful of animated carpet-tacks? Hey, now, quit a tryin' to kiss me! Don't hold on to my neck so tight—this here paint hoss ain't any too shore-footed, let me tell ye. He's liable to dump us both off if we don't watch out."

Two minutes of waiting brought a tired "paint" pony single-footing into camp. A gangling youth of twenty lolled in the saddle. Of the "Muriel" whom he had been addressing, nothing was to be seen.

"Hi, fellows!" shouted the rider, cheerfully. "This here's a letter fer Lieutenant Manning."

He dismounted, unsaddled, dropped the coils of his stake-rope, and got his hobbles from the saddle-horn. While Lieutenant Manning, in command, was reading the letter, the newcomer rubbed solicitously at some dried mud in the loops of the hobbles, showing a consideration for the forelegs of his mount.

"Boys," said the lieutenant, waving his hand to the rangers, "this is Mr. James Hayes. He's a new member of the company. Captain McLean sends him down from El Paso. The boys will see that you have some supper, Hayes, as soon as you get your pony hobbled."

The recruit was received cordially by the rangers. Still, they observed him shrewdly and with suspended judgment. Picking a comrade on the border is done with ten times the care and discretion with which a girl chooses a sweetheart. On your "side-kicker's" nerve, loyalty, aim, and coolness your own life may depend many times.

After a hearty supper Hayes joined the smokers about the fire. His appearance did not settle all the questions in the minds of his brother rangers. They saw simply a loose, lank youth with tow-colored sunburned hair and a berry-brown, ingenuous face that wore a quizzical, good-natured smile.

"Fellows," said the new ranger, "I'm goin' to interduce to you a lady friend of mine. Ain't ever heard anybody call her a beauty, but you'll all admit she's got some fine points about her. Come along, Muriel!"

He held open the front of his blue flannel shirt. Out of it crawled a horned frog. A bright red ribbon was tied jauntily around its spiky neck. It crawled to its owner's knee and sat there motionless.

"This here Muriel," said Hayes, with an oratorical wave of his hand, "has got qualities. She never talks back, she always stays at home, and she's satisfied with one red dress for every day and Sunday, too."

"Look at that blame insect!" said one of the rangers with a grin. "I've seen plenty of them horny frogs, but I never knew anybody to have one for a side-partner. Does the blame thing know you from anybody else?"

"Take it over there and see," said Hayes.

The stumpy little lizard known as the horned frog is harmless. He has the hideousness of the prehistoric monsters whose reduced descendant he is, but he is gentler than the dove.

The ranger took Muriel from Hayes's knee and went back to his seat on a roll of blankets. The captive twisted and clawed and struggled vigorously in his hand. After holding it for a moment or two, the ranger set it upon the ground. Awkwardly, but swiftly, the frog worked its four oddly moving legs until it stopped close by Hayes's foot.

"Well, dang my hide!" said the other ranger. "The little cuss knows you. Never thought them insects had that much sense!"

II   Jimmy Hayes became a favorite in the ranger camp. He had an endless store of good nature, and a mild, perennial quality of humor that is well adapted to camp life. He was never without his horned frog. In the bosom of his shirt during rides, on his knee or shoulder in camp, under his blankets at night, the ugly little beast never left him.

Jimmy was a humorist of a type that prevails in the rural South and West. Unskilled in originating methods of amusing or in witty conceptions, he had hit upon a comical idea and clung to it reverently. It had seemed to Jimmy a very funny thing to have about his person, with which to amuse his friends, a tame horned frog with a red ribbon around its neck. As it was a happy idea, why not perpetuate it?

The sentiments existing between Jimmy and the frog cannot be exactly determined. The capability of the horned frog for lasting affection is a subject upon which we have no symposiums. It is easier to guess Jimmy's feelings. Muriel was his *chef d'œuvre* of wit, and as such he cherished her. He caught flies for her, and shielded her from sudden northers. Yet his care was half selfish, and when the time came she repaid him a thousand fold. Other Muriels have thus overbalanced the light attentions of other Jimmies.

Not at once did Jimmy attain full brotherhood with his comrades. They loved him for his simplicity and drollness, but there hung above him a great sword of suspended judgment. To make merry in camp is not all of a ranger's life. There are horse-thieves to trail, desperate criminals to run down, bravos to battle with, bandits to rout out of the chaparral, peace and order to be compelled at the muzzle of a six-shooter. Jimmy had been " 'most generally a cow-puncher," he said; he was inexperienced in ranger methods of warfare. Therefore the rangers speculated apart and solemnly as to how he would stand fire. For, let it be known, the honor and pride of each ranger company is the individual bravery of its members.

For two months the border was quiet. The rangers lolled, listless, in camp. And then—bringing joy to the rusting guardians of the frontier —Sebastiano Saldar, an eminent Mexican desperado and cattle-thief, crossed the Rio Grande with his gang and began to lay waste the Texas side. There were indications that Jimmy Hayes would soon have the opportunity to show his mettle. The rangers patrolled with alacrity, but Saldar's men were mounted like Lochinvar, and were hard to catch.

One evening, about sundown, the rangers halted for supper after a long ride. Their horses stood panting, with their saddles on. The men were frying bacon and boiling coffee. Suddenly, out of the brush, Sebastiano Saldar and his gang dashed upon them with blazing six-shooters and high-voiced yells. It was a neat surprise. The rangers swore in annoyed tones, and got their Winchesters busy; but the attack was only a spectacular dash of the purest Mexican type. After the florid demonstration the raiders galloped away, yelling, down the river. The rangers mounted and pursued; but in less than two miles the fagged ponies labored so that Lieutenant Manning gave the word to abandon the chase and return to the camp.

Then it was discovered that Jimmy Hayes was missing. Some one remembered having seen him run for his pony when the attack began, but no one had set eyes on him since. Morning came, but no Jimmy. They searched the country around, on the theory that he had been killed or wounded, but without success. Then they followed after Saldar's gang, but it seemed to have disappeared. Manning concluded that the wily Mexican had recrossed the river after his theatric farewell. And, indeed, no further depredations from him were reported.

This gave the rangers time to nurse a soreness they had. As has been said, the pride and honor of the company is the individual bravery of its members. And now they believed that Jimmy Hayes had turned coward at the whiz of Mexican bullets. There was no other deduction. Buck Davis pointed out that not a shot was fired by Saldar's gang after Jimmy was seen running for his horse. There was no way for him to have been shot. No, he had fled from his first fight, and afterward he would not return, aware that the scorn of his comrades would be a worse thing to face than the muzzles of many rifles.

So Manning's detachment of McLean's company, Frontier Battalion, was gloomy. It was the first blot on its escutcheon. Never before in the history of the service had a ranger shown the white feather. All of them had liked Jimmy Hayes, and that made it worse.

Days, weeks, and months went by, and still that little cloud of unforgotten cowardice hung above the camp.

III Nearly a year afterward—after many camping grounds and many hundreds of miles guarded and defended—Lieutenant Manning, with almost the same detachment of men, was sent to a point only a few miles below their old camp on the river to look after some smuggling there. One afternoon, while they were riding through a dense mesquite flat, they came upon a patch of open hog-wallow prairie. There they rode upon the scene of an unwritten tragedy.

In a big hog-wallow lay the skeletons of three Mexicans. Their clothing alone served to identify them. The largest of the figures had once been Sebastiano Saldar. His great, costly sombrero, heavy with gold ornamentation—a hat famous all along the Rio Grande—lay there pierced by three bullets. Along the ridge of the hog-wallow rested the rusting Winchesters of the Mexicans—all pointing in the same direction.

The rangers rode in that direction for fifty yards. There, in a little depression of the ground, with his rifle still bearing upon the three, lay another skeleton. It had been a battle of extermination. There was nothing to identify the solitary defender. His clothing—such as the elements had left distinguishable—seemed to be of the kind that any ranchman or cowboy might have worn.

"Some cow-puncher," said Manning, "that they caught out alone. Good boy! He put up a dandy scrap before they got him. So that's why we didn't hear from Don Sebastiano any more!"

And then, from beneath the weather-beaten rags of the dead man, there wriggled out a horned frog with a faded red ribbon around its neck, and sat upon the shoulder of its long quiet master. Mutely it told the story of the untried youth and the swift "paint" pony—how they had outstripped all their comrades that day in the pursuit of the Mexican raiders, and how the boy had gone down upholding the honor of the company.

The ranger troop herded close, and a simultaneous wild yell arose from their lips. The outburst was at once a dirge, an apology, an epitaph, and a pæan of triumph. A strange requiem, you may say, over the body of a fallen comrade; but if Jimmy Hayes could have heard it he would have understood.

THE DOOR OF UNREST

I sat an hour by sun, in the editor's room of the Montopolis *Weekly Bugle*. I was the editor.

The saffron rays of the declining sunlight filtered through the cornstalks in Micajah Widdup's garden-patch, and cast an amber glory upon my paste-pot. I sat at the editorial desk in my non-rotary revolving chair, and prepared my editorial against the oligarchies. The room, with its one window, was already a prey to the twilight. One by one, with my trenchant sentences, I lopped off the heads of the political hydra, while I listened, full of kindly peace, to the home-coming cowbells and wondered what Mrs. Flanagan was going to have for supper.

Then in from the dusky, quiet street there drifted and perched himself upon a corner of my desk old Father Time's younger brother. His face was beardless and as gnarled as an English walnut. I never saw clothes such as he wore. They would have reduced Joseph's coat to a mono-chrome. But the colors were not the dyer's. Stains and patches and the work of sun and rust were responsible for the diversity. On his coarse shoes was the dust, conceivably, of a thousand leagues. I can describe him no further, except to say that he was little and weird and old—old I began to estimate in centuries when I saw him. Yes, and I remember that there was an odor, a faint odor like aloes, or possibly like myrrh or leather; and I thought of museums.

And then I reached for a pad and pencil, for business is business, and visits of the oldest inhabitants are sacred and honorable, requiring to be chronicled.

"I am glad to see you, sir," I said. "I would offer you a chair, but—you see, sir," I went on, "I have lived in Montopolis only three weeks, and I have not met many of our citizens." I turned a doubtful eye upon his dust-stained shoes, and concluded with a newspaper phrase, "I suppose that you reside in our midst?"

My visitor fumbled in his raiment, drew forth a soiled card, and handed it to me. Upon it was written, in plain but unsteadily formed characters, the name "Michob Ader."

"I am glad you called, Mr. Ader," I said. "As one of our older citizens, you must view with pride the recent growth and enterprise of Montopolis. Among other improvements, I think I can promise that the town will now be provided with a live, enterprising newspa——"

"Do ye know the name on that card?" asked my caller, interrupting me.

"It was not a familiar one to me," I said.

Again he visited the depths of his ancient vestments. This time he brought out a torn leaf of some book or journal, brown and flimsy with age. The heading on the page was the *Turkish Spy* in old-style type; the printing upon it was this:

"There is a man come to Paris in this year 1643 who pretends to have lived these sixteen hundred years. He says of himself that he was a shoemaker in Jerusalem at the time of the Crucifixion; that his name is Michob Ader; and that when Jesus, the Christian Messias, was condemned by Pontius Pilate, the Roman president, he paused to rest while bearing his cross to the place of crucifixion before the door of Michob Ader. The shoemaker struck Jesus with his fist, saying: 'Go; why tarriest thou?' The Messias answered him: 'I indeed am going; but thou shalt tarry until I come'; thereby condemning him to live until the day of judgment. He lives for ever, but at the end of every hundred years he falls into a fit or trance, on recovering from which he finds himself in the same state of youth in which he was when Jesus suffered, being then about thirty years of age.

"Such is the story of the Wandering Jew, as told by Michob Ader, who relates——" Here the printing ended.

I must have muttered aloud something to myself about the Wandering Jew, for the old man spake up, bitterly and loudly.

"'Tis a lie," said he, "like nine tenths of what ye call history. 'Tis a Gentile I am, and no Jew. I am after footing it out of Jerusalem, my son; but if that makes me a Jew, then everything that comes out of a bottle is babies' milk. Ye have my name on the card ye hold; and ye have read the bit of paper they call the *Turkish Spy* that printed the news when I stepped into their office on the 12th day of June, in the year 1643, just as I have called upon ye to-day."

I laid down my pencil and pad. Clearly it would not do. Here was an item for the local column of the *Bugle* that—but it would not do. Still, fragments of the impossible "personal" began to flit through my conventionalized brain. "Uncle Michob is as spry on his legs as a young chap of only a thousand or so." "Our venerable caller relates with pride that George Wash—no, Ptolemy the Great—once dandled him on his knee at his father's house." "Uncle Michob says that our wet spring was nothing in comparison with the dampness that ruined the crops around Mount Ararat when he was a boy——" But no, no—it would not do.

I was trying to think of some conversational subject with which to interest my visitor, and was hesitating between walking matches and the Pliocene Age, when the old man suddenly began to weep poignantly and distressfully.

"Cheer up, Mr. Ader," I said, a little awkwardly; "this matter may blow over in a few hundred years more. There has already been a decided reaction in favor of Judas Iscariot and Colonel Burr and the celebrated violinist, Signor Nero. This is the age of whitewash. You must not allow yourself to become down-hearted."

Unknowingly, I had struck a chord. The old man blinked belligerently through his senile tears.

"'Tis time," he said, "that the liars be doin' justice to somebody. Yer historians are no more than a pack of old women gabblin' at a wake. A finer man than the Imperor Nero niver wore sandals. Man, I was at the burnin' of Rome. I knowed the Imperor well, for in them days I was a well-known char-actor. In thim days they had rayspect for a man that lived for ever.

"But 'twas of the Imperor Nero I was goin' to tell ye. I struck into Rome, up the Appian Way, on the night of July the 16th, the year 64. I had just stepped down by way of Siberia and Afghanistan; and one foot of me had a frost-bite, and the other a blister burned by the sand of the desert; and I was feelin' a bit blue from doin' patrol duty from the North Pole down to the Last Chance corner in Patagonia, and bein' miscalled a

Jew in the bargain. Well, I'm tellin' ye I was passin' the Circus Maximus, and it was dark as pitch over the way, and then I heard somebody sing out, 'Is that you, Michob?'

"Over ag'inst the wall, hid out amongst a pile of barrels and old dry-goods boxes, was the Imperor Nero wid his togy wrapped around his toes, smokin' a long, black segar.

" 'Have one, Michob?' says he.

" 'None of the weeds for me,' says I—'nayther pipe nor segar. What's the use,' says I, 'of smokin' when ye've got not the ghost of a chance of killin' yeself by doin' it?'

" 'True for ye, Michob Ader, my perpetual Jew,' says the Imperor; 'ye're not always wandering. Sure, 'tis danger gives the spice of our pleasures—next to their bein' forbidden.'

" 'And for what,' says I, 'do ye smoke be night in dark places widout even a cinturion in plain clothes to attend ye?'

" 'Have ye ever heard, Michob,' says the Imperor, 'of predestinarianism?'

" 'I've had the cousin of it,' says I. 'I've been on the trot with pedestrianism for many a year, and more to come, as ye well know.'

" 'The longer word,' says me friend Nero, 'is the tachin' of this new sect of people they call the Christians. 'Tis them that's raysponsible for me smokin' be night in holes and corners of the dark.'

"And then I sets down and takes off a shoe and rubs me foot that is frosted, and the Imperor tells me about it. It seems that since I passed that way before, the Imperor had mandamused the Impress wid a divorce suit, and Misses Poppæa, a cilibrated lady, was ingaged, widout riferences, as housekeeper at the palace. 'All in one day,' says the Imperor, 'she puts up new lace windy-curtains in the palace and joins the anti-tobacco society, and whin I feels the need of a smoke I must be after sneakin' out to these piles of lumber in the dark.' So there in the dark me and the Imperor sat, and I told him of me travels. And when they say the Imperor was an incindiary, they lie. 'Twas that night the fire started that burnt the city. 'Tis my opinion that it began from a stump of segar that he threw down among the boxes. And 'tis a lie that he fiddled. He did all he could for six days to stop it, sir."

And now I detected a new flavor to Mr. Michob Ader. It had not been myrrh or balm of hyssop that I had smelled. The emanation was the odor of bad whiskey—and, worse, still, of low comedy—the sort that small humorists manufacture by clothing the grave and reverend things of legend and history in the vulgar, topical frippery that passes for a certain kind of wit. Michob Ader as an impostor, claiming nineteen hundred years, and playing his part with the decency of respectable lunacy, I could endure; but as a tedious wag, cheapening his egregious story with song-book levity, his importance as an entertainer grew less.

And then, as if he suspected my thoughts, he suddenly shifted his key. "You'll excuse me, sir," he whined, "but sometimes I get a little mixed in my head. I am a very old man; and it is hard to remember everything."

I knew that he was right, and that I should not try to reconcile him with Roman history; so I asked for news concerning other ancients with whom he had walked familiar.

Above my desk hung an engraving of Raphael's cherubs. You could yet make out their forms, though the dust blurred their outlines strangely. "Ye calls them 'cher-rubs,'" cackled the old man. "Babes, ye fancy they are, with wings. And there's one wid legs and a bow and arrow that ye call Cupid—I know where they was found. The great-great-great-grandfather of thim all was a billy-goat. Bein' an editor, sir, do ye happen to know where Solomon's Temple stood?"

I fancied that it was in—in Persia? Well, I did not know.

"'Tis not in history nor in the Bible where it was. But I saw it, meself. The first pictures of cher-rubs and cupids was sculptured upon thim walls and pillars. Two of the biggest, sir, stood in the adytum to form the baldachin over the Ark. But the wings of thim sculptures was intindid for horns. And the faces was the faces of goats. Ten thousand goats there was in and about the temple. And your cher-rubs was billy-goats in the days of King Solomon, but the painters misconstrued the horns into wings.

"And I knew Tamerlane, the lame Timour, sir, very well. I saw him at Keghut and at Zaranj. He was a little man no larger than yerself, with hair the color of an amber pipe stem. They buried him at Samarkand. I was at the wake, sir. Oh, he was a fine-built man in his coffin, six feet long, with black whiskers to his face. And I see 'em throw turnips at the Imperor Vispacian in Africa. All over the world I have tramped, sir, without the body of me findin' any rest. 'Twas so commanded. I saw Jerusalem destroyed, and Pompeii go up in the fireworks; and I was at the coronation of Charlemagne and the lynchin' of Joan of Arc. And everywhere I go there comes storms and revolutions and plagues and fires. 'Twas so commanded. Ye have heard of the Wandering Jew. 'Tis all so, except that divil a bit am I Jew. But history lies, as I have told ye. Are ye quite sure, sir, that ye haven't a drop of whiskey convenient? Ye well know that I have many miles of walking before me."

"I have none," said I, "and, if you please, I am about to leave for my supper."

I pushed my chair back creakingly. This ancient landlubber was becoming as great an affliction as any cross-bowed mariner. He shook a musty effluvium from his piebald clothes, overturned my inkstand, and went on with his insufferable nonsense.

"I wouldn't mind it so much," he complained, "if it wasn't for the work I must do on Good Fridays. Ye know about Pontius Pilate, sir, of course. His body, whin he killed himself, was pitched into a lake on the Alps mountains. Now, listen to the job that 'tis mine to perform on the night of every Good Friday. The ould divil goes down in the pool and drags up Pontius, and the water is bilin' and spewin' like a wash pot. And the ould divil sets the body on top of a throne on the rocks, and thin comes me share of the job. Oh, sir, ye would pity me thin—ye would pray for the poor Wandering Jew that niver was a Jew if ye could see the horror of the thing that I must do. 'Tis I that must fetch a bowl of water and kneel down before it till it washes its hands. I declare to ye that Pontius Pilate, a man dead two hundred years, dragged up with the lake slime coverin' him and fishes wrigglin' inside of hid widout eyes, and in the discomposition of the body, sits there, sir, and washes his hands in the bowl I hold for him on Good Fridays. 'Twas so commanded."

Clearly, the matter had progressed far beyond the scope of the *Bugle's* local column. There might have been employment here for the alienist or for those who circulate the pledge; but I had had enough of it. I got up, and repeated that I must go.

At this he seized my coat, grovelled upon my desk, and burst again into distressful weeping. Whatever it was about, I said to myself that his grief was genuine.

"Come now, Mr. Ader," I said, soothingly; "what is the matter?"

The answer came brokenly through his racking sobs: "Because I would not . . . let the poor Christ . . . rest . . . upon the step."

His hallucination seemed beyond all reasonable answer; yet the effect of it upon him scarcely merited disrespect. But I knew nothing that might assuage it; and I told him once more that both of us should be leaving the office at once.

Obedient at last, he raised himself from my dishevelled desk, and permitted me to half lift him to the floor. The gale of his grief had blown away his words; his freshet of tears had soaked away the crust of his grief. Reminiscence died in him—at least, the coherent part of it.

" 'Twas me that did it," he muttered, as I led him toward the door— "me, the shoemaker of Jerusalem."

I got him to the sidewalk, and in the augmented light I saw that his face was seared and lined and warped by a sadness almost incredibly the product of a single lifetime.

And then high up in the firmamental darkness we heard the clamant cries of some great passing birds. My Wandering Jew lifted his hand, with side-tilted head.

"The Seven Whistlers!" he said, as one introduces well-known friends.

"Wild geese," said I; "but I confess that their number is beyond me."

"They follow me everywhere," he said. " 'Twas so commanded. What ye hear is the souls of the seven Jews that helped with the Crucifiixion. Sometimes they're plovers and sometimes geese, but ye'll flnd them always flyin' where I go."

I stood, uncertain how to take my leave. I looked down the street, shuffled my feet, looked back again—and felt my hair rise. The old man had disappeared.

And then my capillaries relaxed, for I dimly saw him footing it away through the darkness. But he walked so swiftly and silently and contrary to the gait promised by his age that my composure was not all restored, though I knew not why.

That night I was foolish enough to take down some dust-covered volumes from my modest shelves. I searched "Hermippus Redivvus" and "Salathiel" and the "Pepys Collection" in vain. And then in a book called "The Citizen of the World," and in one two centuries old, I came upon what I desired. Michob Ader had indeed come to Paris in the year 1643, and related to the *Turkish Spy* an extraordinary story. He claimed to be the Wandering Jew, and that——

But here I fell asleep, for my editorial duties had not been light that day.

Judge Hoover was the *Bugle's* candidate for congress. Having to confer with him, I sought his home early the next morning; and we walked together down town through a little street with which I was unfamiliar.

"Did you ever hear of Michob Ader?" I asked him, smiling.

"Why, yes," said the judge. "And that reminds me of my shoes he has for mending. Here is his shop now."

Judge Hoover stepped into a dingy, small shop. I looked up at the sign, and saw "Mike O'Bader, Boot and Shoe Maker," on it. Some wild geese passed above, honking clearly. I scratched my ear and frowned, and then trailed into the shop.

There sat my Wandering Jew on his shoemaker's bench, trimming a half sole. He was drabbled with dew, grass-stained, unkempt, and miserable; and on his face was still the unexplained wretchedness; the problematic sorrow, the esoteric woe, that had been written there by nothing less, it seemed, than the stylus of the centuries.

Judge Hoover inquired kindly concerning his shoes. The old shoemaker looked up, and spoke sanely enough. He had been ill, he said, for a few days. The next day the shoes would be ready. He looked at me, and I could see that I had no place in his memory. So out we went, and on our way.

"Old Mike," remarked the candidate, "has been on one of his sprees. He gets crazy drunk regularly once a month. But he's a good shoemaker."

"What is his history?" I inquired.

"Whiskey," epitomized Judge Hoover. "That explains him."

I was silent, but I did not accept the explanation. And so, when I had the chance, I asked old man Sellers, who browsed daily on my exchanges.

"Mike O'Bader," said he, "was makin' shoes in Montopolis when I come here goin' on fifteen year ago. I guess whiskey's his trouble. Once a month he gets off the track, and stays so a week. He's got a rigmarole somethin' about his bein' a Jew peddler that he tells ev'rybody. Nobody won't listen to him any more. When he's sober he ain't sich a fool—he's got a sight of books in the back room of his shop that he reads. I guess you can lay all his trouble to whiskey."

But again I would not. Not yet was my Wandering Jew rightly construed for me. I trust that women may not be allowed a title to all the curiosity in the world. So when Montopolis's oldest inhabitant (some ninety score years younger than Michob Ader) dropped into acquire promulgation in print, I siphoned his perpetual trickle of reminiscence in the direction of the uninterpreted maker of shoes.

Uncle Abner was the Complete History of Montopolis, bound in butternut.

"O'Bader," he quavered, "come here in '69. He was the first shoemaker in the place. Folks generally considers him crazy at times now. But he don't harm nobody. I s'pose drinkin' upset his mind—yes, drinkin' very likely done it. It's a powerful bad thing, drinkin'. I'm an old, old man, sir, and I never see no good in drinkin'."

I felt disappointment. I was willing to admit drink in the case of my shoemaker, but I preferred it as a recourse instead of a cause. Why had he pitched upon his pereptual, strange note of the Wandering Jew? Why his unutterable grief during his aberration? I could not yet accept whiskey as an explanation.

"Did Mike O'Bader ever have a great loss or trouble of any kind?" I asked.

"Lemme see! About thirty years ago there was somethin' of the kind, I recollect. Montopolis, sir, in them days used to be a mighty strict place.

"Well, Mike O'Bader had a daughter then—a right pretty girl. She was too gay a sort for Montopolis, so one day she slips off to another town and runs away with a circus. It was two years before she comes back, all fixed up in fine clothes and rings and jewelry, to see Mike. He wouldn't have nothin' to do with her, so she stays around town awhile, anyway. I reckon the men folks wouldn't have raised no objections, but the women egged 'em on to order her to leave town. But she had plenty of spunk, and told 'em to mind their own business.

"So one night they decided to run her away. A crowd of men and women drove her out of her house, and chased her with sticks and stones. She run to her father's door, callin' for help. Mike opens it, and when he sees who it is he hits her with his fist and knocks her down and shuts the door.

"And then the crowd kept on chunkin' her till she run clear out of town. And the next day they finds her drowned dead in Hunter's mill pond. I mind it all now. That was thirty year ago."

I leaned back in my non-rotary revolving chair and nodded gently, like a mandarin, at my paste-pot.

"When old Mike has a spell," went on Uncle Abner, tepidly garrulous, "he thinks he's the Wanderin' Jew."

"He is," said I, nodding away.

And Uncle Abner cackled insinuatingly at the editor's remarks, for he was expecting at least a "stickful" in the "Personal Notes" of the *Bugle*.

THE DUPLICITY OF HARGRAVES

When Major Pendleton Talbot, of Mobile, sir, and his daughter, Miss Lydia Talbot, came to Washington to reside, they selected for a boarding place a house that stood fifty yards back from one of the quietest avenues. It was an old-fashioned brick building, with a portico upheld by tall white pillars. The yard was shaded by stately locusts and elms, and a catalpa tree in season rained its pink and white blossoms upon the grass. Rows of high box bushes lined the fence and walks. It was the Southern style and aspect of the place that pleased the eyes of the Talbots.

In this pleasant, private boarding house they engaged rooms, including a study for Major Talbot, who was adding the finishing chapters to his book, "Anecdotes and Reminiscences of the Alabama Army, Bench, and Bar."

Major Talbot was of the old, old South. The present day had little interest or excellence in his eyes. His mind lived in that period before the Civil War, when the Talbots owned thousands of acres of fine cotton land and the slaves to till them; when the family mansion was the scene of princely hospitality, and drew its guests from the aristocracy of the South. Out of that period he had brought all of its old pride and scruples of honor, and antiquated and punctilious politeness, and (you would think) its wardrobe.

Such clothes were surely never made within fifty years. The major was tall, but whenever he made that wonderful, archaic genuflexion he called a bow, the corners of his frock coat swept the floor. That garment was a surprise even to Washington, which has long ago ceased to shy at the frocks and broad-brimmed hats of Southern congressmen. One of the boarders christened it a "Father Hubbard," and it certainly was high in the waist and full in the skirt.

But the major, with all his queer clothes, his immense area of plaited, ravelling shirt bosom, and the little black string tie with the bow always slipping on one side, both was smiled at and liked in Mrs Vardeman's select boarding house. Some of the young department clerks would often "string him," as they called it, getting him started upon the subject dearest to him—the traditions and history of his beloved Southland. During his talks he would quote freely from the "Anecdotes and Reminiscences." But they were very careful not to let him see their designs, for in spite of his sixty-eight years, he could make the boldest of them uncomfortable under the steady regard of his piercing gray eyes.

Miss Lydia was a plump, little old maid of thirty-five, with smoothly drawn, tightly twisted hair that made her look still older. Old fashioned, too, she was; but ante-bellum glory did not radiate from her as it did from the major. She possessed a thrifty common sense; and it was she who handled the finances of the family, and met all comers when there were bills to pay. The major regarded board bills and wash bills as contemptible nuisances. They kept coming in so persistently and so often. Why, the major wanted to know, could they not be filed and paid in a lump sum at some convenient period—say when the "Anecdotes and Reminiscences" had been published and paid for? Miss Lydia would calmly go on with her sewing and say, "We'll pay as we go as long as the money lasts, and then perhaps they'll have to lump it."

Most of Mrs. Vardeman's boarders were away during the day, being nearly all department clerks and business men; but there was one of them who was about the house a great deal from morning to night. This was a young man named Henry Hopkins Hargraves—every one in the house addressed him by his full name—who was engaged at one of the popular vaudeville theatres. Vaudeville has risen to such a respectable plane in the last few years, and Mr. Hargraves was such a modest and well-mannered person, that Mrs. Vardeman could find no objection to enrolling him upon her list of boarders.

At the theatre Hargraves was known as an all-round dialect comedian, having a large repertoire of German, Irish, Swede, and black-face specialties. But Mr. Hargraves was ambitious, and often spoke of his great desire to succeed in legitimate comedy.

This young man appeared to conceive a strong fancy for Major Talbot. Whenever that gentleman would begin his Southern reminiscences, or repeat some of the liveliest of the anecdotes, Hargraves could always be found, the most attentive among his listeners.

For a time the major showed an inclination to discourage the advances of the "play actor," as he privately termed him; but soon the young man's agreeable manned and indubitable appreciation of the old gentleman's stories completely won him over.

It was not long before the two were like old chums. The major set apart each afternoon to read to him the manuscript of his book. During the anecdotes Hargraves never failed to laugh at exactly the right point. The major was moved to declare to Miss Lydia one day that young Hargraves possessed remarkable perception and a gratifying respect for the old regime. And when it came to talking of those old days—if Major Talbot liked to talk, Mr. Hargraves was entranced to listen.

Like almost all old people who talk of the past, the major loved to linger over details. In describing the splendid, almost royal, days of the old planters, he would hesitate until he had recalled the name of the Negro who held his horse, or the exact date of certain minor happenings, or the number of bales of cotton raised in such a year; but Hargraves never grew impatient or lost interest. On the contrary, he would advance questions on a variety of subjects connected with the life of that time, and he never failed to extract ready replies.

The fox hunts, the 'possum suppers, the hoe downs and jubilees in the Negro quarters, the banquets in the plantation-house hall, when invitations went for fifty miles around; the occasional feuds with the neighboring gentry; the major's duel with Rathbone Culbertson about Kitty Chalmers, who afterward married a Thwaite of South Carolina; and private yacht races for fabulous sums on Mobile Bay; the quaint beliefs, improvident habits, and loyal virtues of the old slaves—all these were subjects that held both the major and Hargraves absorbed for hours at a time.

Sometimes, at night, when the young man would be coming upstairs to his room after his turn at the theatre was over, the major would appear at the door of his study and beckon archly to him. Going in, Hargraves would find a little table set with a decanter, sugar bowl, fruit, and a big bunch of fresh green mint.

"It occurred to me," the major would begin—he was always ceremonious—"that perhaps you might have found your duties at the—at your place of occupation—sufficiently arduous to enable you, Mr. Hargraves, to appreciate what the poet might well have had in his mind when he wrote, 'tired Nature's sweet restorer,'—one of our Southern juleps."

It was a fascination to Hargraves to watch him make it. He took rank among artists when he began, and he never varied the process. With what delicacy he bruised the mint; with what exquisite nicety he estimated the ingredients; with what solicitous care he capped the compound with the scarlet fruit glowing against the dark green fringe! And then the hospitality and grace with which he offered it, after the selected oat straws had been plunged into its tinkling depths!

After about four months in Washington, Miss Lydia discovered one morning that they were almost without money. The "Anecdotes and Reminiscences" was completed, but publishers had not jumped at the collected gems of Alabama sense and wit. The rental of a small house which they still owned in Mobile was two months in arrears. Their board money for the month would be due in three days. Miss Lydia called her father to a consultation.

"No money?" said he with a surprised look. "It is quite annoying to be called on so frequently for these petty sums. Really, I——"

The major searched his pockets. He found only a two-dollar bill, which he returned to his vest pocket.

"I must attend to this at once, Lydia," he said. "Kindly get me my umbrella and I will go down town immediately. The congressman from our district, General Fulghum, assured me some days ago that he would use his influence to get my book published at an early date. I will go to his hotel at once and see what arrangement has been made."

With a sad little smile Miss Lydia watched him button his "Father Hubbard" and depart, pausing at the door, as he always did, to bow profoundly.

That evening, at dark, he returned. It seemed that Congressman Fulghum had seen the publisher who had the major's manuscript for reading. That person had said that if the anecdotes, etc., were carefully pruned down about one half, in order to eliminate the sectional and class prejudice with which the book was dyed from end to end, he might consider its publication.

The major was in a white heat of anger, but regained his equanimity, according to his code of manners, as soon as he was in Miss Lydia's presence.

"We must have money," said Miss Lydia, with a little wrinkle above her nose. "Give me the two dollars, and I will telegraph to Uncle Ralph for some to-night."

The major drew a small envelope from his upper vest pocket and tossed it on the table.

"Perhaps it was injudicious," he said mildly, "but the sum was so merely nominal that I bought tickets to the theatre to-night. It's new war drama, Lydia. I thought you would be pleased to witness its first production in Washington. I am told that the South has very fair treatment in the play. I confess I should like to see the performance myself."

Miss Lydia threw up her hands in silent despair.

Still, as the tickets were bought, they might as well be used. So that evening, as they sat in the theatre listening to the lively overture, even Miss Lydia was minded to relegate their troubles, for the hour, to second place. The major, in spotless linen, with his extraordinary coat showing only where it was closely buttoned, and his white hair smoothly roached, looked really fine and distinguished. The curtain went up on the first act of "A Magnolia Flower," revealing a typical Southern plantation scene. Major Talbot betrayed some interest.

"Oh, see!" exclaimed Miss Lydia, nudging his arm, and pointing to her programme.

The major put on his glasses and read the line in the cast of characters that her finger indicated.

Col. Webster Calhoun. . . . H. Hopkins Hargraves.

"It's our Mr. Hargraves," said Miss Lydia. "It must be his first appearance in what he calls 'the legitimate.' I'm so glad for him."

Not until the second act did Col. Webster Calhoun appear upon the stage. When he made his entry Major Talbot gave an audible sniff, glared at him, and seemed to freeze solid. Miss Lydia uttered a little ambiguous squeak and crumpled her programme in her hand. For Colonel Calhoun was made up as nearly resembling Major Talbot as one pea does another. The long, thin, white hair, curly at the ends, the aristocratic beak of a nose, the crumpled, wide, ravelling shirt front, the string tie, with the bow nearly under one ear, were almost exactly duplicated. And then, to clinch the imitation, he wore the twin to the major's supposed to be unparalleled coat. High-collared, baggy, empire-waisted, ample-skirted, hanging a foot lower in front than behind, the garment could have been designed from no other pattern. From then on, the major and Miss Lydia sat bewitched, and saw the counterfeit presentment of a haughty Talbot "dragged," as the major afterward expressed it, "through the slanderous mire of a corrupt stage."

Mr. Hargraves had used his opportunities well. He had caught the major's little idosyncrasies of speech, accent, and intonation and his pompous courtliness to perfection—exaggerating all to the purpose of the stage. When he performed that marvelous bow that the major fondly imagined to be the pink of all salutations, the audience sent forth a sudden round of hearty applause.

Miss Lydia sat immovable, not daring to glance toward her father. Sometimes her hand next to him would be laid against her cheek, as if to conceal the smile which, in spite of her disapproval, she could not entirely suppress.

The culmination of Hargraves's audacious imitation took place in the third act. The scene is where Colonel Calhoun entertains a few of the neighboring planters in his "den."

Standing at a table in the centre of the stage, with his friends grouped about him, he delivers that inimitable, rambling, character monologue so famous in "A Magnolia Flower," at the same time that he deftly makes juleps for the party.

Major Talbot, sitting quietly, but white with indignation, heard his best stories retold, his pet theories and hobbies advanced and expanded, and the dream of the "Anecdotes and Reminiscences" served, exaggerated and garbled. His favorite narrative—that of his duel with Rathbone Culbertson—was not omitted, and it was delivered with more fire, egotism, and gusto than the major himself put into it.

The monologue concluded with a quaint, delicious, witty little lecture on the art of concocting a julep, illustrated by the act. Here Major Talbot's delicate but showy science was reproduced to a hair's breadth—from his dainty handling of the fragrant weed—"the one-thousandth part of a grain too much pressure, gentlemen, and you extract the bitterness, instead of the aroma, of this heaven-bestowed plant"—to his solicitous selection of the oaten straws.

At the close of the scene the audience raised a tumultuous roar of appreciation. The portrayal of the type was so exact, so sure and thorough, that the leading characters in the play were forgotten. After repeated calls, Hargraves came before the curtain and bowed, his rather boyish face bright and flushed with the knowledge of success.

At last Miss Lydia turned and looked at the major. His thin nostrils were working like the gills of a fish. He laid both shaking hands upon the arms of his chair to rise.

"We will go, Lydia," he said, chokingly. "This is an abominable—desecration."

Before he could rise, she pulled him back into his seat.

"We will stay it out," she declared. "Do you want to advertise the copy by exhibiting the original coat?" So they remained to the end.

Hargraves's success must have kept him up late that night, for neither at the breakfast nor at the dinner table did he appear.

About three in the afternoon he tapped at the door of Major Talbot's study. The major opened it, and Hargraves walked in with his hands full of the morning papers—too full of his triumph to notice anything unusual in the major's demeanor.

"I put it all over 'em last night, major," he began, exultantly. "I had my inning, and, I think, scored. Here's what the *Post* says:

"His conception and portrayal of the old-time Southern colonel, with his absurd grandiloquence, his eccentric garb, his quaint idioms and phrases, his moth-eaten pride of family, and his really kind heart, fastidious sense of honor, and lovable simplicity, is the best delineation of a character rôle on the boards to-day. The coat worn by Colonel Calhoun is itself nothing less than an evolution of genius. Mr. Hargraves has captured his public.

"How does that sound, major, for a first nighter?"

"I had the honor"—the major's voice sounded ominously frigid—"of witnessing your very remarkable performance, sir, last night."

Hargraves looked disconcerted.

"You were there? I didn't know you ever—I didn't know you cared for the theatre. Oh, I say, Major Talbot," he exclaimed, frankly, "don't you be offended. I admit I did get a lot of pointers from you that helped me out wonderfully in the part. But it's a type, you know—not individual. The way the audience caught on shows that. Half the patrons of that theatre are Southerners. They recognized it."

"Mr. Hargraves," said the major, who had remained standing, "you have put upon me an unpardonable insult. You have burlesqued my person, grossly betrayed my confidence, and misused my hospitality. If I thought you possessed the faintest conception of what is the sign manual of a gentleman, or what is due one, I would call you out, sir, old as I am. I will ask you to leave the room, sir."

The actor appeared to be slightly bewildered, and seemed hardly to take in the full meaning of the old gentleman's words.

"I am truly sorry you took offence," he said, regretfully. "Up here we don't look at things just as you people do. I know men who would buy out half the house to have their personality put on the stage so the public would recognize it."

"They are not from Alabama, sir," said the major, haughtily.

"Perhaps not. I have a pretty good memory, major; let me quote a few lines from your book. In response to a toast at a banquet given in Milledgeville, I believe—you uttered, and intend to have printed these words:

"The Northern man is utterly without sentiment or warmth except in so far as the feelings may be turned to his own commercial profit. He will suffer without resentment any imputation cast upon the honor of himself or his loved ones that does not bear with it the consequence of pecuniary loss. In his charity, he gives with a liberal hand; but it must be heralded with the trumpet and chronicled in brass.

"Do you think that picture is fairer than the one you saw of Colonel Calhoun last night?"

"The description," said the major frowning, "is—not without grounds. Some exag—latitude must be allowed in public speaking."

"And in public acting," replied Hargraves.

"That is not the point," persisted the major, unrelenting. "It was a personal caricature. I positively decline to overlook it, sir."

"Major Talbot," said Hargraves, with a winning smile, "I wish you would understand me. I want you to know that I never dreamed of insulting you. In my profession, all life belongs to me. I take what I want, and what I can, and return it over the footlights. Now, if you will, let's let it go at that. I came in to see you about something else. We've been pretty good friends for some months, and I'm going to take the risk of offending you again. I know you are hard up for money—never mind how I found out; a boarding house is no place to keep such matters secret—and I want you to let me help you out of the pinch. I've been there often enough myself. I've been getting a fair salary all the season, and I've saved some money. You're welcome to a couple hundred—or even more—until you get——"

"Stop!" commanded the major, with his arm outstretched. "It seems that my book didn't lie, after all. You think your money salve will heal all the hurts of honor. Under no circumstances would I accept a loan from a casual acquaintance; and as to you, sir, I would starve before I would consider your insulting offer of a financial adjustment of the circumstances we have discussed. I beg to repeat my request relative to your quitting the apartment."

Hargraves took his departure without another word. He also left the house the same day, moving, as Mrs. Vardeman explained at the supper table, nearer the vicinity of the down-town theatre, where "A Magnolia Flower" was booked for a week's run.

Critical was the situation with Major Talbot and Miss Lydia. There was no one in Washington to whom the major's scruples allowed him to apply for a loan. Miss Lydia wrote a letter to Uncle Ralph, but it was doubtful whether that relative's constricted affairs would permit him to furnish help. The major was forced to make an apologetic address to Mrs. Vardeman regarding the delayed payment for board, referring to "delinquent rentals" and "delayed remittances" in a rather confused strain.

Deliverance came from an entirely unexpected source.

Late one afternoon the door maid came up and announced an old colored man who wanted to see Major Talbot. The major asked that he be sent up to his study. Soon an old darkey appeared in the doorway, with his hat in hand, bowing, and scraping with one clumsy foot. He was quite decently dressed in a baggy suit of black. His big, coarse shoes shone with a metallic lustre suggestive of stove polish. His bushy wool was gray—almost white. After middle life, it is difficult to estimate the age of a Negro. This one might have seen as many years as had Major Talbot.

"I be bound you don't know me, Mars' Pendleton," were his first words.

The major rose and came forward at the old, familiar style of address. It was one of the old plantation darkeys without a doubt; but they had been widely scattered, and he could not recall the voice or face.

"I don't believe I do," he said, kindly—"unless you will assist my memory."

"Don't you 'member Cindy's Mose, Mars' Pendleton, what 'migrated 'mediately after de war?"

"Wait a moment," said the major, rubbing his forehead with the tips of his fingers. He loved to recall everything connected with those beloved days. "Cindy's Mose," he reflected. 'You worked among the horses—breaking the colts. Yes, I remember now. After the surrender, you took the name of—don't prompt me—Mitchell, and went to the West—to Nebraska."

"Yassir, yassir,"—the old man's face stretched with a delighted grin—"dat's him, dat's it. Newbraska. Dat's me—Mose Mitchell. Old Uncle Mose Mitchell, dey calls me now. Old mars', your pa, gimme a pah of dem mule colts when I lef' fur to staht me goin' with. You 'member dem colts, Mars. Pendleton?"

"I don't seem to recall the colts," said the major. "You know I was married the first year of the war and living at the old Follinsbee place. But sit down, sit down, Uncle Mose. I'm glad to see you. I hope you have prospered."

Uncle Mose took a chair and laid his hat carefully on the floor beside it.

"Yassir; of late I done mouty famous. When I first got to Newbraska, dey folks come all roun' me to see dem mule colts. Dey ain't see no mules like dem in Newbraska. I sold dem mules for three hundred dollars. Yassir—three hundred.

"Den I open a blacksmith shop, suh, and made some money and bought some lan'. Me and my old 'oman done raised up seb'm chillun, and all doin' well 'cept two of 'em what died. Fo' year ago a railroad come along and staht a town slam ag'inst my lan', and, suh, Mars' Pendleton, Uncle Mose am worth lem'm thousand dollars in money, property, and lan'."

"I'm glad to hear it," said the major heartily. "Glad to hear it."

"And dat little baby of yo'n, Mars' Pendleton—one what you name Miss Lyddy—I be bound dat little tad done growed up tell nobody wouldn't know her."

The major stepped to the door and called: "Lydia, dear, will you come?"

Miss Lydia, looking quite grown up and a little worried, came in from her room.

"Dar, now! What'd I tell you? I knowed dat baby be plum growed up. You don't 'member Uncle Mose, child?"

"This is Aunt Cindy's Mose, Lydia," explained the major. "He left Sunnymead for the West when you were two years old."

"Well," said Miss Lydia, "I can hardly be expected to remember you, Uncle Mose, at that age. And, as you say, 'I'm 'plum growed up,' and was a blessed long time ago. But I'm glad to see you, even if I can't remember you."

And she was. And so was the major. Something alive and tangible had come to link them with the happy past. The three sat and talked over the olden times, the major and Uncle Mose, correcting or prompting each other as they reviewed the plantation scenes and days.

The major inquired what the old man was doing so far from his home.

"Uncle Mose am a delicate," he explained, "to de grand Baptis' convention in dis city. I never preached none, but bein' a residin' elder in de church, and able fur to pay my own expenses, dey sent me along."

"And how did you know we were in Washington?" inquired Miss Lydia.

"Dey's a cullud man works in de hotel whar I stops, what comes from Mobile. He told me he seen Mars' Pendeleton comin' outen dish here house one mawnin'.

"What I come fur," continued Uncle Mose, reaching into his pocket— "besides de sight of home folks—was to pay Mars' Pendleton what I owes him."

"Owe me?" said the major, in surprise.

"Yassir—three hundred dollars." He handed the major a roll of bills. "When I lef' old mars' says: 'Take dem mule colts, Mose, and, if it be so you gits able, pay fur 'em.' Yas sir—dem was his words. De war had done lef' old mars po' hisself. Old mars' bein' 'long ago dead, de debt descends to Mars' Pendleton. Three hundred dollars. Uncle Mose is plenty able to pay now. When dat railroad buy my lan' I laid off to pay for dem mules. Count de money, Mars' Pendleton. Dat's what I sold dem mules fur. Yassir."

Tears were in Major Talbot's eyes. He took Uncle Mose's hand and laid his other upon his shoulder.

"Dear, faithful old servitor," he said in an unsteady voice, "I don't mind saying to you that 'Mars' Pendleton' spent his last dollar in the world a week ago. We will accept this money, Uncle Mose, since, in a way, it is a sort of payment, as well as a token of the loyalty and devotion of the old régime. Lydia, my dear, take the money. You are better fitted than I to manage its expenditure."

"Take it, honey," said Uncle Mose. "Hit belongs to you. Hit's Talbot money."

After Uncle Mose had gone, Miss Lydia had a good cry—for joy; and the major turned his face to a corner, and smoked his clay pipe volcanically.

The succeeding days saw the Talbots restored to peace and ease. Miss Lydia's face lost its worried look. The major appeared in a new frock coat, in which he looked like a wax figure personifying the memory of his golden age. Another publisher who read the manuscript of the "Anecdotes and Reminiscences" thought that, with a little retouching and toning down of the high lights, he could make a really bright and salable volume of it. Altogether, the situation was comfortable, and not without the touch of hope that is often sweeter than arrived blessings.

One day, about a week after their piece of good luck, a maid brought a letter for Miss Lydia to her room. The postmark showed that it was from New York. Not knowing any one there, Miss Lydia, in a mild flutter of wonder, sat down by her table and opened the letter with her scissors. This was what she read:

Dear Miss Talbot:

I thought you might be glad to learn of my good fortune. I have received and accepted an offer of two hundred dollars per week by a New York stock company to play Colonel Calhoun in "A Magnolia Flower."

There is something else I wanted you to know. I guess you'd better not tell Major Talbot. I was anxious to make him some amends for the great help he was to me in studying the part, and for the bad humor he was in about it. He refused to let me, so I did it anyhow. I could easily spare the three hundred.

Sincerely yours,
H. Hopkins Hargraves

P. S. How did I play Uncle Mose?

Major Talbot, passing through the hall, saw Miss Lydia's door open and stopped.

"Any mail for us this morning, Lydia dear?" he asked.

Miss Lydia slid the letter beneath a fold of her dress.

"The *Mobile Chronicle* came," she said, promptly. "It's on the table in your study."

LET ME FEEL YOUR PULSE

So I went to a doctor.

"How long has it been since you took any alcohol into your system?" he asked.

Turning my head sidewise, I answered, "Oh, quite awhile."

He was a young doctor, somewhere between twenty and forty. He wore heliotrope socks, but he looked like Napoleon. I liked him immensely.

"Now," said he, "I am going to show you the effect of alcohol upon your circulation." I think it was "circulation" he said; though it may have been "advertising."

He bared my left arm to the elbow, brought out a bottle of whiskey, and gave me a drink. He began to look more like Napoleon. I began to like him better.

Then he put a tight compress on my upper arm, stopped my pulse with his fingers, and squeezed a rubber bulb connected with an apparatus on a stand that looked like a thermometer. The mercury jumped up and down without seeming to stop anywhere; but the doctor said it registered two hundred and thirty-seven or one hundred and sixty-five or some such number.

"Now," said he, "you see what alcohol does to the blood-pressure."

"It's marvelous," said I, "but do you think it a sufficient test? Have one on me, and let's try the other arm." But, no!

Then he grasped my hand. I thought I was doomed and he was saying good-bye. But all he wanted to do was to jab a needle into the end of a finger and compare the red drop with a lot of fifty-cent poker chips that he had fastened to a card.

"It's the hæmoglobin test," he explained. "The color of your blood is wrong."

"Well," said I, "I know it should be blue; but this is a country of mix-ups. Some of my ancestors were cavaliers; but they got thick with some people on Nantucket Island, so——"

"I mean," said the doctor, "that the shade of red is too light."

"Oh," I said, "it's a case of matching instead of matches."

The doctor then pounded me severely in the region of the chest. When he did that I don't know whether he reminded me most of Napoleon or Battling or Lord Nelson. Then he looked grave and mentioned a string of grievances that the flesh is heir to—mostly ending in "itis." I immediately paid him fifteen dollars on account.

"Is or are it or some or any of them necessarily fatal?" I asked. I thought my connection with the matter justified my manifesting a certain amount of interest.

"All of them," he answered, cheerfully. "But their progress may be arrested. With care and proper continuous treatment you may live to be eighty-five or ninety."

I began to think of the doctor's bill. "Eighty-five would be sufficient, I am sure," was my comment. I paid him ten dollars more on account.

"The first thing to do," he said, with renewed animation, "is to find a sanitarium where you will get a complete rest for a while, and allow your nerves to get into a better condition. I myself will go with you and select a suitable one."

So he took me to a mad-house in the Catskills. It was on a bare mountain frequented only by infrequent frequenters. You could see nothing but stones and boulders, some patches of snow, and scattered pine trees. The young physician in charge was most agreeable. He gave me a stimulant without applying a compress to the arm. It was luncheon time, and we were invited to partake. There were about twenty inmates at little tables in the dining room. The young physician in charge came to our table and said: "It is a custom with our guests not to regard themselves as patients, but merely as tired ladies and gentlemen taking a rest. Whatever slight maladies they may have are never alluded to in conversation."

My doctor called loudly to a waitress to bring some phosphoglycerate of lime hash, dog-bread, bromo-seltzer pancakes, and nux vomica tea for my repast. Then a sound arose like a sudden wind storm among pine trees. It was produced by every guest in the room whispering loudly, "Neurasthenia!"—except one man with a nose, whom I distinctly heard say, "Chronic alcoholism." I hope to meet him again. The physician in charge turned and walked away.

An hour or so after luncheon he conducted us to the workshop—say fifty yards from the house. Thither the guests had been conducted by the physician in charge's understudy and sponge-holder—a man with feet and a blue sweater. He was so tall that I was not sure he had a face; but the Armour Packing Company would have been delighted with his hands.

"Here," said the physician in charge, "our guests find relaxation from past mental worries by devoting themselves to physical labor—recreation, in reality."

There were turning-lathes, carpenters' outfits, clay-modelling tools, spinning-wheels, weaving-frames, treadmills, bass drums, enlarged-crayon-portrait apparatuses, blacksmith forges, and everything, seemingly, that could interest the paying lunatic guests of a first-rate sanitarium.

"The lady making mud pies in the corner," whispered the physician in charge, "is no other than—Lulu Lulington, the authoress of the novel entitled 'Why Love Loves.' What she is doing now is simply to rest her mind after performing that piece of work."

I had seen the book. "Why doesn't she do it by writing another one instead?" I asked.

As you see, I wasn't as far gone as they thought I was.

"The gentleman pouring water through the funnel," continued the physician in charge, "is a Wall Street broker broken down from overwork."

I buttoned my coat.

Others he pointed out were architects playing with Noah's arks, ministers reading Darwin's "Theory of Evolution," lawyers sawing wood, tired-out society ladies talking Ibsen to the blue-sweatered sponge-holder, a neurotic millionaire lying asleep on the floor, and a prominent artist drawing a little red wagon around the room.

"You look pretty strong," said the physician in charge of me. "I think the best mental relaxation for you would be throwing small boulders over the mountainside and then bringing them up again."

I was a hundred yards away before my doctor overtook me.

"What's the matter?" he asked.

"The matter is," said I, "that there are no aeroplanes handy. So I am going to merrily and hastily jog the foot-pathway to yon station and catch the first unlimited-soft-coal express back to town."

"Well," said the doctor, "perhaps you are right. This seems hardly the suitable place for you. But what you need is rest—absolute rest and exercise."

That night I went to a hotel in the city, and said to the clerk: "What I need is absolute rest and exercise. Can you give me a room with one of those tall folding beds in it, and a relay of bellboys to work it up and down while I rest?"

The clerk rubbed a speck off one of his finger nails and glanced sidewise at a tall man in a white hat sitting in the lobby. That man came over and asked me politely if I had seen the shrubbery at the west entrance. I had not, so he showed it to me and then looked me over.

"I thought you had 'em," he said, not unkindly, "but I guess you're all right. You'd better go see a doctor, old man."

A week afterward my doctor tested my blood pressure again without the preliminary stimulant. He looked to me a little less like Napoleon. And his socks were of a shade of tan that did not appeal to me.

"What you need," he decided, "is sea air and companionship."

"Would a mermaid——" I began; but he slipped on his professional manner.

"I myself," he said, "will take you to the Hotel Bonair off the coast of Long Island and see that you get in good shape. It is a quiet, comfortable resort where you will soon recuperate."

The Hotel Bonair proved to be a nine-hundred-room fashionable hostelry on an island off the main shore. Everybody who did not dress for dinner was shoved into a side dining room and given only a terrapin and champagne table d'hôte. The bay was a great stamping ground for wealthy yachtsmen. The *Corsair* anchored there the day we arrived. I saw Mr. Morgan standing on deck eating a cheese sandwich and gazing longingly at the hotel. Still, it was a very inexpensive place. Nobody could afford to pay their prices. When you went away you simply left your baggage, stole a skiff, and beat it for the mainland in the night.

When I had been there one day I got a pad of monogrammed telegraph blanks at the clerk's desk and began to wire to all my friends for get-away money. My doctor and I played one game of croquet on the golf links and went to sleep on the lawn.

When we got back to town a thought seemed to occur to him suddenly. "By the way," he asked, "how do you feel?"

"Relieved of very much," I replied.

Now a consulting physician is different. He isn't exactly sure whether he is to be paid or not, and this uncertainty insures you either the most careful or the most careless attention. My doctor took me to see a consulting physician. He made a poor guess and gave me careful attention. I liked him immensely. He put me through some coördination exercises.

"Have you a pain in the back of your head?" he asked. I told him I had not.

"Shut your eyes," he ordered, "put your feet close together, and jump backward as far as you can."

I always was a good backward jumper with my eyes shut, so I obeyed. My head struck the edge of the bathroom door, which had been left open and was only three feet away. The doctor was very sorry. He had overlooked the fact that the door was open. He closed it.

"Now touch your nose with your right forefinger," he said.

"Where is it?" I asked.

"On your face," said he.

"I mean my right forefinger," I explained.

"Oh, excuse me," said he. He reopened the bathroom door, and I took my finger out of the crack of it. After I had performed the marvelous digito-nasal feat I said:

"I do not wish to deceive you as to symptoms, Doctor; I really have something like a pain in the back of my head." He ignored the symptom and examined my heart carefully with a latest-popular-air-penny-in-the-slot ear-trumpet. I felt like a ballad. "Now," he said, "gallop like a horse for about five minutes around the room."

I gave the best imitation I could of a disqualified Percheron being led out of Madison Square Garden. Then, without dropping in a penny, he listened to my chest again.

"No glanders in our family, Doc," I said.

The consulting physician held up his forefinger within three inches of my nose. "Look at my finger," he commanded.

"Did you ever try Pears'——" I began; but he went on with his test rapidly.

"Now look across the bay. At my finger. Across the bay. At my finger. At my finger. Across the bay. At my finger. Across the bay. Across the bay. At my finger. Across the bay." This for about three minutes.

He explained that this was a test of the action of the brain. It seemed easy to me. I never once mistook his finger for the bay. I'll bet that if he had used the phrases: "Gaze, as it were, unpreoccupied, outward—or rather laterally—in the direction of the horizon, underlaid, so to speak, with the adjacent fluid inlet," and "Now, returning—or rather, in a manner, withdrawing your attention, bestow it upon my upraised digit"—I'll bet, I say, that Henry James himself could have passed the examination.

After asking me if I had ever had a grand uncle with curvature of the spine or a cousin with swelled ankles, the two doctors retired to the bathroom and sat on the edge of the bath tub for their consultation. I ate an apple, and gazed first at my finger and then across the bay.

The doctors came out looking grave. More: they looked tombstones and Tennessee-papers-please-copy. They wrote out a diet list to which I was to be restricted. It had everything that I had ever heard of to eat on it, except snails. And I never eat a snail unless it overtakes me and bites me first.

"You must follow this diet strictly," said the doctors.

"I'd follow it a mile if I could get one-tenth of what's on it," I answered.

"Of next importance," they went on, "is outdoor air and exercise. And here is a prescription that will be of great benefit to you."

Then all of us took something. They took their hats, and I took my departure.

I went to a druggist and showed him the prescription.

"It will be $2.87 for an ounce bottle," he said.

"Will you give me a piece of your wrapping cord?" said I.

I made a hole in the prescription, ran the cord through it, tied it around my neck, and tucked it inside. All of us have a little superstition, and mine runs to a confidence in amulets.

Of course there was nothing the matter with me, but I was very ill. I couldn't work, sleep, eat, or bowl. The only way I could get any sympathy was to go without shaving for four days. Even then somebody would say: "Old man, you look as hardy as a pine knot. Been up for a jaunt in the Maine Woods, eh?"

Then, suddenly, I remembered that I must have outdoor air and exercise. So I went down South to John's. John is an approximate relative by verdict of a preacher standing with a little book in his hands in a bower of chrysanthemums while a hundred thousand people looked on. John has a country house seven miles from Pineville. It is at an altitude and on the Blue Ridge Mountains in a state too dignified to be dragged into this controversy. John is mica, which is more valuable and clearer than gold.

He met me at Pineville, and we took the trolley car to his home. It is a big, neighborless cottage on a hill surrounded by a hundred mountains. We got off at his little private station, where John's family and Amaryllis met and greeted us. Amaryllis looked at me a trifle anxiously.

A rabbit came bounding across the hill between us and the house. I threw down my suit-case and pursued it hotfoot. After I had run twenty yards and seen it disappear, I sat down on the grass and wept disconsolately.

"I can't catch a rabbit any more," I sobbed. "I'm of no further use in the world. I may as well be dead."

"Oh, what is it—what is it, Brother John?" I heard Amaryllis say.

"Nerves a little unstrung," said John, in his calm way. "Don't worry. Get up, you rabbit-chaser, and come on to the house before the biscuits get cold." It was about twilight, and the mountains came up nobly to Miss Murfree's descriptions of them.

Soon after dinner I announced that I believed I could sleep for a year or two, including legal holidays. So I was shown to a room as big and cool as a flower garden, where there was a bed as broad as a lawn. Soon afterward the remainder of the household retired, and then there fell upon the land a silence.

I had not heard a silence before in years. It was absolute. I raised myself on my elbow and listened to it. Sleep! I thought that if I only could hear a star twinkle or a blade of grass sharpen itself I could compose myself to rest. I thought once that I heard a sound like the sail of a catboat flapping as it veered about in a breeze, but I decided that it was probably only a tack in the carpet. Still I listened.

Suddenly some belated little bird alighted upon the window-sill, and, in what he no doubt considered sleepy tones, enunciated the noise generally translated as "cheep!"

I leaped into the air.

"Hey! what's the matter down there?" called John from his room above mine.

"Oh, nothing," I answered, "except that I accidentally bumped my head against the ceiling."

The next morning I went out on the porch and looked at the mountains. There were forty-seven of them in sight. I shuddered, went into the big hall sitting room of the house, selected "Pancoast's Family Practice of Medicine" from a bookcase, and began to read. John came in, took the book away from me, and led me outside. He has a farm of three hundred acres furnished with the usual complement of barns, mules, peasantry, and harrows with three front teeth broken off. I had seen such things in my childhood, and my heart began to sink.

Then John spoke of alfalfa, and I brightened at once. "Oh, yes," said I, "wasn't she in the chorus of—let's see——"

"Green, you know," said John, "and tender, and you plow it under after the first season."

"I know," said I, "and the grass grows over her."

"Right," said John. "You know something about farming, after all."

"I know something of some farmers," said I, "and a sure scythe will mow them down some day."

On the way back to the house a beautiful and inexplicable creature walked across our path. I stopped irresistibly fascinated, gazing at it. John waited patiently, smoking his cigarette. He is a modern farmer. After ten minutes he said: "Are you going to stand there looking at that chicken all day? Breakfast is nearly ready."

"A chicken?" said I.

"A white Orpington hen, if you want to particularize."

"A white Orpington hen?" I repeated, with intense interest. The fowl walked slowly away with graceful dignity, and I followed like a child after the Pied Piper. Five minutes more were allowed me by John, and then he took me by the sleeve and conducted me to breakfast.

After I had been there a week I began to grow alarmed. I was sleeping and eating well and actually beginning to enjoy life. For a man in my desperate condition that would never do. So I sneaked down to the trolley-car station, took the car for Pineville, and went to see one of the best physicians in town. By this time I knew exactly what to do when I needed medical treatment. I hung my hat on the back of a chair, and said rapidly:

"Doctor, I have cirrhosis of the heart, indurated arteries, neurasthenia, neuritis, acute indigestion, and convalescence. I am going to live on a strict diet. I shall also take a tepid bath at night and a cold one in the morning. I shall endeavor to be cheerful, and fix my mind on pleasant subjects. In the way of drugs I intend to take a phosphorus pill three times a day, preferably after meals, and a tonic composed of the tinctures of gentian, cinchona, calisaya, and cardamon compound. Into each teaspoonful of this I shall mix tincture of nux vomica, beginning with one drop and increasing it a drop each day until the maximum dose is reached. I shall drop this with a medicine-dropper, which can be procured at a trifling cost at any pharmacy. Good-morning."

I took my hat and walked out. After I had closed the door I remembered something that I had forgotten to say. I opened it again. The doctor had not moved from where he had been sitting, but he gave a slightly nervous start when he saw me again.

"I forgot to mention," said I, "that I shall also take absolute rest and exercise."

After this consultation I felt much better. The reëstablishing in my mind of the fact that I was hopelessly ill gave me so much satisfaction that I almost became gloomy again. There is nothing more alarming to a neurasthenic than to feel himself growing well and cheerful.

John looked after me carefully. After I had evinced so much interest in his White Orpington chicken he tried his best to divert my mind, and was particular to lock his hen house of nights. Gradually the tonic mountain air, the wholesome food, and the daily walks among the hills so alleviated my malady that I became utterly wretched and despondent. I heard of a country doctor who lived in the mountains near-by. I went to see him and told him the whole story. He was a gray-bearded man with clear, blue, wrinkled eyes, in a home-made suit of gray jeans.

In order to save time I diagnosed my case, touched my nose with my right forefinger, struck myself below the knee to make my foot kick, sounded my chest, stuck out my tongue, and asked him the price of cemetery lots in Pineville.

He lit his pipe and looked at me for about three minutes. "Brother," he said, after a while, "you are in a mighty bad way. There's a chance for you to pull through, but it's a mighty slim one."

"What can it be?" I asked, eagerly. "I have taken arsenic and gold, phosphorus, exercise, nux vomica, hydrotherapeutic baths, rest, excitement, codein, and aromatic spirits of ammonia. Is there anything left in the pharmacopœia?"

"Somewhere in these mountains," said the doctor, "there's a plant growing—a flowering plant that'll cure you, and it's about the only thing that will. It's of a kind that's as old as the world; but of late it's powerful scarce and hard to find. You and I will have to hunt it up. I'm not engaged in active practice now: I'm getting along in years; but I'll take your case. You'll have to come every day in the afternoon and help me hunt for this plant till we find it. The city doctors may know a lot about new scientific things, but they don't know much about the cures that nature carries around in her saddle bags."

So every day the old doctor and I hunted the cure-all plant among the mountains and valleys of the Blue Ridge. Together we toiled up steep heights so slippery with fallen autumn leaves that we had to catch every sapling and branch within our reach to save us from falling. We waded through gorges and chasms, breast-deep with laurel and ferns; we followed the banks of mountain streams for miles, we wound our way like Indians through brakes of pine—road side, hill side, river side, mountain side we explored in our search for the miraculous plant.

As the old doctor said, it must have grown scarce and hard to find. But we followed our quest. Day by day we plumbed the valleys, scaled the heights, and tramped the plateaus in search of the miraculous plant. Mountain-bred, he never seemed to tire. I often reached home to fatigued to do anything except fall into bed and sleep until morning. This we kept up for a month.

One evening after I had returned from a six-mile tramp with the old doctor, Amaryllis and I took a little walk under the trees near the road. We looked at the mountains drawing their royal-purple robes around them for their night's repose.

"I'm glad you're well again," she said. "When you first came you frightened me. I thought you were really ill."

"Well again!" I almost shrieked. "Do you know that I have only one chance in a thousand to live?"

Amaryllis looked at me in surprise. "Why," said she, "you are as strong as one of the plow-mules, and sleep ten or twelve hours every night, and you are eating us out of house and home. What more do you want?"

"I tell you," said I, "that unless we find the magic—that is, the plant we are looking for—in time, nothing can save me. The doctor tells me so."

"What doctor?"

"Doctor Tatum—the old doctor who lives halfway up Black Oak Mountain. Do you know him?"

"I have known him since I was able to talk. And is that where you go every day—is it he who takes you on these long walks and climbs that have brought back your health and strength? God bless the old doctor."

Just then the old doctor himself drove slowly down the road in his rickety old buggy. I waved my hand at him and shouted that I would be on hand the next day at the usual time. He stopped his horse and called to Amaryllis to come out to him. They talked for five minutes while I waited. Then the old doctor drove on.

When we got to the house Amaryllis lugged out an encyclopædia and sought a word in it. "The doctor said," she told me, "that you needn't call any more as a patient, but he'd be glad to see you any time as a friend. And then he told me to look up my name in the encyclopædia and tell you what it means. It seems to be the name of a genus of flowering plants, and also the name of a country girl in Theocritus and Virgil. What do you suppose the doctor meant by that?"

"I know what he meant," said I. "I know now."

A word to a brother who may have come under the spell of the unquiet Lady Neurasthenia.

The formula was true. Even though gropingly at times, the physicians
of the walled cities had put their fingers upon the specific medicament.

And so for the exercise one is referred to good Doctor Tatum on Black
Oak Mountain—take the road to your right at the Methodist meeting
house in the pine-grove.

Absolute rest and exercise!

What rest more remedial than to sit with Amaryllis in the shade, and,
with a sixth sense, read the wordless Theocritan idyl of the gold-bannered
blue mountains marching orderly into the dormitories of the night?

OCTOBER AND JUNE

The Captain gazed gloomily at his sword that hung upon the wall. In
the closet near by was stored his faded uniform, stained and worn by
weather and service. What a long, long time it seemed since those old
days of war's alarms!

And now, veteran that he was of his country's strenuous times, he had
been reduced to abject surrender by a woman's soft eyes and smiling lips.
As he sat in his quiet room he held in his hand the letter he had just
received from her—the letter that had caused him to wear that look of
gloom. He re-read the fatal paragraph that had destroyed his hope.

> In declining the honor you have done me in asking me to be your wife,
> I feel that I ought to speak frankly. The reason I have for so doing is the
> great difference between our ages. I like you very, very much, but I am sure
> that our marriage would not be a happy one. I am sorry to have to refer
> to this, but I believe that you will appreciate my honesty in giving you the
> true reason.

The Captain sighed, and leaned his head upon his hand. Yes, there
were many years between their ages. But he was strong and rugged, he
had position and wealth. Would not his love, his tender care, and the
advantages he could bestow upon her make her forget the question of
age? Besides, he was almost sure that she cared for him.

The Captain was a man of prompt action. In the field he had been
distinguished for his decisiveness and energy. He would see her and
plead his cause again in person. Age!—what was it to come between him
and the one he loved?

In two hours he stood ready, in light marching order, for his greatest
battle. He took the train for the old Southern town in Tennessee where
she lived.

Theodora Deming was on the steps of the handsome, porticoed old mansion, enjoying the summer twilight, when the Captain entered the gate and came up the gravelled walk. She met him with a smile that was free from embarrassment. As the Captain stood on the step below her, the difference in their ages did not appear so great. He was tall and straight and clear-eyed and browned. She was in the bloom of lovely womanhood.

"I wasn't expecting you," said Theodora; "but now that you've come you may sit on the step. Didn't you get my letter?"

"I did," said the Captain, "and that's why I came. I say, now, Theo, reconsider your answer, won't you?"

Theodora smiled softly upon him. He carried his years well. She was really fond of his strength, his wholesome looks, his manliness—perhaps, if——

"No, no," she said, shaking her head, positively; "it's out of the question. I like you a whole lot, but marrying won't do. My age and yours are—but don't make me say it again—I told you in my letter."

The Captain flushed a little through the bronze on his face. He was silent for a while, gazing sadly into the twilight. Beyond a line of woods that he could see was a field where the boys in blue had once bivouacked on their march toward the sea. How long ago it seemed now! Truly, Fate and Father Time had tricked him sorely. Just a few years interposed between himself and happiness!

Theodora's hand crept down and rested in the clasp of his firm brown one. She felt, at least, that sentiment that is akin to love.

"Don't take it so hard, please," she said, gently. "It's all for the best. I've reasoned it out very wisely all by myself. Some day you'll be glad I didn't marry you. It would be very nice and lovely for a while—but, just think! In only a few short years what different tastes we would have. One of us would want to sit by the fireside and read, and maybe nurse neuralgia or rheumatism of evenings, while the other would be crazy for balls and theatres and late suppers. No, my dear friend. While it isn't exactly January and May, it's a clear case of October and pretty early in June."

"I'd always do what you wanted me to do, Theo. If you wanted to——"

"No, you wouldn't. You think now that you would, but you wouldn't. Please don't ask me any more."

The Captain had lost his battle. But he was a gallant warrior, and when he rose to make his final adieu his mouth was grimly set and his shoulders were squared.

He took the train for the North that night. On the next evening he was back in his room, where his sword was hanging against the wall. He was dressing for dinner, tying his white tie into a very careful bow. And at the same time he was indulging in a pensive soliloquy.

" 'Pon my honor, I believe Theo was right, after all. Nobody can deny that she's a peach, but she must be twenty-eight, at the very kindest calculation."

For you see, the Captain was only nineteen, and his sword had never been drawn except on the parade ground at Chattanooga, which was as near as he ever got to the Spanish-American War.

THE CHURCH WITH AN OVERSHOT-WHEEL

Lakelands is not to be found in the catalogues of fashionable summer resorts. It lies on a low spur of the Cumberland range of mountains on a little tributary of the Clinch River. Lakelands proper is a contented village of two dozen houses situated on a forlorn, narrow-gauge railroad line. You wonder whether the railroad lost itself in the pine woods and ran into Lakelands from fright and loneliness, or whether Lakelands got lost and huddled itself along the railroad to wait for the cars to carry it home.

You wonder again why it was named Lakelands. There are no lakes, and the lands about are too poor to be worth mentioning.

Half a mile from the village stands the Eagle House, a big, roomy old mansion run by Josiah Rankin for the accommodation of visitors who desire the mountain air at inexpensive rates. The Eagle House is delightfully mismanaged. It is full of ancient instead of modern improvements, and it is altogether as comfortably neglected and pleasingly disarranged as your own home. But you are furnished with clean rooms and good and abundant fare: yourself and the piny woods must do the rest. Nature has provided a mineral spring, grape-vine swings, and croquet—even the wickets are wooden. You have Art to thank only for the fiddle-and-guitar music twice a week at the hop in the rustic pavilion.

The patrons of the Eagle House are those who seek recreation as a necessity, as well as a pleasure. They are busy people, who may be likened to clocks that need a fortnight's winding to insure a year's running of their wheels. You will find students there from the lower towns, now and then an artist, or a geologist absorbed in construing the ancient strata of the hills. A few quiet families spend the summers there; and often one or two tired members of that patient sisterhood known to Lakelands as "schoolmarms."

A quarter of a mile from the Eagle House was what would have been described to its guests as "an object of interest" in a catalogue, had the Eagle House issued a catalogue. This was an old, old mill that was no longer a mill. In the words of Josiah Rankin, it was "the only church in the United States, sah, with a overshot-wheel; and the only mill in the world, sah, with pews and a pipe-organ." The guests of the Eagle House attended the old mill church each Sabbath, and heard the preacher liken the purified Christian to bolted flour ground to usefulness between the millstones of experience and suffering.

Every year about the beginning of autumn there came to the Eagle House one Abram Strong, who remained for a time an honored and beloved guest. In Lakelands he was called "Father Abram," because his hair was so white, his face so strong and kind and florid, his laugh so merry, and his black clothes and broad hat so priestly in appearance. Even new guests, after three or four days' acquaintance gave him this familiar title.

Father Abram came a long way to Lakelands. He lived in a big, roaring town in the northwest where he owned mills, not little mills with pews and an organ in them, but great, ugly, mountain-like mills that the freight trains crawled around all day like ants round an ant-heap. And now you must be told about Father Abram and the mill that was a church, for their stories run together.

In days when the church was a mill, Mr. Strong was the miller. There was no jollier, dustier, busier, happier miller in all the land than he. He lived in a little cottage across the road from the mill. His hand was heavy, but his toll was light, and the mountaineers brought their grain to him across many weary miles of rocky roads.

The delight of the miller's life was his little daughter, Aglaia. That was a brave name, truly, for a flaxen-haired toddler; but the mountaineers love sonorous and stately names. The mother had encountered it somewhere in a book, and the deed was done. In her babyhood Aglaia herself repudiated the name, as far as common use went, and persisted in calling herself "Dums." The miller and his wife often tried to coax from Aglaia the source of this mysterious name, but without results. At last they arrived at a theory. In the little garden behind the cottage was a bed of rhododendrons in which the child took a peculiar delight and interest. It may have been that she perceived in "Dums" a kinship to the formidable name of her favorite flowers.

When Aglaia was four years old she and her father used to go through a little performance in the mill every afternoon, that never failed to come off, the weather permitting. When supper was ready her mother would brush her hair and put on a clean apron and send her across to the mill to bring her father home. When the miller saw her coming in the mill door he would come forward, all white with the flour dust, and wave his hand and sing an old miller's song that was familiar in those parts and ran something like this:

"The wheel goes round,   He sings all day,
  The grist is ground,   His work is play,
    The dusty miller's merry.   While thinking of his dearie."

Then Aglaia would run to him laughing, and call: "Da-da, come take Dums home"; and the miller would swing her to his shoulder and march over to supper, singing the miller's song. Every evening this would take place.

One day, only a week after her fourth birthday, Aglaia disappeared. When last seen she was plucking wild flowers by the side of the road in front of the cottage. A little while later her mother went out to see that she did not stray too far away, and she was already gone.

Of course every effort was made to find her. The neighbors gathered and searched the woods and the mountains for miles around. They dragged every foot of the mill race and the creek for a long distance below the dam. Never a trace of her did they find. A night or two before there had been a family of wanderers camped in a grove near by. It was conjectured that they might have stolen the child; but when their wagon was overtaken and searched she could not be found.

The miller remained at the mill for nearly two years; and then his hope of finding her died out. He and his wife moved to the Northwest. In a few years he was the owner of a modern mill in one of the important milling cities in that region. Mrs. Strong never recovered from the shock caused by the loss of Aglaia, and two years after they moved away the miller was left to bear his sorrow alone.

When Abram Strong became prosperous he paid a visit to Lakelands and the old mill. The scene was a sad one for him, but he was a strong man, and always appeared cheery and kindly. It was then that he was inspired to convert the old mill into a church. Lakelands was too poor to build one; and the still poorer mountaineers could not assist. There was no place of worship nearer than twenty miles.

The miller altered the appearance of the mill as little as possible. The big overshot-wheel was left in its place. The young people who came to the church used to cut their initials in its soft and slowly decaying wood. The dam was partly destroyed, and the clear mountain stream rippled unchecked down its rocky bed. Inside the mill the changes were greater. The shafts and millstones and belt and pulleys were, of course, all removed. There were two rows of benches with aisles between, and a little raised platform and pulpit at one end. On three sides overhead was a gallery containing seats, and reached by a stairway inside. There was also an organ—a real pipe organ—in the gallery, that was the pride of the congregation of the Old Mill Church. Miss Phœbe Summers was the organist. The Lakelands boys proudly took turns at pumping it for her at each Sunday's service. The Rev. Mr. Bainbridge was the preacher, and rode down from Squirrel Gap on his old white horse without ever missing a service. And Abram Strong paid for everything. He paid the preacher five hundred dollars a year; and Miss Phœbe two hundred dollars.

Thus, in memory of Aglaia, the old mill was converted into a blessing for the community in which she had once lived. It seemed that the brief life of the child had brought about more good than the three score years and ten of many. But Abram Strong set up yet another monument to her memory.

Out from his mills in the Northwest came the "Aglaia" flour, made from the hardest and finest wheat that could be raised. The country soon found out that the "Aglaia" flour had two prices. One was the highest market price, and the other was—nothing.

Wherever there happened a calamity that left people destitute—a fire, a flood, a tornado, a strike, or a famine, there would go hurrying a generous consignment of the "Aglaia" at its "nothing" price. It was given away cautiously and judiciously, but it was freely given, and not a penny could the hungry ones pay for it. There got to be a saying that whenever there was a disastrous fire in the poor districts of a city the fire chief's buggy reached the scene first, next the "Aglaia" flour wagon, and then the fire engines.

So this was Abram Strong's other monument to Aglaia. Perhaps to a poet the theme may seem too utilitarian for beauty; but to some the fancy will seem sweet and fine that the pure, white, virgin flour, flying on its mission of love and charity, might be likened to the spirit of the lost child whose memory it signalized.

There came a year that brought hard times to the Cumberlands. Grain crops everywhere were light, and there were no local crops at all. Mountain floods had done much damage to property. Even game in the woods was so scarce that the hunters brought hardly enough home to keep their folks alive. Especially about Lakelands was the rigor felt.

As soon as Abram Strong heard of this his messages flew; and the little narrow-gauge cars began to unload "Aglaia" flour there. The miller's orders were to store the flour in the gallery of the Old Mill Church; and that every one who attended the church was to carry home a sack of it.

Two weeks after that Abram Strong came for his yearly visit to the Eagle House, and became "Father Abram" again.

That season the Eagle House had fewer guests than usual. Among them was Rose Chester. Miss Chester came to Lakelands from Atlanta, where she worked in a department store. This was the first vacation outing of her life. The wife of the store manager had once spent a summer at the Eagle House. She had taken a fancy to Rose, and had persuaded her to go there for her three weeks' holiday. The manager's wife gave her a letter to Mrs. Rankin, who gladly received her in her own charge and care.

Miss Chester was not very strong. She was about twenty, and pale and delicate from an indoor life. But one week of Lakelands gave her a brightness and spirit that changed her wonderfully. The time was early September when the Cumberlands are at their greatest beauty. The mountain foliage was growing brilliant with autumnal colors; one breathed aerial champagne, the nights were deliciously cool, causing one to snuggle cosily under the warm blankets of the Eagle House.

Father Abram and Miss Chester became great friends. The old miller learned her story from Mrs. Rankin, and his interest went out quickly to the slender, lonely girl who was making her own way in the world.

The mountain country was new to Miss Chester. She had lived many years in the warm, flat town of Atlanta; and the grandeur and variety of the Cumberlands delighted her. She was determined to enjoy every moment of her stay. Her little hoard of savings had been estimated so carefully in connection with her expenses that she knew almost to a penny what her very small surplus would be when she returned to work.

Miss Chester was fortunate in gaining Father Abram for a friend and companion. He knew every road and peak and slope of the mountains near Lakelands. Through him she became acquainted with the solemn delight of the shadowy, tilted aisles of the pine forests, the dignity of the bare crags, the crystal, tonic mornings, the dreamy, golden afternoons full of mysterious sadness. So her health improved and her spirits grew light. She had a laugh as genial and hearty in its feminine way as the famous laugh of Father Abram. Both of them were natural optimists; and both knew how to present a serene and cheerful face to the world.

One day Miss Chester learned from one of the guests the history of Father Abram's lost child. Quickly she hurried away and found the miller seated on his favorite rustic bench near the chalybeate spring. He was surprised when his little friend slipped her hand into his, and looked at him with tears in her eyes.

"Oh, Father Abram," she said. "I'm so sorry! I didn't know until to-day about your little daughter. You will find her yet some day—Oh, I hope you will."

The miller looked down at her with his strong, ready smile.

"Thank you, Miss Rose," he said, in his usual cheery tones. "But I do no expect to find Aglaia. For a few years I hoped that she had been stolen by vagrants, and that she still lived; but I have lost that hope. I believe that she was drowned."

"I can understand," said Miss Chester, "how the doubt must have made it so hard to bear. And yet you are so cheerful and so ready to make other people's burden light. Good Father Abram!"

"Good Miss Rose!" mimicked the miller, smiling. "Who thinks of others more than you do?"

A whimsical mood seemed to strike Miss Chester.

"Oh, Father Abram," she cried, "wouldn't it be grand if I should prove to be your daughter? Wouldn't it be romantic? And wouldn't you like to have me for a daughter?"

"Indeed, I would," said the miller, heartily. "If Aglaia had lived I could wish for nothing better than for her to have grown up to be just such a little woman as you are. Maybe you are Aglaia," he continued, falling in with her playful mood; "can't you remember when we lived at the mill?"

Miss Chester fell swiftly into serious meditation. Her large eyes were fixed vaguely upon something in the distance. Father Abram was amused at her quick return to seriousness. She sat thus for a long time before she spoke.

"No," she said at length, with a long sigh, "I can't remember anything at all about a mill. I don't think that I ever saw a flour mill in my life until I saw your funny little church. And if I were your little girl I would remember it, wouldn't I? I'm so sorry, Father Abram."

"So am I," said Father Abram, humoring her. "But if you cannot remember that you are my little girl, Miss Rose, surely you can recollect being some one else's. You remember your own parents, of course."

"Oh, yes; I remember them very well—especially my father. He wasn't a bit like you, Father Abram. Oh, I was only making believe. Come, now, you've rested long enough. You promised to show me the pool where you can see the trout playing, this afternoon. I never saw a trout."

Late one afternoon Father Abram set out for the old mill alone. He often went to sit and think of the old days when he lived in the cottage across the road. Time had smoothed away the sharpness of his grief until he no longer found the memory of those times painful. But whenever Abram Strong sat in the melancholy September afternoons on the spot where "Dums" used to run in every day with her yellow curls flying, the smile that Lakelands always saw upon his face was not there.

The miller made his way slowly up the winding, steep road. The trees crowded so close to the edge of it that he walked in their shade, with his hat in his hand. Squirrels ran playfully upon the old rail fence at his right. Quails were calling to their young broods in the wheat stubble. The low sun sent a torrent of pale gold up the ravine that opened to the west. Early September!—it was within a few days only of the anniversary of Aglaia's disappearance.

The old overshot-wheel, half covered with mountain ivy, caught patches of the warm sunlight filtering through the trees. The cottage across the road was still standing, but it would doubtless go down before the next winter's mountain blasts. It was overrun with morning glory and wild gourd vines, and the door hung by one hinge.

Father Abram pushed open the mill door, and entered softly. And then he stood still, wondering. He heard the sound of some one within, weeping inconsolably. He looked, and saw Miss Chester sitting in a dim pew, with her head bowed upon an open letter that her hands held.

Father Abram went to her, and laid one of his strong hands firmly upon hers. She looked up, breathed his name and tried to speak further.

"Not yet, Miss Rose," said the miller kindly. "Don't try to talk yet.

There's nothing as good for you as a nice, quiet little cry when you are feeling blue."

It seemed that the old miller, who had known so much sorrow himself, was a magician in driving it away from others. Miss Chester's sobs grew easier. Presently she took her little plain-bordered handkerchief and wiped away a drop or two that had fallen from her eyes upon Father Abram's big hand. Then she looked up and smiled through her tears. Miss Chester could always smile before her tears had dried, just as Father Abram could smile through his own grief. In that way the two were very much alike.

The miller asked her no questions; but by and by Miss Chester began to tell him.

It was the old story that always seems so big and important to the young, and that brings reminiscent smiles to their elders. Love was the theme, as may be supposed. There was a young man in Atlanta, full of all goodness and the graces, who had discovered that Miss Chester also possessed these qualities above all other people in Atlanta or anywhere else from Greenland to Patagonia. She showed Father Abram the letter over which she had been weeping. It was a manly, tender letter, a little superlative and urgent, after the style of love letters written by young men full of goodness and the graces. He proposed for Miss Chester's hand in marriage at once. Life, he said, since her departure for a three weeks' visit, was not to be endured. He begged for an immediate answer; and if it were favorable he promised to fly, ignoring the narrow-gauge railroad, at once to Lakelands.

"And now where does the trouble come in?" asked the miller when he had read the letter.

"I cannot marry him," said Miss Chester.

"Do you want to marry him?" asked Father Abram.

"Oh, I love him," she answered, "but——" Down went her head and she sobbed again.

"Come, Miss Rose," said the miller; "you can give me your confidence. I do not question you, but I think you can trust me."

"I do trust you," said the girl. "I will tell you why I must refuse Ralph. I am nobody; I haven't even a name; the name I call myself is a lie. Ralph is a noble man. I love him with all my heart, but I can never be his."

"What talk is this?" said Father Abram. "You said that you remember your parents. Why do you say that you have no name? I do not understand."

"I do remember them," said Miss Chester. "I remember them too well. My first recollections are of our life somewhere in the far South. We moved many times to different towns and states. I have picked cotton, and worked in factories, and have often gone without enough food and clothes. My mother was sometimes good to me; my father was always cruel, and beat me. I think they were both idle and unsettled.

"One night when we were living in a little town on a river near Atlanta they had a great quarrel. It was while they were abusing and taunting each other that I learned—oh, Father Abram, I learned that I didn't even have the right to be—don't you understand? I had no right even to a name; I was nobody.

"I ran away that night. I walked to Atlanta and found work. I gave myself the name of Rose Chester, and have earned my own living ever since. Now you know why I cannot marry Ralph—and, oh, I can never tell him why."

Better than any sympathy, more helpful than pity, was Father Abram's depreciation of her woes.

"Why, dear! is that all?" he said. "Fie, fie! I thought something was in the way. If this perfect young man is a man at all he will not care a pinch of bran for your family tree. Dear Miss Rose, take my word for it, it is yourself he cares for. Tell him frankly, just as you have told me, and I'll warrant that he will laugh at your story, and think all the more of you for it."

"I shall never tell him," said Miss Chester, sadly, "And I shall never marry him nor any one else. I have not the right."

But they saw a long shadow come bobbing up the sunlit road. And then came a shorter one bobbing by its side; and presently two strange figures approached the church. The long shadow was made by Miss Phœbe Summers, the organist, come to practice. Tommy Teague, aged twelve, was responsible for the shorter shadow. It was Tommy's day to pump the organ for Miss Phœbe, and his bare toes proudly spurned the dust of the road.

Miss Phœbe, in her lilac-spray chintz dress; with her accurate little curls hanging over each ear, courtesied low to Father Abram, and shook her curls ceremoniously at Miss Chester. Then she and her assistant climbed the steep stairway to the organ loft.

In the gathering shadows below, Father Abram and Miss Chester lingered. They were silent; and it is likely that they were busy with their memories. Miss Chester sat, leaning her head on her hand, with her eyes fixed far away. Father Abram stood in the next pew, looking thoughtfully out of the door at the road and the ruined cottage.

Suddenly the scene was transformed for him back almost a score of years into the past. For, as Tommy pumped away, Miss Phœbe struck a low bass note on the organ and held it to test the volume of air that it contained. The church ceased to exist, so far as Father Abram was concerned. The deep, booming vibration that shook the little frame building was no note from an organ, but the humming of the mill machinery. He felt sure that the old overshot-wheel was turning; that he was back again, a dusty, merry miller in the old mountain mill. And now evening was come, and soon would come Aglaia with flying colors, toddling across the road to take him home to supper. Father Abram's eyes were fixed upon the broken door of the cottage.

And then came another wonder. In the gallery overhead the sacks of flour were stacked in long rows. Perhaps a mouse had been at one of them; anyway, the jar of the deep organ note shook down between the cracks of the gallery floor a stream of flour, covering Father Abram from head to foot with the white dust. And then the old miller stepped into the aisle, and waved his arms and began to sing the miller's song:

"The wheel goes round,
    The grist is ground,
        The dusty miller's merry."

—and then the rest of the miracle happened. Miss Chester was leaning forward from her pew, as pale as the flour itself, her wide-open eyes staring at Father Abram like one in a waking dream. When he began the song she stretched out her arms to him; her lips moved; she called to him in dreamy tones: "Da-da, come take Dums home!"

Miss Phœbe released the low key of the organ. But her work had been well done. The note that she struck had beaten down the doors of a closed memory; and Father Abram held his lost Aglaia close in his arms.

When you visit Lakelands they will tell you more of this story. They will tell you how the lines of it were afterward traced, and the history of the miller's daughter revealed after the gipsy wanderers had stolen her on that September day, attracted by her childish beauty. But you should wait until you sit comfortably on the shaded porch of the Eagle House, and then you can have the story at your ease. It seems best that our part of it should close while Miss Phœbe's deep bass note was yet reverberating softly.

And yet, to my mind, the finest thing of it all happened while Father Abram and his daughter were walking back to the Eagle House in the long twilight, almost too glad to speak.

"Father," she said, somewhat timidly and doubtfully, "have you a great deal of money?"

"A great deal?" said the miller. "Well, that depends. There is plenty unless you want to buy the moon or something equally expensive."

"Would it cost very, very much," asked Aglaia, who had always counted her dimes so carefully, "to send a telegram to Atlanta?"

"Ah," said Father Abram, with a little sigh, "I see. You want to ask Ralph to come."

"I want to ask him to wait," she said, "I have just found my father, and I want it to be just two for a while. I want to tell him he will have to wait."

NEW YORK BY CAMP FIRE LIGHT

Away out in the Creek Nation we learned things about New York.

We were on a hunting trip, and were camped one night on the bank of a little stream. Bud Kingsbury was our skilled hunter and guide, and it was from his lips that we had explanations of Manhattan and the queer folks that inhabit it. Bud had once spent a month in the metropolis, and a week or two at other times, and he was pleased to discourse to us of what he had seen.

Fifty yards away from our camp was pitched the teepee of a wandering family of Indians that had come up and settled there for the night. An old, old Indian woman was trying to build a fire under an iron pot hung upon three sticks.

Bud went over to her assistance, and soon had her fire going. When he came back we complimented him playfully upon his gallantry.

"Oh," said Bud, "don't mention it. It's a way I have. Whenever I see a lady trying to cook things in a pot and having trouble I always go to the rescue. I done the same thing once in a high-toned house in New York City. Heap big society teepee on Fifth Avenue. That Injun lady kind of recalled it to my mind. Yes, I endeavors to be polite and help the ladies out."

The camp demanded the particulars.

"I was manager of the Triangle B Ranch in the Panhandle," said Bud. "It was owned at that time by old man Sterling, of New York. He wanted to sell out, and he wrote for me to come on to New York and explain the ranch to the syndicate that wanted to buy. So I sends to Fort Worth and has a forty-dollar suit of clothes made, and hits the trail for the big village.

"Well, when I got there, old man Sterling and his outfit certainly laid themselves out to be agreeable. We had business and pleasure so mixed up that you couldn't tell whether it was a treat or a trade half the time. We had trolley rides, and cigars, and theatre round-ups, and rubber parties."

"Rubber parties?" said a listener, inquiringly.

"Sure," said Bud. "Didn't you never attend 'em? You walk around and try to look at the tops of the skyscrapers. Well, we sold the ranch, and old man Sterling asks me 'round to his house to take grub on the night before I started back. It wasn't any high-collared affair—just me and the old man and his wife and daughter. But they was a fine-haired outfit all right, and the lilies of the field wasn't in it. They made my Fort Worth clothes carpenter look like a dealer in horse blankets and gee strings. And then the table was all pompous with flowers, and there was a whole kit of tools laid out beside everybody's plate. You'd have thought you was fixed out to burglarize a restaurant before you could get your grub. But I'd been in New York over a week then, and I was getting on to stylish ways. I kind of trailed behind and watched others use the hardware supplies, and then I tackled the chuck with the same weapons. It ain't much trouble to travel with the high-flyers after you find out their gait. I got along fine. I was feeling cool and agreeable, and pretty soon I was talking away fluent as you please, all about the ranch and the West, and telling 'em how the Indians eat grasshopper stew and snakes, and you never saw people so interested.

"But the real joy of that feast was that Miss Sterling. Just a little trick she was, not bigger than two bits' worth of chewing plug; but she had a way about her that seemed to say she was the people, and you believed it. And yet, she never put on any airs, and she smiled at me the same as if I was a millionaire while I was telling about a Creek dog feast and listened like it was news from home.

"By and by, after we had eat oysters and some watery soup and truck that never was in my repertory, a Methodist preacher brings in a kind of camp stove arrangement, all silver, on long legs, with a lamp under it.

"Miss Sterling lights up and begins to do some cooking right on the supper table. I wondered why old man Sterling didn't hire a cook with all the money he had. Pretty soon she dished out some cheesy tasting truck that she said was rabbit, but I swear there had never been a Molly cotton tail in a mile of it.

"The last thing on the programme was lemonade. It was brought around in little flat glass bowls and set by your plate. I was pretty thirsty, and I picked up mine and took a big swig of it. Right there was where the little lady had made a mistake. She had put in the lemon all right, but she'd forgot the sugar. The best housekeepers slip up sometimes. I thought maybe Miss Sterling was just learning to keep house and cook— that rabbit would surely make you think so—and I says to myself, 'Little lady, sugar or no sugar I'll stand by you,' and I raises up by bowl again and drinks the last drop of the lemonade. And then all the balance of 'em picks up their bowls and does the same. And then I gives Miss Sterling the laugh proper, just to carry it off like a joke, so she wouldn't feel bad about the mistake.

"After we all went into the sitting room she sat down and talked to me quite awhile.

"'It was so kind of you, Mr. Kingsbury,' says she, 'to bring my blunder off so nicely. It was so stupid of me to forget the sugar.'

"'Never you mind,' says I, 'some lucky man will throw his rope over a mighty elegant little housekeeper some day, not far from here.'

"'If you mean me, Mr. Kingsbury,' says she laughing out loud, I hope he will be as lenient with my poor housekeeping as you have been.'

" 'Don't mention it,' says I 'Anything to oblige the ladies.' "

Bud ceased his reminiscences. And then some one asked him what he considered the most striking and prominent trait of New Yorkers.

"The most visible and peculiar trait of New York folks," answered Bud, "is New York. Most of 'em has New York on the brain. They have heard of other places, such as Waco, and Paris, and Hot Springs, and London; but they don't believe in 'em. They think that town is all Merino. Now to show you how much they care for their village I'll tell you about one of 'em that strayed out as far as the Triangle B while I was working there.

"This New Yorker come out there looking for a job on the ranch. He said he was a good horseback rider, and there were pieces of tanbark hanging on his clothes yet from his riding school.

"Well, for a while they put him to keeping books in the ranch store, for he was a devil at figures. But he got tired of that, and asked for something more in the line of activity. The boys on the ranch like him all right, but he made us tired shouting New York all the time. Every night he'd tell us about East River and J. P. Morgan and the Eden Musee and Hetty Green and Central Park till we used to throw tin plates and branding irons at him.

"One day this chap gets on a pitching pony, and the pony kind of sidled up his back and went to eating grass while the New Yorker was coming down.

"He come down on his head on a chunk of mesquite wood, and he didn't show any designs toward getting up again. We laid him out in a tent, and he begun to look pretty dead. So Gideon Pease saddles up and burns the wind for old Doc Sleeper's residence in Dogtown, thirty miles away.

"The doctor comes over and he investigates the patient.

" 'Boys,' says he, 'you might as well go to playing seven-up for his saddle and clothes, for his head's fractured and if he lives ten minutes it will be a remarkable case of longevity.'

"Of course we didn't gamble for the poor rooster's saddle—that was one of Doc's jokes. But we stood around feeling solemn, and all of us forgive him for having talked us to death about New York.

"I never saw anybody about to hand in his checks act more peaceful than this fellow. His eyes were fixed 'way up in the air, and he was using rambling words to himself all about sweet music and beautiful streets and white-robed forms, and he was smiling like dying was a pleasure.

" 'He's about gone now,' said Doc. 'Whenever they begin to think they see heaven it's all off.'

"Blamed if that New York man didn't sit right up when he heard the Doc say that.

" 'Say,' says he, kind of disappointed, 'was that heaven? Confound it all, I thought it was Broadway. Some of you fellows get my clothes. I'm going to get up.'

"And I'll be blamed," concluded Bud, "if he wasn't on the train with a ticket for New York in his pocket four days afterward!"

THE ADVENTURES OF SHAMROCK JOLNES

I am so fortunate as to count Shamrock Jolnes, the great New York detective, among my muster of friends. Jolnes is what is called the "inside man" of the city detective force. He is an expert in the use of the typewriter, and it is his duty, whenever there is a "murder mystery" to be solved, to sit at a desk telephone at headquarters and take down the message of "cranks" who 'phone in their confessions to having committed the crime.

But on certain "off" days when confessions are coming in slowly and three or four newspapers have run to earth as many different guilty persons, Jolnes will knock about the town with me, exhibiting, to my great delight and instruction, his marvellous powers of observation and deduction.

The other day I dropped in at Headquarters and found the great detective gazing thoughtfully at a string that was tied tightly around his little finger.

"Good morning, Whatsup," he said, without turning his head. "I'm glad to notice that you've had your house fitted up with electric lights at last."

"Will you please tell me," I said, in surprise, "how you knew that? I am sure that I never mentioned the fact to any one, and the wiring was a rush order not completed until this morning."

"Nothing easier," said Jolnes, genially. "As you came in I caught the odor of the cigar you are smoking. I know an expensive cigar; and I know that not more than three men in New York can afford to smoke cigars and pay gas bills too at the present time. That was an easy one. But I am working just now on a little problem of my own."

"Why have you that string on your finger?" I asked.

"That's the problem," said Jolnes. "My wife tied that on this morning to remind me of something I was to send up to the house. Sit down, Whatsup, and excuse me for a few moments."

The distinguished detective went to a wall telephone, and stood with the receiver to his ear for probably ten minutes.

"Were you listening to a confession?" I asked, when he had returned to his chair.

"Perhaps," said Jolnes, with a smile, "it might be called something of the sort. To be frank with you, Whatsup, I've cut out the dope. I've been increasing the quantity for so long that morphine doesn't have much effect on me any more. I've got to have something more powerful. That telephone I just went to is connected with a room in the Waldorf where there's an author's reading in progress. Now, to get at the solution of this string."

After five minutes of silent pondering, Jolnes looked at me, with a smile, and nodded his head.

"Wonderful man!" I exclaimed; "already?"

"It is quite simple," he said, holding up his finger. "You see that knot? That is to prevent my forgetting. It is, therefore, a forget-me-knot. A forget-me-not is a flower. It was a sack of flour that I was to send home!"

"Beautiful!" I could not help crying out in admiration.

"Suppose we go out for a ramble," suggested Jolnes.

"There is only one case of importance on hand now. Old man McCarty, one hundred and four years old, died from eating too many bananas. The evidence points so strongly to the Mafia that the police have surrounded the Second Avenue Katzenjammer Gambrinus Club No. 2, and the capture of the assassin is only the matter of a few hours. The detective force has not yet been called on for assistance."

Jolnes and I went out and up the street toward the corner, where we were to catch a surface car.

Halfway up the block we met Rheingelder, an acquaintance of ours, who held a City Hall position.

"Good morning, Rheingelder," said Jolnes, halting.

"Nice breakfast that was you had this morning."

Always on the lookout for the detective's remarkable feats of deduction, I saw Jolnes's eyes flash for an instant upon a long yellow splash on the shirt bosom and a smaller one upon the chin of Rheingelder—both undoubtedly made by the yolk of an egg.

"Oh, dot is some of your detectiveness," said Rheingelder, shaking all over with a smile. "Vell, I bet you trinks and cigars all around dot you cannot tell vot I haf eaten for breakfast."

"Done," said Jolnes. "Sausage, pumpernickel, and coffee."

Rheingelder admitted the correctness of the surmise and paid the bet. When we had proceeded on our way I said to Jolnes:

"I thought you looked at the egg spilled on his chin and shirt front."

"I did," said Jolnes. "That is where I began my deduction. Rheingelder is a very economical, saving man. Yesterday eggs dropped in the market to twenty-eight cents per dozen. To-day they are quoted at forty-two. Rheingelder ate eggs yesterday, and to-day he went back to his usual fare. A little thing like this isn't anything, Whatsup; it belongs to the primary arithmetic class."

When we boarded the street car we found the seats all occupied—principally by ladies. Jolnes and I stood on the rear platform.

About the middle of the car there sat an elderly man with a short, gray beard, who looked to be the typical, well-dressed New Yorker. At successive corners other ladies climbed aboard, and soon three or four of them were standing over the man, clinging to straps and glaring meaningly at the man who occupied the coveted seat. But he resolutely retained his place.

"We New Yorkers," I remarked to Jolnes, "have about lost our manners, as far as the exercise of them in public goes."

"Perhaps so," said Jolnes, lightly; "but the man you evidently refer to happens to be a very chivalrous and courteous gentleman from Old Virginia. He is spending a few days in New York with his wife and two daughters, and he leaves for the South to-night."

"You know him, then?" I said, in amazement.

"I never saw him before we stepped on the car," declared the detective, smilingly.

By the gold tooth of the Witch of Endor!" I cried, "if you can construe all that from his appearance you are dealing in nothing else than black art."

"The habit of observation—nothing more," said Jolnes. "If the old gentleman gets off the car before we do, I think I can demonstrate to you the accuracy of my deduction."

Three blocks farther along the gentleman rose to leave the car. Jolnes addressed him at the door:

"Pardon me, sir, but are you not Colonel Hunter, of Norfolk, Virginia?"

"No, suh," was the extremely courteous answer. "My name, suh, is Ellison—Major Winfield R. Ellison, from Fairfax County, in the same state. I know a good many people, suh, in Norfolk—the Goodriches, the Tollivers, and the Crabtrees, suh, but I never had the pleasure of meeting yo' friend, Colonel Hunter. I am happy to say, suh, that I am going back to Virginia to-night, after having spent a week in yo' city with my wife and three daughters. I shall be in Norfolk in about ten days, and if you will give me yo' name, suh, I will take pleasure in looking up Colonel Hunter and telling him that you inquired after him, suh."

"Thank you," said Jolnes; "tell him that Reynolds sent his regards, if you will be so kind."

I glanced at the great New York detective and saw that a look of intense chagrin had come upon his clear-cut features. Failure in the slightest point always galled Shamrock Jolnes.

"Did you say your *three* daughters?" he asked of the Virginia gentleman.

"Yes, suh, my three daughters, all as fine girls as there are in Fairfax County," was the answer.

With that Major Ellison stopped the car and began to descend the step. Shamrock Jolnes clutched his arm.

"One moment, sir," he begged, in an urbane voice in which I alone detected the anxiety—"am I not right in believing that one of the young ladies is an *adopted* daughter?"

"You are, suh," admitted the major, from the ground, "but how the devil you knew it, suh, is mo' than I can tell."

"And mo' than I can tell, too," I said, as the car went on.

Jolnes was restored to his calm, observant serenity by having wrested victory from his apparent failure; so after we got off the car he invited me into a café promising to reveal the process of his latest wonderful feat.

"In the first place," he began after we were comfortably seated, "I knew the gentleman was no New Yorker because he was flushed and uneasy and restless on account of the ladies that were standing, although he did not rise and give them his seat. I decided from his appearance that he was a Southerner rather than a Westerner.

"Next I began to figure out his reason for not relinquishing his seat to a lady when he evidently felt strongly, but not overpoweringly, impelled to do so. I very quickly decided upon that. I noticed that one of his eyes had received a severe jab in one corner, which was red and inflamed, and that all over his face were tiny round marks about the size of the end of an uncut lead pencil. Also upon both of his patent-leather shoes were a number of deep imprints shaped like ovals cut off square at one end.

"Now, there is only one district in New York City where a man is bound to receive scars and wounds and indentations of that sort—and that is along the sidewalks of Twenty-third Street and a portion of Sixth Avenue south of there. I knew from the imprints of trampling French heels on his feet and the marks of countless jabs in the face from umbrellas and parasols carried by women in the shopping district that he had been in conflict with the amazonian troops. And as he was a man of intelligent appearance, I knew he would not have braved such dangers unless he had been dragged thither by his own women folk. Therefore, when he got on the car his anger at the treatment he had received was sufficient to make him keep his seat in spite of his traditions of Southern chivalry."

"That is all very well," I said, "but why did you insist upon daughters—and especially two daughters? Why couldn't a wife alone have taken him shopping?"

"There had to be daughters," said Jolnes, calmly. "If he had only a wife, and she near his own age, he could have bluffed her into going alone. If he had a young wife she would prefer to go alone. So there you are."

"I'll admit that," I said; "but, now, why two daughters? And how, in the name of all the prophets, did you guess that one was adopted when he told you he had three?"

"Don't say guess," said Jolnes, with a touch of pride in his air; "there is no such word in the lexicon of ratiocination. In Major Ellison's button-hole there was a carnation and a rosebud backed by a geranium leaf. No woman ever combined a carnation and a rosebud into a boutonnière. Close your eyes, Whatsup, and give the logic of your imagination a chance. Cannot you see the lovely Adele fastening the carnation to the lapel so that papa may be gay upon the street? And then the romping Edith May dancing up with sisterly jealousy to add her rosebud to the adornment?"

"And then," I cried, beginning to feel enthusiasm, "when he declared that he had three daughters——"

"I could see," said Jolnes, "one in the background who added no flower; and I knew that she must be——"

"Adopted!" I broke in. "I give you every credit; but how did you know he was leaving for the South to-night?"

"In his breast pocket," said the great detective, "something large and oval made a protuberance. Good liquor is scarce on trains, and it is a long journey from New York to Fairfax County."

"Again, I must bow to you," I said. "And tell me this, so that my last shred of doubt will be cleared away; why did you decide that he was from Virginia?"

"It was very faint, I admit," answered Shamrock Jolnes, "but no trained observer could have failed to detect the odor of mint in the car."

THE LADY HIGHER UP

New York City, they said, was deserted; and that accounted, doubtless, for the sounds carrying so far in the tranquil summer air. The breeze was south-by-southwest; the hour was midnight; the theme was a bit of feminine gossip by wireless mythology. Three hundred and sixty-five feet above the heated asphalt the tiptoeing symbolic deity on Manhattan pointed her vacillating arrow straight, for the time, in the direction of her exalted sister on Liberty Island. The lights of the great Garden were out; the benches in the Square were filled with sleepers in postures so strange that beside them the writhing figures in Doré's illustrations of the Inferno would have straightened into tailor's dummies. The statue of Diana on the tower of the Garden—its constancy shown by its weathercock ways, its innocence by the coating of gold that it has acquired, its devotion to style by its single, graceful flying scarf, its candor and artlessness by its habit of ever drawing the long bow, its metropolitanism by its posture of swift flight to catch a Harlem train—remained poised with its arrow pointed across the upper bay. Had that arrow sped truly and horizontally it would have passed fifty feet above the head of the heroic matron whose duty it is to offer a cast-ironical welcome to the oppressed of other lands.

Seaward this lady gazed, and the furrows between steamship lines began to cut steerage rates. The translators, too, have put an extra burden upon her. "Liberty Lighting the World" (as her creator christened her) would have had a no more responsible duty, except for the size of it, than that of an electrician or a Standard Oil magnate. But to "enlighten" the world (as our learned civic guardians "Englished" it) requires abler qualities. And so poor Liberty, instead of having a sinecure as a mere illuminator, must be converted into a Chautauqua schoolma'am, with the oceans for her field instead of the placid, classic lake. With a fireless torch and an empty head must she dispel the shadows of the world, and teach it its A, B, C's.

"Ah, there, Mrs. Liberty!" called a clear, rollicking soprano voice through the still, midnight air.

"Is that you, Miss Diana? Excuse my not turning my head. I'm not as flighty and whirly-whirly as some. And 'tis so hoarse I am I can hardly talk on account of the peanut-hulls left on the stairs in me throat by that last boatload of tourists from Marietta, Ohio. 'Tis after being a fine evening, miss."

"If you don't mind my asking," came the bell-like tones of the golden statue, "I'd like to know where you got that City Hall brogue. I didn't know that Liberty was necessarily Irish."

"If ye'd studied the history of art in its foreign complications ye'd not need to ask," replied the offshore statue. "If ye wasn't so lightheaded and giddy ye'd know that I was made by a Dago and presented to the American people on behalf of the French Government for the purpose of welcomin' Irish immigrants into the Dutch city of New York. 'Tis that I've been doing night and day since I was erected. Ye must know, Miss Diana, that 'tis with statues the same as with people—'tis not their makers nor the purposes for which they were created that influence the operations of their tongues at all—it's the associations with which they become associated, I'm telling ye."

"You're dead right," agreed Diana. "I notice it on myself. If any of the old guys from Olympus were to come along and hand me any hot air in the ancient Greek I couldn't tell it from a conversation between a Coney Island car conductor and a five-cent fare."

"I'm right glad ye've made up your mind to be sociable, Miss Diana," said Mrs. Liberty. " 'Tis a lonesome life I have down here. Is there anything doin' up in the city, Miss Diana, dear?"

"Oh, la, la, la!—no," said Diana. "Notice that 'la, la, la,' Aunt Liberty? Got that from 'Paris by Night' on the roof garden under me. You'll hear that 'la, la, la' at the Café McCann now, along with 'garsong.' The bohemian crowd there have become tired of 'garsong' since O'Rafferty, the head waiter, punched three of them for calling him it. Oh, no; the town's strictly on the bum these nights. Everybody's away. Saw a downtown merchant on the roof garden this evening with his stenographer. Show was so dull he went to sleep. A waiter biting on a dime tip to see if it was good half woke him up. He looks around and sees his little pothooks perpetrator. 'H'm!' says he, 'will you take a letter, Miss De St. Montmorency?' 'Sure, in a minute,' says she, 'if you make it an X.'

"That was the best thing happened on the roof. So you see how dull it is. La, la, la!"

" 'Tis fine ye have it up there in society, Miss Diana. Ye have the cat show and the horse show and the military tournaments where the privates look grand as generals and the generals try to look grand as floor-walkers. And ye have the Sportsmen's Show, where the girl that measures 36, 19, 45 cooks breakfast food in a birch-bark wigwam on the banks of the Grand Canal of Venice conducted by one of the Vanderbilts, Bernard McFadden, and the Reverends Dowie and Duss. And ye have the French ball, where the original Cohens and the Robert Emmet-Sangerbund Society dance the Highland fling one with another. And ye have the grand O'Ryan ball, which is the most beautiful pageant in the world, where the French students vie with the Tyrolean warblers in doin' the cake walk. Ye have the best job for a statue in the whole town, Miss Diana."

" 'Tis weary work," sighed the island statue, "disseminatin' the science of liberty in New York Bay. Sometimes when I take a peep down at Ellis Island and see the gang of immigrants I'm supposed to light up, 'tis tempted I am to blow out the gas and let the coroner write out their naturalization papers."

"Say, it's a shame, ain't it, to give you the worst end of it?" came the sympathetic antiphony of the steeplechase goddess. "It must be awfully lonesome down there with so much water around you. I don't see how you ever keep your hair in curl. And that Mother Hubbard you are wearing went out ten years ago. I think those sculptor guys ought to be held for damages for putting iron or marble clothes on a lady. That's where Mr. St. Gaudens was wise. I'm always a little ahead of the styles; but they're coming my way pretty fast. Excuse my back a moment—I caught a puff of wind from the north—shouldn't wonder if things had loosened up in Esopus. There, now! It's in the West—I should think that gold plank would have calmed the air out in that direction. What were you saying, Mrs. Liberty?"

"A fine chat I've had with ye, Miss Diana, ma'am, but I see one of them European steamers a-sailin' up the Narrows, and I must be attendin' to me duties. 'Tis me job to extend aloft the torch of Liberty to welcome all them that survive the kicks that the steerage stewards give 'em while landin'. Sure 'tis a great country ye can come to for $8.50, and the doctor waitin' to send ye back home free if he sees yer eyes red from cryin' for it."

The golden statue veered in the changing breeze, menacing many points on the horizon with its aureate arrow.

"So long, Aunt Liberty," sweetly called Diana of the Tower. "Some night, when the wind's right, I'll call you up again. But—say! you haven't got such a fierce kick coming about your job. I've kept pretty good watch on the island of Manhattan since I've been up here. That's a pretty sick-looking bunch of liberty chasers they dump down at your end of it; but they don't all stay that way. Every little while up here I see guys signing checks and voting the right ticket, and encouraging the arts and taking a bath every morning, that was shoved ashore by a dock laborer born in the United States who never earned over forty dollars a month. Don't run down your job, Aunt Liberty; you're all right, all right."

THE GREATER CONEY

"Next Sunday," said Dennis Carnahan, "I'll be after going down to see the new Coney Island that's risen like a phœnix bird from the ashes of the old resort. I'm going with Norah Flynn, and we'll fall victims to all the dry goods deceptions, from the red-flannel eruption of Mount Vesuvius to the pink silk ribbons on the race-suicide problems in the incubator kiosk.

"Was I there before? I was. I was there last Tuesday. Did I see the sights? I did not.

"Last Monday I amalgamated myself with the Bricklayers' Union, and in accordance with the rules I was ordered to quit work the same day on account of a sympathy strike with the Lady Salmon Canners' Lodge No. 2, of Tacoma, Washington.

" 'Twas disturbed I was in mind and proclivities by losing me job, bein' already harassed in me soul on account of havin' quarrelled with Norah Flynn a week before by reason of hard words spoken at the Dairymen and Street-Sprinkler Drivers' semi-annual ball, caused by jealousy and prickly heat and that divil, Andy Coghlin.

"So, I says, it will be Coney for Tuesday; and if the chutes and the short change and the green-corn silk between the teeth don't create diversions and get me feeling better, then I don't know at all.

"Ye will have heard that Coney has received moral reconstruction. The old Bowery, where they used to take your tintype by force and give ye knockout drops before having your palm read, is now called the Wall Street of the island. The wienerwurst stands are required by law to keep a news ticker in 'em; and the doughnuts are examined every four years by a retired steamboat inspector. The nigger man's head that was used by the old patrons to throw baseballs at is now illegal; and, by order of the Police Commissioner the image of a man drivin' an automobile has been substituted. I hear that the old immoral amusements have been suppressed. People who used to go down from New York to sit in the sand and dab-ble in the surf now give up their quarters to squeeze through turnstiles and see imitations of city fires and floods painted on canvas. The reprehensible and degradin' resorts that disgraced old Coney are said to be wiped out. The wipin'-out process consists of raisin' the price from 10 cents to 25 cents, and hirin' a blonde named Maudie to sell tickets instead of Mickey, the Bowery Bite. That's what they say—I don't know.

"But to Coney I goes a-Tuesday. I gets off the 'L' and starts for the glitterin' show. 'Twas a fine sight. The Babylonian towers and the Hindoo roof gardens was blazin' with thousands of electric lights, and the streets was thick with people. 'Tis a true thing they say that Coney levels all rank. I see millionaires eatin' popcorn and trampin' along with the crowd; and I see eight-dollar-a-week clothin'-store clerks in red automobiles fightin' one another for who'd squeeze the horn when they come to a corner.

" 'I made a mistake,' I says to myself. 'Twas not Coney I needed. When a man's sad 'tis not scenes of hilarity he wants. 'Twould be far better for him to meditate in a graveyard or to attend services at the Paradise Roof Gardens. 'Tis no consolation when a man's lost his sweetheart to order hot corn and have the waiter bring him the powdered sugar cruet instead of salt and then conceal himself, or to have Zozookum, the gipsy palmist, tell him that he has three children and to look out for another serious calamity; price twenty-five cents.

"I walked far away down on the beach, to the ruins of an old pavilion near one corner of this new private park, Dreamland. A year ago that old pavilion was standin' up straight and the old-style waiters was slammin' a week's supply of clam chowder down in front of you for a nickel and callin' you 'cully' friendly, and vice was rampant, and you got back to New York with enough change to take a car at the bridge. Now they tell me that they serve Welsh rabbits on Surf Avenue, and you get the right change back in the movin'-picture joints.

"I sat down at one side of the old pavilion and looked at the surf spreadin' itself on the beach, and thought about the time me and Norah Flynn sat on that spot last summer. 'Twas before reform struck the island; and we was happy. We had tintypes and chowder in the ribald dives, and the Egyptian Sorceress of the Nile told Norah out of her hand, while I was waitin' in the door, that 'twould be the luck of her to marry a red-headed gossoon with two crooked legs, and I was overrunnin' with joy on account of the illusion. And 'twas there that Norah Flynn put her two hands in mine a year before and we talked of flats and the things she could cook and the love business that goes with such episodes. And that was Coney as we loved it, and as the hand of Satan was upon it, friendly and noisy and your money's worth, with no fence around the ocean and not too many electric lights to show the sleeve of a black serge coat against a white shirtwaist.

"I sat with my back to the parks where they had the moon and the dreams and the steeples corralled, and longed for the old Coney. There wasn't many people on the beach. Lots of them was feedin' pennies to the slot machines to see the 'Interrupted Courtship' in the movin' pictures; and a good many was takin' the air in the Canals of Venice and some was breathin' the smoke of the sea battle by actual warships in a tank filled with real water. A few was down on the sands enjoyin' the moonlight and the water. And the heart of me was heavy for the new morals of the old island, while the bands behind me played and the sea pounded on the bass drum in front.

"And directly I got up and walked along the old pavilion, and there on the other side of, half in the dark, was a slip of a girl sittin' on the tumble-down timbers, and unless I'm a liar she was cryin' by herself there, all alone.

" 'Is it trouble you are in, now, Miss,' says I; 'and what's to be done about it?'

" " 'Tis none of your business at all, Denny Carnahan,' says she, sittin' up straight. And it was the voice of no other than Norah Flynn.

" 'Then it's not,' says I, 'and we're after having a pleasant evening, Miss Flynn. Have ye seen the sights of this new Coney Island, then? I presume ye have come here for that purpose,' says I.

" 'I have,' says she. 'Me mother and Uncle Tim they are waiting beyond. 'Tis an elegant evening I've had. I've seen all the attractions that be.'

" 'Right ye are,' says I to Norah; and I don't know when I've been that amused. After disportin' meself among the most laughable moral improvements of the revised shell games I took meself to the shore for the benefit of the cool air. 'And did ye observe the Durbar, Miss Flynn?'

" 'I did,' says she, reflectin'; 'but 'tis not safe, I'm thinkin', to ride down them slantin' things into the water.'

" 'How did ye fancy the shoot the chutes?' I asks.

" 'True, then, I'm afraid of guns,' says Norah. 'They make such noise in my ears. But Uncle Tim, he shot them, he did, and won cigars. 'Tis a fine time we had this day, Mr. Carnahan.'

" 'I'm glad you've enjoyed yerself,' I says. 'I suppose you've had a roarin' fine time seein' the sights. And how did the incubators and the helter-skelter and the midgets suit the taste of ye?'

" 'I—I wasn't hungry,' says Norah, faint. 'But mother ate a quantity of all of 'em. I'm that pleased with the fine things in the new Coney Island,' says she, 'that it's the happiest day I've seen in a long time, at all.'

" 'Did you see Venice?' says I.

" 'We did,' says she. 'She was a beauty. She was all dressed in red, she was, with——'

"I listened no more to Norah Flynn. I stepped up and gathered her in my arms.

" ' 'Tis a story-teller ye are, Norah Flynn,' says I. 'Ye've seen no more of the greater Coney Island than I have meself. Come, now, tell the truth—ye came to sit by the old pavilion by the waves where you sat last summer and made Dennis Carnahan a happy man. Speak up, and tell the truth.'

"Norah stuck her nose against me vest.

" 'I despise it, Denny,' she says, half cryin'. 'Mother and Uncle Tim went to see the shows, but I came down here to think of you. I couldn't bear the lights and the crowd. Are you forgivin' me, Denny, for the words we had?'

" ' 'Twas me fault,' says I. 'I came here for the same reason meself. Look at the lights, Norah,' I says, turning my back to the sea—'ain't they pretty?'

" 'They are,' says Norah, with her eyes shinin'; 'and do ye hear the bands playin'? Oh, Denny, I think I'd like to see it all.'

" 'The old Coney is gone, darlin',' I says to her. 'Everything moves. When a man's glad it's not scenes of sadness he wants. 'Tis a great Coney we have here, but we couldn't see it till we got in the humor for it. Next Sunday, Norah darlin', we'll see the new place from end to end.' "

LAW AND ORDER

I found myself in Texas recently, revisiting old places and vistas. At a sheep ranch where I had sojourned many years ago, I stopped for a week. And, as all visitors do, I heartily plunged into the business at hand, which happened to be that of dipping the sheep.

Now, this process is so different from ordinary human baptism that it deserves a word of itself. A vast iron cauldron with half the fires of Avernus beneath it is partly filled with water that soon boils furiously. Into that is cast concentrated lye, lime, and sulphur, which is allowed to stew and fume until the witches' broth is strong enough to scorch the third arm of Palladino herself.

Then this concentrated brew is mixed in a long, deep vat with cubic gallons of hot water, and the sheep are caught by their hind legs and flung into the compound. After being thoroughly ducked by means of a forked pole in the hands of a gentleman detailed for that purpose, they are allowed to clamber up an incline into a corral and dry or die, as the state of their constitutions may decree. If you ever caught an able-bodied, two-year-old mutton by the hind legs and felt the 750 volts of kicking that he can send through your arm seventeen times before you can hurl him into the vat, you will, of course, hope that he may die instead of dry.

But this is merely to explain why Bud Oakley and I gladly stretched ourselves on the bank of the near-by *charco* after the dipping, glad for the welcome inanition and pure contact with the earth after our muscle-racking labors. The flock was a small one, and we finished at three in the afternoon so Bud brought from the *morral* on his saddle horn, coffee and a coffee pot and a big hunk of bread and some side bacon. Mr. Mills, the ranch owner and my old friend, rode away to the ranch with his force of Mexican *trabajadores*.

While the bacon was frizzling nicely, there was the sound of horses' hoofs behind us. Bud's six-shooter lay in its scabbard ten feet away from his hand. He paid not the slightest heed to the approaching horseman. This attitude of a Texas ranchman was so different from the old-time custom that I marvelled. Instinctively I turned to inspect the possible foe that menaced us in the rear. I saw a horseman dressed in black, who might have been a lawyer or a parson or an undertaker, trotting peaceably along the road by the *arroyo*.

Bud noticed my precautionary movement and smiled sarcastically and sorrowfully.

"You've been away too long," said he. "You don't need to look around any more when anybody gallops up behind you in this state, unless something hits you in the back; and even then it's liable to be only a bunch of tracts or a petition to sign against the trusts. I never looked at that *hombre* that rode by; but I'll bet a quart of sheep dip that he's some double-dyed son of a popgun out rounding up prohibition votes."

"Times have changed, Bud," said I, oracularly. "Law and order is the rule now in the South and the Southwest."

I caught a cold gleam from Bud's pale blue eyes.

"Not that I——" I began, hastily.

"Of course you don't," said Bud, warmly. "You know better. You've lived here before. Law and order, you say? Twenty years ago we had 'em here. We only had two or three laws, such as against murder before witnesses, and being caught stealing horses, and voting the Republican ticket. But how is it now? All we get is orders; and the laws go out of the state. Them legislators set up there at Austin and don't do nothing but make laws against kerosene oil and schoolbooks being brought into the state. I reckon they was afraid some man would go home some evening after work and light up and get an education and go to work and make laws to repeal aforesaid laws. Me, I'm for the old days when law and order meant what they said. A law was a law, and a order was a order."

"But——" I began.

"I was going on," continued Bud, "while this coffee is boiling to describe to you a case of genuine law and order that I knew of once in the times when cases was decided in the chambers of a six-shooter instead of a supreme court.

"You've heard of old Ben Kirkman, the cattle king? His ranch run from the Nueces to the Rio Grande. In them days, as you know, there was cattle barons and cattle kings. The difference was this: when a cattleman went to San Antone and bought beer for the newspaper reporters and only give them the number of cattle he actually owned, they wrote him up for a baron. When he bought 'em champagne wine and added in the amount of cattle he had stole, they called him a king.

"Luke Summers was one of his range bosses. And down to the king's ranch comes one day a bunch of these Oriental people from New York or Kansas City or thereabouts. Luke was tailed with a squad to ride about with 'em, and see that the rattlesnakes got fair warning when they was coming, and drive the deer out of their way. Among the bunch was a black-eyed girl that wore a number two shoe. That's all I noticed about her. But Luke must have seen more, for he married her one day before the *caballard* started back, and went over on Canada Verde and set up a ranch of his own. I'm skipping over the sentimental stuff on purpose, because I never saw or wanted to see any of it. And Luke takes me along with him because we was old friends and I handles cattle to suit him.

"I'm skipping over much what followed, because I never saw or wanted to see any of it—but three years afterward there was a boy kid stumbling and blubbering around the galleries and floors of Luke's ranch. I never had no use for kids; but it seems they did. And I'm skipping over much what followed until one day out to the ranch drives in hacks and buck-boards a lot of Mrs. Summers's friends from the East—a sister or so and two or three men. One looked like an uncle to somebody; and one looked like nothing; and the other one had on corkscrew pants and spoke in a tone of voice. I never liked a man who spoke in a tone of voice.

"I'm skipping over much what followed; but one afternoon when I rides up to the ranch house to get some orders about a drove of beeves that was to be shipped, I hears something like a popgun go off. I waits at the hitching rack, not wishing to intrude on private affairs. In a little while Luke comes out and gives some orders to some of his Mexican hands, and they go and hitch up sundry and divers vehicles; and mighty soon out comes one of the sisters or so and some of the two or three men. But two of the two or three men carries between 'em the corkscrew man who spoke in a tone of voice, and lays him flat down in one of the wagons. And they all might have been seen wending their way away.

" 'Bud,' says Luke to me, 'I want you to fix up a little and go up to San Antone with me.'

" 'Let me get on my Mexican spurs,' says I, 'and I'm your company.'

"One of the sisters or so seems to have stayed at the ranch with Mrs. Summers and the kid. We rides to Encinal and catches the International, and hits San Antone in the morning. After breakfast Luke steers me straight to the office of a lawyer. They go in a room and talk and then come out.

" 'Oh, there won't be any trouble, Mr. Summers,' says the lawyer. 'I'll acquaint Judge Simmons with the facts to-day and the matter will be put through as promptly as possible. Law and order reigns in this state as swift and sure as any in the country.'

" 'I'll wait for the decree if it won't take over half an hour,' says Luke.

" 'Tut, tut,' says the lawyer man. 'Law must take its course. Come back day after to-morrow at half-past nine.'

"At that time me and Luke shows up, and the lawyer hands him a folded document. And Luke writes him out a check.

"On the sidewalk Luke holds up the paper to me and puts a finger the size of a kitchen door latch on it and says:

" 'Decree of ab-so-lute divorce with cus-to-dy of the child.'

" 'Skipping over much what has happened of which I know nothing,' says I, 'it looks to me like a split. Couldn't the lawyer man have made it a strike for you?'

" 'But,' says he, in a pained style, 'that child is the one thing I have to live for. *She* may go; but the boy is mine!—think of it—I have the cus-to-dy of the child.'

" 'All right,' says I. 'If it's the law, let's abide by it. But I think,' says I, 'that Judge Simmons might have used exemplary clemency, or whatever is the legal term, in our case.'

"You see, I wasn't inveigled much into the desirableness of having infants around a ranch, except the kind that feed themselves and sell for so much on the hoof when they grow up. But Luke was struck with that sort of parental foolishness that I never could understand. All the way riding from the station back to the ranch, he kept pulling that decree out of his pocket and laying his finger on the back of it and reading off to me the sum and substance of it. 'Cus-to-dy of the child, Bud,' says he. 'Don't forget it—cus-to-dy of the child.'

"But when we hits the ranch we finds our decree of court obviated, *nolle prossed,* and remanded for trial. Mrs. Summers and the kid was gone. They tell us that an hour after me and Luke had started for San Antone she had a team hitched and lit out for the nearest station with her trunks and the youngster.

"Luke takes out his decree once more and reads off its emoluments.

" 'It ain't possible, Bud,' says he, 'for this to be. It's contrary to law and order. It's wrote as plain as day here—"Cus-to-dy of the child." '

" 'There is what you might call a human leaning,' says I, 'toward smashing 'em both—not to mention the child.'

" 'Judge Simmons,' goes on Luke, 'is a incorporated officer of the law. She can't take the boy away. He belongs to me by statutes passed and approved by the state of Texas.'

" 'And he's removed from the jurisdiction of mundane mandamuses,' says I, 'by the unearthly statutes of female partiality. Let us praise the

Lord and be thankful for whatever small mercies——' I begins; but I see Luke don't listen to me. Tired as he was, he calls for a fresh horse and starts back again for the station.

"He come back two weeks afterward, not saying much.

" 'We can't get the trail,' says he; 'but we've done all the telegraphing that the wires'll stand, and we've got these city rangers they call detectives on the lookout. In the meantime, Bud,' says he, 'we'll round up them cows on Brush Creek, and wait for the law to take its course.' "

And after that we never alluded to allusions, as you might say.

"Skipping over much what happened in the next twelve years, Luke was made sheriff of Mojada County. He made me his office deputy. Now, don't get in your mind no wrong apparitions of a office deputy doing sums in a book or mashing letters in a cider press. In them days his job was to watch the back windows so nobody didn't plug the sheriff in the rear while he was adding up mileage at his desk in front. And in them days I had qualifications for the job. And there was law and order in Mojada County, and schoolbooks, and all the whiskey you wanted, and the Government built its own battleships instead of collecting nickels from the school children to do it with. And, as I say, there was law and order instead of enactments and restrictions such as disfigure our umpire state to-day. We had our office at Bildad, the county seat, from which we emerged forth on necessary occasions to soothe whatever fracases and unrest that might occur in our jurisdiction.

"Skipping over much what happened while me and Luke was sheriff, I want to give you an idea of how the law was respected in them days. Luke was what you would call one of the most conscious men in the world. He never knew much book law, but he had the inner emoluments of justice and mercy inculcated into his system. If a respectable citizen shot a Mexican or held up a train and cleaned out the safe in the express car, and Luke ever got hold of him, he'd give the guilty party such a reprimand and a cussin' out that he'd probable never do it again. But once let somebody steal a horse (unless it was a Spanish pony), or cut a wire fence, or otherwise impair the peace and indignity of Mojada County, Luke and me would be on 'em with habeas corpuses and smokeless powder and all the modern inventions of equity and etiquette.

"We certainly had our county on a basis of lawfulness. I've known persons of Eastern classification with little spotted caps and buttoned-up shoes to get off the train at Bildad and eat sandwiches at the railroad station without being shot at or even roped and drug about by the citizens of the town.

"Luke had his own ideas of legality and justice. He was kind of training me to succeed him when he went out of office. He was always looking ahead to the time when he'd quit sheriffing. What he wanted to do was to build a yellow house with lattice-work under the porch and have hens scratching in the yard. The one main thing in his mind seemed to be the yard.

"'Bud,' he says to me, 'by instinct and sentiment I'm a contractor. I want to be a contractor. That's what I'll be when I get out of office.'

"'What kind of a contractor?' says I. 'It sounds like a kind of business to me. You ain't going to haul cement or establish branches or work on a railroad, are you?'

"'You don't understand,' says Luke. 'I'm tired of space and horizons and territory and distances and things like that. What I want is reasonable contraction. I want a yard with a fence around it that you can go out and set on after supper and listen to whip-poor-wills,' says Luke.

"That's the kind of a man he was. He was homelike, although he'd had bad luck in such investments. But he never talked about them times on the ranch. It seemed like he'd forgotten about it. I wondered how, with his ideas of yards and chickens and notions of lattice-work, he'd seemed to have got out of his mind that kid of his that had been taken away from him, unlawful, in spite of his decree of court. But he wasn't a man you could ask about such things as he didn't refer to in his own conversation.

"I reckon he'd put all his emotions and ideas into being sheriff. I've read in books about men that was disappointed in these poetic and fine-haired and high-collared affairs with ladies renouncing truck of that kind and wrapping themselves up into some occupation like painting pictures, or herding sheep, or science, or teaching school—something to make 'em forget. Well, I guess that was the way with Luke. But, as he couldn't paint pictures, he took it out in rounding up horse thieves and in making Mojada County a safe place to sleep in if you was well armed and not afraid of requisitions or tarantulas.

"One day there passes through Bildad a bunch of these money investors from the East, and they stopped off there, Bildad being the dinner station on the I. & G. N. They was just coming back from Mexico looking after mines and such. There was five of 'em—four solid parties, with gold watch chains, that would grade up over two hundred pounds on the hoof, and one kid about seventeen or eighteen.

"This youngster had on one of them cowboy suits such as tenderfoots bring West with 'em; and you could see he was aching to wing a couple of Indians or bag a grizzly or two with the little pearl-handled gun he had buckled around his waist.

"I walked down to the depot to keep an eye on the outfit and see that they didn't locate any land or scare the cow ponies hitched in front of Murchison's store or act otherwise unseemly. Luke was away after a gang of cattle thieves down on the Frio, and I always looked after the law and order when he wasn't there.

"After dinner this boy comes out of the dining room while the train was

waiting, and prances up and down the platform ready to shoot all antelope, lions, or private citizens that might endeavor to molest or come too
near him. He was a good-looking kid; only he was like all them tenderfoots—he didn't know a law-and-order town when he saw it.

"By and by along comes Pedro Johnson, the proprietor of the Crystal
Palace *chili-concarne* stand in Bildad. Pedro was a man who liked to
amuse himself; so he kind of herd rides this youngster, laughing at him,
tickled to death. I was too far away to hear, but the kid seems to mention
some remarks to Pedro, and Pedro goes up and slaps him about nine feet
away, and laughs harder than ever. And then the boy gets up quicker
than he fell and jerks out his little pearl-handle, and—bing! bing! bing!
Pedro gets it three times in special and treasured portions of his carcass.
I saw the dust fly off his clothes every time the bullets hit. Sometimes
them little thirty-twos cause worry at close range.

"The engine bell was ringing, and the train starting off slow. I goes up
to the kid and places him under arrest, and takes away his gun. But the
first thing I knew that *caballard* of capitalists makes a break for the train.
One of 'em hesitates in front of me for a second, and kind of smiles and
shoves his hand up against my chin, and I sort of laid down on the platform and took a nap. I never was afraid of guns; but I don't want any
person except a barber to take liberties like that with my face again.
When I woke up, the whole outfit—train, boy, and all—was gone. I asked
about Pedro, and they told me the doctor said he would recover provided
his wounds didn't turn out to be fatal.

"When Luke got back three days later, and I told him about it, he was
mad all over.

" 'Why'n't you telegraph to San Antone,' he asks, 'and have the bunch
arrested there?'

" 'Oh, well,' says I, 'I always did admire telegraphy; but astronomy was
what I had took up just then.' That capitalist sure knew how to gesticulate
with his hands.

"Luke got madder and madder. He investigates and finds in the depot
a card one of the men had dropped that gives the address of some *hombre*
called Scudder in New York City.

" 'Bud,' says Luke, 'I'm going after that bunch. I'm going there and get
the man or boy, as you say he was, and bring him back. I'm sheriff of
Mojada County, and I shall keep law and order in its precincts while I'm
able to draw a gun. And I want you to go with me. No Eastern Yankee
can shoot up a respectable and well-known citizen of Bildad, 'specially
with a thirty-two calibre, and escape the law. Pedro Johnson,' says Luke,
'is one of our most prominent citizens and business men. I'll appoint Sam
Bell acting sheriff with penitentiary powers while I'm away, and you and
me will take a six forty-five northbound to-morrow evening and follow
up this trail.'

" 'I'm your company,' says I. 'I never see this New York, but I'd like to. But, Luke,' says I, 'don't you have to have a dispensation or a habeas corpus or something from the state, when you reach out that far for rich men and malefactors?'

" 'Did I have a requisition,' says Luke, 'when I went over into the Brazos bottoms and brought back Bill Grimes and two more for holding up the International? Did me and you have a search warrant or a posse comitatus when we rounded up them six Mexican cow thieves down in Hidalgo? It's my business to keep order in Mojada County.'

" 'And it's my business as office deputy,' says I, 'to see that business is carried on according to law. Between us both we ought to keep things pretty well cleaned up.'

"So, the next day, Luke packs a blanket and some collars and his mileage book in a haversack, and him and me hits the breeze for New York. It was a powerful long ride. The seats in the cars was too short for six-footers like us to sleep comfortable on; and the conductor had to keep us from getting off at every town that had five-story houses in it. But we got there finally; and we seemed to see right away that he was right about it.

" 'Luke,' says I, 'as office deputy and from a law standpoint, it don't look to me like this place is properly and legally in the jurisdiction of Mojada County, Texas.'

" 'From the standpoint of order,' says he, 'it's amenable to answer for its sins to the properly appointed authorities from Bildad to Jerusalem.'

" 'Amen,' says I. 'But let's turn our trick sudden, and ride. I don't like the looks of this place.'

" 'Think of Pedro Johnson,' says Luke, 'a friend of mine and yours shot down by one of these gilded abolitionists at his very door!'

" 'It was at the door of the freight depot,' says I. 'But the law will not be balked at a quibble like that.'

"We put up at one of them big hotels on Broadway. The next morning I goes down about two miles of stairsteps to the bottom and hunts for Luke. It ain't no use. It looks like San Jacinto day in San Antone. There's a thousand folks milling around in a kind of a roofed-over plaza with marble pavements and trees growing right out of 'em, and I see no more chance of finding Luke than if we was hunting each other in the big pear flat down below Old Fort Ewell. But soon Luke and me runs together in one of the turns of them marble alleys.

" 'It ain't no use, Bud,' says he. 'I can't find no place to eat at. I've been looking for restaurant signs and smelling for ham all over the camp. But I'm used to going hungry when I have to. Now,' says he, 'I'm going out and get a hack and ride down to the address on this Scudder card. You stay here and try to hustle some grub. But I doubt if you'll find it. I wish we'd brought along some cornmeal and bacon and beans. I'll be back when I see this Scudder, if the trail ain't wiped out.'

"So I starts foraging for breakfast. For the honor of old Mojada County I didn't want to seem green to them abolitionists, so every time I turned a corner in them marble halls I went up to the first desk or counter I see and looks around for grub. If I didn't see what I wanted I asked for something else. In about half an hour I had a dozen cigars, five story magazines, and seven or eight railroad timetables in my pockets, and never a smell of coffee or bacon to point out the trail.

"Once a kind lady sitting at a table and playing a game kind of like pushpin told me to go into a closet that she called No. 3. I went in and shut the door, and the blamed thing lit itself. I set down on a stool before a shelf and waited. Thinks I, 'This is a private dining room.' But no waiter never came. When I got to sweating good and hard, I goes out again.

" 'Did you get what you wanted?' says she.

" 'No, ma'am, says I. 'Not a bite.'

" 'Then there's no charge,' says she.

" 'Thanky, ma'am,' says I, and takes up the trail again.

"By and by I thinks I'll shed etiquette; and I picks up one of them boys with blue clothes and yellow buttons in front, and he leads me to what he calls the caffay breakfast room. And the first thing I lays my eyes on when I go in is that boy that had shot Pedro Johnson. He was setting all alone at a little table, hitting a egg with a spoon like he was afraid he'd break it.

"I takes the chair across the table from him; and he looks insulted and makes a move like he was going to get up.

" 'Keep still, son,' says I. 'You're apprehended, arrested, and in charge of the Texas authorities. Go on and hammer that egg some more if it's the inside of it you want. Now, what did you shoot Mr. Johnson, of Bildad, for?'

" 'And may I ask who you are?' says he.

" 'You may,' says I. 'Go ahead.'

" 'I suppose you're on,' says this kid, without batting his eyes. 'But what are you eating? Here, waiter!' he calls out, raising his finger. 'Take this gentleman's order.'

" 'A beefsteak,' says I, 'and some fried eggs and a can of peaches and a quart of coffee will about suffice.'

"We talk awhile about the sundries of life and then he says:

" 'What are you going to do about that shooting? I had a right to shoot that man,' says he. 'He called me names that I couldn't overlook, and then he struck me. He carried a gun, too. What else could I do?'

" 'We'll have to take you back to Texas,' says I.

" 'I'd like to go back,' says the boy, with a kind of a grin—'if it wasn't on an occasion of this kind. It's the life I like. I've always wanted to ride and shoot and live in the open air ever since I can remember.'

" 'Who was this gang of stout parties you took this trip with?' I asks.

" 'My stepfather,' says he, 'and some business partners of his in some Mexican mining and land schemes.'

" 'I saw you shoot Pedro Johnson,' says I, 'and I took that little pop-gun away from you that you did it with. And when I did so I noticed three or four little scars in a row over your right eyebrow. You've been in rookus before, haven't you?'

" 'I've had these scars ever since I can remember,' says he. 'I don't know how they came there.'

" 'Was you ever in Texas before?' says I.

" 'Not that I remember of,' says he. 'But I thought I had when we struck the prairie country. But I guess I hadn't.'

" 'Have you got a mother?' I asks.

" 'She died five years ago,' says he.

"Skipping over the most of what followed—when Luke came back I turned the kid over to him. He had seen Scudder and told him what he wanted; and it seems that Scudder got active with one of these telephones as soon as he left. For in about an hour afterward there comes to our hotel some of these city rangers in everyday clothes that they call detectives, and marches the whole outfit of us to what they call a magistrate's court. They accuse Luke of attempted kidnapping, and ask him what he has to say.

" 'This snipe,' says Luke to the judge, 'shot and wilfully punctured with malice and forethought one of the most respected and prominent citizens of the town of Bildad, Texas, Your Honor. And in so doing laid himself liable to the penitence of law and order. And I hereby make claim and demand restitution of the State of New York City for the said alleged criminal; and I know he done it.'

" 'Have you the usual and necessary requisition papers from the governor of your state?' asks the judge.

" 'My usual papers,' says Luke, 'was taken away from me at the hotel by these gentlemen who represent law and order in your city. They was two Colt's .45's that I've packed for nine years; and if I don't get 'em back, there'll be more trouble. You can ask anybody in Mojada County about Luke Summers. I don't usually need any other kind of papers for what I do.'

"I see the judge looks mad, so I steps up and says:

" 'Your Honor, the aforesaid defendant, Mr. Luke Summers, sheriff of Mojada County, Texas, is as fine a man as ever threw a rope or upheld the statutes and codicils of the greatest state in the Union. But he——'

"The judge hits his table with a wooden hammer and asks who I am.

" 'Bud Oakley,' says I. 'Office deputy of the sheriff's office of Mojada

County, Texas. Representing,' says I, 'the Law. Luke Summers,' I goes on, 'represents Order. And if Your Honor will give me about ten minutes in private talk, I'll explain the whole thing to you, and show you the equitable and legal requisition papers which I carry in my pocket.'

"The judge kind of half smiles and says he will talk with me in his private room. In there I put the whole thing up to him in such language as I had, and when we goes outside, he announces the verdict that the young man is delivered into the hands of the Texas authorities; and calls the next case.

"Skipping over much of what happened on the way back, I'll tell you how the thing wound up in Bildad.

"When we got the prisoner in the sheriff's office, I says to Luke:

"'You remember that kid of yours—that two-year-old that they stole away from you when the bust-up come?'

"Luke looks black and angry. He'd never let anybody talk to him about that business, and he never mentioned it himself.

"'Toe the mark,' says I. 'Do you remember when he was toddling around on the porch and fell down on a pair of Mexican spurs and cut four little holes over his right eye? Look at the prisoner,' says I, 'look at his nose and the shape of his head and—why, you old fool, don't you know your own son?—I knew him,' says I, 'when he perforated Mr. Johnson at the depot.'

"Luke comes over to me shaking all over. I never saw him lose his nerve before.

"'Bud,' says he, 'I've never had that boy out of my mind one day or one night since he was took away. But I never let on. But can we hold him?—Can we make him stay?—I'll make the best man of him that ever put his foot in a stirrup. Wait a minute,' says he, all excited and out of his mind—'I've got something here in my desk—I reckon it'll hold legal yet—I've looked at it a thousand times—"Cus-to-dy of the child," says Luke—"Cus-to-dy of the child." We can hold him on that, can't we? Le'me see if I can find that decree.'

"Luke begins to tear his desk to pieces.

"'Hold on,' says I. 'You are Order and I'm Law. You needn't look for that paper, Luke. It ain't a decree any more. It's requisition papers. It's on file in that Magistrate's office in New York. I took it along when we went, because I was office deputy and knew the law.'

"'I've got him back,' says Luke. 'He's mine again. I never thought——'

"'Wait a minute,' says I. 'We've got to have law and order. You and me have got to preserve 'em both in Mojada County according to our oath and conscience. The kid shot Pedro Johnson, one of Bildad's most prominent and——'

"'Oh, hell!' says Luke. 'That don't amount to anything. That fellow was half Mexican, anyhow.'"

TRANSFORMATION OF MARTIN BURNEY

In behalf of Sir Walter's soothing plant let us look into the case of Martin Burney.

They were constructing the Speedway along the west bank of the Harlem River. The grub-boat of Dennis Corrigan, sub-contractor, was moored to a tree on the bank. Twenty-two men belonging to the little green island toiled there at the sinew-cracking labor. One among them, who wrought in the kitchen of the grub-boat, was of the race of the Goths. Over them all stood the exorbitant Corrigan, harrying them like the captain of a galley crew. He paid them so little that most of the gang, work as they might, earned little more than food and tobacco; many of them were in debt to him. Corrigan boarded them all in the grub-boat, and gave them good grub, for he got it back in work.

Martin Burney was furthest behind of all. He was a little man, all muscles and hands and feet, with a gray-red, stubby beard. He was too light for the work, which would have glutted the capacity of a steam shovel.

The work was hard. Besides that, the banks of the river were humming with mosquitoes. As a child in a dark room fixes his regard on the pale light of a comforting window, these toilers watched the sun that brought around the one hour of the day that tasted less bitter. After the sundown supper they would huddle together on the river bank, and send the mosquitoes whining and eddying back from the malignant puffs of twenty-three reeking pipes. Thus socially banded against the foe, they wrenched out of the hour a few well-smoked drops from the cup of joy.

Each week Burney grew deeper in debt. Corrigan kept a small stock of goods on the boat, which he sold to the men at prices that brought him no loss. Burney was a good customer at the tobacco counter. One sack when he went to work in the morning and one when he came in at night, so much was his account swelled daily. Burney was something of a smoker. Yet it was not true that he ate his meals with a pipe in his mouth, which had been said of him. The little man was not discontented. He had plenty to eat, plenty of tobacco, and a tyrant to curse; so why should not he, an Irishman, be well satisfied?

One morning as he was starting with the others for work he stopped at the pine counter for his usual sack of tobacco.

"There's no more for ye," said Corrigan. "Your account's closed. Ye are a losing investment. No, not even tobaccy, my son. No more tobaccy on account. If ye want to work on and eat, do so, but the smoke of ye has all ascended. 'Tis my advice that ye hunt a new job."

"I have no tobaccy to smoke in my pipe this day, Mr. Corrigan," said Burney, not quite understanding that such a thing could happen to him.

"Earn it," said Corrigan, "and then buy it."

Burney stayed on. He knew of no other job. At first he did not realize that tobacco had got to be his father and mother, his confessor and sweetheart, and wife and child.

For three days he managed to fill his pipe from the other men's sacks, and then they shut him off, one and all. They told him, rough but friendly, that of all things in the world tobacco must be quickest forthcoming to a fellow-man desiring it, but that beyond the immediate temporary need requisition upon the store of a comrade is pressed with great danger to friendship.

Then the blackness of the pit arose and filled the heart of Burney. Sucking the corpse of his deceased dudheen, he staggered through his duties with his barrowful of stones and dirt, feeling for the first time that the curse of Adam was upon him. Other men bereft of a pleasure might have recourse to other delights, but Burney had only two comforts in life. One was his pipe, the other was an ecstatic hope that there would be no Speedways to build on the other side of Jordan.

At meal times he would let the other men go first into the grub-boat, and then he would go down on his hands and knees, grovelling fiercely upon the ground where they had been sitting, trying to find some stray crumbs of tobacco. Once he sneaked down the river bank and filled his pipe with dead willow leaves. At the first whiff of the smoke he spat in the direction of the boat and put the finest curse he ever knew on Corrigan—one that began with the first Corrigans born on earth and ended with the Corrigans that shall hear the trumpet of Gabriel blow. He began to hate Corrigan with all his shaking nerves and soul. Even murder occurred to him in a vague sort of way. Five days he went without the taste of tobacco—he who had smoked all day and thought the night misspent in which he had not awakened for a pipeful or two under the bedclothes.

One day a man stopped at the boat to say that there was work to be had in the Bronx Park, where a large number of laborers were required in making some improvements.

After dinner Burney walked thirty yards down the river bank away from the maddening smell of the others' pipes. He sat down upon a stone. He was thinking he would set out for the Bronx. At least he could earn tobacco there. What if the books did say he owed Corrigan? Any man's work was worth his keep. But then he hated to go without getting even with the hard-hearted screw who had put his pipe out. Was there any way to do it?

Softly stepping among the clods came Tony, he of the race of Goths, who worked in the kitchen. He grinned at Burney's elbow, and that unhappy man, full of race animosity and holding urbanity in contempt, growled at him: "What d'ye want, ye——Dago?"

Tony also contained a grievance—and a plot. He, too, was a Corrigan hater, and had been primed to see it in others.

"How you like-a Mr. Corrigan?" he asked. "You think-a him a nice-a man?"

"To hell with 'm," he said. "May his liver turn to water, and the bones of him crack in the cold of his heart. May dog fennel grow upon his ancestors' graves, and the grandsons of his children be born without eyes. May whiskey turn to clabber in his mouth, and every time he sneezes may he blister the soles of his feet. And the smoke of his pipe—may it make his eyes water, and the drops fall on the grass that his cows eat and poison the butter that he spreads on his bread."

Though Tony remained a stranger to the beauties of this imagery, he gathered from it the conviction that it was sufficiently anti-Corrigan in its tendency. So, with the confidence of a fellow-conspirator, he sat by Burney upon the stone and unfolded his plot.

It was very simple in design. Every day after dinner it was Corrigan's habit to sleep for an hour in his bunk. At such times it was the duty of the cook and his helper, Tony, to leave the boat so that no noise might disturb the autocrat. The cook always spent this hour in walking exercise. Tony's plan was this. After Corrigan should be asleep he (Tony) and Burney would cut the mooring ropes that held the boat to the shore. Tony lacked the nerve to do the deed alone. Then the awkward boat would swing out into a swift current and surely overturn against a rock there was below.

"Come on and do it," said Burney. "If the back of ye aches from the lick he gave ye as the pit of me stomach does for the taste of a bite of smoke, we can't cut the ropes too quick."

"All a-right," said Tony. "But better wait 'bout-a ten minute more. Give-a Corrigan plenty time get good-a sleep."

They waited, sitting upon the stone. The rest of the men were at work out of sight around a bend in the road. Everything would have gone well—except, perhaps, with Corrigan, had not Tony been moved to decorate the plot with its conventional accompaniment. He was of dramatic blood, and perhaps he intuitively divined the appendage to villainous machinations as prescribed by the stage. He pulled from his shirt bosom a long, black, beautiful, venomous cigar, and handed it to Burney.

"You like-a smoke while we wait?" he asked.

Burney clutched it and snapped off the end as a terrier bites at a rat. He laid it to his lips like a long-lost sweetheart. When the smoke began to draw he gave a long, deep sigh, and the bristles of his gray-red mustache curled down over the cigar like the talons of an eagle. Slowly the red faded from the whites of his eyes. He fixed his gaze dreamily upon the hills across the river. The minutes came and went.

" 'Bout time to go now," said Tony. "That damn-a Corrigan he be in the reever very quick."

Burney started out of his trance with a grunt. He turned his head and gazed with a surprised and pained severity at his accomplice. He took the cigar partly from his mouth, but sucked it back again immediately, chewed it lovingly once or twice, and spoke in virulent puffs, from the corner of his mouth:

"What is it, ye yaller haythen? Would ye lay contrivances against the enlightened races of the earth, ye instigator of illegal crimes? Would ye seek to persuade Martin Burney into the dirty tricks of an indecent Dago? Would ye be for murderin' your benefactor, the good man that gives ye food and work? Take that, ye punkin-colored assassin!"

The torrent of Burney's indignation carried with it bodily assault. The toe of his shoe sent the would-be cutter of ropes tumbling from his seat.

Tony arose and fled. His vendetta he again relegated to the files of things that might have been. Beyond the boat he fled and away—away; he was afraid to remain.

Burney, with expanded chest, watched his late co-plotter disappear. Then he, too, departed, setting his face in the direction of the Bronx.

In his wake was a rank and pernicious trail of noisome smoke that brought peace to his heart and drove the birds from the roadside into the deepest thickets.

THE CALIPH AND THE CAD

Surely there is no pastime more diverting than that of mingling, incognito, with persons of wealth and station. Where else but in those circles can one see life in its primitive, crude state unhampered by the conventions that bind the dwellers in a lower sphere?

There was a certain Caliph of Bagdad who was accustomed to go down among the poor and lowly for the solace obtained from the relation of their tales and histories. Is it not strange that the humble and poverty-stricken have not availed themselves of the pleasure they might glean by donning diamonds and silks and playing Caliph among the haunts of the upper world?

There was one who saw the possibilities of thus turning the tables on Haroun al Raschid. His name was Corny Brannigan, and he was a truck driver for a Canal Street importing firm. And if you read further you will learn how he turned upper Broadway into Bagdad and learned something about himself that he did not know before.

Many people would have called Corny a snob—preferably by means of a telephone. His chief interest in life, his chosen amusement, and his sole diversion after working hours, was to place himself in juxtaposition —since he could not hope to mingle—with people of fashion and means. Every evening after Corny had put up his team and dined at a lunch-counter that made immediateness a specialty, he would clothe himself in evening raiment as correct as any you will see in the palm rooms. Then he would betake himself to that ravishing, radiant roadway devoted to Thespis, Thais, and Bacchus.

For a time he would stroll about the lobbies of the best hotels, his soul steeped in blissful content. Beautiful women, cooing like doves, but feathered like birds of Paradise, flicked him with their robes as they passed. Courtly gentlemen attended them, gallant and assiduous. And Corny's heart within him swelled like Sir Lancelot's, for the mirror spoke to him as he passed and said: "Corny, lad, there's not a guy among 'em that looks a bit the sweller than yerself. And you drivin' of a truck and them swearin' off their taxes and playin' the red in art galleries with the best in the land!"

And the mirrors spake the truth. Mr. Corny Brannigan had acquired the outward polish, if nothing more. Long and keen observation of polite · society had gained for him its manner, its genteel air, and—most difficult of acquirement—its repose and ease.

Now and then in the hotels Corny had managed conversation and temporary acquaintance with substantial, if not distinguished, guests. With many of these he had exchanged cards, and the ones he received he carefully treasured for his own use later. Leaving the hotel lobbies, Corny would stroll leisurely about, lingering at the theatre entrance, dropping into the fashionable restaurants as if seeking some friend. He rarely patronized any of these places; he was no bee come to suck honey, but a butterfly flashing his wings among the flowers whose calyces held no sweets for him. His wages were not large enough to furnish him with more than the outside garb of the gentleman. To have been one of the beings he so cunningly imitated, Corny Brannigan would have given his right hand.

One night Corny had an adventure. After absorbing the delights of an hour's lounging in the principal hotels along Broadway, he passed up into the stronghold of Thespis. Cab drivers hailed him as a likely fare, to his prideful content. Languishing eyes were turned upon him as a hopeful source of lobsters and the delectable, ascendant globules of ef-fervescence. These overtures and unconscious compliments Corny swallowed as manna, and hoped Bill, the off horse, would be less lame in the left forefoot in the morning.

Beneath a cluster of milky globes of electric light Corny paused to admire the sheen of his low-cut patent leather shoes. The building occupying the angle was a pretentious café. Out of this came a couple, a lady in a white, cobwebby evening gown, with a lace wrap like a wreath of mist thrown over it, and a man, tall, faultless, assured—too assured. They moved to the edge of the sidewalk and halted. Corny's eye, ever alert for "pointers" in "swell" behavior, took them in with a sidelong glance.

"The carriage is not here," said the lady. "You ordered it to wait?"

"I ordered it for nine-thirty," said the man. "It should be here now."

A familiar note in the lady's voice drew a more especial attention from Corny. It was pitched in a key well known to him. The soft electric shone upon her face. Sisters of sorrow have no quarters fixed for them. In the index to the book of breaking hearts you will find that Broadway follows very soon after the Bowery. This lady's face was sad, and her voice was attuned with it. They waited, as if for the carriage. Corny waited too, for it was out of doors, and he was never tired of accumulating and profiting by knowledge of gentlemanly conduct.

"Jack," said the lady, "don't be angry. I've done everything I could to please you this evening. Why do you act so?"

"Oh, you're an angel," said the man. "Depend upon woman to throw the blame upon a man."

"I'm not blaming you. I'm only trying to make you happy."

"You go about it in a very peculiar way."

"You have been cross with me all the evening without any cause."

"Oh, there isn't any cause except—you make me tired."

Corny took out his card case and looked over his collection. He selected one that read: "Mr. R. Lionel Whyte-Melville, Bloomsbury Square, London." This card he had inveigled from a tourist at the King Edward Hotel. Corny stepped up to the man and presented it with a correctly formal air.

"May I ask why I am selected for the honor?" asked the lady's escort.

Now, Mr. Corny Brannigan had a very wise habit of saying little during his imitations of the Caliph of Bagdad. The advice of Lord Chesterfield: "Wear a black coat and hold your tongue," he believed in without having heard. But now speech was demanded and required of him.

"No gent," said Corny, "would talk to a lady like you done. Fie upon you, Willie! Even if she happens to be your wife you ought to have more respect for your clothes than to chin her back that way. Maybe it ain't my butt-in, but it goes, anyhow—you strike me as bein' a whole lot to the wrong."

The lady's escort indulged in more elegantly expressed but fetching repartee. Corny, eschewing his truck driver's vocabulary, retorted as nearly as he could in polite phrases. Then diplomatic relations were severed; there was a brief but lively set-to with other than oral weapons, from which Corny came forth easily victor.

A carriage dashed up, driven by a tardy and solicitous coachman.

"Will you kindly open the door for me?" asked the lady. Corny assisted her to enter, and took off his hat. The escort was beginning to scramble up from the sidewalk.

"I beg your pardon, ma'am," said Corny, "if he's your man."

"He's no man of mine," said the lady. "Perhaps he—but there's no chance of his being now. Drive home, Michael. If you care to take this—with my thanks."

Three red roses were thrust out through the carriage window into Corny's hand. He took them, and the hand for an instant; and then the carriage sped away.

Corny gathered his foe's hat and began to brush the dust from his clothes.

"Come along," said Corny, taking the other man by the arm.

His late opponent was yet a little dazed by the hard knocks he had received. Corny led him carefully into a saloon three doors away.

"The drinks for us," said Corny, "me and my friend."

"You're a queer feller," said the lady's late escort—"lick a man and then want to set 'em up."

"You're my best friend," said Corny, exultantly. "You don't understand? Well, listen. You just put me wise to somethin'. I been playin' gent a long time, thinkin' it was just the glad rags I had and nothin' else. Say—you're a swell, ain't you? Well, you trot in that class, I guess. I don't; but I found out one thing—I'm a gentleman, by —— and I know it now. What'll you have to drink?"

THE DIAMOND OF KALI

The original news item concerning the diamond of the goddess Kali was handed in to the city editor. He smiled and held it for a moment above the waste-basket. Then he laid it back on his desk and said: "Try the Sunday people; they might work something out of it."

The Sunday editor glanced the item over and said: "H'm!" Afterward he sent for a reporter and expanded his comment.

"You might see General Ludlow," he said, "and make a story out of this if you can. Diamond stories are a drug; but this one is big enough to be found by a scrubwoman wrapped up in a piece of newspaper and tucked under the corner of the hall linoleum. Find out first if the General has a daughter who intends to go on the stage. If not, you can go ahead with the story. Run cuts of the Kohinoor and J. P. Morgan's collection, and work in pictures of the Kimberley mines and Barney Barnato. Fill in with a tabulated comparison of the values of diamonds, radium, and veal cutlets since the meat strike; and let it run to a half page."

On the following day the reporter turned in his story. The Sunday editor let his eye sprint along its lines. "H'm" he said again. This time the copy went into the waste-basket with scarcely a flutter.

The reporter stiffened a little around the lips; but he was whistling softly and contentedly between his teeth when I went over to talk with him about an hour later.

"I don't blame the 'old man,'" said he, magnanimously, "for cutting it out. It did sound like funny business; but it happened exactly as I wrote it. Say, why don't you fish that story out of the w.-b., and use it? Seems to me it's as good as the tommyrot you write."

I accepted the tip, and if you read further you will learn the facts about the diamond of the goddess Kali as vouched for by one of the most reliable reporters on the staff.

Gen. Marcellus B. Ludlow lives in one of those decaying but venerated old red-brick mansions in the West Twenties. The General is a member of an old New York family that does not advertise. He is a globe-trotter by birth, a gentleman by predilection, a millionaire by the mercy of Heaven, and a connoisseur of precious stones by occupation.

The reporter was admitted promptly when he made himself known at the General's residence at about eight thirty on the evening that he received the assignment. In the magnificent library he was greeted by the distinguished traveller and connoisseur, a tall, erect gentleman in the early fifties, with a nearly white mustache, and a bearing so soldierly that one perceived in him scarcely a trace of the national Guardsman. His weather-beaten countenance lit up with a charming smile of interest when the reporter made known his errand.

"Ah, you have heard of my latest find. I shall be glad to show you what I conceive to be one of the six most valuable blue diamonds in existence."

The General opened a small safe in a corner of the library and brought forth a plush-covered box. Opening this, he exposed to the reporter's bewildered gaze a huge and brilliant diamond—nearly as large as a hailstone.

"This stone," said the General, "is something more than a mere jewel. It once formed the central eye of the three-eyed goddess Kali, who is worshipped by one of the fiercest and most fanatical tribes of India. If you will arrange yourself comfortably I will give you a brief history of it for your paper."

General Ludlow brought a decanter of whisky and glasses from a cabinet, and set a comfortable armchair for the lucky scribe.

"The Phansigars, or Thugs, of India," began the General, "are the most dangerous and dreaded of the tribes of North India. They are extremists in religion, and worship the horrid goddess Kali in the form of images. Their rites are interesting and bloody. The robbing and murdering of travellers are taught as a worthy and obligatory deed by their strange religious code. Their worship of the three-eyed goddess Kali is conducted so secretly that no traveller has ever heretofore had the honor of witnessing the ceremonies. That distinction was reserved for myself.

"While at Sakaranpur, between Delhi and Khelat, I used to explore the jungle in every direction in hope of learning something new about these mysterious Phansigars.

"One evening at twilight I was making my way through a teakwood forest, when I came upon a deep circular depression in an open space, in the centre of which was a rude stone temple. I was sure that this was one of the temples of the Thugs, so I concealed myself in the undergrowth to watch.

"When the moon rose the depression in the clearing was suddenly filled with hundreds of shadowy, swiftly gliding forms. Then a door opened in the temple, exposing a brightly illuminated image of the goddess Kali, before which a white-robed priest began a barbarous incantation, while the tribe of worshippers prostrated themselves upon the earth.

"But what interested me most was the central eye of the huge wooden idol. I could see by its flashing brilliancy that it was an immense diamond of the purest water.

"After the rites were concluded the Thugs slipped away into the forest as silently as they had come. The priest stood for a few minutes in the door of the temple enjoying the cool of the night before closing his rather warm quarters. Suddenly a dark, lithe shadow slipped down into the hollow, leaped upon the priest, and struck him down with a glittering knife. Then the murderer sprang at the image of the goddess like a cat and pried out the glowing central eye of Kali with his weapon. Straight toward me he ran with his royal prize. When he was within two paces I rose to my feet and struck him with all my force between the eyes. He rolled over senseless and the magnificent jewel fell from his hand. That is the splendid blue diamond you have just seen—a stone worthy of a monarch's crown."

"That's a corking story," said the reporter. "That decanter is exactly like the one that John W. Gates always sets out during an interview."

"Pardon me," said General Ludlow, "for forgetting hospitality in the excitement of my narrative. Help yourself."

"Here's looking at you," said the reporter.

"What I am afraid of now," said the General, lowering his voice, "is that I may be robbed of the diamond. The jewel that formed an eye of their goddess is their most sacred symbol. Somehow the tribe suspected me of having it; and members of the band have followed me half around the earth. They are the most cunning and cruel fanatics in the world, and their religious vows would compel them to assassinate the unbeliever who has desecrated their sacred treasure.

"Once in Lucknow three of their agents, disguised as servants in a hotel, endeavored to strangle me with a twisted cloth. Again, in London, two Thugs, made up as street musicians, climbed into my window at night and attacked me. They have even tracked me to this country. My life is never safe. A month ago, while I was at a hotel in the Berkshires, three of them sprang upon me from the roadside weeds. I saved myself then by my knowledge of their customs."

"How was that, General?" asked the reporter.

"There was a cow grazing near by," said General Ludlow, "a gentle Jersey cow. I ran to her side and stood. The three Thugs ceased their attack, knelt and struck the ground thrice with their foreheads. Then, after many respectful salaams, they departed."

"Afraid the cow would hook?" asked the reporter.

"No; the cow is a sacred animal to the Phansigars. Next to their goddess they worship the cow. They have never been known to commit any deed of violence in the presence of the animal they reverence."

"It's a mighty interesting story," said the reporter. "If you don't mind I'll take another drink, and then a few notes."

"I will join you," said General Ludlow, with a courteous wave of his hand.

"If I were you," advised the reporter, "I'd take that sparkler to Texas. Get on a cow ranch there, and the Pharisees——"

"Phansigars," corrected the General.

"Oh, yes; the fancy guys would run up against a long horn every time they made a break."

General Ludlow closed the diamond case and thrust it into his bosom.

"The spies of the tribe have found me out in New York," he said, straightening his tall figure. "I'm familiar with the East Indian cast of countenance, and I know that my every movement is watched. They will undoubtedly attempt to rob and murder me here."

"Here?" exclaimed the reporter, seizing the decanter and pouring out a liberal amount of its contents.

"At any moment," said the General. "But as a soldier and a connoisseur I shall sell my life and my diamond as dearly as I can."

At this point of the reporter's story there is a certain vagueness, but it can be gathered that there was a loud crashing at the rear of the house they were in. General Ludlow buttoned his coat closely and sprang for the door. But the reporter clutched him firmly with one hand, while he held the decanter with the other.

"Tell me before we fly," he urged, in a voice thick with some inward turmoil, "do any of your daughters contemplate going on the stage?"

"I have no daughters—fly for your life—the Phansigars are upon us!" cried the General.

The two men dashed out of the front door of the house.

The hour was late. As their feet struck the sidewalk strange men of dark and forbidding appearance seemed to rise up out of the earth and encompass them. One with Asiatic features pressed close to the General and droned in a terrible voice:

"Buy cast clo'!"

Another, dark-whiskered and sinister, sped lithely to his side and began in a whining voice:

"Say, mister, have yer got a dime fer a poor feller what——"

They hurried on, but only into the arms of a black-eyed, dusky-browed being, who held out his hat under their noses, while a confederate of Oriental hue turned the handle of a street organ near by.

Twenty steps farther on General Ludlow and the reporter found themselves in the midst of half a dozen villainous-looking men with high-turned coat collars and faces bristling with unshaven beards.

"Run for it!" hissed the General. "They have discovered the possessor of the diamond of the goddess Kali."

The two men took to their heels. The avengers of the goddess pursued.

"Oh, Lordy!" groaned the reporter, "there isn't a cow this side of Brooklyn. We're lost!"

When near the corner they both fell over an iron object that rose from the sidewalk close to the gutter. Clinging to it desperately, they awaited their fate.

"If I only had a cow!" moaned the reporter—"or another nip from that decanter, General!"

As soon as the pursuers observed where their victims had found refuge they suddenly fell back and retreated to a considerable distance.

"They are waiting for reinforcements in order to attack us," said General Ludlow.

But the reporter emitted a ringing laugh, and hurled his hat triumphantly into the air.

"Guess again," he shouted, and leaned heavily upon the iron object. "Your old fancy guys or thugs, whatever you call 'em, are up to date. Dear General, this is a pump we've stranded upon—same as a cow in New York (hic!) see? Thas'h why the 'nfuriated smoked guys don't attack us—see? Sacred an'mal, the pump in N' York, my dear General!"

But further down in the shadows of Twenty-eighth Street the marauders were holding a parley.

"Come on, Reddy," said one. "Let's go frisk the old 'un. He's been showin' a sparkler as big as a hen egg all around Eighth Avenue for two weeks past."

"Not on your silhouette," decided Reddy. "You see 'em rallyin' round The Pump? They're friends of Bill's. Bill won't stand for nothin' of this kind in his district since he got that bid to Esopus."

This exhausts the facts concerning the Kali diamond. But it is deemed not inconsequent to close with the following brief (paid) item that appeared two days later in a morning paper.

"It is rumored that a niece of Gen. Marcellus B. Ludlow, of New York City, will appear on the stage next season.

"Her diamonds are said to be extremely valuable and of much historic interest."

THE DAY WE CELEBRATE

"In the tropics" ("Hop-along" Bibb, the bird fancier, was saying to me) "the seasons, months, fortnights, week-ends, holidays, dog-days, Sundays, and yesterdays get so jumbled together in the shuffle that you never know when a year has gone by until you're in the middle of the next one."

"Hop-along" Bibb kept his bird store on lower Fourth Avenue. He was an ex-seaman and beachcomber who made regular voyages to southern ports and imported personally conducted invoices of talking parrots and dialectic paroquets. He had a stiff knee, neck, and nerve. I had gone to him to buy a parrot to present, at Christmas, to my Aunt Joanna.

"This one," said I, disregarding his homily on the subdivisions of time —"this one that seems all red, white and blue—to what genus of beasts does he belong? He appeals at once to my patriotism and to my love of discord in color schemes."

"That's a cockatoo from Ecuador," said Bibb. "All he has been taught to say is 'Merry Christmas.' A seasonable bird. He's only seven dollars; and I'll bet many a human has stuck you for money by making the same speech to you."

And then Bibb laughed suddenly and loudly.

"That bird," he exclaimed, "reminds me. He's got his dates mixed. He ought to be saying '*E pluribus unum*,' to match his feathers, instead of trying to work the Santa Claus graft. It reminds me of the time me and Liverpool Sam got our ideas of things tangled up on the coast of Costa Rica on account of the weather and other phenomena to be met with in the tropics.

"We were, as it were, stranded on that section of the Spanish Main with no money to speak of and no friends that should be talked about either. We had stoked and second-cooked ourselves down there on a fruit steamer from New Orleans to try our luck, which was discharged, after we got there, for lack of evidence. There was no work suitable to our instincts; so me and Liverpool began to subsist on the red rum of the country and such fruit as we could reap where we had not sown. It was an alluvial town, called Soledad, where there was no harbor or future or recourse. Between steamers the town slept and drank rum. It only woke up when there were bananas to ship. It was like a man sleeping through dinner until the dessert.

"When me and Liverpool got so low down that the American consul wouldn't speak to us we knew we'd struck bed rock.

"We boarded with a snuff-brown lady named Chica, who kept a rum-shop and a ladies' and gents' restaurant in a street called the *calle de los* Forty-seven Inconsolable Saints. When our credit played out there, Liverpool, whose stomach overshadowed his sensations of *noblesse oblige,* married Chica. This kept us in rice and fried plantain for a month; and then Chica pounded Liverpool one morning sadly and earnestly for fifteen minutes with a casserole handed down from the stone age, and we knew that we had out-welcomed our liver. That night we signed an engagement with Don Jaime McSpinosa, a hybrid banana fancier of the place, to work on his fruit preserves nine miles out of town. We had to do it or be reduced to sea water and broken doses of feed and slumber.

"Now, speaking of Liverpool Sam, I don't malign or inexculpate him to you any more than I would to his face. But in my opinion, when an Englishman gets as low as he can he's got to dodge so that the dregs of other nations don't drop ballast on him out of their balloons. And if he's a Liverpool Englishman, why, fire-damp is what he's got to look out for. Being a natural American, that's my personal view. But Liverpool and me had much in common. We were without decorous clothes or ways and means of existence; and, as the saying goes, misery certainly does enjoy the society of accomplices.

"Our job on old McSpinosa's plantation was chopping down banana stalks and loading the bunches of fruit on the backs of horses. Then a native dressed up in an alligator-hide belt, a machete, and a pair of AA sheeting pajamas, drives 'em over to the coast and piles 'em up on the beach.

"You ever been in a banana grove? It's as solemn as a rathskeller at seven A.M. It's like being lost behind the scenes at one of these mushroom musical shows. You can't see the sky for the foliage above you; and the ground is knee deep in rotten leaves; and it's so still that you can hear the stalks growing again after you chop 'em down.

"At night me and Liverpool herded in a lot of grass huts on the edge of a lagoon, with the red, yellow, and black employés of Don Jaime. There we lay fighting mosquitoes and listening to the monkeys squalling and the alligators grunting and splashing in the lagoon until daylight with only snatches of sleep between times.

"We soon lost all idea of what time of the year it was. It's just about eighty degrees there in December and June and on Fridays and at midnight and election day and any other old time. Sometimes it rains more than at others, and that's all the difference you notice. A man is liable to live along there without noticing any fugiting of tempus until some day the undertaker calls in for him just when he's beginning to think about cutting out the gang and saving up a little to invest in real estate.

"I don't know how long we worked for Don Jaime; but it was through two or three rainy spells, eight or ten hair cuts, and the life of three pairs of sailcloth trousers. All the money we earned went for rum and tobacco; but we ate, and that was something.

"All of a sudden one day me and Liverpool find the trade of committing surgical operations on banana stalks turning to aloes and quinine in our mouths. It's a seizure that often comes upon white men in Latin and geographical countries. We wanted to be addressed again in language and see the smoke of a steamer and read the real estate transfers and gents' outfitting ads in an old newspaper. Even Soledad seemed like a center of civilization to us, so that evening we put our thumbs on our nose at Don Jaime's fruit stand and shook his grass burrs off our feet.

"It was only twelve miles to Soledad, but it took me and Liverpool two days to get there. It was banana grove nearly all the way; and we got twisted time and again. It was like paging the palm room of a New York hotel for a man named Smith.

"When we saw the houses of Soledad between the trees all my disinclination toward this Liverpool Sam rose up in me. I stood him while we were two white men against the banana brindles; but now, when there were prospects of my exchanging even cuss words with an American citizen, I put him back in his proper place. And he was a sight, too, with his rum-painted nose and his red whiskers and elephant feet with leather sandals strapped to them. I suppose I looked about the same.

"'It looks to me,' says I, 'like Great Britain ought to be made to keep such gin-swilling, scurvy, unbecoming mud larks as you at home instead of sending 'em over here to degrade and taint foreign lands. We kicked you out of America once and we ought to put on rubber boots and do it again.'

"'Oh, you go to 'ell,' says Liverpool, which was about all the repartee he ever had.

"Well, Soledad looked fine to me after Don Jaime's plantation. Liverpool and me walked into it side by side, from force of habit, past the calabosa and the Hotel Grande, down across the plaza toward Chica's hut, where we hoped that Liverpool, being a husband of hers, might work his luck for a meal.

"As we passed the two-story little frame house occupied by the American Club, we noticed that the balcony had been decorated all around with wreaths of evergreens and flowers, and the flag was flying from the pole on the roof. Stanzey, the consul, and Arkright, a gold-mine owner, were smoking on the balcony. Me and Liverpool waved our dirty hands toward 'em and smiled real society smiles; but they turned their backs to us and went on talking. And we had played whist once with the two of 'em up to the time when Liverpool held all thirteen trumps for four hands in succession. It was some holiday, we knew; but we didn't know the day nor the year.

"A little further along we saw a reverend man named Pendergast, who had come to Soledad to build a church, standing under a cocoanut palm with his little black alpaca coat and green umbrella.

"'Boys, boys!' says he, through his blue spectacles, 'is it as bad as this? Are you so far reduced?'

"'We're reduced,' says I, 'to very vulgar fractions.'

"'It is indeed sad,' says Pendergast, 'to see my countrymen in such circumstances.'

"'Cut 'arf of that out, old party,' says Liverpool. 'Cawn't you tell a member of the British upper classes when you see one?'

"'Shut up,' I told Liverpool. 'You're on foreign soil now, or that portion of it that's not on you.'

"'And on this day, too!' goes on Pendergast, grievous—'on this most glorious day of the year when we should all be celebrating the dawn of Christian civilization and the downfall of the wicked.'

"'I did notice bunting and bouquets decorating the town, reverend,' says I, 'but I didn't know what it was for. We've been so long out of touch with calendars that we didn't know whether it was summer time or Saturday afternoon.'

"'Here is two dollars,' says Pendergast, digging up two Chili silver wheels and handing 'em to me. 'Go, men, and observe the rest of the day in a befitting manner.'

"Me and Liverpool thanked him kindly, and walked away.

"'Shall we eat?' I asks.

"'Oh 'ell!' says Liverpool. 'What's money for?'

"'Very well, then,' I says, 'since you insist upon it, we'll drink.'

"So we pull up in a rum shop and get a quart of it and go down on the beach under a cocoanut tree and celebrate.

"Not having eaten anything but oranges in two days, the rum has immediate effect; and once more I conjure up great repugnance toward the British nation.

"'Stand up here,' I says to Liverpool, 'you scum of a despot limited monarchy, and have another dose of Bunker Hill. That good man, Mr. Pendergast,' says I, 'said we were to observe the day in a befitting manner, and I'm not going to see his money misapplied.'

"'Oh, you go to 'ell!' says Liverpool, and I started in with a fine left-hander on his right eye.

"Liverpool had been a fighter once, but dissipation and bad company had taken the nerve out of him. In ten minutes I had him lying on the sand waving the white flag.

"'Get up,' says I, kicking him in the ribs, 'and come along with me.'

Liverpool got up and followed behind me because it was his habit, wiping the red off his face and nose. I led him to Reverend Pendergast's shack and called him out.

" 'Look at this, sir,' says I—'look at this thing that was once a proud Britisher. You gave us two dollars and told us to celebrate the day. The star-spangled banner still waves. Hurrah for the stars and eagles!'

" 'Dear me,' says Pendergast, holding up his hands. 'Fighting on this day of all days! On Christmas day, when peace on——'

" 'Christmas, hell!' says I. 'I thought it was the Fourth of July.' "

"Merry Christmas!" said the red, white, and blue cockatoo.

"Take him for six dollars," said Hop-along Bibb. "He's got his dates and colors mixed."

BOOK 3

ROLLING STONES

THE DREAM

This was the last work of O. Henry. The *Cosmopolitan Magazine* had ordered it from him and, after his death, the unfinished manuscript was found in his room. The story as it here appears was published in the *Cosmopolitan* for September, 1910.

Murray dreamed a dream.

Both psychology and science grope when they would explain to us the strange adventures of our immaterial selves when wandering in the realm of "Death's twin brother, sleep." This story will not attempt to be illuminative; it is no more than record of Murray's dream. One of the most puzzling phases of that strange waking sleep is that dreams which seem to cover months or even years may take place within a few seconds or minutes.

Murray was waiting in his cell in the ward of the condemned. An electric arc light in the ceiling of the corridor shone brightly upon his table. On a sheet of white paper an ant crawled wildly here and there as Murray blocked its way with an envelope. The electrocution was set for eight o'clock in the evening. Murray smiled at the antics of the wisest of insects.

There were seven other condemned men in the chamber. Since he had been there Murray had seen three taken out to their fate; one gone mad and fighting like a wolf caught in a trap; one, no less mad, offering up a sanctimonious lip-service to Heaven; the third, a weakling, collapsed and strapped to a board. He wondered with what credit to himself his own heart, foot, and face would meet his punishment; for this was his evening. He thought it must be nearly eight o'clock.

Opposite his own in the two rows of cells was the cage of Bonifacio, the Sicilian slayer of his betrothed and of two officers who came to arrest him. With him Murray had played checkers many a long hour, each calling his move to his unseen opponent across the corridor.

Bonifacio's great booming voice with its indestructible singing quality called out:

"Eh, Meestro Murray; how you feel—all-a right—yes?"

"All right, Bonifacio," said Murray steadily, as he allowed the ant to crawl upon the envelope and then dumped it gently on the stone floor.

"Dat's good-a, Meestro Murray. Men like us, we must-a die like-a men. My time come nex'-a week. All-a right. Remember, Meestro Murray, I beat-a you dat las' game of de check. Maybe we play again some-a time. I don'-a know. Maybe we have to call-a de move damn-a loud to play de check where dey goin' send us."

Bonifacio's hardened philosophy, followed closely by his deafening musical peal of laughter, warmed rather than chilled Murray's numbed heart. Yet, Bonifacio had until next week to live.

The cell-dwellers heard the familiar, loud click of the steel bolts as the door at the end of the corridor was opened. Three men came to Murray's cell and unlocked it. Two were prison guards; the other was "Len"—no; that was in the old days; now the Reverend Leonard Winston, a friend and neighbor from their barefoot days.

"I got them to let me take the prison chaplain's place," he said, as he gave Murray's hand one short, strong grip. In his left hand he held a small Bible, with his forefinger marking a page.

Murray smiled slightly and arranged two or three books and some penholders orderly on his small table. He would have spoken, but no appropriate words seemed to present themselves to his mind.

The prisoners had christened this cellhouse, eighty feet long, twenty-eight feet wide, Limbo Lane. The regular guard of Limbo Lane, an immense, rough, kindly man, drew a pint bottle of whiskey from his pocket and offered it to Murray, saying:

"It's the regular thing, you know. All has it who feel like they need a bracer. No danger of it becoming a habit with 'em, you see."

Murray drank deep into the bottle.

"That's the boy!" said the guard. "Just a little nerve tonic, and everything goes smooth as silk."

They stepped into the corridor, and each one of the doomed seven knew. Limbo Lane is a world on the outside of the world; but it had learned, when deprived of one or more of the five senses, to make another sense supply the deficiency. Each one knew that it was nearly eight, and that Murray was to go to the chair at eight. There is also in the many Limbo Lanes an aristocracy of crime. The man who kills in the open, who beats his enemy or pursuer down, flushed by the primitive emotions and the ardor of combat, holds in contempt the human rat, the spider, and the snake.

So, of the seven condemned only three called their farewells to Murray as he marched down the corridor between the two guards—Bonifacio, Marvin, who had killed a guard while trying to escape from the prison, and Bassett, the train-robber, who was driven to it because the express-messenger wouldn't raise his hands when ordered to do so. The remaining four smoldered, silent, in their cells, no doubt feeling their social ostracism in Limbo Lane society more keenly than they did the memory of their less picturesque offences against the law.

Murray wondered at his own calmness and nearly indifference. In the execution room were about twenty men, a congregation made up of prison officers, newspaper reporters, and lookers-on who had succeeded.

Here, in the very middle of a sentence, the hand of Death interrupted the telling of O. Henry's last story. He had planned to make this story different from his others, the beginning of a new series in a style he had not previously attempted. "I want to show the public," he said, "that I can write something new—new for me, I mean—a story without slang, a straightforward dramatic plot treated in a way that will come nearer my idea of real story-writing." Before starting to write the present story, he outlined briefly how he intended to develop it: Murray, the criminal accused and convicted of the brutal murder of his sweetheart—a murder prompted by jealous rage—at first faces the death penalty, calm, and, to all outward appearances, indifferent to his fate. As he nears the electric chair he is overcome by a revulsion of feeling. He is left dazed, stupefied, stunned. The entire scene in the death-chamber—the witnesses, the spectators, the preparations for execution—become unreal to him. The thought flashes through his brain that a terrible mistake is being made. Why is he being strapped to the chair? What has he done? What crime has he committed? In the few moments while the straps are being adjusted a vision comes to him. He dreams a dream. He sees a little country cottage, bright, sun-lit, nestling in a bower of flowers. A woman is there, and a little child. He speaks with them and finds that they are his wife, his child—and the cottage their home. So, after all, it is a mistake. Some one has frightfully, irretrievably blundered. The accusation, the trial, the conviction, the sentence to death in the electric chair—all a dream. He takes his wife in his arms and kisses the child. Yes, here is happiness. It was a dream. Then—at a sign from the prison warden the fatal current is turned on.

Murray had dreamed the wrong dream.

A RULER OF MEN

I walked the streets of the City of Insolence, thirsting for the sight of a stranger face. For the City is a desert of familiar types as thick and alike as the grains in a sand-storm; and you grow to hate them as you do a friend who is always by you, or one of your kin.

And my desire was granted, for I saw near a corner of Broadway and Twenty-ninth Street, a little flaxen-haired man with a face like a scaly-bark hickory-nut, selling to a fast-gathering crowd a tool that omnigenously proclaimed itself a can-opener, a screw-driver, a button-hook, a nail-file, a shoe-horn, a watch-guard, a potato-peeler, and an ornament to any gentleman's key-ring.

And then a stall-fed cop shoved himself through the congregation of customers. The vender, plainly used to having his seasons of trade thus abruptly curtailed, closed his satchel and slipped like a weasel through the opposite segment of the circle. The crowd scurried aimlessly away like ants from a disturbed crumb. The cop, suddenly becoming oblivious of the earth and its inhabitants, stood still, swelling his bulk and putting his club through an intricate drill of twirls. I hurried after Kansas Bill Bowers, and caught him by an arm.

Without his looking at me or slowing his pace, I found a five-dollar bill crumpled neatly into my hand.

"I wouldn't have thought, Kansas Bill," I said, "that you'd hold an old friend that cheap."

Then he turned his head, and the hickory-nut cracked into a wide smile.

"Give back the money," said he, "or I'll have the cop after you for false pretenses. I thought you was the cop."

"I want to talk to you, Bill," I said. "When did you leave Oklahoma? Where is Reddy McGill now? Why are you selling those impossible contraptions on the street? How did your Big Horn gold-mine pan out? How did you get so badly sunburned? What will you drink?"

"A year ago," answered Kansas Bill, systematically. "Putting up windmills in Arizona. For pin money to buy etceteras with. Salted. Been down in the tropics. Beer."

We foregathered in a propitious place and became Elijahs, while a waiter of dark plumage played the raven to perfection. Reminiscence needs must be had before I could steer Bill into his epic mood.

"Yes," said he, "I mind the time Timoteo's rope broke on that cow's horns while the calf was chasing you. You and that cow! I'd never forget it."

"The tropics," said I, "are a broad territory. What part of Cancer or Capricorn have you been honoring with a visit?"

"Down along China or Peru—or maybe the Argentine Confederacy," said Kansas Bill. "Anyway 'twas among a great race of people, off-colored but progressive. I was there three months."

"No doubt you are glad to be back among the truly great race," I surmised. "Especially among New Yorkers, the most progressive and independent citizens of any country in the world," I continued, with the fatuity of the provincial who has eaten the Broadway lotus.

"Do you want to start an argument?" asked Bill.

"Can there be one?" I answered.

"Has an Irishman humor, do you think?" asked he.

"I have an hour or two to spare," said I, looking at the café clock.

"Not that the Americans aren't a great commercial nation," conceded Bill. "But the fault laid with the people who wrote lies for fiction."

"What was this Irishman's name?" I asked.

"Was that last beer cold enough?" said he.

"I see there is talk of further outbreaks among the Russian peasants," I remarked.

"His name was Barney O'Connor," said Bill.

Thus, because of our ancient prescience of each other's trail of thought, we travelled ambiguously to the point where Kansas Bill's story began:

"I met O'Connor in a boarding-house on the West Side. He invited me to his hall-room to have a drink, and we became like a dog and a cat that had been raised together. There he sat, a tall, fine, handsome man, with his feet against one wall and his back against the other, looking over a map. On the bed and sticking three feet out of it was a beautiful gold sword with tassels on it and rhinestones in the handle.

" 'What's this?' says I (for by that time we were well acquainted). 'The annual parade in vilification of the ex-snakes of Ireland? And what's the line of march? Up Broadway to Forty-second; thence east to McCarty's café; thence——'

" 'Sit down on the wash-stand,' says O'Connor, 'and listen. And cast no perversions on the sword. 'Twas my father's in old Munster. And this map, Bowers, is no diagram of a holiday procession. If ye look again ye'll see that it's the continent known as South America, comprising fourteen green, blue, red, and yellow countries, all crying out from time to time to be liberated from the yoke of the oppressor.'

" 'I know,' says I to O'Connor. 'The idea is a literary one. The ten-cent magazine stole it from "Ridpath's History of the World from the Sand-store Period to the Equator." You'll find it in every one of 'em. It's a continued story of a soldier of fortune, generally named O'Keefe, who gets to be dictator while the Spanish-American populace cries "Cospetto!" and other Italian maledictions. I misdoubt if it's ever been done. You're not thinking of trying that, are you, Barney?' I asks.

" 'Bowers,' says he, 'you're a man of education and courage.'

" 'How can I deny it?' says I. 'Education runs in my family; and I have acquired courage by a hard struggle with life.'

" 'The O'Connors,' says he, 'are a warlike race. There is me father's sword; and here is the map. A life of inaction is not for me. The O'Connors were born to rule. 'Tis a ruler of men I must be.'

" 'Barney,' I says to him, 'why don't you get on the force and settle down to a quiet life of carnage and corruption instead of roaming off to foreign parts? In what better way can you indulge your desire to subdue and maltreat the oppressed?'

" 'Look again at the map,' says he, 'at the country I have the point of me knife on. 'Tis that one I have selected to aid and overthrow with me father's sword.'

" 'I see,' says I. 'It's the green one; and that does credit to your patri-otism, and it's the smallest one; and that does credit to your judgment.'

" 'Do ye accuse me of cowardice?' says Barney, turning pink.

" 'No man,' says I, 'who attacks and confiscates a country singlehanded could be called a coward. The worst you can be charged with is plagiarism or imitation. If Anthony Hope and Roosevelt let you get away with it, nobody else will have any right to kick.'

" 'I'm not joking,' says O'Connor. 'And I've got $1,500 cash to work the scheme with. I've taken a liking to you. Do you want it, or not?'

" 'I'm not working,' I told him; 'but how is it to be? Do I eat during the fomentation of the insurrection, or am I only to be Secretary of War after the country is conquered? Is it to be a pay envelope or only a portfolio?'

" 'I'll pay all expenses,' says O'Connor. 'I want a man I can trust. If we succeed you may pick out any appointment you want in the gift of the government.'

" 'All right, then,' says I. 'You can get me a bunch of draying contracts and then a quick-action consignment to a seat on the Supreme Court bench so I won't be in line for the presidency. The kind of cannon they chasten their presidents with in that country hurt too much. You can consider me on the pay-roll.'

"Two weeks afterward O'Connor and me took a steamer for the small, green, doomed country. We were three weeks on the trip. O'Connor said he had his plans all figured out in advance; but being the commanding general, it consorted with his dignity to keep the details concealed from his army and cabinet, commonly known as William T. Bowers. Three dollars a day was the price for which I joined the cause of liberating an undiscovered country from the ills that threatened or sustained it. Every Saturday night on the steamer I stood in line at parade rest, and O'Connor handed over the twenty-one dollars.

"The town we landed at was named Guayaquerita, so they told me. 'Not for me,' says I. 'It'll be little old Hilldale or Tompkinsville or Cherry Tree Corners when I speak of it. It's a clear case where Spelling Reform ought to butt in and disenvowel it.'

"But the town looked fine from the bay when we sailed in. It was white, with green ruching, and lace ruffles on the skirt when the surf slashed up on the sand. It looked as tropical and dolce far ultra as the pictures of Lake Ronkonkoma in the brochure of the passenger department of the Long Island Railroad.

"We went through the quarantine and custom house indignities; and then O'Connor leads me to a 'dobe house on a street called 'The Avenue of the Dolorous Butterflies of the Individual and Collective Saints.' Ten feet wide it was, and knee-deep in alfalfa and cigar stumps.

" 'Hooligan Alley,' says I, rechristening it.

" ' 'Twill be our headquarters,' says O'Connor. 'My agent here, Don Fernando Pacheco, secured it for us.'

"So in that house O'Connor and me established the revolutionary centre. In the front room we had ostensible things such as fruit, a guitar, and a table with a conch shell on it. In the back room O'Connor had his desk and a large looking-glass and his sword hid in a roll of straw matting. We slept on hammocks that we hung to hooks in the wall; and took our meals at the Hotel Inglés, a beanery run on the American plan by a German proprietor with Chinese cooking served à la Kansas City lunch counter.

"It seems that O'Connor really did have some sort of system planned out beforehand. He wrote plenty of letters; and every day or two some native gent would stroll round to headquarters and be shut up in the back room for half an hour with O'Connor and the interpreter. I noticed that when they went in they were always smoking eight-inch cigars and at peace with the world; but when they came out they would be folding up a ten- or twenty-dollar bill and cursing the government horribly.

"One evening after we had been in Guaya—in this town of Smellville-by-the-Sea—about a month, and me and O'Connor were sitting outside the door helping along old tempus fugit with rum and ice and limes, I says to him:

" 'If you'll excuse a patriot that don't exactly know what he's patronizing, for the question—what is your scheme for subjugating this country? Do you intend to plunge it into bloodshed, or do you mean to buy its votes peacefully and honorably at the polls?'

" 'Bowers,' says he, 'ye're a fine little man and I intend to make great use of ye after the conflict. But ye do not understand statecraft. Already by now we have a network of strategy clutching with invisible fingers at the throat of the tyrant Calderas. We have agents at work in every town in the republic. The Liberal party is bound to win. On our secret lists we have the names of enough sympathizers to crush the administration forces at a single blow.'

" 'A straw vote,' says I, 'only shows which way the hot air blows.'

" 'Who has accomplished this?' goes on O'Connor. 'I have. I have directed everything. The time was ripe when we came, so my agents inform me. The people are groaning under burdens of taxes and levies. Who will be their natural leader when they rise? Could it be any one but meself? 'Twas only yesterday that Zaldas, our representative in the province of Durasnas, tells me that the people, in secret, already call me "El Library Door," which is the Spanish manner of saying "The Liberator." '

" 'Was Zaldas that maroon-colored old Aztec with a paper collar on and unbleached domestic shoes?' I asked.

" 'He was,' says O'Connor.

" 'I saw him tucking a yellow-back into his vest pocket as he came out,' says I. 'It may be,' says I, 'that they call you a library door, but they treat you more like the side door of a bank. But let us hope for the worst.'

" 'It has cost money, of course,' says O'Connor; 'but we'll have the country in our hands inside of a month.'

"In the evenings we walked about in the plaza and listened to the band playing and mingled with the populace at its distressing and obnoxious pleasures. There were thirteen vehicles belonging to the upper classes, mostly rock-aways and old-style barouches, such as the mayor rides in at the unveiling of the new poor-house at Milledgeville, Alabama. Round and round the desiccated fountain in the middle of the plaza they drove, and lifted their high silk hats to their friends. The common people walked around in barefooted bunches, puffing stogies that a Pittsburg millionaire wouldn't have chewed for a dry smoke on Ladies' Day at his club. And the grandest figure in the whole turnout was Barney O'Connor. Six foot two he stood in his Fifth Avenue clothes, with his eagle eye and his black moustache that tickled his ears. He was a born dictator and czar and hero and harrier of the human race. It looked to me that all eyes were turned upon O'Connor, and that every woman there loved him, and every man feared him. Once or twice I looked at him and thought of funnier things that had happened than his winning out in his game; and I began to feel like a Hidalgo de Officio de Grafto de South America myself. And then I would come down again to solid bottom and let my imagination gloat, as usual, upon the twenty-one American dollars due me on Saturday night.

" 'Take note,' says O'Connor to me as thus we walked, 'of the mass of the people. Observe their oppressed and melancholy air. Can ye not see that they are ripe for revolt? Do ye not perceive that they are disaffected?'

" 'I do not,' says I. 'Nor disinfected either. I'm beginning to understand these people. When they look unhappy they're enjoying themselves. When they feel unhappy they go to sleep. They're not the kind of people to take an interest in revolutions.'

" 'They'll flock to our standard,' says O'Connor. 'Three thousand men in this town alone will spring to arms when the signal is given. I am assured of that. But everything is in secret. There is no chance for us to fail.'

"On Hooligan Alley, as I prefer to call the street our headquarters was on, there was a row of flat 'dobe houses with red tile roofs, some straw shacks full of Indians and dogs, and one two-story wooden house with balconies a little farther down. That was where General Tumbalo, the comandante and commander of the military forces, lived. Right across the street was a private residence built like a combination bake-oven and folding-bed. One day, O'Connor and me were passing it, single file, on the flange they called a sidewalk, when out of the window flies a big red rose. O'Connor, who is ahead, picks it up, presses it to his fifth rib, and bows to the ground. By Carrambos! that man certainly had the Irish drama chaunceyized. I looked around expecting to see the little boy and girl in white sateen ready to jump on his shoulder while he jolted their spinal columns and ribs together through a breakdown, and sang: 'Sleep, Little One, Sleep.'

"As I passed the window I glanced inside and caught a glimpse of a white dress and a pair of big, flashy black eyes and gleaming teeth under a dark lace mantilla.

"When we got back to our house O'Connor began to walk up and down the floor and twist his moustaches.

" 'Did ye see her eyes, Bowers?' he asks me.

" 'I did,' says I, 'and I can see more than that. It's all coming out according to the story-books. I knew there was something missing. 'Twas the love interest. What is it that comes in Chapter VII to cheer the gallant Irish adventurer? Why, Love, of course—Love that makes the hat go around. At last we have the eyes of midnight hue and the rose flung from the barred window. Now, what comes next? The underground passage—the intercepted letter—the traitor in camp—the hero thrown into a dungeon—the mysterious message from the señorita—then the outburst —the fighting on the plaza—the——'

" 'Don't be a fool,' says O'Connor, interrupting. 'But that's the only woman in the world for me, Bowers. The O'Connors are as quick to love as they are to fight. I shall wear that rose over me heart when I lead me men into action. For a good battle to be fought there must be some woman to give it power.'

" 'Every time,' I agreed, 'if you want to have a good lively scrap. There's only one thing bothering me. In the novels the light-haired friend of the hero always gets killed. Think 'em all over that you've read, and you'll see that I'm right. I think I'll step down to the Botica Española and lay in a bottle of walnut stain before war is declared.'

" 'How will I find out her name?' says O'Connor, laying his chin in his hand.

" 'Why don't you go across the street and ask her?' says I.

" 'Will ye never regard anything in life seriously?' says O'Connor, looking down at me like a school-master.

" 'Maybe she meant the rose for me,' I said, whistling the Spanish Fandango.

"For the first time since I'd known O'Connor, he laughed. He got up and roared and clapped his knees, and leaned against the wall till the tiles on the roof clattered to the noise of his lungs. He went into the back room and looked at himself in the glass and began and laughed all over from the beginning again. Then he looked at me and repeated himself. That's why I asked you if you thought an Irishman had any humor. He'd been doing farce comedy from the day I saw him without knowing it; and the first time he had an idea advanced to him with any intelligence in it he acted like two twelfths of the sextet in a 'Floradora' road company.

"The next afternoon he comes in with a triumphant smile and begins to pull something like ticker tape out of his pocket.

" 'Great!' says I: 'This is something like home. How is Amalgamated Copper to-day?'

" 'I've got her name,' says O'Connor, and he reads off something like this: 'Doña Isabel Antonia Inez Lolita Carreras y Buencaminos y Monteleon. She lives with her mother,' explains O'Connor. 'Her father was killed in the last revolution. She is sure to be in sympathy with our cause.'

"And sure enough the next day she flung a little bunch of roses clear across the street into our door. O'Connor dived for it and found a piece of paper curled around a step with a line in Spanish on it. He dragged the interpreter out of his corner and got him busy. The interpreter scratched his head, and gave us as a translation three best bets: 'Fortune had got a face like the man fighting'; 'Fortune looks like a brave man'; and 'Fortune favors the brave.' We put our money on the last one.

" 'Do ye see?' says O'Connor. 'She intends to encourage me sword to save her country.'

" 'It looks to me like an invitation to supper,' says I.

"So every day this señorita sits behind the barred windows and exhausts a conservatory or two, one posy at a time. And O'Connor walks like a Dominecker rooster and swells his chest and swears to me he will win her by feats of arms and big deeds on the gory field of battle.

"By and by the revolution began to get ripe. One day O'Connor takes me into the back room and tells me all.

" 'Bowers,' says he, 'at twelve o'clock one week from to-day the struggle will take place. It has pleased ye to find amusement and diversion in this project because ye have not sense enough to perceive that it is easily accomplished by a man of courage, intelligence, and historical superiority, such as meself. The whole world over,' says he, 'the O'Connors have ruled men, women, and nations. To subdue a small and indifferent country like this is a trifle. Ye see what little bare-footed manikins the men of it are. I could lick four of 'em single-handed.'

" 'No doubt,' says I. 'But could you lick six? And suppose they hurled an army of seventeen against you?'

" 'Listen,' says O'Connor, 'to what will occur. At noon next Tuesday 25,000 patriots will rise up in the towns of the republic. The government will be absolutely unprepared. The public buildings will be taken, the regular army made prisoners, and the new administration set up. In the capital it will not be so easy on account of most of the army being stationed there. They will occupy the president's palace and the strongly fortified government buildings and stand a siege. But on the very day of the outbreak a body of our troops will begin a march to the capital from every town as soon as the local victory has been won. The thing is so well planned that it is an impossibility for us to fail. I meself will lead the troops from here. The new president will be Señor Espadas, now Minister of Finance in the present cabinet.'

" 'What do you get?' I asked.

" ' 'Twill be strange,' said O'Connor, smiling, 'if I don't have all the jobs handed to me on a silver salver to pick what I choose. I've been the brains of the scheme, and when the fighting opens I guess I won't be in the rear rank. Who managed it so our troops could get arms smuggled into this country? Didn't I arrange it with a New York firm before I left there? Our financial agents inform me that 20,000 stands of Winchester rifles have been delivered a month ago at a secret place up coast and distributed among the towns. I tell you, Bowers, the game is already won.'

"Well, that kind of talk kind of shook my disbelief in the infallibility of the serious Irish gentleman soldier of fortune. It certainly seemed that the patriotic grafters had gone about the thing in a business way. I looked upon O'Connor with more respect, and began to figure on what kind of uniform I might wear as Secretary of War.

"Tuesday, the day set for the revolution, came around according to schedule. O'Connor said that a signal had been agreed upon for the uprising. There was an old cannon on the beach near the national ware-house. That had been secretly loaded and promptly at twelve o'clock was to be fired off. Immediately the revolutionists would seize their con-cealed arms, attack the comandante's troops in the cuartel, and capture the custom-house and all government property and supplies.

"I was nervous all the morning. And about eleven o'clock O'Connor became infused with the excitement and martial spirit of murder. He geared his father's sword around him, and walked up and down in the back room like a lion in the Zoo suffering from corns. I smoked a couple of dozen cigars, and decided on yellow stripes down the trouser legs of my uniform.

"At half-past eleven O'Connor asks me to take a short stroll through the streets to see if I could notice any signs of the uprising. I was back in fifteen minutes.

"'Did you hear anything?' he asks.

"'I did,' says I. 'At first I thought it was drums. But it wasn't; it was snoring. Everybody in town's asleep.'

"O'Connor tears out his watch.

"'Fools!' says he. 'They've set the time right at the siesta hour when everybody takes a nap. But the cannon will wake 'em up. Everything will be all right, depend upon it.'

"Just at twelve o'clock we heard the sound of a cannon—BOOM!—shaking the whole town.

"O'Connor loosens his sword in its scabbard and jumps for the door. I went as far as the door and stood in it.

"People were sticking their heads out of doors and windows. But there was one grand sight that made the landscape look tame.

"General Tumbalo, the comandante, was rolling down the steps of his residential dugout, waving a five-foot sabre in his hand. He wore his cocked and plumed hat and his dress-parade coat covered with gold braid and buttons. Sky-blue pajamas, one rubber boot, and one red-plush slipper completed his make-up.

"The general had heard the cannon, and he puffed down the side-walk toward the soldiers' barracks as fast as his rudely awakened two hundred pounds could travel.

"O'Connor sees him and lets out a battle-cry and draws his father's sword and rushes across the street and tackles the enemy.

"Right there in the street he and the general gave an exhibition of black-smithing and butchery. Sparks flew from their blades, the general roared, and O'Connor gave the slogan of his race and proclivities.

"Then the general's sabre broke in two; and he took to his ginger-colored heels crying out, 'Policios,' at every jump. O'Connor chased him a block, imbued with the sentiment of man-slaughter, and slicing buttons off the general's coat tails with the paternal weapon. At the corner five barefooted policemen in cotton undershirts and straw hats climbed over O'Connor and subjugated him according to the municipal statutes. They brought him past the late revolutionary headquarters on the way to jail. I stood in the door. A policeman had him by each hand and foot, and they dragged him on his back through the grass like a turtle. Twice they stopped, and the odd policeman took another's place while he rolled a cigarette. The great soldier of fortune turned his head and looked at me as they passed. I blushed, and lit another cigar. The procession passed on, and at ten minutes past twelve everybody had gone back to sleep again.

"In the afternoon the interpreter came around and smiled as he laid his hand on the big red jar we usually kept ice-water in.

" 'The ice-man didn't call to-day,' says I. 'What's the matter with everything, Sancho?'

" 'Ah, yes,' says the liver-colored linguist. 'They just tell me in the town. Verree bad act that Señor O'Connor make fight with General Tumbalo. Yes, General Tumbalo great soldier and big mans.'

" 'What'll they do to Mr. O'Connor?' I asks.

" 'I talk little while presently with the Juez de la Paz—what you call Justice-with-the-peace,' says Sancho. 'He tell me it verree bad crime that one Señor Americano try kill General Tumbalo. He say they keep Señor O'Connor in jail six months; then have trial and shoot him with guns. Verree sorree.'

" 'How about this revolution that was to be pulled off?' I asks.

" 'Oh,' says this Sancho. 'I think too hot weather for revolution. Revolution better in winter-time. Maybe so next winter. *Quién sabe?*'

" 'But the cannon went off,' says I. 'The signal was given.'

" 'That big sound?' says Sancho, grinning. 'The boiler in ice factory he blow up—BOOM! Wake everybody up from siesta. Verree sorree. No ice. Mucho hot day.'

"About sunset I went over to the jail, and they let me talk to O'Connor through the bars.

" 'What's the news, Bowers?' says he. 'Have we taken the town? I've been expecting a rescue party all the afternoon. I haven't heard any firing. Has any word been received from the capital?'

" 'Take it easy, Barney,' says I. 'I think there's been a change of plans. There's something more important to talk about. Have you any money?'

" 'I have not,' says O'Connor. "The last dollar went to pay our hotel bill yesterday. Did our troops capture the custom-house? There ought to be plenty of government money there.'

" 'Segregate your mind from battles,' says I. 'I've been making inquiries. You're to be shot six months from date for assault and battery. I'm expecting to receive fifty years at hard labor for vagrancy. All they furnish you while you're a prisoner is water. You depend on your friends for food. I'll see what I can do.'

"I went away and found a silver Chile dollar in an old vest of O'Connor's. I took him some fried fish and rice for his supper. In the morning I went down to a lagoon and had a drink of water, and then went back to the jail. O'Connor had a porterhouse steak look in his eye.

" 'Barney,' says I, 'I've found a pond full of the finest kind of water. It's the grandest, sweetest, purest water in the world. Say the word and I'll go fetch you a bucket of it and you can throw this vile government stuff out the window. I'll do anything I can for a friend.'

" 'Has it come to this?' says O'Connor, raging up and down his cell. 'Am I to be starved to death and then shot? I'll make those traitors feel the weight of an O'Connor's hand when I get out of this.' And then he comes to the bars and speaks softer. 'Has nothing been heard from Doña Isabel?' he asks. 'Though every one else in the world fail,' says he, 'I trust those eyes of hers. She will find a way to effect my release. Do ye think ye could communicate with her? One word from her—even a rose would make me sorrow light. But don't let her know except with the utmost delicacy, Bowers. These high-bred Castilians are sensitive and proud.'

" 'Well said, Barney,' says I. 'You've given me an idea. I'll report later. Something's got to be pulled off quick, or we'll both starve.'

"I walked out and down to Hooligan Alley, and then on the other side of the street. As I went past the window of Doña Isabel Antonia Concha Regalia, out flies the rose as usual and hits me on the ear.

"The door was open, and I took off my hat and walked in. It wasn't very light inside, but there she sat in a rocking-chair by the window smoking a black cheroot. And when I got closer I saw that she was about thirty-nine, and had never seen a straight front in her life. I sat down on the arm of her chair, and took the cheroot out of her mouth and stole a kiss.

" 'Hullo, Izzy,' I says. 'Excuse my unconventionality, but I feel like I have known you for a month. Whose Izzy is oo?'

"The lady ducked her head under her mantilla, and drew in a long breath. I thought she was going to scream, but with all that intake of air she only came out with: 'Me likee Americanos.'

"As soon as she said that, I knew that O'Connor and me would be doing things with a knife and fork before the day was over. I drew a chair beside her, and inside of half an hour we were engaged. Then I took my hat and said I must go out for a while.

" 'You come back?' says Izzy, in alarm.

" 'Me go bring preacher,' says I. 'Come back twenty minutes. We marry now. How you likee?'

" 'Marry to-day?' says Izzy. 'Good!'

"I went down on the beach to the United States consul's shack. He was a grizzly man, eighty-two pounds, smoked glasses, five foot eleven, pickled. He was playing chess with an india-rubber man in white clothes.

" 'Excuse me for interrupting,' says I, 'but can you tell me how a man could get married quick?'

"The consul gets up and fingers in a pigeonhole.

" 'I believe I had a license to perform the ceremony myself, a year or two ago,' he said. 'I'll look, and——'

"I caught hold of his arm.

" 'Don't look it up,' says I. 'Marriage is a lottery anyway. I'm willing to take the risk about the license if you are.'

"The consul went back to Hooligan Alley with me. Izzy called her ma to come in, but the old lady was picking a chicken in the patio and begged to be excused. So we stood up and the consul performed the ceremony.

"That evening Mrs. Bowers cooked a great supper of stewed goat, tamales, baked bananas, fricasseed red peppers and coffee. Afterward I sat in the rocking-chair by the front window, and she sat on the floor plunking at a guitar and happy, as she should be, as Mrs. William T. B.

"All at once I sprang up in a hurry. I'd forgotten all about O'Connor. I asked Izzy to fix up a lot of truck for him to eat.

" 'That big, oogly man,' said Izzy. 'But all right—he your friend.'

"I pulled a rose out a bunch in a jar, and took the grub-basket around to the jail. O'Connor ate like a wolf. Then he wiped his face with a banana peel and said: 'Have you heard nothing from Doña Isabel yet?'

" 'Hist!' says I, slipping the rose between the bars. 'She send you this. She bids you take courage. At nightfall two masked men brought it to the ruined château in the orange grove. How did you like that goat hash, Barney?'

"O'Connor pressed the rose to his lips.

" 'This is more to me than all the food in the world,' says he. 'But the supper was fine. Where did you raise it?'

" 'I've negotiated a stand-off at a delicatessen hut downtown,' I tells him. 'Rest easy. If there's anything to be done I'll do it.'

"So things went along that way for some weeks. Izzy was a great cook; and if she had had a little more poise of character and smoked a little better brand of tobacco we might have drifted into some sense of responsibility for the honor I had conferred on her. But as time went on I began to hunger for the sight of a real lady standing before me in a street-car. All I was staying in that land of bilk and money for was because I couldn't get away, and I thought it no more than decent to stay and see O'Connor shot.

"One day our old interpreter drops around and after smoking an hour says that the judge of the peace sent him to request me to call on him. I went to his office in a lemon grove on a hill at the edge of the town; and there I had a surprise. I expected to see one of the usual cinnamon-colored natives in congress gaiters and one of Pizzaro's cast-off hats. What I saw was an elegant gentleman of a slightly claybank complexion sitting in an upholstered leather chair, sipping a highball and reading Mrs. Humphry Ward. I had smuggled into my brain a few words of Spanish by the help of Izzy, and I began to remark in a rich Andalusian brogue:

" 'Buenas dias, señor. Yo tengo—yo tengo——'

" 'Oh, sit down, Mr. Bowers,' says he. 'I spent eight years in your country in colleges and law schools. Let me mix you a highball. Lemon peel, or not?'

"Thus we got along. In about half an hour I was beginning to tell him about the scandal in our family when Aunt Elvira ran away with a Cumberland Presbyterian preacher. Then he says to me:

" 'I sent for you, Mr. Bowers, to let you know that you can have your friend Mr. O'Connor now. Of course we had to make a show of punishing him on account of his attack on General Tumbalo. It is arranged that he shall be released to-morrow night. You and he will be conveyed on board the fruit steamer *Voyager*, bound for New York, which lies in the harbor. Your passage will be arranged for.'

" 'One moment, judge,' says I; 'that revolution——'

"The judge lays back in his chair and howls.

" 'Why,' says he presently, 'that was all a little joke fixed up by the boys around the court-room, and one or two of our cut-ups, and a few clerks in the stores. The town is bursting its sides with laughing. The boys made themselves up to be conspirators, and they—what you call it?—stick Señor O'Connor for his money. It is very funny.'

" 'It was,' says I. 'I saw the joke all along. I'll take another highball, if your Honor don't mind.'

"The next evening just at dark a couple of soldiers brought O'Connor down to the beach, where I was waiting under a cocoanut-tree.

" 'Hist!' says I in his ear. 'Doña Isabel has arranged our escape. Not a word!'

"They rowed us in a boat out to a little steamer that smelled of table d'hôte salad oil and bone phosphate.

"The great, mellow, tropical moon was rising as we steamed away. O'Connor leaned on the taffrail or rear balcony of the ship and gazed silently at Guaya—at Buncoville-on-the-Beach. He had the red rose in his hand.

" 'She will wait,' I heard him say. 'Eyes like hers never deceive. But I shall see her again. Traitors cannot keep an O'Connor down forever.'

" 'You talk like a sequel,' says I. 'But in Volume II please omit the light-haired friend who totes the grub to the hero in his dungeon cell.'

"And thus reminiscing, we came back to New York."

There was a little silence broken only by the familiar roar of the streets after Kansas Bill Bowers ceased talking.

"Did O'Connor ever go back?" I asked.

"He attained his heart's desire," said Bill. "Can you walk two blocks? I'll show you."

He led me eastward and down a flight of stairs that was covered by a curious-shaped glowing, pagoda-like structure. Signs and figures on the tiled walls and supporting columns attested that we were in the Grand Central station of the subway. Hundreds of people were on the midway platform.

An uptown express dashed up and halted. It was crowded. There was a rush for it by a still larger crowd.

Towering above every one there a magnificent, broad-shouldered, athletic man leaped into the centre of the struggle. Men and women he seized in either hand and hurled them like manikins toward the open gates of the train.

Now and then some passenger with a shred of soul and self-respect left to him turned to offer remonstrance; but the blue uniform on the towering figure, the fierce and conquering glare of his eye and the ready impact of his ham-like hands glued together the lips that would have spoken complaint.

When the train was full, then he exhibited to all who might observe and admire his irresistible genius as a ruler of men. With his knees, with his elbows, with his shoulders, with his resistless feet he shoved, crushed, slammed, heaved, kicked, flung, pounded the overplus of passengers aboard. Then with the sounds of its wheels drowned by the moans, shrieks, prayers, and curses of its unfortunate crew, the express dashed away.

"That's him. Ain't he a wonder?" said Kansas Bill, admiringly. "That tropical country wasn't the place for him. I wish the distinguished traveler, writer, war correspondent, and playwright, Richmond Hobson Davis, could see him now. O'Connor ought to be dramatized."

THE ATAVISM OF JOHN TOM LITTLE BEAR

I saw a light in Jeff Peters's room over the Red Front Drug Store. I hastened toward it, for I had not known that Jeff was in town. He is a man of the Hadji breed, of a hundred occupations, with a story to tell (when he will) of each one.

I found Jeff repacking his grip for a run down to Florida to look at an orange grove for which he had traded, a month before, his mining claim on the Yukon. He kicked me a chair, with the same old humorous, profound smile on his seasoned countenance. It had been eight months since we had met, but his greeting was such as men pass from day to day. Time is Jeff's servant, and the continent is a big lot across which he cuts to his many roads.

For a while we skirmished along the edges of unprofitable talk which culminated in that unquiet problem of the Philippines.

"All them tropical races," said Jeff, "could be run out better with their own jockeys up. The tropical man knows what he wants. All he wants is a season ticket to the cock-fights and a pair of Western Union climbers to go up the bread-fruit tree. The Anglo-Saxon man wants him to learn to conjugate and wear suspenders. He'll be happiest in his own way."

I was shocked.

"Education, man," I said, "is the watchword. In time they will rise to our standard of civilization. Look at what education has done for the Indian."

"O-ho!" sang Jeff, lighting his pipe (which was a good sign). "Yes, the Indian! I'm looking. I hasten to contemplate the redman as a standard bearer of progress. He's the same as the other brown boys. You can't make an Anglo-Saxon of him. Did I ever tell you about the time my friend John Tom Little Bear bit off the right ear of the arts of culture and education and spun the teetotum back round to where it was when Columbus was a little boy? I did not?

"John Tom Little Bear was an educated Cherokee Indian and an old friend of mine when I was in the Territories. He was a graduate of one of them Eastern football colleges that have been so successful in teaching the Indian to use the gridiron instead of burning his victims at the stake. As an Anglo-Saxon, John Tom was copper-colored in spots. As an Indian, he was one of the whitest men I ever knew. As a Cherokee, he was a gentleman on the first ballot. As a ward of the nation, he was mighty hard to carry at the primaries.

"John Tom and me got together and began to make medicine—how to get up some lawful, genteel swindle which we might work in a quiet way so as not to excite the stupidity of the police or the cupidity of the larger corporations. We had close upon $500 between us, and we pined to make it grow, as all respectable capitalists do.

"So we figured out a proposition which seems to be as honorable as a gold mine prospectus and as profitable as a church raffle. And inside of thirty days you find us swarming into Kansas with a pair of fluent horses and a red camping wagon on the European plan. John Tom is Chief Wish-Heap-Dough, the famous Indian medicine man and Samaritan Sachem of the Seven Tribes. Mr. Peters is business manager and half owner. We needed a third man, so we looked around and found J. Conyngham Binkly leaning against the want column of a newspaper. This Binkly has a disease for Shakespearian rôles, and an hallucination about a 200 nights' run on the New York stage. But he confesses that he never could earn the butter to spread on his William S. rôles, so he is willing to drop to the ordinary baker's kind, and be satisfied with a 200-mile run behind the medicine ponies. Besides Richard III, he could do twenty-seven coon songs and banjo specialties, and was willing to cook, and curry the horses. We carried a fine line of excuses for taking money. One was a magic soap for removing grease spots and quarters from clothes. One was a Sum-wah-tah, the great Indian Remedy made from a prairie herb revealed by the Great Spirit in a dream to his favorite medicine men, the great chiefs McGarrity and Siberstein, bottlers, Chicago. And the other was a frivolous system of pick-pocketing the Kansasters that had the department stores reduced to a decimal fraction. Look ye! A pair of silk garters, a dream book, one dozen clothespins, a gold tooth, and 'When Knighthood Was in Flower' all wrapped up in a genuine Japanese silkarina handkerchief and handed to the handsome lady by Mr. Peters for the trivial sum of fifty cents, while Professor Binkly entertains us in a three-minute round with the banjo.

"'Twas an eminent graft we had. We ravaged peacefully through the State, determined to remove all doubt as to why 'twas called bleeding Kansas. John Tom Little Bear, in full Indian chief's costume, drew crowds away from the parchesi sociables and government ownership conversaziones. While at the football college in the East he had acquired quantities of rhetoric and the art of calisthenics and sophistry in his classes, and when he stood up in the red wagon and explained to the farmers, eloquent, about chilblains and hyperæsthesia of the cranium, Jeff couldn't hand out the Indian Remedy fast enough for 'em.

"One night we was camped on the edge of a little town out west of Salina. We always camped near a stream, and put up a little tent. Sometimes we sold out of the Remedy unexpected, and then Chief Wish-Heap-Dough would have a dream in which the Manitou commanded him to fill up a few bottles of Sum-wah-tah at the most convenient place. 'Twas about ten o'clock, and we'd just got in from a street performance. I was in the tent with a lantern, figuring up the day's profits. John Tom hadn't taken off his Indian make-up, and was sitting by the campfire minding a fine sirloin steak in the pan for the Professor till he finished his hair-raising scene with the trained horses.

"All at once out of dark bushes comes a pop like a fire-cracker, and John Tom gives a grunt and digs out of his bosom a little bullet that has dented itself against his collar-bone. John Tom makes a dive in the direction of the fireworks, and comes back dragging by the collar a kid about nine or ten years young, in a velveteen suit, with a little nickel-mounted rifle in his hand about as big as a fountain-pen.

"'Here, you papoose,' says John Tom, 'what are you gunning for with that howitzer? You might hit somebody in the eye. Come out, Jeff, and mind the steak. Don't let it burn, while I investigate this demon with the pea shooter.'

" 'Cowardly redskin,' says the kid like he was quoting from a favorite author. 'Dare to burn me at the stake and the paleface will sweep you from the prairies like—like everything. Now, you lemme go, or I'll tell mamma.'

"John Tom plants the kid on a camp-stool, and sits down by him. 'Now, tell the big chief,' he says, 'why you try to shoot pellets into your Uncle John's system. Didn't you know it was loaded?'

" 'Are you a Indian?' asks the kid, looking up cute as you please at John Tom's buckskin and eagle feathers. 'I am,' says John Tom. 'Well, then, that's why,' answered the boy, swinging his feet. I nearly let the steak burn watching the nerve of the youngster.

" 'O-ho!' says John Tom, 'I see. You're the Boy Avenger. And you've sworn to rid the continent of the savage redman. Is that about the way of it, son?'

"The kid halfway nodded his head. And then he looked glum. 'Twas indecent to wring his secret from his bosom before a single brave had fallen before his parlor-rifle.

" 'Now, tell us where your wigwam is, papoose,' says John Tom— 'where you live? Your mamma will be worrying about your being out so late. Tell me, and I'll take you home.'

"The kid grins. 'I guess not,' he says. 'I live thousands and thousands of miles over there.' He gyrated his hand toward the horizon. 'I come on the train,' he says, 'by myself. I got off here because the conductor said my ticket had ex-pirated.' He looks at John Tom with sudden suspicion. 'I bet you ain't a Indian,' he says. 'You don't talk like a Indian. You look like one, but all a Indian can say is "heap good" and "paleface die." Say, I bet you are one of them make-believe Indians that sell medicine on the streets. I saw one once in Quincy.'

" 'You never mind,' says John Tom, 'whether I'm a cigar-sign or a Tammany cartoon. The question before the council is what's to be done with you. You've run away from home. You've been reading Howells. You've disgraced the profession of boy avengers by trying to shoot a tame Indian, and never saying: "Die, dog of a redskin! You have crossed the path of the Boy Avenger nineteen times too often." What do you mean by it?'

"The kid thought for a minute. 'I guess I made a mistake,' he says. 'I ought to have gone farther west. They find 'em wild out there in the cañons.' He holds out his hand to John Tom, the little rascal. 'Please excuse me, sir,' says he, 'for shooting at you. I hope it didn't hurt you. But you ought to be more careful. When a scout sees a Indian in his war-dress, his rifle must speak.' Little Bear gave a big laugh with a whoop at the end of it, and swings the kid ten feet high and sets him on his shoulder, and the runaway fingers the fringe and the eagle feathers and is full of the joy the white man knows when he dangles his heels against an inferior race. It is plain that Little Bear and that kid are chums from that on. The little renegade has already smoked the pipe of peace with the savage; and you can see in his eye that he is figuring on a tomahawk and a pair of moccasins, children's size.

"We have supper in the tent. The youngster looks upon me and the Professor as ordinary braves, only intended as a background to the camp scene. When he is seated on a box of Sum-wah-tah, with the edge of the table sawing his neck, and his mouth full of beefsteak, Little Bear calls for his name. 'Roy,' says the kid, with a sirloiny sound to it. But when the rest of it and his post-office address is referred to, he shakes his head. 'I guess not,' he says. 'You'll send me back. I want to stay with you. I like this camping out. At home, we fellows had a camp in our back yard. They called me Roy, the Red Wolf! I guess that'll do for a name. Gimme another piece of beefsteak, please.'

"We had to keep that kid. We knew there was a hullabaloo about him somewheres, and that Mamma, and Uncle Harry, and Aunt Jane, and the Chief of Police were hot after finding his trail, but not another word would he tell us. In two days he was the mascot of the Big Medicine outfit, and all of us had a sneaking hope that his owners wouldn't turn up. When the red wagon was doing business he was in it, and passed up the bottles to Mr. Peters as proud and satisfied as a prince that's abjured a two-hundred-dollar crown for a million-dollar parvenuess. Once John Tom asked him something about his papa. 'I ain't got any papa,' he says. 'He runned away and left us. He made my mamma cry. Aunt Lucy says he's a shape.' 'A what?' somebody asks him. 'A shape,' says the kid; 'some kind of a shape—lemme see—oh, yes, a feendenuman shape. I don't know what it means.' John Tom was for putting our brand on him, and dressing him up like a little chief, with wampum and beads, but I vetoes it. 'Somebody's lost that kid, is my view of it, and they may want him. You let me try him with a few stratagems, and see if I can't get a look at his visiting-card.'

"So that night I goes up to Mr. Roy Blank by the camp-fire, and looks at him contemptuous and scornful. 'Snickenwitzel!' says I, like the word made me sick; 'Snickenwitzel! Bah! Before I'd be named Snickenwitzel!'

" 'What's the matter with you, Jeff?' says the kid, opening his eyes wide.

" 'Snickenwitzel!' I repeats, and I spat the word out. 'I saw a man to-day from your town and he told me your name. I'm not surprised you was ashamed to tell it. Snickenwitzel! Whew!'

" 'Ah, here, now,' says the boy, indignant and wriggling all over, 'what's the matter with you? That ain't my name. It's Conyers. What's the matter with you?'

" 'And that's not the worst of it,' I went on quick, keeping him hot and not giving him time to think. 'We thought you was from a nice, well-to-do family. Here's Mr. Little Bear, a chief of the Cherokee, entitled to wear nine otter tails on his Sunday blanket, and Professor Binkly, who plays Shakespeare and the banjo, and me, that's got hundreds of dollars in that black tin box in the wagon, and we've got to be careful about the company we keep. That man tells me your folks live 'way down in little old Hencoop Alley, where there are no sidewalks, and the goats eat off the table with you.'

"That kid was almost crying now. ' 'Tain't so,' he splutters. 'He—he don't know what he's talking about. We live on Poplar Av'noo. I don't 'sociate with goats. What's the matter with you?'

" 'Poplar Avenue,' says I, sarcastic. 'Poplar Avenue! That's a street to live on! It only runs two blocks and then falls off a bluff. You can throw a keg of nails the whole length of it. Don't talk to me about Poplar Avenue.'

" 'It's—it's miles long,' says the kid. 'Our number's 862 and there are lots of houses after that. What's the matter with—aw, you make me tired, Jeff.'

" 'Well, well, now,' says I. 'I guess that man made a mistake. Maybe it was some other boy he was talking about. If I catch him I'll teach him to go around slandering people.' And after supper I goes up town and telegraphs to Mrs. Conyers, 862 Poplar Avenue, Quincy, Ill., that the kid is safe and sassy with us, and will be held for further orders. In two hours an answer comes to hold him tight, and she'll start for him by next train.

"The next train was due at 6 P.M. the next day, and me and John Tom was at the depot with the kid. You might scour the plains in vain for the big Chief Wish-Heap-Dough. In his place is Mr. Little Bear, in the human habiliments of the Anglo-Saxon sect; and the leather of his shoes is patented and the loop of his necktie is copyrighted. For these things John Tom had grafted on him at college along with metaphysics and the knockout guard for the low tackle. But for his complexion, which is some yellowish, and the black mop of his straight hair, you might have thought here was an ordinary man out of the city directory that subscribes for magazines and pushes the lawn-mower in his shirt-sleeves of evenings.

"Then the train rolled in, and a little woman in a gray dress, with sort of illuminating hair, slides off and looks around quick. And the Boy Avenger sees her, and yells 'Mamma,' and she cries 'O!' and they meet in a clinch, and now the pesky redskin can come forth from their caves on the plains without fear any more of the rifle of Roy, the Red Wolf. Mrs. Conyers comes up and thanks me an' John Tom without the usual extremities you always look for in a woman. She says just enough, in a way to convince, and there is no incidental music by the orchestra. I made a few illiterate requisitions upon the art of conversation, at which the lady smiles friendly, as if she had known me a week. And then Mr. Little

Bear adorns the atmosphere with the various idioms into which education can fracture the wind of speech. I could see the kid's mother didn't quite place John Tom; but it seemed she was apprised of his dialects, and she played up to his lead in the science of making three words do the work of one.

"That kid introduced us, with some footnotes and explanations that made things plainer than a week of rhetoric. He danced around, and punched us in the back, and tried to climb John Tom's leg. 'This is John Tom, mamma,' says he. 'He's an Indian. He sells medicine in a red wagon. I shot him, but he wasn't wild. The other one's Jeff. He's a fakir, too. Come on and see the camp where we live, won't you, mamma?'

"It is plain to see that the life of the woman is in that boy. She has got him again where her arms can gather him, and that's enough. She's ready to do anything to please him. She hesitates the eighth of a second and takes another look at these men. I imagine she says to herself about John Tom, 'Seems to be a gentleman, if his hair don't curl.' And Mr. Peters she disposes of as follows: 'No ladies' man, but a man who knows a lady.'

"So we all rambled down to the camp as neighborly as coming from a wake. And there she inspects the wagon and pats the place with her hand where the kid used to sleep, and dabs around her eyewinkers with her handkerchief. And Professor Binkly gives us 'Trovatore' on one string of the banjo, and is about to slide off into Hamlet's monologue when one of the horses gets tangled in his rope and he must go look after him, and says something about 'foiled again.'

"When it got dark me and John Tom walked back to the Corn Exchange Hotel, and the four of us had supper there. I think the trouble started at that supper, for then was when Mr. Little Bear made an intellectual balloon ascension. I held on to the tablecloth, and listened to him soar. That redman, if I could judge, had the gift of information. He took languages, and did with it all a Roman can do with macaroni. His vocal remarks was all embroidered over with the most scholarly verbs and prefixes. And his syllables was smooth, and fitted nicely to the joints of his idea. I thought I'd heard him talk before, but I hadn't. And it wasn't the size of his words, but the way they come; and 'twasn't his subjects, for he spoke of common things like cathedrals and football and poems and catarrh and souls and freight rates and sculpture. Mrs. Conyers understood his accents, and the elegant sounds went back and forth between 'em. And now and then Jefferson D. Peters would intervene a few shopworn, senseless words to have the butter passed or another leg of the chicken.

"Yes, John Tom Little Bear appeared to be inveigled some in his bosom about that Mrs. Conyers. She was of the kind that pleases. She had the good looks and more, I'll tell you. You take one of those cloak models in a big store. They strike you as being on the impersonal system. They are adapted for the eye. What they run to is inches around and complexion, and the art of fanning the delusion that the sealskin would look just as well on the lady with the warts and the pocket-book. Now, if one of them models was off duty, and you took it, and it would say 'Charlie' when you pressed it, and sit up at the table, why, then you would have something similar to Mrs. Conyers. I could see how John Tom could resist any inclination to hate that white squaw.

"The lady and the kid stayed at the hotel. In the morning, they say, they will start for home. Me and Little Bear left at eight o'clock, and sold Indian Remedy on the courthouse square till nine. He leaves me and the Professor to drive down to camp, while he stays up town. I am not enamored with that plan, for it shows John Tom is uneasy in his composures, and that leads to fire-water, and sometimes to the green-corn dance and costs. Not often does Chief Wish-Heap-Dough get busy with the firewater, but whenever he does there is heap much doing in the lodges of the palefaces who wear blue and carry the club.

"At half-past nine Professor Binkly is rolled in his quilt snoring in blank verse, and I am sitting by the fire listening to the frogs. Mr. Little Bear slides into camp and sits down against a tree. There is no symptoms of firewater.

"'Jeff,' says he, after a long time, 'a little boy came West to hunt Indians.'

"'Well, then?' says I, for I wasn't thinking as he was.

"'And he bagged one,' says John Tom, 'and 'twas not with a gun, and he never had on a velveteen suit of clothes in his life.' And then I began to catch his smoke.

"'I know it,' says I. 'And I'll bet you his pictures are on valentines, and fool men are his game, red and white.'

"'You win on the red,' says John Tom, calm. 'Jeff, for how many ponies do you think I could buy Mrs. Conyers?'

"'Scandalous talk!' I replies. ''Tis not a paleface custom.' John Tom laughs loud and bites into his cigar. 'No,' he answers; ''tis the savage equivalent for the dollars of the white man's marriage settlement. Oh, I know. There's an eternal wall between the races. If I could do it, Jeff, I'd put a torch to every white college that a redman has ever set foot inside. Why don't you leave us alone,' he says, 'to our own ghost-dances and dog-feasts and our dingy squaws to cook our grass-hopper soup and darn our moccasins?'

"'Now, you don't mean disrespect to the perennial blossom entitled education?' says I, scandalized, 'because I wear it in the bosom of my own intellectual shirtwaist. I've had education,' says I, 'and never took any harm from it.'

"'You lasso us,' goes on Little Bear, not noticing my prose insertions, 'and teach us what is beautiful in literature and life, and how to appreciate what is fine in men and women. What have you done to me?' says he. 'You've made me a Cherokee Moses. You've taught me to hate the wigwams and love the white man's ways. I can look over into the promised land and see Mrs. Conyers, but my place is—on the reservation.'

"Little Bear stands up in his chief's dress, and laughs again. 'But, white man Jeff,' he goes on, 'the paleface provides a recourse. 'Tis a temporary one, but it gives a respite and the name of it is whiskey.' And straight off he walks up the path to town again. 'Now,' says I in my mind, 'may the Manitou move him to do only bailable things this night!' For I perceive that John Tom is about to avail himself of the white man's solace.

"Maybe it was 10:30, as I sat smoking, when I hear pit-a-pats on the path, and here comes Mrs. Conyers running, her hair twisted up any way, and a look on her face that says burglars and mice and the flour's-all-out rolled in one. 'Oh, Mr. Peters,' she calls out, as they will, 'oh, oh!' I made a quick think, and I spoke the gist of it out loud. 'Now,' says I, 'we've been brothers, me and that Indian, but I'll make a good one of him in two minutes if——'

" 'No, no,' she says, wild and cracking her knuckles, 'I haven't seen Mr. Little Bear. 'Tis my—husband. He's stolen my boy. Oh,' she says, 'just when I had him back in my arms again! That heartless villain! Every bitterness life knows,' she says, 'he's made me drink. My poor little lamb, that ought to be warm in his bed, carried off by that fiend!'

" 'How did all this happen?' I ask. 'Let's have the facts.'

" 'I was fixing his bed,' she explains, 'and Roy was playing on the hotel porch and he drives up to the steps. I heard Roy scream, and ran out. My husband had him in the buggy then. I begged him for my child. This is what he gave me.' She turns her face to the light. There is a crimson streak running across her cheek and mouth. 'He did that with his whip,' she says.

" 'Come back to the hotel,' says I, 'and we'll see what can be done.'

"On the way she tells me some of the wherefores. When he slashed her with the whip he told her he found out she was coming for the kid, and he was on the same train. Mrs. Conyers had been living with her brother, and they'd watched the boy always, as her husband had tried to steal him before. I judge that man was worse than a street railway promoter. It seems he had spent her money and slugged her and killed her canary bird, and told it around that she had cold feet.

"At the hotel we found a mass meeting of five infuriated citizens chewing tobacco and denouncing the outrage. Most of the town was asleep by ten o'clock. I talks to the lady some quiet, and tells her I will take the one o'clock train for the next town, forty miles east, for it is likely that the esteemed Mr. Conyers will drive there to take the cars. 'I don't know,'

I tells her, 'but what he has legal rights; but if I find him I can give him an illegal left in the eye, and tie him up for a day or two, anyhow, on a disturbal of the peace proposition.'

"Mrs. Conyers goes inside and cries with the landlord's wife, who is fixing some catnip tea that will make everything all right for the poor dear. The landlord comes out on the porch, thumbing his one suspender, and says to me:

"'Ain't had so much excitement in town since Bedford Steegall's wife swallowed a spring lizard. I seen him through the winder hit her with the buggy whip, and everything. What's that suit of clothes cost you you got on? 'Pears like we'd have some rain, don't it? Say, doc, that Indian of yorn's on a kind of a whizz to-night, ain't he? He comes along just before you did, and I told him about this here occurrence. He gives a cur'us kind of a hoot, and trotted off. I guess our constable'll have him in the lock-up 'fore morning.'

"I thought I'd sit on the porch and wait for the one o'clock train. I wasn't feeling saturated with mirth. Here was John Tom on one of his sprees, and this kidnapping business losing sleep for me. But then, I'm always having trouble with other people's trouble. Every few minutes Mrs. Conyers would come out on the porch and look down the road the way the buggy went, like she expected to see that kid coming back on a white pony with a red apple in his hand. Now, wasn't that like a woman? And that brings up cats. 'I saw a mouse go in this hole,' says Mrs. Cat; 'you can go prize up a plank over there if you like; I'll watch this hole.'

"About a quarter to one o'clock the lady comes out again, restless, crying easy, as females do for their own amusement, and she looks down that road again and listens. 'Now, ma'am,' says I, 'there's no use watching cold wheel-tracks. By this time they're halfway to——' 'Hush,' she says, holding up her hand. And I do hear something coming 'flip-flap' in the dark; and then there is the awfullest war-whoop ever heard outside of Madison Square Garden at a Buffalo Bill matinée. And up the steps and on to the porch jumps the disrespectable Indian. The lamp in the hall shines on him, and I fail to recognize Mr. J. T. Little Bear, alumnus of the class of '91. What I see is a Cherokee brave, and the warpath is what he has been traveling. Firewater and other things have got him going. His buckskin is hanging in strings, and his feathers are mixed up like a frizzly hen's. The dust of miles is on his moccasins, and the light in his eye is the kind the aborigines wear. But in his arms he brings that kid, his eyes half closed, with his little shoes dangling and one hand fast around the Indian's collar.

"'Papoose!' says John Tom, and I notice that the flowers of the white man's syntax have left his tongue. He is the original proposition in bear's claws and copper color. 'Me bring,' says he, and he lays the kid in his mother's arms. 'Run fifteen mile,' says John Tom—'Ugh! Catch white man. Bring papoose.'

"The little woman is in extremities of gladness. She must wake up that stir-up trouble youngster and hug him and make proclamation that he is his mamma's own precious treasure. I was about to ask questions, but I looked at Mr. Little Bear, and my eye caught the sight of something in his belt. 'Now go to bed, ma'am,' says I, 'and this gadabout youngster likewise, for there's no more danger, and the kidnapping business is not what it was earlier in the night.'

"I inveigled John Tom down to camp quick, and when he tumbled over asleep I got that thing out of his belt and disposed of it where the eye of education can't see it. For even the football colleges disapprove of the art of scalp-taking in their curriculums.

"It is ten o'clock next day when John Tom wakes up and looks around. I am glad to see the nineteenth century in his eyes again.

" 'What was it, Jeff?' he asks.

" 'Heap firewater,' says I.

"John Tom frowns, and thinks a little. 'Combined,' says he directly, 'with the interesting little physiological shake-up known as reversion to type. I remember now. Have they gone yet?'

" 'On the 7:30 train,' I answers.

" 'Ugh!' says John Tom; 'better so. Paleface, bring big Chief Wish-Heap-Dough a little bromo-seltzer, and then he'll take up the red man's burden again.' "

HELPING THE OTHER FELLOW

"But can thim that helps others help thimselves!"   MULVANEY

This is the story that William Trotter told me on the beach at Aguas Frescas while I waited for the gig of the captain of the fruit steamer *Andador* which was to take me abroad. Reluctantly I was leaving the Land of Always Afternoon. William was remaining, and he favored me with a condensed oral autobiography as we sat on the sands in the shade cast by the Bodega Nacional.

As usual, I became aware that the Man from Bombay had already written the story; but as he had compressed it to an eight-word sentence, I have become an expansionist, and have quoted his phrase above, with apologies to him and best regards to *Terence*.

II   "Don't you ever have a desire to go back to the land of derby hats and starched collars?" I asked him. "You seem to be a handy man and a man of action," I continued, "and I am sure I could find you a comfortable job somewhere in the States."

Ragged, shiftless, barefooted, a confirmed eater of the lotos, William Trotter had pleased me much, and I hated to see him gobbled up by the tropics.

"I've no doubt you could," he said, idly splitting the bark from a section of sugar-cane. "I've no doubt you could do much for me. If every man could so as much for himself as he can for others, every country in the world would be holding millenniums instead of centennials."

There seemed to be a pabulum in W. T.'s words. And then another idea came to me.

I had a brother in Chicopee Falls who owned manufactories—cotton, or sugar, or A. A. sheetings, or something in the commercial line. He was vulgarly rich, and therefore reverenced art. The artistic temperament of the family was monopolized at my birth. I knew that Brother James would honor my slightest wish. I would demand from him a position in cotton, sugar, or sheeting for William Trotter—something say, at two hundred a month or thereabouts. I confided my beliefs and made my large proposition to William. He had pleased me much, and he was ragged.

While we were talking, there was a sound of firing guns—four or five, rattlingly, as if by a squad. The cheerful noise came from the direction of the cuartel, which is a kind of make-shift barracks for the soldiers of the republic.

"Hear that?" said William Trotter. "Let me tell you about it.

"A year ago I landed on this coast with one solitary dollar. I have the same sum in my pocket to-day. I was second cook on a tramp fruiter; and they marooned me here early one morning, without benefit of clergy, just because I poulticed the face of the first mate with cheese omelette at dinner. The fellow had kicked because I'd put horseradish in it instead of cheese.

"When they threw me out of the yawl into three feet of surf, I waded ashore and sat down under a palm-tree. By and by a fine-looking white man with a red face and white clothes, genteel as possible, but somewhat under the influence, came and sat down beside me.

"I had noticed there was a kind of a village back of the beach, and enough scenery to outfit a dozen moving-picture shows. But I thought, of course, it was a cannibal suburb, and I was wondering whether I was to be served with carrots or mushrooms. And, as I say, this dressed-up man sits beside me, and we become friends in the space of a minute or two. For an hour we talked, and he told me all about it.

"It seems that he was a man of parts, conscientiousness, and plausibility, besides being educated and a wreck to his appetites. He told me all about it. Colleges had turned him out, and distilleries had taken him in. Did I tell you his name? It was Clifford Wainwright. I didn't exactly catch the cause of his being cast away on that particular stretch of South America; but I reckon it was his own business. I asked him if he'd ever been second cook on a tramp fruiter, and he said no: so that concluded my line of surmises. But he talked like the encyclopedia from 'A—Berlin' to 'Trilo—Zyria.' And he carried a watch—a silver arrangement with works, and up to date within twenty-four hours, anyhow.

" 'I'm pleased to have met you,' says Wainwright. 'I'm a devotee to the great joss Booze; but my ruminating facilities are unrepaired,' says he— or words to that effect. 'And I hate,' says he, 'to see fools trying to run the world.'

" 'I never touch a drop,' says I, 'and there are many kinds of fools; and the world runs on its own apex, according to science, with no meddling from me.'

" 'I was referring,' says he, 'to the president of this republic. His country is in a desperate condition. Its treasury is empty, it's on the verge of war with Nicamala, and if it wasn't for the hot weather the people would be starting revolutions in every town. Here is a nation,' goes on Wainwright, 'on the brink of destruction. A man of intelligence could rescue it from its impending doom in one day by issuing the necessary edicts and orders. President Gomez knows nothing of statesmanship or policy. Do you know Adam Smith?'

" 'Lemme see,' says I. 'There was a one-eared man named Smith in Fort Worth, Texas, but I think his first name was——'

" 'I am referring to the political economist,' says Wainwright.

" 'S'mother Smith, then,' says I. 'The one I speak of never was arrested.'

"So Wainwright boils some more with indignation at the insensibility of people who are not corpulent to fill public positions; and then he tells me he is going out to the president's summer palace, which is four miles from Aguas Frescas, to instruct him in the art of running steam-heated republics.

" 'Come along with me, Trotter,' says he, 'and I'll show you what brains can do.'

" 'Anything in it?' I asks.

" 'The satisfaction,' says he, 'of redeeming a country of two hundred thousand population from ruin back to prosperity and peace.'

" 'Great,' says I. 'I'll go with you. I'd prefer to eat a live broiled lobster just now; but give me liberty as second choice if I can't be in at the death.'

"Wainwright and me permeates through the town, and he halts at a rum-dispensary.

" 'Have you any money?' he asks.

" 'I have,' says I, fishing out my silver dollar. 'I always go about with adequate sums of money.'

" 'Then we'll drink,' says Wainwright.

" 'Not me,' says I. 'Not any demon rum or any of its ramifications for mine. It's one of my non-weaknesses.'

" 'It's my failing,' says he. 'What's your particular soft point?'

" 'Industry,' says I, promptly. 'I'm hard-working, diligent, industrious, and energetic.'

" 'My dear Mr. Trotter,' says he, 'surely I've known you long enough to tell you you are a liar. Every man must have his own particular weakness, and his own particular strength in other things. Now, you will buy me a drink of rum, and we will call on President Gomez.'

III   "Well, sir," Trotter went on, "we walks the four miles out, through a virgin conservatory of palms and ferns and other roof-garden products, to the president's summer White House. It was blue, and reminded you of what you see on the stage in the third act, which they describe as 'same as the first' on the programs.

"There was more than fifty people waiting outside the iron fence that surrounded the house and grounds. There was generals and agitators and épergnes in gold-laced uniforms, and citizens in diamonds and Panama hats—all waiting to get an audience with the Royal Five-Card Draw. And in a kind of summer-house in front of the mansion we could see a burnt-sienna man eating breakfast out of gold dishes and taking his time. I judged that the crowd outside had come out for their morning orders and requests, and was afraid to intrude.

"But C. Wainwright wasn't. The gate was open, and he walked inside and up to the president's table as confident as a man who knows the head waiter in a fifteen-cent restaurant. And I went with him, because I had only seventy-five cents, and there was nothing else to do.

"The Gomez man rises from his chair, and looks, colored man as he was, like he was about to call out for corporal of the guard, post number one. But Wainwright says some phrases to him in a peculiarly lubricating manner; and the first thing you know we was all three of us seated at the table, with coffee and rolls and iguana cutlets coming as fast as about ninety peons could rustle 'em.

"And then Wainwright begins to talk; but the president interrupts him.

" 'You Yankees,' says he, polite, 'assuredly take the cake for assurance, I assure you'—or words to that effect. He spoke English better than you or me. 'You've had a long walk,' says he, 'but it's nicer in the cool morning to walk than to ride. May I suggest some refreshments?' says he.

" 'Rum,' says Wainwright.

" 'Gimme a cigar,' says I.

"Well, sir, the two talked an hour, keeping the generals and equities all in their good uniforms waiting outside the fence. And while I smoked, silent, I listened to Clifford Wainwright making a solid republic out of the wreck of one. I didn't follow his arguments with any special collocation of international intelligibility; but he had Mr. Gomez's attention glued and riveted. He takes out a pencil and marks the white linen table-cloth all over with figures and estimates and deductions. He speaks more or less disrespectfully of import and export duties and custom-house receipts and taxes and treaties and budgets and concessions and such truck that politics and government require; and when he gets through the Gomez man hops up and shakes his hand and says he's saved the country and the people.

"'You shall be rewarded,' says the President.

"'Might I suggest another—rum?' says Wainwright.

"'Cigar for me—darker brand,' says I.

"Well, sir, the president sent me and Wainwright back to the town in a victoria hitched to two flea-bitten selling-platers—but the best the country afforded.

"I found out afterwards that Wainwright was a regular beachcomber —the smartest man on the whole coast, but kept down by rum. I liked him.

"One day I inveigled him into a walk out a couple of miles from the village, where there was an old grass hut on the bank of a little river. While he was sitting on the grass, talking beautiful of the wisdom of the world that he had learned in books, I took hold of him easy and tied his hands and feet together with leather thongs that I had in my pocket.

"'Lie still,' says I, 'and meditate on the exigencies and irregularities of life till I get back.'

"I went to a shack in Aguas Frescas where a mighty wise girl named Timotea Carrizo lived with her mother. The girl was just about as nice as you ever saw. In the States she would have been called a brunette; but she was better than a brunette—I should say she was what you might term an écru shade. I knew her pretty well. I told her about my friend Wainwright. She gave me a double handful of bark—calisaya, I think it was—and some more herbs that I was to mix with it, and told me what to do. I was to make tea of it and give it to him, and keep him from rum for a certain time. And for two weeks I did it. You know, I liked Wainwright. Both of us was broke; but Timotea sent us goat-meat and plantains and tortillas every day; and at last I got the curse of drink lifted from Clifford Wainwright. He lost his taste for it. And in the cool of the evening him and me would sit on the roof of Timotea's mother's hut, eating harmless truck like coffee and rice and stewed crabs, and playing the accordion.

"About that time President Gomez found out that the advice of C. Wainwright was the stuff he had been looking for. The country was pulling out of debt, and the treasury had enough boodle in it for him to amuse himself occasionally with the night-latch. The people were beginning to take their two-hour siestas again every day—which was the surest sign of prosperity.

"So down from the regular capital he sends for Clifford Wainwright and makes him his private secretary at twenty thousand Peru dollars a year. Yes, sir—so much. Wainwright was on the water-wagon—thanks to me and Timotea—and he was soon in clover with the government gang. Don't forget what done it—calisaya bark with them other herbs mixed—make a tea of it, and give a cupful every two hours. Try it yourself. It takes away the desire.

"As I said, a man can do it a lot more for another party than he can for himself. Wainwright, with his brains, got a whole country out of trouble and on its feet; but what could he do for himself? And without any special brains, but with some nerve and common sense, I put him on his feet because I never had the weakness that he did—nothing but a cigar for mine, thanks. And——"

Trotter paused. I looked at his tattered clothes and at his deeply sun-burnt, hard, thoughtful face.

"Didn't Cartwright ever offer to do anything for you?" I asked.

"Wainwright," corrected Trotter. "Yes, he offered me some pretty good jobs. But I'd have had to leave Aguas Frescas; so I didn't take any of 'em up. Say, I didn't tell you much about that girl—Timotea. We rather hit it off together. She was as good as you find 'em anywhere—Spanish, mostly, with just a twist of lemon-peel on top. What if they did live in a grass hut and went bare-armed?

"A month ago," went on Trotter, "she went away. I don't know where to. But——"

"You'd better come back to the States," I insisted. "I can promise you positively that my brother will give you a position in cotton, sugar, or sheetings—I am not certain which."

"I think she went back with her mother," said Trotter, "to the village in the mountains that they come from. Tell me, what would this job you speak of pay?"

"Why," said I, hesitating over commerce, "I should say fifty or a hundred dollars a month—maybe two hundred."

"Ain't it funny," said Trotter, digging his toes in the sand, "what a chump a man is when it comes to paddling his own canoe? I don't know. Of course, I'm not making a living here. I'm on the bum. But—well, I wish you could have seen that Timotea. Every man has his own weak spot."

The gig from the *Andador* was coming ashore to take out the captain, purser, and myself, the lone passenger.

"I'll guarantee," said I, confidently, "that my brother will pay you seventy-five dollars a month."

"All right, then," said William Trotter. "I'll——"

But a soft voice called across the blazing sands. A girl, faintly lemon-tinted, stood in the Calle Real and called. She was bare-armed—but what of that?

"It's her!" said William Trotter, looking. "She's come back! I'm obliged; but I can't take the job. Thanks, just the same. Ain't it funny how we can't do nothing for ourselves, but we can do wonders for the other fellow? You was about to get me with your financial proposition; but we've all got our weak points. Timotea's mine. And, say!" Trotter had turned to leave, but he retraced the step or two that he had taken. "I like to have left you without saying good-bye," said he. "It kind of rattles you when they go away unexpected for a month and come back the same way. Shake hands. So long! Say, do you remember them gun-shots we heard a while ago up at the cuartel? Well, I knew what they was, but I didn't mention it. It was Clifford Wainwright being shot by a squad of soldiers against a stone wall for giving away secrets of state to that Nicamala republic. Oh, yes, it was rum that did it. He backslided and got his. I guess we all have our weak points, and can't do much toward helping ourselves. Mine's waiting for me. I'd have liked to have that job with your brother, but—we've all got our weak points. So long!"

IV A big black Carib carried me on his back through the surf to the ship's boat. On the way the purser handed me a letter that he had brought for me at the last moment from the post-office in Aguas Frescas. It was from my brother. He requested me to meet him at the St. Charles Hotel in New Orleans and accept a position with his house—in either cotton, sugar, or sheetings, and with five thousand dollars a year as my salary.

When I arrived at the Crescent City I hurried away—far away from the St. Charles to a dim *chambre garnie* in Bienville Street. And there, look-ing down from my attic window from time to time at the old, yellow, absinthe house across the street, I wrote this story to buy my bread and butter.

"Can thim that helps others help thimselves?"

THE MARIONETTES

The policeman was standing at the corner of Twenty-fourth Street and a prodigiously dark alley near where the elevated railroad crosses the street. The time was two o'clock in the morning; the outlook a stretch of cold, drizzling, unsociable blackness until the dawn.

A man, wearing a long overcoat, with his hat tilted down in front, and carrying something in one hand, walked softly but rapidly out of the black alley. The policeman accosted him civilly, but with the assured air that is linked with conscious authority. The hour, the alley's musty reputation, the pedestrian's haste, the burden he carried—these easily combined into the "suspicious circumstances" that required illumination at the officer's hands.

The "suspect" halted readily and tilted back his hat, exposing, in the flicker of the electric lights, an emotionless, smooth countenance with a rather long nose and steady dark eyes. Thrusting his gloved hand into a side pocket of his overcoat, he drew out a card and handed it to the policeman. Holding it to catch the uncertain light, the officer read the name "Charles Spencer James, M.D." The street and number of the address were of a neighborhood so solid and respectable as to subdue even curiosity. The policeman's downward glance at the article carried in the doctor's hand—a handsome medicine case of black leather, with small silver mountings—further endorsed the guarantee of the card.

"All right, doctor," said the officer, stepping aside, with an air of bulky affability. "Orders are to be extra careful. Good many burglars and holdups lately. Bad night to be out. Not so cold, but—clammy."

With a formal inclination of his head, and a word or two corroborative of the officer's estimate of the weather, Doctor James continued his somewhat rapid progress. Three times that night had a patrolman accepted his professional card and the sight of his paragon of a medicine case as vouchers for his honesty of person and purpose. Had any one of those officers seen fit, on the morrow, to test the evidence of that card he would have found it borne out by the doctor's name on a handsome doorplate, his presence, calm and well dressed, in his well-equipped office—provided it were not too early, Doctor James being a late riser—and the testimony of the neighborhood to his good citizenship, his devotion to his family, and his success as a practitioner the two years he had lived among them.

Therefore, it would have much surprised any one of those zealous guardians of the peace could they have taken a peep into that immaculate medicine case. Upon opening it, the first article to be seen would have been an elegant set of the latest conceived tools used by the "box man," as the ingenious safe burglar now denominates himself. Specially designed and constructed were the implements—the short but powerful "jimmy," the collection of curiously fashioned keys, the blued drills and punches of the finest temper—capable of eating their way into chilled steel as a mouse eats into a cheese, and the clamps that fasten like a leech to the polished door of a safe and pull out the combination knob as a dentist extracts a tooth. In a little pouch in the inner side of the "medicine" case was a four-ounce vial of nitroglycerine, now half empty. Underneath the tools was a mass of crumpled banknotes and a few handfuls of gold coin, the money, altogether, amounting to eight hundred and thirty dollars.

To a very limited circle of friends Doctor James was known as "The Swell 'Greek.'" Half of the mysterious term was a tribute to his cool and gentlemanlike manners; the other half denoted, in the argot of the brotherhood, the leader, the planner, the one who, by the power and prestige of his address and position, secured the information upon which they based their plans and desperate enterprises.

Of this elect circle the other members were Skitsie Morgan and Gum Decker, expert "box men," and Leopold Pretzfelder, a jeweller down town, who manipulated the "sparklers" and other ornaments collected by the working trio. All good and loyal men, as loose-tongued as Memnon and as fickle as the North Star.

That night's work had not been considered by the firm to have yielded more than a moderate repayal for their pains. An old-style two-story side-bolt safe in the dingy office of a very wealthy old-style dry-goods firm on a Saturday night should have excreted more than twenty-five hundred dollars. But that was all they found, and they had divided it, the three of them, into equal shares upon the spot, as was their custom. Ten or twelve thousand was what they expected. But one of the proprietors had proved to be just a trifle too old style. Just after dark he had carried home in a shirt box most of the funds on hand.

Doctor James proceeded up Twenty-fourth Street, which was, to all appearance, depopulated. Even the theatrical folk, who affect this district as a place of residence, were long since abed. The drizzle had accumulated upon the street; puddles of it among the stones received the fire of the arc lights, and returned it, shattered into a myriad liquid spangles. A captious wind, shower-soaked and chilling, coughed from the laryngeal flues between the houses.

As the practitioner's foot struck even with the corner of a tall brick residence of more pretension than its fellows the front door popped open, and a bawling negress clattered down the steps to the pavement. Some medley of words came forth from her mouth, addressed, like as not, to herself—the recourse of her race when alone and beset by evil. She looked to be one of that old vassal class of the South—voluble, familiar, loyal, irrepressible; her person pictured it—fat, neat, aproned, kerchiefed.

This sudden apparition, spewed from the silent house, reached the bottom of the steps as Doctor James came opposite. Her brain transferring its energies from sound to sight, she ceased her clamor and fixed her popeyes upon the case the doctor carried.

"Bress de Lawd!" was the benison the sight drew from her. "Is you a doctor, suh?"

"Yes, I am a physician," said Doctor James, pausing.

"Den fo' God's sake come and see Mister Chandler, suh. He done had a fit or sump'n. He layin' jist like he wuz dead. Miss Amy sont me to git a doctor. Lawd knows whar old Cindy'd a skeared one up from, if you, suh, hadn't come along. Ef old Mar's knowed one ten-hundredth part of dese doin's de'd be shootin' gwine on, suh—pistol shootin'—leb'm feet marked off on de ground, and ev'ybody a-duellin'. And dat po' lamb, Miss Amy——"

"Lead the way," said Doctor James, setting his foot upon the step, "if you want me as a doctor. As an auditor I'm not open to engagements."

The negress preceded him into the house and up a flight of thickly carpeted stairs. Twice they came to dimly lighted branching hallways. At the second one the now panting conductress turned down a hall, stopping at a door and opening it.

"I done brought de doctor, Miss Amy."

Doctor James entered the room, and bowed slightly to a young lady standing by the side of a bed. He set his medicine case upon a chair, removed his overcoat, throwing it over the case and the back of the chair, and advanced with quiet self-possession to the bedside.

There lay a man, sprawling as he had fallen—a man dressed richly in the prevailing mode, with only his shoes removed; lying relaxed, and as still as the dead.

There emanated from Doctor James an aura of calm, force and reserve strength that was as manna in the desert to the weak and desolate among his patrons. Always had women, especially, been attracted by something in his sick-room manner. It was not the indulgent suavity of the fashionable healer, but a manner of poise, of sureness, of ability to overcome fate, of deference and protection and devotion. There was an exploring magnetism in his steadfast, luminous brown eyes; a latent authority in the impassive, even priestly, tranquillity of his smooth countenance that outwardly fitted him for the part of confidant and consoler. Sometimes, at his first professional visit, women would tell him where they hid their diamonds at night from the burglars.

With the ease of much practice, Doctor James's unroving eyes estimated the order and quality of the room's furnishings. The appointments were rich and costly. The same glance had secured cognizance of the lady's appearance. She was small and scarcely past twenty. Her face possessed the title to a winsome prettiness, now obscured by (you would say) rather a fixed melancholy than the more violent imprint of a sudden sorrow. Upon her forehead, above one eyebrow, was a livid bruise, suffered, the physician's eye told him, within the past six hours.

Doctor James's fingers went to the man's wrist. His almost vocal eyes questioned the lady.

"I am Mrs. Chandler," she responded, speaking with the plaintive Southern slur and intonation. "My husband was taken suddenly ill about ten minutes before you came. He has had attacks of heart trouble before —some of them were very bad." His clothed state and the late hour seemed to prompt her to further explanation. "He had been out late; to —a supper, I believe."

Doctor James now turned his attention to his patient. In whichever of his "professions" he happened to be engaged he was wont to honor the "case" or the "job" with his whole interest.

The sick man appeared to be about thirty. His countenance bore a look of boldness and dissipation, but was not without a symmetry of feature and the fine lines drawn by a taste and indulgence in humor that gave the redeeming touch. There was an odor of spilled wine about his clothes.

The physician laid back his outer garments, and then, with a pen-knife, slit the shirt-front from collar to waist. The obstacles cleared, he laid his ear to the heart and listened intently.

"Mitral regurgitation?" he said, softly, when he rose. The words ended with the rising inflection of uncertainty. Again he listened long; and this time he said, "Mitral insufficiency," with the accent of an assured diagnosis.

"Madam," he began, in the reassuring tones that had so often allayed anxiety, "there is a probability——" As he slowly turned his head to face the lady, he saw her fall, white and swooning, into the arms of the old negress.

"Po' lamb! po' lamb! Has dey done killed Aunt Cindy's own blessed child? May de Lawd 'stroy wid his wrath dem what stole her away; what break dat angel heart; what left——"

"Lift her feet," said Doctor James, assisting to support the drooping form. "Where is her room? She must be put to bed."

"In here, suh." The woman nodded her kerchiefed head toward a door. "Dat's Miss Amy's room."

They carried her in there, and laid her on the bed. Her pulse was faint, but regular. She passed from the swoon, without recovering consciousness, into a profound slumber.

"She is quite exhausted," said the physician. "Sleep is a good remedy. When she wakes, give her a toddy—with an egg in it, if she can take it. How did she get that bruise upon her forehead?"

"She done got a lick there, suh. De po' lamb fell—— No, suh"—the old woman's racial mutability swept her in a sudden flare of indignation —"old Cindy ain't gwineter lie for dat debble. He done it, suh. May de Lawd wither de hand what—dar now! Cindy promise her sweet lamb she ain't gwine tell. Miss Amy got hurt, suh, on de head."

Doctor James stepped to a stand where a handsome lamp burned, and turned the flame low.

"Stay here with your mistress," he ordered, "and keep quiet so she will sleep. If she wakes, give her the toddy. If she grows any weaker, let me know. There is something strange about it."

"Dar's mo' strange t'ings dan dat 'round here," began the negress, but the physician hushed her in a seldom-employed peremptory, concentrated voice with which he had often allayed hysteria itself. He returned to the other room, closing the door softly behind him. The man on the bed had not moved, but his eyes were open. His lips seemed to form words. Doctor James bent his head to listen. "The money! the money!" was what they were whispering.

"Can you understand what I say?" asked the doctor, speaking low, but distinctly.

The head nodded slightly.

"I am a physician, sent for by your wife. You are Mr. Chandler, I am told. You are quite ill. You must not excite or distress yourself at all."

The patient's eyes seemed to beckon to him. The doctor stooped to catch the same faint words.

"The money—the twenty thousand dollars."

"Where is this money?—in the bank?"

The eyes expressed a negative. "Tell her"—the whisper was growing fainter—"the twenty thousand dollars—her money"—his eyes wandered about the room.

"You have placed this money somewhere?"—Doctor James's voice was toiling like a siren's to conjure the secret from the man's failing intelligence—"Is it in this room?"

He thought he saw a fluttering assent in the dimming eyes. The pulse under his fingers was as fine and small as a silk thread.

There arose in Doctor James's brain and heart the instincts of his other profession. Promptly, as he acted in everything, he decided to learn the whereabouts of this money, and at the calculated and certain cost of a human life.

Drawing from his pocket a little pad of prescription blanks, he scribbled upon one of them a formula suited, according to the best practice, to the needs of the sufferer. Going to the door of the inner room, he softly called the old woman, gave her the prescription, and bade her take it to some drug store and fetch the medicine.

When she had gone, muttering to herself, the doctor stepped to the bedside of the lady. She still slept soundly; her pulse was a little stronger; her forehead was cool, save where the inflammation of the bruise extended, and a slight moisture covered it. Unless disturbed, she would yet sleep for hours. He found the key in the door, and locked it after him when he returned.

Doctor James looked at his watch. He could call half an hour his own, since before that time the old woman could scarcely return from her mission. Then he sought and found water in a pitcher and a glass tumbler. Opening his medicine case he took out the vial containing the nitroglycerine—"the oil," as his brethren of the brace-and-bit term it.

One drop of the faint yellow, thickish liquid he let fall in the tumbler.

He took out his silver hypodermic syringe case, and screwed the needle into its place. Carefully measuring each modicum of water in the graduated glass barrel of the syringe, he diluted the one drop with nearly half a tumbler of water.

Two hours earlier that night Doctor James had, with that syringe, injected the undiluted liquid into a hole drilled in the lock of a safe, and had destroyed, with one dull explosion, the machinery that controlled the movement of the bolts. He now purposed, with the same means, to shiver the prime machinery of a human being—to rend its heart—and each shock was for the sake of the money to follow.

The same means, but in a different guise. Whereas, that was the giant in its rude, primary dynamic strength, this was the courtier, whose no less deadly arms were concealed by velvet and lace. For the liquid in the tumbler and in the syringe that the physician carefully filled was now a solution of glonoin, the most powerful heart stimulant known to medical science. Two ounces had riven the solid door of the iron safe; with one fiftieth part of a minim he was now about to still forever the intricate mechanism of a human life.

But not immediately. It was not so intended. First there would be a quick increase of vitality; a powerful impetus given to every organ and faculty. The heart would respond bravely to the fatal spur; the blood in the veins return more rapidly to its source.

But, as Doctor James well knew, over-stimulation in this form of heart disease means death, as sure as by a rifle shot. When the clogged arteries should suffer congestion from the increased flow of blood pumped into them by the power of the burglar's "oil," they would rapidly become "no thoroughfare," and the fountain of life would cease to flow.

The physician bared the chest of the unconscious Chandler. Easily and skilfully he injected, subcutaneously, the contents of the syringe into the muscles of the region over the heart. True to his neat habits in both professions, he next carefully dried his needle and re-inserted the fine wire that threaded it when not in use.

In three minutes Chandler opened his eyes, and spoke, in a voice faint but audible, inquiring who attended upon him. Doctor James again explained his presence there.

"Where is my wife?" asked the patient.

"She is asleep—from exhaustion and worry," said the doctor. "I would not awaken her, unless——"

"It isn't—necessary." Chandler spoke with spaces between his words caused by his short breath that some demon was driving too fast. "She wouldn't—thank you to disturb her—on my—account."

Doctor James drew a chair to the bedside. Conversation must not be squandered.

"A few minutes ago," he began, in the grave, candid tones of his other profession, "you were trying to tell me something regarding some money. I do not seek your confidence, but it is my duty to advise you that anxiety and worry will work against your recovery. If you have any communication to make about this—to relieve your mind about this—twenty thousand dollars, I think was the amount you mentioned—you would better do so."

Chandler could not turn his head, but he rolled his eyes in the direction of the speaker.

"Did I—say where this—money is?"

"No," answered the physician. "I only inferred, from your scarcely intelligible words, that you felt a solicitude concerning its safety. If it is in this room——"

Doctor James paused. Did he only seem to perceive a flicker of understanding, a gleam of suspicion upon the ironical features of his patient? Had he seemed too eager? Had he said too much? Chandler's next words restored his confidence.

"Where—should it be," he gasped, "but in—the safe—there?"

With his eyes he indicated a corner of the room, where now, for the first time, the doctor perceived a small iron safe, half-concealed by the trailing end of a window curtain.

Rising, he took the sick man's wrist. His pulse was beating in great throbs, with ominous intervals between.

"Lift your arm," said Doctor James.

"You know—I can't move, Doctor."

The physician stepped swiftly to the hall door, opened it, and listened. All was still. Without further circumvention he went to the safe, and examined it. Of a primitive make and simple design, it afforded a little more security than protection against light-fingered servants. To his skill it was a mere toy, a thing of straw and pasteboard. The money was as good as in his hands. With his clamps he could draw the knob, punch the tumblers, and open the door in two minutes. Perhaps, in another way, he might open it in one.

Kneeling upon the floor, he laid his ear to the combination plate, and slowly turned the knob. As he had surmised, it was locked at only a "day com."—upon one number. His keen ear caught the faint warning click as the tumbler was disturbed; he used the clue—the handle turned. He swung the door wide open.

The interior of the safe was bare—not even a scrap of paper rested, within the hollow iron cube.

Doctor James rose to his feet and walked back to the bed.

A thick dew had formed upon the dying man's brow, but there was a mocking, grim smile on his lips and in his eyes.

"I never—saw it before," he said, painfully, "medicine and—burglary wedded! Do you—make the—combination pay—dear Doctor?"

Than that situation afforded, there was never a more rigorous test of Doctor James's greatness. Trapped by the diabolic humor of his victim into a position both ridiculous and unsafe, he maintained his dignity as well as his presence of mind. Taking out his watch, he waited for the man to die.

"You were—just a shade—too—anxious—about that money. But it never was—in any danger—from you, dear Doctor. It's safe. Perfectly safe. It's all—in the hands—of the bookmakers. Twenty—thousand—Amy's money. I played it at the races—lost every—cent of it. I've been a pretty bad boy, Burglar—excuse me—Doctor, but I've been a square sport. I don't think—I ever met—such an—eighteen-carat rascal as you are, Doctor—excuse me—Burglar, in all my rounds. Is it contrary—to the ethics —of your—gang, Burglar, to give a victim—excuse me—patient, a drink of water?"

Doctor James brought him a drink. He could scarcely swallow it. The reaction from the powerful drug was coming in regular, intensifying waves. But his moribund fancy must have one more grating fling.

"Gambler—drunkard—spendthrift—I've been those, but—a doctor-burglar!"

The physician indulged himself to but one reply to the other's caustic taunts. Bending low to catch Chandler's fast crystallizing gaze, he pointed to the sleeping lady's door with a gesture so stern and significant that the prostrate man half-lifted his head, with his remaining strength, to see. He saw nothing; but he caught the cold words of the doctor—the last sounds he was to hear:

"I never yet—struck a woman."

It were vain to attempt to con such men. There is no curriculum that can reckon with them in its ken. They are offshoots from the types whereof men say, "He will do this," or "He will do that." We only know that they exist; and that we can observe them, and tell one another of their bare performances, as children watch and speak of the marionettes.

Yet it were a droll study in egoism to consider these two—one an assassin and a robber, standing above his victim; the other baser in his offences, if a lesser law-breaker, lying, abhorred, in the house of the wife he had persecuted, spoiled, and smitten, one a tiger, the other a dog-wolf —to consider each of them sickening at the foulness of the other; and each flourishing out of the mire of his manifest guilt his own immaculate standard—of conduct, if not of honor.

The one retort of Doctor James must have struck home to the other's remaining shreds of shame and manhood, for it proved the *coup de grâce.* A deep blush suffused his face—an ignominious *rosa mortis;* the respiration ceased, and, with scarcely a tremor, Chandler expired.

Close following upon his last breath came the negress, bringing the medicine. With a hand gently pressing upon the closed eyelids, Doctor

James told her of the end. Not grief, but a hereditary *rapprochement* with death in the abstract, moved her to a dismal, watery sniffling, accompanied by her usual jeremiad.

"Dar now! It's in de Lawd's hands. He am de jedge ob de transgressor, and de suppo't of dem in distress. He gwine hab suppo't us now. Cindy done paid out de last quarter fer dis bottle of physic, and it nebber come to no use."

"Do I understand," asked Doctor James, "that Mrs. Chandler has no money?"

"Money, suh? You know what make Miss Amy fall down and so weak? Stahvation, suh. Nothin' to eat in dis house but some crumbly crackers in three days. Dat angel sell her finger rings and watch mont's ago. Dis fine house, suh, wid de red cyarpets and shiny bureaus, it's all hired and de man talkin' scan'lous about de rent. Dat debble—'scuse me, Lawd— he done in Yo' hands fer jedgment, now—he made way wid everything."

The physician's silence encouraged her to continue. The history that he gleaned from Cindy's disordered monologue was an old one, of illusion, wilfulness, disaster, cruelty, and pride. Standing out from the blurred panorama of her gabble were little clear pictures—an ideal home in the far South; a quickly repented marriage; an unhappy season, full of wrongs and abuse, and, of late, an inheritance of money that promised deliverance; its seizure and waste by the dog-wolf during a two months' absence, and his return in the midst of a scandalous carouse. Unobtruded, but visible between every line, ran a pure white thread through the smudged warp of the story—the simple, all-enduring, sublime love of the old negress, following her mistress unswervingly through everything to the end.

When at last she paused, the physician spoke, asking if the house contained whiskey or liquor of any sort. There was, the old woman informed him, half a bottle of brandy left in the sideboard by the dog-wolf.

"Prepare a toddy as I told you," said Doctor James. "Wake your mistress; have her drink it, and tell her what has happened."

Some ten minutes afterward, Mrs. Chandler entered, supported by old Cindy's arm. She appeared to be a little stronger since her sleep and the stimulant she had taken. Doctor James had covered, with a sheet, the form upon the bed.

The lady turned her mournful eyes once, with a half-frightened look, toward it, and pressed closer to her protector. Her eyes were dry and bright. Sorrow seemed to have done its utmost with her. The fount of tears was dried; feeling itself paralyzed.

Doctor James was standing near the table, his overcoat donned, his hat and medicine case in his hand. His face was calm and impassive—practice had inured him to the sight of human suffering. His lambent brown eyes alone expressed a discreet professional sympathy.

He spoke kindly and briefly, stating that, as the hour was late, and assistance, no doubt, difficult to procure, he would himself send the proper persons to attend to the necessary finalities.

"One matter, in conclusion," said the doctor, pointing to the safe with its still wide-open door. "Your husband, Mrs. Chandler, toward the end, felt that he could not live; and directed me to open that safe, giving me the number upon which the combination is set. In case you may need to use it, you will remember that the number is forty-one. Turn several times to the right; then to the left once; stop at forty-one. He would not permit me to waken you, though he knew the end was near.

"In that safe he said he had placed a sum of money not large—but enough to enable you to carry out his last request. That was that you should return to your old home, and, in after days, when time shall have made it easier, forgive his many sins against you."

He pointed to the table, where lay an orderly pile of banknotes, surmounted by two stacks of gold coins.

"The money is there—as he described it—eight hundred and thirty dollars. I beg to leave my card with you, in case I can be of any service later on."

So, he had thought of her—and kindly—at the last! So late! And yet the lie fanned into life one last spark of tenderness where she had thought all was turned to ashes and dust. She cried aloud "Rob! Rob!" She turned, and, upon the ready bosom of her true servitor, diluted her grief in relieving tears. It is well to think, also, that in the years to follow, the murderer's falsehood shone like a little star above the grave of love, comforting her, and gaining the forgiveness that is good in itself, whether asked for or no.

Hushed and soothed upon the dark bosom, like a child, by a crooning, babbling sympathy, at last she raised her head—but the doctor was gone.

THE MARQUIS AND MISS SALLY

Without knowing it, Old Bill Bascom had the honor of being overtaken by fate the same day with the Marquis of Borodale.

The Marquis lived in Regent Square, London. Old Bill lived on Limping Doe Creek, Hardeman County, Texas. The cataclysm that engulfed the Marquis took the form of a bursting bubble known as the Central and South American Mahogany and Caoutchouc Monopoly. Old Bill's Nemesis was in the no less perilous shape of a band of civilized Indian cattle thieves from the Territory who ran off his entire herd of four hundred head, and shot old Bill dead as he trailed after them. To even up the consequences of the two catastrophes, the Marquis, as soon as he found that all he possessed would pay only fifteen shillings on the pound of his indebtedness, shot himself.

Old Bill left a family of six motherless sons and daughters, who found themselves without even a red steer left to eat or a red cent to buy one with.

The Marquis left one son, a young man, who had come to the States and established a large and well-stocked ranch in the Panhandle of Texas. When this young man learned the news he mounted his pony and rode to town. There he placed everything he owned except his horse, saddle, Winchester, and fifteen dollars in his pockets, in the hands of his lawyers, with instructions to sell and forward the proceeds to London to be applied upon the payment of his father's debts. Then he mounted his pony and rode southward.

One day, arriving about the same time, but by different trails, two young chaps rode up to the Diamond-Cross ranch, on the Little Piedra, and asked for work. Both were dressed neatly and sprucely in cowboy costume. One was a straight-set fellow, with delicate, handsome features, short brown hair, and smooth face, sunburned to a golden brown. The other applicant was stouter and broad-shouldered, with fresh red complexion, somewhat freckled, reddish, curling hair, and a rather plain face, made attractive by laughing eyes and a pleasant mouth.

The superintendent of the Diamond-Cross was of the opinion that he could give them work. In fact, word had reached him that morning that the camp cook—a most important member of the outfit—had straddled his bronco and departed, being unable to withstand the fire of fun and practical jokes of which he was, ex-officio, the legitimate target.

"Can either of you cook?" asked the superintendent.

"I can," said the reddish-haired fellow, promptly. "I've cooked in camp quite a lot. I'm willing to take the job until you've got something else to offer."

"Now, that's the way I like to hear a man talk," said the superintendent, approvingly. "I'll give you a note to Saunders, and he'll put you to work."

Thus the names of John Bascom and Charles Norwood were added to the pay-roll of the Diamond-Cross. The two left for the round-up camp immediately after dinner. Their directions were simple, but sufficient: "Keep down the arroyo for fifteen miles till you get there." Both being strangers from afar, young, spirited, and thus thrown together by chance for a long ride, it is likely that the comradeship that afterward existed so strongly between them began that afternoon as they meandered along the little valley of the Candad Verda.

They reached their destination just after sunset. The main camp of the round-up was comfortably located on the bank of a long water-hole, under a fine mott of timber. A number of small A tents pitched upon grassy spots and the big wall tent for provisions showed that the camp was intended to be occupied for a considerable length of time.

The round-up had ridden in but a few moments before, hungry and tired, to a supperless camp. The boys were engaged in an emulous display of anathemas supposed to fit the case of the absconding cook. While they were unsaddling and hobbling their ponies, the newcomers rode in and inquired for Pink Saunders. The boss of the round-up came forth and was given the superintendent's note.

Pink Saunders, though a boss during working hours, was a humorist in camp, where everybody, from cook to superintendent, is equal. After reading the note he waved his hand toward the camp and shouted, ceremoniously, at the top of his voice, "Gentlemen, allow me to present to you the Marquis and Miss Sally."

At the words both the new arrivals betrayed confusion. The newly employed cook started, with a surprised look on his face, but, immediately recollecting that "Miss Sally" is the generic name for the male cook in every west Texas cow camp, he recovered his composure with a grin at his own expense.

His companion showed little less discomposure, even turning angrily, with a bitten lip, and reaching for his saddle pommel, as if to remount his pony; but "Miss Sally" touched his arm and said, laughingly, "Come now, Marquis; that was quite a compliment from Saunders. It's that distinguished air of yours and aristocratic nose that made him call you that."

He began to unsaddle, and the Marquis, restored to equanimity, followed his example. Rolling up his sleeves, Miss Sally sprang for the grub wagon, shouting:

"I'm the new cook b'thunder! Some of you chaps rustle a little wood for a fire, and I'll guarantee you a hot square meal inside of thirty minutes." Miss Sally's energy and good-humor as he ransacked the grub wagon for coffee, flour, and bacon, won the good opinion of the camp instantly.

And also, in days following, the Marquis, after becoming better acquainted, proved to be a cheerful, pleasant fellow, always a little reserved, and taking no part in the rough camp frolics; but the boys gradually came to respect this reserve—which fitted the title Saunders had given him—and even to like him for it. Saunders had assigned him to a place holding the herd during the cuttings. He proved to be a skilful rider and as good with the lariat or in the branding pen as most of them.

The Marquis and Miss Sally grew to be quite close comrades. After supper was over, and everything cleaned up, you would generally find them together, Miss Sally smoking his brier-root pipe, and the Marquis plaiting a quirt or scraping rawhide for a new pair of hobbles.

The superintendent did not forget his promise to keep an eye on the cook. Several times, when visiting the camp, he held long talks with him. He seemed to have taken a fancy to Miss Sally. One afternoon he rode up, on his way back to the ranch from a tour of the camps and said to him:

"There'll be a man here in the morning to take your place. As soon as he shows up you come to the ranch. I want you to take charge of the ranch accounts and correspondence. I want somebody that I can depend upon to keep things straight when I'm away. The wages'll be all right. The Diamond-Cross'll hold its end up with a man who'll look after its interests."

"All right," said Miss Sally, as quietly as if he had expected the notice all along. "Any objections to my bringing my wife down to the ranch?"

"You married?" said the superintendent, frowning a little. "You didn't mention it when we were talking."

"Because I'm not," said the cook. "But I'd like to be. Thought I'd wait till I got a job under roof. I couldn't ask her to live in a cow camp."

"Right," agreed the superintendent. "A camp isn't quite the place for a married man—but—well, there's plenty of room at the house, and if you suit us as well as I think you will you can afford it. You write to her to come on."

"All right," said Miss Sally again, "I'll ride in as soon as I am relieved to-morrow."

It was a rather chilly night, and after supper the cow-punchers were lounging about a big fire of dried mesquite chunks.

Their usual exchange of jokes and repartee had dwindled almost to silence, but silence in a cow camp generally betokens the brewing of mischief.

Miss Sally and the Marquis were seated upon a log, discussing the relative merits of the lengthened or shortened stirrup in long-distance riding. The Marquis arose presently and went to a tree near by to examine some strips of rawhide he was seasoning for making a lariat. Just as he left a little puff of wind blew some scraps of tobacco from a cigarette that Dry-Creek Smithers was rolling, into Miss Sally's eyes. While the cook was rubbing at them, with tears flowing, "Phonograph" Davis— so called on account of his strident voice—arose and began a speech.

"Fellers and citizens! I desire to perpound a interrogatory. What is the most grievous spectacle what the human mind can contemplate?"

A volley of answers responded to his question.

"A busted flush!"

"A Maverick when you ain't got your branding iron!"

"Yourself!"

"The hole in the end of some other feller's gun!"

"Shet up, you ignoramuses," said Old Taller, the fat cow-puncher. "Phony knows what it is. He's waitin' for to tell us."

"No, fellers and citizens," continued Phonograph. "Them spectacles you've e-numerated air shore grievious, and way up yonder close to the so-lution, but they ain't it. The most grievious spectacle air that"—he pointed to Miss Sally, who was still rubbing his streaming eyes—"a trustin' and a in-veegled female a-weepin' tears on account of her heart bein' busted by a false deceiver. Air we men or air we catamounts to gaze upon the blightin' of our Miss Sally's affections by a a-risto-crat, which has come among us with his superior beauty and his glitterin' title to give the weeps to the lovely critter we air bound to pertect? Air we goin' to act like men, or air we goin' to keep on eatin' soggy chuck from her cryin' so plentiful over the bread-pan?"

"It's a gallopin' shame," said Dry-Creek, with a sniffle. "It ain't human. I've noticed the varmint a-palaverin' round her frequent. And him a Marquis! Ain't that a title, Phony?"

"It's somethin' like a king," the Brushy Creek Kid hastened to explain, "only lower in the deck. Guess it comes in between the Jack and the ten-spot."

"Don't misconstruct me," went on Phonograph, "as undervaluatin' the a-risto-crats. Some of 'em air proper people and can travel right along with the Watson boys. I've herded some with 'em myself. I've viewed the elephant with the Mayor of Fort Worth, and I've listened to the owl with the gen'ral passenger agent of the Katy, and they can keep up with the percession from where you laid the chunk. But when a Marquis monkeys with the innocent affections of a cook-lady, may I inquire what the case seems to call for?"

"The leathers," shouted Dry-Creek Smithers.

"You hear 'er, Charity!" was the Kid's form of corroboration.

"We've got your company," assented the cowpunchers, in chorus.

Before the Marquis realized their intention, two of them seized him by each arm and led him up to the log. Phonograph Davis, self-appointed to carry out the sentence, stood ready, with a pair of stout leather leggings in his hands.

It was the first time they had ever laid hands on the Marquis during their somewhat rude sports.

"What are you up to?" he asked, indignantly, with flashing eyes.

"Go easy, Marquis," whispered Rube Fellows, one of the boys that held him. "It's all in fun. Take it good-natured and they'll let you off light. They're only goin' to stretch you over the log and tan you eight or ten times with the leggin's. 'Twon't hurt much."

The Marquis, with an exclamation of anger, his white teeth gleaming, suddenly exhibited a surprising strength. He wrenched with his arms so violently that the four men were swayed and dragged many yards from the log. A cry of anger escaped him, and then Miss Sally, his eyes cleared of the tobacco, saw, and he immediately mixed with the struggling group.

But at that moment a loud "Hallo!" rang in their ears, and a buckboard drawn by a team of galloping mustangs spun into the campfire's circle of light. Every man turned to look, and what they saw drove from their minds all thoughts of carrying out Phonograph Davis's rather time-worn contribution to the evening's amusement. Bigger game than the Marquis was at hand, and his captors released him and stood staring at the approaching victim.

The buckboard and team belonged to Sam Holly, a cattleman from the Big Muddy. Sam was driving, and with him was a stout, smooth-faced man, wearing a frock coat and a high silk hat. That was the county judge, Mr. Dave Hackett, candidate for reëlection. Sam was escorting him about the country, among the camps, to shake up the sovereign voters.

The men got out, hitched the team to a mesquite, and walked toward the fire.

Instantly every man in camp, except the Marquis, Miss Sally, and Pink Saunders, who had to play host, uttered a frightful yell of assumed terror and fled on all sides into the darkness.

"Heavens alive!" exclaimed Hackett, "are we as ugly as that? How do you do, Mr. Saunders? Glad to see you again. What are you doing to my hat, Holly?"

"I was afraid of this hat," said Sam Holly, meditatively. He had taken the hat from Hackett's head and was holding it in his hand, looking dubiously around at the shadows beyond the firelight where now absolute stillness reigned. "What do you think, Saunders?"

Pink grinned.

"Better elevate it some," he said, in the tone of one giving disinterested advice. "The light ain't none too good. I wouldn't want it on my head."

Holly stepped upon the hub of a hind wheel of the grub wagon and hung the hat upon a limb of a live-oak. Scarcely had his foot touched the ground when the crash of a dozen six-shooters split the air, and the hat fell to the ground riddled with bullets.

A hissing noise was heard as if from a score of rattlesnakes, and the cow-punchers emerged on all sides from the darkness, stepping high, with ludicrously exaggerated caution, and "hist"-ing to one another to observe the utmost prudence in approaching. They formed a solemn, wide circle about the hat, gazing at it in manifest alarm, and seized every few moments by little stampedes of panicky flight.

"It's the varmint," said one in awed tones, "that flits up and down in the low grounds at night, saying, 'Willie-wallo!'"

"It's the venomous Kypootum," proclaimed another. "It stings after it's dead, and hollers after it's buried."

"It's the chief of the hairy tribe," said Phonograph Davis. "But it's stone dead, now, boys."

"Don't you believe it," demurred Dry-Creek. "It's only 'possumin'.' It's the dreaded Highgollacum fantod from the forest. There's only one way to destroy its life."

He led forward Old Taller, the 240-pound cow-puncher. Old Taller placed the hat upright on the ground and solemnly sat upon it, crushing it as flat as a pancake.

Hackett had viewed these proceedings with wide-open eyes. Sam Holly saw that his anger was rising and said to him:

"Here's where you win or lose, Judge. There are sixty votes on the Diamond-Cross. The boys are trying your mettle. Take it as a joke, and I don't think you'll regret it." And Hackett saw the point and rose to the occasion.

Advancing to where the slayers of the wild beast were standing about its remains and declaring it to be at last defunct, he said, with deep earnestness:

"Boys, I must thank you for this gallant rescue. While driving through the arroyo that cruel monster that you have so fearlessly and repeatedly slaughtered sprang upon us from the tree tops. To you I shall consider that I owe my life, and also, I hope, reëlection to the office for which I am again candidate. Allow me to hand you my card."

The cow-punchers, always so sober-faced while engaged in their monkey-shines, relaxed into a grin of approval.

But Phonograph Davis, his appetite for fun not yet appeased, had something more up his sleeve.

"Pardner," he said, addressing Hackett with grave severity, "many a camp would be down on you for turnin' loose a pernicious varmint like that in it; but, bein' as we all escaped without loss of life, we'll overlook it. You can play square with us if you'll do it."

"How's that?" asked Hackett, suspiciously.

"You're authorized to perform the sacred rights and lefts of mattermony, air you not?"

"Well, yes," replied Hackett. "A marriage ceremony conducted by me would be legal."

"A wrong air to be righted in this here camp," said Phonograph, virtuously. "A a-ristocrat have slighted a 'umble but beautchoos female wat's pinin' for his affections. It's the jooty of the camp to drag forth the haughty descendant of a hundred—or maybe a hundred and twenty-five —earls, even so at the p'int of a lariat, and jine him to the weepin' lady. Fellows! round up Miss Sally and the Marquis, there's goin' to be a weddin'."

This whim of Phonograph's was received with whoops of appreciation. The cow-punchers started to apprehend the principals of the proposed ceremony.

"Kindly prompt me," said Hackett, wiping his forehead, though the night was cool, "how far this thing is to be carried. And might I expect any further portions of my raiment to be mistaken for wild animals and killed?"

"The boys are livelier than usual to-night," said Saunders. "The ones they are talking about marrying are two of the boys—a herd rider and the cook. It's another joke. You and Sam will have to sleep here to-night anyway; p'rhaps you'd better see 'em through with it. Maybe they'll quiet down after that."

The matchmakers found Miss Sally seated on the tongue of the grub wagon, calmly smoking his pipe. The Marquis was leaning idly against one of the trees under which the supply tent was pitched.

Into this tent they were both hustled, and Phonograph, as master of ceremonies, gave orders for the preparations.

"You, Dry-Creek and Jimmy, and Ben and Taller—hump yourselves to the wildwood and rustle flowers for the blow-out—mesquite'll do—and get the Spanish dagger blossom at the corner of the horse corral for the bride to pack. You, Limpy, get out that red and yaller blanket of your'n for Miss Sally's skyirt. Marquis, you'll do 'thout fixin'; nobody don't ever look at the groom."

During their absurd preparations, the two principals were left alone for a few minutes in the tent. The Marquis suddenly showed wild perturbation.

"This foolishness must not go on," he said, turning to Miss Sally a face white in the light of the lantern, hanging to the ridge-pole.

"Why not?" said the cook, with an amused smile. "It's fun for the boys; and they've always let you off pretty light in their frolics. I don't mind it."

"But you don't understand," persisted the Marquis, pleadingly. "That man is county judge, and his acts are binding. I can't—oh, you don't know——"

The cook stepped forward and took the Marquis's hands.

"Sally Bascom," he said, "I KNOW!"

"You know!" faltered the Marquis, trembling. "And you—want to——"

"More than I ever wanted anything. Will you—here come the boys!"

The cow-punchers crowded in, laden with armfuls of decorations.

"Perfidious coyote!" said Phonograph, sternly, addressing the Marquis. "Air you willing to patch up the damage you've did this ere slab-sided but trustin' bunch o' calico by single-footin' easy to the altar, or will we have to rope ye, and drag you thar?"

The Marquis pushed back his hat, and leaned jauntily against some high-piled sacks of beans. His cheeks were flushed, and his eyes were shining.

"Go on with the rat killin'," said he.

A little while after a procession approached the tree under which Hackett, Holly, and Saunders were sitting smoking.

Limpy Walker was in the lead, extracting a doleful tune on his concertina. Next came the bride and groom. The cook wore the gorgeous Navajo blanket tied around his waist and carried in one hand the waxen-white Spanish dagger blossom as large as a peck-measure and weighing fifteen pounds. His hat was ornamented with mesquite branches and yellow ratama blooms. A resurrected mosquito bar served as a veil. After them stumbled Phonograph Davis, in the character of the bride's father, weeping into a saddle blanket with sobs that could be heard a mile away. The cow-punchers followed by twos, loudly commenting upon the bride's appearance, in a supposed imitation of the audiences at fashionable weddings.

Hackett rose as the procession halted before him, and after a little lecture upon matrimony, asked:

"What are your names?"

"Sally and Charles," answered the cook.

"Join hands, Charles and Sally."

Perhaps there never was a stranger wedding. For, wedding it was, though only two of those present knew it.

When the ceremony was over, the cow-punchers gave one yell of congratulation and immediately abandoned their foolery for the night. Blankets were unrolled and sleep became the paramount question.

The cook (divested of his decorations) and the Marquis lingered for a moment in the shadow of the grub wagon. The Marquis leaned her head against his shoulder.

"I didn't know what else to do," she was saying. "Father was gone, and we kids had to rustle. I had helped him so much with the cattle that I thought I'd turn cowboy. There wasn't anything else I could make a living at. I wasn't much stuck on it though, after I got here, and I'd have left only——"

"Only what?"

"You know. Tell me something. When did you first—what made you——"

"Oh, it was as soon as we struck the camp, when Saunders bawled out 'The Marquis and Miss Sally!' I saw how rattled you got at the name, and I had my sus——"

"Cheeky!" whispered the Marquis. "And why should you think that I thought he was calling me 'Miss Sally'?"

"Because," answered the cook, calmly, "I was the Marquis. My father was the Marquis of Borodale. But you'll excuse that, won't you, Sally? It really isn't my fault, you know."

A FOG IN SANTONE

The drug clerk looked sharply at the white face half concealed by the high-turned overcoat collar.

"I would rather not supply you," he said, doubtfully. "I sold you a dozen morphine tablets less than an hour ago."

The customer smiles wanly. "The fault is in your crooked streets. I didn't intend to call upon you twice, but I guess I got tangled up. Excuse me."

He draws his collar higher, and moves out slowly. He stops under an electric light at the corner, and juggles absorbedly with three or four little pasteboard boxes. "Thirty-six," he announces to himself. "More than plenty." For a gray mist had swept upon Santone that night, an opaque terror that laid a hand to the throat of each of the city's guests. It was computed that three thousand invalids were hibernating in the town. They had come from far and wide, for here, among these contracted river-side streets, the goddess Ozone has elected to linger.

Purest atmosphere, sir, on earth! You might think from the river winding through our town that we are malarial, but, no, sir! Repeated experiments made both by the Government and local experts show that our air contains nothing deleterious—nothing but ozone, sir, pure ozone. Litmus paper tests made all along the river show—but you can read it all in the prospectuses; or the Santonian will recite it for you, word by word.

We may achieve climate, but weather is thrust upon us. Santone, then, cannot be blamed for this cold gray fog that came and kissed the lips of the three thousand, and then delivered them to the cross. That night the tubercles, whose ravages hope holds in check, multiplied. The writhing fingers of the pale mist did not go thence bloodless. Many of the wooers of ozone capitulated with the enemy that night, turning their faces to the wall in that dumb, isolated apathy that so terrifies their watchers. On the red streams of Hemorrhagia a few souls drifted away, leaving behind pathetic heaps, white and chill as the fog itself. Two or three came to view this atmospheric wraith as the ghost of impossible joys, sent to whisper to them of the egregious folly it is to inhale breath into the lungs, only to exhale it again, and these used whatever came handy to their relief, pistols, gas, or the beneficent muriate.

The purchaser of the morphine wanders into the fog, and at length finds himself upon a little iron bridge, one of the score or more in the heart of the city, under which the small tortuous river flows. He leans on the rail and gasps, for here the mist has concentrated, lying like a footpad to garrot such of the Three Thousand as creep that way. The iron bridge guys rattle to the strain of his cough, a mocking phthisical rattle, seeming to say to him: "Clickety-clack! just a little rusty cold, sir—but not from our river. Litmus paper all along the banks and nothing but ozone. Clacket-y-clack!"

The Memphis man at last recovers sufficiently to be aware of another overcoated man ten feet away, leaning on the rail, and just coming out of a paroxysm. There is a freemasonry among the Three Thousand that does away with formalities and introductions. A cough is your card; a hemorrhage a letter of credit. The Memphis man, being nearer recovered, speaks first.

"Goodall. Memphis—pulmonary tuberculosis—guess last stages." The Three Thousand economize on words. Words are breath and they need breath to write checks for the doctors.

"Hurd," gasps the other. "Hurd; of T'leder. T'leder, Ah-hia. Catarrhal bronkeetis. Name's Dennis, too—doctor says. Says I'll live four weeks if I —take care of myself. Got your walking papers yet?"

"My doctor," says Goodall of Memphis, a little boastingly, "gives me three months."

"Oh," remarks the man from Toledo, filling up great gaps in his conversation with wheezes, "damn the difference. What's months! Expect to—cut mine down to one week—and die in a hack—a four wheeler, not a cough. Be considerable moanin' of the bars when I put out to sea. I've patronized 'em pretty freely since I struck my—present gait. Say, Goodall of Memphis—if your doctor has set your pegs so close—why don't you— get on a big spree and go—to the devil quick and easy—like I'm doing?"

"A spree," says Goodall, as one who entertains a new idea, "I never did such a thing. I was thinking of another way, but——"

"Come on," invites the Ohioan, "and have some drinks. I've been at it—for two days, but the inf—ernal stuff won't bite like it used to. Goodall of Memphis, what's your respiration?"

"Twenty-four."

"Daily—temperature?"

"Hundred and four."

"You can do it in two days. It'll take me a—week. Tank up, friend Goodall—have all the fun you can; then—off you go, in the middle of a jag, and s-s-save trouble and expense. I'm a s-son of a gun if this ain't a health resort—for your whiskers! A Lake Erie fog'd get lost here in two minutes."

"You said something about a drink," says Goodall.

A few minutes later they line up at a glittering bar, and hang upon the arm rest. The bartender, blond, heavy, well-groomed, sets out their drinks, instantly perceiving that he serves two of the Three Thousand. He observes that one is a middle-aged man, well-dressed, with a lined and sunken face; the other a mere boy who is chiefly eyes and overcoat. Disguising well the tedium begotten by many repetitions, the server of drinks begins to chant the sanitary saga of Santone. "Rather a moist night, gentlemen, for our town. A little fog from our river, but nothing to hurt. Repeated Tests."

"Damn your litmus papers," gasps Toledo—"without any—personal offense intended."

"We've heard of 'em before. Let 'em turn red, white, and blue. What we want is a repeated test of that—whiskey. Come again. I paid for the last round, Goodall of Memphis."

The bottle oscillates from one to the other, continues to do so, and is not removed from the counter. The bartender sees two emaciated invalids dispose of enough Kentucky Belle to floor a dozen cowboys, without displaying any emotion save a sad and contemplative interest in the peregrinations of the bottle. So he is moved to manifest a solicitude as to the consequences.

"Not on your Uncle Mark Hanna," responds Toledo, "will we get drunk. We've been—vaccinated with whiskey—and—cod liver oil. What would send you to the police station—only gives us a thirst. S-s-set out another bottle."

It is slow work trying to meet death by that route. Some quicker way must be found. They leave the saloon and plunge again into the mist. The sidewalks are mere flanges at the base of the houses; the streets a cold ravine, the fog filling it like a freshet. Not far away is the Mexican quarter. Conducted as if by wires along the heavy air comes a guitar's tinkle, and the demoralizing voice of some señorita singing:

"En las tardes sombrillos del invierro   Y maldigo mi fausto destino—
    En el prado a Marar me reclino   Una vida la mas infeliz."

The words of it they do not understand—neither Toledo nor Memphis, but words are the least important things in life. The music tears the breasts of the seekers after Nepenthe, inciting Toledo to remark:

"Those kids of mine—I wonder—by God, Mr. Goodall of Memphis, we had too little of that whiskey! No slow music in mine, if you please. It makes you disremember to forget."

Hurd of Toledo here pulls out his watch, and says:

"I'm a son of a gun! Got an engagement for a hack ride out to San Pedro Springs at eleven. Forgot it. A fellow from Noo York, and me, and the Castillo sisters at Rhinegelder's Garden. That Noo York chap's a lucky dog—got one whole lung—good for a year yet. Plenty of money, too. He pays for everything. I can't afford—to miss the jamboree. Sorry you ain't going along. Good-bye, Goodall of Memphis."

He rounds the corner and shuffles away, casting off thus easily the ties of acquaintanceship as the moribund do, the season of dissolution being man's supreme hour of egoism and selfishness. But he turns and calls back through the fog to the other: "I say, Goodall, of Memphis! If you get there before I do, tell 'em Hurd's a-comin' too. Hurd, of T'leder, Ah-hia."

Thus Goodall's tempter deserts him. That youth, uncomplaining and uncaring, takes a spell at coughing, and, recovered, wanders desultorily on down the street, the name of which he neither knows nor recks. At a certain point he perceives swinging doors, and hears, filtering between them, a noise of wind and string instruments. Two men enter from the street as he arrives, and he follows them in. There is a kind of ante-chamber, plentifully set with palms and cactuses and oleanders. At little marble-topped tables some people sit, while soft-shod attendants bring the beer. All is orderly, clean, melancholy, gay, of the German method of pleasure. At his right is the foot of a stairway. A man there holds out his hand. Goodall extends his, full of silver, the man selects therefrom a coin. Goodall goes upstairs and sees there two galleries extending along the sides of a concert hall which he now perceives to lie below and beyond the anteroom he first entered. These galleries are divided into boxes or stalls, which bestow with the aid of hanging lace curtains a certain privacy upon their occupants.

Passing with aimless feet down the aisle contiguous to these saucy and discreet compartments, he is half checked by the sight in one of them of a young woman, alone and seated in an attitude of reflection. This young woman becomes aware of his approach. A smile from her brings him to a standstill, and her subsequent invitation draws him, though hesitating, to the other chair in the box, a little table between them.

Goodall is only nineteen. There are some whom, when the terrible god Phthisis wishes to destroy he first makes beautiful; and the boy is one of these. His face is wax, and an awful pulchritude is born of the menacing flame in his cheeks. His eyes reflect an unearthly vista engendered by the certainty of his doom. As it is forbidden man to guess accurately concerning his fate, it is inevitable that he shall tremble at the slightest lifting of the veil.

The young woman is well-dressed, and exhibits a beauty of distinctly feminine and tender sort; an Eve-like comeliness that scarcely seems predestined to fade.

It is immaterial, the steps by which the two mount to a certain plane of good understanding; they are short and few, as befits the occasion.

A button against the wall of the partition is frequently disturbed and a waiter comes and goes at a signal.

Pensive beauty would nothing of wine; two thick plaits of her blonde hair hang almost to the floor; she is a lineal descendant of the Lorelei. So the waiter brings the brew; effervescent, icy, greenish golden. The orchestra on the stage is playing "Oh, Rachel." The youngsters have exchanged a good bit of information. She calls him "Walter" and he calls her "Miss Rosa."

Goodall's tongue is loosened and he has told her everything about himself, about his home in Tennessee, the old pillared mansion under the oaks, the stables, the hunting; the friends he has; down to the chickens, and the box bushes bordering the walks. About his coming South for the climate, hoping to escape the hereditary foe of his family. All about his three months on a ranch; the deer hunts, the rattlers, and the rollicking in the cow camps. Then of his advent to Santone, where he had indirectly learned, from a great specialist, that his life's calendar probably contains but two more leaves. And then of this death-white, choking night which has come and strangled his fortitude and sent him out to seek a port amid its depressing billows.

"My weekly letter from home failed to come," he told her, "and I was pretty blue. I knew I had to go before long and I was tired of waiting. I went out and bought morphine at every drug store where they would sell me a few tablets. I got thirty-six quarter grains, and was going back to my room and take them, but I met a queer fellow on a bridge, who had a new idea."

Goodall fillips a little pasteboard box upon the table. "I put 'em all together in there."

Miss Rosa, being a woman, must raise the lid, and give a slight shiver at the innocent-looking triturates. "Horrid things! but those little, white bits—they could never kill one!"

Indeed they could. Walter knew better. Nine grains of morphia! Why, half the amount might.

Miss Rosa demands to know about Mr. Hurd, of Toledo, and is told. She laughs like a delighted child. "What a funny fellow! But tell me more about your home and your sisters, Walter. I know enough about Texas and tarantulas and cowboys."

The theme is dear, just now, to his mood, and he lays before her the simplest details of a true home; the little ties and endearments that so fill the exile's heart. Of his sisters, one, Alice, furnishes him a theme he loves to dwell upon.

"She is like you, Miss Rosa," he says. "Maybe not quite so pretty, but just as nice, and good, and——"

"There! Walter," says Miss Rosa, "now talk about something else."

But a shadow falls upon the wall outside, preceding a big, softly treading man, finely dressed, who pauses a second before the curtains and then passes on. Presently comes the waiter with a message: "Mr. Rolfe says ——"

"Tell Rolfe I'm engaged."

"I don't know why it is," says Goodall, of Memphis, "but I don't feel as bad as I did. An hour ago I wanted to die, but since I've met you, Miss Rosa, I'd like so much to live."

The young woman whirls around the table, lays an arm behind his neck and kisses him on the cheek.

"You must, dear boy," she says. "I know what was the matter. It was the miserable foggy weather that has lowered your spirit and mine too— a little. But look, now."

With a little spring she has drawn back the curtains. A window is in the wall opposite, and lo! the mist is cleared away. The indulgent moon is out again, revoyaging the plumbless sky. Roof and parapet and spire are softly pearl enamelled. Twice, thrice the retrieved river flashes back, between the houses, the light of the firmament. A tonic day will dawn, sweet and prosperous.

"Talk of death when the world is so beautiful!" says Miss Rosa, laying her hand on his shoulder. "Do something to please me, Walter. Go home to your rest and say: 'I mean to get better,' and do it."

"If you ask it," says the boy, with a smile, "I will."

The waiter brings full glasses. Did they ring? No; but it is well. He may leave them. A farewell glass. Miss Rosa says: "To your better health, Walter." He says: "To our next meeting."

His eyes look no longer into the void, but gaze upon the antithesis of death. His foot is set in an undiscovered country to-night. He is obedient, ready to go. "Good-night," she says.

"I never kissed a girl before," he confesses, "except my sisters."

"You didn't this time," she laughs, "I kissed you—good-night."

"When shall I see you again?" he persists.

"You promised me to go home," she frowns, "and get well. Perhaps we shall meet again soon. Good-night." He hesitates, his hat in hand. She smiles broadly and kisses him once more upon the forehead. She watches him far down the aisle, then sits again at the table.

The shadow falls once more against the wall. This time the big, softly stepping man parts the curtains and looks in. Miss Rosa's eyes meet his and for half a minute they remain thus, silent, fighting a battle with that king of weapons. Presently the big man drops the curtains and passes on.

The orchestra ceases playing suddenly, and an important voice can be heard loudly talking in one of the boxes farther down the aisle. No doubt some citizen entertains there some visitor to the town, and Miss Rosa leans back in her chair and smiles at some of the words she catches:

"Purest atmosphere—in the world—litmus paper all long—nothing hurtful—our city—nothing but pure ozone."

The waiter returns for the tray and glasses. As he enters, the girl crushes a little empty pasteboard box in her hand and throws it in a corner. She is stirring something in her glass with her hatpin.

"Why, Miss Rosa," says the waiter with the civil familiarity he uses— "putting salt in your beer this early in the night!"

THE FRIENDLY CALL

When I used to sell hardware in the West, I often "made" a little town called Saltillo, in Colorado. I was always certain of securing a small or a larger order from Simon Bell, who kept a general store there. Bell was one of those six-foot, low-voiced products, formed from a union of the West and the South. I liked him. To look at him you would think he should be robbing stage coaches or juggling gold mines with both hands; but he would sell you a paper of tacks or a spool of thread, with ten times more patience and courtesy than any saleslady in a city department store.

I had a twofold object in my last visit to Saltillo. One was to sell a bill of goods; the other to advise Bell of a chance that I knew of by which I was certain he could make a small fortune.

In Mountain City, a town on the Union Pacific, five times larger than Saltillo, a mercantile firm was about to go to the wall. It had a lively and growing custom, but was on the edge of dissolution and ruin. Mismanagement and the gambling habits of one of the partners explained it. The condition of the firm was not yet public property. I had my knowledge of it from a private source. I knew that, if the ready cash were offered, the stock and good will could be bought for about one fourth their value.

On arriving in Saltillo I went to Bell's store. He nodded to me, smiled his broad, lingering smile, went on leisurely selling some candy to a little girl, then came around the counter and shook hands.

"Well," he said (his invariably preliminary jocosity at every call I made), "I suppose you are out here making kodak pictures of the mountains. It's the wrong time of the year to buy any hardware, of course."

I told Bell about the bargain in Mountain City. If he wanted to take advantage of it, I would rather have missed a sale than have him overstocked in Saltillo.

"It sounds good," he said, with enthusiasm. "I'd like to branch out and do a bigger business, and I'm obliged to you for mentioning it. But—well, you come and stay at my house to-night and I'll think about it."

It was then after sundown and time for the larger stores in Saltillo to close. The clerks in Bell's put away their books, whirled the combination of the safe, put on their coats and hats and left for their homes. Bell padlocked the big, double wooden front doors, and we stood, for a moment, breathing the keen fresh mountain air coming across the foothills.

A big man walked down the street and stopped in front of the high porch of the store. His long, black moustache, black eyebrows, and curly black hair contrasted queerly with his light, pink complexion, which belonged, by rights, to a blonde. He was about forty, and wore a white vest, a white hat, a watch chain made of five-dollar gold pieces linked together, and a rather well-fitting two-piece gray suit of the cut that college boys of eighteen are wont to affect. He glanced at me distrustfully, and then at Bell with coldness and, I thought, something of enmity in his expression.

"Well," asked Bell, as if he were addressing a stranger, "did you fix up that matter?"

"Did I!" the man answered, in a resentful tone. "What do you suppose I've been here two weeks for? The business is to be settled tonight. Does that suit you, or have you got something to kick about?"

"It's all right," said Bell. "I knew you'd do it."

"Of course you did," said the magnificent stranger. "Haven't I done it before?"

"You have," admitted Bell. "And so have I. How do you find it at the hotel?"

"Rocky grub. But I ain't kicking. Say—can you give me any pointers about managing that—affair? It's my first deal in that line of business, you know."

"No, I can't," answered Bell, after some thought. "I've tried all kinds of ways. You'll have to try some of your own."

"Tried soft soap?"

"Barrels of it."

"Tried a saddle girth with a buckle on the end of it?"

"Never none. Started to once; and here's what I got."

Bell held out his right hand. Even in the deepening twilight I could see on the back of it a long, white scar, that might have been made by a claw or a knife or some sharp-edged tool.

"Oh, well," said the florid man, carelessly, "I'll know what to do later on."

He walked away without another word. When he had gone ten steps he turned and called to Bell:

"You keep well out of the way when the goods are delivered, so there won't be any hitch in the business."

"All right," answered Bell, "I'll attend to my end of the line."

This talk was scarcely clear in its meaning to me; but as it did not concern me, I did not let it weigh upon my mind. But the singularity of the other man's appearance lingered with me for a while; and as we walked toward Bell's house I remarked to him:

"Your customer seems to be a surly kind of fellow—not one that you'd like to be snowed in with in a camp on a hunting trip."

"He is that," assented Bell, heartily. "He reminds me of a rattlesnake that's been poisoned by the bite of a tarantula."

"He doesn't look like a citizen of Saltillo," I went on.

"No," said Bell, "he lives in Sacramento. He's down here on a little business trip. His name is George Ringo, and he's been my best friend—in fact, the only friend I ever had—for twenty years."

I was too surprised to make any further comment.

Bell lived in a comfortable, plain, square, two-story white house on the edge of the little town. I waited in the parlor—a room depressingly genteel—furnished with red plush, straw matting, looped-up lace curtains, and a glass case large enough to contain a mummy, full of mineral specimens.

While I waited I heard, upstairs, that unmistakable sound instantly recognized the world over—a bickering woman's voice, rising as her anger and fury grew. I could hear, between the gusts, the temperate rumble of Bell's tones, striving to oil the troubled waters.

The storm subsided soon; but not before I had heard the woman say, in a lower, concentrated tone, rather more carrying than her high-pitched railings: "This is the last time. I tell you—the last time. Oh, you *will* understand."

The household seemed to consist of only Bell and his wife and a servant or two. I was introduced to Mrs. Bell at supper.

At first sight she seemed to be a handsome woman, but I soon perceived that her charm had been spoiled. An uncontrolled petulance, I thought, and emotional egotism, an absence of poise and a habitual dissatisfaction had marred her womanhood. During the meal, she showed that false gayety, spurious kindliness and reactionary softness that mark the woman addicted to tantrums. Withal, she was a woman who might be attractive to many men.

After supper, Bell and I took our chairs outside, set them on the grass in the moonlight and smoked. The full moon is a witch. In her light, truthful men dig up for you nuggets of purer gold; while liars squeeze out brighter colors from the tubes of their invention. I saw Bell's broad, slow smile come out upon his face and linger there.

"I reckon you think George and me are a funny kind of friends," he said. "The fact is we never did take much interest in each other's company. But his idea and mine, of what a friend should be, was always synonymous and we lived up to it, strict, all these years. Now, I'll give you an idea of what our idea is.

"A man don't need but one friend. The fellow who drinks your liquor and hangs around you, slapping you on the back and taking up your time, telling you how much he likes you, ain't a friend, even if you did play marbles at school and fish in the same creek with him. As long as you don't need a friend one of that kind may answer. But a friend, to my mind, is one you can deal with on a strict reciprocity basis like me and George have always done.

"A good many years ago, him and me was connected in a number of ways. We put our capital together and run a line of freight wagons in New Mexico, and we mined some and gambled a few. And then, we got into trouble of one or two kinds; and I reckon that got us on a better understandable basis than anything else did, unless it was the fact that we never had much personal use for each other's ways. George is the vainest man I ever see, and the biggest brag. He could blow the biggest geyser in the Yosemite valley back into its hole with one whisper. I am a quiet man, and fond of studiousness and thought. The more we used to see each other, personally, the less we seemed to like to be together. If he ever had slapped me on the back and snivelled over me like I've seen men do to what they called their friends, I know I'd have had a rough-and-tumble with him on the spot. Same way with George. He hated my ways as bad as I did his. When we were mining, we lived in separate tents, so as not to intrude our obnoxiousness on each other.

"But after a long time, we begun to know each of us could depend on the other when we were in a pinch, up to his last dollar, word of honor or perjury, bullet, or drop of blood we had in the world. We never even spoke of it to each other, because that would have spoiled it. But we tried it out, time after time, until we came to know. I've grabbed my hat and jumped a freight and rode 200 miles to identify him when he was about to be hung by mistake, in Idaho, for a train robber. Once, I laid sick of typhoid in a tent in Texas, without a dollar or a change of clothes, and sent for George in Boise City. He came on the next train. The first thing he did before speaking to me, was to hang up a little looking glass on the side of the tent and curl his moustache and rub some hair dye on his head. His hair is naturally a light reddish. Then he gave me the most scientific cussing I ever had, and took off his coat.

"'If you wasn't a Moses-meek little Mary's lamb, you wouldn't have been took down this way,' says he. 'Haven't you got gumption enough not to drink swamp water or fall down and scream whenever you have a little colic or feel a mosquito bite you?' He made me a little mad.

"'You've got the bedside manners of a Piute medicine man,' says I. 'And I wish you'd go away and let me die a natural death. I'm sorry I sent for you.'

"'I've a mind to,' says George, 'for nobody cares whether you live or die. But now I've been tricked into coming, I might as well stay until this little attack of indigestion or nettle rash or whatever it is, passes away.'

"Two weeks afterward, when I was beginning to get around again, the doctor laughed and said he was sure that my friend's keeping me mad all the time did more than his drugs to cure me.

"So that's the way George and me was friends. There wasn't any sentiment about it—it was just give and take, and each of us knew that the other was ready for the call at any time.

"I remember, once, I played a sort of joke on George, just to try him.

I felt a little mean about it afterward, because I never ought to have doubted he'd do it.

"We was both living in a little town in the San Luis valley, running some flocks of sheep and a few cattle. We were partners, but, as usual, we didn't live together. I had an old aunt, out from the East, visiting for the summer, so I rented a little cottage. She soon had a couple of cows and some pigs and chickens to make the place look like home. George lived alone in a little cabin half a mile out of town.

"One day a calf that we had, died. That night I broke its bones, dumped it into a coarse sack and tied it up with wire. I put on an old shirt, tore a sleeve 'most out of it, and the collar half off, tangled up my hair, put some red ink on my hands and splashed some of it over my shirt and face. I must have looked like I'd been having the fight of my life. I put the sack in a wagon and drove out to George's cabin. When I halloed, he come out in a yellow dressing-gown, a Turkish cap, and patent leather shoes. George always was a great dresser.

· "I dumped the bundle to the ground.

" 'Sh-sh!' says I, kind of wild in my way. 'Take that and bury it, George, out somewhere behind your house—bury it just like it is. And don——'

" 'Don't get excited,' says George. 'And for the Lord's sake go and wash your hands and face and put on a clean shirt.'

"And he lights his pipe, while I drove away at a gallop. The next morning he drops around to our cottage, where my aunt was fiddling with her flowers and truck in the front yard. He bends himself and bows and makes compliments as he could do, when so disposed, and begs a rose bush from her, saying he had turned up a little land back of his cabin, and wanted to plant something on it by way of usefulness and ornament. So my aunt, flattered, pulls up one of her biggest by the roots and gives it to him. Afterward I see it growing where he planted it, in a place where the grass had been cleared off and the dirt levelled. But neither George nor me ever spoke of it to each other again."

The moon rose higher, possibly drawing water from the sea, pixies from their dells, and certainly more confidences from Simms Bell, the friend of a friend.

"There come a time, not long afterward," he went on, "when I was able to do a good turn for George Ringo. George had made a little pile of money in beeves and he was up in Denver, and he showed up when I saw him, wearing deer-skin vests, yellow shoes, clothes like the awnings in front of drug stores, and his hair dyed so blue that it looked black in the dark. He wrote me to come up there, quick—that he needed me, and to bring the best outfit of clothes I had. I had 'em on when I got the letter, so I left on the next train. George was——"

Bell stopped for half a minute, listening intently.

"I thought I heard a team coming down the road," he explained.

"George was at a summer resort on a lake near Denver and was putting on as many airs as he knew how. He had rented a little two-room cottage, and had a Chihuahua dog and a hammock and eight different kinds of walking sticks.

" 'Simms,' he says to me, 'there's a widow woman here that's petering the soul out of me with her intentions. I can't get out of her way. It ain't that she ain't handsome and agreeable, in a sort of style, but her attentions is serious, and I ain't ready for to marry nobody and settle down. I can't go to no festivity nor sit on the hotel piazza or mix in any of the society round-ups, but what she cuts me out of the herd and puts her daily brand on me. I like this here place,' goes on George, 'and I'm making a hit here in the most censorious circles, so I don't want to have to run away from it. So I sent for you.'

" 'What do you want me to do?' I asks George.

" 'Why,' says he, 'I want you to head her off. I want you to cut me out. I want you to come to the rescue. Suppose you seen a wildcat about for to eat me, what would you do?'

" 'Go for it,' says I.

" 'Correct,' says George. 'Then go for this Mrs. De Clinton the same.'

" 'How am I to do it?' I asks. 'By force and awfulness or in some gentler and less lurid manner?'

" 'Court her,' George says, 'get her off my trail. Feed her. Take her out in boats. Hang around her and stick to her. Get her mashed on you if you can. Some women are pretty big fools. Who knows but what she might take a fancy to you.'

" 'Had you ever thought,' I asks, 'of repressing your fatal fascinations in her presence; of squeezing a harsh note in the melody of your siren voice, of veiling your beauty—in other words, of giving her the bounce yourself?'

"George sees no essence of sarcasm in my remark. He twists his moustache and looks at the points of his shoes.

" 'Well, Simms,' he said, 'you know how I am about the ladies. I can't hurt none of their feelings. I'm by nature polite and esteemful of their intents and purposes. This Mrs. De Clinton don't appear to be the suitable sort for me. Besides, I ain't a marrying man by all means.'

" 'All right,' said I, 'I'll do the best I can in the case.'

"So I bought a new outfit of clothes and a book on etiquette and made a dead set for Mrs. De Clinton. She was a fine-looking woman, cheerful and gay. At first, I almost had to hobble her to keep her from loping around at George's heels; but finally I got her so she seemed glad to go riding with me and sailing on the lake; and she seemed real hurt on the mornings when I forgot to send her a bunch of flowers. Still, I didn't like the way she looked at George, sometimes, out of the corner of her eye. George was having a fine time now, going with the whole bunch just as he pleased. Yes'm," continued Bell, "she certainly was a fine-looking woman at that time. She's changed some since, as you might have noticed at the supper table."

"What!" I exclaimed.

"I married Mrs. De Clinton," went on Bell. "One evening while we were up at the lake. When I told George about it, he opened his mouth and I thought he was going to break our traditions and say something grateful, but he swallowed it back.

" 'All right,' says he, playing with his dog. 'I hope you won't have too much trouble. Myself, I'm not never going to marry.'

"That was three years ago," said Bell. "We came here to live. For a year we got along medium fine. And then everything changed. For two years I've been having something that rhymes first-class with my name. You heard the row upstairs this evening? That was a merry welcome compared to the usual average. She's tired of me and of this little town life and she rages all day, like a panther in a cage. I stood it until two weeks ago and then I had to send out The Call. I located George in Sacramento. He started the day he got my wire."

Mrs. Bell came out of the house swiftly toward us. Some strong excitement or anxiety seemed to possess her, but she smiled a faint hostess smile, and tried to keep her voice calm.

"The dew is falling," she said, "and it's growing rather late. Wouldn't you gentlemen rather come into the house?"

Bell took some cigars from his pocket and answered: "It's most too fine a night to turn in yet. I think Mr. Ames and I will walk out along the road a mile or so and have another smoke. I want to talk with him about some goods that I want to buy."

"Up the road or down the road?" asked Mrs. Bell.

"Down," said Bell.

I thought she breathed a sigh of relief.

When we had gone a hundred yards and the house became concealed by trees, Bell guided me into the thick grove that lined the road and back through them toward the house again. We stopped within twenty yards of the house, concealed by the dark shadows. I wondered at this maneuver. And then I heard in the distance coming down the road beyond the house, the regular hoofbeats of a team of horses. Bell held his watch in a ray of moonlight.

"On time, within a minute," he said. "That's George's way."

The team slowed up as it drew near the house and stopped in a patch of black shadows. We saw the figure of a woman carrying a heavy valise move swiftly from the other side of the house, and hurry to the waiting vehicle. Then it rolled away briskly in the direction from which it had come.

I looked at Bell inquiringly, I suppose. I certainly asked him no question.

"She's running away with George," said Bell, simply. "He's kept me posted about the progress of the scheme all along. She'll get a divorce in six months and then George will marry her. He never helps anybody halfway. It's all arranged between them."

I began to wonder what friendship was, after all.

When we went into the house, Bell began to talk easily on other subjects; and I took his cue. By and by the big chance to buy out the business in Mountain City came back to my mind and I began to urge it upon him. Now that he was free, it would be easier for him to make the move; and he was sure of a splendid bargain.

Bell was silent for some minutes, but when I looked at him I fancied that he was thinking of something else—that he was not considering the project.

"Why, no, Mr. Ames," he said, after a while, "I can't make that deal. I'm awful thankful to you, though, for telling me about it. But I've got to stay here. I can't go to Mountain City."

"Why?" I asked.

"Missis Bell," he replied, "won't live in Mountain City. She hates the place and wouldn't go there. I've got to keep right on here in Saltillo."

"Mrs. Bell!" I exclaimed, too puzzled to conjecture what he meant.

"I ought to explain," said Bell. "I know George and I know Mrs. Bell. He's impatient in his ways. He can't stand things that fret him, long, like I can. Six months, I give them—six months of married life, and there'll be another disunion. Mrs. Bell will come back to me. There's no other place for her to go. I've got to stay here and wait. At the end of six months, I'll have to grab a satchel and catch the first train. For George will be sending out The Call."

A DINNER AT ——[1]

The Adventures of an Author with His Own Hero

All that day—in fact from the moment of his creation—Van Sweller had conducted himself fairly well in my eyes. Of course I had had to make many concessions; but in return he had been no less considerate. Once or twice we had had sharp, brief contentions over certain points of behavior; but, prevailingly, give and take had been our rule.

His morning toilet provoked our first tilt. Van Sweller went about it confidently.

"The usual thing, I suppose, old chap," he said, with a smile and a

[1]See advertising column, "Where to Dine Well," in the daily newspapers.

yawn. "I ring for a.b. and s., and then I have my tub. I splash a good deal in the water, of course. You are aware that there are two ways in which I can receive Tommy Carmichael when he looks in to have a chat about polo. I can talk to him through the bathroom door, or I can be picking at a grilled bone which my man has brought in. Which would you prefer?"

I smiled with diabolic satisfaction at his coming discomfiture.

"Neither," I said. "You will make your appearance on the scene when a gentleman should—after you are fully dressed, which indubitably private function shall take place behind closed doors. And I will feel indebted to you if, after you do appear, your deportment and manners are such that it will not be necessary to inform the public, in order to appease its apprehension, that you have taken a bath."

Van Sweller slightly elevated his brows.

"Oh, very well," he said, a trifle piqued. "I rather imagine it concerns you more than it does me. Cut the 'tub' by all means, if you think best. But it has been the usual thing, you know."

This was my victory; but after Van Sweller emerged from his apartments in the "Beaujolie" I was vanquished in a dozen small but well-contested skirmishes. I allowed him a cigar; but routed him on the question of naming its brand. But he worsted me when I objected to giving him a "coat unmistakably English in its cut." I allowed him to "stroll down Broadway," and even permitted "passers by" (God knows there's nowhere to pass but by) to "turn their heads and gaze with evident admiration at his erect figure." I demeaned myself, and, as a barber, gave him a "smooth, dark face with its keen, frank eye, and firm jaw."

Later on he looked in at the club and saw Freddy Vavasour, polo team captain, dawdling over grilled bone No. 1.

"Dear old boy," began Van Sweller; but in an instant I had seized him by the collar and dragged him aside with the scantiest courtesy.

"For heaven's sake talk like a man," I said, sternly. "Do you think it is manly to use those mushy and inane forms of address? That man is neither dear nor old nor a boy."

To my surprise Van Sweller turned upon me a look of frank pleasure.

"I am glad to hear you say that," he said, heartily. "I used those words because I have been forced to say them so often. They really are contemptible. Thanks for correcting me, dear old boy."

Still I must admit that Van Sweller's conduct in the park that morning was almost without flaw. The courage, the dash, the modesty, the skill, the fidelity that he displayed atoned for everything.

This is the way the story runs.

Van Sweller has been a gentleman member of the "Rugged Riders," the company that made a war with a foreign country famous. Among his comrades was Lawrence O'Roon, a man whom Van Sweller liked. A strange thing—and a hazardous one in fiction—was that Van Sweller and O'Roon resembled each other mightily in face, form, and general appearance. After the war Van Sweller pulled wires, and O'Roon was made a mounted policeman.

Now, one night in New York there are commemorations and libations by old comrades, and in the morning, Mounted Policeman O'Roon, unused to potent liquids—another premise hazardous in fiction—finds the earth bucking and bounding like a bronco, with no stirrup into which he may insert foot and save his honor and his badge.

Noblesse oblige? Surely. So out along the driveways and bridle paths trots Hudson Van Sweller in the uniform of his incapacitated comrade, as like unto him as one French pea is unto a *petit pois*.

It is, of course, jolly larks for Van Sweller, who has wealth and social position enough for him to masquerade safely even as a police commissioner doing his duty, if he wished to do so. But society, not given to scanning the countenances of mounted policemen, sees nothing unusual in the officer on the beat.

And then comes the runaway.

That is a fine scene—the swaying victoria, the impetuous, daft horses plunging through the line of scattering vehicles, the driver stupidly holding his broken reins, and the ivory-white face of Amy Ffolliott, as she clings desperately with each slender hand. Fear has come and gone: it has left her expression pensive and just a little pleading, for life is not so bitter.

And then the clatter and swoop of Mounted Policeman Van Sweller! Oh, it was—but the story has not yet been printed. When it is you shall learn how he sent his bay like a bullet after the imperilled victoria. A Crichton, a Crœsus, and a Centaur in one, he hurls the invincible combination into the chase.

When the story is printed you will admire the breathless scene where Van Sweller checks the headlong team. And then he looks into Amy Ffolliott's eyes and sees two things—the possibilities of a happiness he has long sought, and a nascent promise of it. He is unknown to her; but he stands in her sight, illuminated by the hero's potent glory, she his and he hers by all the golden, fond, unreasonable laws of love and light literature.

Ay, that is a rich moment. And it will stir you to find Van Sweller in that fruitful nick of time thinking of his comrade O'Roon, who is cursing his gyrating bed and incapable legs in an unsteady room in a West Side hotel while Van Sweller holds his badge and his honor.

Van Sweller hears Miss Ffolliott's voice thrillingly asking the name of her preserver. If Hudson Van Sweller, in policeman's uniform, has saved the life of palpitating beauty in the park—where is Mounted Policeman O'Roon, in whose territory the deed is done? How quickly by a word can the hero reveal himself, thus discarding his masquerade of ineligibility and doubling the romance! But there is his friend!

Van Sweller touches his cap. "It's nothing, Miss," he says, sturdily; "that's what we are paid for—to do our duty." And away he rides. But the story does not end there.

As I have said, Van Sweller carried off the park scene to my decided satisfaction. Even to me he was a hero when he foreswore, for the sake of his friend, the romantic promise of his adventure. It was later in the day, amongst the more exacting conventions that encompass the society hero, when we had our liveliest disagreement. At noon he went to O'Roon's room and found him far enough recovered to return to his post, which he at once did.

At about six o'clock in the afternoon Van Sweller fingered his watch, and flashed at me a brief look full of such shrewd cunning that I suspected him at once.

"Time to dress for dinner, old man," he said, with exaggerated carelessness.

"Very well," I answered, without giving him a clue to my suspicions; "I will go with you to your rooms and see that you do the thing properly. I suppose that every author must be a valet to his own hero."

He affected cheerful acceptance of my somewhat officious proposal to accompany him. I could see that he was annoyed by it, and that fact fastened deeper in my mind the conviction that he was meditating some act of treachery.

When he had reached his apartments he said to me, with a too patronizing air: "There are, as you perhaps know, quite a number of little distinguishing touches to be had out of the dressing process. Some writers rely almost wholly upon them. I suppose that I am to ring for my man, and that he is to enter noiselessly, with an expressionless countenance."

"He may enter," I said, with decision, "and only enter. Valets do not usually enter a room shouting college songs or with St. Vitus's dance in their faces; so the contrary may be assumed without fatuous or gratuitous asseveration."

"I must ask you to pardon me," continued Van Sweller, gracefully, "for annoying you with questions, but some of your methods are a little new to me. Shall I don a full-dress suit with an immaculate white tie—or is there another tradition to be upset?"

"You will wear," I replied, "evening dress, such as a gentleman wears. If it is full, your tailor should be responsible for its bagginess. And I will leave it to whatever erudition you are supposed to possess whether a white tie is rendered any whiter by being immaculate. And I will leave it to the consciences of you and your man whether a tie that is not white, and therefore not immaculate, could possibly form any part of a gentleman's evening dress. If not, then the perfect tie is included and understood in the term 'dress,' and its expressed addition predicates either a redundancy of speech or the spectacle of a man wearing two ties at once."

With this mild but deserved rebuke I left Van Sweller in his dressing-room and waited for him in his library.

About an hour later his valet came out, and I heard him telephone for an electric cab. Then out came Van Sweller, smiling, but with that sly, secretive design in his eye that was puzzling me.

"I believe," he said, easily, as he smoothed a glove, "that I will drop in at ——[1] for dinner."

I sprang up, angrily, at his words. This, then, was the paltry trick he had been scheming to play upon me. I faced him with a look so grim that even his patrician poise was flustered.

"You will never do so," I exclaimed, "with my permission. What kind of a return is this," I continued, hotly, "for the favors I have granted you? I gave you a 'Van' to your name when I might have called you 'Perkins' or 'Simpson.' I have humbled myself so far as to brag of your polo ponies, your automobiles, and the iron muscles that you acquired when you were stroke-oar of your 'varsity eight' or 'eleven,' whichever it is. I created you for the hero of this story; and I will not submit to having you queer it. I have tried to make you a typical young New York gentleman of the highest social station and breeding. You have no reason to complain of my treatment to you. Amy Ffolliott, the girl you are to win, is a prize for any man to be thankful for, and cannot be equalled for beauty—provided the story is illustrated by the right artist. I do not understand why you should try to spoil everything. I had thought you were a gentleman."

"What is it you are objecting to, old man?" asked Van Sweller, in a surprised tone.

"To your dining at ——,[1]" I answered. "The pleasure would be yours, no doubt, but the responsibility would fall upon me. You intend deliberately to make me out a tout for a restaurant. Where you dine to-night has not the slightest connection with the thread of our story. You know very well that the plot requires that you be in front of the Alhambra Opera House at 11:30 where you are to rescue Miss Ffolliott a second time as the fire engine crashes into her cab. Until that time your movements are immaterial to the reader. Why can't you dine out of sight somewhere, as many a hero does, instead of insisting upon an inapposite and vulgar exhibition of yourself?"

"My dear fellow," said Van Sweller, politely, but with a stubborn tightening of his lips, "I'm sorry it doesn't please you, but there's no help for it. Even a character in a story has rights that an author cannot ignore. The hero of a story of New York social life must dine at ——[1] at least once during its action."

" 'Must,' " I echoed, disdainfully; "why 'must'? Who demands it?"

"The magazine editors," answered Van Sweller, giving me a glance of significant warning.

[1] See advertising column, "Where to Dine Well," in the daily newspapers.

"But why?" I persisted.

"To please subscribers around Kankakee, Ill.," said Van Sweller, without hesitation.

"How do you know these things?" I inquired, with sudden suspicion. "You never came into existence until this morning. You are only a character in fiction, anyway. I, myself, created you. How is it possible for you to know anything?"

"Pardon me for referring to it," said Van Sweller, with a sympathetic smile, "but I have been the hero of hundreds of stories of this kind."

I felt a slow flush creeping into my face.

"I thought . . ." I stammered; "I was hoping . . . that is . . . Oh, well, of course an absolutely original conception in fiction is impossible in these days."

"Metropolitan types," continued Van Sweller, kindly, "do not offer a hold for much originality. I've sauntered through every story in pretty much the same way. Now and then the women writers have made me cut some rather strange capers, for a gentleman; but the men generally pass me along from one to another without much change. But never yet, in any story, have I failed to dine at ——.[1]"

"You will fail this time," I said, emphatically.

"Perhaps so," admitted Van Sweller, looking out of the window into the street below, "but if so it will be for the first time. The authors all send me there. I fancy that many of them would have liked to accompany me, but for the little matter of the expense."

"I say I will be touting for no restaurant," I repeated, loudly. "You are subject to my will, and I declare that you shall not appear on record this evening until the time arrives for you to rescue Miss Ffolliott again. If the reading public cannot conceive that you have dined during that interval at some one of the thousands of establishments provided for that purpose that do not receive literary advertisement it may suppose, for aught I care, that you have gone fasting."

"Thank you," said Van Sweller, rather coolly, "you are hardly courteous. But take care! it is at your own risk that you attempt to disregard a fundamental principle in metropolitan fiction—one that is dear alike to author and reader. I shall, of course, attend to my duty when it comes time to rescue your heroine; but I warn you that it will be your loss if you fail to send me to-night to dine at ——.[1]"

"I will take the consequences if there are to be any," I replied. "I am not yet come to be sandwich man for an eating-house."

I walked over to a table where I had left my cane and gloves. I heard the whirr of the alarm in the cab below and I turned quickly. Van Sweller was gone.

[1]See advertising column, "Where to Dine Well," in the daily newspapers.

I rushed down the stairs and out to the curb. An empty hansom was just passing. I hailed the driver excitedly.

"See that auto cab halfway down the block?" I shouted. "Follow it. Don't lose sight of it for an instant, and I will give you two dollars!"

If I only had been one of the characters in my story instead of myself I could easily have offered $10 or $25 or even $100. But $2 was all I felt justified in expending, with fiction at its present rates.

The cab driver, instead of lashing his animal into a foam, proceeded at a deliberate trot that suggested a by-the-hour arrangement.

But I suspected Van Sweller's design; and when we lost sight of his cab I ordered my driver to proceed at once to ——.[1]

I found Van Sweller at a table under a palm, just glancing over the menu, with a hopeful waiter hovering at his elbow.

"Come with me," I said, inexorably. "You will not give me the slip again. Under my eye you shall remain until 11:30."

Van Sweller countermanded the order for his dinner, and rose to accompany me. He could scarcely do less. A fictitious character is but poorly equipped for resisting a hungry but live author who comes to drag him forth from a restaurant. All he said was: "You were just in time; but I think you are making a mistake. You cannot afford to ignore the wishes of the great reading public."

I took Van Sweller to my own rooms—to my room. He had never seen anything like it before.

"Sit on that trunk," I said to him, "while I observe whether the land-lady is stalking us. If she is not, I will get things at a delicatessen store below, and cook something for you in a pan over the gas jet. It will not be so bad. Of course nothing of this will appear in the story."

"Jove! old man!" said Van Sweller, looking about him with interest, "this is a jolly little closet you live in! Where the devil do you sleep?—Oh, that pulls down! And I say—what is this under the corner of the carpet? —Oh, a frying pan! I see—clever idea! Fancy cooking over the gas! What larks it will be!"

"Think of anything you could eat?" I asked; "try a chop, or what?"

"Anything," said Van Sweller, enthusiastically, "except a grilled bone."

Two weeks afterward the postman brought me a large fat envelope. I opened it, and took out something that I had seen before, and this type-written letter from a magazine that encourages society fiction:

Your short story, "The Badge of Policeman O'Roon," is herewith returned.

We are sorry that it has been unfavorably passed upon; but it seems to lack in some of the essential requirements of our publication.

[1] See advertising column, "Where to Dine Well," in the daily newspapers.

The story is splendidly constructed; its style is strong and inimitable, and its action and character-drawing deserve the highest praise. As a story *per se* it has merit beyond anything that we have read for some time. But, as we have said, it fails to come up to some of the standards we have set.

Could you not re-write the story, and inject into it the social atmosphere, and return it to us for further consideration? It is suggested to you that you have the hero, Van Sweller, drop in for luncheon or dinner once or twice at ——[1] or at the ——[1] which will be in line with the changes desired.

Very truly yours,
The Editors

SOUND AND FURY

PERSONS OF THE DRAMA   Mr. Penne   *An Author*
Miss Lore   *An Amanuensis*

SCENE   *Workroom of* Mr. Penne's *popular novel factory.*

MR. PENNE   Good morning, Miss Lore. Glad to see you so prompt. We should finish that June installment for the *Epoch* to-day. Leverett is crowding me for it. Are you quite ready? We will resume where we left off yesterday. (*Dictates.*) "Kate, with a sigh, rose from his knees, and——"

MISS LORE   Excuse me; you mean "rose from *her* knees," instead of "his," don't you?

MR. PENNE   Er—no—"his," if you please. It is the love scene in the garden. (*Dictates.*) "Rose from his knees where, blushing with youth's bewitching coyness, she had rested for a moment after Cortland had declared his love. The hour was one of supreme and tender joy. When Kate—scene that Cortland never——"

MISS LORE   Excuse me; but wouldn't it be more grammatical to say "when Kate *saw*," instead of "seen"?

MR. PENNE   The context will explain. (*Dictates.*) "When Kate—scene that Cortland never forgot—came tripping across the lawn it seemed to him the fairest sight that earth had ever offered to his gaze."

MISS LORE   Oh!

MR. PENNE   (*dictates*)   "Kate had abandoned herself to the joy of her newfound love so completely that no shadow of her former grief was cast upon it. Cortland, with his arm firmly entwined about her waist, knew nothing of her sighs——"

MISS LORE   Goodness! If he couldn't tell her size with his arm around

——

MR. PENNE   (*frowning*)   "Of her sighs and tears of the previous night."

[1]See advertising column, "Where to Dine Well," in the daily newspapers.

MISS LORE Oh!

MR. PENNE (*dictates*) "To Cortland the chief charm of this girl was her look of innocence and unworldliness. Never had nun——"

MISS LORE How about changing that to "never had any"?

MR. PENNE (*emphatically*) "Never had nun in cloistered cell a face more sweet and pure."

MISS LORE Oh!

MR. PENNE (*dictates*) "But now Kate must hasten back to the house lest her absence be discovered. After a fond farewell she turned and sped lightly away. Cortland's gaze followed her. He watched her rise——"

MISS LORE Excuse me, Mr. Penne; but how could he watch her eyes while her back was turned toward him?

MR. PENNE (*with extreme politeness*) Possibly you would gather my meaning more intelligently if you would wait for the conclusion of the sentence. (*Dictates.*) "Watched her rise as gracefully as a fawn as she mounted the eastern terrace."

MISS LORE Oh!

MR. PENNE (*dictates*) "And yet Cortland's position was so far above that of this rustic maiden that he dreaded to consider the social upheaval that would ensue should he marry her. In no uncertain tones the traditional voices of his caste and world cried out loudly to him to let her go. What should follow——"

MISS LORE (*looking up with a start*) I'm sure I can't say, Mr. Penne. Unless (*with a giggle*) you would want to add "Gallegher."

MR. PENNE (*coldly*) Pardon me. I was not seeking to impose upon you the task of a collaborator. Kindly consider the question as a part of the text.

MISS LORE Oh!

MR. PENNE (*dictates*) "On one side was love and Kate; on the other side his heritage of social position and family pride. Would love win? Love, that the poets tell us will last forever!" (*Perceives that* Miss Lore *looks fatigued, and looks at his watch.*) That's a good long stretch. Perhaps we'd better knock off a bit.

(Miss Lore *does not reply.*)

MR. PENNE I said, Miss Lore, we've been at it quite a long time—wouldn't you like to knock off for a while?

MISS LORE Oh! Were you addressing me before? I put what you said down. I thought it belonged in the story. It seemed to fit in all right. Oh, no; I'm not tired.

MR. PENNE Very well, then, we will continue. (*Dictates.*) "In spite of these qualms and doubts, Cortland was a happy man. That night at the club he silently toasted Kate's bright eyes in a bumper of the rarest vintage. Afterward he set out for a stroll with, as Kate on——"

miss lore   Excuse me, Mr. Penne, for venturing a suggestion; but don't you think you might state that in a less coarse manner?

mr. penne (*astounded*)   Wh-wh—I'm afraid I fail to understand you.

miss lore   His condition. Why not say he was "full" or "intoxicated"? It would sound much more elegant than the way you express it.

mr. penne (*still darkly wandering*)   Will you kindly point out, Miss Lore, where I have intimated that Cortland was "full," if you prefer that word?

miss lore (*calmly consulting her stenographic notes*)   It is right here, word for word. (*Reads.*) "Afterwards he set out for a stroll with a skate on."

mr. penne (*with peculiar emphasis*)   Ah! And now will you kindly take down the expurgated phrase? (*Dictates.*) "Afterward he set out for a stroll with, as Kate on one occasion had fancifully told him, her spirit leaning upon his arm."

miss lore   Oh!

mr. penne (*dictates*)   Chapter thirty-four. Heading—"What Kate Found in the Garden." "That fragrant summer morning brought gracious tasks to all. The bees were at the honeysuckle blossoms on the porch. Kate, singing a little song, was training the riotous branches of her favorite woodbine. The sun, himself, had rows——"

miss lore   Shall I say "had risen"?

mr. penne (*very slowly and with desperate deliberation*)   "The—sun—himself — had — rows — of — blushing — pinks — and — hollyhocks — and — hyacinths — waiting — that — he — might — dry — their — dew-drenched — cups."

miss lore   Oh!

mr. penne (*dictates*)   "The earliest trolley, scattering the birds from its pathway like some marauding cat, brought Cortland over from Oldport. He had forgotten his fair——"

miss lore   Hm! Wonder how he got the conductor to——

mr. penne (*very loudly*)   "Forgotten his fair and roseate visions of the night in the practical light of the sober morn."

miss lore   Oh!

mr. penne (*dictates*)   "He greeted her with his usual smile and manner. 'See the waves,' he cried, pointing to the heaving waters of the sea, 'ever wooing and returning to the rock-bound shore.' 'Ready to break,' Kate said, with——"

miss lore   My! One evening he has his arm around her, and the next morning he's ready to break her head! Just like a man!

mr. penne (*with suspicious calmness*)   There are times, Miss Lore, when a man becomes so far exasperated that even a woman—— But suppose we finish the sentence. (*Dictates.*) " 'Ready to break,' Kate said, with the thrilling look of a soul-awakened woman, 'into foam and spray, destroying themselves upon the shore they love so well.' "

MISS LORE   Oh!

MR. PENNE (*dictates*) "Cortland in Kate's presence heard faintly the voice of caution. Thirty years had not cooled his ardor. It was in his power to bestow great gifts upon this girl. He still retained the beliefs that he had at twenty." (*To* Miss Lore, *wearily*) I think that will be enough for the present.

MISS LORE (*wisely*) Well, if he had the twenty that he believed he had, it might buy her a rather nice one.

MR. PENNE (*faintly*) The last sentence was my own. We will discontinue for the day, Miss Lore.

MISS LORE   Shall I come again to-morrow?

MR. PENNE (*helpless under the spell*) If you will be so good.

(*Exit* Miss Lore.)

ASBESTOS CURTAIN

TICTOCQ

These two farcical stories about Tictocq appeared in the *Rolling Stone*. They are reprinted here with all of their local references because, written hurriedly and for neighborly reading, they nevertheless have an interest for the admirer of O. Henry. They were written in 1894.

The Great French Detective, in Austin—*A Successful Political Intrigue*

CHAPTER I   It is not generally known that Tictocq, the famous French detective, was in Austin last week. He registered at the Avenue Hotel under an assumed name, and his quiet and reserved manners singled him out at once for one not to be singled out.

No one knows why he came to Austin, but to one or two he vouchsafed the information that his mission was an important one from the French Government.

One report is that the French Minister of State has discovered an old statute among the laws of the empire, resulting from a treaty between the Emperor Charlemagne and Governor Roberts which expressly provides for the north gate of the Capital grounds being kept open, but this is merely a conjecture.

Last Wednesday afternoon a well-dressed gentleman knocked at the door of Tictocq's room in the hotel.

The detective opened the door.

"Monsieur Tictocq, I believe," said the gentleman.

"You will see on the register that I sign my name Q. X. Jones," said Tictocq, "and gentlemen would understand that I wish to be known as such. If you do not like being referred to as no gentleman, I will give you satisfaction any time after July 1st, and fight Steve O'Donnell, John McDonald, and Ignatius Donnelly in the meantime if you desire."

"I do not mind it in the least," said the gentleman. "In fact, I am accustomed to it. I am Chairman of the Democratic Executive Committee, Platform No. 2, and I have a friend in trouble. I knew you were Tictocq from your resemblance to yourself."

"Entrez vous," said the detective.

The gentleman entered and was handed a chair.

"I am a man of few words," said Tictocq. "I will help your friend if possible. Our countries are great friends. We have given you Lafayette and French fried potatoes. You have given us California champagne and —taken back Ward McAllister. State your case."

"I will be very brief," said the visitor. "In room No. 76 in this hotel is stopping a prominent Populist Candidate. He is alone. Last night some one stole his socks. They cannot be found. If they are not recovered, his party will attribute their loss to the Democracy. They will make great capital of the burglary, although I am sure it was not a political move at all. The socks must be recovered. You are the only man that can do it."

Tictocq bowed.

"Am I to have carte blanche to question every person connected with the hotel?"

"The proprietor has already been spoken to. Everything and everybody is at your service."

Tictocq consulted his watch.

"Come to this room to-morrow afternoon at 6 o'clock with the landlord, the Populist Candidate, and any other witnesses elected from both parties, and I will return the socks."

"Bien, Monsieur; schlafen sie wohl."

"Au revoir."

The Chairman of the Democratic Executive Committee, Platform No. 2, bowed courteously and withdrew.

Tictocq sent for the bell boy.

"Did you go to room 76 last night?"

"Yes, sir."

"Who was there?"

"An old hayseed what come on the 7:25."

"What did he want?"

"The bouncer."

"What for?"
"To put the light out."
"Did you take anything while in the room?"
"No, he didn't ask me."
"What is your name?"
"Jim."
"You can go."

CHAPTER II The drawing-rooms of one of the most magnificent private residences in Austin are a blaze of lights. Carriages line the streets in front, and from gate to doorway is spread a velvet carpet, on which the delicate feet of the guests may tread.

The occasion is the entrée into society of one of the fairest buds in the City of the Violet Crown. The rooms are filled with the culture, the beauty, the youth and fashion of society. Austin society is acknowledged to be the wittiest, the most select, and the highest bred to be found southwest of Kansas City.

Mrs. Rutabaga St. Vitus, the hostess, is accustomed to draw around her a circle of talent and beauty rarely equalled anywhere. Her evenings come nearer approaching the dignity of a salon than any occasion, except, perhaps, a Tony Faust and Marguerite reception at the Iron Front.

Miss St. Vitus, whose advent into society's maze was heralded by such an auspicious display of hospitality, is a slender brunette, with large, lustrous eyes, a winning smile, and a charming ingénue manner. She wears a china silk, cut princesse, with diamond ornaments, and a couple of towels inserted in the back to conceal prominence of shoulder blades. She is chatting easily and naturally on a plush-covered tête-à-tête with Harold St. Clair, the agent for a Minneapolis pants company. Her friend and schoolmate, Elsie Hicks, who married three drummers in one day, a week or two before, and won a wager of two dozen bottles of Budweiser from the handsome and talented young hack-driver, Bum Smithers, is promenading in and out the low French windows with Ethelbert Windup, the popular young candidate for hide inspector, whose name is familiar to every one who reads police court reports.

Somewhere, concealed by shrubbery, a band is playing, and during the pauses in conversation, onions can be smelt frying in the kitchen.

Happy laughter rings out from ruby lips, handsome faces grow tender as they bend over white necks and drooping heads; timid eyes convey things that lips dare not speak, and beneath silken bodice and broadcloth, hearts beat time to the sweet notes of "Love's Young Dream."

"And where have you been for some time past, you recreant cavalier?" says Miss St. Vitus to Harold St. Clair. "Have you been worshipping at another shrine? Are you recreant to your whilom friends? Speak, Sir Knight, and defend yourself."

"Oh, come off," says Harold, in his deep, musical baritone; "I've been having a devil of a time fitting pants on a lot of bow-legged jays from the cotton-patch. Got knobs on their legs, some of 'em big as gourds, and all expect a fit. Did you ever try to measure a bow-legged—I mean—can't you imagine what a jam-swizzled time I have getting pants to fit 'em? Business dull too, nobody wants 'em over three dollars."

"You witty boy," says Miss St. Vitus. "Just as full of bon mots and clever sayings as ever. What do you take now?"

"Oh, beer."

"Give me your arm and let's go into the drawing-room and draw a cork. I'm chewing a little cotton myself."

Arm in arm, the handsome couple pass across the room, the cynosure of all eyes. Luderic Hetherington, the rising and gifted night-watchman at the Lone Star slaughter house, and Mabel Grubb, the daughter of the millionaire owner of the Humped-backed Camel saloon, are standing under the oleanders as they go by.

"She is very beautiful," says Luderic.

"Rats," says Mabel.

A keen observer would have noted all this time the figure of a solitary man who seemed to avoid the company but by adroit changing of his position, and perfectly cool and self-possessed manner, avoided drawing any especial attention to himself.

The lion of the evening is Herr Professor Ludwig von Bum, the pianist.

He had been found drinking beer in a saloon on East Pecan Street by Colonel St. Vitus about a week before, and according to the Austin custom in such cases, was invited home by the colonel, and the next day accepted into society, with large music classes at his service.

Professor von Bum is playing the lovely symphony in G minor from Beethoven's "Songs Without Music." The grand chords fill the room with exquisite harmony. He glays the extremely difficult passages in the obligato home run in a masterly manner, and when he finishes with that grand te deum with arpeggios on the side, there is that complete hush in the room that is dearer to the artist's heart than the loudest applause.

The professor looks around.

The room is empty.

Empty with the exception of Tictocq, the great French detective, who springs from behind a mass of tropical plants to his side.

The professor rises in alarm.

"Hush," says Tictocq: "Make no noise at all. You have already made enough."

Footsteps are heard outside.

"Be quick," says Tictocq: "give me those socks. There is not a moment to spare."

"Vas sagst du?"

"Ah, he confesses," says Tictocq. "No socks will do but those you carried off from the Populist Candidate's room."

The company is returning, no longer hearing the music.

Tictocq hesitates not. He seizes the professor, throws him upon the floor, tears off his shoes and socks, and escapes with the latter through the open window into the garden.

CHAPTER III Tictocq's room in the Avenue Hotel.

A knock is heard at the door.

Tictocq opens it and looks at his watch.

"Ah," he says, "it is just six. Entrez, Messieurs."

The messieurs entrez. There are seven of them; the Populist Candidate who is there by invitation, not knowing for what purpose; the chairman of the Democratic Executive Committee, Platform No. 2; the hotel proprietor, and three or four Democrats and Populists, as near as could be found out.

"I don't know," begins the Populist Candidate, "what in the h——"

"Excuse me," says Tictocq, firmly. "You will oblige me by keeping silent until I make my report. I have been employed in this case, and I have unravelled it. For the honor of France I request that I be heard with attention."

"Certainly," says the chairman; "we will be pleased to listen."

Tictocq stands in the centre of the room. The electric light burns brightly above him. He seems the incarnation of alertness, vigor, cleverness, and cunning.

The company seat themselves in chairs along the wall.

"When informed of the robbery," begins Tictocq, "I first questioned the bell boy. He knew nothing. I went to the police headquarters. They knew nothing. I invited one of them to the bar to drink. He said there used to be a little colored boy in the Tenth Ward who stole things and kept them for recovery by the police, but failed to be at the place agreed upon for arrest one time, and had been sent to jail.

"I then began to think. I reasoned. No man, said I, would carry a Populist's socks in his pocket without wrapping them up. He would not want to do so in the hotel. He would want a paper. Where would he get one? At the *Statesman* office, of course. I went there. A young man with his hair combed down on his forehead sat behind the desk. I knew he was writing society items, for a young lady's slipper, a piece of cake, a fan, a half emptied bottle of cocktail, a bunch of roses, and a police whistle lay on the desk before him.

"Can you tell me if a man purchased a paper here in the last three months?" I said.

"Yes," he replied; "we sold one last night."

"Can you describe the man?"

"Accurately. He had blue whiskers, a wart between his shoulder blades, a touch of colic, and an occupation tax on his breath."

"Which way did he go?"

"Out."

"I then went——"

"Wait a minute," said the Populist Candidate, rising: "I don't see why in the h——"

"Once more I must beg that you will be silent," said Tictocq, rather sharply. "You should not interrupt me in the midst of my report."

"I made one false arrest," continued Tictocq. "I was passing two finely dressed gentlemen on the street, when one of them remarked that he had 'stole his socks.' I handcuffed him and dragged him to a lighted store, when his companion explained to me that he was somewhat intoxicated and his tongue was not entirely manageable. He had been speaking of some business transaction, and what he intended to say was that he had 'sold his stocks.'

"I then released him.

"An hour afterward I passed a saloon, and saw this Professor von Bum drinking beer at a table. I knew him in Paris. I said 'here is my man.' He worshipped Wagner, lived on limburger cheese, beer, and credit, and would have stolen anybody's socks. I shadowed him to the reception at Colonel St. Vitus's, and in an opportune moment I seized him and tore the socks from his feet. There they are."

With a dramatic gesture, Tictocq threw a pair of dingy socks upon the table, folded his arms, and threw back his head.

With a loud cry of rage, the Populist Candidate sprang once more to his feet.

"Gol darn it! I WILL say what I want to. I——"

The two other Populists in the room gazed at him coldly and sternly.

"Is this tale true?" they demanded of the Candidate.

"No, by gosh, it ain't!" he replied, pointing a trembling finger at the Democratic Chairman. "There stands the man who has concocted the whole scheme. It is an infernal, unfair political trick to lose votes for our party. How far has this thing gone?" he added, turning savagely to the detective.

"All the newspapers have my written report on the matter, and the *Statesman* will have it in plate matter next week," said Tictocq, complacently.

"All is lost!" said the Populists, turning toward the door.

"For God's sake, my friends," pleaded the Candidate, following them; "listen to me; I swear before high heaven that I never wore a pair of socks in my life. It is all a devilish campaign lie."

The Populists turn their backs.

"The damage is already done," they said. "The people have heard the story. You have yet time to withdraw decently before the race."

All left the room except Tictocq and the Democrats.

"Let's all go down and open a bottle of fizz on the Finance Committee," said the Chairman of the Executive Committee, Platform No. 2.

TRACKED TO DOOM

or The Mystery of the Rue de Peychaud

'Tis midnight in Paris.

A myriad of lamps that line the Champs Élysées and the Rouge et Noir, cast their reflection in the dark waters of the Seine as it flows gloomily past the Place Vendôme and the black walls of the Convent Notadam.

The great French capital is astir.

It is the hour when crime and vice and wickedness reign.

Hundreds of fiacres drive madly through the streets conveying women, flashing with jewels and as beautiful as dreams, from opera and concert, and the little bijou supper rooms of the Café Tout le Temps are filled with laughing groups, while bon mots, persiflage, and repartee fly upon the air—the jewels of thought and conversation.

Luxury and poverty brush each other in the streets. The homeless gamin, begging a sou with which to purchase a bed, and the spendthrift roué, scattering golden louis d'or, tread the same pavement.

When other cities sleep, Paris has just begun her wild revelry.

The first scene of our story is a cellar beneath the Rue de Peychaud.

The room is filled with smoke of pipes, and is stifling with the reeking breath of its inmates. A single flaring gas jet dimly lights the scene, which is one Rembrandt or Moreland and Keisel would have loved to paint.

A garçon is selling absinthe to such of the motley crowd as have a few sous, dealing it out in niggardly portions in broken teacups.

Leaning against the bar is Carnaignole Cusheau—generally known as the Gray Wolf.

He is the worst man in Paris.

He is more than four feet ten in height, and his sharp, ferocious-looking face and the mass of long, tangled gray hair that covers his face and head, have earned for him the name he bears.

His striped blouse is wide open at the neck and falls outside of his dingy leather trousers. The handle of a deadly looking knife protrudes from his belt. One stroke of its blade would open a box of the finest French sardines.

"Voilà, Gray Wolf," cries Couteau, the bartender. "How many victims to-day? There is no blood upon your hands. Has the Gray Wolf forgotten how to bite?"

"Sacré Bleu, Mille Tonnerre, by George," hisses the Gray Wolf. "Monsieur Couteau, you are bold indeed to speak to me thus.

"By Ventre St. Gris! I have not even dined to-day. Spoils indeed. There is no living in Paris now. But one rich American have I garroted in a fortnight.

"Bah! those Democrats. They have ruined the country. With their income tax and their free trade, they have destroyed the millionaire business. Carrambo! Diable! D—n it!"

"Hist!" suddenly says Chamounix the rag-picker, who is worth 20,-000,000 francs, "some one comes!"

The cellar door opened and a man crept softly down the rickety steps. The crowd watches him with silent awe.

He went to the bar, laid his card on the counter, bought a drink of absinthe, and then drawing from his pocket a little mirror, set it up on the counter and proceeded to don a false beard and hair and paint his face into wrinkles, until he closely resembled an old man seventy-one years of age.

He then went into a dark corner and watched the crowd of people with sharp, ferret-like eyes.

Gray Wolf slipped cautiously to the bar and examined the card left by the newcomer.

"Holy Saint Bridget!" he exclaims. "It is Tictocq, the detective."

Ten minutes later a beautiful woman enters the cellar.

Tenderly nurtured, and accustomed to every luxury that money could procure, she had, when a young vivandière at the Convent of Saint Susan de la Moutarde, run away with the Gray Wolf, fascinated by his many crimes and the knowledge that his business never allowed him to scrape his feet in the hall or snore.

"Parbleau, Marie," snarls the Gray Wolf. "Que voulez vous? Avez-vous le beau cheval de mon frère, ou le joli chien de votre père?"

"No, no, Gray Wolf," shouts the motley group of assassins, rogues, and pickpockets, even their hardened hearts appalled at his fearful words. "Mon Dieu! You cannot be so cruel!"

"Tiens!" shouts the Gray Wolf, now maddened to desperation, and drawing his gleaming knife. "Voilà! Canaille! Tout le monde, carte blanche embonpoint sauve que peut entre nous revenez nous a nous moutons!"

The horrified sans-culottes shrink back in terror as the Gray Wolf seizes Marie by the hair and cuts her into twenty-nine pieces, each exactly the same size.

As he stands with reeking hands above the corpse, amid a deep silence, the old, gray-bearded man who has been watching the scene springs forward, tears off his false beard and locks, and Tictocq, the famous French detective, stands before them.

Spellbound and immovable, the denizens of the cellar gaze at the greatest modern detective as he goes about the customary duties of his office.

He first measures the distance from the murdered woman to a point on the wall, then he takes down the name of the bartender and the day of the month and the year. Then drawing from his pocket a powerful microscope, he examines a little of the blood that stands upon the floor in little pools.

"Mon Dieu!" he mutters, "it is as I feared—human blood."

He then enters rapidly in a memorandum book the result of his investigations, and leaves the cellar.

Tictocq bends his rapid steps in the direction of the headquarters of the Paris gendarmerie, but suddenly pausing, he strikes his hand upon his brow with a gesture of impatience.

"Mille tonnerre," he mutters. "I should have asked the name of that man with the knife in his hand."

It is reception night at the palace of the Duchess Valerie du Bellairs.

The apartments are flooded with a mellow light from paraffine candles in solid silver candelabra.

The company is the most aristocratic and wealthy in Paris.

Three or four brass bands are playing behind a portière between the coal shed, and also behind time. Footmen in gay-laced livery bring in beer noiselessly and carry out apple-peelings dropped by the guests.

Valerie, seventh Duchess du Bellairs, leans back on a solid gold ottoman on eiderdown cushions, surrounded by the wittiest, the bravest, and the handsomest courtiers in the capital.

"Ah, madame," said the Prince Champvilliers, of Palais Royale, corner of Seventy-third Street, "as Montesquiaux says, 'Rien de plus bon tutti frutti'—Youth seems your inheritance. You are to-night the most beautiful, the wittiest in your own salon. I can scarce believe my own senses, when I remember that thirty-one years ago you——"

"Saw it off!" says the Duchess, peremptorily.

The Prince bows low, and drawing a jewelled dagger, stabs himself to the heart.

"The displeasure of your grace is worse than death," he says, as he takes his overcoat and hat from a corner of the mantelpiece and leaves the room.

"Voilà," says Bèebè Françillon, fanning herself languidly. "That is the way with men. Flatter them, and they kiss your hand. Loose but a moment the silken leash that holds them captive through their vanity and self-opinionativeness, and the son-of-a-gun gets on his ear at once. The devil go with him, I say."

"Ah, mon Princesse," sighs the Count Pumpernickel, stooping and whispering with eloquent eyes into her ear. "You are too hard upon us. Balzac says, 'All women are not to themselves what no one else is to another.' Do you not agree with him?"

"Cheese it!" says the Princess. "Philosophy palls upon me. I'll shake you."

"Hosses?" says the Count.

Arm and arm they go out to the salon au Beurre.

Armande de Fleury, the young pianissimo danseuse from the Folies Bergère, is about to sing.

She slightly clears her throat and lays a voluptuous cud of chewing gum upon the piano as the first notes of the accompaniment ring through the salon.

As she prepares to sing, the Duchess du Bellairs grasps the arm of her ottoman in a vicelike grip, and she watches with an expression of almost anguished suspense.

She scarcely breathes.

Then, as Armande de Fleury, before uttering a note, reels, wavers, turns white as snow and falls dead upon the floor, the Duchess breathes a sigh of relief.

The Duchess had poisoned her.

Then the guests crowd about the piano, gazing with bated breath, and shuddering as they look upon the music rack and observe that the song that Armande came so near singing is "Sweet Marie."

Twenty minutes later a dark and muffled figure was seen to emerge from a recess in the mullioned wall of the Arc de Triomphe and pass rapidly northward.

It was no other than Tictocq, the detective.

The network of evidence was fast being drawn about the murderer of Marie Cusheau.

It is midnight on the steeple of the Cathedral of Notadam.

It is also the same time at other given points in the vicinity.

The spire of the Cathedral is 20,000 feet above the pavement, and a casual observer, by making a rapid mathematical calculation, would have readily perceived that this Cathedral is, at least, double the height of others that measure only 10,000 feet.

At the summit of the spire there is a little wooden platform on which there is room for but one man to stand.

Crouching on this precarious footing, which swayed dizzily with every breeze that blew, was a man closely muffled, and disguised as a wholesale grocer.

Old François Beongfallong, the great astronomer, who is studying the sidereal spheres from his attic window in the Rue de Bologny, shudders as he turns his telescope upon the solitary figure upon the spire.

"Sacré Bleu!" he hisses between his new celluloid teeth. "It is Tictocq, the detective. I wonder whom he is following now?"

While Tictocq is watching with lynx-like eyes the hill of Montmartre, he suddenly hears a heavy breathing beside him, and turning gazes into the ferocious eyes of the Gray Wolf.

Carnaignole Cusheau had put on his W. U. Tel. Co. climbers and climbed the steeple.

"Parbleu, monsieur," says Tictocq. "To whom am I indebted for the honor of this visit?"

The Gray Wolf smiled softly and depreciatingly.

"You are Tictocq, the detective?" he said.

"I am."

"Then listen. I am the murderer of Marie Cusheau. She was my wife and she had cold feet and ate onions. What was I to do? Yet life is sweet to me. I do not wish to be guillotined. I have heard that you are on my track. Is it true that the case is in your hands?"

"It is."

"Thank le bon Dieu, then, I am saved."

The Gray Wolf carefully adjusts the climbers on his feet and descends the spire.

Tictocq takes out his notebook and writes in it.

"At last," he says, "I have a clue."

Monsieur le Compte Carnaignole Cusheau, once known as the Gray Wolf, stands in the magnificent drawing-room of his palace on East 47th Street.

Three days after his confession to Tictocq, he happened to look in the pockets of a discarded pair of pants and found twenty million francs in gold.

Suddenly the door opens and Tictocq, the detective, with a dozen gens d'arme, enters the room.

"You are my prisoner," says the detective.

"On what charge?"

"The murder of Marie Cusheau on the night of August 17th."

"Your proofs?"

"I saw you do it, and your own confession on the spire of Notadam."

The Count laughed and took a paper from his pocket.

"Read this," he said, "here is proof that Marie Cusheau died of heart failure."

Tictocq looked at the paper.

It was a check for 100,000 francs.

Tictocq dismissed the gens d'arme with a wave of his hand.

"We have made a mistake, monsieurs," he said, but as he turns to leave the room, Count Carnaignole stops him.

"One moment, monsieur."

The Count Carnaignole tears from his own face a false beard and reveals the flashing eyes and well-known features of Tictocq, the detective.

Then, springing forward, he snatches a wig and false eyebrows from his visitor, and the Gray Wolf, grinding his teeth in rage, stands before him.

The murderer of Marie Cusheau was never discovered.

A SNAPSHOT AT THE PRESIDENT

This is the kind of waggish editorial O. Henry was writing in 1894 for the readers of the *Rolling Stone*. The reader will do well to remember that the paper was for local consumption and that the allusions are to a very special place and time.

(It will be remembered that about a month ago there were special rates offered to the public for a round trip to the City of Washington. The price of the ticket being exceedingly low, we secured a loan of twenty dollars from a public-spirited citizen of Austin, by mortgaging our press and cow, with the additional security of our brother's name and a slight draught on Major Hutchinson for $4,000.

We purchased a round trip ticket, two loaves of Vienna bread, and quite a large piece of cheese, which we handed to a member of our reportorial staff, with instructions to go to Washington, interview President Cleveland, and get a scoop, if possible, on all other Texas papers.

Our reporter came in yesterday morning, via the Manor dirt road, with a large piece of folded cotton bagging tied under each foot.

It seems that he lost his ticket in Washington, and having divided the Vienna bread and cheese with some disappointed office seekers who were coming home by the same route, he arrived home hungry, desiring food, and with quite an appetite.

Although somewhat late, we give his description of his interview with President Cleveland.)

I am chief reporter on the staff of the *Rolling Stone*.

About a month ago the managing editor came into the room where we were both sitting engaged in conversation and said:

"Oh, by the way, go to Washington and interview President Cleveland."

"All right," said I. "Take care of yourself."

Five minutes later I was seated in a palatial drawing-room car bounding up and down quite a good deal on the elastic plush-covered seat.

I shall not linger upon the incidents of the journey. I was given carte blanche to provide myself with every comfort, and to spare no expense that I could meet. For the regalement of my inside the preparations had been lavish. Both Vienna and Germany had been called upon to furnish dainty viands suitable to my palate.

I changed cars and shirts once only on the journey. A stranger wanted me to also change a two-dollar bill, but I haughtily declined.

The scenery along the entire road to Washington is diversified. You find a portion of it on one hand by looking out of the window, and upon turning the gaze upon the other side the eye is surprised and delighted to discovering some more of it.

There were a great many Knights of Pythias on the train. One of them insisted upon my giving him the grip I had with me, but he was unsuccessful.

On arriving in Washington, which city I instantly recognized from reading the history of George, I left the car so hastily that I forgot to fee Mr. Pullman's representative.

I went immediately to the Capitol.

In a spirit of jew d'esprit I had made a globular representation of a "rolling stone." It was of wood, painted a dark color, and about the size of a small cannon ball. I had attached to it a twisted pendant about three inches long to indicate moss. I had resolved to use this in place of a card, thinking people would readily recognize it as an emblem of my paper.

I had studied the arrangement of the Capitol, and walked directly to Mr. Cleveland's private office.

I met a servant in the hall, and held up my card to him smilingly.

I saw his hair rise on his head, and he ran like a deer to the door, and, lying down, rolled down the long flight of steps into the yard.

"Ah," said I to myself, "he is one of our delinquent subscribers."

A little farther along I met the President's private secretary, who had been writing a tariff letter and cleaning a duck gun for Mr. Cleveland.

When I showed him the emblem of my paper he sprang out of a high window into a hothouse filled with rare flowers.

This somewhat surprised me.

I examined myself. My hat was on straight, and there was nothing at all alarming about my appearance.

I went into the President's private office.

He was alone. He was conversing with Tom Ochiltree. Mr. Ochiltree saw my little sphere, and with a loud scream rushed out of the room.

President Cleveland slowly turned his eyes upon me.

He also saw what I had in my hand, and said in a husky voice:

"Wait a moment, please."

He searched his coat pocket, and presently found a piece of paper on which some words were written.

He laid this on his desk and rose to his feet, raised one hand above him, and said in deep tones:

"I die for Free Trade, my country, and—and—all that sort of thing."

I saw him jerk a string, and a camera snapped on another table, taking our picture as we stood.

"Don't die in the House, Mr. President," I said. "Go over into the Senate Chamber."

"Peace, murderer!" he said. "Let your bomb do its deadly work."

"I'm no bum," I said, with spirit. "I represent the *Rolling Stone* of Austin, Texas, and this I hold in my hand does the same thing, but, it seems unsuccessfully."

The President sank back in his chair greatly relieved.

"I thought you were a dynamiter," he said. "Let me see; Texas! Texas!" He walked to a large wall map of the United States, and placing his finger thereon at about the location of Idaho, ran it down in a zigzag, doubtful way until he reached Texas.

"Oh, yes, here it is. I have so many things on my mind, I sometimes forget what I should know well.

"Let's see; Texas? Oh, yes, that's the State where Ida Wells and a lot of colored people lynched a socialist named Hogg for raising a riot at a camp-meeting. So you are from Texas. I know a man from Texas named Dave Culberson. How is Dave and his family? Has Dave got any children?"

"He has a boy in Austin," I said, "working around the Capitol."

"Who is President of Texas now?"

"I don't exactly——"

"Oh excuse me. I forgot again. I thought I heard some talk of its having been made a Republic again."

"Now, Mr. Cleveland," I said, "you answer some of my questions."

A curious film came over the President's eyes. He sat stiffly in his chair like an automaton.

"Proceed," he said.

"What do you think of the political future of this country?"

"I will state that political exigencies demand emergentistical promptitude, and while the United States is indissoluble in conception and invisible in intent, treason and internecine disagreement have ruptured the consanguinity of patriotism, and——"

"One moment, Mr. President," I interrupted; "would you mind changing that cylinder? I could have gotten all that from the American Press Association if I had wanted plate matter. Do you wear flannels? What is your favorite poet, brand of catsup, bird, flower, and what are you going to do when you are out of a job?"

"Young man," said Mr. Cleveland, sternly, "you are going a little too far. My private affairs do not concern the public."

I begged his pardon, and he recovered his good humor in a moment.

"You Texans have a great representative in Senator Mills," he said. "I think the greatest two speeches I ever heard were his address before the Senate advocating the removal of the tariff on salt and increasing it on the chloride of sodium."

"Tom Ochiltree is also from our State," I said.

"Oh, no, he isn't. You must be mistaken," replied Mr. Cleveland, "for he says he is. I really must go down to Texas some time, and see the State. I want to go up into the Panhandle and see if it is really shaped like it is on the map."

"Well, I must be going," said I.

"When you get back to Texas," said the President, rising, "you must write to me. Your visit has awakened in me quite an interest in your State which I fear I have not given the attention it deserves. There are many historical and otherwise interesting places that you have revived in my recollection—the Alamo, where Davy Jones fell; Goliad, Sam Houston's surrender to Montezuma, the petrified boom found near Austin, five-cent cotton and the Siamese Democratic platform born in Dallas. I should so much like to see the gals in Galveston, and go to the wake in Waco. I am glad I met you. Turn to the left as you enter the hall and keep straight on out." I made a low bow to signify that the interview was at an end, and withdrew immediately. I had no difficulty in leaving the building as soon as I was outside.

I hurried downtown in order to obtain refreshments at some place where viands had been placed upon the free list.

I shall not describe my journey back to Austin. I lost my return ticket somewhere in the White House, and was forced to return home in a manner not especially beneficial to my shoes. Everybody was well in Washington when I left, and all send their love.

AN UNFINISHED CHRISTMAS STORY

Now, a Christmas story should be one. For a good many years the ingenious writers have been putting forth tales for the holiday numbers that employed every subtle, evasive, indirect, and strategic scheme they could invent to disguise the Christmas flavor. So far has this new practice been carried that nowadays when you read a story in a holiday magazine the only way you can tell it is a Christmas story is to look at the footnote which reads: ["The incidents in the above story happened on December 25th.—ED."]

There is progress in this; but it is all very sad. There are just as many real Christmas stories as ever, if we would only dig 'em up. Me, I am for the Scrooge and Marley Christmas story, and the Annie and Willie's prayer poem, and the long lost son coming home on the stroke of twelve to the poorly thatched cottage with his arms full of talking dolls and popcorn balls and—Zip! you hear the second mortgage on the cottage go flying off it into the deep snow.

So, this is to warn you that there is no subterfuge about this story— and you might come upon stockings hung to the mantel and plum puddings and hark! the chimes! and wealthy misers loosening up and handing over penny whistles to lame newsboys if you read further.

Once I knocked at a door (I have so many things to tell you I keep on losing sight of the story). It was the front door of a furnished room house in West 'Teenth Street. I was looking for a young illustrator named Paley originally and irrevocably from Terre Haute. Paley doesn't enter even into the first serial rights of this Christmas story; I mention him simply in explaining why I came to knock at the door—some people have so much curiosity.

The door was opened by the landlady. I had seen hundreds like her. And I had smelled before that cold, dank, furnished draught of air that hurried by her to escape immurement in the furnished house.

She was stout, and her face and hands were as white as though she had been drowned in a barrel of vinegar. One hand held together at her throat a buttonless flannel dressing sacque whose lines had been cut by no tape or butterick known to mortal woman. Beneath this a too long, flowered, black sateen skirt was draped about her, reaching the floor in stiff wrinkles and folds.

The rest of her was yellow. Her hair, in some bygone age, had been dipped in the fountain of folly presided over by the merry nymph Hydrogen; but now, except at the roots, it had returned to its natural grim and grizzled white.

Her eyes and teeth and finger nails were yellow. Her chops hung low and shook when she moved. The look on her face was exactly that smileless look of fatal melancholy that you may have seen on the countenance of a hound left sitting on the doorstep of a deserted cabin.

I inquired for Paley. After a long look of cold suspicion the landlady spoke, and her voice matched the dingy roughness of her flannel sacque.

Paley? Was I sure that was the name? And wasn't it, likely, Mr. Sanderson I meant, in the third floor rear? No; it was Paley I wanted. Again that frozen, shrewd, steady study of my soul from her pale-yellow, unwinking eyes, trying to penetrate my mask of deception and rout out my true motives from my lying lips. There was a Mr. Tompkins in the front hall bedroom two flights up. Perhaps it was he I was seeking. He worked of nights; he never came in till seven in the morning. Or if it was really Mr. Tucker (thinly disguised as Paley) that I was hunting I would have to call between five and——

But no; I held firmly to Paley. There was no such name among her lodgers. Click! the door closed swiftly in my face; and I heard through the panels the clanking of chains and bolts.

I went down the steps and stopped to consider. The number of this house was 43. I was sure Paley had said 43—or perhaps it was 45 or 47—I decided to try 47, the second house farther along.

I rang the bell. The door opened; and there stood the same woman. I wasn't confronted by just a resemblance—it was the *same* woman holding together the same old sacque at her throat and looking at me with the same yellow eyes as if she had never seen me before on earth. I saw on the knuckle of her second finger the same red-and-black spot made, probably, by a recent burn against a hot stove.

I stood speechless and gaping while one with moderate haste might have told fifty. I couldn't have spoken Paley's name even if I had remembered it. I did the only thing that a brave man who believes there are mysterious forces in nature that we do not yet fully comprehend could have done in the circumstances. I backed down the steps to the sidewalk and then hurried away frontward, fully understanding how incidents like that must bother the psychical research people and the census takers.

Of course I heard an explanation of it afterward, as we always do about inexplicable things.

The landlady was Mrs. Kannon; and she leased three adjoining houses, which she made into one by cutting arched doorways through the walls. She sat in the middle house and answered the three bells.

I wonder why I have maundered so slowly through the prologue. I have it! it was simply to say to you, in the form of introduction rife through the Middle West: "Shake hands with Mrs. Kannon."

For, it was in her triple house that the Christmas story happened; and it was there where I picked up the incontrovertible facts from the gossip of many roomers and met Stickney—and saw the necktie.

Christmas came that year on Thursday, and snow came with it.

Stickney (Harry Clarence Fowler Stickney to whomsoever his full baptismal cognominal burdens may be of interest) reached his address at six-thirty Wednesday afternoon. "Address" is New Yorkese for "Home." Stickney roomed at 45 West 'Teenth Street, third floor rear hall room. He was twenty years and four months old, and he worked in a cameras-of-all-kinds, photographic supplies and films-developed store. I don't know what kind of work he did in the store; but you must have seen him. He is the young man who always comes behind the counter to wait on you and lets you talk for five minutes, telling him what you want. When you are done, he calls the proprietor at the top of his voice to wait on you, and walks away whistling between his teeth.

I don't want to bother about describing to you his appearance; but, if you are a man reader, I will say that Stickney looked precisely like the young chap that you always find sitting in your chair smoking a cigarette after you have missed a shot while playing pool—not billiards, but pool— when you want to sit down yourself.

There are some to whom Christmas gives no Christmassy essence. Of course, prosperous people and comfortable people who have homes or flats or rooms with meals, and even people who live in apartment houses with hotel service get something of the Christmas flavor. They give one another presents with the cost mark scratched off with a penknife; and they hang holly wreaths in the front windows, and when they are asked whether they prefer light or dark meat from the turkey they say: "Both, please," and giggle and have lots of fun. And the very poorest people have the best time of it. The Army gives 'em a dinner, and the 10 A.M. issue of the Night Final edition of the newspaper with the largest circulation in the city leaves a basket at their door full of an apple, a Lake Ronkonkoma squab, a scrambled eggplant, and a bunch of Kalamazoo bleached parsley. The poorer you are the more Christmas does for you.

But, I'll tell you to what kind of a mortal Christmas seems to be only the day before the twenty-sixth day of December. It's the chap in the big city earning sixteen dollars a week, with no friends and few acquaintances, who finds himself with only fifty cents in his pocket on Christmas eve. He can't accept charity; he can't borrow; he knows no one who would invite him to dinner. I have a fancy that when the shepherds left their flocks to follow the star of Bethlehem there was a bandy-legged young fellow among them who was just learning the sheep business. So they said to him, "Bobby, we're going to investigate this star route and see what's in it. If it should turn out to be the first Christmas day we don't want to miss it. And, as you are not a wise man, and as you couldn't possibly purchase a present to take along, suppose you stay behind and mind the sheep." So as we may say, Harry Stickney was a direct descendant of the shepherd who was left behind to take care of the flocks.

Getting back to facts, Stickney rang the door-bell of 45. He had a habit of forgetting his latchkey.

Instantly the door opened and there stood Mrs. Kannon, clutching her sacque together at the throat and gorgonizing him with her opaque yellow eyes.

(To give you good measure, here is a story within a story. Once a roomer in 47 who had a Scotch habit, not kilts, but a habit of drinking Scotch—began to figure to himself what might happen if two persons should ring the doorbells of 43 and 47 at the same time. Visions of two halves of Mrs. Kannon appearing respectively and simultaneously at the two entrances, each clutching at a side of an open, flapping sacque that could never meet, overpowered him. Bellevue got him.)

"Evening," said Stickney cheerlessly, as he distributed little piles of muddy slush along the hall matting. "Think we'll have snow?"

"You left your key," said——

(Here the manuscript ends.)

THE UNPROFITABLE SERVANT

I am the richer by the acquaintance of four newspaper men. Singly, they are my encyclopedias, friends, mentors, and sometimes bankers. But now and then it happens that all of them will pitch upon the same print-worthy incident of the passing earthly panorama and will send in reportorial constructions thereof to their respective journals. It is then that, for me, it is to laugh. For it seems that to each of them, trained and skilled as he may be, the same occurrence presents a different facet of the cut diamond, life.

One will have it (let us say) that Mme. André Macarté's apartment was looted by six burglars, who descended via the fire-escape and bore away a ruby tiara valued at two thousand dollars and a five-hundred-dollar prize Spitz dog, which (in violation of the expectoration ordinance) was making free with the halls of the Wutta-pesituckquesunoo-wetunquah Apartments.

My second "chiel" will take notes to the effect that while a friendly game of pinochle was in progress in the tenement rooms of Mrs. Andy McCarty, a lady guest named Ruby O'Hara threw a burglar down six flights of stairs, where he was pinioned and held by a two-thousand-dollar English bulldog amid a crowd of five hundred excited spectators.

My third chronicler and friend will gather the news threats of the happening in his own happy way; setting forth on the page for you to read that the house of Antonio Macartini was blown up at 6 A.M., by the Black Hand Society, on his refusing to leave two thousand dollars at a certain street corner, killing a pet five-hundred-dollar Pomeranian belonging to Alderman Rubitara's little daughter (see photo and diagram opposite).

Number four of my history-makers will simply construe from the premises the story that while an audience of two thousand enthusiasts was listening to a Rubinstein concert on Sixth Street, a woman who said she was Mrs. Andrew M. Carter threw a brick through a plate-glass window valued at five hundred dollars. The Carter woman claimed that some one in the building had stolen her dog.

Now, the discrepancies in these registrations of the day's doings need do no one hurt. Surely, one newspaper is enough for any man to prop against his morning water-bottle to fend off the smiling hatred of his wife's glance. If he be foolish enough to read four he is no wiser than a Higher Critic.

I remember (probably as well as you do) having read the parable of the talents. A prominent citizen, about to journey into a far country, first hands over to his servants his goods. To one he gives five talents; to another two; to another one—to every man according to his several ability, as the text has it. There are two versions of this parable, as you well know. There may be more—I do not know.

When the p. c. returns he requires an accounting. Two servants have put their talents out at usury and gained one hundred per cent. Good. The unprofitable one simply digs up the talent deposited with him and hands it out on demand. A pattern of behavior for trust companies and banks, surely! In one version we read that he had wrapped it in a napkin and laid it away. But the commentator informs us that the talent mentioned was composed of 750 ounces of silver—about $900 worth. So the chronicler who mentioned the napkin had either to reduce the amount of the deposit or do a lot of explaining about the size of the napery used in those days. Therefore in his version we note that he uses the word "pound" instead of "talent."

A pound of silver may very well be laid away—and carried away—in a napkin, as any hotel or restaurant man will tell you.

But let us get away from our mutton.

When the returned nobleman finds that the one-talented servant has nothing to hand over except the original fund entrusted to him, he is as angry as a multi-millionaire would be if some one should hide under his bed and make a noise like an assessment. He orders the unprofitable servant cast into outer darkness, after first taking away his talent and giving it to the one-hundred-per-cent. financier, and breathing strange saws, saying: "From him that hath not shall be taken away even that which he hath." Which is the same as to say: "Nothing from nothing leaves nothing."

And now closer draw the threads of parable, precept, allegory, and narrative, leading nowhere if you will, or else weaving themselves into the little fiction story about Cliff McGowan and his one talent. There is but a definition to follow; and then the homely actors trip on.

Talent: A gift, endowment, or faculty; some peculiar ability, power, or accomplishment, natural or acquired. (A metaphor borrowed from the parable in Matt. XXV, 14–30.)

In New York City to-day there are (estimated) 125,000 living creatures training for the stage. This does not include seals, pigs, dogs, elephants, prizefighters, Carmens, mind-readers, or Japanese wrestlers. The bulk of them are in the ranks of the Four Million. Out of this number will survive a thousand.

Nine hundred of these will have attained their fulness of fame when they shall dubiously indicate with the point of a hatpin a blurred figure in a flashlight photograph of a stage tout ensemble with the proud commentary: "That's me."

Eighty, in the pinkest of (male) Louis XIV court costumes, shall welcome the Queen of the (mythical) Pawpaw Isles in a few well-memorized words, turning a tip-tilted nose upon the nine hundred.

Ten, in tiny lace caps, shall dust Ibsen furniture for six minutes after the rising of the curtain.

Nine shall attain the circuits, besieging with muscle, skill, eye, hand, voice, wit, brain, heel, and toe the ultimate high walls of stardom.

One shall inherit Broadway. Sic venit gloria mundi.

Cliff McGowan and Mac McGowan were cousins. They lived on the West Side and were talented. Singing, dancing, imitations, trick bicycle riding, boxing, German and Irish dialect comedy, and a little sleight-of-hand and balancing of wheat straws and wheelbarrows on the ends of their chins came as easy to them as it is for you to fix your rat so it won't show or to dodge a creditor through the swinging-doors of a well-lighted café—according as you may belong to the one or the other division of the greatest prestidigitators—the people. They were slim, pale, consummately self-possessed youths, whose fingernails were always irreproachably (and clothes seams reproachfully) shiny. Their conversation was in sentences so short that they made Kipling's seem as long as court citations.

Having the temperament, they did no work. Any afternoon you could find them on Eighth Avenue either in front of Spinelli's barber shop, Mike Dugan's place, or the Limerick Hotel, rubbing their forefinger nails with dingy silk handkerchiefs. At any time, if you had happened to be standing, undecisive, near a pool-table, and Cliff and Mac had, casually, as it were, drawn near, mentioning something, disinterestedly, about a game, well, indeed, would it have been for you had you gone your way, unresponsive. Which assertion, carefully considered, is a study in tense, punctuation, and advice to strangers.

Of all kinships it is likely that the closest is that of cousin. Between cousins there exist the ties of race, name, and favor—ties thicker than water, and yet not coagulated with the jealous precipitations of brotherhood or the enjoining obligations of the matrimonial yoke. You can bestow upon a cousin almost the interest and affection that you would give to a stranger; you need not feel toward him the contempt and embarrassment that you have for one of your father's sons—it is the closer clan-feelings that sometimes makes the branch of a tree stronger than its trunk.

Thus were the two McGowans bonded. They enjoyed a quiet celebrity in their district, which was a strip west of Eight Avenue with the Pump for its pivot. Their talents were praised in a hundred "joints"; their friendship was famed even in a neighborhood where men had been known to fight off the wives of their friends—when domestic onslaught was being made upon their friends by the wives of their friends. (Thus do the limitations of English force us to repetends.)

So, side by side, grim, sallow, lowering, inseparable, undefeated, the cousins fought their way into the temple of Art—art with a big A, which causes to intervene a lesson in geometry.

One night at about eleven o'clock Del Delano dropped into Mike's place on Eighth Avenue. From that moment, instead of remaining a Place, the café became a Resort. It was as though King Edward had condescended to mingle with ten-spots of a different suit; or Joe Gans had casually strolled in to look over the Tuskegee School; or Mr. Shaw, of England, had accepted an invitation to read selections from "Rena the Snow-Bird" at an unveiling of the proposed monument to James Owen O'Connor at Chinquapin Falls, Mississippi. In spite of these comparisons, you will have to be told why the patronizing of a third-rate saloon on the West Side by the said Del Delano conferred such a specific honor upon the place.

Del Delano could not make his feet behave; and so the world paid him $300 a week to see them misconduct themselves on the vaudeville stage. To make the matter plain to you (and to swell the number of words), he was the best fancy dancer on any of the circuits between Ottawa and Corpus Christi. With his eyes fixed on vacancy and his feet apparently fixed on nothing, he "nightly charmed thousands," as his press-agent incorrectly stated. Even taking night performance and matinée together, he scarcely could have charmed more than eighteen hundred, including those who left after Zora, the Nautch girl, had squeezed herself through a hoop twelve inches in diameter, and those who were waiting for the moving pictures.

But Del Delano was the West Side's favorite; and nowhere is there a more loyal Side. Five years before our story was submitted to the editors, Del had crawled from some Tenth Avenue basement like a lean rat and had bitten his way into the Big Cheese. Patched, half starved, cuffless, and as scornful of the Hook as an interpreter of Ibsen, he had danced his way into health (as you and I view it) and fame in sixteen minutes on Amateur Night at Creary's (Variety) Theatre in Eighth Avenue. A bookmaker (one of the kind that talent wins with instead of losing) sat in the audience, asleep, dreaming of an impossible pick-up among the amateurs. After a snore, a glass of beer from the handsome waiter, and a temporary blindness caused by the diamonds of a transmontane blonde in Box E, the bookmaker woke up long enough to engage Del Delano for a three-weeks' trial engagement fused with a trained-dog short-circuit covering the three Washingtons—Heights, Statue, and Square.

THE UNPROFITABLE SERVANT   1037

By the time this story was read and accepted, Del Delano was drawing his three hundred dollars a week, which, divided by seven (Sunday acts not in costume being permissible), dispels the delusion entertained by most of us that we have seen better days. You can easily imagine the worshipful agitation of Eighth Avenue whenever Del Delano honored it with a visit after his terpsichorean act in a historically great and vilely ventilated Broadway theatre. If the West Side could claim forty-two minutes out of his forty-two weeks' bookings every year, it was an occasion for bonfires and repainting of the Pump. And now you know why Mike's saloon is a Resort, and no longer a simple Place.

Del Delano entered Mike's alone. So nearly concealed in a fur-lined overcoat and a derby two sizes too large for him was Prince Lightfoot that you saw of his face only his pale, hatchet-edged features and a pair of unwinking, cold, light blue eyes. Nearly every man lounging at Mike's bar recognized the renowned product of the West Side. To those who did not, wisdom was conveyed by prodding elbows and growls of one-sided introduction.

Upon Charley, one of the bartenders, both fame and fortune descended simultaneously. He had once been honored by shaking hands with the great Delano at a Seventh Avenue boxing bout. So with lungs of brass he now cried: "Hello, Del, old man; what'll it be?"

Mike, the proprietor, who was cranking the cash register, heard. On the next day he raised Charley's wages five a week.

Del Delano drank a pony beer, paying for it carelessly out of his nightly earnings of $42.85 5/7. He nodded amiably but coldly at the long line of Mike's patrons and strolled past them into the rear room of the café. For he heard in there sounds pertaining to his own art—the light, stirring staccato of a buck-and-wing dance.

In the back room Mac McGowan was giving a private exhibition of the genius of his feet. A few young men sat at tables looking on critically while they amused themselves seriously with beer. They nodded approval at some new fancy steps of Mac's own invention.

At the sight of the great Del Delano, the amateur's feet stuttered, blundered, clicked a few times, and ceased to move. The tongues of one's shoes become tied in the presence of the Master. Mac's sallow face took on a slight flush.

From the uncertain cavity between Del Delano's hat brim and the lapels of his high fur coat collar came a thin puff of cigarette smoke and then a voice:

"Do that last step over again, kid. And don't hold your arms quite so stiff. Now, then!"

Once more Mac went through his paces. According to the traditions of the man dancer, his entire being was transformed into mere feet and legs. His gaze and expression became cataleptic; his body, unbending above the waist, but as light as a cork, bobbed like the same cork dancing on the ripples of a running brook. The beat of his heels and toes pleased you like a snare-drum obligato. The performance ended with an amazing clatter of leather against wood that culminated in a sudden flat-footed stamp, leaving the dancer erect and as motionless as a pillar of the colonial portico of a mansion in a Kentucky prohibition town. Mac felt that he had done his best and that Del Delano would turn his back upon him in derisive scorn.

An approximate silence followed, broken only by the mewing of a café cat and the hubbub and uproar of a few million citizens and transportation facilities outside.

Mac turned a hopeless but nervy eye upon Del Delano's face. In it he read disgust, admiration, envy, indifference, approval, disappointment, praise, and contempt.

Thus, in the countenances of those we hate or love we find what we most desire or fear to see. Which is an assertion equalling in its wisdom and chiaroscuro the most famous sayings of the most foolish philosophers that the world has ever known.

Del Delano retired within his overcoat and hat. In two minutes he emerged and turned his left side to Mac. Then he spoke.

"You've got a foot movement, kid, like a baby hippopotamus trying to sidestep a jab from a humming-bird. And you hold yourself like a truck driver having his picture taken in a Third Avenue photograph gallery. And you haven't got any method or style. And your knees are about as limber as a couple of Yale pass-keys. And you strike the eye as weighing, let us say, 450 pounds while you work. But, say, would you mind giving me your name?"

"McGowan," said the humbled amateur—"Mac McGowan."

Delano the Great slowly lighted a cigarette and continued, through its smoke:

"In other words, you're rotten. You can't dance. But I'll tell you one thing you've got."

"Throw it all off your system while you're at it," said Mac. "What've I got?"

"Genius," said Del Delano. "Except myself, it's up to you to be the best fancy dancer in the United States, Europe, Asia, and the colonial possessions of all three."

"Smoke up!" said Mac McGowan.

"Genius," repeated the Master—"you've got a talent for genius. Your brains are in your feet, where a dancer's ought to be. You've been self-taught until you're almost ruined, but not quite. What you need is a trainer. I'll take you in hand and put you at the top of the profession. There's room there for the two of us. You may beat me," said the Master, casting upon him a cold, savage look combining so much rivalry, affection, justice, and human hate that it stamped him at once as one of the little great ones of the earth—"you may beat me; but I doubt it. I've got the start and the pull. But at the top is where you belong. Your name, you say, is Robinson?"

"McGowan," repeated the amateur, "Mac McGowan."

"It don't matter," said Delano. "Suppose you walk up to my hotel with me. I'd like to talk to you. Your footwork is the worst I ever saw, Madigan—but—well, I'd like to talk to you. You may not think so, but I'm not so stuck up. I came off of the West Side myself. That overcoat cost me eight hundred dollars; but the collar ain't so high but what I can see over it. I taught myself to dance, and I put in most of nine years at it before I shook a foot in public. But I had genius. I didn't go too far wrong in teaching myself as you've done. You've got the rottenest method and style of anybody I ever saw."

"Oh, I don't think much of the few little steps I take," said Mac, with hypocritical lightness.

"Don't talk like a package of self-raising buckwheat flour," said Del Delano. "You've had a talent handed to you by the Proposition Higher Up; and it's up to you to do the proper thing with it. I'd like to have you go up to my hotel for a talk, if you will."

In his rooms in the King Clovis Hotel, Del Delano put on a scarlet house coat bordered with gold braid and set out Appollinaris and a box of sweet crackers.

Mac's eye wandered.

"Forget it," said Del. "Drink and tobacco may be all right for a man who makes his living with his hands; but they won't do if you're depending on your head or your feet. If one end of you gets tangled, so does the other. That's why beer and cigarettes don't hurt piano players and picture painters. But you've got to cut 'em out if you want to do mental or pedal work. Now, have a cracker, and then we'll talk some."

"All right," said Mac. "I take it as an honor, of course, for you to notice my hopping around. Of course I'd like to do something in a professional line. Of course I can sing a little and do card tricks and Irish and German comedy stuff, and of course I'm not so bad on the trapeze and comic bicycle stunts and Hebrew monologues and——"

"One moment," interrupted Del Delano, "before we begin. I said you couldn't dance. Well, that wasn't quite right. You've only got two or three bad tricks in your method. You're handy with your feet, and you belong at the top, where I am. I'll put you there. I've got six weeks continuous in New York; and in four I can shape up your style till the booking agents will fight one another to get you. And I'll do it, too. I'm of, from, and for the West Side. 'Del Delano' looks good on bill-boards, but the family name's Crowley. Now, Mackintosh—McGowan, I mean—you've got your chance—fifty times a better one than I had."

"I'd be a shine to turn it down," said Mac. "And I hope you understand I appreciate it. Me and my cousin Cliff McGowan was thinking of
getting a try-out at Creary's on amateur night a month from tomorrow."

"Good stuff!" said Delano. "I got mine there. Junius T. Rollins, the
booker for Kuhn & Dooley, jumped on the stage and engaged me after my
dance. And the boards were an inch deep in nickels and dimes and quarters. There wasn't but nine penny pieces found in the lot."

"I ought to tell you," said Mac, after two minutes of pensiveness, "that
my Cousin Cliff can beat me dancing. We've always been what you might
call pals. If you'd take him up instead of me, now, it might be better. He's
invented a lot of steps that I can't cut."

"Forget it," said Delano. "Mondays, Wednesdays, Fridays, and Saturdays of every week from now till amateur night, a month off, I'll coach
you. I'll make you as good as I am; and nobody could do more for you.
My act's over every night at 10:15. Half an hour later I'll take you up and
drill you till twelve. I'll put you at the top of the bunch, right where I
am. You've got talent. Your style's bum; but you've got the genius. You
let me manage it. I'm from the West Side myself, and I'd rather see one
of the same gang win out before I would an East-Sider, or any of the Flatbush or Hackensack Meadow kind of butt-iners. I'll see that Junius Rollins is present on your Friday night; and if he don't climb over the footlights and offer you fifty a week as a starter, I'll let you draw it down
from my own salary every Monday night. Now, am I talking on the level
or am I not?"

Amateur night at Creary's Eighth Avenue Theatre is cut by the same
pattern as amateur nights elsewhere. After the regular performance the
humblest talent may, by previous arrangement with the management,
make its début upon the public stage. Ambitious nonprofessionals, mostly
self-instructed, display their skill and powers of entertainment along the
broadest lines. They may sing, dance, mimic, juggle, contort, recite, or
disport themselves along any of the ragged boundary lines of Art. From
the ranks of these anxious tyros are chosen the professionals that adorn or
otherwise make conspicuous the full-blown stage. Press-agents delight in
recounting to open-mouthed and close-eared reporters stories of the humble beginnings of the brilliant stars whose orbits they control.

Such and such a prima donna (they will tell you) made her initial bow
to the public while turning handsprings on an amateur night. One great
matinée favorite made his début on a generous Friday evening singing
coon songs of his own composition. A tragedian famous on two continents
and an island first attracted attention by an amateur impersonation of a
newly landed Scandinavian peasant girl. One Broadway comedian that
turns 'em away got a booking on a Friday night by reciting (seriously)
the graveyard scene in "Hamlet."

Thus they get their chance. Amateur night is a kindly boon. It is charity divested of alms-giving. It is a brotherly hand reached down by members of the best united band of coworkers in the world to raise up less fortunate ones without labelling them beggars. It gives you the chance, if you can grasp it, to step for a few minutes before some badly painted scenery and during the playing by the orchestra of some ten or twelve bars of music, and while the soles of your shoes may be clearly holding to the uppers, to secure a salary equal to a Congressman's or any orthodox minister's. Could an ambitious student of literature or financial methods get a chance like that by spending twenty minutes in a Carnegie library? I do not trow so.

But shall we look in at Creary's? Let us say that the specific Friday night had arrived on which the fortunate Mac McGowan was to justify the flattering predictions of his distinguished patron and, incidentally, drop his silver talent into the slit of the slot-machine of fame and fortune that gives up reputation and dough. I offer, sure of your acquiescence, that we now forswear hypocritical philosophy and bigoted comment, permitting the story to finish itself in the dress of material allegations—a medium more worthy, when held to the line, than the most laborious creations of the word-milliners . . .

(Page of manuscript missing here.)

easily among the wings with his patron, the great Del Delano. For, whatever footlights shone in the City-That-Would-Be-Amused, the freedom of their unshaded side was Del's. And if he should take up an amateur—see? and bring him around—see? and, winking one of his cold blue eyes, say to the manager: "Take it from me—he's got the goods—see?" you wouldn't expect that amateur to sit on an unpainted bench sudorifically awaiting his turn, would you? So Mac strolled around largely with the nonpareil; and the seven waited, clammily, on the bench.

A giant in shirt-sleeves with a grim, kind face in which many stitches had been taken by surgeons from time to time, i. e., with a long stick, looped at the end. He was the man with the Hook. The manager, with his close-smoothed blond hair, his one-sided smile, and his abnormally easy manner, pored with patient condescension over the difficult program of the amateurs. The last of the professional turns—the Grand March of the Happy Huzzard—had been completed; the last wrinkle and darn of their blue silk-olene cotton tights had vanished from the stage. The man in the orchestra who played the kettle-drum, cymbals, triangle, sandpaper, whangdoodle, hoof-beats, and catcalls, and fired the pistol shots, had wiped his brow. The illegal holiday of the Romans had arrived.

While the orchestra plays the famous waltz from "The Dismal Wife," let us bestow two hundred words upon the psychology of the audience.

The orchestra floor was filled by People. The boxes contained Persons. In the galleries was the Foreordained Verdict. The claque was there as it had originated in the Stone Age and was afterward adopted by the

French. Every Micky and Maggie who sat upon Creary's amateur bench, wise beyond their talents, knew that their success or doom lay already meted out to them by that crowded, whistling, roaring mass of Romans in the three galleries. They knew that the winning or the losing of the game for each one lay in the strength of the "gang" aloft that could turn the applause to its favorite. On a Broadway first night a wooer of fame may win it from the ticket buyers over the heads of the cognoscenti. But not so at Creary's. The amateur's fate is arithmetical. The number of his supporting admirers present at his try-out decides it in advance. But how these outlying Friday nights put to a certain shame the Mondays, Tuesdays, Wednesdays, Thursdays, Saturdays, and matinées of the Broadway stage you should know. . . . (Here the manuscript ends.)

ARISTOCRACY VERSUS HASH

The snake reporter of the *Rolling Stone* was wandering up the avenue last night on his way home from the Y. M. C. A. rooms when he was approached by a gaunt, hungry-looking man with wild eyes and dishevelled hair. He accosted the reporter in a hollow, weak voice.

" 'Can you tell me, Sir, where I can find in this town a family of scrubs?'

" 'I don't understand exactly.'

" 'Let me tell you how it is,' said the stranger, inserting his forefinger in the reporter's buttonhole and badly damaging his chrysanthemum. 'I am a representative from Soapstone County, and I and my family are houseless, homeless, and shelterless. We have not tasted food for over a week. I brought my family with me, as I have indigestion and could not get around much with the boys. Some days ago I started out to find a boarding house, as I cannot afford to put up at a hotel. I found a nice aristocratic-looking place, that suited me, and went in and asked for the proprietress. A very stately lady with a Roman nose came in the room. She had one hand laid across her stom—across her waist, and the other held a lace handkerchief. I told her I wanted board for myself and family, and she condescended to take us. I asked for her terms, and she said $300 per week.

" 'I had two dollars in my pocket and I gave her that for a fine teapot that I broke when I fell over the table when she spoke.'

" 'You appear surprised,' says she. 'You will please remembah that I am the widow of Governor Riddle of Georgiah; my family is very highly connected; I give you board as a favah; I nevah considah money any equivalent for the advantage of my society, I——'

" 'Well, I got out of there, and I went to some other places. The next lady was a cousin of General Mahone of Virginia, and wanted four dollars an hour for a back room with a pink motto and a Burnet granite bed in it. The next one was an aunt of Davy Crockett, and asked eight dollars a day for a room furnished in imitation of the Alamo, with prunes for breakfast and one hour's conversation with her for dinner. Another one said she was a descendant of Benedict Arnold on her father's side and Captain Kidd on the other.

" 'She took more after Captain Kidd.

" 'She only had one meal and prayers a day, and counted her society worth $100 a week.

" 'I found nine widows of Supreme Judges, twelve relicts of Governors and Generals, and twenty-two ruins left by various happy Colonels, Professors, and Majors, who valued their aristocratic worth from $90 to $900 per week, with weak-kneed hash and dried apples on the side. I admire people of fine descent, but my stomach yearns for pork and beans instead of culture. Am I not right?' "

" 'Your words,' said the reporter, 'convince me that you have uttered what you have said.'

" 'Thanks. You see how it is. I am not wealthy; I have only my per diem and my per quisites, and I cannot afford to pay for high lineage and moldy ancestors. A little corned beef goes further with me than a coronet, and when I am cold a coat of arms does not warm me.'

" 'I greatly fear,' said the reporter, with a playful hiccough, 'that you have run against a high-toned town. Most all the first-class boarding houses here are run by ladies of the old Southern families, the very first in the land.'

" 'I am now desperate,' said the Representative, as he chewed a tack awhile, thinking it was a clove. 'I want to find a boarding house where the proprietress was an orphan found in a livery stable, whose father was a dago from East Austin, and whose grandfather was never placed on the map. I want a scrubby, ornery, low-down, snuff-dipping, backwoodsy, piebald gang, who never heard of finger bowls or Ward McAllister, but who can get up a mess of hot corn-bread and Irish stew at regular market quotations.'

" 'Is there such a place in Austin?'

"The snake reporter sadly shook his head. 'I do not know,' he said, 'but I will shake you for the beer.'

"Ten minutes later the slate in the Blue Ruin saloon bore two additional characters: 10."

THE PRISONER OF ZEMBLA

So the king fell into a furious rage, so that none durst go near him for fear, and he gave out that since the Princess Ostla had disobeyed him there would be a great tourney, and to the knight who should prove himself of the greatest valor he would give the hand of the princess.

And he sent forth a herald to proclaim that he would do this.

And the herald went about the country making his desire known, blowing a great tin horn and riding a noble steed that pranced and gambolled; and the villagers gazed upon him and said: "Lo, that is one of them tinhorn gamblers concerning which the chroniclers have told us."

And when the day came, the king sat in the grandstand, holding the gage of battle in his hand, and by his side sat the Princess Ostla, looking very pale and beautiful, but with mournful eyes from which she scarce could keep the tears. And the knights which came to the tourney gazed upon the princess in wonder at her beauty, and each swore to win so that he could marry her and board with the king. Suddenly the heart of the princess gave a great bound, for she saw among the knights one of the poor students with whom she had been in love.

The knights mounted and rode in a line past the grandstand, and the king stopped the poor student, who had the worst horse and the poorest caparisons of any of the knights and said:

"Sir Knight, prithee tell me of what that marvellous shacky and rusty-looking armor of thine is made?"

"Oh, king," said the young knight, "seeing that we are about to engage in a big fight, I would call it scrap iron, wouldn't you?"

"Ods Bodkins!" said the king. "The youth hath a pretty wit."

About this time the Princess Ostla, who began to feel better at the sight of her lover, slipped a piece of gum into her mouth and closed her teeth upon it, and even smiled a little and showed the beautiful pearls with which her mouth was set. Whereupon, as soon as the knights perceived this, 217 of them went over to the king's treasurer and settled for their horse feed and went home.

"It seems very hard," said the princess, "that I cannot marry when I chews."

But two of the knights were left, one of them being the princess's lover.

"Here's enough for a fight, anyhow," said the king. "Come hither, O knights, will ye joust for the hand of this fair lady?"

"We joust will," said the knights.

The two knights fought for two hours, and at length the princess's lover prevailed and stretched the other upon the ground. The victorious knight made his horse caracole before the king and bowed low in his saddle.

On the Princess Ostla's cheeks was a rosy flush; in her eyes the light of excitement vied with the soft glow of love; her lips were parted, her lovely hair unbound, and she grasped the arms of her chair and leaned forward with heaving bosom and happy smile to hear the words of her lover.

"You have foughten well, sir knight," said the king. "And if there is any boon you crave you have but to name it."

"Then," said the knight, "I will ask you this: I have bought the patent rights in your kingdom for Schneider's celebrated monkey wrench, and I want a letter from you endorsing it."

"You shall have it," said the king, "but I must tell you that there is not a monkey in my kingdom."

With a yell of rage the victorious knight threw himself on his horse and rode away at a furious gallop.

The king was about to speak, when a horrible suspicion flashed upon him and he fell dead upon the grandstand.

"My God!" he cried. "He has forgotten to take the princess with him!"

A STRANGE STORY

In the northern part of Austin there once dwelt an honest family by the name of Smothers. The family consisted of John Smothers, his wife, himself, their little daughter, five years of age and her parents, making six people toward the population of the city when counted for a special write-up, but only three by actual count.

One night after supper the little girl was seized with a severe colic, and John Smothers hurried downtown to get some medicine.

He never came back.

The little girl recovered and in time grew up to womanhood.

The mother grieved very much over her husband's disappearance, and it was nearly three months before she married again, and moved to San Antonio.

The little girl also married in time, and after a few years had rolled around, she also had a little girl five years of age.

She still lived in the same house where they dwelt when her father had left and never returned.

One night by a remarkable coincidence her little girl was taken with cramp colic on the anniversary of the disappearance of John Smothers, who would now have been her grandfather if he had been alive and had a steady job.

"I will go downtown and get some medicine for her," said John Smith (for it was none other than he whom she had married).

"No, no, dear John," cried his wife. "You, too, might disappear forever, and then forget to come back."

So John Smith did not go, and together they sat by the bedside of little Pansy (for that was Pansy's name).

After a little Pansy seemed to grow worse, and John Smith again attempted to go for medicine, but his wife would not let him.

Suddenly the door opened, and an old man, stooped and bent, with long white hair, entered the room.

"Hello, here is grandpa," said Pansy. She had recognized him before any of the others.

The old man drew a bottle of medicine from his pocket and gave Pansy a spoonful.

She got well immediately.

"I was a little late," said John Smothers, "as I waited for a street car."

FICKLE FORTUNE OR HOW GLADYS HUSTLED

"Press me no more, Mr. Snooper," said Gladys Vavasour-Smith. "I can never be yours."

"You have led me to believe different, Gladys," said Bertram D. Snooper.

The setting sun was flooding with golden light the oriel windows of a magnificent mansion situated in one of the most aristocratic streets west of the brick yard.

Bertram D. Snooper, a poor but ambitious and talented young lawyer, had just lost his first suit. He had dared to aspire to the hand of Gladys Vavasour-Smith, the beautiful and talented daughter of one of the oldest and proudest families in the county. The bluest blood flowed in her veins. Her grandfather had sawed wood for the Hornsbys and an aunt on her mother's side had married a man who had been kicked by General Lee's mule.

The lines about Bertram D. Snooper's hands and mouth were drawn tighter as he paced to and fro, waiting for a reply to the question he intended to ask Gladys as soon as he thought of one.

At last an idea occurred to him.

"Why will you not marry me?" he asked in an inaudible tone.

"Because," said Gladys, firmly, speaking easily with great difficulty, "the progression and enlightenment that the woman of to-day possesses demand that the man shall bring to the marriage altar a heart and body as free from the debasing and hereditary iniquities that now no longer exist except in the chimerical imagination of enslaved custom."

"It is as I expected," said Bertram, wiping his heated brow on the window curtain. "You have been reading books."

"Besides that," continued Gladys, ignoring the deadly charge, "you have no money."

The blood of the Snoopers rose hastily and mantled the cheek of Bertram D. He put on his coat and moved proudly to the door.

"Stay here till I return," he said, "I will be back in fifteen years."

When he had finished speaking he ceased and left the room.

When he had gone, Gladys felt an uncontrollable yearning take possession of her. She said slowly, rather to herself than for publication, "I wonder if there was any of that cold cabbage left from dinner."

She then left the room.

When she did so, a dark-complexioned man with black hair and gloomy, desperate-looking clothes, came out of the fireplace where he had been concealed and stated:

"Aha! I have you in my power at last, Bertram D. Snooper. Gladys Vavasour-Smith shall be mine. I am in the possession of secrets that not a soul in the world suspects. I have papers to prove that Bertram Snooper is the heir to the Tom Bean estate,[1] and I have discovered that Gladys' grandfather who sawed wood for the Hornsbys was also a cook in Major Rhoads Fisher's command during the war. Therefore, the family repudiate her, and she will marry me in order to drag their proud name down in the dust. Ha, ha, ha!"

As the reader has doubtless long also discovered, this man was no other than Henry R. Grasty. Mr. Grasty then proceeded to gloat some more, and then with a sardonic laugh left for New York.

$$* \quad * \quad * \quad * \quad *$$

Fifteen years have elapsed.

Of course, our readers will understand that this is only supposed to be the case.

It really took less than a minute to make the little stars that represent an interval of time.

We could not afford to stop a piece in the middle and wait fifteen years before continuing it.

We hope this explanation will suffice. We are careful not to create any wrong impressions.

Gladys Vavasour-Smith and Henry R. Grasty stood at the marriage altar.

[1]An estate famous in Texas legal history. It took many, many years for adjustment and a large part of the property was, of course, consumed as expenses of litigation.

Mr. Grasty had evidently worked his rabbit's foot successfully, although he was quite a while in doing so.

Just as the preacher was about to pronounce the fatal words on which he would have realized ten dollars and had the laugh on Mr. Grasty, the steeple of the church fell off and Bertram D. Snooper entered.

The preacher fell to the ground with a dull thud. He could ill afford to lose ten dollars. He was hastily removed and a cheaper one secured.

Bertram D. Snooper held a *Statesman* in his hand.

"Aha!" he said, "I thought I would surprise you. I just got in this morning. Here is a paper noticing my arrival."

He handed it to Henry R. Grasty.

Mr. Grasty looked at the paper and turned deadly pale. It was dated three weeks after Mr. Snooper's arrival.

"Foiled again!" he hissed.

"Speak, Bertram D. Snooper," said Gladys, "why have you come between me and Henry?"

"I have just discovered that I am the sole heir to Tom Bean's estate and am worth two million dollars."

With a glad cry Gladys threw herself in Bertram's arms.

Henry R. Grasty drew from his breast pocket a large tin box and opened it, took therefrom 467 pages of closely written foolscap.

"What you say is true, Mr. Snooper, but I ask you to read that," he said, handing it to Bertram Snooper.

Mr. Snooper had no sooner read the document than he uttered a piercing shriek and bit off a large chew of tobacco.

"All is lost," he said.

"What is that document?" asked Gladys, "Governor Hogg's message?"

"It is not as bad as that," said Bertram, "but it deprives me of my entire fortune. But I care not for that, Gladys, since I have won you."

"What is it? Speak, I implore you," said Gladys.

"Those papers," said Henry R. Grasty, "are the proofs of my appointment as administrator of the Tom Bean estate."

With a loving cry Gladys threw herself in Henry R. Grasty's arms.

Twenty minutes later Bertram D. Snooper was seen deliberately to enter a beer saloon on Seventeenth Street.

AN APOLOGY

The person who sweeps the office, translates letters from foreign countries, deciphers communications from graduates of business colleges, and does most of the writing for this paper, has been confined for the past two weeks to the under side of a large red quilt, with a joint caucus of la grippe and measles.

We have missed two issues of the *Rolling Stone,* and are now slightly convalescent, for which we desire to apologize and express our regrets.

Everybody's term of subscription will be extended long enough to cover all missed issues, and we hope soon to report that the goose remains suspended at a favorable altitude. People who have tried to run a funny paper and entertain a congregation of large piebald measles at the same time will understand something of the tact, finesse, and hot sassafras tea required to do so. We expect to get out the paper regularly from this time on, but are forced to be very careful, as improper treatment and deleterious after-effects of measles, combined with the high price of paper and presswork, have been known to cause a relapse. Any one not getting their paper regularly will please come down and see about it, bringing with them a ham or any little delicacy relished by invalids.

LORD OAKHURST'S CURSE

Lord Oakhurst lay dying in the oak chamber in the eastern wing of Oakhurst Castle. Through the open window in the calm of the summer evening, came the sweet fragrance of the early violets and budding trees, and to the dying man it seemed as if earth's loveliness and beauty were never so apparent as on this bright June day, his last day of life.

His young wife, whom he loved with a devotion and strength that the presence of the king of terrors himself could not alter, moved about the apartment, weeping and sorrowful, sometimes arranging the sick man's pillow and inquiring of him in low, mournful tones if anything could be done to give him comfort, and again, with stifled sobs, eating some chocolate caramels which she carried in the pocket of her apron. The servants went to and fro with that quiet and subdued tread which prevails in a house where death is an expected guest, and even the crash of broken china and shivered glass, which announced their approach, seemed to fall upon the ear with less violence and sound than usual.

Lord Oakhurst was thinking of days gone by, when he wooed and won his beautiful young wife, who was then but a charming and innocent girl. How clearly and minutely those scenes rose up at the call of his memory. He seemed to be standing once more beneath the old chestnut grove where they had plighted their troth in the twilight under the stars; while the rare fragrance of the June roses and the smell of supper came gently by on the breeze. There he had told her his love; how that his whole happiness and future joy lay in the hope that he might win her for a bride; that if she would trust her future to his care the devotedness of his lifetime should be hers, and his only thought would be to make her life one long day of sunshine and peanut candy.

How plainly he remembered how she had, with girlish shyness and coyness, at first hesitated, and murmured something to herself about "an old bald-headed galoot," but when he told her that to him life without her would be a blasted mockery, and that his income was £50,000 a year, she threw herself on to him and froze there with the tenacity of a tick on a brindled cow, and said, with tears of joy, "Hen-ery, I am thine."

And now he was dying. In a few short hours his spirit would rise up at the call of the Destroyer and, quitting his poor, weak, earthly frame, would go forth into that dim and dreaded Unknown Land, and solve with certainty that Mystery which revealeth itself not to mortal man.

II A carriage drove rapidly up the avenue and stopped at the door. Sir Everhard FitzArmond, the famous London physician, who had been telegraphed for, alighted and quickly ascended the marble steps. Lady Oakhurst met him at the door, her lovely face expressing great anxiety and grief. "Oh, Sir Everhard, I am so glad you have come. He seems to be sinking rapidly. Did you bring the cream almonds I mentioned in the telegram?"

Sir Everhard did not reply, but silently handed her a package, and, slipping a couple of cloves into his mouth, ascended the stairs that led to Lord Oakhurst's apartment. Lady Oakhurst followed.

Sir Everhard approached the bedside of his patient and laid his hand gently on this sick man's diagnosis. A shade of feeling passed over his professional countenance as he gravely and solemnly pronounced these words: "Madam, your husband has croaked."

Lady Oakhurst at first did not comprehend his technical language, and her lovely mouth let up for a moment on the cream almonds. But soon his meaning flashed upon her, and she seized an ax that her husband was accustomed to keep by his bedside to mangle his servants with, and struck open Lord Oakhurst's cabinet containing his private papers, and with eager hands opened the document which she took therefrom. Then, with a wild, unearthly shriek that would have made a steam piano go out behind a barn and kick itself in despair, she fell senseless to the floor.

Sir Everhard FitzArmond picked up the paper and read its contents. It was Lord Oakhurst's will, bequeathing all his property to a scientific institution which should have for its object the invention of a means for extracting peach brandy from sawdust.

Sir Everhard glanced quickly around the room. No one was in sight. Dropping the will, he rapidly transferred some valuable ornaments and rare specimens of gold and silver filigree work from the centre table to his pockets, and rang the bell for the servants.

III   THE CURSE   Sir Everhard FitzArmond descended the stairway of Oakhurst Castle and passed out into the avenue that led from the doorway to
the great iron gates of the park. Lord Oakhurst had been a great sportsman during his life and always kept a well-stocked kennel of curs, which
now rushed out from their hiding places and with loud yelps sprang upon
the physician, burying their fangs in his lower limbs and seriously damaging his apparel.

Sir Everhard, startled out of his professional dignity and usual indifference to human suffering, by the personal application of feeling, gave vent
to a most horrible and blighting CURSE and ran with great swiftness to
his carriage and drove off toward the city.

BEXAR SCRIP NO. 2692

Whenever you visit Austin you should by all means go to see the General
Land Office.

As you pass up the avenue you turn sharp round the corner of the court
house, and on a steep hill before you you see a mediæval castle.

You think of the Rhine; the "castled crag of Drachenfels"; the Lorelei;
and the vine-clad slopes of Germany. And German it is in every line of its
architecture and design.

The plan was drawn by an old draftsman from the "Vaterland," whose
heart still loved the scenes of his native land, and it is said he reproduced
the design of a certain castle near his birthplace with remarkable fidelity.

Under the present administration a new coat of paint has vulgarized its
ancient and venerable walls. Modern tiles have replaced the limestone
slabs of its floors, worn in hollows by the tread of thousands of feet, and
smart and gaudy fixtures have usurped the place of the timeworn furniture that has been consecrated by the touch of hands that Texas will never
cease to honor.

But even now, when you enter the building, you lower your voice, and
time turns backward for you, for the atmosphere which you breathe is
cold with the exudations of buried generations.

The building is stone with a coating of concrete; the walls are immensely thick; it is cold in the summer and warm in the winter; it is isolated and sombre; standing apart from the other state buildings, sullen
and decaying, brooding on the past.

Twenty years ago it was much the same as now; twenty years from now
the garish newness will be worn off and it will return to its appearance of
gloomy decadence.

People living in other states can form no conception of the vastness and importance of the work performed and the significance of the millions of records and papers composing the archives of this office.

The title deeds, patents, transfers, and legal documents connected with every foot of land owned in the state of Texas are filed here.

Volumes could be filled with accounts of the knavery, the double-dealing, the cross purposes, the perjury, the lies, the bribery, the alteration and erasing, the suppressing and destroying of papers, the various schemes and plots that for the sake of the almighty dollar have left their stains upon the records of the General Land Office.

No reference is made to the employees. No more faithful, competent, and efficient force of men exists in the clerical portions of any government, but there is—or was, for their day is now over—a class of land speculators commonly called land sharks, unscrupulous and greedy, who have left their trail in every department of this office, in the shape of titles destroyed, patents cancelled, homes demolished and torn away, forged transfers and lying affidavits.

Before the modern tiles were laid upon the floors, there were deep hollows in the limestone slabs, worn by the countless feet that daily trod uneasily through its echoing corridors, pressing from file room to business room, from commissioner's sanctum to record books and back again.

The honest but ignorant settler, bent on saving the little plot of land he called home, elbowed the wary land shark who was searching the records for evidence to oust him; the lordly cattle baron, relying on his influence and money, stood at the Commissioner's desk side by side with the pre-emptor, whose little potato patch lay like a minute speck of island in the vast, billowy sea of his princely pastures, and played the old game of "freeze-out," which is as old as Cain and Abel.

The trail of the serpent is through it all.

Honest, earnest men have wrought for generations striving to disentangle the shameful coil that certain years of fraud and infamy have wound. Look at the files and see the countless endorsements of those in authority:

"Transfer doubtful—locked up."

"Certificate a forgery—locked up."

"Signature a forgery."

"Patent refused—duplicate patented elsewhere."

"Field notes forged."

"Certificates stolen from office"—and so on, ad infinitum.

The record books, spread upon long tables in the big room upstairs, are open to the examination of all.

Open them, and you will find the dark and greasy fingerprints of half a century's handling. The quick hand of the land grabber has fluttered the leaves a million times; the damp clutch of the perturbed tiller of the soil has left traces of his calling on the ragged leaves.

Interest centres in the file room.

This is a large room, built as a vault, fireproof, and entered by but a single door.

There is "No Admission" on the portal; and the precious files are handed out by a clerk in charge only on presentation of an order signed by the Commissioner or chief clerk.

In years past too much laxity prevailed in its management, and the files were handled by all comers, simply on their request, and returned at their will or not at all.

In those days most of the mischief was done. In the file room, there are about —— files, each in a paper wrapper, and comprising the title papers of a particular tract of land.

You ask the clerk in charge for the papers relating to any survey in Texas. They are arranged simply in districts and numbers.

He disappears from the door, you hear the sliding of a tin box, the lid snaps, and the file is in your hand.

Go up there some day and call for Bexar Scrip No. 2692.

The file clerk stares at you for a second, says shortly:

"Out of file."

It has been missing twenty years.

The history of that file has never been written before.

Twenty years ago there was a shrewd land agent living in Austin who devoted his undoubted talents and vast knowledge of land titles, and the laws governing them, to the locating of surveys made by illegal certificates or improperly made, and otherwise of no value through non-compliance with the statutes, or whatever flaws his ingenious and unscrupulous mind could unearth.

He found a fatal defect in the title of the land as on file in Bexar Scrip No. 2692 and placed a new certificate upon the survey in his own name.

The law was on his side.

Every sentiment of justice, of right, and humanity was against him.

The certificate by virtue of which the original survey had been made was missing.

It was not to be found in the file, and no memorandum or date on the wrapper to show that it had ever been filed.

Under the law the land was vacant, unappropriated public domain and open to location.

The land was occupied by a widow and her only son, and she supposed her title good.

The railroad had surveyed a new line through the property, and it had doubled in value.

Sharp, the land agent, did not communicate with her in any way until he had filed his papers, rushed his claim through the departments and into the patent room for patenting.

Then he wrote her a letter, offering her the choice of buying from him or vacating at once.

He received no reply.

One day he was looking through some files and came across the missing certificate. Some one, probably an employee of the office, had by mistake, after making some examination, placed it in the wrong file, and curiously enough another inadvertence, in there being no record of its filing on the wrapper, had completed the appearance of its having never been filed.

Sharp called for the file in which it belonged and scrutinized it carefully, fearing he might have overlooked some endorsement regarding its return to the office.

On the back of the certificate was plainly endorsed the date of filing, according to law, and signed by the chief clerk.

If this certificate should be seen by the examining clerk, his own claim, when it came up for patenting, would not be worth the paper on which it was written.

Sharp glanced furtively around. A young man, or rather a boy about eighteen years of age, stood a few feet away regarding him closely with keen black eyes.

Sharp, a little confused, thrust the certificate into the file where it properly belonged and began gathering up the other papers.

The boy came up and leaned on the desk beside him.

"A right interesting office, sir!" he said. "I have never been in here before. All those papers, now, they are about lands, are they not? The titles and deeds, and such things?"

"Yes," said Sharp. "They are supposed to contain all the title papers."

"This one, now," said the boy, taking up Bexar Scrip No. 2692, "what land does this represent the title of? Ah, I see 'Six hundred and forty acres in B—— county? Absalom Harris, original grantee.' Please tell me, I am so ignorant of these things, how can you tell a good survey from a bad one? I am told that there are a great many illegal and fraudulent surveys in this office. I suppose this one is all right?"

"No," said Sharp. "The certificate is missing. It is invalid."

"That paper I just saw you place in that file I suppose is something else —field notes, or a transfer probably?"

"Yes," said Sharp, hurriedly, "corrected field notes. Excuse me, I am a little pressed for time."

The boy was watching him with bright, alert eyes.

It would never do to leave the certificate in the file; but he could not take it out with that inquisitive boy watching him.

He turned to the file room, with a dozen or more files in his hands, and accidentally dropped part of them on the floor. As he stooped to pick them up he swiftly thrust Bexar Scrip No. 2692 in the inside breast pocket of his coat.

This happened at just half-past four o'clock, and when the file clerk took the files he threw them in a pile in his room, came out and locked the door.

The clerks were moving out of the doors in long, straggling lines.

It was closing time.

Sharp did not desire to take the file from the Land Office.

The boy might have seen him place the file in his pocket, and the penalty of the law for such an act was very severe.

Some distance back from the file room was the draftsman's room now entirely vacated by its occupants.

Sharp dropped behind the outgoing stream of men, and slipped slyly into this room.

The clerks trooped noisily down the iron stairway, singing, whistling, and talking.

Below, the night watchman awaited their exit, ready to close and bar the great doors to the south and east.

It is his duty to take careful note each day that no one remains in the building after the hour of closing.

Sharp waited until all sounds had ceased.

It was his intention to linger until everything was quiet, and then to remove the certificate from the file, and throw the latter carelessly on some draftsman's desk, as if it had been left there during the business of the day.

He knew also that he must remove the certificate from the office or destroy it, as the chance finding of it by a clerk would lead to its immediately being restored to its proper place, and the consequent discovery that his location over the old survey was absolutely worthless.

As he moved cautiously along the stone floor the loud barking of the little black dog, kept by the watchman, told that his sharp ears had heard the sounds of his steps.

The great, hollow rooms echoed loudly, move as lightly as he could.

Sharp sat down at a desk and laid the file before him.

In all his queer practices and cunning tricks he had not yet included any act that was down-right criminal.

He had always kept on the safe side of the law, but in the deed he was about to commit there was no compromise to be made with what little conscience he had left.

There is no well-defined boundary line between honesty and dishonesty.

The frontiers of one blend with the outside limits of the other, and he who attempts to tread this dangerous ground may be sometimes in the one domain and sometimes in the other; so the only safe road is the broad highway that leads straight through and has been well defined by line and compass.

Sharp was a man of what is called high standing in the community. That is, his word in a trade was as good as any man's; his check was as good as so much cash, and so regarded; he went to church regularly; went in good society and owed no man anything.

He was regarded as a sure winner in any land trade he chose to make, but that was his occupation.

The act he was about to commit now would place him forever in the ranks of those who chose evil for their portion—if it was found out.

More than that, it would rob a widow and her son of property soon to be of great value, which, if not legally theirs, was theirs certainly by every claim of justice.

But he had gone too far to hesitate.

His own survey was in the patent room for patenting. His own title was about to be perfected by the State's own hand.

The certificate must be destroyed.

He leaned his head on his hands for a moment, and as he did so a sound behind him caused his heart to leap with guilty fear, but before he could rise, a hand came over his shoulder and grasped the file.

He rose quickly, as white as paper, rattling his chair loudly on the stone floor.

The boy who had spoken to him earlier stood contemplating him with contemptuous and flashing eyes, and quietly placed the file in the left breast pocket of his coat.

"So, Mr. Sharp, by nature as well as by name," he said, "it seems that I was right in waiting behind the door in order to see you safely out. You will appreciate the pleasure I feel in having done so when I tell you my name is Harris. My mother owns the land on which you have filed, and if there is any justice in Texas she shall hold it. I am not certain, but I think I saw you place a paper in this file this afternoon, and it is barely possible that it may be of value to me. I was also impressed with the idea that you desired to remove it again, but had not the opportunity. Anyway, I shall keep it until to-morrow and let the Commissioner decide."

Far back among Mr. Sharp's ancestors there must have been some of the old berserker blood, for his caution, his presence of mind left him, and left him possessed of a blind, devilish, unreasoning rage that showed itself in a moment in the white glitter of his eye.

"Give me that file, boy," he said, thickly, holding out his hand.

"I am no such fool, Mr. Sharp," said the youth. "This file shall be laid before the Commissioner to-morrow for examination. If he finds—— Help! Help!"

Sharp was upon him like a tiger and bore him to the floor. The boy was strong and vigorous, but the suddenness of the attack gave him no chance to resist. He struggled up again to his feet, but it was an animal, with blazing eyes and cruel-looking teeth, that fought him, instead of a man.

Mr. Sharp, a man of high standing and good report, was battling for his reputation.

Presently there was a dull sound, and another, and still one more, and a blade flashing white and then red, and Edward Harris dropped down like some stuffed effigy of a man, that boys make for sport, with limbs all crumpled and lax, on the stone floor of the Land Office.

The old watchman was deaf and heard nothing.

The little dog barked at the foot of the stairs until his master made him come into his room.

Sharp stood there for several minutes holding in his hand his bloody clasp knife, listening to the cooing of the pigeons on the roof, and the loud ticking of the clock above the receiver's desk.

A map rustled on the wall and his blood turned to ice; a rat ran across some strewn papers, and his scalp prickled, and he could scarcely moisten his dry lips with his tongue.

Between the file room and the draftsman's room there is a door that opens on a small dark spiral stairway that winds from the lower floor to the ceiling at the top of the house.

This stairway was not used then, nor is it now.

It is unnecessary, inconvenient, dusty, and dark as night, and was a blunder of the architect who designed the building.

This stairway ends above at the tent-shaped space between the roof and the joists.

That space is dark and forbidding, and being useless is rarely visited.

Sharp opened this door and gazed for a moment up this narrow cobwebbed stairway.

After dark that night a man opened cautiously one of the lower windows of the Land Office, crept out with great circumspection and disappeared in the shadows.

One afternoon, a week after this time, Sharp lingered behind again after the clerks had left and the office closed.

The next morning the first comers noticed a broad mark in the dust on the upstairs floor, and the same mark was observed below stairs near a window.

It appeared as if some heavy and rather bulky object had been dragged along through the limestone dust. A memorandum book with "E. Harris" written on the flyleaf was picked up on the stairs, but nothing particular was thought of any of these signs.

Circulars and advertisements appeared for a long time in the papers asking for information concerning Edward Harris, who left his mother's home on a certain date and had never been heard of since.

After a while these things were succeeded by affairs of more recent interest, and faded from the public mind.

Sharp died two years ago, respected and regretted. The last two years of his life were clouded with a settled melancholy for which his friends could assign no reason.

The bulk of his comfortable fortune was made from the land he obtained by fraud and crime.

The disappearance of the file was a mystery that created some commotion in the Land Office, but he got his patent.

It is a well-known tradition in Austin and vicinity that there is a buried treasure of great value somewhere on the banks of Shoal Creek, about a mile west of the city.

Three young men living in Austin recently became possessed of what they thought was a clue of the whereabouts of the treasure, and Thursday night they repaired to the place after dark and plied the pickaxe and shovel with great diligence for about three hours.

At the end of that time their efforts were rewarded by the finding of a box buried about four feet below the surface, which they hastened to open.

The light of a lantern disclosed to their view the fleshless bones of a human skeleton with clothing still wrapping its uncanny limbs.

They immediately left the scene and notified the proper authorities of their ghastly find.

On closer examination, in the left breast pocket of the skeleton's coat, there was found a flat, oblong packet of papers, cut through and through in three places by a knife blade, and so completely soaked and clotted with blood that it had become an almost indistinguishable mass.

With the aid of a microscope and the exercise of a little imagination this much can be made out of the letters at the top of the papers:
B—x a— ——rip N—2—92.

QUERIES AND ANSWERS

COLLEGE GRADUATE   Can you inform me where I can buy an interest in a newspaper of some kind? I have some money and would be glad to invest it in something of the sort, if some one would allow me to put in my capital against his experience.

Telegraph us your address at once, day message. Keep telegraphing every ten minutes at our expense until we see you. Will start on first train after receiving your wire.

G. F.   Who was the author of the line, "Breathes there a man with soul so dead"?

This was written by a visitor to the State Saengerfest of 1892 while conversing with a member who had just eaten a large slice of limburger cheese.

GEOLOGIST Where can I get the "Testimony of the Rocks"?
See the reports of the campaign committees after the election in November.

SCHOLAR Please state what the seven wonders of the world are. I know five of them, I think, but can't find out the other two.
The Temple of Diana, at Lexington, Ky.; the Great Wall of China; Judge Von Rosenberg (the Colossus of Roads); the Hanging Gardens at Albany; a San Antonio Sunday school; Mrs. Frank Leslie, and the Populist party.

CONSTANT READER What day did Christmas come on in the year 1847?
The 25th of December.

IGNORANT What does an F. F. V. mean?
What does he mean by what? If he takes you by the arm and tells you how much you are like a brother of his in Richmond, he means Feel For Your Vest, for he wants to borrow a five. If he holds his head high and don't speak to you on the street he means that he already owes you ten and is Following a Fresh Victim.

R. Please decide a bet for us. My friend says that the sentence, "The negro bought the watermelon *of* the farmer" is correct, and I say it should be "The negro bought the watermelon from the farmer." Which is correct?
Neither. It should read, "The negro stole the watermelon from the farmer."

HUNTER When do the Texas game laws go into effect?
When you sit down at the table.

LAND AGENT Do you know where I can trade a section of fine Panhandle land for a pair of pants with a good title?
We do not. You can't raise anything on land in that section. A man can always raise a dollar on a good pair of pants.

ADVERTISER Name in order the three best newspapers in Texas.
Well, the Galveston *News* runs about second, and the San Antonio *Express* third. Let us hear from you again.

PROSPECTOR Has a married woman any rights in Texas?
Hush, Mr. Prospector. Not quite so loud. if you please. Come up to the

office some afternoon, and if everything seems quiet, come inside, and look at our eye, and our suspenders hanging on to one button, and feel the lump on the top of our head. Yes, she has some rights of her own, and everybody else's she can scoop in.

Who was the author of the sayings, "A public office is a public trust," and "I would rather be right than President"?
Eli Perkins.

INQUISITIVE   Is the Lakeside Improvement Company making anything out of their own town tract on the lake?
Yes, lots.

BOOK **9**

POEMS

THE PEWEE

In the hush of the drowsy afternoon,
When the very wind on the breast of June
Lies settled, and hot white tracery
Of the shattered sunlight filters free
Through the unstinted leaves to the pied cool sward;
On a dead tree branch sings the saddest bard
      Of the birds that be;
        'Tis the lone Pewee.
Its note is a sob, and its note is pitched
In a single key, like a soul bewitched
      To a mournful minstrelsy.

"Peewee, Pewee," doth it ever cry;
A sad, sweet minor threnody
That threads the aisles of the dim hot grove
Like a tale of a wrong or a vanished love;
And the fancy comes that the wee dun bird
Perchance was a maid, and her heart was stirred
    By some lover's rhyme
    In a golden time,
And broke when the world turned false and cold;
And her dreams grew dark and her faith grew cold
    In some fairy far-off clime.

And her soul crept into the Pewee's breast;
And forever she cries with a strange unrest
For something lost, in the afternoon;
For something missed from the lavish June;
For the heart that died in the long ago;
For the livelong pain that pierceth so:
    Thus the Pewee cries,
    While the evening lies
Steeped in the languorous still sunshine,
Rapt, to the leaf and the bough and the vine
    Of some hopeless paradise.

NOTHING TO SAY

"You can tell your paper," the great man said,
  "I refused an interview.
I have nothing to say on the question, sir;
  Nothing to say to you."

And then he talked till the sun went down
  And the chickens went to roost;
And he seized the collar of the poor young man,
  And never his hold he loosed.

And the sun went down and the moon came up,
  And he talked till the dawn of day;
Though he said, "On this subject mentioned by you,
  I have nothing whatever to say."

And down the reporter dropped to sleep
 And flat on the floor he lay;
And the last he heard was the great man's words,
 "I have nothing at all to say."

THE MURDERER

"I push my boat among the reeds;
 I sit and stare about;
Queer slimy things crawl through the weeds,
 Put to a sullen rout.
I paddle under cypress trees;
 All fearfully I peer
Through oozy channels when the breeze
 Comes rustling at my ear.

"The long moss hangs perpetually;
 Gray scalps of buried years;
Blue crabs steal out and stare at me,
 And seem to gauge my fears;
I start to hear the eel swim by;
 I shudder when the crane
Strikes at his prey; I turn to fly
 At drops of sudden rain.

"In every little cry of bird
 I hear a tracking shout;
From every sodden leaf that's stirred
 I see a face frown out;
My soul shakes when the water rat
 Cowed by the blue snake flies;
Black knots from tree holes glimmer at
 Me with accusive eyes.

"Through all the murky silence rings
 A cry not born of earth;
And endless, deep, unechoing thing
 That owns not human birth,
I see no colors in the sky
 Save red, as blood is red;
I pray to God to still that cry
 From pallid lips and dead.

"One spot in all that stagnant waste
   I shun as moles shun light,
And turn my prow to make all haste
   To fly before the night.
A poisonous mound hid from the sun,
   Where crabs hold revelry;
Where eels and fishes feed upon
   The Thing that once was He.

"At night I steal along the shore;
   Within my hut I creep;
But awful stars blink through the door,
   To hold me from my sleep.
The river gurgles like his throat,
   In little choking coves,
And loudly dins that phantom note
   From out the awful groves.

"I shout with laughter through the night:
   I rage in greatest glee;
My fears all vanish with the light
   Oh! splendid nights they be!
I see her weep; she calls his name;
   He answers not, nor will;
My soul with joy is all aflame;
   I laugh, and laugh, and thrill.

"I count her teardrops as they fall;
   I flout my daytime fears;
I mumble thanks to God for all
   These gibes and happy jeers.
But, when the warning dawn awakes,
   Begins my wandering;
With stealthy strokes through tangled brakes,
   A wasted, frightened thing."

SOME POSTSCRIPTS

Two Portraits

Wild hair flying, in a matted maze,
Hand firm as iron, eyes all ablaze;

Bystanders timidly, breathlessly gaze,
As o'er the keno board boldly he plays.
                        —That's Texas Bill.

Wild hair flying, in a matted maze,
Hand firm as iron, eyes all ablaze;
Bystanders timidly, breathlessly gaze,
As o'er the keyboard boldly he plays.
                        —That's Paderewski.

A Contribution

There came unto ye editor
    A poet, pale and wan,
And at the table sate him down,
    A roll within his hand.

Ye editor accepted it,
    And thanked his lucky fates;
Ye poet had to yield it up
    To a king full on eights.

The Old Farm

Just now when the whitening blossoms flare
    On the apple trees and the growing grass
Creeps forth, and a balm is in the air;
        With my lighted pipe and well-filled glass
            Of the old farm I am dreaming,
            And softly smiling, seeming
            To see the bright sun beaming
            Upon the old home farm.

And when I think how we milked the cows,
    And hauled the hay from the meadows low;
And walked the furrows behind the plows,
        And chopped the cotton to make it grow
            I'd much rather be here dreaming
            And smiling, only seeming
            To see the hot sun gleaming
            Upon the old home farm.

Vanity

A Poet sang so wondrous sweet
    That toiling thousands paused and listened long;
So lofty, strong and noble were his themes,
    It seemed that strength supernal swayed his song.

He, god-like, chided poor, weak, weeping man,
    And bade him dry his foolish, shameful tears;
Taught that each soul on its proud self should lean,
    And from that rampart scorn all earth-born fears.

The Poet grovelled on a fresh heaped mound,
    Raised o'er the clay of one he'd fondly loved;
And cursed the world, and drenched the sod with tears
    And all the flimsy mockery of his precepts proved.

The Lullaby Boy

The lullaby boy to the same old tune
    Who abandons his drum and toys
For the purpose of dying in early June
    Is the kind the public enjoys.

But, just for a change, please sing us a song,
    Of the sore-toed boy that's fly,
And freckled and mean, and ugly, and bad,
    And positively will not die.

Chanson de Bohème

Lives of great men all remind us
    Rose is red and violet's blue;
Johnny's got his gun behind us
    'Cause the lamb loved Mary too.
—Robert Burns' "Hocht Time in the aud Town."

I'd rather write this, as bad as it is
    Than be Will Shakespeare's shade;
I'd rather be known as an F. F. V.
    Than in Mount Vernon laid.

I'd rather count ties from Denver to Troy
  Then to head Booth's old programme;
I'd rather be special for the New York *World*
  Than to lie with Abraham.

For there's stuff in the can, there's Dolly and Fan
  And a hundred things to choose;
There's a kiss in the ring, and every old thing
  That a real live man can use.

I'd rather fight flies in a boarding house
  Than fill Napoleon's grave,
And snuggle up warm in my three slat bed
  Than be André the brave.
I'd rather distribute a coat of red
  On the town with a wad of dough
Just now, than to have my cognomen
  Spelled "Michael Angelo."

For a small live man, if he's prompt on hand
  When the good things pass around,
While the world's on tap has a better snap
  Than a big man under ground.

Hard to Forget

I'm thinking to-night of the old farm, Ned,
  And my heart is heavy and sad
As I think of the days that by have fled
  Since I was a little lad.
There rises before me each spot I know
  Of the old home in the dell,
The fields, and woods, and meadows below
  That memory holds so well.

The city is pleasant and lively, Ned,
  But what to us is its charm?
To-night all my thoughts are fixed, instead,
  On our childhood's old home farm.
I know you are thinking the same, dear Ned,
  With your head bowed on your arm,
For to-morrow at four we'll be jerked out of bed
  To plow on that darned old farm.

DROP A TEAR IN THIS SLOT

He who, when torrid Summer's sickly glare
Beat down upon the city's parched walls,
Sat him within a room scarce 8 by 9,
And, with tongue hanging out and panting breath,
Perspiring, pierced by pangs of prickly heat,
Wrote variations of the seaside joke
We all do know and always loved so well,
And of cool breezes and sweet girls that lay
In shady nooks, and pleasant windy coves
Anon
Will in that self-same room, with tattered quilt
Wrapped round him, and blue stiffening hands,
All shivering, fireless, pinched by winter's blasts,
Will hale us forth upon the rounds once more,
So that we may expect it not in vain,
The joke of how with curses deep and coarse
Papa puts up the pipe of parlor stove.
So ye
Who greet with tears this olden favorite,
Drop one for him who, though he strives to please
Must write about the things he never sees.

TAMALES

This is the Mexican
Don José Calderon
One of God's countrymen.
Land of the buzzard.
Cheap silver dollar, and
Cacti and murderers.
Why has he left his land?
Land of the lazy man,
Land of the pulque
Land of the bull fight,
Fleas and revolution.

This is the reason,
Hark to the wherefore;
Listen and tremble.
One of his ancestors,
Ancient and garlicky
Probably grandfather,
Died with his boots on.
Killed by the Texans,
Texans with big guns,
At San Jacinto.
Died without benefit

Of priest or clergy;
Died full of minie balls,
Mescal and pepper.

Don José Calderon
Heard of the tragedy.
Heard of it, thought of it,
Vowed a deep vengeance;
Vowed retribution
On the Americans,
Murderous gringos,
Especially Texans.
"Válgame Dios! qué
Ladrones, diablos,
Matadores, mentidores,
Carracos y perros,
Voy a matarles,
Con sólo mis manos,
Toditas sin falta."
Thus swore the Hidalgo
Don José Calderon.
He hied him to Austin.
Bought him a basket,
A barrel of pepper,
And another of garlic;
Also a rope he bought.
That was his stock in trade;
Nothing else had he.
Nor was he rated in
Dun or in Bradstreet,
Though he meant business.
Don José Calderon,
Champion of Mexico,
Don José Calderon,
Seeker of vengeance.

With his stout lariat,
Then he caught swiftly
Tomcats and puppy dogs,
Caught them and cooked them,
Don José Calderon,
Vower of vengeance.
Now on the sidewalk
Sits the avenger

Selling Tamales to
Innocent purchasers.
Dire is thy vengeance,
Oh, José Calderon,
Pitiless Nemesis
Fearful Redresser
Of the wrongs done to thy
Sainted grandfather.

Now the doomed Texans,
Rashly hilarious,
Buy of the deadly wares,
Buy and devour.
Rounders at midnight,
Citizens solid,
Bankers and newsboys,
Bootblacks and preachers,
Rashly importunate,
Courting destruction,
Buy and devour.
Beautiful maidens
Buy and devour,
Gentle society youths
Buy and devour.

Buy and devour
This thing called Tamale;
Made of rat terrier,
Spitz dog and poodle,
Maltese cat, boarding house
Steak and red pepper,
Garlic and tallow,
Corn meal and shucks.
Buy without shame
Sit on store steps and eat,
Stand on the street and eat,
Ride on the cars and eat,
Strewing the shucks around
Over creation.

Dire is thy vengeance,
Don José Calderon,
For the slight thing we did
Killing thy grandfather.

What boots it if we killed
Only one greaser,
Don José Calderon?
This is your deep revenge,
You have greased all of us,
Greased a whole nation

With your Tamales,
Don José Calderon.
Santos Esperitos,
Vicente Camillo,
Quitana de Rios,
De Rosa y Ribera.

SOME LETTERS

Letter to Mr. Gilman Hall, O. Henry's friend and Associate Editor of
Everybody's Magazine.

"the Callie"—
Excavation Road—   Sundy.
my dear mr. hall:
    in your october E'bodys' i read a story in which i noticed some sentences
as follows:
    "Day in, day out, day in, day out, day in, day out, day in, day out, day
in, day out, it had rained, rained, and rained and rained & rained & rained &
rained & rained till the mountains loomed like a chunk of rooined velvet."
    And the other one was: "i don't keer whether you are any good or not,"
she cried. "You're alive! You're alive! You're alive! You're alive! You're
alive! You're alive! You're alive! You're alive! You're alive! You're
alive! You're alive! You're alive! You're alive! You're alive! You're
alive! You're alive!"
    I thought she would never stop saying it, on and on and on and on
and on and on and on and on and on and on and on and on. "You're
alive! You're alive! You're alive! You're alive! You're alive! You're
alive! You're ALIVE!
    "You're alive! You're alive! You're alive! You're alive! You're alive!
You're alive! You're alive! You're ALIVE!
    "YOU'RE ALIVE!"
    Say, bill; do you get this at a rate, or does every word go?
    i want to know, because if the latter is right i'm going to interduce in
compositions some histerical personages that will loom up large as re-
peeters when the words are counted up at the polls.
                              Yours truly
                              O. henry
                    28 West 26th St.,
                                        West of Broadway
Mr. hall,
    part editor
        of everybody's.

Letter to Mrs. Hall, a friend back in North Carolina.

KYNTOEKNEEYOUGH RANCH, November 31, 1883

Dear Mrs. Hall:

As I have not heard from you since the shout you gave when you set out from the station on your way home I guess you have not received some seven or eight letters from me, and hence your silence. The mails are so unreliable that they may all have been lost. If you don't get this you had better send to Washington and get them to look over the dead letter office for the others. I have nothing to tell you of any interest, except that we all nearly froze to death last night, thermometer away below 32 degrees in the shade all night.

You ought by all means to come back to Texas this winter; you would love it more and more; that same little breeze that you looked for so anxiously last summer is with us now, as cold as Callum Bros. suppose their soda water to be.

My sheep are doing finely; they never were in better condition. They give me very little trouble, for I have never been able to see one of them yet. I will proceed to give you all the news about this ranch. Dick has got his new house well under way, the pet lamb is doing finely, and I take the cake for cooking mutton steak and fine gravy. The chickens are doing mighty well, the garden produces magnificent prickly pears and grass; onions are worth two for five cents, and Mr. Haynes has shot a Mexican.

Please send by express to this ranch 75 cooks and 200 washwomen, blind or wooden legged ones preferred. The climate has a tendency to make them walk off every two or three days, which must be overcome. Ed Brockman has quit the store and I think is going to work for Lee among the cows. Wears a red sash and swears so fluently that he has been mistaken often for a member of the Texas Legislature.

If you see Dr. Beall bow to him for me, politely but distantly; he refuses to waste a line upon me. I suppose he is too much engaged in courting to write any letters. Give Dr. Hall my profoundest regards. I think about him invariably whenever he is occupying my thoughts.

Influenced by the contents of the *Bugle,* there is an impression general at this ranch that you are president, secretary, and committee, &c., of the various associations of fruit fairs, sewing societies, church fairs, Presbytery, general assembly conference, medical conventions, and baby shows that go to make up the glory and renown of North Carolina in general, and while I heartily congratulate the aforesaid institutions on their having such a zealous and efficient officer, I tremble lest their requirements leave you not time to favor me with a letter in reply to this, and assure you that if you would so honor me I would highly appreciate the effort. I would rather have a good long letter from you than many *Bugles*. In your letter be certain to refer as much as possible to the advantages of civilized life over the barbarous; you might mention the theatres you see there, the nice things you eat, warm fires, niggers to cook and bring in wood; a special reference to nice beefsteak would be advisable. You know our being reminded of these luxuries make us contented and happy. When we hear of you people at home eating turkeys and mince pies and getting drunk Christmas and having a fine time generally we become more and more reconciled to this country and would not leave it for anything.

I must close now as I must go and dress for the opera. Write soon.

Yours very truly,

W. S. Porter

Dr. Beall, of Greensboro, N. C., was one of Porter's best friends. Between them there was an almost regular correspondence during Porter's first years in Texas.

TO DR. W. P. BEALL

La Salle County, Texas, December 8, 1883

Dear Doctor: I send you a play—a regular high art full orchestra, gilt-edged drama. I send it to you because of old acquaintance and as a revival of old associations. Was I not ever ready in times gone by to generously furnish a spatula and other assistance when you did buy the succulent watermelon? And was it not by my connivance and help that you did oft from the gentle Oscar Mayo skates entice? But I digress. I think that I have so concealed the identity of the characters introduced that no one will be able to place them, as they all appear under fictitious names, although I admit that many of the incidents and scenes were suggested by actual experiences of the author in your city.

You will, of course, introduce the play upon the stage if proper arrangements can be made. I have not yet had an opportunity of ascertaining whether Edwin Booth, John McCullough, or Henry Irving can be secured. However, I will leave all such matters to your judgment and taste. Some few suggestions I will make with regard to the mounting of the piece which may be of value to you. Discrimination will be necessary in selecting a fit person to represent the character of Bill Slax, the tramp. The part is that of a youth of great beauty and noble manners, temporarily under a cloud, and is generally rather difficult to fill properly. The other minor characters, such as damfools, citizens, police, customers, countrymen, &c., can be very easily supplied, especially the first.

Let it be announced in the *Patriot* for several days that in front of

Benbow Hall, at a certain hour, a man will walk a tight rope seventy feet from the ground who has never made the attempt before; that the exhibition will be FREE, and that the odds are 20 to 1 that the man will be killed. A large crowd will gather. Then let the Guildford Grays charge one side, the Reidsville Light Infantry the other, with fixed bayonets, and a man with a hat commence taking up a collection in the rear. By this means they can be readily driven into the hall and the door locked.

I have studied a long time about devising a plan for obtaining pay from the audience and have finally struck upon the only feasible one I think.

After the performance let some one come out on the stage and announce that James Forbis will speak two hours. The result, easily explainable by philosophical and psychological reasons, will be as follows: The minds of the audience, elated and inspired by the hope of immediate departure when confronted by such a terror-inspiring and dismal prospect, will collapse with the fearful reaction which will take place, and for a space of time they will remain in a kind of comatose, farewell-vain-world condition. Now, as this is the time when the interest of the evening is at its highest pitch, let the melodious strains of the orchestra steal forth as a committee appointed by the managers of lawyers, druggists, doctors, and revenue officers, go around and relieve the audience of the price of admission for each one. Where one person has no money let it be made up from another, but on no account let the whole sum taken be more than the just amount at usual rates.

As I said before, the characters in the play are purely imaginary, and therefore not to be confounded with real persons. But lest any one, feeling some of the idiosyncrasies and characteristics apply too forcibly to his own high moral and irreproachable self, should allow his warlike and combative spirits to arise, you might as you go, kind of casually like, produce the impression that I rarely miss my aim with a Colt's forty-five, but if that does not have the effect of quieting the splenetic individual, and he still thirsts for Bill Slax's gore, just inform him that if he comes out here he can't get any whiskey within two days' journey of my present abode, and water will have to be his only beverage while on the warpath. This, I am sure, will avert the bloody and direful conflict.

Accept my lasting regards and professions of respect.

Ever yours,
Bill Slax

TO DR. W. P. BEALL

My dear Doctor: I wish you a happy, &c., and all that sort of thing, don't you know, &c., &c. I send you a few little productions in the way of poetry, &c., which, of course, were struck off in an idle moment. Some of the pictures are not good likenesses, and so I have not labelled them, which you may do as fast [as] you discover whom they represent, as some of them resemble others more than themselves, but the poems are good without exception, and will compare favorably with Baron Alfred's latest on spring.

I have just come from a hunt, in which I mortally wounded a wild hog, and as my boots are full of thorns I can't write any longer than this paper will contain, for it's all I've got, because I'm too tired to write any more for the reason that I have no news to tell.

I see by the *Patriot* that you are Superintendent of Public Health, and assure you that all such upward rise as you make like that will ever be witnessed with interest and pleasure by me, &c., &c. Give my regards to Dr. and Mrs. Hall. It would be uncomplimentary to your powers of perception as well as superfluous to say that I will now close and remain, yours truly,

W. S. Porter

LETTER TO DR. W. P. BEALL

LA SALLE COUNTY, Texas, February 27, 1884

My dear Doctor: Your appreciated epistle of the 18th received. I was very glad to hear from you. I hope to hear again if such irrelevant correspondence will not interfere with your duties as Public Health Eradicator, which I believe is the office you hold under county authority. I supposed the very dramatic Shakespearean comedy to be the last, as I heard nothing from you previous before your letter, and was about to write another of a more exciting character, introducing several bloody single combats, a dynamite explosion, a ladies' oyster supper for charitable purposes, &c., also comprising some mysterious sub rosa transactions known only to myself and a select few, new songs and dances, and the Greensboro Poker Club. Having picked up a few points myself relative to this latter amusement, I feel competent to give a lucid, glittering portrait of the scenes presented under its auspices. But if the former drama has reached you safely, I will refrain from burdening you any more with the labors of general stage manager, &c.

If long hair, part of a sombrero, Mexican spurs, &c., would make a fellow famous, I already occupy a topmost niche in the Temple Frame. If my wild, untamed aspect had not been counteracted by my well-known benevolent and amiable expression of countenance, I would have been arrested long ago by the Rangers on general suspicions of murder and horse stealing. In fact, I owe all my present means of lugubrious living to my desperate and bloodthirsty appearance, combined with the confident and easy way in which I tackle a Winchester rifle. There is a gentleman who lives about fifteen miles from the ranch, who for amusement and recreation, and not altogether without an eye to the profit, keeps a general merchandise store. This gent for the first few months has been trying very earnestly to sell me a little paper, which I would like much to have, but am not anxious to purchase. Said paper is my account, receipted. Occasionally he is absent, and the welcome news coming to my ear, I mount my fiery hoss and gallop wildly up to the store, enter with something of the sang froid, grace, abandon, and recherché nonchalance with which Charles Yates ushers ladies and gentlemen to their seats in the opera-house, and, nervously fingering my butcher knife, fiercely demand goods and chattels of the clerk. This plan always succeeds. This is by way of explanation of this vast and unnecessary stationery of which this letter is composed. I am always in too big a hurry to demur at kind and quality, but when I get to town I will write you on small gilt-edged paper that would suit even the fastidious and discriminating taste of a Logan.

When I get to the city, which will be shortly, I will send you some account of this country and its inmates.

You are right, I have almost forgotten what a regular old, gum-chewing, ice-cream-destroying, opera ticket vortex, ivory-clawing girl looks like. Last summer a very fair specimen of this kind ranged over about Fort Snell, and I used to ride over twice a week on mail days and chew the end of my riding whip while she "Stood on the Bridge" and "Gathered up Shells on the Sea Shore" and wore the "Golden Slippers." But she has vamoosed, and my ideas on the subject are again growing dim.

If you see anybody about to start to Texas to live, especially to this part, if you will take your scalpyouler and sever the jugular vein, cut the brachiopod artery and hamstring him, after he knows what you have done for him he will rise and call you blessed. This country is a silent but eloquent refutation of Bob Ingersoll's theory; a man here gets prematurely insane, melancholy and unreliable and finally dies of lead poisoning, in his boots, while in a good old land like Greensboro a man can die, as they do every day, with all the benefits of the clergy.

W. S. Porter

Austin, Texas, April 21, 1885

Dear Dave: I take my pen in hand to let you know that I am well, and hope these few lines will find you as well as can be expected.

I carried out your parting injunction of a floral nature with all the solemnity and sacredness that I would have bestowed upon a dying man's last request. Promptly at half-past three I repaired to the robbers' den, commonly known as Radams Horticultural and Vegetable Emporium, and secured the high-priced offerings according to promise. I asked if the bouquets were ready, and the polite but piratical gentleman in charge pointed proudly to two objects on the counter reposing in a couple of vases, and said they were.

I then told him I feared there was some mistake, as no buttonhole bouquets had been ordered, but he insisted on his former declaration, and so I brought them away and sent them to their respective destinations.

I thought it a pity to spoil a good deck of cards by taking out only one, so I bundled up the whole deck, and inserted them in the bouquet, but finally concluded it would not be right to *violet* (JOKE) my promise and I *rose* (JOKE) superior to such a mean trick and sent only one as directed.

I have a holiday to-day, as it is San Jacinto day. Thermopylae had its messenger of defeat, but the Alamo had none. Mr. President and fellow citizens, those glorious heroes who fell for their country on the bloody field of San Jacinto, etc.

There is a bazaar to-night in the representatives' hall. You people out in Colorado don't know anything. A bazaar is cedar and tacks and girls and raw-cake and step-ladders and Austin Grays and a bass solo by Bill Stacy, and net profits $2.65.

Albert has got his new uniform and Alf Menille is in town, and the store needs the "fine Italian hand" of the bookkeeper very much, besides some of his plain Anglo-Saxon conversation.

Was interviewed yesterday by Gen'l Smith, Clay's father. He wants Jim S. and me to represent a manufactory in Jeff. City: Convict labor. Says parties in Galveston and Houston are making good thing of it. Have taken him up. Hope to be at work soon. Glad, by jingo! Shake. What'll you have? Claret and sugar? Better come home. Colorado no good.

Strange thing happened in Episcopal Church Sunday. Big crowd. Choir had sung jolly tune and preacher come from behind scenes. Everything quiet. Suddenly fellow comes down aisle. Late. Everybody looks. Disappointment. It is a stranger. Jones and I didn't go. Service proceeds.

Jones talks about his mashes and Mirabeau B. Lamar, daily. Yet there is hope. Cholera infantum; Walsh's crutch; Harvey, or softening of the brain may carry him off yet.

Society notes are few. Bill Stacey is undecided where to spend the summer. Henry Harrison will resort at Wayland and Crisers. Charlie Cook will not go near a watering place if he can help it.

If you don't strike a good thing out West, I hope we will see you soon.

Yours as ever,
W. S. P.

Austin, Texas, April 28, 1885

Dear Dave: I received your letter in answer to mine, which you never got till sometime after you had written.

I snatch a few moments from my arduous labors to reply. The Colorado has been on the biggest boom I have seen since '39. In the pyrotechnical and not strictly grammatical language of the *Statesman*—The cruel, devastating flood swept, on a dreadful holocaust of swollen, turbid waters, surging and dashing in mad fury which have never been equalled in human history. A pitiable sight was seen the morning after the flood. Six hundred men, out of employment, were seen standing on the banks of the river, gazing at the rushing stream, laden with débris of every description. A wealthy New York Banker, who was present, noticing the forlorn appearance of these men, at once began to collect a subscription for them, appealing in eloquent terms for help for these poor sufferers by the flood. He collected one dollar and five horn buttons. The dollar he had given himself. He learned on inquiry that these men had not been at any employment in six years, and all they had lost by the flood was a few fishing poles. The Banker put his dollar in his pocket and stepped up to the Pearl Saloon.

As you will see by this morning's paper, there is to be a minstrel show next Wednesday for benefit of Austin Grays.

I attended the rehearsal last night, but am better this morning, and the doctor thinks I will pull through with careful attention.

The jokes are mostly mildewed, rockribbed, and ancient as the sun. I can give you no better idea of the tout ensemble and sine die of the affair than to state that Scuddy is going to sing a song. . . .

Mrs. Harrell brought a lot of crystallized fruits from New Orleans for you. She wants to know if she shall send them around on Bois d'arc or keep them 'til you return. Answer.

Write to your father. He thinks you are leaving him out, writing to everybody else first. Write.

We have the boss trick here now. Have sold about ten boxes of cigars betting on it in the store.

Take four nickels, and solder them together so the solder will not appear. Then cut out of three of them a square hole like this: (Illustration.) Take about twelve other nickels, and on top of them you lay a small die with the six up, that will fit easily in the hole without being noticed. You lay the four nickels over this, and all presents the appearance of a stack of nickles. You do all this privately so everybody will suppose it is nothing but a stack of five-cent pieces. You then lay another small die on top of the stack with the ace up. You have a small tin cup shaped like this (Illustration) made for the purpose. You let everybody see the ace, and then say you propose to turn the ace into a six. You lay the tin cup carefully over the stack this way, and feel around in your pocket for a pencil and not finding one. . . . [The rest of this letter is lost]

AUSTIN, Texas, May 10, 1885

Dear Dave: I received your two letters and have commenced two or three in reply, but always failed to say what I wanted to, and destroyed them all. I heard from Joe that you would probably remain in Colorado. I hope you will succeed in making a good thing out of it, if you conclude to do so, but would like to see you back again in Austin. If there is anything I can do for you here let me know.

Town is fearfully dull, except for the frequent raids of the Servant Girl Annihilators, who make things lively during the dead hours of the night; if it were not for them, items of interest would be very scarce, as you may see by the *Statesman*.

Our serenading party has developed new and alarming modes of torture for our helpless and sleeping victims. Last Thursday night we loaded up a small organ on a hack and with our other usual instruments made an assault upon the quiet air of midnight that made the atmosphere turn pale.

After going the rounds we were halted on the Avenue by Fritz Hartkopf and ordered into his *salon*. We went in, carrying the organ, etc. A large crowd of bums immediately gathered, prominent among which were to be seen Percy James, Theodore Hillyer, Randolph Burmond, Charlie Hicks, and after partaking freely of lemonade we wended our way down, and were duly halted and treated in the same manner by other hospitable gentlemen.

We were called in at several places while wit and champagne, Rhine Wine, etc., flowed in a most joyous and hilarious manner. It was one of the most recherché and per diem affairs ever known in the city. Nothing occurred to mar the pleasure of the hour, except a trifling incident that might be construed as malapropos and post-meridian by the hypercritical. Mr. Charles Sims on attempting to introduce Mr. Charles Hicks and your humble servant to young ladies, where we had been invited inside, forgot our names and required to be informed on the subject before proceeding.

Yours,
W. S. P.

AUSTIN, Texas, December 22, 1885

Dear Dave: Everything wept at your departure. Especially the clouds. Last night the clouds had a silver lining, three dollars and half's worth. I fulfilled your engagement in grand, tout ensemble style, but there is a sad bonjour look about the thirty-eight cents left in my vast pocket that would make a hired man weep. All day long the heavens wept, and the heavy, somber clouds went drifting about overhead, and the north wind howled in maniacal derision, and the hack drivers danced on the pavements in wild, fierce glee, for they knew too well what the stormy day betokened. The hack was to call for me at eight. At five minutes to eight I went upstairs and dressed in my usual bijou and operatic style, and rolled away to the opera. Emma sang finely. I applauded at the wrong times, and praised her rendering of the chromatic scale when she was performing on "c" flat andante pianissimo, but otherwise the occasion passed off without anything to mar the joyousness of the hour. Everybody was there. Isidor Moses and John Ireland, and Fritz Hartkopf and Prof. Herzog and Bill Stacy and all the bong ton elight. You will receive a draft to-day through the First National Bank of Colorado for $3.65, which you will please honor.

There is no news, or there are no news, either you like to tell. Lavaca Street is very happy and quiet and enjoys life, for Jones was sat on by his Uncle Wash and feels humble and don't sing any more, and the spirit of peace and repose broods over its halls. Martha rings the matin bell, it seems to me before cock crow or ere the first faint streaks of dawn are limned in the eastern sky by the rosy fingers of Aurora. At noon the foul ogre cribbage stalks rampant, and seven-up for dim, distant oysters that only the eye of faith can see.

The hour grows late. The clock strikes! Another day has vanished. Gone into the dim recesses of the past leaving its record of misspent hours, false hopes, and disappointed expectations. May a morrow dawn that will bring recompense and requital for the sorrows of the days gone by, and a new order of things when there will be more starch in cuff and collar, and less in handkerchiefs.

Come with me out into the starlight night. So calm, so serene, ye lights of heaven, so high above earth; so pure and majestic and mysterious; looking down on the mad struggle of life here below, is there no pity in your never-closing eyes for us mortals on which you shine?

Come with me on to the bridge. Ah, see there, far below, the dark, turbid stream. Rushing and whirling and eddying under the dark pillars with ghostly murmur and siren whisper. What shall we find in your depths? The stars do not reflect themselves in your waters, they are too dark and troubled and swift! What shall we find in your depths? Rest?— Peace?—catfish? Who knows? 'Tis but a moment. A leap! A plunge! —and—then oblivion or another world? Who can tell? A man once dived into your depths and brought up a horse collar and a hoop-skirt. Ah! what do we know of the beyond? We know that death comes, and we return no more to our world of trouble and care—but where do we go? Are there lands where no traveler has been? A chaos—perhaps where no human foot had trod—perhaps Bastrop—perhaps New Jersey Who knows? Where do people go who are in McDade? Do they go where they have to fare worse? They cannot go where they have worse fare.

Let us leave the river. The night grows cold. We could pierce the future or pay the toll. Come, the ice factory is deserted! No one sees us. My partner, W. P. Anderson, will never destroy himself. Why? His credit is good. No one will sue a side-partner of mine!

You have heard of a brook murmuring, but you never knew a sewer sighed! But we digress! We will no longer pursue a side issue like this. Au revoir. I will see you later.

Yours truly,

WILLIAM SHAKESPEARE INGOMAR JUNIUS BRUTUS CALLIOPE SIX-HANDED EUCHRE
GROVER CLEVELAND HILL CITY QUARTETTE JOHNSON

AN EARLY PARABLE

In one of his early letters, written from Austin, O. Henry wrote a long parable that was evidently to tell his correspondent some of the local gossip. Here it is:

Once upon a time there was a maiden in a land not far away—a maiden of much beauty and rare accomplishments. She was beloved by all on account of her goodness of heart, and her many charms of disposition. Her father was a great lord, rich and powerful, and a mighty man, and he loved his daughter with exceeding great love, and he cared for her with jealous and loving watchfulness, lest any harm should befall her, or even the least discomfort should mar her happiness and cause any trouble in her smooth and peaceful life. The cunningest masters were engaged to teach her from her youngest days; she played upon the harpsichord the loveliest and sweetest music; she wrought fancy work in divers strange and wonderful forms that might puzzle all beholders as to what manner of things they might be; she sang, and all listeners hearkened thereunto, as to the voice of an angel; she danced stately minuets with the gay knights as graceful as a queen and as light as the thistledown borne above the clover blossoms by the wind; she could paint upon china, rare and unknown flowers the like unto which man never saw in colors, crimson and blue and yellow, glorious to behold; she conversed in unknown tongues whereof no man knew the meaning and sense; and created wild admiration in all, by the ease and grace with which she did play upon a new and strange instrument of wondrous sound and structure which she called a banjo.

She had gone into a strange land, far away beyond the rivers that flowed through her father's dominion—farther than one could see from the highest castle tower—up into the land of ice and snow, where wise men, famous for learning and ancient lore, had gathered together from many lands and countries the daughters of great men. Kings and powerful rulers, railroad men, bankers, mighty men who wished to bring up their children to be wise and versed in all things old and new. Here, the Princess abode for many seasons, and she sat at the feet of old wise men, who could tell of the world's birth, and the stars, and read the meaning of the forms of the rocks that make the high mountains and knew the history of all created things that are; and here she learned to speak strange tongues, and studied the deep mysteries of the past—the secrets of the ancients; Chaldic lore; Etruscan inscription; hidden and mystic sciences, and knew the names of all the flowers and things that grow in fields or wood; even unto the tiniest weed by the brook.

In due time the Princess came back to her father's castle. The big bell boomed from the high tower; the heavy iron gates were thrown open; banners floated all along the battlemented walls, and in the grand hall, servants and retainers hurried to and fro, bearing gold dishes, and great bowls of flaming smoking punch, while oxen were roasted whole and hogsheads of ale tapped on the common by the castle walls, and thither hied them the villagers one and all to make merry at the coming of the dear Princess again. "She will come back so wise and learned," they said, "so far above us that she will not notice us as she did once," but not so: the Princess with a red rose in her hair, and dressed so plain and neat that she looked more like a farmer's daughter than a great king's, came down among them from her father's side with nods of love and welcome on her lips, and a smile upon her face, and took them by the hands as in the old days, and none among them so lowly or so poor but what received a kind word from the gracious Princess, and carried away in their hearts glad feelings that she was still the same noble and gracious lady she always was. Then night came, and torches by thousands lit up the great forest, and musicians played and bonfires glowed, with sparks flying like myriads of stars among the gloomy trees.

In the great castle hall were gathered the brave knights and the fairest ladies in the kingdom. The jolly old King, surrounded by the wise men and officers of state, moved about among his guests, stately and courteous, ravishing music burst forth from all sides, and down the hall moved the fair Princess in the mazy dance, on the arm of a knight who gazed upon her face in rapt devotion and love. Who was he that dared to look thus upon the daughter of the King, sovereign prince of the kingdom, and the heiress of her father's wealth and lands?

He had no title, no proud name to place beside a royal one, beyond that of an honorable knight, but who says that that is not a title that, borne worthily, makes a man the peer of any that wears a crown?

He had loved her long. When a boy they had roamed together in the great forest about the castle, and played among the fountains of the court like brother and sister. The King saw them together often and smiled and went his way and said nothing. The years went on and they were together as much as they could be. The summer days when the court went forth into the forest mounted on prancing steeds to chase the stags with hounds; all clad in green and gold with waving plumes and shining silver and ribbons of gay colors, this knight was by the Princess' side to guide her through the pathless swamps where the hunt ranged, and saw that no harm came to her. And now that she had come back after years of absence, he went to her with fear lest she should have changed from her old self, and would not be to him as she was when they were boy and girl together. But no, there was the same old kindly welcome, the same smiling greeting, the warm pressure of the hand, the glad look in the eyes as of yore. The Knight's heart beat wildly and a dim new-awakened hope arose in him. Was she too far away, after all?

He felt worthy of her, and of any one in fact, but he was without riches, only a knight-errant with his sword for his fortune, and his great love his only title; and he had always refrained from ever telling her anything of his love, for his pride prevented him, and you know a poor girl even though she be a princess cannot say to a man, "I am rich, but, let that be no bar between us, I am yours and will let my wealth pass if you will give up your pride." No princess can say this, and the Knight's pride would not let him say anything of the kind and so you see there was small chance of their ever coming to an understanding.

Well, the feasting and dancing went on, and the Knight and the Princess danced and sang together, and walked out where the moon was making a white wonder of the great fountain, and wandered under the rows of great oaks, but spoke no word of love, though no mortal man knows what thoughts passed in their heads; and she gave long accounts of the wonders she had seen in the far, icy north, in the great school of wise men, and the Knight talked of the wild and savage men he had seen in the Far West, where he had been in battles with the heathen in a wild and dreary land; and she heard with pity his tales of suffering and trials in the desert among wild animals and fierce human kings; and inside the castle the music died away and the lights grew dim and the villagers had long since gone to their homes and the Knight and the Princess still talked of old times, and the moon climbed high in the eastern sky.

One day there came news from a country far to the west where lay the possessions of the Knight. The enemy had robbed him of his treasure, driven away his cattle, and he found it was best to hie him away and rescue his inheritance and goods. He buckled on his sword and mounted his good war-horse. He rode to the postern gate of the castle to make his adieus to the Princess.

When he told her he was going away to the wild western country to do battle with the heathen, she grew pale, and her eyes took on a look of such pain and fear that the Knight's heart leaped and then sank in his bosom, as his pride still kept him from speaking the words that might have made all well.

She bade him farewell in a low voice, and tears even stood in her eyes, but what could she say or do?

The Knight put spurs to his horse, and dashed away over the hills without ever looking back, and the Princess stood looking over the gate at him till the last sight of his plume below the brow of the hill. The Knight was gone. Many suitors flocked about the Princess. Mighty lords and barons of great wealth were at her feet and attended her every journey. They came and offered themselves and their fortunes again and again, but none of them found favor in her eyes. "Will the Princess listen to no one?" they began to say among themselves. "Has she given her heart to some one who is not among us?" No one could say.

A great and mighty physician, young and of wondrous power in his art, telephoned to her every night if he might come down. How his suit prospered no one could tell, but he persevered with great and astonishing diligence. A powerful baron who assisted in regulating the finances of the kingdom and who was a direct descendant of a great prince who was cast into a lion's den, knelt at her feet.

A gay and lively lord who lived in a castle hung with ribbons and streamers and gay devices of all kinds, with other nobles of like character, prostrated themselves before her, but she would listen to none of them.

The Princess rode about in quiet ways in the cool evenings upon a gray palfrey, alone and very quiet, and she seemed to grow silent and thoughtful as time went on and no news came from the western wars, and the Knight came not back again. [Written to his daughter Margaret.]

Toledo, Ohio, Oct. 1, 1900

Dear Margaret: I got your very nice, long letter a good many days ago. It didn't come straight to me, but went to a wrong address first. I was very glad indeed to hear from you, and very, very sorry to learn of your getting your finger so badly hurt. I don't think you were to blame at all, as you couldn't know just how that villainous old "hoss" was going to bite. I do hope that it will heal up nicely and leave your finger strong. I am learning to play the mandolin, and we must get you a guitar, and we will learn a lot of duets together when I come home which will certainly not be later than next summer, and maybe earlier.

I suppose you have started to school again some time ago. I hope you like to go, and don't have to study too hard. When one grows up, a thing they never regret is that they went to school long enough to learn all they could. It makes everything easier for them, and if they like books and study they can always content and amuse themselves that way even if other people are cross and tiresome, and the world doesn't go to suit them.

You mustn't think that I've forgotten somebody's birthday. I couldn't find just the thing I wanted to send, but I know where it can be had, and it will reach you in a few days. So, when it comes you'll know it is for a birthday remembrance.

I think you write the prettiest hand of any little girl (or big one, either) I ever knew. The letters you make are as even and regular as printed ones. The next time you write, tell me how far you have to go to school and whether you go alone or not.

I am busy all the time writing for the papers and magazines all over the country, so I don't have a chance to come home, but I'm going to try to come this winter. If I don't I will by summer *sure,* and then you'll have somebody to boss and make trot around with you.

Write me a letter whenever you have some time to spare, for I am always glad and anxious to hear from you. Be careful when you are on the streets not to feed shucks to strange dogs, or pat snakes on the head or shake hands with cats you haven't been introduced to, or stroke the noses of electric car horses.

Hoping you are well and your finger is getting all right, I am, with much love, as ever,

Papa

My dear Margaret: Here it is summertime, and the bees are blooming and the flowers are singing and the birds making honey, and we haven't been fishing yet. Well, there's only one more month till July, and then we'll go, and no mistake. I thought you would write and tell me about the high water around Pittsburg some time ago, and whether it came up to where you live, or not. And I haven't heard a thing about Easter, and about the rabbit's eggs—but I suppose you have learned by this time that eggs grow on egg plants and are not laid by rabbits.

I would like very much to hear from you oftener, it has been more than a month now since you wrote. Write soon and tell me how you are, and when school will be out, for we want plenty of holidays in July so we can have a good time. I am going to send you something nice the last of this week. What do you guess it will be?

Lovingly,

Papa

The Caledonia

Wednesday

My dear Mr. Jack:

I owe Gilman Hall $175 (or mighty close to it) pussonally—so he tells me. I thought it was only about $30, but he has been keeping the account.

He's just got to have it to-day. *McClure's* will pay me some money on the 15th of June, but I can't get it until then. I was expecting it before this—anyhow before Gilman left, but they stick to the letter.

I wonder if you could give me a check for that much to pay him to-day. If you will I'll hold up my right hand—thus: that I'll have you a *first-class story on your desk before the last of this week.*

I reckon I'm pretty well overdrawn, but I've sure got to see that Hall gets his before he leaves. I don't want anything for myself.

Please, sir, let me know right away, by return boy if you'll do it.

If you can't, I'll have to make a quick dash at the three-ball magazines; and I do hate to tie up with them for a story.

The Same
Sydney Porter

Mr. J. O. H. Cosgrave,
   at this time editor of *Everybody's Magazine.*

A letter to Gilman Hall, written just before the writer's marriage to Miss Sara Lindsay Coleman of Asheville, N. C.

Wednesday

Dear Gilman:

Your two letters received this A.M. Mighty good letters, too, and cheering.

Mrs. Jas. Coleman is writing Mrs. Hall to-day. She is practically the hostess at Wynn Cottage where the hullabaloo will occur.

Say, won't you please do one or two little things for me before you leave, as you have so kindly offered?

(1) Please go to Tiffany's and get a wedding ring, size 5⅛. Sara says the bands worn now are quite narrow—and that's the kind she wants.

(2) And bring me a couple of dress colors, size 16½. I have ties.

(3) And go to a florist's—there is one named Mackintosh (or something like that) on Broadway, East side of street five or six doors north of 26th St., where I used to buy a good many times. He told me he could ship flowers in good shape to Asheville—you might remind him that I used to send flowers to 36 West 17th Street some time ago. I am told by the mistress of ceremonies that I am to furnish two bouquets—one of lilies of the valley and one of pale pink roses. Get plenty of each—say enough lilies to make a large bunch to be carried in the hand and say three or four dozen of the roses.

I note what you say about hard times and will take heed. I'm not going into any extravagances at all, and I'm going to pitch into hard work just as soon as I get the rice grains out of my ear.

I wired you to-day "MS, mailed to-day, please rush one century by wire."

That will exhaust the Reader check—if it isn't too exhausted itself to come. You, of course, will keep the check when it arrives—I don't think they will fall down on it surely. I wrote Howland a pretty sharp letter and ordered him to send it at once care of *Everybody's*.

When this story reaches you it will cut down the overdraft "right smart," but if the house is willing I'd mighty well like to run it up to the limit again, because cash is sure scarce, and I'll have to have something like $300 more to see me through. The story I am sending is a new one; I still have another partly written for you, which I shall finish and turn in before I get back to New York and then we'll begin to clean up all debts.

Just after the wedding we are going to Hot Spring, N. C., only thirty-five miles from Asheville, where there is a big winter resort hotel, and stay there about a week or ten days. Then back to New York.

Please look over the story and arrange for bringing me the $300 when you come—it will still keep me below the allowed limit and thereafter I will cut down instead of raising it.

Just had a 'phone message from S. L. C. saying how pleased she was with your letter to her.

I'm right with you on the question of the "home-like" system of having fun. I think we'll all agree beautifully on that. I've had all the cheap bohemia that I want. I can tell you, none of the "climbers" and the cocktail crowd are going to bring their *vaporings* into my house. It's for the clean, merry life, with your best friends in the game and a general concentration of energies and aims. I am having a cedar-wood club cut from the mountains with knots on it, and I am going to stand in my hallway (when I have one) and edit with it the cards of all callers. You and Mrs. will have latchkeys, of course.

Yes, I think you'd better stay at the hotel—— Of course they'd want you out at Mrs. C's. But suppose we take Mrs. Hall out there, and you and I remain at the B. P. We'll be out at the Cottage every day anyhow, and it'll be scrumptious all round.

I'm simply tickled to death that "you all" are coming.

The protoplasm is in Heaven; all's right with the world. Pippa passes.

Yours as ever,

Bill

Friday

My dear Col. Griffith:

Keep your shirt on. I found I had to re-write the story when it came in. I am sending you part of it so you will have something tangible to remind you that you can't measure the water from the Pierian Spring in spoonfuls.

I've got the story in much better form; and I'll have the rest of it ready this evening.

I'm sorry to have delayed it; but it's best for both of us to have it a little late and a good deal better.

I'll send over the rest before closing time this afternoon or the first thing in the morning.

In its revised form I'm much better pleased with it.

Yours truly,
Sydney Porter

[Mr. Al. Jennings, of Oklahoma City, was an early friend of O. Henry's. Now, in 1912, a prominent attorney, Mr. Jennings, in his youth, held up trains.]

28 W. 26   N. Y. SUNDAY
ALGIE JENNINGS, ESQ., THE WEST
Dear Bill:

Glad you've been sick too. I'm well again. Are you?

Well, as I had nothing to do I thought I would write you a letter; and as I have nothing to say I will close.

How are ye, Bill? How's old Initiative and Referendum? When you coming back to Manhattan? You wouldn't know the old town now. Main Street is building up, and there is talk of an English firm putting up a new hotel. I saw Duffy a few days ago. He looks kind of thoughtful as if he were trying to calculate how much he'd have been ahead on Gerald's board and clothes by now if you had taken him with you. Mrs. Hale is up in Maine for a 3 weeks' vacation.

Say, Bill, I'm sending your MS. back by mail to-day. I kept it a little longer after you sent for it because one of the McClure & Phillips firm wanted to see it first. Everybody says it is full of good stuff, but thinks it should be put in a more connected shape by some skilful writer who has been trained to that sort of work.

It seems to me that you ought to do better with it out there than you could here. If you can get somebody out there to publish it it ought to sell all right. N. Y. is a pretty cold proposition and it can't see as far as the Oklahoma country when it is looking for sales. How about trying Indianapolis or Chicago? Duffy told me about the other MS. sent out by your friend Abbott. Kind of a bum friendly trick, wasn't it?

Why don't you get "Arizona's Hand" done and send it on? Seems to me you could handle a short story all right.

My regards to Mrs. Jennings and Bro. Frank. Write some more.

Still
Bill

N. Y., May 23, '05

Dear Jennings:

Got your letter all right. Hope you'll follow it soon.

I'd advise you not to build any high hopes on your book—just consider that you're on a little pleasure trip, and taking it along as a side line. Mighty few MSS. ever get to be books, and mighty few books pay.

I have to go to Pittsburgh the first of next week to be gone about 3 or 4 days. If you decide to come here any time after the latter part of next week I will be ready to meet you. Let me know in advance a day or two.

Gallot is in Grand Rapids—maybe he will run over for a day or two.

In haste and truly yours,

W. S. P.

[It was hard to get O. Henry to take an interest in his books. He was always eager to be at the undone work, to be writing a new story instead of collecting old ones. This letter came from North Carolina. It shows how much thought he gave always to titles.]

LAND O' THE SKY, MONDAY, 1909

My dear Colonel Steger: As I wired you to-day, I like "Man About Town" for a title.

But I am sending in a few others for you to look at; and if any other suits you better, I'm agreeable. Here they are, in preferred order:

The Venturers.

Transfers.

Merry-Go-Rounds.

Babylonica.

Brickdust from Babel.

Babes in the Jungle.

If none of these hit you right, let me know and I'll get busy again. But I think "Man About Town" is about the right thing. It gives the city idea without using the old hackneyed words.

I am going to write you a letter in a day or so "touchin' on and appertainin' to" other matters and topics. I am still improving and feeling pretty good. Colonel Bingham has put in a new ash-sifter and expects you to come down and see that it works all right.

All send regards to you. You seem to have made quite a hit down here for a Yankee.

Salutations and good wishes.

Yours,

S. P.

[This letter was found unfinished, among his papers after his death. His publishers had discussed many times his writing of a novel, but the following letter constitutes the only record of his own opinions in the matter. The date is surely 1909 or 1910.]

My dear Mr. Steger: My idea is to write the story of a man—an individual, not a type—but a man who, at the same time, I want to represent a "human nature type," if such a person could exist. The story will teach no lesson, inculcate no moral, advance no theory.

I want it to be something that it won't or can't be—but as near as I can make it—the *true* record of a man's thoughts, his description of his mischances and adventures, his *true* opinions of life as he has seen it and his *absolutely honest* deductions, comments, and views upon the different phases of life that he passes through.

I do not remember ever to have read an autobiography, a biography, or a piece of fiction that told the *truth*. Of course, I have read stuff such as Rousseau and Zola and George Moore; and various memoirs that were supposed to be window panes in their respective breasts; but, mostly, all of them were either liars, actors, or posers. (Of course, I'm not trying to belittle the greatness of their literary expression.)

All of us have to be prevaricators, hypocrites, and liars every day of our lives; otherwise the social structure would fall into pieces the first day. We must act in one another's presence just as we must wear clothes. It is for the best.

The trouble about writing the truth has been that the writers have kept in their minds one or another or all of three thoughts that made a handicap—they were trying either to do a piece of immortal literature, or to shock the public or to please editors. Some of them succeeded in all three, but they did not write the *truth*. Most autobiographies are insincere from beginning to end. About the only chance for the truth to be told is in fiction.

It is well understood that "all the truth" cannot be told in print—but how about "nothing but the truth"? That's what I want to do.

I want the man who is telling the story to tell it—not as he would to a reading public or to a confessor—but something in this way: Suppose he were marooned on an island in mid-ocean with no hope of ever being rescued; and, in order to pass away some of the time he should tell a story *to himself* embodying his adventure and experiences and opinions. Having a certain respect for himself (let us hope) he would leave out the "realism" that he would have no chance of selling in the market; he would omit the lies and self-conscious poses, and would turn out to his one auditor something real and true.

So, as truth is not to be found in history, autobiography, press reports (nor at the bottom of an H. G. Wells), let us hope that fiction may be the means of bringing out a few grains of it.

The "hero" of the story will be a man born and "raised" in a somnolent little southern town. His education is about a common school one, but he learns afterward from reading and life. I'm going to try to give him a "style" in narrative and speech—the best I've got in the shop. I'm going to take him through all the main phases of life—wild adventure, city, society, something of the "under world," and among many characteristic planes of the phases. I want him to acquire all the sophistication that experience can give him, and always preserve his individual honest *human* view, and have him tell the *truth* about everything.

It is time to say now, that by the "truth" I don't mean the objectionable stuff that so often masquerades under the name. I mean true opinions, a true estimate of all things as they seem to the "hero." If you find a word or a suggestive line or sentence in any of my copy, you cut it out and deduct it from the royalties.

I want this man to be a man of natural intelligence, of individual character, absolutely open and broad minded; and show how the Creator of the earth has got him in a rat trap—put him here "willy nilly" (you know the Omar verse) : and then I want to show what he does about it. There is always the eternal question from the Primal Source—"What are you going to do about it?"

Please don't think for the half of a moment that the story is going to be anything of an autobiography. I have a distinct character in my mind for the part, and he does not at all [Here the letter ends. He never finished it.]

THE STORY OF "HOLDING UP A TRAIN"

In "Sixes and Sevens" there appears an article entitled "Holding Up a Train." Now the facts were given to O. Henry by a friend who had actually held up trains. To-day he is Mr. Al Jennings, of Oklahoma City, Okla., a prominent attorney. He has permitted the publication of two letters O. Henry wrote him, the first outlining the story as he thought his friend Jennings ought to write it, and the second announcing that, with O. Henry's revision, the manuscript had been accepted.

From W. S. Porter to Al Jennings, September 21st (year not given but probably 1902).

Dear Pard:

In regard to that article—I will give you my idea of what is wanted. Say we take for a title "The Art and Humor of the Hold-Up"—or something like that. I would suggest that in writing you assume a character. We have got to respect the conventions and delusions of the public to a certain extent. An article written as you would naturally write it would be regarded as a fake and an imposition. Remember that the traditions must be preserved wherever they will not interfere with the truth. Write in as simple, plain, and unembellished a style as you know how. Make your sentences short. Put in as much realism and as many facts as possible. Where you want to express an opinion or comment on the matter do it as practically and plainly as you can. Give it *life* and the vitality of *facts*.

Now, I will give you a sort of general synopsis of my idea—of course, everything is subject to your own revision and change. The article, we will say, is written by a *typical* train hoister—one without your education and powers of expression (bouquet) but intelligent enough to convey his ideas from *his standpoint*—not from John Wanamaker's. Yet, in order to please John, we will have to assume a virtue that we do not possess. Comment on the moral side of the proposition as little as possible. Do not claim that holding up trains is the only business a gentleman would engage in, and, on the contrary, do not depreciate a profession that is really only financiering with spurs on. Describe the *facts* and *details*— all that part of the proceedings that the passenger sitting with his hands up in a Pullman looking into the end of a tunnel in the hands of one of the performers does not see. Here is a rough draft of my idea: Begin abruptly, without any philosophizing, with your idea of the best times, places and conditions for the hold-up—compare your opinions of this with those of others—mention some poorly conceived attempts and failures of others, giving your opinion why—as far as possible refer to actual occurrences, and incidents—describe the manner of a hold-up, how many men is best, where they are stationed, how do they generally go into it, nervous? or joking? or solemnly. The details of stopping the train, the duties of each man of the gang—the behavior of the train crew and passengers (here give as many brief odd and humorous incidents as you can think of). Your opinions on going through the passengers, when it is done and when not done. How is the boodle gotten at? How does the express clerk generally take it? Anything done with the mail car? *Under what circumstances will a train robber shoot a passenger or a train man*—suppose a man refuses to throw up his hands? Queer articles found on passengers (a chance here for some imaginative work)—queer and laughable incidents of any kind. Refer whenever apropos to actual hold-ups and facts concerning them of interest. What could two or three brave and determined passengers do if they were to try? Why don't they try? How long does it take to do the business. Does the train man ever stand in with the hold-up? Best means of getting away—how and when is the money divided. How is it mostly spent. Best way to maneuver afterward. How to get caught and how not to. Comment on the methods of officials who try to capture. (Here's your chance to get even.)

These ideas are some that occur to me casually. You will, of course, have many far better. I suggest that you make the article anywhere from 4,000 to 6,000 words. Get as much meat in it as you can, and by the way —stuff it full of western *genuine* slang—(not the eastern story paper kind). Get all the quaint cowboy expressions and terms of speech you can think of.

Information is what we want, clothed in the peculiar western style of the character we want to present. The main idea is to be *natural, direct,* and *concise.*

I hope you will understand what I say. I don't. But try her a whack and send it along as soon as you can, and let's see what we can do. By the way, Mr. "Everybody" pays good prices. I thought I would, when I get your story, put it into the shape my judgment decides upon, and then send both your MS. and mine to the magazine. If he uses mine, we'll whack up shares on the proceeds. If he uses yours, you get the check direct. If he uses neither, we are out only a few stamps.

Sincerely your friend,
W. S. P.

And here is the letter telling his "pard" that the article had been bought by *Everybody's Magazine.* This is dated Pittsburg, October 24th, obviously the same year:

Dear Pard:

You're It. I always told you you were a genius. All you need is to succeed in order to make a success.

I enclose pubʳˢ letter which explains itself. When you see your baby in print don't blame me if you find strange ear marks and brands on it. I slashed it and cut it and added lots of stuff that never happened, but I followed your facts and ideas, and that is what made it valuable. I'll think up some other idea for an article and we'll collaborate again some time —eh?

I have all the work I can do, and am selling it right along. Have averaged about $150 per month since August 1st. And yet I don't overwork—don't think I ever will. I commence about 9 A.M. and generally knock off about 4 or 5 P.M.

As soon as check mentioned in letter comes I'll send you your "sheer" of the boodle.

By the way, please keep my *nom de plume* strictly to yourself. I don't want any one to know just yet.

Give my big regards to Billy. Reason with him and try to convince him that we believe him to be pure merino and of more than average width. With the kindest remembrances to yourself I remain,

Your friend,
W. S. P.

At this time O. Henry was unknown and thought himself lucky to sell a story at any price.

BOOK 10

WHIRLIGIGS

THE WORLD AND THE DOOR

A favorite dodge to get your story read by the public is to assert that it is true, and then add that Truth is stranger than Fiction. I do not know if the yarn I am anxious for you to read is true; but the Spanish purser of the fruit steamer *El Carrero* swore to me by the shrine of Santa Guadalupe that he had the facts from the U. S. vice-consul at La Paz—a person who could not possibly have been cognizant of half of them.

As for the adage quoted above, I take pleasure in puncturing it by affirming that I read in a purely fictional story the other day the line: " 'Be it so,' said the policeman." Nothing so strange has yet cropped out in Truth.

When H. Ferguson Hedges, millionaire promoter, investor, and man-about-New-York, turned his thoughts upon matters convivial, and word of it went "down the line," bouncers took a precautionary turn at the Indian clubs, waiters put ironstone china on his favorite tables, cab drivers crowded close to the curbstone in front of all-night cafés, and careful cashiers in his regular haunts charged up a few bottles to his account by way of preface and introduction.

As a money power a one-millionaire is of small account in a city where the man who cuts your slice of beef behind the free-lunch counter rides to work in his own automobile. But Hedges spent his money as lavishly, loudly, and showily as though he were only a clerk squandering a week's wages. And, after all, the bartender takes no interest in your reserve fund. He would rather look you up on his cash register than in Brad-street.

On the evening that the material allegation of facts begins, Hedges was bidding dull care begone in the company of five or six good fellows—acquaintances and friends who had gathered in his wake.

Among them were two younger men—Ralph Merriam, a broker, and Wade, his friend.

Two deep-sea cabmen were chartered. At Columbus Circle they hove to long enough to revile the statue of the great navigator, unpatriotically rebuking him for having voyaged in search of land instead of liquids. Midnight overtook the party marooned in the rear of a cheap café far uptown.

Hedges was arrogant, overriding, and quarrelsome. He was burly and tough, iron-gray but vigorous, "good" for the rest of the night. There was a dispute—about nothing that matters—and the five-fingered words were passed—the words that represent the glove cast into the lists. Merriam played the rôle of the verbal Hotspur.

Hedges rose quickly, seized his chair, swung it once and smashed wildly down at Merriam's head. Merriam dodged, drew a small revolver and shot Hedges in the chest. The leading roysterer stumbled, fell in a wry heap, and lay still.

Wade, a commuter, had formed that habit of promptness. He juggled Merriam out a side door, walked him to the corner, ran him a block and caught a hansom. They rode five minutes and then got out on a dark corner and dismissed the cab. Across the street the lights of a small saloon betrayed its hectic hospitality.

"Go in the back room of that saloon," said Wade, "and wait. I'll go find out what's doing and let you know. You may take two drinks while I am gone—no more."

At ten minutes to one o'clock Wade returned.

"Brace up, old chap," he said. "The ambulance got there just as I did. The doctor says he's dead. You may have one more drink. You let me run this thing for you. You've got to skip. I don't believe a chair is legally a deadly weapon. You've got to make tracks, that's all there is to it."

Merriam complained of the cold querulously, and asked for another drink. "Did you notice what big veins he had on the back of his hands?" he said. "I never could stand—I never could——"

"Take one more," said Wade, "and then come on. I'll see you through."

Wade kept his promise so well that at eleven o'clock the next morning Merriam, with a new suit case full of new clothes and hair-brushes, stepped quietly on board a little 500-ton fruit steamer at an East River pier. The vessel had brought the season's first cargo of limes from Port Limon, and was homeward bound. Merriam had his bank balance of $2,800 in his pocket in large bills, and brief instructions to pile up as much water as he could between himself and New York. There was no time for anything more.

From Port Limon Merriam worked down the coast by schooner and sloop to Colon, thence across the isthmus to Panama, where he caught a tramp bound for Callao and such intermediate ports as might tempt the discursive skipper from his course.

It was at La Paz that Merriam decided to land—La Paz the Beautiful, a little harborless town smothered in a living green ribbon that banded the foot of a cloud-piercing mountain. Here the little steamer stopped to tread water while the captain's dory took him ashore that he might feel the pulse of the cocoanut market. Merriam went too, with his suit case, and remained.

Kalb, the vice-consul, a Græco-Armenian citizen of the United States, born in Hesse-Darmstadt, and educated in Cincinnati ward primaries, considered all Americans his brothers and bankers. He attached himself to Merriam's elbow, introduced him to every one in La Paz who wore shoes, borrowed ten dollars and went back to his hammock.

There was a little wooden hotel in the edge of a banana grove, facing the sea, that catered to the tastes of the few foreigners that had dropped out of the world into the *triste* Peruvian town. At Kalb's introductory: "Shake hands with ——," he had obediently exchanged manual salutations with a German doctor, one French and two Italian merchants, and three or four Americans who were spoken of as gold men, rubber men, mahogany men—anything but men of living tissue.

After dinner Merriam sat in a corner of the broad front *galería* with Bibb, a Vermonter interested in hydraulic mining, and smoked and drank Scotch "smoke." The moonlit sea, spreading infinitely before him, seemed to separate him beyond all apprehension from his old life. The horrid tragedy in which he had played such a disastrous part now began, for the first time since he stole on board the fruiter, a wretched fugitive, to lose its sharper outlines. Distance lent assuagement to his view. Bibb had opened the flood-gates of a stream of long-dammed discourse, overjoyed to have captured an audience that had not suffered under a hundred repetitions of his views and theories.

"One year more," said Bibb, "and I'll go back to God's country. Oh, I know it's pretty here, and you get *dolce far niente* handed to you in chunks, but this country wasn't made for a white man to live in. You've got to have to plug through snow now and then, and see a game of base-ball and wear a stiff collar and have a policeman cuss you. Still, La Paz is a good sort of a pipe-dreamy old hole. And Mrs. Conant is here. When any of us feels particularly like jumping into the sea we rush around to her house and propose. It's nicer to be rejected by Mrs. Conant than it is to be drowned. And they say drowning is a delightful sensation."

"Many like her here?" asked Merriam.

"Not anywhere," said Bibb, with a comfortable sigh. "She's the only white woman in La Paz. The rest range from a dappled dun to the color of a b-flat piano key. She's been here a year. Comes from—well, you know how a woman can talk—ask 'em to say 'string' and they'll say 'crow's foot' or 'cat's cradle.' Sometimes you'd think she was from Oshkosh, and again from Jacksonville, Florida, and the next day from Cape Cod."

"Mystery?" ventured Merriam.

"M—well, she looks it; but her talk's translucent enough. But that's a woman. I suppose if the Sphinx were to begin talking she'd merely say: 'Goodness me! more visitors coming for dinner, and nothing to eat but the sand which is here.' But you won't think about that when you meet her, Merriam. You'll propose to her too."

To make a hard story soft, Merriam did meet her and propose to her. He found her to be a woman in black with hair the color of a bronze turkey's wings, and mysterious, *remembering* eyes that—well, that looked as if she might have been a trained nurse looking on when Eve was created. Her words and manner, though, were translucent, as Bibb had said. She spoke, vaguely, of friends in California and some of the lower parishes in Louisiana. The tropical climate and indolent life suited her; she had thought of buying an orange grove later on; La Paz, all in all, charmed her.

Merriam's courtship of the Sphinx lasted three months, although he did not know that he was courting her. He was using her as an antidote for remorse, until he found, too late, that he had acquired the habit. During that time he had received no news from home. Wade did not know where he was; and he was not sure of Wade's exact address, and was afraid to write. He thought he had better let matters rest as they were for a while.

One afternoon he and Mrs. Conant hired two ponies and rode out along the mountain trail as far as the little cold river that came tumbling down the foothills. There they stopped for a drink, and Merriam spoke his piece—he proposed, as Bibb had prophesied.

Mrs. Conant gave him one glance of brilliant tenderness, and then her face took on such a strange, haggard look that Merriam was shaken out of his intoxication and back to his senses.

"I beg your pardon, Florence," he said, releasing her hand; "but I'll have to hedge on part of what I said. I can't ask you to marry me, of course. I killed a man in New York—a man who was my friend—shot him down—in quite a cowardly manner, I understand. Of course, the drinking didn't excuse it. Well, I couldn't resist having my say; and I'll always mean it. I'm here as a fugitive from justice, and—I suppose that ends our acquaintance."

Mrs. Conant plucked little leaves assiduously from the low-hanging branch of a lime tree.

"I suppose so," she said, in low and oddly uneven tones; "but that depends upon you. I'll be as honest as you were. I poisoned my husband. I am a self-made widow. A man cannot love a murderess. So I suppose that ends our acquaintance."

She looked up at him slowly. His face turned a little pale, and he stared at her blankly, like a deaf-and-dumb man who was wondering what it was all about.

She took a swift step toward him, with stiffened arms and eyes blazing.

"Don't look at me like that!" she cried, as though she were in acute pain. "Curse me, or turn your back on me, but don't look that way. Am I a woman to be beaten? If I could show you—here on my arms, and on my back are scars—and it has been more than a year—scars that he made in his brutal rages. A holy nun would have risen and struck the fiend down. Yes, I killed him. The foul and horrible words that he hurled at me that last day are repeated in my ears every night when I sleep. And then came his blows, and the end of my endurance. I got the poison that afternoon. It was his custom to drink every night in the library before going to bed a hot punch made of rum and wine. Only from my fair hands would he receive it—because he knew that the fumes of spirits always sickened me. That night when the maid brought it to me I sent her downstairs on an errand. Before taking him his drink I went to my little private cabinet and poured into it more than a teaspoonful of tincture of aconite—enough to kill three men, so I had learned. I had drawn $6,000 that I had in bank, and with that and a few things in a satchel I left the house without any one seeing me. As I passed the library I heard him stagger up and fall heavily on a couch. I took a night train for New Orleans, and from there I sailed to the Bermudas. I finally cast anchor in La Paz. And now what have you to say? Can you open your mouth?"

Merriam came back to life.

"Florence," he said, earnestly, "I want you. I don't care what you've done. If the world——"

"Ralph," she interrupted, almost with a scream, "be my world!"

Her eyes melted; she relaxed magnificently and swayed toward Merriam so suddenly that he had to jump to catch her.

Dear me! in such scenes how the talk runs into artificial prose. But it can't be helped. It's the subconscious smell of the footlights' smoke that's in all of us. Stir the depths of your cook's soul sufficiently and she will discourse in Bulwer-Lyttonese.

Merriam and Mrs. Conant were very happy. He announced their engagement at the Hotel Orilla del Mar. Eight foreigners and four native Astors pounded his back and shouted insincere congratulations at him. Pedrito, the Castilian-mannered barkeep, was goaded to extra duty until his agility would have turned a Boston cherry-phosphate clerk a pale lilac with envy.

They were both very happy. According to the strange mathematics of the god of mutual affinity, the shadows that clouded their pasts when united became only half as dense instead of darker. They shut the world out and bolted the doors. Each was the other's world. Mrs. Conant lived again. The remembering look left her eyes. Merriam was with her every moment that was possible. On a little plateau under a grove of palms and calabash trees they were going to build a fairy bungalow. They were to be married in two months. Many hours of the day they had their heads together over the house plans. Their joint capital would set up a business in fruit or woods that would yield a comfortable support. "Good-night, my world," would say Mrs. Conant every evening when Merriam left her for his hotel. They were very happy. Their love had, circumstantially, that element of melancholy in it that it seems to require to attain its supremest elevation. And it seemed that their mutual great misfortune or sin was a bond that nothing could sever.

One day a steamer hove in the offing. Bare-legged and bare-shouldered La Paz scampered down to the beach, for the arrival of a steamer was their loop-the-loop, circus, Emancipation Day, and four-o'clock tea.

When the steamer was near enough, wise ones proclaimed that she was the *Pájaro,* bound up-coast from Callao to Panama.

The *Pájaro* put on brakes a mile off shore. Soon a boat came bobbing shoreward. Merriam strolled down on the beach to look on. In the shallow water the Carib sailors sprang out and dragged the boat with a mighty rush to the firm shingle. Out climbed the purser, the captain, and two passengers ploughing their way through the deep sand toward the hotel. Merriam glanced toward them with the mild interest due to strangers. There was something familiar to him in the walk of one of the passengers. He looked again, and his blood seemed to turn to strawberry ice cream in his veins. Burly, arrogant, debonair as ever, H. Ferguson Hedges, the man he had killed, was coming toward him ten feet away.

When Hedges saw Merriam his face flushed a dark red. Then he shouted in his old, bluff way: "Hello, Merriam. Glad to see you. Didn't expect to find you out here. Quinby, this is my old friend Merriam, of New York—Merriam, Mr. Quinby."

Merriam gave Hedges and then Quinby an ice-cold hand.

"Br-r-r-r!" said Hedges. "But you've got a frappéed flipper! Man, you're not well. You're as yellow as a Chinaman. Malarial here? Steer us to a bar if there is such a thing, and let's take a prophylactic."

Merriam, still half comatose, led them toward the Hotel Orilla del Mar.

"Quinby and I," explained Hedges, puffing through the slippery sand, "are looking out along the coast for some investments. We've just come up from Concepción and Valparaiso and Lima. The captain of this sub-sidized ferry boat told us there was some good picking around here in silver mines. So we got off. Now, where is that café, Merriam? Oh, in this portable soda-water pavilion?"

Leaving Quinby at the bar, Hedges drew Merriam aside.

"Now, what does this mean?" he said, with gruff kindness. "Are you sulking about that fool row we had?"

"I thought," stammered Merriam—"I heard—they told me you were —that I had——"

"Well, you didn't, and I'm not," said Hedges. "That fool young am-bulance surgeon told Wade I was a candidate for a coffin just because I'd got tired and quit breathing. I laid up in a private hospital for a month; but here I am, kicking as hard as ever. Wade and I tried to find you, but couldn't. Now, Merriam, shake hands and forget it all. I was as much to blame as you were; and the shot really did me good—I came out of the hospital as healthy and fit as a cab horse. Come on; that drink's waiting."

"Old man," said Merriam, brokenly, "I don't know how to thank you —I—well, you know——"

"Oh, forget it," boomed Hedges. "Quinby'll die of thirst if we don't join him."

Bibb was sitting on the shady side of the gallery waiting for the eleven-o'clock breakfast. Presently Merriam came out and joined him. His eye was strangely bright.

"Bibb, my boy," said he, slowly waving his hand, "do you see those mountains and that sea and sky and sunshine?—they're mine, Bibbsy— all mine."

"You go in," said Bibb, "and take eight grains of quinine, right away. It won't do in this climate for a man to get to thinking he's Rockefeller, or James O'Neill either."

Inside, the purser was untying a great roll of newspapers, many of them weeks old, gathered in the lower ports by the *Pájaro* to be dis-tributed at casual stopping-places. Thus do the beneficent voyagers scat-ter news and entertainment among the prisoners of sea and mountains.

Tío Pancho, the hotel proprietor, set his great silver-rimmed *anteojos* upon his nose and divided the papers into a number of smaller rolls. A barefooted *muchacho* dashed in, desiring the post of messenger.

"*Vien venido,*" said Tío Pancho. "This to Señora Conant; that to el Doctor S-S-Schlegel—*Dios!* what a name to say! that to Señor Davis— one for Don Alberto. These two for the *Casa de Huéspedes, Numero 6, en la calle de las Buenas Gracias.* And say to them all, *muchacho,* that the *Pájaro* sails for Panama at three this afternoon. If any have letters to send by the post, let them come quickly, that they may first pass through the *correo.*"

Mrs. Conant received her roll of newspapers at four o'clock. The boy was late in delivering them, because he had been deflected from his duty by an iguana that crossed his path and to which he immediately gave chase. But it made no hardship, for she had no letters to send.

She was idling in a hammock in the *patio* of the house that she occupied, half awake, half happily dreaming of the paradise that she and Merriam had created out of the wrecks of their pasts. She was content now for the horizon of that shimmering sea to be the horizon of her life. They had shut out the world and closed the door.

Merriam was coming to her house at seven, after his dinner at the hotel. She would put on a white dress and an apricot-colored lace mantilla, and they would walk an hour under the cocoanut palms by the lagoon. She smiled contentedly, and chose a paper at random from the roll the boy had brought.

At first the words of a certain headline of a Sunday newspaper meant nothing to her; they conveyed only a visualized sense of familiarity. The largest type ran thus: "Lloyd B. Conant secures divorce." And then the sub headings: "Well-known Saint Louis paint manufacturer wins suit, pleading one year's absence of wife." "Her mysterious disappearance recalled." "Nothing has been heard of her since."

Twisting herself quickly out of the hammock, Mrs. Conant's eye soon traversed the half-column of the *Recall.* It ended thus: "It will be remembered that Mrs. Conant disappeared one evening in March of last year. It was freely rumored that her marriage with Lloyd B. Conant resulted in much unhappiness. Stories were not wanting to the effect that his cruelty toward his wife had more than once taken the form of physical abuse. After her departure a full bottle of tincture of aconite, a deadly poison, was found in a small medicine cabinet in her bedroom. This might have been an indication that she meditated suicide. It is supposed that she abandoned such an intention if she possessed it, and left her home instead."

Mrs. Conant slowly dropped the paper, and sat on a chair, clasping her hands tightly.

"Let me think—O God!—let me think," she whispered. "I took the

bottle with me . . . I threw it out of the window of the train . . . I——
. . . there was another bottle in the cabinet . . . there were two, side by
side—the aconite—and the valerian that I took when I could not sleep
. . . If they found the aconite bottle full, why—but, he is alive, of course
—I gave him a harmless dose of valerian . . . I am not a murderess in
fact . . . Ralph, I—O God, don't let this be a dream!"

She went into the part of the house that she rented from the old
Peruvian man and his wife, shut the door, and walked up and down
her room swiftly and feverishly for half an hour. Merriam's photograph
stood in a frame on a table. She picked it up, looked at it with a smile
of exquisite tenderness, and—dropped four tears on it. And Merriam
only twenty rods away! Then she stood still for ten minutes, looking
into space. She looked into space through a slowly opening door. On her
side of the door was the building material for a castle of Romance—love,
an Arcady of waving palms, a lullaby of waves on the shore of a haven
of rest, respite, peace, a lotus land of dreamy ease and security—a life of
poetry and heart's ease and refuge. Romanticist, will you tell me what
Mrs. Conant saw on the other side of the door? You cannot?—that is,
you will not? Very well; then listen.

*She saw herself go into a department store and buy five spools of silk
thread and three yards of gingham to make an apron for the cook. "Shall
I charge it, ma'am?" asks the clerk. As she walked out a lady whom she
met greeted her cordially. "Oh, where did you get the pattern for those
sleeves, dear Mrs. Conant?" she said. At the corner a policeman helped
her across the street and touched his helmet. "Any callers?" she asked
the maid when she reached home. "Mrs. Waldron," answered the maid,
"and the two Misses Jenkinson." "Very well," she said. "You may bring
me a cup of tea, Maggie."*

Mrs. Conant went to the door and called Angela, the old Peruvian
woman. "If Mateo is there send him to me." Mateo, a half-breed, shuffling
and old but efficient, came.

"Is there a steamer or a vessel of any kind leaving this coast to-night
or to-morrow that I can get passage on?" she asked.

Mateo considered.

"At Punta Reina, thirty miles down the coast, señora," he answered,
"there is a small steamer loading with cinchona and dyewoods. She
sails for San Francisco to-morrow at sunrise. So says my brother, who
arrived in his sloop to-day, passing by Punta Reina."

"You must take me in that sloop to the steamer to-night. Will you do
that?"

"Perhaps——" Mateo shrugged a suggestive shoulder. Mrs. Conant
took a handful of money from a drawer and gave it to him.

"Get the sloop ready behind the little point of land below the town,"
she ordered. "Get sailors, and be ready to sail at six o'clock. In half an

hour bring a cart partly filled with straw into the *patio* here, and take my trunk to the sloop. There is more money yet. Now, hurry."

For one time Mateo walked away without shuffling his feet.

"Angela," cried Mrs. Conant, almost fiercely, "come and help me pack. I am going away. Out with this trunk. My clothes first. Stir your-self. Those dark dresses first. Hurry."

From the first she did not waver from her decision. Her view was clear and final. Her door had opened and let the world in. Her love for Merriam was not lessened; but it now appeared a hopeless and un-realizable thing. The visions of their future that had seemed so blissful and complete had vanished. She tried to assure herself that her renuncia-tion was rather for his sake than for her own. Now that she was cleared of her burden—at least, technically—would not his own weigh too heavily upon him? If she should cling to him, would not the difference forever silently mar and corrode their happiness? Thus she reasoned; but there were a thousand little voices calling to her that she could feel rather than hear, like the hum of distant, powerful machinery—the little voices of the world, that, when raised in unison, can send their insistent call through the thickest door.

Once, while packing, a brief shadow of the lotus dream came back to her. She held Merriam's picture to her heart with one hand, while she threw a pair of shoes into the trunk with her other.

At six o'clock Mateo returned and reported the sloop ready. He and his brother lifted the trunk into the cart, covered it with straw, and con-veyed it to the point of embarkation. From there they transferred it on board in the sloop's dory. Then Mateo returned for additional orders.

Mrs. Conant was ready. She had settled all business matters with Angela, and was impatiently waiting. She wore a long, loose black-silk duster that she often walked about in when the evenings were chilly. On her head was a small round hat, and over it the apricot-colored lace mantilla.

Dusk had quickly followed the short twilight. Mateo led her by dark and grass-grown streets toward the point behind which the sloop was anchored. On turning a corner they beheld the Hotel Orilla del Mar three streets away, nebulously aglow with its array of kerosene lamps.

Mrs. Conant paused, with streaming eyes. "I must, *I must* see him once before I go," she murmured in anguish. But even then she did not falter in her decision. Quickly she invented a plan by which she might speak to him, and yet make her departure without his knowing. She would walk past the hotel, ask some one to call him out, and talk a few moments on some trivial excuse, leaving him expecting to see her at her home at seven.

She unpinned her hat and gave it to Mateo. "Keep this, and wait here till I come," she ordered. Then she draped the mantilla over her head

as she usually did when walking after sunset, and went straight to the
Orilla del Mar.

She was glad to see the bulky, white-clad figure of Tío Pancho standing alone on the gallery.

"Tío Pancho," she said, with a charming smile, "may I trouble you to
ask Mr. Merriam to come out for just a few moments that I may speak
with him?"

Tío Pancho bowed as an elephant bows.

"*Buenas tardes,* Señora Conant," he said, as a cavalier talks. And then
he went on, less at his ease:

"But does not the señora know that Señor Merriam sailed on the
Pájaro for Panama at three o'clock of this afternoon?"

THE THEORY AND THE HOUND

Not many days ago my old friend from the tropics, J. P. Bridger, United
States consul on the island of Ratona, was in the city. We had wassail
and jubilee and saw the Flatiron building, and missed seeing the Bronx-
less menagerie by about a couple of nights. And then, at the ebb tide,
we were walking up a street that parallels and parodies Broadway.

A woman with a comely and mundane countenance passed us, holding in leash a wheezing, vicious, waddling brute of a yellow pug. The
dog entangled himself with Bridger's legs and mumbled his ankles in
a snarling, peevish, sulky bite. Bridger, with a happy smile, kicked the
breath out of the brute; the woman showered us with a quick rain of
well-conceived adjectives that left us in no doubt as to our place in her
opinion, and we passed on. Ten yards farther an old woman with disordered white hair and her bankbook tucked well hidden beneath her
tattered shawl begged. Bridger stopped and disinterred for her a quarter
from his holiday waistcoat.

On the next corner a quarter of a ton of well-clothed man with a rice-
powdered, fat, white jowl, stood holding the chain of a devil-born bulldog whose forelegs were strangers by the length of a dachshund. A little
woman in a last-season's hat confronted him and wept, which was plainly
all she could do, while he cursed her in low, sweet, practised tones.

Bridger smiled again—strictly to himself—and this time he took out a
little memorandum book and made a note of it. This he had no right to
do without due explanation, and I said so.

"It's a new theory," said Bridger, "that I picked up down in Ratona.
I've been gathering support for it as I knock about. The world isn't
ripe for it yet, but—well, I'll tell you; and then you run your mind back
along the people you've known and see what you make of it."

And so I cornered Bridger in a place where they have artificial palms and wine; and he told me the story which is here in my words and on his responsibility.

One afternoon at three o'clock, on the island of Ratona, a boy raced along the beach screaming, *"Pájaro, ahoy!"*

Thus he made known the keenness of his hearing and the justice of his discrimination in pitch.

He who first heard and made oral proclamation concerning the toot of an approaching steamer's whistle, and correctly named the steamer, was a small hero in Ratona—until the next steamer came. Wherefore, there was rivalry among the barefoot youth of Ratona, and many fell victims to the softly blown conch shells of sloops which, as they enter harbor, sound surprisingly like a distant steamer's signal. And some could name you the vessel when its call, in your duller ears, sounded no louder than the sigh of the wind through the branches of the cocoanut palms.

But to-day he who proclaimed the *Pájaro* gained his honors. Ratona bent its ear to listen; and soon the deep-tongued blast grew louder and nearer, and at length Ratona saw above the line of palms on the low "point" the two black funnels of the fruiter slowly creeping toward the mouth of the harbor.

You must know that Ratona is an island twenty miles off the south of a South American republic. It is a port of that republic; and it sleeps sweetly in a smiling sea, toiling not nor spinning; fed by the abundant tropics where all things "ripen, cease and fall toward the grave."

Eight hundred people dream life away in a green-embowered village that follows the horseshoe curve of its bijou harbor. They are mostly Spanish and Indian mestizos, with a shading of San Domingo Negroes, a lightening of pure-blood Spanish officials, and a slight leavening of the froth of three or four pioneering white races. No steamers touch at Ratona save the fruit steamers which take on their banana inspectors there on their way to the coast. They leave Sunday newspapers, ice, quinine, bacon, watermelons, and vaccine matter at the island and that is about all the touch Ratona gets with the world.

The *Pájaro* paused at the mouth of the harbor, rolling heavily in the swell that sent the whitecaps racing beyond the smooth water inside. Already two dories from the village—one conveying fruit inspectors, the other going for what it could get—were halfway out to the steamer.

The inspector's dory was taken on board with them, and the *Pájaro* steamed away for the mainland for its load of fruit.

The other boat returned to Ratona bearing a contribution from the *Pájaro's* store of ice, the usual roll of newspapers, and one passenger— Taylor Plunkett, sheriff of Chatham County, Kentucky.

Bridger, the United States consul at Ratona, was cleaning his rifle in the official shanty under a bread-fruit tree twenty yards from the water of the harbor. The consul occupied a place somewhat near the tail of his political party's procession. The music of the band wagon sounded very faintly to him in the distance. The plums of office went to others. Bridger's share of the spoils—the consulship at Ratona—was little more than a prune—a dried prune from the boarding-house department of the public crib. But $900 yearly was opulence in Ratona. Besides, Bridger had contracted a passion for shooting alligators in the lagoons near his consulate, and he was not unhappy.

He looked up from a careful inspection of his rifle lock and saw a broad man filling his doorway. A broad, noiseless, slow-moving man sunburned almost to the brown of Vandyke. A man of forty-five, neatly clothed in homespun, with scanty light hair, a close-clipped brown-and-gray beard and pale-blue eyes expressing mildness and simplicity.

"You are Mr. Bridger, the consul," said the broad man. "They directed me here. Can you tell me what those big bunches of things like gourds are in those trees that look like feather dusters along the edge of the water?"

"Take that chair," said the consul, reoiling his cleaning rag. "No, the other one—that bamboo thing won't hold you. Why, they're cocoanuts—green cocoanuts. The shell of 'em is always a light green before they're ripe."

"Much obliged," said the other man, sitting down carefully. "I didn't quite like to tell the folks at home they were olives unless I was sure about it. My name is Plunkett. I'm sheriff of Chatham County, Kentucky. I've got extradition papers in my pocket authorizing the arrest of a man on this island. They've been signed by the President of this country, and they're in correct shape. The man's name is Wade Williams. He's in the cocoanut raising business. What he's wanted for is the murder of his wife two years ago. Where can I find him?"

The consul squinted an eye and looked through his rifle barrel.

"There's nobody on the island who calls himself 'Williams,'" he remarked.

"Didn't suppose there was," said Plunkett mildly. "He'll do by any other name."

"Besides myself," said Bridger, "there are only two Americans on Ratona—Bob Reeves and Henry Morgan."

"The man I want sells cocoanuts," suggested Plunkett.

"You see that cocoanut walk extending up to the point?" said the consul, waving his hand toward the open door. "That belongs to Bob Reeves. Henry Morgan owns half the trees to loo'ard on the island."

"One month ago," said the sheriff, "Wade Williams wrote a confidential letter to a man in Chatham County, telling him where he was and how he was getting along. The letter was lost; and the person that found it gave it away. They sent me after him, and I've got the papers. I reckon he's one of your cocoanut men for certain."

"You've got his picture, of course," said Bridger. "It might be Reeves or Morgan, but I'd hate to think it. They're both as fine fellows as you'd meet in an all-day auto ride."

"No," doubtfully answered Plunkett; "there wasn't any picture of Williams to be had. And I never saw him myself. I've been sheriff only a year. But I've got a pretty accurate description of him. About 5 feet 11; dark hair and eyes; nose inclined to be Roman; heavy about the shoulders; strong, white teeth, with none missing; laughs a good deal, talkative; drinks considerably but never to intoxication; looks you square in the eye when talking; age thirty-five. Which one of your men does that description fit?"

The consul grinned broadly.

"I'll tell you what you do," he said, laying down his rifle and slipping on his dingy black alpaca coat. "You come along, Mr. Plunkett, and I'll take you up to see the boys. If you can tell which one of 'em your description fits better than it does the other you have the advantage of me."

Bridger conducted the sheriff out and along the hard beach close to which the tiny houses of the village were distributed. Immediately back of the town rose sudden, small, thickly wooded hills. Up one of these, by means of steps cut in the hard clay, the consul led Plunkett. On the very verge of an eminence was perched a two-room wooden cottage with a thatched roof. A Carib woman was washing clothes outside. The consul ushered the sheriff to the door of the room that overlooked the harbor.

Two men were in the room, about to sit down, in their shirt sleeves, to a table spread for dinner. They bore little resemblance one to the other in detail; but the general description given by Plunkett could have been justly applied to either. In height, color of hair, shape of nose, build, and manners each of them tallied with it. They were fair types of jovial, ready-witted, broad-gauged Americans who had gravitated together for companionship in an alien land.

"Hello, Bridger!" they called in unison at sight of the consul. "Come and have dinner with us!" And then they noticed Plunkett at his heels, and came forward with hospitable curiosity.

"Gentlemen," said the consul, his voice taking an unaccustomed formality, "this is Mr. Plunkett. Mr. Plunkett—Mr. Reeves and Mr. Morgan."

The cocoanut barons greeted the newcomer joyously. Reeves seemed about an inch taller than Morgan, but his laugh was not quite as loud. Morgan's eyes were deep brown; Reeves's were black. Reeves was the host and busied himself with fetching other chairs and calling to the Carib woman for supplemental table ware. It was explained that Morgan lived in a bamboo shack to "loo'ard," but that every day the two friends dined together. Plunkett stood still during the preparations, looking about mildly with his pale-blue eyes. Bridger looked apologetic and uneasy.

At length two other covers were laid and the company was assigned to places. Reeves and Morgan stood side by side across the table from the visitors. Reeves nodded genially as a signal for all to seat themselves. And then suddenly Plunkett raised his hand with a gesture of authority. He was looking straight between Reeves and Morgan.

"Wade Williams," he said quietly, "you are under arrest for murder."

Reeves and Morgan instantly exchanged a quick, bright glance, the quality of which was interrogation, with a seasoning of surprise. Then, simultaneously they turned to the speaker with a puzzled and frank deprecation in their gaze.

"Can't say that we understand you, Mr. Plunkett," said Morgan, cheerfully. "Did you say 'Williams'?"

"What's the joke, Bridgy?" asked Reeves, turning to the consul with a smile.

Before Bridger could answer, Plunkett spoke again.

"I'll explain," he said, quietly. "One of you don't need any explanation, but this is for the other one. One of you is Wade Williams of Chatham County, Kentucky. You murdered your wife on May 5, two years ago, after ill-treating and abusing her continually for five years. I have the proper papers in my pocket for taking you back with me, and you are going. We will return on the fruit steamer that comes back by this island to-morrow to leave its inspectors. I acknowledge, gentlemen, that I'm not quite sure which one of you is Williams. But Wade Williams goes back to Chatham County to-morrow. I want you to understand that."

A great sound of merry laughter from Morgan and Reeves went out over the still harbor. Two or three fishermen in the fleet of sloops anchored there looked up at the house of the *diablos Americanos* on the hill and wondered.

"My dear Mr. Plunkett," cried Morgan, conquering his mirth, "the dinner is getting cold. Let us sit down and eat. I am anxious to get my spoon into that shark-fin soup. Business afterward."

"Sit down, gentlemen, if you please," added Reeves, pleasantly. "I am sure Mr. Plunkett will not object. Perhaps a little time may be of advantage to him in identifying—the gentleman he wishes to arrest."

"No objections, I'm sure," said Plunkett, dropping into his chair heavily. "I'm hungry myself. I didn't want to accept the hospitality of you folks without giving you notice; that's all."

Reeves set bottles and glasses on the table.

"There's cognac," he said, "and anisada, and Scotch 'smoke,' and rye. Take your choice."

Bridger chose rye, Reeves poured three fingers of Scotch for himself, Morgan took the same. The sheriff, against much protestation, filled his glass from the water bottle.

"Here's to the appetite," said Reeves, raising his glass, "of Mr. Williams!" Morgan's laugh and his drink encountering sent him into a choking-splutter. All began to pay attention to the dinner, which was well cooked and palatable.

"Williams!" called Plunkett, suddenly and sharply.

All looked up wonderingly. Reeves found the sheriff's mild eye resting upon him. He flushed a little.

"See here," he said, with some asperity, "my name's Reeves, and I don't want you to——" But the comedy of the thing came to his rescue and he ended with a laugh.

"I suppose, Mr. Plunkett," said Morgan, carefully seasoning an alligator pear, "that you are aware of the fact that you will import a good deal of trouble for yourself into Kentucky if you take back the wrong man—that is, of course, if you take anybody back?"

"Thank you for the salt," said the sheriff. "Oh, I'll take somebody back. It'll be one of you two gentlemen. Yes, I know I'll get stuck for damages if I make a mistake. But I'm going to try to get the right man."

"I'll tell you what you do," said Morgan, leaning forward with a jolly twinkle in his eyes. "You take me. I'll go without any trouble. The cocoanut business hasn't panned out well this year, and I'd like to make some extra money out of your bondsmen."

"That's not fair," chimed in Reeves. "I got only $16 a thousand for my last shipment. Take me, Mr. Plunkett."

"I'll take Wade Williams," said the sheriff, patiently, "or I'll come pretty close to it."

"It's like dining with a ghost," remarked Morgan, with a pretended shiver. "The ghost of a murderer, too! Will somebody pass the toothpicks to the shade of the naughty Mr. Williams?"

Plunkett seemed as unconcerned as if he were dining at his own table in Chatham County. He was a gallant trencherman, and the strange tropic viands tickled his palate. Heavy, commonplace, almost slothful in his movements, he appeared to be devoid of all the cunning and watchfulness of the sleuth. He even ceased to observe, with any sharpness or attempted discrimination, the two men, one of whom he had undertaken with surprising self-confidence to drag away upon the serious charge of wife-murder. Here, indeed, was a problem set before him that if wrongly solved would have amounted to his serious discomfiture, yet there he sat puzzling his soul (to all appearances) over the novel flavor of a broiled iguana cutlet.

The consul felt a decided discomfort. Reeves and Morgan were his friends and pals; yet the sheriff from Kentucky had a certain right to his official aid and moral support. So Bridger sat the silentest around the board and tried to estimate the peculiar situation. His conclusion was that both Reeves and Morgan, quickwitted, as he knew them to be, had conceived at the moment of Plunkett's disclosure of his mission—and in the brief space of a lightning flash—the idea that the other might be the guilty Williams; and that each of them had decided in that moment loyally to protect his comrade against the doom that threatened him. This was the consul's theory, and if he had been a bookmaker at a race of wits for life and liberty he would have offered heavy odds against the plodding sheriff from Chatham County, Kentucky.

When the meal was concluded the Carib woman came and removed the dishes and cloth. Reeves strewed the table with excellent cigars, and Plunkett, with the others, lighted one of these with evident gratification.

"I may be dull," said Morgan, with a grin and a wink at Bridger; "but I want to know if I am. Now, I say this is all a joke of Mr. Plunkett's concocted to frighten two babes-in-the-woods. Is this Williamson to be taken seriously or not?"

"'Williams,'" corrected Plunkett, gravely. "I never got off any jokes in my life. I know I wouldn't travel 2,000 miles to get off a poor one as this would be if I didn't take Wade Williams back with me. Gentlemen!" continued the sheriff, now letting his mild eyes travel impartially from one of the company to another, "see if you can find any joke in this case. Wade Williams is listening to the words I utter now; but out of politeness I will speak of him as a third person. For five years he made his wife lead the life of a dog—No; I'll take that back. No dog in Kentucky was ever treated as she was. He spent the money that she brought him—spent it at races, at the card table, and on horses and hunting. He was a good fellow to his friends, but a cold, sullen demon at home. He wound up the five years of neglect by striking her with his closed hand— a hand as hard as a stone—when she was ill and weak from suffering. She died the next day; and he skipped. That's all there is to it. It's enough. I never saw Williams; but I knew his wife. I'm not a man to tell half. She and I were keeping company when she met him. She went to Louisville on a visit and saw him there. I'll admit that he spoilt my chances in no time. I lived then on the edge of the Cumberland Mountains. I was elected sheriff of Chatham County a year after Wade Williams killed his wife. My official duty sends me out here after him; but I'll admit that there's personal feeling, too. And he's going back with me. Mr.—er— Reeves, will you pass me a match?"

"Awfully imprudent of Williams," said Morgan, putting his feet up against the wall, "to strike a Kentucky lady. Seems to me I've heard they were scrappers."

"Bad, bad Williams," said Reeves, pouring out more "Scotch."

The two men spoke lightly, but the consul saw and felt the tension and the carefulness in their actions and words. "Good old fellows," he said to himself; "they're both all right. Each of 'em is standing by the other like a little brick church."

And then a dog walked into the room where they sat—a black-and-tan hound, long-eared, lazy, confident of welcome.

Plunkett turned his head and looked at the animal, which halted, confidently, within a few feet of his chair.

Suddenly the sheriff, with a deep-mouthed oath, left his seat and bestowed upon the dog a vicious and heavy kick, with his ponderous shoe.

The hound, heart-broken, astonished, with flapping ears and in-curved tail, uttered a piercing yelp of pain and surprise.

Reeves and the consul remained in their chairs, saying nothing, but astonished at the unexpected show of intolerance from the easy-going man from Chatham County.

But Morgan, with a suddenly purpling face, leaped to his feet and raised a threatening arm above the guest.

"You—brute!" he shouted, passionately; "why did you do that?"

Quickly the amenities returned, Plunkett muttered some indistinct apology and regained his seat. Morgan with a decided effort controlled his indignation and also returned to his chair.

And then Plunkett, with the spring of a tiger, leaped around the corner of the table and snapped handcuffs on the paralyzed Morgan's wrists.

"Hound-lover and woman-killer!" he cried; "get ready to meet your God."

When Bridger had finished I asked him:

"Did he get the right man?"

"He did," said the consul.

"And how did he know?" I inquired, being in a kind of bewilderment.

"When he put Morgan in the dory," answered Bridger, "the next day to take him aboard the *Pájaro,* this man Plunkett stopped to shake hands with me and I asked him the same question.

" 'Mr. Bridger,' said he. 'I'm a Kentuckian, and I've seen a great deal of both men and animals. And I never yet saw a man that was overfond of horses and dogs but what was cruel to women.' "

THE HYPOTHESES OF .FAILURE

Lawyer Gooch bestowed his undivided attention upon the engrossing arts of his profession. But one flight of fancy did he allow his mind to entertain. He was fond of likening his suite of office rooms to the bottom of a ship. The rooms were three in number, with a door opening from one to another. These doors could also be closed.

"Ships," Lawyer Gooch would say, "are constructed for safety, with separate, water-tight compartments in their bottoms. If one compartment springs a leak it fills with water; but the good ship goes on unhurt. Were it not for the separating bulkheads one leak would sink the vessel. Now it often happens that while I am occupied with clients, other clients with conflicting interests call. With the assistance of Archibald—an office boy with a future—I cause the dangerous influx to be diverted into separate compartments, while I sound with my legal plummet the depth of each. If necessary, they may be baled into the hallway and permitted to escape by way of the stairs, which we may term the lee scuppers. Thus the good ship of business is kept afloat; whereas if the element that supports her were allowed to mingle freely in her hold we might be swamped—ha, ha, ha!"

The law is dry. Good jokes are few. Surely it might be permitted Lawyer Gooch to mitigate the bore of briefs, the tedium of torts and the prosiness of processes with even so light a levy upon the good property of humor.

Lawyer Gooch's practice leaned largely to the settlement of marital infelicities. Did matrimony languish through complications, he mediated, soothed, and arbitrated. Did it suffer from implications, he readjusted, defended, and championed. Did it arrive at the extremity of duplications, he always got light sentences for his clients.

But not always was Lawyer Gooch the keen, armed, wily belligerent, ready with his two-edged sword to lop off the shackles of Hymen. He had been known to build up instead of demolishing, to reunite instead of severing, to lead erring and foolish ones back into the fold instead of scattering the flock. Often had he by his eloquent and moving appeals sent husband and wife, weeping, back into each other's arms. Frequently he had coached childhood so successfully that, at the psychological moment (and at a given signal), the plaintive pipe of "Papa, won't you turn home adain to me and muvver?" had won the day and upheld the pillars of a tottering home.

Unprejudiced persons admitted that Lawyer Gooch received as big fees from these reyoked clients as would have been paid him had the cases been contested in court. Prejudiced ones intimated that his fees were doubled, because the penitent couples always came back later for the divorce, anyhow.

There came a season in June when the legal ship of Lawyer Gooch (to borrow his own figure) was nearly becalmed. The divorce mill grinds slowly in June. It is the month of Cupid and Hymen.

Lawyer Gooch, then, sat idle in the middle room of his clientless suite. A small anteroom connected—or rather separated—this apartment from the hallway. Here was stationed Archibald, who wrested from visitors their cards or oral nomenclature which he bore to his master while they waited.

Suddenly, on this day, there came a great knocking at the outermost door.

Archibald, opening it, was thrust aside as superfluous by the visitor, who without due reverence at once penetrated to the office of Lawyer Gooch and threw himself with good-natured insolence into a comfortable chair facing that gentleman.

"You are Phineas C. Gooch, attorney-at-law?" said the visitor, his tone of voice and inflection making his words at once a question, an assertion, and an accusation.

Before committing himself by a reply, the lawyer estimated his possible client in one of his brief but shrewd and calculating glances.

The man was of the emphatic type—large-sized, active, bold and debonair in demeanor, vain beyond a doubt, slightly swaggering, ready and at ease. He was well clothed, but with a shade too much ornateness. He was seeking a lawyer; but if that fact would seem to saddle him with troubles they were not patent in his beaming eye and courageous air.

"My name is Gooch," at length the lawyer admitted. Upon pressure he would also have confessed to the Phineas C. But he did not consider it good practice to volunteer information. "I did not receive your card," he continued, by way of rebuke, "so I——"

"I know you didn't," remarked the visitor, coolly; "and you won't just yet. Light up?" He threw a leg over an arm of his chair, and tossed a handful of rich-hued cigars upon the table. Lawyer Gooch knew the brand. He thawed just enough to accept the invitation to smoke.

"You are a divorce lawyer," said the cardless visitor. This time there was no interrogation in his voice. Nor did his words constitute a simple assertion. They formed a charge—a denunciation—as one would say to a dog: "You are a dog." Lawyer Gooch was silent under the imputation.

"You handle," continued the visitor, "all the various ramifications of busted-up connubiality. You are a surgeon, we might say, who extracts Cupid's darts when he shoots 'em into the wrong parties. You furnish patent, incandescent lights for premises where the torch of Hymen has burned so low you can't light a cigar at it. Am I right, Mr. Gooch?"

"I have undertaken cases," said the lawyer, guardedly, "in the line to which your figurative speech seems to refer. Do you wish to consult me professionally, Mr. ——" The lawyer paused, with significance.

"Not yet," said the other, with an arch wave of his cigar, "not just yet. Let us approach the subject with the caution that should have been used in the original act that makes this pow-wow necessary. There exists a matrimonial jumble to be straightened out. But before I give you names I want your honest—well, anyhow, your professional opinion on the merits of the mix-up. I want you to size up the catastrophe—abstractly—you understand? I'm Mr. Nobody; and I've got a story to tell you. Then you say what's what. Do you get my wireless?"

"You want to state a hypothetical case?" suggested Lawyer Gooch.

"That's the word I was after. 'Apothecary' was the best shot I could make at it in my mind. The hypothetical goes. I'll state the case. Suppose there's a woman—a deuced fine-looking woman—who has run away from her husband and home? She's badly mashed on another man who went to her town to work up some real estate business. Now, we may as well call this woman's husband Thomas R. Billings, for that's his name. I'm giving you straight tips on the cognomens. The Lothario chap is Henry K. Jessup. The Billingses lived in a little town called Susanville—a good many miles from here. Now, Jessup leaves Susanville two weeks ago. The next day Mrs. Billings follows him. She's dead gone on this man Jessup; you can bet your law library on that."

Lawyer Gooch's client said this with such unctuous satisfaction that even the callous lawyer experienced a slight ripple of repulsion. He now saw clearly in his fatuous visitor the conceit of the lady-killer, the egoistic complacency of the successful trifler.

"Now," continued the visitor, "suppose this Mrs. Billings wasn't happy at home? We'll say she and her husband didn't gee worth a cent. They've got incompatibility to burn. The things she likes, Billings wouldn't have as a gift with trading-stamps. It's Tabby and Rover with them all the time. She's an educated woman in science and culture, and she reads things out loud at meetings. Billings is not on. He don't appreciate progress and obelisks and ethics, and things of that sort. Old Billings is simply a blink when it comes to such things. The lady is out and out above his class. Now, laywer, don't it look like a fair equalization of rights and wrongs that a woman like that should be allowed to throw down Billings and take the man that can appreciate her?"

"Incompatibility," said Lawyer Gooch, "is undoubtedly the source of much marital discord and unhappiness. Where it is positively proved, divorce would seem to be the equitable remedy. Are you—excuse me—is this man Jessup one to whom the lady may safely trust her future?"

"Oh, you can bet on Jessup," said the client, with a confident wag of his head. "Jessup's all right. He'll do the square thing. Why, he left Susanville just to keep people from talking about Mrs. Billings. But she followed him up, and now, of course, he'll stick to her. When she gets a divorce, all legal and proper, Jessup will do the proper thing."

"And now," said Lawyer Gooch, "continuing the hypothesis, if you prefer, and supposing that my services should be desired in the case, what——"

The client rose impulsively to his feet.

"Oh, dang the hypothetical business," he exclaimed, impatiently. "Let's let her drop, and get down to straight talk. You ought to know who I am by this time. I want that woman to have her divorce. I'll pay for it. The day you set Mrs. Billings free I'll pay you five hundred dollars."

Lawyer Gooch's client banged his fist upon the table to punctuate his generosity.

"If that is the case——" began the lawyer.

"Lady to see you, sir," bawled Archibald, bouncing in from his ante-room. He had orders to always announce immediately any client that might come. There was no sense in turning business away.

Lawyer Gooch took client number one by the arm and led him suavely into one of the adjoining rooms. "Favor me by remaining here a few minutes, sir," said he. "I will return and resume our consultation with the least possible delay. I am rather expecting a visit from a very wealthy old lady in connection with a will. I will not keep you waiting long."

The breezy gentleman seated himself with obliging acquiescence, and took up a magazine. The lawyer returned to the middle office, carefully closing behind him the connecting door.

"Show the lady in, Archibald," he said to the office boy, who was awaiting the order.

A tall lady, of commanding presence and sternly handsome, entered the room. She wore robes—robes; not clothes—ample and fluent. In her eye could be perceived the lambent flame of genius and soul. In her hand was a green bag of the capacity of a bushel, and an umbrella that also seemed to wear a robe, ample and fluent. She accepted a chair.

"Are you Mr. Phineas C. Gooch, the lawyer?" she asked, in formal and unconciliatory tones.

"I am," answered Lawyer Gooch, without circumlocution. He never circumlocuted when dealing with a woman. Women circumlocute. Time is wasted when both sides in debate employ the same tactics.

"As a lawyer, sir," began the lady, "you may have acquired some knowledge of the human heart. Do you believe that the pusillanimous and petty conventions of our artificial social life should stand as an obstacle in the way of a noble and affectionate heart when it finds its true mate among the miserable and worthless wretches in the world that are called men?"

"Madam," said Lawyer Gooch, in the tone that he used in curbing his female clients, "this is an office for conducting the practices of law. I am a lawyer, not a philosopher, nor the editor of an 'Answers to the Lovelorn' column of a newspaper. I have other clients waiting. I will ask you kindly to come to the point."

"Well, you needn't get so stiff around the gills about it," said the lady, with a snap of her luminous eyes and a startling gyration of her umbrella. "Business is what I've come for. I want your opinion in the matter of a suit for divorce, as the vulgar would call it, but which is really only the readjustment of the false and ignoble conditions that the short-sighted laws of man have interposed between a loving——"

"I beg your pardon, madam," interrupted Lawyer Gooch, with some impatience, "for reminding you again that this is a law office. Perhaps Mrs. Wilcox——"

"Mrs. Wilcox is all right," cut in the lady, with a hint of asperity. "And so are Tolstoi, and Mrs. Gertrude Atherton, and Omar Khayyam, and Mr. Edward Bok. I've read 'em all. I would like to discuss with you the divine right of the soul as opposed to the freedom-destroying restrictions of a bigoted and narrow-minded society. But I will proceed to business. I would prefer to lay the matter before you in an impersonal way until you pass upon its merits. That is to describe it as a supposable instance, without——"

"You wish to state a hypothetical case?" said Lawyer Gooch.

"I was going to say that," said the lady, sharply. "Now, suppose there is a woman who is all soul and heart and aspirations for a complete existence. This woman has a husband who is far below her in intellect, in taste—in everything. Bah! he is a brute. He despises literature. He sneers at the lofty thoughts of the world's great thinkers. He thinks only of real estate and such sordid things. He is no mate for a woman with soul. We will say that this unfortunate wife one day meets with her ideal—a man with brain and heart and force. She loves him. Although this man feels the thrill of a new-found affinity he is too noble, too honorable to declare himself. He flies from the presence of his beloved. She flies after him, trampling, with superb indifference, upon the fetters with which an unenlightened social system would bind her. Now, what will a divorce cost? Eliza Ann Timmins, the poetess of Sycamore Gap, got one for three hundred and forty dollars. Can I—I mean can this lady I speak of get one that cheap?"

"Madam," said Lawyer Gooch, "your last two or three sentences delight me with their intelligence and clearness. Can we not now abandon the hypothetical and come down to names and business?"

"I should say so," exclaimed the lady, adopting the practical with admirable readiness. "Thomas R. Billings is the name of the low brute who stands between the happiness of his legal—his legal, but not his spiritual—wife and Henry K. Jessup, the noble man whom nature intended for her mate. I," concluded the client, with an air of dramatic revelation, "am Mrs. Billings!"

"Gentleman to see you, sir," shouted Archibald, invading the room almost at a handspring. Lawyer Gooch arose from his chair.

"Mrs. Billings," he said, courteously, "allow me to conduct you into the adjoining office apartment for a few minutes. I am expecting a very wealthy old gentleman on business connected with a will. In a very short while I will join you, and continue our consultation."

With his accustomed chivalrous manner, Lawyer Gooch ushered his soulful client into the remaining unoccupied room, and came out, closing the door with circumspection.

The next visitor introduced by Archibald was a thin, nervous, irritable-looking man of middle age, with a worried and apprehensive expression of countenance. He carried in one hand a small satchel, which he set down upon the floor beside the chair which the lawyer placed for him. His clothing was of good quality, but it was worn without regard to neatness or style, and appeared to be covered with the dust of travel.

"You make a specialty of divorce cases," he said, in an agitated but businesslike tone.

"I may say," began Lawyer Gooch, "that my practice has not altogether avoided——"

"I know you do," interrupted client number three. "You needn't tell me. I've heard all about you. I have a case to lay before you without necessarily disclosing any connection that I might have with it—that is——"

"You wish," said Lawyer Gooch, "to state a hypothetical case."

"You may call it that. I am a plain man of business. I will be as brief as possible. We will first take up the hypothetical woman. We will say she is married uncongenially. In many ways she is a superior woman. Physically she is considered to be handsome. She is devoted to what she calls literature—poetry and prose, and such stuff. Her husband is a plain man in the business walks of life. Their home has not been happy, although the husband has tried to make it so. Some time ago a man—a stranger—came to the peaceful town in which they lived and engaged in some real estate operations. This woman met him, and became unaccountably infatuated with him. Her attentions became so open that the man felt the community to be no safe place for him, so he left it. She abandoned husband and home, and followed him. She forsook her home, where she was provided with every comfort, to follow this man who had inspired her with such a strange affection. Is there anything more to be deplored," concluded the client, in a trembling voice, "than the wrecking of a home by a woman's uncalculating folly?"

Lawyer Gooch delivered the cautious opinion that there was not.

"This man she has gone to join," resumed the visitor, "is not the man to make her happy. It is a wild and foolish self-deception that makes her think he will. Her husband, in spite of their many disagreements, is the only one capable of dealing with her sensitive and peculiar nature. But this she does not realize now."

"Would you consider a divorce the logical cure in the case you present?" asked Lawyer Gooch, who felt that the conversation was wandering too far from the field of business.

"A divorce!" exclaimed the client, feelingly—almost tearfully. "No, no

—not that. I have read, Mr. Gooch, of many instances where your sympathy and kindly interest led you to act as a mediator between estranged husband and wife, and brought them together again. Let us drop the hypothetical case—I need conceal no longer that it is I who am the sufferer in this said affair—the names you shall have—Thomas R. Billings and Wife—and Henry K. Jessup, the man with whom she is infatuated."

Client number three laid his hand upon Mr. Gooch's arm. Deep emotion was written upon his careworn face. "For Heaven's sake," he said, fervently, "help me in this hour of trouble. Seek out Mrs. Billings, and persuade her to abandon this distressing pursuit of her lamentable folly. Tell her, Mr. Gooch, that her husband is willing to receive her back to his heart and home—promise her anything that will induce her to return. I have heard of your success in these matters. Mrs. Billings cannot be very far away. I am worn out with travel and weariness. Twice during the pursuit I saw her, but various circumstances prevented our having an interview. Will you undertake this mission for me, Mr. Gooch, and earn my everlasting gratitude?"

"It is true," said Lawyer Gooch, frowning slightly at the other's last words, but immediately calling up an expression of virtuous benevolence, "that on a number of occasions I have been successful in persuading couples who sought the severing of their matrimonial bonds to think better of their rash intentions and return to their homes reconciled. But I assure you that the work is often exceedingly difficult. The amount of argument, perseverance, and, if I may be allowed to say it, eloquence that it requires would astonish you. But this is a case in which my sympathies would be wholly enlisted. I feel deeply for you, sir, and I would be most happy to see husband and wife reunited. But my time," concluded the lawyer, looking at his watch as if suddenly reminded of the fact, "is valuable."

"I am aware of that," said the client, "and if you will take the case and persuade Mrs. Billings to return home and leave the man alone that she is following—on that day I will pay you the sum of one thousand dollars. I have made a little money in real estate during the recent boom in Susanville, and I will not begrudge that amount."

"Retain your seat for a few moments, please," said Lawyer Gooch, arising and again consulting his watch. "I have another client waiting in an adjoining room whom I had very nearly forgotten. I will return in the briefest possible space."

The situation was now one that fully satisfied Lawyer Gooch's love of intricacy and complication. He revelled in cases that presented such subtle problems and possibilities. It pleased him to think that he was master of the happiness and fate of the three individuals who sat, unconscious of one another's presence, within his reach. His old figure of the ship glided into his mind. But now the figure failed, for to have filled every compartment of an actual vessel would have been to endanger her safety; while here, with his compartments full, his ship of affairs could but sail on to the advantageous port of a fine, fat fee. The thing for him to do, of course, was to wring the best bargain he could from some one of his anxious cargo.

First he called to the office boy: "Lock the outer door, Archibald, and admit no one." Then he moved, with long, silent strides, into the room in which client number one waited. That gentleman sat, patiently scanning the pictures in the magazine, with a cigar in his mouth and his feet upon a table.

"Well," he remarked, cheerfully, as the lawyer entered, "have you made up your mind? Does five hundred dollars go for getting the fair lady a divorce?"

"You mean that as a retainer?" asked Lawyer Gooch, softly interrogative.

"Hey? No; for the whole job. It's enough, ain't it?"

"My fee," said Lawyer Gooch, "would be one thousand five hundred dollars. Five hundred dollars down, and the remainder upon issuance of the divorce."

A loud whistle came from client number one. His feet descended to the floor.

"Guess we can't close the deal," he said, arising. "I cleaned up five hundred dollars in a little real estate dicker down in Susanville. I'd do anything I could to free the lady, but it outsizes my pile."

"Could you stand one thousand two hundred dollars?" asked the lawyer, insinuatingly.

"Five hundred is my limit, I tell you. Guess I'll have to hunt up a cheaper lawyer." The client put on his hat.

"Out this way, please," said Lawyer Gooch, opening the door that led into the hallway.

As the gentleman flowed out of the compartment and down the stairs, Lawyer Gooch smiled to himself. "Exit Mr. Jessup," he murmured, as he fingered the Henry Clay tuft of hair at his ear. "And now for the forsaken husband." He returned to the middle office, and assumed a businesslike manner.

"I understand," he said to client number three, "that you agree to pay one thousand dollars if I bring about, or am instrumental in bringing about, the return of Mrs. Billings to her home, and her abandonment of her infatuated pursuit of the man for whom she has conceived such a violent fancy. Also that the case is now unreservedly in my hands on that basis. Is that correct?"

"Entirely," said the other, eagerly. "And I can produce the cash any time at two hours' notice."

Lawyer Gooch stood up at his full height. His thin figure seemed to expand. His thumbs sought the armholes of his vest. Upon his face was a look of sympathetic benignity that he always wore during such undertakings.

"Then, sir," he said, in kindly tones, "I think I can promise you an early relief from your troubles. I have that much confidence in my powers of argument and persuasion, in the natural impulses of the human heart towards good, and in the strong influence of a husband's unfaltering love. Mrs. Billings, sir, is here—in that room——" the lawyer's long arm pointed to the door. "I will call her in at once; and our united pleadings——"

Lawyer Gooch paused, for client number three had leaped from his chair as if propelled by steel springs, and clutched at his satchel.

"What the devil," he exclaimed, harshly, "do you mean? That woman in there! I thought I shook her off forty miles back."

He ran to the open window, looked out below, and threw one leg over the sill.

"Stop!" cried Lawyer Gooch, in amazement. "What would you do? Come, Mr. Billings, and face your erring but innocent wife. Our combined entreaties cannot fail to——"

"Billings!" shouted the now thoroughly moved client; "I'll Billings you, you old idiot!"

Turning, he hurled his satchel with fury at the lawyer's head. It struck that astounded peacemaker between the eyes, causing him to stagger backward a pace or two. When Lawyer Gooch recovered his wits he saw that his client had disappeared. Rushing to the window, he leaned out, and saw the recreant gathering himself up from the top of a shed upon which he had dropped from the second-story window. Without stopping to collect his hat he then plunged downward the remaining ten feet to the alley, up which he flew with prodigious celerity until the surrounding building swallowed him up from view.

Lawyer Gooch passed his hand tremblingly across his brow. It was an habitual act with him, serving to clear his thoughts. Perhaps also it now seemed to soothe the spot where a very hard alligator-hide satchel had struck.

The satchel lay upon the floor, wide open, with its contents spilled about. Mechanically Lawyer Gooch stooped to gather up the articles. The first was a collar; and the omniscient eye of the man of law perceived, wonderingly, the initials H. K. J. marked upon it. Then came a comb, a brush, a folded map and a piece of soap. Lastly, a handful of old business letters, addressed—every one of them—to "Henry K. Jessup, Esq."

Lawyer Gooch closed the satchel, and set it upon the table. He hesitated for a moment, and then put on his hat and walked into the office boy's anteroom.

"Archibald," he said mildly, as he opened the hall door, "I am going to the Supreme Court rooms. In five minutes you may step into the inner office, and inform the lady who is waiting there that"—here Lawyer Gooch made use of the vernacular—"that there's nothing doing."

CALLOWAY'S CODE

The New York *Enterprise* sent H. B. Calloway as special correspondent to the Russo-Japanese-Portsmouth war.

For two months Calloway hung about Yokohama and Tokio, shaking dice with the other correspondents for drinks of 'rickshaws—oh, no, that's something to ride in; anyhow, he wasn't earning the salary that his paper was paying him. But that was not Calloway's fault. The little brown men who held the strings of Fate between their fingers were not ready for the readers of the *Enterprise* to season their breakfast bacon and eggs with the battles of the descendants of the gods.

But soon the column of correspondents that were to go out with the First Army tightened their field-glass belts and went down to the Yalu with Kuroki. Calloway was one of these.

Now, this is no history of the battle of Yalu River. That has been told in detail by the correspondents who gazed at the shrapnel smoke rings from a distance of three miles. But, for justice's sake, let it be understood that the Japanese commander prohibited a nearer view.

Calloway's feat was accomplished before the battle. What he did was to furnish the *Enterprise* with the biggest beat of the war. That paper published exclusively and in detail the news of the attack on the lines of the Russian General Zassulitch on the same day that it was made. No other paper printed a word about it for two days afterward, except a London paper, whose account was absolutely incorrect and untrue.

Calloway did this in face of the fact that General Kuroki was making his moves and laying his plans with the profoundest secrecy as far as the world outside his camps was concerned. The correspondents were forbidden to send out any news whatever of his plans; and every message that was allowed on the wires was censored with rigid severity.

The correspondent for the London paper handed in a cablegram describing Kuroki's plans; but as it was wrong from beginning to end the censor grinned and let it go through.

So, there they were—Kuroki on one side of the Yalu with forty-two thousand infantry, five thousand cavalry, and one hundred and twenty-four guns. On the other side Zassulitch waited for him with only twenty-three thousand men, and with a long stretch of river to guard. And Calloway had got hold of some important inside information that he knew would bring the *Enterprise* staff around a cablegram as thick as flies around a Park Row lemonade stand. If he could only get that message past the censor—the new censor who had arrived and taken his post that day!

Calloway did the obviously proper thing. He lit his pipe and sat down on a gun carriage to think it over. And there we must leave him; for the rest of the story belongs to Vesey, a sixteen-dollar-a-week reporter on the *Enterprise*.

Calloway's cablegram was handed to the managing editor at four o'clock in the afternoon. He read it three times; and then drew a pocket mirror from a pigeon-hole in his desk, and looked at his reflection carefully. Then he went over to the desk of Boyd, his assistant (he usually called Boyd when he wanted him), and laid the cablegram before him.

"It's from Calloway," he said. "See what you make of it."

The message was dated at Wi-ju, and these were the words of it:

Foregone preconcerted rash witching goes muffled rumor mine dark silent unfortunate richmond existing great hotly brute select mooted parlous beggars ye angel incontrovertible.

Boyd read it twice.

"It's either a cipher or a sunstroke," said he.

"Ever hear of anything like a code in the office—a secret code?" asked the m. e., who had held his desk for only two years. Managing editors come and go.

"None except the vernacular that the lady specials write in," said Boyd. "Couldn't be an acrostic, could it?"

"I thought of that," said the m. e., "but the beginning letters contain only four vowels. It must be a code of some sort."

"Try 'em in groups," suggested Boyd. "Let's see—'Rash witching goes' not with me it doesn't. 'Muffled rumor mine'—must have an underground wire. 'Dark silent unfortunate richmond'—no reason why he should knock that town so hard. 'Existing great hotly'—no, it doesn't pan out. I'll call Scott."

The city editor came in a hurry, and tried his luck. A city editor must know something about everything; so Scott knew a little about cipher-writing.

"It may be what is called an inverted alphabet cipher," said he. "I'll try that. 'R' seems to be the oftenest used initial letter, with the exception of 'm.' Assuming 'r' to mean 'e,' the most frequently used vowel, we transpose the letters—so."

Scott worked rapidly with his pencil for two minutes; and then showed the first word according to his reading—the word "Scejtzez."

"Great!" cried Boyd. "It's a charade. My first is a Russian General. Go on, Scott."

"No, that won't work," said the city editor. "It's undoubtedly a code. It's impossible to read it without the key. Has the office ever used a cipher code?"

"Just what I was asking," said the m. e. "Hustle everybody up that ought to know. We must get at it some way. Calloway has evidently got hold of something big, and the censor has put the screws on, or he wouldn't have cabled in a lot of chop suey like this."

Throughout the office of the *Enterprise* a dragnet was sent, hauling in such members of the staff as would be likely to know of a code, past or present, by reason of their wisdom, information, natural intelligence, or length of servitude. They got together in a group in the city room, with the m. e. in the centre. No one had heard of a code. All began to explain to the head investigator that newspapers never use a code, anyhow—that is, a cipher code. Of course the Associated Press stuff is a sort of code—an abbreviation, rather—but——

The m. e. knew all that, and said so. He asked each man how long he had worked on the paper. Not one of them had drawn pay from an *Enterprise* envelope for longer than six years. Calloway had been on the paper twelve years.

"Try old Heffelbauer," said the m. e. "He was here when Park Row was a potato patch."

Heffelbauer was an institution. He was half janitor, half handyman about the office, and half watchman—thus becoming the peer of thirteen and one-half tailors. Sent for, he came, radiating his nationality.

"Heffelbauer," said the m. e., "did you ever hear of a code belonging to the office a long time ago—a private code? You know what a code is, don't you?"

"Yah," said Heffelbauer. "Sure I know vat a code is. Yah, apout dwelf or fifteen year ago der office had a code. Der reborters in der city-room haf it here."

"Ah!" said the m. e. "We're getting on the trail now. Where was it kept, Heffelbauer? What do you know about it?"

"Somedimes," said the retainer, "dey keep it in der little room behind der library room."

"Can you find it?" asked the m. e., eagerly. "Do you know where it is?"

"Mein Gott!" said Heffelbauer. "How long you dink a code live? Der reborters call him a maskeet. But von day he butt mit his head der editor, und——"

"Oh, he's talking about a goat," said Boyd. "Get out, Heffelbauer."

Again discomfited, the concerted wit and resource of the *Enterprise* huddled around Calloway's puzzle, considering its mysterious words in vain.

Then Vesey came in.

Vesey was the youngest reporter. He had a thirty-two-inch chest and wore a number fourteen collar; but his bright Scotch plaid suit gave him presence and conferred no obscurity upon his whereabouts. He wore his hat in such a position that people followed him about to see him take it off, convinced that it must be hung upon a peg driven into the back of his head. He was never without an immense, knotted, hard-wood cane with a German-silver tip on its crooked handle. Vesey was the best photograph hustler in the office. Scott said it was because no living human being could resist the personal triumph it was to hand his picture over to Vesey. Vesey always wrote his own news stories, except the big ones, which were sent to the rewrite men. Add to this fact that among all the inhabitants, temples, and groves of the earth nothing existed that could abash Vesey, and his dim sketch is concluded.

Vesey butted into the circle of cipher readers very much as Heffelbauer's "code" would have done, and asked what was up. Some one explained, with the touch of half-familiar condescension that they always used toward him. Vesey reached out and took the cablegram from the m. e.'s hand. Under the protection of some special Providence, he was always doing appalling things like that, and coming off unscathed.

"It's a code," said Vesey. "Anybody got the key?"

"The office has no code," said Boyd, reaching for the message. Vesey held to it.

"Then old Calloway expects us to read it, anyhow," said he. "He's up a tree, or something, and he's made this up so as to get it by the censor. It's up to us. Gee! I wish they had sent me, too. Say—we can't afford to fall down on our end of it. 'Foregone, preconcerted rash, witching'—h'm."

Vesey sat down on a table corner and began to whistle softly, frowning at the cablegram.

"Let's have it, please," said the m.e. "We've got to get to work on it."

"I believe I've got a line on it," said Vesey. "Give me ten minutes."

He walked to his desk, threw his hat into a waste-basket, spread out flat on his chest like a gorgeous lizard, and started his pencil going. The wit and wisdom of the *Enterprise* remained in a loose group, and smiled at one another, nodding their heads toward Vesey. Then they began to exchange their theories about the cipher.

It took Vesey exactly fifteen minutes. He brought to the m. e. a pad with the code-key written on it.

"I felt the swing of it as soon as I saw it," said Vesey. "Hurrah for old Calloway! He's done the Japs and every paper in town that prints literature instead of news. Take a look at that."

Thus had Vesey set forth the reading of the code:

Foregone—conclusion
Preconcerted—arrangement
Rash—act
Witching—hour of midnight
Goes—without saying
Muffled—report
Rumor—hath it
Mine—host
Dark—horse
Silent—majority
Unfortunate—pedestrians[1]
Richmond—in the field

Existing—conditions
Great—White Way
Hotly—contested
Brute—force
Select—few
Mooted—question
Parlous—times
Beggars—description
Ye—correspondent
Angel—unawares
Incontrovertible—fact

"It's simply newspaper English," explained Vesey. "I've been reporting on the *Enterprise* long enough to know it by heart. Old Calloway gives us the cue word, and we use the word that naturally follows it just as we use 'em in the paper. Read it over, and you'll see how pat they drop into their places. Now, here's the message he intended us to get."

Vesey handed out another sheet of paper.

Concluded arrangement to act at hour of midnight without saying. Report hath it that a large body of cavalry and an overwhelming force of infantry will be thrown into the field. Conditions white. Way contested by only a small force. Question the *Times* description. Its correspondent is unaware of the facts.

"Great stuff!" cried Boyd, excitedly. "Kuroki crosses the Yalu to-night and attacks. Oh, we won't do a thing to the sheets that make up with Addison's essays, real estate transfers, and bowling scores!"

"Mr. Vesey," said the m. e., with his jollying-which-you-should-regard-as-a-favor manner, "you have cast a serious reflection upon the literary standards of the paper that employs you. You have also assisted materially in giving us the biggest 'beat' of the year. I will let you know in a day or two whether you are to be discharged or retained at larger salary. Somebody send Ames to me."

Ames was the king-pin, the snowy-petalled marguerite, the star-bright looloo of the rewrite men. He saw attempted murder in the pains of green-apple colic, cyclones in the summer zephyr, lost children in every top-spinning urchin, an uprising of the down-trodden masses in every hurling of a derelict potato at a passing automobile. When not rewriting, Ames sat on the porch of his Brooklyn villa playing checkers with his ten-year-old son.

[1] Mr. Vesey afterward explained that the logical journalistic complement of the word "unfortunate" was once the word "victim." But, since the automobile became so popular, the correct following word is now "pedestrians." Of course, in Calloway's code it meant infantry.

Ames and the "war editor" shut themselves in a room. There was a map in there stuck full of little pins that represented armies and divisions. Their fingers had been itching for days to move those pins along the crooked line of the Yalu. They did so now; and in words of fire Ames translated Calloway's brief message into a front page masterpiece that set the world talking. He told of the secret councils of the Japanese officers; gave Kuroki's flaming speeches in full; counted the cavalry and infantry to a man and a horse; described the quick and silent building of the bridge at Suikauchen, across which the Mikado's legions were hurled upon the surprised Zassulitch, whose troops were widely scattered along the river. And the battle!—well, you know what Ames can do with a battle if you give him just one smell of smoke for a foundation. And in the same story, with seemingly supernatural knowledge, he gleefully scored the most profound and ponderous paper in England for the false and misleading account of the intended movements of the Japanese First Army printed in its issue of *the same date.*

Only one error was made; and that was the fault of the cable operator at Wi-ju. Calloway pointed it out after he came back. The word "great" in his code should have been "gage" and its complemental words "of battle." But it went to Ames "conditions white," and of course he took that to mean snow. His description of the Japanese army struggling through the snowstorm, blinded by whirling flakes, was thrillingly vivid. The artists turned out some effective illustrations that made a hit as pictures of the artillery dragging their guns through the drifts. But, as the attack was made on the first day of May, the "conditions white" excited some amusement. But it made no difference to the *Enterprise,* anyway.

It was wonderful. And Calloway was wonderful in having made the new censor believe that his jargon of words meant no more than a complaint of the dearth of news and a petition for more expense money. And Vesey was wonderful. And most wonderful of all are words, and how they make friends one with another, being oft associated, until not even obituary notices them do part.

On the second day following, the city editor halted at Vesey's desk where the reporter was writing the story of a man who had broken his leg by falling into a coal-hole—Ames having failed to find a murder motive in it.

"The old man says your salary is to be raised to twenty a week," said Scott.

"All right," said Vesey. "Every little helps. Say—Mr. Scott, which would you say—'We can state without fear of successful contradiction,' or, 'On the whole it can be safely asserted'?"

A MATTER OF MEAN ELEVATION

One winter the Alcazar Opera Company of New Orleans made a speculative trip along the Mexican, Central American, and South American coasts. The venture proved a most successful one. The music-loving, impressionable Spanish-Americans deluged the company with dollars and "vivas." The manager waxed plump and amiable. But for the prohibitive climate he would have put forth the distinctive flower of his prosperity— the overcoat of fur, braided, frogged, and opulent. Almost was he persuaded to raise the salaries of his company. But with a mighty effort he conquered the impulse toward such an unprofitable effervescence of joy.

At Macuto, on the coast of Venezuela, the company scored its greatest success. Imagine Coney Island translated into Spanish and you will comprehend Macuto. The fashionable season is from November to March. Down from La Guayra and Caracas and Valencia and other interior towns flock the people for their holiday season. There are bathing and fiestas and bull fights and scandal. And then the people have a passion for music that the bands in the plaza and on the sea beach stir but do not satisfy. The coming of the Alcazar Opera Company aroused the utmost ardor and zeal among the pleasure seekers.

The illustrious Guzman Blanco, President and Dictator of Venezuela, sojourned in Macuto with his court for the season. That potent ruler— who himself paid a subsidy of 40,000 pesos each year to grand opera in Caracas—ordered one of the government warehouses to be cleared for a temporary theatre. A stage was quickly constructed and rough wooden benches made for the audience. Private boxes were added for the use of the President and the notables of the army and Government.

The company remained in Macuto for two weeks. Each performance filled the house as closely as it could be packed. Then the music-mad people fought for room in the open doors and windows, and crowded about, hundreds deep on the outside. Those audiences formed a brilliantly diversified patch of color. The hue of their faces ranged from the clear olive of the pure-blood Spaniards down through the yellow and brown shades of the mestizos to the coal-black Carib and the Jamaica Negro. Scattered among them were little groups of Indians with faces like stone idols, wrapped in gaudy fibre-woven blankets—Indians down from the mountain states of Zamora and Los Andes and Miranda to trade their gold dust in the coast towns.

The spell cast upon these denizens of the interior fastnesses was remarkable. They sat in petrified ecstasy, conspicuous among the excitable Macutians, who wildly strove with tongue and hand to give evidence of their delight. Only once did the sombre rapture of these aboriginals find expression. During the rendition of "Faust," Guzman Blanco, extravagantly pleased by the "Jewel Song," cast upon the stage a purse of gold pieces. Other distinguished citizens followed his lead to the extent of whatever loose coin they had convenient, while some of the fair and fashionable señoras were moved, in imitation, to fling a jewel or a ring or two at the feet of the Marguerite—who was, according to the bills, Mlle Nina Giraud. Then from different parts of the house rose sundry of the stolid hillmen and cast upon the stage little brown and dun bags that fell with soft "thumps" and did not rebound. It was, no doubt, pleasure at the tribute to her art that caused Mlle Giraud's eyes to shine so brightly when she opened these little deerskin bags in her dressing room and found them to contain pure gold dust. If so, the pleasure was rightly hers, for her voice in song, pure, strong, and thrilling with the feeling of the emotional artist, deserved the tribute that it earned.

But the triumph of the Alcazar Opera Company is not the theme: it but leans upon and colors it. There happened in Macuto a tragic thing, an unsolvable mystery, that sobered for a time the gaiety of the happy season.

One evening between the short twilight and the time when she should have whirled upon the stage in the red and black of the ardent Carmen, Mlle Nina Giraud disappeared from the sight and ken of 6,000 pairs of eyes and as many minds in Macuto. There was the usual turmoil and hurrying to seek her. Messengers flew to the little French-kept hotel where she stayed; others of the company hastened here or there where she might be lingering in some *tienda* or unduly prolonging her bath upon the beach. All search was fruitless. Mademoiselle had vanished.

Half an hour passed, and she did not appear. The dictator, unused to the caprices of prime donne, became impatient. He sent an aide from his box to say to the manager that if the curtain did not at once rise he would immediately hale the entire company to the calabosa, though it would desolate his heart, indeed, to be compelled to such an act. Birds in Macuto could be made to sing.

The manager abandoned hope, for the time, of Mlle Giraud. A member of the chorus, who had dreamed hopelessly for years of the blessed opportunity, quickly Carmenized herself and the opera went on.

Afterward, when the lost cantatrice appeared not, the aid of the authorities was invoked. The President at once set the army, the police, and all citizens to the search. Not one clue to Mlle Giraud's disappearance was found. The Alcazar left to fill engagements farther down the coast.

On the way back the steamer stopped at Macuto and the manager made anxious inquiry. Not a trace of the lady had been discovered. The Alcazar could do no more. The personal belongings of the missing lady were stored in the hotel against her possible later reappearance and the opera company continued upon its homeward voyage to New Orleans.

On the *camino real* along the beach the two saddle mules and the four pack mules of Señor Don Johnny Armstrong stood, patiently awaiting the crack of the whip of the *arriero,* Luis. That would be the signal for the start on another long journey into the mountains. The pack mules were loaded with a varied assortment of hardware and cutlery. These articles Don Johnny traded to the interior Indians for the gold dust that they washed from the Andean streams and stored in quills and bags against his coming. It was a profitable business, and Señor Armstrong expected soon to be able to purchase the coffee plantation that he coveted.

Armstrong stood on the narrow sidewalk, exchanging garbled Spanish with old Peralto, the rich native merchant who had just charged him four prices for half a gross of pot-metal hatchets, and abridged English with Rucker, the little German who was Consul for the United States.

"Take with you, señor," said Peralto, "the blessings of the saints upon your journey."

"Better try quinine," growled Rucker through his pipe. "Take two grains every night. And don't make your trip too long, Johnny, because we haf needs of you. It is ein villainous game dot Melville play of whist, and dere is no oder substitute. *Auf wiedersehen,* und keep your eyes dot mule's ear between when you on der edge of der brecipices ride."

The bells of Luis's mule jingled and the pack train filed after the warning note. Armstrong waved a good-bye and took his place at the trail of the procession. Up the narrow street they turned, and passed the two-story wooden Hotel Inglés where Ives and Dawson and Richards and the rest of the chaps were dawdling on the broad piazza, reading week-old newspapers. They crowded to the railing and shouted many friendly and wise and foolish farewells after him. Across the plaza they trotted slowly past the bronze statue of Guzman Blanco, within its fence of bayoneted rifles captured from revolutionists, and out of the town between the rows of thatched huts swarming with the unclothed youth of Macuto. They plunged into the damp coolness of banana groves at length to emerge upon a bright stream, where brown women in scant raiment laundered clothes destructively upon the rocks. Then the pack train, fording the stream, attacked the sudden ascent, and bade adieu to such civilization as the coast afforded.

For weeks Armstrong, guided by Luis, followed his regular route among the mountains. After he had collected an arroba of the precious metal, winning a profit of nearly $5,000, the heads of the lightened mules were turned down-trail again. Where the head of the Guarico River springs from a great gash in the mountainside, Luis halted the train.

"Half a day's journey from here, Señor," said he, "is the village of Tacuzama, which we have never visited. I think many ounces of gold may be procured there. It is worth the trial."

Armstrong concurred, and they turned again upward toward Tacuzama. The trail was abrupt and precipitous, mounting through a dense
forest. As night fell, dark and gloomy, Luis once more halted. Before
them was a black chasm, bisecting the path as far as they could see.

Luis dismounted. "There should be a bridge," he called, and ran
along the cleft a distance. "It is here," he cried, and remounting, led the
way. In a few moments Armstrong heard a sound as though a thunderous drum were beating somewhere in the dark. It was the falling of the
mules' hoofs upon the bridge made of strong hides lashed to poles and
stretched across the chasm. Half a mile further was Tacuzama. The
village was a congregation of rock and mud huts set in that profundity
of an obscure wood. As they rode in a sound inconsistent with that brooding solitude met their ears. From a long, low mud hut that they were
nearing rose the glorious voice of a woman in song. The words were
English, the air familiar to Armstrong's memory, but not to his musical
knowledge.

He slipped from his mule and stole to a narrow window in one end of
the house. Peering cautiously inside, he saw, within three feet of him, a
woman of marvellous, imposing beauty, clothed in a splendid loose robe
of leopard skins. The hut was packed close to the small space in which she
stood with the squatting figures of Indians.

The woman finished her song and seated herself close to the little
window, as if grateful for the unpolluted air that entered it. When she
had ceased several of the audience rose and cast little softly falling bags
at her feet. A harsh murmur—no doubt a barbarous kind of applause and
comment—went through the grim assembly.

Armstrong was used to seizing opportunities promptly. Taking advantage of the noise he called to the woman in a low but distinct voice: "Do
not turn your head this way, but listen. I am an American. If you need
assistance tell me how I can render it. Answer as briefly as you
can."

The woman was worthy of his boldness. Only by a sudden flush of her
pale cheek did she acknowledge understanding of his words. Then she
spoke, scarcely moving her lips.

"I am held a prisoner by these Indians. God knows I need help. In
two hours come to the little hut twenty yards toward the mountainside.
There will be a light and a red curtain in the window. There is always
a guard at the door whom you will have to overcome. For the love of
heaven, do not fail to come."

The story seems to shrink from adventure and rescue and mystery.
The theme is one too gentle for those brave and quickening tones. And
yet it reaches as far back as time itself. It has been named "environment,"
which is as weak a word as any to express the unnamable kinship of man

to nature, that queer fraternity that causes stones and trees and salt water and clouds to play upon our emotions. Why are we made serious and solemn and sublime by mountain heights, grave and contemplative by an abundance of overhanging trees, reduced to inconstancy and monkey capers by the ripples on a sandy beach? Did the protoplasm—but enough. The chemists are looking into the matter, and before long they will have all life in the table of the symbols.

Briefly, then, in order to confine the story within scientific bounds, John Armstrong went to the hut, choked the Indian guard and carried away Mlle Giraud. With her was also conveyed a number of pounds of gold dust she had collected during her six months' forced engagement in Tacuzama. The Carabobo Indians are easily the most enthusiastic lovers of music between the equator and the French Opera House in New Orleans. They are also strong believers that the advice of Emerson was good when he said: "The thing thou wantest, O discontented man—take it, and pay the price." A number of them had attended the performance of the Alcazar Opera Company in Macuto, and found Mlle Giraud's style and technique satisfactory. They wanted her, so they took her one evening suddenly and without any fuss. They treated her with much consideration, exacting only one song recital each day. She was quite pleased at being rescued by Mr. Armstrong. So much for mystery and adventure. Now to resume the theory of the protoplasm.

John Armstrong and Mlle Giraud rode among the Andean peaks, enveloped in their greatness and sublimity. The mightiest cousins, furthest removed, in Nature's great family became conscious of the tie. Among those huge piles of primordial upheaval, amid those gigantic silences and elongated fields of distance the littlenesses of men are precipitated as one chemical throws down a sediment from another. They moved reverently, as in a temple. Their souls were uplifted in unison with the stately heights. They traveled in a zone of majesty and peace.

To Armstrong the woman seemed almost a holy thing. Yet bathed in the white, still dignity of her martyrdom that purified her earthly beauty and gave out, it seemed, an aura of transcendent loveliness, in those first hours of companionship she drew from him an adoration that was half human love, half the worship of a descended goddess.

Never yet since her rescue had she smiled. Over her dress she still wore the robe of leopard skins, for the mountain air was cold. She looked to be some splendid princess belonging to those wild and awesome altitudes. The spirit of the region chimed with hers. Her eyes were always turned upon the somber cliffs, the blue gorges, and the snow-clad turrets, looking a sublime melancholy equal to their own. At times on the journey she sang thrilling te deums and misereres that struck the true note of the hills, and made their route seem like a solemn march down a cathedral aisle.

The rescued one spoke but seldom, her mood partaking of the hush of nature that surrounded them. Armstrong looked upon her as an angel. He could not bring himself to the sacrilege of attempting to woo her as other women may be wooed.

On the third day they had descended as far as the *tierra templada,* the zone of the table lands and foot hills. The mountains were receding in their rear, but still towered, exhibiting yet impressively their formidable heads. Here they met signs of man. They saw the white houses of coffee plantations gleam across the clearings. They struck into a road where they met travelers and pack-mules. Cattle were grazing on the slopes. They passed a little village where the round-eyed *niños* shrieked and called at sight of them.

Mlle Giraud laid aside her leopard-skin robe. It seemed to be a trifle incongruous now. In the mountains it had appeared fitting and natural. And if Armstrong was not mistaken she laid aside with it something of the high dignity of her demeanor. As the country became more populous and significant of comfortable life he saw, with a feeling of joy, that the exalted princess and priestess of the Andean peaks was changing to a woman—an earth woman, but no less enticing. A little color crept to the surface of her marble cheek. She arranged the conventional dress that the removal of the robe now disclosed with the solicitous touch of one who is conscious of the eyes of others. She smoothed the careless sweep of her hair. A mundane interest, long latent in the chilling atmosphere of the ascetic peaks, showed in her eyes.

This thaw in his divinity sent Armstrong's heart going faster. So might an Arctic explorer thrill at his first ken of green fields and liquescent waters. They were on a lower plane of earth and life and were succumbing to its peculiar, subtle influence. The austerity of the hills no longer thinned the air they breathed. About them was the breath of fruit and corn and builded homes, the comfortable smell of smoke and warm earth and the consolations man has placed between himself and the dust of his brother earth from which he sprung. While traversing those awful mountains, Mlle Giraud had seemed to be wrapped in their spirit of reverent reserve. Was this that same woman—now palpitating, warm, eager, throbbing with conscious life and charm, feminine to her fingertips? Pondering over this, Armstrong felt certain misgivings intrude upon his thoughts. He wished he could stop there with this changing creature, descending no farther. Here was the elevation and environment to which her nature seemed to respond with its best. He feared to go down upon the man-dominated levels. Would her spirit not yield still further in that artificial zone to which they were descending?

Now from a little plateau they saw the sea flash at the edge of the green lowlands. Mlle Giraud gave a little, catching sigh.

"Oh, look, Mr. Armstrong, there is the sea! Isn't it lovely? I'm so tired of mountains." She heaved a pretty shoulder in a gesture of repugnance. "Those horrid Indians! Just think of what I suffered! Although I suppose I attained my ambition of becoming a stellar attraction, I wouldn't care to repeat the engagement. It was very nice of you to bring me away. Tell me, Mr. Armstrong—honestly, now—do I look such an awful, awful fright? I haven't looked into a mirror, you know, for months."

Armstrong made answer according to his changed moods. Also he laid his hand upon hers as it rested upon the horn of her saddle. Luis was at the head of the pack train and could not see. She allowed it to remain there, and her eyes smiled frankly into his.

Then at sundown they dropped upon the coast level under the palms and lemons among the vivid greens and scarlets and ochres of the *tierra caliente*. They rode into Macuto, and saw the line of volatile bathers frolicking in the surf. The mountains were very far away.

Mlle Giraud's eyes were shining with a joy that could not have existed under the chaperonage of the mountain-tops. There were other spirits calling to her—nymphs of the orange groves, pixies from the chattering surfs, imps, born of the music, the perfumes, colors and the insinuating presence of humanity. She laughed aloud, musically, at a sudden thought.

"Won't there be a sensation?" she called to Armstrong. "Don't I wish I had an engagement just now, though! What a picnic the press agent would have! 'Held a prisoner by a band of savage Indians subdued by the spell of her wonderful voice'—wouldn't that make great stuff? But I guess I quit the game winner, anyhow—there ought to be a couple of thousand dollars in that sack of gold dust I collected as encores, don't you think?"

He left her at the door of the little Hotel de Buen Descansar, where she had stopped before. Two hours later he returned to the hotel. He glanced in at the open door of the little combined reception room and café.

Half a dozen of Macuto's representative social and official *caballeros* were distributed about the room. Señor Villablanca, the wealthy rubber concessionist, reposed his fat figure on two chairs, with an emollient smile beaming upon his chocolate-colored face. Guilbert, the French mining engineer, leered through his polished nose-glasses. Colonel Mendez, of the regular army, in gold-laced uniform and fatuous grin, was busily extracting corks from champagne bottles. Other patterns of Macutian gallantry and fashion pranced and posed. The air was hazy with cigarette smoke. Wine dripped upon the floor.

Perched upon a table in the centre of the room in an attitude of easy pre-eminence was Mlle Giraud. A chic costume of white lawn and cherry ribbons supplanted her traveling garb. There was a suggestion of lace, and a frill or two, with a discreet, small implication of hand-embroidered pink hosiery. Upon her lap rested a guitar. In her face was the light of resurrection, the peace of elysium attained through fire and suffering. She was singing to a lively accompaniment a little song:

"When you see de big round moon
  Comin' up like a balloon,
  Dis nigger skips fur to kiss de lips
  Of his stylish, black-faced coon."

The singer caught sight of Armstrong.

"Hi! there, Johnny," she called; "I've been expecting you for an hour. What kept you? Gee! but these smoked guys are the slowest you ever saw. They ain't on, at all. Come along in, and I'll make this coffee-colored old sport with the gold epaulettes open one for you right off the ice."

"Thank you," said Armstrong; "not just now, I believe. I've several things to attend to."

He walked out and down the street, and met Rucker coming up from the Consulate.

"Play you a game of billiards," said Armstrong. "I want something to take the taste of the sea level out of my mouth."

"GIRL"

In gilt letters on the ground glass of the door of room No. 962 were the words: "Robbins & Hartley, Brokers." The clerks had gone. It was past five, and with the solid tramp of a drove of prize Percherons, scrub-women were invading the cloud-capped twenty-story office building. A puff of red-hot air flavored with lemon peelings, soft-coal smoke, and train oil came in through the half-open windows.

Robbins, fifty, something of an overweight beau, and addicted to first nights and hotel palm-rooms, pretended to be envious of his partner's commuter's joys.

"Going to be something doing in the humidity line to-night," he said. "You out-of-town chaps will be the people, with your katydids and moon-light and long drinks and things out on the front porch."

Hartley, twenty-nine, serious, thin, good-looking, nervous, sighed and frowned a little.

"Yes," said he, "we always have cool nights in Floralhurst especially in the winter."

A man with an air of mystery came in the door and went up to Hartley.

"I've found where she lives," he announced in the portentous half-whisper that makes the detective at work a marked being to his fellow men.

Hartley scowled him into a state of dramatic silence and quietude. But by that time Robbins had got his cane and set his tie pin to his liking, and with a debonair nod went out to his metropolitan amusements.

"Here is the address," said the detective in a natural tone, being deprived of an audience to foil.

Hartley took the leaf torn out of the sleuth's dingy memorandum book. On it were pencilled the words "Vivienne Arlington, No. 341 East —th Street, care of Mrs. McComus."

"Moved there a week ago," said the detective. "Now, if you want any shadowing done, Mr. Hartley, I can do you as fine a job in that line as anybody in the city. It will be only $7 a day and expenses. Can send in a daily type-written report, covering——"

"You needn't go on," interrupted the broker. "It isn't a case of that kind. I merely wanted the address. How much shall I pay you?"

"One day's work," said the sleuth. "A tenner will cover it."

Hartley paid the man and dismissed him. Then he left the office and boarded a Broadway car. At the first large crosstown artery of travel he took an eastbound car that deposited him in a decaying avenue, whose ancient structures once sheltered the pride and glory of the town.

Walking a few squares, he came to the building that he sought. It was a new flat-house, bearing carved upon its cheap stone portal its sonorous name, "The Vallambrosa." Fire-escapes zigzagged down its front—these laden with household goods, drying clothes, and squalling children evicted by the midsummer heat. Here and there a pale rubber plant peeped from the miscellaneous mass as if wondering to what kingdom it belonged— vegetable, animal, or artificial.

Hartley pressed the "McComus" button. The door latch clicked spasmodically—now hospitably, now doubtfully, as though in anxiety whether it might be admitting friends or duns. Hartley entered and began to climb the stairs after the manner of those who seek their friends in city flathouses—which is the manner of a boy who climbs an apple-tree, stopping when he comes upon what he wants.

On the fourth floor he saw Vivienne standing in an open door. She invited him inside, with a nod and a bright, genuine smile. She placed a chair for him near a window, and poised herself gracefully upon the edge of one of those Jekyll-and-Hyde pieces of furniture that are masked and mysteriously hooded, unguessable bulks by day and inquisitorial racks of torture by night.

Hartley cast a quick, critical, appreciative glance at her before speaking, and told himself that his taste in choosing had been flawless.

Vivienne was about twenty-one. She was of the purest Saxon type. Her hair was a ruddy golden, each filament of the neatly gathered mass shining with its own lustre and delicate graduation of color. In perfect harmony were her ivory-clear complexion and deep sea-blue eyes that looked upon the world with the ingenuous calmness of a mermaid or the pixie of an undiscovered mountain stream. Her frame was strong and yet possessed the grace of absolute naturalness. And yet with all her Northern clearness and frankness of line and coloring, there seemed to be something of the tropics in her—something of languor in the droop of her pose, of love of ease in her ingenious complacency of satisfaction and comfort in the mere act of breathing—something that seemed to claim for her a right as a perfect work of nature to exist and be admired equally with a rare flower or some beautiful, milk-white dove among its sober-hued companions.

She was dressed in a white waist and dark skirt—that discreet masquerade of goose-girl and duchess.

"Vivienne," said Hartley, looking at her pleadingly, "you did not answer my last letter. It was only by nearly a week's search that I found where you had moved to. Why have you kept me in suspense when you knew how anxiously I was waiting to see you and hear from you?"

The girl looked out the window dreamily.

"Mr. Hartley," she said hesitatingly, "I hardly know what to say to you. I realize all the advantages of your offer, and sometimes I feel sure that I could be contented with you. But, again, I am doubtful. I was born a city girl, and I am afraid to bind myself to a quiet suburban life."

"My dear girl," said Hartley, ardently, "have I not told you that you shall have everything that your heart can desire that is in my power to give you? You shall come to the city for the theatres, for shopping, and to visit your friends as often as you care to. You can trust me, can you not?"

"To the fullest," she said, turning her frank eyes upon him with a smile. "I know you are the kindest of men, and that the girl you get will be a lucky one. I learned all about you when I was at the Montgomerys'."

"Ah!" exclaimed Hartley, with a tender, reminiscent light in his eye; "I remember well the evening I first saw you at the Montgomerys'. Mrs. Montgomery was sounding your praises to me all the evening. And she hardly did you justice. I shall never forget that supper. Come, Vivienne, promise me. I want you. You'll never regret coming with me. No one else will ever give you as pleasant a home."

The girl sighed and looked down at her folded hands.

A sudden jealous suspicion seized Hartley.

"Tell me, Vivienne," he asked, regarding her keenly, "is there another —is there some one else?"

A rosy flush crept slowly over her fair cheeks and neck.

"You shouldn't ask that, Mr. Hartley," she said, in some confusion. "But I will tell you. There is one other—but he has no right—I have promised him nothing."

"His name?" demanded Hartley, sternly.

"Townsend."

"Rafford Townsend!" exclaimed Hartley, with a grim tightening of his jaw. "How did that man come to know you? After all I've done for him——"

"His auto has just stopped below," said Vivienne, bending over the window-sill. "He's coming for his answer. Oh, I don't know what to do!"

The bell in the flat kitchen whirred. Vivienne hurried to press the latch button.

"Stay here," said Hartley. "I will meet him in the hall."

Townsend, looking like a Spanish grandee in his light tweeds, Panama hat, and curling black mustache, came up the stairs three at a time. He stopped at sight of Hartley and looked foolish.

"Go back," said Hartley, firmly, pointing downstairs with his fore-finger.

"Hullo!" said Townsend, feigning surprise. "What's up? What are you doing here, old man?"

"Go back," repeated Hartley, inflexibly. "The Law of the Jungle. Do you want the Pack to tear you to pieces? The kill is mine."

"I came here to see a plumber about the bathroom connections," said Townsend, bravely.

"All right," said Hartley. "You shall have that lying plaster to stick upon your traitorous soul. But, go back."

Townsend went downstairs, leaving a bitter word to be wafted up the draught of the stair-case. Hartley went back to his wooing.

"Vivienne," said he, masterfully. "I have got to have you. I will take no more refusals or dilly-dallying."

"When do you want me?" she asked.

"Now. As soon as you can get ready."

She stood calmly before him and looked him in the eye.

"Do you think for one moment," she said, "that I would enter your home while Héloïse is there?"

Hartley cringed as if from an unexpected blow. He folded his arms and paced the carpet once or twice.

"She shall go," he declared, grimly. Drops stood upon his brow. "Why should I let that woman make my life miserable? Never have I seen one day of freedom from trouble since I have known her. You are right, Vivienne. Héloïse must be sent away before I can take you home. But she shall go. I have decided. I will turn her from my doors."

"When will you do this?" asked the girl.

Hartley clinched his teeth and bent his brows together.

"To-night," he said, resolutely. "I will send her away to-night."

"Then," said Vivienne, "my answer is 'yes.' Come for me when you will."

She looked into his eyes with a sweet, sincere light in her own. Hartley could scarcely believe that her surrender was true, it was so swift and complete.

"Promise me," he said, feelingly, "on your word and honor."

"On my word and honor," repeated Vivienne, softly.

At the door he turned and gazed at her happily, but yet as one who scarcely trusts the foundations of his joy.

"To-morrow," he said, with a forefinger of reminder uplifted.

"To-morrow," she repeated with a smile of truth and candor.

In an hour and forty minutes Hartley stepped off the train at Floral-hurst. A brisk walk of ten minutes brought him to the gate of a hand-some two-story cottage set upon a wide and well-tended lawn. Halfway to the house he was met by a woman with jet-black braided hair and flowing white summer gown, who half strangled him without apparent cause.

When they stepped into the hall she said:

"Mamma's here. The auto is coming for her in half an hour. She came to dinner, but there's no dinner."

"I've something to tell you," said Hartley. "I thought to break it to you gently, but since your mother is here we may as well out with it."

He stooped and whispered something at her ear.

His wife screamed. Her mother came running into the hall. The dark-haired woman screamed again—the joyful scream of a well-beloved and petted woman.

"Oh, mamma!" she cried, ecstatically, "what do you think? Vivienne is coming to cook for us! She is the one that stayed with the Montgomerys a whole year. And now, Billy, dear," she concluded, "you must go right down into the kitchen and discharge Héloïse. She has been drunk again the whole day long."

SOCIOLOGY IN SERGE AND STRAW

The season of irresponsibility is at hand. Come, let us twine round our brows wreaths of poison ivy (that is for idiocy), and wander hand in hand with sociology in the summer fields.

Likely as not the world is flat. The wise men have tried to prove that it is round, with indifferent success. They pointed out to us a ship going to sea, and bade us observe that, at length, the convexity of the earth hid from our view all but the vessel's topmast. But we picked up a telescope and looked, and saw the decks and hull again. Then the wise men said: "Oh, pshaw! anyhow, the variation of the intersection of the equator and the ecliptic proves it." We could not see this through our telescope, so we remained silent. But it stands to reason that, if the world were round, the queues of Chinamen would stand straight up from their heads instead of hanging down their backs, as travelers assure us they do.

Another hot-weather corroboration of the flat theory is the fact that all of life, as we know it, moves in little, unavailing circles. More justly than to anything else, it can be likened to the game of baseball. Crack! we hit the ball, and away we go. If we earn a run (in life we call it success) we get back to the home plate and sit upon a bench. If we are thrown out, we walk back to the home plate—and sit upon a bench.

The circumnavigators of the alleged globe may have sailed the rim of a watery circle back to the same port again. The truly great return at the high tide of their attainments to the simplicity of a child. The billionaire sits down at his mahogany to his bowl of bread and milk. When you reach the end of your career, just take down the sign "Goal" and look at the other side of it. You will find "Beginning Point" there. It has been reversed while you were going around the track.

But this is humor, and must be stopped. Let us get back to the serious questions that arise whenever sociology turns summer boarder. You are invited to consider the scene of the story—wild, Atlantic waves, thundering against a wooded and rock-bound shore—in the Greater City of New York.

The town of Fishampton, on the south shore of Long Island, is noted for its clam fritters and the summer residence of the Van Plushvelts.

The Van Plushvelts have a hundred million dollars, and their name is a household word with tradesmen and photographers.

On the fifteenth of June the Van Plushvelts boarded up the front door of their city house, carefully deposited their cat on the sidewalk, instructed the caretaker not to allow it to eat any of the ivy on the walls, and whizzed away in a 40-horse-power to Fishampton to stray alone in the shade— Amaryllis not being in their class. If you are a subscriber to the *Toadies' Magazine,* you have often—— You say you are not? Well, you buy it at a news-stand, thinking that the news-dealer is not wise to you. But he knows about it all. HE knows—HE knows! I say that you have often seen in the *Toadies' Magazine* pictures of the Van Plushvelts' summer home; so it will not be described here. Our business is with young Haywood Van Plushvelt, sixteen years old, heir to the century of millions, darling of the financial gods, and great grandson of Peter Van Plushvelt, former owner of a particularly fine cabbage patch that has been ruined by an intrusive lot of downtown skyscrapers.

One afternoon young Haywood Van Plushvelt strolled out between the granite gate posts of "Dolce far Niente"—that's what they called the place; and it was an improvement on dolce far Rockaway, I can tell you.

Haywood walked down into the village. He was human, after all, and his prospective millions weighed upon him. Wealth had wreaked upon him its direfullest. He was the product of private tutors. Even under his first hobby-horse had tan bark been strewn. He had been born with a gold spoon, lobster fork, and fish-set in his mouth. For which I hope, later, to submit justification, I must ask your consideration of his haberdashery and tailoring.

Young Fortunatus was dressed in a neat suit of dark blue serge, a neat white straw hat, neat low-cut tan shoes, linen of the well-known "immaculate" trade mark, a neat, narrow four-in-hand tie, and carried a slender, neat, bamboo cane.

Down Persimmon Street (there's never tree north of Hagerstown, Md.) came from the village "Smoky" Dodson, fifteen and a half, worst boy in Fishampton. "Smoky" was dressed in a ragged red sweater, wrecked and weather-worn golf cap, run-over shoes, and trousers of the "serviceable" brand. Dust, clinging to the moisture induced by free exercise, darkened wide areas of his face. "Smoky" carried a baseball bat, and a league ball that advertised itself in the rotundity of his trousers pocket. Haywood stopped and passed the time of day.

"Going to play ball?" he asked.

"Smoky's" eyes and countenance confronted him with a frank blue-and-freckled scrutiny.

"Me?" he said, with deadly mildness; "sure not. Can't you see I've got a divin' suit on? I'm goin' up in a submarine balloon to catch butterflies with a two-inch auger."

"Excuse me," said Haywood, with the insulting politeness of his caste, "for mistaking you for a gentleman. I might have known better."

"How might you have known better if you thought I was one?" said "Smoky," unconsciously a logician.

"By your appearance," said Haywood. "No gentleman is dirty, ragged, and a liar."

"Smoky" hooted once like a ferry-boat, spat on his hand, got a firm grip on his baseball bat and then dropped it against the fence.

"Say," said he, "I knows you. You're the pup that belongs in that swell private summer sanitarium for city guys over there. I seen you come out of the gate. You can't bluff nobody because you're rich. And because you got on swell clothes. Arabella! Yah!"

"Ragamuffin!" said Haywood.

"Smoky" picked up a fence-rail splinter and laid it on his shoulder.

"Dare you to knock it off," he challenged.

"I wouldn't soil my hands with you," said the aristocrat.

"'Fraid," said "Smoky" concisely. "Youse city ducks ain't got the sand. I kin lick you with one hand."

"I don't wish to have any trouble with you," said Haywood. "I asked you a civil question; and you replied like a—like a—a cad."

"Wot's a cad?" asked "Smoky."

"A cad is a disagreeable person," answered Haywood, "who lacks manners and doesn't know his place. They sometimes play baseball."

"I can tell you what a mollycoddle is," said "Smoky." "It's a monkey dressed up by its mother and sent out to pick daisies on the lawn."

"When you have the honor to refer to the members of my family," said Haywood, with some dim ideas of a code in his mind, "you'd better leave the ladies out of your remarks."

"Ho! ladies!" mocked the rude one. "I say ladies! I know what them rich women in the city does. They drink cocktails and swear and give parties to gorillas. The papers say so."

Then Haywood knew that it must be. He took off his coat, folded it neatly and laid it on the roadside grass, placed his hat upon it and began to unknot his blue silk tie.

"Hadn't yer better ring fer your maid, Arabella?" taunted "Smoky." "Wot yer going to do—go to bed?"

"I'm going to give you a good trouncing," said the hero. He did not hesitate, although the enemy was far beneath him socially. He remembered that his father once thrashed a cabman, and the papers gave it two columns, first page. And the *Toadies' Magazine* had a special article on Upper Cuts by the Upper Classes, and ran new pictures of the Van Plushvelt country seat, at Fishampton.

"Wot's trouncing?" asked "Smoky," suspiciously. "I don't want your old clothes. I'm no—oh, you mean to scrap! My, my! I won't do a thing to mamma's pet. Criminy! I'd hate to be a hand-laundered thing like you."

"Smoky" waited with some awkwardness for his adversary to prepare for battle. His own decks were always clear for action. When he should spit upon the palm of his terrible right it was equivalent to "You may fire now, Gridley."

The hated patrician advanced, with his shirt sleeves neatly rolled up. "Smoky" waited, in an attitude of ease, expecting the affair to be conducted according to Fishampton's rules of war. These allowed combat to be prefaced by stigma, recrimination, epithet, abuse, and insult gradually increasing in emphasis and degree. After a round of these "you're anothers" would come the chip knocked from the shoulder, or the advance across the "dare" line drawn with a toe on the ground. Next light taps given and taken, these also increasing in force until finally the blood was up and fists going at their best.

But Haywood did not know Fishampton's rules. *Noblesse oblige* kept a faint smile on his face as he walked slowly up to "Smoky" and said:

"Going to play ball?"

"Smoky" quickly understood this to be a putting of the previous question, giving him the chance to make a practical apology by answering it with civility and relevance.

"Listen this time," said he. "I'm goin' skatin' on the river. Don't you see me automobile with Chinese lanterns on it standin' and waitin' for me?"

Haywood knocked him down.

"Smoky" felt wronged. To thus deprive him of preliminary wrangle and objurgation was to send an armored knight full tilt against a crashing lance without permitting him first to caracole around the list to the flourish of trumpets. But he scrambled up and fell upon his foe, head, feet, and fists.

The fight lasted one round of an hour and ten minutes. It was lengthened until it was more like a war or a family feud than a fight. Haywood had learned some of the science of boxing and wrestling from his tutors, but these he discarded for the more instinctive methods of battle handed down by the cave-dwelling Van Plushvelts.

So, when he found himself, during the mêlée, seated upon the kicking and roaring "Smoky's" chest, he improved the opportunity by vigorously kneading handfuls of sand and soil into his adversary's ears, eyes, and mouth, and when "Smoky" got the proper leg hold and "turned" him, he fastened both hands in the Plushvelt hair and pounded the Plushvelt head against the lap of mother earth. Of course, the strife was not incessantly active. There were seasons when one sat upon the other, holding him down, while each blew like a grampus, spat out the more inconveniently large sections of gravel and earth, and strove to subdue the spirit of his opponent with a frightful and soul-paralyzing glare.

At last, it seemed that in the language of the ring, their efforts lacked steam. They broke away, and each disappeared in a cloud as he brushed away the dust of the conflict. As soon as his breath permitted, Haywood walked close to "Smoky" and said:

"Going to play ball?"

"Smoky" looked pensively at the sky, at his bat lying on the ground, and at the "leaguer" rounding his pocket.

"Sure," he said off-handedly. "The 'Yellowjackets' play the 'Long Islands.' I'm cap'n of the 'Long Islands.'"

"I guess I didn't mean to say you were ragged," said Haywood. "But you are dirty, you know."

"Sure," said "Smoky." "Yer get that way knockin' around. Say, I don't believe them New York papers about ladies drinkin' and havin' monkeys dinin' at the table with 'em. I guess they're lies, like they print about people eatin' out of silver plates, and ownin' dogs that cost $100."

"Certainly," said Haywood. "What do you play on your team?"

"Ketcher. Ever play any?"

"Never in my life," said Haywood. "I've never known any fellows except one or two of my cousins."

"Jer like to learn? We're goin' to have a practice game before the match. Wanter come along? I'll put yer in left-field, and yer won't be long ketchin' on."

"I'd like it bully," said Haywood. "I've always wanted to play baseball."

The ladies' maids of New York and the families of Western mine owners with social ambitions will remember well the sensation that was created by the report that the young multi-millionaire, Haywood Van Plushvelt, was playing ball with the village youths of Fishampton. It was conceded that the millennium of democracy had come. Reporters and photographers swarmed to the island. The papers printed half-page pictures of him as short-stop stopping a hot grounder. The *Toadies' Magazine* got out a Bat and Ball number that covered the subject historically, beginning with the vampire bat and ending with the Patriarchs' ball—illustrated with interior views of the Van Plushvelt country seat. Ministers, educators, and sociologists everywhere hailed the event as the tocsin call that proclaimed the universal brotherhood of man.

One afternoon I was reclining under the trees near the shore at Fishampton in the esteemed company of an eminent, bald-headed young sociologist. By way of note it may be inserted that all sociologists are more or less bald, and exactly thirty-two. Look 'em over.

The sociologist was citing the Van Plushvelt case as the most important "uplift" symptom of a generation and as an excuse for his own existence.

Immediately before us were the village baseball grounds. And now came the sportive youth of Fishampton and distributed themselves, shouting, about the diamond.

"There," said the sociologist, pointing, "there is young Plushvelt."

I raised myself (so far a cosycophant with Mary Ann) and gazed.

Young Van Plushvelt sat upon the ground. He was dressed in a ragged red sweater, wrecked and weather-worn golf cap, run-over shoes, and trousers of the "serviceable" brand. Dust clinging to the moisture induced by free exercise, darkened the wide areas of his face.

"That is he," repeated the sociologist. If he had said "him" I could have been less vindictive.

On a bench, with an air, sat the young millionaire's chum.

He was dressed in a neat suit of dark blue serge, a neat white straw hat, neat low-cut tan shoes, linen of the well-known "immaculate" trade mark, a neat, narrow four-in-hand tie, and carried a slender, neat bamboo cane.

I laughed loudly and vulgarly.

"What you want to do," said I to the sociologist, "is to establish a reformatory for the Logical Vicious Circle. Or else I've got wheels. It looks to me as if things are running round and round in circles instead of getting anywhere."

"What do you mean?" asked the man of progress.

"Why, look what he has done to 'Smoky,' " I replied.

"You will always be a fool," said my friend, the sociologist, getting up and walking away.

THE RANSOM OF RED CHIEF

It looked like a good thing: but wait till I tell you. We were down South, in Alabama—Bill Driscoll and myself—when this kidnapping idea struck us. It was, as Bill afterward expressed it, "during a moment of temporary mental apparition"; but we didn't find that out till later.

There was a town down there, as flat as a flannel-cake, and called Summit, of course. It contained inhabitants of as undeleterious and self-satisfied a class of peasantry as ever clustered around a Maypole.

Bill and me had a joint capital of about six hundred dollars, and we needed just two thousand dollars more to pull off a fraudulent town-lot scheme in Western Illinois with. We talked it over on the front steps of the hotel. Philoprogenitoveness, says we, is strong in semi-rural communities; therefore, and for other reasons, a kidnapping project ought to do better there than in the radius of newspapers that send reporters out in plain clothes to stir up talk about such things. We knew that Summit couldn't get after us with anything stronger than constables and, maybe, some lackadaisical bloodhounds and a diatribe or two in the *Weekly Farmers' Budget.* So, it looked good.

We selected for our victim the only child of a prominent citizen named Ebenezer Dorset. The father was respectable and tight, a mortgage fancier and a stern, upright collection-plate passer and forecloser. The kid was a boy of ten, with bas-relief freckles, and hair the color of the cover of the magazine you buy at the news-stand when you want to catch a train. Bill and me figured that Ebenezer would melt down for a ransom of two thousand dollars to a cent. But wait till I tell you.

About two miles from Summit was a little mountain, covered with a dense cedar brake. On the rear elevation of this mountain was a cave. There we stored provisions.

One evening after sundown, we drove in a buggy past old Dorset's house. The kid was in the street, throwing rocks at a kitten on the opposite fence.

"Hey, little boy!" says Bill, "would you like to have a bag of candy and a nice ride?"

The boy catches Bill neatly in the eye with a piece of brick.

"That will cost the old man an extra five hundred dollars," says Bill, climbing over the wheel.

That boy put up a fight like a welter-weight cinnamon bear; but, at last, we got him down in the bottom of the buggy and drove away. We took him up to the cave, and I hitched the horse in the cedar brake. After dark I drove the buggy to the little village, three miles away, where we had hired it, and walked back to the mountain.

Bill was pasting court-plaster over the scratches and bruises on his features. There was a fire burning behind the big rock at the entrance of the cave, and the boy was watching a pot of boiling coffee, with two buzzard tail-feathers stuck in his red hair. He points a stick at me when I come up, and says:

"Ha! cursed paleface, do you dare to enter the camp of Red Chief, the terror of the plains?"

"He's all right now," says Bill, rolling up his trousers and examining some bruises on his shins. "We're playing Indian. We're making Buffalo Bill's show look like magic-lantern views of Palestine in the town hall. I'm Old Hank, the Trapper, Red Chief's captive, and I'm to be scalped at daybreak. By Geronimo! that kid can kick hard."

Yes, sir, that boy seemed to be having the time of his life. The fun of camping out in a cave had made him forget that he was a captive himself. He immediately christened me Snake-eye, the Spy, and announced that, when his braves returned from the warpath, I was to be broiled at the stake at the rising of the sun.

Then we had supper; and he filled his mouth full of bacon and bread and gravy, and began to talk. He made a during-dinner speech something like this:

"I like this fine. I never camped out before; but I had a pet 'possum once, and I was nine last birthday. I hate to go to school. Rats ate up sixteen of Jimmy Talbot's aunt's speckled hen's eggs. Are there any real Indians in these woods? I want some more gravy. Does the trees moving make the wind blow? We had five puppies. What makes your nose so red, Hank? My father has lots of money. Are the stars hot? I whipped Ed Walker twice, Saturday. I don't like girls. You dassent catch toads unless with a string. Do oxen make any noise? Why are oranges round? Have you got beds to sleep on in this cave? Amos Murray has got six toes. A parrot can talk, but a monkey or a fish can't. How many does it take to make twelve?"

Every few minutes he would remember that he was a pesky redskin, and pick up his stick rifle and tiptoe to the mouth of the cave to rubber for the scouts of the hated paleface. Now and then he would let out a war-whoop that made Old Hank the Trapper shiver. That boy had Bill terrorized from the start.

"Red Chief," says I to the kid, "would you like to go home?"

"Aw, what for?" says he. "I don't have any fun at home. I hate to go to school. I like to camp out. You won't take me back home again, Snake-eye, will you?"

"Not right away," says I. "We'll stay here in the cave awhile."

"All right!" says he. "That'll be fine. I never had such fun in all my life."

We went to bed about eleven o'clock. We spread down some wide blankets and quilts and put Red Chief between us. We weren't afraid he'd run away. He kept us awake for three hours, jumping up and reaching for his rifle and screeching: "Hist! pard," in mine and Bill's ears, as the fancied crackle of a twig or the rustle of a leaf revealed to his young imagination the stealthy approach of the outlaw band. At last, I fell into a troubled sleep, and dreamed that I had been kidnapped and chained to a tree by a ferocious pirate with red hair.

Just at daybreak, I was awakened by a series of awful screams from Bill. They weren't yells, or howls, or shouts, or whoops, or yawps, such as you'd expect from a manly set of vocal organs—they were simply indecent, terrifying, humiliating screams, such as women emit when they see ghosts or caterpillars. It's an awful thing to hear a strong, desperate, fat man scream incontinently in a cave at daybreak.

I jumped up to see what the matter was. Red Chief was sitting on Bill's chest, with one hand twined in Bill's hair. In the other he had the sharp case-knife we used for slicing bacon; and he was industriously and realistically trying to take Bill's scalp, according to the sentence that had been pronounced upon him the evening before.

I got the knife away from the kid and made him lie down again. But, from that moment, Bill's spirit was broken. He laid down on his side of the bed, but he never closed an eye again in sleep as long as that boy was with us. I dozed off for a while, but along toward sun-up I remembered that Red Chief had said I was to be burned at the stake at the rising of the sun. I wasn't nervous or afraid; but I sat up and lit my pipe and leaned against a rock.

"What you getting up so soon for, Sam?" asked Bill.

"Me?" says I. "Oh, I got a kind of pain in my shoulder. I thought sitting up would rest it."

"You're a liar!" says Bill. "You're afraid. You was to be burned at sunrise, and you was afraid he'd do it. And he would, too, if he could find a match. Ain't it awful, Sam? Do you think anybody will pay out money to get a little imp like that back home?"

"Sure," said I. "A rowdy kid like that is just the kind that parents dote on. Now, you and the Chief get up and cook breakfast, while I go up on the top of this mountain and reconnoitre."

I went up on the peak of the little mountain and ran my eye over the contiguous vicinity. Over towards Summit I expected to see the sturdy yeomanry of the village armed with scythes and pitchforks beating the countryside for the dastardly kidnappers. But what I saw was a peaceful landscape dotted with one man ploughing with a dun mule. Nobody was dragging the creek; no couriers dashed hither and yon, bringing tidings of no news to the distracted parents. There was a sylvan attitude of somnolent sleepiness pervading that section of the external outward surface of Alabama that lay exposed to my view. "Perhaps," says I to myself, "it has not yet been discovered that the wolves have borne away the tender lambkin from the fold. Heaven help the wolves!" says I, and I went down the mountain to breakfast.

When I got to the cave I found Bill backed up against the side of it, breathing hard, and the boy threatening to smash him with a rock half as big as a cocoanut.

"He put a red-hot boiled potato down my back," explained Bill, "and then mashed it with his foot; and I boxed his ears. Have you got a gun about you, Sam?"

I took the rock away from the boy and kind of patched up the argument. "I'll fix you," says the kid to Bill. "No man ever yet struck the Red Chief but he got paid for it. You better beware!"

After breakfast the kid takes a piece of leather with strings wrapped around it out of his pocket and goes outside the cave unwinding it.

"What's he up to now?" says Bill, anxiously. "You don't think he'll run away, do you, Sam?"

"No fear of it," says I. "He don't seem to be much of a home body. But we've got to fix up some plan about the ransom. There don't seem to be much excitement around Summit on account of his disappearance; but maybe they haven't realized yet that he's gone. His folks may think he's spending the night with Aunt Jane or one of the neighbors. Anyhow, he'll be missed to-day. To-night we must get a message to his father demanding the two thousand dollars for his return."

Just then we heard a kind of war-whoop, such as David might have emitted when he knocked out the champion Goliath. It was a sling that Red Chief had pulled out of his pocket, and he was whirling it around his head.

I dodged, and heard a heavy thud and a kind of a sigh from Bill, like a horse gives out when you take his saddle off. A niggerhead rock the size of an egg had caught Bill just behind his left ear. He loosened himself all over and fell in the fire across the frying pan of hot water for washing the dishes. I dragged him out and poured cold water on his head for half an hour.

By and by, Bill sits up and feels behind his ear and says: "Sam, do you know who my favorite Biblical character is?"

"Take it easy," says I. "You'll come to your senses presently."

"King Herod," says he. "You won't go away and leave me here alone, will you, Sam?"

I went out and caught that boy and shook him until his freckles rattled.

"If you don't behave," says I, "I'll take you straight home. Now, are you going to be good, or not?"

"I was only funning," says he, sullenly. "I didn't mean to hurt Old Hank. But what did he hit me for? I'll behave, Snake-eye, if you won't send me home, and if you'll let me play the Black Scout to-day."

"I don't know the game," says I. "That's for you and Mr. Bill to decide. He's your playmate for the day. I'm going away for a while, on business. Now, you come in and make friends with him and say you are sorry for hurting him, or home you go, at once."

I made him and Bill shake hands, and then I took Bill aside and told him I was going to Poplar Grove, a little village three miles from the cave, and find out what I could about how the kidnapping had been regarded in Summit. Also, I thought it best to send a peremptory letter to old man Dorset that day, demanding the ransom and dictating how it should be paid.

"You know, Sam," says Bill, "I've stood by you without batting an eye in earthquakes, fire and flood—in poker games, dynamite outrages, police raids, train robberies, and cyclones. I never lost my nerve yet till we kidnapped that two-legged skyrocket of a kid. He's got me going. You won't leave me long with him, will you, Sam?"

"I'll be back some time this afternoon," says I. "You must keep the boy amused and quiet till I return. And now we'll write the letter to old Dorset."

Bill and I got paper and pencil and worked on the letter while Red Chief, with a blanket wrapped around him, strutted up and down, guarding the mouth of the cave. Bill begged me tearfully to make the ransom fifteen hundred dollars instead of two thousand. "I ain't attempting," says he, "to decry the celebrated moral aspect of parental affection, but we're dealing with humans, and it ain't human for anybody to give up two thousand dollars for that forty-pound chunk of freckled wildcat. I'm willing to take a chance at fifteen hundred dollars. You can charge the difference up to me."

So, to relieve Bill, I acceded, and we collaborated a letter that ran this way:

Ebenezer Dorset, Esq.:

We have your boy concealed in a place far from Summit. It is useless for you or the most skilful detectives to attempt to find him. Absolutely, the only terms on which you can have him restored to you are these: We demand fifteen hundred dollars in large bills for his return; the money to be left at midnight to-night at the same spot and in the same box as your reply —as hereinafter described. If you agree to these terms, send your answer in writing by a solitary messenger to-night at half-past eight o'clock. After crossing Owl Creek on the road to Poplar Grove, there are three large trees about a hundred yards apart, close to the fence of the wheat field on the right-hand side. At the bottom of the fence-post, opposite the third tree, will be found a small pasteboard box.

The messenger will place the answer in this box and return immediately to Summit.

If you attempt any treachery or fail to comply with our demand as stated, you will never see your boy again.

If you pay the money as demanded, he will be returned to you safe and well within three hours. These terms are final, and if you do not accede to them no further communication will be attempted.

Two Desperate Men

I addressed this letter to Dorset, and put it in my pocket. As I was about to start, the kid comes up to me and says:

"Aw, Snake-eye, you said I could play the Black Scout while you was gone."

"Play it, of course," says I. "Mr. Bill will play with you. What kind of a game is it?"

"I'm the Black Scout," says Red Chief, "and I have to ride to the stockade to warn the settlers that the Indians are coming. I'm tired of playing Indian myself. I want to be the Black Scout."

"All right," says I. "It sounds harmless to me. I guess Mr. Bill will help you foil the pesky savages."

"What am I to do?" asks Bill, looking at the kid suspiciously.

"You are the hoss," says Black Scout. "Get down on your hands and knees. How can I ride to the stockade without a hoss?"

"You'd better keep him interested," said I, "till we get the scheme going. Loosen up."

Bill gets down on his all fours, and a look comes in his eye like a rabbit's when you catch it in a trap.

"How far is it to the stockade, kid?" he asks, in a husky manner of voice.

"Ninety miles," says the Black Scout. "And you have to hump yourself to get there on time. Whoa, now!"

The Black Scout jumps on Bill's back and digs his heels in his side.

"For Heaven's sake," says Bill, "hurry back, Sam, as soon as you can. I wish we hadn't made the ransom more than a thousand. Say, you quit kicking me or I'll get up and warm you good."

I walked over to Poplar Grove and sat around the post-office and store, talking with the chaw-bacons that came in to trade. One whiskerando says that he hears Summit is all upset on account of Elder Ebenezer Dorset's boy having been lost or stolen. That was all I wanted to know. I bought some smoking tobacco, referred casually to the price of black-eyed peas, posted my letter surreptitiously, and came away. The postmaster said the mail-carrier would come by in an hour to take the mail to Summit.

When I got back to the cave Bill and the boy were not to be found. I explored the vicinity of the cave, and risked a yodel or two, but there was no response.

So I lighted my pipe and sat down on a mossy bank to await developments.

In about half an hour I heard the bushes rustle, and Bill wabbled out into the little glade in front of the cave. Behind him was the kid, stepping softly like a scout, with a broad grin on his face. Bill stopped, took off his hat, and wiped his face with a red handkerchief. The kid stopped about eight feet behind him.

"Sam," says Bill, "I suppose you'll think I'm a renegade, but I couldn't help it. I'm a grown person with masculine proclivities and habits of self-defense, but there is a time when all systems of egotism and predominance fail. The boy is gone. I sent him home. All is off. There was martyrs in old times," goes on Bill, "that suffered death rather than give up the particular graft they enjoyed. None of 'em ever was subjugated to such supernatural tortures as I have been. I tried to be faithful to our articles of depredation; but there came a limit."

"What's the trouble, Bill?" I asks him.

"I was rode," says Bill, "the ninety miles to the stockade, not barring an inch. Then, when the settlers was rescued, I was given oats. Sand ain't a palatable substitute. And then, for an hour I had to try to explain to him why there was nothin' in holes, how a road can run both ways, and what makes the grass green. I tell you, Sam, a human can only stand so much. I takes him by the neck of his clothes and drags him down the mountain. On the way he kicks my legs black and blue from the knees down; and I've got to have two or three bites on my thumb and hand cauterized.

"But he's gone"—continues Bill—"gone home. I showed him the road to Summit and kicked him about eight feet nearer there at one kick. I'm sorry we lose the ransom; but it was either that or Bill Driscoll to the madhouse."

Bill is puffing and blowing, but there is a look of ineffable peace and growing content on his rose-pink features.

"Bill," says I, "there isn't any heart disease in your family, is there?"

"No," says Bill, "nothing chronic except malaria and accidents. Why?"

"Then you might turn around," says I, "and have a look behind you."

Bill turns and sees the boy, and loses his complexion and sits down plump on the ground and begins to pluck aimlessly at grass and little sticks. For an hour I was afraid of his mind. And then I told him that my scheme was to put the whole job through immediately and that we would get the ransom and be off with it by midnight if old Dorset fell in with our proposition. So Bill braced up enough to give the kid a weak sort of a smile and a promise to play the Russian in a Japanese war with him as soon as he felt a little better.

I had a scheme for collecting that ransom without danger of being caught by counterplots that ought to commend itself to professional kidnappers. The tree under which the answer was to be left—and the money later on—was close to the road fence with big, bare fields on all sides. If a gang of constables should be watching for any one to come for the note, they could see him a long way off crossing the fields or in the road. But no, sirree! At half-past eight I was up in that tree as well hidden as a tree toad, waiting for the messenger to arrive.

Exactly on time, a half-grown boy rides up the road on a bicycle, locates the pasteboard box at the foot of the fence-post, slips a folded piece of paper into it, and pedals away again back toward Summit.

I waited an hour and then concluded the thing was square. I slid down the tree, got the note, slipped along the fence till I struck the woods, and was back at the cave in another half an hour. I opened the note, got near the lantern, and read it to Bill. It was written with a pen in a crabbed hand, and the sum and substance of it was this:

Two Desperate Men.

Gentlemen: I received your letter to-day by post, in regard to the ransom you ask for the return of my son. I think you are a little high in your demands, and I hereby make you a counter-proposition, which I am inclined to believe you will accept. You bring Johnny home and pay me two hundred and fifty dollars in cash, and I agree to take him off your hands. You had better come at night, for the neighbors believe he is lost, and I couldn't be responsible for what they would do to anybody they saw bringing him back. Very respectfully,

Ebenezer Dorset

"Great pirates of Penzance," says I; "of all the impudent——"

But I glanced at Bill, and hesitated. He had the most appealing look in his eyes I ever saw on the face of a dumb or a talking brute.

"Sam," says he, "what's two hundred and fifty dollars, after all? We've got the money. One more night of this kid will send me to a bed in Bedlam. Besides being a thorough gentleman, I think Mr. Dorset is a spendthrift for making us such a liberal offer. You ain't going to let the chance go, are you?"

"Tell you the truth, Bill," says I, "this little he ewe lamb has somewhat got on my nerves too. We'll take him home, pay the ransom, and make our getaway."

We took him home that night. We got him to go to telling him that his father had bought a silver-mounted rifle and a pair of moccasins for him, and we were to hunt bears the next day.

It was just twelve o'clock when we knocked at Ebenezer's front door.

Just at the moment when I should have been abstracting the fifteen hundred dollars from the box under the tree, according to the original proposition, Bill was counting out two hundred and fifty dollars into Dorset's hand.

When the kid found out we were going to leave him at home he started up a howl like a calliope and fastened himself as tight as a leech to Bill's leg. His father peeled him away gradually, like a porous plaster.

"How long can you hold him?" asks Bill.

"I'm not as strong as I used to be," says old Dorset, "but I think I can promise you ten minutes."

"Enough," says Bill. "In ten minutes I shall cross the Central, Southern, and Middle Western States, and be legging it trippingly for the Canadian border."

And, as dark as it was, and as fat as Bill was, and as good a runner as I am, he was a good mile and a half out of Summit before I could catch up with him.

THE MARRY MONTH OF MAY

Prithee, smite the poet in the eye when he would sing to you praises of the month of May. It is a month presided over by the spirits of mischief and madness. Pixies and flibbertigibbets haunt the budding woods; Puck and his train of midgets are busy in town and country.

In May Nature holds up at us a chiding finger, bidding us remember that we are not gods, but overconceited members of her own great family. She reminds us that we are brothers to the chowder-doomed clam and the donkey; lineal scions of the pansy and the chimpanzee, and but cousins-german to the cooing doves, the quacking ducks, and the housemaids and policemen in the parks.

In May Cupid shoots blindfolded—millionaires marry stenographers; wise professors woo white-aproned gum-chewers behind quick-lunch counters; schoolma'ams make big bad boys remain after school; lads with ladders steal lightly over lawns where Juliet waits in her trellised window with her telescope packed; young couples out for a walk come home married; old chaps put on white spats and promenade near the Normal School; even married men, grown unwontedly tender and sentimental, whack their spouses on the back and growl: "How goes it, old girl?"

This May, who is no goddess, but Circe, masquerading at the dance given in honor of the fair débutante, Summer, puts the kibosh on us all.

Old Mr. Coulson groaned a little, and then sat up straight in his invalid's chair. He had the gout very bad in one foot, a house near Gramercy Park, half a million dollars, and a daughter. And he had a housekeeper. Mrs.

Widdup. The fact and the name deserve a sentence each. They have it.
When May poked Mr. Coulson he became elder brother to the turtle-
dove. In the window near which he sat were boxes of jonquils, of hyacinths, geraniums, and pansies. The breeze brought their odor into the
room. Immediately there was a well-contested round between the breath
of the flowers and the able and active effluvium from gout liniment. The
liniment won easily; but not before the flowers got an uppercut to old
Mr. Coulson's nose. The deadly work of the implacable, false enchantress
May was done.

Across the park to the olfactories of Mr. Coulson came other unmistakable, characteristic, copyrighted smells of spring that belong to the-big-
city-above-the-Subway, alone. The smells of hot asphalt, underground
caverns, gasoline, patchouli, orange peel, sewer gas, Albany grabs, Egyptian cigarettes, mortar and the undried ink on newspapers. The inblowing
air was sweet and mild. Sparrows wrangled happily everywhere outdoors.
Never trust May.

Mr. Coulson twisted the ends of his white mustache, cursed his foot, and
pounded a bell on the table by his side.

In came Mrs. Widdup. She was comely to the eye, fair, flustered, forty,
and foxy.

"Higgins is out, sir," she said, with a smile suggestive of vibratory
massage. "He went to post a letter. Can I do anything for you, sir?"

"It's time for my aconite," said old Mr. Coulson. "Drop it for me. The
bottle's there. Three drops. In water. D— that is, confound Higgins!
There's nobody in this house cares if I die here in this chair for want of
attention."

Mrs. Widdup sighed deeply.

"Don't be saying that, sir," she said. "There's them that would care more
than any one knows. Thirteen drops you said, sir?"

"Three," said old man Coulson.

He took his dose and then Mrs. Widdup's hand. She blushed. Oh, yes,
it can be done. Just hold your breath and compress the diaphragm.

"Mrs. Widdup," said Mr. Coulson, "the springtime's full upon us."

"Ain't that right?" said Mrs. Widdup. "The air's real warm. And
there's bock-beer signs on every corner. And the park's all yaller and pink
and blue with flowers; and I have such shooting pains up my legs and
body."

" 'In the spring,' " quoted Mr. Coulson, curling his mustache, " 'a y—
that is, a man's—fancy lightly turns to thoughts of love.' "

"Lawsy, now!" exclaimed Mrs. Widdup; "ain't that right? Seems like
it's in the air."

" 'In the spring,' " continued old Mr. Coulson, " 'a livelier iris shines
upon the burnished dove.' "

"They do be lively, the Irish," sighed Mrs. Widdup, pensively.

"Mrs. Widdup," said Mr. Coulson, making a face at a twinge of his gouty foot, "this would be a lonesome house without you. I'm an—that is, I'm an elderly man—but I'm worth a comfortable lot of money. If half a million dollars' worth of Government bonds and the true affection of a heart that, though no longer beating with the first ardor of youth, can still throb with genuine——"

The loud noise of an overturned chair near the portières of the adjoining room interrupted the venerable and scarcely suspecting victim of May.

In stalked Miss Van Meeker Constantia Coulson, bony, durable, tall, high-nosed, frigid, well-bred, thirty-five, in-the-neighborhood-of-Gramercy-Parkish. She put up a lorgnette. Mrs. Widdup hastily stooped and arranged the bandages on Mr. Coulson's gouty foot.

"I thought Higgins was with you," said Miss Van Meeker Constantia.

"Higgins went out," explained her father, "and Mrs. Widdup answered the bell. That is better now, Mrs. Widdup, thank you. No; there is nothing else I require."

The housekeeper retired, pink under the cool, inquiring stare of Miss Coulson.

"This spring weather is lovely, isn't it, daughter?" said the old man, consciously conscious.

"That's just it," replied Miss Van Meeker Constantia Coulson, somewhat obscurely. "When does Mrs. Widdup start on her vacation, papa?"

"I believe she said a week from to-day," said Mr. Coulson.

Miss Van Meeker Constantia stood for a minute at the window gazing toward the little park, flooded with the mellow afternoon sunlight. With the eye of a botanist she viewed the flowers—most potent weapons of insidious May. With the cool pulses of a virgin of Cologne she withstood the attack of the ethereal mildness. The arrows of the pleasant sunshine fell back, frostbitten, from the cold panoply of her unthrilled bosom. The odor of the flowers waked no soft sentiments in the unexplored recesses of her dormant heart. The chirp of the sparrows gave her a pain. She mocked at May.

But although Miss Coulson was proof against the season, she was keen enough to estimate its power. She knew that elderly men and thick-waisted women jumped as educated fleas in the ridiculous train of May, the merry mocker of the months. She had heard of foolish old gentlemen marrying their housekeepers before. What a humiliating thing, after all, was this feeling called love!

The next morning at 8 o'clock, when the iceman called, the cook told him that Miss Coulson wanted to see him in the basement.

"Well, ain't I the Olcott and Depew; not mentioning the first name at all?" said the iceman, admiringly, of himself.

As a concession he rolled his sleeves down, dropped his icehooks on a syringa and went back. When Miss Van Meeker Constantia Coulson addressed him he took off his hat.

"There is a rear entrance to this basement," said Miss Coulson, "which can be reached by driving into the vacant lot next door, where they are excavating for a building. I want you to bring in that way within two hours 1,000 pounds of ice. You may have to bring another man or two to help you. I will show you where I want it placed. I also want 1,000 pounds a day delivered the same way for the next four days. Your company may charge the ice on our regular bill. This is for your extra trouble."

Miss Coulson tendered a ten-dollar bill. The iceman bowed, and held his hat in his two hands behind him.

"Not if you'll excuse me, lady. It'll be a pleasure to fix things up for you any way you please."

Alas for May!

About noon Mr. Coulson knocked two glasses off his table, broke the spring of his bell, and yelled for Higgins at the same time.

"Bring an axe," commanded Mr. Coulson, sardonically, "or send out for a quart of prussic acid, or have a policeman come in and shoot me. I'd rather that than be frozen to death."

"It does seem to be getting cold, sir," said Higgins. "I hadn't noticed it before. I'll close the window, sir."

"Do," said Mr. Coulson. "They call this spring, do they? If it keeps up long I'll go back to Palm Beach. House feels like a morgue."

Later Miss Coulson dutifully came in to inquire how the gout was progressing.

" 'Stantia," said the old man, "how is the weather outdoors?"

"Bright," answered Miss Coulson, "but chilly."

"Feels like the dead of winter to me," said Mr. Coulson.

"An instance," said Constantia, gazing abstractedly out of the window, "of 'winter lingering in the lap of spring,' though the metaphor is not in the most refined taste."

A little later she walked down by the side of the little park and on westward to Broadway to accomplish a little shopping.

A little later than that Mrs. Widdup entered the invalid's room.

"Did you ring, sir?" she asked, dimpling in many places. "I asked Higgins to go to the drug store, and I thought I heard your bell."

"I did not," said Mr. Coulson.

"I'm afraid," said Mrs. Widdup, "I interrupted you, sir, yesterday when you were about to say something."

"How comes it, Mrs. Widdup," said old man Coulson, sternly, "that I find it so cold in this house?"

"Cold, sir?" said the housekeeper, "why, now, since you speak of it it do seem cold in this room. But outdoors it's as warm and fine as June, sir.

And how this weather do seem to make one's heart jump out of one's shirt waist, sir. And the ivy all leaved out on the side of the house, and the hand-organs playing, and the children dancing on the sidewalk—'tis a great time for speaking out what's in the heart. You were saying yesterday, sir——"

"Woman!" roared Mr. Coulson; "you are a fool. I pay you to take care of this house. I am freezing to death in my own room, and you come in and drivel to me about ivy and hand-organs. Get me an overcoat at once. See that all doors and windows are closed below. An old, fat, irresponsible, one-sided object like you pratting about springtime and flowers in the middle of winter! When Higgins comes back, tell him to bring me a hot rum punch. And now get out!"

But who shall shame the bright face of May? Rogue though she be and disturber of sane men's peace, no wise virgin's cunning nor cold storage shall make her bow her head in the bright galaxy of months.

Oh, yes, the story was not quite finished.

A night passed, and Higgins helped old man Coulson in the morning to his chair by the window. The cold of the room was gone. Heavenly odors and fragrant mildness entered.

In hurried Mrs. Widdup, and stood by his chair. Mr. Coulson reached his bony hand and grasped her plump one.

"Mrs. Widdup," he said, "this house would be no home without you. I have half a million dollars. If that and the true affection of a heart no longer in its youthful prime, but still not cold could——"

"I found out what made it cold," said Mrs. Widdup, leaning against his chair. " 'Twas ice—tons of it—in the basement and in the furnace room, everywhere. I shut off the registers that it was coming through into your room, Mr. Coulson, poor soul! And now it's May-time again."

"A true heart," went on old man Coulson, a little wanderingly, "that the springtime has brought to life again, and—but what will my daughter say, Mrs. Widdup?"

"Never fear, sir," said Mrs. Widdup, cheerfully, "Miss Coulson, she ran away with the iceman last night, sir!"

A TECHNICAL ERROR

I never cared especially for feuds, believing them to be even more over-rated products of our country than grapefruit, scrapple, or honeymoons. Nevertheless, if I may be allowed, I will tell you of an Indian Territory feud of which I was press-agent, camp-follower, and inaccessory during the fact.

I was on a visit to Sam Durkee's ranch, where I had a great time falling off unmanicured ponies and waving my bare hand at the lower jaws of wolves about two miles away. Sam was a hardened person of about twenty-five, with a reputation for going home in the dark with perfect equanimity, though often with reluctance.

Over in the Creek Nation was a family bearing the name of Tatum. I was told that the Durkees and Tatums had been feuding for years. Several of each family had bitten the grass, and it was expected that more Nebuchadnezzars would follow. A younger generation of each family was growing up, and the grass was keeping pace with them. But I gathered that they had fought fairly; that they had not lain in cornfields and aimed at the division of their enemies' suspenders in the back—partly, perhaps, because there were no cornfields, and nobody wore more than one suspender. Nor had any woman or child of either house ever been harmed. In those days—and you will find it so yet—their women were safe.

Sam Durkee had a girl. (If it were an all-fiction magazine that I expected to sell this story to, I should say, "Mr. Durkee rejoiced in a fiancée.") Her name was Ella Baynes. They appeared to be devoted to each other, and to have perfect confidence in each other, as all couples do who are and have or aren't and haven't. She was tolerably pretty, with a heavy mass of brown hair that helped her along. He introduced me to her, which seemed not to lessen her preference for him; so I reasoned that they were surely soul-mates.

Miss Baynes lived in Kingfisher, twenty miles from the ranch. Sam lived on a gallop between the two places.

One day there came to Kingfisher a courageous young man, rather small, with smooth face and regular features. He made many inquiries about the business of the town, and especially of the inhabitants cognominally. He said he was from Muscogee, and he looked it, with his yellow shoes and crocheted four-in-hand. I met him once when I rode in for the mail. He said his name was Beverly Travers, which seemed rather improbable.

There were active times on the ranch just then, and Sam was too busy to go to town often. As an incompetent and generally worthless guest, it devolved upon me to ride in for little things such as post cards, barrels of flours, baking-powder, smoking-tobacco, and—letters from Ella.

One day, when I was messenger for half a gross of cigarette papers and a couple of wagon tires, I saw the alleged Beverly Travers in a yellow-wheeled buggy with Ella Baynes, driving about town as ostentatiously as the black, waxy mud would permit. I knew that this information would bring no balm of Gilead to Sam's soul, so I refrained from including it in the news of the city that I retailed on my return. But on the next afternoon an elongated ex-cowboy of the name of Simmons, an old-time pal of Sam's, who kept a feed store in Kingfisher, rode out to the ranch and rolled and burned many cigarettes before he would talk. When he did make oration, his words were these:

"Say, Sam, there's been a description of a galoot miscallin' himself Bevel-edged Travels impairing the atmospheric air of Kingfisher for the past two weeks. You know who he was? He was not otherwise than Ben Tatum, from the Creek Nation, son of old Gopher Tatum that your Uncle Newt shot last February. You know what he done this morning? He killed your brother Lester—shot him in the co't-house yard."

I wondered if Sam had heard. He pulled a twig from a mesquite bush, chewed it gravely, and said:

"He did, did he? He killed Lester?"

"The same," said Simmons. "And he did more. He run away with your girl, the same as to say Miss Ella Baynes. I thought you might like to know, so I rode out to impart the information."

"I am much obliged, Jim," said Sam, taking the chewed twig from his mouth. "Yes, I'm glad you rode out. Yes, I'm right glad."

"Well, I'll be ridin' back, I reckon. That boy I left in the feed store don't know hay from oats. He shot Lester in the *back*."

"Shot him in the back?"

"Yes, while he was hitchin' his hoss."

"I'm much obliged, Jim."

"I kind of thought you'd like to know as soon as you could."

"Come in and have some coffee before you ride back, Jim?"

"Why, no, I reckon not; I must get back to the store."

"And you say——"

"Yes, Sam. Everybody seen 'em drive away together in a buckboard, with a big bundle, like clothes, tied up in the back of it. He was drivin' the team he brought over with him from Muscogee. They'll be hard to overtake right away."

"And which——"

"I was goin' on to tell you. They left on the Guthrie road; but there's no tellin' which forks they'll take—you know that."

"All right, Jim; much obliged."

"You're welcome, Sam."

Simmons rolled a cigarette and stabbed his pony with both heels. Twenty yards away he reined up and called back:

"You don't want no—assistance, as you might say?"

"Not any, thanks."

"I didn't think you would. Well, so long!"

Sam took out and opened a bone-handled pocket-knife and scraped a dried piece of mud from his left boot. I thought at first he was going to swear a vendetta on the blade of it, or recite "The Gipsy's Curse." The few feuds I had ever seen or read about usually opened that way. This one seemed to be presented with a new treatment. Thus offered on the stage, it would have been hissed off, and one of Belasco's thrilling melo-dramas demanded instead.

"I wonder," said Sam, with a profoundly thoughtful expression, "if the cook has any cold beans left over!"

He called Wash, the Negro cook, and finding that he had some, ordered him to heat up the pot and make some strong coffee. Then we went into Sam's private room, where he slept, and kept his armory, dogs, and the saddles of his favorite mounts. He took three or four six-shooters out of a bookcase and began to look them over, whistling "The Cowboy's La-ment" abstractedly. Afterward he ordered the two best horses on the ranch saddled and tied to the hitching-post.

Now, in the feud business, in all sections of the country, I have observed that in one particular there is a delicate but strict etiquette belonging. You must not mention the word or refer to the subject in the presence of a feudist. It would be more reprehensible than commenting upon the mole on the chin of your rich aunt. I found, later on, that there is another unwritten rule, but I think that belongs solely to the West.

It yet lacked two hours to supper-time; but in twenty minutes Sam and I were plunging deep into the reheated beans, hot coffee, and cold beef.

"Nothing like a good meal before a long ride," said Sam. "Eat hearty."

I had a sudden suspicion.

"Why did you have two horses saddled?" I asked.

"One, two—one, two," said Sam. "You can count, can't you?"

His mathematics carried with it a momentary qualm and a lesson. The thought had not occurred to him that the thought could possibly occur to me not to ride at his side on that red road to revenge and justice. It was the higher calculus. I was booked for the trail. I began to eat more beans.

In an hour we set forth at a steady gallop eastward. Our horses were Kentucky-bred, strengthened by the mesquite grass of the west. Ben Tatum's steeds may have been swifter, and he had a good lead; but if he had heard the punctual thuds of the hoofs of those trailers of ours, born in the heart of feudland, he might have felt that retribution was creeping up on the hoof-prints of his dapper nags.

I knew that Ben Tatum's card to play was flight—flight until he came within the safer territory of his own henchmen and supporters. He knew that the man pursuing him would follow the trail to any end where it might lead.

During the ride Sam talked of the prospect for rain, of the price of beef, and of the musical glasses. You would have thought he had never had a brother or a sweetheart or an enemy on earth. There are some sub-jects too big even for the words in the "Unabridged." Knowing this phase of the feud code, but not having practised it sufficiently, I overdid the thing by telling some slightly funny anecdotes. Sam laughed at exactly the right place—laughed with his mouth. When I caught sight of his mouth, I wished I had been blessed with enough sense of humor to have suppressed those anecdotes.

Our first sight of them we had in Guthrie. Tired and hungry, we stumbled, unwashed, into a little yellow-pine hotel and sat at a table. In the opposite corner we saw the fugitives. They were bent upon their meal, but looked around at times uneasily.

The girl was dressed in brown—one of these smooth, half-shiny, silky-looking affairs with lace collar and cuffs, and what I believe they call an accordion-pleated skirt. She wore a thick brown veil down to her nose, and a broad-brimmed straw hat with some kind of feathers adorning it. The man wore plain, dark clothes, and his hair was trimmed very short. He was such a man as you might see anywhere.

There they were—the murderer and the woman he had stolen. There we were—the rightful avenger, according to the code, and the supernumerary who writes these words.

For one time, at least, in the heart of the supernumerary there rose the killing instinct. For one moment he joined the force of combatants—orally.

"What are you waiting for, Sam?" I said in a whisper. "Let him have it now!"

Sam gave a melancholy sigh.

"You don't understand; but _he_ does," he said. _"He_ knows. Mr. Tenderfoot, there's a rule out here among white men in the Nation that you can't shoot a man when he's with a woman. I never knew it to be broke yet. You _can't_ do it. You've got to get him in a gang or by himself. That's why. He knows it, too. We all know. So, that's Mr. Ben Tatum! One of the 'pretty men'! I'll cut him out of the herd before they leave the hotel, and regulate his account!"

After supper the flying pair disappeared quickly. Although Sam haunted lobby and stairway and halls half the night, in some mysterious way the fugitives eluded him; and in the morning the veiled lady in the brown dress with the accordion-pleated skirt and the dapper young man with the close-clipped hair, and the buckboard with the prancing nags, were gone.

It is a monotonous story, that of the ride; so it shall be curtailed. Once again we overtook them on a road. We were about fifty yards behind. They turned in the buckboard and looked at us; then drove on without whipping up their horses. Their safety no longer lay in speed. Ben Tatum knew. He knew that the only rock of safety left to him was the code. There is no doubt that, had he been alone, the matter would have been settled quickly with Sam Durkee in the usual way; but he had something at his side that kept still the trigger-finger of both. It seemed likely that he was no coward.

So, you may perceive that woman, on occasions, may postpone instead of precipitating conflict between man and man. But not willingly or consciously. She is oblivious of codes.

Five miles farther, we came upon the future great Western city of Chandler. The horses of pursuers and pursued were starved and weary. There was one hotel that offered danger to man and entertainment to beast; so the four of us met again in the dining room at the ringing of a bell so resonant and large that it had cracked the welkin long ago. The dining room was not as large as the one at Guthrie.

Just as we were eating apple pie—how Ben Davises and tragedy impinge upon each other!—I noticed Sam looking with keen intentness at our quarry where they were seated at a table across the room. The girl still wore the brown dress with lace collar and cuffs, and the veil drawn down to her nose. The man bent over his plate, with his close-cropped head held low.

"There's a code," I heard Sam say, either to me or to himself, "that won't let you shoot a man in the company of a woman; but, by thunder, there ain't one to keep you from killing a woman in the company of a man!"

And, quicker than my mind could follow his argument, he whipped a Colt's automatic from under his left arm and pumped six bullets into the body that the brown dress covered—the brown dress with the lace collar and cuffs and the accordion-pleated skirt.

The young person in the dark sack suit, from whose head and from whose life a woman's glory had been clipped, laid her head on her arms stretched upon the table; while people came running to raise Ben Tatum from the floor in his feminine masquerade that had given Sam the opportunity to set aside, technically, the obligations of the code.

SUITE HOMES AND THEIR ROMANCE

Few young couples in the Big-City-of-Bluff began their married existence with greater promise of happiness than did Mr. and Mrs. Claude Turpin. They felt no especial animosity toward each other; they were comfortably established in a handsome apartment house that had a name and accommodations like those of a sleeping-car; they were living as expensively as the couple on the next floor above who had twice their income; and their marriage had occurred on a wager, a ferry-boat, and first acquaintance, thus securing a sensational newspaper notice of their names attached to pictures of the Queen of Roumania and M. Santos-Dumont.

Turpin's income was $200 per month. On pay day, after calculating the amounts due for rent, instalments on furniture and piano, gas, and bills owed to the florist, confectioner, milliner, tailor, wine merchant, and cab company, the Turpins would find that they still had $200 left to spend. How to do this is one of the secrets of metropolitan life.

The domestic life of the Turpins was a beautiful picture to see. But you couldn't gaze upon it as you could at an oleograph of "Don't Wake Grandma," or "Brooklyn by Moonlight."

You had to blink when you looked at it and you heard a fizzing sound just like the machine with a "scope" at the end of it. Yes; there wasn't much repose about the picture of the Turpins' domestic life. It was something like "Spearing Salmon in the Columbia River," or "Japanese Artillery in Action."

Every day was just like another; as the days are in New York. In the morning Turpin would take bromo-seltzer, his pocket change from under the clock, his hat, no breakfast, and his departure for the office. At noon Mrs. Turpin would get out of bed and humor, put on a kimono, airs, and the water to boil for coffee.

Turpin lunched downtown. He came home at 6 to dress for dinner. They always dined out. They strayed from the chop-house to chop-sueydom, from terrace to table d'hôte, from rathskeller to roadhouse, from café to casino, from Maria's to the Martha Washington. Such is domestic life in the great city. Your vine is the mistletoe; your fig tree bears dates. Your household gods are Mercury and John Howard Payne. For the wedding march you now hear only "Come with the Gypsy Bride." You rarely dine at the same place twice in succession. You tire of the food; and, besides, you want to give them time for the question of that souvenir silver sugar bowl to blow over.

The Turpins were therefore happy. They made many warm and delightful friends, some of whom they remembered the next day. Their home life was an ideal one, according to the rules and regulations of the Book of Bluff.

There came a time when it dawned upon Turpin that his wife was getting away with too much money. If you belong to the near-swell class in the Big City, and your income is $200 per month, and you find at the end of the month, after looking over the bills for current expenses, that you, yourself, have spent $150, you very naturally wonder what has become of the other $50. So you suspect your wife. And perhaps you give her a hint that something needs explanation.

"I say, Vivien," said Turpin, one afternoon when they were enjoying in rapt silence the peace and quiet of their cozy apartment, "you've been creating a hiatus big enough for a dog to crawl through in this month's honorarium. You haven't been paying your dressmaker anything on account, have you?"

There was a moment's silence. No sounds could be heard except the breathing of the fox terrier, and the subdued, monotonous sizzling of Vivien's fulvous locks against the insensate curling irons. Claude Turpin, sitting upon a pillow that he had thoughtfully placed upon the convolutions of the apartment sofa, narrowly watched the riante, lovely face of his wife.

"Claudie, dear," said she, touching her finger to her ruby tongue and testing the unresponsive curling irons, "you do me an injustice. Mme. Toinette has not seen a cent of mine since the day you paid your tailor ten dollars on account."

Turpin's suspicions were allayed for the time. But one day soon there came an anonymous letter to him that read:

Watch your wife. She is blowing in your money secretly. I was a sufferer just as you are. The place is No. 345 Blank Street. A word to the wise, etc.

A Man Who Knows

Turpin took this letter to the captain of police of the precinct that he lived in.

"My precinct is as clean as a hound's tooth," said the captain. "The lid's shut down as close there as it is over the eye of a Williamsburg girl when she's kissed at a party. But if you think there's anything queer at the address, I'll go there with ye."

On the next afternoon at 3, Turpin and the captain crept softly up the stairs of No. 345 Blank Street. A dozen plain-clothes men, dressed in full police uniforms, so as to allay suspicion, waited in the hall below.

At the top of the stairs was a door, which was found to be locked. The captain took a key from his pocket and unlocked it. The two men entered.

They found themselves in a large room, occupied by twenty or twenty-five elegantly clothed ladies. Racing charts hung against the walls, a ticker clicked in one corner; with a telephone receiver to his ear a man was calling out the various positions of the horses in a very exciting race. The occupants of the room looked up at the intruders; but, as if reassured by the sight of the captain's uniform, they reverted their attention to the man at the telephone.

"You see," said the captain to Turpin, "the value of an anonymous letter! No high-minded and self-respecting gentleman should consider one worthy of notice. Is your wife among this assembly, Mr. Turpin?"

"She is not," said Turpin.

"And if she was," continued the captain, "would she be within the reach of the tongue of slander? These ladies constitute a Browning Society. They meet to discuss the meaning of the great poet. The telephone is connected with Boston, whence the parent society transmits frequently its interpretations of the poems. Be ashamed of yer suspicions, Mr. Turpin."

"Go soak your shield," said Turpin. "Vivien knows how to take care of herself in a pool-room. She's not dropping anything on the ponies. There must be something queer going on here."

"Nothing but Browning," said the captain. "Hear that?"

"Thanatopsis by a nose," drawled the man at the telephone.

"That's not Browning; that's Longfellow," said Turpin, who sometimes read books.

"Back to the pasture!" exclaimed the captain. "Longfellow made the pacing-to-wagon record of 7.53 'way back in 1868."

"I believe there's something queer about this joint," repeated Turpin.

"I don't see it," said the captain.

"I know it looks like a pool-room, all right," persisted Turpin, "but that's all a blind. Vivien has been dropping a lot of coin somewhere. I believe there's some underhanded work going on here."

A number of racing sheets were tacked close together, covering a large space on one of the walls. Turpin, suspicious, tore several of them down. A door, previously hidden, was revealed. Turpin placed an ear to the crack and listened intently. He heard the soft hum of many voices, low and guarded laughter, and a sharp, metallic clicking and scraping as if from a multitude of tiny but busy objects.

"My God! It is as I feared!" whispered Turpin to himself. "Summon your men at once!" he called to the captain. "She is in there, I know."

At the blowing of the captain's whistle the uniformed plain-clothes men rushed up the stairs into the pool-room. When they saw the betting paraphernalia distributed around they halted, surprised and puzzled to know why they had been summoned.

But the captain pointed to the locked door and bade them break it down. In a few moments they demolished it with the axes they carried. Into the other room sprang Claude Turpin, with the captain at his heels.

The scene was one that lingered long in Turpin's mind. Nearly a score of women—women expensively and fashionably clothed, many beautiful and of refined appearance—had been seated at little marble-topped tables. When the police burst open the door they shrieked and ran here and there like gayly plumed birds that had been disturbed in a tropical grove. Some became hysterical; one or two fainted; several knelt at the feet of the officers and besought them for mercy on account of their families and social position.

A man who had been seated behind a desk had seized a roll of currency as large as the ankle of a Paradise Roof Gardens chorus girl and jumped out of the window. Half a dozen attendants huddled at one end of the room, breathless from fear.

Upon the tables remained the damning and incontrovertible evidences of the guilt of the habituées of that sinister room—dish after dish heaped high with ice cream, and surrounded by stacks of empty ones, scraped to the last spoonful.

"Ladies," said the captain to his weeping circle of prisoners, "I'll not hold any of yez. Some of yez I recognize as having fine houses and good standing in the community, with hard-working husbands and childer at home. But I'll read ye a bit of a lecture before ye go. In the next room there's a 20-to-1 shot just dropped in under the wire three lengths ahead of the field. Is this the way ye waste your husbands' money instead of helping earn it? Home wid yez! The lid's on the ice-cream freezer in this precinct."

Claude Turpin's wife was among the patrons of the raided room. He led her to their apartment in stern silence. There she wept so remorsefully and besought his forgiveness so pleadingly that he forgot his just anger, and soon he gathered his penitent golden-haired Vivien in his arms and forgave her.

"Darling," she murmured, half sobbingly, as the moonlight drifted through the open window, glorifying her sweet, upturned face, "I know I done wrong. I will never touch ice cream again. I forgot you were not a millionaire. I used to go there every day. But to-day I felt some strange, sad presentiment of evil, and I was not myself. I ate only eleven saucers."

"Say no more," said Claude, gently, as he fondly caressed her waving curls.

"And you are sure that you fully forgive me?" asked Vivien, gazing at him entreatingly with dewy eyes of heavenly blue.

"Almost sure, little one," answered Claude, stooping and lightly touching her snowy forehead with his lips. "I'll let you know later on. I've got a month's salary down on Vanilla to win the three-year-old steeplechase to-morrow; and if the ice-cream hunch is to the good you are It again —see?"

THE WHIRLIGIG OF LIFE

Justice-of-the-peace Benaja Widdup sat in the door of his office smoking his elder-stem pipe. Halfway to the Zenith the Cumberland range rose blue-gray in the afternoon haze. A speckled hen swaggered down the main street of the "settlement," cackling foolishly.

Up the road came a sound of creaking axles, and then a slow cloud of dust, and then a bull-cart bearing Ransie Bilbro and his wife. The cart stopped at the Justice's door, and the two climbed down. Ransie was a narrow six feet of sallow brown skin and yellow hair. The imperturbability of the mountains hung upon him like a suit of armor. The woman was calicoed, angled, snuff-brushed, and weary with unknown desires. Through it all gleamed a faint protest of cheated youth unconscious of its loss.

The Justice of the Peace slipped his feet into his shoes, for the sake of dignity, and moved to let them enter.

"We-all," said the woman, in a voice like the wind blowing through pine boughs, "wants a divo'ce." She looked at Ransie to see if he noted any flaw or ambiguity or evasion or partiality or self-partisanship in her statement of their business.

"A divo'ce," repeated Ransie, with a solemn nod. "We-all can't git along together nohow. It's lonesome enough fur to live in the mount'ins when a man and a woman keers fur one another. But when she's a-spittin' like a wildcat or a-sullenin' like a hoot-owl in the cabin, a man ain't got no call to live with her."

"When he's a no-'count varmint," said the woman, without any especial warmth, "a-traipsin' along of scalawags and moonshiners and a-layin' on his back pizen 'ith co'n whiskey, and a-pesterin' folks with a pack o' hungry, triflin' houn's to feed!"

"When she keeps a-throwin skillet lids," came Ransie's antiphony, "and slings b'ilin' water on the best coon-dog in the Cumberlands, and sets herself again' cookin' a man's victuals, and keeps him awake o' nights accusin' him of a sight of doin's!"

"When he's al'ays a-fightin' the revenues, and gits a hard name in the mount'ins fur a mean man, who's gwine to be able fur to sleep o' nights?"

The Justice of the Peace stirred deliberately to his duties. He placed his one chair and a wooden stool for his petitioners. He opened his book of statutes on the table and scanned the index. Presently he wiped his spectacles and shifted his inkstand.

"The law and the statutes," said he, "air silent on the subjeck of divo'ce as fur as the jurisdiction of this co't air concerned. But, accordin' to equity and the Constitution and the golden rule, it's a bad barg'in that can't run both ways. If a justice of the peace can marry a couple, it's plain that he is bound to be able to divo'ce 'em. This here office will issue a decree of divo'ce and abide by the decision of the Supreme Co't to hold it good."

Ransie Bilbro drew a small tobacco-bag from his trousers pocket. Out of this he shook upon the table a five-dollar note. "Sold a b'arskin and two foxes fur that," he remarked. "It's all the money we got."

"The regular price of a divo'ce in this co't," said the Justice, "air five dollars." He stuffed the bill into the pocket of his homespun vest with a deceptive air of indifference. With much bodily toil and mental travail he wrote the decree upon half a sheet of foolscap, and then copied it upon the other. Ransie Bilbro and his wife listened to his reading of the document that was to give them freedom:

Know all men by these presents that Ransie Bilbro and his wife, Ariela Bilbro, this day personally appeared before me and promises that herein-after they will neither love, honor, nor obey each other, neither for better nor worse, being of sound mind and body, and accept summons for divorce according to the peace and dignity of the State. Herein fail not, so help you God. Benaja Widdup, justice of the peace in and for the county of Piedmont, State of Tennessee.

The Justice was about to hand one of the documents to Ransie. The voice of Ariela delayed the transfer. Both men looked at her. Their dull masculinity was confronted by something sudden and unexpected in the woman.

"Judge, don't you give him that air paper yit. 'Tain't all settled, nohow. I got to have my rights first. I got to have my ali-money. 'Tain't no kind of a way to do fur a man to divo'ce his wife 'thout her havin' a cent fur to do with. I'm a-layin' off to be a-goin' up to brother Ed's up on Hogback Mount'in. I'm bound fur to hev a pa'r of shoes and some snuff and things besides. Ef Rance kin affo'd a divo'ce, let him pay me ali-money."

Ransie Bilbro was stricken to dumb perplexity. There had been no previous hint of alimony. Women were always bringing up startling and unlooked-for issues.

Justice Benaja Widdup felt that the point demanded judicial decision. The authorities were also silent on the subject of alimony. But the woman's feet were bare. The trail to Hogback Mountain was steep and flinty.

"Ariela Bilbro," he asked, in official tones, "how much did you 'low would be good and sufficient ali-money in the case befo' the co't?"

"I 'lowed," she answered, "fur the shoes and all, to say five dollars. That ain't much fur ali-money, but I reckon that'll git me up to brother Ed's."

"The amount," said the Justice, "air not onreasonable. Ransie Bilbro, you air ordered by the co't to pay the plaintiff the sum of five dollars befo' the decree of divo'ce air issued."

"I hain't no mo' money," breathed Ransie, heavily. "I done paid you all I had."

"Otherwise," said the Justice, looking severely over his spectacles, "you air in contempt of co't."

"I reckon if you gimme till to-morrow," pleaded the husband, "I mout be able to rake or scrape it up somewhars. I never looked for to be a-payin' no ali-money."

"The case air adjourned," said Benaja Widdup, "till to-morrow, when you-all will present yo'selves and obey the order of the co't. Followin' of which the decrees of divo'ce will be delivered." He sat down in the door and began to loosen a shoestring.

"We mout as well go down to Uncle Ziah's," decided Ransie, "and spend the night." He climbed into the cart on one side, and Ariela climbed in on the other. Obeying the flat of his rope, the little red bull slowly came around on a tack, and the cart crawled away in the nimbus arising from its wheels.

Justice-of-the-peace Benaja Widdup smoked his elder-stem pipe. Late in the afternoon he got his weekly paper, and read it until the twilight dimmed its lines. Then he lit the tallow candle on his table, and read until the moon rose, marking the time for supper. He lived in the double log cabin on the slope near the girdled poplar. Going home to supper he crossed a little branch darkened by a laurel thicket. The dark figure of a man stepped from the laurels and pointed a rifle at his breast. His hat was pulled down low, and something covered most of his face.

"I want yo' money," said the figure, " 'thout any talk. I'm gettin' nervous, and my finger's a-wabblin on this here trigger."

"I've only got f-f-five dollars," said the Justice, producing it from his vest pocket.

"Roll it up," came the order, "and stick it in the end of this here gun-bar'l."

The bill was crisp and new. Even fingers that were clumsy and trembling found little difficulty in making a spill of it and inserting it (this with less ease) into the muzzle of the rifle.

"Now I reckon you kin be goin' along," said the robber.

The Justice lingered not on his way.

The next day came the little red bull, drawing the cart to the office door. Justice Benaja Widdup had his shoes on, for he was expecting the visit. In his presence Ransie Bilbro handed to his wife a five-dollar bill. The official's eye sharply viewed it. It seemed to curl up as though it had been rolled and inserted into the end of a gun-barrel. But the Justice refrained from comment. It is true that other bills might be inclined to curl. He handed each one a decree of divorce. Each stood awkwardly silent, slowly folding the guarantee of freedom. The woman cast a shy glance full of constraint at Ransie.

"I reckon you'll be goin' back up to the cabin," she said, "along 'ith the bull-cart. There's bread in the tin box settin' on the shelf. I put the bacon in the bilin'-pot to keep the hounds from gettin' it. Don't forget to wind the clock to-night."

"You air a-goin' to your brother Ed's?" asked Ransie, with fine unconcern.

"I was 'lowin' to get along up thar afore night. I ain't sayin' as they'll pester theyselves any to make me welcome, but I hain't nowhar else fur to go. It's a right smart ways, and I reckon I better be goin'. I'll be a-sayin' good-bye, Ranse—that is, if you keer fur to say so."

"I don't know as anybody's a hound dog," said Ransie, in a martyr's voice, "fur to not want to say good-bye—'less you air so anxious to git away that you don't want me to say it."

Ariela was silent. She folded the five-dollar bill and her decree carefully, and placed them in the bosom of her dress. Benaja Widdup watched the money disappear with mournful eyes behind his spectacles.

And then with his next words he achieved rank (as his thoughts ran) with either the great crowd of the world's sympathizers or the little crowd of its great financiers.

"Be kind o' lonesome in the old cabin to-night, Ransie," she said.

Ransie Bilbro stared out at the Cumberlands, clear blue now in the sunlight. He did not look at Ariela.

"I 'low it might be lonesome," he said; "but when folks gits mad and wants a divo'ce, you can't make folks stay."

"There's others wanted a divo'ce," said Ariela, speaking to the wooden stool. "Besides, nobody don't want nobody to stay."

"Nobody never said they didn't."

"Nobody never said they did. I reckon I better start on now to brother Ed's."

"Nobody can't wind that old clock."

"Want me to go along 'ith you in the cart and wind it fur you, Ranse?"

The mountaineer's countenance was proof against emotion. But he reached out a big hand and enclosed Ariela's thin brown one. Her soul peeped out once through her impassive face, hallowing it.

"Them hounds sha'n't pester you no more," said Ransie. "I reckon I been mean and low down. You wind that clock, Ariela."

"My heart hit's in that cabin, Ranse," she whispered, "along 'ith you. I ain't a-goin' to git mad no more. Le's be startin', Ranse, so's we kin git home by sundown."

Justice-of-the-peace Benaja Widdup interposed as they started for the door, forgetting his presence.

"In the name of the State of Tennessee," he said, "I forbid you-all to be a-defyin' of its laws and statutes. This co't is mo' than willin' and full of joy to see the clouds of discord and misunderstandin' rollin' away from two lovin' hearts, but it air the duty of the co't to p'eserve the morals and integrity of the State. The co't reminds you that you air no longer man and wife, but air divo'ced by regular decree, and as such air not entitled to the benefits and 'purtenances of the mattermonal estate."

Ariela caught Ransie's arm. Did those words mean that she must lose him now when they had just learned the lesson of life?

"But the co't air prepared," went on the Justice, "fur to remove the disabilities set up by the decree of divo'ce. The co't air on hand to perform the solemn ceremony of marri'ge, thus fixin' things up and enablin' the parties in the case to resume the honor'ble and elevatin' state of mattermony which they desires. The fee fur performin' said ceremony will be, in this case, to wit, five dollars."

Ariela caught the gleam of promise in his words. Swiftly her hand went to her bosom. Freely as an alighting dove the bill fluttered to the Justice's table. Her sallow cheek colored as she stood hand in hand with Ransie and listened to the reuniting words.

Ransie helped her into the cart, and climbed in beside her. The little red bull turned once more, and they set out, hand-clasped, for the mountains.

Justice-of-the-peace Benaja Widdup sat in his door and took off his shoes. Once again he fingered the bill tucked down in his vest pocket. Once again he smoked his elder-stem pipe. Once again the speckled hen swaggered down the main street of the "settlement," cackling foolishly.

A SACRIFICE HIT

The editor of the *Hearthstone Magazine* has his own ideas about the selection of manuscript for his publication. His theory is no secret; in fact, he will expound it to you willingly sitting at his mahogany desk, smiling benignantly and tapping his knee gently with his gold-rimmed eyeglasses.

"The *Hearthstone*," he will say, "does not employ a staff of readers. We obtain opinions of the manuscripts submitted to us directly from types of the various classes of our readers."

That is the editor's theory; and this is the way he carries it out:

When a batch of MSS. is received the editor stuffs every one of his pockets full of them and distributes them as he goes about during the day. The office employees, the hall porter, the janitor, the elevator man, messenger boys, the waiters at the café where the editor has luncheon, the man at the news-stand where he buys his evening paper, the grocer and the milkman, the guard on the 5:30 uptown elevated train, the ticket-chopper at Sixty—th street, the cook and maid at his home—these are the readers who pass upon MSS. sent in to the *Hearthstone Magazine*. If his pockets are not entirely emptied by the time he reaches the bosom of his family the remaining ones are handed over to his wife to read after the baby goes to sleep. A few days later the editor gathers in the MSS. during his regular rounds and considers the verdict of his assorted readers.

This system of making up a magazine has been very successful; and the circulation, paced by the advertising rates, is making a wonderful record of speed.

The *Hearthstone* Company also publishes books, and its imprint is to be found on several successful works—all recommended, says the editor, by the *Hearthstone's* army of volunteer readers. Now and then (according to talkative members of the editorial staff) the *Hearthstone* has allowed manuscripts to slip through its fingers on the advice of its heterogeneous readers, that afterward proved to be famous sellers when brought out by other houses.

For instance (the gossips say), "The Rise and Fall of Silas Latham" was unfavorably passed upon by the elevator-man; the office-boy unanimously rejected "The Boss"; "In the Bishop's Carriage" was contemptuously looked upon by the street-car conductor; "The Deliverance" was turned down by a clerk in the subscription department whose wife's mother had just begun a two month's visit at his home; "The Queen's Quair" came back from the janitor with the comment: "So is the book."

But nevertheless the *Hearthstone* adheres to its theory and system, and it will never lack volunteer readers; for each one of the widely scattered staff, from the young lady stenographer in the editorial office to the man who shovels in coal (whose adverse decision lost to the *Hearthstone* Company the manuscript of "The Under World"), has expectations of becoming editor of the magazine some day.

This method of the *Hearthstone* was well known to Allen Slayton when he wrote his novelette entitled "Love Is All." Slayton had hung about the editorial offices of all the magazines so persistently that he was acquainted with the inner workings of every one in Gotham.

He knew not only that the editor of the *Hearthstone* handed his MSS. around among different types of people for reading, but that the stories of sentimental love-interest went to Miss Puffkin, the editor's stenographer. Another of the editor's peculiar customs was to conceal invariably the name of the writer from his readers of MSS. so that a glittering name might not influence the sincerity of their reports.

Slayton made "Love Is All" the effort of his life. He gave it six months of the best work of his heart and brain. It was a pure love-story, fine, elevated, romantic, passionate—a prose poem that set the divine blessing of love (I am transposing from the manuscript) high above all earthly gifts and honors, and listed it in the catalogue of heaven's choicest rewards. Slayton's literary ambition was intense. He would have sacrificed all other worldly possessions to have gained fame in his chosen art. He would almost have cut off his right hand, or have offered himself to the knife of the appendicitis fancier to have realized his dream of seeing one of his efforts published in the *Hearthstone*.

Slayton finished "Love Is All," and took it to the *Hearthstone* in person. The office of the magazine was in a large, conglomerate building, presided under by a janitor.

As the writer stepped inside the door on his way to the elevator a potato masher flew through the hall, wrecking Slayton's hat, and smashing the glass of the door. Closely following in the wake of the utensil flew the janitor, a bulky, unwholesome man, suspenderless and sordid, panic-stricken and breathless. A frowsy, fat woman with flying hair followed the missile. The janitor's foot slipped on the tiled floor, he fell in a heap with an exclamation of despair. The woman pounced upon him and seized his hair. The man bellowed lustily.

Her vengeance wreaked, the virago rose and stalked, triumphant as Minerva, back to some cryptic domestic retreat at the rear. The janitor got to his feet, blown and humiliated.

"This is married life," he said to Slayton with a certain bruised humor. "That's the girl I used to lay awake of nights thinking about. Sorry about your hat, mister. Say, don't snitch to the tenants about this, will yer? I don't want to lose me job."

Slayton took the elevator at the end of the hall and went up to the offices of the *Hearthstone*. He left the MS. of "Love Is All" with the editor, who agreed to give him an answer as to its availability at the end of the week.

Slayton formulated his great winning scheme on his way down. It struck him with one brilliant flash, and he could not refrain from admiring his own genius in conceiving the idea. That very night he set about carrying it into execution.

Miss Puffkin, the *Hearthstone* stenographer, boarded in the same house with the author. She was an oldish, thin, exclusive, languishing, sentimental maid; and Slayton had been introduced to her some time before.

The writer's daring and self-sacrificing project was this: he knew that the editor of the *Hearthstone* relied strongly upon Miss Puffkin's judgment in the manuscript of romantic and sentimental fiction. Her taste represented the immense average of mediocre women who devour novels and stories of that type. The central idea and keynote of "Love Is All" was love at first sight—the enrapturing, irresistible, soul-thrilling feeling that compels a man or a woman to recognize his or her spirit-mate as soon as heart speaks to heart. Suppose he should impress this divine truth upon Miss Puffkin personally!—would she not surely indorse her new and rapturous sensations by recommending highly to the editor of the *Hearthstone* the novelette "Love Is All"?

Slayton thought so. And that night he took Miss Puffkin to the theatre. The next night he made vehement love to her in the dim parlor of the boarding-house. He quoted freely from "Love Is All"; and he wound up with Miss Puffkin's head on his shoulder, and visions of literary fame dancing in his head.

But Slayton did not stop at love-making. This, he said to himself, was the turning point of his life; and, like a true sportsman, he "went the limit." On Thursday night he and Miss Puffkin walked over to the Big Church in the Middle of the Block and were married.

Brave Slayton! Chateaubriand died in a garret, Byron courted a widow, Keats starved to death, Poe mixed his drinks, De Quincey hit the pipe, Ade lived in Chicago, James kept on doing it, Dickens wore white socks, De Maupassant wore a strait-jacket, Tom Watson became a Populist, Jeremiah wept, all these authors did these things, for the sake of literature, but thou didst cap them all; thou marriedst a wife for to carve for thyself a niche in the temple of fame!

On Friday morning Mrs. Slayton said she would go over to the *Hearthstone* office, hand in one or two manuscripts that the editor had given her to read, and resign her position as stenographer.

"Was there anything—er—that—er—you particularly fancied in the stories you are going to turn in?" asked Slayton with a thumping heart.

"There was one—a novelette, that I liked so much," said his wife. "I haven't read anything in years that I thought was half as nice and true to life."

That afternoon Slayton hurried down to the *Hearthstone* office. He felt that his reward was close at hand. With a novelette in the *Hearthstone,* literary reputation would soon be his.

The office boy met him at the railing in the outer office. It was not for unsuccessful authors to hold personal colloquy with the editor except at rare intervals.

Slayton, hugging himself internally, was nursing in his heart the exquisite hope of being able to crush the office boy with his forthcoming success.

He inquired concerning his novelette. The office boy went into the sacred precincts and brought forth a large envelope, thick with more than the bulk of a thousand checks.

"The boss told me to tell you he's sorry," said the boy, "but your manuscript ain't available for the magazine."

Slayton stood dazed. "Can you tell me," he stammered, "whether or no Miss Puff—that is my—I mean Miss Puffkin—handed in a novelette this morning that she had been asked to read?"

"Sure she did," answered the office boy, wisely. "I heard the old man say that Miss Puffkin said it was a daisy. The name of it was, 'Married for the Mazuma, or a Working Girl's Triumph.'

"Say, you!" said the office boy, confidentially, "your name's Slayton, ain't it? I guess I mixed cases on you without meanin' to do it. The boss gave me some manuscript to hand around the other day and I got the ones for Miss Puffkin and the janitor mixed. I guess it's all right, though."

And then Slayton looked closer and saw on the cover of his manuscript, under the title "Love Is All," the janitor's comment scribbled with a piece of charcoal:

"The — you say!"

THE ROADS WE TAKE

Twenty miles west of Tucson the "Sunset Express" stopped at a tank to take on water. Besides the aqueous addition the engine of that famous flyer acquired some other things that were not good for it.

While the fireman was lowering the feeding hose, Bob Tidball, "Shark" Dodson, and a quarter-bred Creek Indian called John Big Dog climbed on the engine and showed the engineer three round orifices in pieces of ordnance that they carried. These orifices so impressed the engineer with their possibilities that he raised both hands in a gesture such as accompanies the ejaculation "Do tell!"

At the crisp command of Shark Dodson, who was leader of the attacking force, the engineer descended to the ground and uncoupled the engine and tender. Then John Big Dog, perched upon the coal, sportively held two guns upon the engine driver and the fireman, and suggested that they run the engine fifty yards away and there await further orders.

Shark Dodson and Bob Tidball, scorning to put such low-grade ore as the passengers through the mill, struck out for the rich pocket of the express car. They found the messenger serene in the belief that the "Sunset Express" was taking on nothing more stimulating and dangerous than aqua pura. While Bob was knocking this idea out of his head with the butt-end of his six-shooter Shark Dodson was already dosing the express-car safe with dynamite.

The safe exploded to the tune of $30,000, all gold and currency. The passengers thrust their heads casually out of the windows to look for the thunder-cloud. The conductor jerked at the bell rope, which sagged down loose and unresisting, at his tug. Shark Dodson and Bod Tidball, with their booty in a stout canvas bag, tumbled out of the express car and ran awkwardly in their high-heeled boots to the engine.

The engineer, sullenly angry but wise, ran the engine, according to orders, rapidly away from the inert train. But before this was accomplished the express messenger, recovered from Bob Tidball's persuader to neutrality, jumped out of his car with a Winchester rifle and took a trick in the game. Mr. John Big Dog, sitting on the coal tender, unwittingly made a wrong lead by giving an imitation of a target, and the messenger trumped him. With a ball exactly between his shoulder blades the Creek chevalier of industry rolled off to the ground, thus increasing the share of his comrades in the loot by one-sixth each.

Two miles from the tank the engineer was ordered to stop.

The robbers waved a defiant adieu and plunged down the steep slope into the thick woods that lined the track. Five minutes of crashing through a thicket of chaparral brought them to open woods, where the three horses were tied to low-hanging branches. One was waiting for John Big Dog, who would never ride by night or day again. This animal the robbers divested of saddle and bridle and set free. They mounted the other two with the bag across one pommel, and rode fast and with discretion through the forest and up a primeval, lonely gorge. Here the animal that bore Bob Tidball slipped on a mossy boulder and broke a foreleg. They shot him through the head at once and sat down to hold a council of flight. Made secure for the present by the tortuous trail they had traveled, the question of time was no longer so big. Many miles and hours lay between them and the spryest posse that could follow. Shark Dodson's horse, with trailing rope and dropped bridle, panted and cropped thankfully of the grass along the stream in the gorge. Bob Tidball opened the sack, and drew out double handfuls of the neat packages of currency and the one sack of gold and chuckled with the glee of a child.

"Say, you old double-decked pirate," he called joyfully to Dodson, "you said we could do it—you got a head for financing that knocks the horns off of anything in Arizona."

"What are we going to do about a hoss for you, Bob? We ain't got long to wait here. They'll be on our trail before daylight in the mornin'."

"Oh, I guess that cayuse of yourn'll carry double for a while," answered the sanguine Bob. "We'll annex the first animal we come across. By jingoes, we made a haul, didn't we? Accordin' to the marks on this money there's $30,000—$15,000 apiece!"

"It's short of what I expected," said Shark Dodson, kicking softly at the packages with the toe of his boot. And then he looked pensively at the wet sides of his tired horse.

"Old Bolivar's mighty nigh played out," he said, slowly. "I wish that sorrel of yours hadn't got hurt."

"So do I," said Bob, heartily, "but it can't be helped. Bolivar's got plenty of bottom—he'll get us both far enough to get fresh mounts. Dang it, Shark, I can't help thinkin' how funny it is that an Easterner like you can come out here and give us Western fellows cards and spades in the desperado business. What part of the East was you from, anyway?"

"New York State," said Shark Dodson, sitting down on a boulder and chewing a twig. "I was born on a farm in Ulster County. I ran away from home when I was seventeen. It was an accident my comin' West. I was walkin' along the road with my clothes in a bundle, makin' for New York City. I had an idea of goin' there and makin' lots of money. I always felt like I could do it. I came to a place one evenin' where the road forked and I didn't know which fork to take. I studied about it for half an hour and then I took the left-hand. That night I run into the camp of a Wild West show that was travelin' among the little towns, and I went West with it. I've often wondered if I wouldn't have turned out different if I'd took the other road."

"Oh, I reckon you'd have ended up about the same," said Bob Tidball, cheerfully philosophical. "It ain't the roads we take; it's what's inside of us that makes us turn out the way we do."

Shark Dodson got up and leaned against a tree.

"I'd a good deal rather that sorrel of yourn hadn't hurt himself, Bob," he said again, almost pathetically.

"Same here," agreed Bob; "he sure was a first-rate kind of a crowbait. But Bolivar, he'll pull us through all right. Reckon we'd better be movin' on, hadn't we, Shark? I'll bag the boodle ag'in and we'll hit the trail for higher timber."

Bob Tidball replaced the spoil in the bag and tied the mouth of it tightly with a cord. When he looked up the most prominent object that he saw was the muzzle of Shark Dodson's .45 held upon him without a waver.

"Stop your funnin'," said Bob, with a grin. "We got to be hittin' the breeze."

"Set still," said Shark. "You ain't goin' to hit no breeze, Bob. I hate to tell you, but there ain't any chance for but one of us. Bolivar, he's plenty tired, and he can't carry double."

"We been pards, me and you, Shark Dodson, for three years," Bob said quietly. "We've risked our lives together time and again. I've always give you a square deal, and I thought you was a man. I've heard some queer stories about you shootin' one or two men in a peculiar way, but I never believed 'em. Now if you're just havin' a little fun with me, Shark, put your gun up, and we'll get on Bolivar and vamoose. If you mean to shoot —shoot, you blackhearted son of a tarantula!"

Shark Dodson's face bore a deeply sorrowful look.

"You don't know how bad I feel," he sighed, "about that sorrel of yourn breakin' his leg, Bob."

The expression on Dodson's face changed in an instant to one of cold ferocity mingled with inexorable cupidity. The soul of the man showed itself for a moment like an evil face in the window of a reputable house.

Truly Bob Tidball was never to "hit the breeze" again. The deadly .45 of the false friend cracked and filled the gorge with a roar that the walls hurled back with indignant echoes. And Bolivar, unconscious accomplice, swiftly bore away the last of the holders-up of the "Sunset Express," not put to the stress of "carrying double."

But as Shark Dodson galloped away the woods seemed to fade from his view; the revolver in his right hand turned to the curved arm of a mahogany chair; his saddle was strangely upholstered, and he opened his eyes and saw his feet, not in stirrups, but resting quietly on the edge of a quartered-oak desk.

I am telling you that Dodson, of the firm of Dodson & Decker, Wall Street brokers, opened his eyes. Peabody, the confidential clerk, was standing by his chair, hesitating to speak. There was a confused hum of wheels below, and the sedative buzz of an electric fan.

"Ahem! Peabody," said Dodson, blinking. "I must have fallen asleep. I had a most remarkable dream. What is it, Peabody?"

"Mr. Williams, sir, of Tracy & Williams, is outside. He has come to settle his deal in X. Y. Z. The market caught him short, sir, if you remember."

"Yes, I remember. What is X. Y. Z. quoted at to-day, Peabody?"

"One eighty-five, sir."

"Then that's his price."

"Excuse me," said Peabody, rather nervously, "for speaking of it, but I've been talking to Williams. He's an old friend of yours, Mr. Dodson, and you practically have a corner in X. Y. Z. I thought you might—that is, I thought you might not remember that he sold you the stock at 98. If he settles at the market price it will take every cent he has in the world and his home too to deliver the shares."

The expression on Dodson's face changed in an instant to one of cold ferocity mingled with inexorable cupidity. The soul of the man showed itself for a moment like an evil face in the window of a reputable house.

"He will settle at one eighty-five," said Dodson. "Bolivar cannot carry double."

A BLACKJACK BARGAINER

The most disreputable thing in Yancey Goree's law office was Goree himself, sprawled in his creaky old armchair. The rickety little office, built of red brick, was set flush with the street—the main street of the town of Bethel.

Bethel rested upon the foot-hills of the Blue Ridge. Above it the mountains were piled to the sky. Far below it the turbid Catawba gleamed yellow along its disconsolate valley.

The June day was at its sultriest hour. Bethel dozed in the tepid shade. Trade was not. It was so still that Goree, reclining in his chair, distinctly heard the clicking of the chips in the grand-jury room, where the "court-house gang" was playing poker. From the open back door of the office a well-worn path meandered across the grassy lot to the court-house. The treading out of that path had cost Goree all he ever had —first inheritance of a few thousand dollars, next the old family home, and, latterly, the last shreds of his self-respect and manhood. The "gang" had cleaned him out. The broken gambler had turned drunkard and parasite; he had lived to see this day come when the men who had stripped him denied him a seat at the game. His word was no longer to be taken. The daily bout at cards had arranged itself accordingly, and to him was assigned the ignoble part of the onlooker. The sheriff, the county clerk, a sportive deputy, a gay attorney, and a chalk-faced man hailing "from the valley," sat at table, and the sheared one was thus tacitly advised to go and grow more wool.

Soon wearying of his ostracism, Goree had departed for his office, muttering to himself as he unsteadily traversed the unlucky pathway. After a drink of corn whiskey from a demijohn under the table, he had flung himself into the chair, staring, in a sort of maudlin apathy, out at the mountains immersed in the summer haze. The little white patch he saw away up on the side of Blackjack was Laurel, the village near which he had been born and bred. There, also, was the birthplace of the feud between the Gorees and the Coltranes. Now no direct heir of the Gorees survived except this plucked and singed bird of misfortune. To the Coltranes, also, but one male supporter was left—Colonel Abner Coltrane, a man of substance and standing, a member of the State Legislature, and a contemporary with Goree's father. The feud had been a typical one of the region; it had left a red record of hate, wrong, and slaughter.

But Yancey Goree was not thinking of feuds. His befuddled brain was hopelessly attacking the problem of the future maintenance of himself and his favorite follies. Of late, old friends of the family had seen to it that he had whereof to eat and a place to sleep, but whiskey they would not buy for him, and he must have whiskey. His law business was extinct; no case had been intrusted to him in two years. He had been a borrower and a sponge, and it seemed that if he fell no lower it would be from lack of opportunity. One more chance—he was saying to himself—if he had one more stake at the game, he thought he could win; but he had nothing left to sell, and his credit was more than exhausted.

He could not help smiling, even in his misery, as he thought of the man to whom, six months before, he had sold the old Goree homestead. There had come from "back yan'" in the mountains two of the strangest creatures, a man named Pike Garvey and his wife. "Back yan'," with a wave of the hand toward the hills, was understood among the mountaineers to designate the remotest fastnesses, the unplumbed gorges, the haunts of lawbreakers, the wolf's den, and the boudoir of the bear. In the cabin far up on Blackjack's shoulder, in the wildest part of these retreats, this odd couple had lived for twenty years. They had neither dog nor children to mitigate the heavy silence of the hills. Pike Garvey was little known in the settlements, but all who had dealt with him pronounced him "crazy as a loon." He acknowledged no occupation save that of a squirrel hunter, but he "moonshined" occasionally by way of diversion. Once the "revenues" had dragged him from his lair, fighting silently and desperately like a terrier, and he had been sent to state's prison for two years. Released, he popped back into his hole like an angry weasel.

Fortune, passing over many anxious wooers, made a freakish flight into Blackjack's bosky pockets to smile upon Pike and his faithful partner.

One day a party of spectacled, knickerbockered, and altogether absurd prospectors invaded the vicinity of the Garveys' cabin. Pike lifted his squirrel rifle off the hook and took a shot at them at long range on the chance of their being revenues. Happily he missed, and the unconscious agents of good luck drew nearer, disclosing their innocence of anything resembling law or justice. Later on, they offered the Garveys an enormous quantity of ready, green, crisp money for their thirty-acre patch of cleared land, mentioning, as an excuse for such a mad action, some irrelevant and inadequate nonsense about a bed of mica underlying the said property.

When the Garveys became possessed of so many dollars that they faltered in computing them, the deficiencies of life on Blackjack began to grow prominent. Pike began to talk of new shoes, a hogshead of tobacco to set in the corner, a new lock to his rifle; and, leading Martella to a certain spot on the mountainside, he pointed out to her how a small cannon —doubtless a thing not beyond the scope of their fortune in price—might be planted so as to command and defend the sole accessible trail to the cabin, to the confusion of revenues and meddling strangers forever.

But Adam reckoned without his Eve. These things represented to him the applied power of wealth, but there slumbered in his dingy cabin an ambition that soared far above his primitive wants. Somewhere in Mrs. Garvey's bosom still survived a spot of femininity unstarved by twenty years of Blackjack. For so long a time the sounds in her ears had been the scaly-barks dropping in the woods at noon, and the wolves singing among the rocks at night, and it was enough to have purged her vanities. She had grown fat and sad and yellow and dull. But when the means came, she felt a rekindled desire to assume the perquisites of her sex—to sit at tea tables; to buy inutile things; to whitewash the hideous veracity of life with a little form and ceremony. So she coldly vetoed Pike's proposed system of fortifications, and announced that they would descend upon the world, and gyrate socially.

And thus, at length, it was decided, and the thing done. The village of Laurel was their compromise between Mrs. Garvey's preference for one of the large valley towns and Pike's hankering for primeval solitudes. Laurel yielded a halting round of feeble social distractions comportable with Martella's ambitions, and was not entirely without recommendation to Pike, its contiguity to the mountains presenting advantages for sudden retreat in case fashionable society should make it advisable.

Their descent upon Laurel had been coincident with Yancey Goree's feverish desire to convert property into cash, and they bought the old

Goree homestead, paying four thousand dollars ready money into the spendthrift's shaking hand.

Thus it happened that while the disreputable last of the Gorees sprawled in his disreputable office, at the end of his row, spurned by the cronies whom he had gorged, strangers dwelt in the halls of his fathers.

A cloud of dust was rolling slowly up the parched street, with something traveling in the midst of it. A little breeze wafted the cloud to one side, and a new, brightly painted carryall, drawn by a slothful gray horse, became visible. The vehicle deflected from the middle of the street as it neared Goree's office, and stopped in the gutter directly in front of his door.

On the front seat sat a gaunt, tall man, dressed in black broadcloth, his rigid hands incarcerated in yellow kid gloves. On the back seat was a lady who triumphed over the June heat. Her stout form was armored in a skintight silk dress of the description known as "changeable," being a gorgeous combination of shifting hues. She sat erect, waving a much-ornamented fan, with her eyes fixed stonily far down the street. However Martella Garvey's heart might be rejoicing at the pleasures of her new life, Blackjack had done his work with her exterior. He had carved her countenance to the image of emptiness and inanity; had imbued her with the stolidity of his crags and the reserve of his hushed interiors. She always seemed to hear, whatever her surroundings were, the scaly-barks falling and pattering down the mountainside. She could always hear the awful silence of Blackjack sounding through the stillest of nights.

Goree watched this solemn equipage, as it drove to his door, with only faint interest but when the lank driver wrapped the reins about his whip, and awkwardly descended, and stepped into the office, he rose unsteadily to receive him, recognizing Pike Garvey, the new, the transformed, the recently civilized.

The mountaineer took the chair Goree offered him. They who cast doubts upon Garvey's soundness of mind had a strong witness in the man's countenance. His face was too long, a dull saffron in hue, and immobile as a statue's. Pale-blue, unwinking round eyes without lashes added to the singularity of his gruesome visage. Goree was at a loss to account for the visit.

"Everything all right at Laurel, Mr. Garvey?" he inquired.

"Everything all right, sir, and mighty pleased is Missis Garvey and me with the property. Missis Garvey likes yo' old place, and she likes the neighborhood. Society is what she 'lows she wants, and she is gettin' of it. The Rogerses, the Hapgoods, the Pratts, and the Troys hev been to see Missis Garvey, and she hev et meals to most of thar houses. The best folks hev axed her to differ'nt of doin's. I cyan't say, Mr. Goree, that sech things suits me—fur me, give me them thar." Garvey's huge yellow-gloved hand flourished in the direction of the mountains. "That's whar

I b'long, 'mongst the wild honey bees and the b'ars. But that ain't what I come fur to say, Mr. Goree. Thar's somethin' you got what me and Missis Garvey wants to buy."

"Buy!" echoed Goree. "From me?" Then he laughed harshly. "I reckon you are mistaken about that. I sold out to you, as you yourself expressed it, 'lock, stock, and barrel.' There isn't even a ramrod left to sell."

"You've got it; and we 'uns want it. 'Take the money,' says Missis Garvey, 'and buy it fa'r and squar'.'"

Goree shook his head. "The cupboard's bare," he said.

"We've riz," pursued the mountaineer, undeflected from his object, "a heap. We was pore as possums, and now we could hev folks to dinner every day. We been reco'nized, Missis Garvey says, by the best society. But there's somethin' we need we ain't got. She says it ought to been put in the 'ventory ov the sale, but it 'tain't thar. 'Take the money, then,' she says, 'and buy it fa'r and squar'.'"

"Out with it," said Goree, his racked nerves growing impatient.

Garvey threw his slouch hat upon the table, and leaned forward, fixing his unblinking eyes upon Goree's.

"There's a old feud," he said, distinctly and slowly, "'tween you 'uns and the Coltranes."

Goree frowned ominously. To speak of his feud to a feudist is a serious breach of the mountain etiquette. The man from "back yan'" knew it as well as the lawyer did.

"Na offense," he went on, "but purely in the way of business. Missis Garvey hev studied all about feuds. Most of the quality folks in the mountains hev 'em. The Settles and the Goforths, the Rankins and the Boyds, the Silers and the Galloways, hev all been cyarin' on feuds f'om twenty to a hundred year. The last man to drap was when yo' uncle, Jedge Paisley Goree, 'journed co't and shot Len Coltrane f'om the bench. Missis Garvey and me, we come f'om the po' white trash. Nobody wouldn't pick a feud with we'uns, no mo'n with a fam'ly of treetoads. Quality people everywhar, says Missis Garvey, has feuds. We 'uns ain't quality, but we're buyin' into it as fur as we can. 'Take the money, then,' says Missis Garvey, 'and buy Mr. Goree's feud, fa'r and squar'.'"

The squirrel hunter straightened a leg half across the room, drew a roll of bills from his pocket, and threw them on the table.

"Thar's two hundred dollars, Mr. Goree, what you would call a fa'r price for a feud that's been 'lowed to run down like yourn hev. Thar's only you left to cyar' on yo' side of it, and you'd make mighty po' killin'. I'll take it off yo' hands, and it'll set me and Missis Garvey up among the quality. Thar's the money."

The little roll of currency on the table slowly untwisted itself, writhing and jumping as its folds relaxed. In the silence that followed Garvey's last speech the rattling of the poker chips in the court-house could be plainly heard. Goree knew that the sheriff had just won a pot, for the subdued whoop with which he always greeted a victory floated across the square upon the crinkly heat waves. Beads of moisture stood on Goree's brow. Stooping, he drew the wicker-covered demijohn from under the table, and filled a tumbler from it.

"A little corn liquor, Mr. Garvey? Of course you are joking about—what you spoke of? Opens quite a new market, doesn't it? Feuds, prime, two-fifty to three. Feuds, slightly damaged—two hundred, I believe you said, Mr. Garvey?"

Goree laughed self-consciously.

The mountaineer took the glass Goree handed him, and drank the whiskey without a tremor of the lids of his staring eyes. The lawyer applauded the feat by a look of envious admiration. He poured his own drink, and took it like a drunkard, by gulps, and with shudders at the smell and taste.

"Two hundred," repeated Garvey. "Thar's the money."

A sudden passion flared up in Goree's brain. He struck the table with his fist. One of the bills flipped over and touched his hand. He flinched as if something had stung him.

"Do you come to me," he shouted, "seriously with such a ridiculous, insulting, darn-fool proposition?"

"It's fa'r and squar'," said the squirrel hunter, but he reached out his hand as if to take back the money; and then Goree knew that his own flurry of rage had not been from pride or resentment, but from anger at himself, knowing that he would set foot in the deeper depths that were being opened to him. He turned in an instant from an outraged gentleman to an anxious chafferer recommending his goods.

"Don't be in a hurry, Garvey," he said, his face crimson and his speech thick. "I accept your p-p-proposition, though it's dirt cheap at two hundred. A t-trade's all right when both p-purchaser and b-buyer are s-satisfied. Shall I w-wrap it up for you, Mr. Garvey?"

Garvey rose, and shook out his broadcloth. "Missis Garvey will be pleased. You air out of it, and it stands Coltrane and Garvey. Just a scrap ov writin', Mr. Goree, you bein' a lawyer, to show we traded."

Goree seized a sheet of paper and a pen. The money was clutched in his moist hand. Everything else suddenly seemed to grow trivial and light.

"Bill of sale, by all means. 'Right, title, and interest in and to' . . . 'forever warrant and——' No, Garvey, we'll have to leave out that 'defend,' " said Goree with a loud laugh. "You'll have to defend this title yourself."

The mountaineer received the amazing screed that the lawyer handed him, folded it with immense labor, and placed it carefully in his pocket.

Goree was standing near the window. "Step here," he said, raising his finger, "and I'll show you your recently purchased enemy. There he goes, down the other side of the street."

The mountaineer crooked his long frame to look through the window in the direction indicated by the other. Colonel Abner Coltrane, an erect, portly gentleman of about fifty wearing the inevitable long, double-breasted frock coat of the Southern lawmaker, and an old high silk hat, was passing on the opposite sidewalk. As Garvey looked, Goree glanced at his face. If there be such a thing as a yellow wolf, here was its counterpart. Garvey snarled as his unhuman eyes followed the moving figure, disclosing long amber-colored fangs.

"Is that him? Why, that's the man who sent me to the pen'tentiary once!"

"He used to be district attorney," said Goree, carelessly. "And, by the way, he's a first-class shot."

"I kin hit a squirrel's eye at a hundred yard," said Garvey. "So that thar's Coltrane! I made a better trade than I was thinkin'. I'll take keer of this feud, Mr. Goree, better'n you ever did!"

He moved toward the door, but lingered there, betraying a slight perplexity.

"Anything else to-day?" inquired Goree with frothy sarcasm. "Any family traditions, ancestral ghosts, or skeletons in the closet? Prices as low as the lowest."

"Thar was another thing," replied the unmoved squirrel hunter, "that Missis Garvey was thinkin' of. 'Tain't so much in my line as t'other, but she wanted partic'lar that I should inquire, and ef you was willin', 'pay fur it,' she says, 'fa'r and squar'.' Thar's a buryin' groun', as you know, Mr. Goree, in the yard of yo' old place, under the cedars. Them that lies thar is yo' folks what was killed by the Coltranes. The monyments has the names on 'em. Missis Garvey says a fam'ly buryin' groun' is a sho' sign of quality. She says ef we git the feud, thar's somethin' else ought to go with it. The names on them monyments is 'Goree,' but they can be changed to ourn by——"

"Go! Go!" screamed Goree, his face turning purple. He stretched out both hands toward the mountaineer, his fingers hooked and shaking. "Go, you ghoul! Even a Ch-Chinaman protects the g-graves of his ancestors—go!"

The squirrel hunter slouched out of the door to his carryall. While he was climbing over the wheel Goree was collecting, with feverish celerity, the money that had fallen from his hand to the floor. As the vehicle slowly turned about, the sheep with a coat of newly grown wool was hurrying, in indecent haste, along the path to the courthouse.

At three o'clock in the morning they brought him back to his office, shorn and unconscious. The sheriff, the sportive deputy, the county clerk, and the gay attorney carried him, the chalk-faced man "from the valley" acting as escort.

"On the table," said one of them, and they deposited him there among the litter of his unprofitable books and papers.

"Yance thinks a lot of a pair of deuces when he's liquored up," sighed the sheriff, reflectively.

"Too much," said the gay attorney. "A man has no business to play poker who drinks as much as he does. I wonder how much he dropped to-night."

"Close to two hundred. What I wonder is whar he got it. Yance ain't had a cent fur over a month, I know."

"Struck a client, maybe. Well, let's get home before daylight. He'll be all right when he wakes up, except for a sort of beehive about the cranium."

The gang slipped away through the early morning twilight. The next eye to gaze upon the miserable Goree was the orb of day. He peered through the uncurtained window, first deluging the sleeper in a flood of faint gold, but soon pouring upon the mottled red of his flesh a searching, white, summer heat. Goree stirred, half unconsciously, among the table's débris, and turned his face from the window. His movement dislodged a heavy law book, which crashed upon the floor. Opening his eyes, he saw, bending over him, a man in a black frock coat. Looking higher, he discovered a well-worn silk hat, and beneath it the kindly, smooth face of Colonel Abner Coltrane.

A little uncertain of the outcome, the colonel waited for the other to make some sign of recognition. Not in twenty years had male members of these two families faced each other in peace. Goree's eyelids puckered as he strained his blurred sight toward this visitor, and then he smiled serenely.

"Have you brought Stella and Lucy over to play?" he said, calmly.

"Do you know me, Yancey?" asked Coltrane.

"Of course I do. You brought me a whip with a whistle in the end."

So he had—twenty-four years ago; when Yancey's father was his best friend.

Goree's eyes wandered about the room. The colonel understood. "Lie still, and I'll bring you some," said he. There was a pump in the yard at the rear, and Goree closed his eyes, listening with rapture to the click of its handle and the bubbling of the falling stream. Coltrane brought a pitcher of the cool water, and held it for him to drink. Presently Goree sat up—a most forlorn object, his summer suit of flax soiled and crumpled, his discreditable head tousled and unsteady. He tried to wave one of his hands toward the colonel.

"Ex-excuse—everything, will you?" he said. "I must have drunk too much whiskey last night, and gone to bed on the table." His brows knitted into a puzzled frown.

"Out with the boys a while?" asked Coltrane, kindly.

"No, I went nowhere. I haven't had a dollar to spend in the last two months. Struck the demijohn too often, I reckon, as usual."

Colonel Coltrane touched him on the shoulder.

"A little while ago, Yancey," he began, "you asked me if I had brought Stella and Lucy over to play. You weren't quite awake then, and must have been dreaming you were a boy again. You are awake now, and I want you to listen to me. I have come from Stella and Lucy to their old playmate, and to my old friend's son. They know that I am going to bring you home with me, and you will find them as ready with a welcome as they were in the old days. I want you to come to my house and stay until you are yourself again, and as much longer as you will. We heard of your being down in the world, and in the midst of temptation, and we agreed that you should come over and play at our house once more. Will you come, my boy? Will you drop our old family trouble and come with me?"

"Trouble!" said Goree, opening his eyes wide. "There was never any trouble between us that I know of. I'm sure we've always been the best of friends. But, good Lord, Colonel, how could I go to your home as I am—a drunken wretch, a miserable, degraded spendthrift and gambler——"

He lurched from the table to his armchair, and began to weep maudlin tears, mingled with genuine drops of remorse and shame. Coltrane talked to him persistently and reasonably, reminding him of the simple mountain pleasures of which he had once been so fond, and insisting upon the genuineness of the invitation.

Finally he landed Goree by telling him he was counting upon his help in the engineering and transportation of a large amount of felled timber from a high mountainside to a waterway. He knew that Goree had once invented a device for this purpose—a series of slides and chutes—upon which he had justly prided himself. In an instant the poor fellow, delighted at the idea of his being of use to any one, had paper spread upon the table, and was drawing rapid but pitifully shaky lines in demonstration of what he could and would do.

The man was sickened of the husks; his prodigal heart was turning again toward the mountains. His mind was yet strangely clogged, and his thoughts and memories were returning to his brain one by one, like carrier pigeons over a stormy sea. But Coltrane was satisfied with the progress he had made.

Bethel received the surprise of its existence that afternoon when a Coltrane and a Goree rode amicably together through the town. Side by side they rode, out from the dusty streets and gaping townspeople, down across the creek bridge, and up toward the mountain. The prodigal had brushed and washed and combed himself to a more decent figure, but he was unsteady in the saddle, and he seemed to be deep in the contemplation of some vexing problem. Coltrane left him in his mood, relying upon the influence of changed surroundings to restore his equilibrium.

Once Goree was seized with a shaking fit, and almost came to a collapse. He had to dismount and rest at the side of the road. The colonel, foreseeing such a condition, had provided a small flask of whiskey for the journey but when it was offered to him Goree refused it almost with violence, declaring he would never touch it again. By and by he was recovered, and went quietly enough for a mile or two. Then he pulled up his horse suddenly, and said:

"I lost two hundred dollars last night, playing poker. Now, where did I get that money?"

"Take it easy, Yancey. The mountain air will soon clear it up. We'll go fishing, first thing, at the Pinnacle Falls. The trout are jumping there like bullfrogs. We'll take Stella and Lucy along, and have a picnic on Eagle Rock. Have you forgotten how a hickory-cured-ham sandwich tastes, Yancey, to a hungry fisherman?"

Evidently the colonel did not believe the story of his lost wealth; so Goree retired again into brooding silence.

By late afternoon they had traveled ten of the twelve miles between Bethel and Laurel. Half a mile this side of Laurel lay the old Goree place; a mile or two beyond the village lived the Coltranes. The road was now steep and laborious, but the compensations were many. The tilted aisles of the forest were opulent with leaf and bird and bloom. The tonic air put to shame the pharmacopœia. The glades were dark with mossy shade, and bright with shy rivulets winking from the ferns and laurels. On the lower side they viewed, framed in the near foliage, exquisite sketches of the far valley swooning in its opal haze.

Coltrane was pleased to see that his companion was yielding to the spell of the hills and woods. For now they had but to skirt the base of Painter's Cliff; to cross Elder Branch and mount the hill beyond, and Goree would have to face the squandered home of his fathers. Every rock he passed, every tree, every foot of the roadway, was familiar to him. Though he had forgotten the woods, they thrilled him like the music of *"Home, Sweet Home."*

They rounded the cliff, descended into Elder Branch, and paused there to let the horses drink and splash in the swift water. On the right was a rail fence that cornered there, and followed the road and stream. Inclosed by it was the old apple orchard of the home place; the house was yet concealed by the brow of the steep hill. Inside and along the fence, pokeberries, elders, sassafras, and sumac grew high and dense. At a rustle of their branches, both Goree and Coltrane glanced up, and saw a long, yellow, wolfish face above the fence, staring at them with pale, unwinking eyes. The head quickly disappeared; there was a violent swaying of the bushes, and an ungainly figure ran up through the apple orchard in the direction of the house zigzagging among the trees.

"That's Garvey," said Coltrane; "the man you sold out to. There's no doubt but he's considerably cracked. I had to send him up for moonshining once, several years ago, in spite of the fact that I believed him irresponsible. Why, what's the matter, Yancey?"

Goree was wiping his forehead, and his face had lost its color. "Do I look queer, too?" he asked, trying to smile. "I'm just remembering a few more things." Some of the alcohol had evaporated from his brain. "I recollect now where I got that two hundred dollars."

"Don't think of it," said Coltrane, cheerfully. "Later on we'll figure it all out together."

They rode out of the branch, and when they reached the foot of the hill Goree stopped again.

"Did you ever suspect I was a very vain kind of fellow, Colonel?" he asked. "Sort of foolish proud about appearances?"

The colonel's eyes refused to wander to the soiled, sagging suit of flax and the faded slouch hat.

"It seems to me," he replied, mystified, but humoring him, "I remember a young buck about twenty, with the tightest coat, the sleekest hair, and the prancingest saddle horse in the Blue Ridge."

"Right you are," said Goree, eagerly. "And it's in me yet, though it don't show. Oh, I'm as vain as a turkey gobbler, and as proud as Lucifer. I'm going to ask you to indulge this weakness of mine in a little matter."

"Speak out, Yancey. We'll create you Duke of Laurel and Baron of Blue Ridge, if you choose; and you shall have a feather out of Stella's peacock's tail to wear in your hat."

"I'm in earnest. In a few minutes we'll pass the house up there on the hill where I was born, and where my people have lived for nearly a century. Strangers live there now—and look at me! I am about to show myself to them ragged and poverty-stricken, a wastrel and a beggar. Colonel Coltrane, I'm ashamed to do it. I want you to let me wear your coat and hat until we are out of sight beyond. I know you think it a foolish pride, but I want to make as good a showing as I can when I pass the old place."

"Now, what does this mean?" said Coltrane to himself, as he compared his companion's sane looks and quiet demeanor with his strange request. But he was already unbuttoning the coat, assenting readily, as if the fancy were in no wise to be considered strange.

The coat and hat fitted Goree well. He buttoned the former about him with a look of satisfaction and dignity. He and Coltrane were nearly the same size—rather tall, portly, and erect. Twenty-five years were between them, but in appearance they might have been brothers. Goree looked older than his age; his face was puffy and lined; the colonel had the smooth, fresh complexion of a temperate liver. He put on Goree's disreputable old flax coat and faded slouch hat.

"Now," said Goree, taking up the reins, "I'm all right. I want you to ride about ten feet in the rear as we go by, Colonel, so that they can get a good look at me. They'll see I'm no back number yet, by any means. I guess I'll show up pretty well to them once more, anyhow. Let's ride on."

He set out up the hill at a smart trot, the colonel following, as he had been requested.

Goree sat straight in the saddle, with head erect, but his eyes were turned to the right, sharply scanning every shrub and fence and hiding-place in the old homestead yard. Once he muttered to himself, "Will the crazy fool try it, or did I dream half of it?"

It was when he came opposite the little family burying ground that he saw what he had been looking for—a puff of white smoke, coming from the thick cedars in one corner. He toppled so slowly to the left that Coltrane had time to urge his horse to that side, and catch him with one arm.

The squirrel hunter had not overpraised his aim. He had sent the bullet where he intended, and where Goree had expected that it would pass—through the breast of Colonel Abner Coltrane's black frock coat.

Goree leaned heavily against Coltrane, but he did not fall. The horses kept pace, side by side, and the colonel's arm kept him steady. The little white houses of Laurel shone through the trees, half a mile away. Goree reached out one hand and groped until it rested upon Coltrane's fingers, which held his bridle.

"Good friend," he said, and that was all.

Thus did Yancey Goree, as he rode past his old home, make, considering all things, the best showing that was in his power.

THE SONG AND THE SERGEANT

Half a dozen people supping at a table in one of the upper-Broadway all-night restaurants were making too much noise. Three times the manager walked past them with a politely warning glance; but their argument had waxed too warm to be quelled by a manager's gaze. It was midnight, and the restaurant was filled with patrons from the theatres of that district. Some among the dispersed audiences must have recognized among the quarrelsome sextet the faces of the players belonging to the Carroll Comedy Company.

Four of the six made up the company. Another was the author of the comedietta, "A Gay Coquette," which the quartet of players had been presenting with fair success at several vaudeville houses in the city. The sixth at the table was a person inconsequent in the realm of art, but one at whose bidding many lobsters had perished.

Loudly the six maintained their clamorous debate. But one of the party was silent except when answers were stormed from him by the excited ones. That was the comedian of "A Gay Coquette." He was a young man with a face even too melancholy for his profession. The oral warfare of four immoderate tongues was directed at Miss Clarice Carroll, the twin-kling star of the small aggregation. Excepting the downcast comedian, all members of the party united in casting upon her with vehemence the blame of some momentous misfortune. Fifty times they told her: "It is your fault, Clarice—it is you alone who spoilt the scene. It is only of late that you have acted this way. At this rate the sketch will have to be taken off."

Miss Carroll was a match for any four. Gallic ancestry gave her a vari-ety that could easily mount to fury. Her large eyes flashed a scorching denial at her accusers. Her slender, eloquent arms constantly menaced the tableware. Her high, clear soprano voice rose to what would have been a sceram had it not possessed so pure a musical quality. She hurled back at the attacking four their denunciations in tones sweet, but of too great carrying power for a Broadway restaurant.

Finally they exhausted her patience both as a woman and an artist. She sprang up like a panther, managed to smash half a dozen plates and glasses with one royal sweep of her arm, and defied her critics. They rose and wrangled more loudly. The comedian sighed and looked a trifle sad-der and disinterested. The manager came tripping and suggested peace. He was told to go to the popular synonym for war so promptly that the affair might have happened at The Hague.

Thus was the manager angered. He made a sign with his hand and a waiter slipped out of the door. In twenty minutes the party of six was in a police station, facing a grizzled and philosophical desk sergeant.

"Disorderly conduct in a restaurant," said the policeman who had brought the party in.

The author of "A Gay Coquette" stepped to the front. He wore nose-glasses and evening clothes, even if his shoes had been tans before they met the patent-leather-polish bottle.

"Mr. Sergeant," said he, out of his throat, like Actor Irving, "I would like to protest against this arrest. The company of actors who are per-forming in a little play that I have written, in company with a friend and myself, were having a little supper. We became deeply interested in the discussion as to which one of the cast is responsible for a scene in the sketch that lately has fallen so flat that the piece is about to become a fail-ure. We may have been rather noisy and intolerant of interruption by the restaurant people; but the matter was of considerable importance to all of us. You see that we are sober and are not the kind of people who de-sire to raise disturbances. I hope that the case will not be pressed and that we may be allowed to go."

"Who makes the charge?" asked the sergeant.

"Me," said a white-aproned voice in the rear. "De restaurant sent me to. De gang was raisin' a dough-house and breakin' dishes."

"The dishes were paid for," said the playwright. "They were not broken purposely. In her anger, because we remonstrated with her for spoiling the scene, Miss——"

"It's not true, sergeant," cried the clear voice of Miss Clarice Carroll. In a long coat of tan silk and a red-plumed hat, she bounded before the desk.

"It's not my fault," she cried, indignantly. "How dare they say such a thing! I've played the title rôle ever since it was staged, and if you want to know who made it a success, ask the public—that's all."

"What Miss Carroll says is true in part," said the author. "For five months the comedietta was a drawing card in the best houses. But during the last two weeks it has lost favor. There is one scene in it in which Miss Carroll made a big hit. Now she hardly gets a hand out of it. She spoils it by acting it entirely different from her old way."

"It is not my fault," reiterated the actress.

"There are only two of you in the scene," argued the playwright, hotly, "you and Delmars, here——"

"Then it's his fault," declared Miss Carroll, with a lightning glance of scorn from her dark eyes. The comedian caught it, and gazed with increased melancholy at the panels of the sergeant's desk.

The night was a dull one in that particular police station.

The sergeant's long-blunted curiosity awoke a little.

"I've heard you," he said to the author. And then he addressed the thin-faced and ascetic-looking lady of the company who played "Aunt Turnip-top" in the little comedy.

"Who do you think spoils the scene you are fussing about?" he asked.

"I'm no knocker," said that lady, "and everybody knows it. So, when I say that Clarice falls down every time in that scene I'm judging her art and not herself. She was great in it once. She does it something fierce now. It'll dope the show if she keeps it up."

The sergeant looked at the comedian.

"You and the lady have this scene together, I understand. I suppose there's no use asking you which one of you queers it?"

The comedian avoided the direct rays from the two fixed stars of Miss Carroll's eyes.

"I don't know," he said, looking down at his patent-leather toes.

"Are you one of the actors?" asked the sergeant of a dwarfish youth with a middle-aged face.

"Why, say!" replied the last Thespian witness, "you don't notice any tin spear in my hands, do you? You haven't heard me shout: 'See, the Emperor comes!' since I've been in here, have you? I guess I'm on the stage long enough for 'em not to start a panic by mistaking me for a thin curl of smoke rising above the footlights."

"In your opinion, if you've got one," said the sergeant, "is the frost that gathers on the scene in question the work of the lady or the gentleman who takes part in it?"

The middle-aged youth looked pained.

"I regret to say," he answered, "that Miss Carroll seems to have lost her grip on that scene. She's all right in the rest of the play, but—but I tell you, sergeant, she can do it—she has done it equal to any of 'em—and she can do it again."

Miss Carroll ran forward, glowing and palpitating.

"Thank you, Jimmy, for the first good word I've had in many a day," she cried. And then she turned her eager face toward the desk.

"I'll show you, sergeant, whether I am to blame. I'll show them whether I can do that scene. Come, Mr. Delmars, let us begin. You will let us, won't you, sergeant?"

"How long will it take?" asked the sergeant, dubiously.

"Eight minutes," said the playwright. "The entire play consumes but thirty."

"You may go ahead," said the sergeant. "Most of you seem to side against the little lady. Maybe she had a right to crack up a saucer or two in that restaurant. We'll see how she does the turn before we take that up."

The matron of the police station had been standing near, listening to the singular argument. She came nigher and stood near the sergeant's chair. Two or three of the reserves strolled in, big and yawning.

"Before beginning the scene," said the playwright, "and assuming that you have not seen a production of 'A Gay Coquette,' I will make a brief but necessary explanation. It is a musical-farce-comedy—burlesque-comedietta. As the title implies, Miss Carroll's rôle is that of a gay, rollicking, mischievous, heartless coquette. She sustains that character throughout the entire comedy part of the production. And I have designed the extravaganza features so that she may preserve and present the same coquettish idea.

"Now, the scene in which we take exception to Miss Carroll's acting is called the 'gorilla dance.' She is costumed to represent a wood nymph, and there is great song-and-dance scene with a gorilla—played by Mr. Delmars, the comedian. A tropical-forest stage is set.

"That used to get four and five recalls. The main thing was the acting and the dance—it was the funniest thing in New York for five months. Delmars' song, 'I'll Woo Thee to My Sylvan Home,' while he and Miss Carroll were cutting hide-and-seek capers among the tropical plants, was a winner."

"What's the trouble with the scene now?" asked the sergeant.

"Miss Carroll spoils it right in the middle," said the playwright, wrathfully.

With a wide gesture of her ever-moving arms the actress waved back the little group of spectators, leaving a space in front of the desk for the scene of her vindication or fall. Then she whipped off her long tan cloak and tossed it across the arm of the policeman who still stood officially among them.

Miss Carroll had gone to supper well cloaked, but in the costume of the tropic wood nymph. A skirt of fern leaves touched her knee; she was like a humming bird—green and golden and purple.

And then she danced a fluttering, fantastic dance, so agile and light and mazy in her steps that the other three members of the Carroll Comedy Company broke into applause at the art of it.

And at the proper time Delmars leaped out at her side, mimicking the uncouth, hideous bounds of the gorilla so funnily that the grizzled sergeant himself gave a short laugh like the closing of a padlock. They danced together the gorilla dance, and won a hand from all.

Then began the most fantastic part of the scene—the wooing of the nymph by the gorilla. It was a kind of dance itself—eccentric and prankish, with the nymph in coquettish and seductive retreat, followed by the gorilla as he sang "I'll Woo Thee to My Sylvan Home."

The song was a lyric of merit. The words were nonsense, as befitted the play, but the music was worthy of something better. Delmars struck into it in a rich tenor that owned a quality that shamed the flippant words.

During one verse of the song the wood nymph performed the grotesque evolutions designed for the scene. At the middle of the second verse she stood still, with a strange look on her face, seeming to gaze dreamily into the depths of the scenic forest. The gorilla's last leap had brought him to her feet, and there he knelt, holding her hand, until he had finished the haunting lyric that was set in the absurd comedy like a diamond in a piece of putty.

When Delmars ceased Miss Carroll started, and covered a sudden flow of tears with both hands.

"There!" cried the playwright, gesticulating with violence; "there you have it, sergeant. For two weeks she has spoiled that scene in just that manner at every performance. I have begged her to consider that it is not Ophelia or Juliet that she is playing. Do you wonder now at our impatience? Tears for the gorilla song! The play is lost!"

Out of her bewitchment, whatever it was, the wood nymph flared suddenly, and pointed a desperate finger at Delmars.

"It is you—you have done this," she cried, wildly. "You never sang that song that way until lately. It is your doing."

"I give it up," said the sergeant.

And then the gray-haired matron of the police station came forward from behind the sergeant's chair.

"Must an old woman teach you all?" she said. She went up to Miss Carroll and took her hand.

"The man's wearing his heart out for you, my dear. Couldn't you tell it the first note you heard him sing? All of his monkey flip-flops wouldn't have kept it from me. Must you be deaf as well as blind? That's why you couldn't act your part, child. Do you love him or must he be a gorilla for the rest of his days?"

Miss Carroll whirled around and caught Delmars with a lightning glance of her eye. He came toward her, melancholy.

"Did you hear, Mr. Delmars?" she asked, with a catching breath.

"I did," said the comedian. "It is true. I didn't think there was any use. I tried to let you know with the song."

"Silly!" said the matron; "why didn't you speak?"

"No, no," cried the wood nymph, "his way was the best. I didn't know, but—it was just what I wanted, Bobby."

She sprang like a green grasshopper; and the comedian opened his arms, and—smiled.

"Get out of this," roared the desk sergeant to the waiting waiter from the restaurant. "There's nothing doing here for you."

ONE DOLLAR'S WORTH

The judge of the United States court of the district lying along the Rio Grande border found the following letter one morning in his mail:

Judge:
When you sent me up for four years you made a talk. Among other hard things, you called me a rattlesnake. Maybe I am one—anyhow, you hear me rattling now. One year after I got to the pen, my daughter died of— well, they said it was poverty and the disgrace together. You've got a daughter, Judge, and I'm going to make you know how it feels to lose one. And I'm going to bite that district attorney that spoke against me. I'm free now, and I guess I've turned to rattlesnake all right. I feel like one. I don't say much, but this is my rattle. Look out what I strike.

Yours respectfully,
Rattlesnake

Judge Derwent threw the letter carelessly aside. It was nothing new to receive such epistles from desperate men whom he had been called up to judge. He felt no alarm. Later on he showed the letter to Littlefield, the young district attorney, for Littlefield's name was included in the threat, and the judge was punctilious in matters between himself and his fellow men.

Littlefield honored the rattle of the writer, as far as it concerned himself, with a smile of contempt; but he frowned a little over the reference to the Judge's daughter, for he and Nancy Derwent were to be married in the fall.

Littlefield went to the clerk of the court and looked over the records with him. They decided that the letter might have been sent by Mexico Sam, a half-breed border desperado who had been imprisoned for manslaughter four years before. Then official duties crowded the matter from his mind, and the rattle of the revengeful serpent was forgotten.

Court was in session at Brownsville. Most of the cases to be tried were charges of smuggling, counterfeiting, post-office robberies, and violations of Federal laws along the border. One case was that of a young Mexican, Rafael Ortiz, who had been rounded up by a clever deputy marshal in the act of passing a counterfeit silver dollar. He had been suspected of many such deviations from rectitude, but this was the first time that anything provable had been fixed upon him. Ortiz languished cozily in jail, smoking brown cigarettes and waiting for trial. Kilpatrick, the deputy, brought the counterfeit dollar and handed it to the district attorney in his office in the court-house. The deputy and a reputable druggist were prepared to swear that Ortiz paid for a bottle of medicine with it. The coin was a poor counterfeit, soft, dull-looking, and made principally of lead. It was the day before the morning on which the docket would reach the case of Ortiz, and the district attorney was preparing himself for the trial.

"Not much need of having in high-priced experts to prove the coin's queer, is there, Kil?" smiled Littlefield, as he thumped the dollar down upon the table, where it fell with no more ring than would have come from a lump of putty.

"I guess the Greaser's as good as behind the bars," said the deputy, easing up his holsters. "You've got him dead. If it had been just one time, these Mexicans can't tell good money from bad; but this little yaller rascal belongs to a gang of counterfeiters, I know. This is the first time I've been able to catch him doing the trick. He's got a girl down there in them Mexican jacals on the river bank. I seen her one day when I was watching him. She's as pretty as a red heifer in a flower bed."

Littlefield shoved the counterfeit dollar into his pocket, and slipped his memoranda of the case into an envelope. Just then a bright, winsome face, as frank and jolly as a boy's, appeared in the doorway, and in walked Nancy Derwent.

"Oh, Bob, didn't court adjourn at twelve to-day until to-morrow?" she asked of Littlefield.

"It did," said the district attorney, "and I'm very glad of it. I've got a lot of rulings to look up, and——"

"Now, that's just like you. I wonder you and Father don't turn to law books or rulings or something! I want you to take me out plover-shooting this afternoon. Long Prairie is just alive with them. Don't say no, please! I want to try my new twelve-bore hammerless. I've sent to the livery stable to engage Fly and Bess for the buckboard; they stand fire so nicely. I was sure you would go."

They were to be married in the fall. The glamour was at its height. The plovers won the day—or, rather, the afternoon—over the calf-bound authorities. Littlefield began to put his papers away.

There was a knock at the door. Kilpatrick answered it. A beautiful, dark-eyed girl with a skin tinged with the faintest lemon color walked into the room. A black shawl was thrown over her head and wound once around her neck.

She began to talk in Spanish, a voluble, mournful stream of melancholy music. Littlefield did not understand Spanish. The deputy did, and he translated her talk by portions, at intervals holding up his hands to check the flow of her words.

"She came to see you, Mr. Littlefield. Her name's Joya Treviñas. She wants to see you about—well, she's mixed up with that Rafael Ortiz. She's his—she's his girl. She says he's innocent. She says she made the money and got him to pass it. Don't you believe her, Mr. Littlefield. That's the way with these Mexican girls; they'll lie, steal, or kill for a fellow when they get stuck on him. Never trust a woman that's in love!"

"Mr. Kilpatrick!"

Nancy Derwent's indignant exclamation caused the deputy to flounder for a moment in attempting to explain that he had misquoted his own sentiments, and then he went on with the translation:

"She says she's willing to take his place in the jail if you'll let him out. She says she was down sick with the fever, and the doctor said she'd die if she didn't have medicine. That's why he passed the lead dollar on the drug store. She says it saved her life. This Rafael seems to be her honey, all right; there's a lot of stuff in her talk about love and such things that you don't want to hear."

It was an old story to the district attorney.

"Tell her," said he, "that I can do nothing. The case comes up in the morning, and he will have to make his fight before the court."

Nancy Derwent was not so hardened. She was looking with sympathetic interest at Joya Treviñas and at Littlefield alternately. The deputy repeated the district attorney's words to the girl. She spoke a sentence or two in a low voice, pulled her shawl closely about her face, and left the room.

"What did she say then?" asked the district attorney.

"Nothing special," said the deputy. "She said: 'If the life of the one'—let's see how it went—'Si la vida de ella a quien tu amas—if the life of the girl you love is ever in danger, remember Rafael Ortiz.'"

Kilpatrick strolled out through the corridor in the direction of the marshal's office.

"Can't you do anything for them, Bob?" asked Nancy. "It's such a little thing—just one counterfeit dollar—to ruin the happiness of two lives! She was in danger of death, and he did it to save her. Doesn't the law know the feeling of pity?"

"It hasn't a place in jurisprudence, Nan," said Littlefield, "especially *in re* the district attorney's duty. I'll promise you that the prosecution will not be vindictive; but the man is as good as convicted when the case is called. Witnesses will swear to his passing the bad dollar which I have in my pocket at this moment as 'Exhibit A.' There are no Mexicans on the jury, and it will vote Mr. Greaser guilty without leaving the box."

The plover-shooting was fine that afternoon, and in the excitement of the sport the case of Rafael and the grief of Joya Treviñas was forgotten. The district attorney and Nancy Derwent drove out from the town three miles along a smooth, grassy road, and then struck across a rolling prairie toward a heavy line of timber on Piedra Creek. Beyond this creek lay Long Prairie, the favorite haunt of the plover. As they were nearing the creek they heard the galloping of a horse to their right, and saw a man with black hair and a swarthy face riding toward the woods at a tangent, as if he had come up behind them.

"I've seen that fellow somewhere," said Littlefield, who had a memory for faces, "but I can't exactly place him. Some ranchman, I suppose, taking a short cut home."

They spent an hour on Long Prairie, shooting from the buckboard. Nancy Derwent, an active, outdoor Western girl, was pleased with her twelve-bore. She had bagged within two brace of her companion's score.

They started homeward at a gentle trot. When within a hundred yards of Piedra Creek a man rode out of the timber directly toward them.

"It looks like the man we saw coming over," remarked Miss Derwent.

As the distance between them lessened, the district attorney suddenly pulled up his team sharply, with his eyes fixed upon the advancing horseman. That individual had drawn a Winchester from its scabbard on his saddle and thrown it over his arm.

"Now I know you, Mexico Sam!" muttered Littlefield to himself. "It *was* you who shook your rattles in that gentle epistle."

Mexico Sam did not leave things long in doubt. He had a nice eye in all matters relating to firearms, so when he was within good rifle range, but outside of danger from No. 8 shot, he threw up his Winchester and opened fire upon the occupants of the buckboard.

The first shot cracked the back of the seat within the two-inch space between the shoulders of Littlefield and Miss Derwent. The next went through the dashboard and Littlefield's trouser leg.

The district attorney hustled Nancy out of the buckboard to the ground. She was a little pale, but asked no questions. She had the frontier instinct that accepts conditions in an emergency without superfluous argument. They kept their guns in hand, and Littlefield hastily gathered some handfuls of cartridges from the pasteboard box on the seat and crowded them into his pockets.

"Keep behind the horses, Nan," he commanded. "That fellow is a ruffian I sent to prison once. He's trying to get even. He knows our shot won't hurt him at that distance."

"All right, Bob," said Nancy, steadily. "I'm not afraid. But you come close, too. Whoa, Bess; stand still, now!"

She stroked Bess's mane. Littlefield stood with his gun ready, praying that the desperado would come within range.

But Mexico Sam was playing his vendetta along safe lines. He was a bird of different feather from the plover. His accurate eye drew an imaginary line of circumference around the area of danger from bird-shot, and upon this line he rode. His horse wheeled to the right, and as his victims rounded to the safe side of their equine breastwork he sent a ball through the district attorney's hat. Once he miscalculated in making a detour, and overstepped his margin. Littlefield's gun flashed, and Mexico Sam ducked his head to the harmless patter of the shot. A few of them stung his horse, which pranced promptly back to the safety line.

The desperado fired again. A little cry came from Nancy Derwent. Littlefield whirled, with blazing eyes, and saw the blood trickling down her cheek.

"I'm not hurt, Bob—only a splinter struck me. I think he hit one of the wheel-spokes."

"Lord!" groaned Littlefield. "If I only had a charge of buckshot!"

The ruffian got his horse still, and took careful aim. Fly gave a snort and fell in the harness, struck in the neck. Bess, now disabused of the idea that plover were being fired at, broke her traces and galloped wildly away. Mexican Sam sent a ball neatly through the fullness of Nancy Derwent's shooting jacket.

"Lie down—lie down!" snapped Littlefield. "Close to the horse—flat on the ground—so." He almost threw her upon the grass against the back of the recumbent Fly. Oddly enough, at that moment the words of the Mexican girl returned to his mind:

"If the life of the girl you love is ever in danger, remember Rafael Ortiz."

Littlefield uttered an exclamation.

"Open fire on him, Nan, across the horse's back! Fire as fast as you can! You can't hurt him, but keep him dodging shot for one minute while I try to work a little scheme."

Nancy gave a quick glance at Littlefield, and saw him take out his pocket-knife and open it. Then she turned her face to obey orders, keeping up a rapid fire at the enemy.

Mexico Sam waited patiently until this innocuous fusillade ceased. He had plenty of time, and he did not care to risk the chance of a bird-shot in his eye if it could be avoided by a little caution. He pulled his heavy Stetson low down over his face until the shots ceased. Then he drew a little nearer, and fired with careful aim at what he could see of his victims above the fallen horse.

Neither of them moved. He urged his horse a few steps nearer. He saw the district attorney rise to one knee, and deliberately level his shotgun. He pulled his hat down and awaited the harmless rattle of the tiny pellets.

The shotgun blazed with a heavy report. Mexico Sam sighed, turned limp all over, and slowly fell from his horse—a dead rattlesnake.

At ten o'clock the next morning court opened, and the case of the United States *versus* Rafael Ortiz was called. The district attorney, with his arm in a sling, rose and addressed the court.

"May it please your honor," he said, "I desire to enter a *nolle pros.* in this case. Even though the defendant should be guilty, there is not sufficient evidence in the hands of the government to secure a conviction. The piece of counterfeit coin upon the identity of which the case was built is not now available as evidence. I ask, therefore, that the case be stricken off."

At the noon recess, Kilpatrick strolled into the district attorney's office.

"I've just been down to take a squint at old Mexico Sam," said the deputy. "They've got him laid out. Old Mexico was a tough outfit, I reckon. The boys was wonderin' down there what you shot him with. Some said it must have been nails. I never see a gun carry anything to make holes like he had."

"I shot him," said the district attorney, "with Exhibit A of your counterfeiting case. Lucky thing for me—and somebody else—that it was as bad money as it was! It sliced up into slugs very nicely. Say, Kil, can't you go down to the jacals and find where that Mexican girl lives? Miss Derwent wants to know."

A NEWSPAPER STORY

At 8 A. M. it lay on Giuseppi's news-stand, still damp from the presses. Giuseppi, with the cunning of his ilk, philandered on the opposite corner leaving his patrons to help themselves, no doubt on a theory related to the hypothesis of the watched pot.

This particular newspaper was, according to its custom and design, an educator, a guide, a monitor, a champion, and a household counsellor and *vade mecum.*

From its many excellencies might be selected three editorials. One was in simple and chaste but illuminating language directed to parents and teachers, deprecating corporal punishment for children.

Another was an accusive and significant warning addressed to a notorious labor leader who was on the point of instigating his clients to a troublesome strike.

The third was an eloquent demand that the police force be sustained and aided in everything that tended to increase its efficiency as public guardians and servants.

Besides these more important chidings and requisitions upon the store of good citizenship was a wise prescription or form of procedure laid out by the editor of the heart-to-heart column in the specific case of a young man who had complained of the obduracy of his lady love, teaching him how he might win her.

Again, there was, on the beauty page, a complete answer to a young lady inquirer who desired admonition toward the securing of bright eyes, rosy cheeks, and a beautiful countenance.

One other item requiring special cognizance was a brief "personal," running thus:

> Dear Jack:—Forgive me. You were right. Meet me at corner of Madison and —th at 8:30 this morning. We leave at noon.
>
> Penitent

At 8 o'clock a young man with a haggard look and the feverish gleam of unrest in his eye dropped a penny and picked up the top paper as he passed Giuseppi's stand. A sleepless night had left him a late riser. There was an office to be reached by nine, and a shave and a hasty cup of coffee to be crowded into the interval.

He visited his barber shop and then hurried on his way. He pocketed his paper, meditating a belated perusal of it at the luncheon hour. At the next corner it fell from his pocket, carrying with it his pair of new gloves. Three blocks he walked, missed the gloves and turned back fuming.

Just on the half-hour he reached the corner where lay the gloves and paper. But he strangely ignored that which he had come to seek. He was holding two little hands as tightly as ever he could and looking into two penitent brown eyes, while joy rioted in his heart.

"Dear Jack," she said, "I knew you would be here on time."

"I wonder what she means by that," he was saying to himself; "but it's all right, it's all right."

A big wind puffed out of the west, picked up the paper from the sidewalk, opened it and sent it flying and whirling down a side street. Up that street was driving a skittish bay to a spider-wheel buggy the young man who had written to the heart-to-heart editor for a recipe that he might win her for whom he sighed.

The wind, with a prankish flurry, flapped the flying newspaper against the face of the skittish bay. There was a lengthened streak of bay mingled with the red of running gear that stretched itself out for four blocks. Then a water-hydrant played its part in the cosmogony, the buggy became match wood as foreordained, and the driver rested very quietly where he had been flung on the asphalt in front of a certain brownstone mansion.

They came out and had him inside very promptly. And there was one who made herself a pillow for his head, and cared for no curious eyes, bending over and saying, "Oh, it was you; it was you all the time, Bobby! Couldn't you see it? And if you die, why, so must I, and——"

But in all this wind we must hurry to keep in touch with our paper.

Policeman O'Brine arrested it as a character dangerous to traffic. Straightening its dishevelled leaves with his big, slow fingers, he stood a few feet from the family entrance of the Shandon Bells Café. One headline he spelled out ponderously. "The Papers to the Front in a Move to Help the Police."

But, whist! The voice of Danny, the head bartender, through the crack of the door: "Here's a nip for ye, Mike, ould man."

Behind the widespread, amicable columns of the press Policeman O'Brine receives swiftly his nip of the real stuff. He moves away, stalwart, refreshed, fortified, to his duties. Might not the editor man view with pride the early, the spiritual, the literal fruit that had blessed his labors.

Policeman O'Brine folded the paper and poked it playfully under the arm of a small boy that was passing. That boy was named Johnny, and he took the paper home with him. His sister was named Gladys, and she had written to the beauty editor of the paper asking for the practicable touchstone of beauty. That was weeks ago, and she had ceased to look for an answer. Gladys was a pale girl, with dull eyes and a discontented expression. She was dressing to go up to the avenue to get some braid. Beneath her skirt she pinned two leaves of the paper Johnny had brought. When she walked the rustling sound was an exact imitation of the real thing.

On the street she met the Brown girl from the flat below and stopped to talk. The Brown girl turned green. Only silk at $5 a yard could make the sound that she heard when Gladys moved. The Brown girl, consumed by jealousy, said something spiteful and went her way, with pinched lips.

Gladys proceeded towards the avenue. Her eyes now sparkled like jagerfonteins. A rosy bloom visited her cheeks; a triumphant, subtle, vivifying smile transfigured her face. She was beautiful. Could the beauty editor have seen her then! There was something in her answer in the paper, I believe, about cultivating a kind feeling towards others in order to make plain features attractive.

The labor leader against whom the paper's solemn and weighty editorial injunction was laid was the father of Gladys and Johnny. He picked up the remains of the journal from which Gladys had ravished a cosmetic of silken sounds. The editorial did not come under his eye, but instead it was greeted by one of those ingenious and specious puzzle problems that enthrall alike the simpleton and the sage.

The labor leader tore off half of the page, provided himself with table, pencil, and paper and glued himself to the puzzle.

Three hours later, after waiting vainly for him at the appointed place, other more conservative leaders declared and ruled in favor of arbitration, and the strike with its attendant dangers was averted. Subsequent editions of the paper referred, in colored inks, to the clarion tone of its successful denunciation of the labor leader's intended designs.

The remaining leaves of the active journal also went loyally to the proving of its potency.

When Johnny returned from school he sought a secluded spot and removed the missing columns from the inside of his clothing, where they had been artfully distributed so as to successfully defend such areas as are generally attacked during scholastic castigations. Johnny attended a private school and had had trouble with his teacher. As has been said, there was an excellent editorial against corporal punishment in that morning's issue, and no doubt it had its effect.

After this can any one doubt the power of the press?

TOMMY'S BURGLAR

At ten o'clock P.M. Felicia, the maid, left by the basement door with the policeman to get a raspberry phosphate around the corner. She detested the policeman and objected earnestly to the arrangement. She pointed out, not unreasonably, that she might have been allowed to fall asleep over one of St. George Rathbone's novels on the third floor, but she was overruled. Raspberries and cops were not created for nothing.

The burglar got into the house without much difficulty; because we must have action and not too much description in a 2,000-word story.

In the dining room he opened the slide of his dark lantern. With a brace and centrebit he began to bore into the lock of the silver-closet.

Suddenly a click was heard. The room was flooded with electric light. The dark velvet portières parted to admit a fair-haired boy of eight in pink pajamas, bearing a bottle of olive oil in his hand.

"Are you a burglar?" he asked, in a sweet, childish voice.

"Listen to that," exclaimed the man, in a hoarse voice. "Am I a burglar? Wot do you suppose I have a three days' growth of bristly beard on my face for, and a cap with flaps? Give me the oil, quick, and let me grease the bit, so I won't wake up your mamma, who is lying down with a headache, and left you in charge of Felicia who has been faithless to her trust."

"Oh, dear," said Tommy, with a sigh. "I thought you would be more up-to-date. This oil is for the salad when I bring lunch from the pantry for you. And mamma and papa have gone to the Metropolitan to hear De Reszke. But that isn't my fault. It only shows how long the story has been knocking around among the editors. If the author had been wise he'd have changed it to Caruso in the proofs."

"Be quiet," hissed the burglar, under his breath. "If you raise an alarm I'll wring your neck like a rabbit's."

"Like a chicken's," corrected Tommy. "You had that wrong. You don't wring rabbits' necks."

"Aren't you afraid of me?" asked the burglar.

"You know I'm not," answered Tommy. "Don't you suppose I know fact from fiction? If this wasn't a story I'd yell like an Indian when I saw you; and you'd probably tumble downstairs and get pinched on the sidewalk."

"I see," said the burglar, "that you're on to your job. Go on with the performance."

Tommy seated himself in an armchair and drew his toes up under him.

"Why do you go around robbing strangers, Mr. Burglar? Have you no friends?"

"I see what you're driving at," said the burglar, with a dark frown. "It's the same old story. Your innocence and childish insouciance is going to lead me back into an honest life. Every time I crack a crib where there's a kid around, it happens."

"Would you mind gazing with wolfish eyes at the plate of cold beef that the butler has left on the dining table?" said Tommy. "I'm afraid it's growing late."

The burglar accommodated.

"Poor man," said Tommy. "You must be hungry. If you will please stand in a listless attitude I will get you something to eat."

The boy brought a roast chicken, a jar of marmalade, and a bottle of wine from the pantry. The burglar seized a knife and fork sullenly.

"It's only been an hour," he grumbled, "since I had a lobster and a pint of musty ale up on Broadway. I wish these story writers would let a fellow have a pepsin tablet, anyhow, between feeds."

"My papa writes books," remarked Tommy.

The burglar jumped to his feet quickly.

"You said he had gone to the opera," he hissed, hoarsely and with immediate suspicion.

"I ought to have explained," said Tommy. "He didn't buy the tickets." The burglar sat again and toyed with the wishbone.

"Why do you burgle houses?" asked the boy, wonderingly.

"Because," replied the burglar, with a sudden flow of tears. "God bless my little brown-haired boy Bessie at home."

"Ah," said Tommy, wrinkling his nose, "you got that answer in the wrong place. You want to tell your hard-luck story before you pull out the child stop."

"Oh, yes," said the burglar, "I forgot. Well, once I lived up in Milwaukee, and——"

"Take the silver," said Tommy, rising from his chair.

"Hold on," said the burglar. "But I moved away. I could find no other employment. For a while I managed to support my wife and child by passing confederate money; but, alas! I was forced to give that up because it did not belong to the union. I became desperate and a burglar."

"Have you ever fallen into the hands of the police?" asked Tommy.

"I said 'burglar,' not 'beggar,'" answered the cracksman.

"After you finish your lunch," said Tommy, "and experience the usual change of heart, how shall we wind up the story?"

"Suppose," said the burglar, thoughtfully, "that Tony Pastor turns out earlier than usual to-night, and your father gets in from 'Parsifal' at 10:30. I am thoroughly repentant because you have made me think of my own little boy Bessie, and——"

"Say," said Tommy, "haven't you got that wrong?"

"Not on your colored crayon drawings by B. Cory Kilvert," said the burglar. "It's always a Bessie that I have at home, artlessly prattling to the pale-cheeked burglar's bride. As I was saying, your father opens the front door just as I am departing with admonitions and sandwiches that you have wrapped up for me. Upon recognizing me as an old Harvard classmate he starts back in——"

"Not in surprise?" interrupted Tommy, with wide-open eyes.

"He starts back in the doorway," continued the burglar. And then he rose to his feet and began to shout: "Rah, rah, rah! rah, rah, rah! rah, rah, rah!"

"Well," said Tommy, wonderingly, "that's the first time I ever knew a burglar to give a college yell when he was burglarizing a house, even in a story."

"That's one on you," said the burglar, with a laugh. "I was practising the dramatization. If this is put on the stage that college touch is about the only thing that will make it go."

Tommy looked his admiration.

"You're on, all right," he said.

"And there's another mistake you've made," said the burglar. "You should have gone some time ago and brought me the $9 gold piece your mother gave you on your birthday to take to Bessie."

"But she didn't give it to me to take to Bessie," said Tommy, pouting.

"Come, come!" said the burglar, sternly. "It's not nice of you to take advantage because the story contains an ambiguous sentence. You know what I mean. It's mighty little I get out of these fictional jobs, anyhow. I lose all the loot, and I have to reform every time; and all the swag I'm allowed is the blamed little fol-de-rols and luck-pieces that you kids hand over. Why in one story, all I got was a kiss from a little girl who came in on me when I was opening a safe. And it tasted of molasses candy, too. I've a good notion to tie this table cover over your head and keep on into the silver-closet."

"Oh, no, you haven't," said Tommy, wrapping his arms around his knees. "Because if you did no editor would buy the story. You know you've got to preserve the unities."

"So've you," said the burglar, rather glumly. "Instead of sitting here talking impudence and taking the bread out of a poor man's mouth, what you'd like to be doing is hiding under the bed and screeching at the top of your voice."

"You're right, old man," said Tommy, heartily. "I wonder what they make us do it for? I think the S. P. C. C. ought to interfere. I'm sure it's neither agreeable nor usual for a kid of my age to butt in when a full-grown burglar is at work and offer him a red sled and a pair of skates not to awaken his sick mother. And look how they make the burglars act! You'd think editors would know—but what's the use?"

The burglar wiped his hands on the tablecloth and arose with a yawn.

"Well, let's get through with it," he said. "God bless you, my little boy! you have saved a man from committing a crime this night. Bessie shall pray for you as soon as I get home and give her her orders. I shall never burglarize another house—at least not until the June magazines are out. It'll be your little sister's turn then to run in on me while I am abstracting the U. S. 4 per cent. from the tea urn and buy me off with her coral necklace and a falsetto kiss."

"You haven't got all the kicks coming to you," sighed Tommy, crawling out of his chair. "Think of the sleep I'm losing. But it's tough on both of us, old man. I wish you could get out of the story and really rob somebody. Maybe you'll have the chance if they dramatize us."

"Never!" said the burglar, gloomily. "Between the box office and my better impulses that your leading juveniles are supposed to awaken and the magazines that pay on publication, I guess I'll always be broke."

"I'm sorry," said Tommy, sympathetically. "But I can't help myself any more than you can. It's one of the canons of household fiction that no burglar shall be successful. The burglar must be foiled by a kid like me, or by a young lady heroine, or at the last moment by his old pal, Red Mike, who recognizes the house as one in which he used to be the coachman. You have got the worst end of it in any kind of a story."

"Well, I suppose I must be clearing out now," said the burglar, taking up his lantern and bracebit.

"You have to take the rest of this chicken and the bottle of wine with you for Bessie and her mother," said Tommy, calmly.

"But confound it," exclaimed the burglar, in an annoyed tone, "they don't want it. I've got five cases of Château de Beychsvelle at home that was bottled in 1853. That claret of yours is corked. And you couldn't get either of them to look at a chicken unless it was stewed in champagne. You know, after I get out of the story I don't have so many limitations. I make a turn now and then."

"Yes, but you must take them," said Tommy, loading his arms with the bundles.

"Bless you, young master!" recited the burglar, obedient. "Second-Story Saul will never forget you. And now hurry and let me out, kid. Our 2,000 words must be nearly up."

Tommy led the way through the hall toward the front door. Suddenly the burglar stopped and called to him softly: "Ain't there a cop out there in front somewhere sparking the girl?"

"Yes," said Tommy, "but what——"

"I'm afraid he'll catch me," said the burglar. "You mustn't forget that this is fiction."

"Great head!" said Tommy, turning. "Come out by the back door."

A CHAPARRAL CHRISTMAS GIFT

The original cause of the trouble was about twenty years in growing.

At the end of that time it was worth it.

Had you lived anywhere within fifty miles of Sundown Ranch you would have heard of it. It possessed a quantity of jet-black hair, a pair of extremely frank, deep-brown eyes, and a laugh that rippled across the prairie like the sound of a hidden brook. The name of it was Rosita McMullen; and she was the daughter of old man McMullen of the Sundown Sheep Ranch.

There came riding on red roan steeds—or, to be more explicit, on a paint and flea-bitten sorrel—two wooers. One was Madison Lane, and the other was the Frio Kid. But at that time they did not call him the Frio Kid, for he had not earned the honors of special nomenclature. His name was simply Johnny McRoy.

It must not be supposed that these two were the sum of the agreeable Rosita's admirers. The bronchos of a dozen others champed their bits at the long hitching rack of the Sundown Ranch. Many were the sheeps'-eyes that were cast in those savannas that did not belong to the flocks of Dan McMullen. But of all the cavaliers, Madison Lane and Johnny McRoy galloped far ahead, wherefore they are to be chronicled.

Madison Lane, a young cattleman from the Nueces country, won the race. He and Rosita were married one Christmas day. Armed, hilarious, vociferous, magnanimous, the cowmen and the sheepmen, laying aside their hereditary hatred, joined forces to celebrate the occasion.

Sundown Ranch was sonorous with the cracking of jokes and six-shooters, the shine of buckles and bright eyes, the outspoken congratulations of the herders of kine.

But while the wedding feast was at its liveliest there descended upon it Johnny McRoy, bitten by jealousy, like one possessed.

"I'll give you a Christmas present," he yelled, shrilly, at the door, with his .45 in his hand. Even then he had some reputation as an offhand shot.

His first bullet cut a neat underbit in Madison Lane's right ear. The barrel of his gun moved an inch. The next shot would have been the bride's had not Carson, a sheepman, possessed a mind with triggers somewhat well oiled and in repair. The guns of the wedding party had been hung, in their belts, upon nails in the wall when they sat at table, as a concession to good taste. But Carson, with great promptness, hurled his plate of roast venison and frijoles at McRoy, spoiling his aim. The second bullet then, only shattered the white petals of a Spanish dagger flower suspended two feet above Rosita's head.

The guests spurned their chairs and jumped for their weapons. It was considered an improper act to shoot the bride and groom at a wedding. In about six seconds there were twenty or so bullets due to be whizzing in the direction of Mr. McRoy.

"I'll shoot better next time," yelled Johnny; "and there'll be a next time." He backed rapidly out of the door.

Carson, the sheepman, spurred on to attempt further exploits by the success of his plate throwing, was first to reach the door. McRoy's bullet from the darkness laid him low.

The cattlemen then swept out upon him, calling for vengeance, for, while the slaughter of a sheepman has not always lacked condonement, it was a decided misdemeanor in this instance. Carson was innocent; he was no accomplice at the matrimonial proceedings; nor had any one heard him quote the line "Christmas comes but once a year" to the guests.

But the sortie failed in its vengeance. McRoy was on his horse and away, shouting back curses and threats as he galloped into the concealing chaparral.

That night was the birthnight of the Frio Kid. He became the "bad man" of that portion of the State. The rejection of his suit by Miss Mc-Mullen turned him to a dangerous man. When officers went after him for the shooting of Carson, he killed two of them, and entered upon the life of an outlaw. He became a marvellous shot with either hand. He would turn up in towns and settlements, raise a quarrel at the slightest opportunity, pick off his man, and laugh at the officers of the law. He was so cool, so deadly, so rapid, so inhumanly bloodthirsty that none but faint attempts were ever made to capture him. When he was at last shot and killed by a little one-armed Mexican who was nearly dead himself from fright, the Frio Kid had the deaths of eighteen men on his head. About half of these were killed in fair duels depending upon the quickness of the draw. The other half were men whom he assassinated from absolute wantonness and cruelty.

Many tales are told along the border of his impudent courage and daring. But he was not one of the breed of desperadoes who have seasons of generosity and even of softness. They say he never had mercy on the object of his anger. Yet at this and every Christmastide it is well to give each one credit, if it can be done, for whatever speck of good he may have possessed. If the Frio Kid ever did a kindly act or felt a throb of generosity in his heart it was once at such a time and season, and this is the way it happened.

One who has been crossed in love should never breathe the odor of the blossoms of the ratama tree. It stirs the memory to a dangerous degree.

One December in the Frio country there was a ratama tree in full bloom, for the winter had been as warm as springtime. That way rode the Frio Kid and his satellite and co-murderer, Mexican Frank. The kid reined in his mustang, and sat in his saddle, thoughtful and grim, with dangerously narrowing eyes. The rich, sweet scent touched him somewhere beneath his ice and iron.

"I don't know what I've been thinking about, Mex," he remarked in his usual mild draw, "to have forgot all about a Christmas present I got to give. I'm going to ride over to-morrow night and shoot Madison Lane in his own house. He got my girl—Rosita would have had me if he hadn't cut into the game. I wonder why I happened to overlook it up to now?"

"Ah, shucks, Kid," said Mexican, "don't talk foolishness. You know you can't get within a mile of Mad Lane's house to-morrow night. I see old man Allen day before yesterday, and he says Mad is going to have Christmas doings at his house. You remember how you shot up the festivities when Mad was married, and about the threats you made? Don't you suppose Mad Lane'll kind of keep his eye open for a certain Mr. Kid? You plumb make me tired, Kid, with such remarks."

"I'm going," repeated the Frio Kid, without heat, "to go to Madison Lane's Christmas doings, and kill him. I ought to have done it a long time ago. Why, Mex, just two weeks ago I dreamed me and Rosita was married instead of her and him; and we was living in a house, and I could see her smiling at me, and—oh! h—l, Mex, he got her; and I'll get him—yes, sir, on Christmas Eve he got her, and then's when I'll get him."

"There's other ways of committing suicide," advised Mexican. "Why don't you go and surrender to the sheriff?"

"I'll get him," said the Kid.

Christmas Eve fell as balmy as April. Perhaps there was a hint of far-away frostiness in the air, but it tingled like seltzer, perfumed faintly with late prairie blossoms and the mesquite grass.

When night came the five or six rooms of the ranch-house were brightly lit. In one room was a Christmas tree, for the Lanes had a boy of three, and a dozen or more guests were expected from the nearer ranches.

At nightfall Madison Lane called aside Jim Belcher and three other cowboys employed on his ranch.

"Now, boys," said Lane, "keep your eyes open. Walk around the house and watch the road well. All of you know the 'Frio Kid,' as they call him now, and if you see him, open fire on him without asking any questions. I'm not afraid of his coming around, but Rosita is. She's been afraid he'd come in on us every Christmas since we were married."

The guests had arrived in buckboards and on horseback, and were making themselves comfortable inside.

The evening went along pleasantly. The guests enjoyed and praised Rosita's excellent supper, and afterward the men scattered in groups about the rooms or on the broad "gallery," smoking and chatting.

The Christmas tree, of course, delighted the youngsters, and above all were they pleased when Santa Claus himself in magnificent white beard and furs appeared and began to distribute the toys.

"It's my papa," announced Billy Sampson, aged six. "I've seen him wear 'em before."

Berkly, a sheepman, an old friend of Lane, stopped Rosita as she was passing by him on the gallery, where he was sitting smoking.

"Well, Mrs. Lane," said he, "I suppose by this Christmas you've gotten over being afraid of that fellow McRoy, haven't you? Madison and I have talked about it, you know."

"Very nearly," said Rosita, smiling, "but I am still nervous sometimes. I shall never forget that awful time when he came so near to killing us."

"He's the most cold-hearted villain in the world," said Berkly. "The citizens all along the border ought to turn out and hunt him down like a wolf."

"He has committed awful crimes," said Rosita, "but—I—don't—know. I think there is a spot of good somewhere in everybody. He was not always bad—that I know."

Rosita turned into the hallway between the rooms. Santa Claus, in muffling whiskers and furs, was just coming through.

"I heard what you said through the window, Mrs. Lane," he said. "I was just going down in my pocket for a Christmas present for your husband. But I've left one for you, instead. It's in the room to your right."

"Oh, thank you, kind Santa Claus," said Rosita, brightly.

Rosita went into the room, while Santa Claus stepped into the cooler air of the yard.

She found no one in the room but Madison.

"Where is my present that Santa said he left for me in here?" she asked.

"Haven't seen anything in the way of a present," said her husband, laughing, "unless he could have meant me."

The next day Gabriel Radd, the foreman of the XO Ranch, dropped into the post-office at Loma Alta.

"Well, the Frio Kid's got his dose of lead at last," he remarked to the postmaster.

"That so? How'd it happen?"

"One of old Sanchez's Mexican sheep herders did it!—think of it! the Frio Kid killed by a sheep herder! The Greaser saw him riding along past his camp about twelve o'clock last night, and was so skeered that he up with a Winchester and let him have it. Funniest part of it was that the Kid was dressed all up with white Angora-skin whiskers and a regular Santy Claus rig-out from head to foot. Think of the Frio Kid playing Santy!"

A LITTLE LOCAL COLOR

I mentioned to Rivington that I was in search of characteristic New York scenes and incidents—something typical, I told him, without necessarily having to spell the first syllable with an "i."

"Oh, for your writing business," said Rivington; "you couldn't have applied to a better shop. What I don't know about little old New York wouldn't make a sonnet to a sunbonnet. I'll put you right in the middle of so much local color that you won't know whether you are a magazine cover or in the erysipelas ward. When do you want to begin?"

Rivington is a young-man-about-town and a New Yorker by birth, preference, and incommutability.

I told him that I would be glad to accept his escort and guardianship so that I might take notes of Manhattan's grand, gloomy, and peculiar idiosyncrasies, and that the time of so doing would be at his own convenience.

"We'll begin this very evening," said Rivington, himself interested, like a good fellow. "Dine with me at seven, and then I'll steer you up against metropolitan phases so thick you'll have to have a kinetoscope to record 'em."

So I dined with Rivington pleasantly at his club, in Forty-eleventh Street, and then we set forth in pursuit of the elusive tincture of affairs.

As we came out of the club there stood two men on the sidewalk near the steps in earnest conversation.

"And by what process of ratiocination," said one of them, "do you arrive at the conclusion that the division of society into producing and non-possessing classes predicates failure when compared with competitive systems that are monopolizing in tendency and result inimically to industrial evolution?"

"Oh, come off your perch!" said the other man, who wore glasses. "Your premises won't come out in the wash. You wind-jammers who apply bandy-legged theories to concrete categorical syllogisms and logical conclusions skally-bootin' into the infinitesimal ragbag. You can't pull my leg with an old sophism with whiskers on it. You quote Marx and Hyndman and Kautsky—what are they?—shines! Tolstoi?—his garret is full of rats. I put it to you over the home-plate that the idea of a coöperative commonwealth and an abolishment of competitive systems simply takes the rag off the bush and gives me hyperesthesia of the roopteetoop! The skookum house for yours!"

I stopped a few yards away and took out my little notebook.

"Oh, come ahead," said Rivington, somewhat nervously; "you don't want to listen to that."

"Why, man," I whispered, "this is just what I do want to hear. These slang types are among your city's most distinguishing features. Is this the Bowery variety? I really must hear more of it."

"If I follow you," said the man who had spoken first, "you do not believe it possible to reorganize society on the basis of common interest?"

"Shinny on your own side!" said the man with glasses. "You never heard any such music from my foghorn. What I said was that I did not believe it practicable just now. The guys with wards are not in the frame of mind to slack upon the mazuma, and the man with the portable tin banqueting canister isn't exactly ready to join the Bible class. You can bet your variegated socks that the situation is all spiflicated up from the Battery to breakfast! What the country needs is for some bully old bloke like Cobden or some wise guy like old Ben Franklin to sashay up to the front and biff the nigger's head with the baseball. Do you catch my smoke? What?"

Rivington pulled me by the arm impatiently.

"Please come on," he said. "Let's go see something. This isn't what you want."

"Indeed, it is," I said resisting. "This tough talk is the very stuff that counts. There is a picturesqueness about the speech of the lower order of people that is quite unique. Did you say that this is the Bowery variety of slang?"

"Oh, well," said Rivington, giving it up, "I'll tell you straight. That's one of our college professors talking. He ran down for a day or two at the club. It's a sort of fad with him lately to use slang in his conversation. He thinks it improves language. The man he is talking to is one of New York's famous social economists. Now will you come on? You can't use that, you know."

"No," I agreed; "I can't use that. Would you call that typical of New York?"

"Of course not," said Rivington, with a sigh of relief. "I'm glad you see the difference. But if you want to hear the real old tough Bowery slang I'll take you down where you'll get your fill of it."

"I would like it," I said; "that is, if it's the real thing. I've often read it in books, but I never heard it. Do you think it will be dangerous to go unprotected among those characters?"

"Oh, no," said Rivington; "not at this time of night. To tell the truth, I haven't been along the Bowery in a long time, but I know it as well as I do Broadway. We'll look up some of the typical Bowery boys and get them to talk. It'll be worth your while. They talk a peculiar dialect that you won't hear anywhere else on earth."

Rivington and I went east in a Forty-second Street car and then south on the Third Avenue line.

At Houston Street we got off and walked.

"We are now on the famous Bowery," said Rivington; "the Bowery celebrated in song and story."

We passed block after block of "gents" furnishing stores—the windows full of shirts with prices attached and cuffs inside. In other windows were neckties and no shirts. People walked up and down the sidewalks.

"In some ways," said I, "this reminds me of Kokomono, Ind., during the peach-crating season."

Rivington was nettled.

"Step into one of these saloons or vaudeville shows," said he, "with a large roll of money, and see how quickly the Bowery will sustain its reputation."

"You make impossible conditions," said I, coldly.

By and by Rivington stopped and said we were in the heart of the Bowery. There was a policeman on the corner whom Rivington knew.

"Hallo, Donahue!" said my guide. "How goes it? My friend and I are down this way looking up a bit of local color. He's anxious to meet one of the Bowery types. Can't you put us on to something genuine in that line—something that's got the color, you know?"

Policeman Donahue turned himself about ponderously, his florid face full of good-nature. He pointed with his club down the street.

"Sure!" he said, huskily. "Here comes a lad now that was born on the Bowery and knows every inch of it. If he's ever been above Bleecker Street he's kept it to himself."

A man about twenty-eight or twenty-nine, with a smooth face, was sauntering toward us with his hands in his coat pockets. Policeman Donahue stopped him with a courteous wave of his club.

"Evening, Kerry," he said. "Here's a couple of gents, friends of mine, that want to hear you spiel something about the Bowery. Can you reel 'em off a few yards?"

"Certainly, Donahue," said the young man, pleasantly. "Good evening, gentlemen," he said to us, with a pleasant smile. Donahue walked off on his beat.

"This is the goods," whispered Rivington, nudging me with his elbow. "Look at his jaw!

"Say, cull," said Rivington, pushing back his hat, "wot's doin'? Me and my friend's taking a look down de old line—see? De copper tipped us off dat you was wise to de Bowery. Is dat right?"

I could not help admiring Rivington's power of adapting himself to his surroundings.

"Donahue was right," said the young man, frankly; "I was brought up on the Bowery. I have been newsboy, teamster, pugilist, member of an organized band of 'toughs,' bartender, and a 'sport' in various meanings of the word. The experience certainly warrants the supposition that I have at least a passing acquaintance with a few phases of Bowery life. I will be pleased to place whatever knowledge and experience I have at the service of my friend Donahue's friends."

Rivington seemed ill at ease.

"I say," he said—somewhat entreatingly, "I thought—you're not stringing us, are you? It isn't just the kind of talk we expected. You haven't even said 'Hully gee!' once. Do you really belong on the Bowery?"

"I am afraid," said the Bowery boy, smilingly, "that at some time you have been enticed into one of the dives of literature and had the counterfeit coin of the Bowery passed upon you. The 'argot' to which you doubtless refer was the invention of certain of your literary 'discoverers' who invaded the unknown wilds below Third Avenue and put strange sounds into the mouths of the inhabitants. Safe in their homes far to the north and west, the credulous readers who were beguiled by this new 'dialect' perused and believed. Like Marco Polo and Mungo Park—pioneers indeed, but ambitious souls who could not draw the line of demarcation between discovery and invention—the literary bones of these explorers are dotting the trackless wastes of the subway. While it is true that after the publication of the mythical language attributed to the dwellers along the Bowery certain of its pat phrases and apt metaphors were adopted and, to a limited extent, used in this locality, it was because our people are prompt in assimilating whatever is to their commercial advantage. To the tourists who visited our newly discovered clime, and who expressed a realization of their literary guide books, they supplied the demands of the market.

"But perhaps I am wandering from the question. In what way can I assist you, gentlemen? I beg you will believe that the hospitality of the streets is extended to all. There are, I regret to say, many catch-penny places of entertainment, but I cannot conceive that they would entice you."

I felt Rivington lean somewhat heavily against me.

"Say!" he remarked, with uncertain utterance; "come and have a drink with us."

"Thank you, but I never drink. I find that alcohol, even in the smallest quantities, alters the perspective. And I must preserve my perspective, for I am studying the Bowery. I have lived in it nearly thirty years, and I am just beginning to understand its heartbeats. It is like a great river fed by a hundred alien streams. Each influx brings strange seeds on its flood, strange silt and weeds, and now and then a flower of rare promise. To construe this river requires a man who can build dykes against the overflow, who is a naturalist, a geologist, a humanitarian, a diver, and a strong swimmer. I love my Bowery. It was my cradle and is my inspiration. I have published one book. The critics have been kind. I put my heart in it. I am writing another, into which I hope to put both heart and brain. Consider me your guide, gentlemen. Is there anything I can take you to see, any place to which I can conduct you?"

I was afraid to look at Rivington except with one eye.

"Thanks," said Rivington. "We were looking up . . . that is . . . my friend . . . confound it; it's against all precedent, you know . . . awfully obliged . . . just the same."

"In case," said our friend, "you would like to meet some of our Bowery young men I would be pleased to have you visit the quarters of our East Side Kappa Delta Phi Society, only two blocks east of here."

"Awfully sorry," said Rivington, "but my friend's got me on the jump to-night. He's a terror when he's out after local color. Now, there's nothing I would like better than to drop in at the Kappa Delta Phi, but—some other time!"

We said our farewells and boarded a home-bound car. We had a rabbit on upper Broadway, and then I parted with Rivington on a street corner.

"Well, anyhow," said he, braced and recovered, "it couldn't have happened anywhere but in little old New York."

Which, to say the least, was typical of Rivington.

GEORGIA'S RULING

If you should chance to visit the General Land Office, step into the draughtsmen's room and ask to be shown the map of Salado County. A leisurely German—possibly old Kampfer himself—will bring it to you.

It will be four feet square, on heavy drawing-cloth. The lettering and the figures will be beautifully clear and distinct. The title will be in splendid, undecipherable German text, ornamented with classic Teutonic designs— very likely Ceres or Pomona leaning against the initial letters with cornucopias venting grapes and weiners. You must tell him that this is not the map you wish to see; that he will kindly bring you its official predecessor. He will then say, "Ach, so!" and bring out a map half the size of the first, dim, old, tattered, and faded.

By looking carefully near its northwest corner you will presently come upon the worn contours of Chiquito River, and, maybe, if your eyes are good, discern the silent witness to this story.

The Commissioner of the Land Office was of the old style; his antique courtesy was too formal for his day. He dressed in fine black, and there was a suggestion of Roman drapery in his long coat-skirts. His collars were "undetached" (blame haberdashery for the word); his tie was a narrow, funereal strip, tied in the same knot as were his shoe-strings. His gray hair was a trifle too long behind, but he kept it smooth and orderly. His face was clean-shaven, like the old statesmen's. Most people thought it a stern face, but when its official expression was off, a few had seen altogether a different countenance. Especially tender and gentle it had appeared to those who were about him during the last illness of his only child.

The Commissioner had been a widower for years, and his life, outside his official duties, had been so devoted to little Georgia that people spoke of it as a touching and admirable thing. He was a reserved man, and dignified almost to austerity, but the child had come below it all and rested upon his very heart, so that she scarcely missed the mother's love that had been taken away. There was a wonderful companionship between them, for she had many of his own ways, being thoughtful and serious beyond her years.

One day, while she was lying with the fever burning brightly in her cheeks, she said suddenly:

"Papa, I wish I could do something good for a whole lot of children!"

"What would you like to do, dear?" asked the Commissioner. "Give them a party?"

"Oh, I don't mean those kind. I mean poor children who haven't homes, and aren't loved and cared for as I am. I tell you what, Papa!"

"What, my own child?"

"If I shouldn't get well, I'll leave them you—not *give* you, but just lend you, for you must come to mamma and me when you die too. If you can find time, wouldn't you do something to help them, if I ask you, Papa?"

"Hush, hush dear, dear child," said the Commissioner, holding her hot little hand against his cheek; "you'll get well real soon, and you and I will see what we can do for them together."

But in whatsoever paths of benevolence, thus vaguely premeditated, the Commissioner might tread, he was not to have the company of his beloved. That night the little frail body grew suddenly too tired to struggle further, and Georgia's exit was made from the great stage when she had scarcely begun to speak her little piece before the footlights. But there must be a stage manager who understands. She had given the cue to the one who was to speak after her.

A week after she was laid away, the Commissioner reappeared at the office, a little more courteous, a little paler and sterner, with the black frock-coat hanging a little more loosely from his tall figure.

His desk was piled with work that had accumulated during the four heart-breaking weeks of his absence. His chief clerk had done what he could, but there were questions of law, of fine judicial decisions to be made concerning the issue of patents, the marketing and leasing of school lands, the classification into grazing, agricultural, watered, and timbered, of new tracts to be opened to settlers.

The Commissioner went to work silently and obstinately, putting back his grief as far as possible, forcing his mind to attack the complicated and important business of his office. On the second day after his return he called the porter, pointed to a leather-covered chair that stood near his own, and ordered it removed to a lumber-room at the top of the building. In that chair Georgia would always sit when she came to the office for him of afternoons.

As time passed, the Commissioner seemed to grow more silent, solitary, and reserved. A new phase of mind developed in him. He could not endure the presence of a child. Often when a clattering youngster belonging to one of the clerks would come chattering into the big business-room adjoining his little apartment, the Commissioner would steal softly and close the door. He would always cross the street to avoid meeting the school-children when they came dancing along in happy groups upon the side-walk, and his firm mouth would close into a mere line.

It was nearly three months after the rains had washed the last dead flower-petals from the mound above little Georgia when the "land-shark" firm of Hamlin and Avery filed papers upon what they considered the "fattest" vacancy of the year.

It should not be supposed that all who were termed "land-sharks" deserved the name. Many of them were reputable men of good business character. Some of them could walk into the most august councils of the state and say: "Gentlemen, we would like to have this, and that, and matters go thus." But, next to a three years' drought and the boll-worm, the Actual Settler hated the land-shark. The land-shark haunted the Land Office, where all the land records were kept, and hunted "vacancies"

—that is, tracts of unappropriated public domain, generally invisible upon the official maps, but actually existing "upon the ground." The law entitled any one possessing certain State scrip to file by virtue of same upon any land not previously legally appropriated. Most of the scrip was now in the hands of the land-sharks. Thus, at the cost of a few hundred dollars, they often secured lands worth as many thousands. Naturally, the search for "vacancies" was lively.

But often—very often—the land they thus secured, though legally "unappropriated," would be occupied by happy and contented settlers, who had labored for years to build up their homes, only to discover that their titles were worthless, and to receive peremptory notice to quit. Thus came about the bitter and not unjustifiable hatred felt by the toiling settlers toward the shrewd and seldom merciful speculators who so often turned them forth destitute and homeless from their fruitless labors. The history of the state teems with their antagonism. Mr. Land-shark seldom showed his face on "locations" from which he should have to eject the unfortunate victims of a monstrously tangled land system, but let his emissaries do the work. There was lead in every cabin, moulded into balls for him; many of his brothers had enriched the grass with their blood. The fault of it all lay far back.

When the state was young, she felt the need of attracting newcomers, and of rewarding those pioneers already within her borders. Year after years she issued land scrip—Headrights, Bounties, Veteran Donations, Confederates; and to railroads, irrigation companies, colonies, and tillers of the soil galore. All required of the grantee was that he or it should have the scrip properly surveyed upon the public domain by the county or district surveyor, and the land thus appropriated became the property of him or it, or his or its heirs and assigns, forever.

In those days—and here is where the trouble began—the state's domain was practically inexhaustible, and the old surveyors, with princely—yes, even Western American—liberality, gave good measure and overflowing. Often the jovial man of metes and bounds would dispense altogether with the tripod and chain. Mounted on a pony that could cover something near a "vara" at a step, with a pocket compass to direct his course, he would trot out a survey by counting the beat of his pony's hoofs, mark his corners, and write out his field notes with the complacency produced by an act of duty well performed. Sometimes—and who could blame the surveyor?—when the pony was "feeling his oats," he might step a little higher and farther, and in that case the beneficiary of the scrip might get a thousand or two more acres in his survey than the scrip called for. But look at the boundless leagues the state had to spare! However, no one ever had to complain of the pony under-stepping. Nearly every old survey in the state contained an excess of land.

In later years, when the state became more populous, and land values

increased, this careless work entailed incalculable trouble, endless litigation, a period of riotous land-grabbing, and no little bloodshed. The
land-sharks voraciously attack these excesses in the old surveys, and filed
upon such portions with new scrip as unappropriated public domain.
Wherever the identifications of the old tracts were vague, and the corners
were not to be clearly established, the Land Office would recognize the
newer locations as valid, and issue title to the locators. Here was the
greatest hardship to be found. These old surveys, taken from the pick
of the land, were already nearly all occupied by unsuspecting and peaceful settlers, and thus their titles were demolished, and the choice was
placed before them either to buy their land over at a double price or to
vacate it, with their families and personal belongings, immediately. Land
locators sprang up by hundreds. The country was held up and searched
for "vacancies" at the point of a compass. Hundreds of thousands of
dollars' worth of splendid acres were wrested from their innocent purchasers and holders. There began a vast hegira of evicted settlers in tattered wagons; going nowhere cursing injustice, stunned, purposeless,
homeless, hopeless. Their children began to look up to them for bread,
and cry.

It was in consequence of these conditions that Hamlin and Avery had
filed upon a strip of land about a mile wide and three miles long, comprising about two thousand acres, it being the excess over complement
of the Elias Denny three-league survey on Chiquito River, in one of the
middle-western counties. This two-thousand-acre body of land was
asserted by them to be vacant land, and improperly considered a part of
the Denny survey. They based this assertion and their claim upon the
land upon the demonstrated facts that the beginning corner of the Denny
survey was plainly identified; that its field notes called to run west 5,760
varas, and then called for Chiquito River; thence it ran south, with the
meanders—and so on—and that the Chiquito River was, on the ground,
fully a mile farther west from the point reached by course and distance.
To sum up: there were two thousand acres of vacant land between the
Denny survey proper and Chiquito River.

One sweltering day in July the Commissioner called for the papers in
connection with this new location. They were brought, and heaped, a
foot deep, upon his desk—field notes, statements, sketches, affidavits, connecting lines—documents of every description that shrewdness and money
could call to the aid of Hamlin and Avery.

The firm was pressing the Commissioner to issue a patent upon their
location. They possessed inside information concerning a new railroad
that would probably pass somewhere near this land.

The General Land Office was very still while the Commissioner was
delving into the heart of the mass of evidence. The pigeons could be

heard on the roof of the old, castle-like building, cooing and fretting. The clerks were droning everywhere, scarcely pretending to earn their salaries. Each little sound echoed hollow and loud from the bare, stone-flagged floors, the plastered walls, and the iron-joisted ceiling. The impalpable, perpetual limestone dust that never settled whitened a long streamer of sunlight that pierced the tattered window-awning.

It seemed that Hamlin and Avery had built well. The Denny survey was carelessly made, even for a careless period. Its beginning corner was identical with that of a well-defined old Spanish grant, but its other calls were sinfully vague. The field notes contained no other object that survived—no tree, no natural object save Chiquito River, and it was a mile wrong there. According to precedent, the Office would be justified in giving in its complement by course and distance, and considering the remainder vacant instead of a mere excess.

The Actual Settler was besieging the office with wild protests *in re*. Having the nose of a pointer and the eye of a hawk for the land-shark, he had observed his myrmidons running the lines upon his ground. Making inquiries, he learned that the spoiler had attacked his home, and he left the plow in the furrow and took his pen in hand.

One of the protests the Commissioner read twice. It was from a woman, a widow, the granddaughter of Elias Denny himself. She told how her grandfather had sold most of the survey years before at a trivial price—land that was now a principality in extent and value. Her mother had also sold a part, and she herself had succeeded to this western portion, along Chiquito River. Much of it she had been forced to part with in order to live, and now she owned only about three hundred acres, on which she had her home. Her letter wound up rather pathetically:

"I've got eight children, the oldest fifteen years. I work all day and half the night to till what little land I can and keep us in clothes and books. I teach my children too. My neighbors is all poor and has big families. The drought kills the crops every two or three years and then we has hard times to get enough to eat. There is ten families on this land what the land-sharks is trying to rob us of, and all of them got titles from me. I sold to them cheap, and they ain't paid out yet, but part of them is, and if their land should be took from them I would die. My grandfather was an honest man, and he helped to build up this state, and he taught his children to be honest, and how could I make it up to them who bought from me? Mr. Commissioner, if you let them land-sharks take the roof from over my children and the little from them as they has to live on, whoever again calls this state great or its government just will have a lie in their mouths."

The Commissioner laid this letter aside with a sigh. Many, many such letters he had received. He had never been hurt by them, nor had he ever felt that they appealed to him personally. He was but the state's servant, and must follow its laws. And yet, somehow, this reflection did not always eliminate a certain responsible feeling that hung upon him. Of all the state's officers he was supremest in his department, not even excepting the Governor. Broad, general land laws he followed, it was true, but he had a wide latitude in particular ramifications. Rather than law, what he followed was Rulings: Office Rulings and precedents. In the complicated and new questions that were being engendered by the state's development the Commissioner's ruling was rarely appealed from. Even the courts sustained it when its equity was apparent.

The Commissioner stepped to the door and spoke to a clerk in the other room—spoke as he always did, as if he were addressing a prince of the blood:

"Mr. Weldon, will you be kind enough to ask Mr. Ashe, the state school-land appraiser, to please come to my office as soon as convenient?"

Ashe came quickly from the big table where he was arranging his reports.

"Mr. Ashe," said the Commissioner, "you worked along the Chiquito River, in Salado County, during your last trip, I believe. Do you remember anything of the Elias Denny three-league survey?"

"Yes, sir, I do," the blunt, breezy surveyor answered. "I crossed it on my way back to Block H, on the north side of it. The road runs with the Chiquito River, along the valley. The Denny survey fronts three miles on the Chiquito."

"It is claimed," continued the Commissioner, "that it fails to reach the river by as much as a mile."

The appraiser shrugged his shoulder. He was by birth and instinct an Actual Settler, and the natural foe of the land-shark.

"It has always been considered to extend to the river," he said, dryly.

"But that is not the point I desired to discuss," said the Commissioner. "What kind of country is this valley portion of (let us say, then) the Denny tract?"

The spirit of the Actual Settler beamed in Ashe's face.

"Beautiful," he said, with enthusiasm. "Valley as level as this floor, with just a little swell on, like the sea, and rich as cream. Just enough brakes to shelter the cattle in winter. Black loamy soil for six feet, and then clay. Holds water. A dozen nice little houses on it, with windmills and gardens. People pretty poor, I guess—too far from market—but comfortable. Never saw so many kids in my life."

"They raise flocks?" inquired the Commissioner.

"Ho, ho! I mean two-legged kids," laughed the surveyor; "two-legged, and bare-legged, and tow-headed."

"Children! oh, children!" mused the Commissioner, as though a new view had opened to him; "they raise children!"

"It's a lonesome country, Commissioner," said the surveyor. "Can you blame 'em?"

"I suppose," continued the Commissioner, slowly, as one carefully pursues deductions from a new, stupendous theory, "not all of them are tow-headed. It would not be unreasonable, Mr. Ashe, I conjecture, to believe that a portion of them have brown, or even black, hair."

"Brown and black sure," said Ashe; "also red."

"No doubt," said the commissioner. "Well, I thank you for your courtesy in informing me, Mr. Ashe. I will not detain you any longer from your duties."

Later, in the afternoon, came Hamlin and Avery, big, handsome, genial, sauntering men, clothed in white duck and low-cut shoes. They permeated the whole office with an aura of debonair prosperity. They passed among the clerks and left a wake of abbreviated given names and fat brown cigars.

These were the aristocracy of the land-sharks, who went in for big things. Full of serene confidence in themselves, there was no corporation, no syndicate, no railroad company or attorney general too big for them to tackle. The peculiar smoke of their rare, fat brown cigars was to be perceived in the sanctum of every department of state, in every committee-room of the Legislature, in every bank parlor and every private caucus-room in the state capital. Always pleasant, never in a hurry, seeming to possess unlimited leisure, people wondered when they gave their attention to the many audacious enterprises in which they were known to be engaged.

By and by the two dropped carelessly into the Commissioner's room and reclined lazily in the big, leather-upholstered arm-chairs. They drawled a good-natured complaint of the weather, and Hamlin told the Commissioner an excellent story he had amassed that morning from the Secretary of State.

But the Commissioner knew why they were there. He had half promised to render a decision that day upon their location.

The chief clerk now brought in a batch of duplicate certificates for the Commissioner to sign. As he traced his sprawling signature, "Hollis Summerfield, Comr. Genl. Land Office," on each one, the chief clerk stood, deftly removing them and applying the blotter.

"I notice," said the chief clerk, "you've been going through that Salado County location. Kampfer is making a new map of Salado, and I believe is platting in that section of the county now."

"I will see it," said the Commissioner. A few moments later he went to the draughtsmen's room.

As he entered he saw five or six of the draughtsmen grouped about Kampfer's desk, gargling away at each other in pectoral German, and gazing at something thereupon. At the Commissioner's approach they scattered to their several places. Kampfer, a wizened little German, with long, frizzled ringlets and a watery eye, began to stammer forth some sort of an apology, the Commissioner thought, for the congregation of his fellows about his desk.

"Never mind," said the Commissioner, "I wish to see the map you are making"; and, passing around the old German, seated himself upon the high draughtsman's stool. Kampfer continued to break English in trying to explain.

"Herr Gommissioner, I assure you blenty sat I haf not it bremeditated—sat it wass—sat it itself make. Look you! from se field notes wass it blatted—blease to observe se calls: South, 10 degrees west 1,050 varas; south, 10 degrees each 300 varas; south, 100; south, 9 west, 200; south, 40 degrees west, 400—and so on. Herr Gommissioner, nefer would I have——"

The Commissioner raised one white hand, silently. Kampfer dropped his pipe and fled.

With a hand at each side of his face, and his elbows resting upon the desk, the Commissioner sat staring at the map which was spread and fastened there—staring at the sweet and living profile of little Georgia drawn thereupon—at her face, pensive, delicate, and infantile, outlined in a perfect likeness.

When his mind at length came to inquire into the reason of it, he saw that it must have been, as Kampfer had said, unpremeditated. The old draughtsman had been platting in the Elias Denny survey, and Georgia's likeness, striking though it was, was formed by nothing more than the meanders of Chiquito River. Indeed, Kampfer's blotter, whereon his preliminary work was done, showed the laborious tracings of the calls and the countless pricks of the compasses. Then, over his faint penciling, Kampfer had drawn in India ink with a full, firm pen the similitude of Chiquito River, and forth had blossomed mysteriously the dainty, pathetic profile of the child.

The Commissioner sat for half an hour with his face in his hands, gazing downward, and none dared approach him. Then he arose and walked out. In the business office he paused long enough to ask that the Denny file be brought to his desk.

He found Hamlin and Avery still reclining in their chairs, apparently oblivious of business. They were lazily discussing summer opera, it being their habit—perhaps their pride also—to appear supernaturally indifferent whenever they stood with large interests imperilled. And they stood to win more on this stake than most people knew. They possessed inside information to the effect that a new railroad would, within a year, split this very Chiquito River valley and send land values ballooning all along its route. A dollar under thirty thousand profit on this location, if it should hold good, would be a loss to their expectations. So, while they chatted lightly and waited for the Commissioner to open the subject, there was a quick, side-long sparkle in their eyes, evincing a desire to read their title clear to those fair acres on the Chiquito.

A clerk brought in the file. The Commissioner seated himself and wrote upon it in red ink. Then he rose to his feet and stood for a while looking straight out of the window. The Land Office capped the summit of a bold hill. The eyes of the Commissioner passed over the roofs of many houses set in a packing of deep green, the whole checkered by strips of blinding white streets. The horizon, where his gaze was focussed, swelled to a fair wooded eminence flecked with faint dots of shining white. There was a cemetery, where lay many who were forgotten, and a few who had not lived in vain. And one lay there occupying very small space, whose childish heart had been large enough to desire, while near its last beats, good to others. The Commissioner's lips moved slightly as he whispered to himself: "It was her last will and testament, and I have neglected it so long!"

The big brown cigars of Hamlin and Avery were fireless, but they still gripped them between their teeth and waited, while they marvelled at the absent expression upon the Commissioner's face.

By and by he spoke suddenly and promptly.

"Gentlemen, I have just endorsed the Elias Denny survey for patenting. This office will not regard your location upon a part of it as legal." He paused a moment, and then, extending his hand as those dear old-time ones used to do in debate, he enunciated the spirit of that Ruling that subsequently drove the land-sharks to the wall, and placed the seal of peace and security over the doors of ten thousand homes.

"And, furthermore," he continued, with a clear, soft light upon his face, "it may interest you to know that from this time on this office will consider that when a survey of land made by virtue of a certificate granted by this state to the men who wrested it from the wilderness and the savage—made in good faith, settled in good faith, and left in good faith to their children or innocent purchasers—when such a survey, although overrunning its complement, shall call for any natural object visible to the eye of man, to that object it shall hold and be good and valid. And the children of this state shall lie down to sleep at night, and rumors of disturbers of title shall not disquiet them. For," concluded the Commissioner, "of such is the Kingdom of Heaven."

In the silence that followed, a laugh floated up from the patent-room below. The man who carried down the Denny file was exhibiting it among the clerks.

"Look here," he said, delightedly, "the old man has forgotten his name. He's written 'Patent to original grantee,' and signed it 'Georgia Summerfield, Comr.'"

The speech of the Commissioner rebounded lightly from the impregnable Hamlin and Avery. They smiled, rose gracefully, spoke of the baseball team, and argued feelingly that quite a perceptible breeze had arisen from the east. They lit fresh fat brown cigars, and drifted courteously away. But later they made another tiger-spring for their quarry in the courts. But the courts, according to reports in the papers, "coolly roasted them" (a remarkable performance, suggestive of liquid-air didoes), and sustained the Commissioner's Ruling.

And this Ruling itself grew to be a Precedent, and the Actual Settler framed it, and taught his children to spell from it, and there was sound sleep o' nights from the pines to the sage-brush, and from the chaparral to the great brown river of the north.

But I think, and I am sure the Commissioner never thought otherwise, that whether Kampfer was a snuffy old instrument of destiny, or whether the meanders of the Chiquito accidently platted themselves into that memorable sweet profile or not, there was brought about "something good for a whole lot of children," and the result ought to be called "Georgia's Ruling."

BLIND MAN'S HOLIDAY

Alas for the man and for the artist with the shifting point of perspective! Life shall be a confusion of ways to the one; the landscape shall rise up and confound the other. Take the case of Lorison. At one time he appeared to himself to be the feeblest of fools; at another he conceived that he followed ideals so fine that the world was not yet ready to accept them. During one mood he cursed his folly; possessed by the other, he bore himself with a serene grandeur akin to greatness: in neither did he attain the perspective.

Generations before, the name had been "Larsen." His race had bequeathed him its fine-strung, melancholy temperament, its saving balance of thrift and industry.

From his point of perspective he saw himself an outcast from society, forever to be a shady skulker along the ragged edge of respectability; a denizen *des trois-quarts de monde,* that pathetic spheroid lying between the *haut* and the *demi,* whose inhabitants envy each of their neighbors, and are scorned by both. He was self-condemned to this opinion, as he was self-exiled, through it, to this quaint Southern city a thousand miles from his former home. Here he had dwelt for longer than a year, knowing but few, keeping in a subjective world of shadows which was invaded at times by the perplexing bulks of jarring realities. Then he fell in love with a girl whom he met in a cheap restaurant, and his story begins.

The Rue Chartres, in New Orleans, is a street of ghosts. It lies in the quarter where the Frenchman, in his prime, set up his translated pride and glory; where, also, the arrogant don had swaggered, and dreamed of gold and grants and ladies' gloves. Every flagstone has its grooves worn by footsteps going royally to the wooing and the fighting. Every house has a princely heartbreak; each doorway its untold tale of gallant promise and slow decay.

By night the Rue Chartres is now but a murky fissure, from which the groping wayfarer sees, flung against the sky, the tangled filigree of Moorish iron balconies. The old houses of monsieur stand yet, indomitable against the century, but their essence is gone. The street is one of ghosts to whosoever can see them.

A faint heartbeat of the street's ancient glory still survives in a corner occupied by the Café Carabine d'Or. Once men gathered there to plot against kings, and to warn presidents. They do so yet, but they are not the same kind of men. A brass button will scatter these; those would have set their faces against an army. Above the door hangs the sign board, upon which has been depicted a vast animal of unfamiliar species. In the act of firing upon this monster is represented an unobtrusive human leveling an obtrusive gun, once the color of bright gold. Now the legend above the picture is faded beyond conjecture; the gun's relation to the title is a matter of faith; the menaced animal, wearied of the long aim of the hunter, has resolved itself into a shapeless blot.

The place is known as "Antonio's," as the name, white upon the red-lit transparency, and gilt upon the windows, attests. There is a promise in "Antonio"; a justifiable expectancy of savory things in oil and pepper and wine, and perhaps an angel's whisper of garlic. But the rest of the name is "O'Riley." Antonio O'Riley!

The Carabine d'Or is an ignominious ghost of the Rue Chartres. The Café where Bienville and Conti dined, where a prince has broken bread, is become a "family ristaurant."

Its customers are working men and women, almost to a unit. Occasonally you will see chorus girls from the cheaper theatres, and men who follow avocations subject to quick vicissitudes; but at Antonio's—name rich in Bohemian promise, but tame in fulfillment—manners debonair and gay are toned down to the "family" standard. Should you light a cigarette, mine host will touch you on the "arrum" and remind you that the proprieties are menaced. "Antonio" entices and beguiles from fiery legend without, but "O'Riley" teaches decorum within.

It was at this restaurant that Lorison first saw the girl. A flashy fellow with a predatory eye had followed her in, and had advanced to take the other chair at the little table where she stopped, but Lorison slipped into the seat before him. Their acquaintance began, and grew, and now for two months they had sat at the same table each evening, not meeting by appointment, but as if by a series of fortuitous and happy accidents. After dining, they would take a walk together in one of the little city parks, or among the panoramic markets where exhibits a continuous vaudeville of sights and sounds. Always at eight o'clock their steps led them to a certain street corner, where she prettily but firmly bade him good-night and left him. "I do not live far from here," she frequently said, "and you must let me go the rest of the way alone."

But now Lorison had discovered that he wanted to go the rest of the way with her, or happiness would depart, leaving him on a very lonely corner of life. And at the same time that he made the discovery, the secret of his banishment from the society of the good laid its finger in his face and told him it must not be.

Man is too thoroughly an egoist not to be also an egotist; if he love, the object shall know it. During a lifetime he may conceal it through stress of expediency and honor, but it shall bubble from his dying lips, though it disrupt a neighborhood. It is known, however, that most men do not wait so long to disclose their passion. In the case of Lorison, his particular ethics positively forbade him to declare his sentiments, but he must needs dally with the subject, and woo by innuendo at least.

On this night, after the usual meal at the Carabine d'Or, he strolled with his companion down the dim old street toward the river.

The Rue Chartres perishes in the old Place d'Armes. The ancient Cabildo, where Spanish justice fell like hail, faces it, and the Cathedral, another provincial ghost, overlooks it. Its centre is a little, iron-railed park of flowers and immaculate gravelled walks, where citizens take the air of evenings. Pedestalled high above it, the General sits his cavorting steed, with his face turned stonily down the river toward English Turn, whence come no more Britons to bombard his cotton bales.

Often the two sat in this square, but to-night Lorison guided her past the stone-stepped gate, and still riverward. As they walked, he smiled to himself to think that all he knew of her—except that he loved her—was her name, Norah Greenway, and that she lived with her brother. They had talked about everything except themselves. Perhaps her reticence had been caused by his.

They came, at length, upon the levee, and sat upon a great, prostrate beam. The air was pungent with the dust of commerce. The great river slipped yellowly past. Across it Algiers lay, a longitudinous black bulk against a vibrant electric haze sprinkled with exact stars.

The girl was young and of the piquant order. A certain bright melancholy pervaded her; she possessed an untarnished, pale prettiness doomed to please. Her voice, when she spoke, dwarfed her theme. It was the voice capable of investing little subjects with a large interest. She sat at ease, bestowing her skirts with the little womanly touch, serene as if the begrimed pier were a summer garden. Lorison poked the rotting boards with his cane.

He began by telling her that he was in love with some one to whom he durst not speak of it. "And why not?" she asked, accepting swiftly his fatuous presentation of a third person of straw. "My place in the world," he answered, "is none to ask a woman to share. I am an outcast from honest people; I am wrongly accused of one crime, and am, I believe, guilty of another."

Thence he plunged into the story of his abdication from society. The story, pruned of his moral philosophy, deserves no more than the slightest touch. It is no new tale, that of the gambler's declension. During one night's sitting he lost, and then had imperilled a certain amount of his employer's money, which, by accident, he carried with him. He continued to lose, to the last wager, and then began to gain, leaving the game winner to a somewhat formidable sum. The same night his employer's safe was robbed. A search was had; the winnings of Lorison were found in his room, their total forming an accusative nearness to the sum purloined. He was taken, tried, and, through incomplete evidence, released, smutched with the sinister *devoirs* of a disagreeing jury.

"It is not in the unjust accusation," he said to the girl, "that my burden lies, but in the knowledge that from the moment I staked the first dollar of the firm's money I was a criminal—no matter whether I lost or won. You see why it is impossible for me to speak of love to her."

"It is a sad thing," said Norah, after a little pause, "to think what very good people there are in the world."

"Good?" said Lorison.

"I was thinking of this superior person whom you say you love. She must be a very poor sort of creature."

"I do not understand."

"Nearly," she continued, "as poor a sort of creature as yourself."

"You do not understand," said Lorison, removing his hat and sweeping back his fine, light hair. "Suppose she loved me in return, and were willing to marry me. Think, if you can, what would follow. Never a day would pass but she would be reminded of her sacrifice. I would read a condescension in her smile, a pity even in her affection, that would madden me. No. The thing would stand between us forever. Only equals should mate. I could never ask her to come down upon my lower plane."

An arc light faintly shone upon Lorison's face. An illumination from within also pervaded it. The girl saw the rapt, ascetic look; it was the face either of Sir Galahad or Sir Fool.

"Quite starlike," she said, "is this unapproachable angel. Really too high to be grasped."

"By me, yes."

She faced him suddenly. "My dear friend, would you prefer your star fallen?"

Lorison made a wide gesture. "You push me to the bald fact," he declared; "you are not in sympathy with my argument. But I will answer you so. If I could reach my particular star, to drag it down, I would not do it; but if it were fallen, I would pick it up, and thank Heaven for the privilege."

They were silent for some minutes. Norah shivered, and thrust her hands deep into the pockets of her jacket. Lorison uttered a remorseful exclamation.

"I'm not cold," she said. "I was just thinking. I ought to tell you something. You have selected a strange confidante. But you cannot expect a chance acquaintance, picked up in a doubtful restaurant, to be an angel."

"Norah," cried Lorison.

"Let me go on. You have told me about yourself. We have been such good friends. I must tell you now what I never wanted you to know. I am—worse than you are. I was on the stage . . . I sang in the chorus . . . I was pretty bad, I guess . . . I stole diamonds from the prima donna . . . they arrested me . . . I gave most of them up, and they let me go . . . I drank wine every night . . . a great deal . . . I was very wicked, but——"

Lorison knelt quickly by her side and took her hands.

"Dear Norah!" he said, exultantly. "It is you, it is you I love! You never guessed it, did you? 'Tis you I meant all the time. Now I can speak. Let me make you forget the past. We have both suffered; let us shut out the world, and live for each other. Norah, do you hear me say I love you?"

"In spite of——"

"Rather say because of it. You have come out of your past noble and good. Your heart is an angel's. Give it to me."

"A little while ago you feared the future too much to even speak."

"But for you; not for myself. Can you love me?"

She cast herself, wildly sobbing, upon his breast.

"Better than life—than truth itself—than everything."

"And my own past," said Lorison, with a note of solicitude—"can you forgive and——"

"I answered you that," she whispered, "when I told you I loved you." She leaned away, and looked thoughtfully at him. "If I had not told you about myself, would you have—would you——"

"No," he interrupted; "I would never have let you know I loved you. I would never have asked you this—Norah, will you be my wife?"

She wept again.

"Oh, believe me; I am good now—I am no longer wicked! I will be the best wife in the world. Don't think I am—bad any more. If you do I shall die, I shall die!"

While he was consoling her, she brightened up eager and impetuous.

"Will you marry me to-night?" she said. "Will you prove it that way? I have a reason for wishing it to be to-night. Will you?"

Of one of two things was this exceeding frankness the outcome; either of importunate brazenness or of utter innocence. The lover's perspective contained only the one.

"The sooner," said Lorison, "the happier I shall be."

"What is there to do?" she asked. "What do you have to get? Come! You should know."

Her energy stirred the dreamer to action.

"A city directory first," he cried, gayly, "to find where the man lives who gives licenses to happiness. We will go together and rout him out. Cabs, cars, policemen, telephones, and ministers shall aid us."

"Father Rogan shall marry us," said the girl, with ardor. "I will take you to him."

An hour later the two stood at the open doorway of an immense, gloomy brick building in a narrow and lonely street. The license was tight in Norah's hand.

"Wait here a moment," she said, "till I find Father Rogan."

She plunged into the black hallway, and the lover was left standing, as it were, on one leg outside. His impatience was not greatly taxed. Gazing curiously into what seemed the hallway to Erebus, he was presently reassured by a stream of light that bisected the darkness, far down the passage. Then he heard her call, and fluttered lampward, like the moth. She beckoned him through a doorway into the room whence emanated the light. The room was bare of nearly everything except books, which had subjugated all its space. Here and there little spots of territory had been reconquered. An elderly, bald man, with a superlatively calm, remote eye, stood by a table with a book in his hand, his finger still marking a page. His dress was sombre and appertained to a religious order. His eyes denoted an acquaintance with the perspective.

"Father Rogan," said Norah, "this is *he*."

"The two of ye," said Father Rogan, "want to get married?"

They did not deny it. He married them. The ceremony was quickly done. One who could have witnessed it, and felt its scope, might have trembled at the terrible inadequacy of it to rise to the dignity of its endless chain of results.

Afterward the priest spake briefly, as if by rote, of certain other civil and legal addenda that either might or should, at a later time, cap the ceremony. Lorison tendered a fee, which was declined, and before the door closed after the departing couple Father Rogan's book popped open again where his finger marked it.

In the dark hall Norah whirled and clung to her companion, tearful.

"Will you never, never be sorry?"

At last she was reassured.

At the first light they reached upon the street, she asked the time, just as she had each night. Lorison looked at his watch. Half-past eight.

Lorison thought it was from habit that she guided their steps toward the corner where they always parted. But, arriving there, she hesitated, and then released his arm. A drug store stood on the corner; its bright, soft light shone upon them.

"Please leave me here as usual to-night," said Norah, sweetly. "I must— I would rather you would. You will not object? At six to-morrow evening I will meet you at Antonio's. I want to sit with you there once more. And then—I will go where you say." She gave him a bewildering, bright smile, and walked swiftly away.

Surely it needed all the strength of her charm to carry off this astounding behaviour. It was no discredit to Lorison's strength of mind that his head began to whirl. Pocketing his hands, he rambled vacuously over to the druggist's windows, and began assiduously to spell over the names of the patent medicines therein displayed.

As soon as he had recovered his wits, he proceeded along the street in an aimless fashion. After drifting for two or three squares, he flowed into a somewhat more pretentious thoroughfare, a way much frequented by him in his solitary ramblings. For here was a row of shops devoted to traffic in goods of the widest range of choice—handiworks of art, skill and fancy, products of nature and labor from every zone.

Here, for a time, he loitered among the conspicuous windows, where was set, emphasized by congested floods of light, the cunningest spoil of the interiors. There were few passers, and of this Lorison was glad. He was not of the world. For a long time he had touched his fellow man only at the gear of a levelled cog-wheel—at right angles, and upon a different axis. He had dropped into a distinctly new orbit. The stroke of ill fortune had acted upon him, in effect, as a blow delivered upon the apex of a certain ingenious toy, the musical top, which, when thus buffeted while spinning, gives forth, with scarcely retarded motion, a complete change of key and chord.

Strolling along the pacific avenue, he experienced a singular, supernatural calm, accompanied by an unusual activity of brain. Reflecting upon recent affairs, he assured himself of his happiness in having won for a bride the one he had so greatly desired, yet he wondered mildly at his dearth of active emotion. Her strange behavior in abandoning him without valid excuse on his bridal eve aroused in him only a vague and curious speculation. Again, he found himself contemplating, with complaisant serenity, the incidents of her somewhat lively career. His perspective seemed to have been queerly shifted.

As he stood before a window near a corner, his ears were assailed by a waxing clamor and commotion. He stood close to the window to allow passage to the cause of the hubbub—a procession of human beings, which rounded the corner and headed in his direction. He perceived a salient hue of blue and a glitter of brass about a central figure of dazzling white and silver, and a ragged wake of black, bobbing figures.

Two ponderous policemen were conducting between them a woman dressed as if for the stage, in a short, white, satiny skirt reaching to the knees, pink stockings, and a sort of sleeveless bodice bright with relucent, armor-like scales. Upon her curly light hair was perched, at a rollicking angle, a shining tin helmet. The costume was to be instantly recognized as one of those amazing conceptions to which competition has harried the inventors of the spectacular ballet. One of the officers bore a long cloak upon his arm, which, doubtless, had been intended to veil the candid attractions of their effulgent prisoner, but, for some reason, it had not been called into use, to the vociferous delight of the tail of the procession.

Compelled by a sudden and vigorous movement of the woman, the parade halted before the window by which Lorison stood. He saw that she was young, and, at the first glance, was deceived by a sophistical prettiness of her face, which waned before a more judicious scrutiny. Her look was bold and reckless, and upon her countenance, where yet the contours of youth survived, were the fingermarks of old age's credentialed courier, Late Hours.

The young woman fixed her unshrinking gaze upon Lorison, and called to him in the voice of the wronged heroine in straits:

"Say! You look like a good fellow; come and put up the bail, won't you? I've done nothing to get pinched for. It's all a mistake. See how they're treating me! You won't be sorry, if you'll help me out of this. Think of your sister or your girl being dragged along the streets this way! I say, come along now, like a good fellow."

It may be that Lorison, in spite of the unconvincing bathos of this appeal, showed a sympathetic face, for one of the officers left the woman's side, and went over to him.

"It's all right, sir," he said, in a husky, confidential tone; "she's the right party. We took her after the first act at the Green Light Theatre, on a wire from the chief of police of Chicago. It's only a square or two to the station. Her rig's pretty bad, but she refused to change clothes— or, rather," added the officer, with a smile, "to put on some. I thought I'd explain matters to you so you wouldn't think she was being imposed upon."

"What is the charge?" asked Lorison.

"Grand larceny. Diamonds. Her husband is a jeweler in Chicago. She cleaned his show case of the sparklers, and skipped with a comic opera troupe."

The policeman, perceiving that the interest of the entire group of

spectators was centred upon himself and Lorison—their conference being regarded as a possible new complication—was fain to prolong the
situation—which reflected his own importance—by a little afterpiece of
philosophical comment.

"A gentleman like you, sir," he went on affably, "would never notice
it, but it comes in my line to observe what an immense amount of trouble
is made by that combination—I mean the stage, diamonds, and lightheaded women who aren't satisfied with good homes. I tell you, sir, a
man these days and nights wants to know what his women folks are
up to."

The policeman smiled a good-night, and returned to the side of his
charge, who had been intently watching Lorison's face during the conversation, no doubt for some indication of his intention to render succor.
Now, at the failure of the sign, and at the movement made to continue
the ignominious progress, she abandoned hope, and addressed him thus,
pointedly:

"You damn chalk-faced quitter! You was thinking of giving me a
hand, but you let the cop talk you out of it the first word. You're a
dandy to tie to. Say, if you ever get a girl, she'll have a picnic. Won't
she work you to the queen's taste! Oh, my!" She concluded with a taunting, shrill laugh that rasped Lorison like a saw. The policemen urged
her forward; the delighted train of gaping followers closed up the rear;
and the captive Amazon, accepting her fate, extended the scope of her
maledictions so that none in hearing might seem to be slighted.

Then there came upon Lorison an overwhelming revulsion of his perspective. It may be that he had been ripe for it, that the abnormal condition of mind in which he had for so long existed was already about to
revert to its balance; however, it is certain that the events of the last few
minutes had furnished the channel, if not the impetus, for the change.

The initial determining influence had been so small a thing as the fact
and manner of his having been approached by the officer. That agent
had, by the style of his accost, restored the loiterer to his former place in
society. In an instant he had been transformed from a somewhat rancid
prowler along the fishy side streets of gentility into an honest gentleman,
with whom even so lordly a guardian of the peace might agreeably exchange the compliments.

This, then, first broke the spell, and set thrilling in him a resurrected
longing for the fellowship of his kind, and the rewards of the virtuous.
To what end, he vehemently asked himself, was this fanciful self-accusa-
tion, this empty renunciation, this moral squeamishness through which
he had been led to abandon what was his heritage in life, and not beyond
his deserts? Technically, he was uncondemned; his sole guilty spot was
in thought rather than deed, and cognizance of it unshared by others.
For what good, moral or sentimental, did he slink, retreating like the

hedgehog from his own shadow, to and fro in this musty Bohemia that lacked even the picturesque?

But the thing that struck home and set him raging was the part played by the Amazonian prisoner. To the counterpart of that astounding belligerent—identical, at least, in the way of experience—to one, by her own confession, thus far fallen, had he, not three hours since, been united in marriage. How desirable and natural it had seemed to him then, and how monstrous it seemed now! How the words of diamond thief number two yet burned in his ears: "If you ever get a girl, she'll have a picnic." What did that mean but that women instinctly knew him for one they could hoodwink? Still again there reverberated the policeman's sapient contribution to his agony: "A man these days and nights wants to know what his women folks are up to." Oh, yes, he had been a fool; he had looked at things from the wrong standpoint.

But the wildest note in all the clamor was struck by pain's forefinger, jealousy. Now, at least, he felt that keenest sting—a mounting love unworthily bestowed. Whatever she might be, he loved her; he bore in his own breast his doom. A grating, comic flavor to his predicament struck him suddenly, and he laughed creakingly as he swung down the echoing pavement. An impetuous desire to act, to battle with his fate, seized him. He stopped upon his heel, and smote his palms together triumphantly. His wife was—where? But there was a tangible link; an outlet more or less navigable, through which his derelict ship of matrimony might yet be safely towed—the priest!

Like all imaginative men with pliable natures, Lorison was, when thoroughly stirred, apt to become tempestuous. With a high and stubborn indignation upon him, he retraced his steps to the intersecting street by which he had come. Down this he hurried to the corner where he had parted with—an astringent grimace tinctured the thought—his wife. Thence still back he harked, following through an unfamiliar district his stimulated recollections of the way they had come from that preposterous wedding. Many times he went abroad, and nosed his way back to the trail, furious.

At last, when he reached the dark, calamitous building in which his madness had culminated, and found the black hallway, he dashed down it, perceiving no light or sound. But he raised his voice, hailing loudly; reckless of everything but that he should find the old mischief-maker with the eyes that looked too far away to see the disaster he had wrought. The door opened, and in the stream of light Father Rogan stood, his book in hand, with his finger marking the place.

"Ah!" cried Lorison. "You are the man I want. I had a wife of you a few hours ago. I would not trouble you, but I neglected to note how it was done. Will you oblige me with the information whether the business is beyond remedy?"

"Come inside," said the priest; "there are other lodgers in the house, who might prefer sleep to even a gratified curiosity."

Lorison entered the room and took the chair offered him. The priest's eyes looked a courteous interrogation.

"I must apologize again," said the young man, "for so soon intruding upon you with my marital infelicities, but as my wife has neglected to furnish me with her address, I am deprived of the legitimate recourse of a family row."

"I am quite a plain man," said Father Rogan, pleasantly; "but I do not see how I am to ask you questions."

"Pardon my indirectness," said Lorison; "I will ask one. In this room to-night you pronounced me to be a husband. You afterwards spoke of additional rites or performances that either should or could be effected. I paid little attention to your words then, but I am hungry to hear them repeated now. As matters stand, am I married past all help?"

"You are as legally and as firmly bound," said the priest, "as though it had been done in a cathedral, in the presence of thousands. The additional observances I referred to are not necessary to the strictest legality of the act, but were advised as a precaution for the future—for convenience of proof in such contingencies as wills, inheritances, and the like."

Lorison laughed harshly.

"Many thanks," he said. "Then there is no mistake, and I am the happy benedict. I suppose I should go stand upon the bridal corner, and when my wife gets through walking the streets she will look me up."

Father Rogan regarded him calmly.

"My son," he said, "when a man and woman come to me to be married I always marry them. I do this for the sake of other people whom they might go away and marry if they did not marry each other. As you see, I do not seek your confidence; but your case seems to me to be one not altogether devoid of interest. Very few marriages that have come to my notice have brought such well-expressed regret within so short a time. I will hazard one question: were you not under the impression that you loved the lady you married, at the time you did so?"

"Loved her!" cried Lorison, wildly. "Never so well as now, though she told me she deceived and sinned and stole. Never more than now, when, perhaps, she is laughing at the fool she cajoled and left, with scarcely a word, to return to God only knows what particular line of her former folly."

Father Rogan answered nothing. During the silence that succeeded, he sat with a quiet expectation beaming in his full, lambent eye.

"If you would listen——" began Lorison. The priest held up his hand.

"As I hoped," he said. "I thought you would trust me. Wait but a moment." He brought a long clay pipe, filled and lighted it.

"Now, my son," he said.

Lorison poured a twelvemonth's accumulated confidence into Father Rogan's ear. He told all; not sparing himself or omitting the facts of his past, the events of the night, or his disturbing conjectures and fears.

"The main point," said the priest, when he had concluded, "seems to me to be this—are you reasonably sure that you love this woman whom you have married?"

"Why," exclaimed Lorison, rising impulsively to his feet—"why should I deny it? But look at me—am I fish, flesh, or fowl? That is the main point to me, I assure you."

"I understand you," said the priest, also rising, and laying down his pipe. "The situation is one that has taxed the endurance of much older men than you—in fact, especially much older men than you. I will try to relieve you from it, and this night. You shall see for yourself into exactly what predicament you have fallen, and how you shall, possibly, be extricated. There is no evidence so credible as that of the eyesight."

Father Rogan moved about the room, and donned a soft black hat. Buttoning his coat to his throat, he laid his hand on the doorknob. "Let us walk," he said.

The two went out upon the street. The priest turned his face down it, and Lorison walked with him through a squalid district, where the houses loomed, awry and desolate-looking, high above them. Presently they turned into a less dismal side street, where the houses were smaller, and, though hinting of the most meagre comfort, lacked the concentrated wretchedness of the more populous byways.

At a segregated, two-story house Father Rogan halted, and mounted the steps with the confidence of a familiar visitor. He ushered Lorison into a narrow hallway, faintly lighted by a cobwebbed hanging lamp. Almost immediately a door to the right opened and a dingy Irishwoman protruded her head.

"Good evening to ye, Mistress Geehan," said the priest, unconsciously, it seemed, falling into a delicately flavored brogue. "And is it yourself can tell me if Norah has gone out again, the night, maybe?"

"Oh, it's yer blissid riverence! Sure and I can tell ye the same. The purty darlin' wint out, as usual, but a bit later. And she says: 'Mother Geehan,' says she, 'it's me last noight out, praise the saints, this noight is!' And oh, yer riverence, the swate, beautiful drame of a dress she had this toime! White satin and silk and ribbons, and lace about the neck and arrums—'twas a sin, yer riverence, the gold was spint upon it."

The priest heard Lorison catch his breath painfully and a faint smile flickered across his own clean-cut mouth.

"Well, then, Mistress Geehan," said he, "I'll just step upstairs and see the bit boy for a minute, and I'll take this gentleman up with me."

"He's awake, thin," said the woman. "I've just come down from sitting wid him the last hour, tilling him fine shtories of ould County Ty-rone. 'Tis a greedy gossoon, it is, yer riverence, for me shtories."

"Small the doubt," said Father Rogan. "There's no rocking would put him to slape the quicker, I'm thinking."

Amid the woman's shrill protest against the retort, the two men ascended the steep stairway. The priest pushed open the door of a room near its top.

"Is that you already, sister?" drawled a sweet, childish voice from the darkness.

"It's only ould Father Denny come to see ye, darlin'; and a foine gin-tleman I've brought to make ye a gr-r-and call. And ye resaves us fast aslape in bed! Shame on yez manners!"

"Oh, Father Denny, is that you? I'm glad. And will you light the lamp, please? It's on the table by the door. And quit talking like Mother Gee-han, Father Denny."

The priest lit the lamp, and Lorison saw a tiny, tousled-haired boy, with a thin, delicate face, sitting up in a small bed in a corner. Quickly, also, his rapid glance considered the room and its contents. It was furnished with more than comfort, and its adornments plainly indicated a woman's discerning taste. An open door beyond revealed the blackness of an adjoining room's interior.

The boy clutched both of Father Rogan's hands. "I'm so glad you came," he said; "but why did you come in the night? Did sister send you?"

"Off wid ye! Am I to be sint about, at me age, as was Terence Mc-Shane of Ballymahone? I come on me own r-r-responsibility."

Lorison had also advanced to the boy's bedside. He was fond of children; and the wee fellow, laying himself down to sleep alone in that dark room, stirred his heart.

"Aren't you afraid, little man?" he asked, stooping down beside him.

"Sometimes," answered the boy, with a shy smile, "when the rats make too much noise. But nearly every night, when sister goes out, Mother Geehan stays a while with me, and tells me funny stories. I'm not often afraid, sir."

"This brave little gentleman," said Father Rogan, "is a scholar of mine. Every day from half-past six to half-past eight—when sister comes for him—he stops in my study, and we find out what's in the inside of books. He knows multiplication, division, and fractions; and he's throubling me to begin wid the chronicles of Ciaran of Clonmacnoise, Corurac Mc-Cullenan and Cuan O'Lochain, the gr-r-reat Irish hishtorians." The boy was evidently accustomed to the priest's Celtic pleasantries. A little, appreciative grin was all the attention the insinuation of pedantry received.

Lorison, to have saved his life, could not have put to the child one of those vital questions that were wildly beating about, unanswered, in his own brain. The little fellow was very like Norah; he had the same shining hair and candid eyes.

"Oh, Father Denny," cried the boy, suddenly, "I forgot to tell you! Sister is not going away at night any more! She told me so when she kissed me good-night as she was leaving. And she said she was so happy, and then she cried. Wasn't that queer? But I'm glad; aren't you?"

"Yes, lad. And now, ye omadhaun, go to sleep, and say good-night; we must be going."

"Which shall I do first, Father Denny?"

"Faith, he's caught me again! Wait till I get the sassench into the annals of Tageruach, the hagiographer; I'll give him enough of the Irish idiom to make him more respectful."

The light was out, and the small, brave voice bidding them good-night from the dark room. They groped downstairs, and tore away from the garrulity of Mother Geehan.

Again the priest steered them through the dim ways, but this time in another direction. His conductor was serenely silent, and Lorison followed his example to the extent of seldom speaking. Serene he could not be. His heart beat suffocatingly in his breast. The following of this blind, menacing trail was pregnant with he knew not what humiliating revelation to be delivered at its end.

They came into a more pretentious street, where trade, it could be surmised, flourished by day. And again the priest paused; this time before a lofty building, whose great doors and windows in the lowest floor were carefully shuttered and barred. Its higher apertures were dark, save in the third story, the windows of which were brilliantly lighted. Lorison's ear caught a distant, regular, pleasing thrumming, as of music above. They stood at an angle of the building. Up, along the side nearest them, mounted an iron stairway. At its top was an upright, illuminated parallelogram. Father Rogan had stopped, and stood, musing.

"I will say this much," he remarked, thoughtfully: "I believe you to be a better man than you think yourself to be, and a better man than I thought some hours ago. But do not take this," he added, with a smile, "as much praise. I promised you a possible deliverance from an unhappy perplexity. I will have to modify that promise. I can only remove the mystery that enhanced that perplexity. Your deliverance depends upon yourself. Come."

He led his companion up the stairway. Halfway up, Lorison caught him by the sleeve. "Remember," he gasped, "I love that woman."

"You desired to know."

"I—— Go on."

The priest reached the landing at the top of the stairway. Lorison, behind him, saw that the illuminated space was the glass upper half of a door opening into the lighted room. The rhythmic music increased as they neared it; the stairs shook with the mellow vibrations.

Lorison stopped breathing when he set foot upon the highest step, for the priest stood aside, and motioned him to look through the glass of the door.

His eyes, accustomed to the darkness, met first a blinding glare, and then he made out the faces and forms of many people, amid an extravagant display of splendid robings—billowy laces, brilliant-hued finery, ribbons, silks, and misty drapery. And then he caught the meaning of that jarring hum, and he saw the tired, pale, happy face of his wife, bending, as were a score of others, over her sewing machine—toiling, toiling. Here was the folly she pursued, and the end of his quest.

But not his deliverance, though even then remorse struck him. His shamed soul fluttered once more before it retired to make room for the other and better one. For, to temper his thrill of joy, the shine of the satin and the glimmer of ornaments recalled the disturbing figure of the bespangled Amazon, and the base duplicate histories lit by the glare of footlights and stolen diamonds. It is past the wisdom of him who only sets the scenes, either to praise or blame the man. But this time his love overcame his scruples. He took a quick step, and reached out his hand for the doorknob. Father Rogan was quicker to arrest it and draw him back.

"You use my trust in you queerly," said the priest, sternly. "What are you about to do?"

"I am going to my wife," said Lorison. "Let me pass."

"Listen," said the priest, holding him firmly by the arm. "I am about to put you in possession of a piece of knowledge of which, thus far, you have scarcely proved deserving. I do not think you ever will; but I will not dwell upon that. You see in that room the woman you married, working for a frugal living for herself, and a generous comfort for an idolized brother. This building belongs to the chief costumer of the city. For months the advance orders for the coming Mardi Gras festivals have kept the work going day and night. I myself secured employment here for Norah. She toils here each night from nine o'clock until daylight, and, besides, carries home with her some of the finer costumes, requiring more delicate needlework, and works there part of the day. Somehow, you two have remained strangely ignorant of each other's lives. Are you convinced now that your wife is not walking the streets?"

"Let me go to her," cried Lorison, again struggling, "and beg her forgiveness!"

"Sir," said the priest, "do you owe me nothing? Be quiet. It seems so often that Heaven lets fall its choicest gifts into hands that must be taught to hold them. Listen again. You forgot that repentant sin must not compromise, but look up, for redemption, to the purest and best. You went to her with the fine-spun sophistry that peace could be found in a mutual guilt and she, fearful of losing what her heart so craved, thought it worth the price to buy it with a desperate, pure, beautiful lie. I have known her since the day she was born; she is as innocent and unsullied in life and deed as a holy saint. In that lowly street where she dwells she first saw the light, and she has lived there ever since, spending her days in generous self-sacrifice, for others. Och, ye spalpeen!" continued Father Rogan, raising his finger in kindly anger at Lorison. "What for, I wonder, could she be afther making a fool of hersilf, and shamin' her swate soul with lies, for the like of you!"

"Sir," said Lorison, trembling, "say what you please of me. Doubt it as you must, I will yet prove my gratitude to you, and my devotion to her. But let me speak to her once now, let me kneel for just one moment at her feet, and——"

"Tut, tut!" said the priest. "How many acts of a love drama do you think an old bookworm like me capable of witnessing? Besides, what kind of figures do we cut, spying upon the mysteries of midnight millinery! Go to meet your wife to-morrow, as she ordered you, and obey her thereafter, and maybe some time I shall get forgiveness for the part I have played in this night's work. Off wid yez down the shtairs, now! 'Tis late, and an ould man like me should be takin' his rest."

MADAME BO-PEEP, OF THE RANCHES

"Aunt Ellen," said Octavia, cheerfully, as she threw her black kid gloves carefully at the dignified Persian cat on the window-seat, "I'm a pauper."

"You are so extreme in your statements, Octavia, dear," said Aunt Ellen, mildly, looking up from her paper. "If you find yourself temporarily in need of some small change for bonbons, you will find my purse in the drawer of the writing desk."

Octavia Beaupree removed her hat and seated herself on a footstool near her aunt's chair, clasping her hands about her knees. Her slim and flexible figure, clad in a modish mourning costume, accommodated itself easily and gracefully to the trying position. Her bright and youthful face, with its pair of sparkling, life-enamored eyes, tried to compose itself to the seriousness that the occasion seemed to demand.

"You good auntie, it isn't a case of bonbons it is abject, staring, unpicturesque poverty, with ready-made clothes, gasolined gloves, and probably one-o'clock dinners all waiting with the traditional wolf at the door. I've just come from my lawyer, Auntie, and, 'Please, ma'am, I ain't got nothink 't all. Flowers, lady? Buttonhole, gentleman? Pencils, sir, three for five, to help a poor widow?' Do I do it nicely, Auntie, or, as a breadwinner accomplishment, were my lessons in elocution entirely wasted?"

"Do be serious, my dear," said Aunt Ellen, letting her paper fall to the floor, "long enough to tell me what you mean. Colonel Beaupree's estate ——"

"Colonel Beaupree's estate," interrupted Octavia, emphasizing her words with appropriate dramatic gestures, "is of Spanish castellar architecture. Colonel Beaupree's resources are—wind. Colonel Beaupree's stocks are—water. Colonel Beaupree's income is—all in. The statement lacks the legal technicalities to which I have been listening for an hour, but that is what it means when translated."

"Octavia!" Aunt Ellen was now visibly possessed by consternation. "I can hardly believe it. And it was the impression that he was worth a million. And the De Peysters themselves introduced him!"

Octavia rippled out a laugh, and then became properly grave.

"*De mortuis nil,* Auntie—not even the rest of it. The dear old colonel —what a gold brick he was, after all! I paid for my bargain fairly—I'm all here, am I not?—items: eyes, fingers, toes, youth, old family, unquestionable position in society as called for in the contract—no wild-cat stock here." Octavia picked up the morning paper from the floor. "But I'm not going to 'squeal'—isn't that what they call it when you rail at Fortune because you've lost the game?" She turned the pages of the paper calmly. "'Stock market'—no use for that. 'Society's doings'—that's done. Here is my page—the wish column. A Van Dresser could not be said to 'want' for anything, of course. Chambermaids, cooks, canvassers, stenographers ——"

"Dear," said Aunt Ellen, with a little tremor in her voice, "please do not talk in that way. Even if your affairs are in so unfortunate a condition, there is my three thousand——"

Octavia sprang up lithely, and deposited a smart kiss on the delicate cheek of the prim little elderly maid.

"Blessed auntie, your three thousand is just sufficient to insure your Hyson to be free from willow leaves and keep the Persian in sterilized cream. I know I'd be welcome, but I prefer to strike bottom like Beelzebub rather than hang around like the Peri listening to the music from the side entrance. I'm going to earn my own living. There's nothing else to do. I'm a—— Oh, oh, oh!—I had forgotten. There's one thing saved from the wreck. It's a corral—no, a ranch in—let me see—Texas; an asset, dear old Mr. Bannister called it. How pleased he was to show me something he could describe as unencumbered! I've a description of it among those stupid papers he made me bring away with me from his office. I'll try to find it."

Octavia found her shopping-bag, and drew from it a long envelope filled with typewritten documents.

"A ranch in Texas," sighed Aunt Ellen. "It sounds to me more like a liability than an asset. Those are the places where the centipedes are found, and cowboys, and fandangos."

" 'The Rancho de las Sombras,' " read Octavia from a sheet of violently purple typewriting, "is situated one hundred and ten miles southeast of San Antonio, and thirty-eight miles from its nearest railroad station, Nopal, on the I. and G. N. Ranch consists of 7,680 acres of well-watered land, with title conferred by State patents, and twenty-two sections, or 14,080 acres, partly under yearly running lease and partly bought under State's twenty-year-purchase act. Eight thousand graded merino sheep, with the necessary equipment of horses, vehicles, and general ranch par-aphernalia. Ranch-house built of brick, with six rooms comfortably furnished according to the requirements of the climate. All within a strong barbed-wire fence.

" 'The present ranch manager seems to be competent and reliable, and is rapidly placing upon a paying basis a business that, in other hands, had been allowed to suffer from neglect and misconduct.

" 'This property was secured by Colonel Beaupree in a deal with a Western irrigation syndicate, and the title to it seems to be perfect. With careful management and the natural increase of land values, it ought to be made the foundation for a comfortable fortune for its owner.' "

When Octavia ceased reading, Aunt Ellen uttered something as near a sniff as her breeding permitted.

"The prospectus," she said, with uncompromising metropolitan suspicion, "doesn't mention the centipedes, or the Indians. And you never did like mutton, Octavia. I don't see what advantage you can derive from this—desert."

But Octavia was in a trance. Her eyes were steadily regarding something quite beyond their focus. Her lips were parted, and her face was lighted by the kindling furor of the explorer, the ardent, stirring disquiet of the adventurer. Suddenly she clasped her hands together exultantly.

"The problem solves itself, auntie," she cried. "I'm going to that ranch. I'm going to live on it. I'm going to learn to like mutton, and even concede the good qualities of centipedes—at a respectful distance. It's just what I need. It's a new life that comes when my old one is just ending. It's a release, auntie; it isn't a narrowing. Think of the gallops over those leagues of prairies, with the wind tugging at the roots of your hair, the coming close to the earth and learning over again the stories of the growing grass and the little wild flowers without names! Glorious is what it will be. Shall I be a shepherdess with a Watteau hat, and a crook to keep the bad wolves from the lambs, or a typical Western ranch girl, with short hair, like the pictures of her in the Sunday papers? I think the latter. And they'll have my picture, too, with the wild-cats I've slain, single-handed, hanging from my saddle horn. 'From the Four Hundred to the Flocks' is the way they'll headline it, and they'll print photographs of the old Van Dresser mansion and the church where I was married. They won't have my picture, but they'll get an artist to draw it. I'll be wild and woolly, and I'll grow my own wool."

"Octavia!" Aunt Ellen condensed into the one word all the protests she was unable to utter.

"Don't say a word, auntie. I'm going. I'll see the sky at night fit down on the world like a big butter-dish cover, and I'll make friends again with the stars that I haven't had a chat with since I was a wee child. I wish to go. I'm tired of all this. I'm glad I haven't any money. I could bless Colonel Beaupree for that ranch, and forgive him for all his bubbles. What if the life will be rough and lonely! I—I deserve it. I shut my heart to everything except that miserable ambition. I—oh, I wish to go away, and forget—forget!"

Octavia swerved suddenly to her knees, laid her flushed face in her aunt's lap, and shook with turbulent sobs.

Aunt Ellen bent over her, and smoothed the coppery-brown hair.

"I didn't know," she said, gently; "I didn't know—that. Who was it, dear?"

When Mrs. Octavia Beaupree, née Van Dresser, stepped from the train at Nopal, her manner lost, for the moment, some of that easy certitude which had always marked her movements. The town was of recent establishment, and seemed to have been hastily constructed of undressed lumber and flapping canvas. The element that had congregated about the station, though not offensively demonstrative, was clearly composed of citizens accustomed to and prepared for rude alarms.

Octavia stood on the platform, against the telegraph office, and attempted to choose by intuition from the swaggering, straggling string of loungers, the manager of the Rancho de las Sombras, who had been instructed by Mr. Bannister to meet her there. That tall, serious-looking, elderly man in the blue flannel shirt and white tie she thought must be he. But no, he passed by, removing his gaze from the lady as hers rested on him, according to the Southern custom. The manager, she thought, with some impatience at being kept waiting, should have no difficulty in selecting her. Young women wearing the most recent thing in ash-colored traveling suits were not so plentiful in Nopal!

Thus keeping a speculative watch on all persons of possible managerial aspect, Octavia, with a catching breath and a start of surprise, suddenly became aware of Teddy Westlake hurrying along the platform in the direction of the train—of Teddy Westlake or his sun-browned ghost in cheviot, boots and leather-girdled hat—Theodore Westlake, Jr., amateur polo (almost) champion, all-round butterfly and cucumber of the soil; but a broader, surer, more emphasized and determined Teddy than the one she had known a year ago when last she saw him.

He perceived Octavia at almost the same time, deflected his course, and steered for her in his old, straightforward way. Something like awe came upon her as the strangeness of his metamorphosis was brought into closer range; the rich, red-brown of his complexion brought out so vividly his straw-colored mustache and steel-gray eyes. He seemed more grown-up, and, somehow, farther away. But, when he spoke, the old, boyish Teddy came back again. They had been friends from childhood.

"Why, 'Tave!" he exclaimed, unable to reduce his perplexity to coherence. "How—what—when—where?"

"Train," said Octavia; "necessity; ten minutes ago; home. Your complexion's gone, Teddy. Now, how—what—when—where?"

"I'm working down here," said Teddy. He cast side glances about the station as one does who tries to combine politeness with duty.

"You didn't notice on the train," he asked, "an old lady with gray curls and a poodle, who occupied two seats with her bundles and quarrelled with the conductor, did you?"

"I think not," answered Octavia, reflecting. "And you haven't, by any chance, noticed a big, gray-mustached man in a blue shirt and six-shooters, with little flakes of merino wool sticking in his hair, have you?"

"Lots of 'em," said Teddy, with symptoms of mental delirium under the strain. "Do you happen to know any such individual?"

"No; the description is imaginary. Is your interest in the old lady whom you describe a personal one?"

"Never saw her in my life. She's painted entirely from fancy. She owns the little piece of property where I earn my bread and butter— the Rancho de las Sombras. I drove up to meet her according to arrangements with her lawyer."

Octavia leaned against the wall of the telegraph office. Was this possible? And didn't he know?

"Are you the manager of that ranch?" she asked, weakly.

"I am," said Teddy, with pride.

"I am Mrs. Beaupree," said Octavia, faintly; "but my hair never would curl, and I was polite to the conductor."

For a moment that strange, grown-up look came back, and removed Teddy miles away from her.

"I hope you'll excuse me," he said, rather awkwardly. "You see, I've been down here in the chaparral a year. I hadn't heard. Give me your checks, please, and I'll have your traps loaded into the wagon. José will follow with them. We travel ahead in the buckboard."

Seated by Teddy in a feather-weight buckboard, behind a pair of wild, cream-colored Spanish ponies, Octavia abandoned all thought for the exhilaration of the present. They swept out of the little town and down the level road toward the south. Soon the road dwindled and disappeared, and they struck across a world carpeted with an endless reach of curly mesquite grass. The wheels made no sound. The tireless ponies bounded ahead at an unbroken gallop. The temperate wind, made fragrant by thousands of acres of blue and yellow wild flowers, roared gloriously in their ears. The motion was aërial, ecstatic, with a thrilling sense of perpetuity in its effect. Octavia sat silent, possessed by a feeling of elemental, sensual bliss. Teddy seemed to be wrestling with some internal problem.

"I'm going to call you madama," he announced as the result of his labors. "That is what the Mexicans will call you—they're nearly all Mexicans on the ranch, you know. That seems to me about the proper thing."

"Very well, Mr. Westlake," said Octavia, primly.

"Oh, now," said Teddy, in some consternation, "that's carrying the thing too far, isn't it?"

"Don't worry me with your beastly etiquette. I'm just beginning to live. Don't remind me of anything artificial. If only this air could be bottled! This much alone is worth coming for. Oh, look! there goes a deer!"

"Jack-rabbit," said Teddy, without turning his head.

"Could I—might I drive?" suggested Octavia, panting, with rose-tinted cheeks and the eye of an eager child.

"On one condition. Could I—might I smoke?"

"Forever!" cried Octavia, taking the lines with solemn joy. "How shall I know which way to drive?"

"Keep her sou' by sou'east, and all sail set. You see that black speck on the horizon under that lowermost Gulf cloud? That's a group of live-oaks and a landmark. Steer halfway between that and the little hill to the left. I'll recite you the whole code of driving rules for the Texas prairies: keep the reins from under the horses' feet, and swear at 'em frequent."

"I'm too happy to swear, Ted. Oh, why do people buy yachts or travel in palace-cars, when a buckboard and a pair of plugs and a spring morning like this can satisfy all desire?"

"Now, I'll ask you," protested Teddy, who was futilely striking match after match on the dashboard, "not to call those denizens of the air plugs. They can kick out a hundred miles between daylight and dark." At last he succeeded in snatching a light for his cigar from the flame held in the hollow of his hands.

"Room!" said Octavia, intensely. "That's what produces the effect. I know now what I've wanted—scope—range—room!"

"Smoking-room," said Teddy, unsentimentally. "I love to smoke in a buckboard. The wind blows the smoke into you and out again. It saves exertion."

The two fell so naturally into their old-time goodfellowship that it was only by degrees that a sense of the strangeness of the new relations between them came to be felt.

"Madama," said Teddy, wonderingly, "however did you get it into your head to cut the crowd and come down here? Is it a fad now among the upper classes to trot off to sheep ranches instead of to Newport?"

"I was broke, Teddy," said Octavia, sweetly, with her interest centred upon steering safely between a Spanish dagger plant and a clump of chaparral; "I haven't a thing in the world but this ranch—not even any other home to go to."

"Come, now," said Teddy, anxiously but incredulously, "you don't mean it?"

"When my husband," said Octavia, with a shy slurring of the word, "died three months ago I thought I had a reasonable amount of the world's goods. His lawyer exploded that theory in a sixty-minute fully illustrated lecture. I took to the sheep as a last resort. Do you happen to know of any fashionable caprice among the gilded youth of Manhattan that induces them to abandon polo and club windows to become managers of sheep ranches?"

"It's easily explained in my case," responded Teddy, promptly. "I had to go to work. I couldn't have earned my board in New York, so I chummed a while with old Sandford, one of the syndicate that owned the ranch before Colonel Beaupree bought it, and got a place down here. I wasn't manager at first. I jogged around on ponies and studied the business in detail, until I got all the points in my head. I saw where it was losing and what the remedies were, and then Sandford put me in charge. I get a hundred dollars a month, and I earn it."

"Poor Teddy!" said Octavia, with a smile.

"You needn't. I like it. I save half my wages, and I'm as hard as a water plug. It beats polo."

"Will it furnish bread and tea and jam for another outcast from civilization?"

"The spring shearing," said the manager, "just cleaned up a deficit in last year's business. Wastefulness and inattention have been the rule heretofore. The autumn clip will leave a small profit over all expenses. Next year there will be jam."

When, about four o'clock in the afternoon, the ponies rounded a gentle, brush-covered hill, and then swooped, like a double cream-colored cyclone, upon the Rancho de las Sombras, Octavia gave a little cry of delight. A lordly grove of magnificent live-oaks cast an area of grateful, cool shade, whence the ranch had drawn its name, "de las Sombras"—of the shadows. The house, of red brick, one story, ran low and long beneath the trees. Through its middle, dividing its six rooms in half, extended a broad, arched passageway, picturesque with flowering cactus and hanging red earthen jars. A "gallery," low and broad, encircled the building. Vines climbed about it, and the adjacent ground was, for a space, covered with transplanted grass and shrubs. A little lake, long and narrow, glimmered in the sun at the rear. Farther away stood the shacks of the Mexican workers, the corrals, wool sheds and shearing pens. To the right lay the low hills, splattered with dark patches of chaparral; to the left the unbounded green prairie blending against the blue heavens.

"It's a home, Teddy," said Octavia, breathlessly; "that's what it is— it's a home."

"Not so bad for a sheep ranch," admitted Teddy, with excusable pride. "I've been tinkering on it at odd times."

A Mexican youth sprang from somewhere in the grass, and took charge of the creams. The mistress and the manager entered the house.

"Here's Mrs. MacIntyre," said Teddy, as a placid, neat, elderly lady came out upon the gallery to meet them. "Mrs. Mac, here's the boss. Very likely she will be wanting a hunk of bacon and a dish of beans after her drive."

Mrs. MacIntyre, the housekeeper, as much a fixture on the place as the lake or the live-oaks, received the imputation of the ranch's resources of refreshment with mild indignation, and was about to give it utterances when Octavia spoke.

"Oh, Mrs. MacIntyre, don't apologize for Teddy. Yes, I call him Teddy. So does every one whom he hasn't duped into taking him seriously. You see, we used to cut paper dolls and play jackstraws together ages ago. No one minds what he says."

"No," said Teddy, "no one minds what he says, just so he doesn't do it again."

Octavia cast one of those subtle, sidelong glances toward him from beneath her lowered eyelids—a glance that Teddy used to describe as an upper-cut. But there was nothing in his ingenuous, weather-tanned face to warrant a suspicion that he was making an allusion—nothing. Beyond a doubt, thought Octavia, he had forgotten.

"Mr. Westlake likes his fun," said Mrs. MacIntyre, as she conducted Octavia to her rooms. "But," she added, loyally, "people around here usually pay atention to what he says when he talks in earnest. I don't know what would have become of this place without him."

Two rooms at the east end of the house had been arranged for the occupancy of the ranch's mistress. When she entered them a slight dismay seized her at their bare appearance and the scantiness of their furniture; but she quickly reflected that the climate was a semi-tropical one, and was moved to appreciation of the well-conceived efforts to conform to it. The sashes had already been removed from the big windows, and white curtains waved in the Gulf breeze that streamed through the wide jalousies. The bare floor was amply strewn with cool rugs; the chairs were inviting, deep, dreamy willows; the walls were papered with a light, cheerful olive. One whole side of her sitting room was covered with books on smooth, unpainted pine shelves. She flew to these at once. Before her was a well-selected library. She caught glimpses of titles of volumes of fiction and travel not yet seasoned from the dampness of the press.

Presently, recollecting that she was now in a wilderness given over to mutton, centipedes, and privations, the incongruity of these luxuries struck her, and, with intuitive feminine suspicion, she began turning to the fly-leaves of volume after volume. Upon each one was inscribed in fluent characters the name of Theodore Westlake, Jr.

Octavia, fatigued by her long journey, retired early that night. Lying upon her white, cool bed, she rested deliciously, but sleep coquetted long with her. She listened to faint noises whose strangeness kept her faculties on the alert—the fractious yelping of the coyotes, the ceaseless, low symphony of the wind, the distant booming of the frogs about the lake, the lamentation of a concertina in the Mexicans' quarters. There were many conflicting feelings in her heart—thankfulness and rebellion, peace and disquietude, loneliness and a sense of protecting care, happiness and an old, haunting pain.

She did what any other woman would have done—sought relief in a wholesome tide of unreasonable tears, and her last words, murmured to herself before slumber, capitulating, came softly to woo her, were, "He has forgotten."

The manager of the Rancho de las Sombras was no dilettante. He was a "hustler." He was generally up, mounted, and away of mornings before the rest of the household were awake, making the rounds of the flocks and camps. This was the duty of the major-domo, a stately old Mexican with a princely air and manner, but Teddy seemed to have a great deal of confidence in his own eyesight. Except in the busy seasons, he nearly always returned to the ranch to breakfast at eight o'clock, with Octavia and Mrs. MacIntyre, at the little table set in the central hallway, bringing with him a tonic and breezy cheerfulness full of the health and flavor of the prairies.

A few days after Octavia's arrival he made her get out one of her riding skirts, and curtail it to a shortness demanded by the chaparral brakes.

With some misgivings she donned this and the pair of buckskin leggings he prescribed in addition, and, mounted upon a dancing pony, rode with him to view her possessions. He showed her everything—the flocks of ewes, muttons and grazing lambs, the dipping vats, the shearing pens, the uncouth merino rams in their little pasture, the water-tanks prepared against the summer drought—giving account of his stewardship with a boyish enthusiasm that never flagged.

Where was the old Teddy that she knew so well? This side of him was the same, and it was a side that pleased her; but this was all she ever saw of him now. Where was his sentimentality—those old, varying moods of impetuous love-making, of fanciful, quixotic devotion, of heart-breaking gloom, of alternating, absurd tenderness and haughty dignity? His nature had been a sensitive one, his temperament bordering closely on the artistic. She knew that, besides being a follower of fashion and its fads and sports, he had cultivated tastes of a finer nature. He had written things, he had tampered with colors, he was something of a student in certain branches of art, and once she had been admitted to all his aspirations and thoughts. But now—and she could not avoid the conclusion— Teddy had barricaded against her every side of himself except one—the side that showed the manager of the Rancho de las Sombras and a jolly chum who had forgiven and forgotten. Queerly enough the words of Mr. Bannister's description of her property came into her mind—"all inclosed within a strong barbed-wire fence."

"Teddy's fenced, too," said Octavia to herself.

It was not difficult for her to reason out the cause of his fortifications. It had originated one night at the Hammersmiths' ball. It occurred at a time soon after she had decided to accept Colonel Beaupree and his millions, which was no more than her looks and the entrée she held to the inner circles were worth. Teddy had proposed with all his impetuosity and fire, and she looked him straight in the eyes, and said, coldly and finally: "Never let me hear any such silly nonsense from you again." "You won't," said Teddy, with a new expression around his mouth, and —now Teddy was inclosed within a strong barbed-wire fence.

It was on this first ride of inspection that Teddy was seized by the inspiration that suggested the name of Mother Goose's heroine, and he at once bestowed it upon Octavia. The idea, supported by both a similarity of names and identity of occupations, seemed to strike him as a peculiarly happy one, and he never tired of using it. The Mexicans on the ranch also took up the name, adding another syllable to accommodate their lingual incapacity for the final "p," gravely referring to her as "La Madama Bo-Peepy." Eventually it spread, and "Madame Bo-Peep's ranch" was as often mentioned as the "Rancho de las Sombras."

Came the long, hot season from May to September, when work is scarce on the ranches. Octavia passed the days in a kind of lotus-eater's dream. Books, hammocks, correspondence with a few intimate friends, a renewed interest in her old water-color box and easel—these disposed of the sultry hours of daylight. The evenings were always sure to bring enjoyment. Best of all were the rapturous horseback rides with Teddy, when the moon gave light over the wind-swept leagues, chaperoned by the wheeling night-hawk and the startled owl. Often the Mexicans would come up from their shacks with their guitars and sing the weirdest of heart-breaking songs. There were long, cosy chats on the breezy gallery, and an interminable warfare of wits between Teddy and Mrs. MacIntyre, whose abundant Scotch shrewdness often more than overmatched the lighter humor in which she was lacking.

And the nights came, one after another, and were filed away by weeks and months—nights soft and languorous and fragrant, that should have driven Strephon to Chloe over wires however barbed, that might have drawn Cupid himself to hunt, lasso in hand, among those amorous pastures—but Teddy kept his fences up.

One July night Madame Bo-Peep and her ranch manager were sitting on the east gallery. Teddy had been exhausting the science of prognostication as to the probabilities of a price of twenty-four cents for the autumn clip, and had then subsided into an anæsthetic cloud of Havana smoke. Only as incompetent a judge as a woman would have failed to note long ago that at least a third of his salary must have gone up in the fumes of those imported Regalias.

"Teddy," said Octavia, suddenly, and rather sharply, "what are you working down here on a ranch for?"

"One hundred per," said Teddy, glibly, "and found."

"I've a good mind to discharge you."

"Can't do it," said Teddy, with a grin.

"Why not?" demanded Octavia, with argumentative heat.

"Under contract. Terms of sale respect all unexpired contracts. Mine runs until 12 P.M., December thirty-first. You might get up at midnight on that date and fire me. If you try it sooner I'll be in a position to bring legal proceedings."

Octavia seemed to be considering the prospects of litigation.

"But," continued Teddy, cheerfully, "I've been thinking of resigning anyway."

Octavia's rocking-chair ceased its motion. There were centipedes in this country, she felt sure; and Indians; and vast, lonely, desolate, empty wastes; all within strong barbed-wire fence. There was a Van Dresser pride, but there was also a Van Dresser heart. She must know for certain whether or not he had forgotten.

"Ah, well, Teddy," she said, with a fine assumption of polite interest, "it's lonely down here; you're longing to get back to the old life—to polo and lobsters and theatres and balls."

"Never cared much for balls," said Teddy, virtuously.

"You're getting old, Teddy. Your memory is failing. Nobody ever knew you to miss a dance, unless it occurred on the same night with another one which you attended. And you showed such shocking bad taste, too, in dancing too often with the same partner. Let me see, what was that Forbes girl's name—the one with wall eyes—Mabel, wasn't it?"

"No; Adèle. Mabel was the one with the bony elbows. That wasn't wall in Adèle's eyes. It was soul. We used to talk sonnets together, and Verlaine. Just then I was trying to run a pipe from the Pierian spring."

"You were on the floor with her," said Octavia, undeflected, "five times at the Hammersmiths'."

"Hamersmiths' what?" questioned Teddy, vacuously.

"Ball—ball," said Octavia, viciously. "What were we talking of?"

"Eyes, I thought," said Teddy, after some reflection; "and elbows."

"Those Hammersmiths," went on Octavia, in her sweetest society prattle, after subduing an intense desire to yank a handful of sunburnt, sandy hair from the head lying back contentedly against the canvas of the steamer chair, "had too much money. Mines, wasn't it? It was something that paid something to the ton. You couldn't get a glass of plain water in their house. Everything at that ball was dreadfully overdone."

"It was," said Teddy.

"Such a crowd there was!" Octavia continued conscious that she was talking the rapid drivel of a school-girl describing her first dance. "The balconies were as warm as the rooms. I—lost—something at that ball." The last sentence was uttered in a tone calculated to remove the barbs from miles of wire.

"So did I," confessed Teddy, in a lower voice.

"A glove," said Octavia, falling back as the enemy approached her ditches.

"Caste," said Teddy, halting his firing line without loss. "I hob-nobbed, half evening, with one of Hammersmith's miners, a fellow who kept his hands in his pockets, and talked like an archangel about reduction plants and drifts and levels and sluice-boxes."

"A pearl-gray glove, nearly new," sighed Octavia, mournfully.

"A bang-up chap, that McArdle," maintained Teddy, approvingly. "A man who hated olives and elevators; a man who handled mountains as croquettes, and built tunnels in the air; a man who never uttered a word of silly nonsense in his life. Did you sign those lease-renewal applications yet, madama? They've got to be on file in the land office by the thirty-first."

Teddy turned his head lazily. Octavia's chair was vacant.

A certain centipede, crawling along the lines marked out by fate, expounded the situation. It was early one morning while Octavia and Mrs. MacIntyre were trimming the honeysuckle on the west gallery. Teddy had risen and departed hastily before daylight in response to a word that a flock of ewes had been scattered from their bedding ground during the night by a thunder-storm.

The centipede, driven by destiny, showed himself on the floor of the gallery, and then, the screeches of the two women giving him his cue, he scuttled with all his yellow legs through the open door into the furthermost west room, which was Teddy's. Arming themselves with do-

mestic utensils selected with regard to their length, Octavia and Mrs. Mac-
Intyre, with much clutching of skirts and skirmishing for the position of
rear guard in the attacking force, followed.

Once inside, the centipede seemed to have disappeared, and his
prospective murderers began a thorough but cautious search for their
victim.

Even in the midst of such a dangerous and absorbing adventure Octavia
was conscious of an awed curiosity on finding herself in Teddy's sanctum.
In that room he sat alone, silently communing with those secret thoughts
that he now shared with no one, dreamed there whatever dreams he now
called on no one to interpret.

It was the room of a Spartan or a soldier. In one corner stood a wide,
canvas-covered cot; in another, a small bookcase; in another, a grim stand
of Winchesters and shotguns. An immense table, strewn with letters,
papers, and documents and surmounted by a set of pigeon-holes, occupied one side.

The centipede showed genius in concealing himself in such bare quarters. Mrs. MacIntyre was poking a broom-handle behind the bookcase.
Octavia approached Teddy's cot. The room was just as the manager
had left it in his hurry. The Mexican maid had not yet given it her attention. There was his big pillow with the imprint of his head still in the
centre. She thought the horrid beast might have climbed the cot and
hidden itself to bite Teddy. Centipedes were thus cruel and vindictive
toward managers.

She cautiously overturned the pillow, and then parted her lips to give
the signal for reinforcements at sight of a long, slender, dark object lying
there. But, repressing it in time, she caught up a glove, a pearl-gray glove,
flattened—it might be conceived—by many, many months of nightly pressure beneath the pillow of the man who had forgotten the Hammersmiths' ball. Teddy must have left so hurriedly that morning that he had,
for once, forgotten to transfer it to its resting-place by day. Even managers,
who are notoriously wily and cunning, are sometimes caught up with.

Octavia slid the gray glove into the bosom of her summery morning
gown. It was hers. Men who put themselves within a strong barbed-wire
fence, and remember Hammersmith balls only by the talk of miners
about sluice boxes, should not be allowed to possess such articles.

After all, what a paradise this prairie country was! How it blossomed
like the rose when you found things that were thought to be lost! How
delicious was that morning breeze coming in the windows, fresh and
sweet with the breath of the yellow ratama blooms! Might one not stand,
for a minute, with shining, far-gazing eyes, and dream that mistakes
might be corrected?

Why was Mrs. MacIntyre poking about so absurdly with a broom?

"I've found it," said Mrs. MacIntyre, banging the door. "Here it is."

"Did you lose something?" asked Octavia, with sweetly polite non-interest.

"The little devil!" said Mrs. MacIntyre, driven to violence. "Ye've no forgotten him alretty?"

Between them they slew the centipede. Thus was he rewarded for his agency toward the recovery of things lost at the Hammersmiths' ball.

It seems that Teddy, in due course, remembered the glove, and when he returned to the house at sunset made a secret but exhaustive search for it. Not until evening, upon the moonlit eastern gallery, did he find it. It was upon the hand that he had thought lost to him forever, and so he was moved to repeat certain nonsense that he had been commanded never, never to utter again. Teddy's fences were down.

This time there was no ambition to stand in the way, and the wooing was as natural and successful as should be between ardent shepherd and gentle shepherdess.

The prairies changed to a garden. The Rancho de las Sombras became the Ranch of Light.

A few days later Octavia received a letter from Mr. Bannister, in reply to one she had written to him asking some questions about her business. A portion of the letter ran as follows:

I am at a loss to account for your references to the sheep ranch. Two months after your departure to take up your residence upon it, it was discovered that Colonel Beaupree's title was worthless. A deed came to light showing that he disposed of the property before his death. The matter was reported to your manager, Mr. Westlake, who at once repurchased the property. It is entirely beyond my powers of conjecture to imagine how you have remained in ignorance of this fact. I beg that you will at once confer with that gentleman, who will, at least, corroborate my statement.

Octavia sought Teddy, with battle in her eye.

"What are you working on this ranch for?" she asked once more.

"One hundred——" he began to repeat, but saw in her face that she knew. She held Mr. Bannister's letter in her hand. He knew that the game was up.

"It's my ranch," said Teddy, like a schoolboy detected in evil. "It's a mighty poor manager that isn't able to absorb the boss's business if you give him time."

"Why were you working down here?" pursued Octavia, still struggling after the key to the riddle of Teddy.

"To tell the truth, 'Tave," said Teddy, with quiet candor, "it wasn't for the salary. That about kept me in cigars and sunburn lotions. I was sent south by my doctor. 'Twas that right lung that was going to the bad on account of over-exercise and strain at polo and gymnastics. I needed climate and ozone and rest and things of that sort."

In an instant Octavia was close against the vicinity of the affected organ. Mr. Bannister's letter fluttered to the floor.

"It's—it's well now, isn't it, Teddy?"

"Sound as a mesquite chunk. I deceived you in one thing. I paid fifty thousand for your ranch as soon as I found you had no title. I had just about that much income accumulated at my banker's while I've been herding sheep down here, so it was almost like picking the thing up on a bargain-counter for a penny. There's another little surplus of unearned increment piling up there, 'Tave. I've been thinking of a wedding trip in a yacht with white ribbons tied to the mast, through the Mediterranean, and then up among the Hebrides and down Norway to the Zuyder Zee."

"And I was thinking," said Octavia, softly, "of a wedding gallop with my manager among the flocks of sheep and back to a wedding breakfast with Mrs. MacIntyre on the gallery, with, maybe, a sprig of orange blossom fastened to the red jar above the table."

Teddy laughed, and began to chant:

"Little Bo-Peep has lost her sheep,
And doesn't know where to find 'em.
Let 'em alone, and they'll come home,
And——"

Octavia drew his head down, and whispered in his ear.

But that is one of the tales they brought behind them.

BOOK 11

THE VOICE OF THE CITY

THE VOICE OF THE CITY

THE VOICE OF THE CITY

Twenty-five years ago the school children used to chant their lessons. The manner of their delivery was a singsong recitative between the utterance of an Episcopal minister and the drone of a tired sawmill. I mean no disrespect. We must have lumber and sawdust.

I remember one beautiful and instructive little lyric that emanated from the physiology class. The most striking line of it was this:

"The shin-bone is the long-est bone in the human bod-y."

What an inestimable boon it would have been if all the corporeal and spiritual facts pertaining to man had thus been tunefully and logically inculcated in our youthful minds! But what we gained in anatomy, music, and philosophy was meagre.

The other day I became confused. I needed a ray of light. I turned back to those school days for aid. But in all the nasal harmonies we whined forth from those hard benches I could not recall one that treated of the voice of agglomerated mankind.

In other words, of the composite vocal message of massed humanity. In other words, of the Voice of a Big City.

Now, the individual voice is not lacking. We can understand the song of the poet, the ripple of the brook, the meaning of the man who wants $5 until next Monday, the inscriptions on the tombs of the Pharaohs, the language of flowers, the "step lively" of the conductor, and the prelude of the milk cans at 4 A.M. Certain large-eared ones even assert that they are wise to the vibrations of the tympanum produced by concussion of the air emanating from Mr. H. James. But who can comprehend the meaning of the voice of the city?

I went out for to see.

First, I asked Aurelia. She wore white Swiss and a hat with flowers on it, and ribbons and ends of things fluttered here and there.

"Tell me," I said, stammeringly, for I have no voice of my own, "what does this big—er—enormous—er—whopping city say? It must have a voice of some kind. Does it ever speak to you? How do you interpret its meaning? It is a tremendous mass, but it must have a key."

"Like a Saratoga trunk?" asked Aurelia.

"No," said I. "Please do not refer to the lid. I have a fancy that every city has a voice. Each one has something to say to the one who can hear it. What does the big one say to you?"

"All cities," said Aurelia, judicially, "say the same thing. When they get through saying it there is an echo from Philadelphia. So, they are unanimous."

"Here are 4,000,000 people," said I, scholastically, "compressed upon an island, which is mostly lamb surrounded by Wall Street water. The conjunction of so many units into so small a space must result in an identity—or, or rather a homogeneity—that finds its oral expression through a common channel. It is, as you might say, a consensus of translation, concentrating in a crystallized, general idea which reveals itself in what may be termed the Voice of the City. Can you tell me what it is?"

Aurelia smiled wonderfully. She sat on the high stoop. A spray of insolent ivy bobbed against her right ear. A ray of impudent moonlight flickered upon her nose. But I was adamant, nickel-plated.

"I must go and find out," I said, "what is the Voice of this City. Other cities have voices. It is an assignment. I must have it. New York," I continued, in a rising tone, "had better not hand me a cigar and say: 'Old man, I can't talk for publication.' No other city acts in that way. Chicago says, unhesitatingly, 'I will'; Philadelphia says, 'I should'; New Orleans says, 'I used to'; Louisville says, 'Don't care if I do'; St. Louis says, 'Excuse me'; Pittsburg says, 'Smoke up.' Now, New York——"

Aurelia smiled.

"Very well," said I, "I must go elsewhere and find out."

I went into a palace, tile-floored, cherub-ceilinged, and square with the cop. I put my foot on the brass rail and said to Billy Magnus, the best bartender in the diocese:

"Billy, you've lived in New York a long time—what kind of a song-and-dance does this old town give you? What I mean is, doesn't the gab of it seem to kind of bunch up and slide over the bar to you in a sort of amalgamated tip that hits off the burg in a kind of an epigram with a dash of bitters and a slice of——"

"Excuse me a minute," said Billy, "somebody's punching the button at the side door."

He went away; came back with an empty tin bucket; again vanished with it full; returned and said to me:

"That was Mame. She rings twice. She likes a glass of beer for supper. Her and the kid. If you ever saw that little skeesicks of mine brace up in his high chair and take his beer and—— But, say, what was yours? I get kind of excited when I hear them two rings—was it the baseball score or gin fizz you asked for?"

"Ginger ale," I answered.

I walked up to Broadway. I saw a cop on the corner. The cops take kids up, women across, and men in. I went up to him.

"If I'm not exceeding the spiel limit," I said, "let me ask you. You see New York during its vocative hours. It is the function of you and your brother cops to preserve the acoustics of the city. There must be a civic voice that is intelligible to you. At night during your lonely rounds you must have heard it. What is the epitome of its turmoil and shouting? What does the city say to you?"

"Friend," said the policeman, spinning his club, "it don't say nothing. I get my orders from the man higher up. Say, I guess you're all right. Stand here for a few minutes and keep an eye open for the roundsman."

The cop melted into the darkness of the side street. In ten minutes he had returned.

"Married last Tuesday," he said, half gruffly. "You know how they are. She comes to that corner at nine every night for a—comes to say 'hello!' I generally manage to be there. Say, what was it you asked me a bit ago—what's doing in the city? Oh, there's a roof-garden or two just opened, twelve blocks up."

I crossed a crow's-foot of street-car tracks, and skirted the edge of an umbrageous park. An artificial Diana, gilded, heroic, poised, wind-ruled, on the tower, shimmered in the clear light of her namesake in the sky.

Along came my poet, hurrying, hatted, haired, emitting dactyls, spondees and dactylis. I seized him.

"Bill," said I (in the magazine he is Cleon), "give me a lift. I am on an assignment to find out the Voice of the City. You see, it's a special order. Ordinarily a symposium comprising the views of Henry Clews, John L. Sullivan, Edwin Markham, May Irwin and Charles Schwab would be about all. But this is a different matter. We want a broad, poetic, mystic vocalization of the city's soul and meaning. You are the very chap to give me a hint. Some years ago a man got at the Niagara Falls and gave us its pitch. The note was about two feet below the lowest G on the piano. Now, you can't put New York into a note unless it's better indorsed than that. But give me an idea of what it would say if it should speak. It is bound to be a mighty and far-reaching utterance. To arrive at it we must take the tremendous crash of the chords of the day's traffic, the laughter and music of the night, the solemn tones of Dr. Parkhurst, the rag-time, the weeping, the stealthy hum of cab-wheels, the shout of the press agent, the tinkle of fountains on the roof-gardens, the hullabaloo of the strawberry vender and the covers of *Everybody's Magazine,* the whispers of the lovers in the parks—all these sounds must go into your Voice—not combined, but mixed, and of the mixture an essence made; and of the essence an extract—an audible extract, of which one drop shall form the thing we seek."

"Do you remember," asked the poet, with a chuckle, "that California girl we met at Stiver's studio last week? Well, I'm on my way to see her. She repeated that poem of mine, 'The Tribute of Spring,' word for word. She's the smartest proposition in this town just at present. Say, how does this confounded tie look? I spoiled four before I got one to set right."

"And the Voice that I asked you about?" I inquired.

"Oh, she doesn't sing," said Cleon. "But you ought to hear her recite my 'Angel of the Inshore Wind.'"

I passed on. I cornered a newsboy and he flashed at me prophetic pink papers that outstripped the news by two revolutions of the clock's longest hand.

"Son," I said, while I pretended to chase coins in my penny pocket, "doesn't it sometimes seem to you as if the city ought to be able to talk? All these ups and downs and funny business and queer things happening every day—what would it say, do you think, if it could speak?"

"Quit yer kiddin'," said the boy. "Wot paper yer want? I got no time to waste. It's Mag's birthday, and I want thirty cents to git her a present."

Here was no interpreter of the city's mouth-piece. I bought a paper, and consigned its undeclared treaties, its premediated murders and unfought battles to an ash can.

Again I repaired to the park and sat in the moon shade. I thought and thought, and wondered why none could tell me what I asked for.

And then, as swift as light from a fixed star, the answer came to me. I arose and hurried—hurried as so many reasoners must, back around my circle. I knew the answer and I hugged it in my breast as I flew, fearing lest someone would stop me and demand my secret.

Aurelia was still on the stoop. The moon was higher and the ivy shadows were deeper. I sat at her side and we watched a little cloud tilt at the drifting moon and go asunder quite pale and discomfited.

And then, wonder of wonders and delight of delights! our hands somehow touched, and our fingers closed together and did not part.

After half an hour Aurelia said, with that smile of hers:

"Do you know, you haven't spoken a word since you came back!"

"That," said I, nodding wisely, "is the Voice of the City."

THE COMPLETE LIFE OF JOHN HOPKINS

There is a saying that no man has tasted the full flavor of life until he has known poverty, love, and war. The justness of this reflection commends it to the lover of condensed philosophy. The three conditions embrace about all there is in life worth knowing. A surface thinker might deem that wealth should be added to the list. Not so. When a poor man finds a long-hidden quarter-dollar that has slipped through a rip into his vest lining, he sounds the pleasure of life with a deeper plummet than any millionaire can hope to cast.

It seems that the wise executive power that rules life has thought best to drill man in these three conditions; and none may escape all three. In rural places the terms do not mean so much. Poverty is less pinching; love is temperate; war shrinks to contests about boundary lines and the neighbors' hens. It is in the cities that our epigram gains in truth and vigor; and it has remained for one John Hopkins to crowd the experience into a rather small space of time.

The Hopkins flat was like a thousand others. There was a rubber plant in one window; a flea-bitten terrier sat in the other, wondering when he was to have his day.

John Hopkins was like a thousand others. He worked at $20 per week in a nine-story, red-brick building at either Insurance, Buckle's Hoisting Engines, Chiropody, Loans, Pulleys, Boas Renovated, Waltz Guaranteed in Five Lessons, or Artificial Limbs. It is not for us to wring Mr. Hopkins's avocation from these outward signs that be.

Mrs. Hopkins was like a thousand others. The auriferous tooth, the sedentary disposition, the Sunday afternoon wanderlust, the draught upon the delicatessen store for home-made comforts, the furor for department store marked-down sales, the feeling of superiority to the lady in the third-floor front who wore genuine ostrich tips and had two names over her bell, the mucilaginous hours during which she remained glued to the window sill, the vigilant avoidance of the instalment man, the tireless patronage of the acoustics of the dumb-waiter shaft—all the attributes of the Gotham flat-dweller were hers.

One moment yet of sententiousness and the story moves.

In the Big City large and sudden things happen. You round a corner and thrust the rib of your umbrella into the eye of your old friend from Kootenai Falls. You stroll out to pluck a Sweet William in the park—and lo! bandits attack you—you are ambulanced to the hospital—you marry your nurse; are divorced—get squeezed while short on U. P. S. and D. O. W. N. S.—stand in the bread line—marry an heiress, take out your laundry and pay your club dues—seemingly all in the wink of an eye. You travel the streets, and a finger beckons to you, a handkerchief is dropped for you, a brick is dropped upon you, the elevator cable or your bank breaks, a table d'hôte or your wife disagrees with you, and Fate tosses you about like cork crumbs in wine opened by an un-feed waiter. The City is a sprightly youngster, and you are red paint upon its toy, and you get licked off.

John Hopkins sat, after a compressed dinner, in his glove-fitting straight-front flat. He sat upon a hornblende couch and gazed, with satiated eyes, at Art Brought Home to the People in the shape of "The Storm" tacked against the wall. Mrs. Hopkins discoursed droningly of the dinner smells from the flat across the hall. The flea-bitten terrier gave Hopkins a look of disgust and showed a man-hating tooth.

Here was neither poverty, love, nor war; but upon such barren stems may be grafted those essentials of a complete life.

John Hopkins sought to inject a few raisins of conversation into the tasteless dough of existence. "Putting a new elevator in at the office," he said, discarding the nominative noun, "and the boss has turned out his whiskers."

"You don't mean it!" commented Mrs. Hopkins.

"Mr. Whipples," continued John, "wore his new spring suit down to-day. I liked it fine. It's a gray with——" He stopped, suddenly stricken by a need that made itself known to him. "I believe I'll walk down to the corner and get a five-cent cigar," he concluded.

John Hopkins took his hat and picked his way down the musty halls and stairs of the flat-house.

The evening air was mild, and the streets shrill with the careless cries of children playing games controlled by mysterious rhythms and phrases. Their elders held the doorways and steps with leisurely pipe and gossip. Paradoxically, the fire-escapes supported lovers in couples who made no attempt to fly the mounting conflagration they were there to fan.

The corner cigar store aimed at by John Hopkins was kept by a man named Freshmayer, who looked upon the earth as a sterile promontory.

Hopkins, unknown in the store, entered and called genially for his "bunch of spinach, carfare grade." This imputation deepened the pessimism of Freshmayer; but he set out a brand that came perilously near to filling the order. Hopkins bit off the roots of his purchase, and lighted up at the swinging gas jet. Feeling in his pockets to make payment, he found not a penny there.

"Say, my friend," he explained, frankly, "I've come out without any change. Hand you that nickel first time I pass."

Joy surged in Freshmayer's heart. Here was corroboration of his belief that the world was rotten and man a peripatetic evil. Without a word he rounded the end of his counter and made earnest onslaught upon his customer. Hopkins was no man to serve as a punching-bag for a pessimistic tobacconist. He quickly bestowed upon Freshmayer a colorado-maduro eye in return for the ardent kick that he received from the dealer in goods for cash only.

The impetus of the enemy's attack forced the Hopkins line back to the sidewalk. There the conflict raged; the pacific wooden Indian, with his carven smile, was overturned, and those of the street who delighted in carnage pressed round to view the zealous joust.

But then came the inevitable cop and imminent inconvenience for both the attacker and attacked. John Hopkins was a peaceful citizen, who worked at rebuses of nights in a flat, but he was not without the fundamental spirit of resistance that comes with the battle-rage. He knocked the policeman into a grocer's sidewalk display of goods and gave Freshmayer a punch that caused him temporarily to regret that he had not made it a rule to extend a five-cent line of credit to certain customers. Then Hopkins took spiritedly to his heels down the sidewalk, closely followed by the cigar-dealer and the policeman, whose uniform testified to the reason in the grocer's sign that read: "Eggs cheaper than anywhere else in the city."

As Hopkins ran he became aware of a big, low, red, racing automobile that kept abreast of him in the street. This auto steered in to the side of the sidewalk, and the man guiding it motioned to Hopkins to jump into it. He did so without slackening his speed, and fell into the turkey-red upholstered seat beside the chauffeur. The big machine, with a diminuendo cough, flew away like an albatross down the avenue into which the street emptied.

The driver of the auto sped his machine without a word. He was masked beyond guess in the goggles and diabolic garb of the chauffeur.

"Much obliged, old man," called Hopkins, gratefully. "I guess you've got sporting blood in you, all right, and don't admire the sight of two men trying to soak one. Little more and I'd have been pinched."

The chauffeur made no sign that he had heard. Hopkins shrugged a shoulder and chewed at his cigar, to which his teeth had clung grimly throughout the mêlée.

Ten minutes and the auto turned into the open carriage entrance of a noble mansion of brown stone, and stood still. The chauffeur leaped out, and said:

"Come quick. The lady, she will explain. It is the great honor you will have, monsieur. Ah, that milady could call upon Armand to do this thing! But, no, I am only one chauffeur."

With vehement gestures the chauffeur conducted Hopkins into the house. He was ushered into a small but luxurious reception chamber. A lady, young, and possessing the beauty of visions, rose from a chair. In her eyes smouldered a becoming anger. Her high-arched, thread-like brows were ruffled into a delicious frown.

"Milady," said the chauffeur, bowing low, "I have the honor to relate to you that I went to the house of Monsieur Long and found him to be not at home. As I came back I see this gentleman in combat against— how you say—greatest odds. He is fighting with five—ten—thirty men— gendarmes, *aussi*. Yes, milady, he what you call 'swat' one—three—eight policemans. If that Monsieur Long is out I say to myself this gentleman he will serve milady so well, and I bring him here."

"Very well, Armand," said the lady, "you may go." She turned to Hopkins.

"I sent my chauffeur," she said, "to bring my cousin, Walter Long. There is a man in this house who has treated me with insult and abuse. I have complained to my aunt, and she laughs at me. Armand says you are brave. In these prosaic days men who are both brave and chivalrous are few. May I count upon your assistance?"

John Hopkins thrust the remains of his cigar into his coat pocket. He looked upon this winning creature and felt his first thrill of romance. It was a knightly love, and contained no disloyalty to the flat with the flea-bitten terrier and the lady of his choice. He had married her after a picnic of the Lady Label Stickers' Union, Lodge No. 2, on a dare and a bet of new hats and chowder all around with his friend, Billy McManus. This angel who was begging him to come to her rescue was something too heavenly for chowder, and as for hats—golden, jewelled crowns for her!

"Say," said John Hopkins, "just show me the guy that you've got the grouch at. I've neglected my talents as a scrapper heretofore, but this is my busy night."

"He is in there," said the lady, pointing to a closed door. "Come. Are you sure that you do not falter or fear?"

"Me?" said John Hopkins. "Just give me one of those roses in the bunch you are wearing, will you?"

The lady gave him a red, red rose. John Hopkins kissed it, stuffed it into his vest pocket, opened the door and walked into the room. It was a handsome library, softly but brightly lighted. A young man was there, reading.

"Books on etiquette is what you want to study," said John Hopkins, abruptly. "Get up here, and I'll give you some lessons. Be rude to a lady, will you?"

The young man looked mildly surprised. Then he arose languidly, dextrously caught the arms of John Hopkins and conducted him irresistibly to the front door of the house.

"Beware, Ralph Branscombe," cried the lady, who had followed, "what you do to the gallant man who has tried to protect me."

The young man shoved John Hopkins gently out the door and then closed it.

"Bess," he said calmly, "I wish you would quit reading historical novels. How in the world did that fellow get in here?"

"Armand brought him," said the young lady. "I think you are awfully mean not to let me have that St. Bernard. I sent Armand for Walter. I was so angry with you."

"Be sensible, Bess," said the young man, taking her arm. "That dog isn't safe. He has bitten two or three people around the kennels. Come now, let's go tell auntie we are in good humor again."

Arm in arm, they moved away.

John Hopkins walked to his flat. The janitor's five-year-old daughter was playing on the steps. Hopkins gave her a nice, red rose and walked upstairs.

Mrs. Hopkins was philandering with curl-papers.

"Get your cigar?" she asked, disinterestedly.

"Sure," said Hopkins, "and I knocked around a while outside. It's a nice night."

He sat upon the hornblende sofa, took out the stump of his cigar, lighted it, and gazed at the graceful figures in "The Storm" on the opposite wall.

"I was telling you," said he, "about Mr. Whipple's suit. It's a gray, with an invisible check, and it looks fine."

A LICKPENNY LOVER

There were 3,000 girls in the Biggest Store. Masie was one of them. She was eighteen and a saleslady in the gents' gloves. Here she became versed in two varieties of human beings—the kind of gents who buy their gloves in department stores and the kind of women who buy gloves for unfortunate gents. Besides this wide knowledge of the human species, Masie had acquired other information. She had listened to the promulgated wisdom of the 2,999 other girls and had stored it in a brain that was as secretive and wary as that of a Maltese cat. Perhaps nature, foreseeing that she would lack wise counsellors, had mingled the saving ingredient of shrewdness along with her beauty, as she has endowed the silver fox of the priceless fur above the other animals with cunning.

For Masie was beautiful. She was a deep-tinted blonde, with the calm poise of a lady who cooks butter cakes in a window. She stood behind her counter in the Biggest Store; and as you closed your hand over the tape-line for your glove measure you thought of Hebe; and as you looked again you wondered how she had come by Minerva's eyes.

When the floorwalker was not looking Masie chewed tutti frutti; when he was looking she gazed up as if at the clouds and smiled wistfully.

That is the shopgirl smile, and I enjoin you to shun it unless you are well fortified with callosity of the heart, caramels, and a congeniality for the capers of Cupid. This smile belonged to Masie's recreation hours and not to the store; but the floorwalker must have his own. He is the Shylock of the stores. When he comes nosing around the bridge of his nose is a toll-bridge. It is goo-goo eyes or "git" when he looks toward a pretty girl. Of course not all floorwalkers are thus. Only a few days ago the papers printed news of one over eighty years of age.

One day Irving Carter, painter, millionaire, traveller, poet, automobilist, happened to enter the Biggest Store. It is due to him to add that his visit was not voluntary. Filial duty took him by the collar and dragged him inside, while his mother philandered among the bronze and terra-cotta statuettes.

Carter strolled across to the glove counter in order to shoot a few minutes on the wing. His need for gloves was genuine; he had forgotten to bring a pair with him. But his action hardly calls for apology, because he had never heard of glove-counter flirtations.

As he neared the vicinity of his fate he hesitated, suddenly conscious of this unknown phase of Cupid's less worthy profession.

Three or four cheap fellows, sonorously garbed, were leaning over the counters, wrestling with the mediatorial hand-coverings, while giggling girls played vivacious seconds to their lead upon the strident string of coquetry. Carter would have retreated, but he had gone too far. Masie confronted him behind her counter with a questioning look in eyes as coldly, beautifully, warmly blue as the glint of summer sunshine on an iceberg drifting in Southern seas.

And then Irving Carter, painter, millionaire, etc., felt a warm flush rise to his aristocratically pale face. But not from diffidence. The blush was intellectual in origin. He knew in a moment that he stood in the ranks of the ready-made youths who wooed the giggling girls at other counters. Himself leaned against the oaken trysting place of a cockney Cupid with a desire in his heart for the favor of a glove salesgirl. He was no more than Bill and Jack and Mickey. And then he felt a sudden tolerance for them, and an elating, courageous contempt for the conventions upon which he had fed, and an unhesitating determination to have this perfect creature for his own.

When the gloves were paid for and wrapped Carter lingered for a moment. The dimples at the corners of Masie's damask mouth deepened. All gentlemen who bought gloves lingered in just that way. She curved an arm, showing like Psyche's through her shirt-waist sleeve, and rested an elbow upon the show-case edge.

Carter had never before encountered a situation of which he had not been perfect master. But now he stood far more awkward than Bill or Jack or Mickey. He had no chance of meeting this beautiful girl socially. His mind struggled to recall the nature and habits of shop-girls as he had read or heard of them. Somehow he had received the idea that they sometimes did not insist too strictly upon the regular channels of introduction. His heart beat loudly at the thought of proposing an unconventional meeting with this lovely and virginal being. But the tumult in his heart gave him courage.

After a few friendly and well-received remarks on general subjects, he laid his card by her hand on the counter.

"Will you please pardon me," he said, "if I seem too bold; but I earnestly hope you will allow me the pleasure of seeing you again. There is my name; I assure you that it is with the greatest respect that I ask the favor of becoming one of your fr—— acquaintances. May I not hope for the privilege?"

Masie knew men—especially men who buy gloves. Without hesitation she looked him frankly and smilingly in the eyes, and said:

"Sure. I guess you're right. I don't usually go out with strange gentlemen, though. It ain't quite ladylike. When should you want to see me again?"

"As soon as I may," said Carter. "If you would allow me to call at your home, I——"

Masie laughed musically. "Oh, gee, no!" she said emphatically. "If you could see our flat once! There's five of us in three rooms. I'd just like to see ma's face if I was to bring a gentleman friend there!"

"Anywhere, then," said the enamored Carter, "that will be convenient to you."

"Say," suggested Masie, with a bright-idea look in her peach-blow face; "I guess Thursday night will about suit me. Suppose you come to the corner of Eighth Avenue and Forty-eighth Street at 7:30. I live right near the corner. But I've got to be back home by eleven. Ma never lets me stay out after eleven."

Carter promised gratefully to keep the tryst, and then hastened to his mother, who was looking about for him to ratify her purchase of a bronze Diana.

A salesgirl, with small eyes and an obtuse nose, strolled near Masie, with a friendly leer.

"Did you make a hit with his nobs, Masie?" she asked, familiarly.

"The gentleman asked permission to call," answered Masie, with the grand air, as she slipped Carter's card into the bosom of her waist.

"Permission to call!" echoed small eyes, with a snigger. "Did he say anything about dinner in the Waldorf and a spin in his auto afterward?"

"Oh, cheese it!" said Masie, wearily. "You've been used to swell things, I don't think. You've had a swelled head ever since that hose-cart driver took you out to a chop suey joint. No, he never mentioned the Waldorf; but there's a Fifth Avenue address on his card, and if he buys the supper you can bet your life there won't be no pigtail on the waiter what takes the order."

As Carter glided away from the Biggest Store with his mother in his electric runabout, he bit his lip with a dull pain at his heart. He knew that love had come to him for the first time in all the twenty-nine years of his life. And that the object of it should make so readily an appointment with him at a street corner, though it was a step toward his desires, tortured him with misgivings.

Carter did not know the shopgirl. He did not know that her home is often either a scarcely habitable tiny room or a domicile filled to overflowing with kith and kin. The street corner is her parlor, the park is her drawing room; the avenue is her garden walk; yet for the most part she is as inviolate mistress of herself in them as is my lady inside her tapestried chamber.

One evening at dusk, two weeks after their first meeting, Carter and Masie strolled arm-in-arm into a little, dimly-lit park. They found a bench, tree-shadowed and secluded, and sat there.

For the first time his arm stole gently around her. Her golden-bronze head slid restfully against his shoulder.

"Gee!" sighed Masie, thankfully. "Why didn't you ever think of that before?"

"Masie," said Carter, earnestly, "you surely know that I love you. I ask you sincerely to marry me. You know me well enough by this time to have no doubts of me. I want you, and I must have you. I care nothing for the difference in our stations."

"What is the difference?" asked Masie, curiously.

"Well, there isn't any," said Carter, quickly, "except in the minds of foolish people. It is in my power to give you a life of luxury. My social position is beyond dispute, and my means are ample."

"They all say that," remarked Masie. "It's the kid they all give you.

I suppose you really work in a delicatessen or follow the races. I ain't as green as I look."

"I can furnish you all the proofs you want," said Carter, gently. "And I want you, Masie. I loved you the first day I saw you."

"They all do," said Masie, with an amused laugh, "to hear 'em talk. If I could meet a man that got stuck on me the third time he'd seen me I think I'd get mashed on him."

"Please don't say such things," pleaded Carter. "Listen to me, dear. Ever since I first looked into your eyes you have been the only woman in the world for me."

"Oh, ain't you the kidder!" smiled Masie. "How many other girls did you ever tell that?"

But Carter persisted. And at length he reached the flimsy, fluttering little soul of the shopgirl that existed somewhere deep down in her lovely bosom. His words penetrated the heart whose very lightness was its safest armor. She looked up at him with eyes that saw. And a warm glow visited her cool cheeks. Tremblingly, awfully, her moth wings closed, and she seemed about to settle upon the flower of love. Some faint glimmer of life and its possibilities on the other side of her glove counter dawned upon her. Carter felt the change and crowded the opportunity.

"Marry me, Masie," he whispered, softly, "and we will go away from this ugly city to beautiful ones. We will forget work and business, and life will be one long holiday. I know where I should take you—I have been there often. Just think of a shore where summer is eternal, where the waves are always rippling on the lovely beach and the people are happy and free as children. We will sail to those shores and remain there as long as you please. In one of those far-away cities there are grand and lovely palaces and towers full of beautiful pictures and statues. The streets of the city are water, and one travels about in——"

"I know," said Masie, sitting up suddenly. "Gondolas."

"Yes," smiled Carter.

"I thought so," said Masie.

"And then," continued Carter, "we will travel on and see whatever we wish in the world. After the European cities we will visit India and the ancient cities there, and ride on elephants and see the wonderful temples of the Hindoos and the Brahmins and the Japanese gardens and the camel trains and chariot races in Persia, and all the queer sights of foreign countries. Don't you think you would like it, Masie?"

Masie rose to her feet.

"I think we had better be going home," she said, coolly. "It's getting late."

Carter humored her. He had come to know her varying, thistle-down moods, and that it was useless to combat them. But he felt a certain happy triumph. He had held for a moment, though but by a silken thread, the soul of his wild Psyche, and hope was stronger within him. Once she had folded her wings and her cool hand had closed about his own.

At the Biggest Store the next day Masie's chum, Lulu, waylaid her in an angle of the counter.

"How are you and your swell friend making it?" she asked.

"Oh, him?" said Masie, patting her side curls. "He ain't in it any more. Say, Lu, what do you think that fellow wanted me to do?"

"Go on the stage?" guessed Lulu, breathlessly.

"Nit; he's too cheap a guy for that. He wanted me to marry him and go down to Coney Island for a wedding tour!"

DOUGHERTY'S EYE-OPENER

Big Jim Dougherty was a sport. He belonged to that race of men. In Manhattan it is a distinct race. They are the Caribs of the North—strong, artful, self-sufficient, clannish, honorable within the laws of their race, holding in lenient contempt neighboring tribes who bow to the measure of Society's tape-line. I refer, of course, to the titled nobility of sportdom. There is a class which bears as a qualifying adjective the substantive belonging to a wind instrument made of a cheap and base metal. But the tin mines of Cornwall never produced the material for manufacturing descriptive nomenclature for "Big Jim" Dougherty.

The habitat of the sport is the lobby or the outside corner of certain hotels and combination restaurants and cafés. They are mostly men of different sizes, running from small to large; but they are unanimous in the possession of a recently shaven, blue-black cheek and chin and dark overcoats (in season) with black velvet collars.

Of the domestic life of the sport little is known. It has been said that Cupid and Hymen sometimes take a hand in the game and copper the queen of hearts to lose. Daring theorists have averred—not content with simply saying—that a sport often contracts a spouse, and even incurs descendants. Sometimes he sits in the game of politics; and then at chowder picnics there is a revelation of a Mrs. Sport and little Sports in glazed hats with tin pails.

But mostly the sport is Oriental. He believes his women-folk should not be too patent. Somewhere behind grilles or flower-ornamented fire escapes they await him. There, no doubt, they tread on rugs from Teheran and are diverted by the bulbul and play upon the dulcimer and feed upon sweetmeats. But away from his home the sport is an integer. He does not, as men of other races in Manhattan do, become the convoy in his unoccupied hours of fluttering laces and high heels that tick off delectably the happy seconds of the evening parade. He herds with his own race at corners, and delivers a commentary in his Carib lingo upon the passing show.

"Big Jim" Dougherty had a wife, but he did not wear a button portrait of her upon his lapel. He had a home in one of those brown-stone, iron-railed streets on the west side that look like a recently excavated bowling alley of Pompeii.

To this home of his Mr. Dougherty repaired each night when the hour was so late as to promise no further diversion in the arch domains of sport. By that time the occupant of the monogamistic harem would be in dreamland, the bulbul silenced and the hour propitious for slumber.

"Big Jim" always arose at twelve, meridian, for breakfast, and soon afterward he would return to the rendezvous of his "crowd."

He was always vaguely conscious that there was a Mrs. Dougherty. He would have received without denial the charge that the quiet, neat, comfortable little woman across the table at home was his wife. In fact, he remembered pretty well that they had been married for nearly four years. She would often tell him about the cute tricks of Spot, the canary, and the light-haired lady that lived in the window of the flat across the street.

"Big Jim" Dougherty even listened to this conversation of hers some-times. He knew that she would have a nice dinner ready for him every evening at seven when he came for it. She sometimes went to matinées, and she had a talking machine with six dozen records. Once when her Uncle Amos blew in on a wind from up-state she went with him to the Eden Musée. Surely these things were diversions enough for any woman.

One afternoon Mr. Dougherty finished his breakfast, put on his hat and got away fairly for the door. When his hand was on the knob he heard his wife's voice.

"Jim," she said, firmly, "I wish you would take me out to dinner this evening. It has been three years since you have been outside the door with me."

"Big Jim" was astounded. She had never asked anything like this before. It had the flavor of a totally new proposition. But he was a game sport.

"All right," he said. "You be ready when I come at seven. None of this 'wait two minutes till I primp an hour or two' kind of business, now, Dele."

"I'll be ready," said his wife, calmly.

At seven she descended the stone steps in the Pompeian bowling alley at the side of "Big Jim" Dougherty. She wore a dinner gown made of a stuff that the spiders must have woven, and of a color that a twilight sky must have contributed. A light coat with many admirably unnecessary capes and adorably inutile ribbons floated downward from her shoulders. Fine feathers do make fine birds; and the only reproach in the saying is for the man who refuses to give up his earnings for the ostrich-tip indus-try.

"Big Jim" Dougherty was troubled. There was a being at his side whom he did not know. He thought of the sober-hued plumage that this bird of paradise was accustomed to wear in her cage, and this winged revelation puzzled him. In some way she reminded him of the Delia Cullen that he had married four years before. Shyly and rather awkwardly he stalked at her right hand.

"After dinner I'll take you back home, Dele," said Mr. Dougherty, "and then I'll drop back up to Seltzer's with the boys. You can have swell chuck to-night if you want it. I made a winning on Anaconda yesterday so you can go as far as you like."

Mr. Dougherty had intended to make the outing with his unwonted wife an inconspicuous one. Uxoriousness was a weakness that the precepts of the Caribs did not countenance. If any of his friends of the track, the billiard cloth or the square circle had wives they had never complained of the fact in public. There were a number of table d'hôte places on the cross streets near the broad and shining way; and to one of these he had proposed to escort her, so that the bushel might not be removed from the light of his domesticity.

But while on the way Mr. Dougherty altered those intentions. He had been casting stealthy glances at his attractive companion and he was seized with the conviction that she was no selling plater. He resolved to parade with his wife past Seltzer's café, where at this time a number of his tribe would be gathered to view the daily evening processions. Yes; and he would take her to dine at Hoogley's, the swellest slow-lunch warehouse on the line, he said to himself.

The congregation of smooth-faced tribal gentlemen were on watch at Seltzer's. As Mr. Dougherty and his reorganized Delia passed they stared, momentarily petrified, and then removed their hats—a performance as unusual to them as was the astonishing innovation presented to their gaze by "Big Jim." On the latter gentleman's impassive face there appeared a slight flicker of triumph—a faint flicker, no more to be observed than the expression called there by the draft of little casino to a four-card spade flush.

Hoogley's was animated. Electric lights shone—as, indeed, they were expected to do. And the napery, the glassware, and the flowers also meritoriously performed the spectacular duties required of them. The guests were numerous, well-dressed, and gay.

A waiter—not necessarily obsequious—conducted "Big Jim" Dougherty and his wife to a table.

"Play that menu straight across for what you like, Dele," said "Big Jim." "It's you for a trough of the gilded oats to-night. It strikes me that maybe we've been sticking too fast to home fodder."

"Big Jim's" wife gave her order. He looked at her with respect. She had mentioned truffles; and he had not known that she knew what truffles were. From the wine list she designated an appropriate and desirable brand. He looked at her with some admiration.

She was beaming with the innocent excitement that woman derives from the exercise of her gregariousness. She was talking to him about a hundred things with animation and delight. And as the meal progressed her cheeks, colorless from a life indoors, took on a delicate flush. "Big Jim" looked around the room and saw that none of the women there had her charm. And then he thought of the three years she had suffered immurement, uncomplaining, and a flush of shame warmed him, for he carried fair play as an item in his creed.

But when the Honorable Patrick Corrigan, leader in Dougherty's district and a friend of his, saw them and came over to the table, matters got to the three-quarter stretch. The Honorable Patrick was a gallant man, both in deeds and words. As for the Blarney stone, his previous actions toward it must have been pronounced. Heavy damages for breach of promise could surely have been obtained had the Blarney stone seen fit to sue the Honorable Patrick.

"Jimmy, old man!" he called; he clapped Dougherty on the back; he shone like a midday sun upon Delia.

"Honorable Mr. Corrigan—Mrs. Dougherty," said "Big Jim."

The Honorable Patrick became a fountain of entertainment and admiration. The waiter had to fetch a third chair for him; he made another at the table, and the wineglasses were refilled.

"You selfish old rascal!" he exclaimed, shaking an arch finger at "Big Jim," "to have kept Mrs. Dougherty a secret from us."

And then "Big Jim" Dougherty, who was no talker, sat dumb, and saw the wife who had dined every evening for three years at home, blossom like a fairy flower. Quick, witty, charming, full of light and ready talk, she received the experienced attack of the Honorable Patrick on the field of repartee and surprised, vanquished, delighted him. She unfolded her long-closed petals and around her the room became a garden. They tried to include "Big Jim" in the conversation, but he was without a vocabulary.

And then a stray bunch of politicians and good fellows who lived for sport came into the room. They saw "Big Jim" and the leader, and over they came and were made acquainted with Mrs. Dougherty. And in a few minutes she was holding a salon. Half a dozen men surrounded her, courtiers all, and six found her capable of charming. "Big Jim" sat, grim, and kept saying to himself: "Three years, three years!"

The dinner came to an end. The Honorable Patrick reached for Mrs. Dougherty's cloak; but that was a matter of action instead of words, and Dougherty's big hand got it first by two seconds.

While the farewells were being said at the door the Honorable Patrick smote Dougherty mightily between the shoulders.

"Jimmy, me boy," he declared, in a giant whisper, "the madam is a jewel of the first water. Ye're a lucky dog."

"Big Jim" walked homeward with his wife. She seemed quite as pleased with the lights and show windows in the streets as with the admiration of the men in Hoogley's. As they passed Seltzer's they heard the sound of many voices in the café. The boys would be starting the drinks around now and discussing past performances.

At the door of their home Delia paused. The pleasure of the outing radiated softly from her countenance. She could not hope for Jim of evenings, but the glory of this one would lighten her lonely hours for a long time.

"Thank you for taking me out, Jim," she said, gratefully. "You'll be going back to Seltzer's now, of course."

"To —— with Seltzer's," said "Big Jim," emphatically. "And d—— Pat Corrigan! Does he think I haven't got any eyes?"

And the door closed behind both of them.

"LITTLE SPECK IN GARNERED FRUIT"

The honeymoon was at its full. There was a flat with the reddest of new carpets, tasselled portières and six steins with pewter lids arranged on a ledge above the wainscoting of the dining-room. The wonder of it was yet upon them. Neither of them had ever seen a yellow primrose by the river's brim; but if such a sight had met their eyes at that time it would have seemed like—well, whatever the poet expected the right kind of people to see in it besides a primrose.

The bride sat in the rocker with her feet resting upon the world. She was wrapt in rosy dreams and a kimono of the same hue. She wondered what the people in Greenland and Tasmania and Beloochistan were saying one to another about her marriage to Kid McGarry. Not that it made any difference. There was no welter-weight from London to the Southern Cross that could stand up four hours—no; four rounds—with her bridegroom. And he had been hers for three weeks; and the crook of her little finger could sway him more than the fist of any 142-pounder in the world.

Love, when it is ours, is the other name for self-abnegation and sacrifice. When it belongs to people across the airshaft it means arrogance and self-conceit.

The bride crossed her oxfords and looked thoughtfully at the distemper Cupids on the ceiling.

"Precious," said she, with the air of Cleopatra asking Antony for Rome done up in tissue paper and delivered at residence, "I think I would like a peach."

Kid McGarry arose and put on his coat and hat. He was serious, shaven, sentimental, and spry.

"All right," said he, as coolly as though he were only agreeing to sign articles to fight the champion of England. "I'll step down and cop one out for you—see?"

"Don't be long," said the bride. "I'll be lonesome without my naughty boy. Get a nice, ripe one."

After a series of farewells that would have befitted an imminent voyage to foreign parts, the Kid went down to the street.

Here he not unreasonably hesitated, for the season was yet early spring, and there seemed small chance of wresting anywhere from those chill streets and stores the coveted luscious guerdon of summer's golden prime.

At the Italian's fruit-stand on the corner he stopped and cast a contemptuous eye over the display of papered oranges, highly polished apples, and wan, sun-hungry bananas.

"Gotta da peach?" asked the Kid in the tongue of Dante, the lover of lovers.

"Ah, no," sighed the vender. "Not for one mont-com-a da peach. Too soon. Gotta da nice-a orange. Like-a da orange?"

Scornful, the Kid pursued his quest. He entered the all-night chophouse, café, and bowling-alley of his friend and admirer, Justus O'Callahan. The O'Callahan was about in his institution, looking for leaks.

"I want it straight," said the Kid to him. "The old woman has got a hunch that she wants a peach. Now, if you've got a peach, Cal, get it out quick. I want it and others like it if you've got 'em in plural quantities."

"The house is yours," said O'Callahan. "But there's no peach in it. It's too soon. I don't suppose you could even find 'em at one of the Broadway joints. That's too bad. When a lady fixes her mouth for a certain kind of fruit nothing else won't do. It's too late now to find any of the first-class fruiterers open. But if you think the missis would like some nice oranges I've just got a box of fine ones in that she might——"

"Much obliged, Cal. It's a peach proposition right from the ring of the gong. I'll try further."

The time was nearly midnight as the Kid walked down the West-Side avenue. Few stores were open, and such as were practically hooted at the idea of a peach.

But in her moated flat the bride confidently awaited her Persian fruit. A champion welter-weight not find a peach?—not stride triumphantly over the seasons and the zodiac and the almanac to fetch an Amsden's June or a Georgia cling to his owny-own?

The Kid's eye caught sight of a window that was lighted and gorgeous with nature's most entrancing colors. The light suddenly went out. The Kid sprinted and caught the fruiterer locking his door.

"Peaches?" said he, with extreme deliberation.

"Well, no, sir. Not for three or four weeks yet. I haven't any idea where you might find some. There may be a few in town from under the glass, but they'd be hard to locate. Maybe at one of the more expensive hotels —some place where there's plenty of money to waste. I've got some very fine oranges, though—from a shipload that came in to-day."

The Kid lingered on the corner for a moment, and then set out briskly toward a pair of green lights that flanked the steps of a building down a dark side street.

"Captain around anywhere?" he asked of the desk sergeant of the police station.

At that moment the captain came briskly forward from the rear. He was in plain clothes and had a busy air.

"Hello, Kid," he said to the pugilist. "Thought you were bridal-touring?"

"Got back yesterday. I'm a solid citizen now. Think I'll take an interest in municipal doings. How would it suit you to get into Denver Dick's place to-night, Cap?"

"Past performances," said the captain, twisting his moustache. "Denver was closed up two months ago."

"Correct," said the Kid. "Rafferty chased him out of the Forty-third. He's running in your precinct now, and his game's bigger than ever. I'm down on this gambling business. I can put you against his game."

"In my precinct?" growled the captain. "Are you sure, Kid? I'll take it as a favor. Have you got the entrée? How is it to be done?"

"Hammers," said the Kid. "They haven't got any steel on the doors yet. You'll need ten men. No; they won't let me in the place. Denver has been trying to do me. He thought I tipped him off for the other raid. I didn't, though. You want to hurry. I've got to get back home. The house is only three blocks from here."

Before ten minutes had sped the captain with a dozen men stole with their guide into the hall-way of a dark and virtuous-looking building in which many businesses were conducted by day.

"Third floor, rear," said the Kid, softly. "I'll lead the way."

Two axemen faced the door that he pointed out to them.

"It seems all quiet," said the captain, doubtfully. "Are you sure your tip is straight?"

"Cut away!" said the Kid. "It's on me if it ain't."

The axes crashed through the as yet unprotected door. A blaze of light from within poured through the smashed panels. The door fell, and the raiders sprang into the room with their guns handy.

The big room was furnished with the gaudy magnificence dear to Denver Dick's western ideas. Various well-patronized games were in progress. About fifty men who were in the room rushed upon the police in a grand break for personal liberty. The plain-clothes men had to do a little club-swinging. More than half the patrons escaped.

Denver Dick had graced his game with his own presence that night. He led the rush that was intended to sweep away the smaller body of raiders. But when he saw the Kid his manner became personal. Being in the heavy-weight class he cast himself joyfully upon his slighter enemy, and they rolled down a flight of stairs in each other's arms. On the landing they separated and arose, and then the Kid was able to use some of his professional tactics, which had been useless to him while in the excited clutch of a 200-pound sporting gentleman who was about to lose $20,000 worth of paraphernalia.

After vanquishing his adversary the Kid hurried upstairs and through the gambling-room into a smaller apartment connecting by an arched doorway.

Here was a long table set with choicest chinaware and silver, and lavishly furnished with food of that expensive and spectacular sort of which the devotees of sport are supposed to be fond. Here again was to be perceived the liberal and florid taste of the gentleman with the urban cognominal prefix.

A No. 10 patent leather shoe protruded a few of its inches outside the tablecloth along the floor. The Kid seized this and plucked forth a black man in a white tie and the garb of a servitor.

"Get up!" commanded the Kid. "Are you in charge of this free lunch?"

"Yes, sah, I was. Has they done pinched us ag'in, boss?"

"Looks that way. Listen to me. Are there any peaches in this layout? If there ain't I'll have to throw up the sponge."

"There was three dozen, sah, when the game opened this evenin'; but I reckon the gentlemen done eat 'em all up. If you'd lik to eat a fustrate orange, sah, I kin find you some."

"Get busy," ordered the Kid sternly, "and move whatever peach crop you've got quick or there'll be trouble. If anybody oranges me again to-night, I'll knock his face off."

The raid on Denver Dick's high-priced and prodigal luncheon revealed one lone, last peach that had escaped the epicurean jaws of the followers of chance. Into the Kid's pocket it went, and that indefatigable forager departed immediately with his prize. With scarcely a glance at the scene on the sidewalk below, where the officers were loading their prisoners into the patrol wagons, he moved homeward with long, swift strides.

His heart was light as he went. So rode the knights back to Camelot after perils and high deeds done for their ladies fair. The Kid's lady had commanded him and he had obeyed. True, it was but a peach that she had craved; but it had been no small deed to glean a peach at midnight from that wintry city where yet the February snows lay like iron. She had asked for a peach; she was his bride; in his pocket the peach was warming in his hand that held it for fear that it might fall out and be lost.

On the way the Kid turned in at an all-night drug store and said to the spectacled clerk:

"Say, sport, I wish you'd size up this rib of mine and see if it's broke. I was in a little scrap and bumped down a flight or two of stairs."

The druggist made an examination.

"It isn't broken," was his diagnosis; "but you have a bruise there that looks like you'd fallen off the Flatiron twice."

"That's all right," said the Kid. "Let's have your clothesbrush, please."

The bride waited in the rosy glow of the pink lamp shade. The miracles were not all passed away. By breathing a desire for some slight thing—a flower, a pomegranate, a—oh, yeh, a peach—she could send forth her man into the night, into the world which could not withstand him, and he would do her bidding.

And now he stood by her chair and laid the peach in her hand.

"Naughty boy!" she said fondly. "Did I say a peach? I think I would much rather have had an orange."

Blest be the bride.

THE HARBINGER

Long before the springtide is felt in the dull bosom of the yokel does the city man know that the grass-green goddess is upon her throne. He sits at his breakfast eggs and toast, begirt by stone walls, opens his morning paper and sees journalism leave vernalism at the post.

For, whereas spring's couriers were once the evidence of our finer senses, now the Associated Press does the trick.

The warble of the first robin in Hackensack, the stirring of the maple sap in Bennington, the budding of the pussy willows along Main Street in Syracuse, the first chirp of the bluebird, the swan song of the Blue Point, the annual tornado in St. Louis, the plaint of the peach pessimist from Pompton, N. J., the regular visit of the tame wild goose with a broken leg to the pond near Bilgewater Junction, the base attempt of the Drug Trust to boost the price of quinine foiled in the House by Congressman Jinks, the first tall poplar struck by lightning and the usual stunned picnickers who had taken refuge, the first crack of the ice jam in the Allegheny River, the finding of a violet in its mossy bed by the Correspondent at Round Corners—these are the advance signs of the burgeoning season that are wired into the wise city, while the farmer sees nothing but winter upon his dreary fields.

But these be mere externals. The true harbinger is the heart. When

Strephon seeks his Chloe and Mike his Maggie, then only is spring arrived and the newspaper report of the five-foot rattler killed in Squire Pettigrew's pasture confirmed.

Ere the first violet blew, Mr. Peters, Mr. Ragsdale and Mr. Kidd sat together on a bench in Union Square and conspired. Mr. Peters was the D'Artagnan of the loafers there. He was the dingiest, the laziest, the sorriest brown blot against the green background of any bench in the park. But just then he was the most important of the trio.

Mr. Peters had a wife. This had not heretofore affected his standing with Ragsy and Kidd. But to-day it invested him with a peculiar interest. His friends, having escaped matrimony, had shown a disposition to deride Mr. Peters for his venture on that troubled sea. But at last they had been forced to acknowledge that either he had been gifted with a large foresight or that he was one of Fortune's lucky sons.

For, Mrs. Peters had a dollar. A whole dollar bill, good and receivable by the Government for customs, taxes, and all public dues. How to get possession of that dollar was the question up for discussion by the three musty musketeers.

"How do you know it was a dollar?" asked Ragsy, the immensity of the sum inclining him to scepticism.

"The coalman seen her have it," said Mr. Peters. "She went out and done some washing yesterday. And look what she give me for breakfast —the heel of a loaf and a cup of coffee, and her with a dollar!"

"It's fierce," said Ragsy.

"Say we go up and punch 'er and stick a towel in 'er mouth and cop the coin," suggested Kidd, viciously. "Y' ain't afraid of a woman, are you?"

"She might holler and have us pinched," demurred Ragsy. "I don't believe in slugging no woman in a houseful of people."

"Gent'men," said Mr. Peters, severely, through his russet stubble, "remember that you are speaking of my wife. A man who would lift his hand to a lady except in the way of——"

"Maguire," said Ragsy, pointedly, "has got his bock beer sign out. If we had a dollar we could——"

"Hush up!" said Mr. Peters, licking his lips. "We got to get that casenote somehow, boys. Ain't what's a man's wife's his? Leave it to me. I'll go over to the house and get it. Wait here for me."

"I've seen 'em give up quick, and tell you where it's hid if you kick 'em in the ribs," said Kidd.

"No man would kick a woman," said Peters, virtuously. "A little choking—just a touch on the wind-pipe—that gets away with 'em—and no marks left. Wait for me. I'll bring back that dollar, boys."

High up in a tenement-house between Second Avenue and the river lived the Peterses in a back room so gloomy that the landlord blushed to take the rent for it. Mrs. Peters worked at sundry times, doing odd jobs of scrubbing and washing. Mr. Peters had a pure, unbroken record of five years without having earned a penny. And yet they clung together, sharing each other's hatred and misery, being creatures of habit. Of habit, the power that keeps the earth from flying to pieces; though there is some silly theory of gravitation.

Mrs. Peters reposed her 200 pounds on the safer of the two chairs and gazed stolidly out the one window at the brick wall opposite. Her eyes were red and damp. The furniture could have been carried away on a pushcart, but no pushcart man would have removed it as a gift.

The door opened to admit Mr. Peters. His fox-terrier eyes expressed a wish. His wife's diagnosis located correctly the seat of it, but misread it hunger instead of thirst.

"You'll get nothing more to eat till night," she said, looking out of the window again. "Take your hound-dog's face out of the room."

Mr. Peters' eye calculated the distance between them. By taking her by surprise it might be possible to spring upon her, overthrow her, and apply the throttling tactics of which he had boasted to his waiting comrades. True, it had been only a boast; never yet had he dared to lay violent hands upon her; but with the thoughts of the delicious, cool bock or Culmbacher bracing his nerves, he was near to upsetting his own theories of the treatment due by a gentleman to a lady. But, with his loafer's love for the more artistic and less strenuous way, he chose diplomacy first, the high card in the game—the assumed attitude of success already attained.

"You have a dollar," he said, loftily, but significantly in the tone that goes with the lighting of a cigar—when the properties are at hand.

"I have," said Mrs. Peters, producing the bill from her bosom and crackling it, teasingly.

"I am offered a position in a—in a tea store," said Mr. Peters. "I am to begin work tomorrow. But it will be necessary for me to buy a pair of——"

"You are a liar," said Mrs. Peters, reinterring the note. "No tea store, nor no A B C store, nor no junk shop would have you. I rubbed the skin off both me hands washin' jumpers and overalls to make that dollar. Do you think it come out of them suds to buy the kind you put into you? Skiddoo! Get your mind off of money."

Evidently the poses of Talleyrand were not worth one hundred cents on that dollar. But diplomacy is dexterous. The artistic temperament of Mr. Peters lifted him by the straps of his congress gaiters and set him on new ground. He called up a look of desperate melancholy to his eyes.

"Clara," he said, hollowly, "to struggle further is useless. You have always misunderstood me. Heaven knows I have striven with all my might to keep my head above the waves of misfortune, but——"

"Cut out the rainbow of hope and that stuff about walkin' one by one through the narrow isles of Spain," said Mrs. Peters, with a sigh. "I've heard it so often. There's an ounce bottle of carbolic on the shelf behind the empty coffee can. Drink hearty."

Mr. Peters reflected. What next! The old expedients had failed. The two musty musketeers were awaiting him hard by the ruined château— that is to say, on a park bench with rickety cast-iron legs. His honor was at stake. He had engaged to storm the castle singlehanded and bring back the treasure that was to furnish them wassail and solace. And all that stood between him and the coveted dollar was his wife, once a little girl whom he could—aha!—why not again? Once with soft words he could, as they say, twist her around his little finger. Why not again? Not for years had he tried it. Grim poverty and mutual hatred had killed all that. But Ragsy and Kidd were waiting for him to bring that dollar!

Mr. Peters took a surreptitiously keen look at his wife. Her formless bulk overflowed the chair. She kept her eyes fixed out the window in a strange kind of trance. Her eyes showed that she had been recently weeping.

"I wonder," said Mr. Peters to himself, "if there'd be anything in it."

The window was open upon its outlook of brick walls and drab, barren back yards. Except for the mildness of the air that entered it might have been midwinter yet in the city that turns such a frowning face to besieging spring. But spring doesn't come with the thunder of cannon. She is a sapper and a miner, and you must capitulate.

"I'll try it," said Mr. Peters to himself, making a wry face.

He went up to his wife and put his arm across her shoulders.

"Clara, darling," he said in tones that shouldn't have fooled a baby seal, "why should we have hard words? Ain't you my own tootsum wootsum?"

A black mark against you, Mr. Peters, in the sacred ledger of Cupid. Charges of attempted graft are filed against you, and of forgery and utterance of two of Love's holiest of appellations.

But the miracle of spring was wrought. Into the back room over the back alley between the black walls had crept the Harbinger. It was ridiculous, and yet—— Well, it is a rat trap, and you, madam and sir and all of us, are in it.

Red and fat and crying like Niobe or Niagara, Mrs. Peters threw her arms around her lord and dissolved upon him. Mr. Peters would have striven to extricate the dollar bill from its deposit vault, but his arms were bound to his sides.

"Do you love me, James?" asked Mrs. Peters.

"Madly," said James, "but——"

"You are ill!" exclaimed Mrs. Peters. "Why are you so pale and tired looking?"

"I feel weak," said Mr. Peters. "I——"

"Oh, wait; I know what it is. Wait, James. I'll be back in a minute."

With a parting hug that revived in Mr. Peters recollections of the Terrible Turk, his wife hurried out of the room and down the stairs.

Mr. Peters hitched his thumbs under his suspenders.

"All right," he confided to the ceiling. "I've got her going. I hadn't any idea the old girl was soft any more under the foolish rib. Well, sir; ain't I the Claude Melnotte of the lower East Side? What? It's a 100 to 1 shot that I get the dollar. I wonder what she went out for. I guess she's gone to tell Mrs. Muldoon on the second floor, that we're reconciled. I'll remember this. Soft soap! And Ragsy was talking about slugging her!"

Mrs. Peters came back with a bottle of sarsaparilla.

"I'm glad I happened to have that dollar," she said. "You're all run down, honey."

Mr. Peters had a tablespoonful of the stuff inserted into him. Then Mrs. Peters sat on his lap and murmured:

"Call me tootsum wootsums again, James."

He sat still, held there by his materialized goddess of spring.

Spring had come.

On the bench in Union Square Mr. Ragsdale and Mr. Kidd squirmed, tongue-parched, awaiting D'Artagnan and his dollar.

"I wish I had choked her at first," said Mr. Peters to himself.

WHILE THE AUTO WAITS

Promptly at the beginning of twilight, came again to that quiet corner of that quiet, small park the girl in gray. She sat upon a bench and read a book, for there was yet to come a half hour in which print could be accomplished.

To repeat: Her dress was gray, and plain enough to mask its impeccancy of style and fit. A large-meshed veil imprisoned her turban hat and a face that shone through it with a calm and unconscious beauty. She had come there at the same hour on the day previous, and on the day before that; and there was one who knew it.

The young man who knew it hovered near, relying upon burnt sacrifices to the great joss, Luck. His piety was rewarded, for, in turning a page, her book slipped from her fingers and bounded from the bench a full yard away.

The young man pounced upon it with instant avidity, returning it to its owner with that air that seems to flourish in parks and public places—a compound of gallantry and hope, tempered with respect for the policeman on the beat. In a pleasant voice, he risked an inconsequent remark upon the weather—that introductory topic responsible for so much of the world's unhappiness—and stood poised for a moment, awaiting his fate.

The girl looked him over leisurely; at his ordinary, neat dress and his features distinguished by nothing particular in the way of expression.

"You may sit down, if you like," she said, in a full, deliberate contralto. "Really, I would like to have you do so. The light is too bad for reading. I would prefer to talk."

The vassal of Luck slid upon the seat by her side with complaisance.

"Do you know," he said, speaking the formula with which park chairmen open their meetings, "that you are quite the stunningest girl I have seen in a long time? I had my eye on you yesterday. Didn't know somebody was bowled over by those pretty lamps of yours, did you, honeysuckle?"

"Whoever you are," said the girl, in icy tones, "you must remember that I am a lady. I will excuse the remark you have just made because the mistake was, doubtless, not an unnatural one—in your circle. I asked you to sit down; if the invitation must constitute me your honeysuckle, consider it withdrawn."

"I earnestly beg your pardon," pleaded the young man. His expression of satisfaction had changed to one of penitence and humility. "It was my fault, you know—I mean, there are girls in parks, you know—that is, of course, you don't know, but——"

"Abandon the subject, if you please. Of course I know. Now, tell me about these people passing and crowding, each way, along these paths. Where are they going? Why do they hurry so? Are they happy?"

The young man had promptly abandoned his air of coquetry. His cue was now for a waiting part; he could not guess the rôle he would be expected to play.

"It *is* interesting to watch them," he replied, postulating her mood. "It is the wonderful drama of life. Some are going to supper and some to—er —other places. One wonders what their histories are."

"I do not," said the girl; "I am not so inquisitive. I come here to sit because here, only, can I be near the great, common, throbbing heart of humanity. My part in life is cast where its beats are never felt. Can you surmise why I spoke to you, Mr.——?"

"Parkenstacker," supplied the young man. Then he looked eager and hopeful.

"No," said the girl, holding up a slender finger, and smiling slightly. "You would recognize it immediately. It is impossible to keep one's name out of print. Or even one's portrait. This veil and this hat of my maid furnish me with an *incog*. You should have seen the chauffeur stare at it when he thought I did not see. Candidly, there are five or six names that belong in the holy of holies, and mine, by the accident of birth, is one of them. I spoke to you, Mr. Stackenpot——"

"Parkenstacker," corrected the young man, modestly.

"—Mr. Parkenstacker, because I wanted to talk, for once, with a natural man—one unspoiled by the despicable gloss of wealth and supposed social superiority. Oh! you do not know how weary I am of it—money, money, money! And of the men who surround me, dancing like little marionettes all cut by the same pattern. I am sick of pleasure, of jewels, of travel, of society, of luxuries of all kinds."

"I always had an idea," ventured the young man, hesitatingly, "that money must be a pretty good thing."

"A competence is to be desired. But when you have so many millions that——!" She concluded the sentence with a gesture of despair. "It is the monotony of it," she continued, "that palls. Drives, dinners, theatres, balls, suppers, with the gilding of superfluous wealth over it all. Sometimes the very tinkle of the ice in my champagne glass nearly drives me mad."

Mr. Parkenstacker looked ingenuously interested.

"I have always liked," he said, "to read and hear about the ways of wealthy and fashionable folks. I suppose I am a bit of a snob. But I like to have my information accurate. Now, I had formed the opinion that champagne is cooled in the bottle and not by placing ice in the glass."

The girl gave a musical laugh of genuine amusement.

"You should know," she explained, in an indulgent tone, "that we of the non-useful class depend for our amusement upon departure from precedent. Just now it is a fad to put ice in champagne. The idea was originated by a visiting Prince of Tartary while dining at the Waldorf. It will soon give way to some other whim. Just as at a dinner party this week on Madison Avenue a green kid glove was laid by the plate of each guest to be put on and used while eating olives."

"I see," admitted the young man, humbly. "These special diversions of the inner circle do not become familiar to the common public."

"Sometimes," continued the girl, acknowledging his confession of error by a slight bow, "I have thought that if I ever should love a man it would be one of lowly station. One who is a worker and not a drone. But, doubtless, the claims of caste and wealth will prove stronger than my inclination. Just now I am besieged by two. One is a Grand Duke of a German principality. I think he has, or has had, a wife, somewhere, driven mad by his intemperance and cruelty. The other is an English Marquis, so cold and mercenary that I even prefer the diabolism of the Duke. What is it that impels me to tell you these things, Mr. Packenstacker?"

"Parkenstacker," breathed the young man. "Indeed, you cannot know how much I appreciate your confidences."

The girl contemplated him with a calm, impersonal regard that befitted the difference in their stations.

"What is your line of business, Mr. Parkenstacker?" she asked.

"A very humble one. But I hope to rise in the world. Were you really in earnest when you said that you could love a man of lowly position?"

"Indeed I was. But I said 'might.' There is the Grand Duke and the

Marquis, you know. Yes; no calling could be too humble were the man what I would wish him to be."

"I work," declared Mr. Parkenstacker, "in a restaurant."

The girl shrank slightly.

"Not as a waiter?" she said, a little imploringly. "Labor is noble, but—personal attendance, you know—valets and——"

"I am not a waiter. I am cashier in"—on the street they faced that bounded the opposite side of the park was the brilliant electric sign "RESTAURANT"—"I am cashier in that restaurant you see there."

The girl consulted a tiny watch set in a bracelet of rich design upon her left wrist, and rose, hurriedly. She thrust her book into a glittering reticule suspended from her waist, for which, however, the book was too large.

"Why are you not at work?" she asked.

"I am on the night turn," said the young man; "it is yet an hour before my period begins. May I not hope to see you again?"

"I do not know. Perhaps—but the whim may not seize me again. I must go quickly now. There is a dinner, and a box at the play—and, oh! the same old round. Perhaps you noticed an automobile at the upper corner of the park as you came. One with a white body."

"And red running gear?" asked the young man, knitting his brows reflectively.

"Yes. I always come in that. Pierre waits for me there. He supposes me to be shopping in the department store across the square. Conceive of the bondage of the life wherein we must deceive even our chauffeurs. Good-night."

"But it is dark now," said Mr. Parkenstacker, "and the park is full of rude men. May I not walk——?"

"If you have the slightest regard for my wishes," said the girl, firmly, "you will remain at this bench for ten minutes after I have left. I do not mean to accuse you, but you are probably aware that autos generally bear the monogram of their owner. Again, good-night."

Swift and stately she moved away through the dusk. The young man watched her graceful form as she reached the pavement at the park's edge, and turned up along it toward the corner where stood the automobile. Then he treacherously and unhesitatingly began to dodge and skim among the park trees and shrubbery in a course parallel to her route, keeping her well in sight.

When she reached the corner she turned her head to glance at the motor car, and then passed it, continuing on across the street. Sheltered behind a convenient standing cab, the young man followed her movements closely with his eyes. Passing down the sidewalk of the street opposite the park, she entered the restaurant with the blazing sign. The place was one of those frankly glaring establishments, all white paint and glass, where one may dine cheaply and conspicuously. The girl penetrated the restaurant to some retreat at its rear, whence she quickly emerged without her hat and veil.

The cashier's desk was well to the front. A red-haired girl on the stool climbed down, glancing pointedly at the clock as she did so. The girl in gray mounted in her place.

The young man thrust his hands into his pockets and walked slowly back along the sidewalk. At the corner his foot struck a small, paper-covered volume lying there, sending it sliding to the edge of the turf. By its picturesque cover he recognized it as the book the girl had been reading. He picked it up carelessly, and saw that its title was "New Arabian Nights," the author being of the name of Stevenson. He dropped it again upon the grass, and lounged, irresolute, for a minute. Then he stepped into the automobile, reclined upon the cushions, and said two words to the chauffeur:

"Club, Henri."

A COMEDY IN RUBBER

One may hope, in spite of the metaphorists, to avoid the breath of the deadly upas tree; one may, by great good fortune, succeed in blacking the eye of the basilisk; one might even dodge the attentions of Cerberus and Argus, but no man, alive or dead, can escape the gaze of the Rubberer.

New York is the Caoutchouc City. There are many, of course, who go their ways, making money, without turning to the right or the left, but there is a tribe abroad wonderfully composed, like the Martians, solely of eyes and means of locomotion.

These devotees of curiosity swarm, like flies, in a moment in a struggling, breathless circle about the scene of an unusual occurrence. If a workman opens a manhole, if a street car runs over a man from North Tarrytown, if a little boy drops an egg on his way home from the grocery, if a casual house or two drops into the subway, if a lady loses a nickel through a hole in the lisle thread, if the police drag a telephone and a racing chart forth from an Ibsen Society reading-room, if Senator Depew or Mr. Chuck Connors walks out to take the air—if any of these incidents or accidents takes place, you will see the mad, irresistible rush of the "rubber" tribe to the spot.

The importance of the event does not count. They gaze with equal interest and absorption at a chorus girl or at a man painting a liver pill sign. They will form as deep a cordon around a man with a clubfoot as they will around a balked automobile. They have the furor rubberendi. They are optical gluttons, feasting and fattening on the misfortunes of their fellow beings. They gloat and pore and glare and squint and stare with their fishy eyes like goggle-eyed perch at the hook baited with calamity.

It will seem that Cupid would find these ocular vampires too cold game for his calorific shafts, but have we not yet to discover an immune even among the Protozoa? Yes, beautiful Romance descended upon two of this tribe, and love came into their hearts as they crowded about the prostrate form of a man who had been run over by a brewery wagon.

William Pry was the first on the spot. He was an expert at such gatherings. With an expression of intense happiness on his features, he stood over the victim of the accident, listening to his groans as if to the sweetest music. When the crowd of spectators had swelled to a closely packed circle William saw a violent commotion in the crowd opposite him. Men were hurled aside like ninepins by the impact of some moving body that clove them like the rush of a tornado. With elbows, umbrella, hat-pin, tongue, and fingernails doing their duty, Violet Seymour forced her way through the mob of onlookers to the first row. Strong men who even had been able to secure a seat on the 5:30 Harlem express staggered back like children as she bucked centre. Two large lady spectators who had seen the Duke of Roxburgh married and had often blocked traffic on Twenty-third Street fell back into the second row with ripped shirt-waists when Violet had finished with them. William Pry loved her at first sight.

The ambulance removed the unconscious agent of Cupid. William and Violet remained after the crowd had dispersed. They were true Rubberers. People who leave the scene of an accident with the ambulance have not genuine caoutchouc in the cosmogony of their necks. The delicate, fine flavor of the affair is to be had only in the aftertaste—in gloating over the spot, in gazing fixedly at the houses opposite, in hovering there in a dream more exquisite than the opium-eater's ecstasy. William Pry and Violet Seymour were connoisseurs in casualties. They knew how to extract full enjoyment from every incident.

Presently they looked at each other. Violet had a brown birthmark on her neck as large as a silver half-dollar. William fixed his eyes upon it. William Pry had inordinately bowed legs. Violet allowed her gaze to linger unswervingly upon them. Face to face they stood thus for moments, each staring at the other. Etiquette would not allow them to speak; but in the Caoutchouc City it is permitted to gaze without stint at the trees in the parks and at the physical blemishes of a fellow creature.

At length with a sigh they parted. But Cupid had been the driver of the brewery wagon, and the wheel that broke a leg united two fond hearts.

The next meeting of the hero and heroine was in front of a board fence near Broadway. The day had been a disappointing one. There had been no fights on the street, children had kept from under the wheels of the street cars, cripples and fat men in negligée shirts were scarce; nobody seemed to be inclined to slip on banana peels or fall down with heart disease. Even the sport from Kokomo, Ind., who claims to be a cousin of ex-Mayor Low and scatters nickels from a cab window, had not put in his appearance. There was nothing to stare at, and William Pry had premonitions of ennui.

But he saw a large crowd scrambling and pushing excitedly in front of a billboard. Sprinting for it, he knocked down an old woman and a child carrying a bottle of milk, and fought his way like a demon into the mass of spectators. Already in the inner line stood Violet Seymour with one sleeve and two gold fillings gone, a corset steel puncture and a sprained wrist, but happy. She was looking at what there was to see. A man was painting upon the fence: "Eat Bricklets—They Fill Your Face."

Violet blushed when she saw William Pry. William jabbed a lady in a black silk raglan in the ribs, kicked a boy in the shin, hit an old gentleman on the left ear and managed to crowd nearer to Violet. They stood for an hour looking at the man paint the letters. Then William's love could be repressed no longer. He touched her on the arm.

"Come with me," he said. "I know where there is a bootblack without an Adam's apple."

She looked up at him shyly, yet with unmistakable love transfiguring her countenance.

"And you have saved it for me?" she asked, trembling with the first dim ecstasy of a woman beloved.

Together they hurried to the bootblack's stand. An hour they spent there gazing at the malformed youth.

A window-cleaner fell from the fifth story to the sidewalk beside them. As the ambulance came clanging up William pressed her hand joyously. "Four ribs at least and a compound fracture," he whispered, swiftly. "You are not sorry that you met me, are you, dearest?"

"Me?" said Violet, returning the pressure. "Sure not. I could stand all day rubbering with you."

The climax of the romance occurred a few days later. Perhaps the reader will remember the intense excitement into which the city was thrown when Eliza Jane, a colored woman, was served with a subpœna. The Rubber Tribe encamped on the spot. With his own hands William Pry placed a board upon two beer kegs in the street opposite Eliza Jane's residence. He and Violet sat there for three days and nights. Then it occurred to a detective to open the door and serve the subpœna. He sent for a kinetoscope and did so.

Two souls with such congenial tastes could not long remain apart. As a policeman drove them away with his night stick that evening they plighted their troth. The seeds of love had been well sown, and had grown up, hardy and vigorous, into a—let us call it a rubber plant.

The wedding of William Pry and Violet Seymour was set for June 10. The Big Church in the Middle of the Block was banked high with flowers.

The populous tribe of Rubberers the world over is rampant over weddings. They are the pessimists of the pews. They are the guyers of the groom and the banterers of the bride. They come to laugh at your marriage, and should you escape from Hymen's tower on the back of death's pale steed they will come to the funeral and sit in the same pew and cry over your luck. Rubber will stretch.

The church was lighted. A grosgrain carpet lay over the asphalt to the edge of the sidewalk. Bridesmaids were patting one another's sashes awry and speaking of the bride's freckles. Coachmen tied white ribbons on their whips and bewailed the space of time between drinks. The minister was musing over his possible fee, essaying conjecture whether it would suffice to purchase a new broadcloth suit for himself and a photograph of Laura Jane Libbey for his wife. Yea, Cupid was in the air.

And outside the church, oh, my brothers, surged and heaved the rank and file of the tribe of Rubberers. In two bodies they were, with the grosgrain carpet and cops with clubs between. They crowded like cattle, they fought, they pressed and surged and swayed and trampled one another to see a bit of a girl in a white veil acquire license to go through a man's pockets while he sleeps.

But the hour for the wedding came and went, and the bride and bridegroom came not. And impatience gave way to alarm and alarm brought about search, and they were not found. And then two big policemen took a hand and dragged out of the furious mob of onlookers a crushed and trampled thing, with a wedding ring in its vest pocket and a shredded and hysterical woman beating her way to the carpet's edge, ragged, bruised and obstreperous.

William Pry and Violet Seymour, creatures of habit, had joined in the seething game of the spectators, unable to resist the overwhelming desire to gaze upon themselves entering, as bride and bridegroom, the rose-decked church.

Rubber will out.

ONE THOUSAND DOLLARS

"One thousand dollars," repeated Lawyer Tolman, solemnly and severely, "and here is the money."

Young Gillian gave a decidedly amused laugh as he fingered the thin package of new fifty-dollar notes.

"It's such a confoundedly awkward amount," he explained, genially, to the lawyer. "If it had been ten thousand a fellow might wind up with a lot of fireworks and do himself credit. Even fifty dollars would have been less trouble."

"You heard the reading of your uncle's will," continued Lawyer Tolman, professionally dry in his tones. "I do not know if you paid much attention to its details. I must remind you of one. You are required to render to us an account of the manner of expenditure of this $1,000 as soon as you have disposed of it. The will stipulates that. I trust that you will so far comply with the late Mr. Gillian's wishes."

"You may depend upon it," said the young man, politely, "in spite of the extra expense it will entail. I may have to engage a secretary. I was never good at accounts."

Gillian went to his club. There he hunted out one whom he called Old Bryson.

Old Bryson was calm and forty and sequestered. He was in a corner reading a book, and when he saw Gillian approaching he sighed, laid down his book and took off his glasses.

"Old Bryson, wake up," said Gillian. "I've a funny story to tell you."

"I wish you would tell it to someone in the billiard room," said Old Bryson. "You know how I hate your stories."

"This is a better one than usual," said Gillian, rolling a cigarette; "and I'm glad to tell it to you. It's too sad and funny to go with the rattling of billiard balls. I've just come from my late uncle's firm of legal corsairs. He leaves me an even thousand dollars. Now, what can a man possibly do with a thousand dollars?"

"I thought," said Old Bryson, showing as much interest as a bee shows in a vinegar cruet, "that the late Septimus Gillian was worth something like half a million."

"He was," assented Gillian, joyously, "and that's where the joke comes in. He's left his whole cargo of doubloons to a microbe. That is, part of it goes to the man who invents a new bacillus and the rest to establish a hospital for doing away with it again. There are one or two trifling bequests on the side. The butler and the housekeeper get a seal ring and $10 each. His nephew gets $1,000."

"You've always had plenty of money to spend," observed Old Bryson.

"Tons," said Gillian. "Uncle was the fairy godmother as far as an allowance was concerned."

"Any other heirs?" asked Old Bryson.

"None." Gillian frowned at his cigarette and kicked the upholstered leather of a divan uneasily. "There is a Miss Hayden, a ward of my uncle, who lived in his house. She's a quiet thing—musical—the daughter of somebody who was unlucky enough to be his friend. I forgot to say that she was in on the seal ring and $10 joke, too. I wish I had been. Then I could have had two bottles of brut, tipped the waiter with the ring, and had the whole business off my hands. Don't be superior and insulting, Old Bryson—tell me what a fellow can do with a thousand dollars."

Old Bryson rubbed his glasses and smiled. And when Old Bryson smiled, Gillian knew that he intended to be more offensive than ever.

"A thousand dollars," he said, "means much or little. One man may buy a happy home with it and laugh at Rockefeller. Another could send his wife South with it and save her life. A thousand dollars would buy pure milk for one hundred babies during June, July, and August and save fifty of their lives. You could count upon a half hour's diversion with it at faro in one of the fortified art galleries. It would furnish an education to an ambitious boy. I am told that a genuine Corot was secured for that amount in an auction room yesterday. You could move to a New Hampshire town and live respectably two years on it. You could rent Madison Square Garden for one evening with it, and lecture your audience, if you should have one, on the precariousness of the profession of heir presumptive."

"People might like you, Old Bryson," said Gillian, almost unruffled, "if you wouldn't moralize. I asked you to tell me what I could do with a thousand dollars."

"You?" said Bryson, with a gentle laugh. "Why, Bobby Gillian, there's only one logical thing you could do. You can go buy Miss Lotta Lauriere a diamond pendant with the money, and then take yourself off to Idaho and inflict your presence upon a ranch. I advise a sheep ranch, as I have a particular dislike for sheep."

"Thanks," said Gillian, rising. "I thought I could depend upon you, Old Bryson. You hit on the very scheme. I wanted to chuck the money in a lump, for I've got to turn in an account for it, and I hate itemizing."

Gillian phoned for a cab and said to the driver:

"The stage entrance of the Columbine Theatre."

Miss Lotta Lauriere was assisting nature with a powder puff, almost ready for her call at a crowded matinée, when her dresser mentioned the name of Mr. Gillian.

"Let it in," said Miss Lauriere. "Now, what is it, Bobby? I'm going on in two minutes."

"Rabbit-foot your right ear a little," suggested Gillian, critically. "That's better. It won't take two minutes for me. What do you say to a little thing in the pendant line? I can stand three ciphers with a figure one in front of 'em."

"Oh, just as you say," carolled Miss Lauriere.

"My right glove, Adams. Say, Bobby, did you see that necklace Della Stacey had on the other night? Twenty-two hundred dollars it cost at Tiffany's. But, of course—pull my sash a little to the left, Adams."

"Miss Lauriere for the opening chorus!" cried the call boy without.

Gillian strolled out to where his cab was waiting.

"What would you do with a thousand dollars if you had it?" he asked the driver.

"Open a s'loon," said the cabby promptly and huskily. "I know a place

I could take money in with both hands. It's a four-story brick on a corner. I've got it figured out. Second story—Chinks and chop suey; third floor—manicures and foreign missions; fourth floor—poolroom. If you was thinking of putting up the cap——"

"Oh, no," said Gillian, "I merely asked from curiosity. I take you by the hour. Drive till I tell you to stop."

Eight blocks down Broadway Gillian poked up the trap with his cane and got out. A blind man sat upon a stool on the sidewalk selling pencils. Gillian went out and stood before him.

"Excuse me," he said, "but would you mind telling me what you would do if you had a thousand dollars?"

"You got out of that cab that just drove up, didn't you?" asked the blind man.

"I did," said Gillian.

"I guess you are all right," said the pencil dealer, "to ride in a cab by daylight. Take a look at that, if you like."

He drew a small book from his coat pocket and held it out. Gillian opened it and saw that it was a bank deposit book. It showed a balance of $1,785 to the blind man's credit.

Gillian returned the book and got into the cab.

"I forgot something," he said. "You may drive to the law offices of Tolman & Sharp, at —— Broadway."

Lawyer Tolman looked at him hostilely and inquiringly through his gold-rimmed glasses.

"I beg your pardon," said Gillian, cheerfully, "but may I ask you a question? It is not an impertinent one, I hope. Was Miss Hayden left anything by my uncle's will besides the ring and the $10?"

"Nothing," said Mr. Tolman.

"I thank you very much, sir," said Gillian, and out he went to his cab. He gave the driver the address of his late uncle's home.

Miss Hayden was writing letters in the library. She was small and slender and clothed in black. But you would have noticed her eyes. Gillian drifted in with his air of regarding the world as inconsequent.

"I've just come from old Tolman's," he explained. "They've been going over the papers down there. They found a"—Gillian searched his memory for a legal term—"they found an amendment or a postscript or something to the will. It seemed that the old boy loosened up a little on second thoughts and willed you a thousand dollars. I was driving up this way and Tolman asked me to bring you the money. Here it is. You'd better count it to see if it's right." Gillian laid the money beside her hand on the desk.

Miss Hayden turned white. "Oh!" she said, and again "Oh!"

Gillian half turned and looked out of the window.

"I suppose, of course," he said, in a low voice, "that you know I love you."

"I am sorry," said Miss Hayden, taking up her money.

"There is no use?" asked Gillian, almost light-heartedly.

"I am sorry," she said again.

"May I write a note?" asked Gillian, with a smile. He seated himself at the big library table. She supplied him with paper and pen, and then went back to her secrétaire.

Gillian made out his account of his expenditure of the thousand dollars in these words:

"Paid by the black sheep, Robert Gillian, $1,000 on account of the eternal happiness, owed by Heaven to the best and dearest woman on earth."

Gillian slipped his writing into an envelope, bowed and went his way.

His cab stopped again at the offices of Tolman & Sharp.

"I have expended the thousand dollars," he said, cheerily, to Tolman of the gold glasses, "and I have come to render account of it, as I agreed. There is quite a feeling of summer in the air—do you not think so, Mr. Tolman?" He tossed a white envelope on the lawyer's table. "You will find there a memorandum, sir, of the *modus operandi* of the vanishing of the dollars."

Without touching the envelope, Mr. Tolman went to a door and called his partner, Sharp. Together they explored the caverns of an immense safe. Forth they dragged as trophy of their search a big envelope sealed with wax. This they forcibly invaded, and wagged their venerable heads together over its contents. Then Tolman became spokesman.

"Mr. Gillian," he said, formally, "there was a codicil to your uncle's will. It was intrusted to us privately, with instructions that it be not opened until you had furnished us with a full account of your handling of the $1,000 bequest in the will. As you have fulfilled the conditions, my partner and I have read the codicil. I do not wish to encumber your understanding with its legal phraseology, but I will acquaint you with the spirit of its contents.

"In the event that your disposition of the $1,000 demonstrates that you possess any of the qualifications that deserve reward, much benefit will accrue to you. Mr. Sharp and I are named as the judges, and I assure you that we will do our duty strictly according to justice—with liberality. We are not at all unfavorably disposed toward you, Mr. Gillian. But let us return to the letter of the codicil. If your disposal of the money in question has been prudent, wise, or unselfish, it is in our power to hand you over bonds to the value of $50,000, which have been placed in our hands for that purpose. But if—as our client, the late Mr. Gillian, explicitly provides —you have used this money as you have used money in the past—I quote the late Mr. Gillian—in reprehensible dissipation among disreputable associates—the $50,000 is to be paid to Miriam Hayden, ward of the late Mr. Gillian, without delay. Now, Mr. Gillian, Mr. Sharp and I will examine your account in regard to the $1,000. You submit it in writing, I believe. I hope you will repose confidence in our decision."

Mr. Tolman reached for the envelope. Gillian was a little the quicker in taking it up. He tore the account and its cover leisurely into strips and dropped them into his pocket.

"It's all right," he said, smilingly. "There isn't a bit of need to bother you with this. I don't suppose you'd understand these itemized bets, anyway. I lost the thousand dollars on the races. Good-day to you, gentlemen."

Tolman & Sharp shook their heads mournfully at each other when Gillian left, for they heard him whistling gayly in the hallway as he waited for the elevator.

THE DEFEAT OF THE CITY

Robert Walmsley's descent upon the city resulted in a Kilkenny struggle. He came out of the fight victor by a fortune and a reputation. On the other hand, he was swallowed up by the city. The city gave him what he demanded and then branded him with its brand. It remodelled, cut, trimmed, and stamped him to the pattern it approves. It opened its social gates to him and shut him in on a close-cropped, formal lawn with the select herd of ruminants. In dress, habits, manners, provincialism, routine, and narrowness he acquired that charming insolence, that irritating completeness, that sophisticated crassness, that over-balanced poise that makes the Manhattan gentleman so delightfully small in his greatness.

One of the up-state rural counties pointed with pride to the successful young metropolitan lawyer as a product of its soil. Six years earlier this county had removed the wheat straw from between its huckleberry-stained teeth and emitted a derisive and bucolic laugh as old man Walmsley's freckle-faced "Bob" abandoned the certain three-per-diem meals of the one-horse farm for the discontinuous quick lunch counters of the three-ringed metropolis. At the end of the six years no murder trial, coaching party, automobile accident or cotillion was complete in which the name of Robert Walmsley did not figure. Tailors waylaid him in the street to get a new wrinkle from the cut of his unwrinkled trousers. Hyphenated fellows in the clubs and members of the oldest subpœnaed families were glad to clap him on the back and allow him three letters of his name.

But the Matterhorn of Robert Walmsley's success was not scaled until he married Alicia Van Der Pool. I cite the Matterhorn, for just so high and cool and white and inaccessible was this daughter of the old burghers. The social Alps that ranged about her—over whose bleak passes a thousand climbers struggled—reached only to her knees. She towered in her own atmosphere, serene, chaste, prideful, wading in no fountains, dining no monkeys, breeding no dogs for bench shows. She was a Van Der Pool. Fountains were made to play for her; monkeys were made for other people's ancestors; dogs, she understood, were created to be companions of blind persons and objectionable characters who smoked pipes.

This was the Matterhorn that Robert Walmsley accomplished. If he found, with the good poet with the game foot and artificially curled hair, that he who ascends to mountain tops will find the loftiest peaks most wrapped in clouds and snow, he concealed his chilblains beneath a brave and smiling exterior. He was a lucky man and knew it, even though he were imitating the Spartan boy with an ice-cream freezer beneath his doublet frappéeing the region of his heart.

After a brief wedding tour abroad, the couple returned to create a decided ripple in the calm cistern (so placid and cool and sunless it is) of the best society. They entertained at their red brick mausoleum of ancient greatness in an old square that is a cemetery of crumbled glory. And Robert Walmsley was proud of his wife; although while one of his hands shook his guests' the other held tightly to his alpenstock and thermometer.

One day Alicia found a letter written to Robert by his mother. It was an unerudite letter, full of crops and motherly love and farm notes. It chronicled the health of the pig and the recent red calf, and asked concerning Robert's in return. It was a letter direct from the soil, straight from home, full of biographies of bees, tales of turnips, pæans of new-laid eggs, neglected parents and the slump in dried apples.

"Why have I not been shown your mother's letters?" asked Alicia. There was always something in her voice that made you think of lorgnettes, of accounts at Tiffany's, of sledges smoothly gliding on the trail from Dawson to Forty Mile, of the tinkling of pendent prisms on your grandmothers' chandeliers, of snow lying on a convent roof; of a police sergeant refusing bail. "Your mother," continued Alicia, "invites us to make a visit to the farm. I have never seen a farm. We will go there for a week or two, Robert."

"We will," said Robert, with the grand air of an associate Supreme Justice concurring in an opinion. "I did not lay the invitation before you because I thought you would not care to go. I am much pleased at your decision."

"I will write to her myself," answered Alicia, with a faint foreshadowing of enthusiasm. "Félice shall pack my trunks at once. Seven, I think, will be enough. I do not suppose that your mother entertains a great deal. Does she give many house parties?"

Robert arose, and as attorney for rural places filed a demurrer against six of the seven trunks. He endeavored to define, picture, elucidate, set forth and describe a farm. His own words sounded strange in his ears. He had not realized how thoroughly urbsidized he had become.

A week passed and found them landed at the little country station five hours out from the city. A grinning, stentorian, sarcastic youth driving a mule to a spring wagon hailed Robert savagely.

"Hallo, Mr. Walmsley. Found your way back at last, have you? Sorry I couldn't bring in the automobile for you, but dad's bull-tonguing the ten-acre clover patch with it to-day. Guess you'll excuse my not wearing a dress suit over to meet you—it ain't six o'clock yet, you know."

"I'm glad to see you, Tom," said Robert, grasping his brother's hand. "Yes, I've found my way at last. You've a right to say 'at last.' It's been over two years since the last time. But it will be oftener after this, my boy."

Alicia, cool in the summer heat as an Arctic wraith, white as a Norse snow maiden in her flimsy muslin and fluttering lace parasol, came round the corner of the station; and Tom was stripped of his assurance. He became chiefly eyesight clothed in blue jeans, and on the homeward drive to the mule alone did he confide in language the inwardness of his thoughts.

They drove homeward. The low sun dropped a spendthrift flood of gold upon the fortunate fields of wheat. The cities were far away. The road lay curling around wood and dale and hill like a ribbon lost from the robe of careless summer. The wind followed like a whinnying colt in the track of Phœbus's steeds.

By and by the farmhouse peeped gray out of its faithful grove; they saw the long lane with its convoy of walnut trees running from the road to the house; they smelled the wild rose and the breath of cool, damp willows in the creek's bed. And then in unison all the voices of the soil began a chant addressed to the soul of Robert Walmsley. Out of the tilted aisles of the dim wood they came hollowly; they chirped and buzzed from the parched grass; they trilled from the ripples of the creek ford; they floated up in clear Pan's pipe notes from the dimming meadows; the whippoorwills joined in as they pursued midges in the upper air; slow-going cow-bells struck out a homely accompaniment—and this was what each one said: "You've found your way back at last, have you?"

The old voices of the soil spoke to him. Leaf and bud and blossom conversed with him in the old vocabulary of his careless youth—the inanimate things, the familiar stones and rails, the gates and furrows and roofs and turns of road had an eloquence, too, and a power in the transformation. The country had smiled and he had felt the breath of it, and his heart was drawn as if in a moment back to his old love. The city was far away.

This rural atavism, then, seized Robert Walmsley and possessed him. A queer thing he noticed in connection with it was that Alicia, sitting at his side, suddenly seemed to him a stranger. She did not belong to this recurrent phase. Never before had she seemed so remote, so colorless and high—so intangible and unreal. And yet he had never admired her more than when she sat there by him in the rickety spring wagon, chiming no more with his mood and with her environment than the Matterhorn chimes with a peasant's cabbage garden.

That night when the greetings and the supper were over, the entire family, including Buff, the yellow dog, bestrewed itself upon the front porch. Alicia, not haughty but silent, sat in the shadow dressed in an exquisite pale-gray tea gown. Robert's mother discoursed to her happily concerning marmalade and lumbago. Tom sat on the top step; Sisters Millie and Pam on the lowest step to catch the lightning bugs. Mother had the willow rocker. Father sat in the big armchair with one of its arms gone. Buff sprawled in the middle of the porch in everybody's way. The twilight pixies and pucks stole forth unseen and plunged other poignant shafts of memory into the heart of Robert. A rural madness entered his soul. The city was far away.

Father sat without his pipe, writhing in his heavy boots, a sacrifice to rigid courtesy. Robert shouted: "No, you don't!" He fetched the pipe and lit it; he seized the old gentleman's boots and tore them off. The last one slipped suddenly, and Mr. Robert Walmsley, of Washington Square, tumbled off the porch backward with Buff on top of him, howling fearfully. Tom laughed sarcastically.

Robert tore off his coat and vest and hurled them into a lilac bush.

"Come out here, you landlubber," he cried to Tom, "and I'll put grass seed on your back. I think you called me a 'dude' a while ago. Come along and cut your capers."

Tom understood the invitation and accepted it with delight. Three times they wrestled on the grass, "side holds," even as the giants of the mat. And twice was Tom forced to bite grass at the hands of the distinguished lawyer. Dishevelled, panting, each still boasting of his own prowess, they stumbled back to the porch. Millie cast a pert reflection upon the qualities of a city brother. In an instant Robert had secured a horrid katydid in his fingers and bore down upon her. Screaming wildly, she fled up the lane pursued by the avenging glass of form. A quarter of a mile and they returned, she full of apology to the victorious "dude." The rustic mania possessed him unabatedly.

"I can do up a cowpenful of you slow hayseeds," he proclaimed, vaingloriously. "Bring on your bulldogs, your hired men, and your log-rollers."

He turned handsprings on the grass that prodded Tom to envious sarcasm. And then, with a whoop, he clattered to the rear and brought back Uncle Ike, a battered colored retainer of the family, with his banjo, and strewed sand on the porch and danced "Chicken in the Bread Tray" and did buck-and-wing wonders for half an hour longer. Incredibly wild and boisterous things he did. He sang, he told stories that set all but one shrieking, he played the yokel, the humorous clodhopper; he was mad, mad with the revival of the old life in his blood.

He became so extravagant that once his mother sought gently to reprove him. Then Alicia moved as though she were about to speak, but she did not. Through it all she sat immovable, a slim, white spirit in the dusk that no man might question or read.

By and by she asked permission to ascend to her room, saying that she was tired. On her way she passed Robert. He was standing in the door, the figure of vulgar comedy, with ruffled hair, reddened face and unpardonable confusion of attire—no trace there of the immaculate Robert Walmsley, the courted clubman and ornament of select circles. He was doing a conjuring trick with some household utensils, and the family, now won over to him without exception, was beholding him with worshipful admiration.

As Alicia passed in Robert started suddenly. He had forgotten for the moment that she was present. Without a glance at him she went on upstairs.

After that the fun grew quiet. An hour passed in talk, and then Robert went up himself.

She was standing by the window when he entered their room. She was still clothed as when they were on the porch. Outside and crowding against the window was a giant apple tree, full blossomed.

Robert sighed and went near the window. He was ready to meet his fate. A confessed vulgarian, he foresaw the verdict of justice in the shape of that still, whiteclad form. He knew the rigid lines that a Van Der Pool would draw. He was a peasant gamboling indecorously in the valley, and the pure, cold, white, unthawed summit of the Matterhorn could not but frown on him. He had been unmasked by his own actions. All the polish, the poise, the form that the city had given him had fallen from him like an ill-fitting mantle at the first breath of a country breeze. Dully he awaited the approaching condemnation.

"Robert," said the calm, cool voice of his judge, "I thought I married a gentleman."

Yes, it was coming. And yet, in the face of it, Robert Walmsley was eagerly regarding a certain branch of the apple tree upon which he used to climb out of that very window. He believed he could do it now. He wondered how many blossoms there were on the tree—ten millions? But here was someone speaking again:

"I thought I married a gentleman," the voice went on, "but——"

Why had she come and was standing so close by his side?

"But I find that I have married"—was this Alicia talking?—"something better—a man—Bob, dear, kiss me, won't you?"

The city was far away.

THE SHOCKS OF DOOM

There is an aristocracy of the public parks and even of the vagabonds who use them for their private apartments. Vallance felt rather than knew this, but when he stepped down out of his world into chaos his feet brought him directly to Madison Square.

Raw and astringent as a schoolgirl—of the old order—young May breathed austerely among the budding trees. Vallance buttoned his coat, lighted his last cigarette and took his seat upon a bench. For three minutes he mildly regretted the last hundred of his last thousand that it had cost him when the bicycle cop put an end to his last automobile ride. Then he felt in every pocket and found not a single penny. He had given up his apartment that morning. His furniture had gone toward certain debts. His clothes, save what were upon him, had descended to his man-servant for back wages. As he sat, there was not in the whole city for him a bed or a broiled lobster or a streetcar fare or a carnation for his buttonhole unless he should obtain them by sponging on his friends or by false pretenses. Therefore he had chosen the park.

And all this was because an uncle had disinherited him, and cut down his allowance from liberality to nothing. And all that was because his nephew had disobeyed him concerning a certain girl, who comes not into the story—therefore, all readers who brush their hair towards its roots may be warned to read no further. There was another nephew, of a different branch, who had once been the prospective heir and favorite. Being without grace or hope, he had long ago disappeared in the mire. Now dragnets were out for him; he was to be rehabilitated and restored. And so Vallance fell grandly as Lucifer to the lowest pit, joining the tattered ghosts in the little park.

Sitting there he leaned far back on the hard bench and laughed a jet of cigarette smoke up to the lowest tree branches. The sudden severing of all his life's ties had brought him a free, thrilling, almost joyous elation. He felt precisely the sensation of the aëronaut when he cuts loose his parachute and lets his balloon drift away.

The hour was nearly ten. Not many loungers were on the benches. The park-dweller, though a stubborn fighter against autumnal coolness, is slow to attack the advance line of spring's chilly cohorts.

Then arose one from a seat near the leaping fountain, and came and sat himself at Vallance's side. He was either young or old; cheap lodging-houses had flavored him mustily; razors and combs had passed him by; in him drink had been bottled and sealed in the devil's bond. He begged a match, which is the form of introduction among park benchers, and then he began to talk.

"You're not one of the regulars," he said to Vallance. "I know tailored clothes when I see 'em. You just stopped for a moment on your way through the park. Don't mind my talking to you for a while? I've got to be with somebody. I'm afraid—I'm afraid. I've told two or three of those bummers over there about it. They think I'm crazy. Say—let me tell you —all I've had to eat to-day was a couple of bretzels and an apple. To-morrow I'll stand in line to inherit three millions; and that restaurant you see over there with the autos around it will be too cheap for me to eat in. Don't believe it, do you?"

"Without the slightest trouble," said Vallance, with a laugh. "I lunched there yesterday. To-night I couldn't buy a five-cent cup of coffee."

"You don't look like one of us. Well, I guess those things happen. I used to be a high-flyer myself—some years ago. What knocked you out of the game?"

"I—oh, I lost my job," said Vallance.

"It's undiluted Hades, this city," went on the other. "One day you're eating from China; the next you are eating in China—a chop-suey joint. I've had more than my share of hard luck. For five years I've been little better than a panhandler. I was raised up to live expensively and do noth-ing. Say—I don't mind telling you—I've got to talk to somebody, you see, because I'm afraid—I'm afraid. My name's Ide. You wouldn't think that old Paulding, one of the millionaires on Riverside Drive, was my uncle, would you? Well, he is. I lived in his house once, and had all the money I wanted. Say, haven't you got the price of a couple of drinks about you —er—what's your name——"

"Dawson," said Vallance. "No; I'm sorry to say that I'm all in finan-cially."

"I've been living for a week in a coal cellar on Division Street," went on Ide, "with a crook they call 'Blinky' Morris. I didn't have anywhere else to go. While I was out to-day a chap with some papers in his pocket was there, asking for me. I didn't know but what he was a fly cop, so I didn't go around again till after dark. There was a letter there he had left for me. Say—Dawson, it was from a big downtown lawyer, Mead. I've seen his sign on Ann Street. Paulding wants me to play the prodigal nephew—wants me to come back and be his heir again and blow in his money. I'm to call at the lawyer's office at ten to-morrow and step into my old shoes again—heir to three million, Dawson, and $10,000 a year pocket money. And—I'm afraid—I'm afraid."

The vagrant leaped to his feet and raised both trembling arms above his head. He caught his breath and moaned hysterically.

Vallance seized his arm and forced him back to the bench.

"Be quiet!" he commanded with something like disgust in his tones.

"One would think you had lost a fortune, instead of being about to acquire one. Of what are you afraid?"

Ide cowered and shivered on the bench. He clung to Vallance's sleeve, and even in the dim glow of the Broadway lights the latest disinherited one could see drops on the other's brow wrung out by some strange terror.

"Why, I'm afraid something will happen to me before morning. I don't know what—something to keep me from coming into that money. I'm afraid a tree will fall on me—I'm afraid a cab will run over me, or a stone drop on me from a housetop, or something. I never was afraid before. I've sat in this park a hundred nights as calm as a graven image without knowing where my breakfast was to come from. But now it's different. I love money, Dawson—I'm happy as a god when it's trickling through my fingers, and people are bowing to me, with the music and the flowers and fine clothes all around. As long as I knew I was out of the game I didn't mind. I was even happy sitting here ragged and hungry, listening to the fountain jump and watching the carriages go up the avenue. But it's in reach of my hand again now—almost—and I can't stand it to wait twelve hours, Dawson—I can't stand it. There are fifty things that could happen to me—I could go blind—I might be attacked with heart disease—the world might come to an end before I could——"

Ide sprang to his feet again, with a shriek. People stirred on the benches and began to look. Vallance took his arm.

"Come and walk," he said, soothingly. "And try to calm yourself. There is no need to become excited or alarmed. Nothing is going to happen to you. One night is like another."

"That's right," said Ide. "Stay with me, Dawson—that's a good fellow. Walk around with me awhile. I never went to pieces like this before, and I've had a good many hard knocks. Do you think you could hustle something in the way of a little lunch, old man? I'm afraid my nerve's too far gone to try any panhandling."

Vallance led his companion up almost deserted Fifth Avenue, and then westward along the Thirties toward Broadway. "Wait here a few minutes," he said, leaving Ide in a quiet and shadowed spot. He entered a familiar hotel, and strolled toward the bar quite in his old assured way.

"There's a poor devil outside, Jimmy," he said to the bartender, "who says he's hungry and looks it. You know what they do when you give them money. Fix up a sandwich or two for him; and I'll see that he doesn't throw it away."

"Certainly, Mr. Vallance," said the bartender. "They ain't all fakes. Don't like to see anybody go hungry."

He folded a liberal supply of the free lunch into a napkin. Vallance went with it and joined his companion. Ide pounced upon the food ravenously. "I haven't had any free lunch as good as this in a year," he said. "Aren't you going to eat any, Dawson?"

"I'm not hungry—thanks," said Vallance.

"We'll go back to the Square," said Ide. "The cops won't bother us there. I'll roll up the rest of this ham and stuff for our breakfast. I won't eat any more; I'm afraid I'll get sick. Suppose I'd die of cramps or some-thing to-night, and never get to touch that money again! It's eleven hours yet till time to see that lawyer. You won't leave me, will you, Dawson? I'm afraid something might happen. You haven't any place to go, have you?"

"No," said Vallance, "nowhere to-night. I'll have a bench with you."

"You take it cool," said Ide, "if you've told it to me straight. I should think a man put on the bum from a good job just in one day would be tearing his hair."

"I believe I've already remarked," said Vallance, laughing, "that I would have thought that a man who was expecting to come into a fortune on the next day would be feeling pretty easy and quiet."

"It's funny business," philosophized Ide, "about the way people take things, anyhow. Here's your bench, Dawson, right next to mine. The light don't shine in your eyes here. Say, Dawson, I'll get the old man to give you a letter to somebody about a job when I get back home. You've helped me a lot to-night. I don't believe I could have gone through the night if I hadn't struck you."

"Thank you," said Vallance. "Do you lie down or sit up on these when you sleep?"

For hours Vallance gazed almost without winking at the stars through the branches of the trees and listened to the sharp slapping of horses' hoofs on the sea of asphalt to the south. His mind was active but his feelings were dormant. Every emotion seemed to have been eradicated. He felt no regrets, no fears, no pain or discomfort. Even when he thought of the girl, it was as of an inhabitant of one of those remote stars at which he gazed. He remembered the absurd antics of his companion and laughed softly, yet without a feeling of mirth. Soon the daily army of milk wagons made of the city a roaring drum to which they marched. Vallance fell asleep on his comfortless bench.

At ten o'clock on the next day the two stood at the door of Lawyer Mead's office in Ann Street.

Ide's nerves fluttered worse than ever when the hour approached; and Vallance could not decide to leave him a possible prey to the dangers he dreaded.

When they entered the office, Lawyer Mead looked at them wonder-ingly. He and Vallance were old friends. After his greeting, he turned to Ide, who stood with white face and trembling limbs before the expected crisis.

"I sent a second letter to your address last night, Mr. Ide," he said. "I learned this morning that you were not there to receive it. It will inform you that Mr. Paulding has reconsidered his offer to take you back into favor. He has decided not to do so, and desires you to understand that no change will be made in the relations existing between you and him."

Ide's trembling suddenly ceased. The color came back to his face, and he straightened his back. His jaw went forward half an inch, and a gleam came into his eye. He pushed back his battered hat with one hand, and extended the other, with levelled fingers, toward the lawyer. He took a long breath and then laughed sardonically.

"Tell old Paulding he may go to the devil," he said, loudly and clearly, and turned and walked out of the office with a firm and lively step.

Lawyer Mead turned on his heel to Vallance and smiled.

"I am glad you came in," he said, genially. "Your uncle wants you to return home at once. He is reconciled to the situation that led to his hasty action, and desires to say that all will be as——"

"Hey, Adams!" cried Lawyer Mead, breaking his sentence, and calling to his clerk. "Bring a glass of water—Mr. Vallance has fainted."

THE PLUTONIAN FIRE

There are a few editor men with whom I am privileged to come in contact. It has not been long since it was their habit to come in contact with me. There is a difference.

They tell me that with a large number of the manuscripts that are submitted to them come advices (in the way of a boost) from the author asseverating that the incidents in the story are true. The destination of such contributions depends wholly upon the question of the inclosure of stamps. Some are returned, the rest are thrown on the floor in a corner on top of a pair of gum shoes, an overturned statuette of the Winged Victory, and a pile of old magazines containing a picture of the editor in the act of reading the latest copy of *Le Petit Journal,* right side up—you can tell by the illustrations. It is only a legend that there are waste baskets in editors' offices.

Thus the truth is held in disrepute. But in time truth and science and nature will adapt themselves to art. Things will happen logically, and the villain be discomfited instead of being elected to the board of directors. But in the meantime fiction must not only be divorced from fact, but must pay alimony and be awarded custody of the press dispatches.

This preamble is to warn you off the grade crossing of a true story. Being that, it shall be told simply, with conjunctions substituted for adjectives wherever possible, and whatever evidences of style may appear in it shall be due to the linotype man. It is a story of the literary life in a great city, and it should be of interest to every author within a 20-mile radius of Gosport, Ind., whose desk holds a MS. story beginning thus: "While the cheers following his nomination were still ringing through the old court-house, Harwood broke away from the congratulating handclasps of his henchmen and hurried to Judge Creswell's house to find Ida."

Pettit came up out of Alabama to write fiction. The Southern papers had printed eight of his stories under an editorial caption identifying the author as the son of "the gallant Major Pettingill Pettit, our former County Attorney and hero of the battle of Lookout Mountain."

Pettit was a rugged fellow, with a kind of shame-faced culture, and my good friend. His father kept a general store in a little town called Hosea. Pettit had been raised in the pine-woods and broom-sedge fields adjacent thereto. He had in his gripsack two manuscript novels of the adventures in Picardy of one Gaston Laboulaye, Vicompte de Montrepos, in the year 1329. That's nothing. We all do that. And some day when we make a hit with the little sketch about a newsy and his lame dog, the editor prints the other one for us—or "on us," as the saying is—and then —and then we have to get a big valise and peddle those patent air-draft gas burners. At $1.25 everybody should have 'em.

I took Pettit to the red-brick house which was to appear in an article entitled "Literary Landmarks of Old New York," some day when we got through with it. He engaged a room there, drawing on the general store for his expenses. I showed New York to him, and he did not mention how much narrower Broadway is than Lee Avenue in Hosea. This seemed a good sign, so I put the final test.

"Suppose you try your hand at a descriptive article," I suggested, "giving your impressions of New York as seen from the Brooklyn Bridge. The fresh point of view, the——"

"Don't be a fool," said Pettit. "Let's go have some beer. On the whole, I rather like the city."

We discovered and enjoyed the only true Bohemia. Every day and night we repaired to one of those palaces of marble and glass and tile-work, where goes on a tremendous and sound epic of life. Valhalla itself could not be more glorious and sonorous. The classic marble on which we ate, the great, light-flooded, vitreous front, adorned with snow-white scrolls; the grand Wagnerian din of clanking cups and bowls, the flashing staccato of brandishing cutlery, the piercing recitative of the white-aproned grub-maidens at the morgue-like banquet tables; the recurrent leit-motif of the cash-register—it was gigantic, triumphant welding of art and sound, a deafening, soul-uplifting pageant of heroic and emblematic life. And the beans were only ten cents. We wondered why our fellow-artists cared to dine at sad little tables in their so-called Bohemian restaurants; and we shuddered lest they should seek out our resorts and make them conspicuous with their presence.

Pettit wrote many stories, which the editors returned to him. He wrote love stories, a thing I have always kept free from, holding the belief that the well-known and popular sentiment is not properly a matter for publication, but something to be privately handled by the alienists and florists. But the editors had told him that they wanted love stories, because they said the women read them.

Now, the editors are wrong about that, of course. Women do not read the love stories in the magazines. They read the poker-game stories and the recipes for cucumber lotion. The love stories are read by fat cigar drummers and little ten-year-old girls. I am not criticizing the judgment of editors. They are mostly very fine men, but a man can be but one man, with individual opinions and tastes. I knew two associate editors of a magazine who were wonderfully alike in almost everything. And yet one of them was very fond of Flaubert, while the other preferred gin.

Pettit brought me his returned manuscripts, and we looked them over together to find out why they were not accepted. They seemed to me pretty fair stories, written in a good style, and ended, as they should, at the bottom of the last page.

They were well constructed and the events were marshalled in orderly and logical sequence. But I thought I detected a lack of living substance —it was much as if I gazed at a symmetrical array of presentable clam-shells from which the succulent and vital inhabitants had been removed. I intimated that the author might do well to get better acquainted with his theme.

"You sold a story last week," said Pettit, "about a gun fight in an Arizona mining town in which the hero drew his Colt's .45 and shot seven bandits as fast as they came in the door. Now, if a six-shooter could——"

"Oh, well," said I, "that's different. Arizona is a long way from New York. I could have a man stabbed with a lariat or chased by a pair of chaparreras if I wanted to, and it wouldn't be noticed until the usual error-sharp from around McAdams Junction isolates the erratum and writes in to the papers about it. But you are up against another proposition. This thing they call love is as common around New York as it is in Sheboygan during the young onion season. It may be mixed here with a little commercialism—they read Byron, but they look up Bradstreet's, too, while they're among the Bs, and Brigham also if they have time—but it's pretty much the same old internal disturbance everywhere. You can fool an editor with a fake picture of a cowboy mounting a pony with his left hand on the saddle horn, but you can't put him up a tree with a love story. So, you've got to fall in love and then write the real thing."

Pettit did. I never knew whether he was taking my advice or whether he fell an accidental victim.

There was a girl he had met at one of these studio contrivances—a glorious, impudent, lucid, open-minded girl with hair the color of Culm-bacher, and a good-natured way of despising you. She was a New York girl.

Well (as the narrative style permits us to say infrequently), Pettit went to pieces. All those pains, those lover's doubts, those heart-burnings and tremors of which he had written so unconvincingly were his. Talk about Shylock's pound of flesh! Twenty-five pounds Cupid got from Pettit. Which is the usurer?

One night Pettit came to my room exalted. Pale and haggard but exalted. She had given him a jonquil.

"Old Hoss," said he, with a new smile flickering around his mouth, "I believe I could write that story to-night—the one, you know, that is to win out. I can feel it. I don't know whether it will come out or not, but I can feel it."

I pushed him out of my door. "Go to your room and write it," I ordered. "Else I can see your finish. I told you this must come first. Write it to-night and put it under my door when it is done. Put it under my door to-night when it is finished—don't keep it until tomorrow."

I was reading my bully old pal Montaigne at two o'clock when I heard the sheets rustle under my door. I gathered them up and read the story.

The hissing of geese, the languishing cooing of doves, the braying of donkeys, the chatter of irresponsible sparrows—these were in my mind's ear as I read. "Suffering Sappho!" I exclaimed to myself. "Is this the divine fire that is supposed to ignite genius and make it practical and wage-earning?"

The story was sentimental drivel, full of whimpering soft-heartedness and gushing egoism. All the art that Pettit had acquired was gone. A perusal of its buttery phrases would have made a cynic of a sighing chamber-maid.

In the morning Pettit came to my room. I read him his doom mercilessly. He laughed idiotically.

"All right, Old Hoss," he said, cheerily, "make cigar-lighters of it. What's the difference? I'm going to take her to lunch at Claremont to-day."

There was about a month of it. And then Pettit came to me bearing an invisible mitten, with the fortitude of a dish-rag. He talked of the grave and South America and prussic acid; and I lost an afternoon getting him straight. I took him out and saw that large and curative doses of whiskey were administered to him. I warned you this was a true story—'ware your white ribbons if you follow this tale. For two weeks I fed him whiskey and Omar, and read to him regularly every evening the column in the evening paper that reveals the secrets of female beauty. I recommend the treatment.

After Pettit was cured he wrote more stories. He recovered his old-time facility and did work just short of good enough. Then the curtain rose on the third act.

A little, dark-eyed, silent girl from New Hampshire, who was studying applied design, fell deeply in love with him. She was the intense sort, but externally *glacée,* such as New England sometimes fools us with. Pettit liked her mildly, and took her about a good deal. She worshipped him, and now and then bored him.

There came a climax when she tried to jump out of a window, and he had to save her by some perfunctory, unmeant wooing. Even I was shaken by the depths of the absorbing affection she showed. Home, friends, traditions, creeds went up like thistle-down in the scale against her love. It was really discomposing.

One night again Pettit sauntered in, yawning. As he had told me before, he said he felt that he could do a great story, and as before I hunted him to his room and saw him open his inkstand. At one o'clock the sheets of paper slid under my door.

I read that story, and I jumped up, late as it was, with a whoop of joy. Old Pettit had done it. Just as though it lay there, red and bleeding, a woman's heart was written into the lines. You couldn't see the joining, but art, exquisite art, and pulsing nature had been combined into a love story that took you by the throat like the quinsy. I broke into Pettit's room and beat him on the back and called him names—names high up in the galaxy of the immortals that we admired. And Pettit yawned and begged to be allowed to sleep.

On the morrow, I dragged him to an editor. The great man read, and rising, gave Pettit his hand. That was a decoration, a wreath of bay, and a guarantee of rent.

And then old Pettit smiled slowly. I call him Gentleman Pettit now to myself. It's a miserable name to give a man, but it sounds better than it looks in print.

"I see," said old Pettit, as he took up his story and began tearing it into small strips. "I see the game now. You can't write with ink, and you can't write with your own heart's blood, but you can write with the heart's blood of someone else. You have to be a cad before you can be an artist. Well, I am for old Alabam and the Major's store. Have you got a light, Old Hoss?"

I went with Pettit to the depot and died hard.

"Shakespeare's sonnets?" I blurted, making a last stand. "How about him?"

"A cad," said Pettit. "They give it to you, and you sell it—love, you know. I'd rather sell ploughs for father."

"But," I protested, "you are reversing the decision of the world's greatest——"

"Good-by, Old Hoss," said Pettit.

"Critics," I continued. "But—say if the Major can use a fairly good sales-man and book-keeper down there in the store, let me know, will you?"

NEMESIS AND THE CANDY MAN

"We sail at eight in the morning on the *Celtic*," said Honoria, plucking a loose thread from her lace sleeve.

"I heard so," said young Ives dropping his hat, and muffing it as he tried to catch it, "and I came around to wish you a pleasant voyage."

"Of course you heard it," said Honoria, coldly sweet, "since we have had no opportunity of informing you ourselves."

Ives looked at her pleadingly, but with little hope.

Outside in the street a high-pitched voice chanted, not unmusically, a commercial gamut of "Cand-ee-ee-ee-s! Nice, fresh cand-ee-ee-ee-ees!"

"It's our old candy man," said Honoria, leaning out of the window and beckoning. "I want some of his motto kisses. There's nothing in the Broadway shops half so good."

The candy man stopped his pushcart in front of the old Madison Ave-nue home. He had a holiday and festival air unusual to street peddlers. His tie was new and bright red, and a horseshoe pin, almost life-size, glit-tered speciously from its folds. His brown, thin face was crinkled into a semi-foolish smile. Striped cuffs with dog-head buttons covered the tan on his wrists.

"I do believe he's going to get married," said Honoria, pityingly. "I never saw him taken that way before. And to-day is the first time in months that he has cried his wares, I am sure."

Ives threw a coin to the sidewalk. The candy man knows his customers. He filled a paper bag, climbed the old-fashioned stoop and handed it in.

"I remember——" said Ives.

"Wait," said Honoria.

She took a small portfolio from the drawer of a writing desk and from the portfolio a slip of flimsy paper one-quarter of an inch by two inches in size.

"This," said Honoria, inflexibly, "was wrapped about the first one we opened."

"It was a year ago," apologized Ives, as he held out his hand for it.

"As long as skies above are blue
    To you, my love, I will be true."

This he read from a slip of flimsy paper.

"We were to have sailed a fortnight ago," said Honoria, gossipingly. "It has been such a warm summer. The town is quite deserted. There is nowhere to go. Yet I am told that one or two of the roof gardens are amusing. The singing—and the dancing—on one or two seem to have met with approval."

Ives did not wince. When you are in the ring you are not surprised when your adversary taps you on the ribs.

"I followed the candy man that time," said Ives, irrelevantly, "and gave him five dollars at the corner of Broadway."

He reached for the paper bag in Honoria's lap, took out one of the square, wrapped confections and slowly unrolled it.

"Sara Chillingworth's father," said Honoria, "has given her an automobile."

"Read that," said Ives, handing over the slip that had been wrapped around the square of candy.

"Life teaches us—how to live,
    Love teaches us—to forgive."

Honoria's cheeks turned pink.

"Honoria!" cried Ives, starting up from his chair.

"Miss Clinton," corrected Honoria, rising like Venus from the bead on the surf. "I warned you not to speak that name again."

"Honoria," repeated Ives, "you must hear me. I know I do not deserve your forgiveness, but I must have it. There is a madness that possesses one sometimes for which his better nature is not responsible. I throw everything else but you to the winds. I strike off the chains that have bound me. I renounce the siren that lured me from you. Let the bought verse of that street peddler plead for me. It is you only whom I can love. Let your love forgive, and I swear to you that mine will be true 'as long as skies above are blue.' "

On the west side, between Sixth and Seventh avenues, an alley cuts the block in the middle. It perishes in a little court in the centre of the block. The district is theatrical; the inhabitants, the bubbling froth of half a dozen nations. The atmosphere is Bohemian, the language polyglot, the locality precarious.

In the court at the rear of the alley lived the candy man. At seven o'clock he pushed his cart into the narrow entrance, rested it upon the irregular stone slats and sat upon one of the handles to cool himself. There was a great draught of cool wind through the alley.

There was a window above the spot where he always stopped his pushcart. In the cool of the afternoon, Mlle. Adèle, drawing card of the Aërial Roof Garden, sat at the window and took the air. Generally her ponderous mass of dark auburn hair was down, that the breeze might have the felicity of aiding Sidonie, the maid, in drying and airing it. About her shoulders—the point of her that the photographers always made the most of—was loosely draped a heliotrope scarf. Her arms to the elbow were bare—there were no sculptors there to rave over them—but even the stolid bricks in the walls of the alley should not have been so insensate as to disapprove. While she sat thus Felice, another maid, anointed and bathed the small feet that twinkled and so charmed the nightly Aërial audiences.

Gradually Mademoiselle began to notice the candy man stopping to mop his brow and cool himself beneath her window. In the hands of her maids she was deprived for the time of her vocation—the charming and binding to her chariot of man. To lose time was displeasing to Mademoiselle. Here was the candy man—no fit game for her darts, truly—but of the sex upon which she had been born to make war.

After casting upon him looks of unseeing coldness for a dozen times, one afternoon she suddenly thawed and poured down upon him a smile that put to shame the sweets upon his cart.

"Candy man," she said, cooingly, while Sidonie followed her impulsive dive, brushing the heavy auburn hair, "don't you think I am beautiful?"

The candy man laughed harshly, and looked up, with his thin jaw set, while he wiped his forehead with a red-and-blue handkerchief.

"Yer'd make a dandy magazine cover," he said grudgingly. "Beautiful or not is for them that cares. It's not my line. If yer lookin' for bouquets apply elsewhere between nine and twelve. I think we'll have rain."

Truly, fascinating a candy man is like killing rabbits in a deep snow; but the hunter's blood is widely diffused. Mademoiselle tugged a great coil of hair from Sidonie's hands and let it fall out the window.

"Candy man, have you a sweetheart anywhere with hair as long and soft as that? And with an arm so round?" She flexed an arm like Galatea's after the miracle across the window-sill.

The candy man cackled shrilly as he arranged a stock of butterscotch that had tumbled down.

"Smoke up!" said he, vulgarly. "Nothin' doin' in the complimentary line. I'm too wise to be bamboozled by a switch of hair and a newly massaged arm. Oh, I guess you'll make good in the calcium, all right, with plenty of powder and paint on and the orchestra playing 'Under the Old Apple Tree.' But don't put on your hat and chase downstairs to fly to the Little Church Around the Corner with me. I've been up against peroxide and make up boxes before. Say, all joking aside—don't you think we'll have rain?"

"Candy man," said Mademoiselle, softly, with her lips curving and her chin dimpling, "don't you think I'm pretty?"

The candy man grinned.

"Savin' money, ain't yer?" said he, "by bein' yer own press agent. I smoke, but I haven't seen yer mug on any of the five-cent cigar boxes. It'd take a new brand of woman to get me goin,' anyway. I know 'em from sidecombs to shoelaces. Gimme a good day's sales and steak-and-onions at seven and a pipe and an evenin' paper back there in the court, and I'll not trouble Lillian Russell herself to wink at me, if you please."

Mademoiselle pouted.

"Candy man," she said, softly and deeply, "yet you shall say that I am beautiful. All men say so and so shall you."

The candy man laughed and pulled out his pipe.

"Well," said he, "I must be goin' in. There is a story in the evening paper that I am readin'. Men are divin' in the seas for a treasure, and pirates are watchin' them from behind a reef. And there ain't a woman on land or water or in the air. Good-evenin'." And he trundled his pushcart down the alley and back to the musty court where he lived.

Incredibly to him who has not learned woman, Mademoiselle sat at the window each day and spread her nets for the ignominious game. Once she kept a grand cavalier waiting in her reception chamber for half an hour while she battered in vain the candy man's tough philosophy. His rough laugh chafed her vanity to its core. Daily he sat on his cart in the breeze of the alley while her hair was being ministered to, and daily the shafts of her beauty rebounded from his dull bosom pointless and ineffectual. Unworthy pique brightened her eyes. Pride-hurt she glowed upon him in a way that would have sent her higher adorers into an egoistic paradise. The candy man's hard eyes looked upon her with a half-concealed derision that urged her to the use of the sharpest arrow in her beauty's quiver.

One afternoon she leaned far over the sill, and she did not challenge and torment him as usual.

"Candy man," said she, "stand up and look into my eyes."

He stood up and looked into her eyes, with his harsh laugh like the sawing of wood. He took out his pipe, fumbled with it, and put it back into his pocket with a trembling hand.

"That will do," said Mademoiselle, with a slow smile. "I must go now to my *masseuse*. Good-evening."

The next evening at seven the candy man came and rested his cart under the window. But was it the candy man? His clothes were a bright new check. His necktie was a flaming red, adorned by a glittering horseshoe pin, almost lifesize. His shoes were polished; the tan of his cheeks had paled—his hands had been washed. The window was empty, and he waited under it with his nose upward, like a hound hoping for a bone.

Mademoiselle came, with Sidonie carrying her load of hair. She looked at the candy man and smiled a slow smile that faded away into ennui. Instantly she knew that the game was bagged; and so quickly she wearied of the chase. She began to talk to Sidonie.

"Been a fine day," said the candy man, hollowly. "First time in a month I've felt first-class. Hit it up down old Madison, hollering out like I useter. Think it'll rain to-morrow?"

Mademoiselle laid two round arms on the cushion on the window-sill, and a dimpled chin upon them.

"Candy man," said she, softly, "do you not love me?"

The candy man stood up and leaned against the brick wall.

"Lady," said he, chokingly, "I've got $800 saved up. Did I say you wasn't beautiful? Take it every bit and buy a collar for your dog with it."

A sound as of a hundred silvery bells tinkled in the room of Mademoiselle. The laughter filled the alley and trickled back into the court, as strange a thing to enter there as sunlight itself. Mademoiselle was amused. Sidonie, a wise echo, added a sepulchral but faithful contralto. The laughter of the two seemed at last to penetrate the candy man. He fumbled with his horseshoe pin. At length Mademoiselle, exhausted, turned her flushed, beautiful face to the window.

"Candy man," said she, "go away. When I laugh Sidonie pulls my hair. I can but laugh while you remain there."

"Here is a note for Mademoiselle," said Félice, coming to the window in the room.

"There is no justice," said the candy man, lifting the handle of his cart and moving away.

Three yards he moved, and stopped. Loud shriek after shriek came from the window of Mademoiselle. Quickly he ran back. He heard a body thumping upon the floor and a sound as though heels beat alternately upon it.

"What is it?" he called.

Sidonie's severe head came into the window.

"Mademoiselle is overcome by bad news," she said. "One whom she loved with all her soul has gone—you may have heard of him—he is Monsieur Ives. He sails across the ocean to-morrow. Oh, you men!"

SQUARING THE CIRCLE

At the hazard of wearying youth this tale of vehement emotions must be prefaced by a discourse on geometry.

Nature moves in circles; Art in straight lines. The natural is rounded; the artificial is made up of angles. A man lost in the snow wanders, in spite of himself, in perfect circles; the city man's feet, denaturalized by rectangular streets and floors, carry him ever away from himself.

The round eyes of childhood typify innocence; the narrow line of the flirt's optic proves the invasion of art. The horizontal mouth is the mark of determined cunning; who has not read Nature's most spontaneous lyric in lips rounded for the candid kiss?

Beauty is Nature in perfection; circularity is its chief attribute. Behold the full moon, the enchanting gold ball, the domes of splendid temples, the huckleberry pie, the wedding ring, the circus ring, the ring for the waiter, and the "round" of drinks.

On the other hand, straight lines show that Nature has been deflected. Imagine Venus's girdle transformed into a "straight front!"

When we began to move in straight lines and turn sharp corners our natures begin to change. The consequence is that Nature, being more adaptive than Art, tries to conform to its sterner regulations. The result is often a rather curious product—for instance: A prize chrysanthemum, wood alcohol whiskey, a Republican Missouri, cauliflower *au gratin,* and a New Yorker.

Nature is lost quickest in a big city. The cause is geometrical, not moral. The straight lines of its streets and architecture, the rectangularity of its laws and social customs, the undeviating pavements, the hard, severe, depressing, uncompromising rules of all its ways—even of its recreation and sports—coldly exhibit a sneering defiance of the curved line of Nature.

Wherefore, it may be said that the big city has demonstrated the problem of squaring the circle. And it may be added that this mathematical introduction precedes an account of the fate of a Kentucky feud that was imported to the city that has a habit of making its importations conform to its angles.

The feud began in the Cumberland Mountains between the Folwell and the Harkness families. The first victim of the homespun vendetta was a 'possum dog belonging to Bill Harkness. The Harkness family evened up this dire loss by laying out the chief of the Folwell clan. The Folwells were prompt at repartee. They oiled up their squirrel rifles and made it feasible for Bill Harkness to follow his dog to a land where the 'possums come down when treed without the stroke of an ax.

The feud flourished for forty years. Harknesses were shot at the plough, through their lamp-lit cabin windows, coming from camp-meetings, asleep, in duello, sober and otherwise, singly and in family groups, prepared and unprepared. Folwells had the branches of their family tree lopped off in similar ways, as the traditions of their country prescribed and authorized.

By and by the pruning left but a single member of each family. And then Cal Harkness, probably reasoning that further pursuance of the controversy would give a too decided personal flavor to the feud, suddenly disappeared from the relieved Cumberlands, baulking the avenging hand of Sam, the ultimate opposing Folwell.

A year afterward Sam Folwell learned that his hereditary, unsuppressed enemy was living in New York City. Sam turned over the big iron washpot in the yard, scraped off some of the soot, which he mixed with lard and shined his boots with the compound. He put on his store clothes of butternut dyed black, a white shirt and collar, and packed a carpet-sack with Spartan *lingerie*. He took his squirrel rifle from its hooks, but put it back again with a sigh. However ethical and plausible the habit might be in the Cumberlands, perhaps New York would not swallow his pose of hunting squirrels among the skyscrapers along Broadway. An ancient but reliable Colt's revolver that he resurrected from a bureau drawer seemed to proclaim itself the pink of weapons for metropolitan adventure and vengeance. This and a hunting-knife in a leather sheath, Sam packed in the carpet-sack. As he started, muleback, for the lowland railroad station the last Folwell turned in his saddle and looked grimly at the little cluster of white-pine slabs in the clump of cedars that marked the Folwell burying-ground.

Sam Folwell arrived in New York in the night. Still moving and living in the free circles of nature, he did not perceive the formidable, pitiless, restless, fierce angles of the great city waiting in the dark to close about the rotundity of his heart and brain and mould him to the form of its millions of reshaped victims. A cabby picked him out of the whirl, as Sam himself had often picked a nut from a bed of wind-tossed autumn leaves, and whisked him away to a hotel commensurate to his boots and carpet-sack.

On the next morning the last of the Folwells made his sortie into the city that sheltered the last Harkness. The Colt was thrust beneath his coat and secured by a narrow leather belt; the hunting-knife hung between his shoulder-blades, with the haft an inch below his coat collar. He knew this much—that Cal Harkness drove an express wagon somewhere in that town, and that he, Sam Folwell, had come to kill him. And as he stepped upon the sidewalk the red came into his eye and the feud-hate into his heart.

The clamor of the central avenues drew him thitherward. He had half expected to see Cal coming down the street in his shirt-sleeves with a jug and a whip in his hand, just as he would have seen him in Frankfort or Laurel City. But an hour went by and Cal did not appear. Perhaps he was waiting in ambush, to shoot him from a door or a window. Sam kept a sharp eye on doors and windows for a while.

About noon the city tired of playing with its mouse and suddenly squeezed him with its straight lines.

Sam Folwell stood where two great, rectangular arteries of the city cross. He looked four ways, and saw the world hurled from its orbit and reduced by spirit level and tape to an edged and cornered plane. All life moved on tracks, in grooves, according to system, within boundaries, by rote. The root of life was the cube root; the measure of existence was square measure. People streamed by in straight rows; the horrible din and crash stupefied him.

Sam leaned against the sharp corner of a stone building. Those faces passed him by thousands, and one of them were turned toward him. A sudden foolish fear that he had died and was a spirit, and that they could not see him, seized him. And then the city smote him with loneliness.

A fat man dropped out of the stream and stood a few feet distant, waiting for his car. Sam crept to his side and shouted above the tumult into his ear:

"The Rankinses' hogs weighed more'n ourn a whole passel, but the mast in thar neighborhood was a fine chance better than what it was down——"

The fat man moved away unostentatiously, and bought roasted chestnuts to cover his alarm.

Sam felt the need of a drop of mountain dew. Across the street men passed in and out through swinging doors. Brief glimpses could be had of a glistening bar and its bedeckings. The feudist crossed and essayed to enter. Again had Art eliminated the familiar circle. Sam's hand found no door-knob—it slid, in vain, over a rectangular brass plate and polished oak with nothing even so large as a pin's head upon which his fingers might close.

Abashed, reddened, heartbroken, he walked away from the bootless door and sat upon a step. A locust club tickled him in the ribs.

"Take a walk for yourself," said the policeman. "You've been loafing around here long enough."

At the next corner a shrill whistle sounded in Sam's ear. He wheeled around and saw a black-browed villain scowling at him over peanuts heaped on a steaming machine. He started across the street. An immense engine, running without mules, with the voice of a bull and the smell of a smoky lamp, whizzed past, grazing his knee. A cab-driver bumped him with a hub and explained to him that kind words were invented to be used on other occasions. A motorman clanged his bell wildly and, for once in his life, corroborated a cab-driver. A large lady in a changeable silk waist dug an elbow into his back, and a newsy pensively pelted him with banana rinds, murmuring, "I hates to do it—but if anybody seen me let it pass!"

Cal Harkness, his day's work over and his express wagon stabled, turned the sharp edge of the building that, by the cheek of architects, is modelled upon a safety razor. Out of the mass of hurrying people his eye picked up, three yards away, the surviving bloody and implacable foe of his kith and kin.

He stopped short and wavered for a moment, being unarmed and sharply surprised. But the keen mountaineer's eye of Sam Folwell had picked him out.

There was a sudden spring, a ripple in the stream of passers-by and the sound of Sam's voice crying:

"Howdy, Cal! I'm durned glad to see ye."

And in the angles of Broadway, Fifth Avenue, and Twenty-third Street the Cumberland feudists shook hands.

ROSES, RUSES AND ROMANCE

Ravenel—Ravenel, the traveller, artist and poet, threw his magazine to the floor. Sammy Brown, broker's clerk, who sat by the window, jumped.

"What is it, Ravvy?" he asked. "The critics been hammering your stock down?"

"Romance is dead," said Ravenel, lightly. When Ravenel spoke lightly he was generally serious. He picked up the magazine and fluttered its leaves.

"Even a Philistine, like you, Sammy," said Ravenel, seriously (a tone that insured him to be speaking lightly), "ought to understand. Now, here is a magazine that once printed Poe and Lowell and Whitman and Bret Harte and Du Maurier and Lanier and—well, that gives you the idea. The current number has this literary feast to set before you: an article on the stokers and coal bunkers of battleships, an exposé of the methods employed in making liverwurst, a continued story of a Standard Preferred International Baking Powder deal in Wall Street, a 'poem' on the bear that the President missed, another 'story' by a young woman who spent a week as a spy making overalls on the East Side, another 'fiction' story that reeks of the 'garage' and certain make of automobile. Of course, the title contains the words 'Cupid' and 'Chauffeur'—an article on naval strategy, illustrated with cuts of the Spanish Armada, and the new Staten Island ferryboats; another story of a political boss who won the love of a Fifth Avenue belle by blackening her eye and refusing to vote for an iniquitous ordinance (it doesn't say whether it was in the Street Cleaning Department or Congress), and nineteen pages by the editors bragging about the circulation. The whole thing, Sammy, is an obituary on Romance."

Sammy Brown sat comfortably in the leather armchair by the open window. His suit was a vehement brown with visible checks, beautifully matched in shade by the ends of four cigars that his vest pocket poorly concealed. Light tan were his shoes, gray his socks, sky-blue his apparent linen, snowy and high and adamantine his collar, against which a black butterfly had alighted and spread his wings. Sammy's face—least important—was round and pleasant and pinkish, and in his eyes you saw no haven for fleeing Romance.

That window of Ravenel's apartment opened upon an old garden full of ancient trees and shrubbery. The apartment-house towered above one side of it; a high brick wall fended it from the street; opposite Ravenel's window an old, old mansion stood, half-hidden in the shade of the summer foliage. The house was a castle besieged. The city howled and roared and shrieked and beat upon its double doors, and shook white, fluttering checks above the wall, offering terms of surrender. The gray dust settled upon the trees; the siege was pressed hotter, but the drawbridge was not lowered. No further will the language of chivalry serve. Inside lived an old gentleman who loved his home and did not wish to sell it. That is all the romance of the besieged castle.

Three or four times every week came Sammy Brown to Ravenel's apartment. He belonged to the poet's club, for the former Browns had been conspicuous, though Sammy had been vulgarized by Business. He had no tears for departed Romance. The song of the ticker was the one that reached his heart, and when it came to matters equine and batting scores he was something of a pink edition. He loved to sit in the leather armchair by Ravenel's window. And Ravenel didn't mind particularly. Sammy seemed to enjoy his talk; and then the broker's clerk was such a perfect embodiment of modernity and the day's sordid practicality that Ravenel rather liked to use him as a scapegoat.

"I'll tell you what's the matter with you," said Sammy, with the shrewdness that business had taught him. "The magazine has turned down some of your poetry stunts. That's why you are sore at it."

"That would be a good guess in Wall Street or in a campaign for the presidency of a woman's club," said Ravenel, quietly. "Now, there is a poem—if you will allow me to call it that—of my own in this number of the magazine."

"Read it to me," said Sammy, watching a cloud of pipe-smoke he had just blown out the window.

Ravenel was no greater than Achilles. No one is. There is bound to be a spot. The Somebody-or-Other must take hold of us somewhere when she dips us in the Something-or-Other that makes us invulnerable. He read aloud this verse in the magazine:

THE FOUR ROSES

"One rose I twined within your hair—
    (White rose, that spake of worth);
And one you placed upon your breast—
    (Red rose, love's seal of birth).
You plucked another from its stem—
    (Tea rose, that means for aye);
And one you gave—that bore for me
    The thorns of memory."

"That's a crackerjack," said Sammy, admiringly.

"There are five more verses," said Ravenel, patiently sardonic. "One naturally pauses at the end of each. Of course——"

"Oh, let's have the rest, old man," shouted Sammy, contritely, "I didn't mean to cut you off. I'm not much of a poetry expert, you know. I never saw a poem that didn't look like it ought to have terminal facilities at the end of every verse. Reel off the rest of it."

Ravenel sighed, and laid the magazine down. "All right," said Sammy, cheerfully, "we'll have it next time. I'll be off now. Got a date at five o'clock."

He took a last look at the shaded green garden and left, whistling in an off key an untuneful air from a roofless farce comedy.

The next afternoon Ravenel, while polishing a ragged line of a new sonnet, reclined by the window overlooking the besieged garden of the unmercenary baron. Suddenly he sat up, spilling two rhymes and a syllable or two.

Through the trees one window of the old mansion could be seen clearly. In its window, draped in flowing white, leaned the angel of all his dreams of romance and poesy. Young, fresh as a drop of dew, graceful as a spray of clematis, conferring upon the garden hemmed in by the roaring traffic the air of a princess's bower, beautiful as any flower sung by poet—thus Ravenel saw her for the first time. She lingered for a while, and then disappeared within, leaving a few notes of a birdlike ripple of song to reach his entranced ears through the rattle of cabs and the snarling of the electric cars.

Thus, as if to challenge the poet's flaunt at romance and to punish him for his recreancy to the undying spirit of youth and beauty, this vision had dawned upon him with a thrilling and accusive power. And so metabolic was the power that in an instant the atoms of Ravenel's entire world were redistributed. The laden drays that passed the house in which she lived rumbled a deep double-bass to the tune of love. The newsboys' shouts were the notes of singing birds; that garden was the pleasance of the Capulets; the janitor was an ogre; himself a knight, ready with sword, lance or lute.

Thus does Romance show herself amid forests of brick and stone when she gets lost in the city, and there has to be sent out a general alarm to find her again.

At four in the afternoon Ravenel looked out across the garden. In the window of his hopes were set four small vases, each containing a great, full-blown rose—red and white. And, as he gazed, she leaned above them, shaming them with her loveliness and seeming to direct her eyes pensively toward his own window. And then, as though she had caught his respectful but ardent regard, she melted away, leaving the fragrant emblems on the window-sill.

Yes, emblems!—he would be unworthy if he had not understood. She had read his poem, "The Four Roses"; it had reached her heart; and this was its romantic answer. Of course she must know that Ravenel, the poet, lived there across her garden. His picture, too, she must have seen in the magazines. The delicate, tender, modest, flattering message could not be ignored.

Ravenel noticed beside the roses a small flower-pot containing a plant. Without shame he brought his opera-glasses and employed them from the cover of his window-curtain. A nutmeg geranium!

With the true poetic instinct he dragged a book of useless information from his shelves, and tore open the leaves at "The Language of Flowers."

"Geranium, Nutmeg—I expect a meeting." So! Romance never does things by halves. If she comes back to you she brings gifts and her knitting, and will sit in your chimney-corner if you will let her.

And now Ravenel smiled. The lover smiles when he thinks he has won. The woman who loves ceases to smile with victory. He ends a battle; she begins hers. What a pretty idea to set the four roses in her window for him to see! She must have a sweet, poetic soul. And now to contrive the meeting.

A whistling and slamming of doors preluded the coming of Sammy Brown.

Ravenel smiled again. Even Sammy Brown was shone upon by the far-flung rays of the renaissance. Sammy, with his ultra clothes, his horse-shoe pin, his plump face, his trite slang, his uncomprehending admiration of Ravenel—the broker's clerk made an excellent foil to the new, bright unseen visitor to the poet's sombre apartment.

Sammy went to his old seat by the window, and looked out over the dusty green foliage in the garden. Then he looked at his watch, and rose hastily.

"By grabs!" he exclaimed. "Twenty after four! I can't stay, old man; I've got a date at 4:30."

"Why did you come, then," asked Ravenel, with sarcastic jocularity, "if you had an engagement at that time? I thought you business men kept better account of your minutes and seconds than that."

Sammy hesitated in the doorway and turned pinker.

"Fact is, Ravvy," he explained, as to a customer whose margin is exhausted, "I didn't know I had it until I came. I'll tell you, old man—there's a dandy girl in that old house next door that I'm dead gone on. I put it straight—we're engaged. The old man says 'nit'—but that don't go. He keeps her pretty close. I can see Edith's window from yours here. She gives me a tip when she's going shopping, and I meet her. It's 4:30 to-day. Maybe I ought to have explained sooner, but I know it's all right with you—so long."

"How do you get your 'tip,' as you call it?" asked Ravenel, losing a little spontaneity from his smile.

"Roses," said Sammy, briefly. "Four of 'em to-day. Means four o'clock at the corner of Broadway and Twenty-third."

"But the geranium?" persisted Ravenel, clutching at the end of flying Romance's trailing robe.

"Means half-past," shouted Sammy from the hall. "See you to-morrow."

THE CITY OF DREADFUL NIGHT

"During the recent warmed-over spell," said my friend Carney, driver of express wagon No. 8,606, "a good many opportunities was had of observing human nature through peekaboo waists.

"The Park Commissioner and the Commissioner of Polis and the Forestry Commission gets together and agrees to let the people sleep in the parks until the Weather Bureau gets the thermometer down again to a living basis. So they draws up open-air resolutions and has them O.K.'d by the Secretary of Agriculture, Mr. Comstock and the Village Improvement Mosquito Exterminating Society of South Orange, N. J.

"When the proclamation was made opening up to the people by special grant the public parks that belong to 'em, there was a general exodus into Central Park by the communities existing along its borders. In ten minutes after sundown you'd have thought that there was an undress rehearsal of a potato famine in Ireland and a Kishineff massacre. They come by families, gangs, clambake societies, clans, clubs and tribes from all sides to enjoy a cool sleep on the grass. Them that didn't have oil stoves brought along plenty of blankets, so as not to be upset with the cold and discomforts of sleeping outdoors. By building fires of the shade trees and huddling together in the bridle paths, and burrowing under the grass where the ground was soft enough, the likes of 5,000 head of people successfully battled against the night air in Central Park alone.

"Ye know I live in the elegant furnished apartment house called the Beersheba Flats, over against the elevated portion of the New York Central Railroad.

"When the order come to the flats that all hands must turn out and sleep in the park, according to the instructions of the consulting committee of the City Club and the Murphy Draying, Returfing and Sodding Company, there was a look of a couple of fires and an eviction all over the place.

"The tenants began to pack up feather beds, rubber boots, strings of garlic, hot-water bags, portable canoes and scuttles of coal to take along for the sake of comfort. The sidewalk looked like a Russian camp in Oyama's line of march. There was wailing and lamenting up and down stairs from Danny Geoghegan's flat on the top floor to the apartments of Missis Goldensteinupski on the first.

" 'For why, says Danny, coming down and raging in his blue yarn socks to the janitor, 'should I be turned out of me comfortable apartments to lay in the dirty grass like a rabbit? 'Tis like Jerome to stir up trouble wid small matters like this instead of——'

" 'Whist!' says Officer Reagan on the sidewalk, rapping with his club. ' 'Tis not Jerome. 'Tis by order of the Polis Commissioner. Turn out every one of yez and hike yerselves to the park.'

"Now, 'twas a peaceful and happy home that all of us had in them same Beersheba Flats. The O'Dowds and the Steinowitzes and the Callahans and the Cohens and the Spizzinellis and the McManuses and the Spiegelmayers and the Joneses—all the nations of us, we lived like one big family together. And when the hot nights come along we kept a line of childher reaching from the front door to Kelly's on the corner, passing along the cans of beer from one to another without the trouble of running after it. And with no more clothing on than is provided for in the statutes, sitting in all the windies, with a cool growler in every one, and your feet out in the air, and the Rosenstein girls singing on the fire escape of the sixth floor, and Patsy Rourke's flute going in the eighth, and the ladies calling each other synonyms out the windies, and now and then a breeze sailing in over Mister Depew's Central—I tell you the Beersheba Flats was a summer resort that made the Catskills look like a hole in the ground. With his person full of beer and his feet out the windy and his old woman frying pork chops over a charcoal furnace and the childher dancing in cotton slips on the sidewalk around the organ-grinder and the rent paid for a week—what does a man want better on a hot night than that? And then comes this ruling of the polis driving people out o' their comfortable homes to sleep in parks—'twas for all the world like a ukase of them Russians—'twill be heard from again at next election time.

"Well, then, Officer Reagan drives the whole lot of us to the park and turns us in by the nearest gate. 'Tis dark under the trees, and all the childher sets up to howling that they want to go home.

" 'Ye'll pass the night in this stretch of woods and scenery,' says Officer Reagan. ' 'Twill be fine and imprisonment for insoolting the Park Commissioner and the Chief of the Weather Bureau if ye refuse. I'm in charge of thirty acres between here and the Agyptian Monument, and I advise ye to give no trouble. 'Tis sleeping on the grass yez all have been condemned to by the authorities. Yez'll be permitted to leave in the morning, but ye must retoorn be night. Me orders was silent on the subject of bail. but I'll find out if 'tis required and there'll be bondsmen at the gate.'

"There being no lights except along the automobile drives, us 179 tenants of the Beersheba Flats prepared to spend the night as best we could in the raging forest. Them that brought blankets and kindling wood was best off. They got fires started and wrapped the blankets round their heads and laid down, cursing, in the grass. There was nothing to see, nothing to drink, nothing to do. In the dark we had no way of telling friend or foe, except by feeling the noses of 'em. I brought along me last winter overcoat, me tooth-brush, some quinine pills and the red quilt off the bed in me flat. Three times during the night somebody rolled on me quilt and stuck his knees against the Adam's apple of me. And three times I judged his character by running me hand over his face, and three times I rose up and kicked the intruder down the hill to the gravelly walk below. And then someone with a flavor of Kelly's whiskey snuggled up to me, and I found his nose turned up the right way, and I says: 'Is that you, then, Patsey?' and he says, 'It is, Carney. How long do you think it'll last?'

"'I'm no weather-prophet,' says I, 'but if they bring out a strong anti-Tammany ticket next fall it ought to get us home in time to sleep on a bed once or twice before they line us up at the polls.'

"'A-playing of my flute in the airshaft,' says Patsey Rourke, 'and a-perspiring in me own windy to the joyful noise of the passing trains and the smell of liver and onions and a-reading of the latest murder in the smoke of the cooking is well enough for me,' says he. 'What is this herding us in grass for, not to mention the crawling things with legs that walk up the trousers of us, and the Jersey snipes that peck at us, masquerading under the name and denomination of mosquitoes. What is it all for, Carney, and the rint going on just the same over at the flats?'

"''Tis the great annual Municipal Free Night Outing Lawn Party,' says I, 'given by the polis, Hetty Green and the Drug Trust. During the heated season they hold a week of it in the principal parks. 'Tis a scheme to reach that portion of the people that's not worth taking up to North Beach for a fish fry.'

"'I can't sleep on the ground,' says Patsey, 'wid any benefit. I have the hay fever and the rheumatism, and me ear is full of ants.'

"Well, the night goes on, and the ex-tenants of the Flats groans and stumbles around in the dark, trying to find rest and recreation in the forest. The childher is screaming with the coldness, and the janitor makes hot tea for 'em and keeps the fires going with the signboards that point to the Tavern and the Casino. The tenants try to lay down on the grass by families in the dark, but you're lucky if you can sleep next to a man from the same floor or believing in the same religion. Now and then a Murphy, accidental, rolls over on the grass of a Rosenstein, or a Cohen tries to crawl under the O'Grady bush, and then there's a feeling of noses and somebody is rolled down the hill to the driveway and stays there. There is some hair-pulling among the women folks and everybody spanks the nearest howling kid to him by the sense of feeling only, regardless of its parentage and ownership. 'Tis hard to keep up the social distinctions in the dark that flourish by daylight in the Beersheba Flats. Mrs. Rafferty, that despises the asphalt that a Dago treads on, wakes up in the morning with her feet in the bosom of Antonio Spizzinelli. And Mike O'Dowd, that always threw peddlers downstairs as fast as he came up 'em, has to unwind old Isaacstein's whiskers from around his neck, and wake up the the whole gang at daylight. But here and there some few got acquainted and overlooked the discomforts of the elements. There was five engagements to be married announced at the flats the next morning.

"About midnight I gets up and wrings the dew out of my hair, and goes to the side of the driveway and sits down. At one side of the park I could see the lights in the streets and houses; and I was thinking how happy them folks was who could chase the duck and smoke their pipes at their windows, and keep cool and pleasant like nature intended for 'em to.

"Just then an automobile stops by me, and a fine-looking, well-dressed man steps out.

" 'Me man,' says he, 'can you tell me why all these people are lying around on the grass in the park? I thought it was against the rules.'

" ' 'Twas an ordinance,' says I, 'just passed by the Polis Department and ratified by the Turf Cutters' Association, providing that all persons not carrying a license number of their rear axles shall keep in the public parks until further notice. Fortunately, the orders comes this year during a spell of fine weather, and the mortality, except on the borders of the lake and along the automobile drives, will not be any greater than usual.'

" 'Who are these people on the side of the hill?' asks the man.

" 'Sure,' says I, 'none others than the tenants of the Beersheba Flats— a fine home for any man, especially on hot nights. May daylight come soon!'

" 'They come here by night,' says he, 'and breathe in the pure air and the fragrance of the flowers and trees. They do that,' says he, 'coming every night from the burning heat of dwellings of brick and stone.'

" 'And wood,' says I. 'And marble and plaster and iron.'

" 'The matter will be attended to at once,' says the man, putting up his book.

" 'Are ye the Park Commissioner?' I asks.

" 'I own the Beersheba Flats,' says he. 'God bless the grass and the trees that give extra benefits to a man's tenants. The rents shall be raised fifteen per cent to-morrow. Good-night,' says he."

THE EASTER OF THE SOUL

It is hardly likely that a goddess may die. Then Eastre, the old Saxon goddess of spring, must be laughing in her muslin sleeve at people who believe that Easter, her namesake, exists only among certain strips of Fifth Avenue pavement after church service.

Aye! It belongs to the world. The ptarmigan in Chilkoot Pass discards his winter white feathers for brown; the Patagonian Beau Brummell oils his chignon and clubs him another sweetheart to drag to his skull-strewn flat. And down in Chrystie Street——

Mr. "Tiger" McQuirk arose with a feeling of disquiet that he did not understand. With a practised foot he rolled three of his younger brothers like logs out of his way as they lay sleeping on the floor. Before a foot-square looking glass that hung by the window he stood and shaved himself. If that may seem to you a task too slight to be thus impressively chronicled, I bear with you; you do not know of the areas to be accomplished in traversing the cheek and chin of Mr. McQuirk.

McQuirk, senior, had gone to work long before. The big son of the house was idle. He was a marble-cutter, and the marble-cutters were out on a strike.

"What ails ye?" asked his mother, looking at him curiously; "are ye not feeling well the morning, maybe now?"

"He's thinking along of Annie Maria Doyle," impudently explained younger brother Tim, ten years old.

"Tiger" reached over the hand of a champion and swept the small McQuirk from his chair.

"I feel fine," said he, "beyond a touch of the I-don't-know-what-you-call-its. I feel like there was going to be earthquakes or music or a trifle of chills and fever or maybe a picnic. I don't know how I feel. I feel like knocking the face off a policeman, or else maybe like playing Coney Island straight across the board from pop-corn to the elephant houdahs."

"It's the spring in yer bones," said Mrs. McQuirk. "It's the sap risin'. Time was when I couldn't keep me feet still nor me head cool when the earthworms began to crawl out in the dew of the mornin'. 'Tis a bit of tea will do ye good, made from pipsissewa and gentian bark at the druggist's."

"Back up!" said Mr. McQuirk, impatiently. "There's no spring in sight. There's snow yet on the shed in Donovan's backyard. And yesterday they puts open cars on the Sixth Avenue lines, and the janitors have quit ordering coal. And that means six weeks more of winter, by all the signs that be."

After breakfast Mr. McQuirk spent fifteen minutes before the corrugated mirror, subjugating his hair and arranging his green-and-purple ascot with its amethyst tombstone pin—eloquent of his chosen calling.

Since the strike had been called it was this particular striker's habit to hie himself each morning to the corner saloon of Flaherty Brothers, and there establish himself upon the sidewalk, with one foot resting on the bootblack's stand, observing the panorama of the street until the pace of time brought twelve o'clock and the dinner hour. And Mr. "Tiger" McQuirk, with his athletic seventy inches, well trained in sport and battle; his smooth, pale, solid, amiable face—blue where the razor had travelled; his carefully considered clothes and air of capability, was himself a spectacle not displeasing to the eye.

But on this morning Mr. McQuirk did not hasten immediately to his post of leisure and observation. Something unusual that he could not quite grasp was in the air. Something disturbed his thoughts, ruffled his senses, made him at once languid, irritable, elated, dissatisfied and sportive. He was no diagnostician, and he did not know that Lent was breaking up physiologically in his system.

Mrs. McQuirk had spoken of spring. Sceptically "Tiger" looked about him for signs. Few they were. The organ-grinders were at work; but they were always precocious harbingers. It was near enough spring for them to go penny-hunting when the skating ball dropped at the park. In the milliners' windows Easter hats, grave, gay, and jubilant, blossomed. There were green patches among the sidewalk débris of the grocers. On a third-story window-sill the first elbow cushion of the season—old gold stripes on a crimson ground—supported the kimonoed arms of a pensive brunette. The wind blew cold from the East River, but the sparrows were flying to the eaves with straws. A second-hand store, combining foresight with faith, had set out an ice-chest and baseball goods.

And then "Tiger's" eye, discrediting these signs, fell upon one that bore a bud of promise. From a bright, new lithograph the head of Capricornus confronted him, betokening the forward and heady brew.

Mr. McQuirk entered the saloon and called for his glass of bock. He threw his nickel on the bar, raised the glass, set it down without tasting and strolled toward the door.

"What's the matter, Lord Bolinbroke?" inquired the sarcastic bartender; "want a chiny vase or a gold-lined épergne to drink it out of—hey?"

"Say," said Mr. McQuirk, wheeling and shooting out a horizontal hand and a forty-five-degree chin, "you know your place only, when it comes for givin' titles. I've changed me mind about drinkin'—see? You got your money, ain't you? Wait till you get stung before you get the droop to your lip, will you?"

Thus Mr. McQuirk added mutability of desires to the strange humors that had taken possession of him.

Leaving the saloon, he walked away twenty steps and leaned in the open doorway of Lutz, the barber. He and Lutz were friends, masking their sentiments behind abuse and bludgeons of repartee.

"Irish loafer," roared Lutz, "how do you do? So, not yet haf der bolicemans or der catcher of dogs done deir duty!"

"Hello, Dutch," said Mr. McQuirk. "Can't get your mind off of frankfurters, can you?"

"Bah!" exclaimed the German, coming and leaning in the door. "I haf a soul above frankfurters to-day. Dere is springtime in der air. I can feel it coming in ofer der mud of der streets and das ice in der river. Soon will dere be bicnics in der islands, mit kegs of beer under der trees."

"Say," said Mr. McQuirk, setting his hat on one side, "is everybody kiddin' me about gentle Spring? There ain't any more spring in the air than there is in a horsehair sofa in a Second Avenue furnished room. For me the winter underwear yet and the buckwheat cakes."

"You haf no boetry," said Lutz. "True, it is yedt cold, und in der city we haf not many of der signs; but dere are dree kinds of beoble dot should always feel der approach of spring first—dey are boets, lovers, and poor vidows."

Mr. McQuirk went on his way, still possessed by the strange perturbation that he did not understand. Something was lacking to his comfort, and it made him half angry because he did not know what it was.

Two blocks away he came upon a foe, one Conover, whom he was bound in honor to engage in combat.

Mr. McQuirk made the attack with the characteristic suddenness and fierceness that had gained for him the endearing sobriquet of "Tiger." The defence of Mr. Conover was so prompt and admirable that the conflict was protracted until the onlookers unselfishly gave the warning cry of "Cheese it—the cop!" The principals escaped easily by running through the nearest open doors into the communicating backyards at the rear of the houses.

Mr. McQuirk emerged into another street. He stood by a lamp-post for a few minutes engaged in thought and then he turned and plunged into a small notion and news shop. A red-haired young woman, eating gum-drops, came and looked freezingly at him across the ice-bound steppes of the counter.

"Say, lady," he said, "have you got a song book with this in it? Let's see how it leads off—

"When the springtime comes we'll wander in the dale, love,
   And whisper of those days of yore——

"I'm having a friend," explained Mr. McQuirk, "laid up with a broken leg, and he sent me after it. He's a devil for songs and poetry when he can't get out to drink."

"We have not," replied the young woman, with unconcealed contempt. "But there is a new song out that begins this way:

"Let us sit together in the old arm-chair,
   And while the firelight flickers we'll be comfortable there."

There will be no profit in following Mr. "Tiger" McQuirk through his further vagaries of that day until he comes to stand knocking at the door of Annie Maria Doyle. The goddess Eastre, it seems, had guided his footsteps aright at last.

"Is that you now, Jimmy McQuirk?" she cried, smiling through the opened door (Annie Maria had never accepted the "Tiger"). "Well, whatever!"

"Come out in the hall," said Mr. McQuirk. "I want to ask your opinion of the weather—on the level."

"Are you crazy, sure?" said Annie Maria.

"I am," said the "Tiger." "They've been telling me all day there was spring in the air. Were they liars? Or am I?"

"Dear me!" said Annie Maria—"haven't you noticed it? I can almost smell the violets. And the green grass. Of course, there ain't any yet—it's just a kind of feeling, you know."

"That's what I'm getting at," said Mr. McQuirk. "I've had it. I didn't recognize it at first. I thought maybe it was en-wee, contracted the other day when I stepped above Fourteenth Street. But the katzenjammer I've got don't spell violets. It spells yer own name, Annie Maria, and it's you I want. I go to work next Monday, and I make four dollars a day. Spiel up, old girl—do we make a team?"

"Jimmy," sighed Annie Maria, suddenly disappearing in his overcoat, "don't you see that spring is all over the world right this minute?"

But you yourself remember how that day ended. Beginning with so fine a promise of vernal things, late in the afternoon the air chilled and an inch of snow fell—even so late in March. On Fifth Avenue the ladies drew their winter furs close about them. Only in the florists' windows could be perceived any signs of the morning smile of the coming goddess Eastre.

At six o'clock Herr Lutz began to close his shop. He heard a well-known shout: "Hello, Dutch!"

"Tiger" McQuirk, in his shirt-sleeves, with his hat on the back of his head, stood outside in the whirling snow, puffing at a black cigar.

"Donnerwetter!" shouted Lutz, "der vinter, he has come back again yet!"

"Yer a liar, Dutch," called back Mr. McQuirk, with friendly geniality, "it's spring-time, by the watch."

THE FOOL-KILLER

Down South whenever any one perpetrates some particularly monumental piece of foolishness everybody says: "Send for Jesse Holmes."

Jesse Holmes is the Fool-Killer. Of course he is a myth, like Santa Claus and Jack Frost and General Prosperity and all those concrete conceptions that are supposed to represent an idea that Nature had failed to embody. The wisest of the Southrons cannot tell you whence comes the Fool-Killer's name; but few and happy are the households from the Roanoke to the Rio Grande in which the name of Jesse Holmes has not been pronounced or invoked. Always with a smile, and often with a tear, is he summoned to his official duty. A busy man is Jesse Holmes.

I remember the clear picture of him that hung on the walls of my fancy during my barefoot days when I was dodging his oft-threatened devoirs. To me he was a terrible old man, in gray clothes, with a long, ragged, gray beard, and reddish, fierce eyes. I looked to see him come stumping up the road in a cloud of dust, with a white oak staff in his hand and his shoes tied with leather thongs. I may yet——

But this is a story, not a sequel.

I have taken notice with regret that few stories worth reading have been written that did not contain drink of some sort. Down go the fluids, from Arizona Dick's three fingers of red pizen to the inefficacious Oolong that nerves Lionel Monstresser to repartee in the "Dotty Dialogues." So, in such good company I may introduce an absinthe drip—one absinthe drip, dripped through a silver dripper, orderly, opalescent, cool, green-eyed—deceptive.

Kerner was a fool. Besides that, he was an artist and my good friend. Now, if there is one thing on earth utterly despicable to another, it is an artist in the eyes of an author whose story he has illustrated. Just try it once. Write a story about a mining camp in Idaho. Sell it. Spend the money, and then, six months later, borrow a quarter (or a dime), and buy the magazine containing it. You find a full-page wash drawing of your hero, Black Bill, the cowboy. Somewhere in your story you employed the word "horse." Aha! the artist has grasped the idea. Black Bill has on the regulation trousers of the M. F. H. of the Westchester County Hunt. He carries a parlor rifle, and wears a monocle. In the distance is a section of Forty-second Street during a search for a lost gas-pipe, and the Taj Mahal, the famous mausoleum in India.

Enough! I hated Kerner, and one day I met him and we became friends. He was young and gloriously melancholy because his spirits were so high and life had so much in store for him. Yes, he was almost riotously sad. That was his youth. When a man begins to be hilarious in a sorrowful way you can bet a million that he is dyeing his hair. Kerner's hair was plentiful and carefully matted as an artist's thatch should be. He was a cigaretteur, and he audited his dinners with red wine. But, most of all, he was a fool. And, wisely, I envied him, and listened patiently while he knocked Velasquez and Tintoretto. Once he told me that he liked a story of mine that he had come across in an anthology. He described it to me, and I was sorry that Mr. Fitz James

O'Brien was dead and could not learn of the eulogy of his work. But mostly Kerner made few breaks and was a consistent fool.

I'd better explain what I mean by that. There was a girl. Now, a girl, as far as I am concerned, is a thing that belongs in a seminary or an album; but I conceded the existence of the animal in order to retain Kerner's friendship. He showed me her picture in a locket—she was a blonde or a brunette—I have forgotten which. She worked in a factory for eight dollars a week. Lest factories quote this wage by way of vindication, I will add that the girl had worked for five years to reach that supreme elevation of remuneration, beginning at $1.50 per week.

Kerner's father was worth a couple of millions. He was willing to stand for art, but he drew the line at the factory girl. So Kerner disinherited his father and walked out to a cheap studio and lived on sausages for breakfast and on Farroni for dinner. Farroni had the artistic soul and a line of credit for painters and poets, nicely adjusted. Sometimes Kerner sold a picture and bought some new tapestry, a ring and a dozen silk cravats, and paid Farroni two dollars on account.

One evening Kerner had me to dinner with himself and the factory girl. They were to be married as soon as Kerner could slosh paint profitably. As for the ex-father's two millions—pouf!

She was a wonder. Small and halfway pretty, and as much at her ease in that cheap café as though she were only in the Palmer House, Chicago, with a souvenir spoon already safely hidden in her shirt waist. She was natural. Two things I noticed about her especially. Her belt buckle was exactly in the middle of her back, and she didn't tell us that a large man with a ruby stick-pin had followed her up all the way from Fourteenth Street. Was Kerner such a fool? I wondered. And then I thought of the quantity of striped cuffs and blue glass beads that $2,000,000 can buy for the heathen, and I said to myself that he was. And then Elise—certainly that was her name—told us, merrily, that the brown spot on her waist was caused by her landlady knocking at the door while she (the girl—confound the English language) was heating an iron over the gas jet, and she hid the iron under the bedclothes until the coast was clear, and there was a piece of chewing gum stuck to it when she began to iron the waist and—well, I wondered how in the world the chewing gum came to be there—don't they ever stop chewing it?

A while after that—don't be impatient, the absinthe drip is coming now—Kerner and I were dining at Farroni's. A mandolin and a guitar were being attacked; the room was full of smoke in nice, long crinkly layers just like the artists draw the steam from a plum pudding on Christmas posters and a lady in a blue silk and gasolined gauntlets was beginning to hum an air from the Catskills.

"Kerner," said I, "you are a fool."

"Of course," said Kerner, "I wouldn't let her go on working. Not my wife. What's the use to wait? She's willing. I sold that water color of the Palisades yesterday. We could cook on a two-burner gas stove. You know the ragouts I can throw together? Yes, I think we will marry next week."

"Kerner," said I, "you are a fool."

"Have an absinthe drip?" said Kerner, grandly. "To-night you are a guest of Art in paying quantities. I think we will get a flat with a bath."

"I never tried one—I mean an absinthe drip," said I.

The waiter brought it and poured the water slowly over the ice in the dipper.

"It looks exactly like the Mississippi River water in the big bend below Natchez," said I, fascinated, gazing at the be-muddled drip.

"There are such flats for eight dollars a week," said Kerner.

"You are a fool," said I, and began to sip the filtration. "What you need," I continued, "is the official attention of one Jesse Holmes."

Kerner, not being a Southerner, did not comprehend, so he sat, sentimental, figuring on his flat in his sordid, artistic way, while I gazed into the green eyes of the sophisticated Spirit of Wormwood.

Presently I noticed casually that a procession of bacchantes limned on the wall immediately below the ceiling had begun to move, traversing the room from right to left in a gay and spectacular pilgrimage. I did not confide my discovery to Kerner. The artistic temperament is too high-strung to view deviations from the natural laws of the art of kalsomining. I sipped my absinthe drip and sawed wormwood.

One absinthe drip is not much—but I said again to Kerner, kindly: "You are a fool." And then, in the vernacular: "Jesse Holmes for yours."

And then I looked around and saw the Fool-Killer, as he had always appeared to my imagination, sitting at a nearby table, and regarding us with his reddish, fatal, relentless eyes. He was Jesse Holmes from top to toe; he had the long, gray, ragged beard, the gray clothes of ancient cut, the executioner's look, and the dusty shoes of one who had been called from afar. His eyes were turned fixedly upon Kerner. I shuddered to think that I had invoked him from his assiduous southern duties. I thought of flying, and then I kept my seat, reflecting that many men had escaped his ministrations when it seemed that nothing short of an appointment as Ambassador to Spain could save them from him. I had called my brother Kerner a fool and was in danger of hell fire. That was nothing; but I would try to save him from Jesse Holmes.

The Fool-Killer got up from his table and came over to ours. He rested his hands upon it, and turned his burning, vindictive eyes upon Kerner, ignoring me.

"You are a hopeless fool," he said to the artist. "Haven't you had enough of starvation yet? I offer you one more opportunity. Give up this girl and come back to your home. Refuse, and you must take the consequences."

The Fool-Killer's threatening face was within a foot of his victim's; but to my horror, Kerner made not the slightest sign of being aware of his presence.

"We will be married next week," he muttered absent-mindedly. "With my studio furniture and some second-hand stuff we can make out."

"You have decided your own fate," said the Fool-Killer, in a low but terrible voice. "You may consider yourself as one dead. You have had your last chance."

"In the moonlight," went on Kerner, softly, "we will sit under the skylight with our guitar and sing away the false delights of pride and money."

"On your own head be it," hissed the Fool-Killer, and my scalp prickled when I perceived that neither Kerner's eyes nor his ears took the slightest cognizance of Jesse Holmes. And then I knew that for some reason the veil had been lifted for me alone, and that I had been elected to save my friend from destruction at the Fool-Killer's hand. Something of the fear and wonder of it must have showed itself in my face.

"Excuse me," said Kerner, with his wan, amiable smile; "was I talking to myself? I think it is getting to be a habit with me."

The Fool-Killer turned and walked out of Farroni's.

"Wait here for me," said I, rising; "I must speak to that man. Had you no answer for him? Because you are a fool must you die like a mouse under his foot? Could you not utter one squeak in your own defence?"

"You are drunk," said Kerner, heartlessly. "No one addressed me."

"The destroyer of your mind," said I, "stood above you just now and marked you for his victim. You are not blind or deaf."

"I recognize no such person," said Kerner. "I have seen no one but you at this table. Sit down. Hereafter you shall have no more absinthe drips."

"Wait here," said I, furious; "if you don't care for your own life, I will save it for you."

I hurried out and overtook the man in gray halfway down the block. He looked as I had seen him in my fancy a thousand times—truculent, gray and awful. He walked with the white oak staff, and but for the street-sprinkler the dust would have been flying under his tread.

I caught him by the sleeve and steered him to a dark angle of a building. I knew he was a myth, and I did not want a cop to see me conversing with vacancy, for I might land in Bellevue minus my silver matchbox and diamond ring.

"Jesse Holmes," said I, facing him with apparent bravery, "I know you. I have heard of you all my life. I know now what a scourge you have been to your country. Instead of killing fools you have been murdering the youth and genius that are necessary to make a people live and grow great. You are a fool yourself, Holmes; you began killing off the brightest and best of your countrymen three generations ago, when the old and obsolete standards of society and honor and orthodoxy were narrow and bigoted. You proved that when you put your murderous mark upon my friend Kerner—the wisest chap I ever knew in my life."

The Fool-Killer looked at me grimly and closely.

"You're a queer jag," said he curiously. "Oh, yes; I see who you are now. You were sitting with him at the table. Well, if I'm not mistaken, I heard you call him a fool, too."

"I did," said I. "I delight in doing so. It is from envy. By all the standards that you know he is the most egregious and grandiloquent and gorgeous fool in all the world. That's why you want to kill him."

"Would you mind telling me who or what you think I am?" asked the old man.

I laughed boisterously and then stopped suddenly, for I remembered that it would not do to be seen so hilarious in the company of nothing but a brick wall.

"You are Jesse Holmes, the Fool-Killer," I said, solemnly, "and you are going to kill my friend Kerner. I don't know who rang you up, but if you do kill him I'll see that you get pinched for it. That is," I added, despairingly, "if I can get a cop to see you. They have a poor eye for mortals, and I think it would take the whole force to round up a myth murderer."

"Well," said the Fool-Killer, briskly, "I must be going. You had better go home and sleep it off. Good-night."

At this I was moved at a sudden fear for Kerner to a softer and more pleading mood. I leaned against the gray man's sleeve and besought him:

"Good Mr. Fool-Killer, please don't kill little Kerner. Why can't you go back South and kill Congressmen and clay-eaters and let us alone? Why don't you go up on Fifth Avenue and kill millionaires that keep their money locked up and won't let young fools marry because one of 'em lives on the wrong street? Come and have a drink, Jesse. Will you never get on to your job?"

"Do you know this girl that your friend has made himself a fool about?" asked the Fool-Killer.

"I have the honor," said I, "and that's why I called Kerner a fool. He is a fool because he has waited so long before marrying her. He is a fool because he has been waiting in the hopes of getting the consent of some absurd two-million-dollar-fool parent or something of the sort."

"Maybe," said the Fool-Killer—"maybe I—I might have looked at it differently. Would you mind going back to the restaurant and bringing your friend Kerner here?"

"Oh, what's the use, Jesse," I yawned. "He can't see you. He didn't know you were talking to him at the table. You are a fictitious character, you know."

"Maybe he can this time. Will you go fetch him?"

"All right," said I, "but I've a suspicion that you're not strictly sober, Jesse. You seem to be wavering and losing your outlines. Don't vanish before I get back."

I went back to Kerner and said:

"There's a man with an invisible homicidal mania waiting to see you outside. I believe he wants to murder you. Come along. You won't see him, so there's nothing to be frightened about."

Kerner looked anxious.

"Why," said he, "I had no idea one absinthe would do that. You'd better stick to Wurzburger. I'll walk home with you."

I led him to Jesse Holmes's.

"Rudolph," said the Fool-Killer, "I'll give in. Bring her up to the house. Give me your hand, boy."

"Good for you, dad," said Kerner, shaking hands with the old man. "You'll never regret it after you know her."

"So, you did see him when he was talking to you at the table?" I asked Kerner.

"We hadn't spoken to each other in a year," said Kerner. "It's all right now."

I walked away.

"Where are you going?" called Kerner.

"I am going to look for Jesse Holmes," I answered, with dignity and reserve.

TRANSIENTS IN ARCADIA

There is a hotel on Broadway that has escaped discovery by the summer-resort promoters. It is deep and wide and cool. Its rooms are finished in dark oak of a low temperature. Home-made breezes and deep-green shrubbery give it the delights without the inconveniences of the Adirondacks. One can mount its broad staircases or glide dreamily upward in its aërial elevators, attended by guides in brass buttons, with a serene joy that Alpine climbers have never attained. There is a chef in its kitchen who will prepare for you brook trout better than the White Mountains ever served, sea food that would turn Old Point Comfort—"by Gad, sah!" —green with envy, and Maine venison that would melt the official heart of the game warden.

A few have found out this oasis in the July desert of Manhattan. During that month you will see the hotel's reduced array of guests scattered luxuriously about in the cool twilight of its lofty dining-room, gazing at one another across the snowy waste of unoccupied tables, silently congratulatory.

Superfluous, watchful, pneumatically moving waiters hover near, supplying every want before it is expressed. The temperature is perpetual April. The ceiling is painted in water colors to counterfeit a summer sky across which delicate clouds drift and do not vanish as those of nature do to our regret.

The pleasing, distant roar of Broadway is transformed in the imagination of the happy guests to the noise of a waterfall filling the woods with its restful sound. At every strange footstep the guests turn an anxious ear, fearful lest their retreat be discovered and invaded by the restless pleasure-seekers who are forever hounding Nature to her deepest lairs.

Thus in the depopulated caravansary the little band of connoisseurs jealously hide themselves during the heated season, enjoying to the uttermost the delights of mountain and seashore that art and skill have gathered and served to them.

In this July came to the hotel one whose card that she sent to the clerk for her name to be registered read "Mme. Héloise D'Arcy Beaumont."

Madame Beaumont was a guest such as the Hotel Lotus loved. She possessed the fine air of the élite, tempered and sweetened by a cordial graciousness that made the hotel employés her slaves. Bell-boys fought for the honor of answering her ring; the clerks, but for the question of ownership, would have deeded to her the hotel and its contents; the other guests regarded her as the final touch of feminine exclusiveness and beauty that rendered the entourage perfect.

This super-excellent guest rarely left the hotel. Her habits were consonant with the customs of the discriminating patrons of the Hotel Lotus. To enjoy that delectable hostelry one must forego the city as though it were leagues away. By night a brief excursion to the nearby roofs is in order; but during the torrid day one remains in the umbrageous fastnesses of the Lotus as a trout hangs poised in the pellucid sanctuaries of his favorite pool.

Though alone in the Hotel Lotus, Madame Beaumont preserved the state of a queen whose loneliness was of position only. She breakfasted at ten, a cool, sweet, leisurely, delicate being who glowed softly in the dimness like a jasmine flower in the dusk.

But at dinner was Madame's glory at its height. She wore a gown as beautiful and immaterial as the mist from an unseen cataract in a mountain gorge. The nomenclature of this gown is beyond the guess of the scribe. Always pale-red roses reposed against its lace-garnished front. It was a gown that the head-waiter viewed with respect and met at the door. You thought of Paris when you saw it, and maybe of mysterious countesses, and certainly of Versailles and rapiers and Mrs. Fiske and rouge-et-noir. There was an untraceable rumor in the Hotel Lotus that Madame was a cosmopolite, and that she was pulling with her slender white hands certain strings between the nations in the favor of Russia. Being a citizeness of the world's smoothest roads it was small wonder that she was quick to recognize in the refined purlieus of the Hotel Lotus the most desirable spot in America for a restful sojourn during the heat of midsummer.

On the third day of Madame Beaumont's residence in the hotel a young man entered and registered himself as a guest. His clothing—to speak of his points in approved order—was quietly in the mode; his features good and regular; his expression that of a poised and sophisticated man of the world. He informed the clerk that he would remain three or four days, inquired concerning the sailing of European steamships, and sank into the blissful inanition of the nonpareil hotel with the contented air of a traveller in his favorite inn.

The young man—not to question the veracity of the register—was Harold Farrington. He drifted into the exclusive and calm current of life in the Lotus so tactfully and silently that not a ripple alarmed his fellow-seekers after rest. He ate in the Lotus and of its patronym, and was lulled into blissful peace with the other fortunate mariners. In one day he acquired his table and his waiter and the fear lest the panting chasers after repose that kept Broadway warm should pounce upon and destroy this contiguous but covert haven.

After dinner on the next day after the arrival of Harold Farrington Madame Beaumont dropped her handkerchief in passing out. Mr. Farrington recovered and returned it without the effusiveness of a seeker after acquaintance.

Perhaps there was a mystic freemasonry between the discriminating guests of the Lotus. Perhaps they were drawn one to another by the fact of their common good fortune in discovering the acme of summer resorts in a Broadway hotel. Words delicate in courtesy and tentative in departure from formality passed between the two. And, as if in the expedient atmosphere of a real summer resort, an acquaintance grew, flowered and fructified on the spot as does the mystic plant of the conjuror. For a few moments they stood on a balcony upon which the corridor ended, and tossed the feathery ball of conversation.

"One tires of the old resorts," said Madame Beaumont, with a faint but sweet smile. "What is the use to fly to the mountains or the seashore to escape noise and dust when the very people that make both follow us there?"

"Even on the ocean," remarked Farrington sadly, "the Philistines be upon you. The most exclusive steamers are getting to be scarcely more than ferry boats. Heaven help us when the summer resorter discovers that the Lotus is further away from Broadway than Thousand Islands or Mackinac."

"I hope our secret will be safe for a week, anyhow," said Madame, with a sigh and a smile. "I do not know where I would go if they should descend upon the dear Lotus. I know of but one place so delightful in summer, and that is the castle of Count Polinski, in the Ural Mountains."

"I hear that Baden-Baden and Cannes are almost deserted this season," said Farrington. "Year by year the old resorts fall in disrepute. Perhaps many others, like ourselves, are seeking out the quiet nooks that are overlooked by the majority."

"I promise myself three days more of this delicious rest," said Madame Beaumont. "On Monday the *Cedric* sails."

Harold Farrington's eyes proclaimed his regret. "I too must leave on Monday," he said, "but I do not go abroad."

Madame Beaumont shrugged one round shoulder in a foreign gesture.

"One cannot hide here forever, charming though it may be. The château has been in preparation for me longer than a month. Those house parties that one must give—what a nuisance! But I shall never forget my week in the Hotel Lotus."

"Nor shall I," said Farrington in a low voice, "and I shall never *forgive* the *Cedric.*"

On Sunday evening, three days afterward, the two sat at a little table on the same balcony. A discreet waiter brought ices and small glasses of claret cup.

Madame Beaumont wore the same beautiful evening gown that she had worn each day at dinner. She seemed thoughtful. Near her hand on the table lay a small chatelaine purse. After she had eaten her ice she opened the purse and took out a one-dollar bill.

"Mr. Farrington," she said, with the smile that had won the Hotel Lotus, "I want to tell you something. I'm going to leave before breakfast in the morning, because I've got to go back to my work. I'm behind the hosiery counter at Casey's Mammoth Store, and my vacation's up at eight o'clock to-morrow. That paper dollar is the last cent I'll see till I draw my eight dollars salary next Saturday night. You're a real gentleman, and you've been good to me, and I wanted to tell you before I went.

"I've been saving up out of my wages for a year just for this vacation. I wanted to spend one week like a lady if I never do another one. I wanted to get up when I please instead of having to crawl out at seven every morning; and I wanted to live on the best and be waited on and ring bells for things just like rich folks do. Now I've done it, and I've had the happiest time I ever expect to have in my life. I'm going back to my work and my little hall bedroom satisfied for another year. I wanted to tell you about it, Mr. Farrington, because I—I thought you kind of liked me, and I—I liked you. But, oh, I couldn't help deceiving you up till now, for it was all just like a fairy tale to me. So I talked about Europe and the things I've read about in other countries, and made you think I was a great lady.

"This dress I've got on—it's the only one I have that's fit to wear—I bought from O'Dowd & Levinsky on the instalment plan.

"Seventy-five dollars is the price, and it was made to measure. I paid $10 down, and they're to collect $1 a week till it's paid for. That'll be about all I have to say, Mr. Farrington, except that my name is Mamie Siviter instead of Madame Beaumont, and I thank you for your attentions. This dollar will pay the instalment due on the dress to-morrow. I guess I'll go up to my room now."

Harold Farrington listened to the recital of the Lotus's loveliest guest with an impassive countenance. When she had concluded he drew a small book like a checkbook from his coat pocket. He wrote upon a blank form in this with a stub of pencil, tore out the leaf, tossed it over to his companion and took up the paper dollar.

"I've got to go to work, too, in the morning," he said, "and I might as well begin now. There's a receipt for the dollar instalment. I've been a collector for O'Dowd & Levinsky for three years. Funny, ain't it, that you and me both had the same idea about spending our vacation? I've always wanted to put up at a swell hotel, and I saved up out of my twenty per, and did it. Say, Mame, how about a trip to Coney Saturday night on the boat—what?"

The face of the pseudo Madame Héloise D'Arcy Beaumont beamed.

"Oh, you bet I'll go, Mr. Farrington. The store closes at twelve on Saturdays. I guess Coney'll be all right even if we did spend a week with the swells."

Below the balcony the sweltering city growled and buzzed in the July night. Inside the Hotel Lotus the tempered, cool shadows reigned, and the solicitous waiter single-footed near the low windows, ready at a nod to serve Madame and her escort.

At the door of the elevator Farrington took his leave, and Madame Beaumont made her last ascent. But before they reached the noiseless cage he said: "Just forget that 'Harold Farrington,' will you?—McManus is the name—James McManus. Some call me Jimmy."

"Good-night, Jimmy," said Madame.

THE RATHSKELLER AND THE ROSE

Miss Posie Carrington had earned her success. She began life handicapped by the family name of "Boggs," in the small town known as Cranberry Corners. At the age of eighteen she had acquired the name of "Carrington" and a position in the chorus of a metropolitan burlesque company. Thence upward she had ascended by the legitimate and delectable steps of "broiler," member of the famous "Dickey-bird" octette, in the successful musical comedy, "Fudge and Fellows," leader of the potato-bug dance in "Fol-de-Rol," and at length to the part of the maid " 'Tointette" in "The King's Bath-Robe," which captured the critics and gave her her chance. And when we come to consider Miss Carrington she is in the heydey of flattery, fame and fizz; and that astute manager Herr Timothy Goldstein has her signature to iron-clad papers that she will star the coming season in Dyde Rich's new play, "Paresis by Gaslight."

Promptly there came to Herr Timothy a capable twentieth-century young character actor by the name of Highsmith, who besought engagement as "Sol Haytosser," the comic and chief male character part in "Paresis by Gaslight."

"My boy," said Goldstein, "take the part if you can get it. Miss Carrington won't listen to any of my suggestions. She has turned down half a dozen of the best imitators of the rural dub in the city. She declares she won't set a foot on the stage unless 'Haytosser' is the best that can be raked up. She was raised in a village, you know, and when a Broadway orchid sticks a straw in his hair and tries to call himself a clover blossom she's on, all right. I asked her, in a sarcastic vein, if she thought Denman Thompson would make any kind of a show in the part. 'Oh, no,' says she. 'I don't want him or John Drew or Jim Corbett or any of these swell actors that don't know a turnip from a turnstile. I want the real article.' So, my boy, if you want to play 'Sol Haytosser' you will have to convince Miss Carrington. Luck be with you."

Highsmith took the train the next day for Cranberry Corners. He remained in that forsaken and inanimate village three days. He found the Boggs family and corkscrewed their history unto the third and fourth generation. He amassed the facts and the local color of Cranberry Corners. The village had not grown as rapidly as had Miss Carrington. The actor estimated that it had suffered as few actual changes since the departure of its solitary follower of Thespis as had a stage upon which "four years is supposed to have elapsed." He absorbed Cranberry Corners and returned to the city of chameleon changes.

It was in the rathskeller that Highsmith made the hit of his histrionic career. There is no need to name the place; there is but one rathskeller where you could hope to find Miss Posie Carrington after a performance of "The King's Bath-Robe."

There was a jolly small party at one of the tables that drew many eyes. Miss Carrington, petite, marvellous, bubbling, electric, fame-drunken, shall be named first. Herr Goldstein follows, sonorous, curly-haired, heavy, a trifle anxious, as some bear that had caught, somehow, a butterfly in his claws. Next, a man condemned to a newspaper, sad, courted, armed, analyzing for press agent's dross every sentence that was poured over him, eating his à la Newburg in the silence of greatness. To conclude, a youth with parted hair, a name that is ochre to red journals and gold on the back of a supper check. These sat at a table while the musicians played, while waiters moved in the mazy performance of their duties with their backs toward all who desired their service, and all was bizarre and merry because it was nine feet below the level of the sidewalk.

At 11.45 a being entered the rathskeller. The first violin perceptibly flatted a C that should have been natural; the clarionet blew a bubble instead of a grace note; Miss Carrington giggled and the youth with parted hair swallowed an olive seed.

Exquisitely and irreproachably rural was the new entry. A lank, disconcerted, hesitating young man it was, flaxen-haired, gaping of mouth, awkward, stricken to misery by the lights and company. His clothing was butternut, with bright blue tie, showing four inches of bony wrist and white-socked ankle. He upset a chair, sat in another one, curled a foot around a table leg and cringed at the approach of a waiter.

"You may fetch me a glass of lager beer," he said, in response to the discreet questioning of the servitor.

The eyes of the rathskeller were upon him. He was as fresh as a collard and as ingenuous as a hay rake. He let his eye rove about the place as one who regards, big-eyed, hogs in the potato patch. His gaze rested at length upon Miss Carrington. He rose and went to her table with a lateral, shining smile and a blush of pleased trepidation.

"How're ye, Miss Posie?" he said in accents not to be doubted. "Don't ye remember me—Bill Summers—the Summerses that lived back of the blacksmith shop? I reckon I've growed up some since ye left Cranberry Corners.

" 'Liza Perry 'lowed I might see ye in the city while I was here. You know 'Liza married Benny Stanfield, and she says——"

"Ah, say!" interrupted Miss Carrington, brightly, "Lize Perry is never married—what! Oh, the freckles of her!"

"Married in June," grinned the gossip, "and livin' in the old Tatum Place. Ham Riley perfessed religion; old Mrs. Blithers sold her place to Cap'n Spooner; the youngest Waters girl run away with a music teacher; the courthouse burned up last March; your uncle Wiley was elected constable; Matilda Hoskins died from runnin' a needle in her hand, and Tom Beedle is courtin' Sallie Lathrop—they say he don't miss a night but what he's settin' on their porch."

"The wall-eyed thing!" exclaimed Miss Carrington, with asperity. "Why, Tom Beedle once—say, you folks, excuse me a while—this is an old friend of mine—Mr.—what was it? Yes, Mr. Summers—Mr. Goldstein, Mr. Ricketts, Mr.—— Oh, what's yours? 'Johnny' 'll do—come over here and tell me some more."

She swept him to an isolated table in a corner. Herr Goldstein shrugged his fat shoulders and beckoned to the waiter. The newspaper man brightened a little and mentioned absinthe. The youth with parted hair was plunged into melancholy. The guests of the rathskeller laughed, clinked glasses and enjoyed the comedy that Posie Carrington was treating them to after her regular performance. A few cynical ones whispered "press agent" and smiled wisely.

Posie Carrington laid her dimpled and desirable chin upon her hands, and forgot her audience—a faculty that had won her laurels for her.

"I don't seem to recollect any Bill Summers," she said thoughtfully, gazing straight into the innocent blue eyes of the rustic young man. "But I know the Summerses, all right. I guess there ain't many changes in the old town. You see any of my folks lately?"

And then Highsmith played his trump. The part of "Sol Haytosser" called for pathos as well as comedy. Miss Carrington should see that he could do that as well.

"Miss Posie," said "Bill Summers," "I was up to your folkses house jist two or three days ago. No, there ain't many changes to speak of. The lilac bush by the kitchen window is over a foot higher, and the elm in the front yard died and had to be cut down. And yet it don't seem the same place that it used to be."

"How's ma?" asked Miss Carrington.

"She was settin' by the front door, crocheting a lamp-mat when I saw her last," said "Bill." "She's older'n she was, Miss Posie. But everything in the house looked jest the same. Your ma asked me to set down. 'Don't touch that willow rocker, William,' says she. 'It ain't been moved since Posie left; and that's the apron she was hemmin' layin' over the arm of of it, jist as she flung it. I'm in hopes,' she goes on, 'that Posie'll finish runnin' out that hem some day.'"

Miss Carrington beckoned peremptorily to a waiter.

"A pint of extra dry," she ordered, briefly; "and give the check to Goldstein."

"The sun was shinin' in the door," went on the chronicler from Cranberry, "and your ma was settin' right in it. I asked her if she hadn't better move back a little. 'William,' says she, 'when I get sot down and lookin' down the road, I can't bear to move. Never a day,' says she, 'but what I set here every minute that I can spare and watch over them palin's for Posie. She went away down that road in the night, for we seen her little shoe tracks in the dust, and somethin' tells me she'll come back that way ag'in when she's weary of the world and begins to think about her old mother.'

"When I was comin' away," concluded "Bill," "I pulled this off'n the bush by the front steps. I thought maybe I might see you in the city, and I knowed you'd like somethin' from the old home."

He took from his coat pocket a rose—a drooping, yellow, velvet, odorous rose, that hung its head in the foul atmosphere of that tainted rathskeller like a virgin bowing before the hot breath of the lions in a Roman arena.

Miss Carrington's penetrating but musical laugh rose above the orchestra's rendering of "Bluebells."

"Oh, say!" she cried, with glee, "ain't those poky places the limit? I just know that two hours at Cranberry Corners would give me the horrors now. Well, I'm awful glad to have seen you, Mr. Summers. I guess I'll hustle around to the hotel now and get my beauty sleep."

She thrust the yellow rose into the bosom of her wonderful, dainty, silken garments, stood up and nodded imperiously at Herr Goldstein.

Her three companions and "Bill Summers" attended her to her cab. When her flounces and streamers were all safely tucked inside she dazzled them with au revoirs from her shining eyes and teeth.

"Come around to the hotel and see me, Bill, before you leave the city," she called as the glittering cab rolled away.

Highsmith, still in his make-up, went with Herr Goldstein to a café booth.

"Bright idea, eh?" asked the smiling actor. "Ought to land 'Sol Haytosser' for me, don't you think? The little lady never once tumbled."

"I didn't hear your conversation," said Goldstein, "but your make-up and acting was O. K. Here's to your success. You'd better call on Miss Carrington early to-morrow and strike her for the part. I don't see how she can keep from being satisfied with your exhibition of ability."

At 11.45 A.M. on the next day Highsmith, handsome, dressed in the latest mode, confident, with a fuchsia in his buttonhole, sent up his card to Miss Carrington in her select apartment hotel.

He was shown up and received by the actress's French maid.

"I am sorree," said Mlle. Hortense, "but I am to say this to all. It is with great regret. Mees Carrington have cancelled all engagements on the stage and have returned to live in that—how you call that town? Cranberry Cornaire!"

THE CLARION CALL

Half of this story can be found in the records of the Police Department; the other half belongs behind the business counter of a newspaper office.

One afternoon two weeks after Millionaire Norcross was found in his apartment murdered by a burglar, the murderer, while strolling serenely down Broadway, ran plump against Detective Barney Woods.

"Is that you, Johnny Kernan?" asked Woods, who had been near-sighted in public for five years.

"No less," cried Kernan, heartily. "If it isn't Barney Woods, late and early of old Saint Jo! You'll have to show me! What are you doing East? Do the green-goods circulars get out that far?"

"I've been in New York some years," said Woods. "I'm on the city detective force."

"Well, well!" said Kernan, breathing smiling joy and patting the detective's arm.

"Come into Muller's," said Woods, "and let's hunt a quiet table. I'd like to talk to you awhile."

It lacked a few minutes to the hour of four. The tides of trade were not yet loosed, and they found a quiet corner of the café. Kernan, well dressed, slightly swaggering, self-confident, seated himself opposite the little detective, with his pale, sandy mustache, squinting eyes, and ready-made cheviot suit.

"What business are you in now?" asked Woods. "You know you left Saint Jo a year before I did."

"I'm selling shares in a copper mine," said Kernan. "I may establish an office here. Well, well! and so old Barney is a New York detective. You always had a turn that way. You were on the police in Saint Jo after I left there, weren't you?"

"Six months," said Woods. "And now there's one more question, Johnny. I've followed your record pretty close ever since you did that hotel job in Saratoga, and I never knew you to use your gun before. Why did you kill Norcross?"

Kernan stared for a few moments with concentrated attention at the slice of lemon in his high-ball; and then he looked at the detective with a sudden crooked, brilliant smile.

"How did you guess it, Barney?" he asked, admiringly. "I swear I thought the job was as clean and as smooth as a peeled onion. Did I leave a string hanging out anywhere?"

Woods laid upon the table a small gold pencil intended for a watch-charm.

"It's the one I gave you the last Christmas we were in Saint Jo. I've got your shaving mug yet. I found this under a corner of the rug in Norcross's room. I warn you to be careful what you say. I've got it put on to you, Johnny. We were old friends once, but I must do my duty. You'll have to go to the chair for Norcross."

Kernan laughed.

"My luck stays with me," said he. "Who'd have thought old Barney was on my trail!" He slipped one hand inside his coat. In an instant Woods had a revolver against his side.

"Put it away," said Kernan, wrinkling his nose. "I'm only investigating.

Aha! It takes nine tailors to make a man, but one can do a man up. There's a hole in that vest pocket. I took that pencil off my chain and slipped it in there in case of a scrap. Put up your gun, Barney, and I'll tell you why I had to shoot Norcross. The old fool started down the hall after me, popping at the buttons on the back of my coat with a peevish little .22 and I had to stop him. The old lady was a darling. She just lay in bed and saw her $12,000 diamond necklace go without a chirp, while she begged like a panhandler to have back a little thin gold ring with a garnet worth about $3. I guess she married old Norcross for his money, all right. Don't they hang onto the little trinkets from the Man Who Lost Out, though? There were six rings, two brooches and a chatelaine watch. Fifteen thousand would cover the lot."

"I warned you not to talk," said Woods.

"Oh, that's all right," said Kernan. "The stuff is in my suit case at the hotel. And now I'll tell you why I'm talking. Because it's safe. I'm talking to a man I know. You owe me a thousand dollars, Barney Woods, and even if you wanted to arrest me your hand wouldn't make the move."

"I haven't forgotten," said Woods. "You counted out twenty fifties without a word. I'll pay it back some day. That thousand saved me and— well, they were piling my furniture out on the sidewalk when I got back to the house."

"And so," continued Kernan, "you being Barney Woods, born as true as steel, and bound to play a white man's game, can't lift a finger to arrest the man you're indebted to. Oh, I have to study men as well as Yale locks and window fastenings in my business. Now, keep quiet while I ring for the waiter. I've had a thirst for a year or two that worries me a little. If I'm ever caught the lucky sleuth will have to divide honors with the old boy Booze. But I never drink during business hours. After a job I can crook elbows with my old friend Barney with a clear conscience. What are you taking?"

The waiter came with the little decanters and the siphon and left them alone again.

"You've called the turn," said Woods, as he rolled the little gold pencil about with a thoughtful forefinger. "I've got to pass you up. I can't lay a hand on you. If I'd a-paid that money back—but I didn't, and that settles it. It's a bad break I'm making, Johnny, but I can't dodge it. You helped me once, and it calls for the same."

"I knew it," said Kernan, raising his glass, with a flushed smile of self-appreciation. "I can judge men. Here's to Barney, for—'he's a jolly good fellow.'"

"I don't believe," went on Woods quietly, as if he were thinking aloud, "that if accounts had been square between you and me, all the money in all the banks in New York could have bought you out of my hands to-night."

"I know it couldn't," said Kernan. "That's why I knew I was safe with you."

"Most people," continued the detective, "look sideways at my business. They don't class it among the fine arts and the professions. But I've always taken a kind of fool pride in it. And here is where I go 'busted.' I guess I'm a man first and a detective afterward. I've got to let you go, and then I've got to resign from the force. I guess I can drive an express wagon. Your thousand dollars is further off than ever, Johnny."

"Oh, you're welcome to it," said Kernan, with a lordly air. "I'd be willing to call the debt off, but I know you wouldn't have it. It was a lucky day for me when you borrowed it. And now, let's drop the subject. I'm off to the West on a morning train. I know a place out there where I can negotiate the Norcross sparks. Drink up, Barney, and forget your troubles. We'll have a jolly time while the police are knocking their heads together over the case. I've got one of my Sahara thirsts on to-night. But I'm in the hands—the unofficial hands—of my old friend Barney, and I won't even dream of a cop."

And then, as Kernan's ready finger kept the button and the waiter working, his weak point—a tremendous vanity and arrogant egotism, began to show itself. He recounted story after story of his successful plunderings, ingenious plots and infamous transgressions until Woods, with all his familiarity with evil-doers, felt growing within him a cold abhorrence toward the utterly vicious man who had once been his benefactor.

"I'm disposed of, of course," said Woods, at length. "But I advise you to keep under cover for a spell. The newspapers may take up this Norcross affair. There has been an epidemic of burglaries and manslaughter in town this summer."

The word sent Kernan into a high glow of sullen and vindictive rage.

"To h—l with the newspapers," he growled. "What do they spell but brag and blow and boodle in box-car letters? Suppose they do take up a case—what does it amount to? The police are easy enough to fool; but what do the newspapers do? They send a lot of pin-head reporters around to the scene; and they make for the nearest saloon and have beer while they take photos of the bartender's oldest daughter in evening dress to print as the fiancée of the young man in the tenth story, who thought he heard a noise below on the night of the murder. That's about as near as the newspapers ever come to running down Mr. Burglar."

"Well, I don't know," said Woods, reflecting. "Some of the papers have done good work in that line. There's the *Morning Mars,* for instance. It warmed up two or three trails, and got the man after the police had let 'em get cold."

"I'll show you," said Kernan, rising, and expanding his chest. "I'll show you what I think of newspapers in general, and your *Morning Mars* in particular."

Three feet from their table was the telephone booth. Kernan went inside and sat at the instrument, leaving the door open. He found a number in the book, took down the receiver and made his demand upon Central. Woods sat still, looking at the sneering, cold, vigilant face waiting close to the transmitter, and listened to the words that came from the thin, truculent lips curved into a contemptuous smile.

"That the *Morning Mars?* . . . I want to speak to the managing editor. . . . Why, tell him it's someone who wants to talk to him about the Norcross murder.

"You the editor? . . . All right. . . . I am the man who killed old Norcross. . . . Wait! Hold the wire; I'm not the usual crank . . . Oh, there isn't the slightest danger. I've just been discussing it with a detective friend of mine. I killed the old man at 2.30 A.M. two weeks ago tomorrow. . . . Have a drink with you? Now, hadn't you better leave that kind of talk to your funny man? Can't you tell whether a man's guying you or whether you're being offered the biggest scoop your dull dishrag of a paper ever had? . . . Well, that's so; it's a bobtail scoop—but you can hardly expect me to 'phone in my name and address. . . . Why! Oh, because I heard you make a specialty of solving mysterious crimes that stump the police. . . . No, that's not all. I want to tell you that your rotten, lying penny sheet is of no more use in tracking an intelligent murderer or highway man than a blind poodle would be. . . . What? . . . Oh, no, this isn't a rival newspaper office; you're getting it straight. I did the Norcross job, and I've got the jewels in my suit case at—'the name of the hotel could not be learned'—you recognize that phrase, don't you? I thought so. You've used it often enough. Kind of rattles you, doesn't it, to have the mysterious villain call up your great, big, all-powerful organ of right and justice and good government and tell you what a helpless old gas-bag you are? . . . Cut that out; you're not that big a fool—no, you don't think I'm a fraud. I can tell it by your voice. . . . Now, listen, and I'll give you a pointer that will prove it to you. Of course you've had this murder case worked over by your staff of bright young blockheads. Half of the second button on old Mrs. Norcross's nightgown is broken off. I saw it when I took the garnet ring off her finger. I thought it was a ruby. . . . Stop that! It won't work."

Kernan turned to Woods with a diabolic smile.

"I've got him going. He believes me now. He didn't quite cover the transmitter with his hand when he told somebody to call up Central on another 'phone and get our number. I'll give him just one more dig and then we'll make a 'get-away.'

"Hello! . . . Yes. I'm here yet. You didn't think I'd run from such a little subsidized, turncoat rag of a newspaper, did you? . . . Have me inside of forty-eight hours? Say, will you quit being funny? Now, you let grown men alone and attend to your business of hunting up divorce cases and street-car accidents and printing the filth and scandal that you make your living by. Good-by, old boy—sorry I haven't time to call on you. I'd feel perfectly safe in your sanctum asinorum. Tra-la!

"He's as mad as a cat that's lost a mouse," said Kernan, hanging up the receiver and coming out. "And now, Barney, my boy, we'll go to a show and enjoy ourselves until a reasonable bedtime. Four hours' sleep for me, and then the west-bound."

The two dined in a Broadway restaurant. Kernan was pleased with himself. He spent money like a prince of fiction. And then a weird and gorgeous musical comedy engaged their attention. Afterward there was a late supper in a grill-room, with champagne, and Kernan at the height of his complacency.

Half-past three in the morning found them in a corner of an all-night café, Kernan still boasting in a vapid and rambling way, Woods thinking moodily over the end that had come to his usefulness as an upholder of the law.

But, as he pondered, his eye brightened with a speculative light.

"I wonder if it's possible," he said to himself, "I won-der if it's pos-si-ble!"

And then outside the café the comparative stillness of the early morning was punctured by faint, uncertain cries that seemed mere fireflies of sound, some growing louder, some fainter, waxing and waning amid the rumble of milk wagons and infrequent cars. Shrill cries they were when near—well-known cries that conveyed many meanings to the ears of those of the slumbering millions of the great city who waked to hear them. Cries that bore upon their significant, small volume the weight of a world's woe and laughter and delight and stress. To some, cowering beneath the protection of a night's ephemeral cover, they brought news of the hideous, bright day; to others, wrapped in happy sleep, they announced a morning that would dawn blacker than sable night. To many of the rich they brought a besom to sweep away what had been theirs while the stars shone; to the poor they brought—another day.

All over the city the cries were starting up, keen and sonorous, heralding the chances that the slipping of one cogwheel in the machinery of time had made; apportioning to the sleepers while they lay at the mercy of fate, the vengeance, profit, grief, reward and doom that the new figure in the calendar had brought them. Shrill and yet plaintive were the cries, as if the young voices grieved that so much evil and so little good was in their irresponsible hands. Thus echoed in the streets of the helpless city the transmission of the latest decrees of the gods, the cries of the newsboys—the Clarion Call of the Press.

Woods flipped a dime to the waiter, and said:

"Get me a *Morning Mars.*"

When the paper came he glanced at its first page, and then tore a leaf out of his memorandum book and began to write on it with the little gold pencil.

"What's the news?" yawned Kernan.

Woods flipped over to him the piece of writing:

The New York *Morning Mars*

Please pay to the order of John Kernan the one thousand dollars reward coming to me for his arrest and conviction.

Barnard Woods

"I kind of thought they would do that," said Woods, "when you were jollying 'em so hard. Now, Johnny, you'll come to the police station with me."

EXTRADITED FROM BOHEMIA

From near the village of Harmony, at the foot of the Green Mountains, came Miss Medora Martin to New York with her color-box and easel.

Miss Medora resembled the rose which the autumnal frosts had spared the longest of all her sister blossoms. In Harmony, when she started alone to the wicked city to study art, they said she was a mad, reckless, headstrong girl. In New York, when she first took her seat at a West Side boarding-house table, the boarders asked: "Who is the nice-looking old maid?"

Medora took heart, a cheap hall bedroom, and two art lessons a week from Professor Angelini, a retired barber who had studied his profession in a Harlem dancing academy. There was no one to set her right, for here in the big city they do it unto all of us. How many of us are badly shaved daily and taught the two-step imperfectly by ex-pupils of Bastien Le Page and Gérôme? The most pathetic sight in New York—except the manners of the rush-hour crowds—is the dreary march of the hopeless army of Mediocrity. Here Art is no benignant goddess, but a Circe who turns her wooers into mewing Toms and Tabbies who linger about the doorsteps of her abode, unmindful of the flying brickbats and boot-jacks of the critics. Some of us creep back to our native villages to the skim-milk of "I told you so"; but most of us prefer to remain in the cold courtyard of our mistress's temple, snatching the scraps that fall from her divine table d'hôte. But some of us grow weary at last of the fruitless service. And then there are two fates open to us. We can get a job driving a grocer's wagon, or we can get swallowed up in the Vortex of Bohemia. The latter sounds good; but the former really pans out better. For, when the grocer pays us off we can rent a dress suit and—the capitalized system of humor describes it best—Get Bohemia On the Run.

Miss Medora chose the Vortex and thereby furnishes us with our little story.

Professor Angelini praised her sketches excessively. Once, when she had made a neat study of a horse-chestnut tree in the park, he declared she would become a second Rosa Bonheur. Again—a great artist has his moods—he would say cruel and cutting things. For example, Medora had spent an afternoon patiently sketching the statue and the architecture at Columbus Circle. Tossing it aside with a sneer, the professor informed her that Giotto had once drawn a perfect circle with one sweep of his hand.

One day it rained, the weekly remittance from Harmony was overdue, Medora had a headache, the professor had tried to borrow two dollars from her, her art dealer had sent back all her water-colors unsold and—Mr. Binkley asked her out to dinner.

Mr. Binkley was the gay boy of the boarding-house. He was forty-nine, and owned a fish-stall in a downtown market. But after six o'clock he wore an evening suit and whooped things up connected with the beaux arts. The young men said he was an "Indian." He was supposed to be an accomplished habitué of the inner circles of Bohemia. It was no secret that he had once loaned $10 to a young man who had had a drawing printed in *Puck*. Often has one thus obtained his entrée into the charmed circle, while the other obtained both his entrée and roast.

The other boarders enviously regarded Medora as she left at Mr. Binkley's side at nine o'clock. She was as sweet as a cluster of dried autumn grasses in her pale blue—oh—er—that very thin stuff—in her pale blue Comstockized silk waist and box-pleated voile skirt, with a soft pink glow on her thin cheeks and the tiniest bit of rouge powder on her face, with her handkerchief and room key in her brown walrus, pebble-grain hand-bag.

And Mr. Binkley looked imposing and dashing with his red face and gray mustache, and his tight dress coat, that made the back of his neck roll up just like a successful novelist's.

They drove in a cab to the Café Terence, just off the most glittering part of Broadway, which, as everyone knows, is one of the most popular and widely patronized, jealously exclusive Bohemian resorts in the city.

Down between the rows of little tables tripped Medora, of the Green Mountains, after her escort. Thrice in a lifetime may woman walk upon clouds—once when she trippeth to the altar, once when she first enters Bohemian halls, the last when she marches back across her first garden with the dead hen of her neighbor in her hand.

There was a table set, with three or four about it. A waiter buzzed around it like a bee, and silver and glass shone upon it. And, preliminary to the meal, as the prehistoric granite strata heralded the protozoa, the bread of Gaul, compounded after the formula of the recipe for the eternal hills, was there set forth to the hand and tooth of a long-suffering city, while the gods lay beside their nectar and home-made biscuits and smiled, and the dentists leaped for joy in their gold-leafy dens.

The eye of Binkley fixed a young man at his table with the Bohemian gleam, which is a compound of the look of the Basilisk, the shine of a bubble of Würzburger, the inspiration of genius and the pleading of a panhandler.

The young man sprang to his feet. "Hello, Bink, old boy!" he shouted. "Don't tell me you were going to pass our table. Join us—unless you've another crowd on hand."

"Don't mind, old chap," said Binkley, of the fish-stall. "You know how I like to butt up against the fine arts. Mr. Vandyke—Mr. Madder—er—Miss Martin, one of the elect also in art—er——"

The introduction went around. There were also Miss Elise and Miss 'Toinette. Perhaps they were models, for they chattered of the St. Regis decorations and Henry James—and they did it not badly.

Medora sat in transport. Music—wild, intoxicating music made by troubadours direct from a rear basement room in Elysium—set her thoughts to dancing. Here was a world never before penetrated by her warmest imagination or any of the lines controlled by Harriman. With the Green Mountains' external calm upon her she sat, her soul flaming in her with the fire of Andalusia. The tables were filled with Bohemia. The room was full of the fragrance of flowers—both mille and cauli. Questions and corks popped; laughter and silver rang; champagne flashed in the pail, wit flashed in the pan.

Vandyke ruffled his long, black locks, disarranged his careless tie and leaned over to Madder.

"Say, Maddy," he whispered, feelingly, "sometimes I'm tempted to pay this Philistine his ten dollars and get rid of him."

Madder ruffled his long, sandy locks and disarranged his careless tie.

"Don't think of it, Vandy," he replied. "We are short, and Art is long."

Medora ate strange viands and drank elderberry wine that they poured in her glass. It was just the color of that in the Vermont home. The waiter poured something in another glass that seemed to be boiling, but when she tasted it it was not hot. She had never felt so lighthearted before. She thought lovingly of Green Mountain farm and its fauna. She leaned, smiling, to Miss Elise.

"If I were at home," she said, beamingly, "I could show you the cutest little calf!"

"Nothing for you in the White Lane," said Miss Elise. "Why don't you pad?"

The orchestra played a wailing waltz that Medora had learned from the hand-organs. She followed the air with nodding head in a sweet soprano hum. Madder looked across the table at her, and wondered in what strange waters Binkley had caught her in his seine. She smiled at him, and they raised glasses and drank of the wine that boiled when it was cold.

Binkley had abandoned art and was prating of the unusual spring catch of shad. Miss Elise arranged the palette-and-maul-stick tie pin of Mr. Vandyke. A Philistine at some distant table was maundering volubly either about Jerome or Gérôme. A famous actress was discoursing excitably about monogrammed hosiery. A hose clerk from a department store was loudly proclaiming his opinions of the drama. A writer was abusing Dickens. A magazine editor and a photographer were drinking a dry brand at a reserved table. A 36-25-42 young lady was saying to an eminent sculptor: "Fudge for your Prax Italys! Bring one of your Venus Anno Dominus down to Cohen's and see how quickly she'd be turned down for a cloak model. Back to the quarries with your Greeks and Dagos!"

Thus went Bohemia.

At eleven Mr. Binkley took Medora to the boarding-house and left her, with a society bow, at the foot of the hall stairs. She went up to her room and lit the gas.

And then, as suddenly as the dreadful genie arose in vapor from the copper vase of the fisherman, arose in that room the formidable shape of the New England Conscience. The terrible thing that Medora had done was revealed to her in its full enormity. She had sat in the presence of the ungodly and looked upon the wine both when it was red and effervescent.

At midnight she wrote this letter:

Mr. Beriah Hoskins, Harmony, Vermont

Dear Sir: Henceforth, consider me as dead to you forever. I have loved you too well to blight your career by bringing into it my guilty and sin-stained life. I have succumbed to the insidious wiles of this wicked world and have been drawn into the vortex of Bohemia. There is scarcely any depth of glittering iniquity that I have not sounded. It is hopeless to combat my decision. There is no rising from the depths to which I have sunk. Endeavor to forget me. I am lost forever in the fair but brutal maze of awful Bohemia. Farewell.

Once your Medora

On the next day Medora formed her resolutions. Beelzebub, flung from heaven, was no more cast down. Between her and the apple blossoms of Harmony there was a fixed gulf. Flaming cherubim warded her from the gates of her lost paradise. In one evening, by the aid of Binkley and Mumm, Bohemia had gathered her into its awful midst.

There remained to her but one thing—a life of brilliant but irremediable error. Vermont was a shrine that she never would dare to approach again. But she would not sink—there were great and compelling ones in history upon whom she would model her meteoric career—Camille, Lola Montez, Royal Mary, Zaza—such a name as one of these would that of Medora Martin be to future generations.

For two days Medora kept to her room. On the third she opened a magazine at the portrait of the King of Belgium, and laughed sardonically. If that far-famed breaker of women's hearts should cross her path, he would have to bow before her cold and imperious beauty. She would not spare the old or the young. All America—all Europe should do homage to her sinister but compelling charm.

As yet she could not bear to think of the life she had once desired— a peaceful one in the shadow of the Green Mountains with Beriah at her side, and orders for expensive oil paintings coming in by each mail from New York. Her one fatal misstep had shattered that dream.

On the fourth day Medora powdered her face and rouged her lips. Once she had seen Carter in "Zaza." She stood before the mirror in a reckless attitude and cried: *"Zut! zut!"* She rhymed it with "nut," but with the lawless word Harmony seemed to pass away forever. The Vortex had her. She belonged to Bohemia for evermore. And never would Beriah——

The door opened and Beriah walked in.

"'Dory," said he, "what's all that chalk and pink stuff on your face, honey?"

Medora extended an arm.

"Too late," she said solemnly. "The die is cast. I belong to another world. Curse me if you will—it is your right. Go, and leave me in the path I have chosen. Bid them all at home never to mention my name again. And sometimes, Beriah, pray for me when I am revelling in the gaudy, but hollow, pleasures of Bohemia."

"Get a towel, 'Dory," said Beriah, "and wipe that paint off your face. I came as soon as I got your letter. Them pictures of yours ain't amounting to anything. I've got tickets for both of us back on the evening train. Hurry and get your things in your trunk."

"Fate was too strong for me, Beriah. Go while I am strong to bear it."

"How do you fold this easel, 'Dory?—now begin to pack, so we have time to eat before train time. The maples is all out in full-grown leaves, 'Dory—you just ought to see 'em!"

"Not this early, Beriah?"

"You ought to see 'em, 'Dory; they're like an ocean of green in the morning sunlight!"

"Oh, Beriah!"

On the train she said to him suddenly:

"I wonder why you came when you got my letter."

"Oh, shucks!" said Beriah. "Did you think you could fool me? How could you be run away to that Bohemia country like you said when your letter was postmarked New York as plain as day?"

A PHILISTINE IN BOHEMIA

George Washington, with his right arm upraised, sits his iron horse at the lower corner of Union Square, forever signalling the Broadway cars to stop as they round the curve into Fourteenth Street. But the cars buzz on, heedless, as they do at the beck of a private citizen, and the great General must feel, unless his nerves are iron, that rapid transit gloria mundi.

Should the General raise his left hand as he has raised his right it would point to a quarter of the city that forms a haven for the oppressed and suppressed of foreign lands. In the cause of national or personal freedom they have found a refuge here, and the patriot who made it for them sits his steed, overlooking their district, while he listens through his left ear to vaudeville that caricatures the posterity of his protégés. Italy, Poland, the former Spanish possessions and the polyglot tribes of Austria-Hungary have spilled here a thick lather of their effervescent sons. In the eccentric cafés and lodging-houses of the vicinity they hover over their native wines and political secrets. The colony changes with much frequency. Faces disappear from the haunts to be replaced by others. Whither do these uneasy birds flit? For half of the answer observe carefully the suave foreign air and foreign courtesy of the next waiter who serves you table d'hôte. For the other half, perhaps if the barber shops had tongues (and who will dispute it?) they could tell their share.

Titles are as plentiful as finger rings among these transitory exiles. For lack of proper exploitation a stock of title goods large enough to supply the trade of upper Fifth Avenue is here condemned to a mere pushcart traffic. The new-world landlords who entertain these off-shoots of nobility are not dazzled by coronets and crests. They have doughnuts to sell instead of daughters. With them it is a serious matter of trading in flour and sugar instead of pearl powder and bonbons.

These assertions are deemed fitting as an introduction to the tale, which is of plebeians and contains no one with even the ghost of a title.

Katy Dempsey's mother kept a furnished-room house in this oasis of the aliens. The business was not profitable. If the two scraped together enough to meet the landlord's agent on rent day and negotiate for the ingredients of a daily Irish stew they called it success. Often the stew lacked both meat and potatoes. Sometimes it became as bad as consommé with music.

In this mouldy old house Katy waxed plump and pert and wholesome and as beautiful and freckled as a tiger lily. She was the good fairy who was guilty of placing the damp clean towels and cracked pitchers of freshly laundered Croton in the lodgers' rooms.

You are informed (by virtue of the privileges of astronomical discovery) that the star lodger's name was Mr. Brunelli. His wearing a yellow tie and paying his rent promptly distinguished him from the other lodgers. His raiment was splendid, his complexion olive, his mustache fierce, his manners a prince's, his rings and pins as magnificent as those of a travelling dentist.

He had breakfast served in his room, and he ate it in a red dressing gown with green tassels. He left the house at noon and returned at midnight. Those were mysterious hours, but there was nothing mysterious about Mrs. Dempsey's lodgers except the things that were not mysterious. One of Mr. Kipling's poems is addressed to "Ye who hold the unwritten clue to all save all unwritten things." The same "readers" are invited to tackle the foregoing assertion.

Mr. Brunelli, being impressionable and a Latin, fell to conjugating the verb "amare," with Katy in the objective case, though not because of antipathy. She talked it over with her mother.

"Sure, I like him," said Katy. "He's more politeness than twinty candidates for Alderman, and he makes me feel like a queen whin he walks at me side. But what is he, I dinno? I've me suspicions. The marnin'll coom whin he'll throt out the picture av his baronial halls and ax to have the week's rint hung up in the ice chist along wid all the rist of 'em."

" 'Tis thrue," admitted Mrs. Dempsey, "that he seems to be a sort iv a Dago and too coolchured in his spache for a rale gintleman. But ye may be misjudgin' him. Ye should niver suspect any wan of bein' of noble descint that pays cash and pathronizes the laundry rig'lar."

"He's the same thricks of spakin' and blarneyin' wid his hands," sighed Katy, "as the Frinch nobleman at Mrs. Toole's that ran away wid Mr. Toole's Sunday pants and left the photograph of the Bastile, his grandfather's chat-taw, as security for tin weeks' rint."

Mr. Brunelli continued his calorific wooing. Katy continued to hesitate. One day he asked her out to dine and she felt that a dénouement was in the air. While they are on their way, with Katy in her best muslin, you must take as an entr'acte a brief peep at New York's Bohemia.

'Tonio's restaurant is in Bohemia. The very location of it is secret. If you wish to know where it is ask the first person you meet. He will tell you in a whisper. 'Tonio discountenances custom; he keeps his house-front black and forbidding; he gives you a pretty bad dinner; he locks his door at the dining hour; but he knows spaghetti as the boarding-house knows cold veal; and—he has deposited many dollars in a certain Banco di —— something with many gold vowels in the name on its windows.

To this restaurant Mr. Brunelli conducted Katy. The house was dark and the shades were lowered; but Mr. Brunelli touched an electric button by the basement door, and they were admitted.

Along a long, dark, narrow hallway they went and then through a shining and spotless kitchen that opened directly upon a backyard.

The walls of houses hemmed three sides of the yard; a high board fence, surrounded by cats, the other. A wash of clothes was suspended high upon a line stretched from diagonal corners. Those were property clothes, and were never taken in by 'Tonio. They were there that wits with defective pronunciation might make puns in connection with the ragout.

A dozen and a half little tables set upon the bare ground were crowded with Bohemia-hunters, who flocked there because 'Tonio pretended not to want them and pretended to give them a good dinner. There was a sprinkling of real Bohemians present who came for a change because they were tired of the real Bohemia, and a smart shower of the men who originate the bright sayings of Congressmen and the little nephew of the well-known general passenger agent of the Evansville and Terre Haute Railroad Company.

Here is a bon mot that was manufactured at 'Tonio's:

"A dinner at 'Tonio's," said a Bohemian, "always amounts to twice the price that is asked for it."

Let us assume that an accommodating voice inquires:

"How so?"

"The dinner costs you 40 cents; you give 10 cents to the waiter, and it makes you feel like 30 cents."

Most of the diners were confirmed table d'hôters—gastronomic adventurers, forever seeking the El Dorado of a good claret, and consistently coming to grief in California.

Mr. Brunelli escorted Katy to a little table embowered with shrubbery in tubs, and asked her to excuse him for a while.

Katy sat, enchanted by a scene so brilliant to her. The grand ladies, in splendid dresses and plumes and sparkling rings; the fine gentlemen who laughed so loudly, the cries of "Garsong" and "We, monseer," and "Hello, Mame!" that distinguished Bohemia; the lively chatter, the cigarette smoke, the interchange of bright smiles and eye-glances—all this display and magnificence overpowered the daughter of Mrs. Dempsey and held her motionless.

Mr. Brunelli stepped into the yard and seemed to spread his smile and bow over the entire company. And everywhere there was a great clapping of hands and a few cries of "Bravo!" and "'Tonio! 'Tonio!" whatever those words might mean. Ladies waved their napkins at him, gentlemen almost twisted their necks off, trying to catch his nod.

When the ovation was concluded Mr. Brunelli, with a final bow, stepped nimbly into the kitchen and flung off his coat and waistcoat.

Flaherty, the nimblest "garsong" among the waiters, had been assigned to the special service of Katy. She was a little faint from hunger, for the Irish stew on the Dempsey table had been particularly weak that day. Delicious odors from unknown dishes tantalized her. And Flaherty began to bring to her table course after course of ambrosial food that the gods might have pronounced excellent.

But even in the midst of her Lucullian repast Katy laid down her knife and fork. Her heart sank as lead, and a tear fell upon her filet mignon. Her haunting suspicions of the star lodger rose again, fourfold. Thus courted and admired and smiled upon by that fashionable and gracious assembly, what else could Mr. Brunelli be but one of these dazzling titled patricians, glorious of name but shy of rent money, concerning whom experience had made her wise? With a sense of his ineligibility growing within her there was mingled a torturing conviction that his personality was becoming more pleasing to her day by day. And why had he left her to dine alone?

But here he was coming again, now coatless, his snowy shirt-sleeves rolled high above his Jeffersonian elbows, a white yachting cap perched upon his jetty curls.

"'Tonio! 'Tonio" shouted many; and "The spaghetti!" shouted the rest.

Never at 'Tonio's did a waiter dare to serve a dish of spaghetti until 'Tonio came to test it, to prove the sauce and add the needful dash of seasoning that gave it perfection.

From table to table moved 'Tonio, like a prince in his palace, greeting his guests. White, jewelled hands signalled him from every side.

A glass of wine with this one and that, smiles for all, a jest and repartee for any that might challenge—truly few princes could be so agreeable a host! And what artist could ask for further appreciation of his handiwork? Katy did not know that the proudest consummation of a New Yorker's ambition is to shake hands with a spaghetti chef or to receive a nod from a Broadway head-waiter.

At last the company thinned, leaving but a few couples and quartettes lingering over new wine and old stories. And then came Mr. Brunelli to Katy's secluded table, and drew a chair close to hers.

Katy smiled at him dreamily. She was eating the last spoonful of a raspberry roll with Burgundy sauce.

"You have seen!" said Mr. Brunelli, laying one hand upon his collar bone. "I am Antonio Brunelli! Yes; I am the great 'Tonio! You have not suspect that! I loave you, Katy, and you shall marry with me. Is it not so? Call me 'Antonio,' and say that you will be mine."

Katy's head dropped to the shoulder that was now freed from all suspicion of having received the knightly accolade.

"Oh, Andy," she sighed, "this is great! Sure, I'll marry wid ye. But why didn't ye tell me ye was the cook? I was near turnin' ye down for bein' one of thim foreign counts!"

FROM EACH ACCORDING TO HIS ABILITY

Vuyning left his club, cursing it softly, without any particular anger. From ten in the morning until eleven it had bored him immeasurably. Kirk with his fish story, Brooks with his Porto Rico cigars, old Morrison with his anecdote about the widow, Hepburn with his invariable luck at billiards—all these afflictions had been repeated without change of bill or scenery. Besides these morning evils Miss Allison had refused him again on the night before. But that was a chronic trouble. Five times she had laughed at his offer to make her Mrs. Vuyning. He intended to ask her again the next Wednesday evening.

Vuyning walked along Forty-fourth Street to Broadway, and then drifted down the great sluice that washes out the dust of the gold-mines of Gotham. He wore a morning suit of light gray, low, dull kid shoes, a plain, finely woven straw hat, and his visible linen was the most delicate possible shade of heliotrope. His necktie was the blue-gray of a November sky, and its knot was plainly the outcome of a lordly carelessness combined with an accurate conception of the most recent dictum of fashion.

Now, to write of a man's haberdashery is a worse thing than to write a historical novel "around" Paul Jones, or to pen a testimonial to a hay-fever cure.

Therefore, let it be known that the description of Vuyning's apparel is germane to the movements of the story, and not to make room for the new fall stock of goods.

Even Broadway that morning was a discord in Vuyning's ears; and in his eyes it paralleled for a few dreamy, dreary minutes a certain howling, scorching, seething, malodorous slice of street that he remembered in Morocco. He saw the struggling mass of dogs, beggars, fakirs, slave-drivers and veiled women in carts without horses, the sun blazing brightly among the bazaars, the piles of rubbish from ruined temples in the street

—and then a lady passing jabbed the ferrule of a parasol in his side and brought him back to Broadway.

Five minutes of his stroll brought him to a certain corner, where a number of silent, pale-faced men are accustomed to stand, immovably, for hours, busy with the file blades of their penknives, with their hat brims on a level with their eyelids. Wall Street speculators, driving home in their carriages, love to point out these men to their visiting friends and tell them of this rather famous lounging-place of the "crooks." On Wall Street the speculators never use the file blades of their knives.

Vuyning was delighted when one of this company stepped forth and addressed him as he was passing. He was hungry for something out of the ordinary, and to be accosted by this smooth-faced, keen-eyed, low-voiced, athletic member of the under world, with his grim yet pleasant smile, had all the taste of an adventure to the convention-weary Vuyning.

"Excuse me, friend," said he. "Could I have a few minutes' talk with you—on the level?"

"Certainly," said Vuyning, with a smile. "But, suppose we step aside to a quieter place. There is a divan—a café over here that will do. Schrumm will give us a private corner."

Schrumm established them under a growing palm, with two seidls between them. Vuyning made a pleasant reference to meteorological conditions, thus forming a hinge upon which might be swung the door leading from the thought repository of the other.

"In the first place," said his companion, with the air of one who presents his credentials, "I want you to understand that I am a crook. Out West I am known as Rowdy the Dude. Pickpocket, supper man, second-story man, yeggman, boxman, all-round burglar, card-sharp and slickest con man west of the Twenty-third Street ferry landing—that's my history. That's to show I'm on the square—with you. My name's Emerson."

"Confound old Kirk with his fish stories," said Vuyning to himself, with silent glee as he went through his pockets for a card. "It's pronounced 'Vining,'" he said, as he tossed it over to the other. "And I'll be as frank with you. I'm just a kind of a loafer, I guess, living on my daddy's money. At the club they call me 'Left-at-the-Post.' I never did a day's work in my life; and I haven't the heart to run over a chicken when I'm motoring. It's a pretty shabby record, altogether."

"There's one thing you can do," said Emerson, admiringly; "you can carry duds. I've watched you several times pass on Broadway. You look the best-dressed man I've seen. And I'll bet you a gold mine I've got $50 worth more gent's furnishings on my frame than you have. That's what I wanted to see you about. I can't do the trick. Take a look at me. What's wrong?"

"Stand up," said Vuyning.

Emerson arose, and slowly revolved.

"You've been 'outfitted,'" declared the clubman. "Some Broadway window-dresser has misused you. That's an expensive suit, though, Emerson."

"A hundred dollars," said Emerson.

"Twenty too much," said Vuyning. "Six months old in cut, one inch too long, and half an inch too much lapel. Your hat is plainly dated one year ago, although there's only a sixteenth of an inch lacking in the brim to tell the story. That English poke in your collar is too short by the distance between Troy and London. A plain gold link cuff-button would take all the shine out of those pearl ones with diamond settings. Those tan shoes would be exactly the articles to work into the heart of a Brooklyn school-ma'am on a two weeks' visit to Lake Ronkonkoma. I think I caught a glimpse of a blue silk sock embroidered with russet lilies of the valley when you—improperly—drew up your trousers as you sat down. There are always plain ones to be had in stores. Have I hurt your feelings, Emerson?"

"Double the ante!" cried the criticized one, greedily. "Give me more of it. There's a way to tote the haberdashery, and I want to get wise to it. Say, you're the right kind of a swell. Anything else to the queer about me?"

"Your tie," said Vuyning, "is tied with absolute precision and correctness."

"Thanks," gratefully—"I spent over half an hour at it before I——"

"Thereby," interrupted Vuyning, "completing your resemblance to a dummy in a Broadway store window."

"Yours truly," said Emerson, sitting down again. "It's bully of you to put me wise. I knew there was something wrong, but I couldn't just put my finger on it. I guess it comes by nature to know how to wear clothes."

"Oh, I suppose," said Vuyning, with a laugh, "that my ancestors picked up the knack while they were peddling clothes from house to house a couple of hundred years ago. I'm told they did that."

"And mine," said Emerson, cheerfully, "were making their visits at night, I guess, and didn't have a chance to catch on to the correct styles."

"I tell you what," said Vuyning, whose ennui had taken wings, "I'll take you to my tailor. He'll eliminate the mark of the beast from your exterior. That is, if you care to go on further in the way of expense."

"Play 'em to the ceiling," said Emerson, with a boyish smile of joy. "I've got a roll as big around as a barrel of black-eyed peas and as loose as the wrapper of a two-for-fiver. I don't mind telling you that I was not touring among the Antipodes when the burglar-proof safe of the Farmers' National Bank of Butterville, Ia., flew open some moonless nights ago to the tune of $16,000."

"Aren't you afraid," asked Vuyning, "that I'll call a cop and hand you over?"

"You tell me," said Emerson, coolly, "why I didn't keep them."

He laid Vuyning's pocketbook and watch—the Vuyning 100-year-old family watch—on the table.

"Man," said Vuyning, revelling, "did you ever hear the tale Kirk tells about the six-pound trout and the old fisherman?"

"Seems not," said Emerson, politely. "I'd like to."

"But you won't," said Vuyning. "I've heard it scores of times. That's why I won't tell you. I was just thinking how much better this is than a club. Now, shall we go to my tailor?"

"Boys, and elderly gents," said Vuyning, five days later at his club, standing up against the window where his coterie was gathered, and keeping out the breeze, "a friend of mine from the West will dine at our table this evening."

"Will he ask if we have heard the latest from Denver?" said a member, squirming in his chair.

"Will he mention the new twenty-three-story Masonic Temple, in Quincy, Ill.?" inquired another, dropping his nose-glasses.

"Will he spring one of those Western Mississippi River catfish stories, in which they use yearling calves for bait?" demanded Kirk fiercely.

"Be comforted," said Vuyning. "He has none of the little vices. He is a burglar and safe-blower, and a pal of mine."

"Oh, Mary Ann!" said they. "Must you always adorn every statement with your alleged humor?"

It came to pass that at eight in the evening a calm, smooth, brilliant, affable man sat at Vuyning's right hand during dinner. And when the ones who pass their lives in city streets spoke of skyscrapers or of the little Czar on his far, frozen throne, or of insignificant fish from inconsequential streams, this big, deep-chested man, faultlessly clothed, and eyed like an Emperor, disposed of their Lilliputian chatter with a wink of his eyelash.

And then he painted for them with hard, broad strokes a marvellous lingual panorama of the West. He stacked snow-topped mountains on the table, freezing the hot dishes of the waiting diners. With a wave of his hand he swept the clubhouse into a pine-crowned gorge, turning the waiters into a grim posse, and each listener into a blood-stained fugitive, climbing with torn fingers upon the ensanguined rocks. He touched the table and spake, and the five panted as they gazed on barren lava beds, and each man took his tongue between his teeth and felt his mouth bake at the tale of a land empty of water and food. As simply as Homer sang, while he dug a tine of his fork leisurely into the tablecloth, he opened a new world to their view, as does one who tells a child of the Looking-Glass Country.

As one of his listeners might have spoken of tea too strong at a Madison

Square "afternoon," so he depicted the ravages of "redeye" in a border town when the caballeros of the lariat and "forty-five" reduced ennui to a minimum.

And then, with a sweep of his white, unringed hands, he dismissed Melpomene, and forthwith Diana and Amaryllis footed it before the mind's eye of the clubmen.

The savannas of the continent spread before them. The wind, humming through a hundred leagues of sage brush and mesquite, closed their ears to the city's staccato noises. He told them of camps, of ranches marooned in a sea of fragrant prairie blossoms, of gallops in the stilly night that Apollo would have forsaken his daytime steeds to enjoy; he read them the great, rough epic of the cattle and the hills that had not been spoiled by the hand of man, the mason. His words were a telescope to the city men, whose eyes had looked upon Youngstown, O., and whose tongues had called it "West."

In fact, Emerson had them "going."

The next morning at ten he met Vuyning, by appointment, at a Forty-second Street café.

Emerson was to leave for the West that day. He wore a suit of dark cheviot that looked to have been draped upon him by an ancient Grecian tailor who was a few thousand years ahead of the styles.

"Mr. Vuyning," said he, with the clear, ingenuous smile of the successful "crook," "it's up to me to go the limit for you any time I can do so. You're the real thing; and if I can ever return the favor, you bet your life I'll do it."

"What was that cow-puncher's name?" asked Vuyning, "who used to catch a mustang by the nose and mane, and throw him till he put the bridle on?"

"Bates," said Emerson.

"Thanks," said Vuyning. "I thought it was Yates. Oh, about that toggery business—I'd forgotten that."

"I've been looking for some guy to put me on the right track for years," said Emerson. "You're the goods, duty free, and halfway to the warehouse in a red wagon."

"Bacon, toasted on a green willow switch over red coals, ought to put broiled lobsters out of business," said Vuyning. "And you say a horse at the end of a thirty-foot rope can't pull a ten-inch stake out of wet prairie? Well, good-bye, old man, if you must be off."

At one o'clock Vuyning had luncheon with Miss Allison by previous arrangement.

For thirty minutes he babbled to her, unaccountably, of ranches, horses, cañons, cyclones, round-ups, Rocky Mountains, and beans and bacon. She looked at him with wondering and half-terrified eyes.

"I was going to propose again to-day," said Vuyning, cheerily, "but I won't. I've worried you often enough. You know dad has a ranch in Colorado. What's the good of staying here? Jumping jonquils! but it's great out there. I'm going to start next Tuesday."

"No, you won't," said Miss Allison.

"What?" said Vuyning.

"Not alone," said Miss Allison, dropping a tear upon her salad. "What do you think?"

"Betty!" exclaimed Vuyning, "what do you mean?"

"I'll go too," said Miss Allison, forcibly.

Vuyning filled her glass with Apollinaris.

"Here's to Rowdy the Dude!" he gave—a toast mysterious.

"Don't know him," said Miss Allison; "but if he's your friend, Jimmy—here goes!"

THE MEMENTO

Miss Lynnette D'Armande turned her back on Broadway. This was but tit for tat, because Broadway had often done the same thing to Miss D'Armande. Still, the "tats" seemed to have it, for the ex-leading lady of the "Reaping the Whirlwind" company had everything to ask of Broadway, while there was no vice-versa.

So Miss Lynnette D'Armande turned the back of her chair to her window that overlooked Broadway, and sat down to stitch in time the lisle-thread heel of a black silk stocking. The tumult and glitter of the roaring Broadway beneath her window had no charm for her; what she greatly desired was the stifling air of a dressing-room on that fairyland street and the roar of an audience gathered in that capricious quarter. In the meantime, those stockings must not be neglected. Silk does wear out so, but—after all, isn't it just the only goods there is?

The Hotel Thalia looks on Broadway as Marathon looks on the sea. It stands like a gloomy cliff above the whirlpool where the tides of two great thoroughfares clash. Here the player-bands gather at the end of their wanderings to loosen the buskin and dust the sock. Thick in the streets around it are booking-offices, theatres, agents, schools, and the lobster-palaces to which those thorny paths lead.

Wandering through the eccentric halls of the dim and fusty Thalia, you seem to have found yourself in some great ark or caravan about to sail, or fly, or roll away on wheels. About the house lingers a sense of unrest, of expectation, of transientness, even of anxiety and apprehension. The halls are a labyrinth. Without a guide, you wander like a lost soul in a Sam Lloyd puzzle.

Turning any corner, a dressing-sack or a *cul-de-sac* may bring you up short. You meet alarming tragedians stalking in bath-robes in search of rumored bathrooms. From hundreds of rooms come the buzz of talk, scraps of new and old songs, and the ready laughter of the convened players.

Summer has come; their companies have disbanded, and they take their rest in their favorite caravansary, while they besiege the managers for engagements for the coming season.

At this hour of the afternoon the day's work of tramping the rounds of the agents' offices is over. Past you, as you ramble distractedly through the mossy halls, flit audible visions of houris, with veiled, starry eyes, flying tag-ends of things and a swish of silk, bequeathing to the dull hallways an odor of gaiety and a memory of *frangipanni*. Serious young comedians, with versatile Adam's apples, gather in doorways and talk of Booth. Far-reaching from somewhere comes the smell of ham and red cabbage, and the crash of dishes on the American plan.

The indeterminate hum of life in the Thalia is enlivened by the discreet popping—at reasonable and salubrious intervals—of beer-bottle corks. Thus punctuated, life in the genial hostel scans easily—the comma being the favorite mark, semicolons frowned upon, and periods barred.

Miss D'Armande's room was a small one. There was room for her rocker between the dresser and the wash-stand if it were placed longitudinally. On the dresser were its usual accoutrements, plus the ex-leading lady's collected souvenirs of road engagements and photographs of her dearest and best professional friends.

At one of these photographs she looked twice or thrice as she darned, and smiled friendlily.

"I'd like to know where Lee is just this minute," she said, half-aloud.

If you had been privileged to view the photograph thus flattered, you would have thought at the first glance that you saw the picture of a many-petalled white flower, blown through the air by a storm. But the floral kingdom was not responsible for that swirl of petalous whiteness.

You saw the filmy, brief skirt of Miss Rosalie Ray as she made a complete heels-over-head turn in her wistaria-entwined swing, far out from the stage, high above the heads of the audience. You saw the camera's inadequate representation of the graceful, strong kick, with which she, at this exciting moment, sent flying, high and far, the yellow silk garter that each evening spun from her agile limb and descended upon the delighted audience below.

You saw, too, amid the black-clothed, mainly masculine patrons of select vaudeville a hundred hands raised with the hope of staying the flight of the brilliant aërial token.

Forty weeks of the best circuits this act had brought Miss Rosalie Ray, for each of two years. She did other things during her twelve minutes—

a song and dance, imitations of two or three actors who are but imitations of themselves, and a balancing feat with a step-ladder and feather-duster; but when the blossom-decked swing was let down from the flies, and Miss Rosalie sprang smiling into the seat, with the golden circlet conspicuous in the place whence it was soon to slide and become a soaring and coveted guerdon—then it was that the audience rose in its seat as a single man—or presumably so—and indorsed the specialty that made Miss Ray's name a favorite in the booking-offices.

At the end of two years Miss Ray suddenly announced to her dear friend, Miss D'Armande, that she was going to spend the summer at an antediluvian village on the north shore of Long Island, and that the stage would see her no more.

Seventeen minutes after Miss Lynnette D'Armande had expressed her wish to know the whereabouts of her old chum, there were sharp raps at her door.

Doubt not that it was Rosalie Ray. At the shrill command to enter she did so, with something of a tired flutter, and dropped a heavy hand-bag on the floor. Upon my word, it was Rosalie, in a loose, travel-stained automobileless coat, closely tied brown veil with yard-long flying ends, gray walking suit, and tan oxfords with lavender over-gaiters.

When she threw off her veil and hat, you saw a pretty enough face, now flushed and disturbed by some unusual emotion, and restless, large eyes with discontent marring their brightness. A heavy pile of dull auburn hair, hastily put up, was escaping in crinkly, waving strands and curling, small locks from the confining combs and pins.

The meeting of the two was not marked by the effusion vocal, gymnastical, osculatory, and catechetical that distinguishes the greetings of their unprofessional sisters in society. There was a brief clinch, two simultaneous labial dabs, and they stood on the same footing of the old days. Very much like the short salutations of soldiers or of travellers in foreign wilds are the welcomes between the strollers at the corners of their criss-cross roads.

"I've got the hall-room two flights up above yours," said Rosalie, "but I came straight to see you before going up. I didn't know you were here till they told me."

"I've been in since the last of April," said Lynnette. "And I'm going on the road with a 'Fatal Inheritance' Company. We open next week in Elizabeth. I thought you'd quit the stage, Lee. Tell me about yourself."

Rosalie settled herself with a skilful wriggle on the top of Miss D'Armande's wardrobe trunk, and leaned her head against the papered wall. From long habit, thus can peripatetic leading ladies and their sisters make themselves as comfortable as though the deepest armchairs embraced them.

"I'm going to tell you, Lynn," she said, with a strangely sardonic and yet carelessly resigned look on her youthful face. "And then to-morrow I'll strike the old Broadway trail again, and wear some more paint off the chairs in the agents' offices. If anybody had told me any time in the last three months up to four o'clock this afternoon that I'd ever listen to that 'Leave-your-name-and-address' rot of the booking bunch again, I'd have given 'em the real Mrs. Fiske laugh. Loan me a handkerchief, Lynn. Gee! but those Long Island trains are fierce. I've got enough soft-coal cinders on my face to go on and play *Topsy* without using the cork. And, speaking of corks—got anything to drink, Lynn?"

Miss D'Armande opened a door of the washstand and took out a bottle.

"There's nearly a pint of Manhattan. There's a cluster of carnations in the drinking glass, but——"

"Oh, pass the bottle. Save the glass for company. Thanks! That hits the spot. The same to you. My first drink in three months!

"Yes, Lynn, I quit the stage at the end of last season. I quit it because I was sick of the life. And especially because my heart and soul were sick of men—of the kind of men we stage people have to be up against. You know what the game is to us—it's a fight against 'em all the way down the line from the manager who wants us to try his new motor-car to the bill-posters who want to call us by our front names.

"And the men we have to meet after the show are the worst of all. The stage-door kind, and the manager's friends who take us to supper and show their diamonds and talk about seeing 'Dan' and 'Dave' and 'Charlie' for us. They're beasts, and I hate 'em.

"I tell you, Lynn, it's the girls like us on the stage that ought to be pitied. It's girls from good homes that are honestly ambitious and work hard to rise in the profession, but never do get there. You hear a lot of sympathy sloshed around on chorus girls and their fifteen dollars a week. Piffle! There ain't a sorrow in the chorus that a lobster cannot heal.

"If there's any tears to shed, let 'em fall for the actress that gets a salary of from thirty to forty-five dollars a week for taking a leading part in a bum show. She knows she'll never do any better; but she hangs on for years, hoping for the 'chance' that never comes.

"And the fool plays we have to work in! Having another girl roll you around the stage by the hind legs in a 'Wheelbarrow Chorus' in a musical comedy is dignified drama compared with the idiotic things I've had to do in the thirty-centers.

"But what I hated most was the men—the men leering and blathering at you across tables, trying to buy you with Würzburger or Extra Dry, according to their estimate of your price. And the men in the audiences, clapping, yelling, snarling, crowding, writhing, gloating—like a lot of wild beasts, with their eyes fixed on you, ready to eat you up if you come in reach of their claws. Oh, how I hate 'em!

"Well, I'm not telling you much about myself, am I, Lynn?

"I had two hundred dollars saved up, and I cut the stage the first of the summer. I went over on Long Island and found the sweetest little village that ever was, called Soundport, right on the water. I was going to spend the summer there, and study up on elocution, and try to get a class in the fall. There was an old widow lady with a cottage near the beach who sometimes rented a room or two just for company, and she took me in. She had another boarder, too—the Reverend Arthur Lyle.

"Yes, he was the head-liner. You're on, Lynn. I'll tell you all of it in a minute. It's only a one-act play.

"The first time he walked on, Lynn, I felt myself going; the first lines he spoke, he had me. He was different from the men in audiences. He was tall and slim, and you never heard him come in the room, but you *felt* him. He had a face like a picture of a knight—like one of that Round Table bunch—and a voice like a 'cello solo. And his manners!

"Lynn, if you'd take John Drew in his best drawing-room scene and compare the two, you'd have John arrested for disturbing the peace.

"I'll spare you the particulars; but in less than a month Arthur and I were engaged. He preached at a little one-night stand of a Methodist church. There was to be a parsonage the size of a lunch-wagon, and hens and honeysuckles when we were married. Arthur used to preach to me a good deal about Heaven, but he never could get my mind quite off those honeysuckles and hens.

"No; I didn't tell him I'd been on the stage. I hated the business and all that went with it; I'd cut it out forever, and I didn't see any use of stirring things up. I was a good girl, and I didn't have anything to confess, except being an elocutionist, and that was about all the strain my conscience would stand.

"Oh, I tell you, Lynn, I was happy. I sang in the choir and attended the sewing society, and recited that 'Annie Laurie' thing with the whistling stunt in it, 'in a manner bordering upon the professional,' as the weekly village paper reported it. And Arthur and I went rowing, and walking in the woods, and clamming, and that poky little village seemed to me the best place in the world. I'd have been happy to live there always, too, if——

"But one morning old Mrs. Gurley, the widow lady, got gossipy while I was helping her string beans on the back porch, and began to gush information, as folks who rent out their rooms usually do. Mr. Lyle was her idea of a saint on her earth—as he was mine, too. She went over all .his virtues and graces, and wound up by telling me that Arthur had had an extremely romantic love-affair, not long before, that had ended unhappily. She didn't seem to be on to the details, but she knew that he had been hit pretty hard. He was paler and thinner, she said, and he had some kind of a remembrance or keepsake of the lady in a little rosewood box that he kept locked in his desk drawer in his study.

"'Several times,' says she, 'I've seen him gloomerin' over that box of evenings, and he always locks it up right away if anybody comes into the room.'

"Well, you can imagine how long it was before I got Arthur by the wrist and led him down stage and hissed in his ear.

"That same afternoon we were lazying around in a boat among the waterlilies at the edge of the bay.

"'Arthur,' says I, 'you never told me you'd had another love-affair. But Mrs. Gurley did,' I went on, to let him know I knew. I hate to hear a man lie.

"'Before you came,' says he, looking me frankly in the eye, 'there was a previous affection—a strong one. Since you know of it, I will be perfectly candid with you.'

"'I am waiting,' says I.

"'My dear Ida,' says Arthur—of course I went by my real name, while I was in Soundport—'this former affection was a spiritual one, in fact. Although the lady aroused my deepest sentiments, and was, as I thought, my ideal woman, I never met her, and never spoke to her. It was an ideal love. My love for you, while no less ideal, is different. You wouldn't let that come between us.'

"'Was she pretty?' I asked.

"'She was very beautiful,' said Arthur.

"'Did you see her often?' I asked.

"'Something like a dozen times,' says he.

"'Always from a distance?' says I.

"'Always from quite a distance,' says he.

"'And you loved her?' I asked.

"'She seemed my ideal of beauty and grace—and soul,' says Arthur.

"'And this keepsake that you keep under lock and key, and moon over at times, is that a remembrance from her?'

"'A memento,' says Arthur, 'that I have treasured.'

"'Did she send it to you?'

"'It came from her,' says he.

"'In a roundabout way?' I asked.

"'Somewhat roundabout,' says he, 'and yet rather direct.'

"'Why didn't you ever meet her?' I asked. 'Were your positions in life so different?'

"'She was far above me,' says Arthur. 'Now, Ida,' he goes on, 'this is all of the past. You're not going to be jealous, are you?'

"'Jealous!' says I. 'Why, man, what are you talking about? It makes me think ten times as much of you as I did before I knew about it.'

"And it did, Lynn—if you can understand it. That ideal love was a new one on me, but it struck me as being the most beautiful and glorious thing I'd ever heard of. Think of a man loving a woman he'd never even spoken to, and being faithful just to what his mind and heart pictured her! Oh, it sounded great to me. The men I'd always known come at you with either diamonds, knock-out drops, or a raise of salary—and their ideals!—well, we'll say no more.

"Yes, it made me think more of Arthur than I did before. I couldn't be jealous of that far-away divinity that he used to worship, for I was going to have him myself. And I began to look upon him as a saint on earth, just as old lady Gurley did.

"About four o'clock this afternoon a man came to the house for Arthur to go and see somebody that was sick among his church bunch. Old lady Gurley was taking her afternoon snore on the couch, so that left me pretty much alone.

"In passing by Arthur's study I looked in, and saw his bunch of keys hanging in the drawer of his desk, where he'd forgotten 'em. Well, I guess we're all to the Mrs. Bluebeard now and then, ain't we, Lynn? I made up my mind I'd have a look at that memento he kept so secret. Not that I cared what it was—it was just curiosity.

"While I was opening the drawer I imagined one or two things it might be. I thought it might be a dried rosebud she'd dropped down to him from a balcony, or maybe a picture of her he'd cut out of a magazine, she being so high up in the world.

"I opened the drawer, and there was the rosewood casket about the size of a gent's collar box. I found the little key in the bunch that fitted it, and raised the lid.

"I took one look at that memento, and then I went to my room and packed my trunk. I threw a few things into my grip, gave my hair a flirt or two with a side-comb, put on my hat, and went in and gave the old lady's foot a kick. I'd tried awfully hard to use proper and correct language while I was there for Arthur's sake, and I had the habit down pat, but it left me then.

" 'Stop sawing gourds,' says I, 'and sit up and take notice. The ghost's about to walk. I'm going away from here, and I owe you eight dollars. The expressman will call for my trunk.'

"I handed her the money.

" 'Dear me, Miss Crosby!' said she. 'Is anything wrong? I thought you were pleased here. Dear me, young women are so hard to understand, and so different from what you expect 'em to be.'

" 'You're damn right,' says I. 'Some of 'em are. But you can't say that about men. *When you know one man you know 'em all!* That settles the human race question.'

"And then I caught the four-thirty-eight, soft-coal unlimited; and here I am."

"You didn't tell me what was in that box, Lee," said Miss D'Armande, anxiously.

"One of those yellow silk garters that I used to kick off my leg into the audience during that old vaudeville swing act of mine. Is there any of the cocktail left, Lynn?"

BOOK *12*

THE TRIMMED LAMP

THE TRIMMED LAMP

Of course there are two sides to the question. Let us look at the other. We often hear "shop-girls" spoken of. No such persons exist. There are girls who work in shops. They make their living that way. But why turn their occupation into an adjective? Let us be fair. We do not refer to the girls who live on Fifth Avenue as "marriage-girls."

Lou and Nancy were chums. They came to the big city to find work because there was not enough to eat at their homes to go around. Nancy was nineteen; Lou was twenty. Both were pretty, active country girls who had no ambition to go on the stage.

The little cherub that sits up aloft guided them to a cheap and respectable boarding-house. Both found positions and became wage-earners. They remained chums. It is at the end of six months that I would beg you to step forward and be introduced to them. Maddlesome Reader: My Lady Friends, Miss Nancy and Miss Lou. While you are shaking hands please take notice—cautiously—of their attire. Yes, cautiously; for they are as quick to resent a stare as a lady in a box at the horse show is.

Lou is a piece-work ironer in a hand laundry. She is clothed in a badly fitting purple dress, and her hat plume is four inches too long; but her ermine muff and scarf cost $25, and its fellow beasts will be ticketed in the windows at $7.98 before the season is over. Her cheeks are pink, and her light blue eyes bright. Contentment radiates from her.

Nancy you would call a shop-girl—because you have the habit. There is no type; but a perverse generation is always seeking a type; so this is what the type should be. She has the high-ratted pompadour and the exaggerated straight-front. Her skirt is shoddy, but has the correct flare. No furs protect her against the bitter spring air, but she wears her short broadcloth jacket as jauntily as though it were Persian lamb! On her face and in her eyes, remorseless type-seeker, is the typical shop-girl expression. It is a look of silent but contemptuous revolt against cheated womanhood; of sad prophecy of the vengeance to come. When she laughs her loudest the look is still there. The same look can be seen in the eyes of Russian peasants; and those of us left will see it some day on Gabriel's face when he comes to blow us up. It is a look that should wither and abash man; but he has been known to smirk at it and offer flowers—with a string tied to them.

Now lift your hat and come away, while you receive Lou's cheery "See you again," and the sardonic, sweet smile of Nancy that seems, somehow, to miss you and go fluttering like a white moth up over the housetops to the stars.

The two waited on the corner for Dan. Dan was Lou's steady company. Faithful? Well, he was on hand when Mary would have had to hire a dozen subpœna servers to find her lamb.

"Ain't you cold, Nancy?" said Lou. "Say, what a chump you are for working in that old store for $8 a week! I made $18.50 last week. Of course ironing ain't as swell work as selling lace behind a counter, but it pays. None of us ironers make less than $10. And I don't know that it's any less respectful work, either."

"You can have it," said Nancy, with uplifted nose. "I'll take my eight a week and hall bedroom. I like to be among nice things and swell people. And look what a chance I've got! Why, one of our glove girls married a Pittsburg—a steel maker, or blacksmith or something—the other day worth a million dollars. I'll catch a swell myself some time. I ain't bragging on my looks or anything; but I'll take my chances where there's big prizes offered. What show would a girl have in a laundry?"

"Why, that's where I met Dan," said Lou, triumphantly. "He came in for his Sunday shirt and collars and saw me at the first board, ironing. We all try to get to work at the first board. Ella Maginnis was sick that day, and I had her place. He said he noticed my arms first, how round and white they was. I had my sleeves rolled up. Some nice fellows come into laundries. You can tell 'em by their bringing their clothes in suit cases, and turning in the door sharp and sudden."

"How can you wear a waist like that, Lou?" said Nancy, gazing down at the offending article with sweet scorn in her heavy-lidded eyes. "It shows fierce taste."

"This waist?" said Lou, with wide-eyed indignation. "Why, I paid $16 for this waist. It's worth twenty-five. A woman left it to be laundered, and never called for it. The boss sold it to me. It's got yards and yards of hand embroidery on it. Better talk about that ugly, plain thing you've got on."

"This ugly, plain thing," said Nancy, calmly, "was copied from one that Mrs. Van Alstyne Fisher was wearing. The girls say her bill in the store last year was $12,000. I made mine, myself. It cost me $1.50. Ten feet away you couldn't tell it from hers."

"Oh, well," said Lou, good-naturedly, "if you want to starve and put on airs, go ahead. But I'll take my job and good wages; and after hours give me something as fancy and attractive to wear as I am able to buy."

But just then Dan came—a serious young man with a ready-made necktie, who had escaped the city's brand of frivolity—an electrician earning $30 per week who looked upon Lou with the sad eyes of Romeo, and thought her embroidered waist a web in which any fly should delight to be caught.

"My friend, Mr. Owens—shake hands with Miss Danforth," said Lou.

"I'm mighty glad to know you, Miss Danforth," said Dan, with outstretched hand. "I've heard Lou speak of you so often."

"Thanks," said Nancy, touching his fingers with the tips of her cool ones, "I've heard her mention you—a few times."

Lou giggled.

"Did you get that handshake from Mrs. Van Alstyne Fisher, Nance?" she asked.

"If I did, you can feel safe in copying it," said Nancy.

"Oh, I couldn't use it at all. It's too stylish for me. It's intended to set off diamond rings, that high shake is. Wait till I get a few and then I'll try it."

"Learn it first," said Nancy, wisely, "and you'll be more likely to get the rings."

"Now, to settle this argument," said Dan, with his ready, cheerful smile, "let me make a proposition. As I can't take both of you up to Tiffany's and do the right thing, what do you say to a little vaudeville? I've got the tickets. How about looking at stage diamonds since we can't shake hands with the real sparklers?"

The faithful squire took his place close to the curb; Lou next, a little peacocky in her bright and pretty clothes; Nancy on the inside, slender, and soberly clothed as the sparrow, but with the true Van Alstyne Fisher walk—thus they set out for their evening's moderate diversion.

I do not suppose that many look upon a great department store as an educational institution. But the one in which Nancy worked was something like that to her. She was surrounded by beautiful things that breathed of taste and refinement. If you live in an atmosphere of luxury, luxury is yours whether your money pays for it, or another's.

The people she served were mostly women whose dress, manners, and position in the social world were quoted as criterions. From them Nancy began to take toll—the best from each according to her view.

From one she would copy and practise a gesture, from another an eloquent lifting of an eyebrow, from others, a manner of walking, of carrying a purse, of smiling, of greeting a friend, of addressing "inferiors in station." From her best beloved model, Mrs. Van Alstyne Fisher, she made requisition for that excellent thing, a soft, low voice as clear as silver and as perfect in articulation as the notes of a thrush. Suffused in the aura of this high social refinement and good breeding, it was impossible for her to escape a deeper effect of it. As good habits are said to be better than good principles, so, perhaps, good manners are better than good habits. The teachings of your parents may not keep alive your New England conscience; but if you sit on a straight-back chair and repeat the words "prisms and pilgrims" forty times the devil will flee from you. And when Nancy spoke in the Van Alstyne Fisher tones she felt the thrill of *noblesse oblige* to her very bones.

There was another source of learning in the great departmental school. Whenever you see three or four shop-girls gather in a bunch and jingle their wire bracelets as an accompaniment to apparently frivolous conversation, do not think that they are there for the purpose of criticizing the way Ethel does her back hair. The meeting may lack the dignity of the deliberative bodies of man; but it has all the importance of the occasion on which Eve and her first daughter first put their heads together to make Adam understand his proper place in the household. It is Woman's Conference for Common Defense and Exchange of Strategical Theories of Attack and Repulse upon and against the World, which is a Stage, and Man, its Audience who Persists in Throwing Bouquets Thereupon. Woman, the most helpless of the young of any animal—with the fawn's grace but without its fleetness; with the bird's beauty but without its power of flight; with the honey-bee's burden of sweetness but without its —— Oh, let's drop that simile—some of us may have been stung.

During this council of war they pass weapons one to another, and exchange stratagems that each has devised and formulated out of the tactics of life.

"I says to 'im," says Sadie, "ain't you the fresh thing! Who do you suppose I am, to be addressing such a remark to me? And what do you think he says back to me?"

The heads, brown, black, flaxen, red, and yellow bob together; the answer is given; and the parry to the thrust is decided upon, to be used by each thereafter in passages-at-arms with the common enemy, man.

Thus Nancy learned the art of defense; and to women successful defense means victory.

The curriculum of a department store is a wide one. Perhaps no other college could have fitted her as well for her life's ambition—the drawing of a matrimonial prize.

Her station in the store was a favored one. The music room was near enough for her to hear and become familiar with the works of the best composers—at least to acquire the familiarity that passed for appreciation in the social world in which she was vaguely trying to set a tentative and aspiring foot. She absorbed the educating influence of art wares, of costly and dainty fabrics, of adornments that are almost culture to women.

The other girls soon became aware of Nancy's ambition. "Here comes your millionaire, Nancy," they would call to her whenever any man who looked the rôle approached her counter. It got to be a habit of men, who were hanging about while their women folk were shopping, to stroll over to the handkerchief counter and dawdle over the cambric squares. Nancy's imitation high-bred air and genuine dainty beauty was what attracted. Many men thus came to display their graces before her. Some of them may have been millionaires; others were certainly no more than their sedulous apes. Nancy learned to discriminate. There was a window at the end of the handkerchief counter; and she could see the rows of vehicles waiting for the shoppers in the street below. She looked and perceived that automobiles differ as well as do their owners.

Once a fascinating gentleman bought four dozen handkerchiefs, and wooed her across the counter with a King Cophetua air. When he had gone one of the girls said:

"What's wrong, Nance, that you didn't warm up to that fellow? He looks the swell article, all right, to me."

"Him?" said Nancy, with her coolest, sweetest, most impersonal, Van Alstyne Fisher smile; "not for mine. I saw him drive up outside. A 12 H. P. machine and an Irish chauffeur! And you saw what kind of handkerchiefs he bought—silk! And he's got dactylis on him. Give me the real thing or nothing, if you please."

Two of the most "refined" women in the store—a forelady and a cashier —had a few "swell gentlemen friends" with whom they now and then dined. Once they included Nancy in an invitation. The dinner took place in a spectacular café whose tables are engaged for New Year's Eve a year in advance. There were two "gentlemen friends"—one without any hair on his head—high living ungrew it; and we can prove it—the other a young man whose worth and sophistication he impressed upon you in two convincing ways—he swore that all the wine was corked; and he wore diamond cuff buttons. This young man perceived irresistible excellencies in Nancy. His taste ran to shop-girls; and here was one that added the voice and manners of her high social world to the franker charms of her own caste. So, on the following day, he appeared in the store and made her a serious proposal of marriage over a box of hemstitched, grass-bleached Irish linens. Nancy declined. A brown pompadour ten feet away had been using her eyes and ears. When the rejected suitor had gone she heaped carboys of upbraidings and horror upon Nancy's head.

"What a terrible little fool you are! That fellow's a millionaire—he's a nephew of old Van Skittles himself. And he was talking on the level, too. Have you gone crazy, Nance?"

"Have I?" said Nancy. "I didn't take him, did I? He isn't a millionaire so hard that you could notice it, anyhow. His family only allows him $20,000 a year to spend. The bald-headed fellow was guying him about it the other night at supper."

The brown pompadour came nearer and narrowed her eyes.

"Say, what do you want?" she inquired, in a voice hoarse for lack of chewing-gum. "Ain't that enough for you? Do you want to be a Mormon, and marry Rockefeller and Gladstone Dowie and the King of Spain and the whole bunch? Ain't $20,000 a year good enough for you?"

Nancy flushed a little under the level gaze of the black, shallow eyes.

"It wasn't altogether the money, Carrie," she explained. "His friend caught him in a rank lie the other night at dinner. It was about some girl he said he hadn't been to the theater with. Well, I can't stand a liar. Put everything together—I don't like him; and that settles it. When I sell out it's not going to be on any bargain day. I've got to have something that sits up in a chair like a man, anyhow. Yes. I'm looking out for a catch; but it's got to be able to do something more than make a noise like a toy bank."

"The physiopathic ward for yours!" said the brown pompadour, walking away.

These high ideas, if not ideals—Nancy continued to cultivate on $8 per week. She bivouacked on the trail of the great unknown "catch" eating her dry bread and tightening her belt day by day. On her face was the faint, soldierly, sweet, grim smile of the preordained man-hunter. The store was her forest; and many times she raised her rifle at game that seemed broad-antlered and big; but always some deep unerring instinct —perhaps of the huntress, perhaps of the woman—made her hold her fire and take up the trail again.

Lou flourished in the laundry. Out of her $18.50 per week she paid $6 for her room and board. The rest went mainly for clothes. Her opportunities for bettering her taste and manners were few compared with Nancy's. In the steaming laundry there was nothing but work, work and her thoughts of the evening pleasures to come. Many costly and showy fabrics passed under her iron; and it may be that her growing fondness for dress was thus transmitted to her through the conducting metal.

When the day's work was over Dan awaited her outside, her faithful shadow in whatever light she stood.

Sometimes he cast an honest and troubled glance at Lou's clothes that increased in conspicuity rather than in style; but this was no disloyalty; he deprecated the attention they called to her in the streets.

And Lou was no less faithful to her chum. There was a law that Nancy should go with them on whatsoever outings they might take. Dan bore the extra burden heartily and in good cheer. It might be said that Lou furnished the color, Nancy the tone, and Dan the weight of the distraction-seeking trio. The escort, in his neat but obviously ready-made suit, his ready-made tie and unfailing, genial, ready-made wit never startled or clashed. He was of that good kind that you are likely to forget while they are present, but remember distinctly after they are gone.

To Nancy's superior taste the flavor of these ready-made pleasures was sometimes a little bitter: but she was young; and youth is a gourmand, when it cannot be a gourmet.

"Dan is always wanting me to marry him right away," Lou told her once. "But why should I? I'm independent. I can do as I please with the money I earn; and he never would agree for me to keep on working afterward. And say, Nance, what do you want to stick to that old store for, and half starve and half dress yourself? I could get you a place in the laundry right now if you'd come. It seems to me that you could afford to be a little less stuck-up if you could make a good deal more money."

"I don't think I'm stuck-up, Lou," said Nancy, "but I'd rather live on half rations and stay where I am. I suppose I've got the habit. It's the chance that I want. I don't expect to be always behind a counter. I'm learning something new every day. I'm right up against refined and rich people all the time—even if I do only wait on them; and I'm not missing any pointers that I see passing around."

"Caught your millionaire yet?" asked Lou with her teasing laugh.

"I haven't selected one yet," answered Nancy. "I've been looking them over."

"Goodness! the idea of picking over 'em! Don't you ever let one get by you, Nance—even if he's a few dollars shy. But of course you're joking—millionaires don't think about working girls like us."

"It might be better for them if they did," said Nancy, with cool wisdom. "Some of us could teach them how to take care of their money."

"If one was to speak to me," laughed Lou, "I know I'd have a duck-fit."

"That's because you don't know any. The only difference between swells and other people is you have to watch 'em closer. Don't you think that red silk lining is just a little bit too bright for that coat, Lou?"

Lou looked at the plain, dull olive jacket of her friend.

"Well, no, I don't—but it may seem so beside that faded-looking thing you've got on."

"This jacket," said Nancy, complacently, "has exactly the cut and fit of one that Mrs. Van Alstyne Fisher was wearing the other day. The material cost me $3.98. I suppose hers cost about $100 more."

"Oh, well," said Lou, lightly, "it don't strike me as millionaire bait. Shouldn't wonder if I catch one before you do, anyway."

Truly it would have taken a philosopher to decide upon the values of the theories held by the two friends. Lou, lacking that certain pride and fastidiousness that keeps stores and desks filled with girls working for the barest living, thumped away gaily with her iron in the noisy and stifling laundry. Her wages supported her even beyond the point of comfort; so that her dress profited until sometimes she cast a sidelong glance of impatience at the neat but inelegant apparel of Dan—Dan the constant, the immutable, the undeviating.

As for Nancy, her case was one of tens of thousands. Silk and jewels and laces and ornaments and the perfume and music of the fine world of good-breeding and taste—these were made for woman; they are her equitable portion. Let her keep near them if they are a part of life to her, and if she will. She is no traitor to herself, as Esau was; for she keeps her birthright and the pottage she earns is often very scant.

In this atmosphere Nancy belonged; and she throve in it and ate her frugal meals and schemed over her cheap dresses with a determined and contented mind. She already knew woman; and she was studying man, the animal, both as to his habits and eligibility. Some day she would bring down the game that she wanted; but she promised herself it would be what seemed to her the biggest and the best, and nothing smaller.

Thus she kept her lamp trimmed and burning to receive the bridegroom when he should come.

But another lesson she learned, perhaps unconsciously. Her standard of values began to shift and change. Sometimes the dollar-mark grew blurred in her mind's eye, and shaped itself into letters that spelled such words as "truth" and "honor" and now and then just "kindness." Let us make a likeness of one who hunts the moose or elk in some mighty wood. He sees a little dell, mossy and embowered, where a rill trickles, babbling to him of rest and comfort. At these times the spear of Nimrod himself grows blunt.

So, Nancy wondered sometimes if Persian lamb was always quoted at its market value by the hearts that it covered.

One Thursday evening Nancy left the store and turned across Sixth Avenue westward to the laundry. She was expected to go with Lou and Dan to a musical comedy.

Dan was just coming out of the laundry when she arrived. There was a queer, strained look on his face.

"I thought I would drop around to see if they had heard from her," he said.

"Heard from who?" asked Nancy. "Isn't Lou there?"

"I thought you knew," said Dan. "She hasn't been here or at the house where she lived since Monday. She moved all her things from there. She told one of the girls in the laundry she might be going to Europe."

"Hasn't anybody seen her anywhere?" asked Nancy.

Dan looked at her with his jaws set grimly, and a steely gleam in his steady gray eyes.

"They told me in the laundry," he said, harshly, "that they saw her pass yesterday—in an automobile. With one of the millionaires, I suppose, that you and Lou were forever busying your brains about."

For the first time Nancy quailed before a man. She laid her hand that trembled slightly on Dan's sleeve.

"You've no right to say such a thing to me, Dan—as if I had anything to do with it!"

"I didn't mean it that way," said Dan, softening. He fumbled in his vest pocket.

"I've got the tickets for the show to-night," he said, with a gallant show of lightness. "If you——"

Nancy admired pluck whenever she saw it.

"I'll go with you, Dan," she said.

Three months went by before Nancy saw Lou again.

At twilight one evening the shop-girl was hurrying home along the border of a little quiet park. She heard her name called, and wheeled about in time to catch Lou rushing into her arms.

After the first embrace they drew their heads back as serpents do, ready to attack or to charm, with a thousand questions trembling on their swift tongues. And then Nancy noticed that prosperity had descended upon Lou, manifesting itself in costly furs, flashing gems, and creations of the tailor's art.

"You little fool!" cried Lou, loudly and affectionately. "I see you are still working in that store, and as shabby as ever. And how about that big catch you were going to make—nothing doing yet, I suppose?"

And then Lou looked, and saw that something better than prosperity had descended upon Nancy—something that shone brighter than gems in her eyes and redder than a rose in her cheeks, and that danced like electricity anxious to be loosed from the tip of her tongue.

"Yes, I'm still in the store," said Nancy, "but I'm going to leave it next week. I've made my catch—the biggest catch in the world. You won't mind now Lou, will you?—I'm going to be married to Dan—to Dan!—he's my Dan now—why, Lou!"

Around the corner of the park strolled one of those new-crop, smooth-faced young policemen that are making the force more endurable—at least to the eye. He saw a woman with an expensive fur coat and diamond-ringed hands crouching down against the iron fence of the park sobbing turbulently, while a slender, plainly dressed working girl leaned close, trying to console her. But the Gibsonian cop, being of the new order, passed on, pretending not to notice, for he was wise enough to know that these matters are beyond help so far as the power he represents is concerned, though he rap the pavement with his nightstick till the sound goes up to the furthermost stars.

A MADISON SQUARE ARABIAN NIGHT

To Carson Chalmers, in his apartment near the square, Phillips brought the evening mail. Besides the routine correspondence there were two items bearing the same foreign postmark.

One of the incoming parcels contained a photograph of a woman. The other contained an interminable letter, over which Chalmers hung, absorbed, for a long time. The letter was from another woman; and it contained poisoned barbs, sweetly dipped in honey, and feathered with innuendos concerning the photographed woman.

Chalmers tore this letter into a thousand bits and began to wear out his expensive rug by striding back and forth upon it. Thus an animal from the jungle acts when it is caged, and thus a caged man acts when he is housed in a jungle of doubt.

By and by the restless mood was overcome. The rug was not an enchanted one. For sixteen feet he could travel along it; three thousand miles was beyond its power to aid.

Phillips appeared. He never entered; he invariably appeared, like a well-oiled genie.

"Will you dine here, sir, or out?" he asked.

"Here," said Chalmers, "and in half an hour." He listened glumly to the January blasts making on Æolian trombone of the empty street.

"Wait," he said to the disappearing genie. "As I came home across the end of the square I saw many men standing there in rows. There was one mounted upon something, talking. Why do those men stand in rows, and why are they there?"

"They are homeless men, sir," said Phillips. "The man standing on the box tries to get lodging for them for the night. People come around to listen and give him money. Then he sends as many as the money will pay for to some lodging-house. That is why they stand in rows; they get sent to bed in order as they come."

"By the time dinner is served," said Chalmers, "have one of those men here. He will dine with me."

"W-w-which——" began Phillips, stammering for the first time during his service.

"Choose one at random," said Chalmers. "You might see that he is reasonably sober—and a certain amount of cleanliness will not be held against him. That is all."

It was an unusual thing for Carson Chalmers to play the Caliph. But on that night he felt the inefficacy of conventional antidotes to melancholy. Something wanton and egregious, something high-flavored and Arabian, he must have to lighten his mood.

On the half hour Phillips had finished his duties as slave of the lamp. The waiters from the restaurant below had whisked aloft the delectable dinner. The dining table, laid for two, glowed cheerily in the glow of the pink-shaded candles.

And now Phillips, as though he ushered a cardinal—or held in charge a burglar—wafted in the shivering guest who had been haled from the line of mendicant lodgers.

It is a common thing to call such men wrecks; if the comparison be used here it is the specific one of a derelict come to grief through fire. Even yet some flickering combustion illuminated the drifting hulk. His face and hands had been recently washed—a rite insisted upon by Phillips as a memorial to the slaughtered conventions. In the candle-light he stood, a flaw in the decorous fittings of the apartment. His face was a sickly white, covered almost to the eyes with a stubble the shade of a red Irish setter's coat. Phillips's comb had failed to control the pale brown hair, long matted and conformed to the contour of a constantly worn hat. His eyes were full of hopeless, tricky defiance like that seen in a cur's that is cornered by his tormentors. His shabby coat was buttoned high, but a quarter inch of redeeming collar showed above it. His manner was singularly free from embarrassment when Chalmers rose from his chair across the round dining table.

"If you will oblige me," said the host, "I will be glad to have your company at dinner."

"My name is Plumer," said the highway guest, in harsh and aggressive tones. "If you're like me, you like to know the name of the party you're dining with."

"I was going on to say," continued Chalmers somewhat hastily, "that mine is Chalmers. Will you sit opposite?"

Plumer, of the ruffled plumes, bent his knee for Phillips to slide the chair beneath him. He had an air of having sat at attended boards before. Phillips set out the anchovies and olives.

"Good!" barked Plumer; "going to be in courses, is it? All right, my jovial ruler of Bagdad. I'm your Scheherezade all the way to the toothpicks. You're the first Caliph with a genuine Oriental flavor I've struck since frost. What luck! And I was forty-third in line. I finished counting, just as your welcome emissary arrived to bid me to the feast. I had about as much chance of getting a bed to-night as I have of being the next President. How will you have the sad story of my life, Mr. Al Raschid—a chapter with each course or the whole edition with the cigars and coffee?"

"The situation does not seem a novel one to you," said Chalmers with a smile.

"By the chin whiskers of the prophet—no!" answered the guest. "New York's as full of cheap Haroun al Raschids as Bagdad is of fleas. I've been held up for my story with a loaded meal pointed at my head twenty times. Catch anybody in New York giving you something for nothing! They spell curiosity and charity with the same set of building blocks. Lots of 'em will stake you to a dime and chop-suey; and a few of 'em will play Caliph to the tune of a top sirloin; but every one of 'em will stand over you till they screw your autobiography out of you with foot notes, appendix and unpublished fragments. Oh, I know what to do when I see victuals coming toward me in little old Bagdad-on-the-Subway. I strike the asphalt three times with my forehead and get ready to spiel yarns for my supper. I claim descent from the late Tommy Tucker, who was forced to hand out vocal harmony for his pre-digested wheaterina and spoopju."

"I do not ask your story," said Chalmers. "I tell you frankly that it was a sudden whim that prompted me to send for some stranger to dine with me. I assure you you will not suffer through any curiosity of mine."

"Oh, fudge!" exclaimed the guest, enthusiastically tackling his soup; "I don't mind it a bit. I'm a regular Oriental magazine with a red cover and the leaves cut when the Caliph walks abroad. In fact, we fellows in the bed line have a sort of union rate for things of this sort. Somebody's always stopping and wanting to know what brought us down so low in the world. For a sandwich and a glass of beer I tell 'em that drink did it. For corned beef and cabbage and a cup of coffee I give 'em the hard-hearted-landlord—six-months-in-the-hospital-lost-job story. A sirloin steak and a quarter for a bed gets the Wall Street tragedy of the swept-away fortune and the gradual descent. This is the first spread of this kind I've stumbled against. I haven't got a story to fit it. I'll tell you what, Mr. Chalmers, I'm going to tell you the truth for this, if you'll listen to it. It'll be harder for you to believe than the made-up ones."

An hour later the Arabian guest lay back with a sigh of satisfaction while Phillips brought the coffee and cigars and cleared the table.

"Did you ever hear of Sherrard Plumer?" he asked, with a strange smile.

"I remember the name," said Chalmers. "He was a painter, I think, of a good deal of prominence a few years ago."

"Five years," said the guest. "Then I went down like a chunk of lead. I'm Sherrard Plumer! I sold the last portrait I painted for $2,000. After that I couldn't have found a sitter for a gratis picture."

"What was the trouble?" Chalmers could not resist asking.

"Funny thing," answered Plumer, grimly. "Never quite understood it myself. For a while I swam like a cork. I broke into the swell crowd and got commissions right and left. The newspapers called me a fashionable painter. Then the funny things began to happen. Whenever I finished a picture people would come to see it, and whisper and look queerly at one another.

"I soon found out what the trouble was. I had a knack of bringing out in the face of a portrait the hidden character of the original. I don't know how I did it—I painted what I saw—but I know it did me. Some of my sitters were fearfully enraged and refused their pictures. I painted the portrait of a very beautiful and popular society dame. When it was finished her husband looked at it with a peculiar expression on his face, and the next week he sued for divorce.

"I remember one case of a prominent banker who sat to me. While I had his portrait on exhibition in my studio an acquaintance of his came in to look at it. 'Bless me,' says he, 'does he really look like that?' I told him it was considered a faithful likeness. 'I never noticed that expression about his eyes before,' said he; 'I think I'll drop downtown and change my bank account.' He did drop down, but the bank account was gone and so was Mr. Banker.

"It wasn't long till they put me out of business. People don't want their secret meannesses shown up in a picture. They can smile and twist their own faces and deceive you, but the picture can't. I couldn't get an order for another picture, and I had to give up. I worked as a newspaper artist for a while, and then for a lithographer, but my work with them got me into the same trouble. If I drew from a photograph my drawing showed up characteristics and expressions that you couldn't find in the photo, but I guess they were in the original, all right. The customers raised lively rows, especially the women, and I never could hold a job long. So I began to rest·my weary head upon the breast of Old Booze for comfort. And pretty soon I was in the free-bed line and doing oral fiction for hand-outs among the food bazaars. Does the truthful statement weary thee, O Caliph? I can turn on the Wall Street disaster stop if you prefer, but that requires a tear, and I'm afraid I can't hustle one up after that good dinner."

"No, no," said Chalmers, earnestly, "you interest me very much. Did all of your portraits reveal some unpleasant trait, or were there some that did not suffer from the ordeal of your peculiar brush?"

"Some? Yes," said Plumer. "Children generally, a good many women and a sufficient number of men. All people aren't bad, you know. When they were all right the pictures were all right. As I said, I don't explain it, but I'm telling you facts."

On Chalmer's writing-table lay the photograph that he had received.

that day in the foreign mail. Ten minutes later he had Plumer at work making a sketch from it in pastels. At the end of an hour the artist rose and stretched wearily. "It's done," he yawned. "You'll excuse me for being so long. I got interested in the job. Lordy! but I'm tired. No bed last night, you know. Guess it'll have to be good-night now, O Commander of the Faithful!"

Chalmers went as far as the door with him and slipped some bills into his hand.

"Oh! I'll take 'em," said Plumer. "All that's included in the fall. Thanks. And for the very good dinner. I shall sleep on feathers to-night and dream of Bagdad. I hope it won't turn out to be a dream in the morning. Farewell, most excellent Caliph!"

Again Chalmers paced restlessly upon his rug. But his beat lay as far from the table whereon lay the pastel sketch as the room would permit. Twice, thrice, he tried to approach it, but failed. He could see the dun and gold and brown of the colors, but there was a wall about it built by his fears that kept him at a distance. He sat down and tried to calm himself. He sprang up and rang for Phillips.

"There is a young artist in this building," he said—"a Mr. Reineman —do you know which is his apartment?"

"Top floor, front, sir," said Phillips.

"Go up and ask him to favor me with his presence here for a few minutes."

Reineman came at once. Chalmers introduced himself.

"Mr. Reineman," said he, "there is a little pastel sketch on yonder table. I would be glad if you will give me your opinion of it as to its artistic merits and as a picture."

The young artist advanced to the table and took up the sketch. Chalmers half turned away, leaning upon the back of a chair.

"How—do—you find it?" he asked, slowly.

"As a drawing," said the artist, "I can't praise it enough. It's the work of a master—bold and fine and true. It puzzles me a little; I haven't seen any pastel work near as good in years."

"The face, man—the subject—the original—what would you say of that?"

"The face," said Reineman, "is the face of one of God's own angels. May I ask who——"

"My wife!" shouted Chalmers, wheeling and pouncing upon the astonished artist, gripping his hand and pounding his back. "She is traveling in Europe. Take that sketch, boy, and paint the picture of your life from it and leave the price to me."

THE RUBAIYAT OF A SCOTCH HIGHBALL

This document is intended to strike somewhere between a temperance lecture and the "Bartender's Guide." Relative to the latter, drink shall swell the theme and be set forth in abundance. Agreeably to the former, not an elbow shall be crooked.

Bob Babbitt was "off the stuff." Which means—as you will discover by referring to the unabridged dictionary of Bohemia—that he had "cut out the booze," that he was "on the water wagon." The reason for Bob's sudden attitude of hostility toward the "demon rum"—as the white ribboners miscall whiskey (see the "Bartender's Guide"), should be of interest to reformers and saloon-keepers.

There is always hope for a man who, when sober, will not concede or acknowledge that he was ever drunk. But when a man will say (in the apt words of the phrase-distiller), "I had a beautiful skate on last night," you will have to put stuff in his coffee as well as pray for him.

One evening on his way home Babbitt dropped in at the Broadway bar that he liked best. Always there were three or four fellows there from the downtown offices whom he knew. And then there would be highballs and stories, and he would hurry home to dinner a little late but feeling good, and a little sorry for the poor Standard Oil Company. On this evening as he entered he heard some one say: "Babbitt was in last night as full as a boiled owl."

Babbitt walked to the bar, and saw in the mirror that his face was as white as chalk. For the first time he had looked Truth in the eyes. Others had lied to him; he had dissembled with himself. He was a drunkard, and had not known it. What he had fondly imagined was a pleasant exhilaration had been maudlin intoxication. His fancied wit had been drivel, his gay humors nothing but the noisy vagaries of a sot. But, never again!

"A glass of seltzer," he said to the bartender.

A little silence fell upon the group of his cronies, who had been expecting him to join them.

"Going off the stuff, Bob?" one of them asked politely and with more formality than the highballs ever called forth.

"Yes," said Babbitt.

Some one of the group took up the unwashed thread of a story he had been telling; the bartender shoved over a dime and a nickel change from the quarter, ungarnished with his customary smile; and Babbitt walked out.

Now, Babbitt had a home and a wife—but that is another story. And I will tell you that story, which will show you a better habit and a worse story than you could find in the man who invented the phrase.

It began away up in Sullivan County, where so many rivers and so much trouble begins—or begin; how would you say that? It was July, and Jessie was a summer boarder at the Mountain Squint Hotel, and Bob, who was just out of college, saw her one day—and they were married in September. That's the tabloid novel—one swallow of water, and it's gone.

But those July days!

Let the exclamation point expound it, for I shall not. For particulars you might read up on "Romeo and Juliet," and Abraham Lincoln's thrilling sonnet about "You can fool some of the people," &c., and Darwin's works.

But one thing I must tell you about. Both of them were made over Omar's Rubaiyat. They knew every verse of the old bluffer by heart—not consecutively, but picking 'em out here and there as you fork the mushrooms in a fifty-cent steak à la Bordelaise. Sullivan County is full of rocks and trees; and Jessie used to sit on them, and—please be good—used to sit on the rocks; and Bob had a way of standing behind her with his hands over her shoulders holding her hands, and his face close to hers, and they would repeat over and over their favorite verses of the old tentmaker. They saw only the poetry and philosophy of the lines then—indeed, they agreed that the Wine was only an image, and that what was meant to be celebrated was some divinity, or maybe Love or Life. However, at that time neither of them had tasted the stuff that goes with a sixty-cent *table d'hôte*.

Where was I? Oh, they married and came to New York. Bob showed his college diploma, and accepted a position filling inkstands in a lawyer's office at $15 a week. At the end of two years he had worked up to $50, and gotten his first taste of Bohemia—the kind that won't stand the borax and formaldehyde tests.

They had two furnished rooms and a little kitchen. To Jess, accustomed to the mild but beautiful savor of a country town, the dreggy Bohemia was sugar and spice. She hung fish seines on the walls of her rooms, and bought a rakish-looking sideboard, and learned to play the banjo. Twice or thrice a week they dined at French or Italian *tables d'hôte* in a cloud of smoke, and brag and unshorn hair. Jess learned to drink a cocktail in order to get the cherry. At home she smoked a cigarette after dinner. She learned to pronounce Chianti, and leave her olive stones for the waiter to pick up. Once she essayed to say la, la, la! in a crowd but got only as far as the second one. They met one or two couples while dining out and became friendly with them. The sideboard was stocked with Scotch and rye and a liqueur. They had their new friends in to dinner and all were laughing at nothing by 1 A.M. Some plastering fell in the room below them, for which Bob had to pay $4.50. Thus they footed it merrily on the ragged frontiers of the country that has no boundary lines or government.

And soon Bob fell in with his cronies and learned to keep his foot on the little rail six inches above the floor for an hour or so every afternoon before he went home. Drink always rubbed him the right way, and he would reach his rooms as jolly as a sandboy. Jessie would meet him at the door, and generally they would dance some insane kind of a rigadoon about the floor by way of greeting. Once when Bob's feet became confused and he tumbled headlong over a foot-stool Jessie laughed so heartily and long that he had to throw all the couch pillows at her to make her hush.

In such wise life was speeding for them on the day when Bob Babbitt first felt the power that the giftie gi'ed him.

But let us get back to our lamb and mint sauce.

When Bob got home that evening he found Jessie in a long apron cutting up a lobster for the Newburg. Usually when Bob came in mellow from his hour at the bar his welcome was hilarious, though somewhat tinctured with Scotch smoke.

By screams and snatches of song and certain audible testimonials of domestic felicity was his advent proclaimed. When she heard his foot on the stairs the old maid in the hall room always stuffed cotton into her ears. At first Jessie had shrunk from the rudeness and flavor of these spiritual greetings, but as the fog of the false Bohemia gradually encompassed her she came to accept them as love's true and proper greeting.

Bob came in without a word, smiled, kissed her neatly but noiselessly, took up a paper and sat down. In the hall room the old maid held her two plugs of cotton poised, filled with anxiety.

Jessie dropped lobster and knife and ran to him with frightened eyes.

"What's the matter, Bob, are you ill?"

"Not at all, dear."

"Then what's the matter with you?"

"Nothing."

Hearken, brethren. When She-who-has-a-right-to-ask interrogates you concerning a change she finds in your mood answer her thus: Tell her that you, in a sudden rage, have murdered your grandmother; tell her that you have robbed orphans and that remorse has stricken you; tell her your fortune is swept away; that you are beset by enemies, by bunions, by any kind of malevolent fate; but do not, if peace and happiness are worth as much as a grain of mustard seed to you—do not answer her "Nothing."

Jessie went back to the lobster in silence. She cast looks of darkest suspicion at Bob. He had never acted that way before.

When dinner was on the table she set out the bottle of Scotch and the glasses. Bob declined. "Tell you the truth, Jess," he said. "I've cut out the drink. Help yourself, of course. If you don't mind I'll try some of the seltzer straight."

"You've stopped drinking?" she said, looking at him steadily and unsmilingly. "What for?"

"It wasn't doing me any good," said Bob. "Don't you approve of the idea?"

Jessie raised her eyebrows and one shoulder slightly.

"Entirely," she said with a sculptured smile. "I could not conscientiously advise any one to drink or smoke, or whistle on Sunday."

The meal was finished almost in silence. Bob tried to make talk, but his efforts lacked the stimulus of previous evenings. He felt miserable, and once or twice his eye wandered toward the bottle, but each time the scathing words of his bibulous friend sounded in his ear, and his mouth set with determination.

Jessie felt the change deeply. The essence of their lives seemed to have departed suddenly. The restless fever, the false gayety, the unnatural excitement of the shoddy Bohemia in which they lived had dropped away in the space of the popping of a cork. She stole curious and forlorn glances at the dejected Bob, who bore the guilty look of at least a wife-beater or a family tyrant.

After dinner the colored maid who came in daily to perform such chores cleared away the things. Jessie, with an unreadable countenance, brought back the bottle of Scotch and the glasses and a bowl of cracked ice and set them on the table.

"May I ask," she said, with some of the ice in her tones, "whether I am to be included in your sudden spasm of goodness? If not, I'll make one for myself. It's rather chilly this evening, for some reason."

"Oh, come now, Jess," said Bob, good-naturedly, "don't be too rough on me. Help yourself, by all means. There's no danger of your overdoing it. But I thought there was with me; and that's why I quit. Have yours, and then let's get out the banjo and try over that new quick-step."

"I've heard," said Jessie in the tones of the oracle, "that drinking alone is a pernicious habit. No, I don't think I feel like playing this evening. If we are going to reform we may as well abandon the evil habit of banjo-playing, too."

She took up a book and sat in her little willow rocker on the other side of the table. Neither of them spoke for half an hour.

And then Bob laid down his paper and got up with a strange, absent look on his face and went behind her chair and reached over her shoulders, taking her hands in his, and laid his face close to hers.

In a moment to Jessie the walls of the seine-hung room vanished, and she saw the Sullivan County hills and rills. Bob felt her hands quiver in his as he began the verse from Old Omar:

"Come, fill the Cup, and in the Fire of Spring
    The Winter Garment of Repentance fling:

The Bird of Time has but a little way
To fly—and Lo! the Bird is on the Wing!"

And then he walked to the table and poured a stiff drink of Scotch into a glass.

But in that moment a mountain breeze had somehow found its way in and blown away the mist of the false Bohemia.

Jessie leaped and with one fierce sweep of her hand sent the bottle and glasses crashing to the floor. The same motion of her arm carried it around Bob's neck, where it met its mate and fastened tight.

"Oh, my God, Bobbie—not that verse—I see now. I wasn't always such a fool, was I? The other one, boy—the one that says: 'Remould it to the Heart's Desire.' Say that one—'to the Heart's Desire.' "

"I know that one," said Bob. "It goes:

"Ah! Love, could you and I with Him conspire
To grasp this sorry Scheme of Things entire
Would not we——"

"Let me finish it," said Jessie.

"Would not we shatter it to bits—and then
Remould it nearer to the heart's Desire!"

"It's shattered all right," said Bob, crunching some glass under his heel.

In some dungeon below the accurate ear of Mrs. Pickens, the landlady, located the smash.

"It's that wild Mr. Babbitt coming home soused again," she said. "And he's got such a nice little wife, too!"

THE PENDULUM

"Eighty-first Street—let 'em out, please," yelled the shepherd in blue.

A flock of citizen sheep scrambled out and another flock scrambled aboard. Ding-ding! The cattle cars of the Manhattan Elevated rattled away, and John Perkins drifted down the stairway of the station with the released flock.

John walked slowly toward his flat. Slowly, because in the lexicon of his daily life there was no such word as "perhaps." There are no surprises awaiting a man who has been married two years and lives in a flat. As he walked John Perkins prophesied to himself with gloomy and down-trodden cynicism the foregone conclusions of the monotonous day.

Katy would meet him at the door with a kiss flavored with cold cream and butter-scotch. He would remove his coat, sit upon a macadamized lounge and read, in the evening paper, of Russians and Japs slaughtered by the deadly linotype. For dinner there would be pot roast, a salad flavored with a dressing warranted not to crack or injure the leather, stewed rhubarb and the bottle of strawberry marmalade blushing at the certificate of chemical purity on its label. After dinner Katy would show him the new patch in her crazy quilt that the iceman had cut for her off the end of his four-in-hand. At half-past seven they would spread newspapers over the furniture to catch the pieces of plastering that fell when the fat man in the flat overhead began to take his physical culture exercises. Exactly at eight Hickey & Mooney, of the vaudeville team (unbooked) in the flat across the hall, would yield to the gentle influence of delirium tremens and begin to overturn chairs under the delusion that Hammerstein was pursuing them with a five-hundred-dollar-a-week contract. Then the gent at the window across the air-shaft would get out his flute; the nightly gas leak would steal forth to frolic in the highways; the dumbwaiter would slip off its trolley; the janitor would drive Mrs. Zanowitski's five children once more across the Yalu; the lady with the champagne shoes and the Skye terrier would trip downstairs and paste her Thursday name over her bell and letter-box—and the evening routine of the Frogmore flats would be under way.

John Perkins knew these things would happen. And he knew that at a quarter past eight he would summon his nerve and reach for his hat, and that his wife would deliver this speech in a querulous tone:

"Now, where are you going, I'd like to know, John Perkins?"

"Thought I'd drop up to McCloskey's," he would answer, "and play a game or two of pool with the fellows."·

Of late such had been John Perkins's habit. At ten or eleven he would return. Sometimes Katy would be asleep; sometimes waiting up, ready to melt in the crucible of her ire a little more gold plating from the wrought steel chains of matrimony. For these things Cupid will have to answer when he stands at the bar of justice with his victims from the Frogmore flats.

To-night John Perkins encountered a tremendous upheaval of the commonplace when he reached his door. No Katy was there with her affectionate, confectionate kiss. The three rooms seemed in portentous disorder. All about lay her things in confusion. Shoes in the middle of the floor, curling tongs, hair bows, kimonos, powder box, jumbled together on dresser and chairs—this was not Katy's way. With a sinking heart John saw the comb with a curling cloud of her brown hair among its teeth. Some unusual hurry and perturbation must have possessed her, for she always carefully placed these combings in the little blue vase on the mantel to be some day formed into the coveted feminine "rat."

Hanging conspicuously to the gas jet by a string was a folded paper. John seized it. It was a note from his wife running thus:

Dear John:

I just had a telegram saying mother is very sick. I am going to take the 4:30 train. Brother Sam is going to meet me at the depot there. There is cold mutton in the icebox. I hope it isn't her quinzy again. Pay the milk-man 50 cents. She had it bad last spring. Don't forget to write to the company about the gas meter, and your good socks are in the top drawer. I will write to-morrow.

Hastily,

Katy

Never during their two years of matrimony had he and Katy been separated for a night. John read the note over and over in a dumbfounded way. Here was a break in a routine that had never varied, and it left him dazed.

There on the back of a chair hung, pathetically empty and formless, the red wrapper with black dots that she always wore while getting the meals. Her week-day clothes had been tossed here and there in her haste. A little paper bag of her favorite butter-scotch lay with its string yet un-wound. A daily paper sprawled on the floor, gaping rectangularly where a railroad time-table had been clipped from it. Everything in the room spoke of a loss, of an essence gone, of its soul and life departed. John Perkins stood among the dead remains with a queer feeling of desolation in his heart.

He began to set the rooms tidy as well as he could. When he touched her clothes a thrill of something like terror went through him. He had never thought what existence would be without Katy. She had become so thoroughly annealed into his life that she was like the air he breathed—necessary but scarcely noticed. Now, without warning, she was gone, vanished, as completely absent as if she had never existed. Of course it would be only for a few days, or at most a week or two, but it seemed to him as if the very hand of death had pointed a finger at his secure and uneventful home.

John dragged the cold mutton from the ice-box, made coffee, and sat down to a lonely meal face to face with the strawberry marmalade's shameless certificate of purity. Bright among withdrawn blessings now appeared to him the ghosts of pot roasts and the salad with tan polish dressing. His home was dismantled. A quinzied mother-in-law had knocked his lares and penates sky-high. After his solitary meal John sat at a front window.

He did not care to smoke. Outside the city roared to him to come join in its dance of folly and pleasure. The night was his. He might go forth unquestioned and thrum the strings of jollity as free as any gay bachelor there. He might carouse and wander and have his fling until dawn if he liked; and there would be no wrathful Katy waiting for him, bearing the chalice that held the dregs of his joy. He might play pool at Mc-Closkey's with his roistering friends until Aurora dimmed the electric bulbs if he chose. The hymeneal strings that had curbed him always when the Frogmore flats had palled upon him were loosened. Katy was gone.

John Perkins was not accustomed to analyzing his emotions. But as he sat in his Katy-bereft 10 x 12 parlor he hit unerringly upon the keynote of his discomfort. He knew now that Katy was necessary to his happiness. His feeling for her, lulled into unconsciousness by the dull round of domesticity, had been sharply stirred by the loss of her presence. Has it not been dinned into us by proverb and sermon and fable that we never prize the music till the sweet-voiced bird has flown—or in other no less florid and true utterances?

"I'm a double-dyed dub," mused John Perkins, "the way I've been treating Katy. Off every night playing pool and bumming with the boys instead of staying home with her. The poor girl here all alone with nothing to amuse her, and me acting that way! John Perkins, you're the worst kind of a shine. I'm going to make it up for the little girl. I'll take her out and let her see some amusement. And I'll cut out the McCloskey gang right from this minute."

Yes, there was the city roaring outside for John Perkins to come dance in the train of Momus. And at McCloskey's the boys were knocking the balls idly into the pockets against the hour for the nightly game. But no primrose way nor clicking cue could woo the remorseful soul of Perkins the bereft. The thing that was his, lightly held and half scorned, had been taken away from him, and he wanted it. Backward to a certain man named Adam, whom the cherubim bounced from the orchard, could Perkins, the remorseful, trace his descent.

Near the right hand of John Perkins stood a chair. On the back of it stood Katy's blue shirtwaist. It still retained something of her contour. Midway of the sleeves were fine, individual wrinkles made by the movements of her arms in working for his comfort and pleasure. A delicate but impelling odor of bluebells came from it. John took it and looked long and soberly at the unresponsive grenadine. Katy had never been unresponsive. Tears:—yes, tears—came into John Perkins's eyes. When she came back things would be different. He would make up for all his neglect. What was life without her?

The door opened. Katy walked in carrying a little hand satchel. John stared at her stupidly.

"My! I'm glad to get back," said Katy. "Ma wasn't sick to amount to anything. Sam was at the depot, and said she just had a little spell, and got all right soon after they telegraphed. So I took the next train back. I'm just dying for a cup of coffee."

Nobody heard the click and rattle of the cogwheels as the third-floor-front of the Frogmore flats buzzed its machinery back into the Order of

Things. A band slipped, a spring was touched, the gear was adjusted and the wheels revolve in their old orbit.

John Perkins looked at the clock. It was 8.15. He reached for his hat and walked to the door.

"Now, where are you going, I'd like to know, John Perkins?" asked Katy, in a querulous tone.

"Thought I'd drop up to McCloskey's," said John, "and play a game or two of pool with the fellows."

TWO THANKSGIVING DAY GENTLEMEN

There is one day that is ours. There is one day when all we Americans who are not self-made go back to the old home to eat salcratus biscuits and marvel how much nearer to the porch the old pump looks than it used to. Bless the day. President Roosevelt gives it to us. We hear some talk of the Puritans, but don't just remember who they were. Bet we can lick 'em, anyhow, if they try to land again. Plymouth Rocks? Well, that sounds more familiar. Lots of us have had to come down to hens since the Turkey Trust got its work in. But somebody in Washington is leaking out advance information to 'em about these Thanksgiving proclamations.

The big city east of the cranberry bogs has made Thanksgiving Day an institution. The last Thursday in November is the only day in the year on which it recognizes the part of America lying across the ferries. It is the one day that is purely American. Yes, a day of celebration, exclusively American.

And now for the story which is to prove to you that we have traditions on this side of the ocean that are becoming older at a much rapider rate than those of England are—thanks to our git-up and enterprise.

Stuffy Pete took his seat on the third bench to the right as you enter Union Square from the east, at the walk opposite the fountain. Every Thanksgiving Day for nine years he had taken his seat there promptly at 1 o'clock. For every time he had done so things had happened to him— Charles Dickensy things that swelled his waistcoat above his heart, and equally on the other side.

But to-day Stuffy Pete's appearance at the annual trysting place seemed to have been rather the result of habit than of the yearly hunger which, as the philanthropists seem to think, afflicts the poor at such extended intervals.

Certainly Pete was not hungry. He had just come from a feast that had left him of his powers barely those of respiration and locomotion. His eyes were like two pale gooseberries firmly imbedded in a swollen and gravy-smeared mask of putty. His breath came in short wheezes; a senatorial roll of adipose tissue denied a fashionable set to his upturned coat collar. Buttons that had been sewed upon his clothes by kind Salvation fingers a week before flew like pop-corn, strewing the earth around him. Ragged he was, with a split shirt front open to the wishbone; but the November breeze, carrying fine snowflakes, brought him only a grateful coolness. For Stuffy Pete was overcharged with the caloric produced by a super-bountiful dinner, beginning with oysters and ending with plum pudding, and including (it seemed to him) all the roast turkey and baked potatoes and chicken salad and squash pie and ice cream in the world. Wherefore he sat, gorged, and gazed upon the world with after-dinner contempt.

The meal had been an unexpected one. He was passing a red brick mansion near the beginning of Fifth Avenue, in which lived two old ladies of ancient family and a reverence for traditions. They even denied the existence of New York, and believed that Thanksgiving Day was declared solely for Washington Square. One of their traditional habits was to station a servant at the postern gate with orders to admit the first hungry wayfarer that came along after the hour of noon had struck, and banquet him to a finish. Stuffy Pete happened to pass by on his way to the park, and the seneschals gathered him in and upheld the custom of the castle.

After Stuffy Pete had gazed straight before him for ten minutes he was conscious of a desire for a more varied field of vision. With a tremendous effort he moved his head slowly to the left. And then his eyes bulged out fearfully, and his breath ceased, and the rough-shod ends of his short legs wriggled and rustled on the gravel.

For the Old Gentleman was coming across Fourth Avenue toward his bench.

Every Thanksgiving Day for nine years the Old Gentleman had come there and found Stuffy Pete on his bench. That was a thing that the Old Gentleman was trying to make a tradition of. Every Thanksgiving Day for nine years he had found Stuffy there, and had led him to a restaurant and watched him eat a big dinner. They do those things in England unconsciously. But this is a young country, and nine years is not so bad. The Old Gentleman was a stanch American patriot, and considered himself a pioneer in American tradition. In order to become picturesque we must keep on doing one thing for a long time without ever letting it get away from us. Something like collecting the weekly dimes in industrial insurance. Or cleaning the streets.

The Old Gentleman moved, straight and stately, toward the Institution that he was rearing. Truly, the annual feeding of Stuffy Pete was nothing national in its character, such as the Magna Charta or jam for breakfast was in England. But it was a step. It was almost feudal. It showed, at least, that a Custom was not impossible to New Y—ahem!—America.

The Old Gentleman was thin and tall and sixty. He was dressed all in black, and wore the old-fashioned kind of glasses that won't stay on your nose. His hair was whiter and thinner than it had been last year, and he seemed to make more use of his big, knobby cane with the crooked handle.

As his established benefactor came up Stuffy wheezed and shuddered like some woman's over-fat pug when a street dog bristles up at him. He would have flown, but all the skill of Santos-Dumont could not have separated him from his bench. Well had the myrmidons of the two old ladies done their work.

"Good morning," said the Old Gentleman. "I am glad to perceive that the vicissitudes of another year have spared you to move in health about the beautiful world. For that blessing alone this day of thanksgiving is well proclaimed to each of us. If you will come with me, my man, I will provide you with a dinner that should make your physical being accord with the mental."

That is what the Old Gentleman said every time. Every Thanksgiving Day for nine years. The words themselves almost formed an Institution. Nothing could be compared with them except the Declaration of Independence. Always before they had been music in Stuffy's ears. But now he looked up at the Old Gentleman's face with tearful agony in his own. The fine snow almost sizzled when it fell upon his perspiring brow. But the Old Gentleman shivered a little and turned his back to the wind.

Stuffy had always wondered why the Old Gentleman spoke his speech rather sadly. He did not know that it was because he was wishing every time that he had a son to succeed him. A son who would come there after he was gone—a son who would stand proud and strong before some subsequent Stuffy, and say: "In memory of my father." Then it would be an Institution.

But the Old Gentleman had no relatives. He lived in rented rooms in one of the decayed old family brownstone mansions in one of the quiet streets east of the park. In the winter he raised fuchsias in a little conservatory the size of a steamer trunk. In the spring he walked in the Easter parade. In the summer he lived at a farmhouse in the New Jersey hills, and sat in a wicker armchair, speaking of a butterfly, the ornithoptera amphrisius, that he hoped to find some day. In the autumn he fed Stuffy a dinner. These were the Old Gentleman's occupations.

Stuffy Pete looked up at him for a half minute, stewing and helpless in his own self-pity. The Old Gentleman's eyes were bright with the giving-pleasure. His face was getting more lined each year, but his little black necktie was in as jaunty a bow as ever, and his linen was beautiful and white, and his gray mustache was curled gracefully at the ends. And then Stuffy made a noise that sounded like peas bubbling in a pot. Speech was intended; and as the Old Gentleman had heard the sounds nine times before, he rightly construed them into Stuffy's old formula of acceptance.

"Thankee, sir. I'll go with ye, and much obliged. I'm very hungry, sir."

The coma of repletion had not prevented from entering Stuffy's mind the conviction that he was the basis of an Institution. His Thanksgiving appetite was not his own; it belonged by all the sacred rights of established custom, if not by the actual Statute of Limitations, to this kind old gentleman who had preëmpted it. True, America is free; but in order to establish tradition some one must be a repetend—a repeating decimal. The heroes are not all heroes of steel and gold. See one here that wielded only weapons of iron, badly silvered, and tin.

The Old Gentleman led his annual protégé southward to the restaurant, and to the table where the feast had always occurred. They were recognized.

"Here comes de old guy," said a waiter, "dat blows dat same bum to a meal every Thanksgiving."

The Old Gentleman sat across the table glowing like a smoked pearl at his corner-stone of future ancient Tradition. The waiters heaped the table with holiday food—and Stuffy, with a sigh that was mistaken for hunger's expression, raised knife and fork and carved for himself a crown of imperishable bay.

No more valiant hero ever fought his way through the ranks of an enemy. Turkey, chops, soups, vegetables, pies, disappeared before him as fast as they could be served. Gorged nearly to the uttermost when he entered the restaurant, the smell of food had almost caused him to lose his honor as a gentleman, but he rallied like a true knight. He saw the look of beneficent happiness on the Old Gentleman's face—a happier look than even the fuchsias and the ornithoptera amphrisius had ever brought to it—and he had not the heart to see it wane.

In an hour Stuffy leaned back with a battle won.

"Thankee kindly, sir," he puffed like a leaky steam pipe; "thankee kindly for a hearty meal."

Then he arose heavily with glazed eyes and started toward the kitchen. A waiter turned him about like a top, and pointed him toward the door. The Old Gentleman carefully counted out $1.30 in silver change, leaving three nickels for the waiter.

They parted as they did each year at the door, the Old Gentleman going south, Stuffy north.

Around the first corner Stuffy turned, and stood for one minute. Then he seemed to puff out his rags as an owl puffs out his feathers, and fell to the sidewalk like a sunstricken horse.

When the ambulance came the young surgeon and the driver cursed softly at his weight. There was no smell of whiskey to justify a transfer to the patrol wagon, so Stuffy and his two dinners went to the hospital.

There they stretched him on a bed and began to test him for strange diseases, with the hope of getting a chance at some problem with the bare steel.

And lo! an hour later another ambulance brought the Old Gentleman. And they laid him on another bed and spoke of appendicitis, for he looked good for the bill.

But pretty soon one of the young doctors met one of the young nurses whose eyes he liked, and stopped to chat with her about the cases.

"That nice old gentleman over there, now," he said, "you wouldn't think that was a case of almost starvation. Proud old family, I guess. He told me he hadn't eaten a thing for three days."

THE ASSESSOR OF SUCCESS

Hastings Beauchamp Morley sauntered across Union Square with a pitying look at the hundreds that lolled upon the park benches. They were a motley lot, he thought; the men with stolid, animal, unshaven faces; the women wriggling and self-conscious, twining and untwining their feet that hung four inches above the gravelled walks.

Were I Mr. Carnegie or Mr. Rockefeller I would put a few millions in my inside pocket and make an appointment with all the Park Commissioners (around the corner, if necessary) and arrange for benches in all the parks of the world low enough for women to sit upon, and rest their feet upon the ground. After that I might furnish libraries to towns that would pay for 'em, or build sanitariums for crank professors, and call 'em colleges, if I wanted to.

Women's rights societies have been laboring for many years after equality with man. With what result? When they sit on a bench they must twist their ankles together and uncomfortably swing their highest French heels clear of earthly support. Begin at the bottom, ladies. Get your feet on the ground, and then rise to theories of mental equality.

Hastings Beauchamp Morley was carefully and neatly dressed. That was the result of an instinct due to his birth and breeding. It is denied us to look further into a man's bosom than the starch on his shirt front; so it is left to us only to recount his walks and conversation.

Morley had not a cent in his pockets; but he smiled pityingly at a hundred grimy, unfortunate ones who had no more, and who would have no more when the sun's first rays yellowed the tall paper-cutter building on the west side of the square. But Morley would have enough by then. Sundown had seen his pockets empty before; but sunrise had always seen them lined.

First he went to the house of a clergyman off Madison Avenue and presented a forged letter of introduction that holily purported to issue from a pastorate in Indiana. This netted him $5 when backed up by a realistic romance of a delayed remittance.

On the sidewalk, twenty steps from the clergyman's door, a pale-faced, fat man huskily enveloped him with a raised red fist and the voice of a bell buoy, demanding payment of an old score.

"Why, Bergman, man," sang Morley, dulcetly, "is this you? I was just on my way up to your place to settle up. That remittance from my aunt arrived only this morning. Wrong address was the trouble. Come up to the corner and I'll square up. Glad to see you. Saves me a walk."

Four drinks placated the emotional Bergman. There was an air about Morley when he was backed by money in hand that would have stayed off a call loan at Rothschilds'. When he was penniless his bluff was pitched half a tone lower, but few were competent to detect the difference in the notes.

"You gum to mine blace and bay me tomorrow, Mr. Morley," said Bergman. "Oxcuse me dat I dun you on der street. But I haf not seen you in dree mont'. Pros't!"

Morley walked away with a crooked smile on his pale, smooth face. The credulous, drink-softened German amused him. He would have to avoid Twenty-ninth Street in the future. He had not been aware that Bergman ever went home by that route.

At the door of a darkened house two squares to the north Morley knocked with a peculiar sequence of raps. The door opened to the length of a six-inch chain, and the pompous, important black face of an African guardian imposed itself in the opening. Morley was admitted.

In a third-story room, in an atmosphere opaque with smoke, he hung for ten minutes above a roulette wheel. Then downstairs he crept, and was out-sped by the important Negro, jingling in his pocket the 40 cents in silver that remained to him of his five-dollar capital. At the corner he lingered, undecided.

Across the street was a drug store, well lighted, sending forth gleams from the German silver and crystal of its soda fountain and glasses. Along came a youngster of five, headed for the dispensary, stepping high with the consequence of a big errand, possibly one to which his advancing age had earned him promotion. In his hand he clutched something tightly, publicly, proudly, conspicuously.

Morley stopped him with his winning smile and soft speech.

"Me?" said the youngster. "I'm doin' to the drug 'tore for Mamma. She dave me a dollar to buy a bottle of med'cin."

"Now, now, now!" said Morley. "Such a big man you are to be doing errands for Mamma. I must go along with my little man to see that the cars don't run over him. And on the way we'll have some chocolates. Or would he rather have lemon drops?"

Morley entered the drug store leading the child by the hand. He presented the prescription that had been wrapped around the money.

On his face was a smile, predatory, parental, politic, profound.

"Aqua pura, one pint," said he to the druggist. "Sodium chloride, ten grains. Fiat solution. And don't try to skin me, because I know all about the number of gallons of H_2O in the Croton reservoir, and I always use the other ingredient on my potatoes."

"Fifteen cents," said the druggist, with a wink, after he had compounded the order. "I see you understand pharmacy. A dollar is the regular price."

"To gulls," said Morley, smilingly.

He settled the wrapped bottle carefully in the child's arms and escorted him to the corner. In his own pocket he dropped the 85 cents accruing to him by virtue of his chemical knowledge.

"Look out for the cars, sonny," he said, cheerfully, to his small victim.

Two street cars suddenly swooped in opposite directions upon the youngster. Morley dashed between them and pinned the infantile messenger by the neck, holding him in safety. Then from the corner of his street he sent him on his way, swindled, happy, and sticky with vile, cheap candy from the Italian's fruit stand.

Morley went to a restaurant and ordered a sirloin and a pint of inexpensive Château Breuille. He laughed noiselessly, but so genuinely that the waiter ventured to premise that good news had come his way.

"Why, no," said Morley, who seldom held conversation with any one. "It is not that. It is something else that amuses me. Do you know what three diversions of people are easiest to over-reach in transactions of all kinds?"

"Sure," said the waiter, calculating the size of the tip promised by the careful knot of Morley's tie; "there's the buyers from the dry goods stores in the South during August, and honeymooners from Staten Island, and——"

"Wrong!" said Morley, chuckling happily. "The answer is just—men, women, and children. The world—well, say New York and as far as summer boarders can swim out from Long Island—is full of greenhorns. Two minutes longer on the broiler would have made this steak fit to be eaten by a gentleman, François."

"If yez t'inks it's on de bum," said the waiter, "Oi'll——"

Morley lifted his hand in protest—slightly martyred protest.

"It will do," he said, magnanimously. "And now, green Chartreuse, frappé and a demitasse."

Morley went out leisurely and stood on a corner where two tradeful arteries of the city cross. With a solitary dime in his pocket, he stood on the curb watching with confident, cynical, smiling eyes the tides of people that flowed past him. Into that stream he must cast his net and draw fish for his further sustenance and need. Good Izaak Walton had not the half of his self-reliance and bait-lore.

A joyful party of four—two women and two men—fell upon him with cries of delight. There was a dinner party on—where had he been for a fortnight past?—what luck to thus run upon him! They surrounded and engulfed him—he must join them—tra la la—and the rest.

One with a white hat plume curving to the shoulder touched his sleeve, and cast at the others a triumphant look that said: "See what I can do with him?" and added her queen's command to the invitations.

"I leave you to imagine," said Morley, pathetically, "how it desolates me to forego the pleasure. But my friend Carruthers, of the New York Yacht Club, is to pick me up here in his motor car at 8."

The white plume tossed, and the quartet danced like midges around an arc light down the frolicsome way.

Morley stood, turning over and over the dime in his pocket and laughing gleefully to himself.

"'Front,'" he chanted under his breath; "'front' does it. It is trumps in the game. How they take it in! Men, women, and children—forgeries, water-and-salt lies—how they all take it in!"

An old man with an ill-fitting suit, a straggling gray beard, and a corpulent umbrella hopped from the conglomeration of cabs and street cars to the sidewalk at Morley's side.

"Stranger," said he, "excuse me for troubling you, but do you know anybody in this here town named Solomon Smothers? He's my son, and I've come down from Ellenville to visit him. Be darned if I know what I done with his street and number."

"I do not, sir," said Morley, half closing his eyes to veil the joy in them. "You had better apply to the police."

"The police!" said the old man. "I ain't done nothin' to call in the police about. I just come down to see Ben. He lives in a five-story house, he writes me. If you know anybody by that name and could——"

"I told you I did not," said Morley, coldly. "I know no one by the name of Smithers, and I advise you to——"

"Smothers not Smithers," interrupted the old man, hopefully. "A heavy-set man, sandy complected, about twenty-nine, two front teeth out, above five-foot——"

"Oh, 'Smothers!'" exclaimed Morley. "Sol Smothers? Why, he lives in the next house to me. I thought you said 'Smithers.'"

Morley looked at his watch. You must have a watch. You can do it for a dollar. Better go hungry than forego a gunmetal or the ninety-eight-cent one that the railroads—according to these watchmakers—are run by.

"The Bishop of Long Island," said Morley, "was to meet me here at 8 to dine with me at the Kingfishers' Club. But I can't leave the father of my friend Sol Smothers alone on the street. By St. Swithin, Mr. Smothers, we Wall Street men have to work! Tired is no name for it! I was about to step across to the other corner and have a glass of ginger ale with a dash of sherry when you approached me. You must let me take you to Sol's house, Mr. Smothers. But before we take the car I hope you will join me in——"

An hour later Morley seated himself on the end of a quiet bench in Madison Square, with a twenty-five-cent cigar between his lips and $140 in deeply creased bills in his inside pocket. Content, light-hearted, ironical, keenly philosophic, he watched the moon drifting in and out amidst a maze of flying clouds. An old, ragged man with a low-bowed head sat at the other end of the bench.

Presently the old man stirred and looked at his bench companion. In Morley's appearance he seemed to recognize something superior to the usual nightly occupants of the benches.

"Kind sir," he whined, "if you could spare a dime or even a few pennies to one who——"

Morley cut short his stereotyped appeal by throwing him a dollar.

"God bless you!" said the old man. "I've been trying to find work for—"

"Work!" echoed Morley with his ringing laugh. "You are a fool, my friend. The world is a rock to you, no doubt; but you must be an Aaron and smite it with your rod. Then things better than water will gush out of it for you. That is what the world is for. It gives to me whatever I want from it."

"God has blessed you," said the old man. "It is only work that I have known. And now I can get no more."

"I must go home," said Morley, rising and buttoning his coat. "I stopped here only for a smoke. I hope you may find work."

"May your kindness be rewarded this night," said the old man.

"Oh," said Morley, "you have your wish already. I am satisfied. I think good luck follows me like a dog. I am for yonder bright hotel across the square for the night. And what a moon that is lighting up the city to-night. I think no one enjoys the moonlight and such little things as I do. Well, a good-night to you."

Morley walked to the corner where he would cross to his hotel. He blew slow streams of smoke from his cigar heavenward. A policeman passing saluted to his benign nod. What a fine moon it was.

The clock struck nine as a girl just entering womanhood stopped on the corner waiting for the approaching car. She was hurrying as if home-ward from employment or delay. Her eyes were clear and pure, she was dressed in simple white, she looked eagerly for the car and neither to the right nor the left.

Morley knew her. Eight years before he had sat on the same bench with her at school. There had been no sentiment between them—nothing but the friendship of innocent days.

But he turned down the side street to a quiet spot and laid his suddenly burning face against the cool iron of a lamp-post, and said dully:

"God! I wish I could die."

THE BUYER FROM CACTUS CITY

It is well that hay fever and colds do not obtain in the healthful vicinity of Cactus City, Texas, for the dry goods emporium of Navarro & Platt, situated there, is not to be sneezed at.

Twenty thousand people in Cactus City scatter their silver coin with liberal hands for the things that their hearts desire. The bulk of this semi-precious metal goes to Navarro & Platt. Their huge brick building covers enough ground to graze a dozen head of sheep. You can buy of them a rattlesnake-skin necktie, an automobile, or an eighty-five dollar, latest style, lady's tan coat in twenty different shades. Navarro & Platt first introduced pennies west of the Colorado River. They had been ranchmen with business heads, who saw that the world did not necessarily have to cease its revolutions after free grass went out.

Every Spring, Navarro, senior partner, fifty-five, half-Spanish, cosmopolitan, able, polished, had "gone on" to New York to buy goods. This year he shied at taking up the long trail. He was undoubtedly growing older; and he looked at his watch several times a day before the hour came for his siesta.

"John," he said, to his junior partner, "you shall go on this year to buy the goods."

Platt looked tired.

"I'm told," said he, "that New York is a plumb dead town; but I'll go. I can take a whirl in San Antone for a few days on my way and have some fun."

Two weeks later a man in a Texas full dress suit—black frock coat, broad-brimmed soft white hat, and lay-down collar 3-4 inch high, with black, wrought-iron necktie—entered the wholesale cloak and suit establishment of Zizzbaum & Son, on lower Broadway.

Old Zizzbaum had the eye of an osprey, the memory of an elephant, and a mind that unfolded from him in three movements like the puzzle of the carpenter's rule. He rolled to the front like a brunette polar bear, and shook Platt's hand.

"And how is the good Mr. Navarro in Texas?" he said. "The trip was too long for him this year, so? We welcome Mr. Platt instead."

"A bull's eye," said Platt, "and I'd give forty acres of unirrigated Pecos County land to know how you did it."

"I knew," grinned Zizzbaum, "just as I know that the rainfall in El Paso for the year was 28.5 inches, or an increase of 15 inches, and that therefore Navarro & Platt will buy a $15,000 stock of suits this spring instead of $10,000, as in a dry year. But that will be to-morrow. There is first a cigar in my private office that will remove from your mouth the taste of the ones you smuggled across the Rio Grande and like—because they are smuggled."

It was late in the afternoon and business for the day had ended. Zizzbaum left Platt with a half-smoked cigar, and came out of the private office to Son, who was arranging his diamond scarfpin before a mirror, ready to leave.

"Abey," he said, "you will have to take Mr. Platt around to-night and show him things. They are customers for ten years. Mr. Navarro and I we played chess every moment of spare time when he came. That is good, but Mr. Platt is a young man and this is his first visit to New York. He should amuse easily."

"All right," said Abey, screwing the guard tightly on his pin. "I'll take him on. After he's seen the Flatiron and the head waiter at the Hotel Astor and heard the phonograph play 'Under the Old Apple Tree' it'll be half-past ten, and Mr. Texas will be ready to roll up in his blanket. I've got a supper engagement at 11:30, but he'll be all to the Mrs. Winslow before then."

The next morning at 10 Platt walked into the store ready to do business. He had a bunch of hyacinths pinned on his lapel. Zizzbaum himself waited on him. Navarro & Platt were good customers, and never failed to take their discount for cash.

"And what did you think of our little town?" asked Zizzbaum, with the fatuous smile of the Manhattanite.

"I shouldn't care to live in it," said the Texan. "Your son and I knocked around quite a little last night. You've got good water, but Cactus City is better lit up."

"We've got a few lights on Broadway, don't you think, Mr. Platt?"

"And a good many shadows," said Platt. "I think I like your horses best. I haven't seen a crowbait since I've been in town."

Zizzbaum led him upstairs to show the samples of suits.

"Ask Miss Asher to come," he said to a clerk.

Miss Asher came, and Platt, of Navarro & Platt, felt for the first time the wonderful bright light of romance and glory descend upon him. He stood still as a granite cliff above the cañon of the Colorado, with his wide-open eyes fixed upon her. She noticed his look and flushed a little, which was contrary to her custom.

Miss Asher was the crack model of Zizzbaum & Son. She was of the blond type known as "medium," and her measurements even went the required 38-25-42 standard a little better. She had been at Zizzbaum's two years, and knew her business. Her eye was bright, but cool; and had she chosen to match her gaze against the optic of the famed basilisk, that fabulous monster's gaze would have wavered and softened first. Incidentally, she knew buyers.

"Now, Mr. Platt," said Zizzbaum, "I want you to see these princess gowns in the light shades. They will be the thing in your climate. This first, if you please, Miss Asher."

Swiftly in and out of the dressing-room the prize model flew, each time wearing a new costume and looking more stunning with every change. She posed with absolute self-possession before the stricken buyer, who stood, tongue-tied and motionless, while Zizzbaum orated oilily of the styles. On the model's face was her faint, impersonal professional smile that seemed to cover something like weariness or contempt.

When the display was over Platt seemed to hesitate. Zizzbaum was a little anxious, thinking that his customer might be inclined to try elsewhere. But Platt was only looking over in his mind the best building sites in Cactus City, trying to select one on which to build a house for his wife-to-be—who was just then in the dressing-room taking off an evening gown of lavender and tulle.

"Take your time, Mr. Platt," said Zizzbaum. "Think it over to-night. You won't find anybody else meet our prices on goods like these. I'm afraid you're having a dull time in New York, Mr. Platt. A young man like you—of course, you miss the society of the ladies. Wouldn't you like a nice young lady to take out to dinner this evening? Miss Asher, now, is a very nice young lady; she will make it agreeable for you."

"Why, she doesn't know me," said Platt, wonderingly. "She doesn't know anything about me. Would she go? I'm not acquainted with her."

"Would she go?" repeated Zizzbaum, with uplifted eyebrows. "Sure, she would go. I will introduce you. Sure, she would go."

He called Miss Asher loudly.

She came, calm and slightly contemptuous, in her white shirt waist and plain black skirt.

"Mr. Platt would like the pleasure of your company to dinner this evening," said Zizzbaum, walking away.

"Sure," said Miss Asher, looking at the ceiling. "I'd be much pleased. Nine-eleven West Twentieth Street. What time?"

"Say seven o'clock."

"All right, but please don't come ahead of time. I room with a school teacher, and she doesn't allow any gentleman to call in the room. There isn't any parlor, so you'll have to wait in the hall. I'll be ready."

At half-past seven Platt and Miss Asher sat at a table in a Broadway restaurant. She was dressed in a plain, filmy black. Platt didn't know that it was all a part of her day's work.

With the unobtrusive aid of a good waiter he managed to order a respectable dinner, minus the usual Broadway preliminaries.

Miss Asher flashed upon him a dazzling smile.

"Mayn't I have something to drink?" she asked.

"Why, certainly," said Platt. "Anything you want."

"A dry Martini," she said to the waiter.

When it was brought and set before her Platt reached over and took it away.

"What is this?" he asked.

"A cocktail, of course."

"I thought it was some kind of tea you ordered. This is liquor. You can't drink this. What is your first name?"

"To my intimate friends," said Miss Asher, freezingly, "it is 'Helen.' "

"Listen, Helen," said Platt, leaning over the table. "For many years every time the spring flowers blossomed out on the prairies I got to thinking of somebody that I'd never seen or heard of. I knew it was you the minute I saw you yesterday. I'm going back home to-morrow, and you're going with me. I know it, for I saw it in your eyes when you first looked at me. You needn't kick, for you've got to fall into line. Here's a little trick I picked out for you on my way over."

He flicked a two-carat diamond solitaire ring across the table. Miss Asher flipped it back to him with her fork.

"Don't get fresh," she said, severely.

"I'm worth a hundred thousand dollars," said Platt. "I'll build you the finest house in west Texas."

"You can't buy me, Mr. Buyer," said Miss Asher, "if you had a hundred million. I didn't think I'd have to call you down. You didn't look like the others to me at first, but I see you're all alike."

"All who?" asked Platt.

"All you buyers. You think because we girls have to go out to dinner with you or lose our jobs that you're privileged to say what you please. Well, forget it. I thought you were different from the others, but I see I was mistaken."

Platt struck his fingers on the table with a gesture of sudden, illuminating satisfaction.

"I've got it!" he exclaimed, almost hilariously—"the Nicholson place, over on the north side. There's a big grove of live oaks and a natural lake. The old house can be pulled down and the new one set further back."

"Put out your pipe," said Miss Asher. "I'm sorry to wake you up, but you fellows might as well get wise, once for all, to where you stand. I'm supposed to go to dinner with you and help jolly you along so you'll trade with old Zizzy, but don't expect to find me in any of the suits you buy."

"Do you mean to tell me," said Platt, "that you go out this way with customers, and they all—they all talk to you like I have?"

"They all make plays," said Miss Asher. "But I must say that you've got 'em beat in one respect. They generally talk diamonds, while you've actually dug one up."

"How long have you been working, Helen?"

"Got my name pat, haven't you? I've been supporting myself for eight years. I was a cash girl and a wrapper and then a shop girl until I was grown, and then I got to be a suit model. Mr. Texas Man, don't you think a little wine would make this dinner a little less dry?"

"You're not going to drink wine any more, dear. It's awful to think how —— I'll come to the store to-morrow and get you. I want you to pick out an automobile before we leave. That's all we need to buy here."

"Oh, cut that out. If you knew how sick I am of hearing such talk."

After the dinner they walked down Broadway and came upon Diana's little wooded park. The trees caught Platt's eye at once, and he must turn along under the winding walk beneath them. The lights shone upon two bright tears in the model's eyes.

"I don't like that," said Platt. "What's the matter?"

"Don't you mind," said Miss Asher. "Well, it's because—well, I didn't think you were that kind when I first saw you. But you are all alike. And now will you take me home, or will I have to call a cop?"

Platt took her to the door of her boarding-house. They stood for a minute in the vestibule. She looked at him with such scorn in her eyes that even his heart of oak began to waver. His arm was halfway around her waist, when she struck him a stinging blow on the face with her open hand.

As he stepped back a ring fell from somewhere and bounded on the tiled floor. Platt groped for it and found it.

"Now, take your useless diamond and go, Mr. Buyer," she said.

"This was the other one—the wedding ring," said the Texan, holding the smooth gold band on the palm of his hand.

Miss Asher's eyes blazed upon him in the half darkness.

"Was that what you meant?—did you——"

Somebody opened the door from inside the house.

"Good-night," said Platt. "I'll see you at the store to-morrow."

Miss Asher ran up to her room and shook the school teacher until she sat up in bed ready to scream "Fire!"

"Where is it?" she cried.

"That's what I want to know," said the model. "You've studied geography, Emma, and you ought to know. Where is a town called Cac—Cac—Carac—Caracas City, I think they called it?"

"How dare you wake me up for that?" said the school teacher. "Caracas is in Venezuela, of course."

"What's it like?"

"Why, it's principally earthquakes and Negroes and monkeys and malarial fever and volcanoes."

"I don't care," said Miss Asher, blithely; "I'm going there tomorrow."

THE BADGE OF POLICEMAN O'ROON

It cannot be denied that men and women have looked upon one another for the first time and become instantly enamored. It is a risky process, this love at first sight, before she has seen him in Bradstreet or he has seen her in curl papers. But these things do happen; and one instance must form a theme for this story—though not, thank Heaven, to the overshadowing of more vital and important subjects, such as drink, policemen, horses, and earldoms.

During a certain war a troop calling itself the Gentle Riders rode into history and one or two ambuscades. The Gentle Riders were recruited from the aristocracy of the wild men of the West and the wild men of the aristocracy of the East. In khaki there is little telling them one from another, so they became good friends and comrades all around.

Ellsworth Remsen, whose old Knickerbocker descent atoned for his modest rating at only ten millions, ate his canned beef gayly by the camp-fires of the Gentle Riders. The war was a great lark to him, so that he scarcely regretted polo and planked shad.

One of the troopers was a well-set-up, affable, cool young man, who called himself O'Roon. To this young man Remsen took an especial liking. The two rode side by side during the famous mooted up-hill charge that was disputed so hotly at the time by the Spaniards and afterward by the Democrats.

After the war Remsen came back to his polo and shad. One day a well-set-up, affable, cool young man disturbed him at his club, and he and O'Roon were soon pounding each other and exchanging opprobrious epithets after the manner of long-lost friends. O'Roon looked seedy and out of luck and perfectly contented. But it seemed that his content was only apparent.

"Get me a job, Remsen," he said. "I've just handed a barber my last shilling."

"No trouble at all," said Remsen. "I know a lot of men who have banks and stores and things downtown. Any particular line you fancy?"

"Yes," said O'Roon, with a look of interest. "I took a walk in your Central Park this morning. I'd like to be one of those bobbies on horseback. That would be about the ticket. Besides, it's the only thing I could do. I can ride a little and the fresh air suits me. Think you could land that for me?"

Remsen was sure that he could. And in a very short time he did. And they who were not above looking at mounted policemen might have seen a well-set-up, affable, cool young man on a prancing chestnut steed attending to his duties along the driveways of the park.

And now at the extreme risk of wearying old gentlemen who carry leather fob chains, and elderly ladies who—but no! grandmother herself yet thrills at foolish, immortal Romeo—there must be a hint of love at first sight.

It came just as Remsen was strolling into Fifth Avenue from his club a few doors away.

A motor car was creeping along foot by foot, impeded by a freshet of vehicles that filled the street. In the car was a chauffeur and an old gentleman with snowy side whiskers and a Scotch plaid cap which could not be worn while automobiling except by a personage. Not even a wine agent would dare do it. But these two were of no consequence—except, perhaps, for the guiding of the machine and the paying for it. At the old gentleman's side sat a young lady more beautiful than pomegranate blossoms, more exquisite than the first quarter moon viewed at twilight through the tops of oleanders. Remsen saw her and knew his fate. He could have flung himself under the very wheels that conveyed her, but he knew that would be the last means of attracting the attention of those who ride in motor cars. Slowly the auto passed, and, if we place the poets above the autoists, carried the heart of Remsen with it. Here was a large city of millions, and many women who at a certain distance appear to resemble pomegranate blossoms. Yet he hoped to see her again; for each one fancies that his romance has its own tutelary guardian and divinity.

Luckily for Remsen's peace of mind there came a diversion in the guise of a reunion of the Gentle Riders of the city. There were not many of them—perhaps a score—and there was wassail and things to eat, and speeches and the Spaniard was bearded again in recapitulation. And when daylight threatened them the survivors prepared to depart. But some remained upon the battlefield. One of these was Trooper O'Roon, who was not seasoned to potent liquids. His legs declined to fulfil the obligations they had sworn to the police department.

"I'm stewed, Remsen," said O'Roon to his friend. "Why do they build hotels that go round and round like catherine wheels? They'll take away my shield and break me. I can think and talk con-con-consec-sec-secutively, but I s-s-stammer with my feet. I've got to go on duty in three hours. The jig is up, Remsen. The jig is up, I tell you."

"Look at me," said Remsen, who was his smiling self, pointing to his own face; "whom do you see here?"

"Goo' fellow," said O'Roon, dizzily. "Goo' old Remsen."

"Not so," said Remsen. "You see Mounted Policeman O'Roon. Look at your face—no; you can't do that without a glass—but look at mine, and think of yours. How much alike are we? As two French *table d'hôte* dinners. With your badge, on your horse, in your uniform, will I charm nurse-maids and prevent the grass from growing under people's feet in the Park this day. I will have your badge and your honor, besides having the jolliest lark I've been blessed with since we licked Spain."

Promptly on time the counterfeit presentment of Mounted Policeman O'Roon single-footed into the Park on his chestnut steed. In a uniform two men who are unlike will look alike; two who somewhat resemble each other in feature and figure will appear as twin brothers. So Remsen trotted down the bridle paths, enjoying himself hugely, so few real pleasures do ten-millionaires have.

Along the driveway in the early morning spun a victoria drawn by a pair of fiery bays. There was something foreign about the affair, for the Park is rarely used in the morning, except by unimportant people who love to be healthy, poor, and wise. In the vehicle sat an old gentleman with snowy side-whiskers and a Scotch plaid cap which could not be worn while driving except by a personage. At his side sat the lady of Remsen's heart—the lady who looked like pomegranate blossoms and the gibbous moon.

Remsen met them coming. At the instant of their passing her eyes looked into his, and but for the ever coward's heart of a true lover he could have sworn that she flushed a faint pink. He trotted on for twenty yards, and then wheeled his horse at the sound of runaway hoofs. The bays had bolted.

Remsen sent his chestnut after the victoria like a shot. There was work cut out for the impersonator of Policeman O'Roon. The chestnut ranged alongside the off bay thirty seconds after the chase began, rolled his eye back at Remsen, and said in the only manner open to policemen's horses:

"Well, you duffer, are you going to do your share? You're not O'Roon, but it seems to me if you'd lean to the right you could reach the reins of that foolish slow-running bay—ah! you're all right; O'Roon couldn't have done it more neatly!"

The runaway team was tugged to an inglorious halt by Remsen's tough muscles. The driver released his hands from the wrapped reins, jumped from his seat and stood at the heads of the team. The chestnut, approving his new rider, danced and pranced, reviling equinely the subdued bays. Remsen, lingering, was dimly conscious of a vague, impossible, unnecessary old gentleman in a Scotch cap who talked incessantly about something. And he was acutely conscious of a pair of violet eyes that would have drawn Saint Pyrites from his iron pillar—or whatever the allusion is—and of the lady's smile and look—a little frightened, but a look that, with the ever coward heart of a true lover, he could not yet construe.

They were asking his name and bestowing upon him well-bred thanks for his heroic deed, and the Scotch cap was especially babbling and insistent. But the eloquent appeal was in the eyes of the lady.

A little thrill of satisfaction ran through Remsen, because he had a name to give which, without undue pride, was worthy of being spoken in high places, and a small fortune which, with due pride, he could leave at his end without disgrace.

He opened his lips to speak and closed them again.

Who was he? Mounted Policeman O'Roon. The badge and the honor of his comrade were in his hands. If Ellsworth Remsen, ten-millionaire and Knickerbocker, had just rescued pomegranate blossoms and Scotch cap from possible death, where was Policeman O'Roon? Off his beat, exposed, disgraced, discharged. Love had come, but before that there had been something that demanded precedence—the fellowship of men on battlefields fighting an alien foe.

Remsen touched his cap, looked between the chestnut's ears, and took refuge in vernacularity.

"Don't mention it," he said, stolidly. "We policemen are paid to do these things. It's our duty."

And he rode away—rode away cursing *noblesse oblige,* but knowing he could never have done anything else.

At the end of the day Remsen sent the chestnut to his stable and went to O'Roon's room. The policeman was again a well-set-up, affable, cool young man who sat by the window smoking cigars.

"I wish you and the rest of the police force and all badges, horses, brass buttons, and men who can't drink two glasses of *brut* without getting upset were at the devil," said Remsen, feelingly.

O'Roon smiled with evident satisfaction.

"Good old Remsen," he said, affably, "I know all about it. They trailed me down and cornered me here two hours ago. There was a little row at home, you know, and I cut sticks just to show them. I don't believe I told you that my Governor was the Earl of Ardsley. Funny you should bob against them in the Park. If you damaged that horse of mine I'll never forgive you. I'm going to buy him and take him back with me. Oh, yes, and I think my sister—Lady Angela, you know—wants particularly for you to come up to the hotel with me this evening. Didn't lose my badge, did you, Remsen? I've got to turn that in at Headquarters when I resign."

BRICKDUST ROW

Blinker was displeased. A man of less culture and poise and wealth would have sworn. But Blinker always remembered that he was a gentleman—

a thing that no gentleman should do. So he merely looked bored and sardonic while he rode in a hansom to the centre of disturbance, which was the Broadway office of Lawyer Oldport, who was agent for the Blinker estate.

"I don't see," said Blinker, "why I should be always signing confounded papers. I am packed, and was to have left for the North Woods this morning. Now I must wait until to-morrow morning. I hate night trains. My best razors are, of course, at the bottom of some unidentifiable trunk. It is a plot to drive me to bay rum and a monologuing, thumb-handed barber. Give me a pen that doesn't scratch. I hate pens that scratch."

"Sit down," said double-chinned, gray Lawyer Oldport. "The worst has not been told you. Oh, the hardships of the rich! The papers are not yet ready to sign. They will be laid before you to-morrow at eleven. You will miss another day. Twice shall the barber tweak the helpless nose of a Blinker. Be thankful that your sorrows do not embrace a haircut."

"If," said Blinker, rising, "the act did not involve more signing of papers I would take my business out of your hands at once. Give me a cigar, please."

"If," said Lawyer Oldport, "I had cared to see an old friend's son gulped down at one mouthful by sharks I would have ordered you to take it away long ago. Now, let's quit fooling, Alexander. Besides the grinding task of signing your name some thirty times to-morrow, I must impose upon you the consideration of a matter of business—of business, and I may say humanity or right. I spoke to you about this five years ago, but you would not listen—you were in a hurry for a coaching trip, I think. The subject has come up again. The property——"

"Oh, property!" interrupted Blinker. "Dear Mr. Oldport, I think you mentioned to-morrow. Let's have it all at one dose to-morrow—signatures and property and snappy rubber bands and that smelly sealing-wax and all. Have luncheon with me? Well, I'll try to remember to drop in at eleven to-morrow. Morning."

The Blinker wealth was in lands, tenements, and hereditaments, as the legal phrase goes. Lawyer Oldport had once taken Alexander in his little pulmonary gasoline runabout to see the many buildings and rows of buildings that he owned in the city. For Alexander was sole heir. They had amused Blinker very much. The houses looked so incapable of producing the big sums of money that Lawyer Oldport kept piling up in banks for him to spend.

In the evening Blinker went to one of his clubs, intending to dine. Nobody was there except some old fogies playing whist who spoke to him with grave politeness and glared at him with savage contempt. Everybody was out of town. But here he was kept in like a schoolboy to write his name over and over on pieces of paper. His wounds were deep.

Blinker turned his back on the fogies, and said to the club steward who

had come forward with some nonsense about cold fresh salmon roe:
"Symons, I'm going to Coney Island." He said it as one might say:
"All's off, I'm going to jump into the river."

The joke pleased Symons. He laughed within a sixteenth of a note of
the audibility permitted by the laws governing employees.

"Certainly, sir," he tittered. "Of course, sir, I think I can see you at
Coney, Mr. Blinker."

Blinker got a paper and looked up the movements of Sunday steamboats. Then he found a cab at the first corner and drove to a North River
pier. He stood in line, as democratic as you or I, and bought a ticket, and
was trampled upon and shoved forward until, at last, he found himself
on the upper deck of the boat staring brazenly at a girl who sat alone
upon a camp stool. But Blinker did not intend to be brazen; the girl was
so wonderfully good looking that he forgot for one minute that he was
the prince incog, and behaved just as he did in society.

She was looking at him, too, and not severely. A puff of wind threatened Blinker's straw hat. He caught it warily and settled it again. The
movement gave the effect of a bow. The girl nodded and smiled, and
in another instant he was seated at her side. She was dressed all in white,
she was paler than Blinker imagined milkmaids and girls of humble stations to be, but she was as tidy as a cherry blossom, and her steady, supremely frank gray eyes looked out from the intrepid depths of an un-
shadowed and untroubled soul.

"How dare you raise your hat to me?" she asked, with a smile-re-
deemed severity.

"I didn't," Blinker said, but he quickly covered the mistake by extending it to "I didn't know how to keep from it after I saw you."

"I do not allow gentlemen to sit by me to whom I have not been introduced," she said with a sudden haughtiness that deceived him. He
rose reluctantly, but her clear, teasing laugh brought him down to his
chair again.

"I guess you weren't going far," she declared, with beauty's magnificent self-confidence.

"Are you going to Coney Island?" asked Blinker.

"Me?" She turned upon him wide-open eyes full of bantering surprise.
"Why, what a question! Can't you see that I'm riding a bicycle in the
park?" Her drollery took the form of impertinence.

"And I'm laying bricks on a tall factory chimney," said Blinker. "Mayn't
we see Coney together? I'm all alone and I've never been there before."

"It depends," said the girl, "on how nicely you behave. I'll consider
your application until we get there."

Blinker took pains to provide against the rejection of his application.
He strove to please. To adopt the metaphor of his nonsensical phrase, he
laid brick upon brick on the tall chimney of his devoirs until, at length,

the structure was stable and complete. The manners of the best society come around finally to simplicity; and as the girl's way was that naturally, they were on a mutual plane of communication from the beginning.

He learned that she was twenty, and her name was Florence; that she trimmed hats in a millinery shop; that she lived in a furnished room with her best chum Ella, who was cashier in a shoe store; and that a glass of milk from the bottle on the window-sill and an egg that boils itself while you twist up your hair makes a breakfast good enough for any one. Florence laughed when she heard "Blinker."

"Well," she said. "It certainly shows that you have imagination. It gives the 'Smiths' a chance for a little rest, anyhow."

They landed at Coney, and were dashed on the crest of a great human wave of mad pleasure-seekers into the walks and avenues of Fairyland gone into vaudeville.

With a curious eye, a critical mind, and a fairly withheld judgment Blinker considered the temples, pagodas and kiosks of popularized delights. Hoi polloi trampled, hustled, and crowded him. Basket parties bumped him; sticky children tumbled, howling, under his feet, candying his clothes. Insolent youths strolling among the booths with hard-won canes under one arm and easily won girls on the other, blew defiant smoke from cheap cigars into his face. The publicity gentlemen with megaphones, each before his own stupendous attraction, roared like Niagara in his ears. Music of all kinds that could be tortured from brass, reed, hide, or string, fought in the air to gain space for its vibrations against its competitors. But what held Blinker in awful fascination was the mob, the multitude, the proletariat shrieking, struggling, hurrying, panting, hurling itself in incontinent frenzy, with unabashed abandon, into the ridiculous sham palaces of trumpery and tinsel pleasures. The vulgarity of it, its brutal overriding of all the tenets of repression and taste that were held by his caste, repelled him strongly.

In the midst of his disgust he turned and looked down at Florence by his side. She was ready with her quick smile and upturned, happy eyes, as bright and clear as the water in trout pools. The eyes were saying that they had the right to be shining and happy, for was their owner not with her (for the present) Man, her Gentleman Friend and holder of the keys to the enchanted city of fun.

Blinker did not read her look accurately, but by some miracle he suddenly saw Coney aright.

He no longer saw a mass of vulgarians seeking gross joys. He now looked clearly upon a hundred thousand true idealists. Their offenses were wiped out. Counterfeit and false though the garish joys of these spangled temples were, he perceived that deep under the gilt surface they offered saving and apposite balm and satisfaction to the restless human heart. Here, at least, was the husk of Romance, the empty but shining casque of Chivalry, the breath-catching though safe-guarded dip and flight of Adventure, the magic carpet that transports you to the realms of fairy-land, though its journey be through but a few poor yards of space. He no longer saw a rabble, but his brothers seeking the ideal. There was no magic of poesy here or of art; but the glamour of their imagination turned yellow calico into cloth of gold and the megaphone into the silver trumpets of joy's heralds.

Almost humbled, Blinker rolled up the shirt sleeves of his mind and joined the idealists.

"You are the lady doctor," he said to Florence. "How shall we go about doing this jolly conglomeration of fairy tales, incorporated?"

"We will begin there," said the Princess, pointing to a fun pagoda on the edge of the sea, "and we will take them all in, one by one."

They caught the eight o'clock returning boat and sat, filled with pleasant fatigue, against the rail in the bow, listening to the Italians' fiddle and harp. Blinker had thrown off all care. The North Woods seemed to him an uninhabitable wilderness. What a fuss he had made over signing his name—pooh! he could sign it a hundred times. And her name was as pretty as she was—"Florence," he said it to himself a great many times.

As the boat was nearing its pier in the North River a two-funnelled, drab, foreign-looking sea-going steamer was dropping down toward the bay. The boat turned its nose in towards its slip. The steamer veered as if to seek mid-stream, and then yawed, seemed to increase its speed and struck the Coney boat on the side near the stern, cutting into it with a terrifying shock and crash.

While the six hundred passengers on the boat were mostly tumbling about the decks in a shrieking panic the captain was shouting at the steamer that it should not back off and leave the rent exposed for the water to enter. But the steamer tore its way out like a savage sawfish and cleaved its heartless way, full speed ahead.

The boat began to sink at its stern, but moved slowly toward the slip. The passengers were a frantic mob, unpleasant to behold.

Blinker held Florence tightly until the boat had righted itself. She made no sound or sign of fear. He stood on a camp stool, ripped off the slats above his head and pulled down a number of the life preservers. He began to buckle one around Florence. The rotten canvas split and the fraudulent granulated cork came pouring out in a stream. Florence caught a handful of it and laughed gleefully.

"It looks like breakfast food," she said. "Take it off. They're no good."

She unbuckled it and threw it on the deck. She made Blinker sit down and sat by his side and put her hand in his. "What'll you bet we don't reach the pier all right?" she said, and began to hum a song.

And now the captain moved among the passengers and compelled order. The boat would undoubtedly make her slip, he said, and ordered the women and children to the bow, where they could land first. The boat, very low in the water at the stern, tried gallantly to make his promise good.

"Florence," said Blinker, as she held him close by an arm and hand, "I love you."

"That's what they all say," she replied, lightly.

"I am not one of 'they all,' " he persisted. "I never knew any one I could love before. I could pass my life with you and be happy every day. I am rich. I can make things all right for you."

"That's what they all say," said the girl again, weaving the words into her little, reckless song.

"Don't say that again," said Blinker in a tone that made her look at him in frank surprise.

"Why shouldn't I say it?" she asked, calmly. "They all do."

"Who are 'they'?" he asked, jealous for the first time in his existence.

"Why, the fellows I know."

"Do you know so many?"

"Oh, well, I'm not a wall flower," she answered with modest complacency.

"Where do you see these—these men? At your home?"

"Of course not. I meet them just as I did you. Sometimes on the boat, sometimes in the park, sometimes on the street. I'm a pretty good judge of a man. I can tell in a minute if a fellow is one who is likely to get fresh."

"What do you mean by 'fresh'?"

"Who try to kiss you—me, I mean."

"Do any of them try that?" asked Blinker, clenching his teeth.

"Sure. All men do. You know that."

"Do you allow them?"

"Some. Not many. They won't take you out anywhere unless you do."

She turned her head and looked searchingly at Blinker. Her eyes were as innocent as a child's. There was a puzzled look in them, as though she did not understand him.

"What's wrong about my meeting fellows?" she asked, wonderingly.

"Everything," he answered, almost savagely. "Why don't you entertain your company in the house where you live? Is it necessary to pick up Tom, Dick, and Harry on the streets?"

She kept her absolutely ingenuous eyes upon his.

"If you could see the place where I live you wouldn't ask that. I live in Brickdust Row. They call it that because there's red dust from the bricks crumbling over everything. I've lived there for more than four years. There's no place to receive company. You can't have anybody come to your room. What else is there to do? A girl has got to meet the men, hasn't she?"

"Yes," he said hoarsely. "A girl has got to meet a—has got to meet the men."

"The first time one spoke to me on the street," she continued, "I ran home and cried all night. But you get used to it. I meet a good many nice fellows at church. I go on rainy days and stand in the vestibule until one comes up with an umbrella. I wish there was a parlor, so I could ask you to call, Mr. Blinker—are you really sure it isn't 'Smith,' now?"

The boat landed safely. Blinker had a confused impression of walking with the girl through quiet crosstown streets until she stopped at a corner and held out her hand.

"I live just one more block over," she said. "Thank you for a very pleasant afternoon."

Blinker muttered something and plunged northward till he found a cab. A big, gray church loomed slowly at his right. Blinker shook his fist at it through the window.

"I gave you a thousand dollars last week," he cried under his breath, "and she meets them in your very doors. There is something wrong; there is something wrong."

At eleven the next day Blinker signed his name thirty times with a new pen provided by Lawyer Oldport.

"Now let me get to the woods," he said, surlily.

"You are not looking well," said Lawyer Oldport. "The trip will do you good. But listen, if you will, to that little matter of business of which I spoke to you yesterday, and also five years ago. There are some buildings, fifteen in number, of which there are new five-year leases to be signed. Your father contemplated a change in the lease provisions, but never made it. He intended that the parlors of these houses should not be sub-let, but that the tenants should be allowed to use them for reception rooms. These houses are in the shopping districts, and are mainly tenanted by young working girls. As it is they are forced to seek companionship outside. This row of red brick——"

Blinker interrupted him with a loud, discordant laugh.

"Brickdust Row for an even hundred," he cried. "And I own it. Have I guessed right?"

"The tenants have some such name for it," said Lawyer Oldport.

Blinker arose and jammed his hat down to his eyes.

"Do what you please with it," he said, harshly. "Remodel it, burn it, raze it to the ground. But, man, it's too late, I tell you. It's too late. It's too late. It's too late."

THE MAKING OF A NEW YORKER

Besides many things, Raggles was a poet. He was called a tramp; but that was only an elliptical way of saying that he was a philosopher, an artist, a traveller, a naturalist, and a discoverer. But most of all he was a poet. In all his life he never wrote a line of verse; he lived his poetry. His Odyssey would have been a Limerick, had it been written. But, to linger with the primary proposition, Raggles was a poet.

Raggles's specialty, had he been driven to ink and paper, would have been sonnets to the cities. He studied cities as women study their reflections in mirrors; as children study the glue and sawdust of a dislocated doll; as the men who write about wild animals study the cages in the zoo. A city to Raggles was not merely a pile of bricks and mortar, peopled by a certain number of inhabitants; it was a thing with soul characteristic and distinct; an individual conglomeration of life, with its own peculiar essence, flavor, and feeling. Two thousand miles to the north and south, east and west, Raggles wandered in poetic fervor, taking the cities to his breast. He footed it on dusty roads, or sped magnificently in freight cars, counting time as of no account. And when he had found the heart of a city and listened to its secret confession, he strayed on, restless, to another. Fickle Raggles!—but perhaps he had not met the civic corporation that could engage and hold his critical fancy.

Through the ancient poets we have learned that the cities are feminine. So they were to poet Raggles; and his mind carried a concrete and clear conception of the figure that symbolized and typified each one that he had wooed.

Chicago seemed to swoop down upon him with a breezy suggestion of Mrs. Partington, plumes and patchouli, and to disturb his rest with a soaring and beautiful song of future promise. But Raggles would awake to a sense of shivering cold and a haunting impression of ideals lost in a depressing aura of potato salad and fish.

Thus Chicago affected him. Perhaps there is a vagueness and inaccuracy in the description; but that is Raggles's fault. He should have recorded his sensations in magazine poems.

Pittsburg impressed him as the play of "Othello" performed in the Russian language in a railroad station by Dockstader's minstrels. A royal and generous lady this Pittsburg, though—homely, hearty, with flushed face, washing the dishes in a silk dress and white kid slippers, and bidding Raggles sit before the roaring fireplace and drink champagne with his pigs' feet and fried potatoes.

New Orleans had simply gazed down upon him from a balcony. He could see her pensive, starry eyes and catch the flutter of her fan, and that was all. Only once he came face to face with her. It was at dawn, when she was flushing the red bricks of the banquette with a pail of water. She laughed and hummed a chansonette and filled Raggles's shoes with ice-cold water. Allons!

Boston construed herself to the poetic Raggles in an erratic and singular way. It seemed to him that he had drunk cold tea and that the city was a white, cold cloth that had been bound tightly around his brow to spur him to some unknown but tremendous mental effort. And, after all, he came to shovel snow for a livelihood; and the cloth, becoming wet, tightened its knots and could not be removed.

Indefinite and unintelligible ideas, you will say; but your disapprobation should be tempered with gratitude, for these are poets' fancies—and suppose you had come upon them in verse!

One day Raggles came and laid siege to the heart of the great city of Manhattan. She was the greatest of all; and he wanted to learn her note in the scale; to taste and appraise and classify and solve and label her and arrange her with the other cities that had given him up the secret of their individuality. And here we cease to be Raggles's translator and become his chronicler.

Raggles landed from a ferry-boat one morning and walked into the core of the town with the blasé air of a cosmopolite. He was dressed with care to play the rôle of an "unidentified man." No country, race, class, clique, union, party clan, or bowling association could have claimed him. His clothing, which had been donated to him piece-meal by citizens of different height, but same number of inches around the heart, was not yet as uncomfortable to his figure as those specimens of raiment, self-measured, that are railroaded to you by transcontinental tailors with a suit case, suspenders, silk handkerchief and pearl studs as a bonus. Without money—as a poet should be—but with the ardor of an astronomer discovering a new star in the chorus of the milky way, or a man who has seen ink suddenly flow from his fountain pen, Raggles wandered into the great city.

Late in the afternoon he drew out of the roar and commotion with a look of dumb terror on his countenance. He was defeated, puzzled, discomfited, frightened. Other cities had been to him as long primer to read; as country maidens quickly to fathom; as send-price-of-subscription-with-answer rebuses to solve; as oyster cocktails to swallow; but here was one as cold, glittering, serene, impossible as a four-carat diamond in a window to a lover outside fingering damply in his pocket his ribbon-counter salary.

The greetings of the other cities he had known—their homespun kindliness, their human gamut of rough charity, friendly curses, garrulous curiosity, and easily estimated credulity or indifference. This city of

Manhattan gave him no clue; it was walled against him. Like a river of adamant it flowed past him in the streets. Never an eye was turned upon him; no voice spoke to him. His heart yearned for the clap of Pittsburg's sooty hand on his shoulder; for Chicago's menacing but social yawp in his ear; for the pale and eleemosynary stare through the Bostonian eye-glass—even for the precipitate but unmalicious boot-toe of Louisville or St. Louis.

On Broadway Raggles, successful suitor of many cities, stood, bashful, like any country swain. For the first time he experienced the poignant humiliation of being ignored. And when he tried to reduce this brilliant, swiftly changing, ice-cold city to a formula he failed utterly. Poet though he was, it offered him no color similes, no points of comparison, no flaw in its polished facets, no handle by which he could hold it up and view its shape and structure, as he familiarly and often contemptuously had done with other towns. The houses were interminable ramparts loop-holed for defence; the people were bright but bloodless spectres passing in sinister and selfish array.

The thing that weighed heaviest on Raggles's soul and clogged his poet's fancy was the spirit of absolute egotism that seemed to saturate the people as toys are saturated with paint. Each one that he considered appeared a monster of abominable and insolent conceit. Humanity was gone from them; they were toddling idols of stone and varnish, worship-ping themselves and greedy for though oblivious of worship from their fellow graven images. Frozen, cruel, implacable, impervious, cut to an identical pattern, they hurried on their ways like statues brought by some miracle to motion, while soul and feeling lay unaroused in the reluctant marble.

Gradually Raggles became conscious of certain types. One was an elderly gentleman with a snow-white, short beard, pink, unwrinkled face, and stony, sharp blue eyes, attired in the fashion of a gilded youth, who seemed to personify the city's wealth, ripeness and frigid unconcern. Another type was a woman, tall, beautiful, clear as a steel engraving, goddess-like, calm, clothed like the princesses of old, with eyes as coldly blue as the reflection of sunlight on a glacier. And another was a by-product of this town of marionettes—a broad, swaggering, grim, threaten-ingly sedate fellow, with a jowl as large as a harvested wheat field, the complexion of a baptized infant, and the knuckles of a prize-fighter. This type leaned against cigar signs and viewed the world with frappéd contumely.

A poet is a sensitive creature, and Raggles soon shriveled in the bleak embrace of the undecipherable. The chill, sphinx-like, ironical, illegible, unnatural, ruthless expression of the city left him downcast and bewil-dered. Had it no heart? Better the woodpile, the scolding of vinegar-faced housewives at back doors, the kindly spleen of bartenders behind provincial free-lunch counters, the amiable truculence of rural constables, the kicks, arrests, and happy-go-lucky chances of the other vulgar, loud, crude cities than this freezing heartlessness.

Raggles summoned his courage and sought alms from the populace. Unheeding, regardless, they passed on without the wink of an eyelash to testify that they were conscious of his existence. And then he said to himself that this fair but pitiless city of Manhattan was without a soul; that its inhabitants were mannikins moved by wires and springs, and that he was alone in a great wilderness.

Raggles started to cross the street. There was a blast, a roar, a hissing and a crash as something struck him and hurled him over and over six yards from where he had been. As he was coming down like the stick of a rocket the earth and all the cities thereof turned to a fractured dream.

Raggles opened his eyes. First an odor made itself known to him—an odor of the earliest spring flowers of Paradise. And then a hand soft as a falling petal touched his brow. Bending over him was the woman clothed like the princess of old, with blue eyes, now soft and humid with human sympathy. Under his head on the pavement were silks and furs. With Raggles's hat in his hand and with his face pinker than ever from a vehement outburst of oratory against reckless driving, stood the elderly gentleman who personified the city's wealth and ripeness. From a near-by café hurried the by-product with the vast jowl and baby complexion, bearing a glass full of crimson fluid that suggested delightful possibilities.

"Drink dis, sport," said the by-product, holding the glass to Raggles's lips.

Hundreds of people huddled around in a moment, their faces wearing the deepest concern. Two flattering and gorgeous policemen got into the circle and pressed back the overplus of Samaritans. An old lady in a black shawl spoke loudly of camphor; a newsboy slipped one of his papers beneath Raggles's elbow, where it lay on the muddy pavement. A brisk young man with a notebook was asking for names.

A bell clanged importantly, and the ambulance cleaned a lane through the crowd. A cool surgeon slipped into the midst of affairs.

"How do you feel, old man?" asked the surgeon, stooping easily to his task. The princess of silks and satins wiped a red drop or two from Raggles's brow with a fragrant cobweb.

"Me?" said Raggles, with a seraphic smile, "I feel fine."

He had found the heart of his new city.

In three days they let him leave his cot for the convalescent ward in the hospital. He had been in there an hour when the attendants heard sounds of conflict. Upon investigation they found that Raggles had assaulted and damaged a brother convalescent—a glowering transient whom a freight train collision had sent in to be patched up.

"What's all this about?" inquired the head nurse.

"He was runnin' down me town," said Raggles.

"What town?" asked the nurse.

"Noo York," said Raggles.

VANITY AND SOME SABLES

When "Kid" Brady was sent to the ropes by Molly McKeever's blue-black eyes he withdrew from the Stovepipe Gang. So much for the power of a colleen's blanderin' tongue and stubborn true-heartedness. If you are a man who read this, may such an influence be sent you before 2 o'clock to-morrow; if you are a woman, may your Pomeranian greet you this morning with a cold nose—a sign of doghealth and your happiness.

The Stovepipe Gang borrowed its name from a sub-district of the city called the "Stovepipe," which is a narrow and natural extension of the familiar district known as "Hell's Kitchen." The "Stovepipe" strip of town runs along Eleventh and Twelfth avenues on the river, and bends a hard and sooty elbow around little, lost homeless De Witt Clinton park. Consider that a stovepipe is an important factor in any kitchen and the situation is analyzed. The chefs in "Hell's Kitchen" are many, and the "Stovepipe" gang wears the cordon blue.

The members of this unchartered but widely known brotherhood appeared to pass their time on street corners arrayed like the lilies of the conservatory and busy with nail files and penknives. Thus displayed as a guarantee of good faith, they carried on an innocuous conversation in a 200-word vocabulary, to the casual observer as innocent and immaterial as that heard in the clubs seven blocks to the east.

But off exhibition the "Stovepipes" were not mere street corner ornaments addicted to posing and manicuring. Their serious occupation was the separating of citizens from their coin and valuables. Preferably this was done by weird and singular tricks without noise or bloodshed; but whenever the citizen honored by their attentions refused to impoverish himself gracefully, his objections came to be spread finally upon some police station blotter or hospital register.

The police held the "Stovepipe" gang in perpetual suspicion and respect. As the nightingale's liquid note is heard in the deepest shadows, so along the "Stovepipe's" dark and narrow confines the whistle for reserves punctures the dull ear of night. Whenever there was smoke in the "Stovepipe" the tasselled men in blue knew there was a fire in "Hell's Kitchen."

"Kid" Brady promised Molly to be good. "Kid" was the vainest, the strongest, the wariest, and the most successful plotter in the gang. Therefore, the boys were sorry to give him up.

But they witnessed his fall to a virtuous life without protest. For, in the Kitchen it is considered neither unmanly nor improper for a guy to do as his girl advises.

Black her eyes for love's sake, if you will; but it is all-to-the-good business to do a thing when she wants you to do it.

"Turn off the hydrant," said the Kid, one night when Molly, tearful, besought him to amend his ways. "I'm going to cut out the gang. You for mine, and the simple life on the side. I'll tell you, Moll—I'll get work; and in a year we'll get married. I'll do it for you. We'll get a flat and a flute, and a sewing machine and a rubber plant and live as honest as we can."

"Oh, Kid," sighed Molly, wiping the powder off his shoulder with her handkerchief, "I'd rather hear you say that than to own all of New York. And we can be happy on so little!"

The Kid looked down at his speckless cuffs and shining patent leathers with a suspicion of melancholy.

"It'll hurt hardest in the rags department," said he. "I've kind of always liked to rig out swell when I could. You know how I hate cheap things, Moll. This suit set me back sixty-five. Anything in the wearing apparel line has got to be just so, or it's to the misfit parlors for it, for mine. If I work I won't have so much coin to hand over to the little man with the big shears."

"Never mind, Kid. I'll like you just as much in a blue jumper as I would in a red automobile."

Before the Kid had grown large enough to knock out his father he had been compelled to learn the plumber's art. So now back to this honorable and useful profession he returned. But it was as an assistant that he engaged himself; and it is the master plumber and not the assistant, who wears diamonds as large as hailstones and looks contemptuously upon the marble colonnades of Senator Clark's mansion.

Eight months went by as smoothly and surely as though they had "elapsed" on a theatre program. The Kid worked away at his pipes and solder with no symptoms of backsliding. The Stovepipe gang continued its piracy on the high avenues, cracked policeman's heads, held up late travellers, invented new methods of peaceful plundering, copied Fifth Avenue's cut of clothes and neckwear fancies, and comported itself according to its lawless bylaws. But the Kid stood firm and faithful to his Molly, even though the polish was gone from his fingernails and it took him 15 minutes to tie his purple silk ascot so that the worn places would not show.

One evening he brought a mysterious bundle with him to Molly's house.

"Open that, Moll!" he said in his large, quiet way. "It's for you."

Molly's eager fingers tore off the wrappings. She shrieked aloud, and in rushed a sprinkling of little McKeevers, and Ma McKeever, dishwashy, but an undeniable relative of the late Mrs. Eve.

Again Molly shrieked, and something dark and long and sinuous flew and enveloped her neck like an anaconda.

"Russian sables," said the Kid, pridefully, enjoying the sight of Molly's round cheek against the clinging fur. "The real thing. They don't grow anything in Russia too good for you, Moll."

Molly plunged her hands into the muff, over-turned a row of the family infants, and flew to the mirror. Hint for the beauty column. To make bright eyes, rosy cheeks, and a bewitching smile: Recipe—one set Russian sables. Apply.

When they were alone Molly became aware of a small cake of the ice of common sense floating down the full tide of her happiness.

"You're a bird, all right, Kid," she admitted, gratefully. "I never had any furs on before in my life. But ain't Russian sables awful expensive? Seems to me I've heard they were."

"Have I ever chucked any bargain-sale stuff at you, Moll?" asked the Kid, with calm dignity. "Did you ever notice me leaning on the remnant counter or peering in the window of the five-and-ten? Call that scarf $250 and the muff $175 and you won't make any mistake about the price of Russian sables. The swell goods for me. Say, they look fine on you, Moll."

Molly hugged the sables to her bosom in rapture. And then her smile went away little by little, and she looked the Kid straight in the eye sadly and steadily.

He knew what every look of hers meant; and he laughed with a faint flush upon his face.

"Cut it out," he said, with affectionate roughness. "I told you I was done with that. I bought 'em and paid for 'em, all right, with my own money."

"Out of the money you worked for, Kid? Out of $75 a month?"

"Sure. I been saving up."

"Let's see—saved $425 in eight months, Kid?"

"Ah, let up," said the Kid, with some heat. "I had some money when I went to work. Do you think I've been holding 'em up again? I told you I'd quit. They're paid for on the square. Put 'em on and come out for a walk."

Molly calmed her doubts. Sables are soothing. Proud as a queen she went forth in the streets at the Kid's side. In all that region of low-lying streets Russian sables had never been seen before. The word sped, and the doors and windows blossomed with heads eager to see the swell furs Kid Brady had given his girl. All down the street there were "Oh's" and "Ah's" and the reported fabulous sum paid for the sables was passed from lip to lip, increasing as it went. At her right elbow sauntered the

Kid with the air of a prince. Work had not diminished his love of pomp and show and his passion for the costly and genuine. On a corner they saw a group of the Stovepipe Gang loafing, immaculate. They raised their hats to the Kid's girl and went on with their calm, unaccented palaver.

Three blocks behind the admired couple strolled Detective Ransom, of the Central office. Ransom was the only detective on the force who could walk abroad with safety in the Stovepipe district. He was fair dealing and unafraid and went there with the hypothesis that the inhabitants were human. Many liked him, and now and then would tip off to him something that he was looking for.

"What's the excitement down the street?" asked Ransom of a pale youth in a red sweater.

"Dey're out rubberin' at a set of buffalo robes Kid Brady staked his girl to," answered the youth. "Some say he paid $900 for de skins. Dey're swell all right enough."

"I hear Brady has been working at his old trade for nearly a year," said the detective. "He doesn't travel with the gang any more, does he?"

"He's workin', all right," said the red sweater, "but—say, sport, are you trailin' anything in the fur line? A job in a plumbin' shop don't match wid dem skins de Kid's girl's got on."

Ransom overtook the strolling couple on an empty street near the river bank. He touched the Kid's arm from behind.

"Let me see you a moment, Brady," he said, quietly. His eye rested for a second on the long fur scarf thrown stylishly back over Molly's left shoulder. The Kid, with his old-time police-hating frown on his face, stepped a yard or two aside with the detective.

"Did you go to Mrs. Hethcote's on West 7—th Street yesterday to fix a leaky water pipe?" asked Ransom.

"I did," said the Kid. "What of it?"

"The lady's $1,000 set of Russian sables went out of the house about the same time you did. The description fits the ones this lady has on."

"To h—Harlem with you," cried the Kid, angrily. "You know I've cut out that sort of thing, Ransom. I bought them sables yesterday at——"

The Kid stopped short.

"I know you've been working straight lately," said Ransom. "I'll give you every chance. I'll go with you where you say you bought the furs and investigate. The lady can wear 'em along with us and nobody'll be on. That's fair, Brady."

"Come on," agreed the Kid, hotly. And then he stopped suddenly in his tracks and looked with an odd smile at Molly's distressed and anxious face.

"No use," he said, grimly. "They're the Hethcote sables, all right. You'll have to turn 'em over, Moll, but they ain't too good for you if they cost a million."

Molly, with anguish in her face, hung upon the Kid's arm.

"Oh, Kiddy, you've broke my heart," she said. "I was so proud of you —and now they'll do you—and where's our happiness gone?"

"Go home," said the Kid, wildly. "Come on, Ransom—take the furs. Let's get away from here. Wait a minute—I've a good mind to—— No, I'll be d— if I can do it—run along, Moll—I'm ready, Ransom."

Around the corner of a lumber-yard came Policeman Kohen on his way to his beat along the river. The detective signed to him for assistance. Kohen joined the group. Ransom explained.

"Sure," said Kohen. "I hear about those saples dat vas stole. You say you have dem here?"

Policeman Kohen took the end of Molly's late scarf in his hands and looked at it closely.

"Once," he said, "I sold furs in Sixth Avenue. Yes, dese are saples. Dey came from Alaska. Dis scarf is vort $12 and dis muff——"

"Biff!" came the palm of the Kid's powerful hand upon the policeman's mouth. Kohen staggered and rallied. Molly screamed. The detective threw himself upon Brady and with Kohen's aid got the nippers on his wrist.

"The scarf is vort $12 and the muff is vort $9," persisted the policeman. "Vot is dis talk about $1,000 saples?"

The Kid sat upon a pile of lumber and his face turned dark red.

"Correct, Solomonski!" he declared, viciously. "I paid $21.50 for the set. I'd rather have got six months and not have told it. Me, the swell guy that wouldn't look at anything cheap! I'm a plain bluffer. Moll—my salary couldn't spell sables in Russian."

Molly cast herself upon his neck.

"What do I care for all the sables and money in the world," she cried. "It's my Kiddy I want. Oh, you dear, stuck-up, crazy blockhead!"

"You can take dose nippers off," said Kohen to the detective. "Before I leaf de station de report come in dat de lady vind her saples—hanging in her wardrobe. Young man, I excuse you dat punch in my vace—dis von time."

Ransom handed Molly her furs. Her eyes were smiling upon the Kid. She wound the scarf and threw the end over her left shoulder with a duchess's grace.

"A gouple of young vools," said Policeman Kohen to Ransom; "come on away."

THE SOCIAL TRIANGLE

At the stroke of six Ikey Snigglefritz laid down his goose. Ikey was a tailor's apprentice. Are there tailors' apprentices nowadays?

At any rate, Ikey toiled and snipped and basted and pressed and patched and sponged all day in the steamy fetor of a tailor-shop. But when work was done Ikey hitched his wagon to such stars as his firmament let shine.

It was Saturday night, and the boss laid twelve begrimed and begrudged dollars in his hand. Ikey dabbled discreetly in water, donned coat, hat and collar with its frazzled tie, and chalcedony pin, and set forth in pursuit of his ideals.

For each of us, when our day's work is done, must seek our ideal, whether it be love or pinochle or lobster à la Newburg, or the sweet silence of the musty bookshelves.

Behold Ikey as he ambles up the street beneath the roaring "El" between the rows of reeking sweatshops. Pallid, stooping, insignificant, squalid, doomed to exist forever in penury of body and mind, yet, as he swings his cheap cane and projects the noisome inhalations from his cigarette you perceive that he nurtures in his narrow bosom the bacillus of society.

Ikey's legs carried him to and into that famous place of entertainment known as the Café Maginnis—famous because it was the rendezvous of Billy McMahan, the greatest man, the most wonderful man, Ikey thought, that the world had ever produced.

Billy McMahan was the district leader. Upon him the Tiger purred, and his hand held manna to scatter. Now, as Ikey entered, McMahan stood, flushed and triumphant and mighty, the centre of a huzzaing concourse of his lieutenants and constituents. It seems there had been an election; a signal victory had been won; the city had been swept back into line by a resistless besom of ballots.

Ikey slunk along the bar and gazed, breath-quickened, at his idol.

How magnificent was Billy McMahan, with his great, smooth, laughing face; his gray eye, shrewd as a chicken hawk's; his diamond ring, his voice like a bugle call, his prince's air, his plump and active roll of money, his clarion call to friend and comrade—oh, what a king of men he was! How he obscured his lieutenants, though they themselves loomed large and serious, blue of chin and important of mien, with hands buried deep in the pockets of their short overcoats! But Billy—oh, what small avail are words to paint for you his glory as seen by Ikey Snigglefritz!

The Café Maginnis rang to the note of victory. The white-coated bartenders threw themselves featfully upon bottle, cork and glass. From a score of clear Havanas the air received its paradox of clouds. The leal and the hopeful shook Billy McMahan's hand. And there was born suddenly in the worshipful soul of Ikey Snigglefritz an audacious, thrilling impulse.

He stepped forward into the little cleared space in which majesty moved, and held out his hand.

Billy McMahan grasped it unhesitatingly, shook it and smiled.

Made mad now by the gods who were about to destroy him, Ikey threw away his scabbard and charged upon Olympus.

"Have a drink with me, Billy," he said familiarly, "you and your friends?"

"Don't mind if I do, old man," said the great leader, "just to keep the ball rolling."

The last spark of Ikey's reason fled.

"Wine," he called to the bartender, waving a trembling hand.

The corks of three bottles were drawn; the champagne bubbled in the long row of glasses set upon the bar. Billy McMahan took his and nodded, with his beaming smile at Ikey. The lieutenants and satellites took theirs and growled "Here's to you." Ikey took his nectar in delirium. All drank.

Ikey threw his week's wages in a crumpled roll upon the bar.

"C'rect," said the bartender, smoothing the twelve one-dollar notes. The crowd surged around Billy McMahan again. Some one was telling how Brannigan fixed 'em over in the Eleventh. Ikey leaned against the bar a while, and then went out.

He went down Hester Street and up Chrystie, and down Delancey to where he lived. And there his women folk, a bibulous mother and three dingy sisters, pounced upon him for his wages. And at his confession they shrieked and objurgated him in the pithy rhetoric of the locality.

But even as they plucked at him and struck him Ikey remained in his ecstatic trance of joy. His head was in the clouds; the star was drawing his wagon. Compared with what he had achieved the loss of wages and the bray of women's tongues were slight affairs.

He had shaken the hand of Billy McMahan.

Billy McMahan had a wife, and upon her visiting cards was engraved the name "Mrs. William Darragh McMahan." And there was a certain vexation attendant upon these cards; for, small as they were, there were houses in which they could not be inserted. Billy McMahan was a dictator in politics, a four-walled tower in business, a mogul, dread, loved and obeyed among his own people. He was growing rich; the daily papers had a dozen men on his trail to chronicle his every word of wisdom; he had been honored in caricature holding the Tiger cringing in leash.

But the heart of Billy was sometimes sore within him. There was a race of men from which he stood apart but that he viewed with the eye of Moses looking over into the promised land. He, too, had ideals, even as had Ikey Snigglefritz; and sometimes, hopeless of attaining them, his own solid success was as dust and ashes in his mouth. And Mrs. William Darragh McMahan wore a look of discontent upon her plump but pretty face, and the very rustle of her silks seemed a sigh.

There was a brave and conspicuous assemblage in the dining saloon of a noted hostelry where Fashion loves to display her charms. At one table sat Billy McMahan and his wife. Mostly silent they were, but the accessories they enjoyed little needed the indorsement of speech. Mrs. McMahan's diamonds were outshone by few in the room. The waiter bore the costliest brands of wine to their table. In evening dress, with an expression of gloom upon his smooth and massive countenance, you would look in vain for a more striking figure than Billy's.

Four tables away sat alone a tall, slender man, about thirty, with thoughtful, melancholy eyes, a Van Dyke beard and peculiarly white, thin hands. He was dining on filet mignon, dry toast and apollinaris. That man was Cortlandt Van Duyckink, a man worth eighty millions, who inherited and held a sacred seat in the exclusive inner circle of society.

Billy McMahan spoke to no one around him, because he knew no one. Van Duyckink kept his eyes on his plate because he knew that every one present was hungry to catch his. He could bestow knighthood and prestige by a nod, and he was chary of creating a too extensive nobility.

And then Billy McMahan conceived and accomplished the most startling and audacious act of his life. He rose deliberately and walked over to Cortlandt Van Duyckink's table and held out his hand.

"Say, Mr. Van Duyckink," he said, "I've heard you was talking about starting some reforms among the poor people down in my district. I'm McMahan, you know. Say, now, if that's straight I'll do all I can to help you. And what I says goes in that neck of the woods, don't it? Oh, say, I rather guess it does."

Van Duyckink's rather somber eyes lighted up. He rose to his lank height and grasped Billy McMahan's hand.

"Thank you, Mr. McMahan," he said, in his deep, serious tones. "I have been thinking of doing some work of that sort. I shall be glad of your assistance. It pleases me to have become acquainted with you."

Billy walked back to his seat. His shoulder was tingling from the accolade bestowed by royalty. A hundred eyes were now turned upon him in envy and new admiration. Mrs. William Darragh McMahan trembled with ecstasy, so that her diamonds smote the eye almost with pain. And now it was apparent that at many tables there were those who suddenly remembered that they enjoyed Mr. McMahan's acquaintance. He saw smiles and bows about him. He became enveloped in the aura of dizzy greatness. His campaign coolness deserted him.

"Wine for that gang!" he commanded the waiter, pointing with his finger. "Wine over there. Wine to those three gents by that green bush. Tell 'em it's on me. D——n it! Wine for everybody!"

The waiter ventured to whisper that it was perhaps inexpedient to carry out the order, in consideration of the dignity of the house and its custom.

"All right," said Billy, "if it's against the rules. I wonder if 'twould do to send my friend Van Duyckink a bottle? No? Well, it'll flow all right at the caffy to-night, just the same. It'll be rubber boots for anybody who comes in there any time up to 2 A. M."

Billy McMahan was happy.

He had shaken the hand of Cortlandt Van Duyckink.

The big pale-gray auto with its shining metal work looked out of place moving slowly among the push carts and trash-heaps on the lower east side. So did Cortlandt Van Duyckink, with his aristocratic face and white, thin hands, as he steered carefully between the groups of ragged, scurrying youngsters in the streets. And so did Miss Constance Schuyler, with her dim, ascetic beauty, seated at his side.

"Oh, Cortlandt," she breathed, "isn't it sad that human beings have to live in such wretchedness and poverty? And you—how noble it is of you to think of them, to give your time and money to improve their condition!"

Van Duyckink turned his solemn eyes upon her.

"It is little," he said, sadly, "that I can do. The question is a large one, and belongs to society. But even individual effort is not thrown away. Look, Constance! On this street I have arranged to build soup kitchens, where no one who is hungry will be turned away. And down this other street are the old buildings that I shall cause to be torn down and there erect others in place of those death-traps of fire and disease."

Down Delancey slowly crept the pale-gray auto. Away from it toddled coveys of wondering, tangle-haired, barefooted, unwashed children. It stopped before a crazy brick structure, foul and awry.

Van Duyckink alighted to examine at a better perspective one of the leaning walls. Down the steps of the building came a young man who seemed to epitomize its degradation, squalor and infelicity—a narrow-chested, pale, unsavory young man, puffing at a cigarette.

Obeying a sudden impulse, Van Duyckink stepped out and warmly grasped the hand of what seemed to him a living rebuke.

"I want to know you people," he said, sincerely. "I am going to help you as much as I can. We shall be friends."

As the auto crept carefully away Cortlandt Van Duyckink felt an unaccustomed glow about his heart. He was near to being a happy man.

He had shaken the hand of Ikey Snigglefritz.

THE PURPLE DRESS

We are to consider the shade known as purple. It is a color justly in repute among the sons and daughters of man. Emperors claim it for their especial dye. Good fellows everywhere seek to bring their noses to the genial hue that follows the commingling of the red and blue. We say of princes that they are born to the purple; and no doubt they are, for the colic tinges their faces with the royal tint equally with the snub-nosed countenance of a woodchopper's brat. All women love it—when it is the fashion.

And now purple is being worn. You notice it on the streets. Of course other colors are quite stylish as well—in fact, I saw a lovely thing the other day in olive-green albatross, with a triple-lapped flounce skirt trimmed with insert squares of silk, and a draped fichu of lace opening over a shirred vest and double puff sleeves with a lace band holding two gathered frills—but you see lots of purple too. Oh, yes, you do; just take a walk down Twenty-third Street any afternoon.

Therefore Maida—the girl with the big brown eyes and cinnamon-colored hair in the Bee-Hive Store—said to Grace—the girl with the rhinestone brooch and peppermint-pepsin flavor to her speech—"I'm going to have a purple dress—a tailor-made purple dress—for Thanks-giving."

"Oh, are you," said Grace, putting away some 7½ gloves into the 6¾ box. "Well, it's me for red. You see more red on Fifth Avenue. And the men all seem to like it."

"I like purple best," said Maida. "And old Schlegel has promised to make it for $8. It's going to be lovely. I'm going to have a plaited skirt and a blouse coat trimmed with a band of galloon under a white cloth collar with two rows of——"

"Sly boots!" said Grace with an educated wink.

"——soutache braid over a surpliced white vest; and a plaited basque and——"

"Sly boots—sly boots!" repeated Grace.

"——plaited gigot sleeves with a drawn velvet ribbon over an inside cuff. What do you mean by saying that?"

"You think Mr. Ramsay likes purple. I heard him say yesterday he thought some of the dark shades of red were stunning."

"I don't care," said Maida. "I prefer purple, and them that don't like it can just take the other side of the street."

Which suggests the thought that after all, the followers of purple may be subject to slight delusions. Danger is near when a maiden thinks she can wear purple regardless of complexions and opinions; and when emperors think their purple robes will wear forever.

Maida had saved $18 after eight months of economy; and this had bought the goods for the purple dress and paid Schlegel $4 on the making of it. On the day before Thanksgiving she would have just enough to pay the remaining $4. And then for a holiday in a new dress—can earth offer anything more enchanting?

Old Bachman, the proprietor of the Bee-Hive Store, always gave a Thanksgiving dinner to his employees. On every one of the subsequent 364 days, excusing Sundays, he would remind them of the joys of the past banquet and the hopes of the coming ones, thus inciting them to increased enthusiasm in work. The dinner was given in the store on one of the long tables in the middle of the room. They tacked wrapping paper over the front windows; and the turkeys and other good things were brought in the back way from the restaurant on the corner. You will perceive that the Bee-Hive was not a fashionable department store, with escalators and pompadours. It was almost small enough to be called an emporium; and you could actually go in there and get waited on and walk out again. And always at the Thanksgiving dinners Mr. Ramsay——

Oh, bother! I should have mentioned Mr. Ramsay first of all. He is more important than purple or green, or even the red cranberry sauce. Mr. Ramsay was the head clerk; and as far as I am concerned I am for him. He never pinched the girls' arms when he passed them in dark corners of the store; and when he told them stories when business was dull and the girls giggled and said: "Oh, pshaw!" it wasn't G. Bernard they meant at all. Besides being a gentleman, Mr. Ramsay was queer and original in other ways. He was a health crank, and believed that people should never eat anything that was good for them. He was violently opposed to anybody being comfortable, and coming in out of snow storms, or wearing overshoes, or taking medicine, or coddling themselves in any way. Every one of the ten girls in the store had little pork-chop-and-fried-onion dreams every night of becoming Mrs. Ramsay. For, next year old Bachman was going to take him in for a partner. And each one of them knew that if she should catch him she would knock those cranky health notions of his sky high before the wedding cake indigestion was over.

Mr. Ramsay was master of ceremonies at the dinners. Always they had two Italians in to play a violin and harp and had a little dance in the store.

And here were two dresses being conceived to charm Ramsay—one purple and the other red. Of course, the other eight girls were going to have dresses too, but they didn't count. Very likely they'd wear some shirt-waist-and-black-skirt-affairs—nothing as resplendent as purple or red.

Grace had saved her money, too. She was going to buy her dress ready-made. Oh, what's the use of bothering with a tailor—when you've got a figger it's easy to get a fit—the ready-made are intended for a perfect figger—except I have to have 'em all taken in at the waist—the average figger is so large waisted.

The night before Thanksgiving came. Maida hurried home, keen and bright with the thoughts of the blessed morrow. Her thoughts were of purple, but they were white themselves—the joyous enthusiasm of the young for the pleasures that youth must have or wither. She knew purple would become her, and—for the thousandth time she tried to assure herself that it was purple Mr. Ramsay said he liked and not red. She was going home first to get the $4 wrapped in a piece of tissue paper in the bottom drawer of her dresser, and then she was going to pay Schlegel and take the dress home herself.

Grace lived in the same house. She occupied the hall room above Maida's.

At home Maida found clamor and confusion. The landlady's tongue clattering sourly in the halls like a churn dasher dabbing in buttermilk. And then Grace came down to her room crying with eyes as red as any dress.

"She says I've got to get out," said Grace. "The old beast. Because I owe her $4. She's put my trunk in the hall and locked the door. I can't go anywhere else. I haven't got a cent of money."

"You had some yesterday," said Maida.

"I paid it on my dress," said Grace. "I thought she'd wait till next week for the rent."

Sniffle, sniffle, sob, sniffle.

Out came—out it had to come—Maida's $4.

"You blessed darling," cried Grace, now a rainbow instead of sunset. "I'll pay the mean old thing and then I'm going to try on my dress. I think it's heavenly. Come up and look at it. I'll pay the money back, a dollar a week—honest I will."

Thanksgiving.

The dinner was to be at noon. At a quarter to twelve Grace switched into Maida's room. Yes, she looked charming. Red was her color. Maida sat by the window in her old cheviot skirt and blue waist darning a st——. Oh, doing fancy work.

"Why, goodness me! ain't you dressed yet?" shrilled the red one. "How does it fit in the back? Don't you think these velvet tabs look awful swell? Why ain't you dressed, Maida?"

"My dress didn't get finished in time," said Maida. "I'm not going to the dinner."

"That's too bad. Why, I'm awfully sorry, Maida. Why don't you put on anything and come along—it's just the store folks, you know, and they won't mind."

"I was set on my purple," said Maida. "If I can't have it I won't go at all. Don't bother about me. Run along or you'll be late. You look awful nice in red."

At her window Maida sat through the long morning and past the time of the dinner at the store. In her mind she could hear the girls shrieking over a pull-bone, could hear old Bachman's roar over his own deeply-concealed jokes, could see the diamonds of fat Mrs. Bachman, who came to the store only on Thanksgiving days, could see Mr. Ramsay moving about, alert, kindly, looking to the comfort of all.

At four in the afternoon, with an expressionless face and a lifeless air she slowly made her way to Schlegel's shop and told him she could not pay the $4 due on the dress.

"Gott!" cried Schlegel, angrily. "For what do you look so glum? Take him away. He is ready. Pay me some time. Haf I not seen you pass mine shop every day in two years? If I make clothes is it that I do not know how to read beoples because? You will pay me some time when you can. Take him away. He is made goot; and if you look bretty in him all right. So. Pay me when you can."

Maida breathed a millionth part of the thanks in her heart, and hurried away with her dress. As she left the shop a smart dash of rain struck upon her face. She smiled and did not feel it.

Ladies who shop in carriages, you do not understand. Girls whose wardrobes are charged to the old man's account, you cannot begin to comprehend—you could not understand why Maida did not feel the cold dash of the Thanksgiving rain.

At five o'clock she went out upon the street wearing her purple dress. The rain had increased, and it beat down upon her a steady, wind-blown pour. People were scurrying home and to cars with close-held umbrellas and tight buttoned raincoats. Many of them turned their heads to marvel at this beautiful, serene happy-eyed girl in the purple dress walking through the storm as though she were strolling in a garden under summer skies.

I say you do not understand it, ladies of the full purse and varied wardrobe. You do not know what it is to live with a perpetual longing for pretty things—to starve eight months in order to bring a purple dress and a holiday together. What difference if it rained, hailed, blew, snowed, cycloned?

Maida had no umbrella nor overshoes. She had her purple dress and she walked abroad. Let the elements do their worst. A starved heart must have one crumb during a year. The rain ran down and dripped from her fingers.

Some one turned a corner and blocked her way. She looked up into Mr. Ramsay's eyes, sparkling with admiration and interest.

"Why, Miss Maida," said he, "you look simply magnificent in your new dress. I was greatly disappointed not to see you at our dinner. And of all the girls I ever knew, you show the greatest sense and intelligence. There is nothing more healthful and invigorating than braving the weather as you are doing. May I walk with you?"

And Maida blushed and sneezed.

THE FOREIGN POLICY OF COMPANY 99

John Byrnes, hose-cart driver of Engine Company No. 99, was afflicted with what his comrades called Japanitis.

Byrnes had a war map spread permanently upon a table in the second story of the engine-house, and he could explain to you at any hour of the day or night the exact positions, conditions and intentions of both the Russian and Japanese armies. He had little clusters of pins stuck in the map which represented the opposing forces, and these he moved about from day to day in conformity with the war news in the daily papers.

Wherever the Japs won a victory John Byrnes would shift his pins, and then he would execute a war dance of delight, and the other firemen would hear him yell: "Go it, you blamed little, sawed-off, huckleberry-eyed, monkey-faced hot tamales! Eat 'em up, you little sleight-o'-hand, bow-legged bull terriers—give 'em another of them Yalu looloos, and you'll eat rice in St. Petersburg. Talk about your Russians—say, wouldn't they give you painsky when it comes to a scrapovitch?"

Not even on the fair island of Nippon was there a more enthusiastic champion of the Mikado's men. Supporters of the Russian cause did well to keep clear of Engine House No. 99.

Sometimes all thoughts of the Japs left John Byrnes's head. That was when the alarm of fire had sounded and he was strapped in his driver's seat on the swaying cart, guiding Erebus and Joe, the finest team in the whole department—according to the crew of 99.

Of all the codes adopted by man for regulating his actions toward his fellow-mortals, the greatest are these—the code of King Arthur's Knights of the Round Table, the Constitution of the United States and the un-written rules of the New York Fire Department. The Round Table methods are no longer practicable since the invention of street cars and breach-of-promise suits, and our Constitution is being found more and more unconstitutional every day, so the code of our firemen must be considered in the lead, with the Golden Rule and Jeffries's new punch trying for place and show.

The Constitution says that one man is as good as another; but the Fire Department says he is better. This is a too generous theory, but the law will not allow itself to be construed otherwise. All of which comes perilously near to being a paradox, and commends itself to the attention of the S. P. C. A.

One of the transatlantic liners dumped out at Ellis Island a lump of protozoa which was expected to evolve into an American citizen. A steward kicked him down the gangway, a doctor pounced upon his eyes like a raven, seeking for trachoma or ophthalmia; he was hustled ashore and ejected into the city in the name of Liberty—perhaps, theoretically, thus inoculating against kingocracy with a drop of its own virus. This hypodermic injection of Europeanism wandered happily into the veins of the city with the broad grin of a pleased child. It was not burdened with baggage, cares or ambitions. Its body was lithely built and clothed in a sort of foreign fustian; its face was brightly vacant, with a small, flat nose, and was mostly covered by a thick, ragged, curling beard like the coat of a spaniel. In the pocket of the imported Thing were a few coins—denarii—scudi—kopecks—pfennigs—pilasters—whatever the financial nomenclature of his unknown country may have been.

Prattling to himself, always broadly grinning, pleased by the roar and movement of the barbarous city into which the steamship cut-rates had shunted him, the alien strayed away from the sea, which he hated, as far as the district covered by Engine Company No. 99. Light as a cork, he was kept bobbing along by the human tide, the crudest atom in all the silt of the stream that emptied into the reservoir of Liberty.

While crossing Third Avenue he slowed his steps, enchanted by the thunder of the elevated trains above him and the soothing crash of the wheels on the cobbles. And then there was a new, delightful chord in the uproar—the musical clanging of a gong and a great shining juggernaut belching fire and smoke, that people were hurrying to see.

This beautiful thing, entrancing to the eye, dashed past, and the protoplasmic immigrant stepped into the wake of it with his broad, enraptured, uncomprehending grin. And so stepping, stepped into the path of No. 99's flying hose-cart, with John Byrnes gripping, with arms of steel, the reins over the plunging backs of Erebus and Joe.

The unwritten constitutional code of the fireman has no exceptions or amendments. It is a simple thing—as simple as the rule of three. There was the heedless unit in the right of way; there was the hose-cart, and the iron pillar of the elevated railroad.

John Byrnes swung all his weight and muscle on the left rein. The team and cart swerved that way and crashed like a torpedo into the pillar. The men on the cart went flying like skittles. The driver's strap burst, the pillar rang with the shock, and John Byrnes fell on the car track with a broken shoulder twenty feet away, while Erebus—beautiful, raven-black, best-loved Erebus—lay whickering in his harness with a broken leg.

In consideration for the feelings of Engine Company No. 99 the details will be lightly touched. The company does not like to be reminded of that day. There was a great crowd, and hurry calls were sent in; and while the ambulance gong was clearing the way the men of No. 99 heard the crack of the S. P. C. A. agent's pistol, and turned their heads away, not daring to look toward Erebus again.

When the firemen got back to the engine-house they found that one of them was dragging by the collar the cause of their desolation and grief. They set it in the middle of the floor and gathered grimly about it. Through its whiskers the calamitous object chattered effervescently and waved its hands.

"Sounds like a seidlitz powder," said Mike Dowling, disgustedly, "and it makes me sicker than one. Call that a man!—that hoss was worth a steamer full of such two-legged animals. It's a immigrant—that's what it is."

"Look at the doctor's chalk mark on its coat," said Reilly, the desk man. "It's just landed. It must be a kind of a Dago or a Hun or one of them Finns, I guess. That's the kind of truck that Europe unloads onto us."

"Think of a thing like that getting in the way and laying John up in hospital and spoiling the best fire team in the city," groaned another fireman. "It ought to be taken down to the dock and drowned."

"Somebody go around and get Sloviski," suggested the engine driver, "and let's see what nation is responsible for this conglomeration of hair and head noises."

Sloviski kept a delicatessen store around the corner on Third Avenue, and was reputed to be a linguist.

One of the men fetched him—a fat, cringing man, with a discursive eye and the odors of many kinds of meats upon him.

"Take a whirl at this importation with your jaw-breakers, Sloviski," requested Mike Dowling. "We can't quite figure out whether he's from the Hackensack bottoms or Hongkong-on-the-Ganges."

Sloviski addressed the stranger in several dialects, that ranged in rhythm and cadence from the sounds produced by a tonsillitis gargle to the opening of a can of tomatoes with a pair of scissors. The immigrant replied in accents resembling the uncorking of a bottle of ginger ale.

"I have you his name," reported Sloviski. "You shall not pronounce it. Writing of it in paper is better." They gave him paper, and he wrote, "Demetre Svangvsk."

"Looks like short hand," said the desk man.

"He speaks some language," continued the interpreter, wiping his forehead, "of Austria and mixed with a little Turkish. And, den, he have some Magyar words and a Polish or two, and many like the Roumanian, but not without talk of one tribe in Bessarabia. I do not quite understand."

"Would you call him a Dago or a Polocker, or what?" asked Mike, frowning at the polyglot description.

"He is a"—answered Sloviski—"he is a—I dink he come from—I dink he is a fool," he concluded, impatient at his linguistic failure, "and if you pleases I will go back at mine delicatessen."

"Whatever he is, he's a bird," said Mike Dowling; "and you want to watch him fly."

Taking by the wing the alien fowl that had fluttered into the nest of Liberty, Mike led him to the door of the engine-house and bestowed upon him a kick hearty enough to convey the entire animus of Company 99. Demetre Svangvsk hustled away down the sidewalk, turning once to show his ineradicable grin to the aggrieved firemen.

In three weeks John Byrnes was back at his post from the hospital. With great gusto he proceeded to bring his war map up to date. "My money on the Japs every time," he declared. "Why, look at them Russians—they're nothing but wolves. Wipe 'em out, I say—and the little old jiu-jitsu gang are just the cherry blossoms to do the trick, and don't you forget it!"

The second day after Byrnes's reappearance came Demetre Svangvsk, the unidentified, to the engine-house, with a broader grin than ever. He managed to convey the idea that he wished to congratulate the hose-cart driver on his recovery and to apologize for having caused the accident. This he accomplished by so many extravagant gestures and explosive noises that the company was diverted for half an hour. Then they kicked him out again, and on the next day he came back grinning. How or where he lived no one knew. And then John Byrnes's nine-year-old son, Chris, who brought him convalescent delicacies from home to eat, took a fancy to Svangvsk, and they allowed him to loaf about the door of the engine-house occasionally.

One afternoon the big drab automobile of the Deputy Fire Commissioner buzzed up to the door of No. 99 and the Deputy stepped inside for an informal inspection. Then men kicked Svangvsk out a little harder than usual and proudly escorted the Deputy around 99, in which everything shone like my lady's mirror.

The Deputy respected the sorrow of the company concerning the loss of Erebus, and he had come to promise it another mate for Joe that would do him credit. So they let Joe out of his stall and showed the Deputy how deserving he was of the finest mate that could be in horsedom.

While they were circling around Joe confabbing, Chris climbed into the Deputy's auto and threw the power full on. The men heard a monster puffing and a shriek from the lad, and sprang out too late. The big auto shot away, luckily taking a straight course down the street. The boy knew nothing of its machinery; he sat clutching the cushions and howling. With the power on nothing could have stopped that auto except a brick house, and there was nothing for Chris to gain by such a stoppage.

Demetre Svangvsk was just coming in again with a grin for another kick when Chris played his merry little prank. While the others sprang for the door Demetre sprang for Joe. He glided upon the horse's bare back like a snake and shouted something at him like the crack of a dozen whips. One of the firemen afterward swore that Joe answered him back in the same language. Ten seconds after the auto started the big horse was eating up the asphalt behind it like a strip of macaroni.

Some people two blocks and a half away saw the rescue. They said that the auto was nothing but a drab noise with a black speck in the middle of it for Chris, when a big bay horse with a lizard lying on its back cantered up alongside of it, and the lizard reached over and picked the black speck out of the noise.

Only fifteen minutes after Svangvsk's last kicking at the hands—or rather the feet—of Engine Company No. 99 he rode Joe back through the door with the boy safe, but acutely conscious of the licking he was going to receive.

Svangvsk slipped to the floor, leaned his head against Joe's and made a noise like a clucking hen. Joe nodded and whistled loudly through his nostrils, putting to shame the knowledge of Sloviski, of the delicatessen.

John Byrnes walked up to Svangvsk, who grinned, expecting to be kicked. Byrnes gripped the outlander so strongly by the hand that Demetre grinned anyhow, conceiving it to be a new form of punishment.

"The heathen rides like a Cossack," remarked a fireman who had seen a Wild West show—"they're the greatest riders in the world."

The word seemed to electrify Svangvsk. He grinned wider than ever.

"Yas—yas—me Cossack," he spluttered, striking his chest.

"Cossack!" repeated John Byrnes, thoughtfully, "ain't that a kind of a Russian?"

"They're one of the Russian tribes, sure," said the desk man, who read books between fire alarms.

Just then Alderman Foley, who was on his way home and did not know of the runaway, stopped at the door of the engine-house and called to Byrnes.

"Hello there, Jimmy, me boy—how's the war coming along? Japs still got the bear on the trot, have they?"

"Oh, I don't know," said John Byrnes, argumentatively, "them Japs haven't got any walkover. You wait till Kuropatkin gets a good whack at 'em and they won't be knee-high to a puddle-ducksky."

THE LOST BLEND

Since the bar has been blessed by the clergy, and cocktails open the dinners of the elect, one may speak of the saloon. Teetotalers need not listen, if they choose; there is always the slot restaurant, where a dime dropped into the cold bouillon aperture will bring forth a dry Martini.

Con Lantry worked on the sober side of the bar in Kenealy's café. You and I stood, one-legged like geese, on the other side and went into voluntary liquidation with our week's wages. Opposite danced Con, clean, temperate, clear-headed, polite, white-jacketed, punctual, trustworthy, young, responsible, and took our money.

The saloon (whether blessed or cursed) stood in one of those little "places" which are parallelograms instead of streets, and inhabited by laundries, decayed Knickerbocker families and Bohemians who have nothing to do with either.

Over the café lived Kenealy and his family. His daughter Katherine had eyes of dark Irish—but why should you be told? Be content with your Geraldine or your Eliza Ann. For Con dreamed of her; and when she called softly at the foot of the back stairs for the pitcher of beer for dinner, his heart went up and down like a milk punch in the shaker. Orderly and fit are the rules of Romance; and if you hurl the last shilling of your fortune upon the bar for whiskey, the bartender shall take it, and marry his boss's daughter, and good will grow out of it.

But not so Con. For in the presence of woman he was tongue-tied and scarlet. He who would quell with his eye the sonorous youth whom the claret punch made loquacious, or smash with lemon squeezer the obstreperous, or hurl gutterward the cantankerous without a wrinkle coming to his white lawn tie, when he stood before a woman he was voiceless, incoherent, stuttering, buried beneath a hot avalanche of bashfulness and misery. What then was he before Katherine? A trembler, with no word to say for himself, a stone without blarney, the dumbest lover that ever babbled of the weather in the presence of his divinity.

There came to Kenealy's two sunburned men, Riley and McQuirk. They had conference with Kenealy; and then they took possession of a back room which they filled with bottles and siphons and jugs and druggist's measuring glasses. All the appurtenances and liquids of a saloon were there, but they dispensed no drinks. All day long the two sweltered in there, pouring and mixing unknown brews and decoctions from the liquors in their store. Riley had the education, and he figured on reams of paper, reducing gallons to ounces and quarts to fluid drams. McQuirk, a morose man with a red eye, dashed each unsuccessful completed mixture into the waste pipe with curses gentle, husky and deep. They labored heavily and untiringly to achieve some mysterious solution like two alchemists striving to resolve gold from the elements.

Into this back room one evening when his watch was done sauntered Con. His professional curiosity had been stirred by these occult bartenders at whose bar none drank, and who daily drew upon Kenealy's store of liquors to follow their consuming and fruitless experiments.

Down the back stairs came Katherine with her smile like sunrise on Gweebarra Bay.

"Good evening, Mr. Lantry," says she. "And what is the news to-day, if you please?"

"It looks like r-rain," stammered the shy one, backing to the wall.

"It couldn't do better," said Katherine. "I'm thinking there's nothing the worse off for a little water." In the back room Riley and McQuirk toiled like bearded witches over their strange compounds. From fifty bottles they drew liquids carefully measured after Riley's figures, and shook the whole together in a great glass vessel. Then McQuirk would dash it out, with gloomy profanity, and they would begin again.

"Sit down," said Riley to Con, "and I'll tell you.

"Last summer me and Tim concludes that an American bar in this nation of Nicaragua would pay. There was a town on the coast where there's nothing to eat but quinine and nothing to drink but rum. The natives and foreigners lay down with chills and get up with fevers; and a good mixed drink is nature's remedy for all such tropical inconveniences.

"So we lays in a fine stock of wet goods in New York, and bar fixtures and glassware, and we sails for that Santa Palma town on a lime steamer. On the way me and Tim sees flying fish and play seven-up with the captain and steward, and already begins to feel like the high-ball kings of the tropics of Capricorn.

"When we gets in five hours of the country that we was going to introduce to long drinks and short change the captain calls us over to the starboard binnacle and recollects a few things.

"'I forgot to tell you, boys,' says he, 'that Nicaragua slapped an import duty of 48 per cent. ad valorem on all bottled goods last month. The President took a bottle of Cincinnati hair tonic by mistake for tabasco sauce, and he's getting even. Barrelled goods is free.'

"'Sorry you didn't mention it sooner,' says we. And we bought two forty-two gallon casks from the captain, and opened every bottle we had and dumped the stuff altogether in the casks. That 48 per cent. would have ruined us; so we took the chances on making that $1,200 cocktail rather than throw the stuff away.

"Well, when we landed we tapped one of the barrels. The mixture was something heartrending. It was the color of a plate of Bowery pea soup, and it tasted like one of those coffee substitutes your aunt makes

you take for the heart trouble you get by picking losers. We gave a nigger four fingers of it to try it, and he lay under a cocoanut tree three days
beating the sand with his heels and refused to sign a testimonial.

"But the other barrel! Say, bartender, did you ever put on a straw hat
with a yellow band around it and go up in a balloon with a pretty girl
with $8,000,000 in your pocket all at the same time? That's what thirty
drops of it would make you feel like. With two fingers of it inside you
you would bury your face in your hands and cry because there wasn't
anything more worth while around for you to lick than little Jim Jeffries.
Yes, sir, that stuff in that second barrel was distilled elixir of battle, money
and high life. It was the color of gold and as clear as glass, and it shone
after dark like the sunshine was still in it. A thousand years from now
you'll get a drink like that across the bar.

"Well, we started up business with that one line of drinks, and it was
enough. The piebald gentry of that country stuck to it like a hive of bees.
If that barrel had lasted that country would have become the greatest
on earth. When we opened up of mornings we had a line of generals
and colonels and ex-presidents and revolutionists a block long waiting to
be served. We started in at 50 cents silver a drink. The last ten gallons
went easy at $5 a gulp. It was wonderful stuff. It gave a man courage and
ambition and nerve to do anything; at the same time he didn't care
whether his money was tainted or fresh from the Ice Trust. When that
barrel was half gone Nicaragua had repudiated the National debt, removed the duty on cigarettes and was about to declare war on the United
States and England.

" 'Twas by accident we discovered this king of drinks, and 'twill be by
good luck if we strike it again. For ten months we've been trying. Small
lots at a time, we've mixed barrels of all the harmful ingredients known
to the profession of drinking. Ye could have stocked ten bars with the
whiskies, brandies, cordials, bitters, gins and wines me and Tim have
wasted. A glorious drink like that to be denied the world! 'Tis a sorrow
and a loss of money. The United States as a nation would welcome a
drink of that sort, and pay for it."

All the while McQuirk had been carefully measuring and pouring together small quantities of various spirits, as Riley called them, from his
latest pencilled prescription. The completed mixture was of a vile, mottled
chocolate color. McQuirk tasted it, and hurled it, with appropriate epithets, into the waste sink.

" 'Tis a strange story, even if true," said Con. "I'll be going now along
to my supper."

"Take a drink," said Riley. "We've all kinds except the lost blend."

"I never drink," said Con, "anything stronger than water. I am just
after meeting Miss Katherine by the stairs. She said a true word, 'There's
not anything,' says she, 'but is better off for a little water.'"

When Con had left them Riley almost felled McQuirk by a blow on the back.

"Did ye hear that?" he shouted. "Two fools are we. The six dozen bottles of 'pollinaris we had on the ship—ye opened them yourself—which barrel did ye pour them in—which barrel, ye mudhead?"

"I mind," said McQuirk, slowly, " 'twas in the second barrel we opened. I mind the blue piece of paper pasted on the side of it."

"We've got it now," cried Riley. " 'Twas that we lacked. 'Tis the water that does the trick. Everything else we had right. Hurry, man, and get two bottles of 'pollinaris from the bar, while I figure out the proportionments with me pencil."

An hour later Con strolled down the sidewalk toward Kenealy's café. Thus faithful employees haunt, during their recreation hours, the vicinity where they labor, drawn by some mysterious attraction.

A police patrol wagon stood at the side door. Three able cops were half carrying, half hustling Riley and McQuirk up its rear steps. The eyes and faces of each bore the bruises and cuts of sanguinary and assiduous conflict. Yet they whooped with strange joy, and directed upon the police the feeble remnants of their pugnacious madness.

"Began fighting each other in the back room," explained Kenealy to Con. "And singing! That was worse. Smashed everything pretty much up. But they're good men. They'll pay for everything. Trying to invent some new kind of cocktail, they was. I'll see they come out all right in the morning."

Con sauntered into the back room to view the battlefield. As he went through the hall Katherine was just coming down the stairs.

"Good evening again, Mr. Lantry," said she. "And is there no news from the weather yet?"

"Still threatens r-rain," said Con, slipping past with red in his smooth, pale cheek.

Riley and McQuirk had indeed waged a great and friendly battle. Broken bottles and glasses were everywhere. The room was full of alcohol fumes; the floor was variegated with spirituous puddles.

On the table stood a 32-ounce glass graduated measure. In the bottom of it were two tablespoonfuls of liquid—a bright golden liquid that seemed to hold the sunshine a prisoner in its auriferous depths.

Con smelled it. He tasted it. He drank it.

As he returned through the hall Katherine was just going up the stairs.

"No news yet, Mr. Lantry?" she asked with her teasing laugh.

Con lifted her clear from the floor and held her there.

"The news is," he said, "that we're to be married."

"Put me down, sir!" she cried indignantly, "or I will—— Oh, Con, oh, wherever did you get the nerve to say it?"

A HARLEM TRAGEDY

Harlem.

Mrs. Fink had dropped into Mrs. Cassidy's flat one flight below.

"Ain't it a beaut?" said Mrs. Cassidy.

She turned her face proudly for her friend Mrs. Fink to see. One eye was nearly closed, with a great, greenish-purple bruise around it. Her lip was cut and bleeding a little and there were red finger-marks on each side of her neck.

"My husband wouldn't ever think of doing that to me," said Mrs. Fink, concealing her envy.

"I wouldn't have a man," declared Mrs. Cassidy, "that didn't beat me up at least once a week. Shows he thinks something of you. Say! but that last dose Jack gave me wasn't no homeopathic one. I can see stars yet. But he'll be the sweetest man in town for the rest of the week to make up for it. This eye is good for theater tickets and a silk shirt waist at the very least."

"I should hope," said Mrs. Fink, assuming complacency, "that Mr. Fink is too much of a gentleman ever to raise his hand against me."

"Oh, go on, Maggie!" said Mrs. Cassidy, laughing and applying witch hazel, "you're only jealous. Your old man is too frappéed and slow to ever give you a punch. He just sits down and practises physical culture with a newspaper when he comes home—now ain't that the truth?"

"Mr. Fink certainly peruses of the papers when he comes home," acknowledged Mrs. Fink, with a toss of her head; "but he certainly don't ever make no Steve O'Donnell out of me just to amuse himself—that's a sure thing."

Mrs. Cassidy laughed the contented laugh of the guarded and happy matron. With the air of Cornelia exhibiting her jewels, she drew down the collar of her kimono and revealed another treasured bruise, maroon-colored, edged with olive and orange—a bruise now nearly well, but still to memory dear.

Mrs. Fink capitulated. The formal light in her eye softened to envious admiration. She and Mrs. Cassidy had been chums in the downtown paper-box factory before they had married, one year before. Now she and her man occupied the flat above Mame and her man. Therefore she could not put on airs with Mame.

"Don't it hurt when he soaks you?" asked Mrs. Fink, curiously.

"Hurt!"—Mrs. Cassidy gave a soprano scream of delight. "Well, say —did you ever have a brick house fall on you?—well, that's just the way it feels—just like when they're digging you out of the ruins. Jack's got

a left that spells two matinées and a new pair of Oxfords—and his right!
—well, it takes a trip to Coney and six pairs of openwork silk lisle threads
to make that good."

"But what does he beat you for?" inquired Mrs. Fink, with wide-open
eyes.

"Silly!" said Mrs. Cassidy, indulgently. "Why, because he's full. It's
generally on Saturday nights."

"But what cause do you give him?" persisted the seeker after knowledge.

"Why, didn't I marry him? Jack comes in tanked up; and I'm here,
ain't I? Who else has he got a right to beat? I'd just like to catch him
once beating anybody else! Sometimes it's because supper ain't ready;
and sometimes it's because it is. Jack ain't particular about causes. He
just lushes till he remembers he's married, and then he makes for home
and does me up. Saturday nights I just move the furniture with sharp
corners out of the way, so I won't cut my head when he gets his work in.
He's got a left swing that jars you! Sometimes I take the count in the
first round; but when I feel like having a good time during the week
or want some new rags I come up again for more punishment. That's
what I done last night. Jack knows I've been wanting a black silk waist
for a month, and I didn't think just one black eye would bring it. Tell
you what, Mag, I'll bet you the ice cream he brings it to-night."

Mrs. Fink was thinking deeply.

"My Mart," she said, "never hit me a lick in his life. It's just like you
said, Mame; he comes in grouchy and ain't got a word to say. He never
takes me out anywhere. He's a chair-warmer at home for fair. He buys
me things, but he looks so glum about it that I never appreciate 'em."

Mrs. Cassidy slipped an arm around her chum.

"You poor thing!" she said. "But everybody can't have a husband like
Jack. Marriage wouldn't be no failure if they was all like him. These discontented wives you hear about—what they need is a man to come home
and kick their slats in once a week, and then make it up in kisses, and
chocolate creams. That'd give 'em some interest in life. What I want is
a masterful man that slugs you when he's jagged and hugs you when he
ain't jagged. Preserve me from the man that ain't got the sand to do
neither!"

Mrs. Fink sighed.

The hallways were suddenly filled with sound. The door flew open at
the kick of Mr. Cassidy. His arms were occupied with bundles. Mame
flew and hung about his neck. Her sound eye sparkled with the love
light that shines in the eye of the Maori maid when she recovers con-
sciousness in the hut of the wooer who has stunned and dragged her
there.

"Hello, old girl!" shouted Mr. Cassidy. He shed his bundles and lifted her off her feet in a mighty hug. "I got tickets for Barnum & Bailey's, and if you'll bust the string of one of them bundles I guess you'll find that silk waist—why, good evening, Mrs. Fink—I didn't see you at first. How's old Mart coming along?"

"He's very well, Mr. Cassidy—thanks," said Mrs. Fink. "I must be going along up now. Mart'll be home for supper soon. I'll bring you down the pattern you want to-morrow, Mame."

Mrs. Fink went up to her flat and had a little cry. It was a meaningless cry, the kind of cry that only a woman knows about, a cry from no particular cause, altogether an absurd cry; the most transient and the most hopeless cry in the repertory of grief. Why had Martin never thrashed her? He was as big and strong as Jack Cassidy. Did he not care for her at all? He never quarrelled; he came home and lounged about silent, glum, idle. He was a fairly good provider, but he ignored the spices of life.

Mrs. Fink's ship of dreams was becalmed. Her captain ranged between plum duff and his hammock. If only he would shiver his timbers or stamp his foot on the quarter-deck now and then! And she had thought to sail so merrily, touching at ports in the Delectable Isles! But now, to vary the figure, she was ready to throw up the sponge, tired out, without a scratch to show for all those tame rounds with her sparring partner. For one moment she almost hated Mame—Mame, with her cuts and bruises, her salve of presents and kisses; her stormy voyage with her fighting, brutal, loving mate.

Mr. Fink came home at 7. He was permeated with the curse of domesticity. Beyond the portals of his cozy home he cared not to roam, to roam. He was the man who had caught the street car, the anaconda that had swallowed its prey, the tree that lay as it had fallen.

"Like the supper, Mart?" asked Mrs. Fink, who had striven over it.

"M-m-m-yep," grunted Mr. Fink.

After supper he gathered his newspapers to read. He sat in his stocking feet.

Arise, some new Dante, and sing me the befitting corner of perdition for the man who sitteth in the house in his stockinged feet. Sisters in Patience who by reason of ties or duty have endured it in silk, yarn, cotton, lisle thread or woollen—does not the new canto belong?

The next day was Labor Day. The occupations of Mr. Cassidy and Mr. Fink ceased for one passage of the sun. Labor, triumphant, would parade and otherwise disport itself.

Mrs. Fink took Mrs. Cassidy's pattern down early. Mame had on her new silk waist. Even her damaged eye managed to emit a holiday gleam. Jack was fruitfully penitent, and there was a hilarious scheme for the day afoot, with parks and picnics and Pilsener in it.

A rising, indignant jealousy seized Mrs. Fink as she returned to her flat above. Oh, happy Mame, with her bruises and her quick-following

balm! But was Mame to have a monopoly of happiness? Surely Martin
Fink was as good a man as Jack Cassidy. Was his wife to go always un-
belabored and uncaressed? A sudden, brilliant breathless idea came to
Mrs. Fink. She would show Mame that there were husbands as able to
use their fists and perhaps to be as tender afterward as any Jack.

The holiday promised to be a nominal one with the Finks. Mrs. Fink
had the stationary washtubs in the kitchen filled with a two-weeks' wash
that had been soaking overnight. Mr. Fink sat in his stockinged feet
reading a newspaper. Thus Labor Day presaged to speed.

Jealousy surged high in Mrs. Fink's heart and higher still surged an
audacious resolve. If her man would not strike her—if he would not so
far prove his manhood, his prerogative and his interest in conjugal affairs, he must be prompted to do his duty.

Mr. Fink lit his pipe and peacefully rubbed an ankle with a stockinged toe. He reposed in the state of matrimony like a lump of unblended
suet in a pudding. This was his level Elysium—to sit at ease vicariously
girdling the world in print amid the wifely splashing of suds and the
agreeable smells of breakfast dishes departed and dinner ones to come.
Many ideas were far from his mind; but the furthest one was the thought
of beating his wife.

Mrs. Fink turned on the hot water and set the washboards in the suds.
Up from the flat below came the gay laugh of Mrs. Cassidy. It sounded
like a taunt, a flaunting of her own happiness in the face of the unslugged
bride above. Now was Mrs. Fink's time.

Suddenly she turned like a fury upon the man reading.

"You lazy loafer!" she cried, "must I work my arms off washing and
toiling for the ugly likes of you? Are you a man or are you a kitchen
hound?"

Mr. Fink dropped his paper, motionless from surprise. She feared
that he would not strike—that the provocation had been insufficient. She
leaped at him and struck him fiercely in the face with her clenched
hand. In that instant she felt a thrill of love for him such as she had not
felt for many a day. Rise up, Martin Fink, and come into your kingdom!
Oh, she must feel the weight of his hand now—just to show that he cared
—just to show that he cared!

Mr. Fink sprang to his feet—Maggie caught him again on the jaw
with a wide swing of her other hand. She closed her eyes in that fearful, blissful moment before his blow should come—she whispered his
name to herself—she leaned to the expected shock, hungry for it.

In the flat below Mr. Cassidy, with a shamed and contrite face, was
powdering Mame's eye in preparation for their junket. From the flat
above came the sound of a woman's voice, high-raised, a bumping, a
stumbling and a shuffling, a chair overturned—unmistakable sounds of
domestic conflict.

"Mart and Mag scrapping?" postulated Mr. Cassidy. "Didn't know they ever indulged. Shall I trot up and see if they need a sponge holder?"

One of Mrs. Cassidy's eyes sparkled like a diamond. The other twinkled at least like paste.

"Oh, oh," she said, softly and without apparent meaning in the feminine ejaculatory manner. "I wonder if—wonder if! Wait, Jack, till I go up and see."

Up the stairs she sped. As her foot struck the hallway above out from the kitchen door of her flat wildly flounced Mrs. Fink.

"Oh, Maggie," cried Mrs. Cassidy, in a delighted whisper; "did he? Oh, did he?"

Mrs. Fink ran and laid her face upon her chum's shoulder and sobbed hopelessly.

Mrs. Cassidy took Maggie's face between her hands and lifted it gently. Tear-stained it was, flushing and paling, but its velvety, pink-and-white, becomingly freckled surface was unscratched, unbruised, unmarred by the recreant fist of Mr. Fink.

"Tell me, Maggie," pleaded Mame, "or I'll go in there and find out. What was it? Did he hurt you—what did he do?"

Mrs. Fink's face went down again despairingly on the bosom of her friend.

"For God's sake don't open that door, Mame," she sobbed. "And don't ever tell nobody—keep it under your hat. He—he never touched me, and—he's—oh, Gawd—he's washin' the clothes—he's washin' the clothes!"

"THE GUILTY PARTY"

A red-haired, unshaven, untidy man sat in a rocking chair by a window. He had just lighted a pipe, and was puffing blue clouds with great satisfaction. He had removed his shoes and donned a pair of blue, faded carpet-slippers. With the morbid thirst of the confirmed daily news drinker, he awkwardly folded back the pages of an evening paper, eagerly gulping down the strong, black headlines, to be followed as a chaser by the milder details of the smaller type.

In an adjoining room a woman was cooking supper. Odors from strong bacon and boiling coffee contended against the cut-plug fumes from the vespertine pipe.

Outside was one of those crowded streets of the east side, in which, as twilight falls, Satan sets up his recruiting office. A mighty host of children danced and ran and played in the street. Some in rags, some in clean white and beribboned, some wild and restless as young hawks, some gentle-faced and shrinking, some shrieking rude and sinful words, some listening, awed, but soon, grown familiar, to embrace—here were the children playing in the corridors of the House of Sin. Above the playground forever hovered a great bird. The bird was known to humorists as the stork. But the people of Chrystie Street were better ornithologists. They called it a vulture.

A little girl of twelve came up timidly to the man reading and resting by the window, and said:

"Papa, won't you play a game of checkers with me if you aren't too tired?"

The red-haired, unshaven, untidy man sitting shoeless by the window answered, with a frown.

"Checkers. No, I won't. Can't a man who works hard all day have a little rest when he comes home? Why don't you go out and play with the other kids on the sidewalk?"

The woman who was cooking came to the door.

"John," she said, "I don't like for Lizzie to play in the street. They learn too much there that ain't good for 'em. She's been in the house all day long. It seems that you might give up a little of your time to amuse her when you come home."

"Let her go out and play like the rest of 'em if she wants to be amused," said the red-haired, unshaven, untidy man, "and don't bother me."

"You're on," said Kid Mullaly. "Fifty dollars to $25 I take Annie to the dance. Put up."

The Kid's black eyes were snapping with the fire of the baited and challenged. He drew out his "roll" and slapped five tens upon the bar. The three or four young fellows who were thus "taken" more slowly produced their stake. The bartender, ex-officio stakeholder, took the money, laboriously wrapped it, recorded the bet with an inch-long pencil and stuffed the whole into a corner of the cash register.

"And, oh, what'll be done to you'll be a plenty," said a bettor, with anticipatory glee.

"That's my lookout," said the "Kid," sternly. "Fill 'em up all around, Mike."

After the round Burke, the Kid's sponge, sponge-holder, pal, mentor and Grand Vizier, drew him out to the bootblack stand at the saloon corner where all the official and important matters of the Small Hours Social Club were settled. As Tony polished the light tan shoes of the club's President and Secretary for the fifth time that day, Burke spake words of wisdom to his chief.

"Cut that blonde out, Kid," was his advice, "or there'll be trouble. What do you want to throw down that girl of yours for? You'll never find one that'll freeze to you like Liz has. She's worth a hallful of Annies."

"I'm no Annie admirer!" said the Kid, dropping a cigarette ash on his polished toe, and wiping it off on Tony's shoulder. "But I want to teach Liz a lesson. She thinks I belong to her. She's been bragging that I daren't speak to another girl. Liz is all right—in some ways. She's drinking a little too much lately. And she uses language that a lady oughtn't."

"You're engaged, ain't you?" asked Burke.

"Sure. We'll get married next year, maybe."

"I saw you make her drink her first glass of beer," said Burke. "That was two years ago, when she used to come down to the corner of Chrystie bareheaded to meet you after supper. She was a quiet sort of a kid then, and couldn't speak without blushing."

"She's a little spitfire, sometimes, now," said the Kid. "I hate jealousy. That's why I'm going to the dance with Annie. It'll teach her some sense."

"Well, you better look a little out," were Burke's last words. "If Liz was my girl and I was to sneak out to a dance coupled up with an Annie, I'd want a suit of chain armor on under my gladsome rags, all right."

Through the land of the stork-vulture wandered Liz. Her black eyes searched the passing crowds fierily but vaguely. Now and then she hummed bars of foolish little songs. Between times she set her small, white teeth together, and spake crisp words that the east side has added to language.

Liz's skirt was green silk. Her waist was a large brown-and-pink plaid, well-fitting and not without style. She wore a cluster ring of huge imitation rubies, and a locket that banged her knees at the bottom of a silver chain. Her shoes were run down over twisted high heels, and were strangers to polish. Her hat would scarcely have passed into a flour barrel.

The "Family Entrance" of the Blue Jay Café received her. At a table she sat, and punched the button with the air of milady ringing for her carriage. The waiter came with his large-chinned, low-voiced manner of respectful familiarity. Liz smoothed her silken skirt with a satisfied wriggle. She made the most of it. Here she could order and be waited upon. It was all that her world offered her of the prerogative of woman.

"Whiskey, Tommy," she said as her sisters further uptown murmur, "Champagne, James."

"Sure, Miss Lizzie. What'll the chaser be?"

"Seltzer. And say, Tommy, has the Kid been around to-day?"

"Why, no, Miss Lizzie, I haven't saw him to-day."

Fluently came the "Miss Lizzie," for the Kid was known to be one who required rigid upholdment of the dignity of his fiancée.

"I'm lookin' for 'm," said Liz, after the chaser had sputtered under her nose. "It's got to me that he says he'll take Annie Karlson to the dance. Let him. The pink-eyed white rat! I'm lookin' for 'm. You know me, Tommy. Two years me and the Kid's been engaged. Look at that ring. Five hundred, he said it cost. Let him take her to the dance. What'll I do? I'll cut his heart out. Another whiskey, Tommy."

"I wouldn't listen to no such reports, Miss Lizzie," said the waiter smoothly, from the narrow opening above his chin. "Kid Mullaly's not the guy to throw a lady like you down. Seltzer on the side?"

"Two years," repeated Liz, softening a little to sentiment under the magic of the distiller's art. "I always used to play out on the street of evenin's 'cause there was nothin' doin' for me at home. For a long time I just sat on doorsteps and looked at the lights and the people goin' by. And then the Kid came along one evenin' and sized me up, and I was mashed on the spot for fair. The first drink he made me take, I cried all night at home, and got a lickin' for makin' a noise. And now—say, Tommy, you ever see this Annie Karlson? If it wasn't for peroxide the chloroform limit would have put her out long ago. Oh, I'm lookin' for 'm. You tell the Kid if he comes in. Me? I'll cut his heart out. Leave it to me. Another whiskey, Tommy."

A little unsteadily, but with watchful and brilliant eyes, Liz walked up the avenue. On the doorstep of a brick tenement a curly-haired child sat, puzzling over the convolutions of a tangled string. Liz flopped down beside her, with a crooked, shifting smile on her flushed face. But her eyes had grown clear and artless of a sudden.

"Let me show you how to make a cat's-cradle, kid," she said, tucking her green silk skirt under her rusty shoes.

And while they sat there the lights were being turned on for the dance in the hall of the Small Hours Social Club. It was a bi-monthly dance, a dress affair in which the members took great pride and bestirred themselves huskily to further and adorn.

At 9 o'clock the President, Kid Mullaly, paced the floor with a lady on his arm. As the Loreley's was her hair golden. Her "yes" was softened to a "yah," but its quality of assent was patent to the most Milesian ears. She stepped upon her own train and blushed, and—she smiled into the eyes of Kid Mullaly.

And then, as the two stood in the middle of the waxed floor, the thing happened to prevent which many lamps are burning nightly in many studies and libraries.

Out from the circle of spectators in the hall leaped Fate in a green silk skirt, under the *nom de guerre* of "Liz." Her eyes were hard and blacker than jet. She did not scream or waver. Most unwomanly, she cried out one oath—the Kid's own favorite oath—and in his own deep voice; and then while the Small Hours Social Club went frantically to pieces, she made good her boast to Tommy, the waiter—made good as far as the length of her knife blade and the strength of her arm permitted.

And next came the primal instinct of self-preservation—or was it self-annihilation, the instinct that society has grafted on the natural branch?

Liz ran out and down the street swift and true as a woodcock flying through a grove of saplings at dusk.

And then followed the big city's biggest shame, its most ancient and rotten surviving canker, its pollution and disgrace, its blight and perversion, its forever infamy and guilt, fostered, unreproved and cherished, handed down from a long-ago century of the basest barbarity—the Hue and Cry. Nowhere but in the big cities does it survive, and here most of all, where the ultimate perfection of culture, citizenship and alleged superiority joins, bawling, in the chase.

They pursued—a shrieking mob of fathers, mothers, lovers and maidens—howling, yelling, calling, whistling, crying for blood. Well may the wolf in the big city stand outside the door. Well may his heart, the gentler, falter at the siege. Knowing her way, and hungry for her surcease, she darted down the familiar ways until at last her feet struck the dull solidity of the rotting pier. And then it was but a few more panting steps—and good mother East River took Liz to her bosom, smoothed her muddily but quickly, and settled in five minutes the problem that keeps lights burning o' nights in thousands of pastorates and colleges.

It's mighty funny what kind of dreams one has sometimes. Poets call them visions, but a vision is only a dream in blank verse. I dreamed the rest of this story.

I thought I was in the next world. I don't know how I got there; I suppose I had been riding on the Ninth Avenue elevated or taking patent medicine or trying to pull Jim Jeffries's nose, or doing some such little injudicious stunt. But, anyhow, there I was, and there was a great crowd of us outside the court-room where the judgments were going on. And every now and then a very beautiful and imposing court-officer angel would come outside the door and call another case.

While I was considering my own worldly sins and wondering whether there would be any use of my trying to prove an alibi by claiming that I lived in New Jersey, the bailiff angel came to the door and sang out: "Case No. 99,852,743."

Up stepped a plain-clothes man—there were lots of 'em there, dressed exactly like preachers and hustling us spirits around just like cops do on earth—and by the arm he dragged—whom, do you think? Why, Liz!

The court officer took her inside and closed the door. I went up to Mr. Fly-Cop and inquired about the case.

"A very sad one," says he, laying the points of his manicured fingers together. "An utterly incorrigible girl. I am Special Terrestrial Officer the Reverend Jones. The case was assigned to me. The girl murdered her fiancé and committed suicide. She had no defense. My report to the court relates the facts in detail, all of which are substantiated by reliable witnesses. The wages of sin is death. Praise the Lord."

The court officer opened the door and stepped out.

"Poor girl," said Special Terrestrial Officer the Reverend Jones, with a tear in his eye. "It was one of the saddest cases that I ever met with. Of course she was——"

"Discharged," said the court officer. "Come here, Jonesy. First thing you know you'll be switched to the pot-pie squad. How would you like to be on the missionary force in the South Sea Islands—hey? Now, you quit making these false arrests, or you'll be transferred—see? The guilty party you've got to look for in this case is a red-haired, unshaven, untidy man, sitting by the window reading, in his stocking feet, while his children play in the streets. Get a move on you."

Now, wasn't that a silly dream?

ACCORDING TO THEIR LIGHTS

Somewhere in the depths of the big city, where the unquiet dregs are forever being shaken together, young Murray and the Captain had met and become friends. Both were at the lowest ebb possible to their fortunes; both had fallen from at least an intermediate Heaven of respectability and importance, and both were typical products of the monstrous and peculiar social curriculum of their over-weening and bumptious civic alma mater.

The Captain was no longer a captain. One of those sudden moral cataclysms that sometimes sweep the city had hurled him from a high and profitable position in the Police Department, ripping off his badge and buttons and washing into the hands of his lawyers the solid pieces of real estate that his frugality had enabled him to accumulate. The passing of the flood left him low and dry. One month after his dishabilitation a saloon-keeper plucked him by the neck from his free-lunch counter as a tabby plucks a strange kitten from her nest, and cast him asphaltward. This seems low enough. But after that he acquired a pair of cloth-top, button Congress gaiters and wrote complaining letters to the newspapers. And then he fought the attendant at the Municipal Lodging House who tried to give him a bath. When Murray first saw him he was holding the hand of an Italian woman who sold apples and garlic on Essex Street, and quoting the words of a song book ballad.

Murray's fall had been more Luciferian, if less spectacular. All the pretty, tiny little kickshaws of Gotham had once been his. The megaphone man roars out at you to observe the house of his uncle on a grand and revered avenue. But there had been an awful row about something, and the prince had been escorted to the door by the butler, which, in said avenue, is equivalent to the impact of the avuncular shoe. A weak Prince Hal, without inheritance or sword, he drifted downward to meet his humorless Falstaff, and to pick the crusts of the streets with him.

One evening they sat on a bench in a little downtown park. The great bulk of the Captain, which starvation seemed to increase—drawing irony instead of pity to his petitions for aid—was heaped against the arm of the bench in a shapeless mass. His red face, spotted by tufts of vermilion, week-old whiskers and topped by a sagging white straw hat, looked, in the gloom, like one of those structures that you may observe in a dark Third Avenue window, challenging your imagination to say whether it be something recent in the way of ladies' hats or a strawberry shortcake. A tight-drawn belt—last relic of his official spruceness—made a deep furrow in his circumference. The Captain's shoes were buttonless. In a smothered bass he cursed his star of ill-luck.

Murray, at his side, was shrunk into his dingy and ragged suit of blue serge. His hat was pulled low; he sat quiet and a little indistinct, like some ghost that had been dispossessed.

"I'm hungry," growled the Captain—"by the top sirloin of the Bull of Bashan, I'm starving to death. Right now I could eat a Bowery restaurant clear through to the stovepipe in the alley. Can't you think of nothing, Murray? You sit there with your shoulders scrunched up, giving an imitation of Reginald Vanderbilt driving his coach—what good are them airs doing you now? Think of some place we can get something to chew."

"You forget, my dear captain," said Murray, without moving, "that our last attempt at dining was at my suggestion."

"You bet it was," groaned the Captain, "you bet your life it was. Have you got any more like that to make—hey?"

"I admit we failed," sighed Murray. "I was sure Malone would be good for one more free lunch after the way he talked baseball with me the last time I spent a nickel in his establishment."

"I had this hand," said the Captain, extending the unfortunate member—"I had this hand on the drumstick of a turkey and two sardine sandwiches when them waiters grabbed us."

"I was within two inches of the olives," said Murray. "Stuffed olives. I haven't tasted one in a year."

"What'll we do?" grumbled the Captain. "We can't starve."

"Can't we?" said Murray, quietly. "I'm glad to hear that. I was afraid we could."

"You wait here," said the Captain, rising heavily and puffily to his feet. "I'm going to try to make one more turn. You stay here till I come back, Murray. I won't be over half an hour. If I turn the trick I'll come back flush."

He made some elephantine attempts at smartening his appearance. He gave his fiery mustache a heavenward twist; he dragged into sight a pair of black-edged cuffs, deepened the crease in his middle by tightening his belt another hole, and set off, jaunty as a zoo rhinoceros, across the south end of the park.

When he was out of sight Murray also left the park, hurrying swiftly eastward. He stopped at a building whose steps were flanked by two green lights.

"A police captain named Maroney," he said to the desk sergeant, "was dismissed from the force after being tried under charges three years ago. I believe sentence was suspended. Is this man wanted now by the police?"

"Why are ye asking?" inquired the sergeant, with a frown.

"I thought there might be a reward standing," explained Murray, easily. "I know the man well. He seems to be keeping himself pretty shady at present. I could lay my hands on him at any time. If there should be a reward——"

"There's no reward," interrupted the sergeant, shortly. "The man's not wanted. And neither are ye. So, get out. Ye are frindly with um, and ye would be selling um. Out with ye quick, or I'll give ye a start."

Murray gazed at the officer with serene and virtuous dignity.

"I would be simply doing my duty as a citizen and gentleman," he said, severely, "if I could assist the law in laying hold of one of its offenders."

Murray hurried back to the bench in the park. He folded his arms and shrank within his clothes to his ghost-like presentment.

Ten minutes afterward the Captain arrived at the rendezvous, windy and thunderous as a dog-day in Kansas. His collar had been torn away; his straw hat had been twisted and battered; his shirt with oxblood stripes split to the waist. And from head to knee he was drenched with some vile and ignoble greasy fluid that loudly proclaimed to the nose its component leaven of garlic and kitchen stuff.

"For Heaven's sake, Captain," sniffed Murray, "I doubt that I would have waited for you if I had suspected you were so desperate as to resort to swill barrels. I——"

"Cheese it," said the Captain, harshly. "I'm not hogging it yet. It's all on the outside. I went around on Essex and proposed marriage to that Catrina that's got the fruit shop there. Now, that business could be built up. She's a peach as far as a Dago could be. I thought I had that senoreena mashed sure last week. But look what she done to me! I guess I got too fresh. Well there's another scheme queered."

"You don't mean to say," said Murray, with infinite contempt, "that you would have married that woman to help yourself out of your disgraceful troubles!"

"Me?" said the Captain. "I'd marry the Empress of China for one bowl of chop suey. I'd commit murder for a plate of beef stew. I'd steal a wafer from a waif. I'd be a Mormon for a bowl of chowder."

"I think," said Murray, resting his head on his hands, "that I would play Judas for the price of one drink of whiskey. For thirty pieces of silver I would——"

"Oh, come now!" exclaimed the Captain in dismay. "You wouldn't do that, Murray? I always thought that Kike's squeal on his boss was about the lowest-down play that ever happened. A man that gives his friend away is worse than a pirate."

Through the park stepped a large man scanning the benches where the electric light fell.

"Is that you, Mac?" he said, halting before the derelicts. His diamond stick-pin dazzled. His diamond-studded fob chain assisted. He was big and smooth and well fed. "Yes, I see it's you," he continued. "They told me at Mike's that I might find you over here. Let me see you a few minutes, Mac."

The Captain lifted himself with a grunt of alacrity. If Charlie Finnegan had come down in the bottomless pit to seek him there must be something doing. Charlie guided him by an arm into a patch of shadow.

"You know, Mac," he said, "they're trying Inspector Pickering on graft charges."

"He was my inspector," said the Captain.

"O'Shea wants the job," went on Finnegan. "He must have it. It's for the good of the organization. Pickering must go under. Your testimony will do it. He was your 'man higher up' when you were on the force. His share of the boodle passed through your hands. You must go on the stand and testify against him."

"He was"—began the Captain.

"Wait a minute," said Finnegan. A bundle of yellowish stuff came out of his inside pocket. "Five hundred dollars in it for you. Two-fifty on the spot, and the rest——"

"He was my friend, I say," finished the Captain. "I'll see you and the gang, and the city, and the party in the flames of Hades before I'll take the stand against Dan Pickering. I'm down and out; but I'm no traitor to a man that's been my friend." The Captain's voice rose and boomed like a split trombone. "Get out of this park, Charlie Finnegan, where us thieves and tramps and boozers are your betters; and take your dirty money with you."

Finnegan drifted out by another walk. The Captain returned to his seat.

"I couldn't avoid hearing," said Murray, drearily. "I think you are the biggest fool I ever saw."

"What would you have done?" asked the Captain.

"Nailed Pickering to the cross," said Murray.

"Sonny," said the Captain, huskily and without heat. "You and me are different. New York is divided into two parts—above Forty-second Street, and below Fourteenth. You come from the other part. We both act according to our lights."

An illuminated clock above the trees retailed the information that it lacked the half hour of twelve. Both men rose from the bench and moved away together as if seized by the same idea. They left the park, struck through a narrow cross street, and came into Broadway, at this hour as dark, echoing and de-peopled as a byway in Pompeii.

Northward they turned; and a policeman who glanced at their unkempt and slinking figures withheld the attention and suspicion that he would have granted them at any other hour and place. For on every street in that part of the city other unkempt and slinking figures were shuffling and hurrying toward a converging point—a point that is marked by no monument save that groove on the pavement worn by tens of thousands of waiting feet.

At Ninth Street a tall man wearing an opera hat alighted from a Broadway car and turned his face westward. But he saw Murray, pounced upon him and dragged him under a street light. The Captain lumbered slowly to the corner, like a wounded bear, and waited, growling.

"Jerry!" cried the hatted one. "How fortunate! I was to begin a search for you to-morrow. The old gentleman has capitulated. You're to be restored to favor. Congratulate you. Come to the office in the morning and get all the money you want. I've liberal instructions in that respect."

"And the little matrimonial arrangement?" said Murray, with his head turned sidewise.

"Why—er—well, of course, your uncle understands—expects that the engagement between you and Miss Vanderhurst shall be——"

"Good night," said Murray, moving away.

"You madman!" cried the other, catching his arm. "Would you give up two millions on account of——"

"Did you ever see her nose, old man?" asked Murray, solemnly.

"But, listen to reason, Jerry. Miss Vanderhurst is an heiress, and——"

"Did you ever see it?"

"Yes, I admit that her nose isn't——"

"Good night!" said Murray. "My friend is waiting for me. I am quoting him when I authorize you to report that there is 'nothing doing.' Good night."

A wriggling line of waiting men extended from a door in Tenth Street far up Broadway, on the outer edge of the pavement. The Captain and Murray fell in at the tail of the quivering millipede.

"Twenty feet longer than it was last night," said Murray, looking up at his measuring angle of Grace Church.

"Half an hour," growled the Captain, "before we get our punk."

The city clocks began to strike 12; the Bread Line moved forward slowly, its leathern feet sliding on the stones with the sound of a hissing serpent, as they who had lived according to their lights closed up in the rear.

A MIDSUMMER KNIGHT'S DREAM

> "The knights are dead;
> Their swords are rust.
> Except a few who have to hust-
> Le all the time
> To raise the dust."

Dear Reader: It was summertime. The sun glared down upon the city with pitiless ferocity. It is difficult for the sun to be ferocious and exhibit compunction simultaneously. The heat was—oh, bother thermometers! —who cares for standard measures, anyhow? It was so hot that——

The roof gardens put on so many extra waiters that you could hope to get your gin fizz now—as soon as all the other people got theirs. The hospitals were putting in extra cots for bystanders. For when little woolly dogs loll their tongues out and say "woof, woof!" at the fleas that bite 'em, and nervous old black bombazine ladies screech "Mad dog!" and policemen begin to shoot, somebody is going to get hurt. The man from Pompton, N. J., who always wears an overcoat in July, had turned up in a Broadway hotel drinking hot Scotches and enjoying his annual ray from the calcium. Philanthropists were petitioning the Legislature to pass a bill requiring builders to make tenement fire-escapes more commodious, so that families might die all together of the heat instead of one or two at a time. So many men were telling you about the number of baths they took each day that you wondered how they got along after the real lessee of the apartment came back to town and thanked 'em for taking such good care of it. The young man who called loudly for cold beef and beer in the restaurant, protesting that roast pullet and Burgundy was really too heavy for such weather, blushed when he met your eye, for you had heard him all winter calling, in modest tones, for the same ascetic viands. Soup, pocketbooks, shirt waists, actors, and baseball excuses grew thinner. Yes, it was summertime.

A man stood at Thirty-fourth Street waiting for a downtown car. A man of forty, gray-haired, pink-faced, keen, nervous, plainly dressed, with a harassed look around the eyes. He wiped his forehead and laughed loudly when a fat man with an outing look stopped and spoke with him.

"No, siree," he shouted with defiance and scorn. "None of your old mosquito-haunted swamps and skyscraper mountains without elevators for me. When I want to get away from hot weather I know how to do it. New York, sir, is the finest summer resort in the country. Keep in the shade and watch your diet, and don't get too far away from an electric fan. Talk about your Adirondacks and your Catskills! There's more solid comfort in the borough of Manhattan than in all the rest of the country together. No, siree! No tramping up perpendicular cliffs and being waked up at 4 in the morning by a million flies, and eating canned goods straight from the city for me. Little old New York will take a few select summer boarders; comforts and conveniences of home—that's the ad. that I answer every time."

"You need a vacation," said the fat man, looking closely at the other. "You haven't been away from town in years. Better come with me for two weeks, anyhow. The trout in the Beaverkill are jumping at anything now that looks like a fly. Harding writes me that he landed a three-pound brown last week."

"Nonsense!" cried the other man. "Go ahead, if you like, and boggle around in rubber boots wearing yourself out trying to catch fish. When I want one I go to a cool restaurant and order it. I laugh at you fellows whenever I think of you hustling around in the heat in the country thinking you are having a good time. For me Father Knickerbocker's little improved farm with the big shady lane running through the middle of it."

The fat man sighed over his friend and went his way. The man who thought New York was the greatest summer resort in the country boarded a car and went buzzing down to his office. On the way he threw away his newspaper and looked up at a ragged patch of sky above the housetops.

"Three pounds!" he muttered, absently. "And Harding isn't a liar. I believe, if I could—but it's impossible—they've got to have another month—another month at least."

In his office the upholder of urban midsummer joys dived, head foremost, into the swimming pool of business. Adkins, his clerk, came and added a spray of letters, memoranda and telegrams.

At 5 o'clock in the afternoon the busy man leaned back in his office chair, put his feet on the desk and mused aloud:

"I wonder what kind of bait Harding used."

She was all in white that day; and thereby Compton lost a bet to Gaines. Compton had wagered she would wear light blue, for she knew that was his favorite color, and Compton was a millionaire's son, and that almost laid him open to the charge of betting on a sure thing. But white was her choice, and Gaines held up his head with twenty-five's lordly air.

The little summer hotel in the mountains had a lively crowd that year. There were two or three young college men and a couple of artists and a young naval officer on one side. On the other there were enough beauties among the young ladies for the correspondent of a society paper to refer to them as a "bevy." But the moon among the stars was Mary Sewell. Each one of the young men greatly desired to arrange matters so that he could pay her millinery bills, and fix the furnace, and have her do away with the "Sewell" part of her name forever. Those who could stay only a week or two went away hinting at pistols and blighted hearts. But Compton stayed like the mountains themselves, for he could afford it. And Gaines stayed because he was a fighter and wasn't afraid of millionaires' sons, and—well, he adored the country.

"What do you think, Miss Mary?" he said once. "I knew a duffer in New York who claimed to like it in the summer time. Said you could keep cooler there than you could in the woods. Wasn't he an awful silly? I don't think I could breathe on Broadway after the 1st of June."

"Mamma was thinking of going back week after next," said Miss Mary with a lovely frown.

"But when you think of it," said Gaines, "there are lots of jolly places in town in the summer. The roof gardens, you know, and the—er—the roof gardens."

Deepest blue was the lake that day—the day when they had the mock tournament, and the men rode clumsy farm horses around in a glade in the woods and caught curtain rings on the end of a lance. Such fun!

Cool and dry as the finest wine came the breath of the shadowed forest. The valley below was a vision seen through an opal haze. A white mist from hidden falls blurred the green of a hand's breadth of tree tops halfway down the gorge. Youth made merry hand-in-hand with young summer. Nothing on Broadway like that.

The villagers gathered to see the city folks pursue their mad drollery. The woods rang with the laughter of pixies and naiads and sprites. Gaines caught most of the rings. His was the privilege to crown the queen of the tournament. He was the conquering knight—as far as the rings went. On his arm he wore a white scarf. Compton wore light blue. She had declared her preference for blue, but she wore white that day.

Gaines looked about for the queen to crown her. He heard her merry laugh, as if from the clouds. She had slipped away and climbed Chimney

Rock, a little granite bluff, and stood there, a white fairy among the laurels, fifty feet above their heads.

Instantly he and Compton accepted the implied challenge. The bluff was easily mounted at the rear, but the front offered small hold to hand or foot. Each man quickly selected his route and began to climb. A crevice, a bush, a slight projection, a vine or tree branch—all of these were aids that counted in the race. It was all foolery—there was no stake; but there was youth in it, cross reader, and light hearts, and something else that Miss Clay writes so charmingly about.

Gaines gave a great tug at the root of a laurel and pulled himself to Miss Mary's feet. On his arm he carried the wreath of roses; and while the villagers and summer boarders screamed and applauded below he placed it on the queen's brow.

"You are a gallant knight," said Miss Mary.

"If I could be your true knight always," began Gaines, but Miss Mary laughed him dumb, for Compton scrambled over the edge of the rock one minute behind time.

What a twilight that was when they drove back to the hotel! The opal of the valley turned slowly to purple, the dark woods framed the lake as a mirror, the tonic air stirred the very soul in one. The first pale stars came out over the mountain tops where yet a faint glow of——

"I beg your pardon, Mr. Gaines," said Adkins.

The man who believed New York to be the finest summer resort in the world opened his eyes and kicked over the mucilage bottle on his desk.

"I—I believe I was asleep," he said.

"It's the heat," said Adkins. "It's something awful in the city these——"

"Nonsense!" said the other. "The city beats the country ten to one in summer. Fools go out tramping in muddy brooks and wear themselves out trying to catch little fish as long as your finger. Stay in town and keep comfortable—that's my idea."

"Some letters just came," said Adkins. "I thought you might like to glance at them before you go."

Let us look over his shoulder and read just a few lines of one of them:

My dear, dear Husband: Just received your letter ordering us to stay another month. . . . Rita's cough is almost gone. . . . Johnny has simply gone wild like a little Indian. . . . Will be the making of both children . . . work so hard, and I know that your business can hardly afford to keep us here so long . . . best man that ever . . . you always pretend that you like the city in summer . . . trout fishing that you used to be so fond of . . . and all to keep us well and happy . . . come to you if it were not doing the babies so much good. . . . I stood last evening on Chimney Rock in exactly the same spot where I was when you put the wreath of roses on my head . . . through all the world . . . when you said you would be my true knight . . . fifteen years ago, dear, just think! . . . have always been that to me . . . ever and ever,

Mary

The man who said he thought New York the finest summer resort in the country dropped into a café on his way home and had a glass of beer under an electric fan.

"Wonder what kind of a fly old Harding used," he said to himself.

THE LAST LEAF

In a little district west of Washington Square the streets have run crazy and broken themselves into small strips called "places." These "places" make strange angles and curves. One street crosses itself a time or two. An artist once discovered a valuable possibility in this street. Suppose a collector with a bill for paints, paper and canvas should, in traversing this route, suddenly meet himself coming back, without a cent having been paid on account!

So, to quaint old Greenwich Village the art people soon came prowling, hunting for north windows and eighteenth-century gables and Dutch attics and low rents. Then they imported some pewter mugs and a chafing dish or two from Sixth Avenue, and became a "colony."

At the top of a squatty, three-story brick Sue and Johnsy had their studio. "Johnsy" was familiar for Joanna. One was from Maine; the other from California. They had met at the *table d'hôte* of an Eighth Street "Delmonico's," and found their tastes in art, chicory salad and bishop sleeves so congenial that the joint studio resulted.

That was in May. In November a cold, unseen stranger, whom the doctors called Pneumonia, stalked about the colony, touching one here and there with his icy fingers. Over on the east side this ravager strode boldly, smiting his victims by scores, but his feet trod slowly through the maze of the narrow and moss-grown "places."

Mr. Pneumonia was not what you would call a chivalric old gentleman. A mite of a little woman with blood thinned by California zephyrs was hardly fair game for the red-fisted, short-breathed old duffer. But Johnsy he smote; and she lay, scarcely moving, on her painted iron bedstead, looking through the small Dutch window-panes at the blank side of the next brick house.

One morning the busy doctor invited Sue into the hallway with a shaggy, gray eyebrow.

"She has one chance in—let us say, ten," he said, as he shook down the mercury in his clinical thermometer. "And that chance is for her to want to live. This way people have of lining-up on the side of the undertaker makes the entire pharmacopœia look silly. Your little lady has made up her mind that she's not going to get well. Has she anything on her mind?"

"She—she wanted to paint the Bay of Naples some day," said Sue.

"Paint?—bosh! Has she anything on her mind worth thinking about twice—a man, for instance?"

"A man?" said Sue, with a jew's-harp twang in her voice. "Is a man worth—but, no, doctor; there is nothing of the kind."

"Well, it is the weakness, then," said the doctor. "I will do all that science, so far as it may filter through my efforts, can accomplish. But whenever my patient begins to count the carriages in her funeral procession I subtract 50 per cent. from the curative power of medicines. If you will get her to ask one question about the new winter styles in cloak sleeves I will promise you a one-in-five chance for her, instead of one in ten."

After the doctor had gone Sue went into the workroom and cried a Japanese napkin to a pulp. Then she swaggered into Johnsy's room with her drawing board, whistling ragtime.

Johnsy, lay, scarcely making a ripple under the bedclothes, with her face toward the window. Sue stopped whistling, thinking she was asleep.

She arranged her board and began a pen-and-ink drawing to illustrate a magazine story. Young artists must pave their way to Art by drawing pictures for magazine stories that young authors write to pave their way to Literature.

As Sue was sketching a pair of elegant horseshow riding trousers and a monocle on the figure of the hero, an Idaho cowboy, she heard a low sound, several times repeated. She went quickly to the bedside.

Johnsy's eyes were open wide. She was looking out the window and counting—counting backward.

"Twelve," she said, and a little later "eleven"; and then "ten," and "nine"; and then "eight" and "seven," almost together.

Sue looked solicitously out of the window. What was there to count? There was only a bare, dreary yard to be seen, and the blank side of the brick house twenty feet away. An old, old ivy vine, gnarled and decayed at the roots, climbed half way up the brick wall. The cold breath of autumn had stricken its leaves from the vine until its skeleton branches clung, almost bare, to the crumbling bricks.

"What is it, dear?" asked Sue.

"Six," said Johnsy, in almost a whisper. "They're falling faster now. Three days ago there were almost a hundred. It made my head ache to count them. But now it's easy. There goes another one. There are only five left now."

"Five what, dear? Tell your Sudie."

"Leaves. On the ivy vine. When the last one falls I must go, too. I've known that for three days. Didn't the doctor tell you?"

"Oh, I never heard of such nonsense," complained Sue, with magnificent scorn. "What have old ivy leaves to do with your getting well? And you used to love that vine, so, you naughty girl. Don't be a goosey. Why, the doctor told me this morning that your chances for getting well real soon were—let's see exactly what he said—he said the chances were ten to one! Why, that's almost as good a chance as we have in New York when we ride on the street cars or walk past a new building. Try to take some broth now, and let Sudie go back to her drawing, so she can sell the editor man with it, and buy port wine for her sick child, and pork chops for her greedy self."

"You needn't get any more wine," said Johnsy, keeping her eyes fixed out the window. "There goes another. No, I don't want any broth. That leaves just four. I want to see the last one fall before it gets dark. Then I'll go, too."

"Johnsy, dear," said Sue, bending over her, "will you promise me to keep your eyes closed, and not look out the window until I am done working? I must hand those drawings in by to-morrow. I need the light, or I would draw the shade down."

"Couldn't you draw in the other room?" asked Johnsy, coldly.

"I'd rather be here by you," said Sue. "Besides, I don't want you to keep looking at those silly ivy leaves."

"Tell me as soon as you have finished," said Johnsy, closing her eyes, and lying white and still as a fallen statue, "because I want to see the last one fall. I'm tired of waiting. I'm tired of thinking. I want to turn loose my hold on everything, and go sailing down, down, just like one of those poor, tired leaves."

"Try to sleep," said Sue. "I must call Behrman up to be my model for the old hermit miner. I'll not be gone a minute. Don't try to move 'til I come back."

Old Behrman was a painter who lived on the ground floor beneath them. He was past sixty and had a Michael Angelo's Moses beard curling down from the head of a satyr along the body of an imp. Behrman was a failure in art. Forty years he had wielded the brush without getting near enough to touch the hem of his Mistress's robe. He had been always about to paint a masterpiece, but had never yet begun it. For several years he had painted nothing except now and then a daub in the line of commerce or advertising. He earned a little by serving as a model to those young artists in the colony who could not pay the price of a professional. He drank gin to excess, and still talked of his coming masterpiece. For the rest he was a fierce little old man, who scoffed terribly at softness in any one, and who regarded himself as especial mastiff-in-waiting to protect the two young artists in the studio above.

Sue found Behrman smelling strongly of juniper berries in his dimly lighted den below. In one corner was a blank canvas on an easel that had been waiting there for twenty-five years to receive the first line of the masterpiece. She told him of Johnsy's fancy, and how she feared she would, indeed, light and fragile as a leaf herself, float away, when her slight hold upon the world grew weaker.

Old Behrman, with his red eyes plainly streaming, shouted his contempt and derision for such idiotic imaginings.

"Vass!" he cried. "Is dere people in de world mit der foolishness to die because leafs dey drop off from a confounded vine? I haf not heard of such a thing. No, I will not bose as a model for your fool hermit-dunderhead. Vy do you allow dot silly pusiness to come in der brain of her? Ach, dot poor leetle Miss Yohnsy."

"She is very ill and weak," said Sue, "and the fever has left her mind morbid and full of strange fancies. Very well, Mr. Behrman, if you do not care to pose for me, you needn't. But I think you are a horrid old— old flibbertigibbet."

"You are just like a woman!" yelled Behrman. "Who said I will not bose? Go on. I come mit you. For half an hour I haf peen trying to say dot I am ready to bose. Gott! dis is not any blace in which one so goot as Miss Yohnsy shall lie sick. Some day I vill baint a masterpiece, and ve shall all go away. Gott! yes."

Johnsy was sleeping when they went upstairs. Sue pulled the shade down to the window-sill, and motioned Behrman into the other room. In there they peered out the window fearfully at the ivy vine. Then they looked at each other for a moment without speaking. A persistent, cold rain was falling, mingled with snow. Behrman, in his old blue shirt, took his seat as the hermit miner on an upturned kettle for a rock.

When Sue awoke from an hour's sleep the next morning she found Johnsy with dull, wide-open eyes staring at the drawn green shade.

"Pull it up; I want to see," she ordered, in a whisper.

Wearily Sue obeyed.

But, lo! after the beating rain and fierce gusts of wind that had endured through the livelong night, there yet stood out against the brick wall one ivy leaf. It was the last on the vine. Still dark green near its stem, but with its serrated edges tinted with the yellow of dissolution and decay, it hung bravely from a branch some twenty feet above the ground.

"It is the last one," said Johnsy. "I thought it would surely fall during the night. I heard the wind. It will fall to-day, and I shall die at the same time."

"Dear, dear!" said Sue, leaning her worn face down to the pillow, "think of me, if you won't think of yourself. What would I do?"

But Johnsy did not answer. The lonesomest thing in all the world is a soul when it is making ready to go on its mysterious, far journey. The fancy seemed to possess her more strongly as one by one the ties that bound her to friendship and to earth were loosed.

The day wore away, and even through the twilight they could see the lone ivy leaf clinging to its stem against the wall. And then, with the coming of the night the north wind was again loosed, while the rain still beat against the windows and pattered down from the low Dutch eaves.

When it was light enough Johnsy, the merciless, commanded that the shade be raised.

The ivy leaf was still there.

Johnsy lay for a long time looking at it. And then she called to Sue, who was stirring her chicken broth over the gas stove.

"I've been a bad girl, Sudie," said Johnsy. "Something has made that last leaf stay there to show me how wicked I was. It is a sin to want to die. You may bring me a little broth now, and some milk with a little port in it, and—no; bring me a hand-mirror first, and then pack some pillows about me, and I will sit up and watch you cook."

An hour later she said:

"Sudie, some day I hope to paint the Bay of Naples."

The doctor came in the afternoon, and Sue had an excuse to go into the hallway as he left.

"Even chances," said the doctor, taking Sue's thin, shaking hand in his. "With good nursing you'll win. And now I must see another case I have downstairs. Behrman, his name is—some kind of an artist, I believe. Pneumonia, too. He is an old, weak man, and the attack is acute. There is no hope for him; but he goes to the hospital to-day to be made more comfortable."

The next day the doctor said to Sue: "She's out of danger. You've won. Nutrition and care now—that's all."

And that afternoon Sue came to the bed where Johnsy lay, contentedly knitting a very blue and very useless woollen shoulder scarf, and put one arm around her, pillows and all.

"I have something to tell you, white mouse," she said. "Mr. Behrman died of pneumonia to-day in the hospital. He was ill only two days. The janitor found him on the morning of the first day in his room downstairs helpless with pain. His shoes and clothing were wet through and icy cold. They couldn't imagine where he had been on such a dreadful night. And then they found a lantern, still lighted, and a ladder that had been dragged from its place, and some scattered brushes, and a palette with green and yellow colors mixed on it, and—look out the window, dear, at the last ivy leaf on the wall. Didn't you wonder why it never fluttered or moved when the wind blew? Ah, darling, it's Behrman's masterpiece— he painted it there the night that the last leaf fell."

THE COUNT AND THE WEDDING GUEST

One evening when Andy Donovan went to dinner at his Second Avenue boarding-house, Mrs. Scott introduced him to a new boarder, a young lady, Miss Conway. Miss Conway was small and unobtrusive. She wore a plain, snuffy-brown dress, and bestowed her interest, which seemed languid, upon her plate. She lifted her diffident eyelids and shot one perspicuous, judicial glance at Mr. Donovan, politely murmured his name, and returned to her mutton. Mr. Donovan bowed with the grace and beaming smile that were rapidly winning for him social, business and political advancement, and erased the snuffy-brown one from the tablets of his consideration.

Two weeks later Andy was sitting on the front steps enjoying his cigar. There was a soft rustle behind and above him and Andy turned his head—and had his head turned.

Just coming out of the door was Miss Conway. She wore a night-black dress of *crêpe de—crêpe de*—oh, this thin black goods. Her hat was black, and from it drooped and fluttered an ebon veil, filmy as a spider's web. She stood on the top step and drew on black silk gloves. Not a speck of white or a spot of color about her dress anywhere. Her rich golden hair was drawn, with scarcely a ripple, into a shining, smooth knot low on her neck. Her face was plain rather than pretty, but it was now illuminated and made almost beautiful by her large gray eyes that gazed above the houses across the street into the sky with an expression of the most appealing sadness and melancholy.

Gather the idea, girls—all black, you know, with the preference for *crêpe de*—oh, *crêpe de Chine*—that's it. All black, and that sad, faraway look, and the hair shining under the black veil (you have to be a blonde, of course), and try to look as if, although your young life had been blighted just as it was about to give a hop-skip-and-a-jump over the threshold of life, a walk in the park might do you good, and be sure to happen out the door at the right moment, and—oh, it'll fetch 'em every time. But it's fierce, now, how cynical I am, ain't it?—to talk about mourning costumes this way.

Mr. Donovan suddenly reinscribed Miss Conway upon the tablets of his consideration. He threw away the remaining inch and a quarter of his cigar, that would have been good for eight minutes yet, and quickly shifted his center of gravity to his low-cut patent leathers.

"It's a fine, clear evening, Miss Conway," he said; and if the Weather Bureau could have heard the confident emphasis of his tones it would have hoisted the square white signal, and nailed it to the mast.

"To them that has the heart to enjoy it, it is, Mr. Donovan," said Miss Conway, with a sigh.

Mr. Donovan, in his heart, cursed fair weather. Heartless weather! It should hail and blow and snow to be consonant with the mood of Miss Conway.

"I hope none of your relatives—I hope you haven't sustained a loss?" ventured Mr. Donovan.

"Death has claimed," said Miss Conway, hesitating—"not a relative, but one who—but I will not intrude my grief upon you, Mr. Donovan."

"Intrude?" protested Mr. Donovan. "Why, say, Miss Conway, I'd be delighted, that is, I'd be sorry—I mean I'm sure nobody could sympathize with you truer than I would."

Miss Conway smiled a little smile. And oh, it was sadder than her expression in repose.

" 'Laugh, and the world laughs with you; weep, and they give you the laugh,' " she quoted. "I have learned that, Mr. Donovan. I have no friends or acquaintances in this city. But you have been kind to me. I appreciate it highly."

He had passed her the pepper twice at the table.

"It's tough to be alone in New York—that's a cinch," said Mr. Donovan. "But, say—whenever this little old town does loosen up and get friendly it goes the limit. Say you took a little stroll in the park, Miss Conway—don't you think it might chase away some of your mullygrubs? And if you'd allow me——"

"Thanks, Mr. Donovan. I'd be pleased to accept of your escort if you think the company of one whose heart is filled with gloom could be anyways agreeable to you."

Through the open gates of the iron-railed, old, downtown park, where the elect once took the air, they strolled, and found a quiet bench.

There is this difference between the grief of youth and that of old age; youth's burden is lightened by as much of it as another shares; old age may give and give, but the sorrow remains the same.

"He was my fiancé," confided Miss Conway, at the end of an hour. "We were going to be married next spring. I don't want you to think that I am stringing you, Mr. Donovan, but he was a real Count. He had an estate and a castle in Italy. Count Fernando Mazzini was his name. I never saw the beat of him for elegance. Papa objected, of course, and once we eloped, but Papa overtook us, and took us back. I thought sure Papa and Fernando would fight a duel. Papa has a livery business—in P'kipsee, you know.

"Finally, Papa came 'round, all right, and said we might be married next spring. Fernando showed him proofs of his title and wealth, and then went over to Italy to get the castle fixed up for us. Papa's very proud and, when Fernando wanted to give me several thousand dollars for my trousseau he called him down something awful. He wouldn't even let me take a ring or any presents from him. And when Fernando sailed I came to the city and got a position as cashier in a candy store.

"Three days ago I got a letter from Italy, forwarded from P'kipsee, saying that Fernando had been killed in a gondola accident.

"That is why I am in mourning. My heart, Mr. Donovan, will remain forever in his grave. I guess I am poor company, Mr. Donovan, but I cannot take any interest in no one. I should not care to keep you from gayety and your friends who can smile and entertain you. Perhaps you would prefer to walk back to the house?"

Now, girls, if you want to observe a young man hustle out after a pick and shovel, just tell him that your heart is in some other fellow's grave. Young men are grave-robbers by nature. Ask any widow. Something must be done to restore that missing organ to weeping angels in *crêpe de Chine*. Dead men certainly get the worst of it from all sides.

"I'm awful sorry," said Mr. Donovan, gently. "No, we won't walk back to the house just yet. And don't say you haven't no friends in this city, Miss Conway. I'm awful sorry, and I want you to believe I'm your friend, and that I'm awful sorry."

"I've got his picture here in my locket," said Miss Conway, after wiping her eyes with her handkerchief. "I never showed it to anybody; but I will to you, Mr. Donovan, because I believe you to be a true friend."

Mr. Donovan gazed long and with much interest at the photograph in the locket that Miss Conway opened for him. The face of Count Mazzini was one to command interest. It was a smooth, intelligent, bright, almost a handsome face—the face of a strong, cheerful man who might well be a leader among his fellows.

"I have a larger one, framed, in my room," said Miss Conway. "When we return I will show you that. They are all I have to remind me of Fernando. But he ever will be present in my heart, that's a sure thing."

A subtle task confronted Mr. Donovan—that of supplanting the unfortunate Count in the heart of Miss Conway. This his admiration for her determined him to do. But the magnitude of the undertaking did not seem to weigh upon his spirits. The sympathetic but cheerful friend was the rôle he essayed; and he played it so successfully that the next half-hour found them conversing pensively across two plates of ice-cream, though yet there was no diminution of the sadness in Miss Conway's large gray eyes.

Before they parted in the hall that evening she ran upstairs and brought down the framed photograph wrapped lovingly in a white silk scarf. Mr. Donovan surveyed it with inscrutable eyes.

"He gave me this the night he left for Italy," said Miss Conway. "I had the one for the locket made from this."

"A fine-looking man," said Mr. Donovan, heartily. "How would it suit you, Miss Conway, to give me the pleasure of your company to Coney next Sunday afternoon?"

A month later they announced their engagement to Mrs. Scott and the other boarders. Miss Conway continued to wear black.

A week after the announcement the two sat on the same bench in the downtown park, while the fluttering leaves of the trees made a dim kineto-scopic picture of them in the moonlight. But Donovan had worn a look of abstracted gloom all day. He was so silent to-night that love's lips could not keep back any longer the question that love's heart propounded.

"What's the matter, Andy, you are so solemn and grouchy to-night?"

"Nothing, Maggie."

"I know better. Can't I tell? You never acted this way before. What is it?"

"It's nothing much, Maggie."

"Yes it is; and I want to know. I'll bet it's some other girl you are thinking about. All right. Why don't you go get her if you want her? Take your arm away, if you please."

"I'll tell you then," said Andy, wisely, "but I guess you won't understand it exactly. You've heard of Mike Sullivan, haven't you? 'Big Mike' Sullivan, everybody calls him."

"No, I haven't," said Maggie. "And I don't want to, if he makes you act like this. Who is he?"

"He's the biggest man in New York," said Andy, almost reverently. "He can about do anything he wants to with Tammany or any other old thing in the political line. He's a mile high and as broad as East River. You say anything against Big Mike, and you'll have a million men on your collarbone in about two seconds. Why, he made a visit over to the old country awhile back, and the kings took to their holes like rabbits.

"Well, Big Mike's a friend of mine. I ain't more than deuce-high in the district as far as influence goes, but Mike's as good a friend to a little man, or a poor man as he is to a big one. I met him to-day on the Bowery, and what do you think he does? Comes up and shakes hands. 'Andy,' says he, 'I've been keeping cases on you. You've been putting in some good licks over on your side of the street, and I'm proud of you. What'll you take to drink?' He takes a cigar and I take a highball. I told him I was going to get married in two weeks. 'Andy,' says he, 'send me an invitation, so I'll keep in mind of it, and I'll come to the wedding.' That's what Big Mike says to me; and he always does what he says.

"You don't understand it, Maggie, but I'd have one of my hands cut off to have Big Mike Sullivan at our wedding. It would be the proudest day of my life. When he goes to a man's wedding, there's a guy being married that's made for life. Now, that's why I'm maybe looking sore to-night."

"Why don't you invite him, then, if he's so much to the mustard?" said Maggie, lightly.

"There's a reason why I can't," said Andy, sadly. "There's a reason why he mustn't be there. Don't ask me what it is, for I can't tell you."

"Oh, I don't care," said Maggie. "It's something about politics, of course. But it's no reason why you can't smile at me."

"Maggie," said Andy, presently, "do you think as much of me as you did of your—as you did of the Count Mazzini?"

He waited a long time, but Maggie did not reply. And then, suddenly she leaned against his shoulder and began to cry—to cry and shake with sobs, holding his arm tightly, and wetting the *crêpe de Chine* with tears.

"There, there, there!" soothed Andy, putting aside his own trouble. "And what is it, now?"

"Andy," sobbed Maggie, "I've lied to you, and you'll never marry me, or love me any more. But I feel that I've got to tell. Andy, there never was so much as the little finger of a count. I never had a beau in my life. But all the other girls had; and they talked about 'em; and that seemed to make the fellows like 'em more. And, Andy, I look swell in black— you know I do. So I went out to a photograph store and bought that picture, and had a little one made for my locket, and made up all that story about the Count and about his being killed, so I could wear black. And nobody can love a liar, and you'll shake me, Andy, and I'll die for shame. Oh, there never was anybody I liked but you—and that's all."

But instead of being pushed away, she found Andy's arm folding her closer. She looked up and saw his face cleared and smiling.

"Could you—could you forgive me, Andy?"

"Sure," said Andy. "It's all right about that. Back to the cemetery for the Count. You've straightened everything out, Maggie. I was in hopes you would before the wedding-day. Bully girl!"

"Andy," said Maggie, with a somewhat shy smile, after she had been thoroughly assured of forgiveness, "did you believe all that story about the Count?"

"Well, not to any large extent," said Andy, reaching for his cigar case; "because it's Big Mike Sullivan's picture you've got in that locket of yours."

THE COUNTRY OF ELUSION

The cunning writer will choose an indefinable subject; for he can then set down his theory of what it is; and next, at length, his conception of what it is not—and lo! his paper is covered. Therefore let us follow the prolix and unmapable trail into that mooted country, Bohemia.

Grainger, sub-editor of *Doc's Magazine,* closed his roll-top desk, put on his hat, walked into the hall, punched the "down" button, and waited for the elevator.

Grainger's day had been trying. The chief had tried to ruin the magazine a dozen times by going against Grainger's ideas for running it. A lady whose grandfather had fought with McClellan had brought a portfolio of poems in person.

Grainger was curator of the Lion's House of the magazine. That day he had "lunched" an Arctic explorer, a short-story writer, and the famous conductor of a slaughter-house exposé. Consequently his mind was in a whirl of icebergs, Maupassant, and trichinosis.

But there was a surcease and a recourse; there was Bohemia. He would seek distraction there; and, let's see—he would call by for Mary Adrian.

Half an hour later he threaded his way like a Brazilian orchid-hunter through the palm forest in the tiled entrance hall of the "Idealia" apartment-house. One day the christeners of apartment-houses and the cognominators of sleeping-cars will meet, and there will be some jealous and sanguinary knifing.

The clerk breathed Grainger's name so languidly into the house telephone that it seemed it must surely drop, from sheer inertia, down to the janitor's regions. But, at length, it soared dilatorily up to Miss Adrian's ear. Certainly, Mr. Grainger was to come up immediately.

A colored maid with an Eliza-crossing-the-ice expression opened the door of the apartment for him. Grainger walked sideways down the narrow hall. A bunch of burnt-umber hair and a sea-green eye appeared in the crack of a door. A long, white, undraped arm came out, barring the way.

"So glad you came, Ricky, instead of any of the others," said the eye. "Light a cigarette and give it to me. Going to take me to dinner? Fine. Go into the front room till I finish dressing. But don't sit in your usual chair. There's pie in it—meringue. Kappelman threw it at Reeves last evening while he was reciting. Sophy has just come to straighten up. Is it lit? Thanks. There's Scotch on the mantel—oh, no, it isn't—that's chartreuse. Ask Sophy to find you some. I won't be long."

Grainger escaped the meringue. As he waited his spirits sank still lower. The atmosphere of the room was as vapid as a zephyr wandering over a Vesuvian lava-bed. Relics of some feast lay about the room, scattered in places where even a prowling cat would have been surprised to find them. A straggling cluster of deep red roses in a marmalade jar bowed their heads over tobacco ashes and unwashed goblets. A chafing-dish stood on the piano; a leaf of sheet music supported a stack of sandwiches in a chair.

Mary came in, dressed and radiant. Her gown was of that thin, black fabric whose name through the change of a single vowel seems to summon visions ranging between the extremes of man's experiences. Spelled with an "*é*" it belongs to Gallic witchery and diaphanous dreams: with an "*a*" it drapes lamentation and woe.

That evening they went to the Café André. And, as people would confide to you in a whisper that André's was the only truly Bohemian restaurant in town, it may be well to follow them.

André began his professional career as a waiter in a Bowery ten-cent eating-house. Had you seen him there you would have called him tough—to yourself. Not aloud, for he would have "soaked" you as quickly as he would have soaked his thumb in your coffee. He saved money and started a basement *table d'hôte* in Eighth (or Ninth) Street. One afternoon André drank too much absinthe. He announced to his startled family that he was the Grand Lama of Thibet, therefore requiring an empty audience hall in which to be worshiped. He moved all the tables and chairs from the restaurant into the back yard, wrapped a red tablecloth around himself, and sat on a step-ladder for a throne. When the diners began to arrive, Madame, in a flurry of despair, laid cloths and ushered them, trembling, outside. Between the tables clothes-lines were stretched, bearing the family wash. A party of Bohemia hunters greeted the artistic innovation with shrieks and acclamations of delight. That week's washing was not taken in for two years. When André came to his senses he had the menu printed on stiffly starched cuffs, and served the ices in little wooden tubs. Next he took down his sign and darkened the front of the house. When you went there to dine you fumbled for an electric button and pressed it. A lookout slid open a panel in the door, looked at you suspiciously, and asked if you were acquainted with Senator Herodotus Q. McMilligan, of the Chickasaw Nation. If you were you were admitted and allowed to dine. If you were not, you were admitted and allowed to dine. There you have one of the abiding principles of Bohemia. When André had accumulated $20,000 he moved uptown, near Broadway, in the fierce light that beats upon the thrown-down. There we find him and leave him, with customers in pearls and automobile veils, striving to catch his excellently graduated nod of recognition.

There is a large round table in the northeast corner of André's at which six can sit. To this table Grainger and Mary Adrian made their way. Kappelman and Reeves were already there. And Miss Tooker, who designed the May cover for the *Ladies' Notathome Magazine*. And Mrs. Pothunter, who never drank anything but black-and-white highballs, being in mourning for her husband, who—oh, I've forgotten what he did —died, like as not.

Spaghetti-weary reader, wouldst take one penny-in-the-slot peep into the fair land of Bohemia? Then look; and when you think you have seen it you have not. And it is neither thimbleriggery nor astigmatism.

The walls of the Café André were covered with original sketches by the artists who furnished much of the color and sound of the place. Fair woman furnished the theme for the bulk of the drawings. When you say "sirens and siphons" you come near to estimating the alliterative atmosphere of André's.

First, I want you to meet my friend, Miss Adrian. Miss Tooker and Mrs. Pothunter you already know. While she tucks in the fingers of her elbow gloves you shall have her daguerreotype. So faint and uncertain shall the portrait be:

Age, somewhere between twenty-seven and high-neck evening dresses. Camaraderie in large bunches—whatever the fearful word may mean. Habitat—anywhere from Seattle to Tierra del Fuego. Temperament uncharted—she let Reeves squeeze her hand after he recited one of his poems; but she counted the change after sending him out with a dollar to buy some pickled pigs' feet. Deportment 75 out of a possible 100. Morals 100.

Mary was one of the princesses of Bohemia. In the first place, it was a royal and a daring thing to have been named Mary. There are twenty Fifines and Héloïses to one Mary in the Country of Elusion.

Now her gloves are tucked in. Miss Tooker has assumed a June poster pose; Mrs. Pothunter has bitten her lips to make the red show; Reeves has several times felt his coat to make sure that his latest poem is in the pocket. (It had been neatly typewritten; but he has copied it on the back of letters with a pencil.) Kappelman is underhandedly watching the clock. It is ten minutes to nine. When the hour comes it is to remind him of a story. Synopsis: A French girl says to her suitor: "Did you ask my father for my hand at nine o'clock this morning, as you said you would?" "I did not," he replies. "At nine o'clock I was fighting a duel with swords in the Bois de Boulogne." "Coward!" she hisses.

The dinner was ordered. You know how long the Bohemian feast of reason keeps up with the courses. Humor with the oysters; wit with the soup; repartee with the entrée; brag with the roast; knocks for Whistler and Kipling with the salad; songs with the coffee, the slapsticks with the cordials.

Between Miss Adrian's eyebrows was the pucker that shows the intense strain it requires to be at ease in Bohemia. Pat must come each sally, *mot*, and epigram. Every second of deliberation upon a reply costs you a bay leaf. Fine as a hair, a line began to curve from her nostrils to her mouth. To hold her own not a chance must be missed. A sentence addressed to her must be as a piccolo, each word of it a stop, which she must be prepared to seize upon and play. And she must always be quicker than a Micmac Indian to paddle the light canoe of conversation away from the rocks in the rapids that flow from the Pierian spring. For, plodding reader, the handwriting on the wall in the banquet hall of Bohemia is "*laisser faire.*" The gray ghost that sometimes peeps through the rings of smoke is that of slain old King Convention. Freedom is the tyrant that holds them in slavery.

As the dinner waned, hands reached for the pepper cruet rather than for the shaker of Attic salt. Miss Tooker, with an elbow to business, leaned across the table toward Grainger, upsetting her glass of wine.

"Now, while you are fed and in good humor," she said, "I want to make a suggestion to you about a new cover."

"A good idea," said Grainger, mopping the tablecloth with his napkin. "I'll speak to the waiter about it."

Kappelman, the painter, was the cut-up. As a piece of delicate Athenian wit he got up from his chair and waltzed down the room with a waiter. The dependent, no doubt an honest, pachydermatous, worthy, tax-paying, art-despising biped, released himself from the unequal encounter, carried his professional smile back to the dumbwaiter and dropped it down the shaft to eternal oblivion. Reeves began to make Keats turn in his grave. Mrs. Pothunter told the story of the men who met the widow on the train. Miss Adrian hummed what is still called a *chanson* in the cafés of Bridgeport. Grainger edited each individual effort with his assistant editor's smile, which meant: "Great! but you'll have to send them in through the regular channels. If I were the chief now—but you know how it is."

And soon the head waiter bowed before them, desolated to relate that the closing hour had already become chronologically historical; so out all trooped into the starry midnight, filling the street with gay laughter, to be barked at by hopeful cabmen and enviously eyed by the dull inhabitants of an uninspired world.

Grainger left Mary at the elevator in the trackless palm forest of the Idealia. After he had gone she came down again carrying a small handbag, 'phoned for a cab, drove to the Grand Central Station, boarded a 12.55 commuter's train, rode four hours with her burnt-umber head bobbing against the red-plush back of the seat, and landed during a fresh, stinging, glorious sunrise at a deserted station, the size of a peach crate, called Crocusville.

She walked a mile and clicked the latch of a gate. A bare, brown cottage stood twenty yards back; an old man with a pearl-white, Calvinistic face and clothes dyed blacker than a raven in a coal-mine was washing his hands in a tin basin on the front porch.

"How are you, Father?" said Mary timidly.

"I am as well as Providence permits, Mary Ann. You will find your mother in the kitchen."

In the kitchen a cryptic, gray woman kissed her glacially on the forehead, and pointed out the potatoes which were not yet peeled for breakfast. Mary sat in a wooden chair and decorticated spuds, with a thrill in her heart.

For breakfast there were grace, cold bread, potatoes, bacon, and tea.

"You are pursuing the same avocation in the city concerning which you have advised us from time to time by letter, I trust," said her father.

"Yes," said Mary. "I am still reviewing books for the same publication."

After breakfast she helped wash the dishes, and then all three sat in straight-back chairs in the barefloored parlor.

"It is my custom," said the old man, "on the Sabbath day to read aloud from the great work entitled the 'Apology for Authorized and Set Forms of Liturgy,' by the ecclesiastical philosopher and revered theologian Jeremy Taylor."

"I know it," said Mary blissfully, folding her hands.

For two hours the numbers of the great Jeremy rolled forth like the notes of an oratorio played on the violoncello. Mary sat gloating in the new sensation of racking physical discomfort that the wooden chair brought her. Perhaps there is no happiness in life so perfect as the martyr's. Jeremy's minor chords soothed her like the music of tom-tom. "Why, oh why," she said to herself, "does some one not write words to it?"

At eleven they went to church in Crocusville. The back of the pine bench on which she sat had a penitential forward tilt that would have brought St. Simeon down, in jealousy, from his pillar. The preacher singled her out, and thundered upon her vicarious head the damnation of the world. At each side of her an adamant parent held her rigidly to the bar of judgment. An ant crawled upon her neck, but she dared not move. She lowered her eyes before the congregation—a hundred-eyed Cerberus that watched the gates through which her sins were fast thrusting her. Her soul was filled with a delirious, almost a fanatic joy. For she was out of the clutch of the tyrant, Freedom. Dogma and creed pinioned her with beneficent cruelty, as steel braces bind the feet of a crippled child. She was hedged, adjured, shackled, shored up, strait-jacketed, silenced, ordered. When they came out the minister stopped to greet them. Mary could only hang her head and answer "Yes, sir," and "No, sir," to his questions. When she saw that the other women carried their hymn-books at their waists with their left hands, she blushed and moved hers there, too, from her right.

She took the three-o'clock train back to the city. At nine she sat at the round table for dinner in the Café André. Nearly the same crowd was there.

"Where have you been to-day?" asked Mrs. Pothunter. "I 'phoned to you at twelve."

"I have been away in Bohemia," answered Mary, with a mystic smile.

There! Mary has given it away. She has spoiled my climax. For I was to have told you that Bohemia is nothing more than the little country in which you do not live. If you try to obtain citizenship in it, at once the court and retinue pack the royal archives and treasure and move away beyond the hills. It is a hillside that you turn your head to peer at from the windows of the Through Express.

At exactly half-past eleven Kappelman, deceived by a new softness and slowness of *riposte* and parry in Mary Adrian, tried to kiss her. Instantly she slapped his face with such strength and cold fury that he shrank down, sobered, with the flaming red print of a hand across his leering features. And all sounds ceased, as when the shadows of great wings come upon a flock of chattering sparrows. One had broken the paramount law of sham-Bohemia—the law of *"Laisser faire."* The shock came not from the blow delivered, but from the blow received. With the effect of a schoolmaster entering the play-room of his pupils was that blow administered. Women pulled down their sleeves and laid prim hands against their ruffled side locks. Men looked at their watches. There was nothing of the effect of a brawl about it; it was purely the still panic produced by the sound of the ax of the fly cop, Conscience, hammering at the gambling-house doors of the Heart.

With their punctilious putting on of cloaks, with their exaggerated pretense of not having seen or heard, with their stammering exchange of unaccustomed formalities, with their false show of a light-hearted exit I must take leave of my Bohemian party. Mary has robbed me of my climax; and she may go.

But I am not defeated. Somewhere there exists a great vault miles broad and miles long—more capacious than the champagne caves of France. In that vault are stored the anti-climaxes that should have been tagged to all the stories that have been told in the world. I shall cheat that vault of one deposit.

Minnie Brown, with her aunt, came from Crocusville down to the city to see the sights. And because she had escorted me to fishless trout streams and exhibited to me open-plumbed waterfalls and broken my camera while I Julyed in her village, I must escort her to the hives containing the synthetic clover honey of town.

Especially did the custom-made Bohemia charm her. The spaghetti wound its tendrils about her heart; the free red wine drowned her belief in the existence of commercialism in the world; she was dazed and enchanted by the rugose wit that can be churned out of California claret.

But one evening I got her away from the smell of halibut and linoleum long enough to read to her the manuscript of this story, which then ended before her entrance into it. I read it to her because I knew that all the printing-presses in the world were running to try to please her and some others. And I asked her about it. "I didn't quite catch the trains," said she. "How long was Mary in Crocusville?"

"Ten hours and five minutes," I replied.

"Well, then the story may do," said Minnie. "But if she had stayed there a week Kappelman would have got his kiss."

THE FERRY OF UNFULFILMENT

At the street corner, as solid as granite in the "rush-hour" tide of humanity, stood the Man from Nome. The Arctic winds and sun had stained him berry-brown. His eye still held the azure glint of the glaciers.

He was as alert as a fox, as tough as a caribou cutlet and as broad-gauged as the aurora borealis. He stood sprayed by a Niagara of sound— the crash of the elevated trains, clanging cars, pounding of rubberless tires and the antiphony of the cab and truck-drivers indulging in scarifying repartee. And so, with his gold dust cashed in to the merry air of a hundred thousand, and with the cakes and ale of one week in Gotham turning bitter on his tongue, the Man from Nome sighed to set foot again in Chilkoot, the exit from the land of street noises and Dead Sea apple pies.

Up Sixth Avenue, with the tripping, scurrying, chattering, bright-eyed, homing tide came the Girl from Sieber-Mason's. The Man from Nome looked and saw, first, that she was supremely beautiful after his own conception of beauty; and next, that she moved with exactly the steady grace of a dog sled on a level crust of snow. His third sensation was an instantaneous conviction that he desired her greatly for his own. Thus quickly do men from Nome make up their minds. Besides, he was going back to the North in a short time and to act quickly was no less necessary.

A thousand girls from the great department store of Sieber-Mason flowed along the side-walk, making navigation dangerous to men whose feminine field of vision for three years has been chiefly limited to Siwash and Chilkat squaws. But the Man from Nome, loyal to her who had resurrected his long-cached heart, plunged into the stream of pulchritude and followed her.

Down Twenty-third Street she glided swiftly, looking to neither side; no more flirtatious than the bronze Diana above the Garden. Her fine brown hair was neatly braided; her neat waist and unwrinkled black skirt were eloquent of the double virtues—taste and economy. Ten yards behind followed the smitten Man from Nome.

Miss Claribel Colby, the Girl from Sieber-Mason's, belonged to that sad company of mariners known as Jersey commuters. She walked into the waiting-room of the ferry, and up the stairs, and by a marvellous swift, little run, caught the ferry-boat that was just going out. The Man from Nome closed up his ten yards in three jumps and gained the deck close beside her.

Miss Colby chose a rather lonely seat on the outside of the upper cabin. The night was not cold, and she desired to be away from the curious eyes and tedious voices of the passengers. Besides, she was extremely weary and drooping from lack of sleep. On the previous night she had graced the annual ball and oyster fry of the West Side Wholesale Fish Dealers' Assistants' Social Club No. 2, thus reducing her usual time of sleep to only three hours.

And the day had been uncommonly troublous. Customers had been inordinately trying; the buyer in her department had scolded her roundly for letting her stock run down; her best friend, Mamie Tuthill, had snubbed her by going to lunch with that Dockery girl.

The Girl from Sieber-Mason's was in that relaxed, softened mood that often comes to the independent feminine wage-earner. It is a mood most propitious for the man who would woo her. Then she has yearnings to be set in some home and heart; to be comforted, and to hide behind some strong arm and rest, rest. But Miss Claribel Colby was also very sleepy.

There came to her side a strong man, browned and dressed carelessly in the best of clothes with his hat in his hand.

"Lady," said the Man from Nome, respectfully, "excuse me for speaking to you, but I—I—saw you on the street, and—and——"

"Oh, gee!" remarked the girl from Sieber-Mason's, glancing up with the most capable coolness. "Ain't there any way to ever get rid of you mashers? I've tried everything from eating onions to using hatpins. Be on your way, Freddie."

"I'm not one of that kind, lady," said the Man from Nome—"honest, I'm not. As I say, I saw you on the street, and I wanted to know you so bad I couldn't help followin' after you. I was afraid I wouldn't ever see you again in this big town unless I spoke; and that's why I done so."

Miss Colby looked once shrewdly at him in the dim light on the ferry-boat. No; he did not have the perfidious smirk or the brazen swagger of the lady-killer. Sincerity and modesty shone through his boreal tan. It seemed to her that it might be good to hear a little of what he had to say.

"You may sit down," she said, laying her hand over a yawn with ostentatious politeness; "and—mind—don't get fresh or I'll call the steward."

The Man from Nome sat by her side. He admired her greatly. He more than admired her. She had exactly the looks he had tried so long in vain to find in a woman. Could she ever come to like him? Well, that was to be seen. He must do all in his power to stake his claim, anyhow.

"My name's Blayden," said he—"Henry Blayden."

"Are you real sure it ain't Jones?" asked the girl, leaning toward him, with delicious, knowing raillery.

"I'm down from Nome," he went on with anxious seriousness. "I scraped together a pretty good lot of dust up there, and brought it down with me."

"Oh, say!" she rippled, pursuing persiflage with engaging lightness, "then you must be on the White Wings force. I thought I'd seen you somewhere."

"You didn't see me on the street to-day when I saw you."

"I never look at fellows on the street."

"Well, I looked at you; and I never looked at anything before that I thought was half as pretty."

"Shall I keep the change?"

"Yes, I reckon so. I reckon you could keep anything I've got. I reckon I'm what you would call a rough man, but I could be awful good to anybody I liked. I've had a rough time of it up yonder, but I beat the game. Nearly 5,000 ounces of dust was what I cleaned up while I was there."

"Goodness!" exclaimed Miss Colby, obligingly sympathetic. "It must be an awful dirty place, wherever it is."

And then her eyes closed. The voice of the Man from Nome had a monotony in its very earnestness. Besides, what dull talk was this of brooms and sweeping and dust? She leaned her head against the wall.

"Miss," said the Man from Nome, with deeper earnestness and monotony, "I never saw anybody I liked as well as I do you. I know you can't think that way of me right yet; but can't you give me a chance? Won't you let me know you, and see if I can't make you like me?"

The head of the Girl from Sieber-Mason's slid over gently and rested upon his shoulder. Sweet sleep had won her, and she was dreaming rapturously of the Wholesale Fish Dealers' Assistants' ball.

The gentleman from Nome kept his arms to himself. He did not suspect sleep, and yet he was too wise to attribute the movement to surrender. He was greatly and blissfully thrilled, but he ended by regarding the head upon his shoulder as an encouraging preliminary, merely advanced as a harbinger of his success, and not to be taken advantage of.

One small speck of alloy discounted the gold of his satisfaction. Had he spoken too freely of his wealth? He wanted to be liked for himself.

"I want to say, Miss," he said, "that you can count on me. They know me in the Klondike from Juneau to Circle City and down the whole length of the Yukon. Many a night I've laid in the snow up there where I worked like a slave for three years, and wondered if I'd ever have anybody to like me. I didn't want all that dust just myself. I thought I'd meet just the right one some time, and I done it to-day. Money's a mighty good thing to have, but to have the love of the one you like best is better still. If you was ever to marry a man, Miss, which would you rather he'd have?"

"Cash!"

The word came sharply and loudly from Miss Colby's lips, giving evidence that in her dreams she was now behind her counter in the great department store of Sieber-Mason.

Her head suddenly bobbed over sideways. She awoke, sat straight, and rubbed her eyes. The Man from Nome was gone.

"Gee! I believe I've been asleep," said Miss Colby. "Wonder what became of the White Wings!"

THE TALE OF A TAINTED TENNER

Money talks. But you may think that the conversation of a little old ten-dollar bill in New York would be nothing more than a whisper. Oh, very well! Pass up this *sotto voce* autobiography of an X if you like. If you are one of the kind that prefers to listen to John D's checkbook roar at you through a megaphone as it passes by, all right. But don't forget that small change can say a word to the point now and then. The next time you tip your grocer's clerk a silver quarter to give you extra weight of his boss's goods read the four words above the lady's head. How are they for repartee?

I am a ten-dollar Treasury note, series of 1901. You may have seen one in a friend's hand. On my face, in the centre, is a picture of the bison Americanus, miscalled a buffalo by fifty or sixty millions of Americans. The heads of Capt. Lewis and Capt. Clark adorn the ends. On my back is the graceful figure of Liberty or Ceres or Maxine Elliott standing in the centre of the stage on a conservatory plant. My references is—or are— Section 3,588, Revised Statutes. Ten cold, hard dollars—I don't say whether silver, gold, lead or iron—Uncle Sam will hand you over his counter if you want to cash me in.

I beg you will excuse any conversational breaks that I make—thanks, I knew you would—got that sneaking little respect and agreeable feeling toward even an X, haven't you? You see, a tainted bill doesn't have much chance to acquire a correct form of expression. I never knew a really cultured and educated person that could afford to hold a ten-spot any longer than it would take to do an Arthur Duffy to the nearest That's All! sign or delicatessen store.

For a six-year-old, I've had a lively and gorgeous circulation. I guess I've paid as many debts as the man who dies. I've been owned by a good many kinds of people. But a little old ragged, damp, dingy five-dollar silver certificate gave me a jar one day. I was next to it in the fat and bad-smelling purse of a butcher.

"Hey, you Sitting Bull," says I, "don't scrouge so. Anyhow, don't you think it's about time you went in on a customs payment and got reissued? For a series of 1899 you're a sight."

"Oh, don't get crackly just because you're a Buffalo bill," says the fiver. "You'd be limp, too, if you'd been stuffed down in a thick cotton-and-lisle-thread under an elastic all day, and the thermometer not a degree under 85 in the store."

"I never heard of a pocketbook like that," says I. "Who carried you?"

"A shopgirl," says the five-spot.

"What's that?" I had to ask.

"You'll never know till their millennium comes," says the fiver.

Just then a two-dollar bill behind me with a George Washington head, spoke up to the fiver:

"Aw, cut out yer kicks. Ain't lisle thread good enough for yer? If you was under all cotton like I'd been to-day, and choked up with factory dust till the lady with the cornucopia on me sneezed half a dozen times, you'd have some reason to complain."

That was the next day after I arrived in New York. I came in a $500 package of tens to a Brooklyn bank from one of its Pennsylvania correspondents—and I haven't made the acquaintance of any of the five and two spot's friends' pocketbooks yet. Silk for mine, every time.

I was lucky money. I kept on the move. Sometimes I changed hands twenty times a day. I saw the inside of every business; I fought for my owner's every pleasure. It seemed that on Saturday nights I never missed being slapped down on a bar. Tens were always slapped down, while ones and twos were slid over to the bartenders folded. I got in the habit of looking for mine, and I managed to soak in a little straight or some spilled Martini or Manhattan whenever I could. Once I got tied up in a great greasy roll of bills in a pushcart peddler's jeans. I thought I never would get in circulation again, for the future department store owner lived on eight cents' worth of dog meat and onions a day. But this peddler got into trouble one day on account of having his cart too near a crossing, and I was rescued. I always will feel grateful to the cop that got me. He changed me at a cigar store near the Bowery that was running a crap game in the back room. So it was the Captain of the precinct, after all, that did me the best turn, when he got his. He blew me for wine and the next evening in a Broadway restaurant; and I really felt as glad to get back again as an Astor does when he sees the lights of Charing Cross.

A tainted ten certainly does get action on Broadway. I was alimony once, and got folded in a little dogskin purse among a lot of dimes. They were bragging about the busy times there were in Ossining whenever three girls got hold of one of them during the ice cream season. But it's Slow Moving Vehicles Keep to the Right for the little Bok tips when you think of the way we bison plasters refuse to stick to anything during the rush lobster hour.

The first I ever heard of tainted money was one night when a good thing with a Van to his name threw me over with some other bills to buy a stack of blues.

About midnight a big, easy-going man with a fat face like a monk's and the eye of a janitor with his wages raised took me and a lot of other notes and rolled us into what is termed a "wad" among the money tainters.

"Ticket me for five hundred," said he to the banker, "and look out for everything, Charlie. I'm going out for a stroll in the glen before the moonlight fades from the brow of the cliff. If anybody finds the roof in their way there's $60,000 wrapped in a comic supplement in the upper left-hand corner of the safe. Be bold; everywhere be bold, but be not bowled over. 'Night."

I found myself between two $20 gold certificates. One of 'em says to me:

"Well, old shorthorn, you're in luck to-night. You'll see something of life. Old Jack's going to make the Tenderloin look like a hamburg steak."

"Explain," says I. "I'm used to joints, but I don't care for filet mignon with the kind of sauce you serve."

"'Xcuse me," said the twenty. "Old Jack is the proprietor of this gambling house. He's going on a whiz to-night because he offered $50,000 to a church and it refused to accept it because they said his money was tainted."

"What is a church?" I asked.

"Oh, I forgot," says the twenty, "that I was talking to a tenner. Of course, you don't know. You're too much to put into the contribution basket, and not enough to buy anything at a bazaar. A church is—a large building in which penwipers and tidies are sold at $20 each."

I don't care much about chinning with gold certificates. There's a streak of yellow in 'em. All is not gold that quitters.

Old Jack certainly was a gilt-edged sport. When it came his time to loosen up he never referred the waiter to an actuary.

By and by it got around that he was smiting the rock in the wilderness; and all along Broadway things with cold noses and hot gullets fell in on our trail. The third Jungle Book was there waiting for somebody to put covers on it. Old Jack's money may have had a taint to it, but all the same he had orders for his Camembert piling up on him every minute. First his friends rallied round him; and then the fellows that his friends knew by sight; and then a few of his enemies buried the hatchet; and finally he was buying souvenirs for so many Neapolitan fisher maidens and butterfly octettes that the head waiters were 'phoning all over town for Julian Mitchell to please come around and get them into some kind of order.

At last we floated into an uptown café that I knew by heart. When the hod-carriers' union in jackets and aprons saw us coming the chief goal kicker called out: "Six—eleven—forty-two—nineteen—twelve" to his men, and they put on nose guards till it was clear whether we meant Port Arthur or Portsmouth. But Old Jack wasn't working for the furniture and glass factories that night. He sat down quiet and sang "Ramble" in a half-hearted way. His feelings had been hurt, so the twenty told me, because his offer to the church had been refused.

But the wassail went on; and Brady himself couldn't have hammered the thirst mob into a better imitation of the real penchant for the stuff that you screw out of a bottle with a napkin.

Old Jack paid the twenty above me for a round, leaving me on the outside of his roll. He laid the roll on the table and sent for the proprietor.

"Mike," says he, "here's money that the good people have refused. Will it buy of your wares in the name of the devil? They say it's tainted."

"It will," says Mike, "and I'll put it in the drawer next to the bills that was paid to the parson's daughter for kisses at the church fair to build a new parsonage for the parson's daughter to live in."

At 1 o'clock when the hod-carriers were making ready to close up the front and keep the inside open, a woman slips in the door of the restaurant and comes up to Old Jack's table. You've seen the kind—black shawl, creepy hair, ragged skirt, white face, eyes a cross between Gabriel's and a sick kitten's—the kind of woman that's always on the lookout for an automobile or the mendicancy squad—and she stands there without a word and looks at the money.

Old Jack gets up, peels me off the roll and hands me to her with a bow.

"Madam," says he, just like actors I've heard, "here is a tainted bill. I am a gambler. This bill came to me to-night from a gentleman's son. Where he got it I do not know. If you will do me the favor to accept it, it is yours."

The woman took me with a trembling hand.

"Sir," said she, "I counted thousands of this issue of bills into packages when they were virgin from the presses. I was a clerk in the Treasury Department. There was an official to whom I owed my position. You say they are tainted now. If you only knew—but I won't say any more. Thank you with all my heart, sir—thank you—thank you."

Where do you suppose that woman carried me almost at a run? To a bakery. Away from Old Jack and a sizzling good time to a bakery. And I got changed, and she does a Sheridan-twenty-miles-away with a dozen rolls and a section of jelly cake as big as a turbine water-wheel. Of course I lost sight of her then, for I was snowed up in the bakery, wondering whether I'd get changed at the drug store the next day in an alum deal or paid over to the cement works.

A week afterward I butted up against one of the one-dollar bills the baker had given the woman for change.

"Hello, E35039669," says I, "weren't you in the change for me in a bakery last Saturday night?"

"Yep," says the solitaire in his free and easy style.

"How did the deal turn out?" I asked.

"She blew E17051431 for milk and round steak," says the one-spot. "She kept me till the rent man came. It was a bum room with a sick kid in it. But you ought to have seen him go for the bread and tincture of formaldehyde. Half-starved, I guess. Then she prayed some. Don't get stuck up, tenner. We one-spots hear ten prayers, where you hear one. She said something about 'who giveth to the poor.' Oh, let's cut out the slum talk. I'm certainly tired of the company that keeps me. I wish I was big enough to move in society with you tainted bills."

"Shut up," says I, "there's no such thing. I know the rest of it. There's a 'lendeth to the Lord' somewhere in it. Now look on my back and read what you see there."

"This note is a legal tender at its face value for all debts public and private."

"This talk about tainted money makes me tired," says I.

ELSIE IN NEW YORK

No, bumptious reader, this story is not a continuation of the Elsie series. But if your Elsie had lived over here in our big city there might have been a chapter in her books not very different from this.

Especially for the vagrant feet of youth are the roads of Manhattan beset "with pitfall and with gin." But the civic guardians of the young have made themselves acquainted with the snares of the wicked, and most of the dangerous paths are patrolled by their agents, who seek to turn straying ones away from the peril that menaces them. And this will tell you how they guided my Elsie safely through all peril to the goal that she was seeking.

Elsie's father had been a cutter for Fox & Otter, cloaks and furs, on lower Broadway. He was an old man, with a slow and limping gait, so a pot-hunter of a newly licensed chauffeur ran him down one day when livelier game was scarce. They took the old man home, where he lay on his bed for a year and then died, leaving $2.50 in cash and a letter from Mr. Otter offering to do anything he could to help his faithful old employee. The old cutter regarded this letter as a valuable legacy to his daughter, and he put it into her hands with pride as the shears of the dread Cleaner and Repairer snipped off his thread of life.

That was the landlord's cue; and forth he came and did his part in the great eviction scene. There was no snowstorm ready for Elsie to steal out into, drawing her little red woollen shawl about her shoulders, but she went out, regardless of the unities. And as for the red shawl—back to Blaney with it! Elsie's fall tan coat was cheap, but it had the style and fit of the best at Fox & Otter's. And her lucky stars had given her good looks, and eyes as blue and innocent as the new shade of note paper, and she had $1 left of the $2.50. And the letter from Mr. Otter. Keep your eye on the letter from Mr. Otter. That is the clue. I desire that everything be made plain as we go. Detective stories are so plentiful now that they do not sell.

And so we find Elsie, thus equipped, starting out in the world to seek her fortune. One trouble about the letter from Mr. Otter was that it did not bear the new address of the firm, which had moved about a month before. But Elsie thought she could find it. She had heard that policemen, when politely addressed, or thumbscrewed by an investigation committee, will give up information and addresses. So she boarded a downtown car at One Hundred and Seventy-seventh Street and rode south to Forty-second, which she thought must surely be the end of the island. There she stood against the wall undecided, for the city's roar and dash was new to her. Up where she lived was rural New York, so far out that the milkmen awaken you in the morning by the squeaking of pumps instead of the rattling of cans.

A kind-faced, sunburned, young man in a soft-brimmed hat went past Elsie into the Grand Central Depot. That was Hank Ross, of the Sunflower Ranch, in Idaho, on his way home from a visit to the East. Hank's heart was heavy, for the Sunflower Ranch was a lonesome place, lacking the presence of a woman. He had hoped to find one during his visit who would congenially share his prosperity and home, but the girls of Gotham had not pleased his fancy. But, as he passed in, he noted, with a jumping of his pulses, the sweet, ingenuous face of Elsie and her pose of doubt and loneliness. With true and honest Western impulse he said to himself that here was his mate. He could love her, he knew; and he would surround her with so much comfort, and cherish her so carefully that she would be happy, and make two sunflowers grow on the ranch where there grew but one before.

Hank turned and went back to her. Backed by his never-before-questioned honesty of purpose, he approached the girl and removed his soft-brimmed hat. Elsie had but time to sum up his handsome frank face with one shy look of modest admiration when a burly cop hurled himself upon the ranchman, seized him by the collar and backed him against the wall. Two blocks away a burglar was coming out of an apartment-house with a bag of silverware on his shoulder; but that is neither here nor there.

"Carry on yez mashin' tricks right before me eyes will yez?" shouted the cop. "I'll teach yez to speak to ladies on me beat that ye're not acquainted with. Come along."

Elsie turned away with a sigh as the ranchman was dragged away. She had liked the effect of his light blue eyes against his tanned complexion. She walked southward, thinking herself already in the district where her father used to work, and hoping to find some one who could direct her to the firm of Fox & Otter.

But did she want to find Mr. Otter? She had inherited much of the old cutter's independence. How much better it would be if she could find work and support herself without calling on him for aid!

Elsie saw a sign "Employment Agency" and went in. Many girls were sitting against the wall in chairs. Several well-dressed ladies were looking them over. One white-haired, kind-faced old lady in rustling black silk hurried up to Elsie.

"My dear," she said in a sweet, gentle voice, "are you looking for a position? I like your face and appearance so much. I want a young woman who will be half maid and half companion to me. You will have a good home and I will pay you $30 a month."

Before Elsie could stammer forth her gratified acceptance, a young woman with gold glasses on her bony nose and her hands in her jacket pockets seized her arm and drew her aside.

"I am Miss Ticklebaum," said she, "of the Association for the Prevention of Jobs Being Put Up on Working Girls Looking for Jobs. We prevented forty-seven girls from securing positions last week. I am here to protect you. Beware of any one who offers you a job. How do you know that this woman does not want to make you work as a breaker-boy in a coal mine or murder you to get your teeth? If you accept work of any kind without permission of our association you will be arrested by one of our agents."

"But what am I to do?" asked Elsie. "I have no home or money. I must do something. Why am I not allowed to accept this kind lady's offer?"

"I do not know," said Miss Ticklebaum. "That is the affair of our Committee on the Abolishment of Employers. It is my duty simply to see that you do not get work. You will give me your name and address and report to our secretary every Thursday. We have 600 girls on the waiting list who will in time be allowed to accept positions as vacancies occur on our roll of Qualified Employers, which now comprise twenty-seven names. There is prayer, music and lemonade in our chapel the third Sunday of every month."

Elsie hurried away after thanking Miss Ticklebaum for her timely warning and advice. After all, it seemed that she must try to find Mr. Otter.

But after walking a few blocks she saw a sign, "Cashier wanted," in the window of a confectionery store. In she went and applied for the place, after casting a quick glance over her shoulder to assure herself that the job-preventer was not on her trail.

The proprietor of the confectionery was a benevolent old man with a peppermint flavor, who decided, after questioning Elsie pretty closely, that she was the very girl he wanted. Her services were needed at once, so Elsie, with a thankful heart, drew off her tan coat and prepared to mount the cashier's stool.

But before she could do so a gaunt lady wearing steel spectacles and black mittens stood before her, with a long finger pointing, and exclaimed: "Young woman, hesitate!"

Elsie hesitated.

"Do you know," said the black-and-steel lady, "that in accepting this position you may this day cause the loss of a hundred lives in agonizing physical torture and the sending as many souls to perdition?"

"Why, no," said Elsie, in frightened tones. "How could I do that?"

"Rum," said the lady—"the demon rum. Do you know why so many lives are lost when a theatre catches fire? Brandy balls. The demon rum lurking in brandy balls. Our society women while in theatres sit grossly intoxicated from eating these candies filled with brandy. When the fire fiend sweeps down upon them they are unable to escape. The candy stores are the devil's distilleries. If you assist in the distribution of these insidious confections you assist in the destruction of the bodies and souls of your fellow-beings, and in the filling of our jails, asylums and almshouses. Think, girl, ere you touch the money for which brandy balls are sold."

"Dear me," said Elsie, bewildered. "I didn't know there was rum in brandy balls. But I must live by some means. What shall I do?"

"Decline the position," said the lady, "and come with me. I will tell you what to do."

After Elsie had told the confectioner that she had changed her mind about the cashiership she put on her coat and followed the lady to the sidewalk, where awaited an elegant victoria.

"Seek some other work," said the black-and-steel lady, "and assist in crushing the hydra-headed demon rum." And she got into the victoria and drove away.

"I guess that puts it up to Mr. Otter again," said Elsie, ruefully, turning down the street. "And I'm sorry, too, for I'd much rather make my way without help."

Near Fourteenth Street Elsie saw a placard tacked on the side of a doorway that read: "Fifty girls, neat sewers, wanted immediately on theatrical costumes. Good pay."

She was about to enter, when a solemn man, dressed all in black, laid his hand on her arm.

"My dear girl," he said, "I entreat you not to enter that dressing-room of the devil."

"Goodness me!" exclaimed Elsie, with some impatience. "The devil seems to have a cinch on all the business in New York. What's wrong about the place?"

"It is here," said the solemn man, "that the regalia of Satan—in other words, the costumes worn on the stage—are manufactured. The stage is the road to ruin and destruction. Would you imperil your soul by lending the work of your hands to its support? Do you know, my dear girl, what the theatre leads to? Do you know where actors and actresses go after the curtain of the playhouse has fallen upon them for the last time?"

"Sure," said Elsie. "Into vaudeville. But do you think it would be wicked for me to make a little money to live on by sewing? I must get something to do pretty soon."

"The flesh-pots of Egypt," exclaimed the reverend gentleman, uplifting his hands. "I beseech you, my child, to turn away from this place of sin and iniquity."

"But what will I do for a living?" asked Elsie. "I don't care to sew for this musical comedy, if it's as rank as you say it is; but I've got to have a job."

"The Lord will provide," said the solemn man. "There is a free Bible class every Sunday afternoon in the basement of the cigar store next to the church. Peace be with you. Amen. Farewell."

Elsie went on her way. She was soon in the downtown district where factories abound. On a large brick building was a gilt sign, "Posey & Trimmer, Artificial Flowers." Below it was hung a newly stretched canvas bearing the words, "Five hundred girls wanted to learn trade. Good wages from the start. Apply one flight up."

Elsie started toward the door, near which were gathered in groups some twenty or thirty girls. One big girl with a black straw hat tipped down over her eyes stepped in front of her.

"Say, you'se," said the girl, "are you'se goin' in there after a job?"

"Yes," said Elsie; "I must have work."

"Now don't do it," said the girl. "I'm chairman of our Scab Committee. There's 400 of us girls locked out just because we demanded 50 cents a week raise in wages, and ice water, and for the foreman to shave off his mustache. You're too nice a looking girl to be a scab. Wouldn't you please help us along by trying to find a job somewhere else, or would you'se rather have your face pushed in?"

"I'll try somewhere else," said Elsie.

She walked aimlessly eastward on Broadway, and there her heart leaped to see the sign, "Fox & Otter," stretching entirely across the front of a tall building. It was as though an unseen guide had led her to it through the byways of her fruitless search for work.

She hurried into the store and sent in to Mr. Otter by a clerk her name and the letter he had written her father. She was shown directly into his private office.

Mr. Otter arose from his desk as Elsie entered and took both hands with a hearty smile of welcome. He was a slightly corpulent man of nearly middle age, a little bald, gold spectacled, polite, well dressed, radiating.

"Well, well, and so this is Beatty's little daughter! Your father was one of our most efficient and valued employees. He left nothing? Well, well. I hope we have not forgotten his faithful services. I am sure there is a vacancy now among our models. Oh, it is easy work—nothing easier."

Mr. Otter struck a bell. A long-nose clerk thrust a portion of himself inside the door.

"Send Miss Hawkins in," said Mr. Otter. Miss Hawkins came.

"Miss Hawkins," said Mr. Otter, "ring for Miss Beatty to try on one of those Russian sable coats and—let's see—one of those latest model black tulle hats with white tips."

Elsie stood before the full-length mirror with pink cheeks and quick breath. Her eyes shone like faint stars. She was beautiful. Alas! she was beautiful.

I wish I could stop this story here. Confound it! I will. No; it's got to run it out. I didn't make it up. I'm just repeating it.

I'd like to throw bouquets at the wise cop and the lady who rescues Girls from Jobs, and the prohibitionist who is trying to crush brandy balls, and the sky pilot who objects to costumes for stage people (there are others), and all the thousands of good people who are at work protecting young people from the pitfalls of a great city; and then wind up by pointing out how they were the means of Elsie reaching her father's benefactor and her kind friend and rescuer from poverty. This would make a fine Elsie story of the old sort. I'd like to do this; but there's just a word or two to follow.

While Elsie was admiring herself in the mirror, Mr. Otter went to the telephone booth and called up some number. Don't ask me what it was.

"Oscar," said he, "I want you to reserve the same table for me this evening. . . . What? Why, the one in the Moorish room to the left of the shrubbery. . . . Yes; two. . . . Yes, the usual brand; and the '85 Johannisburger with the roast. If it isn't the right temperature I'll break your neck. . . . No; not her . . . No, indeed . . . A new one—a peacherino, Oscar, a peacherino!"

Tired and tiresome reader, I will conclude, if you please, with a paraphrase of a few words that you will remember were written by him—by him of Gad's Hill, before whom, if you doff not your hat, you shall stand with a covered pumpkin—aye, sir, a pumpkin.

Lost, Your Excellency. Lost, Associations, and Societies. Lost, Right Reverends and Wrong Reverends of every order. Lost, Reformers and Lawmakers, born with heavenly compassion in your hearts, but with the reverence of money in your souls. And lost thus around us every day.

BOOK 13

STRICTLY BUSINESS

STRICTLY BUSINESS

I suppose you know all about the stage and stage people. You've been touched with and by actors, and you read the newspaper criticisms and the jokes in the weeklies about the Rialto and the chorus girls and the long-haired tragedians. And I suppose that a condensed list of your ideas about the mysterious stageland would boil down to something like this:

Leading ladies have five husbands, paste diamonds, and figures no better than your own (madam) if they weren't padded. Chorus girls are inseparable from peroxide, Panhards, and Pittsburg. All shows walk back to New York on tan oxford and railroad ties. Irreproachable actresses reserve the comic-landlady part for their mothers on Broadway and their step-aunts on the road. Kyrle Bellew's real name is Boyle O'Kelley. The ravings of John McCullough in the phonograph were stolen from the first sale of the Ellen Terry memoirs. Joe Weber is funnier than E. H. Sothern; but Henry Miller is getting older than he was.

All theatrical people on leaving the theatre at night drink champagne and eat lobsters until noon the next day. After all, the moving pictures have got the whole bunch pounded to a pulp.

Now, few of us know the real life of the stage people. If we did, the profession might be more overcrowded than it is. We look askance at the players with an eye full of patronizing superiority—and we go home and practise all sorts of elocution and gestures in front of our looking glasses.

Latterly there has been much talk of the actor people in a new light. It seems to have been divulged that instead of being motoring baccha-nalians and diamond-hungry *loreleis* they are businesslike folk, students and ascetics with childer and homes and libraries, owning real estate, and conducting their private affairs in as orderly and unsensational a manner as any of us good citizens who are bound to the chariot wheels of the gas, rent, coal, ice, and wardmen.

Whether the old or the new report of the sock-and-buskiners be the true one is a surmise that has no place here. I offer you merely this little story of two strollers; and for proof of its truth I can show you only the dark patch above the cast-iron handle of the stage-entrance door of Kee-tor's old vaudeville theatre made there by the petulant push of gloved hands too impatient to finger the clumsy thumb-latch—and where I last saw Cherry whisking through like a swallow into her nest, on time to the minute, as usual, to dress for her act.

The vaudeville team of Hart & Cherry was an inspiration. Bob Hart had been roaming through the Eastern and Western circuits for four years with a mixed-up act comprising a monologue, three lightning changes with songs, a couple of imitations of celebrated imitators, and a buck-and-wing dance that had drawn a glance of approval from the bass-viol player in more than one house—than which no performer ever received more satisfactory evidence of good work.

The greatest treat an actor can have is to witness the pitiful performance with which all other actors desecrate the stage. In order to give himself this pleasure he will often forsake the sunniest Broadway corner between Thirty-fourth and Forty-fourth to attend a matinée offering by his less gifted brothers. Once during the lifetime of a minstrel joke one comes to scoff and remains to go through with that most difficult exercise of Thes-pian muscles—the audible contact of the palm of one hand against the palm of the other.

One afternoon, Bob Hart presented his solvent, serious, well-known vaudevillian face at the box-office window of a rival attraction and got his d. h. coupon for an orchestra seat.

A, B, C, and D glowed successively on the announcement spaces and passed into oblivion, each plunging Mr. Hart deeper into gloom. Others of the audience shrieked, squirmed, whistled and applauded; but Bob Hart, "All the Mustard and a Whole Show in Himself," sat with his face as long and his hands as far apart as a boy holding a hank of yarn for his grandmother to wind into a ball.

But when H came on, "The Mustard" suddenly sat up straight. H was the happy alphabetical prognosticator of Winona Cherry, in Character Songs and Impersonations. There were scarcely more than two bits to Cherry; but she delivered the merchandise tied with a pink cord and charged to the old man's account. She first showed you a deliciously dewy and ginghamy country girl with a basket of property daisies who informed you ingenuously that there were other things to be learned at the old log school-house besides cipherin' and nouns, especially "When the Teach-er Kept Me in." Vanishing, with a quick flirt of gingham apron-strings, she reappeared in considerably less than a "trice" as a fluffy "Parisienne"—so near does Art bring the old red mill to the Moulin Rouge. And then——

But you know the rest. And so did Bob Hart; but he saw somebody else. He thought he saw that Cherry was the only professional on the short order stage that he had seen who seemed exactly to fit the part of "Helen Grimes" in the sketch he had written and kept tucked away in the tray of his trunk. Of course Bob Hart, as well as every other normal actor, grocer, newspaper man, professor, curb broker, and farmer, has a play tucked away somewhere. They tuck 'em in trays of trunks, trunks of trees, desks, haymows, pigeonholes, inside pockets, safe-deposit vaults, handboxes, and coal cellars, waiting for Mr. Frohman to call. They belong among the fifty-seven different kinds.

But Bob Hart's sketch was not destined to end in a pickle jar. He called it "Mice Will Play." He had kept it quiet and hidden away ever since he wrote it, waiting to find a partner who fitted his conception of "Helen Grimes." And here was "Helen" herself, with all the innocent abandon, the youth, the sprightliness, and the flawless stage of art that his critical taste demanded.

After the act was over Hart found the manager in the box office, and got Cherry's address. At five the next afternoon he called at the musty old house in the West Forties and sent up his professional card.

By daylight, in a secular shirtwaist and plain voile skirt, with her hair curbed and her Sister of Charity eyes, Winona Cherry might have been playing the part of Prudence Wise, the deacon's daughter, in the great (unwritten) New England drama not yet entitled anything.

"I know your act, Mr. Hart," she said after she had looked over his card carefully. "What did you wish to see me about?"

"I saw you work last night," said Hart. "I've written a sketch that I've been saving up. It's for two; and I think you can do the other part. I thought I'd see you about it."

"Come in the parlor," said Miss Cherry. "I've been wishing for something of the sort. I think I'd like to act instead of doing turns."

Bob Hart drew his cherished "Mice Will Play" from his pocket, and read it to her.

"Read it again, please," said Miss Cherry.

And then she pointed out to him clearly how it could be improved by introducing a messenger instead of a telephone call, and cutting the dialogue just before the climax while they were struggling with the pistol, and by completely changing the lines and business of Helen Grimes at the point where her jealousy overcomes her. Hart yielded to all her strictures without argument. She had at once put her finger on the sketch's weaker points. That was her woman's intuition that he had lacked. At the end of their talk Hart was willing to stake the judgment, experience, and savings of his four years of vaudeville that "Mice Will Play" would blossom into a perennial flower in the garden of the circuits. Miss Cherry was slower to decide. After many puckerings of her smooth young brow and tappings on her small, white teeth with the end of a lead pencil she gave out her dictum.

"Mr. Hart," said she, "I believe your sketch is going to win out. That Grimes part fits me like a shrinkable flannel after its first trip to a handless hand laundry. I can make it stand out like the colonel of the Forty-fourth Regiment at a Little Mothers' Bazaar. And I've seen you work. I know what you can do with the other part. But business is business. How much do you get a week for the stunt you do now?"

"Two hundred," answered Hart.

"I get one hundred for mine," said Cherry. "That's about the natural discount for a woman. But I live on it and put a few simoleons every week under the loose brick in the old kitchen hearth. The stage is all right. I love it; but there's something else I love better—that's a little country home, some day, with Plymouth Rock chickens and six ducks wandering around the yard.

"Now, let me tell you, Mr. Hart, I am STRICTLY BUSINESS. If you want me to play the opposite part in your sketch, I'll do it. And I believe we can make it go. And there's something else I want to say: There's no nonsense in my make-up; I'm *on the level,* and I'm on the stage for what it pays me, just as other girls work in stores and offices. I'm going to save my money to keep me when I'm past doing my stunts. No Old Ladies' Home or Retreat for Imprudent Actresses for me.

"If you want to make this a business partnership, Mr. Hart, with all nonsense cut out of it, I'm in on it. I know something about vaudeville teams in general; but this would have to be one in particular. I want you to know that I'm on the stage for what I can cart away from it every pay-day in a little manila envelope with nicotine stains on it, where the cashier has licked the flap. It's kind of a hobby of mine to want to cravenette myself for plenty of rainy days in the future. I want you to know just how I am. I don't know what an all-night restaurant looks like; I drink only weak tea; I never spoke to a man at a stage entrance in my life and I've got money in five savings banks."

"Miss Cherry," said Bob Hart in his smooth, serious tones, "you're in on your own terms. I've got 'strictly business' pasted in my hat and stenciled on my make-up box. When I dream of nights I always see a five-room bungalow on the north shore of Long Island with a Jap cooking clam broth and duckling in the kitchen, and me with the title deeds to the place in my pongee coat pocket, swinging in a hammock on the side porch, reading Stanley's 'Explorations into Africa.' And nobody else around. You never was interested in Africa, was you, Miss Cherry?"

"Not any," said Cherry. "What I'm going to do with my money is to bank it. You can get four per cent. on deposits. Even at the salary I've been earning, I've figured out that in ten years I'd have an income of about $50 a month just from the interest alone. Well, I might invest some of the principal in a little business—say, trimming hats or a beauty parlor, and make more."

"Well," said Hart, "you've got the proper idea all right, all right, anyhow. There are mighty few actors that amount to anything at all who couldn't fix themselves for the wet days to come if they'd save their money instead of blowing it. I'm glad you've got the correct business idea of it, Miss Cherry. I think the same way; and I believe this sketch will more than double what both of us earn now when we get it shaped up."

The subsequent history of "Mice Will Play" is the history of all successful writings for the stage. Hart & Cherry cut it, pieced it, remodeled it, performed surgical operations on the dialogue and business, changed the lines, restored 'em, added more, cut 'em out, renamed it, gave it back the old name, rewrote it, substituted a dagger for the pistol, restored the pistol—put the sketch through all the known processes of condensation and improvement.

They rehearsed it by the old-fashioned boarding-house clock in the rarely used parlor until its warning click at five minutes to the hour would occur every time exactly half a second before the click of the unloaded revolver that Helen Grimes used in rehearsing the thrilling climax of the sketch.

Yes, that was a thriller and a piece of excellent work. In the act a real 32-caliber revolver was used loaded with a real cartridge. Helen Grimes, who is a Western girl of decidedly Buffalo Billish skill and daring, is tempestuously in love with Frank Desmond, the private secretary and confidential prospective son-in-law of her father, "Arapahoe" Grimes, quarter-million-dollar cattle king, owning a ranch that, judging by the scenery, is in either the Bad Lands or Amagansett, L. I. Desmond (in private life Mr. Bob Hart) wears puttees and Meadow Brook Hunt riding trousers, and gives his address as New York, leaving you to wonder why he comes to the Bad Lands or Amagansett (as the case may be) and at the same time to conjecture mildly why a cattleman should want puttees about his ranch with a secretary in 'em.

Well, anyhow, you know as well as I do that we all like that kind of play, whether we admit it or not—something along in between "Blue-beard, Jr.," and "Cymbeline" played in the Russian.

There were only two parts and a half in "Mice Will Play." Hart and Cherry were the two, of course; and the half was a minor part always played by a stage hand, who merely came in once in a Tuxedo coat and a panic to announce that the house was surrounded by Indians, and to turn down the gas fire in the grate by the manager's orders.

There was another girl in the sketch—a Fifth Avenue society swelless —who was visiting the ranch and who had sirened Jack Valentine when he was a wealthy clubman on lower Third Avenue before he lost his money. This girl appeared on the stage only in the photographic state— Jack had her Sarony stuck up on the mantel of the Amagan—of the Bad Lands droring room. Helen was jealous, of course.

And now for the thriller. Old "Arapahoe" Grimes dies of angina pectoris one night—so Helen informs us in a stage-ferryboat whisper over the footlights—while only his secretary was present. And that same day he was known to have had $647,000 in cash in his (ranch) library just received for the sale of a drove of beeves in the East (that accounts for the prices we pay for steak!). The cash disappears at the same time. Jack Valentine was the only person with the ranchman when he made his (alleged) croak.

"Gawd knows I love him; but if he has done this deed—" you sabe, don't you? And then there are some mean things said about the Fifth Avenue girl—who doesn't come on the stage—and can we blame her, with the vaudeville trust holding down prices until one actually must be but-toned in the back by a call boy, maids cost so much?

But, wait. Here's the climax. Helen Grimes, chaparralish as she can be, is goaded beyond imprudence. She convinces herself that Jack Valentine is not only a falsetto, but a financier. To lose at one fell swoop $647,000 and a lover in riding trousers with angles in the sides like the variations on the chart of a typhoid-fever patient is enough to make any perfect lady mad. So, then!

They stand in the (ranch) library, which is furnished with mounted elk heads (didn't the Elks have a fish fry in Amagansett once?), and the dénouement begins. I know of no more interesting time in the run of a play unless it be when the prologue ends.

Helen thinks Jack has taken the money. Who else was there to take it? The box-office manager was at the front on his job; the orchestra hadn't left their seats; and no man could get past "Old Jimmy," the stage doorman, unless he could show a Skye terrier or an automobile as a guarantee of eligibility.

Goaded beyond imprudence (as before said), Helen says to Jack Valentine: "Robber and thief—and worse yet, stealer of trusting hearts, this should be your fate!"

With that out she whips, of course, the trusty 32-caliber.

"But I will be merciful," goes on Helen. "You shall live—that will be your punishment. I will show you how easily I could have sent you to the death that you deserve. There is *her* picture on the mantel. I will send through her more beautiful face the bullet that should have pierced your craven heart."

And she does it. And there's no fake blank cartridges or assistants pulling strings. Helen fires. The bullet—the actual bullet—goes through the face of the photograph—and then strikes the hidden spring of the sliding panel in the wall—and lo! the panel slides, and there is the missing $647,000 in convincing stacks of currency and bags of gold. It's great. You know how it is. Cherry practised for two months at a target on the roof of her boarding house. It took good shooting. In the sketch she had to hit a brass disk only three inches in diameter, covered by wall paper in the panel; and she had to stand in exactly the same spot every night, and the photo had to be in exactly the same spot, and she had to shoot steady and true every time.

Of course old "Arapahoe" had tucked the funds away there in the secret place; and, of course, Jack hadn't taken anything except his salary (which really might have come under the head of "obtaining money under"; but that is neither here nor there); and, of course, the New York girl was really engaged to a concrete house contractor in the Bronx; and, necessarily, Jack and Helen ended in a half-Nelson—and there you are.

After Hart and Cherry had gotten "Mice Will Play" flawless, they had a tryout at a vaudeville house that accommodates. The sketch was a house wrecker. It was one of those rare strokes of talent that inundates a theatre from the roof down. The gallery wept; and the orchestra seats, being dressed for it, swam in tears.

After the show the booking agents signed blank checks and pressed fountain pens upon Hart and Cherry. Five hundred dollars a week was what it panned out.

That night at 11:30 Bob Hart took off his hat and bade Cherry goodnight at her boarding-house door.

"Mr. Hart," said she thoughtfully, "come inside just a few minutes. We've got our chance now to make good and to make money. What we want to do is to cut expenses every cent we can and save all we can."

"Right," said Bob. "It's business with me. You've got your scheme for banking yours; and I dream every night of that bungalow with the Jap cook and nobody around to raise trouble. Anything to enlarge the net receipts will engage my attention."

"Come inside just a few minutes," repeated Cherry, deeply thoughtful. "I've got a proposition to make to you that will reduce our expenses a lot and help you to work out your own future and help me to work out mine—and all on business principles."

"Mice Will Play" had a tremendously successful run in New York for ten weeks—rather neat for a vaudeville sketch—and then it started on the circuits. Without following it, it may be said that it was a solid drawing card for two years without a sign of abated popularity.

Sam Packard, manager of one of Keetor's New York houses, said of Hart & Cherry:

"As square and high-toned a little team as ever came over the circuit. It's a pleasure to read their names on the booking list. Quiet, hard workers, no Johnny and Mabel nonsense, on the job to the minute, straight home after their act, and each of 'em as gentlemanlike as a lady. I don't expect to handle any attractions that give me less trouble or more respect for the profession."

And now, after so much cracking of a nut-shell, here is the kernel of the story:

At the end of its second season "Mice Will Play" came back to New York for another run at the roof gardens and summer theatres. There was never any trouble in booking it at the top-notch price. Bob Hart had his bungalow nearly paid for, and Cherry had so many savings deposit bank books that she had begun to buy sectional bookcases on the instalment plan to hold them.

I tell you these things to assure you, even if you can't believe it, that many, very many of the stage people are workers with abiding ambitions—just the same as the man who wants to be president, or the grocery clerk who wants a home in Flatbush, or a lady who is anxious to flop out of the Count-pan into the Prince-fire. And I hope I may be allowed to say, without chipping into the contribution basket, that they often move in a mysterious way their wonders to perform.

But, listen.

At the first performance of "Mice Will Play" in New York at the new Westphalia (no hams alluded to) Theatre, Winona Cherry was nervous. When she fired at the photograph of the Eastern beauty on the mantel, the bullet, instead of penetrating the photo and then striking the disk, went into the lower left side of Bob Hart's neck. Not expecting to get it there, Hart collapsed neatly, while Cherry fainted in a most artistic manner.

The audience, surmising that they viewed a comedy instead of a tragedy in which the principals were married or reconciled, applauded with great enjoyment. The Cool Head, who always graces such occasions, rang the curtain down, and two platoons of scene shifters respectively and more or less respectfully removed Hart & Cherry from the stage. The next turn went on, and all went as merry as an alimony bell.

The stage hands found a young doctor at the stage entrance who was waiting for a patient with a decoction of Am. B'ty roses. The doctor examined Hart carefully and laughed heartily.

"No headlines for you, Old Sport," was his diagnosis. "If it had been two inches to the left it would have undermined the carotid artery as far as the Red Front Drug Store in Flatbush and Back Again. As it is, you just get the property man to bind it up with a flounce torn from any one of the girls' Valenciennes and go home and get it dressed by the parlor-floor practitioner on your block, and you'll be all right. Excuse me; I've got a serious case outside to look after."

After that Bob Hart looked up and felt better. And then to where he lay come Vincente, the Tramp Juggler, great in his line. Vincente, a solemn man from Brattleboro, Vt., named Sam Griggs at home, sent toys and maple sugar home to two small daughters from every town he played. Vincente had moved on the same circuits with Hart & Cherry, and was their peripatetic friend.

"Bob," said Vincente in his serious way, "I'm glad it's no worse. The little lady is wild about you."

"Who?" asked Hart.

"Cherry," said the juggler. "We didn't know how bad you were hurt; and we kept her away. It's taking the manager and three girls to hold her."

"It was an accident, of course," said Hart. "Cherry's all right. She wasn't feeling in good trim or she couldn't have done it. There's no hard feelings. She's strictly business. The doctor says I'll be on the job again in three days. Don't let her worry."

"Man," said Sam Griggs severely, puckering his old, smooth, lined face, "are you a chess automaton or a human pincushion? Cherry's crying her heart out for you—calling 'Bob, Bob,' every second, with them holding her hands and keeping her from coming to you."

"What's the matter with her?" asked Hart, with wide-open eyes. "The sketch'll go on again in three days. I'm not hurt bad, the doctor says. She won't lose out half a week's salary. I know it was an accident. What's the matter with her?"

"You seem to be blind, or a sort of a fool," said Vincente. "The girl loves you and is almost mad about your hurt. What's the matter with *you*? Is she nothing to you? I wish you could hear her call you."

"Loves me?" asked Bob Hart, rising from the stack of scenery on which he lay. "Cherry loves me? Why, it's impossible."

"I wish you could see her and hear her," said Griggs.

"But, man," said Bob Hart, sitting up, "it's impossible. It's impossible, I tell you. I never dreamed of such a thing."

"No human being," said the Tramp Juggler, "could mistake it. She's wild for love of you. How have you been so blind?"

"But, my God," said Bob Hart, rising to his feet, *"it's too late.* It's too late. I tell you, Sam; *it's too late.* It can't be. You must be wrong. It's *impossible.* There's some mistake."

"She's crying for you," said the Tramp Juggler. "For love of you she's fighting three, and calling your name so loud they don't dare to raise the curtain. Wake up, man."

"For love of me?" said Bob Hart with staring eyes. "Don't I tell you it's too late? It's too late, man. Why, *Cherry and I have been married two years!"*

THE GOLD THAT GLITTERED

A story with a moral appended is like the bill of a mosquito. It bores you, and then injects a stinging drop to irritate your conscience. Therefore let us have the moral first and be done with it. All is not gold that glitters, but it is a wise child that keeps the stopper in his bottle of testing acid.

Where Broadway skirts the corner of the square presided over by George the Veracious is the Little Rialto. Here stands the actors of that quarter, and this is their shibboleth: " 'Nit,' says I to Frohman, 'you can't touch me for a kopeck less than two-fifty per,' and out I walks."

Westward and southward from the Thespian glare are one or two streets where a Spanish-American colony has huddled for a little tropical warmth in the nipping North. The centre of life in this precinct is "El Refugio," a café and restaurant that caters to the volatile exiles from the South. Up from Chili, Bolivia, Colombia, the rolling republics of Central America and the ireful islands of the Western Indies flit the cloaked and sombreroed señores, who are scattered like burning lava by the political eruptions of their several countries. Hither they come to lay counterplots, to bide their time, to solicit funds, to enlist filibusterers, to smuggle out arms and ammunitions, to play the game at long taw. In El Refugio they find the atmosphere in which they thrive.

In the restaurant of El Refugio are served compounds delightful to the palate of the man from Capricorn or Cancer. Altruism must halt the story thus long. Oh, diner, weary of the culinary subterfuges of the Gallic chef, hie thee to El Refugio! There only will you find a fish—bluefish, shad, or pompano from the Gulf—baked after the Spanish method. Tomatoes give it color, individuality, and soul; chili colorado bestows upon it zest, originality, and fervor; unknown herbs furnish piquancy and mystery, and—but its crowning glory deserves a new sentence. Around it, above it, beneath it, in its vicinity—but never in it—hovers an ethereal aura, an effluvium so rarefied and delicate that only the Society for Physical Research could note its origin. Do not say that garlic is in the fish at El Refugio. It is not otherwise than as if the spirit of Garlic, flitting past, has wafted one kiss that lingers in the parsley-crowned dish as haunting as those kisses in life, "by hopeless fancy feigned on lips that are for others." And then, when Conchito, the waiter, brings you a plate of brown frijoles and a carafe of wine that has never stood still between Oporto and El Refugio—ah, Dios!

One day a Hamburg-American liner deposited upon Pier No. 55 Gen. Perrico Ximenes Villablanca Falcon, a passenger from Cartagena. The General was between a claybank and a bay in complexion, had a 42-inch waist and stood 5 feet 4 with his Du Barry heels. He had the mustache of a shooting-gallery proprietor, he wore the full dress of a Texas congressman, and had the important aspect of an uninstructed delegate.

Gen. Falcon had enough English under his hat to enable him to inquire his way to the street in which El Refugio stood. When he reached that neighborhood he saw a sign before a respectable red-brick house that read, "Hotel Español." In the window was a card in Spanish, "Aqui se habla Español." The General entered, sure of a congenial port.

In the cozy office was Mrs. O'Brien, the proprietress. She had blonde —oh, unimpeachably blonde hair. For the rest she was amiability, and ran largely to inches around. Gen. Falcon brushed the floor with his broad-brimmed hat, and emitted a quantity of Spanish, the syllables sounding like firecrackers gently popping their way down the string of a bunch.

"Spanish or Dago?" asked Mrs. O'Brien, pleasantly.

"I am a Colombian, madam," said the General proudly. "I speak the Spanish. The advisement in your window say the Spanish he is spoken here. How is that?"

"Well, you've been speaking it, ain't you?" said the madam. "I'm sure I can't."

At the Hotel Español General Falcon engaged rooms and established himself. At dusk he sauntered out upon the streets to view the wonders of this roaring city of the North. As he walked he thought of the wonderful golden hair of Mme. O'Brien. "It is here," said the General to himself, no doubt in his own language, "that one shall find the most beautiful señoras in the world. I have not in my Colombia viewed among our beauties one so fair. It is not for the General Falcon to think of beauty. It is my country that claims my devotion."

At the corner of Broadway and the Little Rialto the General became involved. The street cars bewildered him, and the fender of one upset him against a pushcart laden with oranges. A cab driver missed him an inch with a hub, and poured barbarous execrations upon his head. He scrambled to the sidewalk and skipped again in terror when the whistle of a peanut-roaster puffed a hot scream into his ear. "Válgame Dios! What devil's city is this?"

As the General fluttered out of the streamers of passers like a wounded snipe he was marked simultaneously as game by two hunters. One was "Bully" McGuire, whose system of sport required the use of a strong arm and the misuse of an eight-inch piece of lead pipe. The other Nimrod of the asphalt was "Spider" Kelley, a sportsman with more refined methods.

In pouncing upon their self-evident prey, Mr. Kelley was a shade the quicker. His elbow fended accurately the onslaught of Mr. McGuire.

"G'wan!" he commanded harshly. "I saw it first." McGuire slunk away, awed by superior intelligence.

"Pardon me," said Mr. Kelley, to the General, "but you got balled up in the shuffle, didn't you? Let me assist you." He picked up the General's hat and brushed the dust from it.

The ways of Mr. Kelley could not but succeed. The General, bewildered and dismayed by the resounding streets, welcomed his deliverer as a caballero with a most disinterested heart.

"I have a desire," said the General, "to return to the hotel of O'Brien, in which I am stop. Caramba! señor, there is a loudness and rapidness of going and coming in the city of this Nueva York."

Mr. Kelley's politeness would not suffer the distinguished Colombian to brave the dangers of the return unaccompanied. At the door of the Hotel Español they paused. A little lower down on the opposite side of the street shone the modest illuminated sign of El Refugio. Mr. Kelley, to whom few streets were unfamiliar, knew the place exteriorly as a "Dago joint." All foreigners Mr. Kelley classed under the two heads of "Dagoes" and Frenchmen. He proposed to the General that they repair thither and substantiate their acquaintance with a liquid foundation.

An hour later found General Falcon and Mr. Kelley seated at a table in the conspirator's corner of El Refugio. Bottles and glasses were between them. For the tenth time the General confided the secret of his mission to the Estados Unidos. He was here, he declared, to purchase arms— 2,000 stands of Winchester rifles—for the Colombian revolutionists. He had drafts in his pocket drawn by the Cartagena Bank on its New York correspondent for $25,000. At other tables other revolutionists were shouting their political secrets to their fellow-plotters; but none was as loud as the General. He pounded the table; he hallooed for some wine; he roared to his friend that his errand was a secret one, and not to be hinted at to a living soul. Mr. Kelley himself was stirred to sympathetic enthusiasm. He grasped the General's hand across the table.

"Monseer," he said, earnestly, "I don't know where this country of yours is, but I'm for it. I guess it must be a branch of the United States, though, for the poetry guys and the schoolmarms call us Columbia, too, sometimes. It's a lucky thing for you that you butted into me to-night. I'm the only man in New York that can get this gun deal through for you. The Secretary of War of the United States is me best friend. He's in the city now, and I'll see him for you to-morrow. In the meantime, monseer, you keep them drafts tight in your inside pocket. I'll call for you to-morrow, and take you to see him. Say! that ain't the District of Columbia you're talking about, is it?" concluded Mr. Kelley, with a sudden qualm. "You can't capture that with no 2,000 guns—it's been tried with more."

"No, no, no!" exclaimed the General. "It is the Republic of Colombia— it is a g-r-reat republic on the top side of America of the South. Yes. Yes."

"All right," said Mr. Kelley, reassured. "Now suppose we trek along home and go by-by. I'll write to the Secretary to-night and make a date with him. It's a ticklish job to get guns out of New York. McClusky himself can't do it."

They parted at the door of the Hotel Español. The General rolled his eyes at the moon and sighed.

"It is a great country, your Nueva York," he said. "Truly the cars in the streets devastate one, and the engine that cooks the nuts terribly makes a squeak in the ear. But, ah, Señor Kelley—the señoras with hair of much goldness, and admirable fatness—they are magníficas! Muy magníficas!"

Kelley went to the nearest telephone booth and called up McCrary's café, far up on Broadway. He asked for Jimmy Dunn.

"Is that Jimmy Dunn?" asked Kelley.

"Yes," came the answer.

"You're a liar," sang back Kelley, joyfully. "You're the Secretary of War. Wait there till I come up. I've got the finest thing down here in the way of a fish you ever baited for. It's a Colorado-maduro, with a gold band around it and free coupons enough to buy a red hall lamp and a statuette of Psyche rubbering in the brook. I'll be up on the next car."

Jimmy Dunn was an A. M. of Crookdom. He was an artist in the confidence line. He never saw a bludgeon in his life; and he scorned knock-out drops. In fact, he would have set nothing before an intended victim but the purest of drinks, if it had been possible to procure such a thing in New York. It was the ambition of "Spider" Kelley to elevate himself into Jimmy's class.

These two gentlemen held a conference that night at McCrary's. Kelley explained.

"He's as easy as a gum shoe. He's from the Island of Colombia, where there's a strike, or a feud, or something going on, and they've sent him up here to buy 2,000 Winchesters to arbitrate the thing with. He showed me two drafts for $10,000 each, and one for $5,000 on a bank here. 'S truth, Jimmy, I felt real mad with him because he didn't have it in thousand-dollar bills, and hand it to me on a silver waiter. Now, we've got to wait till he goes to the bank and gets the money for us."

They talked it over for two hours, and then Dunn said: "Bring him to No. — Broadway, at four o'clock to-morrow afternoon."

In due time Kelley called at the Hotel Español for the General. He found that wily warrior engaged in delectable conversation with Mrs. O'Brien.

"The Secretary of War is waitin' for us," said Kelley.

The General tore himself away with an effort.

"Ay, señor," he said, with a sigh, "duty makes a call. But, señor, the señoras of your Estados Unidos—how beauties! For exemplification, take you la Madame O'Brien—que magnifica! She is one goddess—one Juno— what you call one ox-eyed Juno."

Now Mr. Kelley was a wit; and better men have been shriveled by the fire of their own imagination.

"Sure!" he said with a grin; "but you mean a peroxide Juno, don't you?"

Mrs. O'Brien heard, and lifted an auriferous head. Her businesslike eye rested for an instant upon the disappearing form of Mr. Kelley. Except in street cars one should never be unnecessarily rude to a lady.

When the gallant Colombian and his escort arrived at the Broadway address, they were held in an anteroom for half an hour, and then admitted into a well-equipped office where a distinguished looking man, with a smooth face, wrote at a desk. General Falcon was presented to the Secretary of War of the United States, and his mission made known by his old friend, Mr. Kelley.

"Ah—Colombia!" said the Secretary, significantly, when he was made to understand; "I'm afraid there will be a little difficulty in that case. The President and I differ in our sympathies there. He prefers the established government, while I——" The Secretary gave the General a mysterious but encouraging smile. "You, of course, know, General Falcon, that since the Tammany war, an act of Congress has been passed requiring all manufactured arms and ammunition exported from this country to pass through the War Department. Now, if I can do anything for you I will be glad to do so to oblige my old friend Mr. Kelley. But it must be in absolute secrecy, as the President, as I have said, does not regard favorably the efforts of your revolutionary party in Colombia. I will have my orderly bring a list of the available arms now in the warehouse."

The Secretary struck a bell, and an orderly with the letters A. D. T. on his cap stepped promptly into the room.

"Bring me Schedule B of the small arms inventory," said the Secretary.

The orderly quickly returned with a printed paper. The Secretary studied it closely.

"I find," he said, "that in Warehouse 9, of Government stores, there is a shipment of 2,000 stands of Winchester rifles that were ordered by the Sultan of Morocco, who forgot to send the cash with his order. Our rule is that legal-tender money must be paid down at the time of purchase.

My dear Kelley, your friend, General Falcon, shall have this lot of arms, if he desires it, at the manufacturer's price. And you will forgive me, I am sure, if I curtail our interview. I am expecting the Japanese Minister and Charles Murphy every moment!"

As one result of this interview, the General was deeply grateful to his esteemed friend, Mr. Kelley. As another, the nimble Secretary of War was extremely busy during the next two days buying empty rifle cases and filling them with bricks, which were then stored in a warehouse rented for that purpose. As still another, when the General returned to the Hotel Español, Mrs. O'Brien went up to him, plucked a thread from his lapel, and said:

"Say, señor, I don't want to 'butt in,' but what does that monkey-faced, cat-eyed, rubber-necked tin horn tough want with you?"

"Sangre de mi vida!" exclaimed the General. "Impossible it is that you speak of my good friend, Señor Kelley."

"Come into the summer garden," said Mrs. O'Brien. "I want to have a talk with you."

Let us suppose that an hour has elapsed.

"And you say," said the General, "that for the sum of $18,000 can be purchased the furnishment of the house and the lease of one year with this garden so lovely—so resembling unto the patios of my cara Colombia?"

"And dirt cheap at that," sighed the lady.

"Ah, Dios!" breathed General Falcon. "What to me is war and politics? This spot is one paradise. My country it have other brave heroes to continue the fighting. What to me should be glory and the shooting of mans? Ah! no. It is here I have found one angel. Let us buy the Hotel Español and you shall be mine, and the money shall not be waste on guns."

Mrs. O'Brien rested her blond pompadour against the shoulder of the Colombian patriot.

"Oh, señor," she sighed, happily, "ain't you terrible!"

Two days later was the time appointed for the delivery of the arms to the General. The boxes of supposed rifles were stacked in the rented warehouse, and the Secretary of War sat upon them, waiting for his friend Kelley to fetch the victim.

Mr. Kelley hurried, at the hour, to the Hotel Español. He found the General behind the desk adding up accounts.

"I have decide," said the General, "to buy not guns. I have to-day buy the insides of this hotel, and there shall be marrying of the General Perrico Ximenes Villablanca Falcon with la Madame O'Brien."

Mr. Kelley almost strangled.

"Say, you old bald-headed bottle of shoe polish," he spluttered, "you're a swindler—that's what you are! You've bought a boarding house with money belonging to your infernal country, wherever it is."

"Ah," said the General, footing up a column, "that is what you call politics. War and revolution they are not nice. Yes. It is not best that one shall always follow Minerva. No. It is of quite desirable to keep hotels and be with that Juno—that ox-eyed Juno. Ah! what hair of the gold it is that she have!"

Mr. Kelley choked again.

"Ah, Señor Kelley!" said the General, feelingly and finally, "is that you have never eaten of the corned beef hash that Madame O'Brien she make?"

BABES IN THE JUNGLE

Montague Silver, the finest street man and art grafter in the West, says to me once in Little Rock: "If you ever lose your mind, Billy, and get too old to do honest swindling among grown men, go to New York. In the West a sucker is born every minute; but in New York they appear in chunks of roe—you can't count 'em!"

Two years afterwards I found that I couldn't remember the names of the Russian admirals, and I noticed some gray hairs over my left ear; so I knew the time had arrived for me to take Silver's advice.

I struck New York about noon one day, and took a walk up Broadway. And I run against Silver himself, all encompassed up in a spacious kind of haberdashery, leaning against a hotel and rubbing the half-moons on his nails with a silk handkerchief.

"Paresis or superannuated?" I asked him.

"Hello, Billy," says Silver; "I'm glad to see you. Yes, it seemed to me that the West was accumulating a little too much wiseness. I've been saving New York for dessert. I know it's a low-down trick to take things from these people. They only know this and that and pass to and fro and think ever and anon. I'd hate for my mother to know I was skinning these weak-minded ones. She raised me better."

"Is there a crush already in the waiting rooms of the old doctor that does skin grafting?" I asks.

"Well, no," says Silver; "you needn't back Epidermis to win to-day. I've only been here a month. But I'm ready to begin; and the members of Willie Manhattan's Sunday School class, each of whom has volunteered to contribute a portion of cuticle toward this rehabilitation, may as well send their photos to the *Evening Daily*.

"I've been studying the town," says Silver, "and reading the papers every day, and I know it as well as the cat in the City Hall knows an O'Sullivan. People here lie down on the floor and scream and kick when you are the least bit slow about taking money from them. Come up in my room and I'll tell you. We'll work the town together, Billy, for the sake of old times."

Silver takes me up in a hotel. He has a quantity of irrelevant objects lying about.

"There's more ways of getting money from these metropolitan hayseeds," says Silver, "than there is of cooking rice in Charleston, S. C. They'll bite at anything. The brains of most of 'em commute. The wiser they are in intelligence the less perception of cognizance they have. Why, didn't a man the other day sell J. P. Morgan an oil portrait of Rockefeller, Jr., for Andrea del Sarto's celebrated painting of the young Saint John!

"You see that bundle of printed stuff in the corner, Billy? That's gold mining stock. I started out one day to sell that, but I quit it in two hours. Why? Got arrested for blocking the street. People fought to buy it. I sold the policeman a block of it on the way to the station-house, and then I took it off the market. I don't want people to give me their money. I want some little consideration connected with the transaction to keep my pride from being hurt. I want 'em to guess the missing letter in Chic—go, or draw to a pair of nines before they pay me a cent of money.

"Now there's another little scheme that worked so easy I had to quit it. You see that bottle of blue ink on the table? I tattooed an anchor on the back of my hand and went to a bank and told 'em I was Admiral Dewey's nephew. They offered to cash my draft on him for a thousand, but I didn't know my uncle's first name. It shows, though, what an easy town it is. As for burglars, they won't go in a house now unless there's a hot supper ready and a few college students to wait on 'em. They're slugging citizens all over the upper part of the city and I guess, taking the town from end to end, it's a plain case of assault and Battery."

"Monty," says I, when Silver had slacked up, "you may have Manhattan correctly discriminated in your perorative, but I doubt it. I've only been in town two hours, but it don't dawn upon me that it's ours with a cherry in it. There ain't enough rus in urbe about it to suit me. I'd be a good ·deal much better satisfied if the citizens had a straw or more in their hair, and run more to velveteen vests and buckeye watch charms. They don't look easy to me."

"You've got it, Billy," says Silver. "All emigrants have it. New York's bigger than Little Rock or Europe, and it frightens a foreigner. You'll be all right. I tell you I feel like slapping the people here because they don't send me all their money in laundry baskets, with germicide sprinkled over it. I hate to go down on the street to get it. Who wears the diamonds in this town? Why, Winnie, the Wiretapper's wife, and Bella, the Buncosteerer's bride. New Yorkers can be worked easier than a blue rose on a tidy. The only thing that bothers me is I know I'll break the cigars in my vest pocket when I get my clothes all full of twenties."

"I hope you are right, Monty," says I; "but I wish all the same I had been satisfied with a small business in Little Rock. The crop of farmers is never so short out there but what you can get a few of 'em to sign a petition for a new post office that you can discount for $200 at the county bank. The people here appear to possess instincts of self-preservation and illiberality. I fear me that we are not cultivated enough to tackle this game."

"Don't worry," says Silver. "I've got this Jayville-near-Tarrytown correctly estimated as sure as North River is the Hudson and East river ain't a river. Why, there are people living in four blocks of Broadway who never saw any kind of building except a skyscraper in their lives! A good, live hustling Western man ought to get conspicuous enough here inside of three months to incur either Jerome's clemency or Lawson's displeasure."

"Hyperbole aside," says I, "do you know of any immediate system of buncoing the community out of a dollar or two except by applying to the Salvation Army or having a fit on Miss Helen Gould's doorsteps?"

"Dozens of 'em," says Silver. "How much capital have you got, Billy?"

"A thousand," I told him.

"I've got $1,200," says he. "We'll pool and do a big business. There's so many ways we can make a million that I don't know how to begin."

The next morning Silver meets me at the hotel and he is all sonorous and stirred with a kind of silent joy.

"We're to meet J. P. Morgan this afternoon," says he. "A man I know in the hotel wants to introduce us. He's a friend of his. He says he likes to meet people from the West."

"That sounds nice and plausible," says I. "I'd like to know Mr. Morgan."

"It won't hurt us a bit," says Silver, "to get acquainted with a few finance kings. I kind of like the social way New York has with strangers."

The man Silver knew was named Klein. At three o'clock Klein brought his Wall Street friend to see us in Silver's room. "Mr. Morgan" looked some like his pictures, and he had a Turkish towel wrapped around his left foot, and he walked with a cane.

"Mr. Silver and Mr. Pescud," says Klein. "It sounds superfluous," says he, "to mention the name of the greatest financial——"

"Cut it out, Klein," says Mr. Morgan. "I'm glad to know you gents; I take great interest in the West. Klein tells me you're from Little Rock. I think I've a railroad or two out there somewhere. If either of you guys would like to deal a hand or two of stud poker I——"

"Now, Pierpont," cuts in Klein, "you forget!"

"Excuse me, gents!" says Morgan; "since I've had the gout so bad I sometimes play a social game of cards at my house. Neither of you never knew One-eyed Peters, did you, while you was around Little Rock? He lived in Seattle, New Mexico."

Before we could answer, Mr. Morgan hammered on the floor with his cane and begins to walk up and down, swearing in a loud tone of voice.

"They have been pounding your stocks to-day on the Street, Pierpont?" asks Klein, smiling.

"Stocks! No!" roars Mr. Morgan. "It's that picture I sent an agent to Europe to buy. I just thought about it. He cabled me to-day that it ain't to be found in all Italy. I'd pay $50,000 to-morrow for that picture—yes, $75,000. I give the agent a la carte in purchasing it. I cannot understand why the art galleries will allow a De Vinchy to——"

"Why, Mr. Morgan," says Klein; "I thought you owned all of the De Vinchy paintings."

"What is the picture like, Mr. Morgan?" asks Silver. "It must be as big as the side of the Flatiron Building."

"I'm afraid your art education is on the bum, Mr. Silver," says Morgan. "The picture is 27 inches by 42; and it is called 'Love's Idle Hour.' It represents a number of cloak models doing the two-step on the bank of a purple river. The cablegram said it might have been brought to this country. My collection will never be complete without that picture. Well, so long, gents; us financiers must keep early hours."

Mr. Morgan and Klein went away together in a cab. Me and Silver talked about how simple and unsuspecting great people was; and Silver said what a shame it would be to try to rob a man like Mr. Morgan; and I said I thought it would be rather imprudent, myself. Klein proposes a stroll after dinner; and me and him and Silver walks down toward Seventh Avenue to see the sights. Klein sees a pair of cuff links that instigate his admiration in a pawnshop window, and we all go in while he buys 'em.

After we got back to the hotel and Klein had gone, Silver jumps at me and waves his hands.

"Did you see it?" says he. "Did you see it, Billy?"

"What?" I asks.

"Why, that picture that Morgan wants. It's hanging in the pawnshop, behind the desk. I didn't say anything because Klein was there. It's the article sure as you live. The girls are as natural as paint can make them, all measuring 36 and 25 and 42 skirts, if they had any skirts, and they're doing a buck-and-wing on the bank of a river with the blues. What did Mr. Morgan say he'd give for it? Oh, don't make me tell you. They can't know what it is in that pawnshop."

When the pawnshop opened the next morning me and Silver was standing there as anxious as if we wanted to soak our Sunday suit to buy a drink. We sauntered inside, and began to look at watch-chains.

"That's a violent specimen of a chromo you've got up there," remarked Silver, casual, to the pawnbroker. "But I kind of enthuse over the girl with the shoulder-blades and red bunting. Would an offer of $2.25 for it cause you to knock over any fragile articles of your stock in hurrying it off the nail?"

The pawnbroker smiles and goes on showing us plate watch-chains.

"That picture," says he, "was pledged a year ago by an Italian gentleman. I loaned him $500 on it. It is called 'Love's Idle Hour,' and it is by Leonardo de Vinchy. Two days ago the legal time expired, and it became an unredeemed pledge. Here is a style of chain that is worn a great deal now."

At the end of half an hour me and Silver paid the pawnbroker $2,000 and walked out with the picture. Silver got into a cab with it and started for Morgan's office. I goes to the hotel and waits for him. In two hours Silver comes back.

"Did you see Mr. Morgan?" I asks. "How much did he pay you for it?"

Silver sits down and fools with a tassel on the table cover.

"I never exactly saw Mr. Morgan," he says, "because Mr. Morgan's been in Europe for a month. But what's worrying me, Billy, is this: The department stores have all got that same picture on sale, framed, for $3.48. And they charge $3.50 for the frame alone—that's what I can't understand."

THE DAY RESURGENT

I can see the artist bite the end of his pencil and frown when it comes to drawing his Easter picture; for his legitimate pictorial conceptions of figures pertinent to the festival are but four in number.

First comes Easter, pagan goddess of spring. Here his fancy may have free play. A beautiful maiden with decorative hair and the proper number of toes will fill the bill. Miss Clarice St. Vavasour, the well-known model, will pose for it in the "Lethergogallagher," or whatever it was that Trilby called it.

Second—the melancholy lady with upturned eyes in a framework of lilies. This is magazine-covery, but reliable.

Third—Miss Manhattan in Fifth Avenue Easter Sunday parade.

Fourth—Maggie Murphy with a new red feather in her old straw hat, happy and self-conscious, in the Grand Street turnout.

Of course, the rabbits do not count. Nor the Easter eggs, since the higher criticism has hard-boiled them.

The limited field of its pictorial possibilities proves that Easter, of all our festival days, is the most vague and shifting in our conception. It belongs to all religions, although the pagans invented it. Going back still further to the first spring, we can see Eve choosing with pride a new green leaf from the tree *ficus carica*.

Now, the object of this critical and learned preamble is to set forth the theorem that Easter is neither a date, a season, a festival, a holiday, nor an occasion. What it is you shall find out if you follow in the footsteps of Danny McCree.

Easter Sunday dawned as it should, bright and early, in its place on the calendar between Saturday and Monday. At 5:24 the sun rose, and at ,0:30 Danny followed its example. He went into the kitchen and washed his face at the sink. His mother was frying bacon. She looked at his hard, smooth, knowing countenance as he juggled with the round cake of soap, and thought of his father when she first saw him stopping a hot grounder between second and third twenty-two years before on a vacant lot in Harlem, where the La Paloma apartment house now stands. In the front room of the flat Danny's father sat by an open window smoking his pipe, with his dishevelled gray hair tossed about by the breeze. He still clung to his pipe, although his sight had been taken from him two years before by a precocious blast of giant powder that went off without permission. Very few blind men care for smoking, for the reason that they cannot see the smoke. Now, could you enjoy having the news read to you from an evening paper unless you could see the color of the headlines?

" 'Tis Easter Day," said Mrs. McCree.

"Scramble mine," said Danny.

After breakfast he dressed himself in the Sabbath morning costume of the Canal Street importing house dray chauffeur—frock coat, striped trousers, patent leathers, gilded trace chain across front of vest, and wing collar, rolled-brim derby and butterfly bow from Schonstein's (between Fourteenth Street and Tony's fruit stand) Saturday night sale.

"You'll be goin' out this day, of course, Danny," said old man McCree, a little wistfully. " 'Tis a kind of holiday, they say. Well, it's fine spring weather. I can feel it in the air."

"Why should I not be going out?" demanded Danny in his grumpiest chest tones. "Should I stay in? Am I as good as a horse? One day of rest my team has a week. Who earns the money for the rent and the breakfast you've just eat, I'd like to know? Answer me that!"

"All right, lad," said the old man. "I'm not complainin'. While me two eyes was good there was nothin' better to my mind than a Sunday out. There's a smell of turf and burnin' brush comin' in the windy. I have me tobaccy. A good fine day and rist to ye, lad. Times I wished your mother had larned to read, so I might hear the rest about the hippopotamus— but let that be."

"Now, what is this foolishness he talks of hippopotamuses?" asked Danny of his mother, as he passed through the kitchen. "Have you been taking him to the Zoo? And for what?"

"I have not," said Mrs. McCree. "He sets by the windy all day. 'Tis little recreation a blind man among the poor gets at all. I'm thinkin' they wander in their minds at times. One day he talks of grease without stoppin' for the most of an hour. I looks to see if there's lard burnin' in the fryin' pan. There is not. He says I do not understand. 'Tis weary days, Sundays, and holidays and all, for a blind man, Danny. There was no better nor stronger than him when he had his two eyes. 'Tis a fine day, son. Injoy yerself ag'inst the morning. There will be cold supper at six."

"Have you heard any talk of a hippopotamus?" asked Danny of Mike, the janitor, as he went out of the door downstairs.

"I have not," said Mike, pulling his shirtsleeves higher. "But 'tis the only subject in the animal, natural and illegal lists of outrages that I've not been complained to about these two days. See the landlord. Or else move out if ye like. Have ye hippopotamuses in the lease? No, then?"

"It was the old man who spoke of it," said Danny. "Likely there's nothing in it."

Danny walked up the street to the Avenue and then struck northward into the heart of the district where Easter—modern Easter, in new, bright raiment—leads the pascal march. Out of towering brown churches came the blithe music of anthems from the living flowers—so it seemed when your eye looked upon the Easter girl.

Gentlemen, frock-coated, silk-hatted, gardeniaed, sustained the background of the tradition. Children carried lilies in their hands. The windows of the brownstone mansions were packed with the most opulent creations of Flora, the sister of the Lady of the Lilies.

Around a corner, white-gloved, pink-gilled, and tightly buttoned, walked Corrigan, the cop, shield to the curb. Danny knew him.

"Why, Corrigan," he asked, "is Easter? I know it comes the first time you're full after the moon rises on the seventeenth of March—but why? Is it a proper and religious ceremony, or does the Government appoint it out of politics?"

" 'Tis an annual celebration," said Corrigan, with the judicial air of the Third Deputy Police Commissioner, "peculiar to New York. It extends up to Harlem. Sometimes they has the reserves out at One Hundred and Twenty-fifth Street. In my opinion 'tis not political."

"Thanks," said Danny. "And say—did you ever hear a man complain of hippopotamuses? When not specially in drink, I mean."

"Nothing larger than sea turtles," said Corrigan, reflecting, "and there was wood alcohol in that."

Danny wandered. The double, heavy incumbency of enjoying simultaneously a Sunday and a festival day was his.

The sorrows of the hand-toiler fit him easily. They are worn so often that they hang with the picturesque lines of the best tailor-made garments.

That is why well-fed artists of pencil and pen find in the griefs of the common people their most striking models. But when the Philistine would disport himself, the grimness of Melpomene, herself, attends upon his capers. Therefore, Danny set his jaw hard at Easter, and took his pleasure sadly.

The family entrance of Dugan's café was feasible; so Danny yielded to the vernal season as far as a glass of bock. Seated in a dark linoleumed, humid back room, his heart and mind still groped after the mysterious meaning of the springtime jubilee.

"Say, Tim," he said to the waiter, "why do they have Easter?"

"Skiddoo!" said Tim, closing a sophisticated eye. "Is that a new one? All right. Tony Pastor's for you last night, I guess. I give it up. What's the answer—two apples or a yard and a half?"

From Dugan's Danny turned back eastward. The April sun seemed to stir in him a vague feeling that he could not construe. He made a wrong diagnosis and decided that it was Katy Conlon.

A block from her house on Avenue A he met her going to church. They pumped hands on the corner.

"Gee! but you look dumpish and dressed up," said Katy. "What's wrong? Come away with me to church and be cheerful."

"What's doing at church?" asked Danny.

"Why, it's Easter Sunday. Silly! I waited till after eleven expectin' you might come around to go."

"What does this Easter stand for, Katy?" asked Danny gloomily. "Nobody seems to know."

"Nobody as blind as you," said Katy with spirit. "You haven't even looked at my new hat. And skirt. Why, it's when all the girls put on new spring clothes. Silly! Are you coming to church with me?"

"I will," said Danny. "If this Easter is pulled off there, they ought to be able to give some excuse for it. Not that the hat ain't a beauty. The green roses are great."

At church the preacher did some expounding with no pounding. He spoke rapidly, for he was in a hurry to get home to his early Sabbath dinner; but he knew his business. There was one word that controlled his theme—resurrection. Not a new creation; but a new life arising out of the old. The congregation had heard it often before. But there was a wonderful hat, a combination of sweet peas and lavender, in the sixth pew from the pulpit. It attracted much attention.

After church Danny lingered on a corner while Katy waited, with pique in her sky-blue eyes.

"Are you coming along to the house?" she asked. "But don't mind me. I'll get there all right. You seem to be studyin' a lot about something. All right. Will I see you at any time specially, Mr. McCree?"

"I'll be around Wednesday night as usual," said Danny, turning and crossing the street.

Katy walked away with the green roses dangling indignantly. Danny stopped two blocks away. He stood still with his hands in his pockets, at the curb on the corner. His face was that of a graven image. Deep in his soul something stirred so small, so fine, so keen and leavening that his hard fibres did not recognize it. It was something more tender than the April day, more subtle than the call of the senses, purer and deeper-rooted than the love of woman—for had he not turned away from green roses and eyes that had kept him chained for a year? And Danny did not know what it was. The preacher, who was in a hurry to go to his dinner, had told him, but Danny had had no libretto with which to follow the drowsy intonation. But the preacher spoke the truth.

Suddenly Danny slapped his leg and gave forth a hoarse yell of delight.

"Hippopotamus!" he shouted to an elevated road pillar. "Well, how is that for a bum guess? Why, blast my skylights! I know what he was driving at now.

"Hippopotamus! Wouldn't that send you to the Bronx! It's been a year since he heard it; and he didn't miss it so very far. We quit at 469 B. C. and this comes next. Well, a wooden man wouldn't have guessed what he was trying to get out of him."

Danny caught a crosstown car and went up to the rear flat that his labor supported.

Old man McCree was still sitting by the window. His extinct pipe lay on the sill.

"Will that be you, lad?" he asked.

Danny flared into the rage of a strong man who is surprised at the outset of committing a good deed.

"Who pays the rent and buys the food that is eaten in this house?" he snapped, viciously. "Have I no right to come in?"

"Ye're a faithful lad," said old man McCree, with a sigh. "Is it evening yet?"

Danny reached up on a shelf and took down a thick book labeled in gilt letters, "The History of Greece." Dust was on it half an inch thick. He laid it on the table and found a place in it marked by a strip of paper. And then he gave a short roar at the top of his voice, and said:

"Was it the hippopotamus you wanted to be read to about then?"

"Did I hear ye open the book?" said old man McCree. "Many and weary be the months since my lad has read it to me. I dinno; but I took a great likings to them Greeks. Ye left off at a place. 'Tis a fine day outside, lad. Be out and take rest from your work. I have gotten used to me chair by the windy and me pipe."

"Pel-Peloponnesus was the place where we left off, and not hippopotamus," said Danny. "The war began there. It kept something doing for thirty years. The headlines say that a guy named Philip of Macedon, in 338 B. C., got to be boss of Greece by getting the decision at the battle of Cher-Cheronœa. I'll read it."

With his hand to his ear, rapt in the Peloponnesian War, old man McCree sat for an hour, listening.

Then he got up and felt his way to the door of the kitchen. Mrs. McCree was slicing cold meat. She looked up. Tears were running from old man McCree's eyes.

"Do ye hear our lad readin' to me?" he said. "There is none finer in the land. My two eyes have come back to me again."

After supper he said to Danny: " 'Tis a happy day, this Easter. And now ye will be off to see Katy in the evening. Well enough."

"Who pays the rent and buys the food that is eaten in this house?" said Danny, angrily. "Have I no right to stay in it? After supper there is yet to come the reading of the battle of Corinth, 146 B. C., when the kingdom, as they say, became an in-integral portion of the Roman Empire. Am I nothing in this house?"

THE FIFTH WHEEL

The ranks of the Bed Line moved closer together; for it was cold, cold. They were alluvial deposit of the stream of life lodged in the delta of Fifth Avenue and Broadway. The Bed Liners stamped their freezing feet, looked at the empty benches in Madison Square whence Jack Frost had evicted them, and muttered to one another in a confusion of tongues. The Flatiron Building with its impious cloud-piercing architecture looming mistily above them on the opposite delta, might well have stood for the tower of Babel, whence these polyglot idlers had been called by the winged walking delegate of the Lord.

Standing on a pine box a head higher than his flock of goats, the Preacher exhorted whatever transient and shifting audience the north wind doled out to him. It was a slave market. Fifteen cents bought you a man. You deeded him to Morpheus; and the recording angel gave you credit.

The Preacher was incredibly earnest and unwearied. He had looked over the list of things one may do for one's fellow man, and had assumed for himself the task of putting to bed all who might apply at his soap box on the nights of Wednesday and Sunday. That left but five nights for other philanthropists to handle; and had they done their part as well, this wicked city might have become a vast Arcadian dormitory where all might snooze and snore the happy hours away, letting problem plays and the rent man and business go to the deuce.

The hour of eight was but a little while past; sightseers in a small, dark mass of pay ore were gathered in the shadow of General Worth's monument. Now and then, shyly, ostentatiously, carelessly, or with conscientious exactness one would step forward and bestow upon the Preacher small bills or silver. Then a lieutenant of Scandinavian coloring and enthusiasm would march away to a lodging house with a squad of the redeemed. All the while the Preacher exhorted the crowd in terms beautifully devoid of eloquence—splendid with the deadly, accusive monotony of truth. Before the picture of the Bed Liners fades you must hear one phrase of the Preacher's—the one that formed his theme that night. It is worthy of being stenciled on all the white ribbons in the world.

"No man ever learned to be a drunkard on five-cent whiskey."

Think of it, tippler. It covers the ground from the sprouting rye to the Potter's Field.

A clean-profiled, erect young man in the rear rank of the bedless emulated the terrapin, drawing his head far down into the shell of his coat collar. It was a well-cut tweed coat; and the trousers still showed signs of having flattened themselves beneath the compelling goose. But, conscientiously, I must warn the milliner's apprentice who reads this, expecting a Reginald Montressor in straits, to peruse no further. The young man was no other than Thomas McQuade, ex-coachman, discharged for drunkenness one month before, and now reduced to the grimy ranks of the one-night bed seekers.

If you live in smaller New York you must know the Van Smuythe family carriage, drawn by the two 1,500-pound, 100 to 1-shot bays. The carriage is shaped like a bath-tub. In each end of it reclines an old lady Van Smuythe holding a black sunshade the size of a New Year's Eve feather tickler. Before his downfall Thomas McQuade drove the Van Smuythe bays and was himself driven by Annie, the Van Smuythe lady's maid. But it is one of the saddest things about romance that a tight shoe or an empty commissary or an aching tooth will make a temporary heretic of any Cupid-worshipper. And Thomas's physical troubles were not few. Therefore, his soul was less vexed with thoughts of his lost lady's maid than it was by the fancied presence of certain non-existent things that his racked nerves almost convinced him were flying, dancing, crawling, and wriggling on the asphalt and in the air above and around the dismal campus of the Bed Line army. Nearly four weeks of straight whiskey and a diet limited to crackers, bologna, and pickles often guarantees a psychozoological sequel. Thus desperate, freezing, angry, beset by phantoms as he was, he felt the need of human sympathy and intercourse.

The Bed Liner standing at his right was a young man of about his own age, shabby but neat.

"What's the diagnosis of your case, Freddy?" asked Thomas, with the free-masonic familiarity of the damned—"Booze? That's mine. You don't look like a pan-handler. Neither am I. A month ago I was pushing the lines over the backs of the finest team of Percheron buffaloes that ever made their mile down Fifth Avenue in 2.85. And look at me now! Say; how do you come to be at this bed bargain-counter rummage sale?"

The other young man seemed to welcome the advances of the airy ex-coachman.

"No," said he, "mine isn't exactly a case of drink. Unless we allow that Cupid is a bartender. I married unwisely, according to the opinion of my unforgiving relatives. I've been out of work for a year because I don't know how to work; and I've been sick in Bellevue and other hospitals for four months. My wife and kid had to go back to her mother. I was turned out of the hospital yesterday. And I haven't a cent. That's my tale of woe."

"Tough luck," said Thomas. "A man alone can pull through all right. But I hate to see the woman and kids get the worst of it."

Just then there hummed up Fifth Avenue a motor car so splendid, so red, so smoothly running, so craftily demolishing the speed regulations that it drew the attention even of the listless Bed Liners. Suspended and pinioned on its left side was an extra tire.

When opposite the unfortunate company the fastenings of this tire became loosed. It fell to the asphalt, bounded and rolled rapidly in the wake of the flying car.

Thomas McQuade scenting an opportunity, darted from his place among the Preacher's goats. In thirty seconds he had caught the rolling tire, swung it over his shoulder, and was trotting smartly after the car. On both sides of the avenue people were shouting, whistling, and waving canes at the red car, pointing to the enterprising Thomas coming up with the lost tire.

One dollar, Thomas had estimated, was the smallest guerdon that so grand an automobilist could offer for the service he had rendered, and save his pride.

Two blocks away the car had stopped. There was a little, brown, muffled chauffeur driving, and an imposing gentleman wearing a magnificent sealskin coat and a silk hat on a rear seat.

Thomas proffered the captured tire with his best ex-coachman manner and a look in the brighter of his reddened eyes that was meant to be suggestive to the extent of a silver coin or two and receptive up to higher denominations.

But the look was not so construed. The sealskinned gentleman received the tire, placed it inside the car, gazed intently at the ex-coachman, and muttered to himself inscrutable words.

"Strange—strange!" said he. "Once or twice even I, myself, have fancied that the Chaldean Chiroscope has availed. Could it be possible?"

Then he addressed less mysterious words to the waiting and hopeful Thomas.

"Sir, I thank you for your kind rescue of my tire. And I would ask you, if I may, a question. Do you know the family of Van Smuythes living in Washington Square North?"

"Oughtn't I to?" replied Thomas. "I lived there. Wish I did yet."

The sealskinned gentleman opened a door of the car.

"Step in, please," he said. "You have been expected."

Thomas McQuade obeyed with surprise but without hesitation. A seat in a motor car seemed better than standing room in the Bed Line. But after the lap-robe had been tucked about him and the auto had sped on its course, the peculiarity of the invitation lingered in his mind.

"Maybe the guy hasn't got any change," was his diagnosis. "Lots of these swell rounders don't lug about any ready money. Guess he'll dump me out when he gets to some joint where he can get cash on his mug. Anyhow, it's a cinch that I've got that open-air bed convention beat to a finish."

Submerged in his greatcoat, the mysterious automobilist seemed, himself, to marvel at the surprises of life. "Wonderful! amazing! strange!" he repeated to himself constantly.

When the car had well entered the crosstown Seventies it swung eastward a half block and stopped before a row of high-stooped, brownstone-front houses.

"Be kind enough to enter my house with me," said the sealskinned gentleman when they had alighted. "He's going to dig up, sure," reflected Thomas, following him inside.

There was a dim light in the hall. His host conducted him through a door to the left, closing it after him and leaving them in absolute darkness. Suddenly a luminous globe, strangely decorated, shone faintly in the centre of an immense room that seemed to Thomas more splendidly appointed than any he had ever seen on the stage or read of in fairy stories.

The walls were hidden by gorgeous red hangings embroidered with fantastic gold figures. At the rear end of the room were draped portières of dull gold spangled with silver crescents and stars. The furniture was of the costliest and rarest styles. The ex-coachman's feet sank into rugs as fleecy and deep as snow-drifts. There were three or four oddly shaped stands or tables covered with black velvet drapery.

Thomas McQuade took in the splendors of this palatial apartment with one eye. With the other he looked for his imposing conductor—to find that he had disappeared.

"B'gee!" muttered Thomas, "this listens like a spook shop. Shouldn't wonder if it ain't one of these Moravian Nights' adventures that you read about. Wonder what became of the furry guy."

Suddenly a stuffed owl that stood on an ebony perch near the illuminated globe slowly raised his wings and emitted from his eyes a brilliant electric glow.

With a fright-born imprecation, Thomas seized a bronze statuette of Hebe from a cabinet near by and hurled it with all his might at the terrifying and impossible fowl. The owl and his perch went over with a crash. With the sound there was a click, and the room was flooded with light from a dozen frosted globes along the walls and ceiling. The gold portières parted and closed, and the mysterious automobilist entered the room. He was tall and wore evening dress of perfect cut and accurate taste. A Vandyke beard of glossy, golden brown, rather long and wavy hair, smoothly parted, and large, magnetic, orientally occult eyes gave him a most impressive and striking appearance. If you can conceive a Russian Grand Duke in a Rajah's throne-room advancing to greet a visiting Emperor, you will gather something of the majesty of his manner. But Thomas McQuade was too near his *d t's* to be mindful of his *p's* and *q's*. When he viewed this silken, polished, and somewhat terrifying host he thought vaguely of dentists.

"Say, doc," said he resentfully, "that's a hot bird you keep on tap. I hope I didn't break anything. But I've nearly got the williwalloos, and when he threw them 32-candle-power lamps of his on me, I took a snapshot at him with that little brass Flatiron Girl that stood on the sideboard."

"That is merely a mechanical toy," said the gentleman with a wave of his hand. "May I ask you to be seated while I explain why I brought you to my house? Perhaps you would not understand nor be in sympathy with the psychological prompting that caused me to do so. So I will come to the point at once by venturing to refer to your admission that you know the Van Smuythe family, of Washington Square North."

"Any silver missing?" asked Thomas tartly. "Any joolry displaced? Of course I know 'em. Any of the old ladies' sunshades disappeared? Well, I know 'em. And then what?"

The Grand Duke rubbed his white hands together softly.

"Wonderful!" he murmured. "Wonderful! Shall I come to believe in the Chaldean Chiroscope myself? Let me assure you," he continued, "that there is nothing for you to fear. Instead, I think I can promise you that very good fortune awaits you. We will see."

"Do they want me back?" asked Thomas, with something of his old professional pride in his voice. "I'll promise to cut out the booze and do the right thing if they'll try me again. But how did you get wise, doc? B'gee, it's the swellest employment agency I was ever in, with its flashlight owls and so forth."

With an indulgent smile the gracious host begged to be excused for two minutes. He went out to the sidewalk and gave an order to the chauffeur, who still waited with the car. Returning to the mysterious apartment, he sat by his guest and began to entertain him so well by his witty and genial converse that the poor Bed Liner almost forgot the cold streets from which he had been so recently and so singularly rescued. A servant brought some tender cold fowl and tea biscuits and a glass of miraculous wine; and Thomas felt the glamor of Arabia envelop him. Thus half an hour sped quickly; and then the honk of the returned motor car at the door suddenly drew the Grand Duke to his feet, with another soft petition for a brief absence.

Two women, well muffled against the cold, were admitted at the front door and suavely conducted by the master of the house down the hall through another door to the left and into a smaller room, which was screened and segregated from the larger front room by heavy double portières. Here the furnishings were even more elegant and exquisitely tasteful than in the other. On a gold-inlaid rosewood table were scattered sheets of white paper and a queer, triangular instrument or toy, apparently of gold, standing on little wheels.

The taller woman threw back her black veil and loosened her cloak. She was fifty, with a wrinkled and sad face. The other, young and plump, took a chair a little distance away and to the rear as a servant or an attendant might have done.

"You sent for me, Professor Cherubusco," said the elder woman, wearily. "I hope you have something more definite than usual to say. I've about lost the little faith I had in your art. I would not have responded to your call this evening if my sister had not insisted upon it."

"Madame," said the professor, with his princeliest smile, "the true Art cannot fail. To find the true psychic and potential branch sometimes requires time. We have not succeeded, I admit, with the cards, the crystal, the stars, the magic formulæ of Zarazin, nor the Oracle of Po. But we have at last discovered the true psychic route. The Chaldean Chiroscope has been successful in our search."

The professor's voice had a ring that seemed to proclaim his belief in his own words. The elderly lady looked at him with a little more interest.

"Why, there was no sense in those words that it wrote with my hands on it," she said. "What do you mean?"

"The words were these," said Professor Cherubusco, rising to his full magnificent height. " 'By the fifth wheel of the chariot he shall come.' "

"I haven't seen many chariots," said the lady, "but I never saw one with five wheels."

"Progress," said the professor—"progress in science and mechanics has accomplished it—though, to be exact, we may speak of it only as an extra tire. Progress in occult art has advanced in proportion. Madame, I repeat that the Chaldean Chiroscope has succeeded. I can not only answer the question that you have propounded, but I can produce before your eyes the proof thereof."

And now the lady was disturbed both in her disbelief and in her poise.

"O professor!" she cried, anxiously—"When?—where? Has he been found? Do not keep me in suspense."

"I beg you will excuse me for a very few minutes," said Professor Cherubusco, "and I think I can demonstrate to you the efficacy of the true Art."

Thomas was contentedly munching the last crumbs of the bread and fowl when the enchanter appeared suddenly at his side.

"Are you willing to return to your old home if you are assured of a welcome and restoration to favor?" he asked, with his courteous, royal smile.

"Do I look bughouse?" answered Thomas. "Enough of the footback life for me. But will they have me again? The old lady is as fixed in her ways as a nut on a new axle."

"My dear young man," said the other, "she has been searching for you everywhere."

"Great!" said Thomas. "I'm on the job. That team of dropsical dromedaries they call horses is a handicap for a first-class coachman like myself; but I'll take the job back, sure, doc. They're good people to be with."

And now a change came o'er the suave countenance of the Caliph of Bagdad. He looked keenly and suspiciously at the ex-coachman.

"May I ask what your name is?" he said shortly.

"You've been looking for me," said Thomas, "and don't know my name? You're a funny kind of sleuth. You must be one of the Central Office gumshoers. I'm Thomas McQuade, of course; and I've been chauffeur of the Van Smuythe elephant team for a year. They fired me a month ago for—well, doc, you saw what I did to your old owl. I went broke on booze, and when I saw the tire drop off your whiz wagon I was standing in that squad of hoboes at the Worth monument waiting for a free bed. Now, what's the prize for the best answer to all this?"

To his intense surprise Thomas felt himself lifted by the collar and dragged, without a word of explanation, to the front door. This was opened, and he was kicked forcibly down the steps with one heavy, disillusionizing, humiliating impact of the stupendous Arabian's shoe.

As soon as the ex-coachman had recovered his feet and his wits he hastened as fast as he could eastward toward Broadway.

"Crazy guy," was his estimate of the mysterious automobilist. "Just wanted to have some fun kiddin', I guess. He might have dug up a dollar, anyhow. Now I've got to hurry up and get back to that gang of bum bed hunters before they all get preached to sleep."

When Thomas reached the end of his two-mile walk he found the ranks of the homeless reduced to a squad of perhaps eight or ten. He took the proper place of a newcomer at the left end of the rear rank. In the file in front of him was the young man who had spoken to him of hospitals and something of a wife and child.

"Sorry to see you back again," said the young man, turning to speak to him. "I hoped you had struck something better than this."

"Me?" said Thomas. "Oh, I just took a run around the block to keep warm! I see the public ain't lending to the Lord very fast tonight."

"In this kind of weather," said the young man, "charity avails itself of the proverb, and both begins and ends at home."

And now the Preacher and his vehement lieutenant struck up a last hymn of petition to Providence and man. Those of the Bed Liners whose windpipes still registered above 32 degrees hopelessly and tunelessly joined in.

In the middle of the second verse Thomas saw a sturdy girl with wind-tossed drapery battling against the breeze and coming straight toward him from the opposite sidewalk. "Annie!" he yelled, and ran toward her.

"You fool, you fool!" she cried, weeping and laughing, and hanging upon his neck, "why did you do it?"

"The Stuff," explained Thomas briefly. "You know. But subsequently nit. Not a drop." He led her to the curb. "How did you happen to see me?"

"I came to find you," said Annie, holding tight to his sleeve. "Oh, you big fool! Professor Cherubusco told us that we might find you here."

"Professor Ch—— Don't know the guy. What saloon does he work in?"

"He's a clearvoyant, Thomas; the greatest in the world. He found you with the Chaldean telescope, he said."

"He's a liar," said Thomas. "I never had it. He never saw me have anybody's telescope."

"And he said you came in a chariot with five wheels or something."

"Annie," said Thomas solicitously, "you're giving me the wheels now. If I had a chariot I'd have gone to bed in it long ago. And without any singing and preaching for a nightcap, either."

"Listen, you big fool. The Missis says she'll take you back. I begged her to. But you must behave. And you can go up to the house to-night; and your old room over the stable is ready."

"Great!" said Thomas earnestly. "You are It, Annie. But when did these stunts happen?"

"To-night at Professor Cherubusco's. He sent his automobile for the Missis, and she took me along. I've been there with her before."

"What's the professor's line?"

"He's a clearvoyant and a witch. The Missis consults him. He knows everything. But he hasn't done the Missis any good yet, though she's paid him hundreds of dollars. But he told us that the stars told him we could find you here."

"What's the old lady want this cherry-buster to do?"

"That's a family secret," said Annie. "And now you've asked enough questions. Come on home, you big fool."

They had moved but a little way up the street when Thomas stopped.

"Got any dough with you, Annie?" he asked.

Annie looked at him sharply.

"Oh, I know what that look means," said Thomas. "You're wrong. Not another drop. But there's a guy that was standing next to me in the bed line over there that's in a bad shape. He's the right kind, and he's got wives or kids or something, and he's on the sick list. No booze. If you could dig up half a dollar for him so he could get a decent bed I'd like it."

Annie's fingers began to wiggle in her purse.

"Sure, I've got money," said she. "Lots of it. Twelve dollars." And then she added, with woman's ineradicable suspicion of vicarious benevolence: "Bring him here and let me see him first."

Thomas went on his mission. The wan Bed Liner came readily enough. As the two drew near, Annie looked up from her purse and screamed:

"Mr. Walter—— Oh—Mr. Walter!"

"Is that you, Annie?" said the young man weakly.

"Oh, Mr. Walter!—and the Missis hunting high and low for you!"

"Does mother want to see me?" he asked, with a flush coming out on his pale cheek.

"She's been hunting for you high and low. Sure, she wants to see you. She wants you to come home. She's tried police and morgues and lawyers and advertising and detectives and rewards and everything. And then she took up clearvoyants. You'll go right home, won't you, Mr. Walter?"

"Gladly, if she wants me," said the young man. "Three years is a long time. I suppose I'll have to walk up, though, unless the street cars are giving free rides. I used to walk and beat that old plug team of bays we used to drive to the carriage. Have they got them yet?"

"They have," said Thomas, feelingly. "And they'll have 'em ten years from now. The life of the royal elephantibus truckhorseibus is one hundred and forty-nine years. I'm the coachman. Just got my re-appointment five minutes ago. Let's all ride up in a surface car—that is—er—if Annie will pay the fares."

On the Broadway car Annie handed each one of the prodigals a nickel to pay the conductor.

"Seems to me you are mighty reckless the way you throw large sums of money around," said Thomas, sarcastically.

"In that purse," said Annie, decidedly, "is exactly $11.85. I shall take every cent of it to-morrow and give it to Professor Cherubusco, the greatest man in the world."

"Well," said Thomas, "I guess he must be a pretty fly guy to pipe off things the way he does. I'm glad his spooks told him where you could find me. If you'll give me his address, some day I'll go up there, myself, and shake his hand."

Presently Thomas moved tentatively in his seat, and thoughtfully felt an abrasion or two on his knees and elbows.

"Say, Annie," said he, confidentially, "maybe it's one of the last dreams of the booze, but I've a kind of a recollection of riding in an automobile with a swell guy that took me to a house full of eagles and arc lights. He fed me on biscuits and hot air, and then kicked me down the front steps. If it was the *d t's,* why am I so sore?"

"Shut up, you fool," said Annie.

"If I could find that funny guy's house," said Thomas, in conclusion, "I'd go up there some day and punch his nose for him."

THE POET AND THE PEASANT

The other day a poet friend of mine, who has lived in close communion with nature all his life, wrote a poem and took it to an editor.

It was a living pastoral, full of the genuine breath of the fields, the song of birds, and the pleasant chatter of trickling streams.

When the poet called again to see about it, with hopes of a beefsteak dinner in his heart, it was handed back to him with the comment:

"Too artificial."

Several of us met over spaghetti and Duchess County chianti, and swallowed indignation with slippery forkfuls.

And we dug a pit for the editor. With us was Conant, a well-arrived writer of fiction—a man who had trod on asphalt all his life and who had never looked upon bucolic scenes except with sensations of disgust from the windows of express trains.

Conant wrote a poem and called it "The Doe and the Brook." It was a fine specimen of the kind of work you would expect from a poet who had strayed with Amaryllis only as far as the florist's windows, and whose sole ornithological discussion had been carried on with a waiter. Conant signed this poem, and we sent it to the same editor.

But this has very little to do with the story.

Just as the editor was reading the first line of the poem, on the next morning, a being stumbled off the West Shore ferryboat, and loped slowly up Forty-second Street.

The invader was a young man with light blue eyes, a hanging lip, and hair the exact color of the little orphan's (afterward discovered to be the earl's daughter) in one of Mr. Blaney's plays. His trousers were corduroy, his coat short-sleeved, with buttons in the middle of his back. One bootleg was outside the corduroys. You looked expectantly, though in vain, at his straw hat for ear holes, its shape inaugurating the suspicion that it had been ravaged from a former equine possessor. In his hand was a valise—description of it is an impossible task; a Boston man would not have carried his lunch and law books to his office in it. And above one ear, in his hair, was a wisp of hay—the rustic's letter of credit, his badge of innocence, the last clinging touch of the Garden of Eden lingering to shame the gold-brick men.

Knowingly, smilingly, the city crowds passed him by. They saw the raw stranger stand in the gutter and stretch his neck at the tall buildings. At this they ceased to smile, and even to look at him. It had been done so often. A few glanced at the antique valise to see what Coney "attraction" or brand of chewing gum he might be thus dinning into his memory. But for the most part he was ignored. Even the newsboys looked bored when he scampered like a circus clown out of the way of cabs and street cars.

At Eighth Avenue stood "Bunco Harry," with his dyed mustache and shiny, good-natured eyes. Harry was too good an artist not to be pained at the sight of an actor overdoing his part. He edged up to the countryman, who had stopped to open his mouth at a jewelry store window, and shook his head.

"Too thick, pal," he said, critically—"too thick by a couple of inches. I don't know what your lay is; but you've got the properties on too thick. That hay, now—why, they don't even allow that on Proctor's circuit any more."

"I don't understand you, mister," said the green one. "I'm not lookin' for any circus. I've just run down from Ulster County to look at the town, bein' that the hayin's over with. Gosh! but it's a whopper. I thought Poughkeepsie was some pumpkins; but this here town is five times as big."

"Oh, well," said "Bunco Harry," raising his eyebrows, "I didn't mean to butt in. You don't have to tell. I thought you ought to tone down a little, so I tried to put you wise. Wish you success at your graft, whatever it is. Come and have a drink, anyhow."

"I wouldn't mind having a glass of lager beer," acknowledged the other.

They went to a café frequented by men with smooth faces and shifty eyes, and sat at their drinks.

"I'm glad I come across you, mister," said Haylocks. "How'd you like to play a game or two of seven-up? I've got the keerds."

He fished them out of Noah's valise—a rare, inimitable deck, greasy with bacon suppers and grimy with the soil of cornfields.

"Bunco Harry," laughed loud and briefly.

"Not for me, sport," he said, firmly. "I don't go against that make-up of yours for a cent. But I still say you've overdone it. The Reubs haven't dressed like that since '79. I doubt if you could work Brooklyn for a key-winding watch with that layout."

"Oh, you needn't think I ain't got the money," boasted Haylocks. He drew forth a tightly rolled mass of bills as large as a teacup, and laid it on the table.

"Got that for my share of grandmother's farm," he announced. "There's

$950 in that roll. Thought I'd come to the city and look around for a likely business to go into."

"Bunco Harry" took up the roll of money and looked at it with almost respect in his smiling eyes.

"I've seen worse," he said, critically. "But you'll never do it in them clothes. You want to get light tan shoes and a black suit and a straw hat with a colored band, and talk a good deal about Pittsburg and freight differentials, and drink sherry for breakfast in order to work off phony stuff like that."

"What's his line?" asked two or three shifty-eyed men of "Bunco Harry" after Haylocks had gathered up his impugned money and departed.

"The queer, I guess," said Harry. "Or else he's one of Jerome's men. Or some guy with a new graft. He's too much hayseed. Maybe that his —I wonder now—oh, no, it couldn't have been real money."

Haylocks wandered on. Thirst probably assailed him again, for he dived into a dark groggery on a side street and bought beer. Several sinister fellows hung upon one end of the bar. At first sight of him their eyes brightened; but when his insistent and exaggerated rusticity became apparent their expressions changed to wary suspicion.

Haylocks swung his valise across the bar.

"Keep that a while for me, mister," he said, chewing at the end of a virulent claybank cigar.

"I'll be back after I knock around a spell. And keep your eye on it, for there's $950 inside of it, though maybe you wouldn't think so to look at me."

Somewhere outside a phonograph struck up a band piece, and Haylocks was off for it, his coat-tail buttons flopping in the middle of his back.

"Divvy, Mike," said the men hanging upon the bar, winking openly at one another.

"Honest, now," said the bartender, kicking the valise to one side. "You don't think I'd fall to that, do you? Anybody can see he ain't no jay. One of McAdoo's come-on squad, I guess. He's a shine if he made himself up. There ain't no parts of the country now where they dress like that since they run rural free delivery to Providence, Rhode Island. If he's got nine-fifty in that valise it's a ninety-eight cent Waterbury that's stopped at ten minutes to ten."

When Haylocks had exhausted the resources of Mr. Edison to amuse he returned for his valise. And then down Broadway he gallivanted, culling the sights with his eager blue eyes. But still and evermore Broadway rejected him with curt glances and sardonic smiles. He was the oldest of the "gags" that the city must endure. He was so flagrantly impossible, so ultra rustic, so exaggerated beyond the most freakish products of the barnyards, the hayfield, and the vaudeville stage, that he excited only weariness and suspicion. And the wisp of hay in his hair was so genuine, so fresh and redolent of the meadows, so clamorously rural that even a shell-game man would have put up his peas and folded his table at the sight of it.

Haylocks seated himself upon a flight of stone steps and once more exhumed his roll of yellow-backs from the valise. The outer one, a twenty, he shucked off and beckoned to a newsboy.

"Son," said he, "run somewhere and get this changed for me. I'm mighty nigh out of chicken feed. I guess you'll get a nickel if you'll hurry up."

A hurt look appeared through the dirt on the newsy's face.

"Aw, watchert'ink! G'wan and get yer funny bill changed yerself. Dey ain't no farm clothes yer got on. G'wan wit yer stage money."

On a corner lounged a keen-eyed steerer for a gambling-house. He saw Haylocks, and his expression suddenly grew cold and virtuous.

"Mister," said the rural one. "I've heard of places in this here town where a fellow could have a good game of old sledge or peg a card at keno. I got $950 in this valise, and I come down from old Ulster to see the sights. Know where a fellow could get action on about $9 or $10? I'm goin' to have some sport, and then maybe I'll buy out a business of some kind."

The steerer looked pained, and investigated a white speck on his left fore-finger nail.

"Cheese it, old man," he murmured, reproachfully. "The Central Office must be bughouse to send you out looking like such a gillie. You couldn't get within two blocks of a sidewalk crap game in them Tony Pastor props. The recent Mr. Scotty from Death Valley has got you beat a cross-town block in the way of Elizabethan scenery and mechanical accessories. Let it be skiddoo for yours. Nay, I know of no gilded halls where one may get a patrol wagon on the ace."

Rebuffed again by the great city that is so swift to detect artificialities, Haylocks sat upon the curb and presented his thoughts to hold a conference.

"It's my clothes," said he; "durned if it ain't. They think I'm a hayseed and won't have nothin' to do with me. Nobody never made fun of this hat in Ulster County. I guess if you want folks to notice you in New York you must dress up like they do."

So Haylocks went shopping in the bazaars where men spake through their noses and rubbed their hands and ran the tape line ecstatically over the bulge in his inside pocket where reposed a red nubbin of corn with an even number of rows. And messengers bearing parcels and boxes streamed to his hotel on Broadway within the lights of Long Acre.

At 9 o'clock in the evening one descended to the sidewalk whom Ulster County would have forsworn. Bright tan were his shoes; his hat the latest block. His light gray trousers were deeply creased; a gay blue silk handkerchief flapped from the breast pocket of his elegant English walking coat. His collar might have graced a laundry window; his blond hair was trimmed close; the wisp of hay was gone.

For an instant he stood, resplendent, with the leisurely air of a boulevardier concocting in his mind the route for his evening pleasures. And then he turned down the gay, bright street with the easy and graceful tread of a millionaire.

But in the instant that he had paused the wisest and keenest eyes in the city had enveloped him in their field of vision. A stout man with gray eyes picked two of his friends with a lift of his eyebrows from the row of loungers in front of the hotel.

"The juicest jay I've seen in six months," said the man with gray eyes. "Come along."

It was half-past eleven when a man galloped into the West Forty-seventh Street Police Station with the story of his wrongs.

"Nine hundred and fifty dollars," he gasped, "all my share of grandmother's farm."

The desk sergeant wrung from him the name Jabez Bulltongue, of Locust Valley farm, Ulster County, and then began to take descriptions of the strong-arm gentlemen.

When Conant went to see the editor about the fate of his poem, he was received over the head of the office boy into the inner office that is decorated with the statuettes by Rodin and J. G. Brown.

"When I read the first line of 'The Doe and the Brook,'" said the editor, "I knew it to be the work of one whose life has been heart to heart with Nature. The finished art of the line did not blind me to that fact. To use a somewhat homely comparison, it was as if a wild, free child of the woods and fields were to don the garb of fashion and walk down Broadway. Beneath the apparel the man would show."

"Thanks," said Conant. "I suppose the check will be round on Thursday, as usual."

The morals of this story have somehow gotten mixed. You can take your choice of "Stay on the Farm" or "Don't Write Poetry."

THE ROBE OF PEACE

Mysteries follow one another so closely in a great city that the reading public and the friends of Johnny Bellchambers have ceased to marvel at his sudden and unexplained disappearance nearly a year ago. This particular mystery has now been cleared up, but the solution is so strange and incredible to the mind of the average man that only a select few who were in close touch with Bellchambers will give it full credence.

Johnny Bellchambers, as is well known, belonged to the intrinsically inner circle of the *élite*. Without any of the ostentation of the fashionable ones who endeavor to attract notice by eccentric display of wealth and show he still was *au fait* in everything that gave deserved lustre to his high position in the ranks of society.

Especially did he shine in the matter of dress. In this he was the despair of imitators. Always correct, exquisitely groomed, and possessed of an unlimited wardrobe, he was conceded to be the best-dressed man in New York, and, therefore, in America. There was not a tailor in Gotham who would not have deemed it a precious boon to have been granted the privilege of making Bellchambers' clothes without a cent of pay. As he wore them, they would have been a priceless advertisement. Trousers were his especial passion. Here nothing but perfection would be noticed. He would have worn a patch as quickly as he would have overlooked a wrinkle. He kept a man in his apartments always busy pressing his ample supply. His friends said that three hours was the limit of time that he would wear these garments without exchanging.

Bellchambers disappeared very suddenly. For three days his absence brought no alarm to his friends, and then they began to operate the usual methods of inquiry. All of them failed. He had left absolutely no trace behind. Then the search for a motive was instituted, but none was found. He had no enemies, he had no debts, there was no woman. There were several thousand dollars in his bank to his credit. He had never showed any tendency toward mental eccentricity; in fact, he was of a particularly calm and well-balanced temperament. Every means of tracing the vanished man was made use of, but without avail. It was one of those cases —more numerous in late years—where men seem to have gone out like the flame of a candle, leaving not even a trail of smoke as a witness.

In May, Tom Eyres and Lancelot Gilliam, two of Bellchambers' old friends, went for a little run on the other side. While pottering around in Italy and Switzerland, they happened, one day, to hear of a monastery in the Swiss Alps that promised something outside of the ordinary tourist-beguiling attractions. The monastery was almost inaccessible to the average sight-seer, being on an extremely rugged and precipitous spur of the mountains. The attractions it possessed but did not advertise were, first, an exclusive and divine cordial made by the monks that was said to far surpass benedictine and chartreuse. Next a huge brass bell so purely and accurately cast that it had not ceased sounding since it was first rung three hundred years ago. Finally, it was asserted that no Englishman had ever set foot within its walls. Eyres and Gilliam decided that these three reports called for investigation.

It took them two days with the aid of two guides to reach the monastery of St. Gondrau. It stood upon a frozen, wind-swept crag with the snow piled about it in treacherous, drifting masses. They were hospitably received by the brothers whose duty it was to entertain the infrequent guest. They drank of the precious cordial, finding it rarely potent and reviving. They listened to the great, ever-echoing bell and learned that they were pioneer travelers, in those gray stone walls, over the Englishman whose restless feet have trodden nearly every corner of the earth.

.At three o'clock on the afternoon they arrived, the two young Gothamites stood with good Brother Cristofer in the great, cold hallway of the monastery to watch the monks march past on their way to the refectory. They came slowly, pacing by twos, with their heads bowed, treading noiselessly with sandaled feet upon the rough stone flags. As the procession slowly filed past, Eyres suddenly gripped Gilliam by the arm. "Look," he whispered, eagerly, "at the one just opposite you now—the one on this side, with his hand at his waist—if that isn't Johnny Bellchambers then I never saw him!"

Gilliam saw and recognized the lost glass of fashion.

"What the deuce," said he, wonderingly, "is old Bell doing here? Tommy, it surely can't be he! Never heard of Bell having a turn for the religious. Fact is, I've heard him say things when a four-in-hand didn't seem to tie up just right that would bring him up for court-martial before any church."

"It's Bell, without a doubt," said Eyres, firmly, "or I'm pretty badly in need of an oculist. But think of Johnny Bellchambers, the Royal High Chancellor of swell togs and the Mahatma of pink teas, up here in cold storage doing penance in a snuff-colored bathrobe! I can't get it straight in my mind. Let's ask the jolly old boy that's doing the honors."

Brother Cristofer was appealed to for information. By that time the monks had passed into the refectory. He could not tell to which one they referred. Bellchambers? Ah, the brothers of St. Gondrau abandoned their worldly names when they took the vows. Did the gentlemen wish to speak with one of the brothers? If they would come to the refectory and indicate the one they wished to see, the reverend abbot in authority would, doubtless, permit it.

Eyres and Gilliam went into the dining hall and pointed out to Brother Cristofer the man they had seen. Yes, it was Johnny Bellchambers. They saw his face plainly now, as he sat among the dingy brothers, never looking up, eating broth from a coarse, brown bowl.

Permission to speak to one of the brothers was granted to the two travelers by the abbot, and they waited in a reception room for him to come. When he did come, treading softly in his sandals, both Eyres and Gilliam looked at him in perplexity and astonishment. It was Johnny Bellchambers, but he had a different look. Upon his smooth-shaven face was an expression of ineffable peace, of rapturous attainment, of perfect and complete happiness. His form was proudly erect, his eyes shone with a serene and gracious light. He was as neat and well-groomed as in the old New York days, but how differently was he clad! Now he seemed clothed in but a single garment—a long robe of rough brown cloth, gathered by a cord at the waist, and falling in straight, loose folds nearly to his feet. He shook hands with his visitors with his old ease and grace of manner. If there was any embarrassment in that meeting it was not manifested by Johnny Bellchambers. The room had no seats; they stood to converse.

"Glad to see you, old man," said Eyres, somewhat awkwardly. "Wasn't expecting to find you up here. Not a bad idea, though, after all. Society's an awful sham. Must be a relief to shake the giddy whirl and retire to—er—contemplation and—er—prayer and hymns, and those things."

"Oh, cut that, Tommy," said Bellchambers, cheerfully. "Don't be afraid that I'll pass around the plate. I go through these thing-um-bobs with the rest of these old boys because they are the rules. I'm Brother Ambrose here, you know. I'm given just ten minutes to talk to you fellows. That's rather a new design in waistcoats you have on, isn't it, Gilliam? Are they wearing those things on Broadway now?"

"It's the same old Johnny," said Gilliam, joyfully. "What the devil— I mean why—— Oh, confound it! what did you do it for, old man?"

"Peel the bathrobe," pleaded Eyres, almost tearfully, "and go back with us. The old crowd'll go wild to see you. This isn't in your line, Bell. I know half a dozen girls that wore the willow on the quiet when you shook us in that unaccountable way. Hand in your resignation, or get a dispensation, or whatever you have to do to get a release from this ice factory. You'll get catarrh here, Johnny—and—— My God! you haven't any socks on!"

Bellchambers looked down at his sandaled feet and smiled.

"You fellows don't understand," he said, soothingly. "It's nice of you to want me to go back, but the old life will never know me again. I have reached here the goal of all my ambitions. I am entirely happy and contented. Here I shall remain for the remainder of my days. You see this robe that I wear?" Bellchambers caressingly touched the straight-hanging garment: "At last I have found something that will not bag at the knees. I have attained——"

At that moment the deep boom of the great brass bell reverberated through the monastery. It must have been a summons to immediate devotions, for Brother Ambrose bowed his head, turned and left the chamber without another word. A slight wave of his hand as he passed through the stone doorway seemed to say a farewell to his old friends. They left the monastery without seeing him again.

And this is the story that Tommy Eyres and Lancelot Gilliam brought back with them from their latest European tour.

THE GIRL AND THE GRAFT

The other day I ran across my old friend Ferguson Pogue. Pogue is a conscientious grafter of the highest type. His headquarters is the Western Hemisphere, and his line of business is anything from speculating in town lots on the Great Staked Plains to selling wooden toys in Connecticut, made by hydraulic pressure from nutmegs ground to a pulp.

Now and then when Pogue has made a good haul he comes to New York for a rest. He says the jug of wine and loaf of bread and Thou in the wilderness business is about as much rest and pleasure to him as sliding down the bumps at Coney would be to President Taft. "Give me," says Pogue, "a big city for my vacation. Especially New York. I'm not much fond of New Yorkers, and Manhattan is about the only place on the globe where I don't find any."

While in the metropolis Pogue can always be found at one of two places. One is a little second-hand bookshop on Fourth Avenue, where he reads books about his hobbies, Mahometanism and taxidermy. I found him at the other—his hall bedroom in Eighteenth Street—where he sat in his stocking feet trying to pluck "The Banks of the Wabash" out of a small zither. Four years he has practised this tune without arriving near enough to cast the longest trout line to the water's edge. On the dresser lay a blued-steel Colt's forty-five and a tight roll of tens and twenties large enough around to belong to the spring rattlesnake-story class. A chambermaid with a room-cleaning air fluttered near by in the hall, unable to enter or to flee, scandalized by the stocking feet, aghast at the Colt's, yet powerless, with her metropolitan instincts, to remove herself beyond the magic influence of the yellow-hued roll.

I sat on his trunk while Ferguson Pogue talked. No one could be franker or more candid in his conversation. Besides his expression the cry of Henry James for lacteal nourishment at the age of one month would have seemed like a Chaldean cryptogram. He told me stories of his profession with pride, for he considered it an art. And I was curious enough to ask him whether he had known any women who followed it.

"Ladies?" said Pogue, with Western chivalry. "Well, not to any great extent. They don't amount to much in special lines of graft, because they're all so busy in general lines. What? Why, they have to. Who's got the money in the world? The men. Did you ever know a man to give a woman a dollar without any consideration? A man will shell out his dust to another man free and easy and gratis. But if he drops a penny in one of the machines run by the Madam Eve's Daughters' Amalgamated Association and the pineapple chewing gum don't fall out when he pulls the lever you can hear him kick to the superintendent four blocks away. Man is the hardest proposition a woman has to go up against. He's a low-grade one, and she has to work overtime to make him pay. Two times out of five she's salted. She can't put in crushers and costly machinery. He'd notice 'em and be onto the game. They have to pan out what they get, and it hurts their tender hands. Some of 'em are natural sluice troughs and can carry out $1,000 to the ton. The dry-eyed ones have to depend on signed letters, false hair, sympathy, the kangaroo walk, cowhide whips, ability to cook, sentimental juries, conversational powers, silk underskirts, ancestry, rouge, anonymous letters, violet sachet powders, witnesses, revolvers, pneumatic forms, carbolic acid, moonlight, cold cream and the evening newspapers."

"You are outrageous, Ferg," I said. "Surely there is none of this 'graft,' as you call it, in a perfect and harmonious matrimonial union!"

"Well," said Pogue, "nothing that would justify you every time in calling up Police Headquarters and ordering out the reserves and a vaudeville manager on a dead run. But it's this way: Suppose you're a Fifth Avenue millionaire, soaring high, on the right side of copper and cappers.

"You come home at night and bring a $9,000,000 diamond brooch to the lady who's staked you for a claim. You hand it over. She says, 'Oh, George!' and looks to see if it's backed. She comes up and kisses you. You've waited for it. You get it. All right. It's graft.

"But I'm telling you about Artemisia Blye. She was from Kansas and she suggested corn in all of its phases. Her hair was as yellow as the silk; her form was as tall and graceful as a stalk on the low grounds during a wet summer; her eyes were as big and startling as bunions, and green was her favorite color.

"On my last trip into the cool recesses of your sequestered city I met a human named Vaucross. He was worth—that is, he had a million. He told me he was in business on the street. 'A sidewalk merchant?' says I, sarcastic. 'Exactly,' says he. 'Senior partner of a paving concern.'

"I kind of took to him. For this reason, I met him on Broadway one night when I was out of heart, luck, tobacco, and place. He was all silk hat, diamonds, and front. He was all front. If you had gone behind him you would have only looked yourself in the face. I looked like a cross between Count Tolstoy and a June lobster. I was out of luck. I had—but let me lay my eyes on that dealer again.

"Vaucross stopped and talked to me a few minutes and then he took me to a high-toned restaurant to eat dinner. There was music, and then some Beethoven, and Bordelaise sauce, and cussing in French and frangipani, and some hauteur and cigarettes. When I am flush I know them places.

"I declare, I must have looked as bad as a magazine artist sitting there without any money and my hair all rumpled like I was booked to read a chapter from 'Elsie's School Days' at a Brooklyn Bohemian smoker. But Vaucross treated me like a bear hunter's guide. He wasn't afraid of hurting the waiter's feelings.

" 'Mr. Pogue,' he explains to me, 'I am using you.'

" 'Go on,' says I; 'I hope you don't wake up.'

"And then he tells me, you know, the kind of man he was. He was a New Yorker. His whole ambition was to be noticed. He wanted to be conspicuous. He wanted people to point him out and bow to him, and tell others who he was. He said it had been the desire of his life always. He didn't have but a million, so he couldn't attract attention by spending money. He said he tried to get into public notice one time by planting a little public square on the east side with garlic for free use of the poor; but Carnegie heard of it, and covered it over at once with a library in the Gaelic language. Three times he had jumped in the way of automobiles; but the only result was five broken ribs and a notice in the papers that an unknown man, five feet ten, with four amalgam-filled teeth, supposed to be the last of the famous Red Leary gang, had been run over.

" 'Ever try the reporters?' I asked him.

" 'Last month,' says Mr. Vaucross, 'my expenditure for lunches to reporters was $124.80.'

" 'Get anything out of that?' I asks.

" 'That reminds me,' says he; 'add $8.50 for pepsin. Yes, I got indigestion.'

" 'How am I supposed to push along your scramble for prominence?' I inquires. 'Contrast?'

" 'Something of that sort to-night,' says Vaucross. 'It grieves me; but I am forced to resort to eccentricity.' And here he drops his napkin in his soup and rises up and bows to a gent who is devastating a potato under a palm across the room.

" 'The Police Commissioner,' says my climber, gratified. 'Friend,' says I, in a hurry, 'have ambitions but don't kick a rung out of your ladder. When you use me as a stepping stone to salute the police you spoil my appetite on the grounds that I may be degraded and incriminated. Be thoughtful.'

"At the Quaker City squab en casserole the idea about Artemisia Blye comes to me.

" 'Suppose I can manage to get you in the papers,' says I—'a column or two every day in all of 'em and your picture in most of 'em for a week. How much would it be worth to you?'

" 'Ten thousand dollars,' says Vaucross, warm in a minute. 'But no murder,' says he; 'and I won't wear pink pants at a cotillion.'

" 'I wouldn't ask you to,' says I. 'This is honorable, stylish, and uneffeminate. Tell the waiter to bring a demi tasse and some other beans, and I will disclose to you the opus moderandi.'

"We closed the deal an hour later in the rococo rouge en noise room. I telegraphed that night to Miss Artemisia in Salina. She took a couple of photographs and an autograph letter to an elder in the Fourth Presbyterian Church in the morning, and got some transportation and $80. She stopped in Topeka long enough to trade a flashlight interior and a valentine to the vice-president of a trust company for a mileage book and a package of five-dollar notes with $250 scrawled on the band.

"The fifth evening after she got my wire she was waiting, all décolleté and dressed up, for me and Vaucross to take her to dinner in one of these New York feminine apartment houses where a man can't get in unless he plays bezique and smokes depilatory powder cigarettes.

"'She's a stunner,' says Vaucross when he saw her. 'They'll give her a two-column cut sure.'

"This was the scheme the three of us concocted. It was business straight through. Vaucross was to rush Miss Blye with all the style and display and emotion he could for a month. Of course, that amounted to nothing as far as his ambitions were concerned. The sight of a man in a white tie and patent leather pumps pouring greenbacks through the large end of a cornucopia to purchase nutriment and heartsease for tall willowy blondes in New York is as common a sight as blue turtles in delirium tremens. But he was to write her love letters—the worst kind of love letters, such as your wife publishes after you are dead—every day. At the end of the month he was to drop her, and she would bring suit for $100,000 for breach of promise.

"Miss Artemisia was to get $10,000. If she won the suit that was all; and if she lost she was to get it anyhow. There was a signed contract to that effect.

"Sometimes they had me out with 'em, but not often. I couldn't keep up to their style. She used to pull out his notes and criticize them like bills of lading.

"'Say, you!' she'd say. 'What do you call this—Letter to a Hardware Merchant from His Nephew on Learning that His Aunt Has Nettlerash? You Eastern duffers know as much about writing love letters as a Kansas grasshopper does about tugboats. "My dear Miss Blye!"—wouldn't that put pink icing and a little red sugar bird on your bridal cake? How long do you expect to hold an audience in a court-room with that kind of stuff? You want to get down to business, and call me "Tweedlums Babe" and "Honeysuckle," and sign yourself "Mamma's Own Big Bad Puggy Wuggy Boy" if you want any limelight to concentrate upon your sparse gray hairs. Get snappy.'

"After that Vaucross dipped his pen in the indelible tabasco. His notes read like something or other in the original. I could see a jury sitting up, and women tearing one another's hats to hear 'em read. And I could see piling up for Mr. Vaucross as much notoriousness as Archbishop Cranmer or the Brooklyn Bridge or cheese-on-salad ever enjoyed. He seemed mighty pleased at the prospects.

"They agreed on a night; and I stood on Fifth Avenue outside a solemn restaurant and watched 'em. A process-server walked in and handed Vaucross the papers at his table. Everybody looked at 'em; and he looked as proud as Cicero. I went back to my room and lit a five-cent cigar, for I knew the $10,000 was as good as ours.

"About two hours later somebody knocked at my door. There stood Vaucross and Miss Artemisia, and she was clinging—yes, sir, clinging— to his arm. And they tells me they'd been out and got married. And they articulated some trivial cadences about love and such. And they laid down a bundle on the table and said 'Good-night,' and left.

"And that's why I say," concluded Ferguson Pogue, "that a woman is too busy occupied with her natural vocation and instinct of graft such as is given her for self-preservation and amusement to make any great success in special lines."

"What was in the bundle that they left?" I asked, with my usual curiosity.

"Why," said Ferguson, "there was a scalper's railroad ticket as far as Kansas City and two pairs of Mr. Vaucross's old pants."

THE CALL OF THE TAME

When the inauguration was accomplished—the proceedings were made smooth by the presence of the Rough Riders—it is well known that a herd of those competent and loyal ex-warriors paid a visit to the big city. The newspaper reporters dug out of their trunks the old broad-brimmed hats and leather belts that they wear to North Beach fish fries, and mixed with the visitors. No damage was done beyond the employment of the wonderful plural "tenderfeet" in each of the scribe's stories. The Westerners mildly contemplated the skyscrapers as high as the third story, yawned at Broadway, hunched down in the big chairs in hotel corridors, and altogether looked as bored and dejected as a member of Ye Ancient and Honorable Artillery separated during a sham battle from his valet.

Out of this sightseeing delegation of good King Teddy's Gentlemen of the Royal Bear-hounds dropped one Greenbrier Nye, of Pin Feather, Ariz.

The daily cyclone of Sixth Avenue's rush hour swept him away from the company of his pardners true. The dust from a thousand rustling skirts filled his eyes. The mighty roar of trains rushing across the sky deafened him. The lightning-flash of twice ten hundred beaming eyes confused his vision.

The storm was so sudden and tremendous that Greenbrier's first impulse was to lie down and grab a root. And then he remembered that the disturbance was human, and not elemental; and he backed out of it with a grin into a doorway.

The reporters had written that but for the wide-brimmed hats the West was not visible upon these gauchos of the North. Heaven sharpen their eyes! The suit of black diagonal, wrinkled in impossible places; the bright blue four-in-hand, factory tied; the low, turned-down collar, pattern of the days of Seymour and Blair, white glazed as the letters on the window of the open-day-and-night-except-Sunday restaurants; the out-curve at the knees from the straddle grip; the peculiar spread of the half-closed right thumb and fingers from the stiff hold upon the circling lasso; the deeply absorbed weather tan that the hottest sun of Cape May can never equal; the seldom-winking blue eyes that unconsciously divided the rushing crowds into fours, as though they were being counted out of a corral; the segregated loneliness and solemnity of expression, as of an emperor or of one whose horizons have not intruded upon him nearer than a day's ride —these brands of the West were set upon Greenbrier Nye. Oh, yes; he wore a broad-brimmed hat, gentle reader—just like those the Madison Square Post Office mail carriers wear when they go up to Bronx Park on Sunday afternoons.

Suddenly Greenbrier Nye jumped into the drifting herd of metropolitan cattle, seized upon a man, dragged him out of the stream and gave him a buffet upon his collar-bone that sent him reeling against a wall.

The victim recovered his hat, with the angry look of a New Yorker who has suffered an outrage and intends to write to the Trib. about it. But he looked at his assailant, and knew that the blow was in consideration of love and affection after the manner of the West, which greets its friends with contumely and uproar and pounding fists, and receives its enemies in decorum and order, such as the judicious placing of the welcoming bullet demands.

"God in the mountains!" cried Greenbrier, holding fast to the foreleg of his cull. "Can this be Longhorn Merritt?"

The other man was—oh, look on Broadway any day for the pattern— business man—latest rolled-brim derby—good barber, business, digestion, and tailor.

"Greenbrier Nye!" he exclaimed, grasping the hand that had smitten him. "My dear fellow! So glad to see you! How did you come to—oh, to be sure—the inaugural ceremonies—I remember you joined the Rough Riders. You must come and have luncheon with me, of course."

Greenbrier pinned him sadly but firmly to the wall with a hand the size, shape and color of a McClellan saddle.

"Longy," he said, in a melancholy voice that disturbed traffic, "what have they been doing to you? You act just like a citizen. They done made you into an inmate of the city directory. You never made no such Johnny

Branch execration of yourself as that out on the Gila. 'Come and have lunching with me!' You never defined grub by any such terms of reproach in them days."

"I've been living in New York seven years," said Merritt. "It's been eight since we punched cows together in Old Man Garcia's outfit. Well, let's go to a café, anyhow. It sounds good to hear it called 'grub' again."

They picked their way through the crowd to a hotel, and drifted, as by a natural law, to the bar.

"Speak up," invited Greenbrier.

"A dry Martini," said Merritt.

"Oh, Lord!" cried Greenbrier; "and yet me and you once saw the same pink Gila monsters crawling up on the walls of the same hotel in Cañon Diablo! A dry—but let that pass. Whiskey straight—and they're on you."

Merritt smiled, and paid.

They lunched in a small extension of the dining room that connected with the café. Merritt dextrously diverted his friend's choice, that hovered over ham and eggs, to a purée of celery, a salmon cutlet, a partridge pie, and a desirable salad.

"On the day," said Greenbrier, grieved and thunderous, "when I can't hold but one drink before eating when I meet a friend I ain't seen in eight years at a 2 by 4 table in a thirty-cent town at 1 o'clock on the third day of the week, I want nine broncos to kick me forty times over a 640-acre section of land. Get them statistics?"

"Right, old man," laughed Merritt. "Waiter, bring an absinthe frappé and—what's yours, Greenbrier?"

"Whiskey straight," mourned Nye. "Out of the neck of a bottle you used to take it, Longy—straight out of the neck of a bottle on a galloping pony—Arizona redeye, not this ab—oh, what's the use? They're on you."

Merritt slipped the wine card under his glass.

"All right. I suppose you think I'm spoiled by the city. I'm as good a Westerner as you are, Greenbrier; but, somehow, I can't make up my mind to go back out there. New York is comfortable—comfortable. I make a good living, and I live it. No more wet blankets and riding herd in snowstorms, and bacon and cold coffee, and blowouts once in six months for me. I reckon I'll hang out here in the future. We'll take in the theatre to-night, Greenbrier, and after that we'll dine at——"

"I'll tell you what you are, Merritt," said Greenbrier, laying one elbow in his salad and the other in his butter. "You are a concentrated, effete, unconditional, short-sleeved, gotch-eared Miss Sally Walker. God made you perpendicular and suitable to ride straddle and use cuss words in the original. Wherefore you have suffered His handiwork to elapse by removing yourself to New York and putting on little shoes tied with strings, and making faces when you talk. I've seen you rope and tie a steer in 49½. If you was to see one now you'd write to the Police Commissioner about it. And these flapdoodle drinks that you inoculate your system with—these little essences of cowslip with acorns in 'em, and paregoric flip—they ain't anyways in assent with the cordiality of manhood. I hate to see you this way."

"Well, Greenbrier," said Merritt, with apology in his tone, "in a way you are right. Sometimes I do feel like I was being raised on the bottle. But, I tell you, New York is comfortable—comfortable. There's something about it—the sights and the crowds, and the way it changes every day, and the very air of it that seems to tie a one-mile-long stake rope around a man's neck, with the other end fastened somewhere about Thirty-fourth Street. I don't know what it is."

"God knows," said Greenbrier, sadly, "and I know. The East has gobbled you up. You was venison, and now you're veal. You put me in mind of a japonica in a window. You've been signed, sealed, and diskivered. Requiescat in hoc signo. You make me thirsty."

"A green chartreuse here," said Merritt to the waiter.

"Whiskey straight," sighed Greenbrier, "and they're on you, you renegade of the round-ups."

"Guilty, with an application for mercy," said Merritt. "You don't know how it is, Greenbrier. It's so comfortable here that——"

"Please loan me your smelling salts," pleaded Greenbrier. "If I hadn't seen you once bluff three bluffers from Mazatzal City with an empty gun in Phœnix——"

Greenbrier's voice died away in pure grief.

"Cigars!" he called harshly to the waiter, to hide his emotion.

"A pack of Turkish cigarettes for mine," said Merritt.

"They're on you," chanted Greenbrier, struggling to conceal his contempt.

At seven they dined in the Where-to-Dine-Well column.

That evening a galaxy had assembled there. Bright shone the lights o'er fair women and br—— Let it go, anyhow—brave men. The orchestra played charmingly. Hardly had a tip from a diner been placed in its hands by a waiter when it would burst forth into soniferousness. The more beer you contributed to it the more Meyerbeer it gave you. Which is reciprocity.

Merritt put forth exertions on the dinner. Greenbrier was his old friend, and he liked him. He persuaded him to drink a cocktail.

"I take the horehound tea," said Greenbrier, "for old times' sake. But I'd prefer whiskey straight. They're on you."

"Right!" said Merritt. "Now, run your eye down that bill of fare and see if it seems to hitch on any of the items."

"Lay me on my lava bed!" said Greenbrier, with bulging eyes. "All these specimens of nutriment in the grub wagon! What's this? Horse with the heaves? I pass. But look along! Here's truck for twenty round-ups all spelled out in different sections. Wait till I see."

The viands ordered, Merritt turned to the wine list.

"This medoc isn't bad," he suggested.

"You're the doc," said Greenbrier. "I'd rather have whiskey straight. It's on you."

Greenbrier looked around the room. The waiter brought things and took dishes away. He was observing. He saw a New York restaurant crowd enjoying itself.

"How was the range when you left the Gila?" asked Merritt.

"Fine," said Greenbrier. "You see that lady in the red speckled silk at that table? Well, she could warm over her beans at my campfire. Yes, the range was good. She looks as nice as a white mustang I see once on Black River."

When the coffee came, Greenbrier put one foot on the seat of the chair next to him.

"You said it was a comfortable town, Longy," he said, meditatively. "Yes, it's a comfortable town. It's different from the plains in a blue norther. What did you call that mess in the crock with the handle, Longy? Oh, yes, squabs in a cash roll. They're worth the roll. That white mustang had just such a way of turning his head and shaking his mane —look at her, Longy. If I thought I could sell out my ranch at a fair price, I believe I'd——

"Gyar—song!" he suddenly cried, in a voice that paralyzed every knife and fork in the restaurant.

The waiter dived toward the table.

"Two more of them cocktail drinks," ordered Greenbrier.

Merritt looked at him and smiled significantly.

"They're on me," said Greenbrier, blowing a puff of smoke to the ceiling.

THE UNKNOWN QUANTITY

The poet Longfellow—or was it Confucius, the inventor of wisdom?—remarked:

Life is real, life is earnest;
And things are not what they seem.

As mathematics are—or is: thanks, old subscriber!—the only just rule by which questions of life can be measured, let us, by all means, adjust our theme to the straight edge and the balanced column of the great goddess Two-and-Two-Makes-Four. Figures—unassailable sums in addition—shall be set over against whatever opposing element there may be.

A mathematician, after scanning the above two lines of poetry, would say: "Ahem! young gentlemen, if we assume that X plus—that is, that life is real—then things (all of which life includes) are real. Anything that is real is what it seems. Then if we consider the proposition that 'things are not what they seem,' why——"

But this is heresy, and not poesy. We woo the sweet nymph Algebra; we would conduct you into the presence of the elusive, seductive, pursued, satisfying, mysterious X.

Not long before the beginning of this century, Septimus Kinsolving, an old New Yorker, invented an idea. He originated the discovery that bread is made from flour and not from wheat futures. Perceiving that the flour crop was short, and that the Stock Exchange was having no perceptible effect on the growing wheat, Mr. Kinsolving cornered the flour market.

The result was that when you or my landlady (before the war she never had to turn her hand to anything; Southerners accommodated) bought a five-cent loaf of bread you laid down an additional two cents, which went to Mr. Kinsolving as a testimonial to his perspicacity.

A second result was that Mr. Kinsolving quit the game with $2,000,000 prof—er—rake-off.

Mr. Kinsolving's son Dan was at college when the mathematical experiment in breadstuffs was made. Dan came home during vacation, and found the old gentleman in a red dressing-gown reading "Little Dorrit" on the porch of his estimable red brick mansion in Washington Square. He had retired from business with enough extra two-cent pieces from bread buyers to reach, if laid side by side, fifteen times around the earth and lap as far as the public debt of Paraguay.

Dan shook hands with his father, and hurried over to Greenwich Village to see his old high-school friend, Kenwitz. Dan had always admired Kenwitz. Kenwitz was pale, curly-haired, intense, serious, mathematical, studious, altruistic, socialistic, and the natural foe of oligarchies. Kenwitz had foregone college, and was learning watch-making in his father's jewelry store. Dan was smiling, jovial, easy-tempered and tolerant alike of kings and rag-pickers. The two foregathered joyously, being opposites. And then Dan went back to college, and Kenwitz to his mainsprings—and to his private library in the rear of the jewelry shop.

Four years later Dan came back to Washington Square with the accumulations of B.A. and two years of Europe thick upon him. He took a filial look at Septimus Kinsolving's elaborate tombstone in Greenwood, and a tedious excursion through typewritten documents with the family lawyer; and then, feeling himself a lonely and hopeless millionaire, hurried down to the old jewelry store across Sixth Avenue.

Kenwitz unscrewed a magnifying glass from his eye, routed out his parent from a dingy rear room, and abandoned the interior of watches for outdoors. He went with Dan, and they sat on a bench in Washington Square. Dan had not changed much; he was stalwart, and had a dignity that was inclined to relax into a grin. Kenwitz was more serious, more intense, more learned, philosophical, and socialistic.

"I know about it now," said Dan, finally. "I pumped it out of the eminent legal lights that turned over to me poor old dad's collection of bonds and boodle. It amounts to $2,000,000, Ken. And I am told that he squeezed it out of the chaps that pay their pennies for loaves of bread at the little bakeries around the corner. You've studied economics, Ken, and you know all about monopolies, and the masses, and octopuses and the rights of laboring people. I never thought about those things before. Football and trying to be white to my fellow-man were about the extent of my college curriculum.

"But since I came back and found out how Dad made his money I've been thinking. I'd like awfully well to pay back those chaps who had to give too much money for bread. I know it would buck the line of my income for a good many yards; but I'd like to make it square with 'em. Is there any way it can be done, old Ways and Means?"

Kenwitz's big black eyes glowed fierily. His thin, intellectual face took on almost a sardonic cast. He caught Dan's arm with the grip of a friend and a judge.

"You can't do it!" he said, emphatically. "One of the chief punishments of you men of ill-gotten wealth is that when you do repent you find that you have lost the power to make reparation or restitution. I admire your good intentions, Dan, but you can't do anything. Those people were robbed of their precious pennies. It's too late to remedy the evil. You can't pay them back."

"Of course," said Dan, lighting his pipe, "we couldn't hunt up every one of the duffers and hand 'em back the right change. There's an awful lot of 'em buying bread all the time. Funny taste they have—I never cared for bread especially, except for a toasted cracker with the Roquefort. But we might find a few of 'em and chuck some of Dad's cash back where it came from. I'd feel better if I could. It seems tough for people to be held up for a soggy thing like bread. One wouldn't mind standing a rise in broiled lobsters or deviled crabs. Get to work and think, Ken. I want to pay back all of that money I can."

"There are plenty of charities," said Kenwitz, mechanically.

"Easy enough," said Dan, in a cloud of smoke. "I suppose I could give the city a park, or endow an asparagus bed in a hospital. But I don't want Paul to get away with the proceeds of the gold brick we sold Peter. It's the bread shorts I want to cover, Ken."

The thin fingers of Kenwitz moved rapidly.

"Do you know how much money it would take to pay back the losses of consumers during that corner in flour?" he asked.

"I do not," said Dan, stoutly. "My lawyer tells me that I have two millions."

"If you had a hundred millions," said Kenwitz, vehemently, "you couldn't repair a thousandth part of the damage that has been done. You cannot conceive of the accumulated evils produced by misapplied wealth. Each penny that was wrung from the lean purses of the poor reacted a thousandfold to their harm. You do not understand. You do not see how hopeless is your desire to make restitution. Not in a single instance can it be done."

"Back up, philosopher!" said Dan. "The penny has no sorrow that the dollar cannot heal."

"Not in one instance," repeated Kenwitz. "I will give you one, and let us see. Thomas Boyne had a little bakery over there in Varick Street. He sold bread to the poorest people. When the price of flour went up he had had to raise the price of bread. His customers were too poor to pay it, Boyne's business failed, and he lost his $1,000 capital—all he had in the world."

Dan Kinsolving struck the park bench a mighty blow with his fist.

"I accept the instance," he cried. "Take me to Boyne. I will repay his thousand dollars and buy him a new bakery."

"Write your check," said Kenwitz, without moving, "and then begin to write checks in payment of the train of consequences. Draw the next one for $50,000. Boyne went insane after his failure and set fire to the building from which he was about to be evicted. The loss amounted to that much. Boyne died in an asylum."

"Stick to the instance," said Dan. "I haven't noticed any insurance companies on my charity list."

"Draw your next check for $100,000," went on Kenwitz. "Boyne's son fell into bad ways after the bakery closed, and was accused of murder. He was acquitted last week after a three-years' legal battle, and the state draws upon taxpayers for that much expense."

"Back to the bakery!" exclaimed Dan, impatiently. "The Government doesn't need to stand in the bread line."

"The last item of the instance is—come and I will show you," said Kenwitz, rising.

The socialistic watchmaker was happy. He was a millionaire-baiter by nature and a pessimist by trade. Kenwitz would assure you in one breath that money was but evil and corruption, and that your brand-new watch needed cleaning and a new racket-wheel.

He conducted Kinsolving southward out of the square and into ragged, poverty-haunted Varick Street. Up the narrow stairway of a squalid brick tenement he led the penitent offspring of the Octopus. He knocked on a door, and a clear voice called to them to enter.

In that almost bare room a young woman sat sewing at a machine. She nodded to Kenwitz as to a familiar acquaintance. One little stream of sunlight through the dingy window burnished her heavy hair to the color of an ancient Tuscan's shield. She flashed a rippling smile at Kenwitz and a look of somewhat flustered inquiry.

Kinsolving stood regarding her clear and pathetic beauty in heart-throbbing silence. Thus they came into the presence of the last item of the Instance.

"How many this week, Miss Mary?" asked the watchmaker. A mountain of coarse gray shirts lay upon the floor.

"Nearly thirty dozen," said the young woman, cheerfully. "I've made almost $4. I'm improving, Mr. Kenwitz. I hardly know what to do with so much money." Her eyes turned, brightly soft, in the direction of Dan. A little pink spot came out on her round, pale cheek.

Kenwitz chuckled like a diabolic raven.

"Miss Boyne," he said, "let me present Mr. Kinsolving, the son of the man who put bread up five years ago. He thinks he would like to do something to aid those who were inconvenienced by that act."

The smile left the young woman's face. She rose and pointed her forefinger toward the door. This time she looked Kinsolving straight in the eye, but it was not a look that gave delight.

The two men went down into Varick Street. Kenwitz, letting all his pessimism and rancor and hatred of the Octopus come to the surface, gibed at the moneyed side of his friend in an acrid torrent of words. Dan appeared to be listening, and then turned to Kenwitz and shook hands with him warmly.

"I'm obliged to you, Ken, old man," he said, vaguely—"a thousand times obliged."

"Mein Gott! you are crazy!" cried the watchmaker, dropping his spectacles for the first time in years.

Two months afterward Kenwitz went into a large bakery on lower Broadway with a pair of gold-rimmed eye-glasses that he had mended for the proprietor.

A lady was giving an order to a clerk as Kenwitz passed her.

"These loaves are ten cents," said the clerk.

"I always get them at eight cents uptown," said the lady. "You need not fill the order. I will drive by there on my way home."

The voice was familiar. The watchmaker paused.

"Mr. Kenwitz!" cried the lady, heartily. "How do you do?"

Kenwitz was trying to train his socialistic and economic comprehension on her wonderful fur boa and the carriage waiting outside.

"Why, Miss Boyne!" he began.

"Mrs. Kinsolving," she corrected. "Dan and I were married a month ago."

THE THING'S THE PLAY

Being acquainted with a newspaper reporter who had a couple of free passes, I got to see the performance a few nights ago at one of the popular vaudeville houses.

One of the numbers was a violin solo by a striking-looking man not much past forty, but with very gray thick hair. Not being afflicted with a taste for music, I let the system of noises drift past my ears while I regarded the man.

"There was a story about that chap a month or two ago," said the reporter. "They gave me the assignment. It was to run a column and was to be on the extremely light and joking order. The old man seems to like the funny touch I give to local happenings. Oh, yes, I'm working on a farce comedy now. Well, I went down to the house and got all the details; but I certainly fell down on that job. I went back and turned in a comic write-up of an east side funeral instead. Why? Oh, I couldn't seem to get hold of it with my funny hooks, somehow. Maybe you could make a one-act tragedy out of it for a curtain-raiser. I'll give you the details."

After the performance my friend, the reporter, recited to me the facts over the Würzburger.

"I see no reason," said I, when he had concluded, "why that shouldn't make a rattling good funny story. Those three people couldn't have acted in a more absurd and preposterous manner if they had been real actors in a real theatre. I'm really afraid that all the stage is a world, anyhow, and all the players merely men and women. 'The thing's the play,' is the way I quote Mr. Shakespeare."

"Try it," said the reporter.

"I will," said I; and I did, to show him how he could have made a humorous column of it for his paper.

There stands a house near Abingdon Square. On the ground floor there has been for twenty-five years a little store where toys and notions and stationery are sold.

One night twenty years ago there was a wedding in the rooms above the store. The Widow Mayo owned the house and store. Her daughter Helen was married to Frank Barry. John Delaney was best man. Helen was eighteen, and her picture had been printed in a morning paper next to the headlines of a "Wholesale Female Murderess" story from Butte, Mont. But after your eye and intelligence had rejected the connection, you seized your magnifying glass and read beneath the portrait her description as one of a series of Prominent Beauties and Belles of the lower west side.

Frank Barry and John Delaney were "prominent" young beaux of the same side, and bosom friends, whom you expected to turn upon each other every time the curtain went up. One who pays his money for orchestra seats and fiction expects this. That is the first funny idea that has turned up in the story yet. Both had made a great race for Helen's hand. When Frank won, John shook his hand and congratulated him—honestly, he did.

After the ceremony Helen ran upstairs to put on her hat. She was getting married in a traveling dress. She and Frank were going to Old Point Comfort for a week. Downstairs the usual horde of gibbering cave-dwellers were waiting with their hands full of old Congress gaiters and paper bags of hominy.

Then there was a rattle of the fire-escape, and into her room jumps the mad and infatuated John Delaney, with a damp curl drooping upon his forehead, and made violent and reprehensible love to his lost one, entreating her to flee or fly with him to the Riviera, or the Bronx, or any old place where there are Italian skies and *dolce far niente*.

It would have carried Blaney off his feet to see Helen repulse him. With blazing and scornful eyes she fairly withered him by demanding whatever he meant by speaking to respectable people that way.

In a few moments she had him going. The manliness that had possessed him departed. He bowed low, and said something about "irresistible impulse" and "forever carry in his heart the memory of"—and she suggested that he catch the first fire-escape going down.

"I will away," said John Delaney, "to the furthermost parts of the earth. I cannot remain near you and know that you are another's. I will to Africa, and there amid other scenes strive to for——"

"For goodness sake, get out," said Helen. "Somebody might come in."

He knelt upon one knee, and she extended him one white hand that he might give it a farewell kiss.

Girls, was this choice boon of the great little god Cupid ever vouchsafed you—to have the fellow you want hard and fast, and have the one you don't want come with a damp curl on his forehead and kneel to you and babble of Africa and love which, in spite of everything, shall forever bloom, an amaranth, in his heart? To know your power, and to feel the sweet security of your own happy state; to send the unlucky one, broken-hearted, to foreign climes, while you congratulate yourself as he presses his last kiss upon your knuckles, that your nails are well manicured—say, girls, it's galluptious—don't ever let it get by you.

And then, of course—how did you guess?—the door opened and in stalked the bridegroom, jealous of slow-tying bonnet strings.

The farewell kiss was imprinted upon Helen's hand, and out of the window and down the fire-escape sprang John Delaney, Africa bound.

A little slow music, if you please—faint violin, just a breath in the clarinet and a touch of the 'cello. Imagine the scene. Frank, white-hot, with the cry of a man wounded to death bursting from him. Helen, rushing and clinging to him, trying to explain. He catches her wrists and tears them from his shoulders—once, twice, thrice he sways her this way and that—the stage manager will show you how—and throws her from him to the floor a huddled, crushed, moaning thing. Never, he cries, will he look upon her face again, and rushes from the house through the staring groups of astonished guests.

And now, because it is the Thing instead of the Play, the audience must stroll out into the real lobby of the world and marry, die, grow gray, rich, poor, happy, or sad during the intermission of twenty years which must precede the rising of the curtain again.

Mrs. Barry inherited the shop and the house. At thirty-eight she could have bested many an eighteen-year-old at a beauty show on points and general results. Only a few people remembered her wedding comedy, but she made of it no secret. She did not pack it in lavender or moth balls, nor did she sell it to a magazine.

One day a middle-aged, money-making lawyer who bought his legal cap and ink of her, asked her across the counter to marry him.

"I'm really much obliged to you," said Helen, cheerfully, "but I married another man twenty years ago. He was more goose than a man, but I think I love him yet. I have never seen him since about half an hour after the ceremony. Was it copying ink that you wanted or just writing fluid?"

The lawyer bowed over the counter with oldtime grace and left a respectful kiss on the back of her hand. Helen sighed. Parting salutes, however romantic, may be overdone. Here she was at thirty-eight, beautiful and admired; and all that she seemed to have got from her lovers were reproaches and adieus. Worse still, in the last one she had lost a customer, too.

Business languished, and she hung out a Room to Let card. Two large rooms on the third floor were prepared for desirable tenants. Roomers came, and went regretfully, for the house of Mrs. Barry was the abode of neatness, comfort, and taste.

One day came Ramonti, the violinist, and engaged the front room above. The discord and clatter uptown offended his nice ear; so a friend had sent him to this oasis in the desert of noise.

Ramonti, with his still youthful face, his dark eyebrows, his short, pointed, foreign, brown beard, his distinguished head of gray hair, and his artist's temperament—revealed in his light, gay, and sympathetic manner—was a welcome tenant in the old house near Abingdon Square.

Helen lived on the floor above the store. The architecture of it was singular and quaint. The hall was large and almost square. Up one side of it and then across the end of it ascended an open stairway to the floor above. This hall space she had furnished as a sitting room and office combined. There she kept her desk and wrote her business letters; and there she sat of evenings by a warm fire and a bright red light and sewed or read. Ramonti found the atmosphere so agreeable that he spent much time there, describing to Mrs. Barry the wonders of Paris, where he had studied with a particularly notorious and noisy fiddler.

Next comes lodger No. 2, a handsome, melancholy man in the early 40's, with a brown, mysterious beard, and strangely pleading, haunting eyes. He, too, found the society of Helen a desirable thing. With the eyes of Romeo and Othello's tongue, he charmed her with tales of distant climes and wooed her by respectful innuendo.

From the first Helen felt a marvelous and compelling thrill in the presence of this man. His voice somehow took her swiftly back to the days of her youth's romance. This feeling grew, and she gave way to it, and led her to an instinctive belief that he had been a factor in that romance. And then with a woman's reasoning (oh, yes, they do, sometimes) she leaped over common syllogisms and theory, and logic, and was sure that her husband had come back to her. For she saw in his eyes love, which no woman can mistake, and a thousand tons of regret and remorse, which aroused pity which is perilously near to love requited, which is the *sine qua non* in the house that Jack built.

But she made no sign. A husband who steps around the corner for twenty years and then drops in again should not expect to find his slippers laid out too conveniently near nor a match ready lighted for his cigar. There must be expiation, explanation, and possibly execration. A little purgatory, and then, maybe, if he were properly humble, he might be trusted with a harp and crown. And so she made no sign that she knew or suspected.

And my friend, the reporter, could see nothing funny in this! Sent out on an assignment to write up a roaring, hilarious, brilliant joshing story of—but I will not knock a brother—let us go on with the story.

One evening Ramonti stopped in Helen's hall-office-reception-room and told his love with the tenderness and ardor of the enraptured artist. His words were a bright flame of the divine fire that glows in the heart of a man who is a dreamer and a doer combined.

"But before you give me an answer," he went on, before she could accuse him of suddenness, "I must tell you that 'Ramonti' is the only name I have to offer you. My manager gave me that. I do not know who I am or where I came from. My first recollection is of opening my eyes in a hospital. I was a young man, and I had been there for weeks. My life before that is a blank to me. They told me that I was found lying in the street with a wound on my head and was brought there in an ambulance. They thought I must have fallen and struck my head upon the stones. There was nothing to show who I was. I have never been able to remember. After I was discharged from the hospital, I took up the violin. I have had success. Mrs. Barry—I do not know your name except that— I love you; the first time I saw you I realized that you were the one woman in the world for me—and"—oh, a lot of stuff like that.

Helen felt young again. First a wave of pride and a sweet little thrill of vanity went all over her; and then she looked Ramonti in the eyes, and a tremendous throb went through her heart. She hadn't expected that throb. It took her by surprise. The musician had become a big factor in her life, and she hadn't been aware of it.

"Mr. Ramonti," she said sorrowfully (this was not on the stage, remember; it was in the old home near Abingdon Square), "I'm awfully sorry, but I'm a married woman."

And then she told him the sad story of her life, as a heroine must do, sooner or later, either to a theatrical manager or to a reporter.

Ramonti took her hand, bowed low and kissed it, and went up to his room.

Helen sat down and looked mournfully at her hand. Well she might. Three suitors had kissed it, mounted their red roan steeds and ridden away.

In an hour entered the mysterious stranger with the haunting eyes. Helen was in the willow rocker, knitting a useless thing in cotton-wool. He ricocheted from the stairs and stopped for a chat. Sitting across the table from her, he also poured out his narrative of love. And then he said: "Helen, do you not remember me? I think I have seen it in your eyes. Can you forgive the past and remember the love that has lasted for twenty years? I wronged you deeply—I was afraid to come back to you —but my love overpowered my reason. Can you, will you, forgive me?"

Helen stood up. The mysterious stranger held one of her hands in a strong and trembling clasp.

There she stood, and I pity the stage that it has not acquired a scene like that and her emotions to portray.

For she stood with a divided heart. The fresh, unforgettable, virginal love for her bridegroom was hers; the treasured, sacred, honored memory of her first choice filled half her soul. She leaned to that pure feeling. Honor and faith and sweet, abiding romance bound her to it. But the other half of her heart and soul was filled with something else—a later, fuller, nearer influence. And so the old fought against the new.

And while she hesitated, from the room above came the soft, racking, petitionary music of a violin. The hag, music, bewitches some of the noblest. The daws may peck upon one's sleeve without injury but whoever wears his heart upon his tympanum gets it not far from the neck.

The music and the musician called her, and at her side honor and the old love held her back.

"Forgive me," he pleaded.

"Twenty years is a long time to remain away from the one you say you love," she declared, with a purgatorial touch.

"How could I tell?" he begged. "I will conceal nothing from you. That night when he left I followed him. I was mad with jealousy. On a dark street I struck him down. He did not rise. I examined him. His head had struck a stone. I did not intend to kill him. I was mad with love and jealousy. I hid near by and saw an ambulance take him away. Although you married him, Helen——"

"*Who Are You?*" cried the woman, with wide-open eyes, snatching her hand away.

"Don't you remember me, Helen—the one who has always loved you the best? I am John Delaney. If you can forgive——"

But she was gone, leaping, stumbling, hurrying, flying up the stairs toward the music and him who had forgotten, but who had known her for his in each of his two existences, and as she climbed up she sobbed, cried, and sang: "Frank! Frank! Frank!"

Three mortals thus juggling with years as though they were billiard balls, and my friend, the reporter, couldn't see anything funny in it!

A RAMBLE IN APHASIA

My wife and I parted on that morning in precisely our usual manner. She left her second cup of tea to follow me to the front door. There she plucked from my lapel the invisible strand of lint (the universal act of woman to proclaim ownership) and bade me take care of my cold. I had no cold. Next came her kiss of parting—the level kiss of domesticity flavored with Young Hyson. There was no fear of the extemporaneous, of variety spicing her infinite custom. With the deft touch of long malpractice, she dabbed awry my well-set scarf pin; and then, as I closed the door, I heard her morning slippers pattering back to her cooling tea.

When I set out I had no thought or premonition of what was to occur. The attack came suddenly.

For many weeks I had been toiling, almost night and day, at a famous railroad law case that I won triumphantly but a few days previously. In fact, I had been digging away at the law almost without cessation for many years. Once or twice good Doctor Volney, my friend and physician, had warned me.

"If you don't slacken up, Bellford," he said, "you'll go suddenly to pieces. Either your nerves or your brain will give way. Tell me, does a week pass in which you do not read in the papers of a case of aphasia—of some man lost, wandering nameless, with his past and his identity blotted out—and all from that little brain clot made by overwork or worry?"

"I always thought," said I, "that the clot in those instances was really to be found on the brains of the newspaper reporters."

Doctor Volney shook his head.

"The disease exists," he said. "You need a change or a rest. Court-room, office, and home—there is the only route you travel. For recreation you—read law books. Better take warning in time."

"On Thursday nights," I said, defensively, "my wife and I play crib-bage. On Sundays she reads to me the weekly letter from her mother. That law books are not a recreation remains yet to be established."

That morning as I walked I was thinking of Doctor Volney's words. I was feeling as well as I usually did—possibly in better spirits than usual.

I woke with stiff and cramped muscles from having slept long on the incommodious seat of a day coach. I leaned my head against the seat and tried to think. After a long time I said to myself: "I must have a name of some sort." I searched my pockets. Not a card; not a letter; not a paper or monogram could I find. But I found in my coat pocket nearly $3,000 in bills of large denomination. "I must be some one, of course," I repeated to myself, and began to consider.

The car was well crowded with men, among whom, I told myself, there must have been some common interest, for they intermingled freely, and seemed in the best good humor and spirits. One of them— a stout, bespectacled gentleman enveloped in a decided odor of cinna-mon and aloes—took the vacant half of my seat with a friendly nod, and unfolded a newspaper. In the intervals between his periods of reading, we conversed, as travelers will, on current affairs. I found myself able to sustain the conversation on such subjects with credit, at least to my memory. By and by my companion said:

"You are one of us, of course. Fine lot of men the West sends in this time. I'm glad they held the convention in New York; I've never been East before. My name's R. P. Bolder—Bolder & Son, of Hickory Grove, Missouri."

Though unprepared, I rose to the emergency, as men will when put to it.

Now must I hold a christening, and be at once babe, parson, and parent. My senses came to the rescue of my slower brain. The insistent odor of drugs from my companion supplied one idea; a glance at his newspaper, where my eye met a conspicuous advertisement, assisted me further.

"My name," said I, glibly, "is Edward Pinkhammer. I am a druggist, and my home is in Cornopolis, Kansas."

"I knew you were a druggist," said my fellow traveler, affably. "I saw the callous spot on your right forefinger where the handle of the pestle rubs. Of course, you are a delegate to our National Convention."

"Are all these men druggists?" I asked, wonderingly.

"They are. This car came through from the West. And they're your old-time druggists, too—none of your patent tablet-and-granule phar-mashootists that use slot machines instead of a prescription desk. We percolate our own paregoric and roll our own pills, and we ain't above handling a few garden seeds in the spring, and carrying a side line of confectionery and shoes. I tell you, Hampinker, I've got a idea to spring on this convention—new ideas is what they want. Now, you know the shelf bottles of tartar emetic and Rochelle salt Ant. et. Pot. Tart. and Sod. et. Pot. Tart.—one's poison, you know, and the other's harmless. It's easy to mistake one label for the other. Where do druggists mostly keep 'em? Why, as far apart as possible, on different shelves. That's wrong. I say keep 'em side by side, so when you want one you can always compare it with the other and avoid mistakes. Do you catch the idea?"

"It seems to me a very good one," I said.

"All right! When I spring it on the convention you back it up. We'll make some of these Eastern orange-phosphate-and-massage-cream professors that think they're the only lozenges in the market look like hypodermic tablets."

"If I can be of any aid," I said, warming, "the two bottles of—er——"

"Tartrate of antimony and potash, and tartrate of soda and potash."

"Shall henceforth sit side by side," I concluded, firmly.

"Now, there's another thing," said Mr. Bolder. "For an excipient in manipulating a pill mass which do you prefer—the magnesia carbonate or the pulverized glycerrhiza radix?"

"The—er—magnesia," I said. It was easier to say than the other word.

Mr. Bolder glanced at me distrustfully through his spectacles.

"Give me the glycerrhiza," said he. "Magnesia cakes."

"Here's another one of these fake aphasia cases," he said, presently, handing me his newspaper, and laying his finger upon an article. "I don't believe in 'em. I put nine out of ten of 'em down as frauds. A man gets sick of his business and his folks and wants to have a good time. He skips out somewhere, and when they find him he pretends to have lost his memory—don't know his own name, and won't even recognize the strawberry mark on his wife's left shoulder. Aphasia! Tut! Why can't they stay at home and forget?"

I took the paper and read, after the pungent headlines, the following:

Denver, June 12.—Elwyn C. Bellford, a prominent lawyer, is mysteriously missing from his home since three days ago, and all efforts to locate him have been in vain. Mr. Bellford is a well-known citizen of the highest standing, and has enjoyed a large and lucrative law practice. He is married and owns a fine home and the most extensive private library in the State. On the day of his disappearance, he drew quite a large sum of money from his bank. No one can be found who saw him after he left the bank. Mr. Bellford was a man of singularly quiet and domestic tastes, and seemed to find his happiness in his home and profession. If any clue at all exists to his strange disappearance, it may be found in the fact that for some months he has been deeply absorbed in an important law case in connection with the Q. Y. and Z. Railroad Company. It is feared that overwork may have affected his mind. Every effort is being made to discover the whereabouts of the missing man.

"It seems to me you are not altogether uncynical, Mr. Bolder," I said, after I had read the despatch. "This has the sound, to me, of a genuine case. Why should this man, prosperous, happily married, and respected, choose suddenly to abandon everything? I know that these lapses of memory do occur, and that men do find themselves adrift without a name, a history, or a home."

"Oh, gammon and jalap!" said Mr. Bolder. "It's larks they're after. There's too much education nowadays. Men know about aphasia, and they use it for an excuse. The women are wise, too. When it's all over they look you in the eye, as scientific as you please, and say: 'He hypnotized me.'"

Thus Mr. Bolder diverted, but did not aid me with his comments and philosophy.

We arrived in New York about ten at night. I rode in a cab to a hotel, and I wrote my name "Edward Pinkhammer" in the register. As I did so I felt pervade me a splendid, wild, intoxicating buoyancy—a sense of unlimited freedom, of newly attained possibilities. I was just born into the world. The old fetters—whatever they had been—were stricken from my hands and feet. The future lay before me a clear road such as an infant enters, and I could set out upon it equipped with a man's learning and experience.

I thought the hotel clerk looked at me five seconds too long. I had no baggage.

"The Druggists' Convention," I said. "My trunk has somehow failed to arrive." I drew out a roll of money.

"Ah!" said he, showing an auriferous tooth, "we have quite a number of the Western delegates stopping here." He struck a bell for the boy.

I endeavored to give color to my rôle.

"There is an important movement on foot among us Westerners," I said, "in regard to a recommendation to the convention that the bottles containing the tartrate of antimony and potash, and the tartrate of sodium and potash be kept in a contiguous position on the shelf."

"Gentleman to three-fourteen," said the clerk, hastily. I was whisked away to my room.

The next day I bought a trunk and clothing, and began to live the life of Edward Pinkhammer. I did not tax my brain with endeavors to solve problems of the past.

It was a piquant and sparkling cup that the great island city held up to my lips. I drank it gratefully. The keys of Manhattan belong to him who is able to bear them. You must be either the city's guest or its victim.

The following few days were as gold and silver. Edward Pinkhammer, yet counting back to his birth by hours only, knew the rare joy of having come upon so diverting a world full-fledged and unrestrained. I sat entranced on the magic carpets provided in theatres and roof-gardens, that transported one into strange and delightful lands full of frolicsome music, pretty girls, and grotesque, drolly extravagant parodies upon human kind. I went here and there at my own dear will, bound by no limits of space, time, or comportment. I dined in weird cabarets, at weirder *tables d'hôte* to the sound of Hungarian music and the wild shouts of mercurial artists and sculptors. Or, again, where the night life quivers in the electric glare like a kinetoscopic picture, and the millinery of the world, and its jewels, and the ones whom they adorn, and the men who make all three possible are met for good cheer and the spectacular effect. And among all these scenes that I have mentioned I learned one thing that I never knew before. And that is that the key to liberty is not in the hands of License, but Convention holds it. Comity has a toll-gate at which you must pay, or you may not enter the land of Freedom. In all the glitter, the seeming disorder, the parade, the abandon, I saw this law, unobtrusive, yet like iron, prevail. Therefore, in Manhattan you must obey these unwritten laws, and then you will be freest of the free. If you decline to be bound by them, you put on shackles.

Sometimes, as my mood urged me, I would seek the stately, softly murmuring palm rooms, redolent with high-born life and delicate restraint, in which to dine. Again I would go down to the waterways in steamers packed with vociferous, bedecked, unchecked love-making clerks and shop-girls to their crude pleasures on the island shores. And there was always Broadway—glistening, opulent, wily, varying, desirable Broadway—growing upon one like an opium habit.

One afternoon as I entered my hotel a stout man with a big nose and a black mustache blocked my way in the corridor. When I would have passed around him, he greeted me with offensive familiarity.

"Hallo, Bellford!" he cried, loudly. "What the deuce are you doing in New York? Didn't know anything could drag you away from that old book den of yours. Is Mrs. B. along or is this a little business run alone, eh?"

"You have made a mistake, sir," I said, coldly, releasing my hand from his grasp. "My name is Pinkhammer. You will excuse me."

The man dropped to one side, apparently astonished. As I walked to the clerk's desk I heard him call to a bell boy and say something about telegraph blanks.

"You will give me my bill," I said to the clerk, "and have my baggage brought down in half an hour. I do not care to remain where I am annoyed by confidence men."

I moved that afternoon to another hotel, a sedate, old-fashioned one on lower Fifth Avenue.

There was a restaurant a little way off Broadway where one could be served almost *al fresco* in a tropic array of screening flora. Quiet and luxury and a perfect service made it an ideal place in which to take luncheon or refreshment. One afternoon I was there picking my way to a table among the ferns when I felt my sleeve caught.

"Mr. Bellford!" exclaimed an amazingly sweet voice.

I turned quickly to see a lady seated alone—a lady of about thirty, with exceedingly handsome eyes, who looked at me as though I had been her very dear friend.

"You were about to pass me," she said, accusingly. "Don't tell me you did not know me. Why should we not shake hands—at least once in fifteen years?"

I shook hands with her at once. I took a chair opposite her at the table. I summoned with my eyebrows a hovering waiter. The lady was philandering with an orange ice. I ordered a *crème de menthe*. Her hair was reddish bronze. You could not look at it, because you could not look away from her eyes. But you were conscious of it as you are conscious of sunset while you look into the profundities of a wood at twilight.

"Are you sure you know me?" I asked.

"No," she said, smiling, "I was never sure of that."

"What would you think," I said, a little anxiously, "if I were to tell you that my name is Edward Pinkhammer from Cornopolis, Kansas?"

"What would I think?" she repeated with a merry glance. "Why, that you had not brought Mrs. Bellford to New York with you, of course. I do wish you had. I would have liked to see Marian." Her voice lowered slightly—"You haven't changed much, Elwyn."

I felt her wonderful eyes searching mine and my face more closely.

"Yes, you have," she amended, and there was a soft, exultant note in her latest tones; "I see it now. You haven't forgotten. You haven't forgotten for a year or a day or an hour. I told you you never could."

I poked my straw anxiously in the *crème de menthe*.

"I'm sure I beg your pardon," I said, a little uneasy at her gaze. "But that is just the trouble. I have forgotten. I've forgotten everything."

She flouted my denial. She laughed deliciously at something she seemed to see in my face.

"I've heard of you at times," she went on. "You're quite a big lawyer out West—Denver, isn't it, or Los Angeles? Marian must be very proud of you. You knew, I suppose, that I married six months after you did. You may have seen it in the papers. The flowers alone cost two thousand dollars."

She had mentioned fifteen years. Fifteen years is a long time.

"Would it be too late," I asked, somewhat timorously, "to offer you congratulations?"

"Not if you dare do it," she answered, with such fine intrepidity that I was silent, and began to crease patterns on the cloth with my thumb nail.

"Tell me one thing," she said, leaning toward me rather eagerly—"a thing I have wanted to know for many years—just from a woman's curiosity, of course—have you ever dared since that night to touch, smell, or look at white roses—at white roses wet with rain and dew?"

I took a sip of *crème de menthe*.

"It would be useless, I suppose," I said, with a sigh, "for me to repeat that I have no recollection at all about these things. My memory is completely at fault. I need not say how much I regret it."

The lady rested her arms upon the table, and again her eyes disdained my words and went traveling by their own route direct to my soul. She laughed softly, with a strange quality in the sound—it was a laugh of happiness—yes, and of content—and of misery. I tried to look away from her.

"You lie, Elwyn Bellford," she breathed, blissfully. "Oh, I know you lie!"

I gazed dully into the ferns.

"My name is Edward Pinkhammer," I said. "I came with the delegates to the Druggists' National Convention. There is a movement on foot for arranging a new position for the bottles of tartrate and antimony and tartrate of potash, in which, very likely, you would take little interest."

A shining landau stopped before the entrance. The lady rose. I took her hand, and bowed.

"I am deeply sorry," I said to her, "that I cannot remember. I could explain, but fear you would not understand. You will not concede Pinkhammer; and I really cannot at all conceive of the—the roses and other things."

"Good-bye, Mr. Bellford," she said, with her happy, sorrowful smile, as she stepped into her carriage.

I attended the theatre that night. When I returned to my hotel, a quiet man in dark clothes, who seemed interested in rubbing his finger nails with a silk handkerchief, appeared, magically, at my side.

"Mr. Pinkhammer," he said, casually, giving the bulk of his attention to his forefinger, "may I request you to step aside with me for a little conversation? There is a room here."

"Certainly," I answered.

He conducted me into a small, private parlor. A lady and a gentleman were there. The lady, I surmised, would have been unusually good-looking had her features not been clouded by an expression of keen worry and fatigue. She was of a style of figure and possessed coloring and features that were agreeable to my fancy. She was in a traveling dress; she fixed upon me an earnest look of extreme anxiety, and pressed an unsteady hand to her bosom. I think she would have started forward, but the gentleman arrested her movement with an authoritative motion of his hand. He then came, himself, to meet me. He was a man of forty, a little gray about the temples, and with a strong, thoughtful face.

"Bellford, old man," he said, cordially, "I'm glad to see you again. Of course we know everything is all right. I warned you, you know, that you were overdoing it. Now, you'll go back with us, and be yourself again in no time."

I smiled ironically.

"I have been 'Bellforded' so often," I said, "that it has lost its edge. Still, in the end, it may grow wearisome. Would you be willing at all to entertain the hypothesis that my name is Edward Pinkhammer, and that I never saw you before in my life?"

Before the man could reply a wailing cry came from the woman. She sprang past his detaining arm. "Elwyn!" she sobbed, and cast herself upon me, and clung tight. "Elwyn," she cried again, "don't break my heart. I am your wife—call my name once—just once. I could see you dead rather than this way."

I unwound her arms respectfully, but firmly.

"Madame," I said, severely, "pardon me if I suggest that you accept a resemblance too precipitately. It is a pity," I went on, with an amused laugh, as the thought occurred to me, "that this Bellford and I could not be kept side by side upon the same shelf like tartrates of sodium and antimony for purposes of identification. In order to understand this allusion," I concluded airily, "it may be necessary for you to keep an eye on the proceedings of the Druggists' National Convention."

The lady turned to her companion, and grasped his arm.

"What is it, Doctor Volney? Oh, what is it?" she moaned.

He led her to the door.

"Go to your room for a while," I heard him say. "I will remain and talk with him. His mind? No, I think not—only a portion of the brain. Yes, I am sure he will recover. Go to your room and leave me with him."

The lady disappeared. The man in dark clothes also went outside, still manicuring himself in a thoughtful way. I think he waited in the hall.

"I would like to talk with you a while, Mr. Pinkhammer, if I may," said the gentleman who remained.

"Very well, if you care to," I replied, "and will excuse me if I take it comfortably; I am rather tired." I stretched myself upon a couch by a window and lit a cigar. He drew a chair near by.

"Let us speak to the point," he said, soothingly. "Your name is not Pinkhammer."

"I know that as well as you do," I said coolly. "But a man must have a name of some sort. I can assure you that I do not extravagantly admire the name of Pinkhammer. But when one christens one's self suddenly, the fine names do not seem to suggest themselves. But, suppose it had been Scheringhausen or Scroggins! I think I did very well with Pinkhammer."

"Your name," said the other man, seriously, "is Elwyn C. Bellford. You are one of the first lawyers in Denver. You are suffering from an attack of aphasia, which has caused you to forget your identity. The cause of it was over-application to your profession, and perhaps a life too bare of natural recreation and pleasures. The lady who has just left the room is your wife."

"She is what I would call a fine-looking woman," I said, after a judicial pause. "I particularly admire the shade of brown in her hair."

"She is a wife to be proud of. Since your disappearance, nearly two weeks ago, she has scarcely closed her eyes. We learned that you were in New York through a telegram sent by Isidore Newman, a traveling man from Denver. He said that he had met you in a hotel here, and that you did not recognize him."

"I think I remember the occasion," I said. "The fellow called me 'Bellford,' if I am not mistaken. But don't you think it about time, now, for you to introduce yourself?"

"I am Robert Volney—Doctor Volney. I have been your close friend for twenty years and your physician for fifteen. I came with Mrs. Bellford to trace you as soon as we got the telegram. Try, Elwyn, old man—try to remember!"

"What's the use to try?" I asked, with a little frown. "You say you are a physician. Is aphasia curable? When a man loses his memory does it return slowly, or suddenly?"

"Sometimes gradually and imperfectly; sometimes as suddenly as it went."

"Will you undertake the treatment of my case, Doctor Volney?" I asked.

"Old friend," said he, "I'll do everything in my power, and will have done everything that science can do to cure you."

"Very well," said I. "Then you will consider that I am your patient. Everything is in confidence now—professional confidence."

"Of course," said Doctor Volney.

I got up from the couch. Someone had set a vase of white roses on the centre table—a cluster of white roses, freshly sprinkled and fragrant. I threw them far out of the window, and then I laid myself upon the couch again.

"It will be best, Bobby," I said, "to have this cure happen suddenly. I'm rather tired of it all, anyway. You may go now and bring Marian in. But, oh, Doc," I said, with a sigh, as I kicked him on the shin—"good old Doc—it was glorious!"

A MUNICIPAL REPORT

> The cities are full of pride,
> Challenging each to each—
> This from her mountainside,
> That from her burthened beach.
>   R. KIPLING

Fancy a novel about Chicago or Buffalo, let us say, of Nashville, Tennessee! There are just three big cities in the United States that are "story cities"—New York, of course, New Orleans, and, best of the lot, San Francisco.—FRANK NORRIS.

East is East, and West is San Francisco, according to Californians. Californians are a race of people; they are not merely inhabitants of a State. They are the Southerners of the West. Now, Chicagoans are no less loyal to their city; but when you ask them why, they stammer and speak of lake fish and the new Odd Fellows Building. But Californians go into detail.

Of course they have, in the climate, an argument that is good for half an hour while you are thinking of your coal bills and heavy underwear. But as soon as they come to mistake your silence for conviction, madness comes upon them, and they picture the city of the Golden Gate as the Bagdad of the New World. So far, as a matter of opinion, no refutation is necessary. But dear cousins all (from Adam and Eve descended), it is a rash one who will lay his finger on the map and say: "In this town there can be no romance—what could happen here?" Yes, it is a bold and a rash deed to challenge in one sentence history, romance, and Rand and McNally.

NASHVILLE.—A city, port of delivery, and the capital of the State of Tennessee, is on the Cumberland River and on the N. C. & St. L. and the L. & N. railroads. This city is regarded as the most important educational centre in the South.

I stepped off the train at 8 P. M. Having searched thesaurus in vain for adjectives, I must, as a substitution, hie me to comparison in the form of a recipe.

Take of London fog 30 parts; malaria 10 parts; gas leaks 20 parts; dewdrops gathered in a brick yard at sunrise, 25 parts; odor of honeysuckle 15 parts. Mix.

The mixture will give you an approximate conception of a Nashville drizzle. It is not so fragrant as a moth-ball nor as thick as pea-soup; but 'tis enough—'twill serve.

I went to a hotel in a tumbril. It required strong self-suppression for me to keep from climbing to the top of it and giving an imitation of Sidney Carton. The vehicle was drawn by beasts of a bygone era and driven by something dark and emancipated.

I was sleepy and tired, so when I got to the hotel I hurriedly paid it the fifty cents it demanded (with approximate lagniappe, I assure you). I knew its habits; and I did not want to hear it prate about its old "marster" or anything that happened "befo' de wah."

The hotel was one of the kind described as "renovated." That means $20,000 worth of new marble pillars, tiling, electric lights and brass cuspidors in the lobby, and a new L. & N. time table and a lithograph of Lookout Mountain in each one of the great rooms above. The management was without reproach, the attention full of exquisite Southern courtesy, the service as slow as the progress of a snail and as goodhumored as Rip Van Winkle. The food was worth traveling a thousand miles for. There is no other hotel in the world where you can get such chicken livers *en brochette.*

At dinner I asked a Negro waiter if there was anything doing in town. He pondered gravely for a minute, and then replied: "Well, boss, I don't really reckon there's anything at all doin' after sundown."

Sundown had been accomplished; it had been drowned in the drizzle long before. So that spectacle was denied me. But I went forth upon the streets in the drizzle to see what might be there.

It is built on undulating grounds; and the streets are lighted by electricity at a cost of $32,470 per annum.

As I left the hotel there was a race riot. Down upon me charged a company of freedmen, or Arabs, or Zulus, armed with—no, I saw with relief that they were not rifles, but whips. And I saw dimly a caravan of black, clumsy vehicles; and at the reassuring shouts, "Kyar you anywhere in the town, boss, fuh fifty cents," I reasoned that I was merely a "fare" instead of a victim.

I walked through long streets, all leading uphill. I wondered how those streets ever came down again. Perhaps they didn't until they were "graded." On a few of the "main streets" I saw lights in stores here and there; saw street cars go by conveying worthy burghers hither and yon; saw people pass engaged in the art of conversation, and heard a burst of semi-lively laughter issuing from a soda-water and ice-cream parlor. The streets other than "main" seemed to have enticed upon their borders houses consecrated to peace and domesticity. In many of them lights shone behind discreetly drawn window shades, in a few pianos tinkled orderly and irreproachable music. There was, indeed, little "doing." I wished I had come before sundown. So I returned to my hotel.

In November, 1864, the Confederate General Hood advanced against Nashville, where he shut up a National force under General Thomas. The latter then sallied forth and defeated the Confederates in a terrible conflict.

All my life I have heard of, admired, and witnessed the fine marksmanship of the South in its peaceful conflicts in the tobacco-chewing regions. But in my hotel a surprise awaited me. There were twelve bright, new, imposing, capacious brass cuspidors in the great lobby, tall enough to be called urns and so wide-mouthed that the crack pitcher of a lady baseball team should have been able to throw a ball into one of them at five paces distant. But, although a terrible battle had raged and was still raging, the enemy had not suffered. Bright, new, imposing, capacious, untouched, they stood. But, shades of Jefferson Brick! the tile floor—the beautiful tile floor! I could not avoid thinking of the battle of Nashville, and trying to draw, as is my foolish habit, some deductions about hereditary marksmanship.

Here I first saw Major (by misplaced courtesy) Wentworth Caswell. I knew him for a type the moment my eyes suffered from the sight of him. A rat has no geographical habitat. My old friend, A. Tennyson, said, as he so well said almost everything:

Prophet, curse me the blabbing lip,
And curse me the British vermin, the rat.

Let us regard the word "British" as interchangeable *ad lib*. A rat is a rat.

This man was hunting about the hotel lobby like a starved dog that had forgotten where he had buried a bone. He had a face of great acreage, red, pulpy, and with a kind of sleepy massiveness like that of Buddha. He possessed one single virtue—he was very smoothly shaven. The mark of the beast is not indelible upon a man until he goes about with a stubble. I think that if he had not used his razor that day I would have repulsed his advances, and the criminal calendar of the world would have been spared the addition of one murder.

I happened to be standing within five feet of a cuspidor when Major Caswell opened fire upon it. I had been observant enough to perceive that the attacking force was using Gatlings instead of squirrel rifles, so I sidestepped so promptly that the major seized the opportunity to apologize to a noncombatant. He had the blabbing lip. In four minutes he had become my friend and had dragged me to the bar.

I desire to interpolate here that I am a Southerner. But I am not one by profession or trade. I eschew the string tie, the slouch hat, the Prince Albert, the number of bales of cotton destroyed by Sherman, and plug chewing. When the orchestra plays "Dixie" I do not cheer. I slide a little lower on the leather-cornered seat and, well, order another Würzburger and wish that Longstreet had—but what's the use?

Major Caswell banged the bar with his fist, and the first gun at Fort Sumter re-echoed. When he fired the last one at Appomattox I began to hope. But then he began on family trees, and demonstrated that Adam was only a third cousin of a collateral branch of the Caswell family. Genealogy disposed of, he took up, to my distaste, his private family matters. He spoke of his wife, traced her descent back to Eve, and profanely denied any possible rumor that she may have had relations in the land of Nod.

By this time I began to suspect that he was trying to obscure by noise the fact that he had ordered the drinks, on the chance that I would be bewildered into paying for them. But when they were down he crashed a silver dollar loudly upon the bar. Then, of course, another serving was obligatory. And when I had paid for that I took leave of him brusquely; for I wanted no more of him. But before I had obtained my release he had prated loudly of an income that his wife received, and showed a handful of silver money.

When I got my key at the desk the clerk said to me courteously: "If that man Caswell has annoyed you, and if you would like to make a complaint, we will have him ejected. He is a nuisance, a loafer, and without any known means of support, although he seems to have some money most the time. But we don't seem to be able to hit upon any means of throwing him out legally."

"Why, no," said I, after some reflection; "I don't see my way clear to making a complaint. But I would like to place myself on record as asserting that I do not care for his company. Your town," I continued, "seems to be a quiet one. What manner of entertainment, adventure, or excitement, have you to offer to the stranger within your gates?"

"Well, sir," said the clerk, "there will be a show here next Thursday. It is—I'll look it up and have the announcement sent up to your room with the ice water. Good-night."

After I went up to my room I looked out the window. It was only about ten o'clock, but I looked upon a silent town. The drizzle continued, spangled with dim lights, as far apart as currants in a cake sold at the Ladies' Exchange.

"A quiet place," I said to myself, as my first shoe struck the ceiling of the occupant of the room beneath mine. "Nothing of the life here that gives color and good variety to the cities in the East and West. Just a good, ordinary, hum-drum, business town."

Nashville occupies a foremost place among the manufacturing centres of the country. It is the fifth boot and shoe market in the United States, the largest candy and cracker manufacturing city in the South, and does an enormous wholesale drygoods, grocery, and drug business.

I must tell you how I came to be in Nashville, and I assure you the digression brings as much tedium to me as it does to you. I was traveling elsewhere on my own business, but I had a commission from a Northern literary magazine to stop over there and establish a personal connection between the publication and one of its contributors, Azalea Adair.

Adair (there was no clue to the personality except the handwriting) had sent in some essays (lost art!) and poems that had made the editors swear approvingly over their one o'clock luncheon. So they had commissioned me to round up said Adair and corner by contract his or her output at two cents a word before some other publisher offered her ten or twenty.

At nine o'clock the next morning, after my chicken livers *en brochette* (try them if you can find that hotel), I strayed out into the drizzle, which was still on for an unlimited run. At the first corner I came upon Uncle Cæsar. He was a stalwart Negro, older than the pyramids, with gray wool and a face that reminded me of Brutus, and a second afterwards of the late King Cettiwayo. He wore the most remarkable coat that I ever had seen or expect to see. It reached to his ankles and had once been a Confederate gray in colors. But rain and sun and age had so variegated it that Joseph's coat, beside it, would have faded to a pale monochrome. I must linger with that coat, for it has to do with the story—the story that is so long in coming, because you can hardly expect anything to happen in Nashville.

Once it must have been the military coat of an officer. The cape of it had vanished, but all adown its front it had been frogged and tasseled magnificently. But now the frogs and tassels were gone. In their stead had been patiently stitched (I surmised by some surviving "black mammy") new frogs made of cunningly twisted common hempen twine. This twine was frayed and disheveled. It must have been added to the coat as a substitute for vanished splendors, with tasteless but painstaking devotion, for it followed faithfully the curves of the long-missing frogs. And, to complete the comedy and pathos of the garment, all its buttons were gone save one. The second button from the top alone remained. The coat was fastened by other twine strings tied through the buttonholes and other holes rudely pierced in the opposite side. There was never such a weird garment so fantastically bedecked and of so many mottled hues. The lone button was the size of a half-dollar, made of yellow horn and sewed on with coarse twine.

This Negro stood by a carriage so old that Ham himself might have started a hack line with it after he left the ark with the two animals hitched to it. As I approached he threw open the door, drew out a feather duster, waved it without using it, and said in deep, rumbling tones:

"Step right in, suh; ain't a speck of dust in it—jus' got back from a funeral, suh."

I inferred that on such gala occasions carriages were given an extra cleaning. I looked up and down the street and perceived that there was little choice among the vehicles for hire that lined the curb. I looked in my memorandum book for the address of Azalea Adair.

"I want to go to 861 Jessamine Street," I said, and was about to step into the hack. But for an instant the thick, long, gorilla-like arm of the Negro barred me. On his massive and saturnine face a look of sudden suspicion and enmity flashed for a moment. Then, with quickly returning conviction, he asked, blandishingly: "What are you gwine there for, boss?"

"What is that to you?" I asked, a little sharply.

"Nothin', suh, jus' nothin'. Only it's a lonesome kind of part of town and few folks ever has business out there. Step right in. The seats is clean—jes' got back from a funeral, suh."

A mile and a half it must have been to our journey's end. I could hear nothing but the fearful rattle of the ancient hack over the uneven brick paving; I could smell nothing but the drizzle, now further flavored with coal smoke and something like a mixture of tar and oleander blossoms. All I could see through the streaming windows were two rows of dim houses.

The city has an area of 10 square miles; 181 miles of streets, of which 137 miles are paved; a system of waterworks that cost $2,000,000, with 77 miles of mains.

Eight-sixty-one Jessamine Street was a decayed mansion. Thirty yards back from the street it stood, outmerged in a splendid grove of trees and untrimmed shrubbery. A row of box bushes overflowed and almost hid the paling fence from sight; the gate was kept closed by a rope noose that encircled the gate post and the first paling of the gate. But when you got inside you saw that 861 was a shell, a shadow, a ghost of former grandeur and excellence. But in the story, I have not yet got inside.

When the hack had ceased from rattling and the weary quadrupeds came to a rest I handed my jehu his fifty cents with an additional quarter, feeling a glow of conscious generosity as I did so. He refused it.

"It's two dollars, suh," he said.

"How's that?" I asked. "I plainly heard you call out at the hotel. 'Fifty cents to any part of the town.'"

"It's two dollars, suh," he repeated obstinately. "It's a long ways from the hotel."

"It is within the city limits and well within them," I argued. "Don't think that you have picked up a greenhorn Yankee. Do you see those hills over there?" I went on, pointing toward the east (I could not see them, myself, for the drizzle); "well, I was born and raised on their other side. You old fool nigger, can't you tell people from other people when you see 'em?"

The grim face of King Cettiwayo softened. "Is you from the South, suh? I reckon it was them shoes of yourn fooled me. They is somethin' sharp in the toes for a Southern gen'l'man to wear."

"Then the charge is fifty cents, I suppose?" said I, inexorably.

His former expression, a mingling of cupidity and hostility, returned, remained ten seconds, and vanished.

"Boss," he said, "fifty cents is right; but I *needs* two dollars, suh; I'm *obleeged* to have two dollars. I ain't *demandin'* it now, suh; after I knows whar you's from; I'm jus sayin' that I *has* to have two dollars to-night and business is mighty po'."

Peace and confidence settled upon his heavy features. He had been luckier than he had hoped. Instead of having picked up a greenhorn, ignorant of rates, he had come upon an inheritance.

"You confounded old rascal," I said, reaching down to my pocket, "you ought to be turned over to the police."

For the first time I saw him smile. He knew; *he knew;* HE KNEW.

I gave him two one-dollar bills. As I handed them over I noticed that one of them had seen parlous times. Its upper right-hand corner was missing, and it had been torn through in the middle, but joined again. A strip of blue tissue paper, pasted over the split, preserved its negotiability.

Enough of the African bandit for the present: I left him happy, lifted the rope, and opened the creaky gate.

The house, as I said, was a shell. A paint brush had not touched it in twenty years. I could not see why a strong wind should not have bowled it over like a house of cards until I looked again at the trees that hugged it close—the trees that saw the battle of Nashville and still drew their protecting branches around it against storm and enemy and cold.

Azalea Adair, fifty years old, white-haired, a descendant of the cavaliers, as thin and frail as the house she lived in, robed in the cheapest and cleanest dress I ever saw, with an air as simple as a queen's, received me.

The reception room seemed a mile square, because there was nothing in it except some rows of books, on unpainted white-pine bookshelves, a cracked marble-topped table, a rag rug, a hairless horsehair sofa, and two or three chairs. Yes, there was a picture on the wall, a colored crayon drawing of a cluster of pansies. I looked around for the portrait of Andrew Jackson and the pine-cone hanging basket but they were not there.

Azalea Adair and I had conversation, a little of which will be repeated to you. She was a product of the old South, gently nurtured in the sheltered life. Her learning was not broad, but was deep and of splendid originality in its somewhat narrow scope. She had been educated at home, and her knowledge of the world was derived from inference and by inspiration. Of such is the precious, small group of essayists made. While she talked to me I kept brushing my fingers, trying, unconsciously, to rid them guiltily of the absent dust from the half-calf backs of Lamb, Chaucer, Hazlitt, Marcus Aurelius, Montaigne, and Hood. She was exquisite, she was a valuable discovery. Nearly everybody nowadays knows too much—oh, so much too much—of real life.

I could perceive clearly that Azalea Adair was very poor. A house and a dress she had, not much else, I fancied. So, divided between my duty to the magazine and my loyalty to the poets and essayists who fought Thomas in the valley of the Cumberland, I listened to her voice which was like a harpsichord's, and found that I could not speak of contracts. In the presence of the nine Muses and the three Graces one hesitated to lower the topic to two cents. There would have to be another colloquy after I had regained my commercialism. But I spoke of my mission, and three o'clock of the next afternoon was set for the discussion of the business proposition.

"Your town," I said, as I began to make ready to depart (which is the time for smooth generalities) "seems to be a quiet, sedate place. A home town, I should say, where few things out of the ordinary ever happen."

It carries on an extensive trade in stoves and hollow ware with the West and South, and its flouring mills have a daily capacity of more than 2,000 barrels.

Azalea Adair seemed to reflect.

"I have never thought of it that way," she said, with a kind of sincere intensity that seemed to belong to her. "Isn't it in the still, quiet places that things do happen? I fancy that when God began to create the earth on the first Monday morning one could have leaned out one's window and heard the drops of mud splashing from His trowel as He built up the everlasting hills. What did the noisiest project in the world—I mean the building of the tower of Babel—result in finally? A page and a half of Esperanto in the *North American Review*."

"Of course," said I, platitudinously, "human nature is the same everywhere; but there is more color—er—more drama and movement and— er—romance in some cities than in others."

"On the surface," said Azalea Adair. "I have traveled many times around the world in a golden airship wafted on two wings—print and dreams. I have seen (on one of my imaginary tours) the Sultan of Turkey bowstring with his own hands one of his wives who had uncovered her face in public. I have seen a man in Nashville tear up his theatre tickets because his wife was going out with her face covered—with rice powder. In San Francisco's Chinatown I saw the slave girl Sing Yee dipped slowly, inch by inch, in boiling almond oil to make her swear she would never see her American lover again. She gave in when the boiling oil had reached three inches above her knee. At a euchre party in East Nashville the other night I saw Kitty Morgan cut dead by seven of her schoolmates and lifelong friends because she had married a house painter. The boiling oil was sizzling as high as her heart; but I wish you could have seen the fine little smile that she carried from table to table. Oh, yes, it is a hum-drum town. Just a few miles of red brick houses and mud and stores and lumber yards."

Some one had knocked hollowly at the back of the house. Azalea Adair breathed a soft apology and went to investigate the sound. She came back in three minutes with brightened eyes, a faint flush on her cheeks, and ten years lifted from her shoulders.

"You must have a cup of tea before you go," she said, "and a sugar cake."

She reached and shook a little iron bell. In shuffled a small Negro girl about twelve, barefoot, not very tidy, glowering at me with thumb in mouth and bulging eyes.

Azalea Adair opened a tiny, worn purse and drew out a dollar bill, a dollar bill with the upper right-hand corner missing, torn in two pieces and pasted together again with a strip of blue tissue paper. It was one of those bills I had given the piratical Negro—there was no doubt of it.

"Go up to Mr. Baker's store on the corner, Impy," she said, handing the girl the dollar bill, "and get a quarter of a pound of tea—the kind he always sends me—and ten cents' worth of sugar cakes. Now, hurry. The supply of tea in the house happens to be exhausted," she explained to me.

Impy left by the back way. Before the scrape of her hard, bare feet had died away on the back porch, a wild shriek—I was sure it was hers— filled the hollow house. Then the deep, gruff tones of an angry man's voice mingled with the girl's further squeals and unintelligible words.

Azalea Adair rose without surprise or emotion and disappeared. For two minutes I heard the hoarse rumble of the man's voice; then some-thing like an oath and a slight scuffle, and she returned calmly to her chair.

"This is a roomy house," she said, "and I have a tenant for part of it.

I am sorry to have to rescind my invitation to tea. It is impossible to get the kind I always use at the store. Perhaps to-morrow Mr. Baker will be able to supply me."

I was sure that Impy had not had time to leave the house. I inquired concerning street-car lines and took my leave. After I was well on my way I remembered that I had not learned Azalea Adair's name. But to-morrow would do.

That same day I started in on the course of iniquity that this uneventful city forced upon me. I was in the town only two days, but in that time I managed to lie shamelessly by telegraph, and to be an accomplice—after the fact, if that is the correct legal term—to a murder.

As I rounded the corner nearest my hotel the Afrite coachman of the polychromatic, nonpareil coat seized me, swung open the dungeony door of his peripatetic sarcophagus, flirted his feather duster and began his ritual: "Step right in, boss. Carriage is clean—jus' got back from a funeral. Fifty cents to any——"

And then he knew me and grinned broadly. " 'Scuse me, boss; you is de gen'l'man what rid out with me dis mawnin'. Thank you kindly, suh."

"I am going out to 861 again to-morrow afternoon at three," said I, "and if you will be here, I'll let you drive me. So you know Miss Adair?" I concluded, thinking of my dollar bill.

"I belonged to her father, Judge Adair, suh," he replied.

"I judge that she is pretty poor," I said. "She hasn't much money to speak of, has she?"

For an instant I looked again at the fierce countenance of King Cetti-wayo, and then he changed back to an extortionate old Negro hack driver.

"She ain't gwine to starve, suh," he said, slowly. "She has reso'ces, suh; she has reso'ces."

"I shall pay you fifty cents for the trip," said I.

"Dat is puffeckly correct, suh," he answered, humbly. "I jus' *had* to have dat two dollars dis mawnin', boss."

I went to the hotel and lied by electricity. I wired the magazine: "A. Adair holds out for eight cents a word."

The answer that came back was: "Give it to her quick, you duffer."

Just before dinner "Major" Wentworth Caswell bore down upon me with the greetings of a long-lost friend. I have seen few men whom I have so instantaneously hated, and of whom it was so difficult to be rid. I was standing at the bar when he invaded me; therefore I could not wave the white ribbon in his face. I would have paid gladly for the drinks, hoping thereby, to escape another; but he was one of those despicable, roaring, advertising bibbers who must have brass bands and fireworks attend upon every cent that they waste in their follies.

With an air of producing millions he drew two one-dollar bills from a pocket and dashed one of them upon the bar. I looked once more at the dollar bill with the upper right-hand corner missing, torn through the middle, and patched with a strip of blue tissue paper. It was my dollar again. It could have been no other.

I went up to my room. The drizzle and the monotony of a dreary, eventless Southern town had made me tired and listless. I remember that just before I went to bed I mentally disposed of the mysterious dollar bill (which might have formed the clue to a tremendously fine detective story of San Francisco) by saying to myself sleepily: "Seems as if a lot of people here own stock in the Hack-Drivers' Trust. Pays dividends promptly, too. Wonder if——" Then I fell asleep.

King Cettiwayo was at his post the next day, and rattled my bones over the stones out to 861. He was to wait and rattle me back again when I was ready.

Azalea Adair looked paler and cleaner and frailer than she had looked on the day before. After she had signed the contract at eight cents per word she grew still paler and began to slip out of her chair. Without much trouble I managed to get her up on the antediluvian horsehair sofa and then I ran out to the sidewalk and yelled to the coffee-colored Pirate to bring a doctor. With a wisdom that I had not suspected in him, he abandoned his team and struck off up the street afoot, realizing the value of speed. In ten minutes he returned with a grave, gray-haired, and capable man of medicine. In a few words (worth much less than eight cents each) I explained to him my presence in the hollow house of mystery. He bowed with stately understanding, and turned to the old Negro.

"Uncle Cæsar," he said, calmly, "run up to my house and ask Miss Lucy to give you a cream pitcher full of fresh milk and half a tumbler of port wine. And hurry back. Don't drive—run. I want you to get back sometime this week."

It occurred to me that Dr. Merriman also felt a distrust as to the speeding powers of the land-pirate's steeds. After Uncle Cæsar was gone, lumberingly, but swiftly, up the street, the doctor looked me over with great politeness and as much careful calculation until he had decided that I might do.

"It is only a case of insufficient nutrition," he said. "In other words, the result of poverty, pride, and starvation. Mrs. Caswell has many devoted friends who would be glad to aid her, but she will accept nothing except from that old Negro, Uncle Cæsar, who was once owned by her family."

"Mrs. Caswell!" said I, in surprise. And then I looked at the contract and saw that she had signed it "Azalea Adair Caswell."

"I thought she was Miss Adair," I said.

"Married to a drunken, worthless loafer, sir," said the doctor. "It is said that he robs her even of the small sums that her old servant contributes toward her support."

When the milk and wine had been brought the doctor soon revived Azalea Adair. She sat up and talked of the beauty of the autumn leaves that were then in season and their height of color. She referred lightly to her fainting seizure as the outcome of an old palpitation of the heart. Impy fanned her as she lay on the sofa. The doctor was due elsewhere, and I followed him to the door. I told him that it was within my power and intentions to make a reasonable advance of money to Azalea Adair on future contributions to the magazine, and he seemed pleased.

"By the way," he said, "perhaps you would like to know that you have had royalty for a coachman. Old Cæsar's grandfather was a king in Congo. Cæsar himself has royal ways, as you may have observed."

As the doctor was moving off I heard Uncle Cæsar's voice inside: "Did he git bofe of dem two dollars from you, Mis' Zalea?"

"Yes, Cæsar," I heard Azalea Adair answer, weakly. And then I went in and concluded business negotiations with our contributor. I assumed the responsibility of advancing fifty dollars, putting it as a necessary formality in binding our bargain. And then Uncle Cæsar drove me back to the hotel.

Here ends all of the story as far as I can testify as a witness. The rest must be only bare statements of facts.

At about six o'clock I went out for a stroll. Uncle Cæsar was at his corner. He threw open the door of his carriage, flourished his duster, and began his depressing formula: "Step right in, suh. Fifty cents to anywhere in the city—hack's puffickly clean, suh—jus' got back from a funeral——"

And then he recognized me. I think his eyesight was getting bad. His coat had taken on a few more faded shades of color, the twine strings were more frayed and ragged, the last remaining button—the button of yellow horn—was gone. A motley descendant of kings was Uncle Cæsar!

About two hours later I saw an excited crowd besieging the front of the drug store. In a desert where nothing happens this was manna; so I wedged my way inside. On an extemporized couch of empty boxes and chairs was stretched the mortal corporeality of Major Wentworth Caswell. A doctor was testing him for the mortal ingredient. His decision was that it was conspicuous by its absence.

The erstwhile Major had been found dead on a dark street and brought by curious and ennuied citizens to the drug store. The late human being had been engaged in terrific battle—the details showed that. Loafer and reprobate though he had been, he had been also a warrior. But he had lost. His hands were yet clinched so tightly that his fingers would not be opened. The gentle citizens who had known him stood about and searched their vocabularies to find some good words, if it were possible, to speak of him. One kind-looking man said, after much thought: "When 'Cas' was about fo'teen he was one of the best spellers in the school."

While I stood there the fingers of the right hand of "the man that was," which hung down the side of a white pine box, relaxed, and dropped something at my feet. I covered it with one foot quietly, and a little later on I picked it up and pocketed it. I reasoned that in his last struggle his hand must have seized that object unwittingly and held it in a death grip.

At the hotel that night the main topic of conversation, with the possible exceptions of politics and prohibition, was the demise of Major Caswell. I heard one man say to a group of listeners:

"In my opinion, gentlemen, Caswell was murdered by some of these no-account niggers for his money. He had fifty dollars this afternoon which he showed to several gentlemen in the hotel. When he was found the money was not on his person."

I left the city the next morning at nine, and as the train was crossing the bridge over the Cumberland River I took out of my pocket a yellow horn overcoat button the size of a fifty-cent piece, with frayed ends of coarse twine hanging from it, and cast it out of the window into the slow, muddy waters below.

I wonder what's doing in Buffalo!

PSYCHE AND THE PSKYSCRAPER

If you are a philosopher you can do this thing: you can go to the top of a high building, look down upon your fellow men 300 feet below, and despise them as insects. Like the irresponsible black waterbugs on summer ponds, they crawl and circle and hustle about idiotically without aim or purpose. They do not even move with the admirable intelligence of ants, for ants always know when they are going home. The ant is of a lowly station, but he will often reach home and get his slippers on while you are left at your elevated station.

Man, then, to the housetopped philosopher, appears to be but a creeping, contemptible beetle. Brokers, poets, millionaires, bootblacks, beauties, hod-carriers, and politicians become little black specks dodging bigger black specks in streets no wider than your thumb.

From this high view the city itself becomes degraded to an unintelligible mass of distorted buildings and impossible perspectives; the revered ocean is a duck pond; the earth itself a lost golf ball. All the minutiæ of life are gone. The philosopher gazes into the infinite heavens above him, and allows his soul to expand in the influence of his new view. He feels that he is the heir to Eternity and the child of Time. Space, too, should be his by the right of his immortal heritage, and he thrills at the thought that some day his kind shall traverse those mysterious aerial roads between planet and planet. The tiny world beneath his feet upon which this towering structure of steel rests as a speck of dust upon a Himalayan mountain—it is but one of a countless number of such whirling atoms. What are the ambitions, the achievements, the paltry conquests and loves of those restless black insects below compared with the serene and awful immensity of the universe that lies above and around their insignificant city?

It is guaranteed that the philosopher will have these thoughts. They have been expressly compiled from the philosophies of the world and set down with the proper interrogation point at the end of them to represent the invariable musings of deep thinkers on high places. And when the philosopher takes the elevator down his mind is broader, his heart is at peace, and his conception of the cosmogony of creation is as wide as the buckle of Orion's summer belt.

But if your name happened to be Daisy, and you worked in an Eighth Avenue candy store and lived in a little cold hall bedroom, five feet by eight, and earned $6 per week, and ate ten-cent lunches and were nineteen years old, and got up at 6.30 and worked till 9, and never had studied philosophy, maybe things wouldn't look that way to you from the top of a skyscraper.

Two sighed for the hand of Daisy, the unphilosophical. One was Joe, who kept the smallest store in New York. It was about the size of a tool-box of the D. P. W., and was stuck like a swallow's nest against a corner of a down-town skyscraper. Its stock consisted of fruit, candies, newspapers, song books, cigarettes, and lemonade in season. When stern winter shook his congealed locks and Joe had to move himself and the fruit inside, there was exactly room in the store for the proprietor, his wares, a stove the size of a vinegar cruet, and one customer.

Joe was not of the nation that keeps us forever in a furore with fugues and fruit. He was a capable American youth who was laying by money, and wanted Daisy to help him spend it. Three times he had asked her.

"I got money saved up, Daisy," was his love song; "and you know how bad I want you. That store of mine ain't very big, but——"

"Oh, ain't it?" would be the antiphony of the unphilosophical one. "Why, I heard Wanamaker's was trying to get you to sublet part of your floor space to them for next year."

Daisy passed Joe's corner every morning and evening.

"Hello, Two-by-Four!" was her usual greeting. "Seems to me your store looks emptier. You must have sold a package of chewing gum."

"Ain't much room in here, sure," Joe would answer, with his slow grin, "except for you, Daise. Me and the store are waitin' for you whenever you'll take us. Don't you think you might before long?"

"Store!"—a fine scorn was expressed by Daisy's uptilted nose—"sardine box! Waitin' for me, you say? Gee! you'd have to throw out about a hundred pounds of candy before I could get inside of it, Joe."

"I wouldn't mind an even swap like that," said Joe, complimentary.

Daisy's existence was limited in every way. She had to walk sideways between the counter and the shelves in the candy store. In her own hall bedroom coziness had been carried close to cohesiveness. The walls were so near to one another that the paper on them made a perfect Babel of noise. She could light the gas with one hand and close the door with the other without taking her eyes off the reflection of her brown pompadour in the mirror. She had Joe's picture in a gilt frame on the dresser and sometimes—but her next thought would always be of Joe's funny little store tacked like a soap box to the corner of that great building, and away would go her sentiment in a breeze of laughter.

Daisy's other suitor followed Joe by several months. He came to board in the house where she lived. His name was Dabster, and he was a philosopher. Though young, attainments stood out upon him like continental labels on a Passaic (N. J.) suit-case. Knowledge he had kidnapped from cyclopedias and handbooks of useful information; but as for wisdom, when she passed he was left sniffing in the road without so much as the number of her motor car. He could and would tell you the proportions of water and muscle-making properties of peas and veal, the shortest verse in the Bible, the number of pounds of shingle nails required to fasten 256 shingles laid four inches to the weather, the population of Kankakee, Ill., the theories of Spinoza, the name of Mr. H. McKay Twombly's second hall footman, the length of the Hoosac Tunnel, the best time to set a hen, the salary of the railway post-office messenger between Driftwood and Red Bank Furnace, Pa., and the number of bones in the forelegs of a cat.

This weight of learning was no handicap to Dabster. His statistics were the sprigs of parsley with which he garnished the feast of small talk that he would set before you if he conceived that to be your taste. And again he used them as breastworks in foraging at the boarding-house. Firing at you a volley of figures concerning the weight of a lineal foot of bar-iron 5 x 2¾ inches, and the average annual rainfall at Fort Snelling, Minn., he would transfix with his fork the best piece of chicken on the dish while you were trying to rally sufficiently to ask him weakly why does a hen cross the road.

Thus, brightly armed, and further equipped with a measure of good looks, of a hair-oily, shopping-district-at-three-in-the-afternoon kind, it seems that Joe, of the Lilliputian emporium, had a rival worthy of his steel. But Joe carried no steel. There wouldn't have been room in his store to draw it if he had.

One Saturday afternoon, about four o'clock, Daisy and Mr. Dabster stopped before Joe's booth. Dabster wore a silk hat, and—well, Daisy was a woman, and that hat had no chance to get back in its box until Joe had seen it. A stick of pineapple chewing gum was the ostensible object of the call. Joe supplied it through the open side of his store. He did not pale or falter at sight of the hat.

"Mr. Dabster's going to take me on top of the building to observe the view," said Daisy, after she had introduced her admirers. "I never was on a skyscraper. I guess it must be awful nice and funny up there."

"H'm!" said Joe.

"The panorama," said Mr. Dabster, "exposed to the gaze from the top of a lofty building is not only sublime, but instructive. Miss Daisy has a decided pleasure in store for her."

"It's windy up there, too, as well as here," said Joe. "Are you dressed warm enough, Daise?"

"Sure thing! I'm all lined," said Daisy, smiling shyly at his clouded brow. "You look just like a mummy in a case, Joe. Ain't you just put in an invoice of a pint of peanuts or another apple? Your stock looks awful over-stocked."

Daisy giggled at her favorite joke; and Joe had to smile with her.

"Your quarters are somewhat limited, Mr.—er—er," remarked Dabster, "in comparison with the size of this building. I understand the area of its side to be about 340 by 100 feet. That would make you occupy a proportionate space as if half of Beloochistan were placed upon a territory as large as the United States east of the Rocky Mountains, with the province of Ontario and Belgium added."

"Is that so, sport?" said Joe, genially. "You are Weisenheimer on figures, all right. How many square pounds of baled hay do you think a jackass could eat if he stopped brayin' long enough to keep still a minute and five eighths?"

A few minutes later Daisy and Mr. Dabster stepped from an elevator to the top floor of the skyscraper. Then up a short, steep stairway and out upon the roof. Dabster led her to the parapet so she could look down at the black dots moving in the street below.

"What are they?" she asked, trembling. She had never been on a height like this before.

And then Dabster must needs play the philosopher on the tower, and conduct her soul forth to meet the immensity of space.

"Bipeds," he said, solemnly. "See what they become even at the small elevation of 340 feet—mere crawling insects going to and fro at random."

"Oh, they ain't anything of the kind," exclaimed Daisy, suddenly— "they're folks! I saw an automobile. Oh, gee! are we that high up?"

"Walk over this way," said Dabster.

He showed her the great city lying like an orderly array of toys far below, starred here and there, early as it was, by the first beacon lights of the winter afternoon. And then the bay and sea to the south and east vanishing mysteriously into the sky.

"I don't like it," declared Daisy, with troubled blue eyes. "Say we go down."

But the philosopher was not to be denied his opportunity. He would let her behold the grandeur of his mind, the half-nelson he had on the infinite, and the memory he had for statistics. And then she would never more be content to buy chewing gum at the smallest store in New York. And so he began to prate of the smallness of human affairs, and how that even so slight a removal from earth made man and his works look like one tenth part of a dollar thrice computed. And that one should consider the sidereal system and the maxims of Epictetus and be comforted.

"You don't carry me with you," said Daisy. "Say, I think it's awful to be up so high that folks look like fleas. One of them we saw might have been Joe. Why, Jimmy! we might as well be in New Jersey! Say, I'm afraid up here!"

The philosopher smiled fatuously.

"The earth," said he, "is itself only as a grain of wheat in space. Look up there."

Daisy gazed upward apprehensively. The short day was spent and the stars were coming out above.

"Yonder star," said Dabster, "is Venus, the evening star. She is 66,000,000 miles from the sun."

"Fudge!" said Daisy, with a brief flash of spirit, "where do you think I come from—Brooklyn? Susie Price, in our store—her brother sent her a ticket to go to San Francisco—that's only three thousand miles."

The philosopher smiled indulgently.

"Our world," he said, "is 91,000,000 miles from the sun. There are eighteen stars of the first magnitude that are 211,000 times farther from us than the sun is. If one of them should be extinguished it would be three years before we would see its light go out. There are six thousand stars of the sixth magnitude. It takes thirty-six years for the light of one of them to reach the earth. With an eighteen-foot telescope we can see 43,000,000 stars, including those of the thirteenth magnitude, whose light takes 2,700 years to reach us. Each of these stars——"

"You're lyin'," cried Daisy, angrily. "You're tryin' to scare me. And you have; I want to go down!"

She stamped her foot.

"Arcturus——" began the philosopher, soothingly, but he was interrupted by a demonstration out of the vastness of the nature that he was endeavoring to portray with his memory instead of his heart. For to the heart-expounder of nature, the stars were set in the firmament expressly to give soft light to lovers wandering happily beneath them; and if you stand tiptoe some September night with your sweetheart on your arm you can almost touch them with your hand. Three years for their light to reach us, indeed!

Out of the west leaped a meteor, lighting the roof of the skyscraper almost to midday. Its fiery parabola was limned against the sky toward the east. It hissed as it went, and Daisy screamed.

"Take me down," she cried, vehemently, "you—you mental arith-metic!"

Dabster got her to the elevator, and inside of it. She was wild-eyed, and she shuddered when the express made its debilitating drop.

Outside the revolving door of the skyscraper the philosopher lost her. She vanished; and he stood, bewildered without figures or statistics to aid him.

Joe had a lull in trade, and by squirming among his stock succeeded in lighting a cigarette and getting one cold foot against the attenuated stove.

The door was burst open, and Daisy, laughing, crying, scattering fruit and candies, tumbled into his arms.

"Oh, Joe, I've been up on the skyscraper. Ain't it cozy and warm and home-like in here! I'm ready for you, Joe, whenever you want me."

A BIRD OF BAGDAD

Without doubt much of the spirit and genius of the Caliph Harun Al Rashid descended to the Margrave August Michael von Paulsen Quigg.

Quigg's restaurant is in Fourth Avenue—that street that the city seems to have forgotten in its growth. Fourth Avenue—born and bred in the Bowery—staggers northward full of good resolutions.

Where it crosses Fourteenth Street it struts for a brief moment proudly in the glare of the museums and cheap theatres. It may yet become a fit mate for its high-born sister boulevard to the west, or its roaring, polyglot, broad-waisted cousin to the east. It passes Union Square; and here the hoofs of the dray horses seem to thunder in unison, recalling the tread of marching hosts—Hooray! But now come the silent and terrible mountains—buildings square as forts, high as the clouds, shutting out the sky, where thousands of slaves bend over desks all day. On the ground floors are only little fruit shops and laundries and book shops, where you see copies of "Littell's Living Age" and G. W. M. Reynold's novels in the windows. And next—poor Fourth Avenue!—the street glides into medi-æval solitude. On each side are the shops devoted to "Antiques."

Let us say it is night. Men in rusty armor stand in the windows and menace the hurrying cars with raised iron gauntlets. Hauberks and helms, blunderbusses, Cromwellian breastplates, matchlocks, creeses, and the swords and daggers of an army of dead-and-gone gallants gleam dully in the ghostly light. Here and there from a corner saloon (lit with Jack-o'-lanterns or phosphorus) stagger forth shuddering, homebound citizens, nerved by the tankards within to their fearsome journey adown that eldritch avenue lined with the blood-stained weapons of the fighting dead. What street could live inclosed by these mortuary relics, and trod by these spectral citizens in whose sunken hearts scarce one good whoop or tra-la-la remained?

Not Fourth Avenue. Not after the tinsel but enlivening glories of the Little Rialto—not after the echoing drum-beats of Union Square. There need be no tears, ladies and gentlemen; 'tis but the suicide of a street. With a shriek and a crash Fourth Avenue dives headlong into the tunnel at Thirty-fourth and is never seen again.

Near the sad scene of the thoroughfare's dissolution stood the modest restaurant of Quigg. It stands there yet if you care to view its crumbling red-brick front, its show window heaped with oranges, tomatoes, layer cakes, pies, canned asparagus—its papier-mâché lobster and two Maltese kittens asleep on a bunch of lettuce—if you care to sit at one of the little tables upon whose cloth has been traced in the yellowest of coffee stains the trail of the Japanese advance—to sit there with one eye on your umbrella and the other upon the bogus bottle from which you drop the counterfeit sauce foisted upon us by the cursed charlatan who assumes to be our dear old lord and friend, the "Nobleman in India."

Quigg's title came through his mother. One of her ancestors was a Margravine of Saxony. His father was a Tammany brave. On account of the dilution of his heredity he found that he could neither become a reigning potentate nor get a job in the City Hall. So he opened a restaurant. He was a man full of thought and reading. The business gave him a living, though he gave it little attention. One side of his house bequeathed to him a poetic and romantic nature. The other gave him the restless spirit that made him seek adventure. By day he was Quigg, the restaurateur. By night he was the Margrave—the Caliph—the Prince of Bohemia—going about the city in search of the odd, the mysterious, the inexplicable, the recondite.

One night at 9, at which hour the restaurant closed, Quigg set forth upon his quest. There was a mingling of the foreign, the military, and the artistic in his appearance as he buttoned his coat high up under his short-trimmed brown and gray beard and turned westward toward the more central life conduits of the city. In his pocket he had stored an assortment of cards, written upon, without which he never stirred out of doors. Each of those cards was good at his own restaurant for its face value. Some called simply for a bowl of soup or sandwiches and coffee; others entitled their bearers to one, two, three, or more days of full meals;

a few were for single regular meals; a very few were, in effect, meal tickets good for a week.

Of riches and power Margrave Quigg had none; but he had a Caliph's heart—it may be forgiven him if his head fell short of the measure of Harun Al Rashid's. Perhaps some of the gold pieces in Bagdad had put less warmth and hope into the complainants among the bazaars than had Quigg's beef stew among the fishermen and one-eyed calenders of Manhattan.

Continuing his progress in search of romance to divert him, or of distress that he might aid, Quigg became aware of a fast-gathering crowd that whooped and fought and eddied at a corner of Broadway and the crosstown street that he was traversing. Hurrying to the spot he beheld a young man of an exceedingly melancholy and preoccupied demeanor engaged in the pastime of casting silver money from his pockets in the middle of the street. With each motion of the generous one's hand the crowd huddled upon the falling largesse with yells of joy. Traffic was suspended. A policeman in the centre of the mob stooped often to the ground as he urged the blockaders to move on.

The Margrave saw at a glance that here was food for his hunger after knowledge concerning abnormal workings of the human heart. He made his way swiftly to the young man's side and took his arm. "Come with me at once," he said, in a low but commanding voice that his waiters had learned to fear.

"Pinched," remarked the young man, looking up at him with expressionless eyes. "Pinched by a painless dentist. Take me away, flatty, and give me gas. Some lay eggs and some lay none. When is a hen?"

Still deeply seized by some inward grief, but tractable, he allowed Quigg to lead him away and down the street to a little park.

There, seated on a bench, he upon whom a corner of the great Caliph's mantle had descended, spake with kindness and discretion, seeking to know what evil had come upon the other, disturbing his soul and driving him to such ill-considered and ruinous waste of his substance and stores.

"I was doing the Monte Cristo act as adapted by Pompton, N. J., wasn't I?" asked the young man.

"You were throwing small coins into the street for the people to scramble after," said the Margrave.

"That's it. You buy all the beer you can hold, and then you throw chicken feed to—— Oh, curse that word chicken, and hens, feathers, roosters, eggs, and everything connected with it!"

"Young sir," said the Margrave, kindly, but with dignity, "though I do not ask your confidence, I invite it. I know the world and I know humanity. Man is my study, though I do not eye him as the scientist eyes a beetle or as the philanthropist gazes at the objects of his bounty—

through a veil of theory and ignorance. It is my pleasure and distraction to interest myself in the peculiar and complicated misfortunes that life in a great city visits upon my fellow men. You may be familiar with the history of that glorious and immortal ruler, the Caliph Harun Al Rashid, whose wise and beneficent excursions among his people in the city of Bagdad secured him the privilege of relieving so much of their distress. In my humble way I walk in his footsteps. I seek for romance and adventure in city streets—not in ruined castles or in crumbling palaces. To me the greatest marvels of magic are those that take place in men's hearts when acted upon by the furious and diverse forces of a crowded population. In your strange behavior this evening I fancy a story lurks. I read in your act something deeper than the wanton wastefulness of a spendthrift. I observe in your countenance the certain traces of consuming grief or despair. I repeat—I invite your confidence. I am not without some powers to alleviate and advise. Will you not trust me?"

"Gee, how you talk!" exclaimed the young man, a gleam of admiration supplanting for a moment the dull sadness of his eyes. "You've got the Astor Library skinned to a synopsis of preceding chapters. I mind that old Turk you speak of. I read 'The Arabian Nights' when I was a kid. He was a kind of Bill Devery and Charlie Schwab rolled into one. But, say, you might wave enchanted dishrags and make copper bottles smoke up coon giants all night without ever touching me. My case won't yield to that kind of treatment."

"If I could hear your story," said the Margrave, with his lofty, serious smile.

"I'll spiel it in about nine words," said the young man, with a deep sigh, "but I don't think you can help me any. Unless you're a peach at guessing it's back to the Bosphorus for you on your magic linoleum."

The Story of the Young Man and the Harness Maker's Riddle

"I work in Hildebrant's saddle and harness shop down in Grant Street. I've worked there five years. I get $18 a week. That's enough to marry on, ain't it? Well, I'm not going to get married. Old Hildebrant is one of these funny Dutchmen—you know the kind—always getting off bum jokes. He's got about a million riddles and things that he faked from Rogers Brothers' great-grandfather. Bill Watson works there, too. Me and Bill have to stand for them chestnuts day after day. Why do we do it? Well, jobs ain't to be picked off every Anheuser bush—— And then there's Laura.

"What? The old man's daughter. Comes in the shop every day. About nineteen, and the picture of the blonde that sits on the palisades of the Rhine and charms the clam-diggers into the surf. Hair the color of straw matting, and eyes as black and shiny as the best harness blacking—think of that!

"Me? Well, it's either me or Bill Watson. She treats us both equal. Bill is all to the psychopathic about her; and me?—well, you saw me plating the road-bed of the Great Maroon Way with silver to-night. That was on account of Laura. I was spiflicated, Your Highness, and I wot not of what I wouldst.

"How? Why, old Hildebrant says to me and Bill this afternoon: 'Boys, one riddle have I for you gehabt haben. A young man who cannot riddles antworten, he is not so good by business for ein family to provide—is not that—hein?' And he hands us a riddle—conundrum, some calls it—and he chuckles interiorly and gives both of us till to-morrow morning to work out the answer to it. And he says whichever of us guesses the repartee end of it goes to his house o' Wednesday night to his daughter's birthday party. And it means Laura for whichever of us goes, for she's naturally aching for a husband, and it's either me or Bill Watson, for old Hildebrant likes us both, and wants her to marry somebody that'll carry on the business after he's stitched his last pair of traces.

"The riddle? Why, it was this: 'What kind of a hen lays the longest?' Think of that! What kind of a hen lays the longest? Ain't it like a Dutchman to risk a man's happiness on a fool proposition like that? Now, what's the use? What I don't know about hens would fill several incubators. You say you're giving imitations of the old Arab guy that gave away—libraries in Bagdad. Well, now, can you whistle up a fairy that'll solve this hen query, or not?"

When the young man ceased the Margrave arose and paced to and fro by the park bench for several minutes. Finally he sat again, and said, in grave and impressive tones:

"I must confess, sir, that during the eight years that I have spent in search of adventure and in relieving distress I have never encountered a more interesting or a more perplexing case. I fear that I have overlooked hens in my researches and observations. As to their habits, their time and manner of laying, their many varieties and crossbreedings, their span of life, their——"

"Oh, don't make an Ibsen drama of it!" interrupted the young man, flippantly. "Riddles—especially old Hildebrant's riddles—don't have to be worked out seriously. They are light themes such as Sim Ford and Harry Thurston Peck like to handle. But, somehow, I can't strike just the answer. Bill Watson may, and he may not. To-morrow will tell. Well, Your Majesty, I'm glad anyhow that you butted in and whiled the time away. I guess Mr. Al Rashid himself would have bounced back if one of his constituents had conducted him up against this riddle. I'll say goodnight. Peace fo' yours, and what-you-may-call-its of Allah."

The Margrave, with a gloomy air, held out his hand.

"I cannot express my regret," he said, sadly. "Never before have I found myself unable to assist in some way. 'What kind of a hen lays the longest?' It is a baffling problem. There is a hen, I believe, called the Plymouth Rock that——"

"Cut it out," said the young man. "The Caliph trade is a mighty serious one. I don't suppose you'd even see anything funny in a preacher's defense of John D. Rockefeller. Well, good-night, Your Nibs."

From habit the Margrave began to fumble in his pockets. He drew forth a card and handed it to the young man.

"Do me the favor to accept this, anyhow," he said. "The time might come when it might be of use to you."

"Thanks!" said the young man, pocketing it carelessly. "My name is Simmons."

Shame to him who would hint that the reader's interest shall altogether pursue the Margrave August Michael von Paulsen Quigg. I am indeed astray if my hand fail in keeping the way where my peruser's heart would follow. Then let us, on the morrow, peep quickly in at the door of Hildebrant, harness maker.

Hildebrant's 200 pounds reposed on a bench, silver buckling a raw leather martingale.

Bill Watson came in first.

"Vell," said Hildebrant, shaking all over with the vile conceit of the joke-maker, "haf you guessed him? 'Vat kind of a hen lays der longest?'"

"Er—why, I think so," said Bill, rubbing a servile chin. "I think so, Mr. Hildebrant—the one that lives the longest—— Is that right?"

"Nein!" said Hildebrant, shaking his head, violently. "You haf not guessed der answer."

Bill passed on and donned a bed-tick apron and bachelorhood.

In came the young man of the Arabian Nights' fiasco—pale, melancholy, hopeless.

"Vell," said Hildebrant, "haf you guessed him? 'Vat kind of a hen lays der longest?'"

Simmons regarded him with dull savagery in his eye. Should he curse this mountain of pernicious humor—curse him and die? Why should—— But there was Laura.

Dogged, speechless, he thrust his hands into his coat pockets and stood. His hand encountered the strange touch of the Margrave's card. He drew it out and looked at it, as men about to be hanged look at a crawling fly. There was written on it in Quigg's bold, round hand:

"Good for one roast chicken to bearer."

Simmons looked up with a flashing eye.

"A dead one!" said he.

"Goot!" roared Hildebrant, rocking the table with giant glee. "Dot is right! You gome at mine house at 8 o'clock to der party."

COMPLIMENTS OF THE SEASON

There are no more Christmas stories to write. Fiction is exhausted; and newspaper items, the next best, are manufactured by clever young journalists who have married early and have an engagingly pessimistic view of life. Therefore, for seasonable diversion, we are reduced to two very questionable sources—facts and philosophy. We will begin with—whichever you choose to call it.

Children are pestilential little animals with which we have to cope under a bewildering variety of conditions. Especially when childish sorrows overwhelm them are we put to our wits' ends. We exhaust our paltry store of consolation; and then beat them, sobbing, to sleep. Then we grovel in the dust of a million years, and ask God why. Thus we call out of the rat-trap. As for the children, no one understands them except old maids, hunchbacks, and shepherd dogs.

Now come the facts in the case of the Rag-Doll, the Tatterdemalion, and the Twenty-fifth of December.

On the tenth of that month the Child of the Millionaire lost her rag-doll. There were many servants in the Millionaire's palace on the Hudson, and these ransacked the house and grounds, but without finding the lost treasure. The Child was a girl of five, and one of those perverse little beasts that often wound the sensibilities of wealthy parents by fixing their affections upon some vulgar, inexpensive toy instead of upon diamond-studded automobiles and pony phaetons.

The Child grieved sorely and truly, a thing inexplicable to the Millionaire, to whom the rag-doll market was about as interesting as Bay State Gas; and to the Lady, the Child's mother, who was all form—that is, nearly all, as you shall see.

The Child cried inconsolably, and grew hollow-eyed, knock-kneed, spindling, and cory-kilverty in many other respects. The Millionaire smiled and tapped his coffers confidently. The pick of the output of the French and German toymakers was rushed by special delivery to the mansion; but Rachel refused to be comforted. She was weeping for her rag child, and was for a high protective tariff against all foreign foolishness. Then doctors with the finest bedside manners and stop-watches were called in. One by one they chattered futilely about peptomanganate of iron and sea voyages and hypophosphites until their stop-watches showed that Bill Rendered was under the wire for show or place. Then, as men, they advised that the rag-doll be found as soon as possible and restored to its mourning parent. The Child sniffed at therapeutics, chewed a thumb, and wailed for her Betsy. And all this time cablegrams were coming from Santa Claus saying that he would soon be here and enjoining us to show a true Christian spirit and let up on the poolrooms and tontine policies and platoon systems long enough to give him a welcome. Everywhere the spirit of Christmas was diffusing itself. The banks were refusing loans, the pawnbrokers had doubled their gang of helpers, people bumped your shins on the streets with red sleds, Thomas and Jeremiah bubbled before you on the bars while you waited on one foot, holly-wreaths of hospitality were hung in windows of the stores, they who had 'em were getting out their furs. You hardly knew which was the best bet in balls—three, high, moth, or snow. It was no time at which to lose the rag-doll of your heart.

If Doctor Watson's investigating friend had been called in to solve this mysterious disappearance he might have observed on the Millionaire's wall a copy of "The Vampire." That would have quickly suggested, by induction, "A rag and a bone and a hank of hair." "Flip," a Scotch terrier, next to the rag-doll in the Child's heart, frisked through the halls. The hank of hair! Aha! X, the unfound quantity, represented the rag-doll. But, the bone? Well, when dogs find bones they—— Done! it were an easy and a fruitful task to examine Flip's forefeet. Look, Watson! Earth— dried earth between the toes. Of course, the dog—but Sherlock was not there. Therefore it devolves. But topography and architecture must intervene.

The Millionaire's palace occupied a lordly space. In front of it was a lawn close-mowed as a South Island man's face two days after a shave. At one side of it, and fronting on another street, was a pleasaunce trimmed to a leaf, and the garage and stables. The Scotch pup had ravished the rag-doll from the nursery, dragged it to a corner of the lawn, dug a hole, and buried it after the manner of careless undertakers. There you have the mystery solved, and no checks to write for the hypodermical wizard or fi'-pun notes to toss to the sergeant. Then let's get down to the heart of the thing, tiresome readers—the Christmas heart of the thing.

Fuzzy was drunk—not riotously or helplessly or loquaciously, as you or I might get, but decently, appropriately, and inoffensively, as becomes a gentleman down on his luck.

Fuzzy was a soldier of misfortune. The road, the haystack, the park bench, the kitchen door, the bitter round of eleemosynary beds-with-shower-bath-attachment, the petty pickings and ignobly garnered largesse of great cities—these formed the chapters of his history.

Fuzzy walked toward the river, down the street that bounded one side of the Millionaire's house and grounds. He saw a leg of Betsy, the lost rag-doll, protruding, like the clue to a Lilliputian murder mystery, from its untimely grave in a corner of the fence. He dragged forth the maltreated infant, tucked it under his arm, and went on his way crooning a road song of his brethren that no doll that has been brought up to the sheltered life should hear. Well for Betsy that she had no ears. And well that she had no eyes save unseeing circles of black; for the faces of Fuzzy and the Scotch terrier were those of brothers, and the heart of no rag-doll could withstand twice to become the prey of such fearsome monsters.

Though you may never know it Grogan's saloon stands near the river and near the foot of the street down which Fuzzy traveled. In Grogan's, Christmas cheer was already rampant.

Fuzzy entered with his doll. He fancied that as a mummer at the feast of Saturn he might earn a few drops from the wassail cup.

He set Betsy on the bar and addressed her loudly and humorously, seasoning his speech with exaggerated compliments and endearments as one entertaining his lady friend. The loafers and bibbers around caught the farce of it, and roared. The bartender gave Fuzzy a drink. Oh, many of us carry rag-dolls.

"One for the lady?" suggested Fuzzy, impudently, and tucked another contribution to Art beneath his waistcoat.

He began to see possibilities in Betsy. His first-night had been a success. Visions of a vaudeville circuit about town dawned upon him.

In a group near the stove sat "Pigeon" McCarthy, Black Riley, and "One-ear" Mike, well and unfavorably known in the tough shoe-string district that blackened the left bank of the river. They passed a newspaper back and forth among themselves. The item that each solid and blunt forefinger pointed out was an advertisement headed "One Hundred Dollars Reward." To earn it one must return the rag-doll lost, strayed, or stolen from the Millionaire's mansion. It seemed that grief still ravaged, unchecked, in the bosom of the too faithful Child. Flip, the terrier, capered and shook his absurd whisker before her, powerless to distract. She wailed for her Betsy in the faces of walking, talking, mama-ing, and eye-closing French Mabelles and Violettes. The advertisement was a last resort.

Black Riley came from behind the stove and approached Fuzzy in his one-sided parabolic way.

The Christmas mummer, flushed with success, had tucked Betsy under his arm, and was about to depart to the filling of impromptu dates elsewhere.

"Say, 'Bo," said Black Riley to him, "where did you cop out dat doll?"

"This doll?" asked Fuzzy, touching Betsy with his forefinger to be sure that she was the one referred to. "Why, this doll was presented to me by the Emperor of Beloochistan. I have seven hundred others in my country home in Newport. This doll——"

"Cheese the funny business," said Riley. "You swiped it or picked it up at de house on de hill where—but never mind dat. You want to take fifty cents for de rags, and take it quick. Me brother's kid at home might be wantin' to play wid it. Hey—what?"

He produced the coin.

Fuzzy laughed a gurgling, insolent, alcoholic laugh in his face. Go to the office of Sarah Bernhardt's manager and propose to him that she be released from a night's performance to entertain the Tackytown Lyceum and Literary Coterie. You will hear the duplicate of Fuzzy's laugh.

Black Riley gauged Fuzzy quickly with his blueberry eye as a wrestler does. His hand was itching to play the Roman and wrest the rag Sabine from the extemporaneous merry-andrew who was entertaining an angel unaware. But he refrained. Fuzzy was fat and solid and big. Three inches of well-nourished corporeity, defended from the winter winds by dingy linen, intervened between his vest and trousers. Countless small, circular wrinkles running around his coat-sleeves and knees guaranteed the quality of his bone and muscle. His small, blue eyes, bathed in the moisture of altruism and wooziness, looked upon you kindly, yet without abashment. He was whiskerly, whiskyly, fleshily formidable. So, Black Riley temporized.

"Wot'll you take for it, den?" he asked.

"Money," said Fuzzy, with husky firmness, "cannot buy her."

He was intoxicated with the artist's first sweet cup of attainment. To set a faded-blue, earth-stained rag-doll on a bar, to hold mimic converse with it, and to find his heart leaping with the sense of plaudits earned and his throat scorching with free libations poured in his honor—could base coin buy him from such achievements? You will perceive that Fuzzy had the temperament.

Fuzzy walked out with the gait of a trained sea-lion in search of other cafés to conquer.

Though the dusk of twilight was hardly yet apparent, lights were beginning to spangle the city like pop-corn bursting in a deep skillet. Christmas Eve, impatiently expected, was peeping over the brink of the hour. Millions had prepared for its celebration. Towns would be painted red. You, yourself, have heard the horns and dodged the capers of the Saturnalians.

"Pigeon" McCarthy, Black Riley, and "One-ear" Mike held a hasty converse outside Grogan's. They were narrow-chested, pallid striplings, not fighters in the open, but more dangerous in their ways of warfare than the most terrible of Turks. Fuzzy, in a pitched battle, could have eaten the three of them. In a go-as-you-please encounter he was already doomed.

They overtook him just as he and Betsy were entering Costigan's Casino. They deflected him, and shoved the newspaper under his nose. Fuzzy could read—and more.

"Boys," said he, "you are certainly damn true friends. Give me a week to think it over."

The soul of the real artist is quenched with difficulty.

The boys carefully pointed out to him that advertisements were soulless, and that the deficiencies of the day might not be supplied by the morrow.

"A cool hundred," said Fuzzy, thoughtfully and mushily.

"Boys," said he, "you are true friends. I'll go up and claim the reward. The show business is not what it used to be."

Night was falling more surely. The three tagged at his sides to the foot of the rise on which stood the Millionaire's house. There Fuzzy turned upon them acrimoniously.

"You are a pack of putty-faced beagle-hounds," he roared. "Go away."

They went away—a little way.

In "Pigeon" McCarthy's pocket was a section of one-inch gas-pipe eight inches long. In one end of it and in the middle of it was a lead slug. One-half of it was packed tight with solder. Black Riley carried a slung-shot, being a conventional thug. "One-ear" Mike relied upon a pair of brass knucks—an heirloom in the family.

"Why fetch and carry," said Black Riley, "when some one will do it for ye? Let him bring it out to us. Hey—what?"

"We can chuck him in the river," said "Pigeon" McCarthy, "with a stone tied to his feet."

"Youse guys make me tired," said "One-ear" Mike sadly. "Ain't progress ever appealed to none of yez? Sprinkle a little gasoline on 'em, and drop 'im on the Drive—well?"

Fuzzy entered the Millionaire's gate and zigzagged toward the softly glowing entrance of the mansion. The three goblins came up to the gate and lingered—one on each side of it, one beyond the roadway. They fingered their cold metal and leather, confident.

Fuzzy rang the door-bell, smiling foolishly and dreamily. An atavistic instinct prompted him to reach for the button of his right glove. But he wore no gloves; so his left hand dropped, embarrassed.

The particular menial whose duty it was to open doors to silks and laces shied at first sight of Fuzzy. But a second glance took in his passport, his card of admission, his surety of welcome—the lost rag-doll of the daughter of the house dangling under his arm.

Fuzzy was admitted into a great hall, dim with the glow from unseen lights. The hireling went away and returned with a maid and the Child. The doll was restored to the mourning one. She clasped her lost darling to her breast; and then, with the inordinate selfishness and candor of childhood, stamped her foot and whined hatred and fear of the odious being who had rescued her from the depths of sorrow and despair. Fuzzy wriggled himself into an ingratiatory attitude and essayed the idiotic smile and blattering small talk that is supposed to charm the budding intellect of the young. The Child bawled, and was dragged away, hugging her Betsy close.

There came the Secretary, pale, poised, polished, gliding in pumps, and worshipping pomp and ceremony. He counted out into Fuzzy's hand ten ten-dollar bills; then dropped his eye upon the door, transferred it to James, its custodian, indicated the obnoxious earner of the reward with the other, and allowed his pumps to waft him away to secretarial regions.

James gathered Fuzzy with his own commanding optic and swept him as far as the front door.

When the money touched Fuzzy's dingy palm his first instinct was to take to his heels; but a second thought restrained him from that blunder of etiquette. It was his; it had been given him. It—and, oh, what an elysium it opened to the gaze of his mind's eye! He had tumbled to the foot of the ladder; he was hungry, homeless, friendless, ragged, cold, drifting; and he held in his hand the key to a paradise of the mud-honey that he craved. The fairy doll had waved a wand with her rag-stuffed hand; and now wherever he might go the enchanted palaces with shining foot-rests and magic red fluids in gleaming glassware would be open to him.

He followed James to the door.

He paused there as the flunky drew open the great mahogany portal for him to pass into the vestibule.

Beyond the wrought-iron gates in the dark highway Black Riley and his two pals casually strolled, fingering under their coats the inevitably fatal weapons that were to make the reward of the rag-doll theirs.

Fuzzy stopped at the Millionaire's door and bethought himself. Like little sprigs of mistletoe on a dead tree, certain living green thoughts and memories began to decorate his confused mind. He was quite drunk, mind you, and the present was beginning to fade. Those wreaths and festoons of holly with their scarlet berries making the great hall gay—where had he seen such things before? Somewhere he had known polished floors and odors of fresh flowers in winter, and—some one was singing a song in the house that he thought he had heard before. Some one singing and playing a harp. Of course, it was Christmas—Fuzzy thought he must have been pretty drunk to have overlooked that.

And then he went out of the present, and there came back to him out of some impossible, vanished, and irrevocable past a little, pure-white, transient, forgotten ghost—the spirit of *noblesse oblige*. Upon a gentleman certain things devolve.

James opened the outer door. A stream of light went down the graveled walk to the iron gate. Black Riley, McCarthy, and "One-ear" Mike saw, and carelessly drew their sinister cordon closer about the gate.

With a more imperious gesture than James's master had ever used or could ever use, Fuzzy compelled the menial to close the door. Upon a gentleman certain things devolve. Especially at the Christmas season.

"It is cust—customary," he said to James, the flustered, "when a gentleman calls on Christmas Eve to pass the compliments of the season with the lady of the house. You und'stand? I shall not move shtep till I pass compl'ments season with lady the house. Und'stand?"

There was an argument. James lost. Fuzzy raised his voice and sent it through the house unpleasantly. I did not say he was a gentleman. He was simply a tramp being visited by a ghost.

A sterling silver bell rang. James went back to answer it, leaving Fuzzy in the hall. James explained somewhere to some one.

Then he came and conducted Fuzzy to the library.

The Lady entered a moment later. She was more beautiful and holy than any picture that Fuzzy had seen. She smiled, and said something about a doll. Fuzzy didn't understand that; he remembered nothing about a doll.

A footman brought in two small glasses of sparkling wine on a stamped sterling-silver waiter. The Lady took one. The other was handed to Fuzzy.

As his fingers closed on the slender glass stem his disabilities dropped from him for one brief moment. He straightened himself; and Time, so disobliging to most of us, turned backward to accommodate Fuzzy.

Forgotten Christmas ghosts whiter than the false beards of the most opulent Kris Kringle were rising in the fumes of Grogan's whisky. What had the Millionaire's mansion to do with a long wainscoted Virginia hall, where the riders were grouped around a silver punch-bowl drinking the ancient toast of the House? And why should the patter of the cab horses' hoofs on the frozen street be in any wise related to the sound of the saddled hunters stamping under the shelter of the west veranda? And what had Fuzzy to do with any of it?

The Lady, looking at him over her glass, let her condescending smile fade away like a false dawn. Her eyes turned serious. She saw something beneath the rags and Scotch terrier whiskers that she did not understand. But it did not matter.

Fuzzy lifted his glass and smiled vacantly.

"P-pardon, lady," he said, "but couldn't leave without exchangin' comp'ments sheason with lady th' house. 'Gainst princ'ples gen'leman do sho."

And then he began the ancient salutation that was a tradition in the House when men wore lace ruffles and powder.

"The blessings of another year——"

Fuzzy's memory failed him. The Lady prompted:

"—Be upon this hearth."

"—The guest——" stammered Fuzzy.

"—And upon her who——" continued the Lady, with a leading smile.

"Oh, cut it out," said Fuzzy, ill-manneredly. "I can't remember. Drink hearty."

Fuzzy had shot his arrow. They drank. The Lady smiled again the smile of her caste. James enveloped Fuzzy and re-conducted him toward the front door. The harp music still softly drifted through the house.

Outside, Black Riley breathed on his cold hands and hugged the gate.

"I wonder," said the Lady to herself, musing, "who—but there were so many who came. I wonder whether memory is a curse or a blessing to them after they have fallen so low."

Fuzzy and his escort were nearly at the door. The Lady called: "James!"

James stalked back obsequiously, leaving Fuzzy waiting unsteadily, with his brief spark of the divine fire gone.

Outside, Black Riley stamped his cold feet and got a firmer grip on his section of gas-pipe.

"You will conduct this gentleman," said the Lady, "downstairs. Then tell Louis to get out the Mercedes and take him to whatever place he wishes to go."

A NIGHT IN NEW ARABIA

The great city of Bagdad-on-the-Subway is caliph-ridden. Its palaces, bazaars, khans, and byways are thronged with Al Rashids in divers disguises, seeking diversion and victims for their unbridled generosity. You can scarcely find a poor beggar whom they are willing to let enjoy the spoils unsuccored, nor a wrecked unfortunate upon whom they will not reshower the means of fresh misfortune. You will hardly find anywhere a hungry one who has not had the opportunity to tighten his belt in gift libraries, nor a poor pundit who has not blushed at the holiday basket of celery-crowned turkey forced resoundingly through his door by the eleemosynary press.

So then, fearfully through the Harun-haunted streets creep the one-eyed calenders, the Little Hunchback and the Barber's Sixth Brother, hoping to escape the ministrations of the roving horde of caliphoid sultans.

Entertainment for many Arabian nights might be had from the histories of those who have escaped the largesse of the army of Commanders of the Faithful. Until dawn you might sit on the enchanted rug and listen to such stories as are told of the powerful genie Roc-Ef-El-Er who sent the Forty Thieves to soak up the oil plant of Ali Baba; of the good Caliph Kar-Neg-Ghe, who gave away palaces; of the Seven Voyages of Sailbad, the Sinner, who frequented wooden excursion steamers among the islands; of the Fisherman and the Bottle; of the Barmecides' Boarding house; of Aladdin's rise to wealth by means of his Wonderful Gas-meter.

But now, there being ten sultans to one Scheherazade, she is held too valuable to be in fear of the bowstring. In consequence the art of narrative languishes. And, as the lesser caliphs are hunting the happy poor and the resigned unfortunate from cover to cover in order to heap upon them strange mercies and mysterious benefits, too often comes the report from Arabian headquarters that the captive refused "to talk."

This reticence, then, in the actors who perform the sad comedies of their philanthropy-scourged world, must, in a degree, account for the shortcomings of this painfully gleaned tale, which shall be called

The Story of the Caliph Who Alleviated His Conscience

Old Jacob Spraggins mixed for himself some Scotch and lithia water at his $1,200 oak sideboard. Inspiration must have resulted from its imbibition, for immediately afterward he struck the quartered oak soundly with his fist and shouted to the empty dining room:

"By the coke ovens of hell, it must be that ten thousand dollars! If I can get that squared, it'll do the trick."

Thus, by the commonest artifice of the trade, having gained your interest, the action of the story will now be suspended, leaving you grumpily to consider a sort of doll biography beginning fifteen years before.

When old Jacob was young Jacob he was a breaker boy in a Pennsylvania coal mine. I don't know what a breaker boy is; but his occupation seems to be standing by a coal dump with a wan look and a dinner-pail to have his picture taken for magazine articles. Anyhow, Jacob was one. But, instead of dying of overwork at nine, and leaving his helpless parents and brothers at the mercy of the union strikers' reserve fund, he hitched up his galluses, put a dollar or two in a side proposition now and then, and at forty-five was worth $20,000,000.

There now! it's over. Hardly had time to yawn, did you? I've seen biographies that—— But let us dissemble.

I want you to consider Jacob Spraggins, Esq., after he had arrived at the seventh stage of his career. The stages meant art, first, humble origin; second, deserved promotion; third, stockholder; fourth, capitalist; fifth, trust magnate; sixth, rich malefactor; seventh, caliph; eight, x. The eighth stage shall be left to the higher mathematics.

At fifty-five Jacob retired from active business. The income of a czar was still rolling in on him from coal, iron, real estate, oil, railroads, manufactories, and corporations, but none of it touched Jacob's hands in a raw state. It was a sterilized increment, carefully cleaned and dusted and fumigated until it arrived at its ultimate stage of untainted, spotless checks in the white fingers of his private secretary. Jacob built a three-million-dollar palace on a corner lot fronting on Nabob Avenue, city of New Bagdad, and began to feel the mantle of the late H. A. Rashid descending upon him. Eventually Jacob slipped the mantle under his collar, tied it in a neat four-in-hand, and became a licensed harrier of our Mesopotamian proletariat.

When a man's income becomes so large that the butcher actually sends him the kind of steak he orders he begins to think about his soul's salvation. Now, the various stages or classes of rich men must not be forgotten. The capitalist can tell you to a dollar the amount of his wealth. The trust magnate "estimates" it. The rich malefactor hands you a cigar and denies that he has bought the P. D. & Q. The caliph merely smiles and talks about Hammerstein and the musical lasses. There is a record of tremendous altercation at breakfast in a "Where-to-Dine-Well" tavern between a magnate and his wife, the rift within the loot being that the wife calculated their fortune at a figure $3,000,000 higher than did her future *divorcé*. Oh, well, I, myself, heard a similar quarrel between a man and his wife because he found fifty cents less in his pockets than he thought he had. After all, we are all human—Count Tolstoi, R. Fitzsimmons, Peter Pan, and the rest of us.

Don't lose heart because the story seems to be degenerating into a sort of moral essay for intellectual readers.

There will be dialogue and stage business pretty soon.

When Jacob first began to compare the eyes of the needle with the camels in the zoo he decided upon organized charity. He had his secretary send a check for one million to the Universal Benevolent Association of the globe. You may have looked down through a grating in front of a decayed warehouse for a nickel that you had dropped through. But that is neither here nor there. The Association acknowledged receipt of his favor of the 24th ult. with enclosure as stated. Separated by a double line, but still mighty close to the matter under the caption of "Oddities of the Day's News" in an evening paper, Jacob Spraggins read that one "Jasper Spargyous" had "donated $100,000 to the U. B. A. of G." A camel may have a stomach for each day in the week; but I dare not venture to accord him whiskers, for fear of the Great Displeasure at Washington; but if he have whiskers, surely not one of them will seem to have been inserted in the eye of a needle by that effort of that rich man to enter the K. of H. The right is reserved to reject any and all bids; signed, S. Peter, secretary and gatekeeper.

Next, Jacob selected the best endowed college he could scare up and presented it with a $200,000 laboratory. The college did not maintain a scientific course, but it accepted the money and built an elaborate lavatory instead, which was no diversion of funds so far as Jacob ever discovered.

The faculty met and invited Jacob to come over and take his A B C degree. Before sending the invitations they smiled, cut out the C, added the proper punctuation marks, and all was well.

While walking on the campus before being capped and gowned, Jacob saw two professors strolling near by. Their voices, long adapted to indoor acoustics, undesignedly reached his ear.

"There goes the latest *chevalier d'industrie*," said one of them, "to buy a sleeping powder from us. He gets his degree to-morrow."

"*In foro conscientiæ*," said the other. "Let's 'eave 'arf a brick at 'im."

Jacob ignored the Latin, but the brick pleasantry was not too hard for him. There was no mandragora in the honorary draught of learning that he had bought. That was before the passage of the Pure Food and Drugs Act.

Jacob wearied of philanthropy on a large scale.

"If I could see folks made happier," he said to himself—"If I could see 'em myself and hear 'em express their gratitude for what I done for 'em it would make me feel better. This donatin' funds to institutions and societies is about as satisfactory as dropping money into a broken slot machine."

So Jacob followed his nose, which led him through unswept streets to the homes of the poorest.

"The very thing!" said Jacob. "I will charter two river steamboats, pack them full of these unfortunate children and—say ten thousand dolls and drums and a thousand freezers of ice cream, and give them a delightful outing up the Sound. The sea breezes on that trip ought to blow the taint off some of this money that keeps coming in faster than I can work it off my mind."

Jacob must have leaked some of his benevolent intentions, for an immense person with a bald face and a mouth that looked as if it ought to have a "Drop Letters Here" sign over it hooked a finger around him and set him in a space between a barber's pole and a stack of ash cans. Words came out of the postoffice slit—smooth, husky words with gloves on 'em, but sounding as if they might turn to bare knuckles any moment.

"Say, Sport, do you know where you are at? Well, dis is Mike O'Grady's district you're buttin' into—see? Mike's got de stomach-ache privilege for every kid in dis neighborhood—see? And if dere's any picnics or red balloons to be dealt out here, Mike's money pays for 'em—see? Don't you butt in, or something'll be handed to you. Youse d—— settlers and reformers with your social ologies and your millionaire detectives have got dis district in a hell of a fix, anyhow. With your college students and professors rough-housing de sodawater stands and dem rubber-neck coaches fillin' de streets, de folks down here are 'fraid to go out of de houses. Now, you leave 'em to Mike. Dey belongs to him, and he knows how to handle 'em. Keep on your own side of de town. Are you some wiser now, uncle, or do you want to scrap wit' Mike O'Grady for de Santa Claus belt in dis district?"

Clearly, that spot in the moral vineyard was preëmpted. So Caliph

Spraggins menaced no more the people in the bazaars of the East Side. To keep down his growing surplus he doubled his donations to organized charity, presented the Y. M. C. A. of his native town with a $10,000 collection of butterflies, and sent a check to the famine sufferers in China big enough to buy new emerald eyes and diamond-filled teeth for all their gods. But none of these charitable acts seemed to bring peace to the caliph's heart. He tried to get a personal note into his benefactions by tipping bellboys and waiters $10 and $20 bills. He got well snickered at and derided for that by the minions who accept with respect gratuities commensurate to the service performed. He sought out an ambitious and talented but poor young woman, and bought for her the star part in a new comedy. He might have gotten rid of $50,000 more of his cumbersome money in this philanthropy if he had not neglected to write letters to her. But she lost the suit for lack of evidence, while his capital still kept piling up, and his *optikos needleorum camelibus*—or rich man's disease—was unrelieved.

In Caliph Spraggins's $3,000,000 home lived his sister Henrietta, who used to cook for the coal miners in a twenty-five-cent eating house in Coketown, Pa., and who now would have offered John Mitchell only two fingers of her hand to shake. And his daughter Celia, nineteen, back from boarding-school and from being polished off by private instructors in the restaurant languages and those études and things.

Celia is the heroine. Lest the artist's delineation of her charms on this very page humbug your fancy, take from me her authorized description. She was a nice-looking, awkward, loud, rather bashful, brown-haired girl, with a sallow complexion, bright eyes, and a perpetual smile. She had a wholesome, Spraggins-inherited love for plain food, loose clothing, and the society of the lower classes. She had too much health and youth to feel the burden of wealth. She had a wide mouth that kept the peppermint-pepsin tablets rattling like hail from the slot-machine wherever she went, and she could whistle hornpipes. Keep this picture in mind; and let the artist do his worst.

Celia looked out of her window one day and gave her heart to the grocer's young man. The receiver thereof was at that moment engaged in conceding immortality to his horse and calling down upon him the ultimate fate of the wicked; so he did not notice the transfer. A horse should stand still when you are lifting a crate of strictly new-laid eggs out of the wagon.

Young lady reader, you would have liked that grocer's young man yourself. But you wouldn't have given him your heart, because you are saving it for a riding-master, or a shoe-manufacturer with a torpid liver, or something quiet but rich in gray tweeds at Palm Beach. Oh, I know about it. So I am glad the grocer's young man was for Celia, and not for you.

The grocer's young man was slim and straight and as confident and easy in his movements as the man in the back of the magazines who wears the new frictionless roller suspenders. He wore a gray bicycle cap on the back of his head, and his hair was straw-colored and curly, and his sunburned face looked like one that smiled a good deal when he was not preaching the doctrine of everlasting punishment to delivery-wagon horses. He slung imported A1 fancy groceries about as though they were only the stuff he delivered at boarding-houses; and when he picked up his whip, your mind instantly recalled Mr. Tackett and his air with the buttonless foils.

Tradesmen delivered their goods at a side gate at the rear of the house. The grocer's wagon came about ten in the morning. For three days Celia watched the driver when he came, finding something new each time to admire in the lofty and almost contemptuous way he had of tossing around the choicest gifts of Pomona, Ceres, and the canning factories. Then she consulted Annette.

To be explicit, Annette McCorkle, the second housemaid who deserves a paragraph herself. Annette Fletcherized large numbers of romantic novels which she obtained at a free public library branch (donated by one of the biggest caliphs in the business). She was Celia's sidekicker and chum, though Aunt Henrietta didn't know it, you may hazard a bean or two.

"Oh, canary-bird seed!" exclaimed Annette. "Ain't it a corkin' situation? You a heiress, and fallin' in love with him on sight! He's a sweet boy, too, and above his business. But he ain't suspectible like the common run of grocers' assistants. He never pays no attention to me."

"He will to me," said Celia.

"Riches——" began Annette, unsheathing the not unjustifiable feminine sting.

"Oh, you're not so beautiful," said Celia, with her wide, disarming smile. "Neither am I; but he shan't know that there's any money mixed up with my looks, such as they are. That's fair. Now, I want you to lend me one of your caps and an apron, Annette."

"Oh, marshmallows!" cried Annette. "I see. Ain't it lovely? It's just like 'Lurline, the Left-Handed; or, A Buttonhole Maker's Wrongs.' I'll bet he'll turn out to be a count."

There was a long hallway (or "passageway," as they call it in the land of the Colonels) with one side latticed, running along the rear of the house. The grocer's young man went through this to deliver his goods. One morning he passed a girl in there with shining eyes, sallow complexion, and wide, smiling mouth, wearing a maid's cap and apron. But as he was cumbered with a basket of Early Drumhead lettuce and Trophy tomatoes and three bunches of asparagus and six bottles of the most expensive Queen olives, he saw no more than that she was one of the maids.

But on his way out he came up behind her, and she was whistling "Fisher's Hornpipe" so loudly and clearly that all the piccolos in the world should have disjointed themselves and crept into their cases for shame.

The grocer's young man stopped and pushed back his cap until it hung on his collar button behind.

"That's out o' sight, Kid," said he.

"My name is Celia, if you please," said the whistler, dazzling him with a three-inch smile.

"That's all right. I'm Thomas McCleod. What part of the house do you work in?"

"I'm the—the second parlor maid."

"Do you know the 'Falling Waters'?"

"No," said Celia, "we don't know anybody. We got rich too quick—that is, Mr. Spraggins did."

"I'll make you acquainted," said Thomas McCleod. "It's a strathspey—a first cousin to a hornpipe."

If Celia's whistling put the piccolos out of commission, Thomas Mc-Cleod's surely made the biggest flutes hunt their holes. He could actually whistle *bass*.

When he stopped Celia was ready to jump into his delivery wagon and ride with him clear to the end of the pier and on to the ferryboat of the Charon line.

"I'll be around to-morrow at 10:15," said Thomas, "with some spinach and a case of carbonic."

"I'll practice that what-you-may-call-it," said Celia. "I can whistle a fine second."

The processes of courtship are personal, and do not belong to general literature. They should be chronicled in detail only in advertisements of iron tonics and in the secret by-laws of the Woman's Auxiliary of the Ancient Order of the Rat Trap. But genteel writing may contain a description of certain stages of its progress without intruding upon the province of the X-ray or of park policemen.

A day came when Thomas McCleod and Celia lingered at the end of the latticed "passage."

"Sixteen a week isn't much," said Thomas, letting his cap rest on his shoulder blades.

Celia looked through the lattice-work and whistled a dead march. Shopping with Aunt Henrietta the day before, she had paid that much for a dozen handkerchiefs.

"Maybe I'll get a raise next month," said Thomas. "I'll be around to-morrow at the same time with a bag of flour and the laundry soap."

"All right," said Celia. "Annette's married cousin pays only $20 a month for a flat in the Bronx."

Never for a moment did she count on the Spraggins money. She knew Aunt Henrietta's invincible pride of caste and pa's mightiness as a Colossus of cash, and she understood that if she chose Thomas she and her grocer's young man might go whistle for their living.

Another day came, Thomas violating the dignity of Nabob Avenue with "The Devil's Dream," whistled keenly between his teeth.

"Raised to eighteen a week yesterday," he said. "Been pricing flats around Morningside. You want to start untying those apron strings and unpinning that cap, old girl."

"Oh, Tommy!" said Celia, with her broadest smile. "Won't that be enough? I got Betty to show me how to make a cottage pudding. I guess we could call it a flat pudding if we wanted to."

"And tell no lie," said Thomas.

"And I can sweep and polish and dust—of course, a parlor maid learns that. And we could whistle duets of evenings."

"The old man said he'd raise me to twenty at Christmas if Bryan couldn't think of any harder name to call a Republican than a 'postponer,'" said the grocer's young man.

"I can sew," said Celia; "and I know that you must make the gas company's man show his badge when he comes to look at the meter; and I know how to put up quince jam and window curtains."

"Bully! you're all right, Cele. Yes, I believe we can pull it off on eighteen."

As he was jumping into the wagon the second parlor maid braved discovery by running swiftly to the gate.

"And, oh, Tommy, I forgot," she called, softly, "I believe I could make your neckties."

"Forget it," said Thomas, decisively.

"And another thing," she continued. "Sliced cucumbers at night will drive away cockroaches."

"And sleep, too, you bet," said Mr. McCleod. "Yes, I believe if I have a delivery to make on the West Side this afternoon I'll look in at a furniture store I know over there."

It was just as the wagon dashed away that old Jacob Spraggins struck the sideboard with his fist and made the mysterious remark about ten thousand dollars that you perhaps remember. Which justifies the reflection that some stories, as well as life, and puppies thrown into wells, move around in circles. Painfully but briefly we must shed light on Jacob's words.

The foundation of his fortune was made when he was twenty. A poor coal-digger (ever hear of a rich one?) had saved a dollar or two and bought a small tract of land on a hillside on which he tried to raise corn. Not a nubbin. Jacob, whose nose was a divining-rod, told him there was a vein of coal beneath. He bought the land from the miner for $125 and sold it a month afterward for $10,000. Luckily the miner had enough left of his sale money to drink himself into a black coat opening in the back, as soon as he heard the news.

And so, forty years afterward, we find Jacob illuminated with the sudden thought that if he could make restitution of this sum of money to the heirs or assigns of the unlucky miner, respite and Nepenthe might be his.

And now must come swift action, for we have here some four thousand words and not a tear shed and never a pistol, joke, safe, nor bottle cracked.

Old Jacob hired a dozen private detectives to find the heirs, if any existed, of the old miner, Hugh McLeod.

Get the point? Of course I know as well as you do that Thomas is going to be the heir. I might have concealed the name; but why always hold back your mystery till the end? I say, let it come near the middle so people can stop reading there if they want to.

After the detectives had trailed false clues about three thousand dollars —I mean miles—they cornered Thomas at the grocery and got his confession that Hugh McLeod had been his grandfather, and that there were no other heirs. They arranged a meeting for him and old Jacob one morning in one of their offices.

Jacob liked the young man very much. He liked the way he looked straight at him when he talked, and the way he threw his bicycle cap over the top of a rose-colored vase on the centre-table.

There was a slight flaw in Jacob's system of restitution. He did not consider that the act, to be perfect, should include confession. So he represented himself to be the agent of the purchaser of the land who had sent him to refund the sale price for the ease of his conscience.

"Well, sir," said Thomas, "this sounds to me like an illustrated postcard from South Boston with 'We're having a good time here' written on it. I don't know the game. Is this ten thousand dollars money, or do I have to save so many coupons to get it?"

Old Jacob counted out to him twenty five-hundred-dollar bills.

That was better, he thought, than a check. Thomas put them thoughtfully into his pocket.

"Grandfather's best thanks," he said, "to the party who sends it."

Jacob talked on, asking him about his work, how he spent his leisure time, and what his ambitions were. The more he saw and heard of Thomas, the better he liked him. He had not met many young men in Bagdad so frank and wholesome.

"I would like to have you visit my house," he said. "I might help you in investing or laying out your money. I am a very wealthy man. I have a daughter about grown, and I would like for you to know her. There are not many young men I would care to have call on her."

"I'm obliged," said Thomas. "I'm not much at making calls. It's generally the side entrance for mine. And, besides, I'm engaged to a girl that has the Delaware peach crop killed in the blossom. She's a parlor maid in a house where I deliver goods. She won't be working there much longer, though. Say, don't forget to give your friend my grandfather's best regards. You'll excuse me now; my wagon's outside with a lot of green stuff that's got to be delivered. See you again, sir."

At eleven Thomas delivered some bunches of parsley and lettuce at the Spraggins mansion. Thomas was only twenty-two; so, as he came back, he took out the handful of five-hundred-dollar bills and waved them carelessly. Annette took a pair of eyes as big as creamed onions to the cook.

"I told you he was a count," she said, after relating. "He never would carry on with me."

"But you say he showed money," said the cook.

"Hundreds of thousands," said Annette. "Carried around loose in his pockets. And he never would look at me."

"It was paid to me to-day," Thomas was explaining to Celia outside. "It came from my grandfather's estate. Say, Cele, what's the use of waiting now? I'm going to quit the job to-night. Why can't we get married next week?"

"Tommy," said Celia, "I'm no parlor maid. I've been fooling you. I'm Miss Spraggins—Celia Spraggins. The newspapers say I'll be worth forty million dollars some day."

Thomas pulled his cap down straight on his head for the first time since we have known him.

"I suppose then," said he, "I suppose then you'll not be marrying me next week. But you *can* whistle."

"No," said Celia, "I'll not be marrying you next week. My father would never let me marry a grocer's clerk. But I'll marry you to-night, Tommy, if you say so."

Old Jacob Spraggins came home at 9:30 P.M., in his motor car. The make of it you will have to surmise sorrowfully; I am giving you unsubsidized fiction; had it been a street car I could have told you its voltage and the number of flat wheels it had. Jacob called for his daughter; he had bought a ruby necklace for her, and wanted to hear her say what a kind, thoughtful, dear old dad he was.

There was a brief search in the house for her, and then came Annette, glowing with the pure flame of truth and loyalty well mixed with envy and histrionics.

"Oh, sir," said she, wondering if she should kneel, "Miss Celia's just this minute running away out of the side gate with a young man to be married. I couldn't stop her, sir. They went in a cab."

"What young man?" roared old Jacob.

"A millionaire, if you please, sir—a rich nobleman in disguise. He carries his money with him, and the red peppers and the onions was only to blind us, sir. He never did seem to take to me."

Jacob rushed out in time to catch his car. The chauffeur had been delayed by trying to light a cigarette in the wind.

"Here, Gaston, or Mike, or whatever you call yourself, scoot around the corner quicker than blazes and see if you can see a cab. If you do, run it down."

There was a cab in sight a block away. Gaston, or Mike, with his eyes half shut and his mind on his cigarette, picked up the trail, neatly crowded the cab to the curb, and pocketed it.

"What t'ell you doin'?" yelled the cabman.

"Pa!" shrieked Celia.

"Grandfather's remorseful friend's agent!" said Thomas. "Wonder what's on his conscience now."

"A thousand thunders!" said Gaston, or Mike. "I have no other match."

"Young man," said old Jacob, severely, "how about that parlor maid you were engaged to?"

A couple of years afterward old Jacob went into the office of his private secretary.

"The amalgamated Missionary Society solicits a contribution of $30,000 toward the conversion of the Koreans," said the secretary.

"Pass 'em up," said Jacob.

"The University of Plumville writes that its yearly endowment fund of $50,000 that you bestowed upon it is past due."

"Tell 'em it's been cut out."

"The Scientific Society of Clam Cove, Long Island, asks for $10,000 to buy alcohol to preserve specimens."

"Waste basket."

"The Society for Providing Healthful Recreation for Working Girls wants $20,000 from you to lay out a golf course."

"Tell 'em to see an undertaker."

"Cut 'em all out," went on Jacob. "I've quit being a good thing. I need every dollar I can scrape or save. I want you to write to the directors of every company that I'm interested in and recommend a 10 per cent. cut in salaries. And say—I noticed half a cake of soap lying in a corner of the hall as I came in. I want you to speak to the scrub-woman about waste. I've got no money to throw away. And say—we've got vinegar pretty well in hand, haven't we?"

"The Globe Spice & Seasons Company," said the secretary, "controls the market at present."

"Raise vinegar two cents a gallon. Notify all our branches."

Suddenly Jacob Spraggins's plump red face relaxed into a pulpy grin.

He walked over to the secretary's desk and showed a small red mark on his thick forefinger.

"Bit it," he said, "darned if he didn't, and he ain't had the tooth three weeks—Jaky McLeod, my Celia's kid. He'll be worth a hundred millions by the time he is twenty-one if I can pile it up for him."

As he was leaving, old Jacob turned at the door, and said:

"Better make that vinegar raise three cents instead of two. I'll be back in an hour and sign the letters."

The true history of the Caliph Harun Al Rashid relates that toward the end of his reign he wearied of philanthropy, and caused to be beheaded all his former favorites and companions of his "Arabian Nights" rambles. Happy are we in these days of enlightenment when the only death warrant the caliphs can serve on us is in the form of a trademan's bill.

THE GIRL AND THE HABIT

Habit—a tendency or aptitude acquired by custom or frequent repetition.

The critics have assailed every source of inspiration save one. To that one we are driven for our moral theme. When we levied upon the masters of old they gleefully dug up the parallels to our columns. When we strove to set forth real life they reproached us for trying to imitate Henry George, George Washington, Washington Irving, and Irving Bacheller. We wrote of the West and the East, and they accused us of both Jesse and Henry James. We wrote from our heart—and they said something about a disordered liver. We took a text from Matthew or—er—yes, Deuteronomy, but the preachers were hammering away at the inspiration idea before we could get into type. So, driven to the wall, we go for our subject-matter to the reliable, old, moral, unassailable vade mecum—the unabridged dictionary.

Miss Merriam was cashier at Hinkle's. Hinkle's is one of the big downtown restaurants. It is in what the papers call the "financial district." Each day from 10 o'clock to 2 Hinkle's was full of hungry customers—messenger boys, stenographers, brokers, owners of mining stock, promoters, inventors with patents pending—and also people with money.

The cashiership at Hinkle's was no sinecure. Hinkle egged and toasted and griddle-caked and coffeed a good many customers; and he lunched (as good a word as "dined") many more. It might be said that Hinkle's breakfast crowd was a contingent, but his luncheon patronage amounted to a horde.

Miss Merriam sat at a stool at her desk inclosed on three sides by a strong, high fencing of woven brass wire. Through an arched opening at the bottom you thrust your waiter's check and the money, while your heart went pit-a-pat.

For Miss Merriam was lovely and capable. She could take 45 cents out of a $2 bill and refuse an offer of marriage before you could—— Next! —lost your chance—please don't shove. She could keep cool and collected while she collected your check, give you the correct change, win your heart, indicate the toothpick stand, and rate you to a quarter of a cent better than Bradstreet could do a thousand in less time than it takes to pepper an egg with one of Hinkle's casters.

There is an old and dignified allusion to the "fierce light that beats upon a throne." The light that beats upon the young lady cashier's cage is also something fierce. The other fellow is responsible for the slang.

Every male patron of Hinkle's from the A. D. T. boys up to the curbstone brokers, adored Miss Merriam. When they paid their checks they wooed her with every wile known to Cupid's art. Between the meshes of the brass railing went smiles, winks, compliments, tender vows, invitations to dinner, sighs, languishing looks, and merry banter that was wafted pointedly back by the gifted Miss Merriam.

There is no coign of vantage more effective than the position of young lady cashier. She sits there, easily queen of the court of commerce; she is duchess of dollars and devoirs, countess of compliments and coin, leading lady of love and luncheon. You take from her a smile and a Canadian dime, and you go your way uncomplaining. You count the cheery word or two that she tosses you as misers count their treasures; and you pocket the change for a five uncomputed. Perhaps the brass-bound inaccessibility multiplies her charms—anyhow, she is a shirt-waisted angel, immaculate, trim, manicured, seductive, bright-eyed, ready, alert—Psyche, Circe, and Ate in one, separating you from your circulating medium after your sirloin medium.

The young men who broke bread at Hinkle's never settle with the cashier without an exchange of badinage and open compliment. Many of them went to greater lengths and dropped promissory hints of theatre tickets and chocolates. The older men spoke plainly of orange blossoms, generally withering the tentative petals by after-allusions to Harlem flats. One broker, who had been squeezed by copper, proposed to Miss Merriam more regularly than he ate.

During a brisk luncheon hour Miss Merriam's conversation, while she took money for checks, would run something like this:

"Good morning, Mr. Haskins—sir?—it's natural, thank you—don't be quite so fresh . . . Hello, Johnny—ten, fifteen, twenty—chase along now or they'll take the letters off your cap . . . Beg pardon—count it again, please—Oh, don't mention it . . . Vaudeville?—thanks; not on your moving picture—I was to see Carter in Hedda Gabler on Wednesday night with Mr. Simmons . . . 'Scuse me, I thought that was a quarter . . . Twenty-five and seventy-five's a dollar—got that ham-and-cabbage habit yet. I see, Billy . . . Who are you addressing?—say—you'll get all that's coming to you in a minute . . . Oh, fudge! Mr. Bassett—you're always fooling—no—? Well, maybe I'll marry you some day—three, four, and sixty-five is five . . . Kindly keep them remarks to yourself if you please . . . Ten cents?—'scuse me; the check calls for seventy—well, maybe it is a one instead of a seven . . . Oh, do you like it that way, Mr. Saunders? —some prefer a pomp; but they say this Cleo de Merody does suit re-fined features . . . and ten is fifty . . . Hike along there, buddy; don't take this for a Coney Island ticket booth . . . Huh?—why, Macy's—don't it fit nice? Oh, no, it isn't too cool—these light-weight fabrics is all the go this season . . . Come again, please—that's the third time you've tried to—what?—forget it—that lead quarter is an old friend of mine . . . Sixty-five—must have had your salary raised, Mr. Wilson . . . I seen you on Sixth Avenue Tuesday afternoon, Mr. De Forest—swell?—oh, my!— who is she? . . . What's the matter with it?—why, it ain't money—what? —Columbian half?—well, this ain't South America . . . Yes, I like the mixed best—Friday?—awfully sorry, but I take my jiu-jitsu lesson on Fri-day—Thursday, then . . . Thanks—that's sixteen times I've been told that this morning—I guess I must be beautiful . . . Cut that out, please— who do you think I am? . . . Why, Mr. Westbrook—do you really think so?—the idea!—one—eighty and twenty's a dollar—thank you ever so much; but I don't ever go automobile riding with gentlemen—your aunt? —well, that's different—perhaps . . . Please don't get fresh—your check was fifteen cents, I believe—kindly step aside and let . . . Hello, Ben— coming around Thursday evening?—there's a gentleman going to send around a box of chocolates, and . . . forty and sixty is a dollar, and one is two . . ."

About the middle of one afternoon the dizzy goddess Vertigo—whose other name is Fortune—suddenly smote an old, wealthy, and eccentric banker while he was walking past Hinkle's, on his way to a street car. A wealthy and eccentric banker who rides in street cars is—move up, please; there are others.

A Samaritan, a Pharisee, a man and a policeman who were first on the spot lifted Banker McRamsey and carried him into Hinkle's restaurant. When the aged but indestructible banker opened his eyes he saw a beau-tiful vision bending over him with a pitiful, tender smile, bathing his forehead with beef tea and chafing his hands with something frappé out of a chafing-dish. Mr. McRamsey sighed, lost a vest button, gazed with deep gratitude upon his fair preserveress, and then recovered con-sciousness.

To the Seaside Library all who are anticipating a romance! Banker

McRamsey had an aged and respected wife, and his sentiments toward Miss Merriam were fatherly. He talked to her for half an hour with interest—not the kind that went with his talks during business hours. The next day he brought Mrs. Ramsey down to see her. The old couple were childless—they had only a married daughter living in Brooklyn.

To make a short story shorter, the beautiful cashier won the hearts of the good old couple. They came to Hinkle's again and again; they invited her to their old-fashioned but splendid home in one of the East Seventies. Miss Merriam's winning loveliness, her sweet frankness and impulsive heart took them by storm. They said a hundred times that Miss Merriam reminded them so much of their lost daughter. The Brooklyn matron, née McRamsey, had the figure of Buddha and a face like the ideal of an art photographer. Miss Merriam was a combination of curves, smiles, rose leaves, pearls, satin, and hair-tonic posters. Enough of the fatuity of parents.

A month after the worthy couple became acquainted with Miss Merriam, she stood before Hinkle one afternoon and resigned her cashiership.

"They're going to adopt me," she told the bereft restaurateur. "They're funny old people, but regular dears. And the swell home they have got! Say, Hinkle, there isn't any use of talking—I'm on the à la carte to wear brown duds and goggles in a whiz wagon, or marry a duke at least. Still, I somehow hate to break out of the old cage. I've been cashiering so long I feel funny doing anything else. I'll miss joshing the fellows awfully when they line up to pay for the buckwheats and. But I can't let this chance slide. And they're awfully good, Hinkle; I know I'll have a swell time. You owe me nine-sixty-two and a half for the week. Cut out the half if it hurts you, Hinkle."

And they did. Miss Merriam became Miss Rosa McRamsey. And she graced the transition. Beauty is only skin-deep, but the nerves lie very near to the skin. Nerve—but just here will you oblige by perusing again the quotation with which this story begins?

The McRamseys poured out money like domestic champagne to polish their adopted one. Milliners, dancing masters, and private tutors got it. Miss—er—McRamsey was grateful, loving, and tried to forget Hinkle's. To give ample credit to the adaptability of the American girl, Hinkle's did fade from her memory and speech most of the time.

Not every one will remember when the Earl of Hitesbury came to East Seventy—— Street, America. He was only a fair-to-medium earl, without debts, and he created little excitement. But you will surely remember the evening when the Daughters of Benevolence held their bazaar in the W——f-A——a Hotel. For you were there, and you wrote a note to Fannie on the hotel paper, and mailed it, just to show her that—you did not? Very well; that was the evening the baby was sick, of course.

At the Bazaar the McRamseys were prominent. Miss Mer—er—Mc-Ramsey was exquisitely beautiful. The Earl of Hitesbury had been very attentive to her since he dropped in to have a look at America. At the charity bazaar the affair was supposed to be going to be pulled off to a finish. An earl is as good as a duke. Better. His standing may be lower, but his outstanding accounts are also lower.

Our ex-young-lady-cashier was assigned to a booth. She was expected to sell worthless articles to nobs and snobs at exorbitant prices. The proceeds of the bazaar were to be used for giving to the poor children of the slums a Christmas din—— Say! did you ever wonder where they get the other 364?

Miss McRamsey—beautiful, palpitating, excited, charming, radiant—fluttered about in her booth. An imitation brass network, with a little arched opening, fenced her in.

Along came the Earl, assured, delicate, accurate, admiring—admiring greatly, and faced the open wicket.

"You look chawming, you know—'pon my word you do—my deah," he said, beguilingly.

Miss McRamsey whirled around.

"Cut that joshing out," she said, coolly and briskly. "Who do you think you are talking to? Your check, please. Oh, Lordy!——"

Patrons of the bazaar became aware of a commotion and pressed around a certain booth. The Earl of Hitesbury stood near by pulling a pale blond and puzzled whisker.

"Miss McRamsey has fainted," some one explained.

PROOF OF THE PUDDING

Spring winked a vitreous optic at Editor Westbrook of the *Minerva Magazine,* and deflected him from his course. He had lunched in his favorite corner of a Broadway hotel, and was returning to his office when his feet became entangled in the lure of the vernal coquette. Which is by way of saying that he turned eastward in Twenty-sixth Street, safely forded the spring freshet of vehicles in Fifth Avenue, and meandered along the walks of budding Madison Square.

The lenient air and the settings of the little park almost formed a pastorale, the color motif was green—the presiding shade at the creation of man and vegetation.

The callow grass between the walks was the color of verdigris, a poisonous green, reminiscent of the horde of derelict humans that had breathed upon the soil during the summer and autumn. The bursting tree buds looked strangely familiar to those who had botanized among the garnishings of the fish course of a forty-cent dinner. The sky above was of that pale aquamarine tint that hall-room poets rhyme with "true" and "Sue" and "coo." The one natural and frank color visible was the ostensible green of the newly painted benches—a shade between the color of a pickled cucumber and that of a last year's fast-black cravenette raincoat. But, to the city-bred eye of Editor Westbrook, the landscape appeared a masterpiece.

And now, whether you are of those who rush in, or of the gentle concourse that fears to tread, you must follow in a brief invasion of the editor's mind.

Editor Westbrook's spirit was contented and serene. The April number of the *Minerva* had sold its entire edition before the tenth day of the month—a newsdealer in Keokuk had written that he could have sold fifty copies more if he had had 'em. The owners of the magazine had raised his (the editor's) salary; he had just installed in his home a jewel of a recently imported cook who was afraid of policemen; and the morning papers had published in full a speech he had made at a publishers' banquet. Also there were echoing in his mind the jubilant notes of a splendid song that his charming young wife had sung to him before he left his up-town apartment that morning. She was taking enthusiastic interest in her music of late, practising early and diligently. When he had complimented her on the improvement in her voice she had fairly hugged him for joy at his praise. He felt, too, the benign, tonic medicament of the trained nurse, Spring, tripping softly adown the wards of the convalescent city.

While Editor Westbrook was sauntering between the rows of park benches (already filling with vagrants and the guardians of lawless childhood) he felt his sleeve grasped and held. Suspecting that he was about to be panhandled, he turned a cold and unprofitable face, and saw that his captor was—Dawe—Shackleford Dawe, dingy, almost ragged, the genteel scarcely visible in him through the deeper lines of the shabby.

While the editor is pulling himself out of his surprise a flashlight biography of Dawe is offered.

He was a fiction writer and one of Westbrook's old acquaintances. At one time they might have called each other old friends. Dawe had some money in those days, and lived in a decent apartment house near Westbrook's. The two families often went to theatres and dinners together. Mrs. Dawe and Mrs. Westbrook became "dearest" friends. Then one day a little tentacle of the octopus, just to amuse itself, ingurgitated Dawe's capital, and he moved to the Gramercy Park neighborhood where one, for a few groats per week, may sit upon one's trunk under eight-branched chandeliers and opposite Carrara marble mantels and watch the mice play upon the floor. Dawe thought to live by writing fiction. Now and then he sold a story. He submitted many to Westbrook. The *Minerva* printed one or two of them; the rest were returned. Westbrook sent a careful and conscientious personal letter with each rejected manuscript, pointing out in detail his reasons for considering it unavailable. Editor Westbrook had his own clear conception of what constituted good fiction. So had Dawe. Mrs. Dawe was mainly concerned about the constituents of the scanty dishes of food that she managed to scrape together. One day Dawe had been spouting to her about the excellencies of certain French writers. At dinner they sat down to a dish that a hungry school-boy could have encompassed at a gulp. Dawe commented.

"It's Maupassant hash," said Mrs. Dawe. "It may not be art, but I do wish you would do a five-course Marion Crawford serial with an Ella Wheeler Wilcox sonnet for dessert. I'm hungry."

As far as this from success was Shackleford Dawe when he plucked Editor Westbrook's sleeve in Madison Square. That was the first time the editor had seen Dawe in several months.

"Why, Shack, is this you?" said Westbrook, somewhat awkwardly, for the form of his phrase seemed to touch upon the other's changed appearance.

"Sit down for a minute," said Dawe, tugging at his sleeve. "This is my office. I can't come to yours, looking as I do. Oh, sit down—you won't be disgraced. Those half-plucked birds on the other benches will take you for a swell porch-climber. They won't know you are only an editor."

"Smoke, Shack?" said Editor Westbrook, sinking cautiously upon the virulent green bench. He always yielded gracefully when he did yield.

Dawe snapped at the cigar as a kingfisher darts at a sunperch, or a girl pecks at a chocolate cream.

"I have just——" began the editor.

"Oh, I know; don't finish," said Dawe. "Give me a match. You have just ten minutes to spare. How did you manage to get past my office-boy and invade my sanctum? There he goes now, throwing his club at a dog that couldn't read the 'Keep off the Grass' signs."

"How goes the writing?" asked the editor.

"Look at me," said Dawe, "for your answer. Now don't put on that embarrassed, friendly-but-honest look and ask me why I don't get a job as a wine agent or a cab driver. I'm in the fight to a finish. I know I can write good fiction and I'll force you fellows to admit it yet. I'll make you change the spelling of 'regrets' to 'c-h-e-q-u-e' before I'm done with you."

Editor Westbrook gazed through his noseglasses with a sweetly sorrowful, omniscient, sympathetic, skeptical expression—the copyrighted expression of the editor beleaguered by the unavailable contributor.

"Have you read the last story I sent you—'The Alarum of the Soul'?" asked Dawe.

"Carefully. I hesitated over that story, Shack, really I did. It had some good points. I was writing you a letter to send with it when it goes back to you. I regret——"

"Never mind the regrets," said Dawe, grimly. "There's neither salve nor sting in 'em any more. What I want to know is *why*. Come, now; out with the good points first."

"The story," said Westbrook, deliberately, after a suppressed sigh, "is written around an almost original plot. Characterization—the best you have done. Construction—almost as good, except for a few weak joints which might be strengthened by a few changes and touches. It was a good story, except——"

"I can write English, can't I?" interrupted Dawe.

"I have always told you," said the editor, "that you had a style."

"Then the trouble is the——"

"Same old thing," said Editor Westbrook. "You work up to your climax like an artist. And then you turn yourself into a photographer. I don't know what form of obstinate madness possesses you, Shack, but that is what you do with everything that you write. No. I will retract the comparison with the photographer. Now and then photography, in spite of its impossible perspective, manages to record a fleeting glimpse of truth. But you spoil every dénouement by those flat, drab, obliterating strokes of your brush that I have so often complained of. If you would rise to the literary pinnacle of your dramatic scenes, and paint them in the high colors that art requires, the postman would leave fewer bulky, self-addressed envelopes at your door."

"Oh, fiddles and footlights!" cried Dawe, derisively. "You've got that old sawmill drama king in your brain yet. When the man with the black mustache kidnaps golden-haired Bessie you are bound to have the mother kneel and raise her hands in the spotlight and say: 'May high heaven witness that I will rest neither night nor day till the heartless villain that has stolen me child feels the weight of a mother's vengeance!'"

Editor Westbrook conceded a smile of impervious complacency.

"I think," said he, "that in real life the woman would express herself in those words or in very similar ones."

"Not in a six hundred nights' run anywhere but on the stage," said Dawe, hotly. "I'll tell you what she'd say in real life. She'd say: 'What! Bessie led away by a strange man? Good Lord! It's one trouble after another! Get my other hat, I must hurry around to the police-station. Why wasn't somebody looking after her, I'd like to know? For God's sake, get out of my way or I'll never get ready. Not that hat—the brown one with the velvet bows. Bessie must have been crazy; she's usually shy of strangers. Is that too much powder? Lordy! How I'm upset!'

"That's the way she'd talk," continued Dawe. "People in real life don't fly into heroics and blank verse at emotional crises. They simply can't do it. If they talk at all on such occasions they draw from the same vocabulary that they use every day, and muddle up their words and ideas a little more, that's all."

"Shack," said Editor Westbrook, impressively, "did you ever pick up the mangled and lifeless form of a child from under the fender of a street car, and carry it in your arms and lay it down before the distracted mother? Did you ever do that and listen to the words of grief and despair as they flowed spontaneously from her lips?"

"I never did," said Dawe. "Did you?"

"Well, no," said Editor Westbrook, with a slight frown. "But I can well imagine what she would say."

"So can I," said Dawe.

And now the fitting time had come for Editor Westbrook to play the oracle and silence his opinionated contributor. It was not for an unarrived fictionist to dictate words to be uttered by the heroes and heroines of the *Minerva Magazine,* contrary to the theories of the editor thereof.

"My dear Shack," said he, "if I know anything of life I know that every sudden, deep, and tragic emotion in the human heart calls forth an opposite, concordant, conformable, and proportionate expression of feeling. How much of this inevitable accord between expression and feeling should be attributed to nature, and how much to the influence of art, it would be difficult to say. The sublimely terrible roar of the lioness that has been deprived of her cubs is dramatically as far above her customary whine and purr as the kingly and transcendent utterances of Lear are above the level of his senile vaporings. But it is also true that all men and women have what may be called a sub-conscious dramatic sense that is awakened by a sufficiently deep and powerful emotion—a sense unconsciously acquired from literature and the stage that prompts them to express those emotions in language befitting their importance and histrionic value."

"And in the name of the seven sacred saddle-blankets of Sagittarius, where did the stage and literature get the stunt?" asked Dawe.

"From life," answered the editor, triumphantly.

The story writer rose from the bench and gesticulated eloquently but dumbly. He was beggared for words with which to formulate adequately his dissent.

On a bench near by a frowzy loafer opened his red eyes and perceived that his moral support was due a downtrodden brother.

"Punch him one, Jack," he called hoarsely to Dawe. "W'at's he come makin' a noise like a penny arcade for amongst gen'lemen that comes in the Square to set and think?"

Editor Westbrook looked at his watch with an affected show of leisure.

"Tell me," asked Dawe, with truculent anxiety, "what especial faults in 'The Alarum of the Soul' caused you to throw it down?"

"When Gabriel Murray," said Westbrook, "goes to his telephone and is told that his fiancée has been shot by a burglar, he says—I do not recall the exact words, but——"

"I do," said Dawe. "He says: 'Damn Central; she always cuts me off.' (And then to his friend) 'Say, Tommy, does a thirty-two bullet make a big hole? It's kind of hard luck, ain't it? Could you get me a drink from the sideboard, Tommy? No; straight; nothing on the side.'"

"And again," continued the editor, without pausing for argument, "when Berenice opens the letter from her husband informing her that he has fled with the manicure girl, her words are—let me see——"

"She says," interposed the author: "'Well, what do you think of that!'"

"Absurdly inappropriate words," said Westbrook, "presenting an anti-climax—plunging the story into hopeless bathos. Worse yet; they mirror life falsely. No human being ever uttered banal colloquialisms when confronted by sudden tragedy."

"Wrong," said Dawe, closing his unshaven jaws doggedly. "I say no man or woman ever spouts 'high-falutin' talk when they go up against a real climax. They talk naturally and a little worse."

The editor rose from the bench with his air of indulgence and inside information.

"Say, Westbrook," said Dawe, pinning him by the lapel, "would you have accepted 'The Alarum of the Soul' if you had believed that the actions and words of the characters were true to life in the parts of the story that we discussed?"

"It is very likely that I would, if I believed that way," said the editor. "But I have explained to you that I do not."

"If I could prove to you that I am right?"

"I'm sorry, Shack, but I'm afraid I haven't time to argue any further just now."

"I don't want to argue," said Dawe. "I want to demonstrate to you from life itself that my view is the correct one."

"How could you do that?" asked Westbrook, in a surprised tone.

"Listen," said the writer, seriously. "I have thought of a way. It is important to me that my theory of true-to-life fiction be recognized as correct by the magazines. I've fought for it for three years, and I'm down to my last dollar, with two months' rent due."

"I have applied the opposite of your theory," said the editor, "in selecting the fiction for the *Minerva Magazine*. The circulation has gone up from ninety thousand to——"

"Four hundred thousand," said Dawe. "Whereas it should have been boosted to a million."

"You said something to me just now about demonstrating your pet theory."

"I will. If you'll give me about half an hour of your time I'll prove to you that I am right. I'll prove it by Louise."

"Your wife!" exclaimed Westbrook. "How?"

"Well, not exactly by her, but *with* her," said Dawe. "Now, you know how devoted and loving Louise has always been. She thinks I'm the only genuine preparation on the market that bears the old doctor's signature. She's been fonder and more faithful than ever, since I've been cast for the neglected genius part."

"Indeed, she is a charming and admirable life companion," agreed the editor. "I remember what inseparable friends she and Mrs. Westbrook once were. We are both lucky chaps, Shack, to have such wives. You must bring Mrs. Dawe up some evening soon, and we'll have one of those informal chafing-dish suppers that we used to enjoy so much."

"Later," said Dawe. "When I get another shirt. And now I'll tell you my scheme. When I was about to leave home after breakfast—if you can call tea and oatmeal breakfast—Louise told me she was going to visit her aunt in Eighty-ninth Street. She said she would return home at three o'clock. She is always on time to a minute. It is now——"

Dawe glanced toward the editor's watch pocket.

"Twenty-seven minutes to three," said Westbrook, scanning his time-piece.

"We have just enough time," said Dawe. "We will go to my flat at once. I will write a note, address it to her and leave it on the table where she will see it as she enters the door. You and I will be in the dining room concealed by the portières. In that note I'll say that I have fled from her forever with an affinity who understands the needs of my artistic soul as she never did. When she reads it we will observe her actions and hear her words. Then we will know which theory is the correct one—yours or mine."

"Oh, never!" exclaimed the editor, shaking his head. "That would be inexcusably cruel. I could not consent to have Mrs. Dawe's feelings played upon in such a manner."

"Brace up," said the writer, "I guess I think as much of her as you do. It's for her benefit as well as mine. I've got to get a market for my stories in some way. It won't hurt Louise. She's healthy and sound. Her heart goes as strong as a ninety-eight-cent watch. It'll last for only a minute, and then I'll step out and explain to her. You really owe it to me to give me the chance, Westbrook."

Editor Westbrook at length yielded, though but half willingly. And in the half of him that consented lurked the vivisectionist that is in all of us. Let him who has not used the scalpel rise and stand in his place. Pity 'tis that there are not enough rabbits and guinea-pigs to go around.

The two experimenters in Art left the Square and hurried eastward and then to the south until they arrived in the Gramercy neighborhood. Within its high iron railings the little park had put on its smart coat of vernal green, and was admiring itself in its fountain mirror. Outside the railings the hollow square of crumbling houses, shells of a bygone gentry, leaned as if in ghostly gossip over the forgotten doings of the vanished quality. *Sic transit gloria urbis.*

A block or two north of the Park, Dawe steered the editor again eastward, then, after covering a short distance, into a lofty but narrow flathouse burdened with a floridly over-decorated façade. To the fifth story they toiled, and Dawe, panting, pushed his latch-key into the door of one of the front flats.

When the door opened Editor Westbrook saw, with feelings of pity, how meanly and meagrely the rooms were furnished.

"Get a chair, if you can find one," said Dawe, "while I hunt up pen and ink. Hello, what's this? Here's a note from Louise. She must have left it there when she went out this morning."

He picked up an envelope that lay on the centre-table and tore it open. He began to read the letter that he drew out of it; and once having begun it aloud he so read it through to the end. These are the words that Editor Westbrook heard:

"Dear Shackleford:
    "By the time you get this I will be about a hundred miles away and still a-going. I've got a place in the chorus of the Occidental Opera Co., and we start on the road to-day at twelve o'clock. I didn't want to starve to death, and so I decided to make my own living. I'm not coming back. Mrs. Westbrook is going with me. She said she was tired of living with a combination phonograph, iceberg, and dictionary, and she's not coming back, either. We've been practicing the songs and dances for two months on the quiet. I hope you will be successful, and get along all right! Good-bye.
                                                    "Louise"

Dawe dropped the letter, covered his face with his trembling hands, and cried out in a deep, vibrating voice:

"My God, why hast thou given me this cup to drink? Since she is false, then let Thy Heaven's fairest gifts, faith and love, become the jesting by-words of traitors and fiends!"

Editor Westbrook's glasses fell to the floor. The fingers of one hand fumbled with a button on his coat as he blurted between his pale lips:

"Say, Shack, ain't that a hell of a note? Wouldn't that knock you off your perch, Shack? Ain't it hell, now, Shack—ain't it?"

PAST ONE AT ROONEY'S

Only on the lower East Side of New York do the houses of Capulet and Montagu survive. There they do not fight by the book of arithmetic. If you but bite your thumb at an upholder of your opposing house you have work cut out for your steel. On Broadway you may drag your man along a dozen blocks by his nose, and he will only bawl for the watch; but in the domain of the East Side Tybalts and Mercutios you must observe the niceties of deportment to the wink of an eyelash and to an inch of elbow room at the bar when its patrons include foes of your house and kin.

So, when Eddie McManus, known to the Capulets as Cork McManus, drifted into Dutch Mike's for a stein of beer, and came upon a bunch of Montagus making merry with the suds, he began to observe the strictest parliamentary rules. Courtesy forbade his leaving the saloon with his thirst unslaked; caution steered him to a place at the bar where the mirror supplied the cognizance of the enemy's movements that his indifferent gaze seemed to disdain; experience whispered to him that the finger of trouble would be busy among the chattering steins at Dutch Mike's that night. Close by his side drew Brick Cleary, his Mercutio, companion of his perambulations. Thus they stood, four of the Mulberry Hill Gang and two of the Dry Dock Gang, minding their P's and Q's so solicitously that Dutch Mike kept one eye on his customers and the other on an open space beneath his bar in which it was his custom to seek safety whenever the ominous politeness of the rival associations congealed into the shapes of bullets and old steel.

But we have not to do with the wars of the Mulberry Hills and the Dry Docks. We must to Rooney's where, on the most blighted dead branch of the tree of life, a little pale orchid shall bloom.

Overstrained etiquette at last gave way. It is not known who first overstepped the bounds of punctilio; but the consequences were immediate. Buck Malone, of the Mulberry Hills, with a Dewey-like swiftness, got an eight-inch gun swung round from his hurricane deck. But McManus's simile must be the torpedo. He glided in under the guns and slipped a scant three inches of knife blade between the ribs of the Mulberry Hills cruiser. Meanwhile Brick Cleary, a devotee to strategy, had skimmed across the lunch counter and thrown the switch of the electrics, leaving the combat to be waged by the light of gunfire alone. Dutch Mike crawled from his haven and ran into the street crying for the watch instead of for a Shakespeare to immortalize the Cimmerian shindy.

The cop came and found a prostrate, bleeding Montagu supported by three distrait and reticent followers of the House. Faithful to the ethics of the gangs, no one knew whence the hurt came. There was no Capulet to be seen.

"Raus mit der interrogatories," said Buck Malone to the officer. "Sure I know who done it. I always manages to get a bird's eye view of any guy that comes up an' makes a show case for a hardware store out of me. No. I'm not telling his name. I'll settle with um meself. Wow—ouch! Easy, boys! Yes, I'll attend to his case meself. I'm not making any complaint."

At midnight McManus strolled around a pile of lumber near an East Side dock, and lingered in the vicinity of a certain water plug. Brick Cleary drifted casually to the trysting place ten minutes later. "He'll maybe not croak," said Brick; "and he won't tell, of course. But Dutch Mike did. He told the police he was tired of having his place shot up. It's unhandy just now, because Tim Corrigan's in Europe for a week's end with Kings. He'll be back on the *Kaiser Williams* next Friday. You'll have to duck out of sight till then. Tim'll fix it up all right for us when he comes back."

This goes to explain why Cork McManus went into Rooney's one night and there looked upon the bright, strange face of Romance for the first time in his precarious career.

Until Tim Corrigan should return from his jaunt among Kings and Princes and hold up his big white finger in private offices, it was unsafe for Cork in any of the old haunts of his gang. So he lay, perdu, in the high rear room of a Capulet, reading pink sporting sheets and cursing the slow paddle wheels of the *Kaiser Wilhelm*.

It was on Thursday evening that Cork's seclusion became intolerable to him. Never a hart panted for water fountain as he did for the cool touch of a drifting stein, for the firm security of a foot-rail in the hollow of his shoe, and the quiet, hearty challenges of friendship and repartee along and across the shining bars. But he must avoid the district where he was known. The cops were looking for him everywhere, for news was scarce, and the newspapers were harping again on the failure of the police to suppress the gangs. If they got him before Corrigan came back, the big white finger could not be uplifted; it would be too late then. But Corrigan would be home the next day, so he felt sure there would be small danger in a little excursion that night among the crass pleasures that represented life to him.

At half-past twelve McManus stood in a darkish cross-town street looking up at the name "Rooney's," picked out by incandescent lights against a signboard over a second-story window. He had heard of the place as a tough "hangout"; with its frequenters and its locality he was unfamiliar. Guided by certain unerring indications common to all such resorts, he ascended the stairs and entered the large room over the café.

Here were some twenty or thirty tables, at this time about half-filled with Rooney's guests. Waiters served drinks. At one end a human pianola with drugged eyes hammered the keys with automatic and furious unprecision. At merciful intervals a waiter would roar or squeak a song— songs full of "Mr. Johnsons" and "babes" and "coons"—historical word guaranties of the genuineness of African melodies composed by red waistcoated young gentlemen, natives of the cotton fields and rice swamps of West Twenty-eighth Street.

For one brief moment you must admire Rooney with me as he receives, seats, manipulates, and chaffs his guests. He is twenty-nine. He has Wellington's nose, Dante's chin, the cheek-bones of an Iroquois, the smile of Talleyrand, Corbett's foot work, and the poise of an eleven-year-old East Side Central Park Queen of the May. He is assisted by a lieutenant known as Frank, a pudgy, easy chap, swell-dressed, who goes among the tables seeing that dull care does not intrude. Now, what is there about Rooney's to inspire all this pother? It is more than respectable by daylight; stout ladies with children and mittens and bundles and un-pedigreed dogs drop up of afternoons for a stein and a chat. Even by gas-light the diversions are melancholy i' the mouth—drink and rag-time, and an occasional surprise when the waiter swabs the suds from under your sticky glass. There is an answer. Transmigration! The soul of Sir Walter Raleigh has traveled from beneath his slashed doublet to a kin-dred home under Rooney's visible plaid waistcoat. Rooney's is twenty years ahead of the times. Rooney has removed the embargo. Rooney has spread his cloak upon the soggy crossing of public opinion, and any Elizabeth who treads upon it is as much a queen as another. Attend to the reve-lation of the secret. In Rooney's ladies may smoke!

McManus sat down at a vacant table. He paid for a glass of beer that he ordered, tilted his narrow-brimmed derby to the back of his brick-dust head, twined his feet among the rungs of his chair, and heaved a sigh of contentment from the breathing spaces of his innermost soul; for this mud honey was clarified sweetness to his taste. The sham gaiety, the hec-tic glow of counterfeit hospitality, the self-conscious, joyless laughter, the wine-born warmth, the loud music retrieving the hour from frequent whiles of awful and corroding silence, the presence of well-clothed and frank-eyed beneficiaries of Rooney's removal of the restrictions laid upon the weed, the familiar blended odors of soaked lemon peel, flat beer, and *peau d'Espagne*—all these were manna to Cork McManus, hungry from his week in the desert of the Capulet's high rear room.

A girl, alone, entered Rooney's, glanced around with leisurely swift-ness, and sat opposite McManus at his table. Her eyes rested upon him for two seconds in the look with which woman reconnoitres all men whom she for the first time confronts. In that space of time she will decide upon one of two things—either to scream for the police, or that she may marry him later on.

Her brief inspection concluded, the girl laid on the table a worn red morocco shopping bag with the inevitable top-gallant sail of frayed lace handkerchief flying from a corner of it. After she had ordered a small beer from the immediate waiter she took from her bag a box of cigarettes and lighted one with slightly exaggerated ease of manner. Then she looked again in the eyes of Cork McManus and smiled.

Instantly the doom of each was sealed.

The unqualified desire of a man to buy clothes and build fires for a woman for a whole lifetime at first sight of her is not uncommon among that humble portion of humanity that does not care for Bradstreet or coats-of-arms or Shaw's plays. Love at first sight has occurred a time or two in high life; but, as a rule, the extempore mania is to be found among unsophisticated creatures such as the dove, the blue-tailed dingbat, and the ten-dollar-a-week clerk. Poets, subscribers to all fiction magazines, and schatchens, take notice.

With the exchange of the mysterious magnetic current came to each of them the instant desire to lie, pretend, dazzle, and deceive, which is the worst thing about the hypocritical disorder known as love.

"Have another beer?" suggested Cork. In his circle the phrase was considered to be a card, accompanied by a letter of introduction and references.

"No, thanks," said the girl, raising her eyebrows and choosing her conventional words carefully. "I—merely dropped in for—a slight refreshment." The cigarette between her fingers seemed to require explanation. "My aunt is a Russian lady," she concluded, "and we often had a post perannual cigarette after dinner at home."

"Cheese it!" said Cork, whom society airs oppressed. "Your fingers are as yellow as mine."

"Say," said the girl, blazing upon him with low-voiced indignation, "what do you think I am? Say, who do you think you are talking to? What?"

She was pretty to look at. Her eyes were big, brown, intrepid, and bright. Under her flat sailor hat, planted jauntily on one side, her crinkly, tawny hair parted and was drawn back, low and massy, in a thick, pendent knot behind. The roundness of girlhood still lingered in her chin and neck, but her cheeks and fingers were thinning slightly. She looked upon the world with defiance, suspicion, and sullen wonder. Her smart short tan coat was soiled and expensive. Two inches below her black dress dropped the lowest flounce of a heliotrope silk underskirt.

"Beg your pardon," said Cork, looking at her admiringly. "I didn't mean anything. Sure, it's no harm to smoke, Maudy."

"Rooney's," said the girl, softened at once by his amends, "is the only place I know where a lady can smoke. Maybe it ain't a nice habit, but aunty let us at home. And my name ain't Maudy, if you please; it's Ruby Delamere."

"That's a swell handle," said Cork, approvingly. "Mine's McManus—Cor—er—Eddie McManus."

"Oh, you can't help that," laughed Ruby. "Don't apologize."

Cork looked seriously at the big clock on Rooney's wall. The girl's ubiquitous eyes took in the movement.

"I know it's late," she said, reaching for her bag; "but you know how you want a smoke when you want one. Ain't Rooney's all right? I never

PAST ONE AT ROONEY'S 1609
saw anything wrong here. This is twice I've been in. I work in a book-bindery on Third Avenue. A lot of us girls have been working overtime three nights a week. They won't let you smoke there, of course. I just dropped in here on my way home for a puff. Ain't it all right in here? If it ain't, I won't come any more."

"It's a little bit late for you to be out alone anywhere," said Cork. "I'm not wise to this particular joint; but anyhow you don't want to have your picture taken in it for a present to your Sunday School teacher. Have one more beer, and then say I take you home."

"But I don't know you," said the girl, with fine scrupulosity. "I don't accept the company of gentlemen I ain't acquainted with. My aunt never would allow that."

"Why," said Cork McManus, pulling his ear, "I'm the latest thing in suitings with side vents and bell skirt when it comes to escortin' a lady. You bet you'll find me all right, Ruby. And I'll give you a tip as to who I am. My governor is one of the hottest cross-buns of the Wall Street push. Morgan's cab horse casts a shoe every time the old man sticks his head out of the window. Me! Well, I'm in trainin' down the Street. The old man's goin' to put a seat on the Stock Exchange in my stockin' my next birthday. But it sounds like a lemon to me. What I like is golf and yachtin' and—er—well, say a corkin' fast ten-round bout between welter-weights with walkin' gloves."

"I guess you can walk to the door with me," said the girl, hesitatingly, but with a certain pleased flutter. "Still I never heard anything extra good about Wall Street brokers, or sports who go to prize fights, either. Ain't you got any other recommendations?"

"I think you're the swellest looker I've had my lamps on in little old New York," said Cork, impressively.

"That'll be about enough of that, now. Ain't you the kidder!" She modified her chiding words by a deep, long, beaming, smile-embellished look at her cavalier. "We'll drink our beer before we go, ha?"

A waiter sang. The tobacco smoke grew denser, drifting and rising in spirals, waves, tilted layers, cumulus clouds, cataracts, and suspended fogs like some fifth element created from the ribs of the ancient four. Laughter and chat grew louder, stimulated by Rooney's liquids and Rooney's gallant hospitality to Lady Nicotine.

One o'clock struck. Downstairs there was a sound of closing and lock-ing doors. Frank pulled down the green shades of the front windows carefully. Rooney went below in the dark hall and stood at the front door, his cigarette cached in the hollow of his hand. Thenceforth who-ever might seek admittance must present a countenance familiar to Rooney's hawk's eye—the countenance of a true sport.

Cork McManus and the bookbindery girl conversed absorbedly, with their elbows on the table. Their glasses of beer were pushed to one side, scarcely touched, with the foam on them sunken to a thin white scum. Since the stroke of one the stale pleasures of Rooney's had become renovated and spiced; not by any addition to the list of distractions, but because from that moment the sweets became stolen ones. The flattest glass of beer acquired the tang of illegality; the mildest claret punch struck a knockout blow at law and order; the harmless and genial company became outlaws, defying authority and rule. For after the stroke of one in such places as Rooney's, where neither bed nor board is to be had, drink may not be set before the thirsty of the city of the four million. It is the law.

"Say," said Cork McManus, almost covering the table with his eloquent chest and elbows, "was that dead straight about you workin' in the bookbindery and livin' at home—and just happenin' in here—and—and all that spiel you gave me?"

"Sure it was," answered the girl with spirit. "Why, what do you think? Do you suppose I'd lie to you? Go down to the shop and ask 'em. I handed it to you on the level."

"On the dead level?" said Cork. "That's the way I want it; because——"

"Because what?"

"I throw up my hands," said Cork. "You've got me goin'. You're the girl I've been lookin' for. Will you keep company with me, Ruby?"

"Would you like me to—Eddie?"

"Surest thing. But I want a straight story about—about yourself, you know. When a fellow has a steady girl—she's got to be all right, you know. She's got to be straight goods."

"You'll find I'll be straight goods, Eddie."

"Of course you will. I believe what you told me. But you can't blame me for wantin' to find out. You don't see many girls smokin' cigarettes in places like Rooney's after midnight that are like you."

The girl flushed a little and lowered her eyes. "I see that now," she said, meekly. "I didn't know how bad it looked. But I won't do it any more. And I'll go straight home every night and stay there. And I'll give up cigarettes if you say so, Eddie—I'll cut 'em out from this minute on."

Cork's air became judicial, proprietary, condemnatory, yet sympathetic. "A lady can smoke," he decided, slowly, "at times and places. Why? Because it's bein' a lady that helps her to pull it off."

"I'm going to quit. There's nothing to it," said the girl. She flicked the stub of her cigarette to the floor.

"At times and places," repeated Cork. "When I call round for you of evenin's we'll hunt out a dark bench in Stuyvesant Square and have a puff or two. But no more Rooney's at one o'clock—see?"

"Eddie, do you really like me?" The girl searched his hard but frank features eagerly with anxious eyes.

"On the dead level."

"When are you coming to see me—where I live?"

"Thursday—day after to-morrow evenin'. That suit you?"

"Fine. I'll be ready for you. Come about seven. Walk to the door with me to-night and I'll show you where I live. Don't forget, now. And don't you go to see any other girls before then, mister! I bet you will, though."

"On the dead level," said Cork, "you make 'em all look like rag-dolls to me. Honest, you do. I know when I'm suited. On the dead level, I do."

Against the front door downstairs repeated heavy blows were delivered. The loud crashes resounded in the room above. Only a trip-hammer or a policeman's foot could have been the author of those sounds. Rooney jumped like a bullfrog to a corner of the room, turned off the electric lights, and hurried swiftly below.

The room was left utterly dark except for the winking red glow of cigars and cigarettes. A second volley of crashes came up from the as-saulted door. A little, rustling, murmuring panic moved among the besieged guests. Frank, cool, smooth, reassuring, could be seen in the rosy glow of the burning tobacco, going from table to table.

"All keep still!" was his caution. "Don't talk or make any noise! Every-thing will be all right. Now, don't feel the slightest alarm. We'll take care of you all."

Ruby felt across the table until Cork's firm hand closed upon hers. "Are you afraid, Eddie?" she whispered. "Are you afraid you'll get a free ride?"

"Nothin' doin' in the teeth-chatterin' line," said Cork. "I guess Rooney's been slow with his envelope. Don't you worry, girly; I'll look out for you all right."

Yet Mr. McManus's case was only skin- and muscle-deep. With the police looking everywhere for Buck Malone's assailant, and with Corrigan still on the ocean wave, he felt that to be caught in a police raid would mean an ended career for him. And just when he had met Ruby, too! He wished he had remained in the high rear room of the true Capulet reading the pink extras.

Rooney seemed to have opened the front door below and engaged the police in conference in the dark hall. The wordless low growl of their voices came up the stairway. Frank made a wireless news station of him-self at the upper door. Suddenly he closed the door, hurried to the extreme rear of the room and lighted a dim gas jet.

"This way, everybody!" he called sharply. "In a hurry; but no noise, please!"

The guests crowded in confusion to the rear. Rooney's lieutenant swung open a panel in the wall, overlooking the back yard, revealing a ladder already placed for the escape.

"Down and out, everybody!" he commanded. "Ladies first! Less talking, please! Don't crowd! There's no danger."

Among the last, Cork and Ruby waited their turn at the open panel. Suddenly she swept him aside and clung to his arm fiercely.

"Before we go out," she whispered in his ear—"before anything happens, tell me again, Eddie, do you l— do you really like me?"

"On the dead level," said Cork, holding her close with one arm, "when it comes to you, I'm all in."

When they turned they found they were lost and in darkness. The last of the fleeing customers had descended. Halfway across the yard they bore the ladder, stumbling, giggling, hurrying to place it against an adjoining low building over the roof of which lay their only route to safety.

"We may as well sit down," said Cork, grimly. "Maybe Rooney will stand the cops off, anyhow."

They sat at a table; and their hands came together again.

A number of men then entered the dark room, feeling their way about. One of them, Rooney himself, found the switch and turned on the electric light. The other man was a cop of the old régime—a big cop, a thick cop, a fuming, abrupt cop—not a pretty cop. He went up to the pair at the table and sneered familiarly at the girl.

"What are youse doin' in here?" he asked.

"Dropped in for a smoke," said Cork, mildly.

"Had any drinks?"

"Not later than one o'clock."

"Get out—quick!" ordered the cop. Then, "Sit down!" he countermanded.

He took off Cork's hat roughly and scrutinized him shrewdly. "Your name's McManus."

"Bad guess," said Cork. "It's Peterson."

"Cork McManus, or something like that," said the cop. "You put a knife into a man in Dutch Mike's saloon a week ago."

"Aw, forget it!" said Cork, who perceived a shade of doubt in the officer's tones. "You've got my mug mixed with somebody else's."

"Have I? Well, you'll come to the station with me, anyhow, and be looked over. The description fits you all right." The cop twisted his fingers under Cork's collar. "Come on!" he ordered roughly.

Cork glanced at Ruby. She was pale, and her thin nostrils quivered. Her quick eye danced from one man's face to the other as they spoke or moved. What hard luck! Cork was thinking—Corrigan on the briny; and Ruby met and lost almost within an hour! Somebody at the police station would recognize him, without a doubt. Hard luck!

But suddenly the girl sprang up and hurled herself with both arms extended against the cop. His hold on Cork's collar was loosened and he stumbled back two or three paces.

"Don't go so fast, Maguire!" she cried in shrill fury. "Keep your hands off my man! You know me, and you know I'm givin' you good advice. Don't you touch him again! He's not the guy you are lookin' for—I'll stand for that."

"See here, Fanny," said the cop, red and angry, "I'll take you, too, if you don't look out! How do you know this ain't the man I want? What are you doing in here with him?"

"How do I know?" said the girl, flaming red and white by turns. "Because I've known him a year. He's mine. Oughtn't I to know? And what am I doin' here with him? That's easy."

She stooped low and reached down somewhere into a swirl of flirted draperies, heliotrope and black. An elastic snapped, she threw on the table toward Cork a folded wad of bills. The money slowly straightened itself with little leisurely jerks.

"Take that, Jimmy, and let's go," said the girl. "I'm declarin' the usual dividends, Maguire," she said to the officer. "You had your usual five-dollar graft at the usual corner at ten."

"A lie!" said the cop, turning purple. "You go on my beat again and I'll arrest you every time I see you."

"No, you won't," said the girl. "And I'll tell you why. Witnesses saw me give you the money to-night, and last week, too. I've been getting fixed for you."

Cork put the wad of money carefully into his pocket and said: "Come on, Fanny; let's have some chop suey before we go home."

"Clear out, quick, both of you, or I'll——"

The cop's bluster trailed away into inconsequentiality.

At the corner of the street the two halted. Cork handed back the money without a word. The girl took it and slipped it slowly into her hand-bag. Her expression was the same she had worn when she entered Rooney's that night—she looked upon the world with defiance, suspicion, and sullen wonder.

"I guess I might as well say good-by here," she said, dully. "You won't want to see me again, of course. Will you—shake hands—Mr. McManus?"

"I mightn't have got wise if you hadn't give the snap away," said Cork. "Why did you do it?"

"You'd have been pinched if I hadn't. That's why. Ain't that reason enough?" Then she began to cry. "Honest, Eddie, I was goin' to be the best girl in the world. I hated to be what I am; I hated men; I was ready almost to die when I saw you. And you seemed different from everybody else. And when I found you liked me, too, why, I thought I'd make you believe I was good, and I was goin' to be good. When you asked to come to my house and see me, why, I'd have died rather than do anything wrong after that. But what's the use of talking about it? I'll say good-by, if you will, Mr. McManus."

Cork was pulling at his ear. "I knifed Malone," said he. "I was the one the cop wanted."

"Oh, that's all right," said the girl, listlessly. "It didn't make any difference about that."

"That was all hot air about Wall Street. I don't do nothin' but hang out with a tough gang on the East Side."

"That was all right, too," repeated the girl. "It didn't make any difference."

Cork straightened himself, and pulled his hat down low. "I could get a job at O'Brien's," he said aloud, but to himself.

"Good-by," said the girl.

"Come on," said Cork, taking her arm. "I know a place."

Two blocks away he turned with her up the steps of a red brick house facing a little park.

"What house is this?" she asked, drawing back. "Why are you going in there?"

A street lamp shone brightly in front. There was a brass name-plate at one side of the closed front doors. Cork drew her firmly up the steps. "Read that," said he.

She looked at the name on the plate, and gave a cry between a moan and a scream. "No, no, no, Eddie! Oh, my God, no! I won't let you do that—not now! Let me go! You shan't do that! You can't—you mustn't! Not after you know! No, no! Come away quick! Oh, my God! Please, Eddie, come!"

Half fainting, she reeled, and was caught in the bend of his arm. Cork's right hand felt for the electric button and pressed it long.

Another cop—how quickly they scent trouble when trouble is on the wing!—came along, saw them, and ran up the steps. "Here! What are you doing with that girl?" he called, gruffly.

"She'll be all right in a minute," said Cork. "It's a straight deal."

"Reverend Jeremiah Jones," read the cop from the door-plate with true detective cunning.

"Correct," said Cork. "On the dead level, we're goin' to get married."

THE VENTURERS

Let the story wreck itself on the spreading rails of the *Non Sequitur* Limited, if it will; first you must take your seat in the observation car *"Raison d'être"* for one moment. It is for no longer than to consider a brief essay on the subject—let us call it: "What's Around the Corner."

Omne mundus in duas partes divisum est—men who wear rubbers and pay poll-taxes, and men who discover new continents. There are no more continents to discover; but by the time overshoes are out of date and the poll has developed into an income tax, the other half will be paralleling the canals of Mars with radium railways.

Fortune, Chance, and Adventure are given as synonyms in the dictionaries. To the knowing each has a different meaning. Fortune is a prize to be won. Adventure is the road to it. Chance is what may lurk in the shadows at the roadside. The face of Fortune is radiant and alluring; that of Adventure flushed and heroic. The face of Chance is the beautiful countenance—perfect because vague and dream-born—that we see in our tea-cups at breakfast while we growl over our chops and toast.

The VENTURER is one who keeps his eye on the hedgerows and wayside groves and meadows while he travels the road to Fortune. That is the difference between him and the Adventurer. Eating the forbidden fruit was the best record ever made by a Venturer. Trying to prove that it happened is the highest work of the Adventuresome. To be either is disturbing to the cosmogony of creation. So, as bracket-sawed and city-directoried citizens, let us light our pipes, chide the children and the cat, arrange ourselves in the willow rocker under the flickering gas jet at the coolest window and scan this little tale of two modern followers of Chance.

"Did you ever hear that story about the man from the West?" asked Billinger, in the little dark-oak room to your left as you penetrate the interior of the Powhatan Club.

"Doubtless," said John Reginald Forster, rising and leaving the room.

Forster got his straw hat (straws will be in and maybe out again long before this is printed) from the check-room boy, and walked out of the air (as Hamlet says). Billinger was used to having his stories insulted and would not mind. Forster was in his favorite mood and wanted to go away from anywhere. A man, in order to get on good terms with himself, must have his opinions corroborated and his moods matched by some one else. (I had written that "somebody"; but an A. D. T. boy who once took a telegram from me pointed out that I could save money by using the compound word. This is a vice versa case.)

Forster's favorite mood was that of greatly desiring to be a follower of Chance. He was a Venturer by nature, but convention, birth, tradition, and the narrowing influences of the tribe of Manhattan had denied him full privilege. He had trodden all the main-traveled thoroughfares and many of the side roads that are supposed to relieve the tedium of life. But none had sufficed. The reason was that he knew what was to be found at the end of every street. He knew from experience and logic almost precisely to what end each digression from routine must lead. He found a depressing monotony in all the variations that the music of his sphere had grafted upon the tune of life. He had not learned that, although the world was made round, the circle had been squared, and that its true interest is to be found in "What's Around the Corner."

Forster walked abroad aimlessly from the Powhatan, trying not to tax either his judgment or his desire as to what streets he traveled. He would have been glad to lose his way if it were possible; but he had no hope of that. Adventure and Fortune move at your beck and call in the Greater City; but Chance is oriental. She is a veiled lady in a sedan chair, protected by a special traffic squad of dragomans. Crosstown, uptown, and downtown you may move without seeing her.

At the end of an hour's stroll, Forster stood on a corner of a broad, smooth avenue, looking disconsolately across it at a picturesque old hotel softly but brilliantly lit. Disconsolately, because he knew that he must dine; and dining in that hotel was no venture. It was one of his favorite caravansaries, and so silent and swift would be the service and so delicately choice the food, that he regretted the hunger that must be appeased by the "dead perfection" of the place's cuisine. Even the music there seemed to be always playing *da capo*.

Fancy came to him that he would dine at some cheap, even dubious, restaurant lower down in the city, where the erratic chefs from all countries of the world spread their national cookery for the omnivorous American. Something might happen there out of the routine—he might come upon a subject without a predicate, a road without an end, a question without an answer, a cause without an effect, a gulf stream in life's salt ocean. He had not dressed for evening; he wore a dark business suit that would not be questioned even where the waiters served the spaghetti in their shirt sleeves.

So John Reginald Forster began to search his clothes for money; because the more cheaply you dine, the more surely must you pay. All of the thirteen pockets, large and small, of his business suit he explored carefully and found not a penny. His bank book showed a balance of five figures to his credit in the Old Ironsides Trust Company, but——

Forster became aware of a man near by at his left hand who was really regarding him with some amusement. He looked like any business man of thirty or so, neatly dressed and standing in the attitude of one waiting for a street car. But there was no car line on that avenue. So his proximity and unconcealed curiosity seemed to Forster to partake of the nature of a personal intrusion. But, as he was a consistent seeker after "What's Around the Corner," instead of manifesting resentment he only turned a half-embarrassed smile upon the other's grin of amusement.

"All in?" asked the intruder, drawing nearer.

"Seems so," said Forster. "Now, I thought there was a dollar in——"

"Oh, I know," said the other man, with a laugh. "But there wasn't. I've just been through the same process myself, as I was around the corner. I found in an upper vest pocket—I don't know how they got there—exactly two pennies. You know what kind of a dinner exactly two pennies will buy!"

"You haven't dined, then?" asked Forster.

"I have not. But I would like to. Now, I'll make you a proposition. You look like a man who would take up one. Your clothes look neat and respectable. Excuse personalities. I think mine will pass the scrutiny of a head waiter, also. Suppose we go over to that hotel and dine together. We will choose from the menu like millionaires—or, if you prefer, like gentlemen in moderate circumstances dining extravagantly for once. When we have finished we will match with my two pennies to see which of us will stand the brunt of the house's displeasure and vengeance. My name is Ives. I think we have lived in the same station of life—before our money took wings."

"You're on," said Forster, joyfully.

Here was a venture at least within the borders of the mysterious country of Chance—anyhow, it promised something better than the stale infestivity of a table d'hôte.

The two were soon seated at a corner table in the hotel dining room. Ives chucked one of his pennies across the table to Forster.

"Match for which of us gives the order," he said.

Forster lost.

Ives laughed and began to name liquids and viands to the waiter with the absorbed but calm deliberation of one who was to the menu born. Forster, listening, gave his admiring approval of the order.

"I am a man," said Ives, during the oysters, "who has made a lifetime search after the to-be-continued-in-our-next. I am not like the ordinary adventurer who strikes for a coveted prize. Nor yet am I like a gambler who knows he is either to win or lose a certain set stake. What I want is to encounter an adventure to which I can predict no conclusion. It is the breath of existence to me to dare Fate in its blindest manifestations. The world has come to run so much by rote and gravitation that you can enter upon hardly any foot-path of chance in which you do not find signboards informing you of what you may expect at its end. I am like the clerk in the Circumlocution Office who always complained bitterly when any one came in to ask information. 'He wanted to *know!*' was the kick he made to his fellow-clerks. Well, I don't want to know, I don't want to reason, I don't want to guess—I want to bet my hand without seeing it."

"I understand," said Forster, delightedly. "I've often wanted the way I feel put into words. You've done it. I want to take chances on what's coming. Suppose we have a bottle of Moselle with the next course."

"Agreed," said Ives. "I'm glad you catch my idea. It will increase the animosity of the house toward the loser. If it does not weary you, we will pursue the theme. Only a few times have I met a true venturer—one who does not ask a schedule and map from Fate when he begins a journey. But, as the world becomes more civilized and wiser, the more difficult it is to come upon an adventure the end of which you cannot foresee. In the Elizabethan days you could assault the watch, wring knockers from doors, and have a jolly set-to with the blades in any convenient angle of a wall and 'get away with it.' Nowadays, if you speak disrespectfully to a policeman, all that is left to the most romantic fancy is to conjecture in what particular police station he will land you."

"I know—I know," said Forster, nodding approval.

"I returned to New York to-day," continued Ives, "from a three years' ramble around the globe. Things are not much better abroad than they are at home. The whole world seems to be overrun by conclusions. The only thing that interests me greatly is a premise. I've tried shooting big game in Africa. I know what an express rifle will do at so many yards; and when an elephant or a rhinoceros falls to the bullet, I enjoy it about as much as I did when I was kept in after school to do a sum in long division on the blackboard."

"I know—I know," said Forster.

"There might be something in aeroplanes," went on Ives, reflectively. "I've tried ballooning; but it seems to be merely a cut-and-dried affair of wind and ballast."

"Women," suggested Forster, with a smile.

"Three months ago," said Ives, "I was pottering around in one of the bazaars in Constantinople. I noticed a lady, veiled, of course, but with a pair of especially fine eyes visible, who was examining some amber and pearl ornaments at one of the booths. With her was an attendant—a big Nubian, as black as coal. After a while the attendant drew nearer to me by degrees and slipped a scrap of paper into my hand. I looked at it when I got a chance. On it was scrawled hastily in pencil: 'The arched gate of the Nightingale Garden at nine to-night.' Does that appear to you to be an interesting premise, Mr. Forster?"

"Go on," said Forster eagerly.

"I made inquiries and learned that the Nightingale Garden was the property of an old Turk—a grand vizier, or something of the sort. Of course I prospected for the arched gate and was there at nine. The same Nubian attendant opened the gate promptly on time, and I went inside and sat on a bench by a perfumed fountain with the veiled lady. We had quite an extended chat. She was Myrtle Thompson, a lady journalist, who was writing up the Turkish harems for a Chicago newspaper. She said she noticed the New York cut of my clothes in the bazaar and wondered if I couldn't work something into the metropolitan papers about it."

"I see," said Forster. "I see."

"I've canoed through Canada," said Ives, "down many rapids and over many falls. But I didn't seem to get what I wanted out of it because I knew there were only two possible outcomes—I would either go to the bottom or arrive at the sea level. I've played all games at cards; but the mathematicians have spoiled that sport by computing the percentages. I've made acquaintances on trains, I've answered advertisements, I've rung strange door-bells, I've taken every chance that presented itself; but there has always been the conventional ending—the logical conclusion to the premise."

"I know," repeated Forster. "I've felt it all. But I've had few chances to take my chance at chances. Is there any life so devoid of impossibilities as life in this city? There seems to be a myriad of opportunities for testing the undeterminable; but not one in a thousand fails to land you where you expected it to stop. I wish the subways and street cars disappointed one as seldom."

"The sun has risen," said Ives, "on the Arabian nights. There are no more caliphs. The fisherman's vase is turned to a vacuum bottle, warranted to keep any genie boiling or frozen for forty-eight hours. Life moves by rote. Science has killed adventure. There are no more opportunities such as Columbus and the man who ate the first oyster had. The only certain thing is that there is nothing uncertain."

"Well," said Forster, "my experience has been the limited one of a city man. I haven't seen the world as you have; but it seems that we view it with the same opinion. But, I tell you I am grateful for even this little venture of ours into the borders of the haphazard. There may be at least one breathless moment when the bill for the dinner is presented. Perhaps, after all, the pilgrims who traveled without scrip or purse found a keener taste to life than did the knights of the Round Table who rode abroad with a retinue and King Arthur's certified checks in the lining of their helmets. And now, if you've finished your coffee, suppose we match one of your insufficient coins for the impending blow of Fate. What have I up?"

"Heads," called Ives.

"Heads it is," said Forster, lifting his hand. "I lose. We forgot to agree upon a plan for the winner to escape. I suggest that when the waiter comes you make a remark about telephoning to a friend. I will hold the fort and the dinner check long enough for you to get your hat and be off. I thank you for an evening out of the ordinary, Mr. Ives, and wish we might have others."

"If my memory is not at fault," said Ives, laughing, "the nearest police station is in MacDougal Street. I have enjoyed the dinner, too, let me assure you."

Forster crooked his finger for the waiter. Victor, with a locomotive effort that seemed to owe more to pneumatics than to pedestrianism, glided to the table and laid the card, face downward, by the loser's cup. Forster took it up and added the figures with deliberate care. Ives leaned back comfortably in his chair.

"Excuse me," said Forster; "but I thought you were going to ring up Grimes about that theatre party for Thursday night. Had you forgotten about it?"

"Oh," said Ives, settling himself more comfortably, "I can do that later on. Get me a glass of water, waiter."

"Want to be in at the death, do you?" asked Forster.

"I hope you don't object," said Ives, pleadingly. "Never in my life have I seen a gentleman arrested in a public restaurant for swindling it out of a dinner."

"All right," said Forster, calmly. "You are entitled to see a Christian die in the arena as your *pousse-café.*"

Victor came with the glass of water and remained, with the disengaged air of an inexorable collector.

Forster hesitated for fifteen seconds, and then took a pencil from his pocket and scribbled his name on the dinner check. The waiter bowed and took it away.

"The fact is," said Forster, with a little embarrassed laugh, "I doubt whether I'm what they call a 'game sport,' which means the same as a 'soldier of Fortune.' I'll have to make confession. I've been dining at this hotel two or three times a week for more than a year. I always sign my checks." And then, with a note of appreciation in his voice: "It was first-rate of you to stay to see me through with it when you know I had no money, and that you might be scooped in, too."

"I guess I'll confess, too," said Ives, with a grin. "I own the hotel. I don't run it, of course, but I always keep a suite on the third floor for my use when I happen to stray into town."

He called a waiter and said: "Is Mr. Gilmore still behind the desk? All right. Tell him that Mr. Ives is here, and ask him to have my rooms made ready and aired."

"Another venture cut short by the inevitable," said Forster. "Is there a conundrum without an answer in the next number? But let's hold to our subject just for a minute or two, if you will. It isn't often that I meet a man who understands the flaws I pick in existence. I am engaged to be married a month from to-day."

"I reserve comment," said Ives.

"Right; I am going to add to the assertion. I am devotedly fond of the lady; but I can't decide whether to show up at the church or make a sneak for Alaska. It's the same idea, you know, that we were discussing —it does for a fellow as far as possibilities are concerned. Everybody knows the routine—you get a kiss flavored with Ceylon tea after breakfast; you go to the office; you come back home and dress for dinner—

theatre twice a week—bills—moping around most evenings trying to make conversation—a little quarrel occasionally—maybe sometimes a big one, and a separation—or else a settling down into a middle-aged contentment, which is worst of all."

"I know," said Ives, nodding wisely.

"It's the dead certainty of the thing," went on Forster, "that keeps me in doubt. There'll nevermore be anything around the corner."

"Nothing after the 'Little Church,'" said Ives, "I know."

"Understand," said Forster, "that I am in no doubt as to my feelings toward the lady. I may say that I love her truly and deeply. But there is something in the current that runs through my veins that cries out against any form of the calculable. I do not know what I want; but I know that I want it. I'm talking like an idiot, I suppose, but I'm sure of what I mean."

"I understand you," said Ives, with a slow smile. "Well I think I will be going up to my rooms now. If you would dine with me here one evening soon, Mr. Forster, I'd be glad."

"Thursday?" suggested Forster.

"At seven, if it's convenient," answered Ives.

"Seven goes," assented Forster.

At half-past eight Ives got into a cab and was driven to a number in one of the correct West Seventies. His card admitted him to the reception room of an old-fashioned house into which the spirits of Fortune, Chance, and Adventure had never dared to enter. On the walls were the Whistler etchings, the steel engravings by Oh-what's-his-name?, the still-life paintings of the grapes and garden truck with the watermelon seeds spilled on the table as natural as life, and the Greuze head. It was a household. There were even brass andirons. On a table was an album, half-morocco, with oxidized-silver protections on the corners of the lids. A clock on the mantel ticked loudly, with a warning click at five minutes to nine. Ives looked at it curiously, remembering a time-piece in his grandmother's home that gave such a warning.

And then down the stairs into the room came Mary Marsden. She was twenty-four, and I leave her to your imagination. But I must say this much—youth and health and simplicity and courage and greenish-violet eyes are beautiful, and she had all these. She gave Ives her hand with the sweet cordiality of an old friendship.

"You can't think what a pleasure it is," she said, "to have you drop in once every three years or so."

For half an hour they talked. I confess that I cannot repeat the conversation. You will find it in books in the circulating library. When that part of it was over, Mary said:

"And did you find what you wanted while you were abroad?"

"What I wanted?" said Ives.

"Yes. You know you were always queer. Even as a boy you wouldn't play marbles or baseball or any games with rules. You wanted to dive in water where you didn't know whether it was ten inches or ten feet deep. And when you grew up you were just the same. We've often talked about your peculiar ways."

"I suppose I am an incorrigible," said Ives. "I am opposed to the doctrine of predestination, to the rule of three, gravitation, taxes, and everything of the kind. Life has always seemed to me something like a serial story would be if they printed above each instalment a synopsis of *succeeding* chapters."

Mary laughed merrily.

"Bob Ames told us once," she said, "of a funny thing you did. It was when you and he were on a train in the South, and you got off at a town where you hadn't intended to stop just because the brakeman hung up a sign in the end of the car with the name of the next station on it."

"I remember," said Ives. "That 'next station' has been the thing I've always tried to get away from."

"I know it," said Mary. "And you've been very foolish. I hope you didn't find what you wanted not to find, or get off at the station where there wasn't any, or whatever it was you expected wouldn't happen to you during the three years you've been away."

"There was something I wanted before I went away," said Ives.

Mary looked in his eyes clearly, with a slight but perfectly sweet smile.

"There was," she said. "You wanted me. And you could have had me as you very well know."

Without replying, Ives let his gaze wander slowly about the room. There had been no change in it since last he had been in it, three years before. He vividly recalled the thoughts that had been in his mind then. The contents of that room were as fixed, in their way, as the everlasting hills. No change would ever come there except the inevitable ones wrought by time and decay. That silver-mounted album would occupy that corner of that table, those pictures would hang on the walls, those chairs be found in their same places every morn and noon and night while the household hung together. The brass andirons were monuments to order and stability. Here and there were relics of a hundred years ago which were still living mementos and would be for many years to come. One going from and coming back to that house would never need to forecast or doubt. He would find what he left, and leave what he found. The veiled lady, Chance, would never lift her hand to the knocker on the outer door.

And before him sat the lady who belonged in the room. Cool and sweet and unchangeable she was. She offered no surprises. If one should pass his life with her, though she might grow white-haired and wrinkled, he would never perceive the change. Three years he had been away from her, and she was still waiting for him as established and constant as the house itself. He was sure that she had once cared for him. It was the knowledge that she would always do so that had driven him away. Thus his thoughts ran.

"I am going to be married soon," said Mary.

On the next Thursday afternoon Forster came hurriedly to Ives's hotel.

"Old man," said he, "we'll have to put that dinner off for a year or so; I'm going abroad. The steamer sails at four. That was a great talk we had the other night, and it decided me. I'm going to knock around the world and get rid of that incubus that has been weighing on both you and me—the terrible dread of knowing what's going to happen. I've done one thing that hurts my conscience a little; but I know it's best for both of us. I've written to the lady to whom I was engaged and explained everything—told her plainly why I was leaving—that the monotony of matrimony would never do for me. Don't you think I was right?"

"It is not for me to say," answered Ives. "Go ahead and shoot elephants if you think it will bring the element of chance into your life. We've got to decide these things for ourselves. But I tell you one thing, Forster, I've found the way. I've found out the biggest hazard in the world—a game of chance that never is concluded, a venture that may end in the highest heaven or the blackest pit. It will keep a man on edge until the clods fall on his coffin, because he will never know—not until his last day, and not then will he know. It is a voyage without a rudder or compass, and you must be captain and crew and keep watch, every day and night, yourself, with no one to relieve you. I have found the VENTURE. Don't bother yourself about leaving Mary Marsden, Forster. I married her yesterday at noon."

THE DUEL

The gods, lying beside their nectar on 'Lympus and peeping over the edge of the cliff, perceive a difference in cities. Although it would seem that to their vision towns must appear as large or small ant-hills without special characteristics, yet it is not so. Studying the habits of ants from so great a height should be but a mild diversion when coupled with the soft drink that mythology tells us is their only solace. But doubtless they have amused themselves by the comparison of villages and towns; and it will be no news to them (nor, perhaps, to many mortals), that in one particularity New York stands unique among the cities of the world. This shall be the theme of a little story addressed to the man who sits smoking with his Sabbath-slippered feet on another chair, and to the woman who snatches the paper for a moment while boiling greens or a narcotized baby leaves her free. With these I love to sit upon the ground and tell sad stories of the death of kings.

New York City is inhabited by 4,000,000 mysterious strangers; thus beating Bird Centre by three millions and half a dozen nine's. They came here in various ways and for many reasons—Hendrik Hudson, the art schools, green goods, the stork, the annual dress-makers' convention, the Pennsylvania Railroad, love of money, the stage, cheap excursion rates, brains, personal column ads., heavy walking shoes, ambition, freight trains —all these have had a hand in making up the population.

But every man Jack when he first sets foot on the stones of Manhattan has got to fight. He has got to fight at once until either he or his adversary wins. There is no resting between rounds, for there are no rounds. It is slugging from the first. It is a fight to a finish.

Your opponent is the City. You must do battle with it from the time the ferry-boat lands you on the island until either it is yours or it has conquered you. It is the same whether you have a million in your pocket or only the price of a week's lodging.

The battle is to decide whether you shall become a New Yorker or turn the rankest outlander and Philistine. You must be one or the other. You cannot remain neutral. You must be for or against—lover or enemy —bosom friend or outcast. And, oh, the city is a general in the ring. Not only by blows does it seek to subdue you. It woos you to its heart with the subtlety of a siren. It is combination of Delilah, green chartreuse, Beethoven, chloral, and John L. in his best days.

In other cities you may wander and abide as a stranger man as long as you please. You may live in Chicago until your hair whitens, and be a citizen and still prate of beans if Boston mothered you, and without rebuke. You may become a civic pillar in any other town but Knickerbocker's, and all the time publicly sneering at its buildings, comparing them with the architecture of Colonel Telfair's residence in Jackson, Miss., whence you hail, and you will not be set upon. But in New York you must be either a New Yorker or an invader of a modern Troy, concealed in the wooden horse of your conceited provincialism. And this dreary preamble is only to introduce to you the unimportant figures of William and Jack.

They came out of the West together, where they had been friends. They came to dig their fortunes out of the big city.

Father Knickerbocker met them at the ferry, giving one a right-hander on the nose and the other an uppercut with his left, just to let them know that the fight was on.

William was for business; Jack was for Art. Both were young and ambitious; so they countered and clinched. I think they were from Nebraska or possibly Missouri or Minnesota. Anyhow, they were out for success and·scraps and scads, and they tackled the city like two Lochinvars with brass knucks and a pull at the City Hall.

Four years afterward William and Jack met at luncheon. The business man blew in like a March wind, hurled his silk hat at a waiter, dropped into a chair that was pushed under him, seized the bill of fare, and had ordered as far as cheese before the artist had time to do more than nod. After the nod a humorous smile came into his eyes.

"Billy," he said, "you're done for. The city has gobbled you up. It has taken you and cut you to its pattern and stamped you with its brand. You are so nearly like ten thousand men I have seen to-day that you couldn't be picked out from them if it weren't for your laundry marks."

"Camembert," finished William. "What's that? Oh, you've still got your hammer out for New York, have you? Well, little old Noisyville-on-the-Subway is good enough for me. It's giving me mine. And, say, I used to think the West was the whole round world—only slightly flattened at the poles whenever Bryan ran. I used to yell myself hoarse about the free expanse and hang my hat on the horizon, and say cutting things in the grocery to little soap drummers from the East. But I'd never seen New York then, Jack. Me for it from the rathskellers up. Sixth Avenue is the West to me now. Have you heard this fellow Crusoe sing? The desert isle for him, I say, but my wife made me go. Give me May Irwin or E. S. Willard any time."

"Poor Billy," said the artist, delicately fingering a cigarette. "You remember, when we were on our way to the East how we talked about this great, wonderful city, and how we meant to conquer it and never let it get the best of us? We were going to be just the same fellows we had always been, and never let it master us. It has downed you, old man. You have changed from a maverick into a butterick."

"Don't see exactly what you are driving at," said William. "I don't wear an alpaca coat with blue trousers and a seersucker vest on dress occasions, like I used to do at home. You talk about being cut to a pattern—well, ain't the pattern all right? When you're in Rome you've got to do as the Dagoes do. This town seems to me to have other alleged metropolises skinned to flag stations. According to the railroad schedule I've got in my mind, Chicago and Saint Jo and Paris, France, are asterisk stops—which means you wave a red flag and get on every other Tuesday. I like this little suburb of Tarrytown-on-the-Hudson. There's something or somebody doing all the time. I'm clearing $8,000 a year selling automatic pumps, and I'm living like kings-up. Why, yesterday, I was introduced to John W. Gates. I took an auto ride with a wine agent's sister. I saw two men run over by a street car, and I seen Edna May play in the evening. Talk about the West, why, the other night I woke everybody up in the hotel hollering. I dreamed I was walking on a board sidewalk in

Oshkosh. What have you got against this town, Jack? There's only one thing in it that I don't care for, and that's a ferryboat."

The artist gazed dreamily at the cartridge paper on the wall. "This town," said he, "is a leech. It drains the blood of the country. Whoever comes to it accepts a challenge to a duel. Abandoning the figure of the leech, it is a juggernaut, a Moloch, a monster to which the innocence, the genius, and the beauty of the land must pay tribute. Hand to hand every newcomer must struggle with the leviathan. You've lost, Billy. It shall never conquer me. I hate it as one hates sin or pestilence or—the color work in a ten-cent magazine. I despise its very vastness and power. It has the poorest millionaires, the littlest great men, the haughtiest beggars, the plainest beauties, the lowest skyscrapers, the dolefulest pleasures of any town I ever saw. It has caught you, old man, but I will never run beside its chariot wheels. It glosses itself as the Chinaman glosses his collars. Give me the domestic finish. I could stand a town ruled by wealth or one ruled by an aristocracy; but this is one controlled by its lowest ingredients. Claiming culture, it is the crudest; asseverating its pre-eminence, it is the basest; denying all outside values and virtue, it is the narrowest. Give me the pure air and the open heart of the West country. I would go back there to-morrow if I could."

"Don't you like this *filet mignon?*" said William. "Shucks, now, what's the use to knock the town! It's the greatest ever. I couldn't sell one automatic pump between Harrisburg and Tommy O'Keefe's saloon, in Sacramento, where I sell twenty here. And have you seen Sarah Bernhardt in 'Andrew Mack' yet?"

"The town's got you, Billy," said Jack.

"All right," said William. "I'm going to buy a cottage on Lake Ronkonkoma next summer."

At midnight Jack raised his window and sat close to it. He caught his breath at what he saw, though he had seen and felt it a hundred times.

Far below and around lay the city like a ragged purple dream. The irregular houses were like the broken exteriors of cliffs lining deep gulches and winding streams. Some were mountainous; some lay in long, monotonous rows like the basalt precipices hanging over desert cañons. Such was the background of the wonderful, cruel, enchanting, bewildering, fatal, great city. But into this background were cut myriads of brilliant parallelograms and circles and squares through which glowed many colored lights. And out of the violet and purple depths ascended like the city's soul sounds and odors and thrills that make up the civic body. There arose the breath of gaiety unrestrained, of love, of hate, of all the passions that man can know. There below him lay all things, good or bad, that can be brought from the four corners of the earth to instruct, please, thrill, enrich, despoil, elevate, cast down, nurture, or kill. Thus the flavor of it came to him and went into his blood.

There was a knock on his door. A telegram had come for him. It came from the West, and these were its words:

Come back home and the answer will be yes.

Dolly

He kept the boy waiting ten minutes, and then wrote the reply: "Impossible to leave here at present." Then he sat at the window again and let the city put its cup of mandragora to his lips again.

After all, it isn't a story; but I wanted to know which one of the heroes won the battle against the city. So I went to a very learned friend and laid the case before him. What he said was: "Please don't bother me, I have Christmas presents to buy."

So there it rests; and you will have to decide for yourself.

"WHAT YOU WANT"

Night had fallen on that great and beautiful city known as Bagdad-on-the-Subway. And with the night came the enchanted glamour that belongs not to Arabia alone. In different masquerade the streets, bazaars, and walled houses of the occidental city of romance were filled with the same kind of folk that so much interested our interesting old friend, the late Mr. H. A. Rashid. They wore clothes eleven hundred years nearer to the latest styles that H. A. saw in the old Bagdad; but they were about the same people underneath. With the eye of faith, you could have seen the Little Hunchback, Sinbad the Sailor, Fitbad the Tailor, the Beautiful Persian, the one-eyed Calenders, Ali Baba and Forty Robbers on every block, and the Barber and his Six Brothers, and all the old Arabian gang easily.

But let us revenue to our lamb chops.

Old Tom Crowley was a caliph. He had $42,000,000 in preferred stocks and bonds with solid gold edges. In these times, to be called a caliph, you must have money. The old-style caliph business as conducted by Mr. Rashid is not safe. If you hold up a person nowadays in a bazaar or a Turkish bath or a side street, and inquire into his private and personal affairs, the police court'll get you.

Old Tom was tired of clubs, theatres, dinners, friends, music, money, and everything. That's what makes a caliph—you must get to despise everything that money can buy, and then go out and try to want something that you can't pay for.

"I'll take a little trot around town all by myself," thought old Tom, "and try if I can stir up anything new. Let's see—it seems I've read about a king or a Cardiff giant or something in old times who used to go about with false whiskers on, making Persian dates with folks he hadn't been introduced to. That don't listen like a bad idea. I certainly have got a case of humdrumness and fatigue on for the ones I do know. That old Cardiff used to pick up cases of trouble as he ran upon 'em and give 'em gold—sequins, I think it was—and make 'em marry or got 'em good government jobs. Now, I'd like something of that sort. My money is as good as his was even if the magazines do ask me every month where I got it. Yes, I guess I'll do a little Cardiff business to-night, and see how it goes."

Plainly dressed, old Tom Crowley left his Madison Avenue palace, and walked westward and then south. As he stepped to the sidewalk, Fate, who holds the ends of the strings in the central offices of all the enchanted cities, pulled a thread, and a young man twenty blocks away looked at a wall clock, and then put on his coat.

James Turner worked in one of those little hat-cleaning establishments on Sixth Avenue in which a fire alarm rings when you push the door open, and where they clean your hat while you wait—two days. James stood all day at an electric machine that turned hats around faster than the best brands of champagne ever could have done. Overlooking your mild impertinence in feeling a curiosity about the personal appearance of a stranger, I will give you a modified description of him. Weight, 118; complexion, hair and brain, light; height, five feet six; age, about twenty-three; dressed in a $10 suit of greenish-blue serge; pockets containing two keys and sixty-three cents in change.

But do not misconjecture because this description sounds like a General Alarm that James was either lost or a dead one.

Allons!

James stood all day at his work. His feet were tender and extremely susceptible to impositions being put upon or below them. All day long they burned and smarted, causing him much suffering and inconvenience. But he was earning twelve dollars per week, which he needed to support his feet whether his feet would support him or not.

James Turner had his own conception of what happiness was, just as you and I have ours. Your delight is to gad about the world in yachts and motorcars and to hurl ducats at wild fowl. Mine is to smoke a pipe at evenfall and watch a badger, a rattlesnake, and an owl go into their common prairie home one by one.

James Turner's idea of bliss was different; but it was his. He would go directly to his boarding-house when his day's work was done. After his supper of small steak, Bessemer potatoes, stooed (not stewed) apples and infusion of chicory, he would ascend to his fifth-floor-back hall room. Then he would take off his shoes and socks, place the soles of his burning feet against the cold bars of his iron bed, and read Clark Russell's sea yarns. The delicious relief of the cool metal applied to his smarting soles was his nightly joy. His favorite novels never palled upon him; the sea and the adventures of its navigators were his sole intellectual passion. No millionaire was ever happier than James Turner taking his ease.

When James left the hat-cleaning shop he walked three blocks out of his way home to look over the goods of a second-hand bookstall. On the sidewalk stands he had more than once picked up a paper-covered volume of Clark Russell at half price.

While he was bending with a scholarly stoop over the marked-down miscellany of cast-off literature, old Tom the caliph sauntered by. His discerning eye, made keen by twenty years' experience in the manufacture of laundry soap (save the wrappers!), recognized instantly the poor and discerning scholar, a worthy object of his caliphanous mood. He descended the two shallow stone steps that led from the sidewalk, and addressed without hesitation the object of his designed munificence. His first words were no worse than salutatory and tentative.

James Turner looked up coldly with "Sartor Resartus" in one hand and "A Mad Marriage" in the other.

"Beat it," said he. "I don't want to buy any coat hangers or town lots in Hankipoo, New Jersey. Run along, now, and play with your Teddy bear."

"Young man," said the caliph, ignoring the flippancy of the hat cleaner, "I observe that you are of a studious disposition. Learning is one of the finest things in the world. I never had any of it worth mentioning, but I admire to see it in others. I come from the West, where we imagine nothing but facts. Maybe I couldn't understand the poetry and allusions in them books you are picking over, but I like to see somebody else seem to know what they mean. Now, I'd like to make you a proposition. I'm worth about $40,000,000, and I'm getting richer every day. I made the height of it manufacturing Aunt Patty's Silver Soap. I invented the art of making it. I experimented for three years before I got just the right quantity of chloride of sodium solution and caustic potash mixture to curdle properly. And after I had taken some $9,000,000 out of the soap business I made the rest in corn and wheat futures. Now, you seem to have the literary and scholarly turn of character; and I'll tell you what I'll do. I'll pay for your education at the finest college in the world. I'll pay the expense of your rummaging over Europe and the art galleries, and finally set you up in a good business. You needn't make it soap if you have any objections. I see by your clothes and frazzled necktie that you are mighty poor; and you can't afford to turn down the offer. Well, when do you want to begin?"

The hat cleaner turned upon old Tom the eye of the Big City, which is an eye expressive of cold and justifiable suspicion, of judgment suspended as high as Haman was hung, of self-preservation, of challenge, curiosity, defiance, cynicism, and, strange as you may think it, of a childlike yearning for friendliness and fellowship that must be hidden when one walks among the "stranger bands." For in New Bagdad one, in order to survive, must suspect whosoever sits, dwells, drinks, rides, walks, or sleeps in the adjacent chair, house, booth, seat, path, or room.

"Say, Mike," said James Turner, "what's your line, anyway—shoe laces? I'm not buying anything. You better put an egg in your shoe and beat it before incidents occur to you. You can't work off any fountain pens, gold spectacles you found on the street, or trust company certificate house clearings on me. Say, do I look like I'd climbed down one of them missing fire escapes at Helicon Hall? What's vitiating you, anyhow?"

"Son," said the caliph, in his most Harunish tones, "as I said, I'm worth $40,000,000. I don't want to have it all put in my coffin when I die. I want to do some good with it. I seen you handling over these here volumes of literature, and I thought I'd keep you. I've give the missionary societies $2,000,000, but what did I get out of it? Nothing but a receipt from the secretary. Now, you are just the kind of young man I'd like to take up and see what money could make of him."

Volumes of Clark Russell were hard to find that evening at the Old Book Shop. And James Turner's smarting and aching feet did not tend to improve his temper. Humble hat cleaner though he was, he had a spirit equal to any caliph's.

"Say, you old faker," he said, angrily, "be on your way. I don't know what your game is, unless you want change for a bogus $40,000,000 bill. Well, I don't carry that much around with me. But I do carry a pretty fair left-handed punch that you'll get if you don't move on."

"You are a blamed impudent little gutter pup," said the caliph.

Then James delivered his self-praised punch; old Tom seized him by the collar and kicked him thrice; the hat cleaner rallied and clinched; two bookstands were overturned, and the books sent flying. A cop came up, took an arm of each, and marched them to the nearest station house. "Fighting and disorderly conduct," said the cop to the sergeant.

"Three hundred dollars' bail," said the sergeant at once, asseveratingly and inquiringly.

"Sixty-three cents," said James Turner with a harsh laugh.

The caliph searched his pockets and collected small bills and change amounting to four dollars.

"I am worth," he said, "$40,000,000, but——"

"Lock 'em up," ordered the sergeant.

In his cell, James Turner laid himself on his cot ruminating. "Maybe he's got the money, and maybe he ain't. But if he has or he ain't what does he want to go 'round butting into other folks's business for? When a man knows what he wants, and can get it, it's the same as $40,000,000 to him."

Then an idea came to him that brought a pleased look to his face.

He removed his socks, drew his cot close to the door, stretched himself out luxuriously, and placed his tortured feet against the cold bars of the cell door. Something hard and bulky under the blankets of his cot gave one shoulder discomfort. He reached under, and drew out a paper-covered volume by Clark Russell called "A Sailor's Sweetheart." He gave a great sigh of contentment.

Presently to his cell came the doorman and said:

"Say, kid, that old gazabo that was pinched with you for scrapping seems to have been the goods, after all. He 'phoned to his friends, and he's out at the desk now with a roll of yellowbacks as big as a Pullman car pillow. He wants to bail you, and for you to come out and see him."

"Tell him I ain't in," said James Turner.

BOOK *14*

WAIFS AND STRAYS

THE RED ROSES OF TONIA

A trestle burned down on the International Railroad. The southbound from San Antonio was cut off for the next forty-eight hours. On that train was Tonia Weaver's Easter hat.

Espirition, the Mexican, who had been sent forty miles in a buckboard from the Espinosa Ranch to fetch it, returned with a shrugging shoulder and hands empty except for a cigarette. At the small station, Nopal, he had learned of the delayed train and, having no commands to wait, turned his ponies toward the ranch again.

Now, if one supposes that Easter, the Goddess of Spring, cares any more for the after-church parade on Fifth Avenue than she does for her loyal outfit of subjects that assemble at the meeting-house at Cactus, Tex., a mistake has been made. The wives and daughters of the ranchmen of the Frio country put forth Easter blossoms of new hats and gowns as faithfully as is done anywhere, and the Southwest is, for one day, a mingling of prickly pear, Paris, and paradise. And now it was Good Friday, and Tonia Weaver's Easter hat blushed unseen in the desert air of an impotent express car, beyond the burned trestle. On Saturday noon the Rogers girls, from the Shoestring Ranch, and Ella Reeves, from the Anchor-O, and Mrs. Bennett and Ida, from Green Valley, would convene at the Espinosa and pick up Tonia. With their Easter hats and frocks carefully wrapped and bundled against the dust, the fair aggregation would then merrily jog the ten miles to Cactus, where on the morrow they would array themselves, subjugate man, do homage to Easter, and cause jealous agitation among the lilies of the field.

Tonia sat on the steps of the Espinosa ranch house flicking gloomily with a quirt at a tuft of curly mesquite. She displayed a frown and a contumelious lip, and endeavored to radiate an aura of disagreeableness and tragedy.

"I hate railroads," she announced positively. "And men. Men pretend to run them. Can you give any excuse why a trestle should burn? Ida Bennett's hat is to be trimmed with violets. I shall not go one step toward Cactus without a new hat. If I were a man I would get one."

Two men listened uneasily to this disparagement of their kind. One was Wells Pearson, foreman of the Mucho Calor cattle ranch. The other was Thompson Burrows, the prosperous sheepman from the Quintana Valley. Both thought Tonia Weaver adorable, especially when she railed at railroads and menaced men. Either would have given up his epidermis to make for her an Easter hat more cheerfully than the ostrich gives up his tip or the aigrette lays down its life. Neither possessed the ingenuity to conceive a means of supplying the sad deficiency against the coming Sabbath. Pearson's deep brown face and sunburned light hair gave him the appearance of a schoolboy seized by one of youth's profound and insolvable melancholies. Tonia's plight grieved him through and through. Thompson Burrows was the more skilled and pliable. He hailed from somewhere in the East originally; and he wore neckties and shoes, and was not made dumb by woman's presence.

"The big water-hole on Sandy Creek," said Pearson, scarcely hoping to make a hit, "was filled up by that last rain."

"Oh! Was it?" said Tonia sharply. "Thank you for the information. I suppose a new hat is nothing to you, Mr. Pearson. I suppose you think a woman ought to wear an old Stetson five years without a change, as you do. If your old water-hole could have put out the fire on that trestle you might have some reason to talk about it."

"I am deeply sorry," said Burrows, warned by Pearson's fate, "that you failed to receive your hat, Miss Weaver—deeply sorry, indeed. If there was anything I could do——"

"Don't bother," interrupted Tonia, with sweet sarcasm. "If there was anything you could do, you'd be doing it, of course. There isn't."

Tonia paused. A sudden sparkle of hope had come into her eye. Her frown smoothed away. She had an inspiration.

"There's a store over at Lone Elm Crossing on the Neuces," she said, "that keeps hats. Eva Rogers got hers there. She said it was the latest style. They might have some left. But it's twenty-eight miles to Lone Elm."

The spurs of two men who hastily arose jingled; and Tonia almost smiled. The Knights, then, were not all turned to dust; nor were their rowels rust.

"Of course," said Tonia, looking thoughtfully at a white gulf cloud sailing across the cerulean dome, "nobody could ride to Lone Elm and back by the time the girls call by for me to-morrow. So, I reckon I'll have to stay at home this Easter Sunday."

And then she smiled.

"Well, Miss Tonia," said Pearson, reaching for his hat, as guileful as a sleeping babe, "I reckon I'll be trotting along back to Mucho Calor. There's some cutting out to be done on Dry Branch first thing in the morning; and me and Road Runner has got to be on hand. It's too bad your hat got sidetracked. Maybe they'll get that trestle mended yet in time for Easter."

"I must be riding, too, Miss Tonia," announced Burrows, looking at his watch. "I declare, it's nearly five o'clock! I must be out at my lambing camp in time to help pen those crazy ewes."

Tonia's suitors seemed to have been smitten with a need for haste. They bade her a ceremonious farewell, and then shook each other's hands with the elaborate and solemn courtesy of the Southwesterner.

"Hope I'll see you again soon, Mr. Pearson," said Burrows.

"Same here," said the cowman, with the serious face of one whose friend goes upon a whaling voyage. "Be gratified to see you ride over to Mucho Calor any time you strike that section of the range."

Pearson mounted Road Runner, the soundest cow-pony on the Frio, and let him pitch for a minute, as he always did on being mounted, even at the end of a hard day's travel.

"What kind of a hat was that, Miss Tonia," he called, "that you ordered from San Antone? I can't help but be sorry about that hat."

"A straw," said Tonia; "the latest shape, of course; trimmed with red roses. That's what I like—red roses."

"There's no color more becoming to your complexion and hair," said Burrows, admiringly.

"It's what I like," said Tonia. "And of all the flowers give me red roses. Keep all the pinks and blues for yourself. But what's the use, when trestles burn and leave you without anything? It'll be a dry old Easter for me!"

Pearson took off his hat and drove Road Runner at a gallop into the chaparral east of the Espinosa ranch house.

As his stirrups rattled against the brush Burrows's long-legged sorrel struck out down the narrow stretch of open prairie to the southwest.

Tonia hung up her quirt and went into the sitting-room.

"I'm mighty sorry, daughter, that you didn't get your hat," said her mother.

"Oh, don't worry, mother," said Tonia coolly. "I'll have a new hat, all right, in time to-morrow."

When Burrows reached the end of the strip of prairie he pulled his sorrel to the right and let him pick his way daintily across a sacuista flat through which ran the ragged, dry bed of an arroyo. Then up a gravelly hill, matted with bush, the horse scrambled, and at length emerged, with a snort of satisfaction, into a stretch of high, level prairie, grassy and dotted with the lighter green of mesquites in their fresh spring foliage. Always to the right Burrows bore, until in a little while he struck the old Indian trail that followed the Nueces southward, and that passed, twenty-eight miles to the southeast, through Lone Elm.

Here Burrows urged the sorrel into a steady lope. As he settled himself in the saddle for a long ride he heard the drumming of hoofs, the hollow "thwack" of chaparral against wooden stirrups, the whoop of a Comanche; and Wells Pearson burst out of the brush at the right of the trail like a precocious yellow chick from a dark green Easter egg.

Except in the presence of awing femininity melancholy found no place in Pearson's bosom. In Tonia's presence his voice was as soft as a summer bullfrog's in his reedy nest. Now, at his gleesome yawp, rabbits, a mile away, ducked their ears, and sensitive plants closed their fearful fronds.

"Moved your lambing camp pretty far from the ranch, haven't you, neighbor?" asked Pearson, as Road Runner fell in at the sorrel's side.

"Twenty-eight miles," said Burrows, looking a little grim. Pearson's laugh woke an owl one hour too early in his water-elm on the river bank, half a mile away.

"All right for you, sheepman. I like an open game, myself. We're two locoed he-milliners hat-hunting in the wilderness. I notify you, Burr, to mind your corrals. We've got an even start; and the one that gets the headgear will stand some higher at the Espinosa."

"You've got a good pony," said Burrows, eyeing Road Runner's barrel-like body and tapering legs that moved as regularly as the piston-rod of an engine. "It's a race, of course; but you're too much of a horseman to whoop it up this soon. Say we travel together till we get to the home stretch."

"I'm your company," agreed Pearson, "and I admire your sense. If there's hats at Lone Elm, one of 'em shall set on Miss Tonia's brow to-morrow, and you won't be at the crowning. I ain't bragging, Burr, but that sorrel of yours is weak in the fore-legs."

"My horse against yours," offered Burrows, "that Miss Tonia wears the hat I take her to Cactus to-morrow."

"I'll take you up," shouted Pearson. "But oh, it's just like horse-stealing for me! I can use that sorrel for a lady's animal when—when somebody comes over to Mucho Calor, and——"

Burrows's dark face glowered so suddenly that the cowman broke off his sentence. But Pearson could never feel any pressure for long.

"What's all this Easter business about, Burr?" he asked, cheerfully. "Why do the women folks have to have new hats by the almanac or bust all cinches trying to get 'em?"

"It's a seasonable statute out of the testaments," explained Burrows. "It's ordered by the Pope or somebody. And it has something to do with the Zodiac. I don't know exactly, but I think it was invented by the Egyptians."

"It's an all-right jubilee if the heathens did put their brand on it," said Pearson; "or else Tonia wouldn't have anything to do with it. And they pull it off at church, too. Suppose there ain't but one hat in the Lone Elm store, Burr!"

"Then," said Burrows, darkly, "the best man of us'll take it back to the Espinosa."

"Oh, man!" cried Pearson, throwing his hat high and catching it again, "there's nothing like you come off the sheep ranges before. You talk good and collateral to the occasion. And if there's more than one?"

"Then," said Burrows, "we'll pick our choice and one of us'll get back first with his and the other won't."

"There never was two souls," proclaimed Pearson to the stars, "that beat more like one heart than yourn and mine. Me and you might be riding on a unicorn and thinking out of the same piece of mind."

At a little past midnight the riders loped into Lone Elm. The half a hundred houses of the big village were dark. On its only street the big wooden store stood barred and shuttered.

In a few moments the horses were fastened and Pearson was pounding cheerfully on the door of old Sutton, the storekeeper.

The barrel of a Winchester came through a cranny of a solid window shutter, followed by a short inquiry.

"Wells Pearson, of the Mucho Calor, and Burrows, of Green Valley," was the response. "We want to buy some goods in the store. Sorry to wake you up, but we must have 'em. Come on out, Uncle Tommy, and get a move on you."

Uncle Tommy was slow, but at length they got him behind his counter with a kerosene lamp lit, and told him of their dire need.

"Easter hats?" said Uncle Tommy, sleepily. "Why, yes, I believe I have got just a couple left. I only ordered a dozen this spring. I'll show 'em to you."

Now, Uncle Tommy Sutton was a merchant, half asleep or awake. In dusty pasteboard boxes under the counter he had two left-over spring hats. But, alas! for his commercial probity on that early Saturday morn—they were hats of two springs ago, and a woman's eye would have detected the fraud at half a glance. But to the unintelligent gaze of the cowpuncher and the sheepman they seemed fresh from the mint of contemporaneous April.

The hats were of a variety once known as "cart-wheels." They were of stiff straw, colored red, and flat brimmed. Both were exactly alike, and trimmed lavishly around their crowns with full blown, immaculate, artificial white roses.

"That all you got, Uncle Tommy?" said Pearson. "All right. Not much choice here, Burr. Take your pick."

"They're the latest styles," lied Uncle Tommy. "You'd see 'em on Fifth Avenue, if you was in New York."

Uncle Tommy wrapped and tied each hat in two yards of dark calico for a protection. One Burrows tied carefully to his calfskin saddle-thongs; and the other became part of Road Runner's burden. They shouted thanks and farewells to Uncle Tommy, and cantered back into the night on the home stretch.

The horsemen jockeyed with all their skill. They rode more slowly on their way back. The few words they spoke were not unfriendly. Burrows had a Winchester under his left leg slung over his saddle horn. Pearson had a six-shooter belted around him. Thus men rode in the Frio country.

At half-past seven in the morning they rode to the top of a hill and saw the Espinosa Ranch, a white spot under a dark patch of live-oaks, five miles away.

The sight roused Pearson from his drooping pose in the saddle. He knew what Road Runner could do. The sorrel was lathered, and stumbling frequently; Road Runner was pegging away like a donkey engine.

Pearson turned toward the sheepman and laughed. "Good-bye, Burr," he cried, with a wave of his hand. "It's a race now. We're on the home stretch."

He pressed Road Runner with his knees and leaned toward the Espinosa. Road Runner struck into a gallop, with tossing head and snorting nostrils, as if he were fresh from a month in pasture.

Pearson rode twenty yards and heard the unmistakable sound of a Winchester lever throwing a cartridge into the barrel. He dropped flat along his horse's back before the crack of the rifle reached his ears.

It is possible that Burrows intended only to disable the horse—he was a good enough shot to do that without endangering his rider. But as Pearson stooped the ball went through his shoulder and then through Road

Runner's neck. The horse fell and the cowman pitched over his head into the hard road, and neither of them tried to move.

Burrows rode on without stopping.

In two hours Pearson opened his eyes and took inventory. He managed to get to his feet and staggered back to where Road Runner was lying.

Road Runner was lying there, but he appeared to be comfortable. Pearson examined him and found that the bullet had "creased" him. He had been knocked out temporarily, but not seriously hurt. But he was tired, and he lay there on Miss Tonia's hat and ate leaves from a mesquite branch that obligingly hung over the road.

Pearson made the horse get up. The Easter hat, loosed from the saddle-thongs, lay there in its calico wrappings, a shapeless thing from its sojourn beneath the solid carcass of Road Runner. Then Pearson fainted and fell headlong upon the poor hat again, crumpling it under his wounded shoulder.

It is hard to kill a cowpuncher. In half an hour he revived—long enough for a woman to have fainted twice and tried ice-cream for a restorer. He got up carefully and found Road Runner who was busy with the near-by grass. He tied the unfortunate hat to the saddle again, and managed to get himself there, too, after many failures.

At noon a gay and fluttering company waited in front of the Espinosa Ranch. The Rogers girls were there in their new buckboard, and the Anchor-O outfit, and the Green Valley folks—mostly women. And each and every one wore her new Easter hat, even upon the lonely prairies, for they greatly desired to shine forth and do honor to the coming festival.

At the gate stood Tonia, with undisguised tears upon her cheeks. In her hand she held Burrows's Lone Elm hat, and it was at its white roses, hated by her, that she wept. For her friends were telling her, with the ecstatic joy of true friends, that cart-wheels could not be worn, being three seasons passed into oblivion.

"Put on your old hat and come, Tonia," they urged.

"For Easter Sunday?" she answered. "I'll die first." And wept again.

The hats of the fortunate ones were curved and twisted into the style of spring's latest proclamation.

A strange being rode out of the brush among them, and there sat his horse languidly. He was stained and disfigured with the green of the grass and the limestone of rocky roads.

"Hallo, Pearson," said Daddy Weaver. "Look like you've been breaking a mustang. What's that you've got tied to your saddle—a pig in a poke?"

"Oh, come on, Tonia, if you're going," said Betty Rogers. "We mustn't wait any longer. We've saved a seat in the buckboard for you. Never mind the hat. That lovely muslin you've got on looks sweet enough with any old hat."

Pearson was slowly untying the queer thing on his saddle. Tonia looked at him with a sudden hope. Pearson was a man who created hope. He got the thing loose and handed it to her. Her quick fingers tore at the strings.

"Best I could do," said Pearson slowly. "What Road Runner and me done to it will be about all it needs."

"Oh, oh! it's just the right shape," shrieked Tonia. "And red roses! Wait till I try it on!"

She flew in to the glass, and out again, beaming, radiating, blossomed.

"Oh, don't red become her?" chanted the girls in recitative. "Hurry up, Tonia!"

Tonia stopped for a moment by the side of Road Runner.

"Thank you, thank you, Wells," she said, happily. "It's just what I wanted. Won't you come over to Cactus to-morrow and go to church with me?"

"If I can," said Pearson. He was looking curiously at her hat, and then he grinned weakly.

Tonia flew into the buckboard like a bird. The vehicle sped away for Cactus.

"What have you been doing, Pearson?" asked Daddy Weaver. "You ain't looking so well as common."

"Me?" said Pearson. "I've been painting flowers. Them roses was white when I left Lone Elm. Help me down, Daddy Weaver, for I haven't got any more paint to spare."

ROUND THE CIRCLE[1]

"Find yo' shirt all right, Sam?" asked Mrs. Webber, from her chair under the live-oak, where she was comfortably seated with a paper-back volume for company.

"It balances perfeckly, Marthy," answered Sam, with a suspicious pleasantness in his tone. "At first I was about ter be a little reckless and kick 'cause ther buttons was all off, but since I diskiver that the button holes is all busted out, why, I wouldn't go so fur as to say the buttons is any loss to speak of."

"Oh, well," said his wife, carelessly, "put on your necktie—that'll keep it together."

Sam Webber's sheep ranch was situated in the loneliest part of the country between the Nueces and the Frio. The ranch house—a two-room box structure—was on the rise of a gently swelling hill in the midst of a wilderness of high chaparral. In front of it was a small clearing where

[1]This story is especially interesting as an early treatment (1902) of the theme afterward developed with a surer hand in the Pendulum.

stood the sheep pens, shearing shed, and wool house. Only a few feet back of it began the thorny jungle.

Sam was going to ride over to the Chapman ranch to see about buying some more improved merino rams. At length he came out, ready for his ride. This being a business trip of some importance, and the Chapman ranch being almost a small town in population and size, Sam had decided to "dress up" accordingly. The result was that he had transformed himself from a graceful, picturesque frontiersman into something much less pleasing to the sight. The tight white collar awkwardly constricted his muscular, mahogany-colored neck. The buttonless shirt bulged in stiff waves beneath his unbuttoned vest. The suit of "ready-made" effectually concealed the fine lines of his straight, athletic figure. His berry-brown face was set to the melancholy dignity befitting a prisoner of state. He gave Randy, his three-year-old son, a pat on the head, and hurried out to where Mexico, his favorite saddle horse, was standing.

Marthy, leisurely rocking in her chair, fixed her place in the book with her finger, and turned her head, smiling mischievously as she noted the havoc Sam had wrought with his appearance in trying to "fix up."

"Well, ef I must say it, Sam," she drawled, "you look jest like one of them hayseeds in the picture papers, 'stead of a free and independent sheepman of the State o' Texas."

Sam climbed awkwardly into the saddle.

"You're the one ought to be 'shamed to say so," he replied hotly. " 'Stead of 'tendin' to a man's clothes you're al'ays settin' around a-readin' them billy-by-dam yaller-back novils."

"Oh, shet up and ride along," said Mrs. Webber, with a little jerk at the handles of her chair; "you al'ays fussin' 'bout my readin'. I do a-plenty; and I'll read when I wanter. I live in the bresh here like a varmint, never seein' nor hearin' nothin', and what other 'musement kin I have? Not in listenin' to you talk, for it's complain, complain, one day after another. Oh, go on, Sam, and leave me in peace."

Sam gave his pony a squeeze with his knees and "shoved" down the wagon trail that connected his ranch with the old, open Government road. It was eight o'clock, and already beginning to be very warm. He should have started three hours earlier. Chapman ranch was only eighteen miles away, but there was a road for only three miles of the distance. He had ridden over there once with one of the Half-Moon cowpunchers, and he had the direction well-defined in his mind.

Sam turned off the old Government road at the split mesquite, and struck down the arroyo of the Quintanilla. Here was a narrow stretch of smiling valley, upholstered with a rich mat of green, curly mesquite grass; and Mexico consumed those few miles quickly with his long, easy lope. Again, upon reaching Wild Duck Waterhole, must he abandon well-defined ways. He turned now to his right up a little hill, pebble-covered, upon which grew only the tenacious and thorny prickly pear and chaparral. At the summit of this he paused to take his last general view of the landscape for, from now on, he must wind through brakes and thickets of chaparral, pear, and mesquite, for the most part seeing scarcely farther than twenty yards in any direction, choosing his way by the prairie-dweller's instinct, guided only by an occasional glimpse of a far distant hilltop, a peculiarly shaped knot of trees, or the position of the sun.

Sam rode down the sloping hill and plunged into the great pear flat that lies between the Quintanilla and the Piedra.

In about two hours he discovered that he was lost. Then came the usual confusion of mind and the hurry to get somewhere. Mexico was anxious to redeem the situation, twisting with alacrity along the tortuous labyrinths of the jungle. At the moment his master's sureness of the route had failed, his horse had divined the fact. There were no hills now that they could climb to obtain a view of the country. They came upon a few, but so dense and interlaced was the brush that scarcely could a rabbit penetrate the mass. They were in the great, lonely thicket of the Frio bottoms.

It was a mere nothing for a cattleman or a sheepman to be lost for a day or a night. The thing often happened. It was merely a matter of missing a meal or two and sleeping comfortably on your saddle blankets on a soft mattress of mesquite grass. But in Sam's case it was different. He had never been away from his ranch at night. Marthy was afraid of the country—afraid of Mexicans, of snakes, of panthers, even of sheep. So he had never left her alone.

It must have been about four in the afternoon when Sam's conscience awoke. He was limp and drenched, rather from anxiety than the heat or fatigue. Until now he had been hoping to strike the trail that led to the Frio crossing and the Chapman ranch. He must have crossed it at some dim part of it and ridden beyond. If so he was now something like fifty miles from home. If he could strike a ranch—a camp—any place where he could get a fresh horse and inquire the road, he would ride all night to get back to Marthy and the kid.

So, I have hinted, Sam was seized by remorse. There was a big lump in his throat as he thought of the cross words he had spoken to his wife. Surely it was hard enough for her to live in that horrible country without having to bear the burden of his abuse. He cursed himself grimly, and felt a sudden flush of shame that over-glowed the summer heat as he remembered the many times he had flouted and railed at her because she had a liking for reading fiction.

"Ther only so'ce ov amusement ther po' gal's got," said Sam aloud, with a sob, which unaccustomed sound caused Mexico to shy a bit. "A-livin' with a sore-headed kiote like me—a low-down skunk that ought to be licked to death with a saddle cinch—a-cookin' and a-washin' and a-livin' on mutton and beans and me abusin' her fur takin' a squint or two in a little book!"

He thought of Marthy as she had been when he first met her in Dog-town—smart, pretty, and saucy—before the sun had turned the roses in her cheeks brown and the silence of the chaparral had tamed her ambitions.

"Ef I ever speaks another hard word to ther little gal," muttered Sam, "or fails in the love and affection that's comin' to her in the deal, I hopes a wildcat'll t'ar me to pieces."

He knew what he would do. He would write to Garcia & Jones, his San Antonio merchants where he bought his supplies and sold his wool, and have them send down a big box of novels and reading matter for Marthy. Things were going to be different. He wondered whether a little piano could be placed in one of the rooms of the ranch house without the family having to move out of doors.

In nowise calculated to allay his self-reproach was the thought that Marthy and Randy would have to pass the night alone. In spite of their bickerings, when night came Marthy was wont to dismiss her fears of the country, and rest her head upon Sam's strong arm with a sigh of peaceful content and dependence. And were her fears so groundless? Sam thought of roving, marauding Mexicans, of stealthy cougars that sometimes invaded the ranches, of rattlesnakes, centipedes, and a dozen possible dangers. Marthy would be frantic with fear. Randy would cry, and call for "dada" to come.

Still the interminable succession of stretches of brush, cactus, and mesquite. Hollow after hollow, slope after slope—all exactly alike—all familiar by constant repetition, and yet all strange and new. If he could only arrive *somewhere*.

The straight line is Art. Nature moves in circles. A straightforward man is more an artificial product than a diplomatist is. Men lost in the snow travel in exact circles until they sink, exhausted, as their footprints have attested. Also, travellers in philosophy and other mental processes frequently wind up at their starting-point.

It was when Sam Webber was fullest of contrition and good resolves that Mexico, with a heavy sigh, subsided from his regular, brisk trot into a slow, complacent walk. They were winding up an easy slope covered with brush ten or twelve feet high.

"I say now, Mex," demurred Sam, "this here won't do. I know you're plumb tired out, but we got ter git along. Oh, Lordy, ain't there no mo' houses in the world!" He gave Mexico a smart kick with his heels.

Mexico gave a protesting grunt as if to say: "What's the use of that, now we're so near?" He quickened his gait into a languid trot. Rounding a great clump of black chaparral he stopped short. Sam dropped the bridle reins and sat, looking into the back door of his own house, not ten yards away.

Marthy, serene and comfortable, sat in her rocking-chair before the door in the shade of the house, with her feet resting luxuriously upon the steps. Randy, who was playing with a pair of spurs on the ground, looked up for a moment at his father and went on spinning the rowels and singing a little song. Marthy turned her head lazily against the back of the chair and considered the arrivals with emotionless eyes. She held a book in her lap with her finger holding the place.

Sam shook himself queerly, like a man coming out of a dream, and slowly dismounted. He moistened his dry lips.

"I see you are still a-settin'," he said, "a-readin' of them billy-by-dam yaller-back novils."

Sam had travelled round the circle and was himself again.

THE RUBBER PLANT'S STORY

We rubber plants form the connecting link between the vegetable kingdom and the decorations of a Waldorf-Astoria scene in a Third Avenue theatre. I haven't looked up our family tree, but I believe we were raised by grafting a gum overshoe on to a 30-cent table d'hôte stalk of asparagus. You take a white bulldog with a Bourke Cockran air of independence about him and a rubber plant and there you have the fauna and flora of a flat. What the shamrock is to Ireland the rubber plant is to the dweller in flats and furnished rooms. We get moved from one place to another so quickly that the only way we can get our picture taken is with a kinetoscope. We are the vagrant vine and the flitting fig tree. You know the proverb: "Where the rubber plant sits in the window the moving van draws up to the door."

We are the city equivalent to the woodbine and the honeysuckle. No other vegetable except the Pittsburgh stogie can withstand as much handling as we can. When the family to which we belong moves into a flat they set us in the front window and we become lares and penates, flypaper and the peripatetic emblem of "Home Sweet Home." We aren't as green as we look. I guess we are about what you would call the soubrettes of the conservatory. You try sitting in the front window of a $40 flat in Manhattan and looking out into the street all day, and back into the flat at night, and see whether you get wise or not—hey? Talk about the tree of knowledge of good and evil in the garden of Eden—say! suppose there had been a rubber plant there when Eve—but I was going to tell you a story.

The first thing I can remember I had only three leaves and belonged to a member of the pony ballet. I was kept in a sunny window, and was generally watered with seltzer and lemon. I had plenty of fun in those days. I got cross-eyed trying to watch the numbers of the automobiles in the street and the dates on the labels inside at the same time.

Well, then the angel that was molting for the musical comedy lost his last feather and the company broke up. The ponies trotted away and I was left in the window ownerless. The janitor gave me to a refined comedy team on the eighth floor, and in six weeks I had been set in the window of five different flats. I took on experience and put out two more leaves.

Miss Carruthers, of the refined comedy team—did you ever see her cross both feet back of her neck?—gave me to a friend of hers who had made an unfortunate marriage with a man in a store. Consequently I was placed in the window of a furnished room, rent in advance, water two flights up, gas extra after ten o'clock at night. Two of my leaves withered off here. Also, I was moved from one room to another so many times that I got to liking the odor of the pipes the express-men smoked.

I don't think I ever had so dull a time as I did with this lady. There was never anything amusing going on inside—she was devoted to her husband, and, besides leaning out the window and flirting with the iceman, she never did a thing toward breaking the monotony.

When the couple broke up they left me with the rest of their goods at a second-hand store. I was put out in front for sale along with the jobbiest lot you ever heard of being lumped into one bargain. Think of this little cornucopia of wonders, all for $1.89: Henry James's works, six talking machine records, one pair of tennis shoes, two bottles of horse radish, and a rubber plant—that was me!

One afternoon a girl came along and stopped to look at me. She had dark hair and eyes, and she looked slim, and sad around the mouth.

"Oh, oh!" she says to herself. "I never thought to see one up here."

She pulls out a little purse about as thick as one of my leaves and fingers over some small silver in it. Old Koen, always on the lookout, is ready, rubbing his hands. This girl proceeds to turn down Mr. James and the other commodities. Rubber plants or nothing is the burden of her song. And at last Koen and she come together at 39 cents, and away she goes with me in her arms.

She was a nice girl, but not my style. Too quiet and sober looking. Thinks I to myself: "I'll just about land on the fire-escape of a tenement, six stories up. And I'll spend the next six months looking at clothes on the line."

But she carried me to a nice little room only three flights up in quite a decent street. And she put me in the window, of course. And then she went to work and cooked dinner for herself. And what do you suppose she had? Bread and tea and a little dab of jam! Nothing else. Not a single lobster, nor so much as one bottle of champagne. The Carruthers comedy team had both every evening, except now and then when they took a notion for pig's knuckle and kraut.

After she had finished her dinner my new owner came to the window and leaned down close to my leaves and cried softly to herself for a while. It made me feel funny. I never knew anybody to cry that way over a rubber plant before. Of course, I've seen a few of 'em turn on the tears for what they could get out of it, but she seemed to be crying just for the pure enjoyment of it. She touched my leaves like she loved 'em, and she bent down her head and kissed each one of 'em. I guess I'm about the toughest specimen of a peripatetic orchid on earth, but I tell you it made me feel sort of queer. Home never was like that to me before. Generally I used to get chewed by poodles and have shirtwaists hung on me to dry, and get watered with coffee grounds and peroxide of hydrogen.

This girl had a piano in the room, and she used to disturb it with both hands while she made noises with her mouth for hours at a time. I suppose she was practising vocal music.

One day she seemed very much excited and kept looking at the clock. At eleven somebody knocked and she let in a stout, dark man with tousled black hair. He sat down at once at the piano and played while she sang for him. When she finished she laid one hand on her bosom and looked at him. He shook his head, and she leaned against the piano.

"Two years already," she said, speaking slowly—"do you think in two more—or even longer?"

The man shook his head again. "You waste your time," he said, roughly I thought. "The voice is not there." And then he looked at her in a peculiar way. "But the voice is not everything," he went on. "You have looks. I can place you, as I told you if——"

The girl pointed to the door without saying anything, and the dark man left the room. And then she came over and cried around me again. It's a good thing I had enough rubber in me to be water-proof.

About that time somebody else knocked at the door. "Thank goodness," I said to myself. "Here's a chance to get the water-works turned off. I hope it's somebody that's game enough to stand a bird and a bottle to liven things up a little." Tell you the truth, this little girl made me tired. A rubber plant likes to see a little sport now and then. I don't suppose there's another green thing in New York that sees as much of gay life unless it's the chartreuse or the sprigs of parsley around the dish.

When the girl opens the door in steps a young chap in a traveling cap and picks her up in his arms, and she sings out "Oh, Dick!" and stays there long enough to—well, you've been a rubber plant too, sometimes, I suppose.

"Good thing!" says I to myself. "This is livelier than scales and weeping. Now there'll be something doing."

"You've got to go back with me," says the young man. "I've come two thousand miles for you. Aren't you tired of it yet, Bess? You've kept all of us waiting so long. Haven't you found out yet what is best?"

"The bubble burst only to-day," says the girl. "Come here, Dick, and see what I found the other day on the sidewalk for sale." She brings him by the hand and exhibits yours truly. "How one ever got away up here who can tell? I bought it with almost the last money I had."

He looked at me, but he couldn't keep his eyes off her for more than a second.

"Do you remember the night, Bess," he said, "when we stood under one of those on the bank of the bayou and what you told me then?"

"Geewillikins!" I said to myself. "Both of them stand under a rubber plant! Seems to me they are stretching matters somewhat!"

"Do I not," says she, looking up at him and sneaking close to his vest, "and now I say it again, and it is to last forever. Look, Dick, at its leaves, how wet they are. Those are my tears, and it was thinking of you that made them fall."

"The dear old magnolias!" says the young man, pinching one of my leaves. "I love them all."

Magnolia! Well, wouldn't that—say! those innocents thought I was a magnolia! What the—well, wasn't that tough on a genuine little old New York rubber plant?

OUT OF NAZARETH

Okochee, in Georgia, had a boom, and J. Pinkney Bloom came out of it with a "wad." Okochee came out of it with a half-million-dollar debt, a two and a half per cent. city property tax, and a city council that showed a propensity for traveling the back streets of the town. These things came about through a fatal resemblance of the river Cooloosa to the Hudson, as set forth and expounded by a Northern tourist. Okochee felt that New York should not be allowed to consider itself the only alligator in the swamp, so to speak. And then that harmless, but persistent, individual so numerous in the South—the man who is always clamoring for more cotton mills, and is ready to take a dollar's worth of stock, provided he can borrow the dollar—that man added his deadly work to the tourist's innocent praise, and Okochee fell.

The Cooloosa River winds through a range of small mountains, passes Okochee, and then blends its waters trippingly, as fall the mellifluous Indian syllables, with the Chattahoochee.

Okochee rose, as it were, from its sunny seat on the post-office stoop, hitched up its suspender, and threw a granite dam two hundred and forty feet long and sixty feet high across the Cooloosa one mile above the town. Thereupon, a dimpling, sparkling lake backed up twenty miles among the little mountains. Thus in the great game of municipal rivalry did Okochee match that famous drawing card, the Hudson. It was conceded that nowhere could the Palisades be judged superior in the way of scenery and grandeur. Following the picture card was played the ace of commercial importance. Fourteen thousand horsepower would this dam furnish. Cotton mills, factories, and manufacturing plants would rise up as the green corn after a shower. The spindle and the flywheel and turbine would sing the shrewd glory of Okochee. Along the picturesque heights above the lake would rise in beauty the costly villas and the splendid summer residences of capital. The naphtha launch of the millionaire would spit among the romantic coves; the verdured hills would take formal shapes of terrace, lawn, and park. Money would be spent like water in Okochee, and water would be turned into money.

The fate of the good town is quickly told. Capital decided not to invest. Of all the great things promised, the scenery alone came to fulfilment. The wooded peaks, the impressive promontories of solemn granite, the beautiful green slants of bank and ravine did all they could to reconcile Okochee to the delinquency of miserly gold. The sunsets gilded the dreamy draws and coves with a minting that should charm away heartburning. Okochee, true to the instinct of its blood and clime, was lulled by the spell. It climbed out of the arena, loosed its suspender, sat down again on the post-office stoop, and took a chew. It consoled itself by drawling sarcasms at the city council which was not to blame, causing the fathers, as has been said, to seek back streets and figure perspiringly on the sinking fund and the appropriation for interest due.

The youth of Okochee—they who were to carry into the rosy future the burden of the debt—accepted failure with youth's uncalculating joy. For, here was sport, aquatic and nautical, added to the meagre round of life's pleasures. In yachting caps and flowing neckties they pervaded the lake to its limits. Girls wore silk waists embroidered with anchors in blue and pink. The trousers of the young men widened at the bottom, and their hands were proudly calloused by the oft-plied oar. Fishermen were under the spell of a deep and tolerant joy. Sailboats and rowboats furrowed the lenient waves, popcorn and ice-cream booths sprang up about the little wooden pier. Two small excursion steamboats were built, and plied the delectable waters. Okochee philosophically gave up the hope of eating turtle soup with a gold spoon, and settled back, not ill content, to its regular diet of lotus and fried hominy. And out of this slow wreck of great expectations rose up J. Pinkney Bloom with his "wad" and his prosperous, cheery smile.

Needless to say J. Pinkney was no product of Georgia soil. He came out of that flushed and capable region known as the "North." He called himself a "promoter"; his enemies had spoken of him as a "grafter"; Okochee took a middle course, and held him to be no better nor no worse than a "Yank."

Far up the lake—eighteen miles above the town—the eye of this cheerful camp-follower of booms had spied out a graft. He purchased there a precipitous tract of five hundred acres at forty-five cents per acre; and this he laid out and subdivided as the city of Skyland—the Queen City of the Switzerland of the South. Streets and avenues were surveyed; parks designed; corners of central squares reserved for the "proposed" opera house, board of trade, lyceum, market, public schools, and "Exposition Hall." The price of lots ranged from five to five hundred dollars. Positively, no lot would be priced higher than five hundred dollars.

While the boom was growing in Okochee, J. Pinkney's circulars, maps, and prospectuses were flying through the mails to every part of the country. Investors sent in their money by post, and the Skyland Real Estate Company (J. Pinkney Bloom) returned to each a deed, duly placed on record, to the best lot, at the price, on hand that day. All this time the catamount screeched upon the reserved lot of the Skyland Board of Trade, the opossum swung by his tail over the site of the exposition hall, and the owl hooted a melancholy recitative to his audience of young squirrels in opera house square. Later, when the money was coming in fast, J. Pinkney caused to be erected in the coming city half a dozen cheap box houses, and persuaded a contingent of indigent natives to occupy them, thereby assuming the rôle of "population" in subsequent prospectuses, which became, accordingly, more seductive and remunerative.

So, when the dream faded and Okochee dropped back to digging bait and nursing its two and a half per cent. tax, J. Pinkney Bloom (unloving of checks and drafts and the cold interrogatories of bankers) strapped about his fifty-two-inch waist a soft leather belt containing eight thousand dollars in big bills, and said that all was very good.

One last trip he was making to Skyland before departing to other salad fields. Skyland was a regular post-office, and the steamboat, *Dixie Belle,* under contract, delivered the mail bag (generally empty) twice a week. There was a little business there to be settled—the postmaster was to be paid off for his light but lonely services, and the "inhabitants" had to be furnished with another month's homely rations, as per agreement. And then Skyland would know J. Pinkney Bloom no more. The owners of these precipitous, barren, useless lots might come and view the scene of their invested credulity, or they might leave them to their fit tenants, the wild hog and the browsing deer. The work of the Skyland Real Estate Company was finished.

The little steamboat *Dixie Belle* was about to shove off on her regular up-the-lake trip, when a rickety hired carriage rattled up to the pier, and a tall, elderly gentleman, in black, stepped out, signaling courteously but vivaciously for the boat to wait. Time was of the least importance in the schedule of the *Dixie Belle;* Captain MacFarland gave the order, and the boat received its ultimate two passengers. For, upon the arm of the tall, elderly gentleman, as he crossed the gangway, was a little elderly lady, with a gray curl depending quaintly forward of her left ear.

Captain MacFarland was at the wheel; therefore it seemed to J. Pinkney Bloom, who was the only other passenger, that it should be his to play the part of host to the boat's new guests, who were, doubtless, on a scenery-viewing expedition. He stepped forward, with that translucent, child-candid smile upon his fresh, pink countenance, with that air of unaffected sincerity that was redeemed from bluffness only by its exquisite calculation, with that promptitude and masterly decision of manner that so well suited his calling—with all his stock in trade well to the front, he stepped forward to receive Colonel and Mrs. Peyton Blaylock. With the grace of a grand marshal or a wedding usher, he escorted the two passengers to the side of the upper deck, from which the scenery was supposed to present itself to the observer in increased quantity and quality. There, in comfortable steamer chairs, they sat and began to piece together the random lines that were to form an intelligent paragraph in the big history of little events.

"Our home, sir," said Colonel Blaylock, removing his wide-brimmed, rather shapeless black felt hat, "is in Holly Springs—Holly Springs, Georgia. I am very proud to make your acquaintance, Mr. Bloom. Mrs. Blaylock and myself have just arrived in Okochee this morning, sir, on business—business of importance in connection with the recent rapid march of progress in this section of our state."

The Colonel smoothed back, with a sweeping gesture, his long, smooth, gray locks. His dark eyes, still fiery under the heavy black brows, seemed inappropriate to the face of a business man. He looked rather to be an old courtier handed down from the reign of Charles, and re-attired in a modern suit of fine, but raveling and seam-worn, broadcloth.

"Yes, sir," said Mr. Bloom, in his heartiest prospectus voice, "things have been whizzing around Okochee. Biggest industrial revival and waking up to natural resources Georgia ever had. Did you happen to squeeze in on the ground floor in any of the gilt-edged grafts, Colonel?"

"Well, sir," said the Colonel, hesitating in courteous doubt, "if I understand your question, I may say that I took the opportunity to make an investment that I believe will prove quite advantageous—yes, sir, I believe it will result in both pecuniary profit and agreeable occupation."

"Colonel Blaylock," said the little elderly lady, shaking her gray curl and smiling indulgent explanation at J. Pinkney Bloom, "is so devoted to business. He has such a talent for financiering and markets and investments and those kind of things. I think myself extremely fortunate in having secured him for a partner on life's journey—I am so unversed in those formidable but very useful branches of learning."

Colonel Blaylock rose and made a bow—a bow that belonged with silk stockings and lace ruffles and velvet.

"Practical affairs," he said, with a wave of his hand toward the promoter, "are, if I may use the comparison, the garden walks upon which we tread through life, viewing upon either side of us the flowers which brighten that journey. It is my pleasure to be able to lay out a walk or two. Mrs. Blaylock, sir, is one of those fortunate higher spirits whose mission it is to make the flowers grow. Perhaps, Mr. Bloom, you have perused the lines of Lorella, the Southern poetess. That is the name above which Mrs. Blaylock has contributed to the press of the South for many years."

"Unfortunately," said Mr. Bloom, with a sense of the loss clearly written upon his frank face, "I'm like the Colonel—in the walk-making business myself—and I haven't had time to even take a sniff at the flowers. Poetry is a line I never dealt in. It must be nice, though—quite nice."

"It is the region," smiled Mrs. Blaylock, "in which my soul dwells. My shawl, Peyton, if you please—the breeze comes a little chilly from yon verdured hills."

The Colonel drew from the tail pocket of his coat a small shawl of knitted silk and laid it solicitously about the shoulders of the lady. Mrs. Blaylock sighed contentedly, and turned her expressive eyes—still as clear and unworldly as a child's—upon the steep slopes that were slowly slipping past. Very fair and stately they looked in the clear morning air. They seemed to speak in familiar terms to the responsive spirit of Lorella. "My native hills!" she murmured, dreamily. "See how the foliage drinks the sunlight from the hollows and dells."

"Mrs. Blaylock's maiden days," said the Colonel, interpreting her mood to J. Pinkney Bloom, "were spent among the mountains of northern Georgia. Mountain air and mountain scenery recall to her those days. Holly Springs, where we have lived for twenty years, is low and flat. I fear that she may have suffered in health and spirits by so long a residence there. That is one potent reason for the change we are making. My dear, can you not recall those lines you wrote—entitled, I think, 'The Georgia Hills'—the poem that was so extensively copied by the Southern press and praised so highly by the Atlanta critics?"

Mrs. Blaylock turned a glance of speaking tenderness upon the Colonel, fingered for a moment the silvery curl that drooped upon her bosom, then looked again toward the mountains. Without preliminary or affectation or demurral she began, in rather thrilling and more deeply pitched tones, to recite these lines:

"The Georgia hills, the Georgia hills!—
  Oh, heart, why dost thou pine?
Are not these sheltered lowlands fair
  With mead and bloom and vine?
Ah! as the slow-paced river here
  Broods on its natal rills
My spirit drifts, in longing sweet,
  Back to the Georgia hills.

"And through the close-drawn, cur-
 tained night
I steal on sleep's slow wings
Back to my heart's ease—slopes of
 pine—
Where end my wanderings.
Oh, heaven seems nearer from their
 tops—
And farther earthly ills—
Even in dreams, if I may but
 Dream of my Georgia hills.

"The grass upon their orchard sides
 Is a fine couch to me;
The common note of each small bird
 Passes all minstrelsy.
It would not seem so dread a thing
 If, when the Reaper wills,
He might come there and take my
 hand
Up in the Georgia hills."

"That's great stuff, ma'am," said J. Pinkney Bloom, enthusiastically, when the poetess had concluded. "I wish I had looked up poetry more than I have. I was raised in the pine hills myself."

"The mountains ever call to their children," murmured Mrs. Blaylock. "I feel that life will take on the rosy hue of hope again in among these beautiful hills. Peyton—a little taste of the currant wine, if you will be so good. The journey, though delightful in the extreme, slightly fatigues me."

Colonel Blaylock again visited the depths of his prolific coat, and produced a tightly corked, rough, black bottle. Mr. Bloom was on his feet in an instant. "Let me bring a glass, ma'am. You come along, Colonel—there's a little table we can bring, too. Maybe we can scare up some fruit or a cup of tea on board. I'll ask Mac."

Mrs. Blaylock reclined at ease. Few royal ladies have held their royal prerogative with the serene grace of the petted Southern woman. The Colonel, with an air as gallant and assiduous as in the days of his courtship, and J. Pinkney Bloom, with a ponderous agility half professional and half directed by some resurrected, unnamed, long-forgotten sentiment, formed a diversified but attentive court. The currant wine—wine home made from the Holly Springs fruit—went round; and then J. Pinkney began to hear something of Holly Springs life.

It seemed (from the conversation of the Blaylocks) that the Springs was decadent. A third of the population had moved away. Business—and the Colonel was an authority on business—had dwindled to nothing. After carefully studying the field of opportunities open to capital he had sold his little property there for eight hundred dollars and invested it in one of the enterprises opened up by the book in Okochee.

"Might I inquire, sir," said Mr. Bloom, "in what particular line of business you inserted your coin? I know that town as well as I know the regulations for illegal use of the mails. I might give you a hunch as to whether you can make the game go or not."

J. Pinkney, somehow, had a kindly feeling toward these unsophisticated representatives of by-gone days. They were so simple, impractical, and unsuspecting. He was glad that he happened not to have a gold brick or a block of that western Bad Boy Silver Mine stock along with him. He would have disliked to unload on people he liked so well as he did these; but there are some temptations too enticing to be resisted.

"No, sir," said Colonel Blaylock, pausing to arrange the queen's wrap. "I did not invest in Okochee. I have made an exhaustive study of business conditions, and I regard old settled towns as unfavorable fields in which to place capital that is limited in amount. Some months ago, through the kindness of a friend, there came into my hands a map and description of this new town of Skyland that has been built upon the lake. The description was so pleasing, the future of the town set forth in such convincing arguments, and its increasing prosperity portrayed in such an attractive style that I decided to take advantage of the opportunity it offered. I carefully selected a lot in the centre of the business district, although its price was the highest in the schedule—five hundred dollars —and made the purchase at once."

"Are you the man—I mean, did you pay five hundred dollars for a lot in Skyland?" asked J. Pinkney Bloom.

"I did, sir," answered the Colonel, with the air of a modest millionaire explaining his success; "a lot most excellently situated on the same square with the opera house, and only two squares from the board of trade. I consider the purchase a most fortuitous one. It is my intention to erect a small building upon it at once, and open a modest book and stationery store. During past years I have met with many pecuniary reverses, and I now find it necessary to engage in some commercial occupation that will furnish me with a livelihood. The book and stationery business, though an humble one, seems to me not inapt nor altogether uncongenial. I am a graduate of the University of Virginia; and Mrs. Blaylock's really wonderful acquaintance with belles-lettres and poetic literature should go far toward insuring success. Of course, Mrs. Blaylock would not personally serve behind the counter. With the nearly three hundred dollars I have remaining I can manage the building of a house, by giving a lien on the lot. I have an old friend in Atlanta who is a partner in a large book store, and he has agreed to furnish me with a stock of goods on credit, on extremely easy terms. I am pleased to hope, sir, that Mrs. Blaylock's health and happiness will be increased by the change of locality. Already I fancy I can perceive the return of those roses that were once the hope and despair of Georgia cavaliers."

Again followed that wonderful bow, as the Colonel lightly touched the pale cheek of the poetess. Mrs. Blaylock, blushing like a girl, shook her curl and gave the Colonel an arch, reproving tap. Secret of eternal youth —where art thou? Every second the answer comes—"Here, here, here."

Listen to thine own heartbeats, O weary seeker after external miracles.

"Those years," said Mrs. Blaylock, "in Holly Springs were long, long, long. But now is the promised land in sight. Skyland!—a lovely name."

"Doubtless," said the Colonel, "we shall be able to secure comfortable accommodations at some modest hotel at reasonable rates. Our trunks are in Okochee, to be forwarded when we shall have made permanent arrangements."

J. Pinkney Bloom excused himself, went forward, and stood by the captain at the wheel.

"Mac," said he, "do you remember my telling you once that I sold one of those five-hundred-dollar lots in Skyland?"

"Seems I do," grinned Captain MacFarland.

"I'm not a coward, as a general rule," went on the promoter, "but I always said that if I ever met the sucker that bought that lot I'd run like a turkey. Now, you see that old babe-in-the-wood over there? Well, he's the boy that drew the prize. That was the only five-hundred-dollar lot that went. The rest ranged from ten dollars to two hundred. His wife writes poetry. She's invented one about the high grounds of Georgia, that's way up in G. They're going to Skyland to open a book store."

"Well," said MacFarland, with another grin, "it's a good thing you are along, J. P.; you can show 'em around town until they begin to feel at home."

"He's got three hundred dollars left to build a house and store with," went on J. Pinkney, as if he were talking to himself. "And he thinks there's an opera house up there."

Captain MacFarland released the wheel long enough to give his leg a roguish slap.

"You old fat rascal!" he chuckled, with a wink.

"Mac, you're a fool," said J. Pinkney Bloom, coldly. He went back and joined the Blaylocks, where he sat, less talkative, with that straight furrow between his brows that always stood as a signal of schemes being shaped within.

"There's a good many swindles connected with these booms," he said presently. "What if this Skyland should turn out to be one—that is, suppose business should be sort of dull there, and no special sale for books?"

"My dear sir," said Colonel Blaylock, resting his hand upon the back of his wife's chair, "three times I have been reduced to almost penury by the duplicity of others, but I have not yet lost faith in humanity. If I have been deceived again, still we may glean health and content, if not worldly profit. I am aware that there are dishonest schemers in the world who set traps for the unwary, but even they are not altogether bad. My dear, can you recall those verses entitled, 'He Giveth the Increase,' that you composed for the choir of our church in Holly Springs?"

"That was four years ago," said Mrs. Blaylock; "perhaps I can repeat a verse or two.

"The lily springs from the rotting mould;
Pearls from the deep sea slime;
Good will come out of Nazareth
All in God's own time.

"To the hardest heart the softening grace
Cometh, at last, to bless;
Guiding it right to help and cheer
And succor in distress.

"I cannot remember the rest. The lines were not ambitious. They were written to the music composed by a dear friend."

"It's a fine rhyme, just the same," declared Mr. Bloom. "It seems to ring the bell, all right. I guess I gather the sense of it. It means that the rankest kind of a phony will give you the best end of it once in a while."

Mr. Bloom strayed thoughtfully back to the captain, and stood meditating.

"Ought to be in sight of the spires and gilded domes of Skyland now in a few minutes," chirruped MacFarland, shaking with enjoyment.

"Go to the devil," said Mr. Bloom, still pensive.

And now, upon the left bank, they caught a glimpse of a white village, high up on the hills, smothered among green trees. That was Cold Branch —no boom town, but the slow growth of many years. Cold Branch lay on the edge of the grape and corn lands. The big country road ran just back of the heights. Cold Branch had nothing in common with the frisky ambition of Okochee with its impertinent lake.

"Mac," said J. Pinkney suddenly, "I want you to stop at Cold Branch. There's a landing there that they made to use sometimes when the river was up."

"Can't," said the captain, grinning more broadly. "I've got the United States mails on board. Right to-day this boat's in the government service. Do you want to have the poor old captain keelhauled by Uncle Sam? And the great city of Skyland all disconsolate, waiting for its mail? I'm ashamed of your extravagance, J. P."

"Mac," almost whispered J. Pinkney, in his danger-line voice, "I looked into the engine room of the *Dixie Belle* a while ago. Don't you know of somebody that needs a new boiler? Cement and black japan can't hide flaws from me. And then, those shares of building and loan that you traded for repairs—they were all yours, of course. I hate to mention these things, but——"

"Oh, come now, J. P.," said the captain. "You know I was just fooling. I'll put you off at Cold Branch, if you say so."

"The other passengers get off there, too," said Mr. Bloom.

Further conversation was held, and in ten minutes the *Dixie Belle* turned her nose toward a little, cranky wooden pier on the left bank, and the captain, relinquishing the wheel to a roustabout, came to the passenger deck and made the remarkable announcement: "All out for Skyland."

The Blaylocks and J. Pinkney Bloom disembarked, and the *Dixie Belle* proceeded on her way up the lake. Guided by the indefatigable promoter, they slowly climbed the steep hillside, pausing often to rest and admire the view. Finally they entered the village of Cold Branch. Warmly both the Colonel and his wife praised it for its homelike and peaceful beauty. Mr. Bloom conducted them to a two-story building on a shady street that bore the legend, "Pinetop Inn." Here he took his leave, receiving the cordial thanks of the two for his attentions, the Colonel remarking that he thought they would spend the remainder of the day in rest, and take a look at his purchase on the morrow.

J. Pinkney Bloom walked down Cold Branch's main street. He did not know this town, but he knew towns, and his feet did not falter. Presently he saw a sign over a door: "Frank E. Cooly, Attorney-at-Law and Notary Public." A young man was Mr. Cooly, and awaiting business.

"Get your hat, son," said Mr. Bloom, in his breezy way, "and a blank deed, and come along. It's a job for you.

"Now," he continued, when Mr. Cooly had responded with alacrity, "is there a bookstore in town?"

"One," said the lawyer. "Henry Williams's."

"Get there," said Mr. Bloom. "We're going to buy it."

Henry Williams was behind his counter. His store was a small one, containing a mixture of books, stationery, and fancy rubbish. Adjoining it was Henry's home—a decent cottage, vine-embowered and cosy. Henry was lank and soporific, and not inclined to rush his business.

"I want to buy your house and store," said Mr. Bloom. "I haven't got time to dicker—name your price."

"It's worth eight hundred," said Henry, too much dazed to ask more than its value.

"Shut that door," said Mr. Bloom to the lawyer. Then he tore off his coat and vest, and began to unbutton his shirt.

"Wanter fight about it, do yer?" said Henry Williams, jumping up and cracking his heels together twice. "All right, hunky—sail in and cut yer capers."

"Keep your clothes on," said Mr. Bloom. "I'm only going down to the bank."

He drew eight one-hundred-dollar bills from his money belt and planked them down on the counter. Mr. Cooly showed signs of future promise, for he already had the deed spread out, and was reaching across the counter for the ink bottle. Never before or since was such quick action had in Cold Branch.

"Your name, please?" asked the lawyer.

"Make it out to Peyton Blaylock," said Mr. Bloom. "God knows how to spell it."

Within thirty minutes Henry Williams was out of business, and **Mr.** Bloom stood on the brick sidewalk with Mr. Cooly, who held in his hand the signed and attested deed.

"You'll find the party at the Pinetop Inn," said J. Pinkney Bloom. "Get it recorded, and take it down and give it to him. He'll ask you a hell's mint of questions; so here's ten dollars for the trouble you'll have in not being able to answer 'em. Never run much to poetry, did you, young man?"

"Well," said the really talented Cooly, who even yet retained his right mind, "now and then."

"Dig into it," said Mr. Bloom, "it'll pay you. Never heard a poem, now, that run something like this, did you?—

"A good thing out of Nazareth
　　Comes up sometimes, I guess,
　On hand, all right, to help and cheer
　　A sucker in distress."

"I believe not," said Mr. Cooly.

"It's a hymn," said J. Pinkney Bloom. "Now, show me the way to a livery stable, son, for I'm going to hit the dirt road back to Okochee."

CONFESSIONS OF A HUMORIST

There was a painless stage of incubation that lasted twenty-five years, and then it broke out on me, and people said I was It.

But they called it humor instead of measles.

The employees in the store bought a silver inkstand for the senior partner on his fiftieth birthday. We crowded into his private office to present it.

I had been selected for spokesman, and I made a little speech that I had been preparing for a week.

It made a hit. It was full of puns and epigrams and funny twists that brought down the house—which was a very solid one in the wholesale hardware line. Old Marlowe himself actually grinned, and the employees took their cue and roared.

My reputation as a humorist dates from half-past nine o'clock on that morning.

For weeks afterward my fellow clerks fanned the flame of my self-esteem. One by one they came to me, saying what an awfully clever speech that was, old man, and carefully explained to me the point of each one of my jokes.

Gradually I found that I was expected to keep it up. Others might speak sanely on business matters and the day's topics, but from me something gamesome and airy was required.

I was expected to crack jokes about the crockery and lighten up the granite ware with persiflage. I was second bookkeeper, and if I failed to show up a balance sheet without something comic about the footings or could find no cause for laughter in an invoice of plows, the other clerks were disappointed.

By degrees my fame spread, and I became a local "character." Our town was small enough to make this possible. The daily newspaper quoted me. At social gatherings I was indispensable.

I believe I did possess considerable wit and a facility for quick and spontaneous repartee. This gift I cultivated and improved by practice. And the nature of it was kindly and genial, not running to sarcasm or offending others. People began to smile when they saw me coming, and by the time we had met I generally had the word ready to broaden the smile into a laugh.

I had married early. We had a charming boy of three and a girl of five. Naturally, we lived in a vine-covered cottage, and were happy. My salary as bookkeeper in the hardware concern kept at a distance those ills attendant upon superfluous wealth.

At sundry times I had written out a few jokes and conceits that I considered peculiarly happy, and had sent them to certain periodicals that print such things. All of them had been instantly accepted. Several of the editors had written to request further contributions.

One day I received a letter from the editor of a famous weekly publication. He suggested that I submit to him a humorous composition to fill a column of space; hinting that he would make it a regular feature of each issue if the work proved satisfactory, I did so, and at the end of two weeks he offered to make a contract with me for a year at a figure that was considerably higher than the amount paid me by the hardware firm.

I was filled with delight. My wife already crowned me in her mind with the imperishable evergreens of literary success. We had lobster croquettes and a bottle of blackberry wine for supper that night. Here was the chance to liberate myself from drudgery. I talked over the matter very seriously with Louisa. We agreed that I must resign my place at the store and devote myself to humor.

I resigned. My fellow clerks gave me a farewell banquet. The speech I made there coruscated. It was printed in full by the *Gazette*. The next morning I awoke and looked at the clock.

"Late, by George!" I exclaimed, and grabbed for my clothes. Louisa reminded me that I was no longer a slave to hardware and contractors' supplies. I was now a professional humorist.

After breakfast she proudly led me to the little room off the kitchen.

Dear girl! There was my table and chair, writing pad, ink, and pipe tray. And all the author's trappings—the celery stand full of fresh roses and honeysuckle, last year's calendar on the wall, the dictionary, and a little bag of chocolates to nibble between inspirations. Dear girl!

I sat me to work. The wall paper is patterned with arabesques or odalisks or—perhaps—it is trapezoids. Upon one of the figures I fixed my eyes. I bethought me of humor.

A voice startled me—Louisa's voice.

"If you aren't too busy, dear," it said, "come to dinner."

I looked at my watch. Yes, five hours had been gathered in by the grim scythe-man. I went to dinner.

"You mustn't work too hard at first," said Louisa. "Goethe—or was it Napoleon?—said five hours a day is enough for mental labor. Couldn't you take me and the children to the woods this afternoon?"

"I *am* a little tired," I admitted. So we went to the woods.

But I soon got the swing of it. Within a month I was turning out copy as regular as shipments of hardware.

And I had success. My column in the weekly made some stir, and I was referred to in a gossipy way by the critics as something fresh in the line of humorists. I augmented my income considerably by contributing to other publications.

I picked up the tricks of the trade. I could take a funny idea and make a two-line joke of it, earning a dollar. With false whiskers on, it would serve up cold as a quatrain, doubling its producing value. By turning the skirt and adding a ruffle of rhyme you would hardly recognize it as *vers de société* with neatly shod feet and a fashion-plate illustration.

I began to save up money, and we had new carpets, and a parlor organ. My townspeople began to look upon me as a citizen of some consequence instead of the merry trifler I had been when I clerked in the hardware store.

After five or six months the spontaneity seemed to depart from my humor. Quips and droll sayings no longer fell carelessly from my lips. I was sometimes hard run for material. I found myself listening to catch available ideas from the conversation of my friends. Sometimes I chewed my pencil and gazed at the wall paper for hours trying to build up some gay little bubble of unstudied fun.

And then I became a harpy, a Moloch, a Jonah, a vampire, to my acquaintances. Anxious, haggard, greedy, I stood among them like a veritable killjoy. Let a bright saying, a witty comparison, a piquant phrase fall from their lips and I was after it like a hound springing upon a bone. I dared not trust my memory; but, turning aside guiltily and meanly, I would make a note of it in my ever-present memorandum book or upon my cuff for my own future use.

My friends regarded me in sorrow and wonder. I was not the same man. Where once I had furnished them entertainment and jollity, I now preyed upon them. No jests from me ever bid for their smiles now. They were too precious. I could not afford to dispense gratuitously the means of my livelihood.

I was a lugubrious fox praising the singing of my friends, the crows, that they might drop from their beaks the morsels of wit that I coveted.

Nearly every one began to avoid me. I even forgot how to smile, not even paying that much for the sayings I appropriated.

No persons, places, times, or subjects were exempt from my plundering in search of material. Even in church my demoralized fancy went hunting among the solemn aisles and pillars for spoil.

Did the minister give out the long-meter doxology, at once I began: "Doxology—sockdology—sockdolager—meter—meet her."

The sermon ran through my mental sieve, its precepts filtering unheeded, could I but glean a suggestion of a pun or a *bon mot*. The solemnest anthems of the choir were but an accompaniment to my thoughts as I conceived new changes to ring upon the ancient comicalities concerning the jealousies of soprano, tenor, and basso.

My own home became a hunting ground. My wife is a singularly feminine creature, candid, sympathetic, and impulsive. Once her conversation was my delight, and her ideas a source of unfailing pleasure. Now I worked her. She was a gold mine of those amusing but lovable inconsistencies that distinguish the female mind.

I began to market those pearls of unwisdom and humor that should have enriched only the sacred precincts of home. With devilish cunning I encouraged her to talk. Unsuspecting, she laid her heart bare. Upon the cold, conspicuous, common, printed page I offered it to the public gaze.

A literary Judas, I kissed her and betrayed her. For pieces of silver I dressed her sweet confidences in the pantalettes and frills of folly and made them dance in the market place.

Dear Louisa! Of nights I have bent over her cruel as a wolf above a tender lamb, hearkening even to her soft words murmured in sleep, hoping to catch an idea for my next day's grind. There is worse to come.

God help me! Next my fangs were buried deep in the neck of the fugitive sayings of my little children.

Guy and Viola were two bright fountains of childish, quaint thoughts and speeches. I found a ready sale for this kind of humor, and was furnishing a regular department in a magazine with "Funny Fancies of Childhood." I began to stalk them as an Indian stalks the antelope. I would hide behind sofas and doors, or crawl on my hands and knees among the bushes in the yard to eavesdrop while they were at play. I had all the qualities of a harpy except remorse.

Once, when I was barren of ideas, and my copy must leave in the next mail, I covered myself in a pile of autumn leaves in the yard, where I knew they intended to come to play. I cannot bring myself to believe that Guy was aware of my hiding place, but even if he was, I would be loath to blame him for his setting fire to the leaves, causing the destruction of my new suit of clothes, and nearly cremating a parent.

Soon my own children began to shun me as a pest. Often, when I was creeping upon them like a melancholy ghoul, I would hear them say to each other: "Here comes papa," and they would gather their toys and scurry away to some safer hiding place. Miserable wretch that I was!

And yet I was doing well financially. Before the first year had passed I had saved a thousand dollars, and we had lived in comfort.

But at what a cost! I am not quite clear as to what a pariah is, but I was everything that it sounds like. I had no friends, no amusements, no enjoyment of life. The happiness of my family had been sacrificed. I was a bee, sucking sordid honey from life's fairest flowers, dreaded and shunned on account of my sting.

One day a man spoke to me, with a pleasant and friendly smile. Not in months had the thing happened. I was passing the undertaking establishment of Peter Heffelbower. Peter stood in the door and saluted me. I stopped, strangely wrung in my heart by his greeting. He asked me inside.

The day was chill and rainy. We went into the back room, where a fire burned in a little stove. A customer came, and Peter left me alone for a while. Presently I felt a new feeling stealing over me—a sense of beautiful calm and content, I looked around the place. There were rows of shining rosewood caskets, black palls, trestles, hearse plumes, mourning streamers, and all the paraphernalia of the solemn trade. Here was peace, order, silence, the abode of grave and dignified reflections. Here, on the brink of life, was a little niche pervaded by the spirit of eternal rest.

When I entered it, the follies of the world abandoned me at the door. I felt no inclination to wrest a humorous idea from those sombre and stately trappings. My mind seemed to stretch itself to grateful repose upon a couch draped with gentle thoughts.

A quarter of an hour ago I was an abandoned humorist. Now I was a philosopher, full of serenity and ease. I had found a *refuge* from humor, from the hot chase of the shy quip, from the degrading pursuit of the panting joke, from the restless reach after the nimble repartee.

I had not known Heffelbower well. When he came back, I let him talk, fearful that he might prove to be a jarring note in the sweet, dirgelike harmony of his establishment.

But, no. He chimed truly. I gave a long sigh of happiness. Never have I known a man's talk to be as magnificently dull as Peter's was. Compared with it the Dead Sea is a geyser. Never a sparkle or a glimmer of wit marred his words. Commonplaces as trite and as plentiful as blackberries flowed from his lips no more stirring in quality than a last week's tape running from a ticker. Quaking a little, I tried upon him one of my best pointed jokes. It fell back ineffectual, with the point broken. I loved that man from then on.

Two or three evenings each week I would steal down to Heffelbower's and revel in his back room. That was my only joy. I began to rise early and hurry through my work, that I might spend more time in my haven. In no other place could I throw off my habit of extracting humorous ideas from my surroundings. Peter's talk left me no opening had I besieged it ever so hard.

Under this influence I began to improve in spirits. It was the recreation from one's labor which every man needs. I surprised one or two of my former friends by throwing them a smile and a cheery word as I passed them on the streets. Several times I dumfounded my family by relaxing long enough to make a jocose remark in their presence.

I had so long been ridden by the incubus of humor that I seized my hours of holiday with a schoolboy's zest.

My work began to suffer. It was not the pain and burden to me that it had been. I often whistled at my desk, and wrote with far more fluency than before. I accomplished my tasks impatiently, as anxious to be off to my helpful retreat as a drunkard is to get to his tavern.

My wife had some anxious hours in conjecturing where I spent my afternoons. I thought it best not to tell her; women do not understand these things. Poor girl!—she had one shock out of it.

One day I brought home a silver coffin handle for a paper weight and a fine, fluffy hearse plume to dust my papers with.

I loved to see them on my desk, and think of the beloved back room down at Heffelbower's. But Louisa found them, and she shrieked with horror. I had to console her with some lame excuse for having them, but I saw in her eyes that the prejudice was not removed. I had to remove the articles, though, at double-quick time.

One day Peter Heffelbower laid before me a temptation that swept me off my feet. In his sensible, uninspired way he showed me his books, and explained that his profits and his business were increasing rapidly. He had thought of taking in a partner with some cash. He would rather have me than any one he knew. When I left his place that afternoon Peter had my check for the thousand dollars I had in the bank, and I was a partner in his undertaking business.

I went home with feelings of delirious joy, mingled with a certain amount of doubt. I was dreading to tell my wife about it. But I walked on air. To give up the writing of humorous stuff, once more to enjoy the apples of life, instead of squeezing them to a pulp for a few drops of hard cider to make the public feel funny—what a boon that would be!

At the supper table Louisa handed me some letters that had come during my absence. Several of them contained rejected manuscript. Ever since I first began going to Heffelbower's my stuff had been coming back with alarming frequency. Lately I had been dashing off my jokes and articles with the greatest fluency. Previously I had labored like a brick-layer, slowly and with agony.

Presently I opened a letter from the editor of the weekly with which I had a regular contract. The checks for that weekly article were still our main dependence. The letter ran thus:

Dear Sir:

As you are aware, our contract for the year expires with the present month. While regretting the necessity for so doing, we must say that we do not care to renew same for the coming year. We were quite pleased with your style of humor, which seems to have delighted quite a large propor-tion of our readers. But for the past two months we have noticed a decided falling off in its quality.

Your earlier work showed a spontaneous, easy, natural flow of fun and wit. Of late it is labored, studied, and unconvincing, giving painful evi-dence of hard toil and drudging mechanism.

Again regretting that we do not consider your contributions available any longer, we are, yours sincerely,

The Editor

I handed this letter to my wife. After she had read it her face grew extremely long, and there were tears in her eyes.

"The mean old thing!" she exclaimed indignantly. "I'm sure your pieces are just as good as they ever were. And it doesn't take you half as long to write them as it did." And then, I suppose, Louisa thought of the checks that would cease coming. "Oh, John," she wailed, "what will you do now?"

For an answer I got up and began to do a polka step around the supper table. I am sure Louisa thought the trouble had driven me mad; and I think the children hoped it had, for they tore after me, yelling with glee and emulating my steps. I was now something like their old playmate as of yore.

"The theatre for us to-night!" I shouted; "nothing less. And a late, wild, disreputable supper for all of us at the Palace Restaurant. Lumpty-diddle-de-dee-de-dum!"

And then I explained my glee by declaring that I was now a partner in a prosperous undertaking establishment, and that written jokes might go hide their heads in sackcloth and ashes for all me.

With the editor's letter in her hand to justify the deed I had done, my wife could advance no objections save a few mild ones based on the feminine inability to appreciate a good thing such as the little back room of Peter Hef——no, of Heffelbower & Co.'s undertaking establishment.

In conclusion, I will say that to-day you will find no man in our town as well liked, as jovial, and full of merry sayings as I. My jokes are again noised about and quoted; once more I take pleasure in my wife's confidential chatter without a mercenary thought, while Guy and Viola play at my feet distributing gems of childish humor without fear of the ghastly tormentor who used to dog their steps, notebook in hand.

Our business has prospered finely. I keep the books and look after the shop, while Peter attends to outside matters. He says that my levity and high spirits would simply turn any funeral into a regular Irish wake.

THE SPARROWS IN MADISON SQUARE

The young man in straitened circumstances who comes to New York City to enter literature has but one thing to do, provided he has studied carefully his field in advance. He must go straight to Madison Square, write an article about the sparrows there, and sell it to the *Sun* for $15.

I cannot recall either a novel or a story dealing with the popular theme of the young writer from the provinces who comes to the metropolis to win fame and fortune with his pen in which the hero does not get his start that way. It does seem strange that some author, in casting about for startlingly original plots, has not hit upon the idea of having his hero write about the bluebirds in Union Square and sell it to the *Herald*. But a search through the files of metropolitan fiction counts up overwhelmingly for the sparrows and the old Garden Square, and the *Sun* always writes the check.

Of course it is easy to understand why this first city venture of the budding author is always successful. He is primed by necessity to a superlative effort; mid the iron and stone and marble of the roaring city he has found this spot of singing birds and green grass and trees; every tender sentiment in his nature is battling with the sweet pain of homesickness; his genius is aroused as it never may be again; the birds chirp, the tree branches sway, the noise of wheels is forgotten; he writes with his soul in his pen—and he sells it to the *Sun* for $15.

I had read of this custom during many years before I came to New York. When my friends were using their strongest arguments to dissuade me from coming, I only smiled serenely. They did not know of that sparrow graft I had up my sleeve.

When I arrived in New York, and the car took me straight from the ferry up Twenty-third Street to Madison Square, I could hear that $15 check rustling in my inside pocket.

I obtained lodging at an unhyphenated hostelry, and the next morning I was on a bench in Madison Square almost by the time the sparrows were awake. Their melodious chirping, the benignant spring foliage of the noble trees and the clean, fragrant grass reminded me so potently of the old farm I had left that tears almost came into my eyes.

Then, all in a moment, I felt my inspiration. The brave, piercing notes of those cheerful small birds formed a keynote to a wonderful, light, fanciful song of hope and joy and altruism. Like myself, they were creatures with hearts pitched to the tune of woods and fields; as I was, so were they captives by circumstance in the discordant, dull city—yet with how much grace and glee they bore the restraint!

And then the early morning people began to pass through the square to their work—sullen people, with sidelong glances and glum faces, hurrying, hurrying, hurrying. And I got my theme cut out clear from the bird notes, and wrought it into a lesson, and a poem, and a carnival dance, and a lullaby; and then translated it all into prose and began to write.

For two hours my pencil traveled over my pad with scarcely a rest. Then I went to the little room I had rented for two days, and there I cut it to half, and then mailed it, white-hot, to the *Sun*.

The next morning I was up by daylight and spent two cents of my capital for a paper. If the word "sparrow" was in it I was unable to find it.

I took it up to my room and spread it out on the bed and went over it, column by column. Something was wrong.

Three hours afterward the postman brought me a large envelope containing my MS. and a piece of inexpensive paper, about 3 inches by 4—I suppose some of you have seen them—upon which was written in violet ink, "With the *Sun's* thanks."

I went over to the square and sat upon a bench. No; I did not think it necessary to eat any breakfast that morning. The confounded pests of sparrows were making the square hideous with their idiotic "cheep, cheep." I never saw birds so persistently noisy, impudent, and disagreeable in all my life.

By this time, according to all traditions, I should have been standing in the office of the editor of the *Sun*. That personage—a tall, grave, white-haired man—would strike a silver bell as he grasped my hand and wiped a suspicious moisture from his glasses.

"Mr. McChesney," he would be saying when a subordinate appeared, "this is Mr. Henry, the young man who sent in that exquisite gem about the sparrows in Madison Square. You may give him a desk at once. Your salary, sir, will be $80 a week, to begin with."

This was what I had been led to expect by all writers who have evolved romances of literary New York.

Something was decidedly wrong with tradition. I could not assume the blame; so I fixed it upon the sparrows. I began to hate them with intensity and heat.

At that moment an individual wearing an excess of whiskers, two hats, and a pestilential air slid into the seat beside me.

"Say, Willie," he muttered cajolingly, "could you cough up a dime out of your coffers for a cup of coffee this morning?"

"I'm lung-weary, my friend," said I. "The best I can do is three cents."

"And you look like a gentleman, too," said he. "What brung you down —booze?"

"Birds," I said fiercely. "The brown-throated songsters carolling songs of hope and cheer to weary man toiling amid the city's dust and din. The little feathered couriers from the meadows and woods chirping sweetly to us of blue skies and flowering fields. The confounded little squint-eyed nuisances yawping like a flock of steam pianos, and stuffing themselves like aldermen with grass seeds and bugs, while a man sits on a bench and goes without his breakfast. Yes, sir, birds! look at them!"

As I spoke I picked up a dead tree branch that lay by the bench, and hurled it with all my force into a close congregation of the sparrows on the grass. The flock flew to the trees with a babel of shrill cries; but two of them remained prostrate upon the turf.

In a moment my unsavory friend had leaped over the row of benches and secured the fluttering victims, which he thrust hurriedly into his pockets. Then he beckoned me with a dirty forefinger.

"Come on, cully," he said hoarsely. "You're in on the feed."

Weakly I followed my dingy acquaintance. He led me away from the park down a side street and through a crack in a fence into a vacant lot where some excavating had been going on. Behind a pile of old stones and lumber he paused, and took out his birds.

"I got matches," said he. "You got any paper to start a fire with?"

I drew forth my manuscript story of the sparrows, and offered it for burnt sacrifice. There were old planks, splinters, and chips for our fire. My frowsy friend produced from some interior of his frayed clothing half a loaf of bread, pepper, and salt.

In ten minutes each of us was holding a sparrow spitted upon a stick over the leaping flames.

"Say," said my fellow bivouacker, "this ain't so bad when a fellow's hungry. It reminds me of when I struck New York first—about fifteen years ago. I come in from the West to see if I could get a job on a newspaper. I hit the Madison Square Park the first mornin' after, and was sitting around on the benches. I noticed the sparrows chirpin', and the grass and trees so nice and green that I thought I was back in the country again. Then I got some papers out of my pocket, and——"

"I know," I interrupted. "You sent it to the *Sun* and got $15."

"Say," said my friend, suspiciously, "you seem to know a good deal. Where was you? I went to sleep on the bench there, in the sun, and somebody touched me for every cent I had—$15."

HEARTS AND HANDS

At Denver there was an influx of passengers into the coaches on the east-bound B. & M. express. In one coach there sat a very pretty young woman dressed in elegant taste and surrounded by all the luxurious comforts of an experienced traveler. Among the newcomers were two young men, one of handsome presence with a bold, frank countenance and manner; the other a ruffled, glum-faced person, heavily built and roughly dressed. The two were handcuffed together.

As they passed down the aisle of the coach the only vacant seat offered was a reversed one facing the attractive young woman. Here the linked couple seated themselves. The young woman's glance fell upon them with a distant, swift disinterest; then with a lovely smile brightening her countenance and a tender pink tingeing her rounded cheeks, she held out a little gray-gloved hand. When she spoke her voice, full, sweet, and deliberate, proclaimed that its owner was accustomed to speak and be heard.

"Well, Mr. Easton, if you *will* make me speak first, I suppose I must. Don't you ever recognize old friends when you meet them in the West?"

The younger man roused himself sharply at the sound of her voice, seemed to struggle with a slight embarrassment which he threw off instantly, and then clasped her fingers with his left hand.

"It's Miss Fairchild," he said, with a smile. "I'll ask you to excuse the other hand; it's otherwise engaged just at present."

He slightly raised his right hand, bound at the wrist by the shining "bracelet" to the left one of his companion. The glad look in the girl's eyes slowly changed to a bewildered horror. The glow faded from her cheeks. Her lips parted in a vague, relaxing distress. Easton, with a little laugh, as if amused, was about to speak again when the other forestalled him. The glum-faced man had been watching the girl's countenance with veiled glances from his keen, shrewd eyes.

"You'll excuse me for speaking, miss, but, I see you're acquainted with the marshal here. If you'll ask him to speak a word for me when we get to the pen he'll do it, and it'll make things easier for me there. He's taking me to Leavenworth prison. It's seven years for counterfeiting."

"Oh!" said the girl, with a deep breath and returning color. "So that is what you are doing out here? A marshal!"

"My dear Miss Fairchild," said Easton, calmly, "I had to do something. Money has a way of taking wings unto itself, and you know it takes money to keep step with our crowd in Washington. I saw this opening in the West, and—well, a marshalship isn't quite as high a position as that of ambassador, but——"

"The ambassador," said the girl, warmly, "doesn't call any more. He needn't ever have done so. You ought to know that. And so now you are one of these dashing Western heroes, and you ride and shoot and go into all kinds of dangers. That's different from the Washington life. You have been missed from the old crowd."

The girl's eyes, fascinated, went back, widening a little, to rest upon the glittering handcuffs.

"Don't you worry about them, miss," said the other man. "All marshals handcuff themselves to their prisoners to keep them from getting away. Mr. Easton knows his business."

"Will we see you again soon in Washington?" asked the girl.

"Not soon, I think," said Easton. "My butterfly days are over, I fear."

"I love the West," said the girl, irrelevantly. Her eyes were shining softly. She looked away out the car window. She began to speak truly and simply, without the gloss of style and manner: "Mamma and I spent the summer in Denver. She went home a week ago because father was slightly ill. I could live and be happy in the West. I think the air here agrees with me. Money isn't everything. But people always misunderstand things and remain stupid——"

"Say, Mr. Marshal," growled the glum-faced man. "This isn't quite fair. I'm needin' a drink, and haven't had a smoke all day. Haven't you talked long enough? Take me in the smoker now, won't you? I'm half dead for a pipe."

The bound travelers rose to their feet, Easton with the same slow smile on his face.

"I can't deny a petition for tobacco," he said, lightly. "It's the one friend of the unfortunate. Good-bye, Miss Fairchild. Duty calls, you know." He held out his hand for a farewell.

"It's too bad you are not going East," she said, reclothing herself with manner and style. "But you must go on to Leavenworth, I suppose?"

"Yes," said Easton, "I must go on to Leavenworth."

The two men sidled down the aisle into the smoker.

The two passengers in a seat near by had heard most of the conversation. Said one of them: "That marshal's a good sort of chap. Some of these Western fellows are all right."

"Pretty young to hold an office like that, isn't he?" asked the other.

"Young!" exclaimed the first speaker, "why—— Oh! didn't you catch on? Say—did you ever know an officer to handcuff a prisoner to his *right* hand?"

THE CACTUS

The most notable thing about Time is that it is so purely relative. A large amount of reminiscence is, by common consent, conceded to the drowning man; and it is not past belief that one may review an entire courtship while removing one's gloves.

That is what Trysdale was doing, standing by a table in his bachelor apartments. On the table stood a singular-looking green plant in a red earthen jar. The plant was one of the species of cacti, and was provided with long, tentacular leaves that perpetually swayed with the slightest breeze with a peculiar beckoning motion.

Trysdale's friend, the brother of the bride, stood at a sideboard complaining at being allowed to drink alone. Both men were in evening dress. White favors like stars upon their coats shone through the gloom of the apartment.

As he slowly unbuttoned his gloves, there passed through Trysdale's mind a swift, scarifying retrospect of the last few hours. It seemed that in his nostrils was still the scent of the flowers that had been banked in odorous masses about the church, and in his ears the lowpitched hum of a thousand well-bred voices, the rustle of crisp garments, and, most insistently recurring, the drawling words of the minister irrevocably binding her to another.

From this last hopeless point of view he still strove, as if it had become a habit of his mind, to reach some conjecture as to why and how he had lost her. Shaken rudely by the uncompromising fact, he had suddenly found himself confronted by a thing he had never before faced—his own innermost, unmitigated, and unbedecked self. He saw all the garbs of pretence and egoism that he had worn now turn to rags of folly. He shuddered at the thought that to others, before now, the garments of his soul must have appeared sorry and threadbare. Vanity and conceit? These were the joints in his armor. And how free from either she had always been— But why——

As she had slowly moved up the aisle toward the altar he had felt an unworthy, sullen exultation that had served to support him. He had told himself that her paleness was from thoughts of another than the man to whom she was about to give herself. But even that poor consolation had been wrenched from him. For, when he saw that swift, limpid, upward look that she gave the man when he took her hand, he knew himself to be forgotten. Once that same look had been raised to him, and he had gauged its meaning. Indeed, his conceit had crumbled; its last prop was gone. Why had it ended thus? There had been no quarrel between them, nothing——

For the thousandth time he remarshalled in his mind the events of those last few days before the tide had so suddenly turned.

She had always insisted upon placing him upon a pedestal, and he had accepted her homage with royal grandeur. It had been a very sweet incense that she had burned before him; so modest (he told himself); so childlike and worshipful, and (he would once have sworn) so sincere. She had invested him with an almost supernatural number of high attributes and excellencies and talents, and he had absorbed the oblation as a desert drinks the rain that can coax from it no promise of blossom or fruit.

As Trysdale grimly wrenched apart the seam of his last glove, the crowning instance of his fatuous and tardily mourned egoism came vividly back to him.

The scene was the night when he had asked her to come up on his pedestal with him and share his greatness. He could not, now, for the pain of it, allow his mind to dwell upon the memory of her convincing beauty that night—the careless wave of her hair, the tenderness and virginal charm of her looks and words. But they had been enough, and they had brought him to speak. During their conversation she had said:

"And Captain Carruthers tells me that you speak the Spanish language like a native. Why have you hidden this accomplishment from me? Is there anything you do not know?"

Now, Carruthers was an idiot. No doubt he (Trysdale) had been guilty (he sometimes did such things) of airing at the club some old, canting Castilian proverb dug from the hotchpotch at the back of dictionaries. Carruthers, who was one of his incontinent admirers, was the very man to have magnified this exhibition of doubtful erudition.

But, alas! the incense of her admiration had been so sweet and flattering. He allowed the imputation to pass without denial. Without protest, he allowed her to twine about his brow this spurious bay of Spanish scholarship. He let it grace his conquering head, and, among its soft convolutions, he did not feel the prick of the thorn that was to pierce him later.

How glad, how shy, how tremulous she was! How she fluttered like a snared bird when he laid his mightiness at her feet! He could have sworn, and he could swear now, that unmistakable consent was in her eyes, but, coyly, she would give him no direct answer. "I will send you my answer to-morrow," she said; and he, the indulgent, confident victor, smilingly granted the delay.

The next day he waited, impatient, in his rooms for the word. At noon her groom came to the door and left the strange cactus in the red earthen jar. There was no note, no message, merely a tag upon the plant bearing a barbarous foreign or botanical name. He waited until night, but her answer did not come. His large pride and hurt vanity kept him from seeking her. Two evenings later they met at a dinner. Their greetings were conventional, but she looked at him, breathless, wondering, eager. He was courteous, adamant, waiting her explanation. With womanly swiftness she took her cue from his manner, and turned to snow and ice. Thus, and wider from this on, they had drifted apart. Where was his fault? Who had been to blame? Humbled now, he sought the answer amid the ruins of his self-conceit. If——

The voice of the other man in the room, querulously intruding upon his thoughts, aroused him.

"I say, Trysdale, what the deuce is the matter with you? You look unhappy as if you yourself had been married instead of having acted merely as an accomplice. Look at me, another accessory, come two thousand miles on a garlicky, cockroachy banana steamer all the way from South America to connive at the sacrifice—please to observe how lightly my guilt rests upon my shoulders. Only little sister I had, too, and now she's gone. Come now! take something to ease your conscience."

"I don't drink just now, thanks," said Trysdale.

"Your brandy," resumed the other, coming over and joining him, "is abominable. Run down to see me some time at Punta Redonda, and try some of our stuff that old Garcia smuggles in. It's worth the trip. Hallo! here's an old acquaintance. Wherever did you rake up this cactus, Trysdale?"

"A present," said Trysdale, "from a friend. Know the species?"

"Very well. It's a tropical concern. See hundreds of 'em around Punta every day. Here's the name on this tag tied to it. Know any Spanish, Trysdale?"

"No," said Trysdale, with the bitter wraith of a smile—"Is it Spanish?"

"Yes. The natives imagine the leaves are reaching out and beckoning to you. They call it by this name—*Ventomarme*. Name means in English, 'Come and take me.'"

THE DETECTIVE DETECTOR

I was walking in Central Park with Avery Knight, the great New York burglar, highwayman, and murderer.

"But, my dear Knight," said I, "it sounds incredible. You have undoubtedly performed some of the most wonderful feats in your profession known to modern crime. You have committed some marvellous deeds under the very noses of the police—you have boldly entered the homes of millionaires and held them up with an empty gun while you made free with their silver and jewels; you have sandbagged citizens in the glare of Broadway's electric lights; you have killed and robbed with superb openness and absolute impunity—but when you boast that within forty-eight hours after committing a murder you can run down and actually bring me face to face with the detective assigned to apprehend you, I must beg leave to express my doubts—remember, you are in New York."

Avery Knight smiled indulgently.

"You pique my professional pride, doctor," he said in a nettled tone. "I will convince you."

About twelve yards in advance of us a prosperous-looking citizen was rounding a clump of bushes where the walk curved. Knight suddenly drew a revolver and shot the man in the back. His victim fell and lay without moving.

The great murderer went up to him leisurely and took from his clothes his money, watch, and a valuable ring and cravat pin. He then rejoined me smiling calmly, and we continued our walk.

Ten steps and we met a policeman running toward the spot where the shot had been fired. Avery Knight stopped him.

"I have just killed a man," he announced, seriously, "and robbed him of his possessions."

"G'wan," said the policeman, angrily, "or I'll run yez in! Want yer name in the papers, don't yez? I never knew the cranks to come around so quick after a shootin' before. Out of th' park, now, for yours, or I'll fan yez."

"What you have done," I said, argumentatively, as Knight and I walked on, "was easy. But when you come to the task of hunting down the detective that they send upon your trail you will find that you have undertaken a difficult feat."

"Perhaps so," said Knight, lightly. "I will admit that my success depends in a degree upon the sort of man they start after me. If it should be an ordinary plain-clothes man I might fail to gain a sight of him. If they honor me by giving the case to some one of their celebrated sleuths I do not fear to match my cunning and powers of induction against his."

On the next afternoon Knight entered my office with a satisfied look on his keen countenance.

"How goes the mysterious murder?" I asked.

"As usual," said Knight, smilingly. "I have put in the morning at the police station and at the inquest. It seems that a card case of mine containing cards with my name and address was found near the body. They have three witnesses who saw the shooting and gave a description of me. The case has been placed in the hands of Shamrock Jolnes, the famous detective. He left Headquarters at 11:30 on the assignment. I waited at my address until two, thinking he might call there."

I laughed, tauntingly.

"You will never see Jolnes," I continued, "until this murder has been forgotten, two or three weeks from now. I had a better opinion of your shrewdness, Knight. During the three hours and a half that you waited he has got out of your ken. He is after you on true induction theories now, and no wrongdoer has yet been known to come upon him while thus engaged. I advise you to give it up."

"Doctor," said Knight, with a sudden glint in his keen gray eye and a squaring of his chin, "in spite of the record your city holds of something like a dozen homicides without a subsequent meeting of the perpetrator and the sleuth in charge of the case, I will undertake to break that record. To-morrow I will take you to Shamrock Jolnes—I will unmask him before you and prove to you that it is not an impossibility for an officer of the law and a manslayer to stand face to face in your city."

"Do it," said I, "and you'll have the sincere thanks of the Police Department."

On the next day Knight called for me in a cab.

"I've been on one or two false scents, doctor," he admitted. "I know something of detectives' methods, and I followed out a few of them, expecting to find Jolnes at the other end. The pistol being a .45-caliber, I thought surely I would find him at work on the clue in Forty-fifth Street. Then, again, I looked for the detective at the Columbia University, as the man's being shot in the back naturally suggested hazing. But I could not find a trace of him."

"Nor will you," I said, emphatically.

"Not by ordinary methods," said Knight. "I might walk up and down Broadway for a month without success. But you have aroused my pride, doctor; and if I fail to show you Shamrock Jolnes this day, I promise you I will never kill or rob in your city again."

"Nonsense, man," I replied. "When our burglars walk into our houses and politely demand thousands of dollars' worth of jewels, and then dine and bang the piano an hour or two before leaving, how do you, a mere murderer, expect to come in contact with the detective that is looking for you?"

Avery Knight sat lost in thought for a while. At length he looked up brightly.

"Doc," said he, "I have it. Put on your hat, and come with me. In half an hour I guarantee that you shall stand in the presence of Shamrock Jolnes."

I entered a cab with Avery Knight. I did not hear his instructions to the driver, but the vehicle set out at a smart pace up Broadway, turning presently into Fifth Avenue, and proceeding northward again. It was with a rapidly beating heart that I accompanied this wonderful and gifted assassin, whose analytical genius and superb self-confidence had prompted him to make me the tremendous promise of bringing me into the presence of a murderer and the New York detective in pursuit of him simultaneously. Even yet I could not believe it possible.

"Are you sure that you are not being led into some trap?" I asked. "Suppose that your clue, whatever it is, should bring us only into the presence of the Commissioner of Police and a couple of dozen cops!"

"My dear doctor," said Knight, a little stiffly, "I would remind you that I am no gambler."

"I beg your pardon," said I. "But I do not think you will find Jolnes."

The cab stopped before one of the handsomest residences on the avenue. Walking up and down in front of the house was a man with long red whiskers, with a detective's badge showing on the lapel of his coat. Now and then the man would remove his whiskers to wipe his face, and then I would recognize at once the well-known features of the great New York detective. Jolnes was keeping a sharp watch upon the doors and windows of the house.

"Well, doctor," said Knight, unable to repress a note of triumph in his voice, "have you seen?"

"It is wonderful—wonderful!" I could not help exclaiming as our cab started on its return trip. "But how did you do it? By what process of induction——"

"My dear doctor," interrupted the great murderer, "the inductive theory is what the detectives use. My process is more modern. I call it the saltatorial theory. Without bothering with the tedious mental phenomena necessary to the solution of a mystery from slight clues, I jump at once to a conclusion. I will explain to you the method I employed in this case.

"In the first place, I argued that as the crime was committed in New York City in broad daylight, in a public place and under peculiarly atrocious circumstances, and that as the most skilful sleuth available was let loose upon the case, the perpetrator would never be discovered. Do you not think my postulation justified by precedent?"

"Perhaps so," I replied, doggedly. "But if Big Bill Dev——"

"Stop that," interrupted Knight, with a smile, "I've heard that several times. It's too late now. I will proceed.

"If homicides in New York went undiscovered, I reasoned, although the best detective talent was employed to ferret them out, it must be true that the detectives went about their work in the wrong way. And not only in the wrong way, but exactly opposite from the right way. That was my clue.

"I slew the man in Central Park. Now, let me describe myself to you.

"I am tall, with a black beard, and I hate publicity. I have no money to speak of; I do not like oatmeal, and it is the one ambition of my life to die rich. I am of a cold and heartless disposition. I do not care for my fellowmen and I never give a cent to beggars or charity.

"Now, my dear doctor, that is the true description of myself, the man whom that shrewd detective was to hunt down. You who are familiar with the history of crime in New York of late should be able to foretell the result. When I promised you to exhibit to your incredulous gaze the sleuth who was set upon me, you laughed at me because you said that detectives and murderers never met in New York. I have demonstrated to you that the theory is possible."

"But how did you do it?" I asked again.

"It was very simple," replied the distinguished murderer. "I assumed that the detective would go exactly opposite to the clues he had. I have given you a description of myself. Therefore, he must necessarily set to work and trail a short man with a white beard who likes to be in the papers, who is very wealthy, is fond of oatmeal, wants to die poor, and is of an extremely generous and philanthropic disposition. When thus far is reached the mind hesitates no longer. I conveyed you at once to the spot where Shamrock Jolnes was piping off Andrew Carnegie's residence."

"Knight," said I, "you're a wonder. If there was no danger of your reforming, what a rounds man you'd make for the Nineteenth Precinct!"

THE DOG AND THE PLAYLET[1]

Usually it is a cold day in July when you can stroll up Broadway in that month and get a story out of the drama. I found one a few breathless, parboiling days ago, and it seems to decide a serious question in art.

There was not a soul left in the city except Hollis and me—and two or three million sunworshippers who remained at desks and counters. The elect had fled to seashore, lake, and mountain, and had already begun to draw for additional funds. Every evening Hollis and I prowled about the deserted town searching for coolness in empty cafés, dining-rooms, and roofgardens. We knew to the tenth part of a revolution the speed of every electric fan in Gotham, and we followed the swiftest as they varied. Hollis's fiancée, Miss Loris Sherman, had been in the Adirondacks, at Lower Saranac Lake, for a month. In another week he would join her party there. In the meantime, he cursed the city cheerfully and optimistically, and sought my society because I suffered him to show me her photograph during the black coffee every time we dined together.

My revenge was to read to him my one-act play.

It was one insufferable evening when the overplus of the day's heat was being hurled quiveringly back to the heavens by every surcharged brick

[1]This story has been rewritten and published in "Strictly Business" under the title, The Proof of the Pudding.

and stone and inch of iron in the panting town. But with the cunning of the two-legged beasts we had found an oasis where the hoofs of Apollo's steed had not been allowed to strike. Our seats were on an ocean of cool, polished oak; the white linen of fifty deserted tables flapped like seagulls in the artificial breeze; a mile away a waiter lingered for a heliographic signal—we might have roared songs there or fought a duel without molestation.

Out came Miss Loris's photo with the coffee, and I once more praised the elegant poise of the neck, the extremely low-coiled mass of heavy hair, and the eyes that followed one, like those in an oil painting.

"She's the greatest ever," said Hollis, with enthusiasm. "Good as Great Northern Preferred, and a disposition built like a watch. One week more and I'll be happy Johnny-on-the-spot. Old Tom Tolliver, my best college chum, went up there two weeks ago. He writes me that Loris doesn't talk about anything but me. Oh, I guess Rip Van Winkle didn't have all the good luck!"

"Yes, yes," said I, hurriedly, pulling out my typewritten play. "She's no doubt a charming girl. Now, here's that little curtain-raiser you promised to listen to."

"Ever been tried on the stage?" asked Hollis.

"Not exactly," I answered. "I read half of it the other day to a fellow whose brother knows Robert Edeson; but he had to catch a train before I finished."

"Go on," said Hollis, sliding back in his chair like a good fellow. "I'm no stage carpenter, but I'll tell you what I think of it from a first-row balcony standpoint. I'm a theatre bug during the season, and I can size up a fake play almost as quick as the gallery can. Flag the waiter once more, and then go ahead as hard as you like with it. I'll be the dog."

I read my little play lovingly, and, I fear, not without some elocution. There was one scene in it that I believed in greatly. The comedy swiftly rises into thrilling and unexpectedly developed drama. Capt. Marchmont suddenly becomes cognizant that his wife is an unscrupulous adventuress, who has deceived him from the day of their first meeting. The rapid and mortal duel between them from that moment—she with her magnificent lies and siren charm, winding about him like a serpent, trying to recover her lost ground; he with his man's agony and scorn and lost faith, trying to tear her from his heart. That scene I always thought was a crackerjack. When Capt. Marchmont discovers her duplicity by reading on a blotter in a mirror the impression of a note that she has written to the Count, he raises his hand to heaven and exclaims: "O God, who created woman while Adam slept, and gave her to him for a companion, take back Thy gift and return instead the sleep, though it last forever!"

"Rot!" said Hollis, rudely, when I had given those lines with proper emphasis.

"I beg your pardon!" I said as sweetly as I could.

"Come now," went on Hollis, "don't be an idiot. You know very well that nobody spouts any stuff like that these days. That sketch went along all right until you rang in the skyrockets. Cut out that right-arm exercise and the Adam and Eve stunt, and make your captain talk as you or I or Bill Jones would."

"I'll admit," said I, earnestly (for my theory was being touched upon), "that on all ordinary occasions all of us use commonplace language to convey our thoughts. You will remember that up to the moment when the captain makes his terrible discovery all the characters on the stage talk pretty much as they would in real life. But I believe that I am right in allowing him lines suitable to the strong and tragic situation into which he falls."

"Tragic, my eye!" said my friend, irreverently. "In Shakespeare's day he might have sputtered out some high-cockalorum nonsense of that sort, because in those days they ordered ham and eggs in blank verse and discharged the cook with an epic. But not for B'way in the summer of 1905!"

"It is my opinion," said I, "that great human emotions shake up our vocabulary and leave the words best suited to express them on top. A sudden violent grief or loss or disappointment will bring expressions out of an ordinary man as strong and solemn and dramatic as those used in fiction or on the stage to portray those emotions."

"That's where you fellows are wrong," said Hollis. "Plain, everyday talk is what goes. Your captain would very likely have kicked the cat, lit a cigar, stirred up a highball, and telephoned for a lawyer, instead of getting off those Robert Mantell pyrotechnics."

"Possibly, a little later," I continued. "But just at the time—just as the blow is delivered, if something Scriptural or theatrical and deep-tongued isn't wrung from a man in spite of his modern and practical way of speaking, then I'm wrong."

"Of course," said Hollis, kindly, "you've got to whoop her up some degrees for the stage. The audience expects it. When the villain kidnaps little Effie you have to make her mother claw some chunks out of the atmosphere, and scream: 'Me chee-ild, me chee-ild!' What she would actually do would be to call up the police by 'phone, ring for some strong tea, and get the little darling's photo out, ready for the reporters. When you get your villain in a corner—a stage corner—it's all right for him to clap his hand to his forehead and hiss: 'All is lost!' Off the stage he would remark: 'This is a conspiracy against me—I refer you to my lawyers.' "

"I get no consolation," said I, gloomily, "from your concession of an accentuated stage treatment. In my play I fondly hoped that I was following life. If people in real life meet great crises in a commonplace way, they should do the same on the stage."

And then we drifted, like two trout, out of our cool pool in the great hotel and began to nibble languidly at the gay flies in the swift current of Broadway. And our question of dramatic art was unsettled.

We nibbled at the flies, and avoided the hooks, as wise trout do; but soon the weariness of Manhattan in summer overcame us. Nine stories up, facing the south, was Hollis's apartment, and we soon stepped into an elevator bound for that cooler haven.

I was familiar in those quarters, and quickly my play was forgotten, and I stood at a sideboard mixing things, with cracked ice and glasses all about me. A breeze from the bay came in the windows not altogether blighted by the asphalt furnace over which it had passed. Hollis, whistling softly, turned over a late-arrived letter or two on his table, and drew around the coolest wicker armchairs.

I was just measuring the Vermouth carefully when I heard a sound. Some man's voice groaned hoarsely: "False, oh, God!—false, and Love is a lie and friendship but the byword of devils!"

I looked around quickly. Hollis lay across the table with his head down upon his outstretched arms. And then he looked up at me and laughed in his ordinary manner.

I knew him—he was poking fun at me about my theory. And it did seem so unnatural, those swelling words during our quiet gossip, that I half began to believe I had been mistaken—that my theory was wrong.

Hollis raised himself slowly from the table.

"You were right about that theatrical business, old man," he said, quietly, as he tossed a note to me.

I read it.

Loris had run away with Tom Tolliver.

A LITTLE TALK ABOUT MOBS

"I see," remarked the tall gentleman in the frock coat and black slouch hat, "that another street car motorman in your city has narrowly escaped lynching at the hands of an infuriated mob by lighting a cigar and walking a couple of blocks down the street."

"Do you think they would have lynched him?" asked the New Yorker, in the next seat of the ferry station, who was also waiting for the boat.

"Not until after the election," said the tall man, cutting a corner off his plug of tobacco. "I've been in your city long enough to know something about your mobs. The motorman's mob is about the least dangerous of them all, except the National Guard and the Dressmakers' Convention.

"You see, when little Willie Goldstein is sent by his mother for pigs' knuckles, with a nickel tightly grasped in his chubby fist, he always crosses the street car track safely twenty feet ahead of the car; and then suddenly turns back to ask his mother whether it was pale ale or a spool of 80 white cotton that she wanted. The motorman yells and throws himself on the brakes like a football player. There is a horrible grinding and then a ripping sound, and a piercing shriek, and Willie is sitting, with part of his trousers torn away by the fender, screaming for his lost nickel.

"In ten seconds the car is surrounded by 600 infuriated citizens, crying, 'Lynch the motorman! Lynch the motorman!' at the top of their voices. Some of them run to the nearest cigar store to get a rope; but they find the last one has just been cut up and labelled. Hundreds of the excited mob press close to the cowering motorman, whose hand is observed to tremble perceptibly as he transfers a stick of pepsin gum from his pocket to his mouth.

"When the bloodthirsty mob of maddened citizens has closed in on the motorman, some bringing camp stools and sitting quite close to him, and all shouting, 'Lynch him!' Policeman Fogarty forces his way through them to the side of their prospective victim.

"'Hello, Mike,' says the motorman in a low voice, 'nice day. Shall I sneak off a block or so, or would you like to rescue me?'

"'Well, Jerry, if you don't mind,' says the policeman, 'I'd like to disperse the infuriated mob singlehanded. I haven't defeated a lynching mob since last Tuesday; and that was a small one of only 300, that wanted to string up a Dago boy for selling wormy pears. It would boost me some down at the station.'

"'All right, Mike,' says the motorman, 'anything to oblige. I'll turn pale and tremble.'

"And he does so; and Policeman Fogarty draws his club and says, 'G'wan wid yez!' and in eight seconds the desperate mob has scattered and gone about its business, except about a hundred who remain to search for Willie's nickel."

"I never heard of a mob in our city doing violence to a motorman because of an accident," said the New Yorker.

"You are not liable to," said the tall man. "They know the motorman's all right, and that he wouldn't even run over a stray dog if he could help it. And they know that not a man among 'em would tie the knot to hang even a Thomas cat that had been tried and condemned and sentenced according to law."

"Then why do they become infuriated and make threats of lynching?" asked the New Yorker.

"To assure the motorman," answered the tall man, "that he is safe. If they really wanted to do him up they would go into the houses and drop bricks on him from the third-story windows."

"New Yorkers are not cowards," said the other man, a little stiffly.

"Not one at a time," agreed the tall man, promptly. "You've got a fine lot of singlehanded scrappers in your town. I'd rather fight three of you than one; and I'd go up against all the Gas Trust's victims in a bunch before I'd pass two citizens on a dark corner, with my watch chain showing. When you get rounded up in a bunch you lose your nerve. Get you in crowds and you're easy. Ask the 'L' road guards and George B. Cortelyou and the tintype booths at Coney Island. Divided you stand, united you fall. *E pluribus nihil.* Whenever one of your mobs surrounds a man and begins to holler, 'Lynch him!' he says to himself, 'Oh, dear, I suppose I must look pale to please the boys, but I will, forsooth, let my life insurance premium lapse to-morrow. This is a sure tip for me to play Methuselah straight across the board in the next handicap.'

"I can imagine the tortured feelings of a prisoner in the hands of New York policemen when an infuriated mob demands that he be turned over to them for lynching. 'For God's sake, officers,' cries the distracted wretch, 'have ye hearts of stone, that ye will not let them wrest me from ye?'

"'Sorry, Jimmy,' says one of the policemen, 'but it won't do. There's three of us—me and Darrel and the plain-clothes man; and there's only sivin thousand of the mob. How'd we explain it at the office if they took ye? Jist chase the infuriated aggregation around the corner, Darrel, and we'll be moving along to the station.'"

"Some of our gatherings of excited citizens have not been so harmless," said the New Yorker, with a faint note of civic pride.

"I'll admit that," said the tall man. "A cousin of mine who was on a visit here once had an arm broken and lost an ear in one of them."

"That must have been during the Cooper Union riots," remarked the New Yorker.

"Not the Cooper Union," explained the tall man—"but it was a union riot—at the Vanastor wedding."

"You seem to be in favor of lynch law," said the New Yorker, severely.

"No, sir, I am not. No intelligent man is. But, sir, there are certain cases when people rise in their just majesty and take a righteous vengeance for crimes that the law is slow in punishing. I am an advocate of law and order, but I will say to you that less than six months ago I myself assisted at the lynching of one of that race that is creating a wide chasm between your section of country and mine, sir."

"It is a deplorable condition," said the New Yorker, "that exists in the South, but——"

"I am from Indiana, sir," said the tall man, taking another chew; "and I don't think you will condemn my course when I tell you that the colored man in question had stolen $9.60 in cash, sir, from my own brother."

THE SNOW MAN

Editorial Note   Before the fatal illness of William Sydney Porter (known through his literary work as "O. Henry") this American master of short-story writing had begun for *Hampton's Magazine* the story printed below. Illness crept upon him rapidly and he was compelled to give up writing about at the point where the girl enters the story.

When he realized that he could do no more (it was his lifelong habit to write with a pencil, never dictating to a stenographer), O. Henry told in detail the remainder of The Snow Man to Harris Merton Lyon, whom he had often spoken of as one of the most effective short-story writers of the present time. Mr. Porter had delineated all of the characters, leaving only the rounding out of the plot in the final pages to Mr. Lyon.

Housed and windowpaned from it, the greatest wonder to little children is the snow. To men, it is something like a crucible in which their world melts into a white star ten million miles away. The man who can stand the test is a Snow Man; and this is his reading by Fahrenheit, Réaumur, or Moses's carven tablets of stone.

Night had fluttered a sable pinion above the cañon of Big Lost River, and I urged my horse toward the Bay Horse Ranch because the snow was deepening. The flakes were as large as an hour's circular tatting by Miss Wilkins's ablest spinster, betokening a heavy snowfall and less entertainment and more adventure than the completion of the tatting could promise. I knew Ross Curtis of the Bay Horse, and that I would be welcome as a snow-bound pilgrim, both for hospitality's sake and because Ross had few chances to confide in living creatures who did not neigh, bellow, bleat, yelp, or howl during his discourse.

The ranch house was just within the jaws of the cañon where its builder may have fatuously fancied that the timbered and rocky walls on both sides would have protected it from the wintry Colorado winds; but I feared the drift. Even now through the endless, bottomless rift in the hills —the speaking tube of the four winds—came roaring the voice of the proprietor to the little room on the top floor.

At my "hello," a ranch hand came from an outer building and received my thankful horse. In another minute, Ross and I sat by a stove in the dining-room of the four-room ranch house, while the big, simple welcome of the household lay at my disposal. Fanned by the whizzing norther, the fine, dry snow was sifted and bolted through the cracks and knotholes of the logs. The cook room, without a separating door, appended.

In there I could see a short, sturdy, leisurely and weather-beaten man moving with professional sureness about his red-hot stove. His face was stolid and unreadable—something like that of a great thinker, or of one who had no thoughts to conceal. I thought his eye seemed unwarrantably superior to the elements and to the man, but quickly attributed that to the characteristic self-importance of a petty chef. "Camp cook" was the niche that I gave him in the Hall of Types; and he fitted it as an apple fits a dumpling.

Cold it was in spite of the glowing stove; and Ross and I sat and talked, shuddering frequently, half from nerves and half from the freezing draughts. So he brought the bottle and the cook brought boiling water, and we made prodigious hot toddies against the attacks of Boreas. We clinked glasses often. They sounded like icicles dropping from the eaves, or like the tinkle of a thousand prisms of a Louis XIV chandelier that I once heard at a boarders' dance in the parlor of a ten-a-week boarding-house in Gramercy Square. *Sic transit.*

Silence in the terrible beauty of the snow and of the Sphinx and of the stars; but they who believe that all things, from a without-wine table d'hôte to the crucifixion, may be interpreted through music, might have found a nocturne or a symphony to express the isolation of that blotted-out world. The clink of glass and bottle, the æolian chorus of the wind in the house crannies, its deeper trombone through the cañon below, and the Wagnerian crash of the cook's pots and pans, united in a fit, discordant melody, I thought. No less welcome an accompaniment was the sizzling of broiling ham and venison cutlets, indorsed by the solvent fumes of true Java, bringing rich promises of comfort to our yearning souls.

The cook brought the smoking supper to the table. He nodded to me democratically as he cast the heavy plates around as though he were pitching quoits or hurling the discus. I looked at him with some appraisement and curiosity and much conciliation. There was no prophet to tell us when that drifting evil outside might cease to fall; and it is well, when snow-bound, to stand somewhere within the radius of the cook's favorable consideration. But I could read neither favor nor disapproval in the face and manner of our pot-wrestler.

He was about five feet nine inches, and two hundred pounds of commonplace, bull-necked, pink-faced, callous calm. He wore brown duck trousers too tight and too short, and a blue flannel shirt with sleeves rolled above his elbows. There was a sort of grim, steady scowl on his features that looked to me as though he had fixed it there purposely as a protection against the weakness of an inherent amiability that, he fancied, were better concealed. And then I let supper usurp his brief occupancy of my thoughts.

"Draw up, George," said Ross. "Let's all eat while the grub's hot."

"You fellows go on and chew," answered the cook. "I ate mine in the kitchen before sun-down."

"Think it'll be a big snow, George?" asked the ranchman.

George had turned to reënter the cook room. He moved slowly around and, looking at his face, it seemed to me that he was turning over the wisdom and knowledge of centuries in his head.

"It might," was his delayed reply.

At the door of the kitchen he stopped and looked back at us. Both Ross and I held our knives and forks poised and gave him our regard. Some men have the power of drawing the attention of others without speaking a word. Their attitude is more effective than a shout.

"And again it mightn't," said George, and went back to his stove.

After we had eaten, he came in and gathered the emptied dishes. He stood for a moment, while his spurious frown deepened.

"It might stop any minute," he said, "or it might keep up for days."

At the farther end of the cook room I saw George pour hot water into his dishpan, light his pipe, and put the tableware through its required lavation. He then carefully unwrapped from a piece of old saddle blanket a paper-back book, and settled himself to read by his dim oil lamp.

And then the ranchman threw tobacco on the cleared table and set forth again the bottles and glasses; and I saw that I stood in a deep channel through which the long dammed flood of his discourse would soon be booming. But I was half content, comparing my fate with that of the late Thomas Tucker, who had to sing for his supper, thus doubling the burdens of both himself and his host.

"Snow is a hell of a thing," said Ross, by way of a foreword. "It ain't, somehow, it seems to me, salubrious. I can stand water and mud and two inches below zero and a hundred and ten in the shade and medium-sized cyclones, but this here fuzzy white stuff naturally gets me all locoed. I reckon the reason it rattles you is because it changes the look of things so much. It's like you had a wife and left her in the morning with the same old blue cotton wrapper on, and rides in of a night and runs across her all outfitted in a white silk evening frock, waving an ostrich-feather fan, and monkeying with a posy of lily flowers. Wouldn't it make you look for your pocket compass? You'd be liable to kiss her before you collected your presence of mind."

By and by, the flood of Ross's talk was drawn up into the clouds (so it pleased me to fancy) and there condensed into the finer snowflakes of thought; and we sat silent about the stove, as good friends and bitter enemies will do. I thought of Ross's preamble about the mysterious influence upon man exerted by that ermine-lined monster that now covered our little world, and knew he was right.

Of all the curious knickknacks, mysteries, puzzles, Indian gifts, rattraps, and well-disguised blessings that the gods chuck down to us from the Olympian peaks, the most disquieting and evil-bringing is the snow. By scientific analysis it is absolute beauty and purity—so, at the beginning we look doubtfully at chemistry.

It falls upon the world, and lo! we live in another. It hides in a night the old scars and familiar places with which we have grown heart-sick or enamored. So, as quietly as we can, we hustle on our embroidered robes and hie us on Prince Camaralzaman's horse or in the reindeer sleigh into the white country where the seven colors converge. This is when our fancy can overcome the bane of it.

But in certain spots of the earth comes the snow-madness, made known by people turned wild and distracted by the bewildering veil that has obscured the only world they know. In the cities, the white fairy who sets the brains of her dupes whirling by a wave of her wand is cast for the comedy rôle. Her diamond shoe buckles glitter like frost; with a pirouette she invites the spotless carnival.

But in the waste places the snow is sardonic. Sponging out the world of the outliers, it gives no foothold on another sphere in return. It makes of the earth a firmament under foot; it leaves us clawing and stumbling in space in an inimical fifth element whose evil outdoes its strangeness and beauty. There Nature, low comedienne, plays her tricks on man. Though she has put him forth as her highest product, it appears that she has fashioned him with what seems almost incredible carelessness and index- terity. One-sided and without balance, with his two halves unequally fashioned and joined, must he ever jog his eccentric way. The snow falls, the darkness caps it, and the ridiculous man-biped strays in accurate circles until he succumbs in the ruins of his defective architecture.

In the throat of the thirsty the snow is vitriol. In appearance as plausible as the breakfast food of the angels, it is as hot in the mouth as ginger, increasing the pangs of the water-famished. It is a derivative from water, air, and some cold, uncanny fire from which the caloric has been ex- tracted. Good has been said of it; even the poets, crazed by its spell and shivering in their attics under its touch, have indited permanent melodies commemorative of its beauty.

Still, to the saddest overcoated optimist it is a plague—a corroding plague that Pharaoh successfully side-stepped. It beneficently covers the wheat fields, swelling the crop—and the Flour Trust gets us by the throat like a sudden quinsy. It spreads the tail of its white kirtle over the red seams of the rugged north—and the Alaska short story is born. Etio- lated perfidy, it shelters the mountain traveler burrowing from the icy air—and, melting to-morrow, drowns his brother in the valley below.

At its worst it is lock and key and crucible, and the wand of Circe. When it corrals man in lonely ranches, mountain cabins, and forest huts, the snow makes apes and tigers of the hardiest. It turns the bosoms of weaker ones to glass, their tongues to infants' rattles, their hearts to lawlessness and spleen. It is not all from the isolation; the snow is not merely a blockader; it is a Chemical Test. It is a good man who can show a reaction that is not chiefly composed of a drachm or two of potash and magnesia, with traces of Adam, Ananias, Nebuchadnezzar, and the fretful porcupine.

This is no story, you say; well, let it begin.

There was a knock at the door (is the opening not full of context and reminiscence oh, best buyers of best sellers?).

We drew the latch, and in stumbled Étienne Girod (as he afterward named himself). But just then he was no more than a worm struggling for life, enveloped in a killing white chrysalis.

We dug down through snow, overcoats, mufflers, and waterproofs, and dragged forth a living thing with a Van Dyck beard and marvelous diamond rings. We put it through the approved curriculum of snow-rubbing, hot milk, and teaspoonful doses of whiskey, working him up to a graduating class entitled to a diploma of three fingers of rye in half a glassful of hot water. One of the ranch boys had already come from the quarters at Ross's bugle-like yell and kicked the stranger's staggering pony to some sheltered corral where beasts were entertained.

Let a paragraphic biography of Girod intervene.

Étienne was an opera singer originally, we gathered; but adversity and the snow had made him *non compos vocis*. The adversity consisted of the stranded San Salvador Opera Company, a period of hotel second-story work, and then a career as a professional palmist, jumping from town to town. For, like other professional palmists, every time he worked the Heart Line too strongly he immediately moved along the Line of Least Resistance. Though Étienne did not confide this to us, we surmised that he had moved out into the dusk about twenty minutes ahead of a constable, and had thus encountered the snow. In his most sacred blue language he dilated upon the subject of snow; for Étienne was Paris-born and loved the snow with the same passion that an orchid does.

"Mee-ser-rhable!" commented Étienne, and took another three fingers.

"Complete, cast-iron, pussy-footed, blank . . . blank!" said Ross, and followed suit.

"Rotten," said I.

The cook said nothing. He stood in the door weighing our outburst; and insistently from behind that frozen visage I got two messages (*via* the M. A. M. wireless). One was that George considered our vituperation against the snow childish; the other was that George did not love Dagoes. Inasmuch as Étienne was a Frenchman, I concluded I had the message wrong. So I queried the other: "Bright eyes, you don't really mean Dagoes, do you?" and over the wireless came three deathly, psychic taps: "Yes." Then I reflected that to George all foreigners were probably "Dagoes." I had once known another camp cook who had thought Mons.,

Sig., and Millie (Trans-Mississippi for Mlle.) were Italian given names; this cook used to marvel therefore at the paucity of Neo-Roman precognomens, and therefore why not——

I have said that snow is a test of men. For one day, two days, Étienne stood at the window, Fletcherizing his finger nails and shrieking and moaning at the monotony. To me, Étienne was just about as unbearable as the snow; and so, seeking relief, I went out on the second day to look at my horse; slipped on a stone, broke my collarbone, and thereafter underwent not the snow test, but the test of flat-on-the-back. A test that comes once too often for any man to stand.

However, I bore up cheerfully. I was now merely a spectator, and from my couch in the big room I could lie and watch the human interplay with that detached, impassive, impersonal feeling which French writers tell us is so valuable to the littérateur, and American writers to the faro-dealer.

"I shall go crazy in this abominable, mee-ser-rhable place!" was Étienne's constant prediction.

"Never knew Mark Twain to bore me before," said Ross, over and over. He sat by the other window, hour after hour, a box of Pittsburgh stogies of the length, strength, and odor of a Pittsburgh graft scandal deposited on one side of him, and "Roughing It," "The Jumping Frog," and "Life on the Mississippi" on the other. For every chapter he lit a new stogy, puffing furiously. This, in time, gave him a recurrent premonition of cramps, gastritis, smoker's colic, or whatever it is they have in Pittsburg after a too deep indulgence in graft scandals. To fend off the colic, Ross resorted time and again to Old Doctor Still's Amber-Colored U. S. A. Colic Cure. Result, after forty-eight hours—nerves.

"Positive fact I never knew Mark Twain to make me tired before. Positive fact." Ross slammed "Roughing It" on the floor. "When you're snowbound this-away you want tragedy, I guess. Humor just seems to bring out all your cussedness. You read a man's poor, pitiful attempts to be funny and it makes you so nervous you want to tear the book up, get out your bandana, and have a good, long cry."

At the other end of the room, the Frenchman took his finger nails out of his mouth long enough to exclaim: "Humor! Humor at such a time as thees! My God, I shall go crazy in thees abominable——"

"Supper," announced George.

These meals were not the meals of Rabelais who said, "the great God makes the planets and we make the platters neat." By that time, the ranch-house meals were not affairs of gusto; they were mental distraction, not bodily provender. What they were to be later shall never be forgotten by Ross or me or Étienne.

After supper, the stogies and finger nails began again. My shoulder ached wretchedly, and with half-closed eyes I tried to forget it by watching the deft movements of the stolid cook.

Suddenly I saw him cock his ear, like a dog. Then, with a swift step, he moved to the door, threw it open, and stood there.

The rest of us had heard nothing.

"What is it, George?" asked Ross.

The cook reached out his hand into the darkness alongside the jamb. With careful precision he prodded something. Then he made one careful step into the snow. His back muscles bulged a little under the arms as he stooped and lightly lifted a burden. Another step inside the door, which he shut methodically behind him, and he dumped the burden at a safe distance from the fire.

He stood up and fixed us with a solemn eye. None of us moved under that Orphic suspense until,

"A woman," remarked George.

Miss Willie Adams was her name. Vocation, school-teacher. Present avocation, getting lost in the snow. Age, yum-yum (the Persian for twenty). Take to the woods if you would describe Miss Adams. A willow for grace; a hickory for fibre; a birch for the clear whiteness of her skin; her eyes, the blue sky seen through treetops; the silk in cocoons for her hair; her voice, the murmur of the evening June wind in the leaves; her mouth, the berries of the wintergreen; fingers as light as ferns; her toe as small as a deer track. General impression upon the dazed beholder— you could not see the forest for the trees.

Psychology, with a capital P and the foot of a lynx, at this juncture stalks into the ranch house. Three men, a cook, a pretty young woman— all snowbound. Count me out of it, as I did not count, anyway. I never did, with women. Count the cook out, if you like. But note the effect upon Ross and Étienne Girod.

Ross dumped Mark Twain in a trunk and locked the trunk. Also, he discarded the Pittsburgh scandals. Also, he shaved off a three days' beard.

Étienne, being French, began on the beard first. He pomaded it, from a little tube of grease Hongroise in his vest pocket. He combed it with a little aluminum comb from the same vest pocket. He trimmed it with manicure scissors from the same vest pocket. His light and Gallic spirits underwent a sudden, miraculous change. He hummed a blithe San Salvador Opera Company tune; he grinned, smirked, bowed, pirouetted, twiddled, twaddled, twisted, and tooralooed. Gayly, the notorious troubadour, could not have equalled Étienne.

Ross's method of advance was brusque, domineering. "Little woman," he said, "you're welcome here!"—and with what he thought subtle double meaning—"welcome to stay here as long as you like, snow or no snow."

Miss Adams thanked him a little wildly, some of the wintergreen berries creeping into the birch bark. She looked around hurriedly as if seeking escape. But there was none, save the kitchen and the room allotted her. She made an excuse and disappeared into her own room.

Later I, feigning sleep, heard the following:

"Mees Adams, I was almos' to perish-die-of-monotony w'en your fair and beautiful face appear in thees mee-ser-rhable house." I opened my starboard eye. The beard was being curled furiously around a finger, the Svengali eye was rolling, the chair was being hunched closer to the school-teacher's. "I am French—you see—temperamental—nervous! I cannot endure thees dull hours in thees ranch house; but—a woman comes! Ah!" The shoulders gave nine 'rahs and a tiger. "What a difference! All is light and gay; ever'ting smile w'en you smile. You have 'eart, beauty, grace. My 'eart comes back to me w'en I feel your 'eart. So!" He laid his hand upon his vest pocket. From this vantage point he suddenly snatched at the school-teacher's own hand. "Ah! Mees Adams, if I could only tell you how I ad——"

"Dinner," remarked George. He was standing just behind the Frenchman's ear. His eyes looked straight into the school-teacher's eyes. After thirty seconds of survey, his lips moved, deep in the flinty, frozen maelstrom of his face: "Dinner," he concluded, "will be ready in two minutes."

Miss Adams jumped to her feet, relieved. "I must get ready for dinner," she said brightly, and went into her room.

Ross came in fifteen minutes late. After the dishes had been cleaned away, I waited until a propitious time when the room was temporarily ours alone, and told him what had happened.

He became so excited that he lit a stogy without thinking. "Yellerhided, unwashed, palm-readin' skunk," he said under his breath. "I'll shoot him full o' holes if he don't watch out—talkin' that way to my wife!"

I gave a jump that set my collarbone back another week. "Your wife!" I gasped.

"Well, I mean to make her that," he announced.

The air in the ranch house the rest of that day was tense with pent-up emotions, oh, best buyers of best sellers.

Ross watched Miss Adams as a hawk does a hen; he watched Étienne as a hawk does a scarecrow. Étienne watched Miss Adams as a weasel does a henhouse. He paid no attention to Ross.

The condition of Miss Adams, in the rôle of sought-after, was feverish. Lately escaped from the agony and long torture of the white cold, where for hours Nature had kept the little school-teacher's vision locked in and turned upon herself, nobody knows through what profound feminine introspections she had gone. Now, suddenly cast among men, instead of finding relief and security, she beheld herself plunged anew into other discomforts. Even in her own room she could hear the loud voices of her imposed suitors. "I'll blow you full o' holes!" shouted Ross. "Witnesses," shrieked Étienne, waving his hand at the cook and me. She could not have known the previous harassed condition of the men, fretting under indoor conditions. All she knew was, that where she had expected the frank freemasonry of the West, she found the subtle tangle of two men's minds, bent upon exacting whatever romance there might be in her situation.

She tried to dodge Ross and the Frenchman by spells of nursing me. They also came over to help nurse. This combination aroused such a natural state of invalid cussedness on my part that they were all forced to retire. Once she did manage to whisper: "I am so worried here. I don't know what to do."

To which I replied, gently, hitching up my shoulder, that I was a hunch-savant and that the Eighth House under this sign, the Moon being in Virgo, showed that everything would turn out all right.

But twenty minutes later I saw Étienne reading her palm and felt that perhaps I might have to recast her horoscope, and try for a dark man coming with a bundle.

Toward sunset, Étienne left the house for a few moments and Ross, who had been sitting taciturn and morose, having unlocked Mark Twain, made another dash. It was typical Ross talk.

He stood in front of her and looked down majestically at that cool and perfect spot where Miss Adams' forehead met the neat part in her fragrant hair. First, however, he cast a desperate glance at me. I was in a profound slumber.

"Little woman," he began, "it's certainly tough for a man like me to see you bothered this way. You"—gulp—"you have been alone in this world too long. You need a protector. I might say that at a time like this you need a protector the worst kind—a protector who would take a three-ring delight in smashing the saffron-colored kisser off of any yeller-skinned skunk that made himself obnoxious to you. Hem. Hem. I am a lonely man, Miss Adams. I have so far had to carry on my life without the"—gulp—"sweet radiance"—gulp—"of a woman around the house. I feel especially doggoned lonely at a time like this, when I am pretty near locoed from havin' to stall indoors, and hence it was with delight I welcomed your first appearance in this here shack. Since then I have been packed jam full of more different kinds of feelings, ornery, mean, dizzy, and superb, than has fallen my way in years." Miss Adams made a useless movement toward escape. The Ross chin stuck firm. "I don't want to annoy you, Miss Adams, but, by heck, if it comes to that you'll have to be annoyed. And I'll have to have my say. This palm-ticklin' slob of a French-man ought to be kicked off the place and if you'll say the word, off he goes. But I don't want to do the wrong thing. You've got to show a pref-erence. I'm gettin' around to the point, Miss—Miss Willie, in my own brick fashion. I've stood about all I can stand these last two days and somethin's got to happen. The suspense hereabouts is enough to hang a sheepherder. Miss Willie"—he lassooed her hand by main force—"just say the word. You need somebody to take your part all your life long. Will you mar——"

"Supper," remarked George, tersely, from the kitchen door.

Miss Adams hurried away.

Ross turned angrily. "You——"

"I have been revolving it in my head," said George.

He brought the coffee pot forward heavily. Then bravely the big platter of pork and beans. Then somberly the potatoes. Then profoundly the biscuits. "I have been revolving it in my mind. There ain't no use waitin' any longer for Swengalley. Might as well eat now."

From my excellent vantage-point on the couch I watched the progress of that meal. Ross, muddled, glowering, disappointed; Étienne, eternally blandishing, attentive, ogling; Miss Adams, nervous, picking at her food, hesitant about answering questions, almost hysterical; now and then the solid, flitting shadow of the cook, passing behind their backs like a Dreadnaught in a fog.

I used to own a clock which gurgled in its throat three minutes before it struck the hour. I know, therefore, the slow freight of Anticipation. For I have awakened at three in the morning, heard the clock gurgle, and waited those three minutes for the three strokes I knew were to come. *Alors.* In Ross's ranch house that night the slow freight of Climax whistled in the distance.

Étienne began it after supper. Miss Adams had suddenly displayed a lively interest in the kitchen layout and I could see her in there, chatting brightly at George—not with him—the while he ducked his head and rattled his pans.

"My fren'," said Étienne, exhaling a large cloud from his cigarette and patting Ross lightly on the shoulder with a bediamonded hand which hung limp from a yard or more of bony arm, "I see I mus' be frank with you. Firs', because we are rivals; second, because you take these matters so serious. I—I am Frenchman. I love the women"—he threw back his curls, bared his yellow teeth, and blew an unsavory kiss toward the kitchen. "It is, I suppose, a trait of my nation. All Frenchmen love the women—pretty women. Now, look: Here I am!" He spread out his arms. "Cold outside! I detes' the col-l-l'! Snow! I abominate the mees-ser-rhable snow! Two men! This"—pointing to me—"an' this!" Pointing to Ross. "I am distracted! For two whole days I stan' at the window an' tear my 'air! I am nervous, upset, pr-r-ro-foun'ly distress inside my 'ead! An' suddenly—be'old! A woman, a nice, pretty, charming, innocen' young woman! I, naturally, rejoice. I become myself again—gay, light-'earted, 'appy. I address myself to mademoiselle; it passes the time. That, m'sieu', is wot the women are for—pass the time! Entertainment—like the music, like the wine!

"They appeal to the mood, the caprice, the temperamen'. To play with thees woman, follow her through her humor, pursue her—ah! that is the mos' delightful way to sen' the hours about their business."

Ross banged the table. "Shut up, you miserable yeller pup!" he roared. "I object to your pursuin' anything or anybody in my house. Now, you listen to me, you——" He picked up the box of stogies and used it on the table as an emphasizer. The noise of it awoke the attention of the girl in the kitchen. Unheeded, she crept into the room. "I don't know anything about your French ways of lovemakin' an' I don't care. In my section of the country, it's the best man wins. And I'm the best man here, and don't you forget it! This girl's goin' to be mine. There ain't going to be any playing, or philandering, or palm reading about it. I've made up my mind I'll have this girl, and that settles it. My word is the law in this neck o' the woods. She's mine, and as soon as she says she's mine, you pull out." The box made one final, tremendous punctuation point.

Étienne's bravado was unruffled. "Ah! that is no way to win a woman," he smiled, easily. "I make prophecy you will never win 'er that way. No. Not thees woman. She mus' be played along an' then keessed, this charming, delicious little creature. One kees! An' then you 'ave her." Again he displayed his unpleasant teeth. "I make you a bet I will kees her——"

As a cheerful chronicler of deeds done well, it joys me to relate that the hand which fell upon Étienne's amorous lips was not his own. There was one sudden sound, as of a mule kicking a lath fence, and then—through the swinging doors of oblivion for Étienne.

I had seen this blow delivered. It was an aloof, unstudied, almost absent-minded affair. I had thought the cook was rehearsing the proper method of turning a flapjack.

Silently, lost in thought, he stood there scratching his head. Then he began rolling down his sleeves.

"You'd better get your things on, Miss, and we'll get out of here," he decided. "Wrap up warm."

I heard her heave a little sigh of relief as she went to get her cloak, sweater, and hat.

Ross jumped to his feet, and said: "George, what are you goin' to do?"

George, who had been headed in my direction, slowly swivelled around and faced his employer. "Bein' a camp cook, I ain't over-burdened with hosses," George enlightened us. "Therefore, I am going to try to borrow this feller's here."

For the first time in four days my soul gave a genuine cheer. "If it's for Lochinvar purposes, go as far as you like," I said, grandly.

The cook studied me a moment, as if trying to find an insult in my words. "No," he replied. "It's for mine and the young lady's purposes, and we'll go only three miles—to Hicksville. Now let me tell you somethin', Ross." Suddenly I was confronted with the cook's chunky back and I heard a low, curt, carrying voice shoot through the room at my host. George had wheeled just as Ross started to speak. "You're nutty. That's what's the matter with you. You can't stand the snow. You're gettin' nervouser, and nuttier every day. That and this Dago"—he jerked a thumb at the half-dead Frenchman in the corner—"has got you to the point where I thought I better horn in. I got to revolvin' it around in my mind and I seen if somethin' wasn't done, and done soon, there'd be murder around here and maybe"—his head gave an imperceptible list toward the girl's room—"worse."

He stopped, but he held up a stubby finger to keep any one else from speaking. Then he plowed slowly through the drift of his ideas. "About this here woman. I know you, Ross, and I know what you reely think about women. If she hadn't happened in here durin' this here snow, you'd never have given two thoughts to the whole woman question. Likewise, when the storm clears, and you and the boys go hustlin' out, this here whole business'll clear out of your head and you won't think of a skirt again until Kingdom Come. Just because o' this snow here, don't forget you're livin' in the selfsame world you was in four days ago. And you're the same man, too. Now, what's the use o' gettin' all snarled up over four days of stickin' in the house? That there's what I been revolvin' in my mind and this here's the decision I've come to."

He plodded to the door and shouted to one of the ranch hands to saddle my horse.

Ross lit a stogy and stood thoughtful in the middle of the room. Then he began: "I've a durn good notion, George, to knock your confounded head off and throw you into that snowbank, if——"

"You're wrong, mister. That ain't a durned good notion you've got. It's durned bad. Look here!" He pointed steadily out of doors until we were both forced to follow his finger. "You're in here for more'n a week yet." After allowing this fact to sink in, he barked out at Ross: "Can *you* cook?" Then at me: "Can *you* cook?" Then he looked at the wreck of Étienne and sniffed.

There was an embarrassing silence as Ross and I thought solemnly of a foodless week.

"If you just use hoss sense," concluded George, "and don't go for to hurt my feelin's, all I want to do is to take this young gal down to Hicksville; and then I'll head back here and cook fer you."

The horse and Miss Adams arrived simultaneously, both of them very serious and quiet. The horse because he knew what he had before him in that weather; the girl because of what she had left behind.

Then all at once I awoke to a realization of what the cook was doing. "My God, man!" I cried, "aren't you afraid to go out in that snow?"

Behind my back I heard Ross mutter, "Not him."

George lifted the girl daintily up behind the saddle, drew on his gloves, put his foot in the stirrup, and turned to inspect me leisurely.

As I passed slowly in his review, I saw in my mind's eye the algebraic equation of Snow, the equals sign, and the answer in the man before me.

"Snow is my last name," said George. He swung into the saddle and they started cautiously out into the darkening swirl of fresh new currency just issuing from the Snowdrop Mint. The girl, to keep her place, clung happily to the sturdy figure of the camp cook.

I brought three things away from Ross Curtis's ranch house—yea, four. One was the appreciation of snow, which I have so humbly tried here to render; (2) was a collarbone, of which I am extra careful; (3) was a memory of what it is to eat very extremely terribly bad food for a week; and (4) was the cause of (3) a little note delivered at the end of the week and hand-painted in blue pencil on a sheet of meat paper.

"I cannot come back there to that there job. Mrs. Snow say no, George. I been revolvin' it in my mind; considerin' circumstances she's right."